Intermediate Accounting

The Willard J. Graham Series in Accounting
Consulting Editor **Robert N. Anthony** Harvard University

Sixth Edition

Intermediate Accounting

GLENN A. WELSCH, Ph.D., C.P.A.
Professor of Accounting

CHARLES T. ZLATKOVICH, Ph.D., C.P.A.
Professor of Accounting

WALTER T. HARRISON, JR., Ph.D., C.P.A.
Associate Professor of Accounting

all of the
College of Business Administration
The University of Texas at Austin

1982

Richard D. Irwin, Inc.
Homewood, Illinois 60430

ISBN 0-256-02598-3

Library of Congress Catalog Card No. 81–84841

Printed in the United States of America

2 3 4 5 6 7 8 9 0 K 9 8 7 6 5 4 3

Preface

THIS SIXTH EDITION is designed primarily for students who have successfully completed a reasonably adequate course in the fundamentals of financial accounting. It is equally adaptable for use by either semester-system schools or those on the quarter system. Two semesters or three quarters or their equivalent normally will be required for complete coverage of all chapters. While the chapters are arranged in an orderly, logical sequence, variations of the sequence or omission of some materials can provide solid coverage of the materials selected.

This edition continues its innovative thrust in topical coverage and presentation. In preparing this edition, the authors gave special attention to pedagogy and presentation to help the student understand the complex issues discussed. Included are innovative exhibits specially designed to facilitate student comprehension. Typically in the one-page exhibits, Panel A presents the hypothetical situation, Panel B gives the journal entries, and Panel C illustrates the financial statement reporting and disclosures.

Although practical accounting and reporting have become increasingly "rule oriented" and detailed, the authors provide a solid theoretical foundation so the specific material which reflects applications of the rules of generally accepted accounting principles (GAAP) can be understood and viewed in perspective. This edition continues the comprehensive features that have characterized the prior editions. Students who complete most or all of the materials in this edition should have an adequate foundation for advanced courses in accounting and for topics which recur on the theory and practice portions of the Uniform CPA Examination.

Troublesome complexities have been addressed comprehensively. We have increased the number of instructional supplements, and some of the more complex material is covered in these chapter supplements. Where appropriate, alternative viewpoints are presented, and the alternative which reflects GAAP is identified. All salient aspects of each topic are considered, which imposes a comparatively high level of sophistication.

Preferred accounting terminology is used throughout on a consistent basis. Citations and references to pronouncements of standard-setting entities and influential bodies such as the American Accounting Association permeate the 24 chapters. Continuing a feature introduced in the fourth edition, a list of *Accounting Research Bulletins, Accounting Principles Board Opinions* and *Statements,* and of Financial

Accounting Standards Board pronouncements appears in Supplement 1–B to Chapter 1; for each item listed, the issue date and current status is indicated. As newer pronouncements appear subsequent to publication of the text, supplementary booklets will be made available to users at no charge.

A new feature of the sixth edition is citation of the academic literature to incorporate into text discussions the implications of research for financial accounting. The text discussions are augmented by footnote references to the related literature for users who wish to do outside reading on a particular topic.

Another new feature of the sixth edition is the use of many actual examples of financial statement disclosures and articles from the business press, such as *The Wall Street Journal.* These items, which have been woven into the text discussions, relate intermediate accounting to actual practice.

Because we recognize that students learn much of their accounting by solving relevant assignment materials, a wealth of questions, cases, short exercises, and problems accompanies each chapter. The volume of assignment material has been expanded to include more decision cases than the prior edition.

Questions which emphasize definitions and basic relationships are provided for class discussion. We suggest that adopters urge their students to attempt to answer all questions related to a chapter immediately after they have studied it. Exercises focus on specific, limited issues discussed in the chapters. Problems generally provide an overview of several related topics and are more complex than exercises. Decision cases present challenging experiences through open-ended situations designed for class or group discussion. An appropriate selection of materials from Uniform CPA Examinations is provided throughout the assignment materials and the examination book.

For the professor:

1. A comprehensive instructor's manual including several typical assignment schedules and detailed step-by-step computations.
2. A test bank classified by chapter.
3. Transparencies for selected assignment materials.
4. Selected teaching transparencies.

For the student:

5. A student study guide that incorporates for each chapter *(a)* study suggestions, *(b)* a summary of important points with illustrations, *(c)* questions for self-evaluation, and *(d)* answers to the questions for self-paced study.
6. A comprehensive review practice set designed for use during the early part of the first semester. This practice set is included in the study guide (5 above); transaction narrative, forms, and selected key figures are provided with the practice set. The complete solution is given in the instructor's manual (1 above).
7. A complete set of working papers (forms with selected captions provided) for working each exercise and problem.
8. A list of key solution figures (provided upon request of the professor).

Chapters are arranged in a teachable and logical sequence and are grouped to facilitate both rearrangement and division of materials over semester or quarter intervals as follows:

Chapters by	
Semester	**Quarter**
1–12	1–8
13–24	9–16
	17–24

Chapter 1 presents an introductory overview of the foundations of accounting theory based upon the FASB's Conceptual Framework Project. It sets the stage for chapters that follow. Chapters 2 through 4 comprehensively review financial accounting fundamentals and extend the usual topical coverage of traditional introductory financial accounting courses. Present and future value concepts and some of their primary applications are introduced in Chapter 5.

Chapter 6 discusses cash, short-term investments, and accounts receivable. Chapters 7 through 9 discuss inventory. Chapter 10 discusses liabilities. Chapters 11 through 13 deal with operational assets. Corporations are discussed in Chapters 14 and 15. Stocks and bonds (both from issuers and investors' standpoints) are discussed in Chapters 16 and 17. Chapters 18, on pensions, and 19, on leases, provide coverage of two difficult liabilities with which accountants must deal. Chapter 20 is devoted to accounting changes and error corrections, and Chapter 21 combines financial statement analysis and interim and segment reporting. Chapter 22, Part A, is entirely new; it comprehensively treats the complex topics of revenue and expense recognition. Chapter 22, Part B, expands earlier coverage of earnings per share in response to requests from users of the fifth edition. The statement of changes in financial position is presented in Chapter 23. Chapter 24 concludes the book and deals with reporting under changing prices. Part A considers general inflation and Part B discusses current cost; it has been completely rewritten and reflects provisions of *FASB Statement 33.* Users of earlier editions will find that the exposition of complex topics has been enhanced through extensive rewriting and the use of specially designed exhibits throughout.

We are indebted to numerous colleagues and users whose comments and suggestions have led to the improvements reflected in this latest edition. We appreciate the permissions granted by the FASB, American Accounting Association, and American Institute of CPAs to quote from their pronouncements. The AICPA also permitted us to make liberal uses of materials adapted from the Uniform CPA Examinations. We are indebted to The Quaker Oats Company for permission to reproduce their annual report as an appendix to the text.

We are especially appreciative of the contributions of our colleagues and friends M. H. Granof, J. W. Deitrick, D. P. Newman, R. L. Kellogg, D. G. Short, P. A. Langefeld, K. D. Larson, and E. C. Nathan for their valuable suggestions as to content, arrangement, and assignment materials. We are particularly appreciative of the technical and editorial assistance throughout the revision process of Rebacca Gallun. We also express thanks to the following graduate students at The University of Texas at Austin: Petrea Sandlin, Carol H. McGinnis, Mary Anne Keely, Jennifer Phelps, Gary Dixon, Teresa Byrd, Paula Larson, Keith Shriver, Becky Phillip, Mary Jane Sloan, Tom Marsh, Richard Brown, Dave Hanusa, Ann Lynch, and Ron Applewhite.

We especially thank Linda Nelson for her dedication in typing, checking, and performing numerous other tasks that were essential to completion of this edition.

Suggestions and comments on this sixth edition are invited.

Glenn A. Welsch
Charles T. Zlatkovich
Walter T. Harrison, Jr.

Contents

1

Introduction and Theoretical Foundation

PURPOSE OF THE CHAPTER

The purpose of this chapter is to present an overview of accounting and the theoretical foundation underlying external financial accounting as it is currently practiced.

Financial accounting represents the branch of accounting which provides financial information primarily for decision makers outside the entity. This financial information is provided to decision makers via **general-purpose statements** of operating results (i.e., the income statement), financial position (i.e., the balance sheet), and changes in financial position (i.e., statement of changes in financial position [SCFP]), including notes to the financial statements. Consistent with the broad objective of reporting to external parties, this book concentrates on the application of accounting concepts, standards, principles, and procedures.

The authors presume you have completed a course in fundamentals of financial accounting.[1] Satisfactory completion of this textbook prepares you for advanced accounting courses. Emphasis throughout on concepts and principles—the "why" of accounting—enables you to cope with new and complex accounting problems on a conceptual rather than a procedural level.

This chapter is divided into two parts:

Part A—Overview of Accounting—presents a (1) definition of accounting, (2) brief summary of the objectives of external financial reporting by business enterprises, (3) description of professional accounting, and (4) description of the various institutional bodies with the most influence on the form and content of external financial reports.[2]

Part B—Theoretical Foundation of Financial Accounting—presents the theoretical foundation underlying external financial accounting. This part discusses (1) accounting theory, (2) users of accounting information, (3) objectives of financial reporting, (4) qualitative characteristics of accounting information, (5) elements of financial statements, (6) implementation assumptions of accounting, (7) implementation principles of accounting, and (8) constraints on implementation.

---

[1] Refer to books such as G. A. Welsch and R. N. Anthony, *Fundamentals of Financial Accounting,* 3d ed. (Homewood, Ill.: Richard D. Irwin, 1981).

[2] The subject matter of this textbook is directly concerned with accounting for the affairs of business enterprises, although many of the concepts apply to not-for-profit entities as well.

Part A: Overview of Accounting

ACCOUNTING DEFINED

Accounting can be defined broadly as an information processing system designed to **capture** and **measure** the economic essence of events that affect an entity and to **report** their economic effects on that entity to decision makers. This definition serves the two basic groups of decision makers—internal decision makers and external decision makers. These two groups require different kinds of information because of their different relationships with the entity.

Internal decision makers are the managers responsible for planning the future of the entity, implementing the plans, and controlling operations on a day-to-day basis. Because of their intimate relationship with the entity, they can command whatever financial data they may need at dates of their choice. Furthermore, much of the information at their disposal is not intended to be communicated to outsiders. The process of developing and reporting financial information to internal users usually is called **management accounting**, and the reports are referred to as internal management reports. Because of the confidential nature of internal management reports and their focus on internal decision making, there is no requirement (other than as specified by the management) that they conform to generally accepted accounting principles (GAAP).

In contrast, **external** users of financial information make distinctly different types of decisions regarding the entity, such as whether to invest or disinvest and whether to loan cash to it. Among the potential external users are owners, lenders, suppliers, potential investors and creditors, employees, customers, financial analysts and advisors, brokers, underwriters, stock exchanges, lawyers, economists, taxing and regulatory authorities, legislators, financial press and reporting agencies, labor unions, trade associations, business researchers, teachers and students, and the public.[3]

In view of the diverse range of external users of financial data, the accounting profession has developed **general-purpose financial statements** designed to meet their decision-making needs. These statements are developed in a phase of accounting known as **financial accounting.** Financial accounting may be broadly defined as an information processing and reporting function. Its purpose is to record transactions and other events affecting the entity and to report their economic impacts to external decision makers. External users, because of their detachment from the entity, cannot directly command specific financial information from the entity; therefore, they must rely on general-purpose financial statements. To meet their information needs, the accounting profession has developed a network of accounting concepts, standards, principles, and procedures designed to assure that external financial reports are **relevant** and **reliable.**[4]

OBJECTIVES OF EXTERNAL FINANCIAL REPORTING

Fundamentally, the **objective** of external financial statements is to communicate the economic effects of completed transactions and certain other events on the financial position and operations of the entity. Although there are other means of communicating financial information, such as a prospectus (for security offerings), news releases, and management "letters," the primary means are the periodic financial statements. The financial statements do not focus on specific groups of individuals. Rather they report financial information relevant primarily to (1) investment decisions (by investors) and (2) credit decisions (by creditors). To accomplish these two objectives, two general types of financial statements are used:

1. The financial position statement (balance sheet), which reports assets, liabilities, and owners' equity of an entity **at a particular time.**
2. Statements reporting **changes;** the principal change statements are:
   a. The income statement.
   b. The statement of changes in financial position (SCFP).

   Both statements relate to a **period of time.**

[3] Financial Accounting Standards Board, *Statement of Financial Accounting Concepts No. 1,* "Objectives of Financial Reporting by Business Enterprises" (Stamford, Conn., November 1978), p. 11.

[4] FASB, *Statement of Financial Accounting Concepts No. 2,* "Qualitative Characteristics of Accounting Information" (Stamford, Conn., May 1980), identifies **relevance** and **reliability** as the two primary qualitative characteristics that accounting information is designed to possess. These and other qualitative characteristics are discussed in Part B in greater detail.

FASB *Statement of Financial Accounting Concepts No. 1,* states:

> The objectives begin with a broad focus on information that is useful in investment and credit decisions; then narrow that focus to investors' and creditors' primary interest in the prospects of receiving cash from their investments in or loans to business enterprises and the relation of those prospects to the enterprise's prospects; and finally focus on information about an enterprise's economic resources, the claims to those resources, and changes in them, including measures of the enterprise's performance, that is useful in assessing the enterprise's cash flow prospects.[5]

PROFESSIONAL ACCOUNTING

Accounting has a long and interesting history dating back to about 3600 B.C. The first published work describing the double-entry system of accounting was authored by Luca Pacioli in 1494 in Venice. Pacioli's treatise described double-entry accounting in much the same way as it is used today. Since that time, the industrial revolutions in Europe and the United States, the emergence of the corporation as a major form of business entity, and many other factors have affected the practice of accounting. Today professional accountants fulfill an important and unique role in society. The professional accountant is usually a **certified public accountant (CPA).** As with lawyers, physicians, and engineers, accountants are engaged in a wide variety of endeavors. The primary endeavors are the following:

1. Public accounting—An independent CPA offers services including *(a)* auditing, (the attest function), *(b)* tax planning and determination of tax liability, and (c) management advisory (consulting) services. CPAs in public practice have a unique relationship with their clients; such CPAs are **independent** and impartial reviewers of the financial statements. Although **independent accountants** are paid by the client, the independence concept extends their responsibilities to third parties, such as the users of the financial statements.

The primary service rendered by the independent CPA is the attest function which is achieved as the result of an **audit** of the financial statements, including an auditor's report. The auditor's report *(a)* states the scope of the audit examination of the accounts and *(b)* expresses the auditor's professional "opinion" as to whether the financial statements are presented in accordance with generally accepted accounting principles (GAAP). The attest function is particularly important to external statement users because it is intended to protect them against outright misrepresentation and bias on the part of the reporting entity. The attest function lends credibility to the financial statements because of the auditor's independence from the client.

2. Industrial accounting—A large number of CPAs and certified management accountants (CMAs) work in businesses where they serve as accountants, internal auditors, tax specialists, systems experts, controllers, financial vice presidents, and chief executives. As employees, they are **not** in the role of **independent** CPAs.

3. Governmental and nonprofit accounting—CPAs serve at all levels of government and not-for-profit entities: local, state, national, and international. In these capacities, they are **not** in the role of **independent** certified public accountants.

Because of the importance of financial reports to users, there is widespread interest in accounting standards and the way they are established. In recent years, interest in the response of the accounting profession to its public responsibility has increased dramatically. For example, accounting standards for oil and gas companies have been viewed as potentially affecting the national energy policy of the United States because they affect the public's awareness of available reserves of petroleum. Financial information of the type provided by accountants is one of the bases of our economic system, for it helps to ensure an orderly flow of capital from investors and creditors to business enterprises. In such a setting, it is easy to understand why financial accounting standards are of major concern to users of financial statements, and, indeed, to the general public.

ACCOUNTING ORGANIZATIONS

The most influential accounting-related organizations in the United States are the Financial Accounting Standards Board (FASB), the American Institute of Certified Public Accountants (AICPA), the Securities and Exchange Commission (SEC), and the American Accounting Association (AAA).

[5] *FASB Concepts Statement 1,* p. 15.

Financial Accounting Standards Board (FASB)

The FASB is the organization which establishes the accounting standards that comprise "generally accepted accounting principles" (GAAP). The FASB is independent in the sense that it is not affiliated with, nor a part of, any other organization. It became operational on July 1, 1973, when it succeeded the Accounting Principles Board (APB) of the AICPA as the standard-setting body of accounting.

In the 1960s and early 1970s, many complaints arose with respect to the institutional arrangements by which accounting standards were established. These complaints criticized *(a)* lack of participation by organizations other than the AICPA, *(b)* "quality" of the APB *Opinions*, *(c)* failure to develop a "statement of the objectives and principles" underlying external financial reports, and *(d)* insufficient output. Consequently, a committee was appointed to study the issues and problems involved in setting accounting principles and to make recommendations for improving the process and to make it more responsive to the needs of those who rely on financial statements. The committee presented its report in March 1972. Basically, the report recommended, and the AICPA implemented, the following:

1. Financial Accounting Foundation—composed of nine trustees appointed by the Board of Directors of the AICPA. **Responsibilities:** to appoint members of the Financial Accounting Standards Board, to appoint a Financial Accounting Standards Advisory Council, to raise funds to support the new structure, and to periodically review and revise the basic structure.
2. Financial Accounting Standards Board (FASB)—composed of seven full-time members to establish standards of financial accounting and reporting. Four members would be CPAs drawn from public practice. The other three would not need to hold a CPA certificate but should possess extensive experience in the financial reporting field. **Responsibilities:** to establish financial accounting standards, and to direct the research program to support the standard-setting process.
3. Financial Accounting Standards Advisory Council—approximately 35 members. **Responsibilities:** to work closely with the FASB in an advisory capacity; and to establish priorities, establish task forces, and react to proposed standards.
4. Research activities—structured to accomplish specific objectives.[6]

The first official action of the FASB was to continue in force the then-existing body of GAAP, which consisted of (1) the *Accounting Research Bulletins (ARBs)* of the Committee on Accounting Procedure and (2) the *Opinions* of the Accounting Principles Board (APB). Prior to that time the Committee on Accounting Procedure (CAP) and then the APB had been official subentities of the AICPA. To date, the FASB has issued categories of pronouncements designated as:

1. *Statements of Financial Accounting Concepts*—The purpose of this series is to set forth fundamental concepts on which financial accounting and reporting standards will be based.
2. *Statements of Financial Accounting Standards*—The FASB calls its major pronouncements *Statements of Standards* rather than *Opinions*, which was used by the APB. These statements specify accounting principles and procedures on specific accounting issues.
3. *Interpretations*—These interpret *ARBs, APB Opinions,* and *FASB Statements of Financial Accounting Standards.*
4. *Technical Bulletins*—These are prepared by the FASB staff to provide guidance on specific accounting and reporting problems on a timely basis.

Prior to issuing a *Statement,* the FASB usually (1) prepares and distributes a *Discussion Memorandum* which provides an exhaustive analysis of the issues under consideration, (2) holds a public hearing on the issues, and (3) distributes an exposure draft of the proposed statement. This process is designed to elicit wide participation and consideration of all relevant aspects of the accounting issue being considered. After this process is completed, the FASB decides *(a)* whether to issue a statement, and *(b)* if so, the prescribed standards of financial accounting and reporting on the issue. Currently, most meetings of the FASB are open to the public.

Supplement 1–B at the end of this chapter lists the *ARBs,* the *APB Opinions,* and the *FASB Statements* issued to date.

---

[6] *Establishing Financial Accounting Standards, Report of the Study on Establishment of Accounting Principles, American Institute of Certified Public Accountants,* March 1972, p. 105 (chair of the Committee, Francis M. Wheat).

American Institute of Certified Public Accountants (AICPA)

The AICPA is the national professional organization of certified public accountants (CPAs). It is responsive primarily to the needs of CPAs in public practice. Consequently, its efforts and publications focus on the practice of public accounting. Its publications include, but are not limited to, the following:

1. *Journal of Accountancy*—a monthly magazine containing pronouncements, articles, and special sections of interest to independent CPAs.
2. *Accountants' Index*—an annual classified bibliography of the accounting literature published during the year.
3. *Accounting Trends & Techniques*—an annual publication containing a survey of the characteristics of the annual financial reports of 600 corporations.
4. *Accounting Research Studies*—a series of studies that focus on specific accounting problems. These studies provide background information, discussion of alternative solutions, and often recommendations.
5. *Statements on Auditing Standards*—These periodically issued statements relate to specific auditing standards to be followed by independent CPAs.
6. Statements that dealt with specific accounting principles, standards, and procedures:
   a. *Accounting Research Bulletins (ARBs)*—During the period 1938 through 1959, the AICPA's Committee on Accounting Procedure was responsible for "narrowing the areas of differences and inconsistencies" in accounting practice. To this end, the Committee issued 51 *Accounting Research Bulletins* and 4 *Accounting Terminology Bulletins* which continue to be a part of GAAP.
   b. *Opinions of the Accounting Principles Board (APB)*—In 1959, the AICPA established the Accounting Principles Board (APB) to replace its Committee on Accounting Procedure (CAP). The APB designated its pronouncements as *Opinions*. During its existence from 1959 to 1973, the APB issued 31 *Opinions* and 4 *Statements*. In contrast to the *Opinions*, the *Statements* presented recommendations, rather than requirements, for improvement in financial accounting and reporting to external decision makers.[7]

Securities and Exchange Commission (SEC)

A number of government regulatory agencies influence accounting and reporting by businesses. Among these agencies are the Internal Revenue Service, Federal Power Commission, Interstate Commerce Commission, and Securities and Exchange Commission. The SEC exerts a powerful influence on the development of accounting standards.

Because of conditions in the securities market at the beginning of the depression of the 1930s, Congress passed the Securities Act of 1933, the Securities Exchange Act of 1934, and the Public Utility Holding Company Act of 1935. The 1934 Act created the Securities and Exchange Commission and gave it broad authority to regulate virtually all aspects of the issuance and sale of securities in interstate commerce. Congress gave the Commission authority to prescribe external financial reporting requirements for companies under its jurisdiction. To obtain permission to sell an issue of securities (interstate), a company must submit to the SEC a **prospectus,** which becomes a public record. The prospectus, which is prepared only for a new security issuance, reports extensive information about the company, its officers, securities, and financial affairs. The financial portion of the prospectus must be audited by an independent CPA. After receiving permission to sell securities, the company must file with the SEC, as a matter of public record, audited financial statements **each subsequent year** (10-K reports) and unaudited quarterly statements (10-Q reports). In most material respects, the annual 10-K reporting requirements are satisfied by the "published financial statements."

The SEC filing and reporting requirements are published as:

1. *Regulation S-X*—This is the original document issued by the Commission, as amended and supplemented, which prescribes the reporting requirements and forms to be filed with the SEC.
2. *Accounting Series Releases (ASRs)*—These releases are amendments, extensions, and additions to *Regulation S-X*.
3. Special *SEC Releases*.

[7] The contents of these *Bulletins, Opinions,* and *Statements* are listed in Supplement 1–B to this chapter.

4. *Staff Accounting Bulletins (SABs)*—These serve as interpretations of *Regulation S-X* and the *Accounting Series Releases (ASRs).*

Although the SEC has wide statutory authority to prescribe financial accounting and external reporting requirements for "registered" companies, the Commission generally has relied on the accounting profession to set and enforce accounting standards and to regulate the profession. The working relationship between the SEC and the accounting profession has been a positive one, and accounting regulation has remained largely in the private sector. However, on numerous occasions the SEC has forced the accounting profession to move forward in tackling critical problems. These situations generally have been in areas where the SEC concluded that the public interest was not being fully served on a timely basis. In a few instances, the SEC has imposed certain accounting and reporting practices without waiting for the profession to act, such as requiring companies to disclose certain replacement cost data (Chapter 24).

American Accounting Association (AAA)

The AAA is an organization dominated by accounting educators; however, its membership also is open to practicing, industrial, and governmental accountants. Its broad objectives are to develop accounting theory, encourage and sponsor accounting research, and improve education in accounting. The statements of the AAA do not necessarily express GAAP. The Association operates primarily through committees and publishes monographs, committee reports, and a quarterly periodical, *The Accounting Review.* This periodical contains articles and sections on a wide range of subjects largely oriented toward research and accounting education.

Since 1936, the AAA, through its committees, has issued a series of statements on accounting theory. Starting in June 1936 with *A Tentative Statement of Accounting Principles Underlying Corporate Financial Statements,* the Association has maintained an active research program on accounting theory. The 1936 statement was revised and supplemented three times; the latest revision was called *Accounting and Reporting Standards for Corporate Financial Statements, 1957 Revision.* Another statement, prepared by a special AAA committee and published in 1966, was entitled *A Statement of Basic Accounting Theory.* Like prior AAA statements, it dealt primarily with accounting theory, as opposed to accounting practice and procedures. The latest publication in this series is *Statement on Accounting Theory and Theory Acceptance,* developed by the Committee on Concepts and Standards for External Financial Reports of the AAA in 1977.

The statements relating to accounting theory and principles issued by the AAA tend to be **normative** rather than descriptive. That is, they tend to express what accounting **should be,** rather than what it is currently.

Other organizations that have contributed to the standard-setting process are the National Association of Accountants and the Financial Executives Institute.

ESTABLISHMENT OF ACCOUNTING STANDARDS

Until 1964, the accounting profession, through the AICPA, followed a policy of persuasion. The pronouncements of the Committee on Accounting Procedure and the Accounting Principles Board were viewed as **recommendations** of GAAP. They were not binding on the profession; there was no strict requirement for adherence.

Their force depended upon their general acceptance by the accounting profession. Acceptance was encouraged by persuasion, that is, by convincing independent CPAs that these recommendations represented the preferred solution to given accounting problems. By 1964, many leaders of the profession were convinced that persuasion alone was insufficient to reduce the wide range of differences and inconsistencies in accounting and reporting to external decision makers. In numerous instances, identical transactions could be accounted for by any of several different methods. Net income could be doctored by selecting a particular accounting approach from among several which were all deemed "generally accepted."

Consequently, a milestone in the development of accounting practice occurred in October 1964, when the Council (i.e., the governing body) of the AICPA adopted a requirement which was incorporated into the rules of ethics for CPAs as follows:

Rule 203—Accounting principles. A member shall not express an opinion that financial statements are presented in conformity with generally accepted accounting principles if such statements contain any departure from an accounting principle [*] promulgated by the body designated by Council to establish such principles which has a material effect on the statements taken as a whole, unless the member can demonstrate that due to unusual circumstances the financial statements would otherwise have been misleading. In such cases his report must describe the departure, the approximate effects thereof, if practicable, and the reasons why compliance with the principle would result in a misleading statement.

* This requirement includes the *FASB Statements of Financial Accounting Standards* and those *Accounting Research Bulletins (ARBs)* and *APB Opinions* which have not been superseded by action of the FASB.

During 1976 and 1977, a new and powerful force, the Congress, entered the standard-setting arena. As part of a broad look at the professions, the U.S. Senate and House of Representatives had separate subcommittees studying the accounting profession. In December 1976, a Senate subcommittee released the results of a staff study entitled "The Accounting Establishment." Many professional accountants interpreted the staff study as a step toward government control of accounting standard setting and of the accounting profession. However, the subcommittee report, which followed, stated "that the subcommittee members preferred that the profession itself achieve reforms in cooperation with the SEC."

Therefore, standard setting in accounting resides with the FASB in the private sector, but it is influenced by the SEC, a public sector body. Consistent with the free-market tradition of the United States, interested parties are free to influence the outcome of FASB deliberations on the form and content of accounting standards. Among the more prominent of these are (1) corporation managers who care about the effects of standards on the financial statements of the corporations they manage, (2) practicing CPAs who care about the economic consequences of standards for their clients, and (3) various government agencies which are supposed to protect the public interest. Balancing these myriad influences is a difficult task for the FASB.

Given the diversity of these interests, it is not surprising that financial reporting is very complex. Apparently, this complexity is believed by bodies such as the FASB and the SEC to be accompanied by increases in benefits for users of the information, and, indeed, for society as a whole, over simpler reporting modes.[8] The overall benefit of adequate financial reporting can be summarized as an efficient allocation of resources in the economy, in which the more successful companies are better able to raise capital to finance their operations than are the less successful companies. An orderly flow of information is required for capital allocation to be efficient. It appears from the FASB focus on reasonably sophisticated investors that the FASB links such benefits to greater complexity in financial reporting.

The FASB is aware that these benefits are obtained at a cost and that the benefits of financial reporting should exceed the costs. The **private** costs of information gathering, processing, and reporting by corporations and of information analysis by users are identifiable and usually measurable. On the other hand, identification of the **social** costs of accounting standards, such as potentially adverse effects on national fiscal or energy policies, pose difficult problems for standard-setting bodies such as the FASB.[9]

In addition, accounting standards may **provide benefits** to some users of external financial statements (e.g., the Federal Trade Commission, by giving them information about the company revenues by product line) and **impose costs** on other parties (e.g., the **corporation,** by reducing its competitive advantage as a result of reporting revenues by product

[8] However, the existence of **private** benefits from using information does not necessarily imply that the **public** also benefits from the information. In fact, no concept of **social** (i.e., public) benefit has received general acceptance. For a discussion of differences between the private and social benefits of information, see J. Hirshleifer, "The Private and Social Value of Information and the Reward to Inventive Activity," *American Economic Review,* September 1971, pp. 561–74.

[9] For example, part of the debate during 1977–79 over whether the FASB should require all oil and gas companies to use the same method of accounting for exploration costs focused on the resultant decrease in the reported incomes of the small oil and gas companies which had been using a different method. These companies argued that lower reported income would make it more difficult for them to raise the capital needed to finance risky exploration ventures and thus would adversely affect their competitive positions in the oil industry. The alleged effect on national energy policy comes from the belief of many that these smaller companies find a disproportionately large amount of new oil and gas reserves. Thus, the argument went, constriction of the flow of venture capital to these small companies would hinder the attempt of the United States to eliminate dependence on foreign oil.

line). In effect, one aspect of the cost-benefit tradeoff in accounting theory formulation is the potential effects of accounting standards on the distribution of wealth in society. Increasingly, these types of factors are being given more consideration in the establishment of accounting standards.[10]

[10] See *FASB Concepts Statement 2,* pp. 54–58, for a discussion of costs and benefits of financial accounting standards.

Part B: Theoretical Foundation of Financial Accounting

The purpose of this part of the chapter is to present the theoretical foundation underlying external financial accounting and reporting as it is practiced currently. This part should be studied carefully; however, it is unrealistic to expect complete understanding and knowledge of the foundation at this point. This chapter is a reference for study throughout the remaining chapters. As the various concepts, principles, and procedures are discussed in subsequent chapters, you may need to return to this chapter to review the relevant parts.

ACCOUNTING THEORY

A definition of **theory,** appropriate for accounting, is a "coherent set of hypothetical, conceptual, and pragmatic principles forming the general frame of reference for a field of inquiry."[11] Accounting is human-made; it is changed in response to the evolving social and economic environment within which the accounting process is applied. Thus, accounting theory is in a continuous process of evolution. The organizations discussed in Part A of this chapter have been influential in its evolution.

Accounting theory is based upon both inductive and deductive reasoning, economic theory, experience, pragmatism, and general acceptability. Because accounting theory is human-made, it cannot be derived from, or proven by, the laws of nature as can be done in mathematics and the natural sciences.

The FASB is engaged in a broad-based project to formulate a conceptual (i.e., theoretical) framework for financial accounting. To date, the FASB Conceptual Framework consists of concepts statements on:

[11] *Webster's Third New International Dictionary, Unabridged* (Springfield, Mass.: G. C. Merriam, 1961), p. 2371.

1. **The objectives of financial reporting by business enterprises.** A theory needs an objective to provide focus and direction. Otherwise, it would not be clear what purpose accounting information is intended to serve. FASB, *Statement of Financial Accounting Concepts No. 1,* "Objective of Financial Reporting by Business Enterprises," November 1978, is intended to provide this focus. In this textbook, this statement is referred to as *FASB Concepts Statement 1.*
2. **The qualitative characteristics of accounting information.** Accounting information is intended to be useful, and certain characteristics enhance its usefulness. FASB, *Statement of Financial Accounting Concepts No. 2,* "Qualitative Characteristics of Accounting Information," May 1980, presents a hierarchy of qualitative characteristics which are intended to enhance the usefulness of accounting information. In this textbook, this statement is referred to as *FASB Concepts Statement 2.*
3. **The elements of financial statements of business enterprises.** The building blocks of financial statements represent certain enterprise resources (i.e., assets), claims to those resources (i.e., liabilities and owners' equities), and the effects of transactions, events, and circumstances that cause changes in those resources and claims (i.e., revenues, expenses, gains, losses, and other financing and investing activities).

   FASB, *Statement of Financial Accounting Concepts No. 3,* "Elements of Financial Statements of Business Enterprises," December 1980, defines the elements related to measuring the financial position and performance of an enterprise. In this textbook, this statement is referred to as *FASB Concepts Statement 3.*

The three concepts statements listed above are discussed in the remainder of this chapter. Questions involving the recognition, measurement, and display of accounting information will be addressed by the FASB in future phases of the Conceptual Framework Project. The Conceptual Framework Project repre-

EXHIBIT 1–1: Structure of Financial Accounting Theory

Query	Structure	Elaboration
Who?	I. Users of accounting information.	Identification and characteristics of decision makers who use accounting information.
Why?	II. Objectives of financial reporting.	Objective: To provide accounting information useful for projecting cash flows of an enterprise.
	III. Accounting information.	Economic information about a specific business enterprise.
What?	A. Qualitative characteristics (see Exhibit 1–2).	Characteristics of accounting information that make it useful to decision makers (users).
How?	B. Implementation.	Application of the above concepts in the accounting process.
	1. Elements of financial statements. 2. Assumptions. 3. Principles. 4. Constraints. 5. Financial statements required.	Building blocks and guidelines with which financial statements are constructed; the elements and conventions needed to measure the performance of an enterprise.

sents a milestone in theory development by a professional organization because, heretofore, the serious attempts at theory development in accounting have been made by academic rather than professional groups.

Exhibit 1–1 outlines the basic components of the structure of accounting theory. The exhibit begins with the **users** of accounting information and proceeds to the **objectives** of financial reporting and concludes with **accounting information.**

USERS OF ACCOUNTING INFORMATION

A wide diversity of external decision makers use accounting information. At one end of the spectrum is the casual investor who seldom looks at the pictures in the annual financial report and never analyzes the financial statements. At the opposite extreme is the chartered financial analyst (CFA), who, like a CPA, has demonstrated competence in a professional discipline. Because of this diversity, accounting information cannot realistically be directed at users at either extreme, nor can it be directed at any **one** group between the extremes. Rather, the FASB establishes accounting standards to meet the information needs of the large group of external users who "lack the authority to prescribe the information they want and must rely on information management communicates to them," and who "have a reasonable understanding of business and economic activities and are willing to study the information with reasonable diligence." The FASB identifies these users as "investors and creditors" . . . and "also those who advise or represent them."[12] Thus, by selecting these two groups of users as the starting point for the objectives of financial reporting, the FASB defined their conception of the "average prudent investor" to be a reasonably sophisticated decision maker.

OBJECTIVES OF FINANCIAL REPORTING

FASB Concepts Statement 1 sets forth the objectives of financial reporting by business enterprises. The objectives, which are highlighted below, focus on the decision makers (financial statement users) identified in the immediately preceding paragraphs. The objectives state that financial reporting should provide information—

1. That is useful to present and potential investors and creditors and other users in making rational investment, credit, and similar decisions. The information should be comprehensible to those who have a reasonable understanding of business and economic activities and are willing to study the information with reasonable diligence.
2. To help present and potential investors and creditors and other users in assessing the amounts, timing, and uncertainty of prospective cash receipts from dividends or interest and the proceeds from the sale, redemption, or maturity of

[12] *FASB Concepts Statement 1,* pp. vii–ix.

securities or loans. Since investors' and creditors' cash flows are related to enterprise cash flows, financial reporting should provide information to help investors, creditors, and others assess the amounts, timing, and uncertainty of **prospective net cash flows** of the related enterprise.

3. About the economic resources of an enterprise, the claims to those resources (obligations of the enterprise to transfer resources to other entities and owners' equity), and the effects of transactions, events, and circumstances that change its resources and claims to those resources.

In summary, *FASB Concepts Statement 1* assumes an investment decision model which investors and creditors can use to predict the future net cash receipts they can expect from an investment in or loan to a particular business enterprise. (It may be useful for you to think in terms of a discounted cash flow analysis in which the investor or creditor will pay for an investment a price which is equal to the present value of the future net cash receipts expected from the investment or loan.) To project the net cash flows, investors usually need information about (1) the timing and amounts of expected net cash flows of the enterprise and (2) the risk that the business may not actually realize these cash flows.

Accounting earnings[13] of the enterprise are believed by the FASB to be a better predictor of future net cash flows of the enterprise than are cash receipt and cash payment data. Finally, the objectives of financial reporting, as set forth in *FASB Concepts Statement 1,* do not require accounting information to measure directly the value of the business enterprise. That is, balance sheets are not intended to reflect enterprise market value. However, investors may be able to use their own cash flow predictions to **estimate** the market value of the enterprise or the market value of a share of its stock. This value estimation is the role of investment analysis, not accounting. The role of accounting is to provide information useful for the analysis.

[13] The term **earnings** is used but is not defined in *FASB Concepts Statements 1, 2,* or *3.* Footnote 1 of FASB, *Statement of Financial Accounting Concepts No. 3,* "Elements of Financial Statements of Business Enterprises" (Stamford, Conn., December 1980), indicates that **earnings** is not defined in this statement but is reserved for possible use to designate "a component part, as yet undetermined, of comprehensive income." The definition of **comprehensive income** is broader than what is known traditionally as "net income." The definition of **comprehensive income** is given below in the discussion of Elements of Financial Statements.

ACCOUNTING INFORMATION

Decision makers **use** accounting information in the process of trying to attain their investment objectives. Therefore, accounting information must be **useful,** and to be useful such information must possess certain qualities. The following discussion of **accounting information** starts with the **qualitative characteristics** of accounting information. The next level discussed is implementation, which involves the *(a)* **elements of financial statements,** *(b)* implementation **assumptions,** *(c)* implementation **principles,** *(d)* implementation **constraints,** and *(e)* the required **financial statements** of accounting. Exhibit 1–1 outlines this structure.

Qualitative Characteristics of Accounting Information

FASB Concepts Statement 2 identifies those qualities of accounting information which are believed to make the information useful for decision making by statement users. Consistent with the specified objectives of financial reporting, the FASB has developed a hierarchy of the **qualitative characteristics** of accounting information. An adaptation of that hierarchy is presented in Exhibit 1–2.

Two additional terms used in defining the qualitative characteristics are bias and error, which are defined as follows:

1. **Bias** is used in the definitions of reliability, verifiability, and neutrality. Bias in measurement is the tendency of a measure to fall more often on one side than the other of what it represents instead of being equally likely to fall on either side. Bias in accounting measures means a tendency to be consistently too high or too low.

2. **Error** is used in the definitions of reliability and verifiability. Error in accounting usually is defined as deviation from truth or accuracy, as in a mistake, either intentional or unintentional. Another kind of error of concern to decision makers is called statistical measurement error, which is a difference between estimated and actual values.[14]

[14] The definitions of the terms given in Exhibit 1–2 and bias are quoted from *FASB Concepts Statement 2,* Summary of Principal Conclusions. The concepts statement does not define **error** but uses the term in the definitions of two qualitative characteristics; therefore, the above definition of **error** was adapted from *Webster's Third New International Dictionary, Unabridged* (Springfield, Mass.: G. C. Merriam, 1961), p. 772.

EXHIBIT 1–2: A Hierarchy of Qualitative Characteristics of Accounting Information (see Exhibit 1–1, III A)

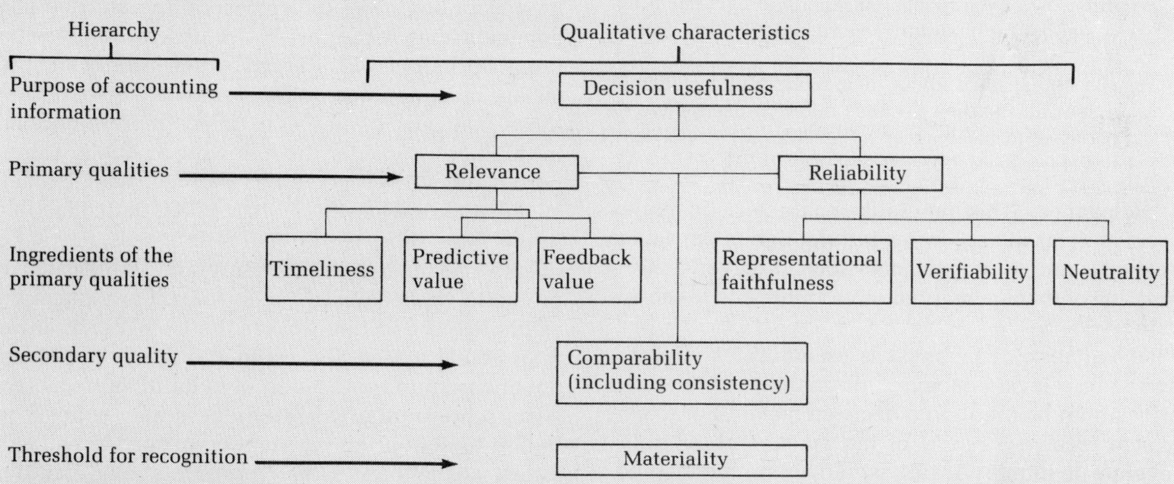

FASB summary definitions:

Relevance: The capacity of information to make a difference in a decision by helping users to form predictions about the outcomes of past, present, and future events (i.e., has predictive value) or to confirm or correct prior expectations (i.e., has feedback value).

Timeliness: Having information available to a decision maker before it loses its capacity to influence decisions.

Predictive value: The quality of information that helps users to increase the likelihood of correctly forecasting the outcome of past or present events.

Feedback value: The quality of information that enables users to confirm or correct prior expectations.

Reliability: The quality of information that assures that information is reasonably free from error and bias and faithfully represents what it purports to represent.

Representational faithfulness: Correspondence or agreement between a measure or description and the phenomenon that it purports to represent (sometimes called validity).

Verifiability: The ability through consensus among measurers to ensure that information represents what it purports to represent or that the chosen method of measurement has been used without error or bias.

Neutrality: Absence in reported information of bias which would be intended to attain a predetermined result or to induce a particular mode of behavior.

Comparability: The quality of information that enables users to identify similarities in and differences between two sets of economic phenomena.

Consistency: Conformity from period to period with unchanging policies and procedures.

Materiality: Defined in subsequent section under caption, Implementation Constraints.

Source: Adapted from FASB *Statement of Financial Accounting Concepts No. 2,* "Qualitative Characteristics of Accounting Information" (Stamford, Conn., May 1980), p. 15.

FASB Concepts Statement 2 identifies **relevance** and **reliability** as the two primary qualities that make accounting information useful for decision making. Ideally, an increase in the reliability of accounting information would be accompanied by an increase in the relevance of the information. Unfortunately, this often is not the case, and many accounting choices involve sacrifices of relevance to gain reliability, or vice versa. For example, in respect to the difficulty of making such trade-off decisions the FASB states:

> In a particular situation, the importance attached to relevance in relation to . . . other . . . qualities of accounting information (for example reliability) will

be different for different information users, and their willingness to trade one quality for another will also differ. . . . Even though considerable agreement exists about the qualitative characteristics that "good" accounting information should have, no consensus can be expected about their relative importance in a specific situation because different users have or perceive themselves to have different needs and, therefore, have different preferences.[15]

Relevance. This qualitative characteristic relates specific items of accounting information to particular business and economic decisions. Relevance is a function of **timeliness, predictive value,** and **feedback value.**

Timeliness. Timeliness is essential for information to be relevant because information obtained too late cannot be useful to a decision maker. For example, to receive a report of the amount of 19J sales revenue on January 1, 19K, would not be **timely** (and, therefore, not relevant) for predicting sales revenue for 19J. However, the 19J information usually would be timely (and relevant) for predicting sales revenue for 19K.

Predictive Value. Users of accounting information are assumed (in *FASB Concepts Statement 1*) to be interested in predicting the cash flows and assessing the risks associated with a particular business enterprise. Therefore, to be relevant to a decision about whether to buy, hold, or sell an investment in the capital stock of a corporation, accounting information must have **predictive value.** That is, the information should aid investors and creditors in predicting net cash flows of a corporation and measuring the risk associated with the corporation's activities. Predictions of net cash flows of the enterprise can perhaps be used in predicting the cash flows to investors through dividends and changes in the market value of their stock investment. Predictions of most types are based largely on historical data.

Feedback Value. The soundness of past decisions affects future predictions. Feedback is the process of reporting information about the outcomes of past decisions to aid a decision maker in making decisions about the future. Therefore, to be useful, accounting information must have **feedback value** because it enhances predictive value.

Reliability. The **reliability** of accounting information is a function of its **representational faithfulness, verifiability,** and **neutrality.**

Representational Faithfulness. **Representational faithfulness** in accounting means agreement between an accounting measure or description and the phenomenon that it purports to represent. Representational faithfulness is affected by uncertainty and precision, bias, and completeness. To understand how these concepts combine to affect representational faithfulness, consider the following example. The reported amount of receivables may represent amounts as collectible when they are, in fact, **not** collectible. In this case, representational faithfulness may suffer due to the inherent **uncertainty and imprecision** of predicting collection of receivables. For example, if estimates of bad debt losses are consistently lower than actual losses, the estimated losses are **biased** downward and representational faithfulness suffers. Also, representational faithfulness may suffer from failure to obtain the information needed to estimate future collections. Thus, representational faithfulness also rests on the **completeness** (or adequacy) of underlying information.

Verifiability. **Verifiability** contributes to usefulness of accounting information because verification provides a degree of assurance that the reported accounting information represents what it purports to represent. Therefore, it is essential that accounting information be verifiable. Verification implies consensus, which is obtained through repeated examinations of an item, such as the credit balance of Allowance for Doubtful Accounts. To illustrate verification by consensus, assume the amounts in this account are recorded in the accounting process, subsequently reviewed by the assistant controller and the controller of the company, and finally, audited by independent outside auditors. Thus, there is a **consensus** that the ending balance in the allowance account represents what it purports to represent.

Neutrality. **Neutrality** means the absence of bias in either direction. In implementing prescribed accounting standards, the primary concern should be the relevance and reliability of the accounting information rather than the effect the information may have on the decisions of a particular individual or group.

Comparability (including consistency). *FASB Concepts Statement 2* summarizes this concept as follows:

Information about a particular enterprise gains greatly in usefulness if it can be compared with similar information about other enterprises and with sim-

[15] *FASB Concepts Statement 2*, par. 45.

> ilar information about the same enterprise for some other period or some other point in time. Comparability between enterprises and consistency in the application of methods over time increases the informational value of comparisons of relative economic opportunities or performance.[16]

Comparisons of accounting information are useful for detecting and explaining similarities and differences among business enterprises. One means of achieving **comparability** would be to require all companies to use identical accounting methods and to report the information in exactly the same format. The FASB has stated that such inflexible standardization may disguise real differences or report false differences among companies. For example, a requirement that all companies use straight-line depreciation may not reveal real differences among companies in the patterns of use of their operational (i.e., fixed) assets.

Consistency is included in comparability because it means conformity from period to period in the application of accounting policies and procedures. Consistency enhances the usefulness of accounting information. However, consistency can be pushed so far that it impedes comparability. To illustrate the potential conflict between consistency and comparability, consider a series of FIFO inventory costs over a 10-year period during which prices increased by 200 percent. If the costs are not restated into dollars of equivalent purchasing power, they would not be comparable over time even though they would reflect consistent application of an accounting method. Comparability is specified by the FASB as a more important qualitative characteristic than consistency; consequently, comparability takes precedence when the two concepts are in conflict. When no conflict exists, consistency enhances comparability.

IMPLEMENTATION

The prior discussion of theoretical foundations began with the users of accounting information and proceeded to the objectives of financial reporting and the qualitative characteristics of accounting information (refer to Exhibit 1–1). Those discussions considered the "who" (i.e., users), the "why" (i.e., objectives), and the "what" (i.e., qualitative characteristics) of accounting. This section on implementation discusses the "how" of accounting; that is, how the qualitative characteristics are **implemented** in terms of the *(a)* elements of accounting information, *(b)* assumptions, *(c)* principles, and *(d)* constraints. This section concludes with a brief description of the required financial statements.

[16] Ibid., Summary of Principal Conclusions.

Elements of Financial Statements

The primary medium used to communicate accounting information about a business enterprise is its periodic financial statements. The building blocks with which financial statements are constructed are called **elements.** *FASB Concepts Statement 3* defines 10 elements. Exhibit 1–3 presents the definitions. The first four elements (revenues, expenses, gains, and losses) relate directly to the income statement; and the next three elements (assets, liabilities, and equity) relate directly to the balance sheet. Thus, the above seven elements are particularly relevant because they provide, for the first time, **authoritative definitions** of the major classifications used on traditional financial statements.

The next two elements (investments by owners and distributions to owners) are related to the balance sheet, although they encompass a **period of time** (as does the income statement and statement of changes in financial position [SCFP]). In contrast, the last element listed in Exhibit 1–3, **comprehensive income,** is unique because *(a)* it does not appear on traditional income statements and *(b)* it holds the potential of extending the concept of income far beyond what currently is reported on traditional income statements.

FASB Concepts Statement 3, paragraph 4, states that "other phases of the conceptual framework project may define additional elements of financial statements as needed." To relate the definitions of the 10 elements to other phases of financial measurement and reporting, the FASB states (par. 16):

> All matters of recognition, measurement, and display have purposely been separated from the definitions of the elements of financial statements in the Board's conceptual framework project. The definitions in this Statement are concerned with the essential characteristics of elements of financial statements. Other phases of the conceptual framework project are concerned with questions such as which financial statements should be provided; which items that qualify under the definitions should be included in those statements; when particular items that qualify as assets, liabilities, revenues, expenses, and so forth

should be formally recognized in the financial statements; which attributes of those items should be measured; which unit of measure should be used; and how the information included should be classified and otherwise displayed.

Implementation Assumptions

Accounting information describes a business enterprise in terms of its **elements** (defined above). The financial statements represent an economic **model** of the business. The purpose of the accounting model is to capture the economic essence of an enterprise in a simplified description. Therefore, the theory of accounting is largely descriptive. As with any descriptive theory, the structure of accounting theory includes assumptions which set certain limits on the way accounting information is presented. Four explicit assumptions used in accounting are the (1) separate entity assumption, (2) continuity assumption, (3) unit-of-measure assumption, and (4) time period assumption. Each assumption is discussed below.

Separate Entity Assumption. Accounting is concerned with specific and separate entities. Thus, each enterprise is considered as an **accounting unit** separate and apart from its owners and from other entities. A corporation and its shareholders are separate entities for accounting purposes. Also, partnerships and sole proprietorships are treated as separate and apart from their owners despite the fact that this distinction is not made in the legal sense.

Under the separate entity assumption, all records and reports are developed from the viewpoint of the particular entity. This provides a basis for clear-cut distinction in analyzing transactions between the enterprise and its owners. For example, the personal residence of an individual owning an unincorporated

EXHIBIT 1–3: Elements of Financial Statements of Business Enterprises (basic definitions)

Income statement (discussed in Chapter 3):

1. **Revenues** are inflows or other enhancements of assets of an entity or settlements of its liabilities (or a combination of both) during a period from delivering or producing goods, rendering services, or other activities that constitute the entity's ongoing major or central operations.
2. **Expenses** are outflows or other using up of assets or incurrences of liabilities (or a combination of both) during a period from delivering or producing goods, rendering services, or carrying out other activities that constitute the entity's ongoing major or central operations.
3. **Gains** are increases in equity (net assets) from peripheral or incidental transactions of an entity and from all other transactions and other events and circumstances affecting the entity during a period except those that result from revenues or investments by owners.
4. **Losses** are decreases in equity (net assets) from peripheral or incidental transactions of an entity and from all other transactions and other events and circumstances affecting the entity during a period except those that result from expenses or distributions to owners.

Balance Sheet (discussed in Chapter 4):

5. **Assets** are probable future economic benefits obtained or controlled by a particular entity as a result of past transactions or events.
6. **Liabilities** are probable future sacrifices of economic benefits arising from present obligations of a particular entity to transfer assets or provide services to other entities in the future as a result of past transactions or events.
7. **Equity** [i.e., owners' equity] is the residual interest in the assets of an entity that remains after deducting its liabilities. In a business enterprise, the equity is the ownership interest.

Other:

8. **Investments by owners** are increases in net assets of a particular enterprise resulting from transfers to it from other entities of something of value to obtain or increase ownership interests (or equity) in it. Assets are most commonly received as investments by owners, but that which is received may also include services or satisfaction or conversion of liabilities of the enterprise. [Discussed in Chapter 14.]
9. **Distributions to owners** are decreases in net assets of a particular enterprise resulting from transfering assets, rendering services, or incurring liabilities by the enterprise to owners. Distributions to owners decrease ownership interests (or equity) in an enterprise. [Discussed in Chapter 15.]
10. **Comprehensive income** is the change in equity (net assets) of an entity during a period from transactions and other events and circumstances from nonowner sources. It includes all changes in equity during a period except those resulting from investments by owners and distributions to owners. [Discussed in Chapter 24.]

Source: FASB, *Statement of Financial Accounting Concepts No. 3,* "Elements of Financial Statements of Business Enterprises," (Stamford, Conn., December 1980), pp. xi and xii.

business is not considered an asset for the business to report, although the residence and the business have a common owner. In this example, although the owner and the business are separate accounting entities, creditors may look to both the personal residence and the business assets for satisfaction of claims against the business.

Continuity Assumption. The continuity assumption frequently is referred to as the "going-concern" assumption. It assumes the business is not expected to liquidate in the foreseeable future. The assumption does not imply that accountancy assumes permanent continuance; rather there is a presumption of continuity for a period of time **sufficient to carry out contemplated operations, contracts, and commitments.** This concept establishes the rationale of accounting on a **nonliquidation basis;** it provides the theoretical foundation for many of the classifications common in accounting. For example, the classification of assets and liabilities as current or long-term relies upon this assumption. If continuity were not assumed, all assets and liabilities would become current, and the current/long-term distinction would lose its significance.

If the particular entity should face probable liquidation, conventional accounting based on the continuity assumption would not be appropriate for reporting the enterprise's elements. Such cases call for **liquidation** accounting, wherein all elements are accounted for at estimated net realizable amounts.

Unit-of-Measure Assumption. The unit-of-measure assumption asserts that accounting will measure and report the results of the economic activities of the entity in terms of money. It recognizes, as does society generally, that the monetary unit is the most effective means of communicating financial information. Thus, money is the common denominator—the meterstick—used in the accounting process.

Unfortunately, use of a monetary unit for measurement purposes poses a problem for accounting. Unlike the meterstick, which is always 1 meter long, the monetary unit (i.e., the dollar) changes in real value or purchasing power. Consequently, during inflation or deflation, dollars of different size (i.e., of different real value) are entered in the accounts and intermingled as if they were of equal purchasing power. Because of the practice of ignoring changes in the purchasing power of the dollar, accounting is said to assume a stable monetary unit. However, in view of the recent high rates of inflation, certain large corporations are required to report selected details of their operating results and financial position in terms of (1) general price level and (2) current cost effects (discussed in Chapter 24) to supplement the basic historical cost financial statements.

Time Period Assumption. Although the results of operations of a specific business enterprise cannot be known with certainty until the business has completed its life span and gone through final liquidation, short-term financial reports are necessary because financial statement users cannot wait until liquidation for financial reports. Thus the environment—the business community and government—has imposed upon accounting a calendar constraint, that is, the necessity for assigning changes in the economic elements of an enterprise to a series of short time periods. These time periods vary; however, the year is the most common period. Some companies adhere to the calendar year, whereas other companies use a business year which ends on the date marked by the lowest point of business activity in each 12-month period—regardless of its relation to the calendar year.

In addition to annual reports, companies also report summarized financial information on an **interim** basis, usually quarterly (discussed in Chapter 21).

The time period assumption recognizes the need of users of accounting information for short-term periodic financial statements. This assumption underlies the use of **accruals** and **deferrals** that distinguish accrual basis accounting from cash basis accounting. If there were no need for periodic reports during the life span of a business, accruals and deferrals of revenues and expenses would not be necessary. To illustrate, assume X Company was organized and $100,000 cash was invested in it. Assets were acquired, liabilities incurred, revenues earned, and expenses paid for a five-year period, at which time the business was liquidated (everything converted to cash) and the resulting cash of $175,000 was returned to the owners. Assuming no distributions to the owners during the five-year period, the company can report with certainty that it earned $75,000 cash income. Under this assumption, accruals or deferrals (adjusting entries in the accounts) would not be necessary to determine the income for the business. However, if the investors required financial statements each year, accruals and deferrals for items such as unpaid wages, uncollected revenues, and depreciation expense would have to be recorded and reported each period.

The need for short-term test readings which accounting renders in the form of financial statements tends to obscure the continuity of business operations. Many continuous and interrelated streams of data are arbitrarily severed in the preparation of annual financial statements. Despite these difficulties, short-term financial reports are of such significance to decision makers that the accounting process is designed to produce them. Adoption of the time period assumption recognizes this need despite the fact that the "actual" results for the short term seldom, if ever, can be determined with absolute precision.

Implementation Principles

Accountants need certain **principles,** which are consistent with the objectives and elements (discussed above), to guide the way they record and report accounting information. The assumptions discussed above provide a part of this guidance by (1) restricting accounting information to separate business entities; (2) assuming continued existence of the enterprise over the foreseeable future; (3) dictating that much, if not most, accounting data be presented in monetary terms; and (4) identifying accounting information with particular time periods.

Accountants also need more specific guidelines as to how to (1) measure (i.e., assign values to) the elements of the financial statements and (2) report financial accounting information. The implementation principles serve this purpose. The implementation principles of accounting can be categorized as follows:

Quantitative principles—focus primarily on measurement:

1. Cost principle.
2. Revenue principle.
3. Matching principle.

Qualitative principles—focus primarily on implementation of the qualitative characteristics:

4. Reporting principle.
5. Reliability principle.
6. Comparability principle.

Throughout this book, we refer to **generally accepted accounting principles (GAAP),** which are the standards of accounting practice. GAAP comprises the implementation assumptions and principles, along with related methods and procedures. The six implementation principles are discussed below.

Cost Principle. The cost principle holds that cost is the appropriate basis for initial accounting recognition of the elements reported on the financial statements. Support for the cost principle is the fact that, at the time of a business transaction, the market value of what is given up in the transaction provides reliable evidence of the market value of the item being acquired in the transaction.

Even though the market value of the item may change over time, the cost principle holds that **subsequent to acquisition,** the original historical cost values must be retained throughout the accounting process. The cost principle recognizes the basic subject matter of accounting as completed exchange transactions which are translated into their effect on the entity in terms of the exchange price at the date of the completed transaction. The cost principle holds that, compared with other alternatives, the historical cost amount established in an arm's-length transaction is the most useful for accounting and reporting. It can be determined objectively at acquisition date; hence, it is not mere conjecture or opinion.

The accountant frequently encounters a problem in measuring cost in **noncash** exchanges. In determining cost, the "cash bargained price" is utilized. Where items other than cash are given, the cost measure of the item acquired in the exchange is the net cash equivalent of the item given in the transaction. If the cash equivalent of what is given cannot be determined reliably, the cost measure of the item acquired is its cash equivalent amount. For example, if capital stock is issued to acquire land, the cost of the land acquired is the cash equivalent price of the stock given up (i.e., its current value). In some cases, however, the cash equivalent price of the item given up (i.e., stock in this example) cannot be determined **reliably.** In such a case, the cash equivalent price of the item received (land in this case) is used as its cost. In some instances, a judgment must be made as to which of the two estimated cash equivalents is the more reliable.

A similar problem is encountered when a debt (i.e., a liability) is given for an asset. Cost in this instance is the **present value** of the amount of cash to be paid in the future, as specified by the terms of the debt. Therefore, the cost principle applies to liabilities as well as to assets. Moreover, because expenses and losses represent expired portions of assets, the cost principle also governs the monetary amounts at which expenses and losses are recorded.

This discussion of the cost principle has focused upon the **reliability** of historical cost as a measure of value. However, subsequent changes in the market value of an item often constitute important information for decision makers. For example, if the sale of an asset is being considered, the more **relevant** value of the asset seldom would be its historical cost. Instead, the decision maker would be more likely to consider the current market value of the asset.[17] Even if sale of the asset is not being considered, the behavior of the decision maker usually should be governed more by the current value of the asset than by its historical cost.[18] Such considerations add complexity because in the absence of an exchange transaction involving the asset, its current value may not be reliably determinable. This example also illustrates the conflict between relevance and reliability because **the most relevant information for a particular decision may possess low reliability, and the most reliable information available may not be relevant to the decision.**

Historical cost accounting emphasizes **reliability** whereas current value accounting emphasizes **relevance.** Accounting practice is evolving to produce information which reflects a balance between these primary characteristics of accounting information. The present evolutionary stage of accounting practice involves the reporting of historical costs, historical costs restated for changes in the general price level (i.e., in constant dollars), and current costs.[19] Although this book emphasizes the historical cost approach, it also discusses and illustrates the approaches used for general price-level and current cost financial statements (Chapter 24).

[17] For simplicity, we ignore income tax considerations which may elevate historical cost to a higher level of importance. Income taxes usually are computed on the difference between the disposal (i.e., selling) amount and the historical cost amount.

[18] This idea is developed by R. J. Chambers, *Accounting, Evaluation and Economic Behavior* (Houston: Scholars Books, 1966); and R. Sterling, *Theory of Measurement of Enterprise Income* (Lawrence: University of Kansas Press, 1970).

[19] "Current cost" is one measure of current value. In general, the current cost of an asset is defined in FASB, *Statement of Financial Accounting Standards No. 33,* "Financial Reporting and Changing Prices" (Stamford, Conn., September 1979), as the **current** cost of acquiring the same service potential as embodied in the asset owned.

Revenue Principle. The revenue principle (1) defines revenue, (2) specifies the measurement of revenue, and (3) pinpoints the timing of revenue recognition. Each of the three facets of the revenue principle is discussed below.

Revenue Defined. Revenue is defined in *FASB Concepts Statement 3* as "inflows or other enhancements of assets of an entity or settlements of its liabilities (or a combination of both) during a period from delivering or producing goods, rendering services, or other activities that constitute the entity's ongoing major or central operations." Revenues "represent actual or expected cash inflows (or the equivalent) that have occurred or will eventuate as a result of the enterprise's **ongoing major or central operations** during the period."[20] (Emphasis supplied.) Revenues are the accomplishments of the **earning process** of a business enterprise during a specific period of time.

Measurement of Revenue. The revenue principle dictates that revenue should be measured as the net cash equivalent price derived in an arm's-length exchange transaction. Thus, revenue is best measured by the net cash exchange value of the product, service, or asset received in the exchange. This principle requires that all discounts be viewed as adjustments of the amount of revenue earned. For example, in determining the net cash exchange value of sales subject to a discount, sales discounts should be subtracted from gross sales revenue in measuring the net amount of sales revenue. It also requires that revenue be measured in noncash transactions by the value of the consideration received except when this value cannot be determined reliably. Then the revenue is measured by the current value of the consideration given up if it can be determined more reliably.

Timing Revenue Recognition. The revenue principle states that revenue should be recognized (i.e., recorded) when *(a)* an exchange transaction involving transfer of goods or services has occurred and *(b)* the **earning process** is essentially complete. The revenue principle requires **accrual basis** accounting rather than cash basis accounting for revenues. For example, completed transactions for the sale of goods or services on credit are recognized as revenue in the period in which the sale or service occurred rather than in the period in which the cash is eventually collected.

[20] *FASB Concepts Statement 3,* par. 64.

The revenue principle also governs the measurement and the timing of the recognition of **gains** as well as revenue. Specific applications of the revenue principle are discussed in the next few paragraphs.

Under the revenue principle, revenue from the sale of **goods** is recognized according to the **sales method** (i.e., at the time of sale) because the earning process usually is complete at the time of sale. At that time, the **relevant** information about the asset inflows to the seller would be known with **reliability.**

The conditions for **completion of the earning process** are *(a)* collection from the buyer is reasonably assured and *(b)* the expenses of making the sale can be determined reliably. Condition *(a)*—reasonable assurance of collection—provides the basis for the conclusion that the transaction provided a "probable future economic benefit" (i.e., an asset) to the seller. Without this condition, the concept of revenue recognition would be altogether lacking in substantive economic content. Condition *(b)*—reliable determination of related expenses—provides the basis for measurement of the net economic benefit of the transaction. Without this condition, measurement of the effect of the revenue would ignore the related expenses and would therefore be partial at best. Condition *(b)* is closely related to the matching principle, which is discussed below.

Exceptional circumstances occasionally require other methods of revenue recognition. One exception relates to installment sales. In the limited case in which sales are made on an extended payment plan, the probability of full collection may be low and/or the expenses of collection cannot be estimated reliably at the time of sale. Under the **installment method** of revenue recognition, revenue is recognized on a proportional basis related to actual cash collections.

Another exception relates to long-term construction contracts. Such contracts may extend over several years, and revenue may be recognized *(a)* when the contract is completed, in accordance with the sales method, or *(b)* as work progresses on the project, under the **percentage-of-completion method.** The percentage of completion of the contract often is determined on the basis of the ratio of cost incurred to estimated total cost of completing the contract.

A third exception to the sales method is the **cost recovery method.** The cost recovery method is applied in the case of highly speculative ventures in which ultimate recovery of the investment is doubtful. Under this method, revenue (or gain) is recognized only after the actual asset inflows from the investment exceed the cost of the investment. After that point, all amounts received are recorded as revenue.

Under the revenue principle, revenue from the sale of **services** is recognized on the basis of performance because performance determines the extent to which the earning process is complete.

Other types of revenue transactions posing problems of revenue recognition are sales of land with minimal down payments and sales of franchises that require a certain level of performance on the part of the purchaser. In these and many other cases, determination of when the earning process is complete and measurement of the amount of revenue are difficult tasks. An extended discussion of revenue recognition is provided in Chapter 22.

Matching Principle. The matching principle states that for any period for which income is reported, revenues should be determined according to the revenue principle; then the expenses incurred in generating that revenue should be determined for the same period. If revenue is carried over from a prior period or deferred to a future period in accordance with the revenue principle, all identifiable elements of expense related to that revenue likewise should be carried over from the prior period or deferred to a future period, as the case may be. Many costs are recorded as assets because they aid in the generation of **future** revenues. The essence of the matching principle is that as the revenues are generated, the assets are sold or consumed, and the costs of the assets sold or consumed are recognized and reported as expenses of the period the related revenue is recognized.

The pattern of expense recognition varies. Some expenses reflect a direct cause-and-effect relationship with revenues. That is, the revenue and expense occurs simultaneously. Examples are cost of goods sold, sales commission expense, and delivery expense. Other expenses are recognized on a **time basis** because their asset counterparts expire over time rather than reflecting direct cause-and-effect relationships with revenues. Examples are depreciation expense of the home office, interest expense, and property tax expense. For still other expenses, no reasonably objective way exists for measuring the expiration of their asset counterparts; for these expenses, conventions are adopted to implement the matching principle. Examples are advertising expense, research and development expense, and goodwill amortization expense.

The matching principle requires the use of **accrual basis** accounting (as opposed to cash basis accounting) to record and report expenses. Thus, **adjusting entries** (discussed in Chapter 2) must be recorded at the end of each period to update certain expenses for the period. Examples are depreciation expense, wage expense, and estimated warranty expense.

To illustrate the matching principle, assume a home appliance was sold for cash during 19B (the annual accounting period) and it was guaranteed for a period of 12 months from date of sale. The sales revenue will be recognized as earned during 19B. The expense of honoring the warranty also should be recognized in 19B, although the actual warranty cost may not be known until the next year. Therefore, at the end of 19B, the warranty expense must be estimated, recorded, and reported. In this way, the warranty expense is **matched** with the 19B revenue to which it is related.

The matching principle is the expense analog to the revenue principle. Because of the wide diversity and large number of types of expenses, it is one of the most pervasive principles of accounting in terms of the number of accounting judgments that it affects. An extended discussion of expense recognition under the matching principle is provided in Chapter 22.

Reporting Principle.[21] The reporting principle asserts that the financial reports of a business enterprise should disclose the relevant information relating to its economic affairs, that is, all the information which "makes a difference" for economic decisions about the enterprise. The theoretical foundation for this principle is **relevance,** which is a **primary** characteristic of accounting information (refer to Exhibit 1–2). Implementation of the relevance concept poses complex practical problems related to the recognition of revenues, expenses, gains, and losses. For example, note disclosures in the financial statements of contingent losses from pending lawsuits tread a thin line between *(a)* disclosing enough information about potential loss to the enterprise for users to draw a reasonable conclusion and *(b)* not disclosing information which might bias the outcome of the lawsuit. Also, for industries with unusual characteristics, it often is difficult to provide statement users with the most relevant accounting information. For example, in the oil and gas industry, the historical cost of oil and gas reserves may not be relevant to most users' decisions. Because of relevance, and without regard for the cost principle, certain oil and gas companies have been required to disclose, in notes to their basic financial statements, the present value of the future cash flows expected from ultimate sale of their oil and gas reserves. Other industries with exceptional reporting practices include railroads (due to government regulation), financial institutions (due to the nature of their assets), and meat packers (due to the difficulty of allocating purchase cost to specific meat products produced).

Without constraints, the reporting principle could force enterprises to disclose a vast amount of information, some of which may not be **reliable.** The reliability principle addresses the issue of the reliability of the information reported.

Reliability Principle. The reliability principle asserts that accounting information should possess *(a)* **representational faithfulness** and *(b)* **verifiability** (Exhibit 1–2).[22] The reliability principle adds balance to the reporting principle because it holds that the accounting information reported in financial statements should be (1) **neutral,** that is, free from upward or downward bias; (2) **verifiable,** that is, its representational faithfulness should be supportable by consensus and not merely by conjecture; and (3) **complete.**

Operationally, the reliability principle means that accounting information should be based on arm's-length exchange transactions to the fullest extent possible. An arm's-length transaction is characterized by an agreement between two or more parties that have adverse interests; for example, the motive of the seller is a high price, whereas the motive of the buyer is a low price. Therefore, assuming the parties are not related, any transaction occurring between them reflects a consensus about the values of the items exchanged.

[21] The reporting principle also is known as the **full-disclosure principle.**

[22] Verifiability is similar to the traditional concept of **objectivity,** which means that accounting data should be based upon objective evidence to the fullest extent possible.

Accountants recognize that many aspects of accounting information involve estimates. For example, depreciation expense is based on *(a)* factual data—the cost of the asset, and *(b)* two estimates—useful life and residual value. Such estimates should be determined in a manner that satisfies the reliability principle.

Traditionally, accounting has been influenced by the concept of **conservatism,** which has characterized accountants' response to the inherent uncertainty of many accounting measurements. Conservatism can be summarized by the statement: "anticipate no profits but anticipate all losses." Also, accountants have traditionally preferred "that possible errors in measurement be in the direction of understatement rather than overstatement of net income and net assets."[23] In summary, conservative judgments in accounting can result in accounting measurements of net income and net assets that reflect a downward bias. *FASB Concepts Statement 2* states that any such bias tends to conflict with representational faithfulness, neutrality, and comparability. An example of the conflict between conservatism and comparability is an unwarranted write-down of asset value to be "conservative." The conservative nature of the write-down boomerangs in future years when the lower asset value is recognized as expense; the lower expense causes reported income to be higher in the future than it would have been with no asset write-down. Therefore, the accounting treatments among the years are inconsistent and this impairs interperiod comparability.

FASB Concepts Statement 2 defines **conservatism** as follows:

> Conservatism is a prudent reaction to uncertainty to try to ensure that uncertainties and risks inherent in business situations are adequately considered. Thus, if two estimates of amounts to be received or paid in the future are about equally likely, conservatism dictates using the less optimistic estimate; however, if two amounts are not equally likely, conservatism does not necessarily dictate using the more pessimistic amount rather than the more likely one.[24]

In this context, *FASB Concepts Statement 2* states that

> Reliability of financial reporting may be enhanced by disclosing the nature and extent of the uncertainty surrounding events and transactions reported to stockholders and others. In assessing the prospect that as yet uncompleted transactions will be concluded successfully, a degree of skepticism is often warranted. The aim must be to put the users of financial information in the best possible position to form their own opinion of the probable outcome of the events reported.[25]

Comparability Principle.[26] The comparability principle asserts that accounting information should be comparable among entities as well as across time for the same entity; therefore, it includes consistency. The theoretical foundation for this principle is **comparability,** which is a **secondary** characteristic of accounting information (refer to Exhibit 1–2).

Quantitative measures usually are easier to **compare** and often have greater information value than qualitative measures. For example, the statement, "The temperature is 35 degrees centigrade (95 degrees Fahrenheit)" has greater information value than the statement, "It is hot," because the measure "35 (95) degrees" permits precise comparison with other measures of heat, whereas the latter statement provides only a vague notion of one's perception of heat.

Likewise, the characterization of an enterprise in terms of its economic elements (i.e., assets, liabilities, . . . income) rests upon the comparability principle because this standardization enhances users' ability to compare companies. To illustrate, consider an attempt to compare Johnson & Johnson Company with Du Pont & Company without their financial statements. The description of a company in common terms of its financial statement elements enhances interfirm comparability, which is an important part of investment analysis.

At a less fundamental level, comparability suffers because companies are permitted to use different accounting methods. For example, in 1979, Johnson & Johnson used the FIFO method of accounting for its inventory, while Du Pont used the LIFO method. Thus, for 1979, the inventory amounts of the two companies were not directly comparable. The resultant breach of interfirm comparability often is justified

---

[23] AICPA, *Statement of the Accounting Principles Board No. 4,* "Basic Concepts and Accounting Principles Underlying Financial Statements" (New York, October 1970), par. 171.

[24] *FASB Concepts Statement 2,* par. 95.

[25] Ibid., par. 97.

[26] The comparability principle includes and, therefore, is broader than the traditional principle of **consistency.**

by appealing to the desire for relevant accounting information; that is, the alternative accounting methods which a company selects may provide relevant information about that company. Some accountants contend that the choice among available accounting methods helps a company "better" measure its elements than if the company were constrained to a single prescribed method. Therefore, based upon the primary importance of relevance and the secondary importance of comparability, it is not surprising that alternative accounting methods are available.

Consistency is included in the comparability principle. In general, consistent application of accounting methods from period to period **enhances the comparability of accounting information** used in trend analysis. For example. LIFO inventory amounts for a company at December 31, 19A, are not comparable with FIFO inventory amounts for the company at December 31, 19B, because of inconsistent use of inventory methods. Also, consistency reduces the potential for manipulation of reported amounts. In some instances a company may have a sound reason for changing from one method to another. On this point the FASB states that "it is possible to make the transition . . . and still retain the capacity to compare the periods before and after the change if the effects of the change . . . are disclosed."[27] Thus, when a company makes an accounting change, *APB Opinion No. 20,* "Accounting Changes," requires it to disclose the effect of the change to facilitate comparability between periods (discussed in Chapter 20).

Implementation Constraints

The goal of accounting information may be summarized as: **Accounting information should help users accomplish their objectives.** Realization of this goal requires that the benefit of using accounting information must exceed the cost of reporting and using it. For example, the attempt to provide relevant accounting information, pursued in isolation, could lead to disclosure of unreliable (albeit relevant) information. The costs associated with bad decisions based upon this unreliable information may exceed the benefits of disclosing the information.

Materiality. A cost-benefit trade-off at the individual company level involves the materiality constraint. **Materiality** is defined in *FASB Concepts Statement 2* as: "The magnitude of an omission or misstatement of accounting information that, in the light of surrounding circumstances, makes it probable that the judgment of a reasonable person relying on the information would have been changed or influenced by the omission or misstatement."[28] Materiality is similar to relevance in that both concepts are defined in terms of what influences a decision maker. In general, the difference between relevance and materiality is that relevance judgments are primarily qualitative in nature, whereas materiality judgments are **primarily quantitative.** This distinction is explained by the FASB as follows:

> A decision not to disclose certain information may be made because investors have no interest in that kind of information (it is not relevant) or because the amounts involved are too small to make a difference (they are not material). But . . . magnitude by itself without regard to the nature of the item and the circumstances in which the judgment has to be made, will not generally be a sufficient basis for a materiality judgment.[29]

Two aspects of this quotation merit emphasis. First, materiality judgments involve quantitative thresholds. That is, reporting an immaterial amount need not be as strict in terms of accounting standards as reporting a material amount. The materiality concept does not mean that an immaterial item may not be accounted for at all. All transactions, events, and circumstances affecting an entity must be accounted for, regardless of their materiality. Also, the materiality concept does not prohibit the exercise of strict care in accounting for immaterial amounts. The cost of exercising strict care often is prohibitive; for this reason, accountants have developed quantitative materiality guidelines to determine when an item is immaterial. An application of the materiality concept is the practice of large companies to expense, at the time of acquisition, the costs of assets (such as office machines) below some materiality threshold, say, $500. The view is that the cost of the theoretically correct accounting for depreciation on such a low-cost asset outweighs the informational benefit relative to the enterprise as a whole. The relative effect of depreciation on periodic income would be so small that the behavior of decision mak-

[27] *FASB Concepts Statement 2,* par. 122.

[28] Ibid., p. xv.

[29] Ibid., par. 125.

ers would not be affected by the method of accounting for the asset.

The second aspect of the above quotation that merits emphasis involves the *(a)* **nature of the item** and *(b)* **circumstances** in which the materiality judgment is made. To illustrate how the nature and circumstances affect the perceived materiality of an item, *FASB Concepts Statement 2* states, "A failure to disclose separately a nonrecurrent item of revenue may be material at a lower threshold than would otherwise be the case if the revenue turns a loss into a profit."[30] The fact that the item of revenue turns a loss into a profit makes the **nonrecurrent** nature of the revenue of material importance to users, whereas it may otherwise not need to be disclosed separately. Based upon this reasoning, it appears that in this particular circumstance, the **nonrecurrent** nature of the revenue should be disclosed even though its amount may be immaterial by other guidelines.

Finally, materiality judgments are situation specific, which means that an amount which is material in one situation may be immaterial in another situation. To illustrate, assume the nonrecurrent revenue in the preceding example did **not** turn a loss into a profit. With this modification the amount of the revenue would have been judged as immaterial, with no need to disclose its nonrecurrent nature. Because of the uniqueness of specific materiality judgments, the FASB is not able to specify **general** materiality guidelines that apply to a wide variety of situations. In practice, materiality guidelines such as "5 percent of net income" or "1 percent of total assets" are often used.

[30] Ibid., par. 128.

Financial Statements Required

The prior discussions concentrated on the **theoretical** foundation of financial accounting and reporting. Application of those concepts is reflected in the periodic financial statements of the enterprise. The financial statements combine the elements (i.e., assets, liabilities, revenues, expenses, etc.) into natural subdivisions. Financial statements are reviewed in greater detail in Chapters 3 and 4.

CONCLUSION

The discussion of the theoretical foundation of financial accounting and reporting in this chapter is intended to provide a frame of reference for study of subsequent chapters. Rather than presenting these concepts piecemeal throughout the text, the authors have chosen to discuss them in this first chapter. Of particular importance are the relationships portrayed in Exhibits 1–1 and 1–2, which summarize the theoretical foundation. The remaining chapters discuss and illustrate numerous examples of the implementation of this foundation. As a result, those chapters continue the emphasis upon the elements, assumptions, principles, and financial statements.

Two supplements are included with this chapter for those with interests in accounting theory development and the official pronouncements. Supplement 1–A briefly discusses a number of alternative approaches to theory development in accounting. Supplement 1–B lists the official pronouncements underlying GAAP.

Supplement 1–A: Approaches to Accounting Theory Development

Accountants have pursued numerous approaches to the development of the theoretical structure of accounting. The different approaches are discussed below under the following categories:

1. Classical approaches.
   a. True income approach.
   b. Inductive approach.
2. Decision usefulness approach.
3. Information economics approach.[31]

CLASSICAL APPROACHES

Classical approaches to theory development in accounting can be divided into two subcategories: the true income approach and the inductive approach.

[31] This supplement is adapted from American Accounting Association Committee on Concepts and Standards for External Financial Reports, *Statement on Theory and Theory Acceptance* (Sarasota, Fla.: AAA, 1977).

The **true income approach** is based upon the belief that a single amount measures the "true" income of an entity for a period of time. This approach is influenced by the concept of economic income, which usually is defined as the amount of wealth an entity can consume during a period and still be as well off at the end of the period as it was at the beginning. In theory, economic income can be measured as the change in the wealth (i.e., owners' equity) of an entity over a period of time, adjusted for investments by, and distributions to, owners during the period. Classical accounting theorists attempt to operationalize the abstract economic concepts of "income" and "wealth."[32] Most theorists in this group advocate the use of current values (versus historical cost) for valuing assets and measuring income; however, they often disagree as to how to measure current values. The reasoning of these theorists starts from the normative position that "true" income exists; they then deduce accounting principles consistent with this normative position. For this reason, the true income approach also is referred to as the "normative deductive" approach.

The **inductive approach** is characterized by the induction of accounting principles from existing accounting practices; thus, it is rationalization of existing practice. Inductive theorists maintain that the accounting information which best serves the needs of decision makers is based upon the actual effects of completed transactions undertaken by the enterprise.[33] Members of this group usually advocate the use of historical cost as the valuation basis of accounting.

DECISION USEFULNESS APPROACH

The **decision usefulness approach** is based upon the decision models of particular users of financial statements. It has a theoretical facet and an empirical facet.

The **theoretical facet** of the decision usefulness approach assumes a particular decision model (or decision maker) and specifies the qualitative characteristics which accounting information must have to be useful for the assumed decision model (or maker). Thus, under the decision usefulness approach, accounting principles are based primarily on these qualitative characteristics. Usually, this facet of accounting theory emphasizes the decisions of **investors** who are assumed to be interested in predicting the **cash flows** and assessing the **risk** of an enterprise.[34]

The **empirical facet** of the decision usefulness approach is based upon empirical research which analyzes actual data to identify *(a)* accounting information which is useful for a particular purpose and *(b)* how that information was actually used by decision makers.

Empirical research on the decision usefulness of accounting information is of two types. One type examines the use of specific items of accounting information by individual decision makers. An example is a study by Libby, who examined the usefulness of selected accounting ratios for the prediction of failure by bank loan officers.[35] A second type of empirical research on decision usefulness examines stock prices to determine how investors at the market level react to selected items of accounting information. Examples were the studies by Collins and Dent and by Dyckman and Smith to determine how the stock market actually reacted to the FASB requirement that oil and gas companies must use the same accounting method.[36]

These examples indicate that empirical research in accounting usually examines the usefulness of specific items of information. As a result, such research cannot respond effectively to global questions such

[32] For example, see W. A. Paton, *Accounting Theory* (New York: Ronald Press, 1922); J. B. Canning, *The Economics of Accountancy* (New York: Ronald Press, 1929); and K. MacNeal, *Truth in Accounting* (Philadelphia: University of Pennsylvania Press, 1939). For a more recent example of the true income approach, see R. T. Sprouse and M. Moonitz, *A Tentative Set of Broad Accounting Principles* (New York: AICPA, 1962).

[33] For example, see A. C. Littleton, *American Accounting Association Monograph No. 5,* "Structure of Accounting Theory" (Evanston, Ill.: AAA, 1953); and Y. Ijiri, *Studies in Accounting Research No. 10,* "Theory of Accounting Measurement" (Sarasota, Fla.: AAA, 1975).

[34] For example, see G. J. Staubus, *A Theory of Income to Investors* (Berkeley: University of California Press, 1961); R. Sterling, *Theory of Measurement of Enterprise Income* (Lawrence: University of Kansas Press, 1970); L. Revsine, *Replacement Cost Accounting* (Englewood Cliffs, N.J.: Prentice-Hall, 1973); *FASB Concepts Statement 1;* and *FASB Concepts Statement 2.*

[35] R. Libby, "Accounting Ratios and the Prediction of Failure: Some Behavioral Evidence," *Journal of Accounting Research,* Spring 1975, pp. 150–61.

[36] D. W. Collins and W. T. Dent, "The Proposed Elimination of Full Cost Accounting in the Extractive Petroleum Industry: An Empirical Assessment of the Market Consequences," *Journal of Accounting & Economics,* March 1979, pp. 3–44; and T. R. Dyckman and A. J. Smith, "Financial Accounting and Reporting by Oil and Gas Producing Companies: A Study of Information Effects," *Journal of Accounting & Economics,* March 1979, pp. 45–75.

as: How useful are accounting ratios? Also, empirical research cannot answer **normative** questions such as: How well **should** bank loan officers be able to predict enterprise failure? Rather, most empirical research of decision usefulness addresses **positive** issues (e.g., how useful **are** accounting ratios for prediction of failure?). Thus, empirical research provides a **positive** base of evidence upon which the **normative** criteria of accounting theory rest; it is the role of theorists to supply the normative criteria (e.g., maximization of net cash flows).

The classical and decision usefulness approaches focus mainly on certain characteristics of accounting information. Important examples are *(a)* correspondence of accounting measures with the economic concepts of wealth and income under the classical approach and *(b)* decision usefulness for particular users under the decision usefulness approach. These approaches do not give explicit recognition to the costs of providing accounting information; rather, they focus entirely on the benefits.

INFORMATION ECONOMICS APPROACH

The information economics approach to accounting theory development is based upon the fundamental premise that accounting provides information. This approach treats accounting information as an economic good and evaluates accounting information in a cost-benefit framework. Ultimately, it involves welfare economics in the identification of those who incur the costs of accounting information and those who receive the benefits.

An example of a welfare economics consideration was the alleged effect of requiring lessees to account for the assets they acquire by lease as though they were purchasing the assets in installments. Lessees argued that requiring them to (1) capitalize leased assets and (2) report the related lease liabilities on their balance sheets would make it unduly difficult for them to obtain additional financing.[37]

The "cost" in this example was the alleged increase in a lessee's difficulty in obtaining financing; this cost would be borne by lessee companies. In contrast, the "benefit" was more realistic accounting for leases; one group of beneficiaries would be investors and creditors who receive and use the relevant lease information. Whether any benefits would extend to the general public is difficult to determine.

In summary, the information economics approach to theory development provides a framework for identifying *(a)* the costs and benefits of alternative reporting systems, *(b)* who bears the costs and who gets the benefits, *(c)* any effects on distributions of wealth, and *(d)* the implications for social welfare.[38]

SUMMARY

The classical approaches to theory development in accounting were popular during the early and mid-1900s. The more recent literature reflects a blend of the decision usefulness and information economics approaches. In particular, *FASB Concepts Statements 1* and *2* seem to be influenced by the decision usefulness approach; however, *FASB Concepts Statement 2* also includes a lengthy discussion (pp. 54–58) of costs and benefits associated with the qualitative characteristics of accounting information. In conclusion, different persons take different approaches to the development of accounting theory, and each approach invariably reflects the individual's normative position. The debate over the "best" approach will continue as long as differences exist in these normative positions.

---

[37] FASB, *Statement of Financial Accounting Standards No. 13,* "Accounting for Leases" (Stamford, Conn., November 1976).

[38] For an example, see J. Demski, "Choice among Financial Reporting Alternatives," *The Accounting Review,* April 1974, pp. 221–32.

Supplement 1-B: List of Official Pronouncements

This supplement is included to help students *(a)* gain an overview of the official pronouncements and *(b)* identify appropriate source documents for numerous accounting issues discussed in this book. Further study of these issues in the source documents often is desirable.

Accounting Research Bulletins (ARBs), **Accounting Procedures Committee, AICPA *(ARBs* discontinued in 1959)**

ARB No.	Contents	Status, January 1, 1982
43.	Restatement and Revisions of *Accounting Research Bulletins Nos. 1–42,* June, 1953	Generally continued in force by *APB Opinion No. 6* (as amended)
	Ch. 1. Prior Opinions	Amended
	Ch. 2. Form of Statements	Amended and partially superseded
	Ch. 3. Working Capital	Amended and partially superseded
	Ch. 4. Inventory Pricing	Amended
	Ch. 5. Intangible Assets	Superseded by *APB Opinions Nos. 16 and 17*
	Ch. 6. Contingency Reserves	Superseded by *FASB Statement No. 5*
	Ch. 7. Capital Accounts	Amended and partially superseded
	Ch. 8. Income and Earned Surplus	Superseded by *APB Opinion No. 9*
	Ch. 9. Depreciation	Amended and partially superseded
	Ch. 10. Taxes	Amended and partially superseded
	Ch. 11. Government Contracts	Amended
	Ch. 12. Foreign Operations and Foreign Exchange	Amended by *FASB Statement No. 8*
	Ch. 13. Compensation (Pension Plans)	Amended and partially superseded
	Ch. 14. Disclosure of Long-Term Leases in Financial Statements	Superseded by *APB Opinion No. 5*
	Ch. 15. Unamortized Discount, Issue Cost, and Redemption Premium on Bonds Refunded	Superseded by *APB Opinion No. 26*
44.	Declining-Balance Depreciation; Revised July 1958	Amended
45.	Long-Term Construction-Type Contracts, October 1955	Unchanged
46.	Discontinuance of Dating Earned Surplus, February 1956	Unchanged
47.	Accounting for Costs of Pension Plans, September 1956	Superseded by *APB Opinion No. 8*
48.	Business Combinations, January 1957	Superseded by *APB Opinion No. 16*
49.	Earnings per Share, April 1958	Superseded by *APB Opinion No. 9*
50.	Contingencies, October 1958	Superseded by *FASB Statement No. 5*
51.	Consolidated Financial Statements, August 1959	Amended and partially superseded

Accounting Terminology Bulletins, **Committee on Terminology, AICPA (*Bulletins* discontinued in 1959)**

ATB No.	Contents	Status, January 1, 1982
1.	Review and Resume (of the eight original terminology bulletins), June 1953	Partially superseded
2.	Proceeds, Revenue, Income, Profit, and Earnings	Amended
3.	Book Value	Unchanged
4.	Cost, Expense, and Loss	Amended

Accounting Principles Board (APB) Opinions, **AICPA (*Opinions* discontinued in 1973)**

1.	New Depreciation Guidelines and Rules, November 1962	Unchanged
2.	Accounting for the "Investment Credit," December 1962	Amended and interpreted
	Addendum to *Opinion No. 2*—Accounting Principles for Regulated Industries, December 1962	Unchanged
3.	The Statement of Source and Application of Funds, October 1963	Superseded by *APB Opinion No. 19*
4.	Accounting for the "Investment Credit" (Amending No. 2), March 1964	Unchanged, but interpreted
5.	Reporting of Leases in Financial Statements of Lessee, September 1964	Superseded
6.	Status of *Accounting Research Bulletins*, October 1965	Amended and partially superseded
7.	Accounting for Leases in Financial Statements of Lessors, May 1966	Superseded
8.	Accounting for the Cost of Pension Plans, November 1966	Amended and interpreted
9.	Reporting the Results of Operations, December 1966	Amended and partially superseded
10.	Omnibus Opinion—1966, December 1966	Amended and partially superseded
11.	Accounting for Income Taxes, December 1967	Amended, partially superseded, and interpreted
12.	Omnibus Opinion—1967; December 1967	Amended and partially superseded
13.	Amending Paragraph 6 of *APB Opinion No. 9*, Application to Commercial Banks, March 1969	Unchanged
14.	Accounting for Convertible Debt and Debt Issued with Stock Purchase Warrants, March 1969	Unchanged
15.	Earnings per Share, May 1969	Amended and interpreted
16.	Business Combinations, August 1970	Amended and interpreted
17.	Intangible Assets, August 1970	Amended, and interpreted
18.	The Equity Method of Accounting for Investments in Common Stock, March 1971	Amended and partially superseded and interpreted
19.	Reporting Changes in Financial Position, March 1971	Unchanged
20.	Accounting Changes, July 1971	Amended and interpreted
21.	Interest on Receivables and Payables, August 1971	Unchanged, but interpreted
22.	Disclosure of Accounting Policies, April 1972	Unchanged
23.	Accounting for Income Taxes—Special Areas, April 1972	Amended and interpreted
24.	Accounting for Income Taxes—Equity Method Investments, April 1972	Unchanged but interpreted
25.	Accounting for Stock issued to Employees, October 1972	Unchanged
26.	Early Extinguishment of Debt, October 1972	Amended and interpreted
27.	Accounting for Lease Transactions by Manufacturer or Dealer Lessors, November 1972	Superseded
28.	Interim Financial Reporting, May 1973	Partially superseded and interpreted
29.	Accounting for Nonmonetary Transactions, May 1973	Unchanged but interpreted
30.	Reporting the Results of Operations, June 1973	Amended and partially superseded
31.	Disclosure of Lease Commitments by Lessees, June 1973	Superseded

***Accounting Principles Board (APB) Statements,* AICPA (*Statements* discontinued in 1973)**

APB No.	**Contents**
1.	Statement by the Accounting Principles Board, April 1962
2.	Disclosure of Supplemental Financial Information by Diversified Companies, September 1967
3.	Financial Statements Restated for General Price-Level Changes, June 1969
4.	Basic Concepts and Accounting Principles Underlying Financial Statements of Business Enterprises, October 1970

Financial Accounting Standards Board (FASB), *Statements of Financial Accounting Standards* (1973 to date)

FASB No.	**Contents**	**Status, January 1, 1982**
1.	Disclosure of Foreign Currency, December 1973	Amended by *FASB Statement No. 8*
2.	Accounting for Research and Development Costs, October 1974	Unchanged, but interpreted
3.	Reporting Accounting Changes in Interim Financial Statements, December 1974 (Amending *APB Opinion No. 23*)	Unchanged
4.	Reporting Gains and Losses from Extinguishment of Debt, March 1975	Unchanged
5.	Accounting for Contingencies	Amended and interpreted
6.	Classification of Short-Term Obligations Expected to Be Refinanced, May 1975	Unchanged, but interpreted
7.	Accounting and Reporting by Development Stage Enterprises, June 1975	Unchanged, but interpreted
8.	Accounting for the Translation of Foreign Currency Transactions and Foreign Currency Financial Statements, October 1975	Superseded
9.	Accounting for Income Taxes—Oil and Gas Producing Companies (an Amendment of *APB Opinions Nos. 11* and *23*), October 1975	Superseded
10.	Extension of "Grandfather" Provisions for Business Combinations (an Amendment of *APB Opinion No. 16*), October 1975	Unchanged
11.	Accounting for Contingencies—Transition Method (an Amendment of *FASB Statement No. 5*), December 1975	Unchanged
12.	Accounting for Certain Marketable Securities, December 1975	Unchanged, but interpreted
13.	Accounting for Leases, November 1976	Amended, partially superseded, and interpreted
14.	Financial Reporting for Segments of a Business Enterprise, December 1976	Amended and partially superseded
15.	Accounting by Debtors and Creditors for Troubled Debt Restructurings, June 1977	Unchanged
16.	Prior Period Adjustments, June 1977	Unchanged
17.	Accounting for Leases—Initial Direct Costs, November 1977	Unchanged
18.	Financial Reporting for Segments of a Business Enterprise—Interim Financial Statements, November 1977	Unchanged
19.	Financial Accounting and Reporting by Oil and Gas Producing Companies, December 1977	Amended, partially suspended (see *FASB No. 25* below), and interpreted
20.	Accounting for Forward Exchange Contracts, December 1977	Unchanged
21.	Suspension of the Reporting of Earnings per Share and Segment Information by Nonpublic Enterprises, April 1978	Unchanged
22.	Changes in the Provisions of Lease Agreements Resulting from Refundings of Tax-Exempt Debt, June 1978	Unchanged
23.	Inception of the Lease, August 1978	Unchanged
24.	Reporting Segment Information in Financial Statements That Are Presented in Another Enterprise's Financial Report, December 1978	Unchanged
25.	Suspension of Certain Accounting Requirements for Oil and Gas Companies, February 1979 (amends *FASB No. 19*)	Unchanged
26.	Profit Recognition on Sales-Type Leases of Real Estate (an amendment of *FASB Statement No. 13*), April 1979	Unchanged
27.	Classification of Renewals or Extensions of Existing Sales-Type or Direct Financing Leases (an amendment of *FASB Statement No. 13*), May 1979	Unchanged

Financial Accounting Standards Board (FASB), *Statements of Financial Accounting Standards* (1973 to date) *(continued)*

FASB No.	Contents	Status, January 1, 1982
28.	Accounting for Sales with Leasebacks (an amendment of *FASB Statement No. 13*), May 1979	Unchanged, but interpreted
29.	Determining Contingent Rentals (an amendment of *FASB Statement No. 13*), June 1979	Unchanged
30.	Disclosure of Information about Major Customers (an amendment of *FASB Statement No. 14*), August 1979	Unchanged
31.	Accounting for Tax Benefits Related to U.K. Tax Legislation concerning Stock Relief, September 1979	Unchanged
32.	Specialized Accounting and Reporting Principles and Practices in AICPA Statements of Position and Guides on Accounting and Auditing Matters (an amendment of *APB Opinion No. 20*), September 1979	Unchanged
33.	Financial Reporting and Changing Prices, September 1979	Amended
	Illustrations of Financial Reporting and Changing Prices, *Statement of Financial Accounting Standards No. 33, December 1979*	Unchanged
34.	Capitalization of Interest Cost, October, 1979	Amended and interpreted
35.	Accounting and Reporting by Defined Benefit Pension Plans, March 1980	Unchanged
36.	Disclosure of Pension Information (an amendment of *APB Opinion No. 8*), May 1980	Unchanged
37.	Balance Sheet Classification of Deferred Income Taxes (an amendment of *APB Opinion No. 11*), July 1980	Unchanged
38.	Accounting for Preacquisition Contingencies of Purchased Enterprises (an amendment of *APB Opinion No. 16*), September 1980	Unchanged
39.	Financial Reporting and Changing Prices: Specialized Assets—Mining and Oil and Gas (a supplement to *FASB Statement No. 33*), October 1980	Unchanged
40.	Financial Reporting and Changing Prices: Specialized Assets—Timberlands and Growing Timber (a supplement to *FASB Statement No. 33*), November 1980	Unchanged
41.	Financial Reporting and Changing Prices: Specialized Assets—Income-Producing Real Estate (a supplement to *FASB Statement No. 33*), November 1980	Unchanged
42.	Determining Materiality for Capitalization of Interest Cost (an amendment for *FASB Statement No. 34*), November 1980	Unchanged
43.	Accounting for Compensated Absences, November 1980	Unchanged
44.	Accounting for Intangible Assets of Motor Carriers (an amendment of Chapter 5 of *ARB No. 43* and an interpretation of *APB Opinions 17* and *30*), December 1980	Unchanged
45.	Accounting for Franchise Fee Revenue	Unchanged
46.	Financial Reporting and Changing Prices: Motion Picture Films, March 1981	Unchanged
47.	Disclosure of Long-Term Obligations, March 1981	Unchanged
48.	Revenue Recognition When Right of Return Exists, June 1981	Unchanged
49.	Accounting for Product Financing Arrangements, June 1981	Unchanged
50.	Financial Reporting in the Record and Music Industry, November 1981	Unchanged
51.	Financial Reporting by Cable Television Companies, November 1981	Unchanged
52.	Foreign Currency Translation, December 1981	Unchanged

***Financial Accounting Standards Board (FASB) Interpretations* (1973 to date)**

FASB No.	Contents	Interpretation of
1.	Accounting Changes Related to the Cost of Inventory June 1974	*APB Opinion No. 20*
2.	Imputing Interest on Debt Arrangements Made under the Federal Bankruptcy Act, June 1974	Superseded
3.	Accounting for the Cost of Pension Plans Subject to the Employment Retirement Income Security Act of 1974, December 1974	*APB Opinion No. 8*
4.	Applicability of *FASB Statement No. 2* to Business Combinations Accounted for by the Purchase Method, February 1975	*FASB Statement No. 2*
5.	Applicability of *FASB Statement No. 2* to Development Stage Enterprises, February 1975	*FASB Statement No. 2*
6.	Applicability of *FASB Statement No. 2* to Computer Software, February 1975	*FASB Statement No. 2*
7.	Applying *FASB Statement No. 7* in Financial Statements of Established Operating Enterprises, October 1975	*FASB Statement No. 7*

Financial Accounting Standards Board (FASB) Interpretations* (1973 to date) *(concluded)

FASB No.	Contents	Interpretation of
8.	Classification of a Short-Term Obligation Repaid Prior to Being Replaced by a Long-Term Security, January 1976	*FASB Statement No. 6*
9.	Applying *APB Opinions No. 16* and *17* When a Savings and Loan Association or a Similar Institution Is Acquired in a Business Combination Accounted for by the Purchase Method, February 1976	*APB Opinions 16* and *17*
10.	Application of *FASB Statement No. 12* to Personal Financial Statements, September 1976	*FASB Statement No. 12*
11.	Changes in Market Value after the Balance Sheet Date, September 1976	*FASB Statement No. 12*
12.	Accounting for Previously Established Allowance Accounts, September 1976	*FASB Statement No. 12*
13.	Consolidation of a Parent and its Subsidiaries having Different Balance Sheet Dates, September 1976	*FASB Statement No. 12*
14.	Reasonable Estimation of the Amount of a Loss, September 1976	*FASB Statement No. 5*
15.	Translation of Unamortized Policy Acquisition Costs by a Stock Life Insurance Company, September 1976	*FASB Statement No. 8*
16.	Clarification of Definitions and Accounting for Marketable Equity Securities That Become Nonmarketable, February 1977	*FASB Statement No. 12*
17.	Applying the Lower of Cost or Market Rule in Translated Financial Statements, February 1977	*FASB Statement No. 8*
18.	Accounting for Income Taxes in Interim Periods, March 1977	*APB Opinion No. 28*
19.	Lessee Guarantee of the Residual Value of Leased Property, October 1977	*FASB Statement No. 13*
20.	Reporting Accounting Changes under AICPA Statements of Position, November 1977	*APB Opinion No. 20*
21.	Accounting for Leases in a Business Combination, April 1978	*FASB Statement No. 13*
22.	Applicability of Indefinite Reversal Criteria to Timing Differences, April 1978	*APB Opinions 11* and *23*
23.	Leases of Certain Property Owned by a Governmental Unit or Authority, August 1978	*FASB Statement No. 13*
24.	Leases Involving Only Part of a Building, September 1978	*FASB Statement No. 13*
25.	Accounting for an Unused Investment Tax Credit, September 1978	*APB Opinions No. 2, 4, 11,* and *16*
26.	Accounting for Purchase of a Leased Asset by the Lessee during the Term of the Lease, September 1978	*FASB Statement No. 13*
27.	Accounting for Loss on a Sublease, November 1978	*FASB No. 13* and *APB Opinion No. 30*
28.	Accounting for Stock Appreciation Rights and Other Variable Stock Option or Award Plans, December 1978	*APB Opinions No. 15* and *25*
29.	Reporting Tax Benefits Realized on Disposition of Investments in Certain Subsidiaries and Other Investees, February 1979	*APB Opinions No. 23* and *24*
30.	Accounting for Involuntary Conversions of Nonmonetary Assets to Monetary Assets, September 1979	*APB Opinion No. 29*
31.	Treatment of Stock Compensation Plans in EPS Computations, February 1980	*APB Opinion No. 15* and *FASB Interpret. No. 28*
32.	Application of Percentage Limitations in Recognizing Investment Tax Credit, March 1980	*APB Opinions, 2, 4,* and *11*
33.	Applying *FASB Statement No. 34* to Oil and Gas Producing Operations Accounted for by the Full Cost Method, August 1980	*FASB Statement No. 34*
34.	Disclosure of Indirect Guarantees of Indebtedness of Others, March 1981	*FASB Statement No. 5*
35.	Criteria for Applying the Equity Method of Accounting for Investments in Common Stock, May 1981	*APB Opinion No. 18*
36.	Accounting for Exploration Wells in Progress at the End of a Period, October, 1981	*FASB Statement No. 19*

Financial Accounting Standards Board (FASB), *Statement of Financial Accounting Concepts* (1978 to date)

FASB No.	Contents	Status, January 1, 1982
1.	Objectives of Financial Reporting by Business Enterprises, November 1978	Unchanged
2.	Qualitative Characteristics of Accounting Information, May 1980	Unchanged
3.	Elements of Financial Statements of Business Enterprises, December 1980	Unchanged
4.	Objectives of Financial Reporting by Nonbusiness Organizations, December 1980	Unchanged

Financial Accounting Standards Board (FASB) *Technical Bulletins*

FASB No.	**Contents**	**Reference**
79–1	Purpose and Scope of FASB Technical Bulletins and Procedures for Issuance—To provide guidance concerning the application of official pronouncements of the FASB, APB, and ARBs, December 28, 1979	
79–2	Computer Software Costs, December 28, 1979	*FASB Statement No. 2* and *FASB Interpretation No. 6*
79–3	Subjective Acceleration Clauses in Long-Term Debt Agreements, December 28, 1979	*FASB Statement No. 6*
79–4	Segment Reporting of Puerto Rican Operations, December 28, 1979	*FASB Statement No. 14*
79–5	Meaning of the Term "Customer" as It Applies to Health Care Facilities, December 28, 1979	*FASB Statement No. 14*
79–6	Valuation Allowances Following Debt Restructure, December 28, 1979	*FASB Statement No. 15*
79–7	Recoveries of a Previous Writedown under a Troubled Debt Restructuring Involving a Modification of Terms, December 28, 1979	*FASB Statement No. 15*
79–8	Applicability of *FASB Statements 21* and *33* to Certain Brokers and Dealers in Securities, December 28, 1979	*FASB Statement No. 21*
79–9	Accounting in Interim Periods for Changes in Income Tax Rates, December 28, 1979	*FASB Interpretation No. 18*
79–10	Fiscal Funding Clauses in Lease Agreements, December 28, 1979	*FASB Statement No. 13*
79–11	Effect of a Penalty on the Term of a Lease, December 28, 1979	*FASB Statement No. 13*
79–12	Interest Rate Used in Calculating the Present Value of Minimum Lease Payments, December 28, 1979	*FASB Statement No. 13*
79–13	Applicability of *FASB Statement No. 13* to Current Value Financial Statements, December 28, 1979	*FASB Statement No. 13*
79–14	Upward Adjustment of Guaranteed Residual Values, December 28, 1979	*FASB Statement No. 13*
79–15	Accounting for Loss on a Sublease Not Involving the Disposal of a Segment, December 28, 1979	*FASB Statement No. 13* and *FASB Interpret. No. 27*
79–16	Effect of a Change in Income Tax Rate on the Accounting for Leveraged Leases, December 28, 1979	*FASB Statement No. 13*
79–17	Reporting Cumulative Effect Adjustment from Retroactive Application of *FASB Statement No. 13,* December 28, 1979	*FASB Statement No. 13*
79–18	Transition Requirement of Certain FASB Amendments and Interpretations of *FASB Statement No. 13,* December 28, 1979	*FASB Statements 17, 22, 23, 26, 27, 28,* and *29;* and *FASB Interpretations 19, 21, 23, 24, 26* and *27* (all related to *FASB Statement No. 13*)
79–19	Investor's Accounting for Unrealized Losses on Marketable Securities Owned by an Equity Method Investee, December 28, 1979	*FASB Statement No. 12* and *APB Opinion No. 18*
80–1	Early Extinguishment of Debt through Exchange for Common or Preferred Stock, December 19, 1980	*APB Opinion No. 26, FASB Statement No. 4,* and *FASB Statement No. 15*
81–1	Disclosure of Interest Rate Futures Contracts and Forward and Standby Contracts, February 6, 1981	*APB Opinion No. 22*
81–2	Accounting for Unused Investment Tax Credits Acquired in a Business Combination Accounted for by the Purchase Method, February 6, 1981	*FASB Statement No. 38* and *FASB Interpret. No. 25*
81–3	Multiemployer Pension Plan Amendments Act of 1980, February 6, 1981	*APB Opinion No. 8, FASB Interpretation No. 3,* and *FASB Statement No. 36*
81–4	Classification as Monetary or Nonmonetary Items, February 6, 1981	*FASB Statement No. 33*
81–5	Offsetting Interest Cost to Be Capitalized with Interest Income, February 6, 1981	*FASB Statement No. 34*
81–6	Applicability of *FASB Statement 15* to Debtors in Bankruptcy Situations, November 30, 1981	*FASB Statement No. 35*

QUESTIONS

PART A

1. Define *accounting.*
2. Explain the distinction between *financial* and *management* accounting. Does this distinction mean that a company should have two accounting systems? Explain.
3. What is meant by *general-purpose financial statements?* What are their basic components?
4. What is the *basic objective* of external financial statements?
5. Explain why the emphasis in financial accounting is on *measurement* and *communication.*
6. What are the *primary endeavors* of certified public accounts (CPAs)?
7. The independent CPA fulfills a unique professional role. Explain the concept of independence and why it is important to society in general.
8. The following statements deal specifically with accounting principles, standards, and procedures. For each, you are to explain its development and its current status.
   a. *Accounting Research Bulletins.*
   b. *Opinions* of the APB.
   c. *FASB Statements of Financial Accounting Standards.*
   d. *FASB Interpretations.*
   e. *FASB Statements of Financial Accounting Concepts.*
9. Explain the developments that led to the establishment of the FASB.
10. Briefly explain the role that the SEC has fulfilled in the establishment of accounting standards. What has been its relationship to the accounting profession in this role?
11. What is the AAA? What role has it fulfilled in the development of accounting theory and standards?
12. Is an approach that is permitted for income tax purposes necessarily "generally accepted" for financial accounting purposes? Explain.

PART B

13. What is the *basic objective* of accounting and what is the *role* of external financial reporting in terms of that objective?
14. Briefly explain the two types of financial statements that are prepared to assist external decision makers.
15. Explain the four basic assumptions that underlie implementation of accounting.
16. What is the basic accounting problem created by the unit-of-measure assumption when there is significant inflation?
17. Explain why the time period assumption causes accruals and deferrals in accounting.
18. Relate the continuity assumption to periodicity of financial statements.
19. Which assumption or principle discussed in this chapter is most affected by the phenomenon of *inflation?* Give reasons for your choice.
20. Relate the continuity assumption to use of the accrual basis of accounting.
21. Explain the *cost principle.* Why is it used in the basic financial statements in preference to a current value model?
22. How is cost measured in noncash transactions?
23. Define the *revenue principle* and explain each of its three aspects: *(a)* definition, *(b)* measurement, and *(c)* realization.
24. How is revenue measured in transactions involving noncash items (exclude credit situations)?
25. Explain the *matching principle.* What is meant by "the expense should follow the revenue"?
26. Explain why the matching principle usually necessitates the use of adjusting entries. Use depreciation expense and unpaid wages as examples.
27. Relate the matching principle to the revenue and cost principles.
28. Explain the *reliability principle.*
29. What is the relationship of comparability to consistency?
30. Explain the *comparability* (including *consistency*) *principle.* Why is it important to the statement user?
31. Explain the *reporting principle.*
32. What is the basic *implementation constraint* on accounting information? Give an example of an implementation constraint.

33. Briefly explain the technical term *generally accepted accounting principles* (GAAP) as used by the accounting profession.

34. What accounting principle or assumption is manifested in each situation below?

    a. Prepayment for an annual license is ratably debited to expense over the next 12 months.
    b. Jerry Jenkins owns a shoe repair shop, a restaurant, and a service station. Different and independent statements are prepared for each business.
    c. Inventories at King Store are valued at lower of cost or market (LCM).
    d. Although the inflation rate for the most recent fiscal year of Clyde's Auto Dealership was 9 percent, no cognizance was taken of it in the year-end statements.
    e. While making a delivery the driver for Cross Appliance Store collided with another vehicle causing both property damage and personal injury. The party sued Cross for damages which could exceed Cross's insurance coverage. Existence of the suit was disclosed on Cross's most recent financial statements.

SUPPLEMENT 1–A

35. Associate the approaches enumerated in the left-hand column with the concepts set forth in the right-hand column.

Approaches to Accounting Theory Development	Related Concepts
______1. Information economics.	*a.* How much wealth an entity can consume during a period and be as well off at the end as at the start.
______2. True income.	*b.* Derivation of principles from existing accounting practices.
______3. Inductive.	*c.* Emphasizes actions of investors who are assumed to be interested in predicting cash flows and assessing risk.
______4. Decision usefulness.	*d.* Costs are measured against benefits.

DECISION CASE 1–1

You and some classmates, Bob, Harold, and Susan, are engaged in a high-level bull session about some accounting topics. During the evening, the following discussion ensues.

Concerning the accrual basis of accounting, Bob says its primary aim is *reliability,* noting that statements prepared on a cash basis are subject to the manipulation and control of management, and would be unreliable in the hands of a management bent on window dressing the results of a given period.

Harold says the thrust of accrual accounting is the *matching principle.* He asserts that by assigning income-determining elements to accounting periods on the basis of passage of time, related revenues and expenses are matched.

Susan partially agrees with Harold, but observes that many expenses and revenues are not time related. She says accrual accounting is widely used because of precedent. She believes that if a new entity were to adopt the cash basis of accounting, the adoption would do violence to *comparability;* in other words, statements of the new entity would not be comparable with those of others in the same industry.

Required:
Analyze separately the positions of Bob, Harold, and Susan. If you believe one of them is partially correct, indicate wherein you agree and why. If you disagree, cite reasons for your disagreement.

DECISION CASE 1–2

Bronson Corporation, at the end of 19X, reported the following (summarized):

Balance Sheet

Total assets	$100,000
Total liabilities	30,000
Total owners' equity	70,000

Income Statement

Sales revenue	$180,000
Expenses	150,000
Net income	30,000

Required:
a. This problem focuses on the concept of materiality.

Define materiality. Do not feel constrained by the definition in the chapter.

b. On the basis of *your definition*, use your best judgment to respond to each of the following examples. For each example make a choice as to materiality, then justify it.

(1) At the beginning of the accounting year, an operational asset, with an estimated useful life of five years and no residual value, was purchased. If the cost is not capitalized, it will be expensed as incurred. The amount in the purchase transaction is material if the amount is (check for "yes" response):

____	$ 100	____	$ 10,000
____	500	____	20,000
____	1,000	____	50,000
____	5,000	____	100,000

(2) At the end of the accounting year, the amount of accrued wages payable is material if the amount is (check for "yes" response):

____	$ 100	____	$ 10,000
____	500	____	20,000
____	1,000	____	50,000
____	5,000	____	100,000

(3) At the end of the accounting year, unearned revenue (cash has been collected) is material if the amount is (check for "yes" response):

____	$ 100	____	$ 10,000
____	500	____	20,000
____	1,000	____	50,000
____	5,000	____	100,000

EXERCISES

PART B ONLY

Exercise 1–1

Give the accounting principle that establishes the dollar valuation in the balance sheet for each of the following items:

a. Inventory.
b. Plant and equipment.
c. Plant site (land).
d. Patent.
e. Unearned rent revenue (rent collected in advance).
f. Accounts receivable.
g. Short-term investments.

Exercise 1–2

Traditional accounting theory is based on the assumption that the "value of money" is relatively stable. If there is a significant change in the price level or in the purchasing power of the dollar, problems arise in interpreting income data as determined under conventional accounting procedures.

Required:
State and explain briefly the nature of such problems as related to inventories and operational assets. You need not attempt to offer specific solutions to these problems.

(AICPA adapted)

Exercise 1–3

On December 31, 19X, the balance sheet for Ark Corporation showed the following (summarized):

Assets		
Current assets*		$ 60,000
Operational assets (net)		235,000
Patent		5,000
		$300,000
Liabilities and Stockholders' Equity		
Current liabilities		$ 30,000
Long-term liabilities		70,000
Contributed capital	$150,000	
Retained earnings	50,000	200,000
		$300,000

* No cash.

On this date the business (including all assets and liabilities) was sold to L. Lentz who paid $320,000 cash which included $35,000 for "goodwill." Assume GAAP were followed. Explain in terms of these principles why the selling price was still $85,000 higher than the sum of owners' equity shown on the balance sheet plus the goodwill.

Exercise 1–4

Explain how each of the following items, as reported on Cate Corporation's balance sheet, violated (if it did) the financial reporting principle.

a. There was no comment or explanation of the fact that the company changed its inventory method from FIFO to LIFO.
b. Owners' equity reported only two amounts: capital stock, $100,000; and retained earnings, $80,000. The cap-

ital stock has a par value of $100,000 and originally sold for $150,000 cash.

c. Although sales amounted to $900,000 and cost of goods sold, $500,000, the first line on the income statement was revenues, $400,000.

d. No earnings per share (EPS) amounts were reported.

e. Although current assets amounted to $200,000 and current liabilities, $180,000, the balance sheet reported, under assets, the following single amount: working capital, $20,000.

f. The income statement showed only the following classifications:

Gross revenues
Costs
Net profit (AICPA adapted)

Exercise 1–5

The general manager of Symon, Inc., received an income statement from the controller. The statement covered the calendar year. The general manager said to the controller, "This statement indicates that a net income of only $250,000 was earned last year. You know the value of the company is much more than it was this time last year."

"You're probably right," replied the controller. "You see, there are factors in accounting which sometimes keep reported operating results from reflecting the change in market value of the company."

Required:
Present a detailed explanation of the accounting theories and principles to which the controller referred. (AICPA adapted)

Exercise 1–6

Accountants frequently refer to a concept of "conservatism." Explain what is meant by conservatism in accounting. Discuss the question of the extent to which it is possible to follow accounting procedures which will result in consistently conservative financial statements over a considerable number of years. Give an example of an application of conservatism in accounting. (AICPA adapted)

Exercise 1–7

In making an audit of Bliss Company, you find certain liabilities, such as taxes, which appear to be overstated. Also some semiobsolete inventory items seem to be undervalued, and the tendency is to expense rather than to capitalize as many items as possible.

In talking with the management about the policies, you are told that "the company has always taken a very conservative view of the business and its future prospects." Management suggests that they do not wish to weaken the company by reporting any more earnings or paying any more dividends than are absolutely necessary, since they do not expect business to continue to be good. They point out that the undervaluation of assets, and so on, does not lose anything for the company and creates reserves for "hard times."

Required:
You are to discuss fully whether the policies followed by the company are appropriate and comment on each of the arguments presented by management. (AICPA adapted)

Exercise 1–8

What is the meaning of *consistency* in the application of accounting principles—for example, as used in the standard form of an independent public accountant's report? Does this concept preclude companies from changing their accounting methods? Discuss. (AICPA adapted)

Exercise 1–9

The financial statements of Phillips Corporation included the following note: "During the current year, plant assets were written down by $6,000,000 because of economic conditions. This resulted in substantial savings to the company. Depreciation and other expenses in future years will be lower as a result; this will benefit profits of future years." Appraise this statement in terms of (1) economic soundness and (2) GAAP.

Exercise 1–10

The following summarized data were taken from the records of Schwarz Company at December 31, 19B, end of the accounting year:

1. Sales: 19B cash sales, $150,000; and 19B credit sales, $110,000.
2. Cash collections during 19B: on 19A credit sales, $30,000; on 19B credit sales, $80,000; and on 19C sales (collected in advance), $20,000.
3. Expenses: 19B cash expenses, $180,000; and 19B credit expenses, $70,000.
4. Cash payments during 19B: for 19A credit expenses, $10,000; for 19B credit expenses, $40,000; and for 19C expenses (paid in advance), $7,000.

Required:
Complete the following statements for 19B as a basis for evaluating the difference between cash and accrual accounting.

	Cash Basis	Accrual Basis
Sales revenue	$______	$______
Expenses	______	______
Net income	______	______

PROBLEMS

PART B ONLY

Problem 1–1

This problem focuses on the revenue principle. Respond to each of the following:

a. Define revenue in accordance with the revenue principle.
b. What should be the dollar amount of revenue recognized under the revenue principle in the case of (1) sales and services for cash and (2) sales and services rendered in exchange for noncash considerations?
c. How should revenue be recognized when there is a highly speculative transaction involving potential revenue?
d. When should revenue be recognized in the case of long-term, low down payment sales and when collectibility is very uncertain?
e. When should revenue be recognized for long-term construction contracts?

Problem 1–2

Poss, Inc. has been involved in a number of transactions necessitating careful interpretation of the revenue principle. For each of the following 19B transactions (1) specify the amount of revenue that should be recognized during 19B and (2) explain the basis for your determination.

a. Regular credit sales amounted to $250,000, of which two thirds was collected by the end of 19B; the balance will be collected in 19C.
b. Regular services were rendered on credit amounting to $190,000, of which three fourths will be collected in 19C.
c. A special item, that had been repossessed from the first purchaser, was sold again for $5,000. A $3,000 cash down payment was received in 19B; the balance is to be paid on a quarterly basis during 19C and 19D. Repossession again would not be a surprise! The item has a new cost of $4,000.
d. On January 1, 19A, the company purchased a $10,000 note. Because it was highly speculative whether the note was collectible, the company was able to acquire it for $1,000 cash. The note specifies 8% simple interest payable each year (disregard interest prior to 19A). The first collection on the note was $1,500 cash on December 31, 19B. Further collections are highly speculative.

Problem 1–3

Appraise each of the following statements for correctness in terms of the appropriate accounting principles, assumptions, and constraints:

a. The accounting entity is considered to be separate and apart from the owners.
b. A transaction involving a very small amount does not need to be recorded because of materiality.
c. The monetary unit is not stable over time.
d. The reporting principle requires the use of notes to the financial statements.
e. LCM should be used in inventories.
f. The cost principle relates only to the income statement.
g. Revenue should be recognized only when the cash is received.
h. Accruals and deferrals are necessary because of the separate entity assumption.
i. Revenue should be recognized as early as possible and expenses as late as possible.

Problem 1–4

Bad Luck Corporation was experiencing a bad year because they were operating at a loss. In order to minimize the loss, they recorded certain transactions as indicated below. Determine for each transaction what accounting principle was violated (if any) and explain the nature of the violation. Also, in each instance indicate the correct accounting treatment by giving the correct entry.

a. At the beginning of the year a new machine costing $80,000 was purchased for cash for use in the business. The estimated useful life was 10 years, and the estimated residual value was $10,000. The following depreciation entry was made at the end of the year:

Depreciation expense	3,500	
Accumulated depreciation		3,500

b. A patent was being amortized over a 17-year useful life. The amortization entry made at the end of the current year was:

Retained earnings	500	
Patent		500

c. Two delivery trucks were repaired (engine tuneup, new tires, brakes relined, front end realigned) at a cost of $350. The following entry was made:

Operational asset—trucks	350	
Cash		350

d. Although the bad debt loss rate did not change, no adjusting entry was made for the estimate of $2,000.
e. Goods for resale (inventory) were being acquired for $1 per unit. However, the company located a good deal and acquired 10,000 units for $7,500 cash. They recorded the purchase as follows:

Inventory	10,000	
Cash		7,500
Revenue		2,500

Problem 1–5

The transactions summarized below were recorded as indicated during the current year. Determine for each transaction what accounting principle was violated (if any) and explain the nature of the violation. Also in each instance indicate how the transaction should have been recorded.

a. The company needed a small structure for temporary storage. A contractor quoted a price of $650,000. The company decided to build it themselves. The cost was $550,000, and construction required three months. The following entry was made:

Operational assets—warehouse	650,000	
Cash		550,000
Revenue		100,000

b. The company owns a plant that is located on a river that floods every few years. As a result, the company suffers a flood loss regularly. During the current year, the flood was severe causing an uninsured loss of $4,800. The following entry was made to recognize the loss:

Retained earnings	4,800	
Cash		4,800

c. The company originally sold and issued 50,000 shares of $100 par value common stock. During the current year, 45,000 of these shares were outstanding and 5,000 were held by the company as treasury stock (they had been repurchased from the shareholders in prior years). Near the end of the current year, the board of directors declared and paid a cash dividend of $2 per share. The dividend was recorded as follows:

Retained earnings	100,000	
Cash		90,000
Investment income		10,000

Problem 1–6

Following is a series of transactions during 19B for McGregor Corporation. Analyze each and then answer the questions.

a. At December 31, 19B, there was an item in the inventory of goods for sale that cost $200. Because it had become obsolete, it was estimated that it could be sold for $65 cash (assume this to be its net realizable value). Accounting for the obsolete item is under consideration.
(1) What accounting principle should govern? Explain.
(2) What amount should be used by the company for this item in the December 31, 19B, inventory? Explain.

b. The corporation acquired a special item of equipment that would be used in operations (an operational asset). The supplier's catalog listed the item at $15,000. Since the corporation was short of cash, it exchanged a small parcel of land that it had acquired 10 years earlier at a cost of $8,000. The land was assessed for tax purposes at $12,000, and a recent appraisal by an independent appraiser showed a market value of $14,000. Accounting for the equipment is under consideration.
(1) What accounting principle should govern at the date of acquisition? Explain.
(2) What amount should be debited to the operational asset account? Explain.
(3) What accounting principle governs the recognition of depreciation on the asset? Explain.

c. During 19B, the company engaged a local attorney to represent it in a dispute with respect to an accident involving a company vehicle. The attorney presented a bill for services for $1,500. Since the company was short of cash, the attorney agreed to accept 100 shares of McGregor common stock (par $10 per share). The last sale of stock was for $17 per share three years earlier. The transaction to record settlement of the attorney's fee is under consideration.
(1) What accounting principle should govern? Explain.
(2) When should the fee be recognized as an expense? Explain.
(3) What amount should be recorded as legal expense? Explain.

d. The corporation sold a large item of equipment which it stocked for sale. The sale was made on December 31, 19B, for $10,000 cash. It is estimated that because of a one-year guarantee on the equipment, during the following year, $300 cash will be spent on the warranty. Recognition of the warranty expense is under consideration.
(1) What accounting principle should govern? Explain.
(2) When should the warranty expense be recognized? Explain.
(3) What amount should be recorded as warranty expense in 19B? In 19C? Explain.

Problem 1–7

The following summarized data were taken from the records of Trippett Corporation at the end of the annual accounting period, December 31, 19B:

Sales for cash	$261,000
Sales on account	84,000
Cash purchases of mdse. for resale	170,000
Credit purchases of mdse. for resale	40,000
Expenses paid in cash (incl. any prepayments)	71,000
Accounts receivable:	
Balance in account on 1/1/19B	23,000
Balance in account on 12/31/19B	30,000
Accounts payable:	
Balance in account on 1/1/19B	14,000
Balance in account on 12/31/19B	16,000

Merchandise inventory:	
Beginning inventory, 1/1/19B	50,000
Ending inventory, 12/31/19B	60,000
Accrued (unpaid) wages at 12/31/19B (none at 1/1/19B)	2,000
Prepaid expenses at 12/31/19B (none at 1/1/19B)	3,000
Operational assets—equipment:	
Cost when acquired	100,000
Annual depreciation	10,000

Required:
Based on the above data, complete the following income statements for 19B in order to evaluate the difference between cash and accrual basis:

	Cash Basis		Accrual Basis	
Sales revenue		$____		$____
Less expenses:				
Cost of goods sold	$____		$____	
Depreciation expense	____		____	
Remaining expenses	____		____	
Total expenses		$____		$____
Pretax income		====		====

Problem 1–8

Appraise each of the following items in financial statements in terms of GAAP. Indicate the principle(s) violated and the violation with respect to each item. Also, in each instance indicate the correct accounting treatment.

a. Inventory (through purchases) was recorded at $14,000 when purchased on credit; terms, 2/10,n/30.

b. Accounts Receivable of $60,000 included amounts due soon from the company president amounting to $50,000.

c. Usual and ordinary repairs on operational assets were recorded as follows: debit Operational Assets, $12,000; credit Cash, $12,000.

d. The company sustained a $20,000 storm damage loss during the current year. The loss was reported as follows:

Income statement: Extraordinary Item—storm loss, $2,000.

Balance sheet: Deferred Charge (under assets), $18,000.

e. Treasury stock (i.e., stock of the company that was sold and subsequently bought back from the shareholders) was reported on the balance sheet as an asset, $18,000.

f. Depreciation expense of $41,000 was deducted directly from Retained Earnings.

g. Income tax expense of $48,000 was deducted directly from Retained Earnings.

2

Review—The Accounting Model and Information Processing

PURPOSE OF THE CHAPTER

The objective of financial accounting is to provide relevant reliable financial information to external decision makers. The periodic financial statements summarize the economic impacts of transactions and other events on an entity. The accounting system must be designed to (1) collect and measure economic data, (2) classify and process the data, and (3) summarize economic effects in financial reports for decision makers. An accounting system must be tailored to the entity's characteristics, such as size, nature of operations, organizational structure, management approaches, and extent of government regulation. However, a fundamental structure, based upon the accounting model, is common to most accounting systems.

The purpose of this chapter is to review and illustrate the accounting model and the information processing cycle which is repeated each accounting period. To accomplish this purpose, the chapter is subdivided as follows:

Part A—The Accounting Model and Information Processing during the Period

Part B—Information Processing at the End of the Period—Adjusting Entries, Worksheet, Closing Entries, and Preparation of the Financial Statements

Supplement 2–A—Control Accounts, Subsidiary Ledgers, and Special Journals

Supplement 2–B—Worksheet for a Manufacturing Company

Part A: The Accounting Model and Information Processing during the Period

THE ACCOUNTING MODEL

In Chapter 1, Part B, we outlined the basic financial statements produced by most accounting systems. The three required financial statements—balance sheet, income statement, and statement of changes in financial position (SCFP)—are derived from the financial statement elements, which are accumulated in terms of the **accounting model.** The accounting model can be expressed as three submodels as follows:

1. Financial position model (the balance sheet):

$$\text{Assets} = \text{Liabilities} + \text{Owners' equity}$$

2. Results of operations model (the income statement):

$$\text{Revenues} - \text{Expenses} + \text{Gains} - \text{Losses} = \text{Net income}$$

3. Funds flow model (SCFP):

$$\text{Funds inflow} - \text{Funds outflow} = \text{Net change in funds}$$

Coupled with the accounting model is the debit-credit concept. This is a mathematical technique used to record increases and decreases in specific elements in the model—assets, liabilities, owners' equity, revenues, expenses, gains, and losses.

Fundamentally, all recognized accounting events are recorded in the accounting system in terms of the **financial position model:** A = L + OE. The debit-credit concept is superimposed on this basic model as follows:

	Assets		=	Liabilities		+	Owners' Equity	
Basic Model								
Debit-Credit Concept	Debit for increases	Credit for decreases		Debit for decreases	Credit for increases		Debit for decreases	Credit for increases

Because investments by owners, revenues, and gains **increase** owners' equity and distributions to owners, expenses, and losses **decrease** owners' equity, the model can be expanded to include them as follows:

Assets		=	Liabilities		+	Owners' Equity	
Debit for increases	Credit for decreases		Debit for decreases	Credit for increases		Debit for decreases: *a.* Distributions to owners. *b.* Expenses. *c.* Losses.	Credit for increases: *a.* Investments by owners. *b.* Revenues. *c.* Gains.

Observe in the above diagram that although the debits are **always** on the left and the credits are **always** on the right, the increases and decreases are in opposite positions on each side of the equation. That is, debits represent increases to assets and decreases to liabilities and owners' equity, whereas credits represent decreases to assets and increases to liabilities and owners' equity. Expenses and losses are recorded as debits, and revenues and gains as credits. This algebraic arrangement forces debits always to equal credits. Thus, the fundamental accounting model always maintains a dual balancing feature, viz:

1. Assets = Liabilities + Owners' equity.
2. Debits = Credits.

Because of this dual feature, the accounting model often is referred to as a **double-entry system.** The two balancing features add reliability to the output of an accounting system by calling attention to those errors which cause the system to be out of balance.

Whether an accounting system is maintained manually, mechanically, or electronically, each entry is recorded in the basic accounting model. Thus, each entry entered in an accounting system maintains the dual-balancing feature singly and on a cumulative basis. The fundamental information processing approach is reviewed in Exhibit 2–1. In particular, note the following: (1) transaction analysis in terms of the basic accounting model—column B, (2) A = L + OE for each entry and cumulatively—column C, and (3) debits equal credits for each entry and cumulatively—column D.

THE ACCOUNTING INFORMATION PROCESSING CYCLE

The accounting system provides a systematic approach for processing information from the capture of raw economic data that affect the entity to the

EXHIBIT 2–1: Information Inputs in an Accounting System

Column A Typical Transaction	Column B Transaction Analysis	Column C Basic Accounting Model (with cumulative balances) A	= L	+ OE	Column D Entry into the Accounting System Accounts	Debit	Credit
1. Service Corporation was organized; owners invested $100,000 cash and received nopar common stock.	Asset increased—cash, $100,000. Owners' equity increased—common stock, $100,000. Liabilities—no effect.	+100,000		+100,000	Cash Common stock	100,000	 100,000
		100,000	-0-	100,000		100,000	100,000
2. Borrowed $50,000 on a note payable.	Asset increased—cash, $50,000. Liabilities increased—notes payable, $50,000. Owners' equity—no effect.	+ 50,000	+50,000		Cash Notes payable	50,000	 50,000
		150,000	50,000	100,000		150,000	150,000
3. Purchased equipment for use in the business, $40,000; paid cash.	Asset increased—equipment $40,000. Asset decreased—cash, $40,000. Liabilities—no effect. Owners' equity—no effect.	+ 40,000 − 40,000			Equipment Cash	40,000	 40,000
		150,000	50,000	100,000		190,000	190,000
4. Services rendered to clients, $20,000 of which $15,000 was collected in cash.	Assets increased—cash, $15,000; accounts receivable, $5,000. Owners' equity increased—revenue, $20,000. Liabilities—no effect.	+ 15,000 +5,000		+ 20,000	Cash Accounts receivable Service revenue	15,000 5,000	 20,000
		170,000	50,000	120,000		210,000	210,000
5. Incurred operating expenses, $11,000, of which $8,000 was paid in cash.	Asset decreased—cash, $8,000. Liability increased—accounts payable $3,000. Owners' equity decreased—expense, $11,000.	− 8,000	+ 3,000	− 11,000	Expenses Cash Accounts payable	11,000	 8,000 3,000
		162,000	53,000	109,000		221,000	221,000
6. Paid $2,000 on accounts payable (5 above).	Asset decreased—cash, $2,000. Liability decreased—accounts payable, $2,000. Owners' equity—no effect.	− 2,000	− 2,000		Accounts payable Cash	2,000	 2,000
		160,000	51,000	109,000		223,000	223,000
7. Depreciation for 1 year on equipment; estimated life, 10 years, no residual value (3 above).	Asset decreased—accumulated depreciation, $4,000. Owners' equity decreased—depreciation expense, $4,000. Liabilities—no effect.	− 4,000		− 4,000	Depreciation expense Accumulated depreciation, equipment	4,000	 4,000
		156,000	51,000	105,000		227,000	227,000

end result, the periodic financial statements. Therefore, an accounting system incorporates an information processing cycle, often called the **accounting cycle,** that is repeated each accounting period. The cycle, diagrammed in Exhibit 2–2, reflects the **sequential order** in which the specific phases usually are accomplished. Each phase will be discussed and illustrated in order.

COLLECTION OF RAW ECONOMIC DATA (PHASE 1)

The accounting system collects raw economic data about **events** affecting the entity that are to be recorded. Two types of events are recognized in an accounting system: (1) exchange transactions between the entity and one or more outside parties, such as the sale of goods, purchase of assets, sale of securities, and payment of wages; and (2) other events that are not exchange transactions but which exert an economic impact on the enterprise and must be recorded. These "nontransaction" events may be external, such as casualties (e.g., floods, fires, hurricanes, etc.) and changes in currency exchange rates. Also, they may be internal, that is, involving no outside parties but rather involving the conversion or use of resources, such as depreciation of operational assets and amortization of intangibles.[1]

Raw economic data are collected by means of **source documents.** Because exchange transactions involve external parties, they almost always generate their own source documents—sale invoices, freight bills, notes signed by debtors, purchase orders, deposit slips, checks, and so on. For nontransaction events, the entity itself must prepare the source documents. Examples of nontransaction events are depreciation computations and issues of raw materials to work in process inventory. The source documents are an important phase of data collection because *(a)* they provide basic data for transaction analysis (and the resulting journal entry) and *(b)* they constitute a "track record" so that the event and the measurement of its effects on the entity subsequently can be **verified.**

[1] For convenience in exposition, the term **transactions** will be used broadly to include both transactions and the other events to be recognized.

TRANSACTION ANALYSIS (PHASE 2)

Transaction analysis is a mental process because it involves an analysis of each transaction to assess its economic impact on the entity in terms of the assets, liabilities, owners' equity, revenues, expenses, gains, and losses of the entity.

Transaction analysis is the basis for developing the **accounting entry,** or entries, that must be recorded in the accounting system. Transaction analysis often requires a high degree of accounting sophistication because the competence with which it is done determines the reliability of the periodic financial statements. Effective transaction analysis depends upon sound knowledge of the theory and structure of accounting discussed in Chapter 1.

JOURNALIZING—THE ORIGINAL DATA INPUT (PHASE 3)

This phase constitutes the original input of economic data into an accounting system. Each transaction is first recorded in a **journal** which is a chronological record (i.e., by order of date) of each transaction in terms of the fundamental accounting model (A = L + OE) and in debit-credit format. Journalizing follows transaction analysis; it records what accounts are increased and decreased and the amount of each change.

Basically, a journal entry lists the date of the transaction, the account(s) debited and the account(s) credited, and their respective amounts. Each entry is recorded so that the integrity of the duality of the system is maintained: A = L + OE and Debits = Credits. Although the journal is not absolutely essential (one could skip it and go directly to the ledger), it is important because it *(a)* maintains a chronological record of the transactions recognized in the system, which is useful for subsequent tracing; and *(b)* shows in one place all aspects of each transaction (i.e., all accounts affected and the amounts).

Manual accounting systems usually have two types of journals: (1) the general journal and (2) several special journals. Each special journal is designed to accommodate like-kind transactions. The commonly used special journals are credit sales, credit purchases, cash receipts, cash payments, and the voucher journal. Special journals are discussed and illustrated in Supplement 2–A of this chapter. Most

EXHIBIT 2–2: Diagram of the Accounting Information Processing Cycle

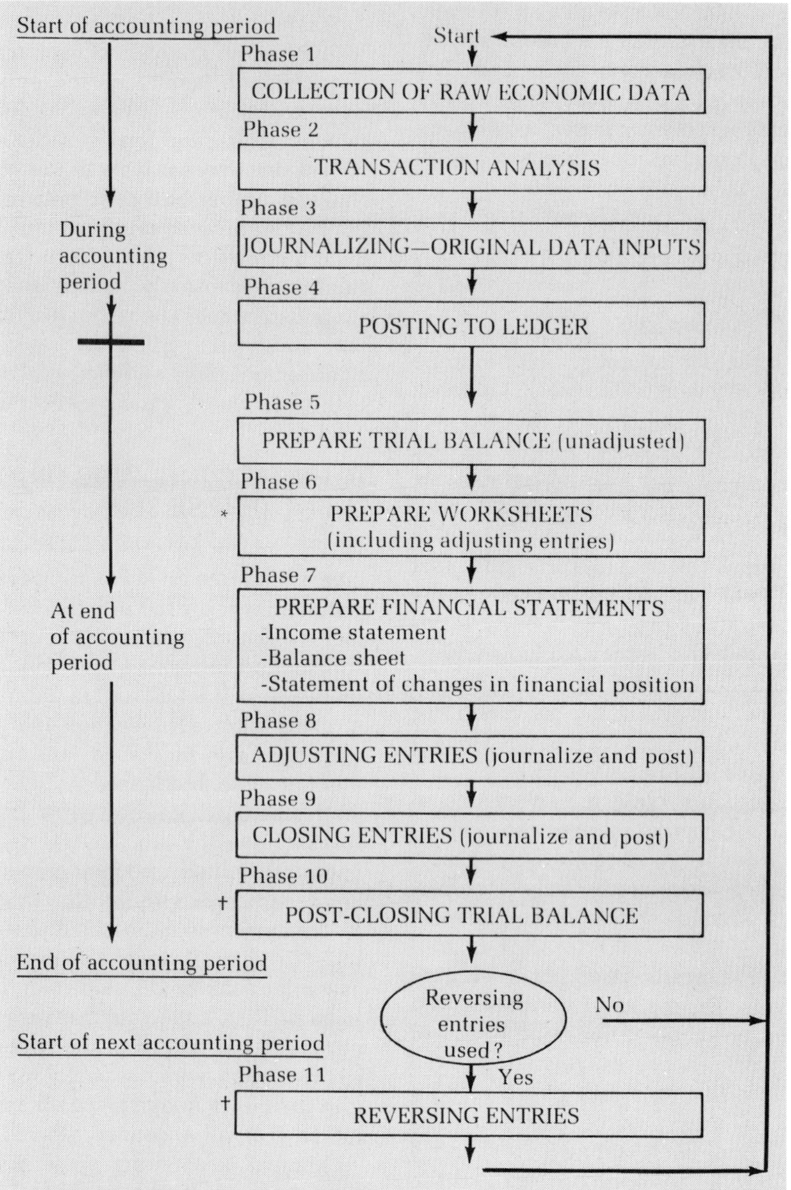

Note: See Exhibit 2–10 for complete summary.

* Worksheets are optional. If not used, prepare an **adjusted** trial balance after Phase 8 as a basis for preparing the financial statements.

† Optional.

accounting systems use at least a general journal. A general journal will be used in the chapters to follow because of its value for instructional purposes. The general journal format, with a typical entry, is shown in Exhibit 2–3.

Many companies use computerized accounting systems that bypass the journal at various stages. For example, the systems of many retailers record, at the cash register, the cash or account receivable received for the sale and the decrease in the specific inventory item—all simultaneously. Thus, they effectively bypass the journal and go directly to the ledger.

POSTING TO THE LEDGER (PHASE 4)

After the initial recording in the journal, the next phase is transfer of the information to the ledger. This transfer process, called **posting,** has the effect of reclassifying the information from the chronological format in the journal to an account classification format in the **ledger.** Posting from the journal to the ledger is illustrated in Exhibit 2–3.

The ledger consists of a large number of separate accounts. There are accounts for each kind of asset (such as cash, accounts receivable, investments, land, buildings, and equipment), liability (such as accounts payable and bonds payable), owners' equity (such as capital stock and retained earnings), revenue, expense, gain, and loss. Posting amounts from the journal to the ledger results in reclassification of the data by accounts, which is compatible with the classifications of information in the financial statements.

PREPARE A TRIAL BALANCE—UNADJUSTED (PHASE 5)

At the end of each period, after all of the regular entries for completed transactions have been journalized and posted to the ledger, a trial balance should be prepared. Since this trial balance is prepared **before** the adjusting entries are made, it is often called the **unadjusted trial balance.** A trial balance is simply a list of all of the accounts in the general ledger and their respective debit or credit balances. A trial balance, prepared after all of the regular entries but before the adjusting entries, serves the following purposes:

1. It verifies that debits equal credits.
2. It provides important information for the development of—
   a. A worksheet.
   b. The end-of-period adjusting entries.

An unadjusted trial balance for Ace Retailers, Inc., is shown in Exhibit 2–4.

As soon as the unadjusted trial balance is completed, the **information processing at the end of the period** can be started. These phases, 6–10 (see Exhibit 2–2), are discussed in Part B of this chapter.

Permanent and Temporary Accounts

The accounts in the ledger often are classified as follows.

1. **Permanent** accounts—These are the balance sheet accounts. They are **permanent** or real, in the sense that they are not closed at the end of each accounting period. They are the asset, liability, and owners' equity accounts. The related contra accounts also are permanent accounts.
2. **Temporary** accounts—These are the income statement accounts. They are **temporary,** or nominal, in the sense that they are closed at the end of each accounting period. They are principally the revenue, expense, gain, and loss accounts.[2]

An account, either permanent or temporary, may be "mixed" at a specific time in the sense that its **balance** may contain both a permanent (i.e., balance sheet) component and a temporary (i.e., income statement) component. To illustrate, assume that on January 1 of the current year, a three-year insurance premium of $600 was paid and debited to a permanent account, Prepaid Insurance. On December 31 of the current year, of the $600, the temporary component, Insurance Expense, is $200 and the permanent component, Prepaid Insurance, is $400 (an asset). An adjusting entry on December 31, debiting Insurance Expense and crediting Prepaid Insurance for $200, is necessary to transfer from the Prepaid Insurance asset account the temporary component of $200 to a temporary account, Insurance Expense.

[2] Revenue, expense, gain, and loss accounts are subaccounts of owners' equity.

EXHIBIT 2–3: General Journal and General Ledger Illustrated

General Journal

Page J-16

Date	Accounts and Explanation	Ledger Folio*	Amount	
19J			Debit	Credit
Jan. 2	Equipment	150	15,000	
	Cash	101		5,000
	Notes payable	215		10,000
	Purchased equipment for use			
	in the business. Paid $5,000			
	cash and gave a $10,000, one-			
	year, note payable with 15%			
	interest payable at maturity.			

* The figures in this column indicate *(a)* that the amount has been posted to the ledger and *(b)* the account number in the ledger to which posted.

General Ledger

Cash — Acct. 101

19J Jan. 1	balance	18,700	19J Jan. 2	J-16†	5,000

Equipment — Acct. 150

19J Jan. 1	balance	62,000			
2	J-16†	15,000			

Notes Payable — Acct. 215

			19J Jan. 2	J-16†	10,000

† This figure indicates the journal page from which the amount was posted.

EXHIBIT 2–4: Unadjusted Trial Balance

ACE RETAILERS, INC.
Unadjusted Trial Balance
December 31, 19J

Account	Debit	Credit
Cash	$ 67,300	
Short-term notes receivable	8,000	
Accounts receivable	45,000	
Allowance for doubtful accts.		$ 1,000
Interest receivable		
Inventory (periodic)	75,000	
Prepaid insurance	600	
Land	8,000	
Building	160,000	
Accum. depr., building		90,000
Equipment	91,000	
Accum. depr., equip.		27,000
Accounts payable		29,000
Income taxes payable		
Interest payable		
Rent revenue collected in adv.		
Bonds payable, 6%		50,000
Common stock, par $10		150,000
Contrib. capital in excess of par		20,000
Retained earnings		31,500
Sales revenue		325,200
Interest revenue		500
Rent revenue		1,800
Purchases	130,000	
Freight on purchases	4,000	
Purchase returns		2,000
Selling expenses*	104,000	
G&A expenses*	23,600	
Interest expense	2,500	
Extraordinary loss	9,000	
Income tax expense		
Totals	$728,000	$728,000

* These broad categories of **expenses** are used to conserve space. They might represent control accounts. Also to conserve space, throughout "general and administrative" is abbreviated **G&A.**

Subsidiary Ledgers and Control Accounts

Most companies use both a **general ledger** and one or more **subsidiary ledgers.** Each subsidiary ledger has a related **control account** in the general ledger. The control account reflects summary information, whereas the subsidiary ledger reflects the details that support the control account. The general ledger contains the control accounts for all assets, liabilities, owners' equity, revenues, expenses, gains, and losses.

Each subsidiary ledger is a device for keeping track of the details of a particular control account in the general ledger. To illustrate, a department store may have 10,000 credit customers. A separate account receivable must be maintained for each customer. Rather than 10,000 different accounts receivable in the general ledger, one controlling account, Accounts Receivable Control, should be used. An accounts receivable subsidiary ledger composed of a separate account for each customer also should be maintained. Each credit sale would *(a)* be posted daily to the customer's account in the subsidiary ledger, and *(b)* the total of all credit sales periodically (e.g., daily or weekly) would be posted to the Accounts Receivable Control account in the general ledger. Thus, at any time when posting is complete, the sum of the balances in the customer accounts in the subsidiary ledger would agree with the single balance in the Accounts Receivable Control account.

Subsidiary ledgers often are used for cash (when there are numerous cash accounts), accounts receivable, accounts payable, operational assets, capital stock (a subsidiary ledger for this account is used when a company handles its own stock transfers; it is a record of each shareholder), revenue, and expense. Subsidiary ledgers and control accounts are discussed and illustrated in Supplement 2–A.

Part B: Information Processing at the End of the Period—Adjusting Entries, Worksheet, Closing Entries, and Preparation of the Financial Statements

As soon as the unadjusted trial balance is available, the following end-of-period procedures can be completed:

1. Develop the adjusting entries.
2. Journalize and post the adjusting and closing entries.
3. Prepare an adjusted trial balance.
4. Prepare the financial statements.

These procedures can be completed in the order listed above. Remember that the adjusting entries must be considered before the financial statements can be developed. However, accountants usually insert another step, preparation of two worksheets, viz: (1) one to facilitate development of the adjusting entries, the income statement, and the balance sheet; and (2) one to facilitate preparation of the statement of changes in financial position (SCFP). These worksheets simply are **facilitating techniques.** They constitute an orderly and systematic approach to completing *(a)* the adjusting and closing entries and *(b)* the financial statements. This is the only reason for using these worksheets (they are not journals, ledgers, or financial statements per se).

PREPARE WORKSHEET (PHASE 6)

A worksheet based on the **unadjusted** trial balance given in Exhibit 2–4 is presented in Exhibit 2–5. This worksheet provides data for the income statement and balance sheet.[3]

[3] If you are not interested in the worksheet technique presented in this chapter, omit the material under the caption "Completion of the Worksheet." However, mastery of techniques for organizing and analyzing a mass of data is essential in any accounting or financial capacity. Experience with traditional accounting worksheet techniques is helpful in acquiring this skill.

The worksheet shown in Exhibit 2–5 was prepared as follows:

1. Enter the ledger account titles and their balances (Exhibit 2–4) on the worksheet, using the accounts column and the first pair of amount columns (Exhibit 2–5).
2. Develop the adjusting entries and record them in the second pair of columns on the worksheet.
3. Extend the unadjusted balances, plus or minus the adjusting amounts, to the Adjusted Trial Balance columns and check for balance (i.e., $748,800 = $748,800).
4. Extend each adjusted amount to the right, line by line, to the pair of columns under the financial statement on which each should be reported: Income Statement, Retained Earnings, or Balance Sheet.
5. Check each pair of columns for equality of debits and credits.

DEVELOPMENT OF ADJUSTING ENTRIES

In accrual accounting, numerous adjustments must be made to the account balances (as reflected in the unadjusted trial balance) at the end of each accounting period. These adjustments are necessary to restate (i.e., adjust) certain income statement and balance sheet accounts because, prior to the adjusting entries, (1) some accounts have a "mixed" balance which includes both permanent and temporary components and (2) certain internal and external events have not yet been entered in the accounts. These adjustments may be classified as follows:

Deferred items—items for which the recognition of expense or revenue comes in an accounting period **after** the entity pays or receives cash, respectively:

1. Prepaid expense—an expense paid in advance of the period(s) in which it is recognized as an expense on the income statement.
2. Revenue collected in advance—a revenue collected in advance of the period(s) in which it is recognized as realized revenue on the income statement (frequently called unearned revenue and sometimes called deferred revenue).

Accrued items—items for which the recognition of expense or revenue comes in an accounting period **before** the entity pays or receives the cash, respectively:

3. Accrued expense—an expense incurred but not yet paid; therefore, it must be recorded.
4. Accrued revenue—a revenue earned but not yet collected; therefore, it must be recorded.

Other items:

5. Estimated items.

Prepaid Expense

A prepaid expense occurs when services or supplies were purchased or otherwise acquired but not consumed or used by the end of the accounting period. To illustrate, Ace Retailers, Inc., on January 1, 19J, paid a three-year insurance premium in advance amounting to $600. At that date, the $600 payment was recorded as a debit to Prepaid Insurance and a credit to Cash. On the unadjusted trial balance of the worksheet, the $600 is reflected as the debit balance of an asset account, Prepaid Insurance. Because $200 of this service was used up in 19J, a $400 balance should remain in the prepaid expense account. Therefore, on December 31, 19J, an adjusting entry must be made as follows (the letter code to the left is used on the worksheet, Exhibit 2–5, for reference in study):

a. December 31, 19J:

Insurance expense (G&A expense)	200	
Prepaid insurance		200

The effects of this entry, which are reflected on the worksheet, are (1) to adjust the asset account to $400, which is reported on the balance sheet; and (2) to record the $200 expense component, which is reported on the income statement.[4]

Revenue Collected in Advance

Precollected or unearned revenue occurs when a company collects cash for revenues that, at the end of the accounting period, have not yet been fully earned. To illustrate, Ace Retailers, Inc., on January 1, 19J, leased to J. R. Jones a small office in their building. At the start, they collected $1,800 cash in advance for 18 months rent. At that time, the collection was recorded as a debit to Cash and a credit to Rent Revenue. On December 31, 19J, the $1,800 balance in the Rent Revenue account included $600 unearned rent revenue. Therefore, the following adjusting entry was made (see Exhibit 2–5):

b. December 31, 19J:

Rent revenue	600	
Rent revenue collected in advance*		600

* Often called Unearned Rent Revenue.

This entry leaves $1,200 in the Rent Revenue account and separates as a liability the $600 unearned rent revenue. The $600 is a liability on December 31, 19J, because Ace owes that amount of "occupancy" to Jones. In 19K, the $600 will be transferred to the Rent Revenue account.[5]

Accrued Expense

An accrued expense is one that has been incurred by the end of the accounting period but has not been paid; therefore, it must be recorded. To illustrate, Ace Retailers, Inc., has a liability for bonds payable of $50,000. These bonds require payments of 6 percent annual interest each October 30. Therefore, on December 31, 19J, accrued (unpaid) interest expense was $\$50{,}000 \times .06 \times 2/12 = \$500$. This accrued interest must be recognized by the following adjusting entry (see Exhibit 2–5):

c. December 31, 19J:

Interest expense	500	
Interest payable		500

This adjusting entry records (1) the expense (interest expense) for income statement purposes and (2) the liability (interest payable) for balance sheet purposes.

Accrued Revenue

An accrued revenue is one that has been earned by the end of the accounting period but has not been collected; therefore, it must be recorded. To illustrate, Ace Retailers, Inc., held short-term notes receivable amounting to $8,000. These notes earn 15 percent annual interest which is received each November

[4] Sometimes a prepaid expense is initially debited to an expense account instead of an asset account, in which case, an adjusting entry also is required. To illustrate, assume the $600 was initially debited to **Insurance Expense.** The adjusting entry would be: debit Prepaid Insurance, $400; credit Insurance Expense, $400. In either case the net effect on the statements is the same.

[5] Alternatively, Ace Retailers, Inc., could have credited Unearned Rent Revenue when it collected $1,800 rent for 18 months. In that case, the year-end adjusting entry would be a debit to Unearned Rent Revenue, $1,200, and a credit to Rent Revenue, $1,200.

EXHIBIT 2–5: Worksheet

ACE RETAILERS, INC.
Worksheet for the Year Ended December 31, 19J

Accounts	Unadjusted Trial Balance		Adjusting Entries		Adjusted Trial Balance		Income Statement		Retained Earnings		Balance Sheet	
	Debit	Credit	Debit	Credit	Debit	Credit	Debit	Credit	Debit	Credit	Debit	Credit
Cash	67,300				67,300						67,300	
Short-term notes receivable	8,000				8,000						8,000	
Accounts receivable	45,000				45,000						45,000	
Allowance for doubtful accounts		1,000		*(f)* 1,200		2,200						2,200
Interest receivable			*(d)* 100		100						100	
Inventory (periodic)	75,000				75,000		75,000	90,000*			90,000	
Prepaid insurance	600			*(a)* 200	400						400	
Land	8,000				8,000						8,000	
Building	160,000				160,000						160,000	
Accum. depr., building		90,000		*(e)* 10,000		100,000						100,000
Equipment	91,000				91,000						91,000	
Accum. depr., equip.		27,000		*(e)* 9,000		36,000						36,000
Accounts payable		29,000				29,000						29,000
Interest payable				*(c)* 500		500						500
Rent revenue collected in advance				*(b)* 600		600						600
Bonds payable, 6%		50,000				50,000						50,000
Common stock, par												

in excess of par		20,000				20,000						20,000
Retained earnings		31,500				31,500				31,500		
Sales revenue		325,200				325,200		325,200				
Interest revenue		500		(d) 100		600		600				
Rent revenue		1,800	(b) 600			1,200		1,200				
Purchases	130,000				130,000		130,000					
Freight on purchases	4,000				4,000		4,000					
Purchase returns		2,000				2,000		2,000				
Selling expenses	104,000		(e) 8,200		113,400		113,400					
			(f) 1,200									
G&A expenses	23,600		(a) 200		34,600		34,600					
			(e) 10,800									
Interest expense	2,500		(c) 500		3,000		3,000					
Extraordinary loss	9,000				9,000		9,000					
	728,000	728,000	21,600	21,600	748,800	748,800	369,000	419,000				
Income tax expense†			(g) 20,000				20,000					
Income taxes payable				(g) 20,000								20,000
Net income to retained earnings							30,000			30,000		
Retained earnings to balance sheet									61,500			61,500
Totals							419,000	419,000	61,500	61,500	469,800	469,800

* This is only one of several techniques for entering the ending inventory on a worksheet.

† ($419,000 − $369,000) .40 = $20,000. There are other ways to reflect income taxes on the worksheet.

30. Since interest revenue was earned for the month of December, an adjusting entry must be made as follows (see Exhibit 2–5):

d. December 31, 19J:

Interest receivable	100	
Interest revenue ($8,000 × .15 × 1/12)		100

This entry records (1) an asset (interest receivable) for balance sheet purposes and (2) a revenue (interest revenue) for income statement purposes.

Adjusting Entries for Estimated Items

Some adjusting entries must be based on **estimated amounts** because they depend upon future conditions and events. Therefore, some revenues and expenses of the period must be estimated. For example, depreciation expense, bad debt expense, and warranty (guarantee) expense must be based on estimates of future useful life, future collectibility, and future expenditures, respectively.

Depreciation Expense. When certain assets, such as a machine, are acquired for use in operating a business (i.e., not for sale), they are "used up" over time through wear and obsolescence. The amount of the **use cost** for machinery is measured each accounting period and recorded as depreciation expense. Depreciation expense always is an estimate because the amount recognized depends upon a known amount, the cost of the asset, and two estimates, useful life and residual value (RV). To illustrate, at the end of 19J, Ace Retailers, Inc., had two assets for which depreciation was computed, viz:

Asset	Computations	Annual Depreciation
Building	$\frac{\text{Cost, \$160,000} - \text{RV, \$10,000}}{\text{Estimated useful life, 15 yrs.}} =$	$10,000
Equipment	$\frac{\text{Cost, \$91,000} - \text{RV, \$1,000}}{\text{Estimated useful life, 10 yrs.}} =$	9,000
Total depreciation expense for the year ..		$19,000

Based on these computations, an adjusting entry is necessary as follows (see Exhibit 2–5):

e. December 31, 19J:

Depreciation expense (selling)	8,200	
Depreciation expense (G&A)	10,800	
Accumulated depreciation (bldg.)		10,000
Accumulated depreciation (equip.)		9,000

Depreciation expense was debited to two expense accounts because the company follows the policy of **allocating** it to the two categories of expense based upon the proportionate use in each function. This entry (1) records the expense for the income statement and (2) reduces the book value of the building and equipment for balance sheet purposes.

Bad Debt Expense. Sales and services billed on credit almost always cause some losses due to uncollectible accounts receivable (i.e., bad debts). The fact that an account will be uncollectible usually is not known for several periods subsequent to the period in which the credit was extended and the sale or service recognized as revenue in accordance with the revenue principle. The matching principle requires that all **expenses** associated with sales and service revenue be recognized in the period in which the revenue is recorded. Because the revenues should be recorded as earned in the period the sales are made or the services performed and the bad debt loss may not be known for several periods later, an estimation of bad debt expense must be recorded by means of an adjusting entry in the period in which the related revenue is recorded. To illustrate, Ace Retailers, Inc., extended credit on sales during 19J amounting to $120,000. Experience by the company indicated an expected average bad debt loss rate of 1 percent of credit sales. Therefore, the following adjusting entry was needed (see Exhibit 2–5):

f. December 31, 19J:

Bad debt expense (selling)	1,200	
Allowance for doubtful accounts		1,200

The credit is made to an "allowance" account rather than directly to Accounts Receivable because the identities of the specific customers involved are not presently known. Bad debt expense is reported on the income statement, and the allowance account is reported on the balance sheet as a deduction from accounts receivable (i.e., it is a contra asset account). When a customer account subsequently is determined to be bad, it is written off by a debit to the allowance account and a credit to Accounts Receivable; this write-off will have no effect on current expenses nor on the net book value of accounts receivable.

COMPLETION OF THE WORKSHEET (PHASE 6 CONTINUED)

After the adjusting entries are entered on the worksheet (in the second pair of columns), it is completed by extending each account balance (i.e., the trial balance amount plus or minus any adjusting amounts) to the next columns as illustrated in Exhibit 2–5. Two pairs of the columns shown on this exhibit are not essential: (1) the Adjusted Trial Balance columns, which are used to ensure accuracy (i.e., a Debits = Credits check **after** the adjusting entries), and (2) the Retained Earnings columns, which can be merged with the balance sheet. Observe in the extending of amounts horizontally that debits are extended as debits and credits as credits. Three additional aspects of the worksheet warrant explanation:

1. Note that the **beginning** inventory amount of $75,000 is extended to the income statement as a debit and that the **ending** inventory of $90,000 is entered as a credit to the income statement and as a debit to the balance sheet.[6] This procedure results from the company's **periodic inventory system** (see Chapter 7). When a company uses the periodic inventory system, the Purchases account is debited for inventory acquisitions and the inventory account is unchanged during the period; thus, prior to the adjusting entries, the inventory account reflects the **beginning inventory** amount. At the end of the accounting period, this balance must be closed and the **ending** inventory amount, determined by physical count and valued at cost, must be recorded. In contrast, when a **perpetual inventory system** is used, purchases and issues are recorded directly in the inventory account on a continuing basis. Therefore, in a perpetual inventory system, the inventory amount in the trial balance will reflect the ending inventory amount and no adjusting or closing entries should be needed for it on the worksheet. The inventory balance is extended directly to the Balance Sheet debit column. When the perpetual inventory system is used, there will be no Purchases account; however, there will be a Cost of Goods Sold account on the worksheet. The Cost of Goods Sold account is extended directly to the Income Statement debit column as an expense.
2. When all of the amounts have been extended, the difference between the debits and credits under the Income Statement column will represent **pretax income.** This amount must be determined to compute income tax expense, for which an adjusting entry must be made. To illustrate, for Ace Retailers, Inc., the computation would be as follows, assuming an average 40 percent income tax rate:

Income Statement column totals (pretax):	
Credit total	$419,000
Debit total	369,000
Pretax income	50,000
Income tax expense ($50,000 × .40)	20,000
Net income	$ 30,000

The adjusting entry for income tax would be as follows:

g. December 31, 19J:

Income tax expense	20,000	
Income tax payable		20,000

3. After the above adjusting entry is made, the extensions can be completed. The amount of net income, $30,000, is entered on the worksheet as a debit to Income Statement and a credit to Retained Earnings. The ending balance of Retained Earnings is then extended to the balance sheet and the last two pairs of columns are summed; in the absence of errors, each pair of columns on the worksheet will balance.

The worksheet can be used as a framework for completing the remaining phases in the cycle.

A worksheet for a manufacturing company, with explanatory comments, is shown in Supplement 2–B to this chapter.

PREPARE FINANCIAL STATEMENTS (PHASE 7)

The income statement, statement of retained earnings, and balance sheet can be prepared directly from

[6] This approach views the two entries for the beginning and ending inventories as **closing** entries.

Another approach is to view them as **adjusting** entries. The technique used on the worksheet for inventories represents only one way; several other ways also are used. The final result is the same.

the completed worksheet. An income statement and balance sheet, taken directly from the worksheet (Exhibit 2–5), are presented in Exhibits 2–6 and 2–7, respectively. Financial statements are discussed in more detail in Chapters 3 and 4.

If a worksheet is not used, adjusting entries should be entered directly in the journal and posted to the ledger. Then an **adjusted trial balance,** taken from the ledger, will provide information for these statements.

The statement of changes in financial position (SCFP) requires a separate analysis, usually on a specially designed worksheet similar to those illustrated in Chapter 23.

JOURNALIZING AND POSTING ADJUSTING ENTRIES (PHASE 8)

The adjusting entries should be entered in the general journal and then posted to the general ledger, dated the last day of the accounting period. The adjusting entries **update** the ledger accounts by separating the account balances into their permanent (i.e., balance sheet) and temporary (i.e., income statement) components. The adjusted temporary accounts are then ready to close. Also, the adjusting entries bring the general ledger accounts into agreement with the financial statements.

If a worksheet, such as Exhibit 2–5, is developed, the adjusting entries can be taken directly from it. They are identical to those illustrated earlier. Note that after the adjusting entries are posted to the general ledger, each account will reflect the account balances shown in Exhibit 2–5 under the caption Adjusted Trial Balance.

EXHIBIT 2–6: Income Statement

ACE RETAILERS, INC.
Income Statement*
For the Year Ended December 31, 19J

Revenues:		
Sales		$325,200
Interest		600
Rent		1,200
Total revenues		327,000
Expenses:		
Cost of goods sold†	$117,000	
Selling	113,400	
G&A	34,600	
Interest	3,000	
Total expenses (excl. income taxes)		268,000
Pretax operating income		59,000
Income taxes ($59,000 × .40)		23,600
Income before extraordinary items		35,400
Extraordinary loss	9,000	
Less tax saving ($9,000 × .40)	3,600	5,400
Net income		$30,000

EPS:	
Income before extraordinary items ($35,400 ÷ 15,000 shares)	$2.36
Extraordinary loss ($5,400 ÷ 15,000 shares)	(.36)
Net income ($30,000 ÷ 15,000 shares)	$2.00

* This is a single-step income statement; various formats are discussed in Chapter 3.

† Computation of cost of goods sold:

Beginning inventory	$ 75,000
Purchases	130,000
Freight on purchases	4,000
Purchase returns	(2,000)
Total goods available for sale	207,000
Less ending inventory	90,000
Cost of goods sold	$117,000

CLOSING ENTRIES (PHASE 9)

The balance sheet accounts are called **permanent** or **real accounts** in the sense that they are not closed out to a zero balance at the end of the accounting period. In contrast, the income statement accounts are called **temporary** or **nominal accounts** because at the end of each accounting period they are closed to a zero balance. The income statement accounts are the **revenue, expense, gain,** and **loss** accounts and are **subaccounts** of owners' equity; revenues and gains increase owners' equity, and expenses and losses decrease owners' equity. These subaccounts are used each period to **classify** and **accumulate** revenue, expense, gain, and loss information to facilitate preparation of the income statement. At the end of the period, when they have served this information **classification** and **accumulation** purpose, each account is closed to Income Summary and in turn the net effect of their balances (i.e., net income or net loss) is transferred from Income Summary to Retained Earnings. The transferring process is referred to as making the closing entries. The purpose is to close the temporary accounts to a zero balance so they will be ready for reuse the next period. A closing entry simply transfers a credit balance to another account as a credit, or it transfers a debit balance to another account as a debit.

EXHIBIT 2–7: Balance Sheet

ACE RETAILERS, INC.
Balance Sheet*
At December 31, 19J

Assets			Liabilities		
Current assets:			Current liabilities:		
Cash		$ 67,300	Accounts payable		$ 29,000
Notes receivable		8,000	Income taxes payable		20,000
Interest receivable		100	Interest payable		500
Accounts receivable	$ 45,000		Rent revenue collected in adv.		600
Allowance for doubtful accts.	2,200	42,800	Total current liabilities		50,100
Inventory		90,000	Long-term liabilities:		
Prepaid insurance†		400	Bonds payable, 6%		50,000
Total current assets		208,600	Total liabilities		100,100
Operational assets:			**Stockholders' Equity**		
Land		8,000	Contributed capital:		
Building	160,000		Common stock, par $10, 15,000 shares issued and outstanding	$150,000	
Accum. depr., building	100,000	60,000			
Equipment	91,000				
Accum. depr., equip.	36,000	55,000	Contrib. capital in excess of par	20,000	
Total operational assets		123,000	Retained earnings	61,500	
			Total stockholders' equity		231,500
Total assets		$331,600	Total liabilities and stockholders' equity		$331,600

* Balance sheets and appropriate supplementary information are discussed in Chapter 4.

† Conceptually, $200 of this amount should not be reported as a current asset since it will extend two years into the future. In practice such differences may not be material in amount, as in this situation; and the conceptual distinction is not necessary (refer to the discussion of materiality in Chapter 1).

Usually a **clearing** or **suspense** account, called Income Summary, is used in the closing process; this account then is closed to Retained Earnings. Sometimes a second clearing account—Cost of Goods Sold—also is used. The clearing accounts are not required; they perform only a facilitating function. Temporary accounts are used the next period to record the revenues, expenses, gains, and losses for that period.

The closing entries can be taken directly from account balances in the **adjusted trial balance,** or if a worksheet such as the one in Exhibit 2–5 is used, they can be taken directly from the Income Statement columns. To illustrate, the closing entries for Ace Retailers, Inc. (with an Income Summary account), would be as follows (refer to Exhibit 2–5):[7]

December 31, 19J:

1. To close the revenue accounts to Income Summary:

Sales revenue	325,200	
Interest revenue	600	
Rent revenue	1,200	
Income summary		327,000

2. To close the purchases and beginning inventory accounts and record the ending inventory:[8]

Inventory (12/31/19J)	90,000	
Purchase returns	2,000	
Income summary	117,000	
Purchases		130,000
Freight on purchases		4,000
Inventory (1/1/19J)		75,000

[7] The closing entries can be grouped in various ways, one of which is illustrated here. Alternatively, a separate closing entry can be made for each temporary account. The net effect of all the approaches to the closing process would be the same.

[8] The Cost of Goods Sold account may be used with a periodic inventory system, in which case these accounts are closed to Cost of Goods Sold which is then closed to Income Summary. If a periodic inventory system is used, the inventory accounts may be updated

3. To close the expense accounts to Income Summary:

Income summary	180,000	
Selling expenses		113,400
G&A expenses		34,600
Interest expense		3,000
Extraordinary loss		9,000
Income tax expense		20,000

4. To close Income Summary account to Retained Earnings:

Income summary	30,000	
Retained earnings		30,000

For review purposes, the closing process is diagrammed in T-account form in Exhibit 2–8. Observe that **after the closing process** each income statement (i.e., temporary) account reflects a zero balance; therefore, each is ready to be used again during the next accounting period.

POST-CLOSING TRIAL BALANCE (PHASE 10)

The purposes of a trial balance usually are *(a)* to verify the equality of the debits and credits and *(b)* to have the account balances handy for other uses. We have discussed two different trial balances up to this point: the **unadjusted** trial balance, taken immediately after the current entries are completed for the accounting period but before the adjusting entries; and the **adjusted** trial balance, which reflects the account balances after the adjusting entries. A third trial balance usually is taken after the closing entries have been posted. It is called the **post-closing trial balance** and is used to verify that the debits and credits are equal at the start of the next accounting period. The post-closing trial balance usually is done on an adding machine (or by computer) rather than by preparing a formal listing.

in the adjusting entries, in which case they would not be included in the closing entries. In either approach, the **beginning** inventory balance must be closed and the **ending** inventory balance recorded. The net effect is the same. To illustrate the use of inventory adjusting entries with a Cost of Goods Sold account, the above entries would be:

Adjusting entries (inventory):

Cost of goods sold	75,000	
Inventory (beginning)		75,000
Inventory (ending)	90,000	
Cost of goods sold		90,000

Closing entry for purchase accounts:

Purchase returns	2,000	
Cost of goods sold	132,000	
Purchases		130,000
Freight on purchases		4,000
Income summary	117,000	
Cost of goods sold		117,000

REVERSING ENTRIES (PHASE 11)

After the adjusting and closing entries are journalized and posted to the general ledger, the accounts are ready for information inputs of the next period. Prior to entering the new information inputs, many companies make **reversing entries.** A reversing entry is dated the first day of the next period and simply reverses or "backs out" an adjusting entry that was made at the end of the period just ended. Reversing entries serve only one purpose, that is, to facilitate (or simplify) a subsequent related entry. Reversing entries are always optional; the same result is obtained whether or not they are used. If used, only certain of the adjusting entries are reversed.

The purpose and application of reversing entries are illustrated in Exhibit 2–9. In the exhibit, a series of entries related to accrued wages is analyzed under two options: (1) with a reversing entry and (2) without a reversing entry. The two options demonstrate the **facilitating** feature of reversing entries and also suggest the kinds of adjusting entries that are candidates for reversal. Although it is impossible to provide rigid rules for selecting adjusting entries to be reversed, some guidelines can be given.

1. Adjusting entries usually reversed—As a general rule, **only adjusting entries for accrued expenses and accrued revenues** that involve frequent cash flows should be reversed. Examples of accrued expenses are unpaid wages, interest, utilities, and other regularly recurring expenses that require subsequent cash disbursements. Examples of accrued revenues are uncollected interest, rent, and other recurring earned revenues that result in subsequent cash collections.
2. Adjusting entries not reversed—As a general rule, adjusting entries for deferred expenses and revenues collected in advance are not reversed. Examples of deferred (i.e., prepaid) expenses are insurance premiums and unused supplies. Examples of revenues collected in advance are precollected rent and magazine subscriptions.
3. Estimated adjusting entries not reversed—Those

EXHIBIT 2–8: Closing Process Diagrammed

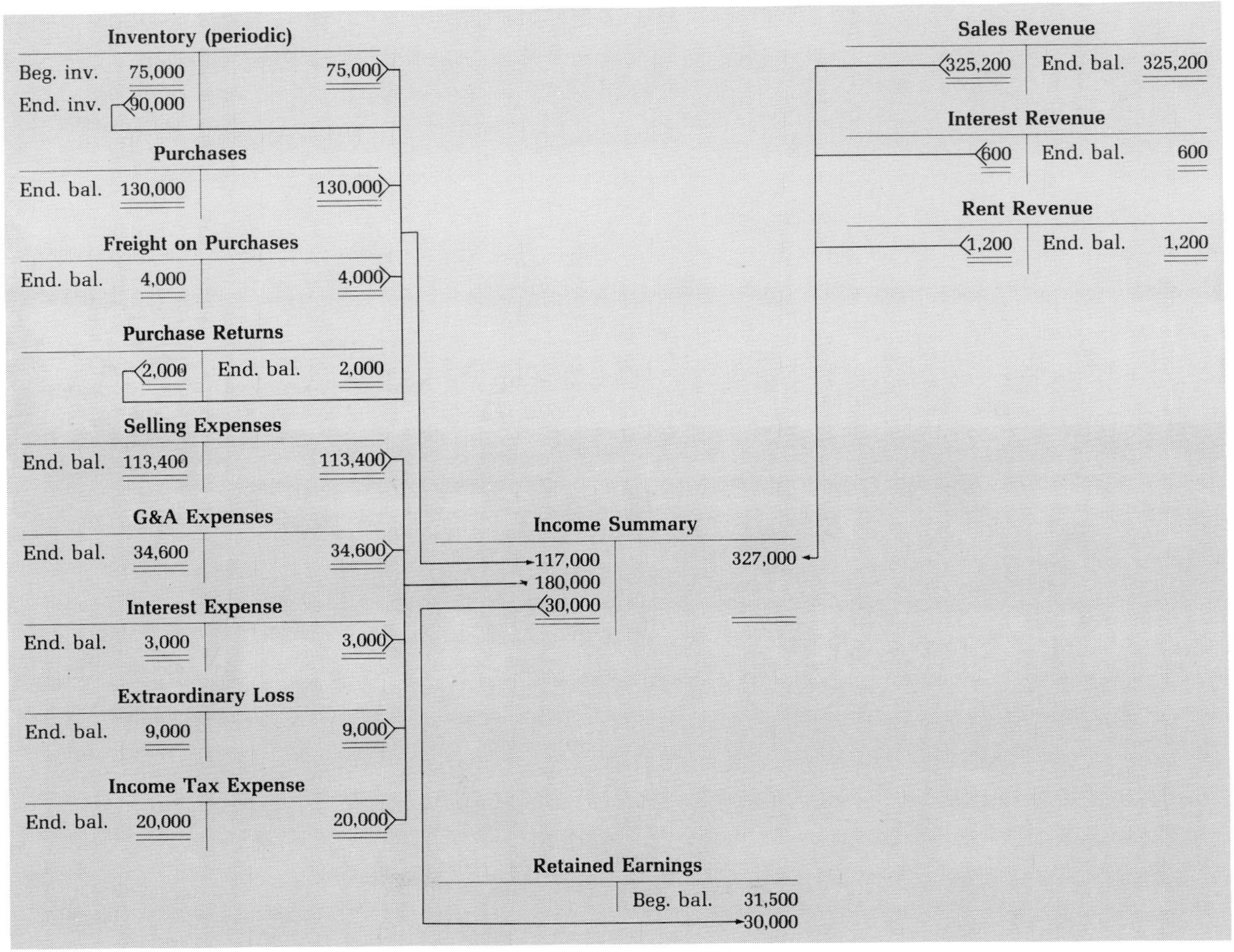

Inventory (periodic)
Beg. inv. 75,000
End. inv. 90,000
75,000
Purchases
End. bal. 130,000
130,000
Freight on Purchases
End. bal. 4,000
4,000
Purchase Returns
2,000
End. bal. 2,000
Selling Expenses
End. bal. 113,400
113,400
G&A Expenses
End. bal. 34,600
34,600
Interest Expense
End. bal. 3,000
3,000
Extraordinary Loss
End. bal. 9,000
9,000
Income Tax Expense
End. bal. 20,000
20,000
Income Summary
117,000
180,000
30,000
327,000
Retained Earnings
Beg. bal. 31,500
30,000
Sales Revenue
325,200
End. bal. 325,200
Interest Revenue
600
End. bal. 600
Rent Revenue
1,200
End. bal. 1,200

EXHIBIT 2–9: Reversing Entries Illustrated

KNOX CORPORATION
Annual Accounting Period Ends December 31, 19A

With Reversing Entry | **Without Reversing Entry**

a. **Adjusting entry**—The last payroll of Knox Corporation was paid on December 28, 19A; the next payroll will be on January 4, 19B. Therefore, at December 31, 19A, accrued (unpaid) wages for three days amounted to $15,000. The following adjusting entry is required:

With Reversing Entry			Without Reversing Entry		
December 31, 19A:			December 31, 19A:		
Wage expense	15,000		Wage expense	15,000	
Wages payable		15,000	Wages payable		15,000

b. **Closing entry**—The revenue and expense accounts are closed to Income Summary.

With Reversing Entry			Without Reversing Entry		
December 31, 19A:			December 31, 19A:		
Income summary*	215,000		Income summary*	215,000	
Wage expense		215,000	Wage expense		215,000

c. At this point the adjusting and closing entries have been journalized and posted to the ledger. The information processing cycle for 19A has been completed. At this time, January 1, 19B, the accountant must decide what adjusting entries are to be **reversed** (if any). **Question:** Would a reversing entry for accrued wages on January 1, 19B, simplify or facilitate making the next payroll entry on January 4, 19B?

With Reversing Entry:

Decision—make a reversing entry, January 1, 19B

Wages payable	15,000	
Wage expense		15,000

(Note that this reverses the adjusting entry made above on 12/31/19A.)

Effect: The Wages Payable account now reflects a zero balance; Wage Expense reflects a **credit** balance of $15,000.

Without Reversing Entry:

Decision—no reversing entry to be made.

Effect: The Wages Payable account continues to reflect a credit balance of $15,000; Wage Expense reflects a zero balance.

d. **Subsequent payroll entry**—Payment of $36,000 payroll on January 4, 19B. This amount includes the $15,000 liability (wages payable) carried over from December 19A.

January 4, 19B, payroll entry (disregarding payroll taxes):

With Reversing Entry			Without Reversing Entry		
Wage expense	36,000		Wages payable	15,000	
Cash		36,000	Wage expense	21,000	
			Cash		36,000

Did the prior reversing entry simplify this subsequent entry? The answer is yes. The last entry, on the left, required only one debit, and, most importantly, preparation of the January 4 payroll entry did not require reference to the December 31, 19A, adjusting entry. To illustrate the importance of not having to refer to the adjusting entry, assume Knox Corporation made 75 adjusting entries of various types and that accountant X supervised the adjusting process. Assume that accountant Z supervises payroll accounting. Therefore, on January 4, 19B, when accountant Z must record the $36,000 payment of the weekly payroll, the credit in the entry is to Cash. Accountant Z realizes that the payroll period spanned two accounting periods and wonders how much of the $36,000 should be debited to Wages Payable from 19A and how much should be debited to 19B Wage Expense. The only way to learn this fact is to scan, possibly all of, the 75 adjusting entries made December 31, 19A. To avoid such a waste of time and cost, accountant X can make a reversing entry at the same time the adjusting entry is made, but postdate it to be effective on January 1, 19B. Then on January 4, 19B, the next payroll date, accountant Z can record the payroll entry by debiting Wage Expense and crediting Cash for $36,000 with no need to refer to the December 31, 19A, adjusting entry. With or without a reversing entry, the Wage Expense account reflects a debit balance of $21,000 and Wages Payable reflects a zero balance. When the payroll processing is computerized, a special routine must be written for the first payment entry which is different from the remaining 51 payroll entries during the year when no reversing entry is made.

* Includes $200,000 wages paid during the period.

EXHIBIT 2–10: Summary of the Accounting Information Processing Cycle

Phase (order)	Identification	Objective
During the period (Phases 1–4):		
1	Collection of raw economic data.	To gather inputs to the accounting system. The inputs are supported by source documents as a basis for *(a)* transaction analysis and *(b)* subsequent verification.
2	Transaction analysis.	To identify, assess, and measure the economic impact on the enterprise of each transaction recognized. To provide the basis for developing the accounting entry to be made in the journal.
3	Journalizing.	To provide a chronological record (i.e., by date) of the entries in the accounting system which reflect the increases and decreases in each account.
4	Posting.	To transfer the economic effects from the journal to the ledger; to reclassify and accumulate the economic effects for each asset, liability, owners' equity, revenue, expense, gain, and loss.
End of the period (Phases 5–11):		
5	Prepare unadjusted trial balance.	To provide, in a convenient form, a listing of the accounts and their balances in the general ledger after all current entries have been posted. It serves to *(a)* check the debit-credit equality and *(b)* provide data for use in developing the worksheet and the adjusting entries.
6*	Prepare worksheets.	To provide an organized and systematic approach at the end of the accounting period for developing *(a)* the adjusting entries, *(b)* the financial statements, and *(c)* the closing entries. One worksheet suffices for the income statement and balance sheet. Another worksheet is needed to develop the statement of changes in financial position.
7	Prepare financial statements.	To provide a vehicle for communicating summarized financial information to external decision makers.
8	Journalize and post adjusting entries.	To update the general ledger and to separate the "mixed" balances into their permanent (i.e., balance sheet) and temporary (i.e., income statement) components so the temporary accounts will be ready for the closing process. This phase brings the general ledger account balances into agreement with their amounts reported on the financial statements.
9	Journalize and post closing entries.	To close the temporary accounts to retained earnings so they will be ready for reuse during the next period for accumulating and classifying revenues and expenses.
10*	Prepare post-closing trial balance.	To verify the debit-credit accuracy of the general ledger after the closing entries are posted.
11*	Reversing entries.	To facilitate subsequent entries by reversing certain adjusting entries. They are journalized and posted on the first day of the new period.

* Optional.

adjusting entries based on estimates where there is no subsequent cash inflow or outflow are not reversed. Examples are depreciation and bad debt expense entries.

Although these general guidelines may be helpful in deciding whether the reversal of a particular adjusting entry would be useful, one must consider *(a)* the original entry, *(b)* the adjusting entry, and *(c)* most importantly, the subsequent related entry. The above rules have exceptions and cannot substitute for judgment.

SUMMARY

Information processing involves the phases or steps used to collect raw economic data, record their economic effects on the entity, classify the information, and, finally, prepare the financial statements and supporting information. In most companies, a large amount of information must be processed daily. This work can be time consuming and costly. Therefore, a well-designed information processing system is needed to provide an efficient flow of information from the collection of raw economic data to the end result, the financial statements. Exhibit 2–10 summarizes the major sequential phases of the information processing cycle in the order they are discussed in this chapter.

Information processing may be done (1) manually, where the work is performed by hand; (2) mechanically, where the information is processed by sorting equipment, tabulating machines, and so on; and (3) electronically, where electronic computers are used. Typically, an accounting system will use each of these approaches in varying degrees depending upon its complexity. Consideration of these information approaches is not within the objectives of this book. For instructional purposes, the manual approach is used because the steps are essentially the same regardless of how the processing is done.

Supplement 2-A: Control Accounts, Subsidiary Ledgers, and Special Journals

An accounting system usually includes application of the information processing devices known as control accounts, subsidiary ledgers, and special journals. This supplement discusses and illustrates these elements of the system.

CONTROL ACCOUNTS AND SUBSIDIARY LEDGERS

The general ledger is the main ledger. It includes an account for each asset, liability, owners' equity, revenue, expense, gain, and loss. To facilitate recordkeeping for accounts that involve a large amount of detail, selected general ledger accounts are designated as **control accounts** to which only summary information is posted. The details related to each control account are maintained in a separate subsidiary ledger (one for each control account). Thus, each control account is supplemented by its specially designated subsidiary ledger. To illustrate, accounts receivable usually is designated as **Accounts Receivable Control** in the general ledger and is supported by a separate **accounts receivable subsidiary ledger** which is composed of individual customer accounts. This arrangement will be illustrated below.

JOURNALS

Both general and special journals are used in most accounting systems. Even when extensive use is made of special journals, a need still exists for a general journal (Exhibit 2–11) in which to record *(a)* those transactions that do not apply to any of the special journals, *(b)* nonrepetitive current transactions, and *(c)* the adjusting, closing, and reversing journal entries. Occasionally there will be a complex entry with characteristics that would, in part, qualify for entry in a special journal and, in part, in the general journal. Such entries may be entered only in the general journal or, alternatively, "split" between the general journal and a special journal.

Special Journals

A special journal serves the same purpose as a general journal except that it is designed to handle **only** one type of transaction because of the large volume of transactions of a particular type. Each special journal, therefore, is designed specifically to simplify the data processing tasks involved in journalizing and posting a particular type of transaction. The format of each special journal and the number used depend upon the types of frequent transactions recorded by the entity. Commonly used special journals are the following:

1. Merchandise sales on credit—designed for credit sales entries only.
2. Merchandise purchases on credit—designed for credit purchases only.
3. Cash receipts—designed for all cash receipts (including cash sales).
4. Cash payments—designed for all cash payments (including cash purchases).
5. Voucher system journals (replaces 2 and 4 above when the voucher system is used)—
   a. Voucher register—designed to record vouch-

ers payable only. A voucher payable is prepared for each cash payment regardless of the purpose of the payment.

b. Check register—designed to record all checks written in payment of vouchers.

Special Journal for Merchandise Sales on Credit. This journal is designed to accommodate entries for credit sales of regular merchandise only. Therefore, it would handle only the following type of entry (cash sales would not be entered in this journal):

January 2, 19J:

Accounts receivable	980	
Sales revenue		980

Credit sale to Adams Company; invoice price, $1,000; terms, 2/10, n/30.[9]

Credit sales should be recorded at net of discount (rather than at gross) amount, as illustrated above. Theoretically, net of discount is correct; however, for various reasons they sometimes are recorded at the gross amount (see Chapter 7). Assuming the initial entry was made net of discount, the subsequent collection entry would be as follows:

Case A—Collection within the discount period:

Cash	980	
Accounts receivable		980

Case B—Collection after the discount period:

Cash	1,000	
Accounts receivable		980
Interest revenue		20

Exhibit 2–12 shows a typical special journal for credit sales for a business that has two sales departments. The general ledger contains an Accounts Receivable Control account. Observe that this special journal provides a convenient format to record all of the relevant data on each credit sale. Also, it can be designed to differentiate sales by department. Clearly, it is easier to enter a credit sale in this format than in the general journal.

The mechanics of posting amounts from the special sales journal to the general and subsidiary ledgers also are simplified. There are two phases of posting a special journal, viz:

1. **Daily posting**—The amount of each credit sale is posted daily to the appropriate individual account in the accounts receivable **subsidiary ledger.** Daily posting is essential so that each customer's account will be up to date when the customer pays. Posting is indicated by entering the account number in the Ledger Folio column. For example, the number 112.13 entered in the Ledger Folio column in Exhibit 2–12 is the account number assigned to Adams Company and signifies that $980 was posted as a debit to that account.
2. **Monthly posting**—At the end of each month, the Amount column is summed. This total is posted to two accounts in the general ledger; that is, in Exhibit 2–12 the $9,360 was posted (1) as a debit to account no. 112 (Accounts Receivable Control) and (2) as a credit to account no. 500 (Sales Revenue Control). The T-accounts shown in Exhibit 2–16 illustrate how these postings are reflected in the general ledger and the subsidiary ledger. Observe that the two ledgers show the **journal page** from which each amount was posted.

Special Journal for Merchandise Purchases on Credit. In situations where there are numerous credit purchases of merchandise for resale, data processing may be facilitated by using a special journal designed only for this type of transaction, viz:

January 3, 19J:

Purchases	990	
Accounts payable (PT Mfg. Co.)		990

Purchased merchandise for resale; invoice price, $1,000; terms, 1/20, n/30.

This transaction, rather than being entered in the general journal, would be entered in the purchases journal as in Exhibit 2–13. In this illustration, the purchases are recorded at net of discount, which is the theoretically correct approach. During the month, each amount would be posted daily as a credit to the accounts of the individual creditors in the **accounts payable subsidiary ledger.**

At the end of the month, the total of the Amount column (i.e., $2,760) would be posted to the general ledger as *(a)* a debit to the Purchases account no. 612[10] and *(b)* a credit to the Accounts Payable Con-

[9] Terms, 2/10, n/30, mean that if the account is paid within 10 days after date of sale, a 2 percent discount is permitted to encourage early payment. If not paid within the 10-day discount period, the full amount is due at the end of 30 days.

[10] This assumes periodic inventory procedures. Alternatively, if perpetual inventory procedures are used, the debit would be to the inventory account.

EXHIBIT 2–11

General Journal — Page J-14

Date 19J	Accounts and Explanation	Ledger Folio	Amounts Debit	Amounts Credit
Jan. 2	Equipment – trucks	140	9,000	
	Notes payable	214		9,000
	Purchased truck for use in the business. Gave $9,000, 60-day note, interest at 10% per year, payable at maturity.			

EXHIBIT 2–12

Special Journal-Merchandise Sales on Credit — Page S-23

Date 19J	Sales Invoice No.	Accounts Receivable (name)	Terms	Ledger Folio	Receivable and Sale Amount	Dept. Sales: Dept. A	Dept. Sales: Dept. B
Jan. 2	93	Adams Co.	2/10, n/30	112.13	980		
3	94	Sayre Corp.	2/10, n/30	112.80	490		
11	95	Cope & Day Co.	Net	112.27	5,734		
27	96	X Y Mfg. Co.	2/10, n/30	112.91	1,960	(Not illustrated; the two totals below would be posted to a sales subsidiary ledger.)	
30	97	Miller, J. B.	2/10, n/30	112.42	196		
31	—	Totals			9,360		
31	—	Posting			(112/500)		

EXHIBIT 2–13

Special Journal-Merchandise Purchases on Credit — P-19

Date 19J	Purchase Order No.	Account Payable (name)	Terms	Ledger Folio	Amount
Jan. 3	41	P. Q. Mfg. Co.	1/20, n/30	210.61	990
7	42	Able Suppliers, Ltd.	Net	210.12	150
31	—	Totals	—	—	6,760
31	—	Posting	—	—	(612/210)

EXHIBIT 2–14

Special Journal-Cash Receipts							Page CR-19
		Debits	Credits				
Date	Explanation	Cash	Account Title	Ledger Folio	Accounts Receivable	Sundry Accounts	Sales Revenue
19J							
Jan. 4	Cash sales	11,200		—			11,200
7	On acct.	4,490	Sayre Corp.	112.80	4,490		
8	Sale of land	10,000	Land	123		4,000	
			Gain on sale of land	510		6,000	
10	On acct.	1,000	Adams Co.	112.13	1,000		
19	Cash sales	43,600		—			43,600
20	On acct.	5,734	Cope & Day Co.	112.27	5,734		
31	Totals	116,224		—	11,224	34,000	71,000
31	Posting	(101)		—	(112)	(NP)*	(500)

* NP—Not posted as one total because the individual amounts are posted as indicated in the Ledger Folio column.

EXHIBIT 2–15

Special Journal-Cash Payments								Page CP-31
			Credits	Debits				
Date	Check No.	Explanation	Cash	Account Name	Ledger Folio	Accounts Payable	Sundry Accounts	Purchases
19J								
Jan. 2	141	Pur. mdse.	3,000		—			3,000
10	142	On acct.	990	P.Q. Mfg. Co.	210.61	990		
15	143	Jan. rent	660	Rent exp.	612		600	
16	144	Pur. mdse.	1,810					1,810
31	—	Totals	98,400		—	5,820	1,600	90,980
31	—	Posting	(101)		—	(210)	(NP)	(612)

trol account no. 210. These two general ledger accounts are not illustrated in Exhibit 2–16.

Special Journal for Cash Receipts. Since a large volume of transactions for cash receipts is typical, a special cash receipts journal is often used. This special journal is designed to accommodate **all** cash receipts including cash sales. Therefore, it must have a column for **cash debit** and several credit columns. Credit columns are designated for recurring credits, and a Sundry Accounts column is used to accommodate infrequent credits. A typical special cash receipts journal is shown in Exhibit 2–14.

During the month, each amount in the Accounts Receivable column is posted daily as a credit to the individual customer accounts in the **accounts receivable subsidiary ledger.** At the end of the month, *(a)* the individual amounts in the Sundry Accounts column are posted as credits to the appropriate general ledger accounts and *(b)* the totals (for Cash, Accounts

EXHIBIT 2–16: General Ledger and Subsidiary Ledger Illustrated

General Ledger (partial)

Cash No. 101

19J Jan. 1	balance	18,000	19J Jan. 31	CP-31	98,400
31	CR-19	116,224			

Accounts Receivable Control No. 112

19J Jan. 1	balance	5,000	19J Jan. 31	CR-19	11,224
31	S-23	9,360			

Equipment No. 140

19J Jan. 2	J-14	9,000			

Notes Payable No. 214

			19J Jan. 2	J-14	9,000

Sales Revenue Control No. 500

			19J Jan. 31	S-23	9,360
			31	CR-19	71,000

Subsidiary Ledger for Accounts Receivable (Accts. No. 112)

Adams Company — Acct. No. 112.13

Date	Folio	Explanation	Debit	Credit	Balance
19J Jan. 1		balance			1,000
2	S-23		980		1,980
10	CR-19			1,000	980

Cope & Day Company — Acct. No. 112.27

Date	Folio	Explanation	Debit	Credit	Balance
Jan. 11	S-23		5,734		5,734
20	CR-19			5,734	-0-

Miller, J.B.—Acct. 112.42

Date	Folio	Explanation	Debit	Credit	Balance
Jan. 30	S-23		196		196

Sayre Corporation—Acct. No. 112.80

Date	Folio	Explanation	Debit	Credit	Balance
Jan. 1		balance			4,000
3	S-23		490		4,490
7	CR-19			4,490	-0-

XY Manufacturing Company—Acct. No. 112.91

Date	Folio	Explanation	Debit	Credit	Balance
Jan. 27	S-23		1,960		1,960

Receivable, and Sales) are posted to the general ledger as indicated by the folio numbers. The total of the Sundry Accounts column is not posted since the individual amounts have already been posted.

Special Journal for Cash Payments. Because of the large volume of cash disbursements, most companies use a special journal designed to accommodate **all** cash payments including cash purchases of merchandise. The special journal must have a column for **cash credits** and a number of debit columns. Debit columns are set up for frequently recurring debits, and a Sundry Accounts column is used for infrequent debits. A typical special cash payments journal, with some common entries, is shown in Exhibit 2–15. Posting follows the same procedures explained above for the cash receipts special journal.

Reconciling a Subsidiary Ledger

The sum of all balances in a subsidiary ledger must agree with the overall balance reflected in the related control account in the general ledger. To assure that this correspondence exists, frequent reconciliations should be made. Clearly, a reconciliation cannot be accomplished unless all posting is complete, both to the control account and to the subsidiary ledger. To illustrate, a reconciliation based upon the information in Exhibit 2–16 for **Accounts Receivable Control** and the **accounts receivable subsidiary ledger** would be as follows:

Reconciliation of Accounts Receivable Subsidiary Ledger (at January 31, 19J)

	Amount
Subsidiary ledger balances:	
112.13 Adams Co.	$ 980
112.42 Miller, J. B.	196
112.91 XY Manufacturing Co.	1,960
Total—agrees with the balance in Accounts Receivable Control ($14,360 − $11,224)	$3,136

The above discussion reviewed the concepts underlying special journals, control accounts, and subsidiary ledgers. Their design and use depend upon the characteristics of the company. They do not involve new accounting principles since they are only data processing techniques. The above discussion also emphasized the four primary efficiencies that may result from their use, viz: (1) journalizing is simplified, (2) posting is simplified, (3) subdivision of work is simplified, and (4) a highly trained person is not needed to maintain a special journal or a subsidiary ledger that involves only one type of transaction.[11]

[11] Voucher system journals are not discussed since they involve essentially the same procedures as illustrated. The voucher system journals are known as *(a)* the voucher register and *(b)* the check register.

Supplement 2-B: Worksheet for a Manufacturing Company

A worksheet for a manufacturing company is somewhat different from that illustrated in Exhibit 2–5 for a merchandising company. Because of the cost accounting procedures generally used for the manufacturing activity, the worksheet should include a pair of columns for **manufacturing.** All of the manufacturing costs, including the raw materials and work in process inventories, are extended to the two manufacturing columns. A worksheet for a manufacturing situation is illustrated in Exhibit 2–17. In studying the exhibit it will be helpful to observe that:

1. Only representative accounts and adjusting entries are included.
2. There are columns for manufacturing; however, the columns for adjusted trial balance and retained earnings have been omitted to demonstrate these simplifications. They were noted as optional in the chapter.
3. Only three typical adjusting entries are included:
   a. Depreciation expense was allocated as follows: factory, 70 percent; distribution, 20 percent, and general 10 percent.
   b. Interest was accrued for two months, $800.
   c. Income tax expense was accrued, $36,000.
4. The entries for factory costs were as follows:

Raw material purchases	70,000	
Direct labor	100,000	
Cash		170,000
Factory overhead	75,000	
Various accounts		75,000

5. The ending inventories at December 31, 19J, were as follows:

Raw materials	$62,000
Work in process	81,000
Finished goods	52,000

A statement of cost of goods manufactured, taken directly from the Manufacturing columns in the worksheet is shown on page 65.

EXHIBIT 2–17

DUNCAN MANUFACTURING COMPANY
Worksheet for the Year Ended December 31, 19J

Accounts	Unadjusted Trial Balance		Adjusting Entries		Manufacturing		Income Statement		Balance Sheet	
	Debit	Credit	Debit	Credit	Debit	Credit	Debit	Credit	Debit	Credit
Cash	32,000								32,000	
Inventory, Jan. 1 (periodic):										
Raw materials	55,000				55,000	62,000*			62,000*	
Work in process	76,000				76,000	81,000*			81,000*	
Finished goods	54,000						54,000	52,000*	52,000*	
Equipment (10-year life)	300,000								300,000	
Accum. depr., equip.		90,000		*(a)* 10,000						100,000
Remaining assets	13,000								13,000	
Accounts payable		15,000								15,000
Interest payable				*(b)* 800						800
Note payable (8% each Nov. 1)		60,000								60,000
Common stock, par $10		200,000								200,000
Retained earnings		74,200								74,200
Sales revenue		474,800						474,800		
Manufacturing costs:										
Raw material purchases	70,000				70,000					
Direct labor	100,000				100,000					
Factory overhead:	75,000		*(a)* 7,000		82,000					
Distribution expenses	70,000		*(a)* 2,000				72,000			
G&A expenses	65,000		*(a)* 1,000				66,000			
Interest expense	4,000		*(b)* 800				4,800			
Cost of goods manufactured						240,000	240,000			
Totals	914,000	914,000	10,800	10,800	383,000	383,000				
Income tax expense			*(c)* 36,000				36,000			
Income taxes payable				*(c)* 36,000						36,000
Net income							54,000			54,000
Totals							526,800	526,800	540,000	540,000

* To record ending inventories.
(a) To record depreciation.
(b) To record accrued interest.
(c) To record income taxes.

DUNCAN MANUFACTURING COMPANY
Statement of Cost of Goods Manufactured
For the Year Ended December 31, 19J

Materials:		
Beginning inventory	$ 55,000	
Purchases	70,000	
Total materials available	125,000	
Less: Ending inventory	62,000	
Cost of materials issued	63,000	
Direct labor	100,000	
Factory overhead	82,000	
Total factory costs	245,000	
Add: Beginning work in process inventory	76,000	
	321,000	
Less: Ending work in process inventory	81,000	
Cost of goods manufactured	$240,000	

Observe on the worksheet that cost of goods manufactured ($240,000) was transferred from the Manufacturing columns to the Income Statement columns (a debit since it is to a manufacturing entity what merchandise purchases is to a trading entity). In other respects, the amounts are extended to the last four columns as explained and illustrated in the chapter (Exhibit 2–5).

QUESTIONS

PART A

1. Explain why an accounting information processing system should be tailored to the characteristics of the entity.

2. What is the *accounting model?* Give the three submodels and briefly explain each.

3. Complete the following matrix by entering "debit" or "credit" in each cell.

Item	Increase	Decrease
Liabilities		
Revenues		
Assets		
Expenses		
Owners' equity		

4. Explain the *dual balancing* feature of the fundamental accounting model.

5. Broadly explain the primary *purpose* of the accounting information processing model.

6. With respect to the collection of raw economic data for the accounting system, why are source documents important? Give some examples of typical source documents.

7. Explain the nature and purpose of *transaction analysis.*

8. What kind of events are recorded in the accounting system? Explain.

9. What is meant by *journalizing?* What purpose does it serve?

10. What is meant by *posting?* What purpose does it serve?

11. Distinguish between permanent, temporary, and mixed accounts.

12. Classify the following accounts, before the adjusting entries, as permanent, temporary, or mixed (explain any assumptions you make):

Accounts Receivable	Prepaid Insurance
Supplies Inventory	Notes Payable
Retained Earnings	Interest Revenue
Patents	Common Stock
Interest Expense	Property Tax Expense

13. Distinguish between the general ledger, control accounts, and subsidiary ledgers. What is the basic purpose of each?

14. Explain the difference between special journals and the general journal.

15. What is a *trial balance?* What are the two primary purposes of a trial balance? Distinguish between unadjusted, adjusted, and post-closing trial balances.

PART B

16. Why is a worksheet a facilitating technique? What does it facilitate?

17. What are the purpose and nature of adjusting entries? Explain why they generally must be made. Explain why the adjusting entries must be considered prior to developing the financial statements.

18. Why are the adjusting entries journalized and posted?

19. What are the purpose and nature of closing entries?

20. What are the purpose and nature of reversing entries? Why are they journalized and posted?

21. X Company owes a $4,000, three-year, 9% note payable. Interest is paid each November 30. Therefore, at the end of the accounting period, December 31, the following adjusting entry was made:

Interest expense	30	
Interest payable		30

Would you recommend using a reversing entry in this situation? Explain.

22. Number the following phases in the accounting information processing cycle to indicate their normal sequence of completion:

_____ Journalize and post reversing entries.
_____ Posting.
_____ Transaction analysis.
_____ Collection of raw data.
_____ Journalize and post adjusting entries.
_____ Journalize and post closing entries.
_____ Prepare financial statements.
_____ Journalize current transactions.
_____ Prepare post-closing trial balance.
_____ Prepare worksheets.
_____ Prepare unadjusted trial balance.

23. In posting a special journal, there are two phases: daily posting and periodic posting. Explain the purpose and nature of each.

24. What circumstances would suggest the need for special journals? Why?

DECISION CASE 2–1

Two inexperienced members of the accounting staff at Cohn Industries have been debating the best procedure for recording expense payments. One would debit all expense payments directly to expense accounts, whereas the other would debit all such payments directly to an asset account. They both agree that given appropriate end-of-period adjusting procedures, the same end result would be obtained. They seek your resolution of their dispute.

Required:
Prepare a tactful response, with supporting arguments.

DECISION CASE 2–2

As the newly engaged independent CPA for Carson Company you have just discovered, while preparing to perform the first audit in the company's history, that the accounting staff records adjusting, closing, and reversing entries directly in the ledger accounts. While the records appear to be in good shape for a company which has never before been audited, you are troubled by the procedures described.

Required:
In expressing your concern to the company's chief accountant, what reasons would you give for your disapproval of the practice described?

EXERCISES

PART A: EXERCISES 2–1 to 2–5

Exercise 2–1

1. Develop a diagram that reflects the dual balancing feature of an accounting information processing system.
2. Explain why expenses are increased with a debit and revenues are increased with a credit.
3. Explain the basis for the designation double-entry system.

Exercise 2–2

The following selected transactions were completed during the current year by Able Corporation:

a. Able Corporation sold 50,000 shares of its own common stock, par $1 per share, for $85,000 cash.
b. Borrowed $20,000 cash on a one-year, 9% note payable (interest is payable at maturity date).

c. Purchased real estate for use in the business at a cash cost of $45,000, which consisted of a small building ($35,000) and the lot on which it was located ($10,000).

d. Purchased merchandise for resale at a cash cost of $28,000. Assume periodic inventory system.

e. Purchased merchandise for resale on credit; terms, 3/10,n/30. If paid within 10 days, the cash payment would be $485; however, if paid after 10 days, the payment would be $500. Since the company takes all discounts, credit purchases are recorded at net. Assume periodic inventory system.

f. Sold merchandise for $12,000; collected 60% in cash and the balance is due in 30 days.

g. Paid the balance due on the purchase in *(e)* within the 10-day period.

Required:
Enter each of the above transactions in a general journal. Use the letter to the left to indicate the date.

Exercise 2–3

The 11 phases that comprise the accounting information processing cycle are listed to the left in scrambled order. To the right is a brief statement of the objective of each phase, also in scrambled order. You are to present two responses.

Required (use separate sheet of paper):

1. In the blanks to the left, number the phases in the usual sequence of completion.
2. In the blanks to the right, use the letters to match each phase with its objective.

Sequence (order)	Phases	Matching (with objective)
____	Journalizing.	____
____	Journalize and post reversing entries.	____
____	Transaction analysis.	____
____	Prepare financial statements.	____
____	Journalize and post closing entries.	____
____	Collection of raw data.	____
____	Posting.	____
____	Journalize and post adjusting entries.	____
____	Prepare worksheets.	____
____	Prepare unadjusted trial balance.	____
____	Prepare post-closing trial balance.	____

Objective

a. Verification after closing entries.
b. Communication to decision makers.
c. Verification before adjusting entries.
d. Transfer from journal to ledger.
e. Based on source documents.
f. Update general ledger by separating "mixed" account balances.
g. Assess economic impact of each transaction.
h. Original input into the accounting system.
i. To facilitate subsequent entries.
j. To obtain a zero balance in the revenue and expense accounts.
k. A logical and systematic technique to aid in completing the end-of-period procedures.

Exercise 2–4

Arby Corporation completed the three transactions given below:

a. January 1, 19A—sold 10,000 shares of its own unissued common stock, par $1 per share, for $46,000 cash.

b. January 3, 19A—purchased a machine costing $50,000. Payment was $10,000 cash plus a $5,000, one-year, 15 percent interest-bearing note payable and a $35,000, three-year, 16 percent interest-bearing note payable.

c. February 1, 19A—sold two lots that would not be needed for $8,500. Received $3,500 cash down payment and a $5,000, 90-day, 15 percent interest-bearing note. The two lots had a book value of $6,500.

Required:

1. Give the general journal entry to record each of the three transactions.
2. Set up T-accounts and post the entries in 1 above. Use a systematic numbering system for posting purposes.

Exercise 2–5

A clerk for Veach Company prepared the following unadjusted trial balance which the clerk was unable to balance:

Account	Debit	Credit
Cash	$ 35,563	
Accounts receivable	31,000	
Allowance for doubtful accts.	(2,000)	
Inventory		$ 18,000
Equipment	181,500	
Accumulated depreciation		12,000
Accounts payable	18,000	
Notes payable		25,000
Common stock, par $10		180,000
Retained earnings (correct)		14,000
Revenues		75,000
Expenses	60,000	
Totals (out of balance by $63)	$324,063	$324,000

Assume you are examining the accounts and have found the following errors:

a. Equipment purchased for $7,500 at year-end was debited to Expenses.

b. Sales on account for $829 were debited to Accounts Receivable for $892 and credited to Revenues for $829.

c. A $6,000 collection on accounts receivable was debited to Cash and credited to Revenues.
d. The inventory amount is understated by $2,000 (cost of goods sold is included in expenses).

Required:
Prepare a corrected trial balance. Show computations.

PART B: EXERCISES 2–6 to 2–15

Exercise 2–6

Dody Corporation started operations January 1, 19C. It is now December 31, 19C, the end of the annual accounting period. A company clerk who maintained the records prepared the following financial statements at December 31, 19C.

Income Statement

Service revenue	$100,000
Expenses:	
Salaries and wages	30,000
Maintenance	5,000
Service	25,000
Other operating	10,000
Total expenses	70,000
Net income	$ 30,000

Balance Sheet

Assets	
Cash	$ 7,500
Note receivable (16%)	1,200
Inventory, supplies	6,000
Equipment	90,000
Other assets	7,300
Total assets	$112,000
Liabilities	
Accounts payable	$ 8,000
Note payable (15%)	24,000
Total liabilities	32,000
Stockholders' Equity	
Capital stock, par $10	50,000
Retained earnings	30,000
Total stockholders' equity	80,000
Total liabilities and stockholders' equity	$112,000

The above statements were presented to a local bank to support a loan request. The bank requested that an outside CPA "examine the situation." The CPA identified the following omissions:

a. Service revenue amounting to $6,000 had been collected but not earned at December 31, 19C.
b. At December 31, 19C, wages earned by employees but not yet paid or recorded amounted to $3,000.
c. A count of the inventory of supplies at December 31, 19C, showed $4,000 supplies on hand.
d. Depreciation on the equipment acquired on January 3, 19C. The estimated residual value was $10,000, and the estimated useful life 10 years.
e. The note receivable received from a customer was dated November 1, 19C; the principal plus interest is payable April 30, 19D.
f. The note payable to the local bank was dated June 1, 19C; the principal plus interest is payable May 31, 19D.
g. Assume an average income tax rate of 20 percent for Dody Corporation and that no income tax has been recorded.

Required (round to nearest dollar):
1. Give the adjusting entries ([*a*] through [*g*]) required to correct the accounts for the above omissions.
2. Correct the above statements to reflect the effects of the adjusting entries you made in 1 above. Key the entries for identification. Use the following format:

Items	Reported Amounts	Changes from Adjusting Entries (Use + and −)	Correct Amounts
Income statement:			
Revenues (detail)			
Expenses (detail)			
Pretax income			
Income tax			
Net income			
EPS			
Balance sheet:			
Assets (detail)			
Liabilities (detail)			
Stockholders' equity (detail)			

3. Reconcile the net change in owners' equity on the income statement with the net change on the balance sheet. Use captions as follows:

	Net Change
Income statement:	
Total revenues	
Total expenses	
Increase or decrease in net income	
Balance sheet:	
Total assets	
Total liabilities	
Increase or decrease in stockholders' equity	

Exercise 2–7

BT Corporation adjusts and closes its accounts each December 31. The following situations require adjusting entries at the current year-end. You are requested to prepare the adjusting entries in the general journal for each situation. Show computations.

a. A machine is to be depreciated for the full year. It cost $157,000, and the estimated useful life is 5 years, with an estimated residual value of $12,000. Assume straight-line depreciation.

b. Credit sales for the current year amounted to $100,000. The estimated bad debt loss rate on credit sales is ½%.

c. Property taxes for the current year have not been recorded or paid. A statement for the calendar year was received near the end of December for $2,400. The taxes are due and will be paid February 1 in the next year.

d. Supplies costing $800 were purchased for use in the offices during the year and debited to Office Supplies Inventory. The inventories of these supplies on hand were as follows: $100 at the end of the prior year, and $175 at the end of the current year.

e. BT rented an office in its building to a tenant for one year, starting on September 1. Rent for one year amounting to $1,200 was collected at that date. The total amount collected was credited to Rent Revenue.

f. BT received a note receivable from a customer dated November 1 of the current year. It is a $10,000, 9% note, due in one year. At the maturity date, BT will collect the face value of the note plus interest for one year.

Exercise 2–8

For each of the following situations, you are to give, in general journal form, the adjusting entry required at the end of the current annual accounting period, December 31. Show computations.

a. At the end of the year, unpaid and unrecorded wages amounted to $3,000.

b. The company owns a building which is to be depreciated for the full year. It cost $254,000, has an estimated useful life of 20 years, and a residual value of $54,000. Accumulated depreciation at the beginning of the current year was $60,000.

c. The company rented some space in its building to a tenant on August 1 of the current year and collected $2,400 cash, which was rent for one year in advance. Rent Revenue was credited for $2,400 on August 1.

d. The company paid a two-year insurance premium in advance on July 1 of the current year amounting to $1,000. The $1,000 was debited to Prepaid Insurance when paid.

e. Credit sales for the current year amounted to $150,000. The estimated bad debt loss rate is ½% of credit sales.

f. On July 1 of the current year, the company received a $10,000, one-year, 14% note from a customer. At maturity date, the company will collect the face amount of $10,000 plus interest for one year.

Exercise 2–9

Ray Company adjusts and closes its accounts each December 31. Below are two typical situations involving adjusting entries.

a. During the current year, office supplies were purchased for cash, $750. The inventory of office supplies at the end of the prior year was $150. At the end of the current year, the inventory showed $200 unused supplies still on hand. Give the adjusting entry assuming at the time of the purchase that in Case A, $750 was debited to Office Supplies Expense, and in Case B, $750 was debited to Office Supplies Inventory.

b. On June 1, the company collected cash, $2,400, which was for rent collected in advance for the next 12 months. Give the adjusting journal entry assuming at the time of the collection that in Case A, $2,400 was credited to Rent Revenue, and in Case B, $2,400 was credited to Rent Revenue Collected in Advance.

Exercise 2–10

a. On January 1, 19A, the Office Supplies Inventory account showed a balance on hand amounting to $350. During 19A, purchases of office supplies amounted to $800. An inventory of office supplies on hand at December 31, 19A, reflected unused supplies amounting to $425. Give the adjusting journal entry that should be made on December 31, 19A, assuming that in Case A the purchases were debited to the Office Supplies Inventory account, and in Case B the purchases were debited to Office Supplies Expense.

b. On January 1, 19A, the Prepaid Insurance account showed a debit balance of $300, which was for coverage for the three months, January–March. On April 1, 19A, the company took out another policy covering a two-year period from that date. The two-year premium amounting to $3,600 was paid and debited to Prepaid Insurance. Give the adjusting journal entry that should be made on December 31, 19A, to adjust for the entire year.

Exercise 2–11

Write a suitable explanation for each of the following journal entries:

a. Wage expense	1,400	
Wages payable		1,400
b. Warranty (guarantee) expense	950	
Estimated warranty liability......		950

c.	Insurance expense	600	
	Prepaid insurance		600
d.	Interest expense	1,200	
	Interest payable		1,200
e.	Interest receivable	900	
	Interest revenue		900
f.	Rent revenue	750	
	Unearned rent revenue		750
g.	Income summary	5,000	
	Retained earnings		5,000

Exercise 2–12

The adjusted trial balance for ABC Company showed the following on December 31, 19E, which is the end of the annual accounting period:

Sales revenue	$92,000
Interest revenue	1,000
Purchases	44,000
Purchase returns	500
Freight-in	1,500
Beginning inventory (periodic)	17,800
Selling expenses	23,000
Administrative expenses	13,000
Interest expense	400
Income tax expense	1,000
Additional data:	
Ending inventory	19,000

Required:

1. Set up T-accounts for each of the above items; enter the balances and diagram the closing entries. Use both Cost of Goods Sold and Income Summary accounts.
2. Explain the manner in which you handled the inventory amounts. Explain an alternate approach.

Exercise 2–13

At the end of the annual accounting period, Ross Corporation made the following adjusting entries:

December 31, 19B:

a.	Wage expense	8,000	
	Wages payable		8,000
b.	Bad debt expense	400	
	Allowance for doubtful accounts		400
c.	Income tax expense	6,000	
	Income tax payable		6,000
d.	Depreciation expense	15,000	
	Accumulated depreciation		15,000

Required:
Journalize the reversing entries that you think would be preferable on January 1, 19C. Explain for each adjusting entry, the analysis you used to decide whether to reverse it.

Exercise 2–14

At the end of the annual accounting period, Crane Corporation made the following adjusting entries:

December 31, 19A:

a.	Property tax expense	600	
	Property taxes payable		600
	(These are paid once each year.)		
b.	Rent receivable	2,000	
	Rent revenue		2,000
	(Rent revenue is collected at various dates each month.)		
c.	Patent amortization expense	4,000	
	Patents		4,000
d.	Warranty expense	600	
	Estimated warranty liability		600
e.	Wage expense	2,000	
	Wages payable		2,000

Required:
Journalize the reversing entries that you think should be made on January 1, 19B. Explain, for each adjusting entry, the analysis you used to determine whether to reverse it.

Exercise 2–15

Complete the following tabulations by entering the appropriate amount in each blank space:

(Relates to Exercise 2–15)

1.

	Owners' Equity at Start of Period	Additional Investment by Owner	Withdrawals by Owner	Owners' Equity at End of Period	Net Income (Loss)
a.	$10,000	$2,000	$1,000	$17,400	$____
b.	28,000	3,000	____	22,000	4,700
c.	____	1,200	800	30,000	(2,200)
d.	15,500	600	____	12,950	(2,000)
e.	18,000	____	2,700	22,000	4,700

(Exercise 2–15 continued)

2.

	Sales	Finished Goods Beginning Inventory	Cost of Goods Manufactured	Finished Goods Ending Inventory	Cost of Goods Sold	Gross Margin	Expenses	Net Income
a.	$____	$25,000	$60,000	$____	$67,000	$23,000	$____	$1,000
b.	80,000	____	48,000	2,000	____	23,000	18,000	____
c.	____	20,000	____	36,000	59,000	18,000	____	8,000

SUPPLEMENT 2–A

Exercise 2–16

Dodd Company uses special journals for credit sales, credit purchases, cash receipts, and cash payments. For each of the following transactions, you are to indicate the appropriate journal.

Transactions	Appropriate Journal
a. Sold common stock of Dodd for cash.	________
b. Purchased merchandise for resale; terms, 2/10, n/60.	________
c. Borrowed $5,000 on 8% note.	________
d. Recorded depreciation expense.	________
e. Sold merchandise for cash.	________
f. Purchased merchandise for cash.	________
g. Purchased equipment for cash.	________
h. Sold operational asset for cash.	________
i. Purchased machinery on credit.	________
j. Collected an account receivable.	________
k. Paid a note payable.	________
l. Recorded accrued wages payable.	________
m. Paid cash dividend on common stock.	________
n. Recorded estimated bad debt expense.	________
o. Recorded amortization expense on patent.	________
p. Sold machinery on credit.	________

Exercise 2–17

Green Wholesalers uses special journals. Following is the special credit sales journal with several representative transactions.

Required:

1. Sum the special journal (below) and post it to the appropriate accounts in the general ledger and the two subsidiary ledgers. Use control accounts and subsidiary ledgers for sales and accounts receivable; assign systematic numbers to the accounts.
2. Prove the correctness of the two subsidiary ledgers.

(Relates to Exercise 2–17)

Special Journal—Merchandise Sales on Credit **Page S-9**

Date	Sales Invoice No.	Account Receivable	Terms	Folio	Amount	Dept. Sales A	Dept. Sales B
19D:							
Jan. 1	21	Fly Corp.	2/10, n/30		498	440	58
5	22	B. T. Co.	2/10, n/30		490	290	200
7	23	Easton Co.	2/10, n/30		294	104	190
11	24	Fly Corp.	2/10, n/30		588	288	300
13	25	Wells Co.	2/10, n/30		686	300	386
18	26	Fly Corp.	2/10, n/30		147	100	47
21	27	Easton Co.	2/10, n/30		784	554	230
28	28	B. T. Co.	2/10, n/30		245	200	45
31	29	Wells Co.	2/10, n/30		637	407	230

Exercise 2–18

Sorensen Retailers uses special journals. Following is a special cash receipts journal with several selected transactions.

Required:

1. Sum the special journal (next page) and post it to the appropriate accounts in the general ledger and subsidiary ledger. Use control accounts and subsidiary ledgers for credit sales and accounts receivable. Assign systematic numbers to the accounts. Assume beginning balances of Riley Corporation, $8,400; Brown, Inc., $1,240; and Watson Company, $10,000.
2. Prove the correctness of the subsidiary ledger.

(Relates to Exercise 2–18)

Special Journal—Cash Receipts							Page CR-8
Date	Explanation	Debits	Credits				
		Cash	Account Title	Folio	Accounts Receivable	Sundry Accounts	Sales
19E:							
Jan. 1	Cash sales	30,000					30,000
2	On account	4,200	Riley Corp.		4,200		
5	Cash sales	10,000					10,000
6	On account	1,240	Brown, Inc.		1,240		
8	Sale of short-term investment	7,000	Short-term investments			4,000	
			Gain on sale of investments			3,000	
11	Cash sales	41,000					41,000
12	Borrowed cash	10,000	Notes payable			10,000	
15	On account	5,500	Watson Co.		5,500		
18	Collected interest	600	Interest revenue			600	
31	Cash sales	52,000					52,000

PROBLEMS

PART A: PROBLEMS 2–1 to 2–2

Problem 2–1

The following selected transactions were completed during the current year by Sollenberger Corporation:

a. Sollenberger sold 10,000 shares of its own common stock, par $10 per share, for $16 per share and received cash in full.

b. Borrowed $50,000 cash on a 16%, one-year note, interest payable at maturity.

c. Purchased equipment for use in operating the business at a net cash cost of $55,000; paid in full.

d. Purchased merchandise for resale at a cash net cost of $20,500; paid cash. Assume a periodic inventory system.

e. Purchased merchandise for resale on credit terms, 2/10, n/60. The merchandise will cost $9,800 if paid within 10 days; after 10 days, the payment will be $10,000. The company always takes the discount; therefore, such purchases are recorded at net. Assume periodic inventory system.

f. Sold merchandise for $48,000; collected $30,000 cash, and the balance is due in one month.

g. Paid $12,000 cash for operating expenses.

h. Paid the balance for the merchandise purchased in *(e)* within 10 days.

i. Collected the balance due on the sale in *(f)*.

j. Paid cash for an insurance premium, $600; the premium was for two years' coverage (debit Prepaid Expense).

Required:

1. Enter each of the above transactions in a general journal. Use the letter to the left to indicate the date.
2. Post each entry to appropriate T-accounts (number them consecutively starting with 101).
3. Prepare an unadjusted trial balance.

Problem 2–2

The following selected transactions were completed during the current year by O'Conner Corporation:

a. At date of organization, sold and issued 50,000 shares of its common stock, par $1 per share, for $80,000 cash.

b. Purchased a plant site for $100,000. The site included a building worth $82,000 and land worth $18,000. Payment was made, $70,000 cash and a $30,000 one-year, 15% note, interest payable at maturity.

c. Borrowed $50,000 cash from the local bank; signed an 18% interest (payable at maturity) note due in six months.

d. Purchased equipment for use in the business for $12,000; paid cash.

e. Purchased goods for resale at a net cost of $80,000; paid $70,000 cash, balance on open account. Assume perpetual inventory system.

f. Sold goods for cash, $62,000 (ignore the cost of goods sold entry).

g. Paid operating expenses, $35,000.
h. Sold goods for cash, $48,000 (ignore the cost of goods sold entry).
i. Purchased goods for cash, $22,000.
j. Paid the $10,000 due from transaction *(e)*.
k. Sold and issued 30,000 shares of its common stock for $50,000.
l. On due date, paid the local bank the note given in entry *(c)* in the amount of $50,000 plus the interest to maturity date.
m. Purchased a two-year insurance policy on the building and equipment. Paid the two-year premium amounting to $1,400.

Required:

1. Journalize the above transactions in a general journal. Use the letters to the left to indicate dates.
2. Set up T-accounts (number them starting with 101) as needed and post the entries from the journal. Use folio notations.
3. Prepare an unadjusted trial balance.

PART B: PROBLEMS 2–3 to 2–15

Problem 2–3

Below are some unrelated adjusting and closing (but no reversing) entries. Write a suitable explanation for each of the following end-of-period entries:

a.	Salary expense	7,000	
	Salaries payable		7,000
b.	Rent revenue	800	
	Unearned rent revenue		800
c.	Income summary	10,000	
	Inventory		10,000
d.	Inventory	12,000	
	Income summary		12,000
e.	Interest receivable	900	
	Interest revenue		900
f.	Supplies expense	400	
	Supplies inventory		400
g.	Income summary	39,000	
	Operating expenses		21,000
	Administrative expenses		16,000
	Interest expense		2,000
h.	Interest expense	750	
	Interest payable		750
i.	Income summary	8,800	
	Retained earnings		8,800
j.	Investment revenue	600	
	Unearned investment revenue		600
k.	Warranty (guarantee) expense	500	
	Estimated warranty liability		500
l.	Income tax expense	3,700	
	Income taxes payable		3,700
m.	Property tax expense	360	
	Property taxes payable		360
n.	Supplies inventory	440	
	Supplies expense		440
o.	Sales revenue	50,000	
	Rent revenue	2,000	
	Interest revenue	1,000	
	Sales returns		1,500
	Income summary		51,500

Problem 2–4

Deitrick Corporation has been in operation since January 1, 19A. It is now December 31, 19B, the end of the annual accounting period. The company has never been audited. The annual statements below were prepared by the company bookkeeper at December 31, 19B (accounts needed in the solution are provided without amounts):

Income Statement

Revenues:	
Service revenue	$250,000
Interest revenue	1,000
Total revenues	251,000
Expenses:	
Salary expense	75,000
Wage expense	60,600
Depreciation expense	
Interest expense	2,400
Other expenses	50,000
Total expenses	188,000
Pretax income	63,000
Income tax expense	
Net income	$ 63,000
EPS	$3.50

Balance Sheet

Assets

Cash	$ 40,000
Note receivable (10%)	12,000
Interest receivable	
Inventory, supplies	2,000
Prepaid insurance	1,500
Equipment	200,000
Accumulated depreciation	(25,000)
Other assets	85,500
Total assets	$316,000

Liabilities

Accounts payable	$ 18,000
Wages payable	
Unearned service revenue	
Interest payable	
Income taxes payable	
Notes payable (16%)	40,000
Total liabilities	58,000
Stockholders' Equity	
Capital stock, par $10	180,000
Retained earnings	78,000
Total stockholders' equity	258,000
Total liabilities and stockholders' equity	$316,000

An outside accountant was engaged to adjust the statements for any items omitted. As a consequence, the following additional information was developed:

a. No depreciation was reported for 19B. The equipment has an eight-year life and no residual value.
b. Prepaid insurance at the end of 19B was $500. Use "Other expenses."
c. Wages unpaid and unrecorded at the end of 19B amounted to $18,000.
d. Interest on the note receivable was last collected at October 31, 19B.
e. The inventory count of supplies at year-end showed $300. Use "Other expenses."
f. On December 31, 19B, service revenues collected but unearned amounted to $6,000.
g. Interest on the note payable is paid each August 31.
h. Assume the income tax rate is 20 percent.

Required:

1. Prepare adjusting entries for the above in general journal form for December 31, 19B.
2. Restate the above statements after taking into account the adjusting entries made in 1 above. Key each adjustment. You need not use additional subclassifications on the statements. Use the following solution format:

Items	Reported Amounts	Changes from Adjusting Entries (use + and −)	Correct Amounts
(list the two statements here)			

3. Reconcile the net changes on the income statement with the net changes on the balance sheet. Use the following format:

	Increase (decrease)
Income statement:	
Change in total revenues	
Change in total expenses	
Change in net income	
Balance sheet:	
Change in total assets	
Change in total liabilities	
Change in owners' equity	

Problem 2–5

R. G. May Company adjusts and closes its books each December 31. It is now December 31, 19A, and the adjusting entries are to be made. You are requested to prepare, in general journal format, the adjusting entry that should be made for each of the following items. Show computations.

a. Credit sales for the year amounted to $200,000. The estimated loss rate on bad debts is ⅜%.
b. Unpaid and unrecorded wages at December 31 amounted to $2,100.
c. The company paid a two-year insurance premium in advance on April 1, 19A, amounting to $3,000, which was debited to Prepaid Insurance.
d. A machine that cost $37,000 is to be depreciated for the full year. The estimated useful life is 10 years, and the residual value, $2,000. Assume straight-line depreciation.
e. The company rented a warehouse on June 1, 19A, for one year. They had to pay the full amount of rent one year in advance on June 1, amounting to $4,800, which was debited to Rent Expense.
f. The company received a 15% note from a customer with a face amount of $6,000. The note was dated September 1, 19A; the principal plus the interest is payable one year later. Notes Receivable was debited, and Sales Revenue credited on September 1, 19A.
g. On December 30, 19A, the property tax bill was received in the amount of $2,000. This amount applied only to 19A and had not been previously recorded. The taxes are due, and will be paid, on January 15, 19B.
h. On April 1, 19A, the company signed a $30,000, 16% note payable. On that date, Cash was debited and Notes Payable credited for $30,000. The note is payable on March 30, 19B, for the face amount plus interest for one year.
i. The company purchased a patent on January 1, 19A, at a cost of $5,950. On that date, Patent was debited and Cash credited for $5,950. The patent has an estimated useful life of 17 years and no residual value.
j. The worksheet is being completed, and pretax income has been computed to be $40,000 after all the above adjustments. Assume an average income tax rate of 31.75%.

Problem 2–6

Willie Mays Company adjusts and closes its accounts each December 31. It is December 31, 19B. You are requested to prepare, in general journal format, the adjusting entry that should be made for each of the following items. Show computations.

a. The company owns a building and the site on which it is situated. The Building account reflects a cost of $267,000; and the Land account, $20,000. The estimated useful life of the building is 20 years, and the residual value, $47,000. Accumulated depreciation to January 1, 19B, was $66,000. Assume straight-line depreciation.

b. Property taxes for the city fiscal year, which ends June 30, 19C, have not been recorded or paid. A tax statement was received near the end of December 19B for $5,000. The taxes are due, and will be paid, on February 15, 19C. Property tax expense for the city fiscal year ended June 30, 19B, was $4,800. No property tax expense has been recorded in 19B.

c. The company received a $6,000, 15% note from a customer on June 1, 19B. On that date, Notes Receivable was debited and Sales Revenue credited for $6,000. The face of the note plus interest for one year is payable on May 30, 19C.

d. At December 31, 19B, the Supplies Inventory account showed a debit balance of $1,600. An inventory of unused supplies taken at year-end reflected $400.

e. Sales for the year amounted to $1,500,000. of which $300,000 was on credit. The estimated bad debt loss rate, based on credit sales, was ⅓% for the year.

f. On August 1, 19B, the company rented some space in its building to a tenant and collected $4,200 cash rent in advance. This was for the 12 months starting August 1, 19B, and was credited to Rent Revenue.

g. At December 31, 19B, unrecorded and unpaid salaries amounted to $7,500.

h. On April 1, 19B, the company borrowed $20,000 on a one-year, 17% note. On that date, Cash was debited and Notes Payable credited for $20,000. At maturity the face amount plus interest for one year must be paid.

i. On January 1, 19B, the company purchased, with cash, a patent for use in the business at a cost of $2,550, which was debited to Patent. The patent has an estimated remaining economic life of 10 years and no residual value.

j. The company uses the periodic inventory system whereby the inventory is physically counted, then valued at unit cost at each year-end. The company considers the inventory entries as adjusting entries. The beginning inventory was $40,000, and the ending inventory (December 31, 19B) was $44,500. You are to give the adjusting entry for each inventory amount assuming a Cost of Goods Sold account is used.

k. The worksheet is being completed; all of the above adjusting entries have been recorded on it. Pretax income has been computed to be $70,000. Assume the average income tax rate is 30%.

Problem 2–7

The following situations relate to the Gray Corporation. The fiscal accounting year ends December 31. The situations relate to the year 19D. Gray Corporation is a manufacturer rather than a retailer. The books are adjusted and closed each December 31.

In each instance, you are to give *only* the adjusting entry (or entries) that would be made on December 31, 19D, incident to adjusting and closing the books and preparation of the annual financial statements. State clearly any assumptions that you make. Give each adjusting entry in general journal format.

a. The company owns a machine that cost $225,000; it was purchased on July 1, 19A. It has an estimated useful life of 15 years and a residual value of $15,000. Straight-line depreciation is used. The machine is still being used.

b. Sales for 19D amounted to $800,000, including $200,000 credit sales. It is estimated, based on experience of the company, that bad debt losses will be ½% of credit sales.

c. At the beginning of 19D, Office Supplies Inventory amounted to $300. During 19D, office supplies amounting to $4,400 were purchased; this amount was debited to Office Supplies Expenses. An inventory of office supplies at the end of 19D showed $250 on the shelves. The January 1 balance of $300 is still reflected in the Office Supplies Inventory account.

d. On July 1, 19D, the company paid a three-year insurance premium amounting to $1,080; this amount was debited to Prepaid Insurance.

e. On October 1, 19D, the company paid rent on some leased office space. The payment of $3,600 cash was for the following 12 months. At the time of payment, Rent Expense was debited for the $3,600.

f. On July 1, 19D, the company borrowed $60,000 from the Sharpstown bank. The loan was for 12 months at 14% interest payable at maturity date.

g. Finished goods inventory on January 1, 19D, was $100,000; and on December 31, 19D, it was $130,000. Assume periodic inventory procedures and that inventory entries are viewed as adjusting entries. Use a Cost of Goods Sold account.

h. The company owned some property (land) that was rented to B. R. Speir on April 1, 19D, for 12 months for $4,200. On April 1, the entire annual rental of $4,200 was credited to Rent Revenue Collected in Advance and Cash was debited.

i. On December 31, 19D, wages earned by employees but not yet paid (nor recorded in the accounts) amounted to $7,000. Disregard payroll taxes.

j. On December 31, 19D, it was discovered that some raw material purchased on the preceding day, although not paid for, was included in the ending inventory.

A purchase had not been recorded. The cost was $950. Assume periodic inventory procedures.

k. On September 1, 19D, the company loaned $12,000 to an outside party. The loan was at 15% per annum and was due in six months; interest is to be paid at maturity. Cash was credited for $12,000, and Notes Receivable debited for the same amount on September 1.

l. On January 1, 19D, factory supplies on hand amounted to $100. During 19D, factory supplies costing $2,000 were purchased and debited to Factory Supplies Inventory. At the end of 19D, a physical inventory count revealed that factory supplies on hand amounted to $300.

m. The company purchased a gravel pit on January 1, 19B, at a cost of $24,000; it was estimated that approximately 60,000 tons of gravel could be removed prior to exhaustion. It was also estimated that the company would take five years to exploit this natural resource. Tons of gravel removed were 19B—2,000; 19C—7,000; and 19D—5,000.

n. At the end of 19D, it was found that postage stamps costing $90 were still on hand (in a "postage" box in the office). When the stamps were purchased, Miscellaneous Expense was debited and Cash credited.

o. At the end of 19D, property taxes for 19D amounting to $2,500 had been assessed on property owned by the company. The taxes are due no later than February 1, 19E. The taxes had not been recorded on the books since payment had not been made.

p. The company borrowed $30,000 from the bank on December 1, 19D. A 60-day note payable was signed that called for 16% interest payable on the due date. As a consequence, on December 1, 19D, Cash was debited and Notes Payable credited for $30,000.

q. On July 1, 19D, the company paid the city a $500 license fee for the next 12 months. On that date, Cash was credited and License Expense debited for $500.

r. On March 1, 19D, the company made a loan to the company president and received a $12,000 note receivable. The loan was due in one year and called for 15% annual interest payable at maturity date.

s. The company owns three company cars used by the executives. A six-month maintenance contract on them was signed on October 1, 19D, whereby a local garage agreed to do "all the required maintenance." The payment was made for the following six months in advance. On October 1, 19D, Cash was credited and Maintenance Expense was debited for $1,800.

Problem 2–8

The adjusted trial balance for Danville Corporation reflected the following on December 31, 19A, end of the annual accounting period:

Cash	$ 27,900	
Accounts receivable	32,000	
Allowance for doubtful accts.		$ 500
Inventory (periodic)	18,000	
Prepaid insurance	600	
Equipment	100,000	
Accum. depr., equip.		20,000
Accounts payable		13,400
Wages payable		800
Income taxes payable		5,000
Bonds payable		20,000
Common stock, par $10		100,000
Retained earnings		12,400
Sales revenue		116,000
Interest revenue		1,000
Sales returns	3,000	
Purchases	70,000	
Freight-in	2,500	
Purchase returns		900
Operating expenses	18,000	
General expenses (incl. interest)	13,000	
Income tax expense	5,000	
	$290,000	$290,000

Inventory, 12/31/19A, $23,000.

Required:

1. Set up T-accounts only for the accounts to be closed and Retained Earnings. Enter the balances. Diagram the closing entries. Use both Cost of Goods Sold and Income Summary accounts.
2. Journalize the closing entries to agree with your diagram.
3. Explain the alternate approach when the Cost of Goods Sold account is not used.

Problem 2–9

The summarized adjusted trial balance for Barrett Corporation reflected the following on December 31, 19A, end of the annual accounting period:

Cash	$60,700	
Inventory (periodic)	12,000	
Accounts receivable	21,000	
Allowance for doubtful accts.		$ 400
Prepaid insurance	300	
Accounts payable		17,600
Wages payable		1,000
Income taxes payable		2,000
Common stock, par $10		50,000
Retained earnings		17,300
Sales revenue		88,000
Sales returns	2,000	
Purchases	45,000	
Freight-in	1,000	
Purchase returns		700
Operating expenses	18,400	
General expenses (incl. interest)	14,600	
Income tax expense	2,000	
	$177,000	$177,000

Inventory (ending), 12/13/19A, $19,800.

Required:

1. Set up T-accounts for Retained Earnings and those accounts that are to be closed. Enter the balances. Diagram the closing entries. Use only the Income Summary account.
2. Journalize the closing entries to agree with your diagram.
3. Explain an alternate approach when the Cost of Goods Sold account is used.

Problem 2–10

The post-closing trial balance of the general ledger of McQueen Corporation at January 1, 19F, reflected the following (McQueen uses the periodic inventory system):

Acct. No.	Account	Debit	Credit
101	Cash	$28,000	
102	Accounts receivable	18,000	
103	Allowance for doubtful accts.		$ 400
104	Inventory (periodic)*	10,000	
105	Equipment (20-year life; no residual value)	20,000	
106	Accum. depr.		6,000
200	Accounts payable		9,000
201	Wages payable		
202	Income taxes payable		
300	Common stock, par $1		50,000
301	Retained earnings		10,600
302	Income summary		
400	Revenues		
500	Operating expenses		
501	Purchases		
600	Income tax expense		
		$76,000	$76,000

* Ending inventory, $17,000 (at 12/31/19F).

The following is a summary of the transactions during 19F (use the number to the left to indicate the date):

Date

1. Sold goods, $90,000, of which $20,000 was on credit.
2. Purchased goods, $40,000, of which $10,000 was on credit.
3. Collected accounts receivable, $35,000.
4. Paid accounts payable, $17,000.
5. Paid operating expenses, $25,800.
6. On January 1, 19F, sold common stock of the company, 2,000 shares at par, collected cash in full.
7. On the last day of the year, purchased a new machine at a cost of $12,000; paid cash. Estimated useful life, 10 years; residual value, $2,000.

Required:

1. Set up T-accounts in the general ledger for the accounts listed above; they are all you will need. Enter the beginning balances.
2. Journalize each of the above transactions in the general journal.
3. Post the journal entries; use folio notations.
4. Prepare an unadjusted trial balance.
5. Journalize and post the adjusting entries. Accrued (unpaid) wages at year-end amounted to $800. Bad debt expense is estimated to be 1% of credit sales for the period. Assume straight-line depreciation. Assume an average 22% corporate income tax rate.
6. Prepare an adjusted trial balance.
7. Prepare an unclassified income statement and balance sheet.
8. Journalize and post the closing entries (use only the Income Summary account).
9. Prepare a post-closing trial balance.

Problem 2–11

The post-closing trial balance of the general ledger of Towson Corporation at December 31, 19I, reflected the following:

Acct. No.	Account	Debit	Credit
101	Cash	$ 27,000	
102	Accounts receivable	21,000	
103	Allowance for doubtful accts.		$ 1,000
104	Inventory (periodic)*	35,000	
105	Prepaid insurance (20 months remaining)	900	
200	Equipment (20-year est. life; no residual value)	50,000	
201	Accum. depr.		22,500
300	Accounts payable		7,500
301	Wages payable		
302	Income taxes payable (for 19I)		4,000
400	Common stock, par $1		80,000
401	Retained earnings		18,900
500	Sales revenue		
600	Purchases		
601	Operating expenses		
602	Income tax expense		
700	Income summary		
		$133,900	$133,900

*Ending inventory, $45,000 (at 12/31/19J).

The following transactions occurred during 19J in the order given (use the number at the left to indicate the date):

Date

1. Sold goods for $30,000, of which $10,000 was on credit.
2. Collected $17,000 on accounts receivable.
3. Paid income taxes payable (19I), $4,000.
4. Purchased merchandise, $40,000, of which $8,000 was on credit.

5. Paid accounts payable, $6,000.
6. Sold goods for cash, $72,000.
7. Paid operating expenses, $19,000.
8. On January 1, 19J, sold and issued 1,000 shares of common stock, par $1, for $1,000 cash.
9. Purchased merchandise, $100,000, of which $27,000 was on credit.
10. Sold goods for $98,000, of which $30,000 was on credit.
11. Collected cash on accounts receivable, $26,000.
12. Paid cash on accounts payable, $28,000.
13. Paid various operating expenses in cash, $18,000.

Required:

1. Set up T-accounts in the general ledger for each of the accounts listed in the above trial balance and enter the December 31, 19I, balances.
2. Journalize each of the transactions listed above for 19J. Use general journal only.
3. Post the journal entries; use folio notations.
4. Prepare an unadjusted trial balance.
5. Journalize the adjusting entries and post them to the ledger. Assume a bad debt rate of ½% of credit sales for the period and an average 40% corporate income tax rate. At December 31, 19J, accrued wages were $300. Assume straight-line depreciation.
6. Prepare an adjusted trial balance.
7. Prepare an unclassified income statement and balance sheet.
8. Journalize and post the closing entries. Do not use a Cost of Goods Sold account.
9. Prepare a post-closing trial balance.

Problem 2–12

Veeder Corporation adjusts and closes its books each December 31. At December 31, 19C, the following unadjusted trial balance has been developed from the general ledger:

	Balances (unadjusted)	
Account	**Debit**	**Credit**
Cash	$139,960	
Accounts receivable	34,000	
Allowance for doubtful accounts		$ 5,400
Inventory (periodic)	62,000	
Prepaid insurance (15 months remaining as of 1/1/19C)	600	
Long-term note receivable (14%)	12,000	
Investment revenue receivable		
Land	27,000	
Building	240,000	
Accum. depr., building		130,000
Equipment	90,000	
Accum. depr., equip.		50,000
Accounts payable		23,000
Salaries payable		
Income taxes payable		
Interest payable		
Unearned rent revenue		
Bonds payable, 10%		120,000
Common stock, par $10		200,000
Contrib. capital in excess of par		10,000
Retained earnings		27,900
Sales revenue		300,000
Investment revenue		1,260
Rent revenue		6,000
Purchases	164,000	
Purchase returns		4,000
Selling expenses	51,000	
G&A expenses	35,000	
Interest expense	7,000	
Extraordinary loss (pretax)	15,000	
Income tax expense		
	$877,560	$877,560

Additional data for adjustments and other purposes:

a. Estimated bad debt loss rate is ½% of credit sales. Ten percent of 19C sales were on credit. Classify as a selling expense.
b. Ending inventory (December 31, 19C), $70,000.
c. Interest on the long-term note receivable was last collected on September 30, 19C.
d. Estimated useful life on the building was 20 years; residual value, $40,000. Allocate 10% to administrative and the balance to selling expenses. Assume straight-line depreciation.
e. Estimated useful life on the equipment was 10 years; residual value, zero. Allocate 10% to administrative and the balance to selling expenses. Assume straight-line depreciation.
f. Unrecorded and unpaid sales salaries payable at December 31, 19C, was $7,500.
g. Interest on the bonds payable was paid last on July 31, 19C.
h. On August 1, 19C, the company rented some space in its building to a tenant and collected $6,000 for 12 months' rent in advance, which was credited to Rent Revenue.
i. Adjust for expired insurance. Assume selling expense.
j. Assume an average 30% corporate income tax rate on all items including the extraordinary loss.

Required:

1. Enter the above unadjusted trial balance on a worksheet. Do not use a Cost of Goods Sold account.
2. Enter the adjusting entries on the worksheet and complete it.
3. Prepare an unclassified income statement and balance sheet.
4. Journalize the closing entries.

Problem 2–13

Royce Corporation currently is completing the end-of-the-period accounting process. At December 31, 19D, the following unadjusted trial balance was developed from the general ledger:

Account	Balances (unadjusted) Debit	Credit
Cash	$ 60,260	
Accounts receivable	38,000	
Allowance for doubtful accts.		$ 2,000
Inventory (periodic)	80,000	
Sales supplies inventory	900	
Long-term note receivable, 14%	12,000	
Equipment	180,000	
Accum. depr., equip.		64,000
Patent	8,400	
Interest receivable		
Accounts payable		23,000
Interest payable		
Income taxes payable		
Property taxes payable		
Unearned rent revenue		
Mortgage payable, 12%		60,000
Common stock, par $10		100,000
Contrib. capital in excess of par		15,000
Retained earnings		32,440
Sales revenue		700,000
Investment revenue		1,120
Rent revenue		3,000
Purchases	400,000	
Freight-in	7,000	
Purchase returns		2,000
Selling expenses	164,400	
G&A expenses	55,000	
Interest expense	6,600	
Income tax expense		
Extraordinary gain (pretax)		10,000
	$1,012,560	$1,012,560

Additional data for adjustments and other purposes:

a. Estimated bad debt loss rate is ¼% of credit sales. Credit sales for the year amounted to $200,000. This is a selling expense.

b. Ending inventory, December 31, 19D, $105,000.

c. Interest on the long-term note receivable was last collected August 31, 19D.

d. Estimated useful life of the equipment is 10 years; residual value, $20,000. Allocate 10% to G & A expenses and the balance to selling expenses. Assume straight-line depreciation.

e. Estimated remaining economic life of the patent is 14 years (from January 1, 19D) and no residual value. Assume straight-line amortization to selling expense (used in sales promotion).

f. Interest on the mortgage payable was last paid on November 30, 19D.

g. On June 1, 19D, the company rented some office space to a tenant for one year and collected $3,000 rent in advance for the year; the entire amount was credited to Rent Revenue.

h. On December 31, 19D, received a statement for calendar year 19D property taxes amounting to $1,300. The amount is due February 15, 19E. Assume it will be paid on that date and that it is a selling expense. None of the amount had been recorded during 19D.

i. Sales supplies on hand at December 31, 19D, amounted to $300 (selling expense).

j. Assume an average 40% corporate income tax rate on all items including the extraordinary gain.

Required:

1. Enter the above unadjusted trial balance on a worksheet. Do not use a Cost of Goods Sold account.
2. Enter the adjusting entries and complete the worksheet.
3. Prepare an unclassified income statement and balance sheet.
4. Journalize the closing entries.

Problem 2–14

At the end of the accounting period, ABC Corporation made the following adjusting entries.

December 31, 19J:

		Debit	Credit
a.	Depreciation expense	7,000	
	Accumulated depreciation		7,000
b.	Bad debt expense	1,000	
	Allowance for doubtful accounts		1,000
c.	Insurance expense	600	
	Prepaid insurance		600
d.	Supplies expense	2,000	
	Supplies inventory		2,000
e.	Wage expense	15,000	
	Wages payable		15,000
f.	Rent receivable	8,000	
	Rent revenue		8,000
g.	Utilities (electric) expense	4,800	
	Utilities payable		4,800
h.	Interest expense	1,800	
	Interest payable		1,800

Required:

1. The first four adjusting entries given above generally are not viewed as candidates for reversal on January 1, 19K. Explain why each is generally not a candidate.

2. The last four adjusting entries shown above generally are viewed as candidates for reversal on January 1, 19K. Give the reversing entry for each and explain why it may be desirable to reverse.
3. The last entry may, or may not, be reversed. In either event, the net effect is the same. Assume the next interest payment is March 31, 19K, for $2,400 (interest for the past 12 months). Prepare entries side by side under the headings With Reversing Entry and Without Reversing Entry and demonstrate that the net effects are the same.

Problem 2–15

Glow Company's annual financial statements contained the following errors:

Item	December 31, 19A	December 31, 19B
a. Ending inventory	$2,000 understated	$1,800 overstated
b. Depr. expense	400 understated	—

c. Three years' insurance premium amounting to $1,500 was prepaid at the start of 19A; although the payment also related to 19B and 19C, the entire amount was expensed in 19A.

d. On December 31, 19B, fully depreciated equipment was sold for $3,200 cash; however, the sale was not recorded until early 19C.

There were no other errors in 19A or 19B, and no corrections have been made for any errors. Ignore any income tax effects.

Required:
1. Compute the dollar amount by which 19B income is misstated.
2. Compute the misstatement of Glow's 19B working capital (excess of current assets over current liabilities).
3. Compute the misstatement of Glow's Retained Earnings balance as of December 31, 19B. Show supporting calculations. (AICPA adapted)

SUPPLEMENT 2–A: PROBLEMS 2–16 to 2–17

Problem 2–16

Baker Company uses special journals for credit sales and credit purchases of merchandise. Below are listed some selected transactions involving merchandise purchases and sales. Amounts given for credit transactions are before any deduction of discount unless otherwise stated. Sales and purchases on credit are recorded net of discount. Assume periodic inventory.

a. Purchased merchandise for cash, $9,800, from X Corporation.
b. Sold merchandise on credit terms, 2/10, n/30, $1,000, to AD Company.
c. Purchased merchandise, $3,000, terms, 2/10, n/30, from Benson Company.
d. Purchased equipment from Roy Company for use in the business for $10,000; paid cash.
e. Collected for merchandise sold in *(b)* within 10 days.
f. Sold merchandise on credit terms, 2/10, n/30, $2,000, to Z Company.
g. Purchased merchandise for cash, $15,000, from AK Company.
h. Sold merchandise for cash, $41,800, to AD Company.
i. Sold merchandise on credit terms, 2/10, n/30, $4,000, to BT Corporation.
j. Purchased merchandise from X Corporation, $1,500; terms, 2/10, n/30.
k. Paid for merchandise purchased in *(c)* above within the discount period.
l. Sold merchandise to VEE Company, $3,300; terms, 2/10, n/60.
m. Purchased merchandise from Benson Company, $4,000; terms, 2/10, n/30.

Required:
1. Design special journals for *(a)* credit sales and *(b)* credit purchases of merchandise similar to those illustrated in the chapter.
2. Enter in the two special journals appropriate transactions from the above list. Enter the remaining entries in the general journal.
3. Set up ledger accounts for Accounts Receivable Control, Accounts Payable Control, Sales Revenue, and Purchases in the general ledger and appropriate subsidiary ledgers for the two control accounts. Use T-account format. Post appropriate amounts to these records. Systematically number the accounts for posting purposes.
4. Prove the accuracy of the accounts receivable and accounts payable records.

Problem 2–17

Reagan Company is a small department store. The accounting system is maintained manually. Control accounts and subsidiary ledgers are used. The following information was selected from the accounting system at January 1, 19J:

Journals	Page No. to Be Used
General journal	J-27
Special journals:	
Merchandise sales on credit	S-13
Mdse. purchases on credit	P-9
Cash receipts	CR-22
Cash payments	CP-34

General Ledger Accounts	Balance 1/1/19J	Acct. No.
Cash	$ 72,000	101
Accounts receivable	38,000	105
Inventory (periodic)	45,000	110
Equipment	25,000	204
Accounts payable	21,000	303
Notes payable	10,000	305
Common stock, par $10	100,000	400
Contributed capital in excess of par		401
Retained earnings	49,000	410
Sales revenue		500
Sales returns		501
Purchases		600
Purchase returns		601
Expenses		700

Subsidiary Ledgers

Accounts receivable (no. 105):		
Ames, C. P.	7,000	105.1
Graves Co.	16,000	105.2
Mason Corp.	5,000	105.3
White Co.	10,000	105.4
Accounts payable (no. 303):		
Buford Wholesale Co.	11,000	303.1
Dawn Suppliers, Inc.	7,000	303.2
Paul Wholesale Co.	3,000	303.3

The following transactions were completed during January 19J.

Date

1. Purchased merchandise for cash, $18,000.
2. Paid $11,000 owed to Buford Wholesale Company within the discount period.
3. Sold merchandise for cash, $26,000.
4. Purchased a new truck for use in the business; paid cash, $4,200.
5. Sold merchandise to XY Corporation on credit; terms, 2/10, n/60; $9,800 if paid within 10 days; otherwise $10,000 (record at net of discount).
6. Paid expenses, $4,500.
7. Purchased merchandise on credit from Sauls Company; terms, 2/10, n/60; $20,000, if paid within 10 days; otherwise add 2% charge.
8. Sold merchandise for cash, $37,000.
8. Collected on accounts receivable within the discount period as follows: Ames, $7,000; Graves, $16,000; and White, $10,000.
9. Purchased merchandise for cash, $21,000.
9. Collected in full from XY Corporation for the sale of January 5.
9. Paid accounts payable within the discount period: Dawn, $7,000; and Paul $2,000.
10. Collected accounts receivable from Mason Corporation, $5,000, within the discount period.
10. Returned merchandise purchased from Paul Wholesale Company because its specifications were incorrect; received a credit for $1,000.
14. Paid expenses, $9,600.
15. Sold merchandise for cash, $11,400.
16. Paid balance due to Sauls within the discount period.
19. Borrowed $30,000 cash on a one-year, 16% interest-bearing note.
22. Sold merchandise on credit terms, 2/10, n/30, as follows (net amount): Ames, $6,000; Graves, $13,000; Mason, $9,000; and White, $4,000.
23. A customer returned merchandise, purchased a few days earlier; since the correct size was unavailable, customer was given a cash refund of $175.
24. Collected the balance due from White Company within the discount period.
25. Returned damaged merchandise to a wholesale supplier and received a cash refund of $450.
26. Purchased merchandise on credit from Buford Wholesale Company: terms, 2/10, n/60; net amount, $35,000.
27. Purchased merchandise on credit from Dawn Suppliers, Inc.: terms, 2/10, n/60; net amount, $12,000.
28. Cash sales, $47,000.
29. Sold merchandise on credit to XY Corporation on the usual terms; net amount, $16,500.
30. Collected in full for the credit sale to Mason on January 22.
31. Sold common stock of Reagan Company to a new shareholder, 1,000 shares for $20,000 cash.

Required:

1. Set up a general journal and special journals for credit sales, credit purchases, cash receipts, and cash payments, similar to those illustrated in Supplement 2–A. Sales and purchases on credit are recorded at net of discount.
2. Set up T-accounts for the general ledger and two subsidiary ledgers, accounts receivable and accounts payable. Enter the beginning balances in the T-accounts.
3. Journalize the above transactions in the appropriate journals.
4. Post to the subsidiary and general ledgers; use folio numbers.
5. Prepare reconciliation of the subsidiary ledgers.
6. Prepare a trial balance from the general ledger.

SUPPLEMENT 2–B: PROBLEM 2–18

Problem 2–18

Bernstein Manufacturing Corporation is in the process of completing the end-of-period accounting process. It is now December 31, 19M, and the following unadjusted trial balance has been developed from the general ledger:

Account	Balance (unadjusted) Debit	Credit
Cash	$ 171,300	
Inventory, Jan. 1 (periodic):		
Raw materials	42,000	
Work in process	60,000	
Finished goods	38,000	
Accounts receivable	18,000	
Allowance for doubtful accts.		$ 450
Factory supplies inventory	6,300	
Plant and equipment	430,000	
Accumulated depreciation		180,000
Remaining assets (not subject to depreciation)	102,000	
Accounts payable		37,000
Wages payable		
Interest payable		
Income taxes payable		
Mortgage payable (9%, each Aug. 31)		40,000
Common stock, par $100		500,000
Retained earnings		42,550
Sales revenue		800,000
Manufacturing costs:		
Raw materials purchases	180,000	
Direct labor	200,000	
Factory overhead	100,000	
Distribution expenses	160,000	
Administrative expenses	90,000	
Interest expense	2,400	
Cost of goods manufactured		
Income tax expense		
	$1,600,000	$1,600,000

Additional data for adjustments and other purposes:

a. Inventories December 31, 19M: raw materials, $45,000; work in process, $54,000; and finished goods, $40,000.

b. Estimated bad debt loss rate is ⅓% of credit sales. Credit sales for the period were $150,000 (Distribution Expense).

c. An inventory of factory supplies taken on December 31, 19M, showed unused supplies amounting to $4,800 (Factory Overhead).

d. Plant and equipment is depreciated over a 20-year life (estimated); residual value is $30,000 (debit Factory Overhead for depreciation).

e. Unrecorded and unpaid administrative wages at December 31, 19M, amounted to $3,500.

f. The most recent interest payment on the mortgage was on August 31, 19M.

g. Assume 40% corporate income tax rate.

Required:

1. Enter the above unadjusted trial balance on a worksheet.
2. Enter the adjusting entries on the worksheet and complete it; assume straight-line depreciation.
3. Prepare a manufacturing statement, single-step income statement, and an unclassified balance sheet.
4. Journalize the closing entries.

3

Review—The Income Statement and Retained Earnings

PERIODIC financial statements are the means by which accounting information is communicated to external decision makers. The financial statements are the following:

1. Income statement.
2. Balance sheet (discussed in Chapter 4).
3. Statement of changes in financial position (SCFP) (discussed in Chapters 4 and 23).

The relationships (sometimes called articulation) among the basic financial statements are illustrated in Exhibit 3–1, which reflects that the income statement and the statement of changes in financial position (SCFP) are the connecting links between the beginning and ending balance sheets. They are designed to explain the **causes** of the changes in financial position during the current period. The income statement explains the changes due to **operations** (i.e., revenues, expenses, gains, and losses), whereas the SCFP explains the reasons for changes in the financial position of the entity in terms of **fund** inflows and outflows during the period.

PURPOSE OF THE CHAPTER

The purpose of this chapter is to discuss the income statement from two perspectives. First is that of decision makers who use income statements. An understanding of the user's perspective is essential for accountants because users' information needs provide the primary focus of external financial reporting. The other perspective is that of those who prepare the financial statements.

This chapter is divided into two parts as follows:

Part A—Concepts Underlying the Income Statement and Its Preparation

Part B—Specific Issues Related to the Income Statement

EXHIBIT 3–1: Relationships among Financial Statements

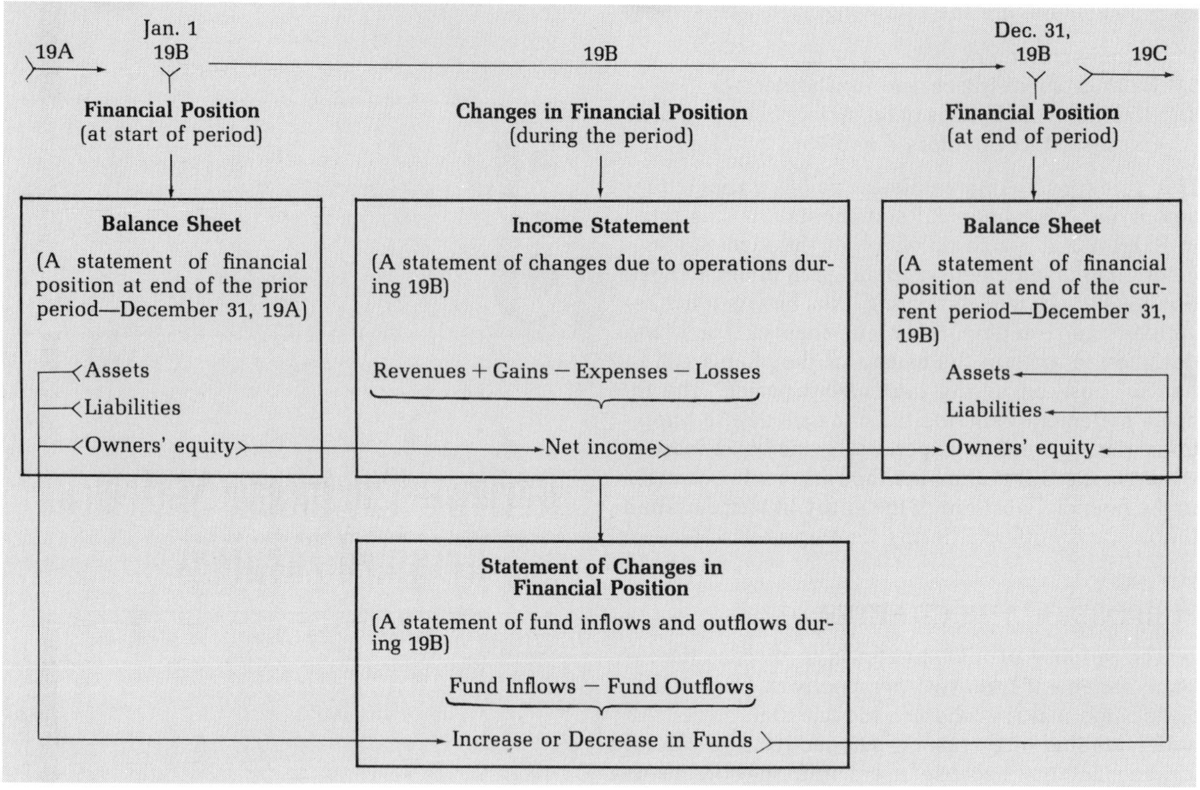

Part A: Concepts Underlying the Income Statement and Its Preparation

CONCEPTS UNDERLYING THE INCOME STATEMENT

The concept of **income** originated in economics, which deals with the allocation of scarce resources among competing uses. One aspect is the competition of business enterprises for investment funds. Businesses need funds to finance their operations, and investors need investments to expand the value of their personal wealth. Therefore, individuals invest in businesses with the expectation of earning a return of **income** on their investments. The income expectation of an investor in a business enterprise is determined in part by the expected income of the enterprise.

The concept of income is subject to different interpretations; however, most definitions of income are derived from the concept of **economic income.** Economists define income of a business enterprise as the amount of "real wealth" the enterprise can consume during a period and remain as well off at the end of that period as it was at the beginning.[1] This definition of income (i.e., economic income) is **not** used to measure accounting income. One primary reason is that economic income is based on the nebulous notion of "real wealth," which involves highly subjective measurements and, hence, is not viewed by

[1] J. R. Hicks, *Value and Capital,* 2d ed. (London: Oxford University Press, 1946), p. 172.

accountants as sufficiently reliable.[2] Another reason is that economic income provides little direction as to how to present the detailed components of income (e.g., how it was earned).[3] Traditionally, detailed information on how income was earned has been viewed as useful to decision makers. Thus, while economic income provides the conceptual basis for income measurement, its practical usefulness for accounting is limited.

Investors define their income (or loss) from an investment in essentially the same way economists define income (or loss). To **investors, investment income** is the change in the market value of an investment during a period, plus any dividends or interest received during that period. To illustrate, assume an investment in one share of stock. Investment income on the share of stock for period 1 can be expressed as follows:

$$II_1 = P_1 - P_0 + D_1$$

where

II_1 = investment income for period 1

P_0 = market price of the share of stock at the beginning of the period (i.e., time 0)

P_1 = market price of the share of stock at the end of the period (i.e., time 1)

D_1 = dividends received during the period ended at time 1

To illustrate this concept of investment income, suppose investor W paid $30 for a share of stock on January 1, received a $1 dividend during January, and on January 31 the price of the stock was $32.[4] In this case, investment income for January would be $3 (i.e., $32 − $30 + $1). If the market price of the stock is $28 on February 28 and no dividend was received during February, the investment loss for February would be $4 (i.e., $28 − $32).[5] This measure of investment income is of fundamental interest to investors because it measures the change in their wealth resulting from the investment.[6]

FASB Concepts Statement 1 states that investors need information which is useful for predicting the expected cash flows from investments in a business enterprise. The equation above indicates that investors need information for predicting future stock prices (P_1) and future dividends (D_1). Accounting income is believed to be useful for predicting future stock prices and dividends, as evidenced by the attention accounting income receives in investment analysis. Many of the models of investment market value are expressed in terms of accounting income.[7]

Accounting income has been shown empirically to be associated with actual stock price movements,[8] and also that the volume of trading in stock increases around the dates of earnings announcements.[9] These empirical findings seem reasonable because it would appear that stock prices **should** react to the factors underlying accounting income.

THE ACCOUNTANT'S PERSPECTIVE OF THE INCOME STATEMENT

The preceding discussions have implied that ideally accounting income should measure the periodic change in the real wealth (i.e., market value) of an

---

[2] For a different opinion on this matter, see R. R. Sterling, *Theory of the Measurement of Enterprise Income* (Lawrence: University of Kansas Press, 1970), chap. 7.

[3] For a suggestion on this point, see L. A. Friedman, "An Exit-Price Income Statement," *The Accounting Review*, January 1978, pp. 18–30.

[4] Technically, the investor realizes income from the dividend when the corporation declares the dividend. This example assumes all dividends are declared and paid by the corporation during the same month.

[5] These income amounts for January and February often are expressed as monthly "holding-period returns" by dividing income by the ending price from the preceding month. The monthly return for January would be 10 percent (i.e., $3/$30). For February, it would be −12.5 percent (i.e., −$4/$32).

[6] This discussion applies also to investors in bonds and other debt instruments. The only change in the above equation needed to make it apply to an investment in bonds or other debt instruments would be to substitute interest in place of dividends. Thus, investment income on a bond equals the change in the price of the bonds plus the interest earned on the bonds.

[7] Refer to textbooks on investment analysis.

[8] R. Ball and P. Brown, "An Empirical Evaluation of Accounting Income Numbers," *Journal of Accounting Research*, Autumn 1968, pp. 159–77; and G. J. Foster, "Quarterly Earnings Data: Time Series Properties and Predictive-Ability Results," *The Accounting Review*, January 1977, pp. 1–21. Ball and Brown found for annual, and Foster for quarterly, earnings announcements that stock prices increased for companies with actual income above their expected level of income, and vice versa for companies with actual income below their expected income. Most of this reaction took place prior to the formal earnings announcements. The prior reactions can be attributed to such events as news releases, investment newsletters, and other elements of the news media which also report investment-related information. Other studies, summarized in R. Ball, "Anomalies in Relationships between Securities' Yields and Yield-Surrogates," *Journal of Financial Economics*, June–September 1978, pp. 103–26, found similar stock market reactions in the weeks following the earnings announcements.

[9] W. H. Beaver, "The Information Content of Annual Earnings Announcements," *Empirical Research in Accounting: Selected Studies, 1968*. Supplement to *Journal of Accounting Research*, 1968, pp. 67–92.

enterprise. However, reliable market values often are difficult to determine because well-developed markets do not exist for many of the assets of businesses.[10] For instance, consider an attempt to determine the market value (i.e., current selling price) of the plant and equipment or the work in process inventory of Ford Motor Company or even the operational (fixed) assets of a small department store. Estimates of the market values of these assets, which would be required to measure the **economic** income of these businesses, may not possess sufficient reliability for external financial reporting. Because of the need for reliability in accounting measurements, accountants have devised a measure of income which possesses the requisite degree of reliability.

Accountants use a **transactions approach** to measure accounting income in which the effects of completed transactions are measured, recorded, and reported in terms of revenues, expenses, gains, and losses. We emphasize that accounting income is a surrogate measure of the change in the market value of a business enterprise, and that accounting income is the result of its **operations** during the period. As such, accounting income is not designed to measure directly changes in market values during the period.

EXHIBIT 3–2: Income Statement Elements

Definition of Element

Revenues are inflows or other enhancements of assets of an enterprise or settlements of its liabilities (or a combination of both) during a period from delivering or producing goods, rendering services, or other activities that constitute the entity's ongoing major or central operations.

Gains are increases in equity (net assets) from peripheral or incidental transactions of an entity and from all other transactions and other events and circumstances affecting the entity during a period except those that result from revenues or investments by owners.

Expenses are outflows or other using up of assets or incurrences of liabilities (or a combination of both) during a period from delivering or producing goods, rendering services, or carrying out other activities that constitute the entity's ongoing major or central operations.

Losses are decreases in equity (net assets) from peripheral or incidental transactions of an entity and from all other transactions and other events and circumstances affecting the entity during a period except those that result from expenses or distributions to owners.

Source: FASB, *Statement of Financial Accounting Concepts No. 3,* "Elements of Financial Statements of Business Enterprises" (Stamford, Conn., December 1980), pars. 63–73.

PREPARING THE INCOME STATEMENT

This part of the chapter presents the definitions of the elements of the income statement. Then it discusses and illustrates various aspects of the income statement.

Definitions of Income Statement Elements

The elements which comprise the income statement are **revenues, expenses, gains,** and **losses.** Combined they measure **net income.** *FASB Concepts Statement 3* defines the income statement elements as given in Exhibit 3–2.

Gains and losses, as defined in Exhibit 3–2, are reported on the income statement in one of three ways, depending upon the circumstances: as "normal" items; as unusual or infrequently occurring items; or as extraordinary items. Extraordinary items and unusual or infrequently occurring items are discussed in Part B of this chapter.

In addition to the terms defined in Exhibit 3–2, other terms used in discussing the income statement are:

1. **Income** is used for a number of subtotals on the income statement, such as **income before income tax, income from continuing operations,** and **income before extraordinary items.**
2. **Earnings** sometimes is used to mean income.
3. **Profit** is used broadly to refer to successful operations during a period. It is not intended to have a technical meaning (see *FASB Concepts Statement 3,* footnote 5).
4. **Cost** is the amount of resources given up or commitments incurred to acquire goods and services which, at time of acquisition, are assets, such as merchandise inventory, prepaid insurance, and operational assets. Upon their expiration or use, most costs become expenses.

Form of Income Statement

The accounting profession has not specified a particular format (i.e., display) that must be used for

[10] For an elaboration of this point, see W. H. Beaver and J. Demski, "The Nature of Income Measurement," *The Accounting Review,* January 1979, pp. 38–46.

the income statement because reasonable flexibility to fit various situations is considered more important than a standard format. The income statement reports all revenues, gains, expenses, and losses for a specific period of time. It is "dated" to indicate that period (e.g., For the Year Ended December 31, 19xx). Also, earnings per common share for the period must be reported on the face of the income statement.

In addition, a number of *ARBs, APB Opinions,* and *FASB Statements* specify certain **disclosure** requirements that influence income statement presentation.

Two different formats are widely used for the income statement, although there are numerous variations of each. These generally are referred to as the single-step and the multiple-step formats. A recent study of 600 major companies reported that 59 percent used the single-step and 41 percent used the multiple-step format.[11]

Single-Step Format. The single-step format focuses on two broad classifications: (1) revenues and gains and (2) expenses and losses. It is called a single-step statement because only one step is involved in arriving at net income when the company has no extraordinary gains or losses (or other types of gains and losses that warrant separate disclosure).[12] An example of a single-step income statement is presented in Exhibit 3–3. Numerous variations exist in practice. For example, income tax expense often is reported as a separate item below Expenses and Losses but preceding Income before extraordinary items.

Multiple-Step Format. The multiple-step format provides multiple classifications and multiple intermediate differences. An example of a multiple-step income statement, using the same data as in Exhibit 3–3, is presented in Exhibit 3–4. The principal differences between the single-step and multiple-step formats are that the multiple-step format (Exhibit 3–4), but not the single-step format (Exhibit 3–3), reports income amounts for the following captions: Gross margin on sales, Income from primary operations, and Income before income tax and Extraordinary items. Graham Company in Exhibits 3–3 and 3–4 is a trading company (e.g., wholesaler or retailer). Supplement 2–B illustrates a manufacturing situation.

EXHIBIT 3–3: Single-Step Income Statement Format

GRAHAM COMPANY
Income Statement
For the Year Ended December 31, 19D

Revenues and gains:		
Sales (less returns and allowances of $20,000)		$670,000
Rent		1,200
Interest and dividends		4,800
Gain on sale of operational assets		6,000
Total revenues and gains		682,000
Expenses and losses:		
Cost of goods sold*	$264,000	
Distribution*	153,500	
Administrative*	73,500	
Depreciation	54,000	
Interest	6,000	
Loss on sale of investments	5,000	
Income taxes	37,800	
Total expenses and losses		593,800
Income before EO† item‡		88,200
Extraordinary item:		
Loss due to earthquake	10,000	
Less: Income tax saving	4,800	5,200
Net income		$ 83,000
EPS of common stock (20,000 shares outstanding):		
Income before extraordinary item		$4.41
Extraordinary loss		(.26)
Net income		$4.15

* These items may be detailed in the statement or separately in the notes to the financial statements.
† Abbreviation for "extraordinary."
‡ Sometimes captioned Income from continuing operations.

Supporting Expense Schedules

Frequently, it is desirable to provide details for the summarized amounts shown on an income statement. This can be done with supplementary schedules. A detailed schedule of operating expenses to supplement the income statements given in Exhibits 3–3 and 3–4 could be as shown in Exhibit 3–5.

[11] AICPA, *Accounting Trends & Techniques, 1980* (New York, 1980). This is an excellent reference to determine how various companies report the multitude of different items on financial statements.

[12] Extraordinary items and earnings per share (EPS) are discussed in Part B. Other income statement items that must be disclosed separately in a manner similar to extraordinary gains and losses include *(a)* cumulative effects of changes in accounting principles and *(b)* gains and losses on discontinued operations. These items are discussed in Chapters 20 and 21, respectively.

EXHIBIT 3–4: Multiple-Step Income Statement Format

GRAHAM COMPANY
Income Statement
For the Year Ended December 31, 19D

Sales revenue			$690,000
Less: Sales returns and allowances			20,000
Net sales			670,000
Cost of goods sold:			
Beginning inventory		$ 52,000	
Purchases of inventory	$268,000		
Freight-in	1,200		
Cost of purchases	269,200		
Less: Purchase returns and allowances	2,700	266,500	
Total goods available for sale		318,500	
Less: Ending Inventory		54,500	
Cost of goods sold			264,000
Gross margin on sales			406,000
Operating expenses:			
Distribution*		153,500	
Administrative*		73,500	
Depreciation		54,000	
Total operating expense			281,000
Income from primary operations			125,000
Other revenues and gains:			
Rent revenue	1,200		
Interest and dividend revenue	4,800		
Gain on sale of operational assets	6,000	12,000	
Other expenses and losses:			
Interest expense	6,000		
Loss on sale of investment	5,000	11,000	1,000
Income before income tax and EO† item			126,000
Income tax expense			37,800
Income before EO† item‡			88,200
Extraordinary item:			
Loss due to earthquake	10,000		
Less: Income tax saving	4,800		5,200
Net income			$ 83,000
EPS of common stock (20,000 shares outstanding):			
Income before extraordinary item			$4.41
Extraordinary loss			(.26)
Net income			$4.15

* These items may be detailed in the statement or separately in the notes to the financial statements.
† Abbreviation for "extraordinary."
‡ Sometimes captioned Income from continuing operations.

DISCLOSURE GUIDELINES

Full disclosure was discussed briefly under the reporting principle in Chapter 1. With respect to the income statement, full disclosure is particularly critical. A limit exists on the extent of disclosure possible in the income statement through parenthetical notation. Therefore, the typical income statement includes a number of **notes to the financial statements.** Frequently, these notes contain schedules and writ-

EXHIBIT 3-5: Expense Schedule

GRAHAM COMPANY
Schedule of Operating Expenses
For the Year Ended December 31, 19B

Operating expenses:		
Distribution expenses:		
Advertising	$58,500	
Salaries	45,000	
Commissions	31,000	
Freight-out	10,000	
Insurance on inventory	1,000	
Other selling expenses	8,000	$153,500
Administrative expenses:		
Office expenses	24,800	
Office payroll	42,100	
Rent	3,600	
Bad debt expense	3,000	73,500
Depreciation expense		54,000
Total operating expense		$281,000

ten explanations to explain more fully amounts reported in the tabular portions of the statements.

APB Opinion No. 22, "Disclosure of Accounting Policies," August 1972, paragraph 8, states that "a description of all significant accounting policies of the reporting entity should be included as an integral part of the financial statements." Examples given are those policies related to the basis of consolidation, depreciation methods, amortization of intangibles, inventory costing, accounting for research and development costs, translation of foreign currencies, recognition of profit on long-term construction contracts, and revenue from leasing transactions.

The primary objective of disclosure notes is the presentation of information that cannot be effectively communicated in another manner. Disclosure notes are an integral part of the financial statements. Generally, pronouncements of the profession on reporting specific items specify that they may, or in some cases must, be disclosed in disclosure notes when it is impractical to present adequately the information in the tabular portions of the statements.

DISCLOSURE OF DEPRECIATION

APB Opinion 12, paragraph 5, requires that *(a)* the amount of depreciation expense for the period and *(b)* the method or methods of depreciation used, be disclosed either in the financial statements or in the notes thereto. This requirement was instituted because depreciation often is a major noncash expense. The amount of depreciation expense depends upon the depreciation policies of the enterprise rather than solely on external transactions; therefore, the amount of depreciation is subject to considerable latitude. Statement users need to know both the amount of depreciation expense and the method of its determination in order to evaluate its impact on income, assets, and cash flows.

In manufacturing enterprises, much of the depreciation expense may be included in the ending inventory and cost of goods sold amounts. Therefore, reporting depreciation by footnote is characteristic for these kinds of companies.

DISCLOSURE OF INCOME TAXES

Income taxes are assessed on profit-making corporations (but not on sole proprietorships or partnerships).[13] Also, stockholders must pay income taxes on dividends received; consequently, it is often pointed out that corporate income is subject to double taxation.

Income taxes paid by corporations are viewed as an expense (as opposed to a distribution of income) and because of their significant amounts, the matching and reporting principles must be fully satisfied. To meet these requirements, *APB Opinion 11,* prescribed two **separate,** and **distinctly different** types of income tax allocations. These are referred to as:

1. **Intraperiod tax allocation**—This is an allocation of total income tax expense for the current **period** to various components on the financial statements for that current period. This kind of allocation is discussed below (and in Chapter 10).
2. **Interperiod tax allocation**—This is an allocation of income taxes on certain taxable items among **periods.** It occurs when there are items of revenue and/or expense on the income statement for the current period that, because of the tax laws, are reported on the income tax return for an earlier or later period. Interperiod tax allocation gives rise to deferred income taxes which appear on

[13] There are certain exceptions. For example, the income of a corporation that qualifies under Subchapter S, Internal Revenue Code, is taxable income to the owners rather than to the corporation. These are generally referred to as "Subchapter S Corporations."

EXHIBIT 3–6: Intraperiod Tax Allocation

Situation

X Corporation accounts for the period reflected the following:

1. Income before income tax and before extraordinary items, $115,000.
2. Extraordinary gain (specified), $40,000 (taxable).
3. Total income tax expense, $57,000. Tax rates: first $25,000, 20%; above $25,000, 40%.

X CORPORATION
Partial Income Statement

Income before income tax and extraordinary items		$115,000
Less: Applicable income tax expense		41,000
Income before extraordinary items		74,000
Extraordinary items:		
Extraordinary gain (specified)	$40,000	
Less: Applicable income tax expense	16,000	
Extraordinary gain, net of applicable income tax		24,000
Net income		$ 98,000

Computation of intraperiod tax allocation:

Tax on ordinary income:		
$25,000 × 20% =	$ 5,000	
$90,000 × 40% =	36,000	$41,000
Tax on extraordinary gain:		
$40,000 × 40% =		16,000
Total income tax allocated		$57,000

Entry for income taxes:

Income tax expense	57,000	
Income tax payable		57,000

the **balance sheet.** This kind of allocation is discussed in Chapter 10.

At this point, we emphasize that although intraperiod and interperiod tax allocation are different types, they are not **mutually exclusive.** Both types are required because each serves a different reporting purpose.

Intraperiod Tax Allocation[14]

The concept underlying **intraperiod** tax allocation is that in accordance with the matching principle, **all income tax consequences should be reported along with the transaction that caused the tax effect.** Thus, total income tax for the current period must be allocated to (1) income before extraordinary items, (2) extraordinary items, and (3) prior period adjustments.[15]

The need for **intraperiod** tax allocations arises because financial statements users need information useful for predicting the future cash flows of an entity. Because extraordinary gains and losses are not as predictable as income before extraordinary items, investors may evaluate a company on the basis of its income **before** extraordinary items. Therefore, it is important to report separately the amounts of income tax expense applicable to (1) income before extraordinary items and (2) extraordinary items.

Exhibit 3–6 illustrates application of intraperiod tax allocation for X Corporation, which had an extraordinary gain. Total income tax expense of $57,000 is allocated between income before extraordinary items (tax, $41,000) and the extraordinary gain (tax, $16,000), which causes Income before extraordinary items to be $74,000. In this example, it would be misleading to allocate total income tax of $57,000 to income before extraordinary items (which would cause Income before extraordinary items to be $58,000) because $16,000 of the income tax expense arose from the extraordinary gain. If an investor were to evaluate X Corporation based on the $58,000 instead of the $74,000 (Exhibit 3–6), the predicted income potential of the company probably would be understated.

[14] Intraperiod tax allocation is discussed in this early chapter because it is used in illustrations and problems prior to Chapter 10, where tax allocation is discussed in detail.

[15] Although rare, certain direct entries to stockholders' equity accounts also may have income tax effects requiring intraperiod tax allocation.

Part B: Specific Issues Directly Related to the Income Statement

EARNINGS PER SHARE (EPS)

Earnings per share (EPS) is the relationship obtained by dividing *(a)* the portion of reported income available to the holders of common stock by *(b)* the outstanding shares of common stock. EPS is not computed for preferred stock. EPS is important for the same reason other income amounts are important; that is, it is useful for predicting the future cash flows of the entity.

EPS is useful because it relates income to a single share of common stock. A usual, although unsophisticated, investment decision model is to multiply EPS by a price-earnings ratio (i.e., Market price ÷ EPS) to derive a rough estimate of the market value of a share of stock. For example, assume RG Company reported EPS of $3 and it was believed that a reasonable price-earnings ratio for RG Company common stock was 8. If the current market price of RG Company common stock were to fall below $24 (i.e., $3 × 8), this could signal a "buy" decision. While this example is oversimplified, it illustrates one of the many uses of EPS by investors.

Reporting EPS was optional prior to the issuance of *APB Opinion 15* in 1969. *Opinion 15* requires companies to report per share data for *(a)* income before extraordinary items and *(b)* net income.[16] EPS is discussed in more detail in Chapter 22.

Calculation of Earnings per Share (EPS)

At this point we will review only the fundamentals of EPS for companies with **simple capital structures.**

To illustrate the calculation of EPS in simple situations, four separate cases are presented in Exhibit 3–7. These cases will provide sufficient background for the discussions prior to Chapter 22.

Case A—This is the simplest case. It involves only common stock with no changes in the number of shares outstanding during the year and no extraordinary items on the income statement. In such a situation calculation of EPS simply involves dividing net income by the number of shares outstanding, as illustrated in Exhibit 3–7.

Case B—A slight complexity occurs when there is an extraordinary gain or loss on the income statement. In this case, EPS amounts would be calculated and reported for *(a)* income before extraordinary items, *(b)* extraordinary items,[17] and *(c)* net income, as illustrated in Exhibit 3–7.

Case C—Another complexity occurs when there is a change during the period in the number of shares outstanding because of the sale and issuance of common stock or the purchase of such shares as treasury stock. This complexity requires calculation of the weighted-average number of shares outstanding during the year. The weighted average, calculated as illustrated in Exhibit 3–7, is divided into the appropriate income amounts.

Case D—Another complexity occurs when the company issues additional shares of its common stock because of a stock dividend or stock split. In these situations the additional shares issued are treated in EPS computations as though they had been outstanding for the entire period, as illustrated in Exhibit 3–7.

Another level of complexity occurs when both common and nonconvertible preferred stock are outstanding. Additional complexities arise when outstanding preferred stock or bonds payable are convertible into common stock. These complexities involve the concepts of common stock equivalents and fully diluted EPS, which are discussed in Chapter 22.

FASB *Statement of Financial Accounting Standards No. 21,* "Suspension of Earnings per Share and Segment Information by Nonpublic Enterprises," exempts corporations that are not publicly held from the EPS disclosure requirement.

[16] Under certain conditions (i.e., complex capital structures), *APB Opinion 15* requires two presentations of EPS on the income statement: (1) primary EPS and (2) fully diluted EPS. Primary EPS relates income to the company's outstanding common stock, and fully diluted EPS relates income to the maximum number of shares of common stock that could conceivably become outstanding. Therefore, fully diluted EPS is an estimate of the company's **minimum** EPS under its existing capital structure.

[17] AICPA, *APB Opinion No. 15,* "Earnings per Share" (New York, May, 1969), does not require reporting of EPS for extraordinary items. EPS for *(a)* income before extraordinary items and *(b)* net income are required. In this textbook, we usually illustrate reporting EPS for the three amounts, for completeness.

EXHIBIT 3–7: Calculation of Earnings per Share (EPS) (simple capital structure)

Assumptions	Calculating and Reporting of EPS	
Case A: Assumptions: 30,000 common shares outstanding throughout the year; net income for the year, $96,000.	Net income	$96,000
	Earnings per common share ($96,000 ÷ 30,000 shares)	$ 3.20
Case B: Assumptions: 30,000 common shares outstanding throughout the year; income before extraordinary item, $96,000; extraordinary loss less applicable tax saving, $21,000; net income for the year, $75,000.	Income before extraordinary item	$96,000
	Extraordinary loss less applicable tax saving	21,000
	Net income	$75,000
	Earnings per common share:	
	Income before extraordinary item	$ 3.20
	Extraordinary loss	(.70)
	Net income	$ 2.50
	$96,000 ÷ 30,000 shares = $3.20 (21,000) ÷ 30,000 shares = (.70) 75,000 ÷ 30,000 shares = 2.50	
Case C: Assumptions: 30,000 common shares outstanding from January 1 through April 1, on which date an additional 10,000 common shares were sold and issued; other data as in Case B.	Income before extraordinary item	$96,000
	Extraordinary loss less applicable tax saving	21,000
	Net income	$75,000
	Earnings per common share:	
	Income before extraordinary item	$ 2.56
	Extraordinary loss	(.56)
	Net income	$ 2.00

Calculation of weighted-average number of shares:

Dates	Months	Shares	Product
Jan. 1–Apr. 1	3	30,000	90,000
Apr. 1–Dec. 31	9	40,000	360,000
	12		450,000

Average: 450,000 ÷ 12 = 37,500.

$96,000 ÷ 37,500 shares = $2.56
(21,000) ÷ 37,500 shares = (.56)
75,000 ÷ 37,500 shares = 2.00

Assumptions	Calculating and Reporting of EPS	
Case D: Assumptions: 30,000 common shares outstanding from January 1 through April 1, on which date an additional 20,000 common shares were issued as a **stock dividend**; other data as in Case B (no additional shares were sold).	Income before extraordinary item	$96,000
	Extraordinary loss less applicable tax saving	21,000
	Net income	$75,000
	Earnings per common share:	
	Income before extraordinary item	$ 1.92
	Extraordinary loss	(.42)
	Net income	$ 1.50

As provided in *APB Opinion 15*, when there is a stock dividend, the divisor is the average number of shares outstanding at year-end (including all stock dividends, as if they had been outstanding for the entire year). In this case, this is 30,000 + 20,000 = 50,000.

$96,000 ÷ 50,000 shares = $1.92
(21,000) ÷ 50,000 shares = (.42)
75,000 ÷ 50,000 shares = 1.50

EXTRAORDINARY ITEMS

Extraordinary items are reported in a separate category on the income statement to alert users of the financial statements about the extraordinary nature of these gains or losses. This separate reporting signals to users that these gains or losses cannot be expected to recur regularly.

Extraordinary items are controversial because they are difficult to define precisely. In the past, companies have classified gains and losses as ordinary or extraordinary, depending upon the particular incentives of the company.[18] For example, a company may have desired to report a high net income amount prior to the issuance of its stock in the hope of receiving a higher price for its stock. This company would have had an incentive to report a loss as "extraordinary" (or a gain as "ordinary") to keep "Income before extraordinary items" as high as possible.

To prevent such manipulation, the APB issued *Opinion 30* (1973), which defined extraordinary items so restrictively as to almost eliminate their existence. Extraordinary items are defined in *APB Opinion 30* as follows:

> Extraordinary items are events and transactions that are distinguished by their unusual nature **and** by the infrequency of their occurrence. Thus, **both** of the following criteria should be met to classify an event or transaction as an extraordinary item:
>
> *a.* **Unusual nature**—The underlying event or transaction should possess a high degree of abnormality and be of a type clearly unrelated to, or only incidentally related to, the ordinary and typical activities of the entity, taking into account the environment in which the entity operates.
>
> *b.* **Infrequency of occurrence**—The underlying event or transaction should be of a type that would not reasonably be expected to recur in the foreseeable future, taking into account the environment in which the entity operates.[19]

Two aspects of the above definition should be emphasized. First, **both** criteria must be met. Thus, an item that meets **either,** but not both, does not qualify as an extraordinary item. Second, in applying the two criteria, the **environment in which the entity operates** often is controlling. For example, earthquake damage usually would be extraordinary—it is unusual and occurs infrequently in most parts of the world. However, if one were to locate a plant on a fault where earthquakes occur regularly, earthquake damage would not be extraordinary in that **particular environment;** the damage would be considered "usual **or** frequent." Thus, whether an event or transaction is extraordinary depends not only on the event but also **on the environment in which it occurs.** The *Opinion* cites three different kinds of events that may be classified as extraordinary: (1) a major casualty, such as an earthquake; (2) expropriation by a foreign government; and (3) prohibition under a newly enacted law or regulation.[20]

The *Opinion* specifically states that the following **should not** be considered as extraordinary items because they result from customary and continuing business activities:

> *a.* Write-down or write-off of receivables, inventories, equipment leased to others, or other intangible assets.
>
> *b.* Gains or losses from exchange or translation of foreign currencies, including those related to major devaluations or revaluations.
>
> *c.* Gains or losses on disposal of a segment of a business.
>
> *d.* Other gains or losses from sale or abandonment of property, plant, or equipment used in the business.
>
> *e.* Effects of a strike, including those against competitors and major suppliers.
>
> *f.* Adjustments of accruals on long-term contracts.[21]

Because of the difficulty in evaluating whether specific gains and losses should be reported as extraordinary items, we have included some specific examples in Supplement 3–A to this chapter. Exhibit 3–8 illustrates the reporting of extraordinary items.

---

[18] Prior to AICPA, *APB Opinion No. 9,* "Reporting the Results of Operations" (New York, December 1966), some companies reported extraordinary gains and losses on the income statement in a manner similar to current practice, under what was known as the **all-inclusive** approach to income reporting. Other companies reported extraordinary items on the statement of retained earnings, under what was known as the **current operating performance** approach to income reporting; in this approach, unusual or nonrecurring items and extraordinary items were *not* reported on the income statement but on the statement of retained earnings. *APB Opinion 9* effectively required the all-inclusive approach.

[19] AICPA, *APB Opinion No. 30,* "Reporting the Results of Operations" (New York, June 1973), par. 20.

[20] Ibid., par. 23.

[21] Ibid., par. 23.

EXHIBIT 3–8: Reporting Extraordinary Items and the Unusual or Infrequent Items

Income Statement		
Revenues (not detailed)		$990,000
Expenses (not detailed)		878,000
Pretax income from continuing operations		112,000
Unusual or infrequent items (Note X):		
Loss on disposal of long-term investment	$43,000	
Gain on disposal of machinery	31,000	12,000
Income before income tax and EO* items		100,000
Income tax expense		48,000
Income before EO* item		52,000
Extraordinary item:		
Loss due to earthquake damage (net of applicable income tax saving of $6,625); (Note Y)		26,500
Net income		$ 25,500
EPS of common stock (10,000 shares outstanding):		
Income before EO item		$ 5.20
Extraordinary loss		(2.65)
Net income		$ 2.55

Notes to financial statements:
Note X—details.
Note Y—details.
* Abbreviation for "extraordinary."

REPORTING UNUSUAL OR INFREQUENT ITEMS

In the discussion above, we referred to items that are **either** unusual or infrequent, but not both. They do not qualify as extraordinary items; however, the prevailing view is that they should be called to the attention of the statement user to fulfill the **full-disclosure** requirement. Therefore, *APB Opinion 30* requires that they be reported separately on the income statement, viz:

> A material event or transaction that is unusual in nature or occurs infrequently, but not both, and therefore does not meet both criteria for classification as an extraordinary item, should be reported as a separate component of income from continuing operations. Such items should not be reported . . . net of income taxes. . . .[22]

Items that are **either** unusual or infrequent, but not both, may be reported as shown in Exhibit 3–8.

Examples of unusual or infrequent items are given in Supplement 3–A to this chapter. One example of an unusual or infrequent item is a gain or loss on discontinued operations (i.e., disposal of a segment of a business). The reporting of this type of item is given special treatment, as specified in *APB Opinion 30,* paragraphs 13–18. This topic is discussed and illustrated in Chapter 21.

PRIOR PERIOD ADJUSTMENTS

Prior period adjustments are reported on the statement of retained earnings. This means that prior period adjustments **never** flow through the income statement, which suggests that they should be defined very carefully. To illustrate the complexity of the determination of whether to classify an item as a prior period adjustment, consider a company which has certain contractual restrictions associated with its bonds payable whereby the company is required to report net income above $100,000 per year over the period the bonds are outstanding. Otherwise, the interest rate on the bonds payable increases from 11 percent to 12 percent. Also, assume income for the current year of $120,000. Finally, assume the company incurred an additional after-tax loss of $25,000 during the current year due to litigation begun two years ago (not included in the $120,000 given above). Should the company report the $25,000 item as a loss on the income statement or as a prior period adjustment to retained earnings? If the company reports the $25,000 item as a loss on the income statement, it will reduce net income to $95,000 (i.e., $120,000 − $25,000) and the bond interest rate will increase. For this reason, the company has an incentive to report the item as a prior period adjustment on the statement of retained earnings rather than on the income statement.

To avoid abuses of the reporting principle such as the type illustrated above, the FASB defined prior period adjustments so narrowly as to almost eliminate their existence. *FASB Statement 16,* paragraph 11, limited prior period adjustments to two categories of items, as follows:

> Items of profit and loss related to the following shall be accounted for and reported as prior period adjustments and excluded from the determination of net income for the current period:

[22] Ibid., par. 26.

a. Correction of an error in the financial statements of a prior period and
b. Adjustments that result from realization of income tax benefits of preacquisition operating loss carryforwards of purchased subsidiaries.

FASB Statement 16 requires all other items of revenue, expense, gain, and loss recognized during the period to be included in the determination of net income for that period.

To illustrate the **recording** of a prior period adjustment for an error correction, assume a machine cost $10,000 (with a 10-year estimated useful life and no residual value) when purchased on January 1, 19A. Further, assume that the cost was erroneously debited to an expense account in 19A. The error was discovered December 29, 19D. The following correcting entry would be required in 19D, assuming any income tax effects are recorded separately.[23]

December 29, 19D:

Machinery	10,000	
Depreciation expense, straight line (for 19D)	1,000	
Accumulated depreciation (19A through 19D)		4,000
Prior period adjustment, error correction		7,000

The Prior Period Adjustment, Error Correction account would be closed directly to Retained Earnings on December 31, 19D. In effect, the adjustment corrects the January 1, 19D (beginning), balance in Retained Earnings. Exhibit 3–9 illustrates the **reporting** of this prior period adjustment.

ACCOUNTING CHANGES

APB Opinion 20 defines three types of accounting changes as follows:

1. **Changes in estimates**—The use of estimates (such as in determining depreciation or bad debt expense) is a natural consequence of the accounting process. From time to time, experience and additional information make it possible for estimates to be improved. For example, an operational asset, after having been used (and depreciated) for 6 years, may realistically be changed from the original 10-year estimated life to a 15-year estimated life. Changes of this type are referred to as "changes in estimates" and are to be distinguished from changes in accounting principle.
2. **Changes in accounting principle**—Because of a change in circumstances, or the development of a new accounting principle, a change in the recording and reporting approach for one or more types of transactions may be desirable or necessary. For example, a change in circumstances may make it desirable to change from straight-line depreciation to sum-of-the-years'-digits (SYD) depreciation. This would be a change in accounting principle, that is, a change from one acceptable principle to another acceptable principle.
3. **Change in the accounting entity** (see Chapter 20).

Accounting changes are important because of the **comparability** principle, which holds that the financial data of an enterprise should be comparable from period to period. When a company changes the estimated useful life of a depreciable asset, changes from one depreciation method to another depreciation method for the asset, or engages in any other type of accounting change, the interperiod comparability of the financial statements of the enterprise suffers. The provisions of *APB Opinion 20* emphasize interperiod comparability.

Accounting changes are discussed and illustrated in detail in Chapter 20. However, because numerous topics discussed in this book utilize changes in accounting **estimates,** they are briefly discussed below.

Changes in Estimates

Revisions of estimates, such as useful lives of depreciable assets, the loss rate for bad debts, and warranty costs, are not considered to be errors. Rather, they are identified as **changes in estimates** and are accorded special treatment. As a company gains experience in such areas as its depreciable assets, receivables, and warranties, it may have a sound basis for revising one or more of its prior estimates. *APB Opinion 20* specifies that in such instances the **prior** accounting results are not to be

---

[23] Any income tax effect of the prior period adjustment could be recorded separately. Assuming the same error was made on the income tax return, the entry to record the income tax effect of the prior period adjustment, assuming a 20 percent income tax rate, would be:

Prior period adjustment, error correction ($7,000 × .20)	1,400	
Income tax payable		1,400

disturbed. Instead, the new estimate should be used over the current and remaining periods. Thus, a change in estimate is made on a **prospective** basis.

To illustrate the accounting for a change in estimate, assume a machine that cost $24,000 is being depreciated on a straight-line basis over a 10-year estimated useful life with no residual value. Early during the 7th year, on the basis of more experience with the machine, it is determined that the total useful life should have been 14 years (and no residual value). Thus, the remaining life becomes eight years from the start of the year in which the revised estimate was made. This is a change in estimate, and at the end of the current year the estimate change would not require a correcting entry but only the normal **adjusting entry** to **record** depreciation on the new basis at the end of the current year as follows:

Depreciation expense	1,200	
Accumulated depreciation, machinery		1,200

Computations:	
Original cost	$24,000
Accumulated depreciation to date ($24,000 × 6/10)	14,400
Difference—depreciated over 8 years remaining life	$ 9,600
Annual depreciation over remaining life: ($9,600 ÷ 8 years)	$ 1,200

Thus, for the year of the change (and for each of the remaining years of the machine's economic life), depreciation expense of $1,200 would be **reported** for the machine.

STATEMENT OF RETAINED EARNINGS

A statement of retained earnings often is presented as a supplement to the income statement and balance sheet because it is needed to comply with the full-disclosure requirement. However, many companies present a **statement of owners' equity** instead, which details all changes in owners' equity, including retained earnings.

The purpose of the statement of retained earnings is to report all changes in retained earnings during the accounting period, to reconcile the beginning and ending balances of retained earnings, and to provide a connecting link between the income statement and the balance sheet. The ending balance of retained earnings is reported on the balance sheet as one element of owners' equity. In accordance with *APB Opinion 9* and *FASB Statement 16,* the major segments of a statement of retained earnings are (1) prior period adjustments, (2) net income or loss for the period, and (3) dividends. An illustrative statement of retained earnings is shown in Exhibit 3–9.

EXHIBIT 3–9: Statement of Retained Earnings Illustrated

GRAHAM COMPANY
Statement of Retained Earnings
For the Year Ended December 31, 19D

Retained earnings, 1/1/19D		$378,800
Prior period adjustments:		
Correction of error from prior period, a credit	$7,000	
Less income tax effect	1,400*	5,600
Balance as adjusted		384,400
Add: Net income, 19D (per income statement, Exhibit 3–3)		83,000
		467,400
Deduct: cash dividends declared in 19D		30,000
Retained earnings, 12/31/19D (Note 7)		$437,400

Notes to financial statements:

Note 7. Retained earnings—Of the $437,400 ending balance in retained earnings, $280,000 is restricted from dividend availability under the terms of the bond indenture. When the bonds are retired, the restriction will be removed.

* This reporting of income tax is an example of intraperiod tax allocation.

Restrictions on Retained Earnings

Restrictions on retained earnings limit the availability of retained earnings for dividends to the unrestricted balance. Restrictions may arise because of **legal requirements,** as in the case of treasury stock held; by **contract,** as in the case of a bond indenture; or by **management decision,** as in the case of "retained earnings appropriated for future plant expansion." When a restriction is removed, the amount is returned to the unrestricted retained earnings balance. In years past, restrictions sometimes were reported as separate items on the statement of retained earnings (or balance sheet); however, in recent years they usually have been reported in notes to the financial statements, as illustrated in Exhibit 3–9. Retained earnings is discussed in detail in Chapter 15.

Combined Statement of Income and Retained Earnings

The income statement and statement of retained earnings may be presented together in the form of a combined statement. The primary advantage is that it brings together related and relevant information for the statement user. The following is a typical format:

Net income (revenues, expenses, gains, and losses not illustrated)	$ 83,000
Retained earnings, 1/1/19D	378,800
Prior period adjustments, net of income tax effect of $1,400 (Note 6)	5,600
Cash dividends during 19D	(30,000)
Retained earnings, 12/31/19D (Note 7)	$437,400

Notes to financial statements:

Note 6. Prior period adjustments—During the year, the company discovered that an expenditure made in 19A was incorrectly expensed. This error caused net income of that period to be understated. The prior period adjustment of $5,600 corrects the error.

Note 7. Restrictions—Of the $437,400 ending balance in Retained Earnings, $280,000 is restricted from dividend availability under the terms of the bond indenture. When the bonds are retired, the restriction will be removed.

ACTUAL FINANCIAL STATEMENTS

Throughout this chapter, hypothetical examples were used for instructional purposes. To enable you to gain confidence in understanding financial statements, the **Appendix following Chapter 24** presents a complete set of actual financial statements for a well-known company. We suggest that you carefully examine these statements and relate them to the topics discussed in this chapter.

Supplement 3-A: Characteristics and Examples of Extraordinary Items*

If it has been determined that the particular event or transaction is not a disposal of a segment of a business, then the criteria for extraordinary items classification should be considered. That is: Does the event or transaction meet **both** criteria of **unusual nature and infrequency of occurrence?**

Discussion. Paragraphs 19–22 of *APB Opinion 30* discuss the criteria of unusual nature and infrequency of occurrence of events or transactions taking into account the environment in which the entity operates. Paragraph 23 specifies certain gains or losses which should not be reported as extraordinary unless they are the direct result of a major casualty, an expropriation, or a prohibition under a newly enacted law or regulation that clearly meets both criteria for extraordinary classification. Events or transactions which would meet both criteria in the circumstances described are:

A large portion of a tobacco manufacturer's crops is destroyed by a hailstorm. Severe damage from hailstorms in the locality where the manufacturer grows tobacco is rare.

A steel fabricating company sells the only land it owns. The land was acquired 10 years ago for future expansion, but shortly thereafter the company abandoned all plans for expansion and held the land for appreciation.

A company sells a block of common stock of a publicly traded company. The block of shares, which represents less than 10 percent of the publicly held company, is the only security investment the company has ever owned.

An earthquake destroys one of the oil refineries owned by a large multinational oil company.

The following are illustrative of events or transactions which do **not** meet both criteria in the circumstances described; therefore, they **should not be reported as extraordinary items:**

A citrus grower's Florida crop is damaged by frost. Frost damage is normally experienced every three or four years. The criterion of infrequency of occurrence taking into account the environment in which the company operates would not be met since the history of losses caused by frost damage provides evidence that such damage may reasonably be expected to recur in the foreseeable future.

A company which operates a chain of warehouses sells the excess land surrounding one of its warehouses. When the company buys property to establish a new warehouse, it usually buys more land

* Source: Excerpts from "Accounting Interpretations—*APB Opinion 30,*" *Journal of Accountancy,* November 1973, pp. 82–84.

than it expects to use for the warehouse with the expectation that the land will appreciate in value. In the past five years, there have been two instances in which the company sold such excess land. The criterion of infrequency of occurrence has not been met since experience indicates that such sales may reasonably be expected to recur in the foreseeable future.

A large diversified company sells a block of shares from its portfolio of securities which it has acquired for investment purposes. This is the first sale from its portfolio of securities. Since the company owns several securities for investment purposes, it should be concluded that sales of such securities are related to its ordinary and typical activities in the environment in which it operates; thus, the criterion of unusual nature would not be met.

A textile manufacturer with only one plant moves to another location. It has not relocated a plant in 20 years and has no plans to do so in the foreseeable future. Notwithstanding the infrequency of occurrence of the event as it relates to this particular company, moving from one location to another is an occurrence which is a consequence of customary and continuing business activities, some of which are finding more favorable labor markets, more modern facilities and proximity to customers or suppliers. Therefore, the criterion of unusual nature has not been met and the moving expenses (and related gains and losses) should not be reported as an extraordinary item. Another example of an event which is a consequence of customary and typical business activities (namely financing) is an unsuccessful public registration, the cost of which should not be reported as an extraordinary item. (For additional examples, see paragraph 23 of *APB Opinion 30*).

QUESTIONS

PART A

1. Explain briefly how the income statement is a connecting link between the beginning and ending balance sheets.

2. Briefly explain the economist's definition of *income.* How does the accountant define income as reflected by the completed transactions approach?

3. How do investors define *investment income?* Is this concept of income closer to economists' or accountants' concept of income? Explain.

4. What links *accounting* income to *investment* income?

5. What is the basis for supposing that accounting income is related to investment income?

6. Define *revenue.* How is revenue distinguished from a "gain"?

7. Define *expense.* How is expense distinguished from a "loss"?

8. Distinguish between *cost* and *expense.*

9. Briefly explain the *two formats* used for income statements. Explain why actual income statements usually are somewhere between these two formats.

10. Explain the *financial reporting principle,* including its full-disclosure aspect. (Refer to Chapter 1.)

11. Explain why the total amount of depreciation expense should be disclosed in the financial statement.

12. Briefly distinguish between *intraperiod* and *interperiod* tax allocation.

13. Explain why the *matching principle* requires intraperiod tax allocation.

PART B

14. Define *earnings per share (EPS).* Why is it required as an integral part of the income statement? What EPS amounts must be reported on the income statement?

15. Define an *extraordinary item.* How should extraordinary items be reported on *(a)* a single-step and *(b)* a multiple-step income statement?

16. How are items that are either unusual or infrequent, but not both, reported on the income statement?

17. Define *prior period adjustments.* How are prior period adjustments recorded and reported on the financial statements?

18. What are the three types of accounting changes discussed in *APB Opinion 20?* Explain what is meant by a change in estimate.

19. Explain the basic approach in recording and reporting *(a)* accounting errors and *(b)* changes in estimates.

20. What items are reported on a statement of retained earnings? Explain how it provides a link between the current income statement and the balance sheet.

21. What is meant by *restrictions* on retained earnings? How are they usually reported?

DECISION CASE 3–1

The president of Round Rock School Supply Company, a wholesaler, presents you with a comparison of distribution costs for two salespersons and wants to know if you think their compensation plan is working to the detriment of the company. The president supplies you with the following data:

	Salesperson	
	McKinney	Sim
Gross sales	$247,000	$142,000
Sales returns	17,000	2,000
Cost of goods sold	180,000	100,000
Reimbursed expenses (e.g., entertainment)	5,500	2,100
Other direct charges (e.g., samples distributed)	4,000	450
Commission rate on gross sales dollars	5%	5%

Required:

1. A salesperson's compensation plan encourages one to work to increase the measure of performance to which compensation is related. List the questionable sales practices by a salesperson that might be encouraged by basing commissions on gross sales.
2. *a.* What evidence can be found in the data that the compensation plan may be working to the detriment of the company?
   b. What other information should the president obtain before reaching definite conclusions about this particular situation? Why?

(AICPA adapted)

DECISION CASE 3–2

J. B. Jacobson opened a small retail cash-and-carry grocery business with an investment of $1,000 cash, $5,000 merchandise, and a lot and building valued at $18,000. Fixtures were obtained by signing a note, payable in equal installments over a 36-month period. Cash is paid for all merchandise purchases, and Jacobson maintains no formal accounting records. When asked how one knew how well one was doing and where one stood, Jacobson made the following statement: "As long as I do not buy or sell anything except merchandise and that remains fairly constant, I can judge my profit or loss by the increase or decrease in my bank balance."

Required:
Evaluate Jacobson's statement in light of the facts known.

DECISION CASE 3–3

GAAP defines income as:

$$\text{Revenues} + \text{Gains} - \text{Expenses} - \text{Losses} = \text{Income}$$

This model requires that revenue and expense be identified and carefully measured. Also, it requires a careful correspondence between revenue and expense.

Required:

1. What principle, or principles, govern identification and measurement of revenues?
2. What principle, or principles, govern identification and measurement of expenses?
3. Identify and explain some of the troublesome problems in applying the principles identified in 1 and 2 above.
4. What guidelines govern identification and measurement of extraordinary items? Do you agree with these guidelines? Explain.
5. What guidelines govern identification and measurement of prior period adjustments? Do you agree with these guidelines? Explain.
6. What guidelines govern reporting of items that are either unusual or infrequent, but not both? Do you agree with these guidelines? Explain.

EXERCISES

PART A: EXERCISES 3–1 to 3–3

Exercise 3–1

For each of the following transactions, state (1) when revenue and/or expense should be recognized and (2) the amount. Explain the basis for your decision. Assume the accounting period ends December 31, 19J.

a. On December 30, 19J, sold $4,000 merchandise; terms, 3/10, n/30.

b. On December 29, 19J, paid $10,000 for advertising in the local paper. The ads related only to a clearance sale that would run from January 1–31, 19K.

c. Performed services each working day for a customer from December 27, 19J, through January 5, 19K. Assume eight working days are involved, of which four were in 19J. Cash collected was $2,000 (in full) on December 27, 19J.

d. Sold a used TV set for $100 on December 28, 19J, and collected $75 cash. The balance is due in six months; however, collection of the balance is very doubtful, and the set will not be worth repossessing again. It is now carried in the inventory of used sets at $60.

e. On December 1, 19J, borrowed $6,000 cash and gave a one-year, 18% note payable for $6,000. Interest is payable at maturity.

Hint: Restudy the revenue, cost, and matching principles in Chapter 1.

Exercise 3–2

The following items were taken from the adjusted trial balance of Ross Manufacturing Corporation at December 31, 19B:

Sales	$900,000
Cost of goods manufactured (including depreciation, $52,000)	550,000
Dividends received on investment in stocks	6,500
Finished goods inventory, 1/1/19B	45,000
Interest expense	4,200
Extraordinary item: Fire loss (pretax)	33,000
Distribution expenses	135,300
Common stock, par $10	200,000
G&A expenses	113,000
Interest revenue	2,500
Finished goods inventory, 12/31/19B	51,300
Income tax, assume average 30% tax rate	?

Required:

1. Prepare a single-step income statement (include EPS).
2. Prepare a multiple-step income statement (include EPS).

Exercise 3–3

The following items were taken from the adjusted trial balance of Star Trading Corporation on December 31, 19K. Assume an average 40% income tax rate on all items (including the casualty loss).

Sales	$640,200
Rent revenue	2,400
Interest revenue	900
Gain on sale of operational assets (assume an ordinary item)	1,000
Distribution expenses	136,000
G&A expenses	110,000
Interest expense	1,500
Depreciation for the period	6,000
Extraordinary item: Casualty loss (pretax)	15,000
Common stock (par $100)	100,000
Cost of goods sold	350,000

Required:

1. Prepare a single-step income statement (include EPS).
2. Prepare a multiple-step income statement (include EPS).

PART B: EXERCISES 3–4 to 3–11

Exercise 3–4

For each of the following transactions, state (1) when revenue and/or expense should be recognized and (2) the amount. Explain the basis for your decision. Assume the annual accounting period ends December 31, 19C.

a. On December 21, 19C, merchandise was sold for $7,000 cash. The buyer took possession of two thirds of the merchandise on that date. The balance will be picked up on January 3, 19D.

b. Services were rendered to a customer starting on December 27, 19C. The services will be completed around January 8, 19D, at which time $8,000 cash in full will be collected. Assume eight working days are involved of which two were in 19C.

c. During 19C, the company sold 10 TV sets and collected $6,000 cash in full. The company gives a one-year guarantee. It is estimated that the average warranty cost per set under the guarantee is $20. Assume by the end of 19C, half of the guarantees on the 10 sets have been satisfied.

d. On December 31, 19C, a used truck was sold by the company. The truck had been used in operating the business and had a book value of $300. The sales price was $500, which was payable six months from date of the sale plus 16% interest per annum.

e. On December 27, 19C, the company received an income tax refund of $1,000 after four years of negotiations with the Internal Revenue Service.

Hint: Restudy the revenue, cost, and matching principles in Chapter 1.

Exercise 3–5

The following pretax amounts were taken from the adjusted trial balance of Roll Corporation on December 31, 19B:

Balance, retained earnings, 1/1/19B	$ 40,000
Sales revenue	291,000
Cost of goods sold	105,000
Distribution expenses	36,000
Administrative expenses	30,000
Extraordinary gain (pretax)	10,000
Prior period adjustment, correction of error from prior period, pretax (a debit)	20,000
Dividends declared	16,000

For problem purposes, assume the income tax rate is 30%. Common shares outstanding during the year were 10,000.

Required:

1. Prepare a multiple-step income statement with intraperiod tax allocation and EPS.
2. Prepare a statement of retained earnings with intraperiod tax allocation.
3. Give the entry to record income taxes payable (assume not yet paid).

Exercise 3–6

The following pretax amounts were taken from the adjusted trial balance of Moon Corporation at December 31, 19C:

Dividends declared	$ 30,000
Sales revenue	300,000
Cost of goods sold	110,000
Operating expenses	60,000
Extraordinary loss (pretax)	12,000
Prior period adjustment, correction of error from prior period, pretax (a credit)	10,000
Common stock (par $5)	150,000
Beginning retained earnings, 1/1/19C	46,000

Required:

1. Prepare a complete single-step income statement assuming the income tax rate is 40% on all items. Include intraperiod tax allocation and EPS.
2. Prepare a statement of retained earnings.
3. Give the entry to record income taxes payable (assume not yet paid).

Exercise 3–7

The following pretax amounts were taken from the adjusted trial balance of Stoner Corporation at December 31, 19J:

Sales revenue	$250,000
Cost of goods sold	115,000
Operating expenses	80,000
Extraordinary gain (pretax)	17,000
Prior period adjustment, correction of error from prior period, pretax (a debit)	32,000

Common stock (par $10):	**Shares**
Outstanding 1/1/19J	15,000
Sold and issued 4/1/19J	5,000
Sold and issued 10/1/19J	7,000
Outstanding 12/31/19J	27,000

Required:
Prepare a complete single-step income statement. Assume an average 30% corporate tax rate on all items (including the extraordinary item and prior period adjustment). Show computation of EPS.

Exercise 3–8

The following pretax amounts were taken from the adjusted trial balance of Deakin Corporation at December 31, 19B:

Sales revenue	$160,000
Service revenue	50,000
Cost of goods sold	100,000
Operating expenses	75,000
Unusual item, gain on sale of operational asset (pretax)	12,000
Extraordinary item, loss (pretax)	20,000
Prior period adjustment, correction of error from prior period, pretax (a debit)	5,000

Common stock (par $1), 10,000 shares outstanding.

Assume an average 40% corporate tax rate on all items.

Required:
Prepare a single-step income statement that meets the full-disclosure requirements with respect to unusual items, extraordinary items, prior period adjustments, intraperiod tax allocation, and EPS.

Exercise 3–9

Price Company has a machine that cost $40,000 when acquired on January 1, 1977. The estimated useful life was 12 years, and the machine had an estimated residual value of $4,000. Straight-line depreciation is used. On December 31, 1982, prior to the adjusting entry, it was decided that the machine should have been depreciated over a 15-year useful life and that the residual value should have been $1,000.

Required:

1. Give the adjusting entry at the end of 1982 for depreciation expense. Show computations.
2. Give the correcting entry required at the end of 1982. If none is required, so state and give the reasons.

Exercise 3–10

It is December 31, 1982, and Tye Company is preparing adjusting entries at the end of the year. The company owns two trucks of different types. The following situations confront the company accountant:

Truck no. 1 cost $7,700 on January 1, 1980. It is being depreciated on a straight-line basis over an estimated useful life of 10 years with a $700 residual value. At December 31, 1982, it has been determined that the useful life should have been 6 years instead of 10, with a revised residual value of $900.

Truck no. 2 cost $4,550 on January 1, 1979. It is being depreciated on a straight-line basis over an estimated useful life of seven years with a $350 residual value. At December 31, 1982, it was discovered that no depreciation had been recorded on this truck for 1979 or 1980.

Required:

1. For each truck, give the required adjusting entry for depreciation expense at December 31, 1982. Show computations.
2. For each truck, give the appropriate correcting entry and show computations. If no correcting entry is needed, give the reasons.

Exercise 3–11

The following pretax amounts were taken from the accounts of Maple Corporation at December 31, 19C:

Sales revenue	$150,000
Cost of goods sold	85,000
Distribution and administrative expenses	45,000
Extraordinary gain (pretax)	15,000
Prior period adjustment, correction of error from prior period, pretax (a debit)	8,000
Interest expense	600
Cash dividends declared and paid	5,000
Retained earnings, 1/1/19C	51,000

Common stock (par $5), 20,000 shares outstanding.

Assume an average 40% tax rate on all items, including the extraordinary gain.

Required:

Prepare a combined single-step income statement and statement of retained earnings, including intraperiod income tax allocation and EPS. Show computations.

PROBLEMS

PART A: PROBLEMS 3–1 to 3–3

Problem 3–1

During the current year, 19J, XY Company completed a number of transactions that posed questions as to when revenue and/or expense should be recognized. The annual accounting period ends December 31. For each of the following selected transactions, state when revenue and/or expense should be recognized and give the basis for your decision.

a. Merchandise (TV sets) was sold on credit during 19J. The terms were 25% down payment plus six monthly payments. The collection experience on such sales, although not as good as on regular credit sales (due at end of month of sale), has been consistently satisfactory.

b. On December 24, 19J, the company sold for $110 a used TV set which had been repossessed and was set up in used goods inventory at $60. At the date of sale, $70 cash was collected with the balance due in six months. There is a high probability that collection will not be made and the TV set probably will not be worth repossessing again.

c. During 19J, the company sold 30 TV sets for a total of $12,000 and collected cash in full. The sets were guaranteed for 12 months from date of sale. It was estimated that the guarantee will cost the company, on the average, $15 per set. At year-end, it was estimated that half of the guarantees were still outstanding.

d. On December 14, 19J, received a $20,000 income tax refund from prior years. The negotiations extended over a three-year period.

e. Services were rendered to a customer starting on December 28, 19J, and will be completed January 6, 19K. Cash in full ($5,000) will be collected at date of completion of the services. Assume eight working days, of which four were in 19J.

f. On July 1, 19J, paid a two-year insurance premium in advance, $600.

g. On December 30, 19J, sold merchandise for $5,000; terms, 2/10, n/30.

h. On December 1, 19J, sold a customer merchandise for $1,000. Collected $600 cash and received a $400, 18% note for the remainder, principal plus interest due in three months.

i. On November 15, 19J, the court assessed damages against the company amounting to $25,000 cash. The suit was filed in 19G as a result of an accident in the company store. Payment in full will be made on January 10, 19K.

j. On December 23, 19J, purchased merchandise for resale that cost $18,000; terms, 2/10, n/30.

Hint: Restudy the revenue, cost, and matching principles in Chapter 1.

Problem 3–2

The following data were taken from the adjusted trial balance of Super Corporation at December 31, 19B:

Merchandise inventory, 1/1/19B	$ 71,000
Purchases	121,400
Sales	395,000
Purchase returns	3,400
Sales returns	5,000
Common stock (par $10)	200,000
Depreciation expense (70% admin.; 30% distribution)	50,000
Rent revenue	4,000
Interest expense	6,000
Investment revenue	2,500
Distribution expenses (exclusive of deprec.)	105,500
G&A expenses (exclusive of deprec.)	46,000
Gain on sale of noncurrent asset (an ordinary gain)	6,000
Loss on sale of long-term investments (ordinary)	3,600
Income tax expense (not incl. EO* item)	?
Extraordinary item: Flood loss (pretax)	10,000
Freight paid on purchases	1,000
Merchandise inventory, 12/31/19B	88,000

* Abbreviation for "extraordinary."

Assume an average 40% income tax rate on all items, including gains and losses on assets sold and extraordinary items.

Required:

1. Prepare a single-step income statement and a schedule of cost of goods sold to support it. Include an EPS presentation.
2. Prepare a multiple-step income statement including EPS.

Problem 3–3

Note: This problem utilizes material from Supplement 2–B. The following information was taken from the adjusted trial balance of Mumm Manufacturing Corporation at December 31, 19D.

Sales	$990,000
Purchases (raw materials)	150,000
Raw materials inventory, 1/1/19D	30,000
Work in process inventory, 1/1/19D	40,000
Finished goods inventory, 1/1/19D	20,000
Sales returns	5,000
Purchase returns	4,000
Freight on purchases	8,000
Distribution expenses	140,000
G&A expenses	92,300
Rent revenue	4,000
Investment revenue	3,000
Gain on sale of noncurrent assets, ordinary item (pretax)	6,000
Interest expense	9,000
Extraordinary loss (pretax)	40,000
Loss on sale of long-term investments, ordinary item (pretax)	10,000
Manufacturing expenses:	
Direct labor	230,000
Factory overhead	190,000
Raw materials inventory, 12/31/19D	24,000
Work in process inventory, 12/31/19D	38,000
Finished goods inventory, 12/31/19D	22,000
Income tax expense	?

Assume an average 40% income tax rate on all items.

Required:

1. Prepare a schedule of cost of goods manufactured to supplement the income statement.
2. Prepare a single-step income statement including EPS. Assume 20,000 shares of common stock outstanding.
3. Prepare a multiple-step income statement including EPS.

PART B: PROBLEMS 3–4 to 3–13

Problem 3–4

Below are listed transactions and amounts that often are reported on the annual financial statements. Indicate how each item usually should be reported. A list of responses is given so you can indicate your response by *code letter*. Enter only one letter for each item. Comment on doubtful items.

Code	Classification
A.	Balance sheet, appropriately classified.
	Income statement:
B.	Revenue
C.	Expense
D.	Unusual or infrequent, but not both
E.	Extraordinary item
	Statement of retained earnings:
F.	Prior period adjustment (an addition or deduction)

G. Addition to retained earnings
H. Deduction from retained earnings
I. Note to the financial statements

1. ______ Estimated warranties payable.
2. ______ Allowance for doubtful accounts.
3. ______ Gain on sale of operational asset.
4. ______ Hurricane damages.
5. ______ Payment of $30,000 additional income tax assessment (on prior year's income).
6. ______ Earthquake damages.
7. ______ Distribution expenses.
8. ______ Total amount of cash and credit sales for the period.
9. ______ Gain on disposal of long-term investments in stocks.
10. ______ Net income for the period.
11. ______ Insurance gain on casualty (fire)—insurance proceeds exceeded the book value of the assets destroyed.
12. ______ Cash dividends declared and paid.
13. ______ Rent collected on office space temporarily leased.
14. ______ Interest expense of the year paid plus interest accrued on liabilities.
15. ______ Dividends received on stocks held as an investment.
16. ______ Damages paid as a result of a lawsuit by an individual injured while shopping in the store; the litigation covered three years.
17. ______ Loss due to expropriation of a plant in a foreign country.
18. ______ A $10,000 bad debt is to be written off—the receivable had been outstanding for five years. Use the allowance method.
19. ______ Adjustment due to correction during current year of an error; the error was made two years earlier.
20. ______ On December 31 of current year, paid rent expense in advance for the next year.
21. ______ Cost of goods sold.
22. ______ Interest collected on November 30 of the current year from a customer on a 90-day note receivable.
23. ______ Year-end bonus of $50,000 paid to employees for performance during the year.

Problem 3–5

During 19D, an independent CPA encountered the following situations that caused serious concern as to proper classification on the financial statements of certain clients. Assume all amounts are material.

a. A client was assessed additional income taxes of $100,000 plus $36,000 interest related to the past three years.

b. A client suffered a casualty loss (a fire) amounting to $500,000. The client occasionally experiences a fire, but this was significantly more than any such loss ever experienced by the client company.

c. A client company paid $175,000 damages assessed by the courts as a result of an injury to a customer, on the company premises, three years earlier.

d. A client sold a large operational asset and reported a gain of $70,000.

e. The major supplier of raw materials to a client company experienced a prolonged strike. As a result, the client company reported a loss of $150,000. This is the first such loss; however, the client has three major suppliers and strikes are not unusual in those industries.

f. A client owns several large blocks of common stock of other corporations. The stock has been held for a number of years and is viewed as a long-term investment. During the past year, 20% of the stock was sold to meet an unusual cash demand. Additional sales of the stock are not anticipated.

Required:

1. For each transaction, indicate how the financial effects should be classified; that is, classify as *(a)* ordinary business operations; *(b)* unusual or infrequent, but not both; *(c)* extraordinary; or *(d)* prior period adjustment.
2. Explain the basis for your decision for each situation.
3. Briefly define each of the four categories (listed in 1 above) and explain how the effects of each should be reported.

Problem 3–6

The following pretax amounts were taken from the adjusted trial balances of Kwik Corporation at December 31, 19B, and 19C:

	19C	19B
Sales and service revenue	$200,000	$170,000
Cost of goods sold	80,000	70,000
Operating expenses	67,000	58,000
Extraordinary item: Casualty loss (pretax)	37,500	-0-
Prior period adjustment, correction of error from prior period, pretax (a credit)		10,000
Cash dividends declared	36,000	4,000
Stock dividend (7/1/19B, see below)		120,000*
Balance, retained earnings, 1/1/19B		160,000

	Shares
Common stock (par $10); shares outstanding:	
1/1/19B	15,000
Stock dividend, 7/1/19B	5,000
12/31/19B	20,000
10/1/19C, sold and issued	10,000
12/31/19C	30,000

* Amount debited to Retained Earnings.

Assume an average 40% income tax rate on all items, including the casualty and prior period adjustment.

Required:

1. Prepare a comparative income statement, using single-step format, with columns for 19C and 19B. Include EPS and intraperiod tax allocation. Show computations.
2. Prepare a comparative statement of retained earnings with columns for 19C and 19B.
3. Give the entry for income taxes at the end of 19B.

Problem 3–7

Young Corporation is undergoing the annual audit by the independent CPA at December 31, 1982. During the audit, the following situations were found that needed attention:

a. On December 29, 1980, an asset that cost $12,000 was debited to operating expenses. The asset has a six-year estimated life and no residual value. The company uses straight-line depreciation.

b. Late in 1982, the company constructed a small warehouse using their own employees. The cost was $90,000. However, before the decision was made to build it themselves, they obtained a $100,000 bid from a contractor. Upon completion of the warehouse, Young Corporation made the following entry in the accounts:

Warehouse (an operational asset)	100,000	
Cash		90,000
Miscellaneous revenue		10,000

c. Prior to recording depreciation expense for 1982, the management decided that a large machine that cost $128,000 should have been depreciated over a useful life of 14 years instead of 20 years. The machine was acquired January 2, 1977. Assume the residual value of $8,000 was not changed. Give the 1982 adjusting entry.

d. During December 1982, the company disposed of an old machine for $6,000 cash. Annual depreciation was $2,000; at the beginning of 1982, the accounts reflected the following:

Machine (cost)	$18,000
Accumulated depreciation	13,000

At date of disposal, the following entry was made:

Cash	6,000	
Machine		6,000

No depreciation has been recorded for 1982.

e. A patent that cost $3,400 is being amortized over its legal life of 17 years at $200 per year. After the 1981 adjusting entry, it had been amortized down to $800. At the end of 1982, it was determined in view of a competitor's patent, that it will have no economic value to the company by the end of 1983. Straight-line amortization is used.

Required:
For each of the above situations, explain what should be done in the accounts. If a journal entry is needed to implement your decision in each case, provide it along with supporting computations. Ignore income tax considerations.

Problem 3–8

The following pretax amounts were taken from the accounts of Striper Corporation at December 31, 19C:

Sales revenue	$540,000
Cost of goods sold	280,000
Distribution expenses	105,000
Administrative expenses	70,000
Interest revenue	1,000
Interest expense	3,000
Unusual item: Gain from sale of noncurrent asset (pretax; an ordinary gain)	19,000
Extraordinary item: Casualty (pretax loss)	30,000
Balance, retained earnings, 1/1/19C	93,000
Cash dividends	15,000
Prior period adjustment, correction of error from prior period, pretax (a debit)	8,000
Common stock (par $1), 50,000 shares outstanding.	
Restriction on retained earnings amounting to $25,000 per indenture agreement on bonds payable.	

Assume an average 35% income tax rate on all items.

Required:
Prepare a combined multiple-step income statement and statement of retained earnings including tax allocation and EPS. Show computations.

Problem 3–9

The following amounts were taken from the accounting records of Poston Corporation at December 31, 19B:

Sales revenue	$240,000
Service revenue	60,000
Cost of goods sold	130,000
Distribution and administrative expenses	125,000
Investment revenue	6,000
Interest expense	4,000

Infrequent item: Loss on sale of long-term investment (pretax)	10,000
Extraordinary item: Earthquake loss (pretax)	27,000
Cash dividends declared	8,000
Prior period adjustment, correction of error from prior period, pretax (a debit)	12,000
Balance, retained earnings, 1/1/19B	78,000

Common stock (par $5), 30,000 shares outstanding.
Restriction on retained earnings, $50,000 per bond payable indenture.

Assume an average 45% income tax rate on all items.

Required:
Prepare a combined single-step income statement and statement of retained earnings, including tax allocation and EPS. Show computations.

Problem 3–10

The following financial statements have come to you for review:

FAST PRODUCTION COMPANY
Profit and Loss Statement
December 31, 19K

Incomes:			
Gross sales		$256,800	
Less: Sales returns		5,120	
Net sales			$251,680
Costs and expenses:			
Cost of goods sold:			
Inventory, Jan. 1		98,500	
Purchases	$132,600		
Less: Purchase returns	2,780	129,820	
		228,320	
Inventory, Dec. 31		102,300	
Cost of goods sold			126,020
Gross profit			125,660
Operating costs:			
Selling		38,000	
G&A:			
General	20,000		
Depreciation	8,800		
Bad debts	1,080	29,880	
Total operating costs			67,880
Income from operations			57,780
Other income:			
Interest income			970
Profit			58,750
Less taxes			28,720
Net			$ 30,030

FAST PRODUCTION COMPANY
Earned Surplus Statement
At December 31, 19K

Balance, at start		$267,600
Corrections:		
Additions:		
Depreciation overstated		3,400
Adjusted		271,000
Additions:		
Profit	$30,030	
Gain on sale of land	8,200	38,230
		309,230
Deductions:		
Dividends	30,000	
Loss on sale of machinery	9,650	39,650
Earned surplus (to balance sheet)		$269,580

Required:
Critically evaluate the above statements. Cite items to support your response. List and explain all of the aspects of the above statements that you would change in order to conform to appropriate reporting, terminology, and format.

Problem 3–11

The following income statement and statement of retained earnings were prepared by the bookkeeper for the Lax Corporation:

LAX CORPORATION
Statement of Profit
December 31, 19J

Sales income (net)		$ 85,000
Service income		46,000
Total		131,000
Cost of sales:		
Inventory	$ 34,000	
Purchases (net)	71,000	
Total	105,000	
Inventory	40,000	65,000
Gross profit		66,000
Costs:		
Salaries, wages, etc.	35,000	
Depreciation and write-offs	7,000	
Rent	3,000	
Taxes	500	
Utilities	2,100	
Promotion	900	
Sundry	6,700	(55,200)
Special items:		
Gain on asset sold		6,000
Inventory theft		(2,800)
Net profit		$ 14,000

LAX CORPORATION
Earned Surplus Statement
December 31, 19J

Balance, earned surplus		$27,000
Add:		
Profit		14,000
Correction of inventory		5,000
Total.........................		46,000
Deduct:		
Fire loss	$13,000	
Dividends	10,000	
Earned surplus to capital	5,000	28,000
Balance		$18,000

Required:
List each item on the above statements that you believe should be changed and give your recommendations on each with respect to appropriate reporting, terminology, and format.

Problem 3–12

The Appendix following Chapter 24 gives an actual set of financial statements. Examine them carefully and respond to the following questions (for 1981 only, unless otherwise specified):

a. Are the statements comparative? Why are comparative statements usually presented?
b. Are the statements consolidated? What do you understand this to mean?
c. Is this a retail, financial, or a manufacturing company? Explain.
d. How many different kinds of revenue were reported? How many different kinds of expenses were reported?
e. How were interest expense and interest revenue reported on the income statement?
f. Was the total amount of depreciation expense separately reported on the income statement? If not, where was it presented?
g. Were any unusual or infrequently occurring (but not both) items reported on the income statement in 1980 or 1981?
h. Were any extraordinary items reported in 1980 or 1981 on the income statement? What were they? Were they net of tax?
i. Was there any indication of an accounting change? If so, explain how it was reported and what type of change it was.
j. How many EPS amounts were reported?
k. What "differences" were reported on the income statement? Gross margin? Income from continuing operations? Income before extraordinary items? Net income? Others (list)?
l. What were the profit margins (net income divided by revenue) for 1980 and 1981?
m. Were income taxes allocated in 1981? Explain.
n. What basis was used for valuing inventories?
o. List all unusual features of the income statement. What aspects of it would you criticize? Explain.
p. How does this company define "funds" in the SCFP? What amount of "funds" was provided from operations in 1981?
q. What was the primary depreciation method used?
r. What amount of the 1981 income tax payable was classified as foreign income taxes?
s. In 1981, what was the total amount of cash dividends declared on *(a)* common stock and *(b)* preferred stock?
t. In 1981, what was the amount of income from foreign activities?
u. What were the total amounts of revenues and net income reported for the first quarter of 1981?
v. Were any prior period adjustments reported in 1980 or 1981? Explain each.
w. Did the auditor's report express any reservations about the financial statements? Explain.
x. Overall, do you believe the balance sheet and the income statement could be improved with respect to format and terminology? Explain each change that you would suggest for consideration.

Problem 3–13

Obtain a set of audited financial statements for the latest year for a company of your choice (from the library or other source) and use it as a basis for responding to each of the questions posed in Problem 3–12.

4

Review—The Balance Sheet and Statement of Changes in Financial Position

THE PRECEDING CHAPTER reviewed the income statement and statement of retained earnings. This chapter reviews the two remaining required financial statements—the balance sheet and the statement of changes in financial position (SCFP). The relationships among the required statements were presented in Exhibit 3–1, which shows the income statement and the SCFP to be the connecting links between successive balance sheets. That is, the income statement and the SCFP are "change" statements; they present the **reasons for the changes** in the financial position of an enterprise that occurred during the period.

PURPOSE OF THE CHAPTER

The purpose of this chapter is to discuss the balance sheet and the SCFP from two perspectives, those of (1) decision makers who use balance sheets and SCFPs and (2) accountants who prepare the financial statements. The chapter is divided into two parts as follows:

Part A—Concepts Underlying the Balance Sheet and Its Preparation

Part B—The Statement of Changes in Financial Position (SCFP) and Additional Reporting Issues

Part A: Concepts Underlying the Balance Sheet and Its Preparation

CONCEPTS UNDERLYING THE BALANCE SHEET

A balance sheet presents the assets, liabilities, and owners' equity of an enterprise at a specific date. Because it presents the current **financial position** of an entity, it also is referred to as the **statement of financial position.** The designation **balance sheet** refers to the fact that the statement "balances" in terms of the fundamental accounting model: Assets = Liabilities + Owners' equity. A balance sheet should be dated at a specific date, such as "At December 31, 19xx," in contrast to an income statement and an SCFP, which are dated to encompass a specific period of time, such as "For the Year Ended December 31, 19xx."

The financial position of an enterprise is represented by the various assets owned, obligations owed, and claims of the owners of the enterprise at a designated date. This information is important to investors and creditors. For example, consider the attempt of an enterprise to borrow money. Critical factors to a potential lender include the (1) composition and market values of the assets owned by the borrower, (2) liquidity of those assets, (3) terms and amounts of existing liabilities of the borrower, and (4) creditor claims (i.e., liens) against the borrower's assets. Balance sheets and the related notes disclose this information, except the current market values of the assets. Without the **information** provided by a borrower's balance sheet, many loans would not be made. The potential lender usually would also analyze the income statement and the SCFP of the borrower to evaluate the potential income performance and net funds generated by the enterprise.

Similarly, investors in capital stock often analyze balance sheet data in making investment decisions. Their direct interest is in future dividends and changes in the market value of their stock investment, rather than the ability of the company to pay its liabilities. However, stock investors also use information about the assets, liabilities, and owners' equities of a company as an indication of its ability to earn income and pay dividends. For example, debt covenants (e.g., bond indentures) often restrict the amount of retained earnings a company may use for dividends (see Exhibit 3–9, Note 7). Also, certain ratios involving balance sheet items, such as the current ratio and the ratio of long-term debt to owners' equity, are used in assessing the risk of a stock investment.

Conventional balance sheets do not report current market values; however, they provide lists of the major categories of assets, liabilities, and owners' equities of a company, for which current market value data may be developed outside the accounting system.

PREPARATION OF THE BALANCE SHEET

Preparation of the balance sheet rests upon (1) the accounting concepts discussed in Chapter 1, (2) the balance sheet elements, and (3) a format that is used widely.

Balance Sheet Elements

The elements of a balance sheet are **assets, liabilities,** and **owners' equity.** Exhibit 4–1 gives definitions of these elements in accordance with *FASB Concepts Statement 3.*

EXHIBIT 4–1: Balance Sheet Elements

Definition of Element

Assets are probable future economic benefits obtained or controlled by a particular entity as a result of past transactions or events.

Liabilities are probable future sacrifices of economic benefits arising from present obligations of a particular entity to transfer assets or provide services to other entities in the future as a result of past transactions or events.

Equity [i.e., **owners' equity**] is the residual interest in the assets of an entity that remains after deducting its liabilities. In a business enterprise, the equity is the ownership interest.

Source: FASB, *Statement of Financial Accounting Concepts No. 3,* "Elements of Financial Statements of Business Enterprises" (Stamford, Conn., December 1980), pars. 19–55.

Measurements (Valuations) on the Balance Sheet

Asset valuations on the balance sheet rarely represent their current market values at the date of the balance sheet. Rather, the assets are reported at their **carrying** or **book value.** Book value is the result of applying the cost and matching principles (with certain exceptions). Generally, it is acquisition cost less accumulated write-offs to date. Cash is reported at its current value; accounts receivable at expected net realizable value (amount of the receivables less the allowance for doubtful accounts). Inventories and marketable equity securities usually are reported after acquisition at lower of cost or market (LCM), and plant and equipment are reported at cost less accumulated depreciation.

Liabilities are reported on the balance sheet at their carrying or book value. The book value of current liabilities usually is measured as the maturity value (versus the present value) of the debt because the difference between the maturity value and the present value of a current liability usually is immaterial. Long-term liabilities are recorded at present value; subsequently, the book value of a long-term liability is its maturity value plus any unamortized premium or less any unamortized discount (liabilities are discussed in Chapters 10 and 17).

Owners' equity is a residual amount. It does not report the current market value of the business; rather, it is a measurement of the owners' interest that follows directly from the measurements used for the assets and liabilities, as determined in accordance with GAAP.

Balance Sheet Format (Display)

The reporting principle (see Chapter 1) requires that a full and complete balance sheet be presented as an integral part of the periodic financial report. Although the format of the balance sheet is not specified, either the **account or report format** is almost always used. These formats are outlined below.

Classifications in the Balance Sheet

To facilitate use by decision makers, balance sheet items usually are grouped according to common characteristics. Assets usually are grouped in decreasing order of liquidity (i.e., nearness to cash), liabilities by time to maturity, and owners' equity in decreasing order of permanency. Classifications of information used in a balance sheet and the array of items under each classification are influenced by the industry and characteristics of the enterprise. For example, the balance sheet of a financial institution, such as a bank, will reflect classifications quite different from those for a manufacturing company. Format and classifications should be designed to accommodate the peculiarities of the enterprise and comply with the reporting principle, which specifies that reporting must be informative and not misleading. Therefore, flexibility in format and classifications generally is considered desirable. Nevertheless, there is a reasonable degree of uniformity. The following classifications are representative of current reporting practices:

Assets:

1. Current assets.
2. Investments and funds.
3. Operational (or fixed) assets—tangible.
4. Operational assets—intangible.
5. Other assets.
6. Deferred charges.

Liabilities:

1. Current liabilities (including short-term deferred credits).
2. Long-term liabilities (including long-term deferred credits).

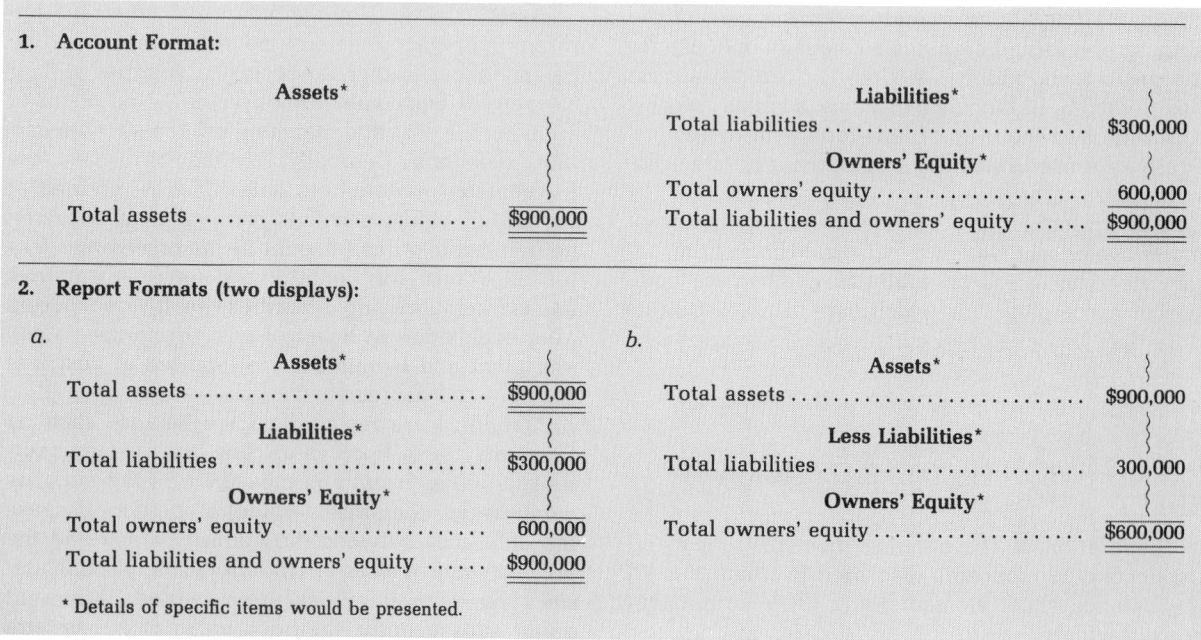

1. Account Format:

Assets*		**Liabilities***	
		Total liabilities	$300,000
		Owners' Equity*	
		Total owners' equity	600,000
Total assets	$900,000	Total liabilities and owners' equity	$900,000

2. Report Formats (two displays):

a.

Assets*	
Total assets	$900,000
Liabilities*	
Total liabilities	$300,000
Owners' Equity*	
Total owners' equity	600,000
Total liabilities and owners' equity	$900,000

b.

Assets*	
Total assets	$900,000
Less Liabilities*	
Total liabilities	300,000
Owners' Equity*	
Total owners' equity	$600,000

* Details of specific items would be presented.

Owners' equity:

1. Contributed capital:
   a. Capital stock.
   b. Contributed capital in excess of the par or stated value of capital stock.
   c. Other contributed capital.
2. Retained earnings.
3. Unrealized losses and gains.

The above classification provides a caption for each balance sheet element—assets, liabilities, and owners' equity. Under each element caption are several subclassifications, as listed above. Exhibit 4–2 presents an illustrative balance sheet to supplement the discussions which follow.

Current Assets. Current assets are cash and other assets, commonly identified as those which are **reasonably expected** to be realized in cash, or to be sold or consumed during the **normal operating cycle** of the business or within one year from the balance sheet date, whichever is longer. The normal operating cycle is defined as the average period of time between the expenditure of cash for goods and services and the date those goods and services are converted back into cash. It is the average length of time from cash expenditure, to inventory, to sale, to accounts receivable, and back to cash.

Current assets usually are presented on the balance sheet in order of decreasing liquidity (i.e., nearness to cash conversion). The major items comprising current assets, in order of liquidity, are cash, short-term investments, receivables, inventories, and prepaid expenses.

Assets which are similar to but **not** classified as current assets include: (1) cash and claims to cash which are **restricted for uses other than current operations,** (2) receivables with an extended maturity date, and (3) long-term prepayments of expenses.

Although the definition of current assets is reasonably clear-cut, problems are encountered in implementation. The phrases "normal operating cycle" and "reasonably expected to be realized in cash" involve judgments. Companies can take advantage of this judgment to incorrectly classify certain items as current assets in order to produce a favorable effect on working capital (i.e., the difference between current assets and current liabilities). For example, a stock investment may be classified as a current or noncurrent asset, depending upon the **stated intention** of management as to the planned holding period. An intention to hold the investment beyond the period specified for current assets would require its classification as a noncurrent asset. Thus, a simple change in **intention** of management may alter the classification of the investments.

Prepaid expenses is another area with considerable variation in classification. A short-term prepayment should be classified as a current asset (i.e., a prepaid expense), whereas a long-term prepayment should be classified as noncurrent (i.e., a deferred charge). Prepaid expenses theoretically are current assets because having "invested" by paying expenses in advance, cash outlays for the next period are reduced.

Some companies and industries have no basis for using a current asset category. For example, financial institutions, such as banks and mutual funds, do not use the current asset caption because it would be pointless in view of the nature of their asset structures.

Current Liabilities. The definition of current liabilities parallels (is dependent upon) the definition of current assets; that is, current liabilities are short-term liabilities "whose liquidation is reasonably expected to require the use of existing resources properly classified as current assets, or the creation of other current liabilities."[1] This definition does not relate to specific current assets (e.g., a specific customer's account receivable); rather, it relates to current assets as a total. This definition includes items such as revenue collected in advance, which entails an obligation to "perform or render the revenue activity" within the next year or operating cycle, whichever is longer. Also included in current liabilities are liabilities whose liquidation is expected to occur within a relatively short period of time, usually one year. Examples include short-term debts arising from acquisition of operational (i.e., fixed) assets, serial maturities of long-term obligations, and obligations arising from cash collections on behalf of a third party. In practice, most companies use one year as the time frame for classifying assets and liabilities as current or long-term because *(a)* the operating cycle usually is less than one year or *(b)* the length of the operating cycle may be difficult to measure reliably.

[1] AICPA, *Accounting Research and Terminology Bulletins, Final Edition* (New York, 1961), p. 21.

EXHIBIT 4–2: Statement of Financial Position

AB CORPORATION
Statement of Financial Position (Balance Sheet)
At December 31, 19J

Assets

Current assets:			
Cash			$ 35,200
Short-term investments (current market value, $21,000)			20,000
Accounts receivable (trade)		$ 43,100	
Less: Allowance for doubtful accounts		1,300	41,800
Merchandise inventory (FIFO, LCM)			120,000
Prepaid expenses:			
Prepaid insurance			3,000
Total current assets			220,000
Investments and funds:			
Investment in stock of Y Corporation (at cost)	$ 77,000		
Less: Allowance to reduce to market value	7,000	70,000	
Plant expansion fund		80,000	150,000
Land, building, and equipment:			
Land		24,000	
Building	200,000		
Less: Accumulated depreciation (straight line)	80,000	120,000	
Equipment and fixtures	140,000		
Less: Accumulated depreciation (straight line)	56,000	84,000	228,000
Intangible assets:			
Patent (cost, $42,500, less accumulated amortization, $17,500)			25,000
Other assets:			
Land held for future building site			37,000
Deferred charges:			
Rearrangement costs			8,000
Total assets			$668,000

Liabilities

Current liabilities:		
Accounts payable (trade)		$ 48,700
Notes payable		30,000
Rent revenue collected in advance		1,800
Wages payable		2,000
Income taxes payable		12,500
Total current liabilities		95,000
Long-term liabilities:		
Bonds payable, 6%, due 19R	175,000	
Less: Unamortized discount	4,000	171,000
Total liabilities		266,000

Current liabilities include the following short-term items:

1. Accounts payable (trade) for goods and services that enter into the operating cycle of the business.
2. Special payables for nonoperating items and services.
3. Short-term notes payable.
4. Current maturities of long-term liabilities.
5. Collections in advance for unearned revenue (such as rent revenue collected in advance).
6. Accrued expenses for payrolls, interest, and taxes (e.g., income and property taxes).

EXHIBIT 4–2 ***(continued)***

Stockholders' Equity		
Contributed capital:		
Preferred stock, par $10, 9% cumulative, nonparticipating, authorized 20,000 shares, issued and outstanding 5,000 shares	50,000	
Common stock, nopar, authorized 100,000 shares, issued and outstanding 75,000 shares	150,000	
Additional contributed capital:		
In excess of par value of preferred stock	40,000	
Total contributed capital	240,000	
Retained earnings (Note A)	169,000	
Total contributed capital and retained earnings	409,000	
Less: Unrealized loss on long-term investment	7,000	
Total stockholders' equity		402,000
Total liabilities and stockholders' equity		$668,000

Notes to financial statements:
Note A. Under the terms of the bond indenture, a part of retained earnings, determined by a formula, is restricted from dividend availability. The formula, computed for 19J, restricts retained earnings in the amount of $61,000. This amount will be increased each year as provided by the bond indenture formula. When the bonds are retired, the restriction will be automatically removed.

Liabilities which are similar to but are not classified as current liabilities include long-term notes, bonds, and obligations that will not be paid out of current assets. For example, bonds payable due during the coming year would not be classified as a current liability if they are to be paid out of a special cash fund classified under the caption Investments and Funds. Similarly, currently maturing bonds payable to be refunded (i.e., paid off by issuing a new series of bonds) should not be classified as a current liability, as specified in *FASB Statement 6*.

Working Capital. Working capital is defined as current assets minus current liabilities. If all of the current assets were converted to cash at their **book value** and all of the current liabilities paid at their book value, working capital would be the amount of cash remaining. Although the concept of working capital is widely used in the business community, no one ever receives or pays working capital as such. For this reason, many investors are more concerned with the amounts of the various items that comprise current assets and current liabilities than with the amount of working capital. In fact, a company may report an excellent working capital position and at the same time have a serious cash deficiency. For these and other reasons, many business persons believe that cash flow statements are more informative than working capital statements. Nevertheless, the amount of working capital and the working capital ratio are viewed as measures of liquidity, that is, the ability of the enterprise to meet its short-term obligations.[2]

To illustrate the computation of working capital, assume AB Corporation (Exhibit 4–2) reported the following:

Current assets	$220,000
Current liabilities	95,000
Difference—working capital	$125,000

Working capital ratio: $220,000 ÷ $95,000 = 2.32

The working capital is $125,000, and the working capital (or current) ratio is 2.32. The ratio indicates that at book value the current assets are 2.32 times the current liabilities, or that for each $1 of current liabilities, there is $2.32 in current assets. Because of the use of working capital as an index of liquidity, the independent auditor sometimes encounters attempts to misclassify some noncurrent assets as current and some current liabilities as noncurrent. These manipulations would make it possible for the company to report a better working capital position than actually exists.

In financial reporting, offsetting of current assets and liabilities is improper because this practice avoids full disclosure and would permit a business to show a more favorable current ratio than actually exists. For example, if AB Corporation were to offset

[2] For a recent criticism of working capital as a measure of liquidity, see R. Greene, "Are More Chryslers in the Offing?" *Forbes*, February 2, 1981, pp. 69–73, esp. p. 72, "Cash Flow Made Easy."

a current liability of $45,000 against current assets, the current ratio would show $175,000 (i.e., $220,000 − $45,000) ÷ $50,000 (i.e., $95,000 − $45,000) = 3.5 instead of the correct ratio of 2.32. In an extreme case, if permitted, AB could increase its current ratio to infinity by offsetting all of its current liabilities against current assets (i.e., $125,000 ÷ $0).

Offsetting is permissible only when a legal right to offset exists. For instance, it would be proper to offset a $5,000 overdraft in one bank account against another account reflecting $8,000 on deposit in **that same bank.**

Investments and Funds. This caption often is labeled Investments. It is reported immediately after current assets. It includes noncurrent assets (other than the operating assets, other assets, and deferred charges) acquired for their financial or investment advantage and funds set aside for future purposes. The long-term items reported under this caption include the following:

1. Long-term investments in securities, such as stocks, bonds, and long-term notes.
2. Investments in subsidiaries, including long-term receivables from subsidiaries.
3. Funds set aside for long-term future use, such as bond sinking funds (to retire bonds payable), expansion funds, stock retirement funds, and long-term savings deposits.
4. Cash surrender value of life insurance policies carried by the company.
5. Long-term investments in tangible assets, such as land and buildings, which are not used in current operations.

The important distinctions are that *(a)* the items are not used in the central operations of the entity and *(b)* management plans long-term retention of them.

Operational Assets. Operational assets are defined as those long-lived assets used in carrying out the operations of the entity; they are not held for resale. Thus, operational assets are different from inventories (e.g., of raw materials, work in process, finished goods, and supplies). Historically, operational assets have been labeled as **fixed assets** because of their relative permanence or long-term nature. Operational assets are subclassified as follows:

1. Tangible—Those assets with physical substance, such as land, buildings, machinery, equipment, furniture, fixtures, and natural resources.
2. Intangible—Those assets that have no physical substance but instead have value solely because of the rights which their ownership confers. Examples are patents, copyrights, trademarks, brand names, leaseholds, and goodwill.

Operational Assets—Tangible. This group of operational assets is reported separately on the balance sheet under various captions depending upon the type of business. Manufacturing enterprises use captions such as **Property, plant, and equipment;** and other enterprises use captions such as **Property and equipment,** or simply **Property.** Companies seldom use the older caption, **Fixed assets.**

Tangible operational assets include items that are *(a)* depreciable, such as buildings, machinery, and fixtures and *(b)* not subject to depreciation, such as land. Therefore, land should be reported separately from depreciable assets.

APB Opinion 12 requires that the balance sheet, or the related notes, report *(a)* balances of major classes of depreciable assets by nature or function; *(b)* accumulated depreciation, either by major classes of depreciable assets or in total; and *(c)* a description of the methods used in computing depreciation for the major classes of operational assets. The term **reserve for depreciation** should not be used to refer to accumulated depreciation because no "reserve" exists. Exhibit 4–2 illustrates reporting of tangible operational assets.

Operational Assets—Intangible. This asset classification is reported separately on the balance sheet usually under the title **Intangible assets.** Major items should be listed separately, and the accumulated amount of **amortization** also should be disclosed. By convention, the contra account, accumulated amortization, seldom is separately listed; this practice contrasts with the usual treatment given tangible operational assets (see Exhibit 4–2). Although deferred charges are "intangible," they differ from "operational assets—intangible" in that the latter represent **exclusive rights** while deferred charges are long-term prepaid expenses.

Other Assets. "Other assets" are those items which cannot be reasonably categorized under the usual asset classifications. Examples include long-term receivables from employees and idle operational assets (such as an idle plant). Items should be analyzed carefully before being reported as other assets because often a logical basis exists for classifying them elsewhere. Items such as deferred strike losses and flood losses intended to be written off in the future sometimes are reported as other assets. This treatment is insupportable inasmuch as no element of future economic benefit is associated with such losses; hence, they are not assets. They should be reported on the income statement as losses of the period in which they occur.

Deferred Charges. Deferred charges represent debit balances derived from expenditures for expense prepayments. Therefore, they are carried forward to be matched with future revenues. Deferred charges are distinguished from prepaid expenses on the basis of the **time** over which they will be amortized; that is, they involve a longer period of time than do prepaid expenses. The following accounts typify those found under the Deferred Charges caption: Machinery Rearrangement Costs, Deferred Income Taxes (discussed in Chapter 10), Organization Costs (alternatively shown under "Intangibles"), Pension Costs Paid in Advance, and Insurance Prepayments (long-term prepayments not properly classified as a current asset). Unfortunately, deferred charges sometimes are reported as "Other assets."

Long-Term Liabilities. A long-term liability is an obligation that will not require the use of current assets for payment during the upcoming operating cycle or during the next year, whichever is longer. Long-term liabilities initially are recorded at their present value. Subsequently, that value will be retained unless *(a)* the debt document does not call for a realistic rate of interest (discussed in Chapter 10) or *(b)* the debt is represented by bonds issued at a premium or discount (discussed in Chapter 17).

All liabilities not appropriately classified as current liabilities are reported under this caption. Typical long-term liabilities are bonds payable, long-term notes payable, long-term lease obligations, and the noncurrent portion of deferred income taxes.

Deferred Credits. Occasionally a company will include the caption, Deferred credits, between long-term liabilities and owners' equity.[3] Deferred credits can be defined only as a catch-all balance sheet classification of long-term credit balance accounts that are difficult to classify elsewhere. Typical deferred credits are long-term deferred income taxes, deferred revenues (i.e., revenues collected in advance), and deferred investment tax credits. Use of this caption is discouraged because items classified as deferred credits usually are liabilities or contra assets and, therefore, should be reported as such. Practically all companies report deferred credits as liabilities (deferred credits are discussed in detail in Chapter 10).

Owners' Equity. Owners' equity represents the residual financial interests in a business. It is the difference between total assets and total liabilities. For a sole proprietorship, it usually is called proprietor's equity (or capital); for a partnership, partners' equity (or capital); and for a corporation, stockholders' or shareholders' equity. Owners' equity is the balance sheet caption used to report the various sources of capital of an entity, such as contributed capital, accumulated earnings, and any unrealized amounts. Primarily because of certain legal requirements, owners' equity is subclassified to reflect detailed **sources.** For a corporation, the following sources commonly are reported:

1. Contributed capital:
   a. Capital stock.
   b. Contributed capital in excess of the par or stated value of capital stock.
   c. Other contributed capital.
2. Retained earnings.
3. Unrealized losses and gains.

Capital Stock. This caption reports the **sources** of owners' equity as represented by the stated or legal capital (i.e., usually the par value of the outstanding capital stock) of the corporation. Legal capital is specified by state law and in the Articles of Incorporation (i.e., the Charter) of the company. Each class of stock, common and preferred, must be reported at the par or stated amount; or in the case of nopar stock, the total amount paid in (these specifications vary depending upon the law of the state

[3] Reporting deferred credits in this way poses an inconsistency because the fundamental accounting model (Assets = Liabilities + Owners' equity) does not include a category between liabilities and owners' equity.

of incorporation). Details of each class of capital stock should be reported separately, including the number of shares authorized, issued, outstanding, and subscribed; conversion features; callability; preferences; and any other special features.

Contributed Capital in Excess of Par or Stated Value. This source sometimes is called **additional paid-in capital** or premium on stock. It reports the amounts received by the corporation in excess of the par or stated value of the capital stock outstanding. These amounts usually arise when the corporation sells its stock at a premium or issues stock dividends. These topics are discussed in detail in Chapters 14 and 15.

Other Contributed Capital. This source of contributed capital arises from such transactions as treasury stock and retirements and conversion of stock (discussed in Chapter 15).

Retained Earnings. Retained earnings (formerly called earned surplus) is the corporation's accumulated earnings, less accumulated losses and dividends to date. It reports the amount of resources (from undistributed earnings) that the corporation has retained for use in the enterprise. In most corporations, over the long term, retained earnings is the major **source** of owners' equity. In the long term, most corporations distribute dividends to the stockholders amounting to less than 50 percent of the earnings, thus establishing a continuing source of internally generated funds. Indirectly, retained earnings represent additional investments by the stockholders because they have foregone dividends equal to the cumulative balance of retained earnings. A negative balance in retained earnings usually is called a **deficit.**

Frequently, a portion of the total amount of retained earnings is **restricted** or **appropriated.** This means that during the period of restriction, the restricted amount is not available for dividends. For example, AB Corporation (Exhibit 4–2) has total retained earnings of $169,000; however, $61,000 of that amount is restricted for a specific period of time. After the restriction is removed, the $61,000 may be used as a basis for the declaration of dividends by the board of directors of the corporation.

A restriction on retained earnings may be **contractual,** as in Exhibit 4–2, in which the bond indenture restricts the amount of retained earnings available for dividend declaration. Alternatively, a restriction may result from a **legal requirement,** as in the case in which state law imposes a restriction equal to the cost of any treasury stock held. Such laws are designed to protect the creditors of the corporation. Finally, the board of directors may exercise its **discretion** and decide to "appropriate" a portion of retained earnings, as in the case of "retained earnings appropriated for future plant expansion."

Restrictions or appropriations of retained earnings may be reported in either of two ways. The predominant way is to report restrictions or appropriations in notes, such as Note A in Exhibit 4–2. An alternative approach is to make an entry in the accounts to reflect the restriction or appropriation. For example, the $61,000 restriction on retained earnings reported by AB Corporation (Exhibit 4–2) could be recorded and reported as follows:

Entry to **record** the appropriation in the accounts:

Retained earnings	61,000	
Retained earnings restricted by bond indenture		61,000

Reporting on the balance sheet then could be as follows:

Retained earnings, unappropriated	$108,000
Retained earnings, restricted by bond indenture	61,000
Total retained earnings	$169,000

Unrealized Capital. This component of owners' equity is used mainly for recording and reporting unrealized losses and loss recoveries resulting from the application of the LCM rule to long-term equity investments in capital stock, under the requirements of *FASB Statement 12.* This *Statement* requires that the cumulative amount of unrealized loss be reported separately as an **unrealized element of owners' equity** (i.e., a reduction in owners' equity as shown in Exhibit 4–2). This topic is discussed in detail in Chapter 16.

Unrealized capital has been used in some situations to accommodate a "gain" arising from the writing up of operational assets (discussed in Chapter 11). This discussion is not intended to imply that write-ups of assets to market value currently are in accordance with GAAP. However, there are a few exceptions, as explained in Chapters 6, 11, 16, and 24.

Part B: Statement of Changes in Financial Position (SCFP) and Additional Reporting Issues

APB Opinion 19 requires that an SCFP, in addition to the income statement and balance sheet, must be included in the annual financial report. The SCFP reports the **sources and uses of funds during the accounting period.** Thus, the SCFP is dated the same as the income statement (e.g., For the Year Ended December 31, 19xx).

CONCEPTS UNDERLYING THE SCFP

On the SCFP, **sources** of funds often are called **financing activities,** and **uses** of funds often are called **investing activities.** *APB Opinion 19* specifies that funds may be measured on the SCFP as either **cash or as working capital.** Therefore, the SCFP must be prepared on either of two bases: (1) cash (which may include short-term investments) or (2) working capital (i.e., current assets minus current liabilities). If the working capital basis is used, the changes in the working capital accounts also must be disclosed in a tabulation as part of the SCFP.

The SCFP is a **change statement,** as diagrammed in Exhibit 3–1, because the financing (i.e., sources) and investing (i.e., uses) activities explain the causes of the changes between the beginning and ending balance sheets, other than those changes explained by the income statement.

The information provided by the SCFP is useful for numerous purposes. One use of the SCFP is that it serves as a statement of cash, or working capital, **inflows** (i.e., sources) and outflows (i.e., uses), which in combination with other information may be useful for predicting future net cash flows to an enterprise. The "Sources of cash (or working capital)" section of the SCFP indicates the relative contributions of cash, or working capital, from continuing operations, extraordinary items, issuances of securities (e.g., bonds payable, capital stock, short-term notes payable), disposals of assets, and other sources. For example, if a company consistently needed to dispose of its operational assets to obtain cash for continuing operations, this could indicate a potential weakness in future operating performance.

The "Uses of cash (or working capital)" section of the SCFP may be particularly useful to decision makers because how a company uses its cash (or working capital) has an impact upon the sources and amounts of its future net cash inflows. For example, if a retailing company were investing heavily in long-term equity or debt securities, this could indicate that the management of the company cannot locate better investment opportunities in retailing. Such an investment strategy could be due to general pessimism about the economy, which may affect the outlook for the retail business; alternatively, it could signal (1) market saturation for the company's products, (2) a long-term shift in the investment strategy of the company, (3) a short-term response to unusually high interest rates, or (4) some combination of these or other factors. The evaluation of this information would depend upon many other factors which are beyond the scope of this example. The SCFP is the only required financial statement which reports the sources and uses of a company's cash or working capital.

In summary, the SCFP reports on changes in the liquidity of an enterprise, as well as its long-term financing and investing activities. Like all accounting information used by decision makers, the information on the SCFP must be used in combination with other information.[4]

INTERPRETATION OF THE SCFP (WORKING CAPITAL BASIS)

Exhibit 4–3 presents an SCFP, working capital basis, which is the basis used most often.[5]

The SCFP has two major captions: (1) Sources of working capital and (2) Uses of working capital.

---

[4] Empirical evidence on the usefulness of SCFP data is provided by G. K. Rakes and W. G. Shenkir, "User Responses to *APB Opinion No. 19*," *Journal of Accountancy,* September 1972, pp. 91–4; and G. Chandra, "A Study of the Consensus on Disclosure Among Public Accountants and Security Analysts," *The Accounting Review,* October 1974, pp. 733–42.

[5] Recent developments in financial reporting, such as the FASB Conceptual Framework Project (which spawned the *FASB Concepts Statements*), strongly suggest a move in the direction of the cash basis.

EXHIBIT 4–3: Statement of Changes in Financial Position

ALLSTAR CORPORATION
Statement of Changes in Financial Position—Working Capital Basis
For the Year Ended December 31, 19M

Sources of working capital (inflow of funds):		
From operations:		
Income before extraordinary items (accrual basis)	$ 80,000	
Add (deduct) adjustments to convert income to working capital basis:		
Depreciation expense	30,000	
Working capital inflow from continuing operations		$110,000
From extraordinary item, net of income tax		20,000
From other sources:		
Sale and issuance of preferred stock	45,000	
Sale of operational assets	25,000	
Total working capital inflow from other sources		70,000
Total working capital inflow from all sources		200,000
Uses of working capital (outflow of funds):		
Purchase of operational assets	100,000	
Purchase of long-term investment in stock of XYZ Corporation	50,000	
Declaration and payment of cash dividends	40,000	
Payment of long-term note payable	30,000	
Total working capital used for all purposes		220,000
Increase (decrease) in working capital during the period		$(20,000)
Financing and investing activities not affecting working capital:		
Common stock issued to retire convertible bonds payable (Note A)		$140,000

Notes to financial statements:

Note A. All of the outstanding 12 percent convertible bonds payable were tendered by bondholders to the company for conversion to nopar common stock in accordance with the conversion provision in the bond indenture. Conversion required the issuance of 10,000 shares of nopar common stock; no cash was paid or received incidental to the conversion.

Changes in working capital accounts:

Account	Balance 12/31/19M	Balance 12/31/19L	Increase (Decrease) in Working Capital
Current assets:			
Cash	$ 23,000	$ 29,000	$ (6,000)
Accounts receivable (net)	67,000	42,000	25,000
Inventories	117,000	81,000	36,000
Prepaid expenses	6,000	8,000	(2,000)
Total current assets	213,000	160,000	53,000
Current liabilities:			
Short-term notes payable	76,000	29,000	(47,000)
Accounts payable	75,000	47,000	(28,000)
Income tax payable	4,000	6,000	2,000
Total current liabilities	155,000	82,000	(73,000)
Working capital	$ 58,000	$ 78,000	$(20,000)

It begins with **sources** which result from (1) continuing operations, (2) extraordinary items, and (3) other sources.

The first source shown in Exhibit 4–3 is inflow from continuing operations, exclusive of extraordinary items (i.e., $110,000). This **source** begins with income (or loss) before extraordinary items. In accrual accounting, income from continuing operations usually includes items which did not use (or provide) working capital (or cash), such as depreciation and amortization expenses. Therefore, such items must be added back to (or deducted from) income from continuing operations. The reason for these adjustments (e.g., depreciation expense of $30,000 in Exhibit 4–3) can be seen by observing that the entry in the accounts to record depreciation expense does not involve a working capital account (i.e., a current asset or current liability), as shown below:

Depreciation expense	30,000	
Accumulated depreciation		30,000

Depreciation Expense is an **expense** account, and Accumulated Depreciation is a contra account to an **operational** (i.e., fixed) asset account; neither is a working capital account. For this reason, Exhibit 4–3 shows depreciation expense as an "adjustment to convert income to a working capital basis." Other nonworking capital expenses include amortization expense and income tax expense associated with long-term deferred income tax (see Chapter 10). In Exhibit 4–3, the sum of depreciation expense and income before extraordinary items is $110,000, which is captioned "Working capital inflow from continuing operations" (exclusive of extraordinary items). Exhibit 4–3 indicates a second source of working capital—the extraordinary item. This transaction increased working capital by $20,000. Therefore, working capital generated by operations, including extraordinary items was $130,000.

The third category of working capital sources in Exhibit 4–3, "other sources," reports two items which increased working capital by $70,000. Thus, "Total working capital inflow from all sources" reported by Allstar Corporation was $200,000.

In Exhibit 4–3, under "Uses of working capital," four typical uses are listed, for a "Total working capital used for all purposes" of $220,000. None of these uses was directly related to the income statement because all sources and uses of working capital related to the **income statement** were reported "From operations" in the two subtotals, "Working capital inflow from continuing operations" ($110,000) and "extraordinary items" ($20,000). Total working capital inflow ($200,000) minus total working capital outflow ($220,000) results in a decrease in working capital during the period of $20,000.

The SCFP must incorporate the **all-resources concept.** This concept means that **all** significant financing and investing activities must be reported in the SCFP regardless of whether working capital (or cash) was directly affected. Thus, **direct exchanges** (i.e., noncash trades) must be reported even though the exchange did not directly affect working capital (or cash). Examples of direct exchanges are the acquisition of property and paying for it by issuing capital stock, the conversion of bonds payable to common stock, and the trade-in of one asset, such as an old machine, for a new machine. Nevertheless, transactions of this type must be included as if working capital (or cash) equal to the market value actually flowed in and out. This type of transaction is illustrated in the final section of Exhibit 4–3 under the caption, "Financing and investing activities not affecting working capital." The transaction was an issuance of common stock to retire bonds payable ($140,000), as explained in Note A of the exhibit. This exchange did not directly affect working capital. In Exhibit 4–3, it was assumed that at the start of the period the company had outstanding 12 percent convertible bonds payable with a maturity amount of $140,000. The bonds carried a conversion agreement which permitted the bondholders to turn them in during 19M and receive, in return, a specified number of shares of the nopar common stock of the company. During 19M, all of the bondholders tendered their bonds and received the requisite number of shares of stock. Thus, debt was retired by the issuance of common stock (a direct exchange of noncash items). Although no working capital flowed in or out of Allstar Corporation, the transaction was reported on the SCFP as if cash had been received for the stock and immediately disbursed to retire the bonds. Therefore, the noncash exchange is reported as a financing activity (i.e., issuance of the common stock) and an investing activity (i.e., retirement of the bonds payable), which did not affect working capital. This was supplemented with an explanatory note to assure full disclosure. Without the all-resources requirement, direct exchanges such as this one would not be reported in the SCFP thereby omitting significant financing and investing activities.

The **sources** of working capital in Exhibit 4–3 can be viewed as **financing** activities. To illustrate, continuing and extraordinary items of Allstar Corporation financed $130,000 of working capital, the sale of preferred stock financed $45,000, and so on. The **uses** of working capital can be viewed as **investing** activities. To illustrate, the purchase of operational assets and long-term investment in stock of XYZ Corporation are investing activities in the sense that the entity invested working capital to acquire them.

An actual SCFP, prepared on the **cash basis,** is shown in the Appendix following Chapter 24. Chapter 23 discusses the preparation and interpretation of the SCFP on both the cash and working capital bases.

ADDITIONAL REPORTING ISSUES

We will conclude the review of information processing and the financial statements with a brief discussion of additional reporting issues that often are encountered.

Terminology

As in all professions, accounting has developed its own jargon. Often the same word or phrase is used to mean different things. In preparing reports, accountants should refrain from using vague terminology. Captions and titles should be selected carefully because the statements will be used by a wide range of decision makers. From time to time, pronouncements such as the *ARBs, APB Opinions,* and *FASB Statements* specifically recommend improved terminology. For example, *FASB Concepts Statement 3* created a new term, **comprehensive income,** which encompasses a wider range of revenues, expenses, gains, and losses than is contemplated by the conventional net income.

An example of careless terminology is the use of the term **reserve** to refer to *(a)* a contra asset account, such as "reserve for depreciation" for accumulated depreciation; *(b)* an estimated liability, such as "reserve for warranties" for estimated warranty liability; and *(c)* an appropriation of retained earnings, such as "reserve for future expansion." *Accounting Terminology Bulletin No. 1* recommended that the term be restricted to the last usage.

Similarly, the terminology bulletin recommended use of the terms **retained earnings** instead of earned surplus and **net income** instead of net profit. *APB Opinion 19* recommended use of the title, **statement of changes in financial position (SCFP),** instead of the vague title, funds flow statement. Confusion of the terms **cost** and **expense,** discussed in Chapter 3, is another example of careless terminology. Throughout this textbook we discuss preferred terminology because the effectiveness of communication depends largely upon the terminology used.

Comparative Statements

To evaluate the financial potentials of an enterprise, one should assemble comparable financial information for two or more periods, because for prediction purposes, trends are much more revealing than information for only one period. In recognition of this fact, *ARB 43* states:

> The presentation of comparative financial statements in annual and other reports enhances the usefulness of such reports and brings out more clearly the nature and trends of current changes affecting the enterprise. Such presentation emphasizes the fact that statements for a series of periods are far more significant than those for a single period and that the accounts for one period are but an installment of what is essentially a continuous history.[6]

Comparative statements for the current and prior year are considered essential to meet the full-disclosure requirement. In 1980, the SEC began requiring three-year comparative statements, in lieu of the customary two-year statements, for "listed" companies. The actual statements shown in the Appendix following Chapter 24 display comparative amounts. In addition to comparative statements, many companies present a special tabulation of selected financial items for time spans of 5 to 20 or more years. Items often included are total revenues, income before extraordinary items, net income, depreciation expense, EPS, dividends, total assets, total owners' equity, and average number of shares of common stock outstanding. These long-term summaries are particularly useful in trend analysis.

Subsequent Events

Certain important events or transactions which occur **subsequent** to the balance sheet date but **prior** to the actual issuance of the financial statements (ordinarily one to four months later) and which have a material effect on the financial statements are called **subsequent events.** Subsequent events must be reported because they involve information that could influence the statement users' interpretation and evaluation of the potentials of the enterprise. Auditing standards define these events and specify that they must be either in the (1) tabular portion of the statements or (2) notes to the statements, depending upon their nature.

The effects of subsequent events should be re-

---

[6] AICPA, *Accounting Research Bulletin No. 43,* "Restatement and Revision of Accounting Research Bulletins" (New York, 1953), chap. 2, sec. A.

ported in the **tabular portion of the statements,** if they *(a)* provide additional evidence about conditions **that existed at balance sheet date,** *(b)* affect estimates inherent in the process of preparing the financial statements, and *(c)* require adjustments to the financial statements resulting from the estimates. An example would be a material loss on an uncollectible receivable because of a customer's deteriorating financial condition. The deteriorating financial condition presumably was occurring at balance sheet date, but recent information made it more evident.

Subsequent events should be **disclosed in the notes** to the statements if they *(a)* result from conditions that did not exist at balance sheet date, *(b)* arose subsequent to the balance sheet date, and *(c)* do not merit adjustment to the current financial statements. Examples listed in *Codification of Statements on Auditing Standards* AU Sec. 560.06, are sale of a bond or capital stock issue, litigation based on an event subsequent to the balance sheet date, inventory losses due to casualty, and losses caused by a condition that arose subsequent to balance sheet date (such as a fire or flood). The fire or flood did not "exist" at the balance sheet date.

This topic is considered in depth in auditing texts and courses.

Full Disclosure

Full disclosure is a particularly important aspect of the **reporting principle** discussed in Part B of Chapter 1. Full disclosure requires complete reporting of all significant information relating to the economic affairs of the enterprise so that the financial statements will not be misleading. Full disclosure requires, in addition to the information reported in the tabular portions of the financial statements, additional information in notes to the financial statements to identify the accounting methods used by the company and other details which cannot be communicated effectively in the tabular portions of the statements. Examples are pension plans, maturity dates on payables and receivables, certain restrictions relating to long-term debt, and the effects of subsequent events and contingencies (e.g., lawsuits pending). A particular note may refer to a single amount on one of the three basic statements or to several amounts on two or more of them, or to a situation that is not directly reflected on any of them. The guideline for deciding when a note is required, other than when specifically required, is largely judgmental within the framework of complete reporting.

A number of *APB Opinions* and *FASB Statements* specifically require certain disclosures in the notes to the financial statements. For example, *APB Opinion No. 22,* "Disclosure of Accounting Policies," specifically requires that information about **important** accounting policies adopted by the enterprise, including their identification and description, must be disclosed "in a separate *Summary of Significant Accounting Policies* preceding the notes to the financial statements or as the initial note." At a minimum, the summary should include policies that involve *(a)* a selection from existing acceptable alternatives, *(b)* principles and methods peculiar to the industry, and *(c)* unusual or innovative applications of GAAP.

Supporting schedules often are incorporated into the notes. Supporting schedules are typical for large and complex companies, and in situations where a particular item involves a number of complex changes during the period. We mentioned in Chapter 3 that when there have been numerous changes in owners' equity, the statement of retained earnings often is replaced with a more comprehensive schedule. For example, the 1981 financial statements of The Quaker Oats Company, given in the Appendix following Chapter 24 presents "Consolidated Statements of Common Shareholders' Equity."

Parenthetical notes are often used in the tabular portions of the financial statements to disclose information such as the method of inventory costing and valuation, for example, Inventory (**FIFO;** applied on LCM basis). **Contra items,** such as accumulated depreciation and allowance for doubtful accounts, are reported as separate line deductions or parenthetically.

The actual statements presented in the Appendix following Chapter 24 include typical disclosures.

Auditors' Report

The auditors' report also is called the accountants' report and the independent accountants' report. It usually follows the financial statements and the notes. The independent auditors' primary function is to express the **auditor's professional opinion** on the financial statements. Although the auditors have sole responsibility for their opinion expressed in the auditors' report, the primary responsibility for the statements (including the supporting notes) rests with the management of the enterprise. The statements are those of the management; the auditors affirm or disaffirm them in the **opinion.**

The auditors' report includes (1) a **scope** paragraph and (2) an **opinion** paragraph. The standard format of the auditors' report is as follows:

(Scope paragraph)

We have examined the balance sheet of X Company as of (at) December 31, 19xx, and the related statements of income, retained earnings and changes in financial position for the year then ended. Our examination was made in accordance with generally accepted auditing standards and, accordingly, included such tests of the accounting records and such other auditing procedures as we considered necessary in the circumstances.

(Opinion paragraph)

In our opinion, the financial statements referred to above present fairly the financial position of X Company as of (at) December 31, 19xx, and the results of its operations and the changes in its financial position for the year then ended, in conformity with generally accepted accounting principles applied on a basis consistent with that of the preceding year.[7]

Signed, CPAs

Eight key elements in the auditors' report have special significance:[8]

1. Date.
2. Salutation.
3. Identification of the statements examined.
4. Statement of scope of the examination.
5. Opinion introduction.
6. Reference to fair presentation in conformity with generally accepted accounting principles.
7. Reference to consistency.
8. Signature of the CPAs.

Upon completion of the audit, the auditors are required to draft the opinion paragraph to communicate their professional opinion by giving one of the following types of opinions on the financial statements.

1. Unqualified opinion—An unqualified opinion is given when the CPA has formed the opinion that the statements (1) "present fairly" results of operations, financial position, and changes in financial position; (2) conform to GAAP, applied on a consistent basis; and (3) meet full-disclosure requirements so that the statements are not misleading.
2. Qualified opinion—A qualified opinion is given when the requirements for an unqualified opinion are not met and the auditor takes exception to the client's financial statements. A qualified opinion must clearly explain the reason for the "exception" and its effect on the financial statements.
3. Adverse opinion—An adverse opinion is given when the financial statements do not "fairly present" (see above). Also, material exceptions require an adverse opinion on the statements as a whole.
4. Disclaimer of opinion—When the auditors have not been able to obtain sufficient competent evidential matter to form an opinion, auditors must state they are unable to express an opinion (i.e., they issue a disclaimer). Auditors must explain the reasons for not giving an opinion.

A comprehensive discussion of the responsibilities of independent auditors is beyond the scope of this book. The above summary is provided to describe auditors' representations (i.e., professional opinion) on the extent to which the financial statements of a client company conform to GAAP.

The auditors' opinion is intended to assure that the financial statements conform to the qualitative characteristics of accounting information (i.e., are relevant, reliable, and comparable), as specified in *FASB Concepts Statement 2,* and otherwise conform to GAAP. The importance of this assurance can be seen in the context of the investment or lending decision of an outside party. For example, without assurance that the financial statements conform to GAAP, the investor or creditor could be misled by the omission of certain liabilities, the inclusion of nonexistent assets, or misclassification of current and long-term items. Likewise, the auditors' report provides assurance that the elements of the company's financial statements conform to the basic definitions of assets, liabilities, and so on, as given in *FASB Concepts Statement 3.* In conclusion, the auditors' report should be read in conjunction with the analysis of the financial statements.

[7] AICPA, *Codification of Statements on Auditing Standards* (New York, 1977), AU Sec. 509.07.

[8] AICPA, *The Auditor's Report—Its Meaning and Significance* (New York, 1967), p. 2.

QUESTIONS

PART A

1. What is a *balance sheet?* Why is it dated differently from an income statement and an SCFP?
2. Define *assets.*
3. Define *liabilities.*
4. Explain, in general terms, why the balance sheet is important to the decision maker.
5. Explain why the balance sheet does not report the current market value of a business.
6. Contrast the two balance sheet formats.
7. Define *current assets* and *current liabilities* emphasizing their interrelationship.
8. Define *working capital.* What is the current ratio?
9. Distinguish between short-term investments and the investments classified as investments and funds. Under what conditions could an investment be moved from current assets to investments and funds and vice versa?
10. What are operational assets? Distinguish between tangible and intangible operational assets.
11. Why is it often necessary to use the caption "Other assets"? Give two examples of items that might be reported under this classification.
12. Explain a *deferred charge* and contrast it with a prepaid expense.
13. Distinguish between *current* and *noncurrent* liabilities. Under what conditions would a noncurrent liability amount be reclassified as a current liability?
14. What is a *deferred credit?* Explain why this classification, reported on a balance sheet between liabilities and owners' equity, is difficult to defend conceptually.
15. What is *owners' equity?* What are the main components of owners' equity?
16. What is a *restriction* on retained earnings? How are restrictions reported?

PART B

17. What is the purpose of the SCFP? What is meant by the all-resources concept?
18. Distinguish between SCFP prepared on *(a)* a cash equivalent basis and *(b)* a working capital basis.
19. Explain the position of the accounting profession with respect to use of the terms *reserves, surplus,* and *net profit.* Why is careful attention to terminology important in financial statements?
20. What are comparative statements? Why are they important?
21. What is meant by subsequent events? Why are they reported? How are they reported?
22. In general, why are notes in the financial statements important? How does the accountant determine when a note should be included?
23. What is the auditors' report? Basically, what does it include? Why is it especially important to the statement user?
24. Are the financial statements the representations of the management of the enterprise, the independent accountant, or both? Explain.

DECISION CASE 4–1

R. Applewhite & Sons is a family corporation operating a chain of seven retail clothing stores in the Southwest. The total owners' equity of $5 million (all shares are outstanding) is owned by R. Applewhite (president and founder) and eight members of the Applewhite family. Except for accounts payable, modest amounts of short-term bank credit, and the usual short-term liabilities, the entire resources of the enterprise came from contributed capital and retained earnings. The general reputation of the company is excellent, and there have never been complaints about slowness in paying its liabilities. The family now has an opportunity to undertake a profitable expansion from 7 to 10 stores and estimates that upward of $2.5 million will be required for the purpose. It will be necessary to borrow this sum, and the issuance of five- to eight-year mortgage notes is contemplated.

Because the business is closely held and has never borrowed to an extent that made issuance of financial statements to outsiders necessary, the only persons who have seen the corporation's statements are members of the family, a few top employees, and some governmental officials, chiefly tax agents. When R. Applewhite was told by a prospective lender that detailed financial statements for the past five years and audited statements for the most recent year as a basis for considering the loan would have to be provided, Applewhite's initial reaction was to "hit the ceiling." After consideration, however, Applewhite became willing to have the audit made and to release balance sheets as of the end of the most recent five years. Applewhite was, as yet, unwilling to release statements of income and changes in financial position, and a majority of the other owners agreed with this stand.

Required:

1. If these five balance sheets are quite detailed, what can prospective lenders ascertain from them?
2. In your opinion would the five balance sheets give enough information to warrant granting a $2.5 million secured intermediate-term loan? Explain the basis for your response.
3. If you were the lending officer of the prospective creditor and sought a compromise in the form of getting some added financial facts without receiving the other statements, what added information would be most useful to you?

EXERCISES: EXERCISES 4–1 to 4–8

PART A

Exercise 4–1

Below left is a list of several different items from a typical balance sheet for a corporation. Below right is a list of brief statements of the valuations usually reported on the balance sheet for the different items.

Required:
Use the code letters to the right to indicate, for each balance sheet item listed, the *usual* valuation reported on the balance sheet. Comment on any doubtful items. Some code letters may be used more than once or not at all.

Balance Sheet Items

1.___Merchandise inventory.
2.___Short-term investments.
3.___Accounts receivable (trade).
4.___Long-term investment in bonds of another company (purchased at a discount).
5.___Plant site (in use).
6.___Plant and equipment (in use).
7.___Patent (in use).
8.___Accounts payable (trade).
9.___Bonds payable (sold at a premium).
10.___Common stock (par $10 per share).
11.___Contributed capital in excess of par.
12.___Retained earnings.
13.___Land (future plant site).
14.___Idle plant (awaiting disposal).
15.___Natural resource.

Valuations Usually Reported

a. Amount payable when due (usually no interest because short-term).
b. LCM.
c. Original cost when acquired.
d. Market value at date of the balance sheet whether it is above or below cost.
e. Original cost less accumulated amortization over estimated economic life.
f. Par value of the issued shares.
g. Face amount of the obligation plus unamortized premium.
h. Realizable value expected.
i. Principal of the asset less unamortized discount.
j. Cost when acquired less accumulated depreciation.
k. Accumulated income less accumulated losses and dividends.
l. Excess of issue price over par or stated value.
m. No valuation reported (explain).
n. Expected net disposal proceeds.
o. Cost less accumulated depletion.
p. None of the above (when this response is used, explain the valuation usually used).

Exercise 4–2

A typical balance sheet has the following captions:

A. Current assets.
B. Investments and funds.
C. Operational assets (land, buildings, and equipment).
D. Intangible assets.
E. Other assets.
F. Deferred charges.
G. Current liabilities.
H. Long-term liabilities.
I. Capital stock.
J. Additional contributed capital.
K. Retained earnings.

Indicate by use of the above letters (use capitals and print) how each of the following items would be classified. When an item is a contra amount (i.e., a deduction) in a caption, place a minus before the lettered response.

1. Accumulated depreciation.
2. Bonds payable (due in 10 years).
3. Accounts payable (trade).
4. Investment in stock of X Company (long term).
5. Plant site (in use).
6. Restriction on retained earnings.
7. Office supplies inventory.
8. Loan to company president (collection not expected for two years).
9. Accumulated income less accumulated dividends.
10. Bond discount unamortized (on bonds payable).
11. Bond sinking fund (to retire long-term bonds).
12. Prepaid insurance.
13. Accounts receivable (trade).
14. Short-term investment.
15. Allowance for doubtful accounts.
16. Building (in use).
17. Common stock (par $10).
18. Interest revenue earned but not collected.
19. Patent.
20. Land (speculative).

Exercise 4–3

Typical balance sheet captions are listed in Exercise 4–2. Indicate, by use of the letters given there (use capitals and print), how each of the following items would be classified. When an item is a contra amount (i.e., a deduction) in a caption, place a minus before the lettered response.

1. Bonds payable (long term).
2. Premium unamortized (on bonds payable).
3. Short-term investments.
4. Cash dividends payable (within six months).
5. Rent revenue collected in advance.
6. Accumulated depreciation.
7. Premium on common stock issued.
8. Idle plant held for final disposal.
9. Deferred costs being amortized over five years.
10. Inventory of supplies.
11. Preferred stock.
12. Discount unamortized on long-term investment in bonds of another company.
13. Installment payment due in six months on long-term note payable.
14. Accrued interest on note payable.
15. Rent revenue receivable.
16. Allowance for doubtful accounts.
17. Investment in bonds of another company (long term).
18. Undeposited cash (for making change).
19. Accounts receivable (trade).
20. Deficit.

Exercise 4–4

The following trial balance was prepared by Aging, Incorporated, as of December 31, 1982. The adjusting entries for 1982 have been made except for any specifically noted below.

Cash	$ 9,000	
Accounts receivable	15,000	
Inventories	12,000	
Equipment	22,400	
Land	6,400	
Building	7,600	
Deferred charges	1,100	
Accounts payable		$ 5,500
Note payable, 18%		8,000
Capital stock (par $10)		38,500
Earned surplus		21,500
	$73,500	$73,500

You ascertain that certain errors and omissions are reflected in the above, including the following:

1. The $15,000 balance in accounts receivable represents the entire amount owed to the company; of this sum, $12,400 is from trade customers, and 5% of that amount is estimated to be uncollectible. The remaining sum owed to the company represents a long-term advance to its president.
2. Inventories include $1,000 of goods incorrectly inventoried at double their cost (i.e., reported at $2,000). No correction has been recorded. Office supplies on hand of $500 are also included in the balance of inventories.
3. When the equipment and building were purchased new in January 1, 1977, they had, respectively, estimated lives of 10 and 25 years. They have been depreciated by the straight-line method on the assumption of zero residual values, and depreciation has been credited directly to the asset accounts.
4. The balance of the Land account includes a $1,000 payment made as a deposit of earnest money on the purchase of an adjoining tract. The option to buy it has not yet been exercised and probably will not be exercised during the coming year.
5. The interest-bearing note matures March 31, 1983, having been drawn July 1, 1982. Interest on it has been ignored.
6. Common stock shares outstanding, 2,500.

Required:
Prepare a correct classified balance sheet using preferred terminology. Use whichever format is specified by your instructor; if not specified, use the format you prefer. Show computation of retained earnings reported on the balance sheet.

Exercise 4–5

Morrow Corporation is preparing the balance sheet at December 31, 19J. The following items are at issue:

a. Note payable, long-term, $80,000. This note will be paid in installments. The first installment of $10,000 will be paid August 1, 19K.

b. Bonds payable, 12%, $200,000; at December 31, 19J, unamortized premium amounted to $6,000.

c. Bond sinking fund, $40,000; this fund is being accumulated to retire the bonds at maturity. There is a restriction on retained earnings required by the bond indenture equal to the balance in the bond sinking fund.

d. Rent revenue collected in advance for the first quarter of 19K, $6,000.

e. After the balance sheet date, but prior to issuance of the 19J balance sheet, one third of the merchandise inventory was destroyed by flood (date, January 13, 19K); estimated loss, $150,000.

Required:
Show, by illustration, how each of these items should be reported on the December 31, 19J, balance sheet.

Exercise 4–6

Based upon the following information, prepare the stockholders' equity section of the balance sheet for Kay Corporation at December 31, 19C.

Retained earnings, unappropriated	$ 80,000
Preferred stock, par $15, authorized 20,000 shares	225,000
Restriction on retained earnings as required by a special contract	60,000
Cash received above par of preferred stock	15,000
Common stock, nopar, 60,000 shares issued (100,000 shares authorized)	200,000

Exercise 4–7

The records of Turner Corporation provided the following selected data on December 31, 19B:

Preferred stock, par $10, 100,000 shares authorized	$300,000
Common stock, nopar 200,000 shares authorized of which 100,000 are outstanding	500,000
Premium on preferred stock	80,000
Earned surplus (free) at start of year	40,000
Reserves at end of 19B for:	
Bad debts	11,000
Depreciation	90,000
Patent amortization	6,000
Warranty obligations	14,000
Income tax obligations	31,000
Future plant expansion	100,000
Retirement of bonds payable (required by the bond indenture)	50,000
Net income for 19B	45,000
Dividends declared and paid in 19B	20,000
Bond sinking fund	50,000

Required:

1. Prepare the stockholders' equity section of the balance sheet using preferred terminology and format.
2. If any of the above items are omitted from the stockholders' equity section, explain how they should be reported.

Exercise 4–8

The following adjusted trial balance was prepared by Perry Corporation at December 31, 19J:

Debits

Cost of goods sold	$230,000
D & A expenses (including interest)	130,000
Income tax expense	41,500
Cash	39,000
Short-term investments	12,000
Accounts receivable	70,000
Merchandise inventory*	72,000
Office supplies inventory	2,000
Investment in bonds of X Corp. (long term), cost (market value, $35,000)	33,000
Land (plant site in use)	10,000
Plant and equipment	120,000
Franchise (less amortization)	8,000
Rearrangement costs†	15,000
Idle equipment held for disposal	7,500
Dividends declared and paid during 19J	40,000
	$830,000

Credits

Sales revenue	$480,000
Accum. depr., plant and equip.	40,000
Accounts payable	50,000
Income taxes payable	11,000
Bonds payable	50,000
Allowance for doubtful accounts	3,000
Premium on bonds payable (unamortized)	1,000
Common stock, par $10 (authorized 50,000 shares)	150,000
Excess of issue price over par of common stock	18,000
Retained earnings, 1/1/19J	27,000
	$830,000

* Perpetual inventory system.

† Amortization period three years; this is the unamortized balance.

Required:

1. Prepare a single-step income statement.
2. Prepare a classified balance sheet.

PART B: EXERCISES 4–9 to 4–13

Exercise 4–9

Following are listed, in scrambled order, the major and minor captions for a balance sheet and an SCFP (cash equivalent basis). Terminology given in the chapter is used.

1. Total assets.
2. Cash from other sources.
3. Contributed capital.
4. Add (deduct) adjustments to revenue to derive cash basis.
5. Retained earnings.
6. Expenses (accrual basis).
7. Current liabilities.
8. From extraordinary items (net of tax).
9. Uses of cash.
10. Unrealized capital.
11. Owners' equity.
12. Total cash expended for all purposes.
13. Operational assets—tangible.
14. Cash generated from revenues.
15. Total cash generated from other sources.
16. Long-term liabilities.
17. Assets.
18. Current assets.
19. Capital stock.
20. Sources of cash (inflows).
21. Other assets.
22. From operations (cash inflow).
23. Revenues (accrual basis).
24. Contributed capital in excess of par.
25. Deferred charges.
26. Total cash generated by operations.
27. Total cash generated from all sources.
28. Liabilities.
29. Investments and funds.
30. Net increase (decrease) in cash.
31. Operational assets—intangible.
32. Cash disbursed for expenses.
33. Total liabilities.
34. Total liabilities and owners' equity.
35. Total owners' equity.
36. Add (deduct) adjustments to expenses to derive cash basis.

Required:
Set up two captions: *(a)* Balance Sheet and *(b)* SCFP. For each caption, list the numbers given above in the order that they normally would be reported on the statements (do not renumber). Example:

a. Balance Sheet: 17, 18, and so on.
b. SCFP: 20, 22, and so on.

Comment on any doubtful items.

Exercise 4–10

Indicate the best answer for each of the following (explain any qualifications):

1. Which of the following is not a current asset?
   a. Office supplies inventory.
   b. Short-term investment.
   c. Petty cash (undeposited cash).
   d. Cash surrender value of life insurance policies.
2. The distinction between current and noncurrent assets and liabilities is based primarily upon —
   a. One year; no exceptions.
   b. One year or operating cycle, whichever is shorter.
   c. One year or operating cycle, whichever is longer.
   d. Operating cycle; no exceptions.
3. Under GAAP, unexpired insurance is a —
   a. Noncurrent asset.
   b. Deferred charge.
   c. Prepaid expense.
   d. Short-term investment.
4. Working capital means—
   a. Excess of current assets over current liabilities.
   b. Current assets.
   c. Capital contributed by stockholders.
   d. Capital contributed by stockholders plus retained earnings.
5. Which of the following is not a current liability?
   a. Accrued interest on notes payable.
   b. Accrued interest on bonds payable.
   c. Rent revenue collected in advance.
   d. Premium on bonds payable (unamortized).
6. A deficit is synonymous with—
   a. A net loss for the current period.
   b. A cash overdraft at the bank.
   c. Negative working capital at the end of the period.
   d. A debit balance in retained earnings at the end of the period.
7. A balance sheet is an expression of the model—
   a. Assets = Liabilities + Owners' equity.
   b. Assets = Liabilities − Owners' equity.
   c. Assets + Liabilities = Owners' equity.
   d. Working capital + Operational assets − Long-term liabilities = Contributed capital.
8. Acceptable usage of the term *reserve* is reflected by—
   a. Deduction from an asset to reflect accumulated depreciation.
   b. Description of a known liability for which the amount is estimated.
   c. Restriction on retained earnings.
   d. Deduction on the income statement for an expected loss.
9. Which terminology essentially is synonymous with "balance sheet"?
   a. Operating statement.
   b. SCFP.

c. Statement of financial value of the business.
d. Statement of resources, obligations, and residual equity.

10. The "operating cycle concept"—
a. Causes the distinction between current and noncurrent items to depend upon whether they will affect cash within one year.
b. Permits some assets to be classed as current even though they are more than one year removed from becoming cash.
c. Is becoming obsolete.
d. Affects the income statement but not the balance sheet.

Exercise 4–11

The following balance sheet has come to your attention:

EASY CORPORATION
Balance Sheet Statement
For Year Ended December 31, 19C

Assets			
Liquid assets:			
Cash		$ 31,000	
Receivables	$ 29,000		
Less: Reserve for bad debts	700	28,300	
Inventories		42,000	
			$101,300
Investments and funds:			
Petty cash fund		200	
Sinking fund		70,000	
			70,200
Permanent assets:			
Land and building	140,000		
Less: Reserve for depreciation	9,000	131,000	
Equipment	84,000		
Less: Reserve for depreciation	29,000	55,000	
			186,000
Deferred charges:			
Prepaid expenses		2,700	
Accrued sinking fund income (interest)		600	
			3,300
Total			$360,800
Obligations			
Short term:			
Accrued interest on mortgage payable		$ 700	
Accounts payable		36,500	
Reserve for income taxes	$ 13,000		
Less: U.S. government bonds	8,000	5,000	
			$ 42,200
Long term:			
Mortgage payable*			74,000
Net Worth			
Capital stock		150,000	
Earned surplus		52,400	
Reserve for contingencies		66,400	
		268,800	
Less: Treasury stock		24,200	
			244,600
Total			$360,800

* The mortgage payable matures 4/18/19D, and is funded by the sinking fund.

Required:
Constructively criticize the above balance sheet. Set up your responses in the following format:

Specific Criticism (list)	Explanation of Criticism	Recommended Treatment
1.		
Etc.		

Exercise 4–12

The ledger of Wicker Manufacturing Company reflects obsolete terminology, but you find its books have been, on the whole, accurately kept. After the most recent closing of the books at December 31, 19B, the following accounts were submitted to you for the preparation of a balance sheet:

Accounts payable	$33,200
Accounts receivable	9,500
Accrued expenses (credit)	800
Bonds payable, 14%	25,000
Capital stock ($100 par)	70,000
Cash	13,000
Earned surplus	xx,xxx
Factory equipment	31,200
Finished goods	12,100
Investments	13,000
Office equipment	9,500
Raw materials	9,600
Reserve for bad debts	500
Reserve for depreciation	9,000
Rent paid in advance (a debit)	3,000
Sinking fund	7,835
Land	15,000
Note receivable	6,600
Work in process	18,300

You ascertain that two thirds of the depreciation relates to factory and one third to office equipment. Of the balance in the Investments account, $4,000 will be converted to cash during the coming year; the remainder represents a long-term investment. Rent paid in advance is for the next year. The land was acquired as a future plant site. The note receivable was signed by the company president on October 1, 19B, and is due in 19D when the principal amount ($6,600) plus 16% interest per annum will be paid to the company. The sinking fund is being accumulated to retire the bonds at maturity.

Required:

1. Prepare a classified balance sheet using preferred terminology.
2. Compute *(a)* the amount of working capital and *(b)* the current ratio.

Exercise 4–13

The following statement has been prepared by Allen Corporation:

ALLEN CORPORATION
Statement of Changes in Financial Position
For the Year Ended December 31, 19B

Sources of funds:		
From operations:		
Net income before EO items*	$ 89,000	
Add (deduct):		
Depreciation expense	114,000	
Amortization of patent	9,000	
Funds generated by continuing operations, excluding EO items		$212,000
From EO item net of income tax (EO loss was $1,000)		17,000
Funds generated by continuing operations and EO items		229,000
From other sources:		
Sale of machinery	12,000	
Issuance of long-term note payable	25,000	
Total funds inflow from other sources		37,000
Total funds inflow from all sources		266,000
Uses of funds:		
Retirement of mortgage note	80,000	
Cash dividends	32,000	
Purchase of long-term investment in stock	23,000	
Purchase of machinery	40,000	
Total funds used for all purposes		175,000
Increase in working capital during the year		$ 91,000
Financing and investing activities not affecting working capital:		
Issuance of common stock for future plant site (Note A)		$195,000

* "Extraordinary" abbreviated "EO" in this statement.

Required:

1. How are funds measured in this statement? Explain.
2. Explain why depreciation expense and amortization of patent were added to net income before extraordinary (EO) items.
3. What was the amount of the EO item? Was it a gain or loss? How much working capital was generated by the transaction that resulted in the EO item? How can the two amounts differ?
4. What was net income for the year? How much did working capital increase from continuing operations? How did management generate more working capital from continuing operations than from income before EO items?
5. Write Note A with respect to the future plant site. Which part of this transaction is the financing activity? Which is the investing activity?
6. Some changes in terminology are needed. Identify them and suggest preferable terminology.

PROBLEMS

PART A: PROBLEMS 4–1 to 4–9

Problem 4–1

Below left is a list of typical items from a balance sheet for a corporation. Below right is a list of brief statements of *valuations* usually reported on a balance sheet for different items.

Required:

Use the code letters to the right to indicate, for each balance sheet item listed, the *usual* valuation reported on the balance sheet. Provide explanatory comments for each doubtful item. Some code letters may be used more than once or not at all.

Balance Sheet Items	Valuations Usually Reported
1.___Cash.	*a.* LCM.
2.___Short-term investments.	*b.* Face amount collectible at maturity.
3.___Accounts receivable (trade).	*c.* Total amount paid in by stockholders when issued.
4.___Notes receivable (short term).	*d.* Cost to acquire the asset.
5.___Merchandise inventory.	*e.* Excess of issue price over par value of stock.
6.___Prepaid expenses (such as prepaid insurance).	*f.* Accumulated income less accumulated losses and dividends.
7.___Long-term investment in bonds of another company (purchased at a premium).	*g.* Cost to acquire, less amortization to date.
8.___Long-term investment in stock of another company (less than 20% of the outstanding shares).	*h.* Estimated net realizable value (amount billed less estimated loss due to uncollectibility).
9.___Plant site (in use).	*i.* Par value of shares issued.
10.___Plant equipment (in use).	*j.* Cost less expired or used portion.
11.___Patent (used in operations).	*k.* Cost at date of investment.
12.___Deferred charge.	*l.* Replacement cost.
13.___Accounts payable (trade).	*m.* Face amount plus unamortized premium.
14.___Income taxes payable.	*n.* Current market value.
15.___Notes payable (short-term).	*o.* Amount payable when due (short term).
16.___Bonds payable (sold at a discount).	*p.* Face amount of the obligation less unamortized discount.
17.___Common stock (nopar).	*q.* Cost to acquire less accumulated depreciation.
18.___Preferred stock (par $10 per share).	*r.* Market value at the date of the balance sheet whether it is above or below cost.
19.___Contributed capital in excess of par.	*s.* No valuation reported (explain).
20.___Retained earnings.	*t.* None of the above (when this response is used, explain the valuation usually used).
21.___Land held for speculation.	
22.___Land held for a future plant site.	
23.___Damaged merchandise (goods held for sale).	

Problem 4–2

Typical balance sheet classifications are as follows:

A. Current assets.
B. Investments and funds.
C. Operational assets (tangible).
D. Intangible assets.
E. Other assets.
F. Deferred charges.
G. Current liabilities.
H. Long-term liabilities.
I. Capital stock.
J. Additional contributed capital.
K. Retained earnings.

Indicate by use of the above letters (use capitals and print), how each of the following items would be classified. When it is a contra item (i.e., a deduction) in a caption, place a minus sign before it. Comment on doubtful items, and if an item is not reported on the balance sheet, write *none*.

1. Cash.
2. Cash set aside to meet long-term purchase commitment.
3. Land (used as plant site).
4. Accrued salaries.
5. Investment in subsidiary (long term; not a controlling interest).
6. Inventory of damaged goods.
7. Idle plant being held for disposal.
8. Investment in bonds of another company.
9. Cash surrender value of life insurance policy.
10. Goodwill.
11. Natural resource (timber tract).
12. Allowance for doubtful accounts.
13. Stock subscriptions receivable (no plans to collect in near future).
14. Organization costs.
15. Discount on bonds payable.
16. Service revenue collected in advance.
17. Accrued interest payable.
18. Accumulated amortization on patent.
19. Prepaid rent expense.
20. Short-term investment (common stock).
21. Rent revenue collected but not earned.
22. Net of accumulated earnings and dividends.
23. Trade accounts payable.
24. Current maturity of long-term debt.
25. Land (held for speculation).
26. Notes payable (short term).
27. Special cash fund accumulated to build plant five years hence.
28. Bonds issued—to be paid within six months out of bond sinking fund.
29. Long-term investment in rental building.
30. Copyright.
31. Accumulated depreciation.
32. Deferred plant rearrangement costs.
33. Franchise.
34. Revenue earned but not collected.
35. Premium on bonds payable (unamortized).
36. Common stock (at par value).

37. Petty cash fund.
38. Deficit.
39. Contributed capital in excess of par.
40. Earnings retained in the business.

(AICPA adapted)

Problem 4–3

The adjusted trial balance for Tallow Corporation, and other related data, at December 31, 19C, are given below in scrambled order. Although the company uses obsolete terminology, the amounts are correct (but certain amounts may have to be reported separately). Assume perpetual inventory.

Additional data:

a. Market value of the short-term marketable securities is $46,000.

b. Merchandise inventory is based on FIFO, LCM.

c. Goodwill is being amortized (i.e., written off) over a 20-year period. The amortization for 19C has already been recorded (as a direct credit to the Goodwill account). Amortization of other intangibles is recorded in this manner except for the patent (a contra account is used for it).

d. Reserve for income taxes represents the estimated taxes payable at the end of 19C. Reserve for estimated damages was recorded by debiting Retained Earnings during 19B. The $10,000 was the estimated amount of damages that would have to be paid as a result of a damage suit against the company. At December 31, 19C, the appeal was still pending. The $10,000 is an appropriation, or restriction, placed on retained earnings by management.

e. Operating expenses as given include interest expense, and revenues include interest and investment revenues.

f. The cash advance from customer was for a special order that will not be completed and shipped until March 19D; the sales price has not been definitely established since it will be based upon cost (no revenue should be recognized for 19C).

Debit

Cash	$ 43,600
Land (used for building site)	29,000
Cost of goods sold	110,500
Short-term securities (stock of S Co.)	42,000
Goodwill (unamortized cost)	12,000
Merchandise inventory	30,000
Office supplies inventory	1,000
Patent	7,000
Operating expenses	55,000
Income tax expense	17,500
Bond discount (unamortized)	7,500
Prepaid insurance	900
Building (at cost)	150,000
Land (held for speculation)	31,000
Accrued interest receivable	300
Accounts receivable (trade)	17,700
Note receivable, 16% (long-term investment)	20,000
Cash surrender value of life insurance policy	9,000
Deferred store rearrangement costs (assume a deferred charge)	6,000
Dividends paid during 19C	15,000
Prior period adjustment (correction of error from prior year—no tax effect)	16,000
	$621,000

Credit

Reserve for bad debts	$ 1,100
Accounts payable (trade)	15,000
Revenues	230,000
Reserve for income taxes	7,500
Note payable (short term)	12,000
Common stock, par $10, authorized 50,000 shares	100,000
Reserve for depreciation, building	90,000
Retained earnings, 1/1/19C	38,000
Accrued wages	2,100
Reserve for estimated damages	10,000
Premium on common stock	15,000
Reserve for patent amortization	4,000
Cash advance from customer	3,000
Accrued property taxes	1,300
Note payable (long-term)	16,000
Rent revenue collected in advance	1,000
Bonds payable, 11% ($25,000 due 6/1/19D)	75,000
	$621,000

Required:

1. Prepare a single-step income statement and a separate statement of retained earnings.
2. Prepare a classified balance sheet including appropriate disclosures. Use preferred terminology and format.

Problem 4–4 (requirement 3 is based on Part B of the chapter)

The adjusted trial balance for Victor Manufacturing Corporation at December 31, 19J, is given below in scrambled order. Debits and credits are not indicated. All amounts are correct. Assume a normal balance situation in each account. Assume a perpetual inventory system.

Work in process inventory	$ 24,000
Accrued interest on notes payable	1,000
Accrued interest receivable	1,200
Accrued income on short-term investments	1,000
Common stock, nopar, authorized 20,000 shares, issued 10,000	150,000
Cash in bank	40,000
Trademarks (unamortized cost)	1,400
Land held for speculation	17,000
Supplies inventory	600
Goodwill (unamortized cost)	20,000

Raw material inventory	13,000
Bond sinking fund	10,000
Accrued property taxes	1,200
Accounts receivable (trade)	19,000
Accrued wages	2,300
Mortgage payable (due in three years)	10,000
Building	130,000
Prepaid rent expenses	1,700
Organization expenses (unamortized cost—assume deferred charge)	7,800
Deposits (cash collected from customers on sales orders to be delivered next quarter; no revenue yet recognized)	1,000
Long-term investment in bonds of K Corp. (at cost)	60,000
Patents (unamortized cost)	12,000
Reserve for bond sinking fund*	10,000
Reserve for depreciation, office equip.	1,600
Reserve for depreciation, building	5,000
Premium on preferred stock	8,000
Cash on hand for change	400
Preferred stock, par $100, authorized 5,000 shares, 10% noncumulative	60,000
Precollected rent income	900
Finished goods inventory	48,000
Note receivable (short term)	4,000
Bonds payable, 12%, (due in 6 years)	50,000
Accounts payable (trade)	17,000
Reserve for bad debts	1,400
Notes payable (short term)	7,000
Office equipment	25,000
Land (used as building site)	8,000
Short-term investments (at cost)	15,500
Retained earnings, unappropriated (1/1/19J)	13,200
Cash dividends declared and paid during 19J	20,000
Revenues during 19J	400,000
Cost of goods sold for 19J	210,000
Expenses for 19J (including income taxes)	90,000
Income taxes payable	40,000

* This is a restriction on retained earnings required by the bond indenture equal to the bond sinking fund which is being accumulated to retire the bonds.

Additional information:

Inventories are based on FIFO, LCM.

Required:

1. Prepare a single-step income statement; use preferred terminology. To compute EPS, deduct $6,000 of net income as an allocation to nonconvertible preferred stock.
2. Prepare a classified balance sheet; use preferred terminology and format. Comment on any items you consider doubtful with respect to classification.
3. Assume that between December 31, 19J, and issuance of the financial statements, a flood damaged the finished goods inventory in an amount estimated to be $20,000. Prepare an appropriate disclosure note to the balance sheet.

Problem 4–5

The following data have been abstracted from the financial statements of Theo's, Inc., a merchandising company.

Balance Sheet Data	12/31/19A	12/31/19B
Trade accounts receivable—net	$ 84,000	$ 78,000
Inventory	150,000	140,000
Payables for merchandise (credit)	(95,000)	(98,000)

Total sales for 19B were $1.2 million and for 19A were $1.1 million. Cash sales were 20% of total sales each year.

Cost of goods sold was $840,000 for 19B.

Variable general and administrative (G&A) expenses for 19B were $120,000. They have varied in proportion to sales and have been paid 50% in the year incurred and 50% the following year.

Fixed G&A expenses, including $35,000 depreciation and $5,000 bad debt expense, totaled $100,000 each year. The amount of such expenses involving cash payments was paid 80% in the year incurred and 20% the following year. Each year (i.e., 19A and 19B) there were a $5,000 bad debt expense and a $5,000 write-off. No unpaid G&A expenses are included in the payables above.

Required:

1. How much cash was collected during 19B resulting from total sales in 19A and 19B?
2. How much cash was disbursed during 19B for purchases of merchandise?
3. How much cash was disbursed during 19B for variable and fixed G&A expenses?

(AICPA adapted)

Problem 4–6

The president of Apple Manufacturing Company is a personal friend of yours and she tells you the company has never had an audit and is contemplating having one principally because it is suspected that the financial statements are not well prepared. As an example the president hands you the following balance sheet for review:

APPLE MANUFACTURING CO., INC.
Balance Sheet
For the Year Ended December 31, 19J

Resources

Liquid assets:	
Cash in banks	$12,500
Receivables from various sources net of reserve for bad debts	5,000
Inventories	6,000
Cash for daily use	500
Total	24,000
Permanent assets:	
Treasury stock	4,000
Fixed assets (net)	26,000
Grand total	$54,000

Obligations and Net Worth

Short-term:	
Trade payables	$ 3,000
Salaries accrued	1,000
Total	4,000
Long-term:	
Mortgage	8,000
Net worth:	
Capital stock	30,000
Earned surplus	12,000
Total	42,000
Grand total	$54,000

Required:

1. List and explain your criticisms of the above balance sheet.
2. Using the above data, prepare a classified balance sheet that meets your specifications. Where amounts needed are missing, use assumed, but realistic, amounts. *Hint:* Total assets is $50,000.

Problem 4–7

The most recent balance sheet of White Corporation appears below:

(Relates to Problem 4–7)

WHITE CORPORATION
Balance Sheet
For the Year Ended December 31, 19B

Assets

Current:			
Cash		$12,000	
Marketable securities		10,000	
Accounts receivable		30,000	
Merchandise		25,000	
Supplies		5,000	
Stock of Co. W (not a controlling interest)		17,000	$ 99,000
Investments:			
Cash surrender value of life insurance		45,000	
Treasury stock (2,500 shares)		37,500	82,500
Tangible:			
Building and land	$56,000		
Less: Reserve for depr.	10,000	46,000	
Equipment	15,000		
Less: Reserve for depr.	10,000	5,000	51,000
Deferred:			
Prepaid expenses		2,000	
Discount on bonds payable		3,000	5,000
Total			$237,500

Liabilities and Capital

Current:		
Accounts payable	$16,000	
Reserve for income tax	17,000	
Customers' accounts with credit balance	100	$ 33,100
Long-term (interest paid at year-end):		
Bonds payable	45,000	
Mortgage	12,000	57,000
Reserve for bad debts		900
Capital:		
Capital stock, authorized 10,000 shares, par $15	112,500	
Earned surplus	25,000	
Capital surplus	9,000	146,500
Total		$237,500

Required:

1. List and explain your criticisms of the above balance sheet.
2. Prepare a correct classified balance sheet. *Hint:* The capital stock was sold above par. Deduct treasury stock from shareholders' equity.

Problem 4–8

The balance sheet shown on page 135, which was submitted to you for review, has been prepared for inclusion in the published annual report of the RGA Company for the year ended December 31, 19J. Additional data are as follows:

1. Reserve for damages was set up by a debit against current fiscal year's income to cover damages possibly payable by the company as a defendant in a lawsuit in progress at the balance sheet date. Suit was subsequently settled for $50,000 prior to issuance of the statement.
2. Reserve for possible future inventory losses was set up in prior years, by action of board of directors, by debits against earned surplus. No change occurred in the account during the current fiscal year.
3. Reserve for contingencies was set up by debits against earned surplus over a period of several years by the board of directors to provide for a possible future recession in general business conditions.
4. Reserve for federal income taxes was set up in a prior year and relates to additional taxes which the Internal Revenue Service contended that the company owed. The company has good evidence that settlement will be effected for the $100,000.
5. Capital surplus consists of the difference between the par value of $10 per share of capital stock and the price at which the stock was actually issued.

Required:

State what changes in classification or terminology you would advocate in the presentation of this balance sheet to make it conform with generally accepted accounting principles and with preferred terminology. State your reasons for your suggested changes.

(AICPA adapted)

Problem 4–9

Sims Corporation has just prepared the annual financial statements dated December 31, 19C. The stockholders' equity section of the balance sheet was as follows:

Stockholders' Equity

Contributed capital:	
Preferred stock, par $10, 5%, nonparticipating, cumulative; authorized 100,000 shares, issued and outstanding 60,000 shares (of which 3,000 are held as treasury stock)	$ 600,000
Common stock, nopar; authorized 500,000 shares, issued and outstanding 200,000 shares	1,249,000
Contributed capital in excess of par, preferred stock	115,000
Total contributed capital	1,964,000
Retained earnings	102,000
Total	2,066,000
Less: Treasury stock (preferred stock, 3,000 shares), at cost	38,000
Total stockholders' equity	$2,028,000

During 19C, the following transactions and data affected stockholders' equity in various ways:

a. Prior period adjustment: Accounting errors made in prior periods (net of tax), a debit	$ 15,000
b. Sold capital stock (1/3/19C):	
(1) Preferred stock 10,000 shares at $10	100,000
(2) Common stock, 11,000 shares at $7.50	82,500
c. Treasury stock acquired, 2,000 shares of preferred at $11 per share	22,000
d. Shares issued for common stock dividend on common stock, 5,000 shares at $7 (debited to retained earnings)	35,000
e. Net income reported	165,000
f. Cash dividends:	
(1) Preferred stock	28,000
(2) Common stock	50,000

g. On 12/31/19C, the board of directors voted to approve appropriation of $70,000 of retained earnings for "Reserve for Future Expansion."

Required:

Based upon the above information prepare a statement to provide full disclosure of the changes in stockholders' equity for Sims Corporation during 19C. The statement, to supplement the balance sheet, should be set up as follows:

a. Caption:

SIMS CORPORATION
Statement of Stockholders' Equity—19C
($000 [deductions in parentheses])

b. List the items *(a)* through *(g)*, given above, to the left (start with the January 1, 19C, balance, and end with the December 31, 19C, items) and set up nine column headings as follows (continued on page 136):

(Relates to Problem 4–8)

RGA COMPANY
Balance Sheet
December 31, 19J

Assets

Current assets:			
Cash			$ 1,900,000
Accounts receivable		$3,900,000	
Less: Reserve for bad debts		50,000	3,850,000
Inventories—at the lower of cost (determined by the first-in, first-out method) or market			3,500,000
Total current assets			9,250,000
Fixed assets:			
Land—at cost		200,000	
Buildings, machinery and fixtures—at cost	$4,200,000		
Less: Reserves for depreciation	1,490,000	2,710,000	2,910,000
Deferred charges and other assets:			
Cash surrender value of life insurance		15,000	
Unamortized discount on first-mortgage note		42,000	
Prepaid expenses		40,000	97,000
Total assets			$12,257,000

Liabilities

Current liabilities:		
Notes payable to bank		$ 750,000
Current maturities of first-mortgage note		600,000
Accounts payable—trade		1,900,000
Reserve for income taxes for the year ended 12/31/19J		700,000
Accrued expenses		550,000
		4,500,000
Funded debt:		
9% first-mortgage note payable in quarterly installments of $150,000	$4,200,000	
Less: Current maturities	600,000	3,600,000
Reserves:		
Reserve for damages	50,000	
Reserve for possible future inventory losses	300,000	
Reserve for contingencies	500,000	
Reserve for additional federal income taxes	100,000	950,000
Capital:		
Capital stock—authorized, issued and outstanding 100,000 shares of $10 par value	1,000,000	
Capital surplus	300,000	
Earned surplus	1,907,000	3,207,000
Total liabilities		$12,257,000

Preferred Stock, Par $10:
1. Shares
2. Amount

Treasury Stock, Preferred:
3. Shares
4. Cost

Common Stock, Nopar:
5. Shares
6. Amount

Contributed Capital in Excess of Par:
7. Amount

Retained Earnings:
8. Amount

Total:
9. Amount

Note. The beginning balances intentionally are not given. You must derive them from the data given.

PART B: PROBLEMS 4–10 to 4–14

Problem 4–10

The following information was taken from the records of Speedo Corporation for the year ended December 31, 19B:

Net income (revenues, $700,000—expenses, $630,000), excluding gain below	$70,000
Depreciation expense	12,000*
Accounts receivable increase	3,000
Amortization expense on patent	4,000
Purchase of operational assets (cash)	88,000
Merchandise inventory increase	7,000
Cash dividends declared and paid	20,000
Gain on sale of operational asset (cash, $25,000—book value, $20,000)	5,000
Sold unissued common stock (cash)	25,000
Acquired future plant site; payment by issuance of 5,000 shares common stock (market value)	24,000
Payment on long-term bonds payable, *not* current portion	25,000
Borrowed on long-term mortgage note	30,000

* Included in the $630,000 total expenses.

Required:
1. Use the above information to prepare an SCFP, working capital basis.
2. Write the disclosure note with respect to the future plant site.

Problem 4–11

Note: This problem goes beyond the material discussed in this chapter.

The following statement has just been prepared by Bryan Corporation:

BRYAN CORPORATION
Statement of Changes in Financial Position
For the Year Ended December 31, 19X

Sources of funds:		
From operations:		
Net income	$130,000	
Add (deduct) adjustments to convert to cash basis:		
Depreciation expense	30,000	
Accounts receivable increase	(15,000)	
Inventory increase	(17,000)	
Accounts payable increase	11,000	
Income taxes payable decrease	(4,000)	
Loss on sale of long-term investment	3,000	
Funds generated from continuing operations		$138,000
From other sources:		
Sale of long-term investment	21,000	
Issuance of common stock to acquire machinery (Note A)	50,000	
Sale of unissued common stock	15,000	
Issuance of long-term note payable	20,000	
Total funds from other sources		106,000
Total funds generated		244,000
Uses of funds:		
Dividends	40,000	
Acquisition of machinery (Note A)	50,000	
Payment on bonds payable	100,000	
Total funds used		190,000
Increase in cash and short-term investments during the year		$ 54,000

Required:
1. How are funds measured in this statement? Explain.
2. What was net income for the year? How much cash was generated from operations? Explain how management generated more cash than net income.
3. What was the primary source of funds? What was the primary use of funds? What sources and uses would you rely upon for predictions of funds flow in this company? Explain.
4. Explain the long-term investment transaction. Why is it reflected in two places?
5. Write Note A with respect to the machinery.
6. Explain the reason for the addition or deduction of each adjustment to net income.
7. Some changes in terminology would be helpful. Identify them and suggest preferable terminology.

Problem 4–12

The Appendix following Chapter 24 gives an actual set of financial statements. Examine them carefully and respond to the following questions. Respond for the latest year (1981) unless directed otherwise.

a. Are they comparative statements? Briefly explain.
b. Are they consolidated statements?
c. On what date does the fiscal year-end?
d. How many years did the long-term summary cover?
e. What was the long-term trend of net income?
f. What was the return on average common shareholders' ending equity for 1980 and 1981?
g. What was the long-term trend of (1) dividends declared per common share and (2) net income per common share?
h. What classifications are used on the balance sheet?
i. What was the amount of (1) cash and (2) working capital reported at the end of the current year?
j. What amounts of income tax obligations and goodwill were reported on the current balance sheet?
k. How many different kinds of capital stock shares are (1) authorized and (2) outstanding?
l. How many different long-term liabilities are outstanding?
m. How much was research and development expense during 1980 and 1981?
n. What was the ratio of net income to average total assets for 1981? Briefly, what does this ratio measure?
o. What percent of total assets was provided by (1) creditors and (2) owners?
p. Was the SCFP prepared on a working capital basis or a cash equivalent basis? How was this made known in the statement?
q. For 1981, what percent of total fund inflows came from (1) operations, (2) extraordinary items, and (3) other sources?
r. What item represented the highest use of funds?
s. By how much did funds increase or decrease during 1979, 1980, and 1981?
t. Were there any new pending legal litigations at the end of the current year? Briefly explain.
u. What kind of opinion did the auditor give? Explain.
v. How much did The Quaker Oats Foundation contribute to educational institutions during 1981?

Problem 4–13

Obtain a set of audited financial statements for the latest year for a company of your choice (from the library or other source) and use it as a basis for responding to each of the questions posed in Problem 4–12. Substitute "current year" for 1981 and preceding year for 1980.

Problem 4–14 (review of Chapters 2, 3, and 4)

On January 1, 19C, Randal Company had the following trial balance:

Acct. No.	Account	Debit	Credit
101	Cash	$ 96,000	
102	Accounts receivable	45,000	
103	Allowance for doubtful accts.		$ 670
104	Office supplies inventory	800	
105	Inventory (periodic)*	60,000	
106	Short-term investments		
107	Investment revenue receivable		
108	Fund to construct future plant	30,000	
109	Machinery	120,000	
110	Accum. depr., machinery		72,000
111	Land (future plant site)	15,000	
112	Patent	4,000	
113	Other assets	55,000	
201	Accounts payable		35,000
202	Interest payable		
203	Income tax payable (19B)		12,330
204	Long-term mortgage note		
301	Common stock (par $10)		150,000
302	Contrib. capital in excess of par		30,000
303	Retained earnings		125,800
400	Income summary		
500	Sales revenue		
501	Investment revenue		
600	Purchases		
601	Freight on purchases		
602	Purchase returns		
700	Selling expenses		
701	G&A expenses		
702	Interest expense		
703	Depreciation expense		
704	Income tax expense		
801	Extraordinary items		
802	Prior period adjustments		
		$425,800	$425,800

* Depending on the worksheet technique used, an additional account for the ending inventory could be used.

19C entries (use numbers to left for date notations):

1. Paid 19B income taxes payable on 3/3/19C in full.
2. Purchases .... $350,000 ($50,000 was on credit)
   Purchase returns .... 1,000 (on acct.)
   Freight on purchases .... 2,000 (cash)
3. The following selling expenses were incurred and paid during 19C:
   Advertising .... $ 10,000
   Salaries 130,000
   Other selling 15,000
4. The following G&A expenses were incurred and paid during 19C:
   Salaries $100,000
   Office supplies (purchased) .... 500 (debit acct. no. 104)
   Rent expense 24,000
5. A 12% mortgage note was dated and signed on 3/1/19C, for $75,000; this amount of cash was received. Interest will be paid annually on this date.
6. A short-term bond investment was acquired for cash on 6/1/19C, at par, $20,000. Interest at 14% is payable annually on June 1.

7. Suffered severe flood loss amounting to $40,000. Assume an extraordinary item and credit cash because this was spent to restore the damaged assets.
8. Correction of accounting error in prior period resulting from understated billing for credit sales to a customer. Received $30,000 cash during 19C. Assume an income tax effect of $6,000.
9. At 12/31/19C, interest on the building fund amounting to $1,500 was added to the fund balance.
10. Cash collections on accounts receivable, $85,000.
11. Cash payments on accounts payable, $65,000.
12. Cash paid for dividends amounting to $2 per share (debit retained earnings).
13. Sales were $700,000 of which 15% was on credit.

Required:

1. Set up a general journal and T-accounts (with account numbers). Enter beginning balances in the ledger accounts. All of the ledger accounts needed are listed in the above trial balance.
2. Journalize and post the current entries. Use posting notations.
3. Set up a worksheet with a minimum of eight columns (or more if you prefer). Develop the unadjusted trial balance from the ledger and enter it into the first two money columns of the worksheet.
4. Enter the following adjusting entries on the worksheet and complete it (label the adjusting entries with the letters to the left).
   a. Bad debt expense is 1% of total credit sales (debit Selling Expense).
   b. Office supplies inventory at December 31, 19C, was determined by count to be $600.
   c. Accrue the short-term investment revenue at 14% per year.
   d. The machinery had an estimated life of 10 years, no residual value; assume straight-line depreciation and a full year's depreciation for 19C.
   e. On January 1, 19C, the patent had eight years remaining life; assume straight-line amortization. Record amortization as general and administrative expenses.
   f. Accrue interest on the mortgage note.
   g. Assume an average income tax rate of 20% on all items.
   h. The ending inventory was $70,000.
5. Prepare a single-step income statement and statement of retained earnings.
6. Prepare a classified balance sheet.
7. Journalize and post the adjusting entries.
8. Journalize and post the closing entries.
9. Prepare a post-closing trial balance.
10. Which adjusting entries would you reverse?

5

Concepts of Future and Present Value

PURPOSE OF THE CHAPTER

This chapter focuses on the time value of money, commonly called interest. **It is the cost of using money over time.** Outflows for the time value of money are identified as interest expense, whereas inflows for the time value of money are identified as interest revenue. Entities at various times make decisions that involve either *(a)* receiving funds, goods, or services currently with a promise to make payments over one or more future periods; or *(b)* disbursing funds as an investment to obtain returns over one or more future periods. In both situations the time value of money is fundamental to the decision-making process and in subsequently measuring and reporting the financial effects of earlier decisions.

Because of the time value of money (aside from inflation or deflation), a dollar has a different value today (often referred to as time zero) than at future or past dates. Therefore, dollar inflows and outflows that occur at significantly different dates cannot simply be aggregated in a meaningful way; rather they must be restated at a common date to reflect the time value of money by applying the concepts of future and/or present value. Restatement for the interest factor is essential in many situations, such as *(a)* when preparing information inputs for decision making (e.g., capital budgeting) and *(b)* for accounting measurement and reporting. Therefore, the accountant's knowledge necessarily must include an understanding of the concepts discussed in this chapter. Discussion of these concepts is presented early in this book because of their widespread use in accounting, as discussed and illustrated in later chapters. Some applications of future and present value concepts in accounting are as follows:

1. Notes receivable and payable—Measuring and reporting those notes that either carry no stated rate of interest or a rate of interest that is not realistic in comparison with the "going" rates (required by *APB Opinion 21*).
2. Assets—Measuring and reporting assets acquired with long-term debt when the interest rate is unspecified (as in a so-called noninterest-bearing note) or unrealistic (required by *APB Opinion 21*).
3. Premium and discount on certain receivables and payables—Measuring the amortization of bond premium and discount for both long-term investments in bonds and bonds payable (required by *APB Opinion 21*).

4. Leases—Measuring and reporting long-term leases (required by *FASB Statement 13* as amended).
5. Pensions—Measuring and reporting numerous aspects of pension plans (required by *APB Opinion 8*).
6. Installment contracts—Measuring and reporting the effects of assets acquired or sold on long-term installment terms (required by *APB Opinion 21*).
7. Sinking funds—Measuring and reporting funds set aside for specific uses in the future (required by GAAP).
8. Depreciation—Measuring depreciation expense by the sinking fund or annuity methods.
9. Capital additions—Evaluation of the probable economic effects of alternative investments in capital assets.
10. Business combinations—Measuring and reporting such items as receivables, debts, and accruals in a business combination by purchase.
11. Goodwill—Estimating the "value" of goodwill.
12. Future commitments of goods and/or services—Measuring and reporting future commitments to furnish or receive goods or services when the interest rate is unspecified or unrealistic (required by GAAP).

The purpose of this chapter is to present the concepts of future and present value in order to build a solid foundation for their applications in subsequent chapters (and in advanced accounting courses) where **specific accounting applications** are discussed and illustrated. The chapter is divided into two parts as follows:

Part A—Basic Concepts and Future and Present Values of 1

Part B—Future and Present Values of Annuities.

Part A: Basic Concepts and Future and Present Values of 1

CONCEPT OF INTEREST

Conceptually, interest is the time value of money. It is measured by the excess of resources (usually cash) received or paid over the amount of resources lent or borrowed at a different date. To illustrate, assume entity A loaned entity B $6,000 cash for one year with the stipulation that $6,900 cash would be paid at maturity date. The interest on this contract would be as follows:

Beginning of year, amount of resources committed		$6,000
End of year, amount of resources returned		6,900
Difference—time value of money (interest) per contract		$ 900
Analysis:		
Actual interest in dollars	$900	
Actual interest as a rate ($900 ÷ $6,000)	15%	

Simple versus Compound Interest

In the above example, the interest was based on the principal amount ($6,000), which would be the usual case in a loan covering one period only. When a loan covers two or more periods, interest may be computed on either a simple or a compound interest basis. **Simple interest** is computed only on the principal amount. For example, assume the above loan contract was for two years with specified **simple** interest of 15 percent per year on the principal amount of $6,000. The amount of interest for the two-year period would be $900 × 2 = $1,800 (i.e., the simple interest amount). In contrast, **compound interest** is computed on the sum of the principal amount plus all interest accumulated on the principal. For example, assume the above loan contract was for two years with specified **compound** interest of 15 percent per year. The amount of compound interest, compounded annually, would be computed as follows for entity A:

	Interest	Amount On Which Interest Is Computed	Cash Flows
Year 1:			
Principal (cash committed)		$6,000	$6,000
Interest ($6,000 × .15)	$ 900		
Year 2:			
Amount subject to interest		6,900	
Interest ($6,900 × .15)	1,035		
Total interest (cash inflow)			1,935
Total cash inflow with compound interest			$7,935

When a choice is available as to whether interest will be simple or compound, at a given interest rate, an investor would prefer compound interest. In the above example, the investor would receive $135 (i.e., $1,935 − $1,800) more interest on a compound interest basis than on a simple interest basis. In contrast, the borrower would have to pay $135 more interest. Simple interest usually is applicable to short-term receivables and payables, and compound interest usually is used for long-term contracts.

Interest Periods

Contracts which call for compound interest usually specify the interest rate on an **annual** basis. The interest periods—those intervals at which interest is accrued and added to the principal—may or may not be as much as one year apart. For example, a contract may call for "interest at 16 percent compounded annually," or for "interest at 16 percent compounded semiannually." In the first instance the rate is 16 percent for one interest period of a year; in the second instance the rate is 8 percent for each interest period of six months. If interest of 16 percent is compounded quarterly, the rate per period (quarter) is 4 percent, and there would be four interest periods per year. If an annual rate is stated and there is no mention of the frequency of compounding, interest is assumed to be compounded annually.[1]

[1] Throughout this chapter and in the problem materials, short-term periods are used to facilitate comprehension. Also, amounts usually are rounded to the nearest dollar for convenience.

Summary of Concepts

Future and present value involve four basic concepts. These four concepts, discussed in the order listed below, may be briefly identified as:

Part A—Values of 1:

1. **Future value of 1**—the future value of $1 at the end of n periods at i compound interest rate.

$$f = (1 + i)^n \text{ (Table 5–1, end of chapter)}$$

2. **Present value of 1**—the present value of $1 due n periods hence, discounted at i compound interest rate.

$$p = \frac{1}{(1 + i)^n} \text{ (Table 5–2, end of chapter)}$$

Part B—Annuities:

3. **Future value of annuity of 1**—the future value of n periodic contributions (rents) of $1 each plus accumulated compound interest at i rate.[2]

$$F_o = \frac{(1 + i)^n - 1}{i} \text{ (Table 5–3, end of chapter)}$$

4. **Present value of annuity of 1**—the present value of n periodic contributions (rents) of $1 each to be received, or paid, each period discounted at i compound interest rate. Stated another way: The amount that must be invested today at i compound interest rate in order to receive n periodic receipts of $1 each in the future.

[2] The subscript "*o*" refers to **ordinary** annuities as contrasted with annuities due. Also, the notations used vary considerably. *FV* and *PV* often are used as abbreviations for future and present value, respectively.

$$P_o = \frac{1 - \frac{1}{(1+i)^n}}{i} \quad \text{(Table 5–4, end of chapter)}$$

FUTURE AND PRESENT VALUE OF 1

To understand these two concepts, a clear distinction between "future value" and "present value" is essential. The fundamental difference is in the time assumption. "Future value" is a concept that looks **forward** from present dollars to future dollars, whereas "present value" is a concept that looks **back** from future dollars to present dollars. This distinction is displayed graphically in Exhibit 5–1. Note in particular the time direction indicated by the arrows.

FUTURE VALUE OF 1

The concept of future value of 1 (the symbol used herein is f) often is called compound interest. The future value is the starting principal plus accumulated compound interest. For example, $1,000 deposited on January 1, 19A, in a savings account, compounded annually at 12 percent interest, would amount (accumulate) to $1,762 at the end of the fifth year (December 31, 19E). The increase of $762 would be accumulated compound interest during the five years. The future value of 1 always will be greater than 1 by the compound interest accumulation.

Calculation of Future Value of 1

It is convenient and customary to use a base figure of 1 in compound interest calculations. In the United States it is natural to think of 1 as one dollar. The figure 1 also could stand for one peso or one of any other unit of currency.

We can determine how much an investment of $1 would be worth in the future if invested for a specified number of periods at a specified compounding rate per period. To illustrate, assume $1 is invested for five years at 12 percent compounded annually. The total principal and compound interest at the end of the five years may be determined by any of the following methods:

1. **By successive interest computations**—Multiply the principal ($1) by the interest rate (.12) and add to the principal the 12 cents interest thus obtained for the first period; the sum ($1.12) is the amount at the end of the first period. This amount then becomes the interest-bearing amount for the second period. This sum is principal plus interest $(1 + i)$ and may be used as the multiplier of the balance at the start of each period to secure the compound amount at the end of that period. Exhibit 5–2 uses this multiplier to illustrate successive interest computations.

2. **By formula**—Substitute into a formula which states that for n interest periods at i rate of interest the future value of 1 is $f = (1 + i)^n$. Substituting, $1 invested at 12 percent annual compound interest for 5 years = $(\$1 + .12)^5$, or $1.76 (see Exhibit 5–2).

3. **By table**—Tables showing the various future and present values may be obtained from numerous sources. Partial tables are presented in this chapter for your convenience. Table 5–1 is based on the formula $f = (1 + i)^n$; therefore it presents the future value of 1 values (for a limited number of periods

EXHIBIT 5–1: Future Value of 1; Present Value of 1

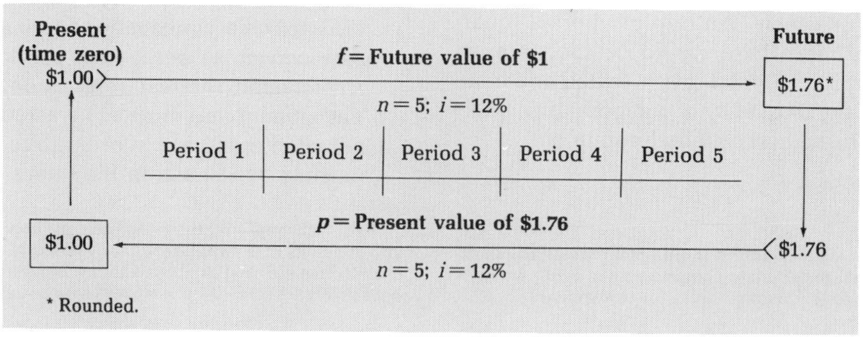

EXHIBIT 5–2: Compound Interest Computations

	By Successive Computations				By Formula
Period	Balance at Start of Period	× Multiplier $(1+i)$	=	Amount at End of Period	Alternate Computation at End $(1+i)^n$
1	$1	1.12		$1.12	$(1.12)^1$ = $1.12
2	1.12	1.12		1.2544	$(1.12)^2$ = 1.2544
3	1.2544	1.12		1.40493	$(1.12)^3$ = 1.40493
4	1.40493	1.12		1.57352	$(1.12)^4$ = 1.57352
5	1.57352	1.12		1.76234	$(1.12)^5$ = 1.76234

and interest rates). Reference to Table 5–1, down the 12 percent column and across on the five-period line, shows the future value of 1 to be 1.76234 (as computed in Exhibit 5–2). Tables facilitate computation of future and present values. Table 5–1 is entitled **Future Value of 1** and the underlying formula is $f = (1 + i)^n$. When the table value is to be applied to a large amount, rounding of **table values** can cause material error in the resulting amount computed. The tables presented in this chapter are carried to five places.

Future Value of a Specified Principal

Because the standard tables are based on 1 (as in Table 5–1), amounts other than 1 are multiplied by the appropriate table value. To illustrate, assume a company deposits $10,000 cash in a fund (or a savings account) that will earn 12 percent compounded annually for six years. How much will be in the fund at the end of the sixth year from the deposit date? We can compute this future value by referring to Table 5–1, Future Value of 1, as follows: $10,000 × $f_{n=6;\,i=12\%}$; that is, $10,000 × 1.97382 = $19,738. The interest revenue earned over the six years would be $9,738.

As another example, assume another company deposits $50,000 cash in a fund which will be needed at the end of 10 years and that the fund will earn 12 percent interest per annum compounded semiannually. Because the interest periods are one-half year, there are 20 interest periods and the semiannual compound interest rate is 6 percent per period. By reference to Table 5–1, the computation of the future value is $50,000 × $f_{n=20;\,i=6\%}$; that is, $50,000 × 3.20714 = $160,357. Interest revenue earned over the 10-year period would be $110,357.

Determination of Other Values Related to Future Value of 1

In each of the two examples given above, **three** values were provided. To restate the first example: *(a)* principal, $10,000; *(b)* interest rate, 12 percent; and *(c)* periods, 6. A fourth value, the future amount, $19,738, was computed. If any three of these four values are known, the other one can be derived from the basic equation:

$$fv = p \times f$$

fv	p	f
Computed future value	Principal amount	Table value for future value of 1

Thus, three types of problems may be encountered as follows:

1. To determine the future value (discussed above—compound amount of a specified principal), that is, $fv = p \times f$.
2. To determine the required interest rate (discussed below—determination of the compound interest rate), that is, $f = fv \div p$. In this case, f, the future value of 1 for a given number of periods, can be identified with the **required interest rate** in the table.
3. To determine the required number of interest periods (discussed below—determination of the number of periods), that is, $f = fv \div p$. In this case, f, the future value of 1 for a given interest rate, can be identified with the **required number of interest periods** in the table.

Determination of the Compound Interest Rate. If the future value to which a given principal sum will accumulate is known and the number of periods is known, the required rate of compound interest can be calculated.

As an example, assume it is desired *(a)* to invest \$5,000, *(b)* at interest compounded annually for 10 years, and *(c)* to accumulate \$15,529. What rate of interest is required? To find the required rate the following steps may be taken:

1. $fv = p \times f$; rearranging terms, $fv \div p = f$; \$15,529 ÷ \$5,000 = 3.10585, the future value to which 1 would accumulate at the unknown interest rate by the end of the 10-year period.
2. Referring to a future value of 1 table (Table 5–1) and reading across the 10-period line, we find the future value 3.10585 under the 12 percent column; thus 12 percent is the required interest rate.

Sometimes it is necessary to interpolate to derive the required rate. Suppose once again \$5,000 is to be invested for 10 years. In this case it is desired to accumulate \$15,000. Here the rate of increase is the same as if \$1 had grown to \$3 (i.e., \$15,000 ÷ \$5,000). Referring to the 10-period line, we find the value under 11 percent is 2.83942; under the next higher rate, 12 percent, it is 3.10585. Therefore, the rate is between 11 percent and 12 percent—a little closer to 12 percent—approximately six tenths of the way between them. We estimate that the required interest rate must be about 11.6 percent. Or more precisely, by interpolation:[3]

$$
\begin{aligned}
11\% &= 2.83942 \\
? &= 3.00000 \quad \rightarrow 3.00000 - 2.83942 = .16058 \quad \rightarrow 3.10585 - 2.83942 = .26643 \\
12\% &= 3.10585
\end{aligned}
$$

$$11\% + \left[\left(\frac{.16058}{.26643}\right) \times (12\% - 11\%)\right] = \underline{\underline{11.603\%}}$$

Determination of Number of Periods. If the future value to which a given sum will accumulate is known and if the interest rate is known, the required number of periods can be calculated from the basic equation, $fv = f \times p$. To use the above example again, assume the following are known: *(a)* investment (i.e., principal), \$5,000; *(b)* accumulation desired, \$15,529; and *(c)* the desired interest rate, 12 percent. To compute the required number of interest periods, the following steps may be taken:

1. $fv = f \times p$; $fv \div p = f$; \$15,529 ÷ \$5,000 = 3.10585, the future value of 1 at 12 percent for the unknown number of interest periods.
2. Referring to future value of 1 table (Table 5–1) and reading down the 12 percent column, we find 3.10585 on the 10-year line; thus the required number of interest periods is 10.

An Accounting Application of Future Value of 1

A typical accounting application of future value of \$1 is to build a fund for a specific future use. Usual situations include a fund to pay a debt at its future maturity date, to construct a major building, expand a plant, or to pay disability benefits. Exhibit 5–3 illustrates the accounting for a typical plant expansion fund by Sonoro Corporation. Panel A gives the hypothetical situation, Panel B presents the fund accumulation schedule, and Panel C gives the related accounting entries.

PRESENT VALUE OF 1

Present value is the "now," or time zero, value of a sum of future dollars discounted back from a specified future date to the present date at a given rate of compound interest. It is the reciprocal of the future value of 1 concept.

Because a future value is discounted, the present value always will be less than the future value. For example, \$1 discounted at 12 percent per annum for one year has a present value of \$0.89286, and discounted for two years it has a present value of \$0.79719.

We have seen that \$1 invested at i interest rate per period has a future value of $(1 + i)^n$ dollars. It follows that the future value $(1 + i)^n$ dollars has a

[3] Linear interpolation is illustrated above. A more precise answer can be obtained by using a calculator and the following procedure:

$$
\begin{aligned}
\$5{,}000\ (1 + i)^{10} &= \$15{,}000 \\
(1 + i)^{10} &= \$15{,}000 \div \$5{,}000 \\
(1 + i) &= (3.0)^{1/10} \\
i &= 11.612\%
\end{aligned}
$$

present value that is less than $(1+i)^n$ due to a reciprocal relationship. To illustrate, assume $1, an interest rate of 12 percent, and 1 period, as shown in Exhibit 5–4.

The reciprocal relationship between the future value of 1 and the present value of 1 provides for an algebraic expression of the computation of present value amounts, viz:

$$\text{Future value of 1, } f = (1+i)^n$$

Therefore, the present value of 1 is:

$$\text{Present value of 1, } p = \frac{1}{f} = \frac{1}{(1+i)^n}$$

This formula is used for computation of all present value of 1 amounts.

EXHIBIT 5–3: Accounting for a Plant Expansion Fund (future value of 1)

Panel A—Hypothetical Situation:

Sonoro Corporation, to assure funds for a planned future expansion, deposited $500,000 cash in a plant expansion fund on January 1, 19A. The bank, serving as trustee, will pay 14 percent interest compounded annually. The funds will be needed on January 1, 19D.

Required:

1. Compute the fund balance at December 31, 19C.
2. Prepare the fund accumulation schedule.
3. Give the accounting entries for the entire period including withdrawal on January 1, 19D.

Panel B—Computation of Fund Balance and Preparation of the Fund Accumulation Schedule:

1. Computation of the fund balance as of December 31, 19C:

$$fv = p \times f$$
$$p \times f = fv$$
$$\$500{,}000 \times f_{n=3;\,i=14\%} = fv$$
$$\$500{,}000 \times 1.48154 \text{ (Table 5–1)} = \underline{\underline{\$740{,}770}}$$

2. Fund accumulation schedule:

Date	Interest Revenue	Fund Balance
1/1/19A deposit		$500,000
12/31/19A	$500,000 × .14 = $70,000	570,000
12/31/19B	570,000 × .14 = 79,800	649,800
12/31/19C	649,800 × .14 = 90,970*	740,770*

* Rounded

Panel C—Entries Related to the Fund:

3. Entries:

a. 1/1/19A deposit of cash:

Plant expansion fund	500,000	
Cash		500,000

b. Each December 31 interest revenue earned:

	12/31/19A		12/31/19B		12/31/19C	
Plant expansion fund	70,000		79,800		90,970	
Investment revenue		70,000		79,800		90,970

c. 1/1/19D withdrawal of fund:

Cash	740,770	
Plant expansion fund		740,770

EXHIBIT 5–4: Reciprocal Relationship between Future Value of 1 and Present Value of 1

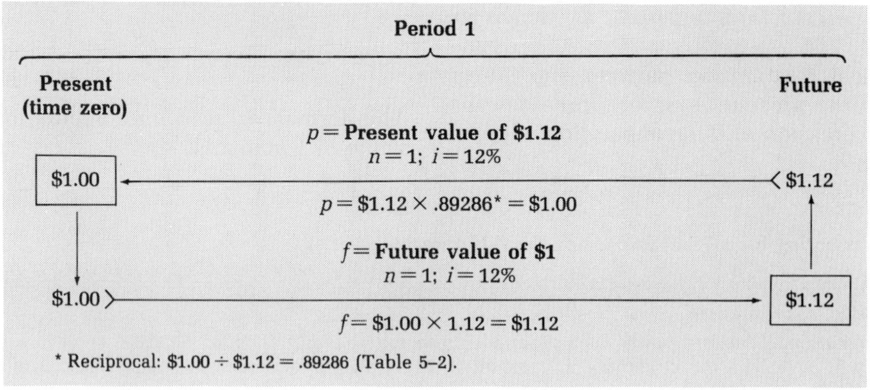

Calculation of Present Value of 1

Present value of 1 amounts can be computed by compound discounting inversely to that shown in Exhibit 5–2 for future amounts. Also, present value amounts can be computed by dividing the values given in Table 5–1, future value of 1, into 1.00. For example, $p_{n=5;\, i=12\%}$ can be computed as follows: 1.00 ÷ 1.76234 (Table 5–1) = .56743 (verifiable in Table 5–2). However, a more convenient approach is to use a table that discounts $1 for various n and i values. A **present value of 1** table for various interest rates and periods is shown as Table 5–2.

An Accounting Application of Present Value of 1

To compute the present value of a future amount, the appropriate amount from Table 5–2 is multiplied by the specified future amount by use of the basic equation:

$$pv = fv \times p$$

- pv: Computed present value
- fv: Future value
- p: Table value for present value of 1

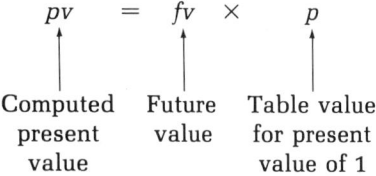

A typical accounting application of present value of 1 is to determine the *(a)* cost of an acquired asset and *(b)* the appropriate accounting entries when the consideration given is a fixed debt payable at a single specified date in the future, which includes all interest amounts. Other examples are in accounting for long-term leases (discussed in Chapter 19). Exhibit 5–5 illustrates the accounting for the acquisition by Blue Corporation of an asset with a specified single amount (i.e., a debt) payable three years later. Panel A presents the hypothetical situation, Panel B illustrates computation of the cost of the asset acquired and preparation of the related debt amortization schedule, and Panel C gives the related accounting entries.

EXHIBIT 5–5: Accounting for an Asset Acquired on Credit (present value of 1)

Panel A—Hypothetical Situation:

Blue Corporation acquired a machine on January 1, 19A. The seller agreed to let Blue Corporation pay for the machine three years after purchase, that is, on December 31, 19C. The amount to be paid at that date is $90,000, which includes all interest amounts. The appropriate interest rate for this type of transaction is 12 percent per year.

Required:

1. Compute the cost of the machine.
2. Prepare the related debt amortization schedule.
3. Give the accounting entries for the entire period including payment of the debt at maturity date.

Panel B—Computation of the Cost of the Acquired Asset and Preparation of the Debt Amortization Schedule:

1. Cost of the acquired asset on January 1, 19A:

$$pv = fv \times p$$
$$fv \times p = pv$$
$$\$90{,}000 \times p_{n=3;\, i=12\%} = pv$$
$$\$90{,}000 \times .71178 \text{ (Table 5–2)} = \underline{\underline{\$64{,}060}}$$

2. Debt amortization schedule:

Date	Interest Expense Incurred	Liability Balance
1/1/19A		$64,060
12/31/19A	$64,060 × .12 = $7,687	71,747
12/31/19B	71,747 × .12 = 8,610	80,357
12/31/19C	80,357 × .12 = 9,643	90,000

Panel C—Entries Related to the Acquisition and Debt:

3. Entries:

a. 1/1/19A acquisition of the machine:

Machine	64,060	
Liability		64,060

b. Each December 31, to record interest expense incurred:

	12/31/19A		12/31/19B		12/31/19C	
Interest expense	7,687		8,610		9,643	
Liability		7,687		8,610		9,643

c. 12/31/19C payment of the liability:

Liability	90,000	
Cash		90,000

Part B: Future and Present Values of Annuities

ANNUITIES DEFINED

Annuities differ from the future value of 1 and present value of 1 concepts in one respect, the concept of an **annuity.** The term annuity means a series of payments, or receipts, of **equal amounts for a series of equal time periods at a constant interest rate.** There is one equal amount (often called a rent) for each equal time period. In contrast, future value of 1 and present value of 1 involve a single amount only at the beginning (present) or at a future specified date. The monthly payments on an auto loan, for example, constitute an annuity; there is an equal cash payment each month by one party and an equal cash receipt each month by the other party. In annuity formulas, tables, and discussions, ***n* refers to the number of rents,** not to the number of interest periods. The future and present values of an ordinary annuity are displayed graphically on a **time scale** in Exhihit 5–6.

In Exhibit 5–6 observe that there are five **equal** rents—one in each period ($n = 5$)—and the rents are at the **end** of each period. The **future value of ordinary annuity of 1** is a future concept, and the future value of the five rents of $1 each, at 12 percent per rent interval, is $6.35. The future value will always be greater than the sum of the rents by the amount of the compound interest accumulation. Because the rents for an **ordinary** annuity are assumed to be on the **last day of each period,** observe that for the future value of an annuity of 1, the future amount is calculated as of the date of the last rent; thus, the last payment coincides with the end of the annuity term. This assumption means that because

EXHIBIT 5–6: Ordinary Annuities Illustrated on a Time Scale

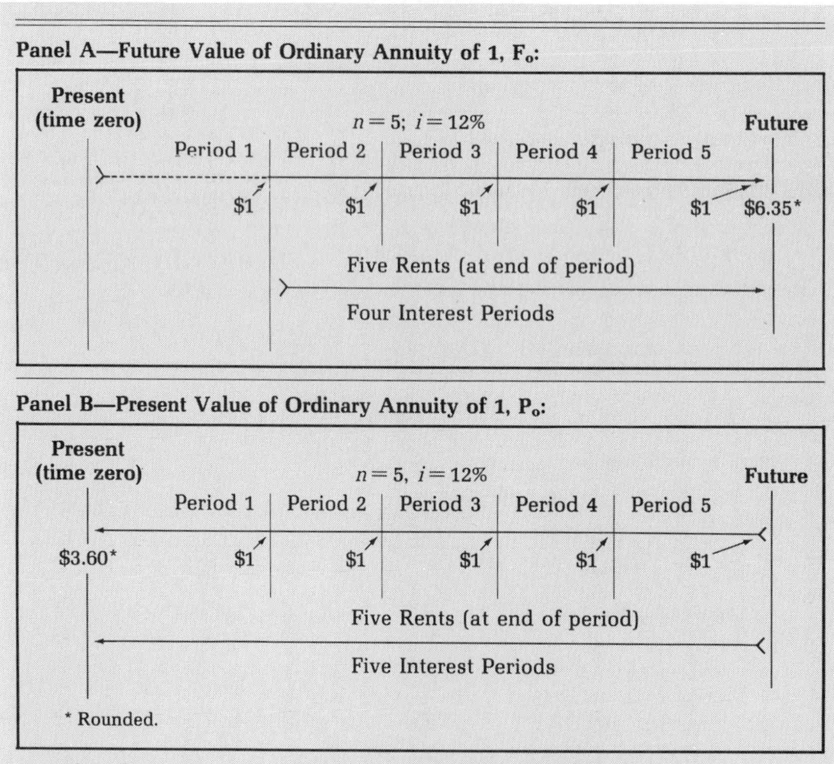

The subscript "o" in F_o and P_o denotes an ordinary annuity.

there is no interest after the last rent, there is one more rent than **interest** periods. The illustration above involves five rents ($n = 5$); however, the future value annuity earns interest for only four periods ($j = 4$), or $n = 5$ and $j = 4$. In contrast, in the present value illustration, it is $n = 5$ and $j = 5$. These effects are a consequence of the end-of-the-period assumption for the rents in ordinary annuities.[4]

The **present value of annuity of 1** is a present (i.e., time zero) concept. As shown in Exhibit 5–6, Panel B, the present value of the five rents of $1 each at 12 percent per rent interval is $3.60. The present value will always be **less** than the sum of the rents by the amount of the compound interest discounting. Note that the present value of an ordinary annuity of 1, as shown in Exhibit 5–6, Panel B, is assumed to be at the **beginning** of the first period (i.e., time zero) and the rents are assumed to be at the end of each period. This assumption means that there is the same number of interest discount periods as rents.

While the term annuity may imply equal **annual** rents to some, we should note that equal rents over equal time intervals of any length, such as monthly, quarterly, semiannually, or annually, constitute an annuity.

FUTURE VALUE OF AN ORDINARY ANNUITY

The **future value of an annuity is the future sum of all its rents plus the compound interest on each.** For example, suppose you deposit $100 per year for five years (periods) in a fund which earns compound interest at 12 percent per annum. At the date of the last deposit, the first rent will have earned compound interest for four years, the second for three years, the third for two years, the fourth for one year, and the fifth will earn no interest. On this ordinary annuity there will be no interest accumulation on the fifth rent because we are computing the future value as of the date of deposit of this rent. Applying principles we learned in Part A on future value of 1, the accumulation at the **date of the last deposit** will consist of the following:

Date of Deposit— End of	Future Value at End of Year 5 of Each Deposit
Year 1	$\$100 \times (1.12)^4 =$ $157.35
Year 2	$100 \times (1.12)^3 =$ 140.49
Year 3	$100 \times (1.12)^2 =$ 125.44
Year 4	$100 \times (1.12)^1 =$ 112.00
Year 5	$100 \times (1.12)^0 =$ 100.00
Future value of ordinary annuity	$635.28

The symbol used to denote the future value of an ordinary annuity of 1 is F_o. The formula to compute the future value of an ordinary annuity of 1 is based upon the formula for a future value of 1 (Table 5–1) because the amount of an annuity of 1, as illustrated above, is the sum of a series of computations of the future value of 1. The formula for the future value of an ordinary annuity is:

$$F_o = \frac{(1 + i)^n - 1}{i}$$

Note in the heading of Table 5–3 that this is the indicated formula for those table values. Observe that the notation n refers to the number of **periodic rents** and **not** to the number of interest periods; i refers to the interest rate per period (and not to the annual rate except when the periods are one year in length). The values given in Table 5–3 are at the **date of the last rent** (i.e., the rents are at the end of each period); therefore, they are for **ordinary** annuities, as is indicated in the title of the table.

An Accounting Application of Future Value of an Ordinary Annuity

Tables of future value of annuity of 1 are commonly used to calculate the future value of a series of rents at a specific rate of compound interest. In most situations the following are known: (1) the amount of the equal rents; (2) the number of rents, n; and (3) the constant interest rate per period, i. To determine the **future value** in a specific situation, the appropriate value from Table 5–3 is multiplied by the amount of the periodic rent, using the basic equation:

$$FV = R \times F_o$$

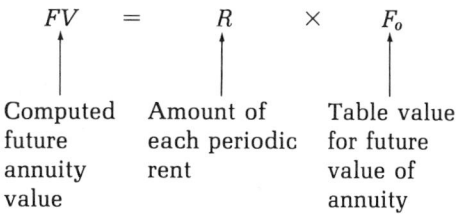

FV	R	F_o
Computed future annuity value	Amount of each periodic rent	Table value for future value of annuity

[4] The notation j is used to denote the number of **interest periods.** In contrast to ordinary annuities, annuities due (see footnotes 9 and 10) assume the rents are at the beginning of each period. Annuities due are discussed in a subsequent section of this chapter.

EXHIBIT 5–7: Accounting for a Facility Expansion Fund (future value of an ordinary annuity of 1)

Panel A—Hypothetical Situation:

Hill Corporation plans to expand its office building three years from now. To assure sufficient cash for this purpose, the company has decided to set up a building fund by making three equal annual contributions of $80,000 cash on each December 31, starting in 19A. The funds will be needed on December 31, 19C, the date of the last deposit. The fund will be deposited with a trustee and will earn 14 percent per year compounded annually.

Required:

1. What will be the balance of the fund on December 31, 19C; that is, immediately after the last deposit?
2. Prepare the fund accumulation schedule.
3. Prepare the accounting entries for the entire period.

Panel B—Computation of Fund Balance and Preparation of the Fund Accumulation Schedule:

1. Computation of the fund balance as of December 31, 19C:

$$FV = R \times F_o$$
$$R \times F_o = FV$$
$$\$80{,}000 \times F_{o_{n=3;\, i=14\%}} = FV$$
$$\$80{,}000 \times 3.43960 \text{ (Table 5–3)} = \$275{,}168$$

2. Fund accumulation schedule:

Date	Cash Deposits	Interest Revenue Earned	Fund Increases	Fund Balance
12/31/19A	$80,000		$80,000	$ 80,000
12/31/19B		$ 80,000 × .14 = $11,200	11,200	91,200
12/31/19B	80,000		80,000	171,200
12/31/19C		171,200 × .14 = 23,968	23,968	195,168
12/31/19C	80,000		80,000	275,168*

* Balance on date of last deposit (i.e., an ordinary annuity). Assumes that interest is added to the fund each December 31.

Panel C—Entries Related to the Fund:

3. Entries:

a. Deposits in the fund:

	12/31/19A		12/31/19B		12/31/19C	
Building fund	80,000		80,000		80,000	
Cash		80,000		80,000		80,000

b. Interest revenue earned on the fund:

	12/31/19B		12/31/19C	
Building fund	11,200		23,968	
Interest revenue		11,200		23,968

A typical accounting application of future value of an ordinary annuity is the accumulation of a fund by making equal annual contributions to it. The fund might be used in the future to construct, or expand a facility. Exhibit 5–7 illustrates the accounting for a typical facility expansion by Hill Corporation. Panel A presents the hypothetical situation, Panel B illustrates computation of the fund balance and preparation of the fund accumulation schedule, and Panel C gives the related accounting entries.

Determination of Other Values Related to Future Value of an Annuity

In the immediately preceding example, **three** values were given: (1) periodic rents, $80,000; (2) number of periodic rents, 3; and (3) the periodic interest rate, 14 percent. A fourth value, the future accumulation in a building fund, $275,168, was computed. If any three of these four values are known, the other one can be derived from the basic equation $FV = R \times F_o$. Thus, as illustrated for the future value of 1, four types of potential problems involve the future value of an annuity of 1, viz:

1. To determine the future value of a number of periodic rents (discussed immediately above), that is, $FV = R \times F_o$.
2. To determine the required interest rate, that is, $F_o = FV \div R$.[5]
   Example (based on above data):
   Given:
   a. Periodic rents, $80,000.
   b. Number of rents, 3.
   c. Future accumulation desired, $275,168.
   To derive the required interest rate:
   i. $FV = R \times F_o$; rearranging terms, $FV \div R = F_o$; $275,168 ÷ $80,000 = 3.4396 (table value for 3 rents at unknown interest rate).
   ii. Reference to Table 5–3, **line** for 3 rents, indicates the required interest rate to be 14 percent.
3. To determine the required number of periodic rents, that is, $F_o = FV \div R$.
   Example (based on above data):
   Given:
   a. Periodic rents, $80,000.
   b. Future accumulation desired, $275,168.
   c. Interest rate, 14 percent per period.
   To derive the required number of rents:
   i. $FV = R \times F_o$; rearranging terms, $FV \div R = F_o$; $275,168 ÷ $80,000 = 3.4396 (table value for annuity of rents of 1 each at 14 percent for unknown number of rents).
   ii. Reference to Table 5–3, **column** for 14 percent interest indicates the required number of rents to be 3.
4. To determine the required amount of each rent, that is, $R = FV \div F_o$.
   Example (based on above data):
   Given:
   a. Number of rents, 3.
   b. Interest rate per period, 14 percent.
   c. Future accumulation desired, $275,168.
   To derive the required amount of each rent:
   i. Reference to Table 5–3, **column** for 14 percent and **line** for 3 rents, gives the value, 3.43960.
   ii. $FV = F_o \times R$; rearranging terms, $FV \div F_o = R$; $275,168 ÷ 3.43960 = $80,000 (the required amount of each periodic rent).

PRESENT VALUE OF AN ORDINARY ANNUITY

The **present value of an annuity** is the equivalent value **now** (i.e., at time zero) of a series of future dollars (i.e., equal periodic rents) discounted back from a series of specific future dates to the present date at a specified constant rate of compound interest per period (i.e., compound discounting). For example, $1 (the equal periodic rent) due at the **end** of each of three periods in the future (total sum due $3), when discounted back at 14 percent compound interest, has a present value of $2.32. Alternatively, $2.32 deposited today at 14 percent compound interest per period would pay back $1 at the end of each of the three future periods. Significantly, the rents in the present value of an **ordinary** annuity are assumed to be at the **end** of each period; hence, in contrast to the future value of an ordinary annuity of 1, the **present value** of an ordinary annuity has the same number of interest periods as rents. That is, $n = 3$ and $j = 3$.[6]

The symbol often used to denote the present value of an ordinary annuity of n rents of 1 each is P_o. As before, n indicates the number of periodic **rents** and i the rate of discounting each rent interval. Table 5–4 gives the present values of ordinary annuities of n rents of 1 each for a number of rents and interest rates. Observe the heading of the statement and the underlying formula:

$$P_o = \frac{1 - \dfrac{1}{(1+i)^n}}{i}$$

[5] In the following examples, the data used above, with one "given" changed in each instance, are used to demonstrate the correctness of the answer and the computational approach.

[6] In both instances an **ordinary** annuity is assumed; annuities due are discussed in the next section.

Tables of present value of an annuity of n rents of 1 each usually are used to compute the present value of a series of future rents. In most situations the following are known: (1) the amount of the equal periodic rents; (2) the number of rents, n; and (3) the constant interest rate per period. To determine the present value in a specific situation, the appropriate value from Table 5–4 is multiplied by the amount of the periodic rent, using the basic equation:

$$PV = R \times P_o$$

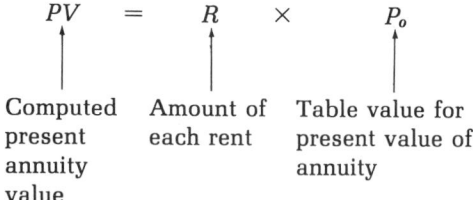

PV	R	P_o
Computed present annuity value	Amount of each rent	Table value for present value of annuity

An Accounting Application of Present Value of an Ordinary Annuity

To illustrate a typical accounting application, assume Delphi Corporation is negotiating the purchase of a certain natural resource. It is estimated that the resource will produce a net cash inflow of \$200,000 per year for the next three years. Assume that the inflow will be at the end of each year and that the "going" rate of compound interest is 16 percent per year. **Question:** What is the maximum amount that should be paid today (i.e., at the present time) for the natural resource assuming complete exhaustion at the end of three years and no residual value?

Solution:

This situation requires computation of the present value of the three future equal rents as follows:

$$R \times P_0 = PV$$

$$\$200{,}000 \times P_{o_{n=3;\ i=16\%}} = PV$$

$$\$200{,}000 \times 2.24589 \text{ (Table 5–4)} = \underline{\underline{\$449{,}178}}$$ [7]

If purchased at this price, the acquisition entry would be as follows:

Natural resource (identified)	449,178	
Cash (and/or debt)..............		449,178

DETERMINATION OF OTHER VALUES RELATED TO PRESENT VALUE OF AN ANNUITY

In the immediately preceding example, **three** values were given: (1) the periodic rent or contribution, R; (2) the number of periodic contributions, n; and (3) the periodic discount rate, i. A fourth value, the present value, P (\$449,178), was computed. If **any** three of these four values are known, the other one can be derived, using the basic equation, $PV = R \times P_o$. Thus, as illustrated for the future value of an annuity of 1, four types of potential problems use the present value of an annuity, viz:

1. To determine the present value of a series of future rents (discussed and illustrated immediately above), that is, $PV = R \times P_o$.
2. To determine the required interest rate; that is, $P_o = PV \div R$.

   Example (based on above data):

   Given:

   a. Periodic rents, \$200,000.
   b. Number of periodic rents, 3.
   c. Present value of the future rents, \$449,178.

   To derive the required interest rate:

   a. $PV = R \times P_o$; rearranging terms, $PV \div R = P_o$; \$449,178 ÷ \$200,000 = 2.24589 (table value for annuity of 3 rents at unknown interest rate).
   b. Reference to Table 5–4, **line** for 3 rents, indicates the required interest rate to be 16 percent.
3. To determine the required number of periodic rents, that is, $P_o = PV \div R$.

   Example (based on above data):

   Given:

   a. Periodic rents, \$200,000.
   b. Interest rate, 16 percent.
   c. Present value of the future rents, \$449,178.

   To derive the required number of periodic rents:

---

[7] As with future value of an ordinary annuity, the **present value** of an ordinary annuity is the sum of the present values of the individual rents:

Date of Rent	Amount of Rent	Present Value of \$1 (Table 5–2)	Present Value of Each Rent
End of year 1 ..	\$200,000 ×	$1/(1.16)^1 = .86207 =$	\$172,414
End of year 2 ..	200,000 ×	$1/(1.16)^2 = .74316 =$	148,632
End of year 3 ..	200,000 ×	$1/(1.16)^3 = .64066 =$	128,132
Present value of ordinary annuity (at start of year 1)			\$449,178

a. $PV = R \times P_o$; rearranging terms, $PV \div R = P_o$; \$449,178 ÷ \$200,000 = 2.24589 (table value at 16 percent for annuity of the required number of rents).
b. Reference to Table 5–4, **column** for 16 percent, indicates that 3 periodic rents are required.

4. To determine the required amount of each rent, that is, $R = PV \div P_o$.
Example (based on above data):
Given:
a. Number of periodic rents, 3.
b. Interest rate per period, 16 percent.
c. Present value of the future rents, \$449,178.
To derive the required amount of each rent:
a. Table 5–4 value at 16 percent, 3 rents = 2.24589.
b. $PV = R \times P_o$; rearranging terms, $PV \div P_o = R$; \$449,178 ÷ 2.24589 = \$200,000 (the periodic rent).

An accounting application to derive the required rent for the **present** value of annuity is presented in Exhibit 5–8. Panel A presents the hypothetical situation, Panel B illustrates the computation of the required equal periodic rents and preparation of the debt amortization schedule, and Panel C gives the related accounting entries.

ANNUITIES DUE

Discussion of annuities to this point has been confined to **ordinary** annuities. For ordinary annuities, the rents are assumed to be paid or received at the **end** of each period. In contrast, for annuities **due,** the rents are assumed to be paid or received at the **beginning** of each period.

FUTURE VALUE OF AN ANNUITY DUE

In the case of the future value of an **ordinary** annuity, the **future** amount is calculated as of the date of the last rent because the rents are assumed to occur at the end of each period. In contrast, the future value of an annuity **due** is calculated for one interest period after the date of the last rent since the rents are assumed to occur at the beginning of each period. The contrast between the two timing assumptions is shown graphically in Exhibit 5–9, Panel A, and detailed in Panel B (p. 155).[8]

The definitions of the future value of an **ordinary annuity** and the future value of an **annuity due** result from differences in their basic assumptions. These definitional differences are reflected in Exhibit 5–9, Panel B, which reveals different assumptions about their timing of rents (item 1), number of interest periods (item 3), and point in time of the future value (item 4). An understanding of the difference between an ordinary annuity and an annuity due is important in solving annuity problems. Care must be exercised to select the one that fits the specific situation.

Ordinary annuity tables are more common than annuity due tables. In situations where only an ordinary annuity table is available and an annuity **due** amount is needed, the conversion is straightforward. For an annuity of n rents, conversion from an ordinary annuity to an annuity due amount can be accomplished in either of two ways, viz:

1. Multiply the future value of ordinary annuity amount by $(1 + i)$. That is, $F_d = F_o \times (1 + i)$. For example, the **annuity due** amounts shown in Exhibit 5–9, Panel A, were computed as follows:

Interest	Rents	Amount of Future Value of Ordinary Annuity (Table 5–3)	×	Multiplier $(1+i)$	=	Future Value of Annuity Due
12%	1	1.00000	×	(1.12)	=	1.12000
12	2	2.12000	×	(1.12)	=	2.37440
12	3	3.37440	×	(1.12)	=	3.77933
12	4	4.77933	×	(1.12)	=	5.35285

2. Read the amount from the future value of an ordinary annuity table for **one greater** rent than the number of rents specified in the annuity due problem; then **subtract** the numeral 1 from it.[9] This procedure has the effect of adding interest to the ordinary annuity amount for one additional pe-

[8] The subscript "*o*" is an ordinary annuity and "*d*" an annuity due. The terms **ordinary** and **due** were coined by mathematicians; many accountants prefer more descriptive terminology:

1. Instead of "ordinary"—"end-of-period annuities," or "annuities in arrears."
2. Instead of "due"—"beginning-of-period annuities," or "annuities in advance."

[9] Frequently expressed as $(n + 1 \text{ rents}) - 1$. This method, as well as the one above, serves to increase the number of interest periods by 1 for an annuity due but maintain the same number of rents.

EXHIBIT 5–8: Computation of Equal Periodic Rents (present value of ordinary annuity)

Panel A—Hypothetical Situation:

Voss Corporation purchased an asset resulting in the incurrence of a $70,000 debt on January 1, 19A. The liability is to be paid in three equal installments on each December 31, starting at the end of 19A. The interest rate is 18 percent, and each equal installment is to include both interest and principal.

Required:

1. Compute the required amount of each equal annual installment.
2. Prepare a debt amortization schedule.
3. Give the journal entries for the period of the debt.

Panel B—Computation of the Required Periodic Payment and Preparation of the Debt Amortization Schedule:

1. Computation of the required periodic payment:

$$PV = R \times P_o$$
$$PV \div P_o = R$$
$$\$70{,}000 \div P_{o_{n=3;\, i=18\%}} = R$$
$$\$70{,}000 \div 2.17427 \text{ (Table 5–4)} = \underline{\underline{\$32{,}195}} \text{ (the periodic rent)}$$

2. Debt amortization schedule:

Date	Cash Payment	Interest Expense	Payment on Principal	Unpaid Principal
1/1/19A				$70,000
12/31/19A	$32,195[a]	$12,600[b]	$19,595[c]	50,405[d]
12/31/19B	32,195	9,073	23,122	27,283
12/31/19C	32,195	4,912*	27,283	-0-

[a] Computed above.
Successive computations:
[b] $70,000 × .18 = $12,600.
[c] $32,195 − $12,600 = $19,595.
[d] $70,000 − $19,595 = $50,405.
* Rounded

Panel C—Entries Related to the Debt:

3. Entries:

a. 1/1/19A to record the debt:

Asset	70,000	
Liability		70,000

b. Each December 31 to record payment (per above schedule):

	12/31/19A		12/31/19B		12/31/19C	
Interest expense	12,600		9,073		4,912	
Liability	19,595		23,122		27,283	
Cash		32,195		32,195		32,195

riod to derive the annuity due amount. To illustrate, for $n = 4$; $i = 12\%$:

From Table 5–3 (*FV* of ordinary annuity), $n = 5$; $i = 12\%$	6.35285
Subtract the numeral 1	−1.00000
Difference—*FV* of annuity *due*, $n = 4$; $i = 12\%$	5.35285

Future Values of Ordinary Annuity and Annuity Due Compared

In applying the concepts of future and present value, it is helpful to analyze the situation or problem graphically in a manner similar to the graphic illustrations in this chapter. This initial step will indicate

EXHIBIT 5–9: Future Value of Ordinary Annuity Distinguished from Future Value of Annuity Due

Panel A—Future Value of Ordinary Annuity and Annuity Due Illustrated:

Future Value of Ordinary Annuity, F_o (rents at end of period):

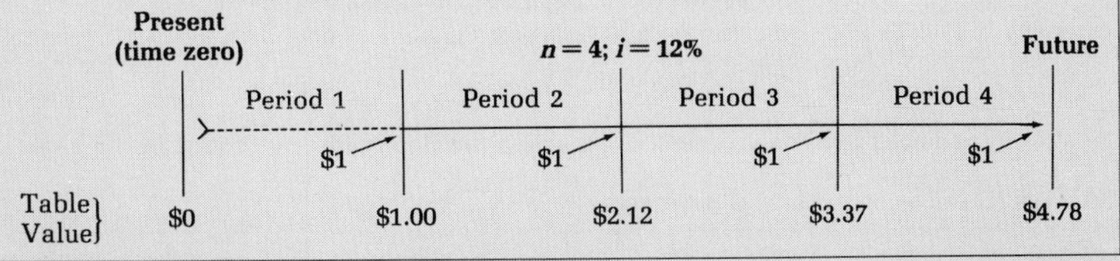

Future Value of Annuity Due, F_d (rents at beginning of period):

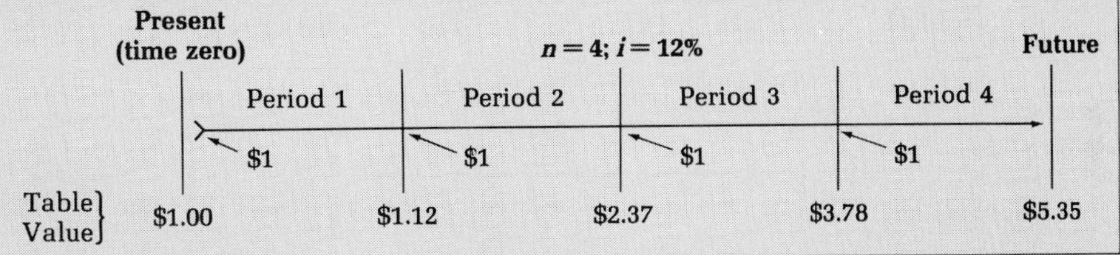

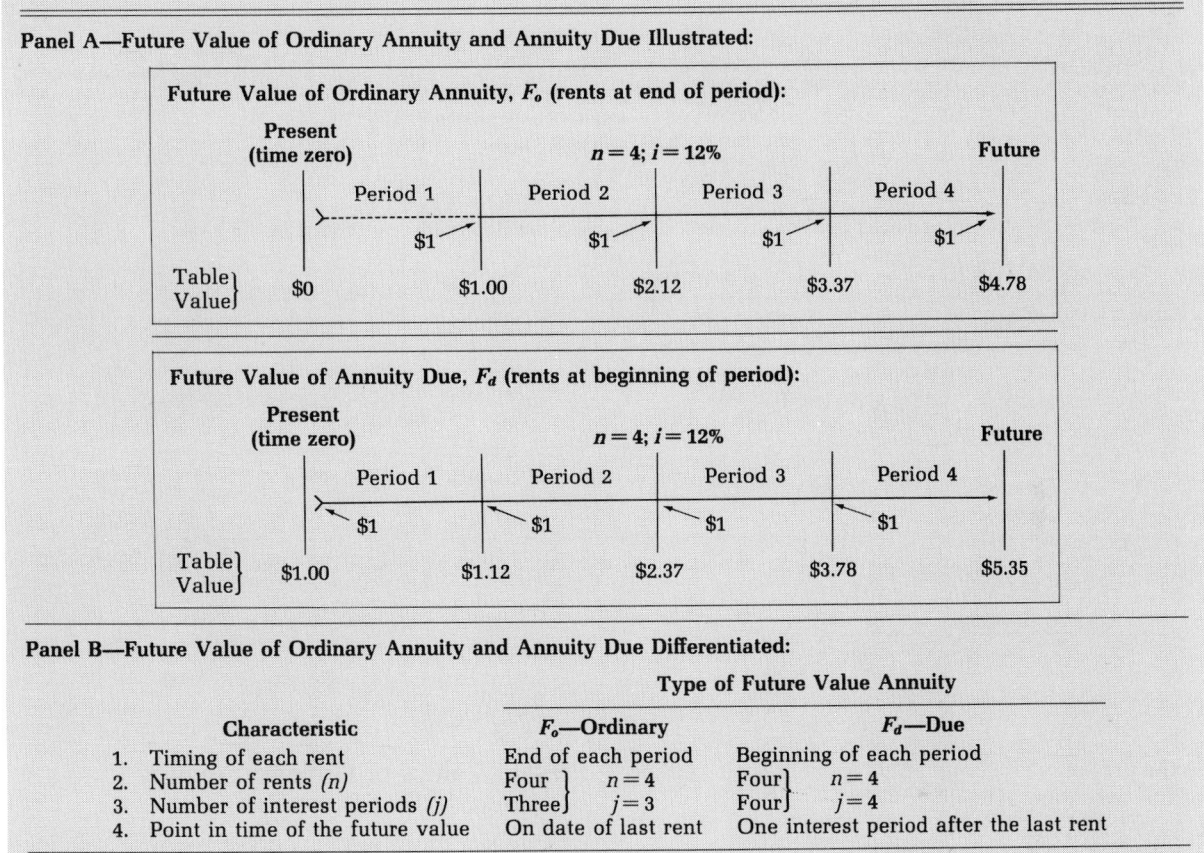

Panel B—Future Value of Ordinary Annuity and Annuity Due Differentiated:

	Type of Future Value Annuity	
Characteristic	**F_o—Ordinary**	**F_d—Due**
1. Timing of each rent	End of each period	Beginning of each period
2. Number of rents *(n)*	Four $n = 4$	Four $n = 4$
3. Number of interest periods *(j)*	Three $j = 3$	Four $j = 4$
4. Point in time of the future value	On date of last rent	One interest period after the last rent

the appropriate future or present value concept to apply. Two examples are given below with explanation of the solution approaches. These examples illustrate different situations requiring computation of the future value of **ordinary** annuity and future value of annuity **due.** Exhibit 5–10 illustrates the solution to a problem involving the future value of an **ordinary** annuity, and Exhibit 5–11 illustrates the solution to a problem involving the future value of an annuity **due.**

PRESENT VALUE OF AN ANNUITY DUE

In the case of present value of an **ordinary annuity,** the rents are assumed to be at the end of the period; therefore, the present value is calculated as of one period prior to the first rent. In contrast, the present value of an **annuity due** assumes the rents are at the beginning of each period; therefore, the present value is calculated on the date of the first rent. The contrast between the two timing assumptions for present value of an annuity is shown graphically in Exhibit 5–12, Panel A, and detailed in Panel B (p. 158).

The definitions of the present value of an **ordinary annuity** and the present value of an **annuity due** result from different basic assumptions. These definitional differences are presented in Exhibit 5–12, Panel B, items 1, 3, and 4.

Often an ordinary annuity table is available but not an annuity due table. In such situations the present value of an ordinary annuity may be converted

EXHIBIT 5–10: Future Value of Ordinary Annuity Problem Illustrated

Panel A—Hypothetical Situation:

On January 1, 19A, Dawson Corporation entered into a contract with a company that required Dawson to pay $50,000 cash on December 31, 19C. Dawson was to deposit three equal annual dollar amounts in a bank account starting December 31, 19A, so that the $50,000 would be available on December 31, 19C. On that date the bank would pay the other company in full. The bank agreed to add 12 percent annual compound interest to the fund each December 31.

Required:

1. Diagram the annuity required by the agreement to establish the debt payment fund with the bank.
2. What kind of annuity is indicated?
3. Compute the amount of the equal annual payments.

Panel B—Solution:

1. Diagram of the **ordinary annuity** ($n = 3$; $i = 12\%$):

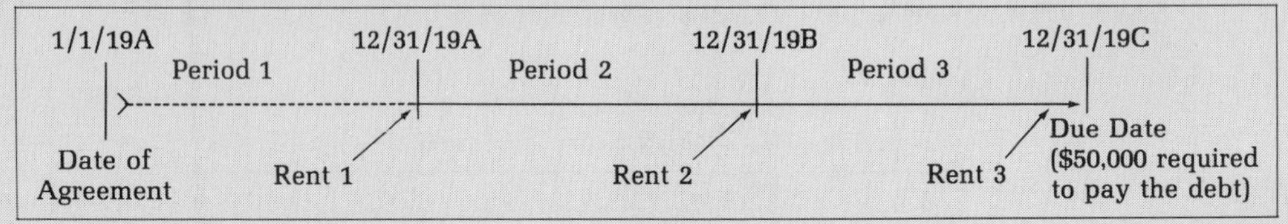

2. Because the rents are at the end of the period, this is the future value of an **ordinary** annuity; that is, the future value is at the date of the last rent.

3. $$\text{Rent} = \frac{\text{Future value}}{F_{o\,n=3;\,i=12\%}} = \frac{\$50{,}000}{3.3744 \text{ (Table 5–3)}} = \underline{\underline{\$14{,}817}}$$

to the present value of an annuity due by using either of the two approaches, viz:

1. Multiply the present value ordinary annuity by $(1 + i)$. For example, the present value of an annuity due for $n = 4$; $i = 10\%$ is 3.16987 (from Table 5–4) × 1.10 = 3.48685.
2. Read the present value of an ordinary annuity table for **one less** than the number of rents specified in the annuity due problem; then **add** the numeral 1 to it.[10] To illustrate for $n = 4$; $i = 10\%$:

From Table 5–4 (present value of ordinary annuity) $n = 3$; $i = 10\%$	2.48685
Add the numeral 1	1.00000
Summation—present value of annuity due, $n = 4$; $i = 10\%$	3.48685

[10] Frequently expressed as $(n - 1 \text{ rents}) + 1$. Either method serves to reduce the discount period by one for an annuity due but maintains the same number of rents.

Present Values of Ordinary Annuity and Annuity Due Compared

Two situations are now presented with solutions to illustrate the different situations in which the present value of an ordinary annuity and present value of an annuity due are applied. Careful attention to the timing of the rents is necessary to determine which type of annuity should be applied to each situation or problem. Exhibit 5–13 (p. 159) illustrates the solution to a problem involving the present value of an **ordinary annuity;** Exhibit 15–14 (p. 160) illustrates the solution to a problem involving an **annuity due.**

In summary, another useful way to view the distinction between an ordinary annuity and an annuity due is to focus on the date the annuity amount is needed. Annuities can be shifted from an ordinary annuity to an annuity due (or vice versa) simply by shifting the date when the desired value is needed.

The **future value of an ordinary annuity** is at the date of the last rent; thus, there is no interest after

EXHIBIT 5–11: Future Value of Annuity Due Problem Illustrated

Panel A—Hypothetical Situation:

On January 1, 19A, Cotter Corporation decided to create a fund by making three annual deposits of $60,000 each on January 1, 19A, 19B, and 19C. The fund will be held by a trustee who will increase the fund on a 10 percent annual compound interest basis. The fund will be needed on December 31, 19C.

Required:

1. Diagram the annuity created in this situation.
2. What kind of annuity is indicated?
3. Compute the balance in the fund on December 31, 19C, and prepare a fund accumulation schedule.

Panel B—Solution:

1. Diagram of the **annuity due** ($n = 3$; $i = 10\%$):

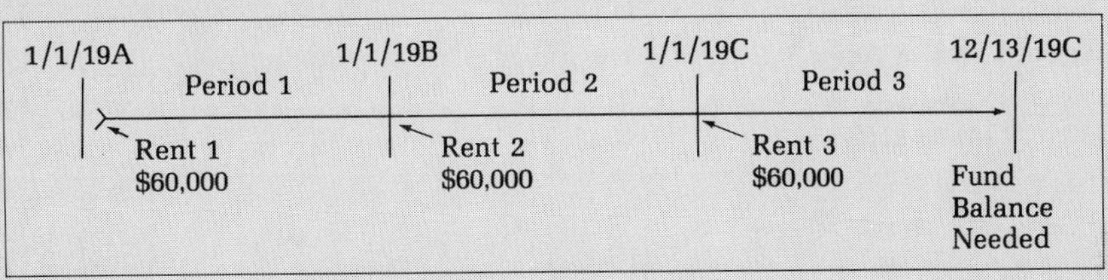

2. Because the rents are paid at the beginning of each period and the amount desired in the fund is one interest period after the last rent, it is a **future value of annuity due.**
3. Fund balance as of December 31, 19C:

$$FV = R \times F_d$$
$$R \times F_d = FV$$
$$\$60{,}000 \times [3.3100 \text{ (Table 5–3)} \times 1.10 = 3.64100] = FV$$
$$\$60{,}000 \times 3.64100 = \underline{\underline{\$218{,}460}} \text{ (fund balance)}$$

The **fund accumulation schedule for this future value of annuity due,** $n = 3$; $i = 10\%$, would be as follows:

Date	Cash Deposits	Interest Revenue Earned	Fund Increases	Fund Balance
1/1/19A	$60,000		$60,000	$ 60,000
12/31/19A		$ 60,000 × .10 = $ 6,000	6,000	66,000
1/1/19B	60,000		60,000	126,000
12/31/19B		126,000 × .10 = 12,600	12,600	138,600
1/1/19C	60,000		60,000	198,600
12/31/19C		198,600 × .10 = 19,860	19,860	218,460

the last rent. In contrast, the **future value of an annuity due** is at the end of the interest period following the last rent; thus, there is interest after the last rent. Therefore, the difference between the future value of an **ordinary** annuity and of an annuity **due** is interest for one period; there is the same number of rents for each, but one **more** period's interest for the future value of an annuity due. For example:

Future value of **ordinary annuity** of 4 rents at 10% (Table 5–3)	4.64100
Multiply by 1.10 (add 1 period interest, 10%)	× 1.10
Future value of **annuity due** of 4 rents..........	5.10510

These relationships reverse for the **present value** concept. The present value of an ordinary annuity

EXHIBIT 5–12: Present Value of Ordinary Annuity Distinguished from Present Value of Annuity Due

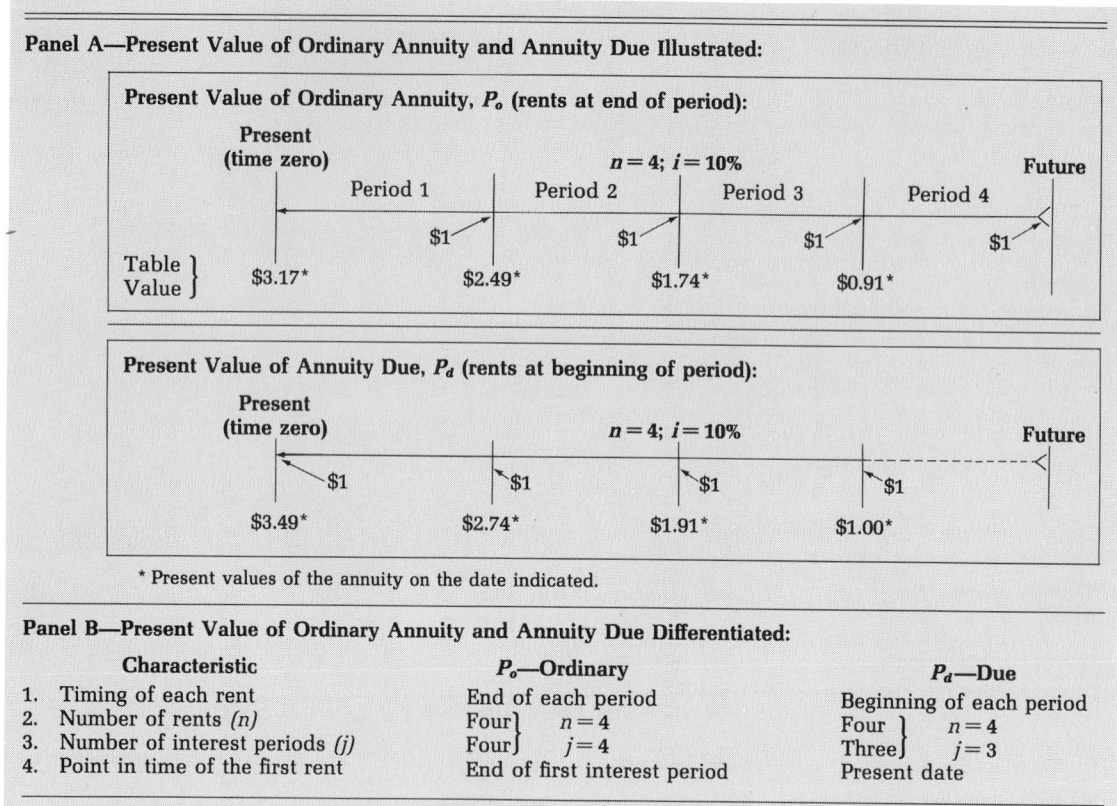

Panel A—Present Value of Ordinary Annuity and Annuity Due Illustrated:

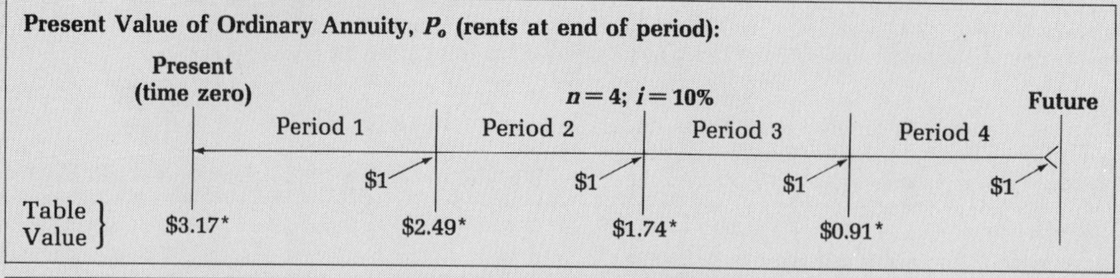

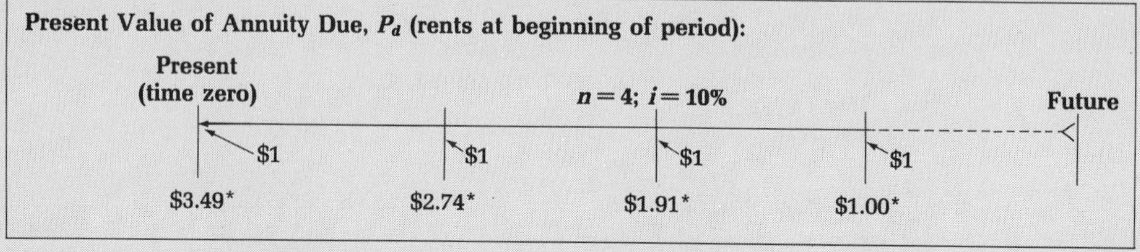

* Present values of the annuity on the date indicated.

Panel B—Present Value of Ordinary Annuity and Annuity Due Differentiated:

Characteristic	**P_o—Ordinary**	**P_d—Due**
1. Timing of each rent	End of each period	Beginning of each period
2. Number of rents *(n)*	Four } $n = 4$	Four } $n = 4$
3. Number of interest periods *(j)*	Four } $j = 4$	Three } $j = 3$
4. Point in time of the first rent	End of first interest period	Present date

is at the present date which is the beginning of the period of the first rent; thus, there is interest discounting for one period on the first rent. In contrast, the present value of an annuity due is at the date of the first rent; thus, there is no interest discounting on the first rent. Therefore, the difference between the present value of an ordinary annuity and of an annuity due is interest discounting for one period; there is the same number of rents for each, but one **fewer** period's interest for the present value of an annuity due. For example:

Present value of **ordinary annuity** of 5 rents at 10% (Table 5–4)	3.79079
Multiply by 1.10 (to deduct 1 period interest discount, 10%)	× 1.10
Present value of **annuity due** of 5 rents	4.16987

The result (4.16987) is 1.00000 **more** than the present value of an ordinary annuity of 4 rents at 10 percent (i.e., 3.16987 per Table 5–4), which is logical because the first rent is not discounted in an annuity due.

USING MULTIPLE TABLE VALUES

The accountant often encounters situations which require the use of two or more tables. These situations may involve annuities with a change in rent amounts. Problems with these characteristics can be solved readily if one understands the concepts underlying future and present value.

To illustrate, assume ST Construction Company is negotiating to purchase 4 acres of land with a deposit of gravel suitable for exploitation. The buyer and the seller are negotiating the price. ST Company has completed an extensive study that provided the following estimates:

EXHIBIT 5–13: Present Value of Ordinary Annuity Problem Illustrated

Panel A—Hypothetical Situation:

On January 1, 19J, Brown Corporation owed a $30,000 debt which was due. The creditor agreed to let Brown pay the debt in four equal annual payments on December 31, 19J, 19K, 19L, and 19M. Interest at 12 percent per year is payable on the unpaid principal. Each equal payment includes interest and principal.

Required:

1. Diagram the annuity represented by the required annual payments.
2. What kind of annuity is represented?
3. Compute the amount of the equal annual rent on the debt.

Panel B—Solution:

1. Diagram of the **ordinary annuity** ($n = 4$; $i = 12\%$):

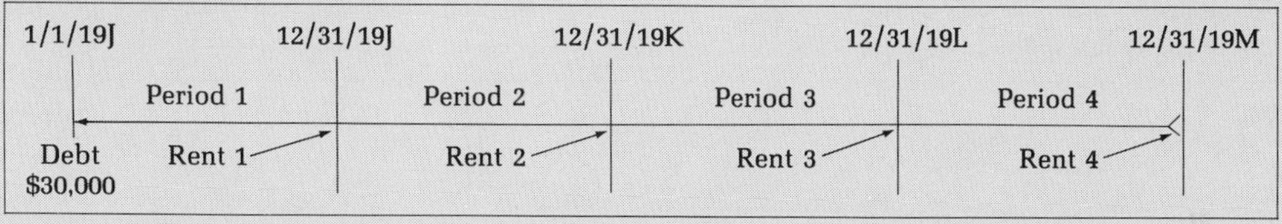

2. Because the payments are to be made at the end of each period, this is an **ordinary annuity,** and the **present value** (i.e., the principal of the debt) is one period prior to the date of the first rent.
3. The amount of each equal annual rent is computed as follows:

$$PV = R \times P_o$$
$$PV \div P_o = R$$
$$\$30{,}000 \div P_{o_{n=4;\ i=12\%}} = R$$
$$\$30{,}000 \div 3.03735 \text{ (Table 5–4)} = \underline{\underline{\$9{,}877}} \text{ (periodic payment)}$$

Expected net cash revenues over life of resource:	
End of year 1	$ 5,000
End of years 2–5 (per year)	30,000
End of years 6–9 (per year)	40,000
End of year 10 (last year—resource exhausted)	10,000
Estimated sales value of 4 acres after exploitation and net of land-leveling costs (end of 10th year)	2,000

Required:

Assuming the above estimates are realistic, compute the amount ST Construction Company should be willing to offer for the land assuming it expects a 12 percent return on the investment. Assume all amounts are at year-end and that the above amounts are net of income taxes.

Solution:

This problem requires computation of the present value of the future expected cash inflows.

The amount that should be offered is the sum of the present values of the net cash revenues for the various years. The complexity in this situation arises because *(a)* $5,000 for year 1, $10,000 for year 10, and the $2,000 estimated value at the end of year 10 involve use of the present value of 1 concept; *(b)* the equal annual revenues for years 2–5 and 6–9 involve the use of the present value of ordinary annuity concept; and *(c)* the net cash revenues for years 2–5, 6–9, and 10 necessarily omit years 1, 1–5, and 1–9, respectively.

Complex situations such as this demonstrate the need to diagram most future and present value situations in terms of *(a)* the timing of the resource flows (rents), *(b)* the interest assumptions, and *(c)* the value (solution) to be derived. Moreover, this problem also illustrates the three basic decisions to solving all future and present value problems:

1. Identification of whether the focus is on future value or on present value.
2. Identification of whether the situation involves a single sum or a series of rents (an annuity).
3. If the situation involves an annuity, do the rents occur at the end of each period (an ordinary an-

EXHIBIT 5–14: Present Value of Annuity Due Problem Illustrated

Panel A—Hypothetical Situation:

J. Doe was injured while working for X Corporation. On January 1, 19J, an agreement was reached whereby X Corporation would deposit $100,000 with the City Bank as trustee for the benefit of Doe. The bank agreed to pay 12 percent compound interest per year on the fund balance while making five equal annual payments to Doe from the principal plus interest earned. The payments are to be made on each January 1, starting immediately, until the fund (principal plus all interest accumulations) is fully expended.

Required:

1. Diagram the annuity represented by the payments.
2. What kind of annuity is represented?
3. Compute the amount of each equal annual payment to Doe.

Panel B—Solution:

1. Diagram of the **annuity due** ($n = 5$; $i = 12\%$):

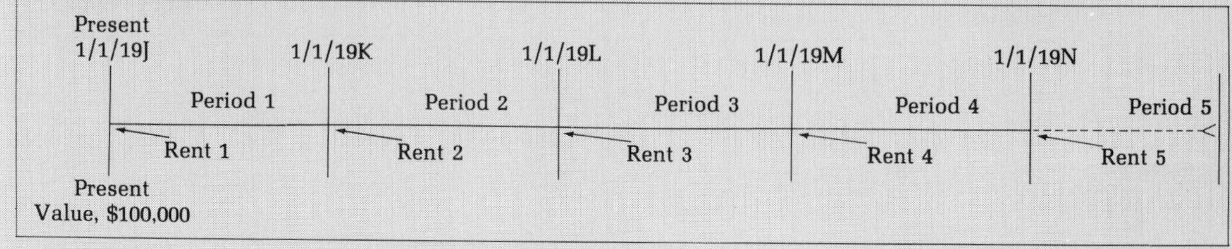

2. Because the rents are at the beginning of the period (the first one starts immediately), this is an **annuity due.** Since the $100,000 is deposited at the beginning, that amount represents the **present value** of the annuity due, on which the amount of the equal rents is based.
3. The amount of each annual rent is computed as follows:

$$PV = R \times P_d$$
$$PV \div P_d = R$$
$$\$100{,}000 \div P_{d_{n=5;\ i=12\%}} = R$$
$$\$100{,}000 \div [3.60478 \text{ (Table 5–4)} \times 1.12 = 4.03735] = \underline{\underline{\$24{,}769}}$$

nuity) or at the beginning of each period (an annuity due)?

For ST Company, the focus is on present value (the amount the company should be willing to pay for the land at the present date). For years 2–5 and 6–9 equal periodic rents are specified; therefore, an annuity situation is involved. Because the problem states that the equal revenue amounts are at year-end, ordinary annuities must be used.

Because of its complexities, this problem is best solved in five steps, one for each element in the solution, as follows:

Step 1 involves preparation of a "timing" diagram, which reveals the *(a)* timing of the resource flows, *(b)* interest assumption, and *(c)* value to be derived (the present value). Exhibit 5–15 presents a diagram which indicates all of the timing data needed.

Step 2 involves computation of the present value of the $5,000 at 12 percent for one year. Thus,

$$\$5{,}000 \times p_{n=1;\ i=12\%} =$$
$$\$5{,}000 \times .89286 \text{ (Table 5–2)} = \underline{\underline{\$4{,}464}}$$

Step 3 can be viewed as the present value of ordinary annuity with rents at the end of years 2–5 (step 3*a* below). Then the present value of the ordinary annuity must be discounted for one period at 12 percent (step 3*b* below). This involves a two-stage computation as follows:

a. $$\$30{,}000 \times P_{o_{n=4;\ i=12\%}} =$$
$$\$30{,}000 \times 3.03735 \text{ (Table 5–4)} = \$91{,}121$$

b. $$\$91{,}121 \times p_{n=1;\ i=12\%} =$$
$$\$91{,}121 \times .89286 \text{ (Table 5–2)} = \underline{\underline{\$81{,}358}}$$

Step 4 is similar to step 3 except the present value of the annuity is computed for rents at the end

EXHIBIT 5–15: Using Multiple Table Values—Diagrammatic Solution

Panel A—Hypothetical Situation:
See caption, Using Multiple Table Values.

Panel B—Diagrammatic Solution:

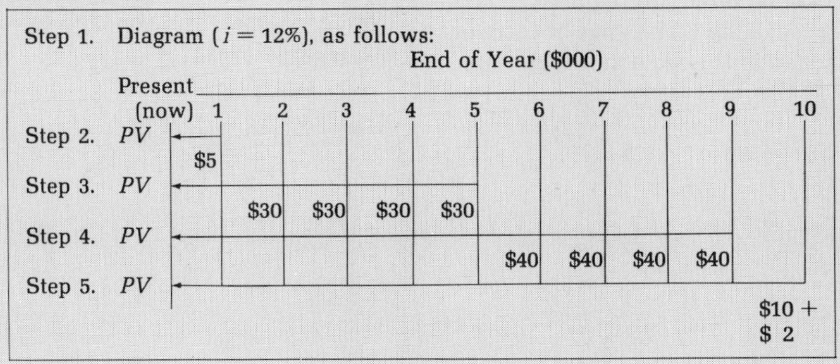

of years 6–9; then this present value is discounted for five periods. Thus,

$$\$40{,}000 \times P_{o_{n=4;\, i=12\%}} =$$
$$\$40{,}000 \times 3.03735 \text{ (Table 5–4)} = \$121{,}494$$

$$\$121{,}494 \times p_{n=5;\, i=12\%} =$$
$$\$121{,}494 \times .56743 \text{ (Table 5–2)} = \underline{\underline{\$68{,}939}}$$

Step 5 is the present value of the single amount $12,000 for 10 periods at 12 percent, as follows:

$$\$12{,}000 \times p_{n=10;\, i=12\%} =$$
$$\$12{,}000 \times .32197 \text{ (Table 5–2)} = \underline{\underline{\$3{,}864}}$$

Finally, the sum of the present values from steps 2–5 is the indicated offering price for the land:

Year End	Estimated Net Cash Revenue	Computed Present Value of Net Cash Revenue at 12 percent
1	$ 5,000	$ 4,464
2–5	$30,000 × 4 = 120,000	81,358
6–9	40,000 × 4 = 160,000	68,939
10	12,000	3,864
Total net cash revenue	$297,000	
Offering price		$158,625

A streamlined solution is as follows:

Year 1:
$\$5{,}000 \times p_{n=1;\, i=12\%} = \$5{,}000 \times .89286$ .... $ 4,464

Years 2–5:
$\$30{,}000 \times P_{o_{n=5-1;\, i=12\%}} = \$30{,}000 \times (3.60478 - .89286)$ ... 81,358

Years 6–9:
$\$40{,}000 \times P_{o_{n=9-5;\, i=12\%}} = \$40{,}000 \times (5.32825 - 3.60478)$ .. 68,939

Year 10:
$(\$10{,}000 + \$2{,}000) \times p_{n=10;\, i=12\%} = \$12{,}000 \times .32197$ 3,864

Offering price $158,625

SUMMARY

This chapter has presented the concepts of future and present value and has illustrated their relevance to certain accounting problems. At the beginning of the chapter the primary accounting applications were listed. These applications often are required to conform to GAAP. Because of the wide range of accounting applications, accountants need a thorough understanding of them. Future and present value concepts also have considerable relevance in financial analyses, capital budgeting, and alternative choice problems which accountants often encounter in public, private, or governmental accounting. Throughout the later chapters, and in subsequent business administration courses, the concepts of compound interest are widely used.

TABLE 5–1: Future Value of 1, $f = (1 + i)^n$

Periods	2%	2½%	3%	4%	5%	6%	7%	8%	9%	10%
1	1.02000	1.02500	1.03000	1.04000	1.05000	1.06000	1.07000	1.08000	1.09000	1.10000
2	1.04040	1.05063	1.06090	1.08160	1.10250	1.12360	1.14490	1.16640	1.18810	1.21000
3	1.06121	1.07689	1.09273	1.12486	1.15763	1.19102	1.22504	1.25971	1.29503	1.33100
4	1.08243	1.10381	1.12551	1.16986	1.21551	1.26248	1.31080	1.36049	1.41158	1.46410
5	1.10408	1.13141	1.15927	1.21665	1.27628	1.33823	1.40255	1.46933	1.53862	1.61051
6	1.12616	1.15969	1.19405	1.26532	1.34010	1.41852	1.50073	1.58687	1.67710	1.77156
7	1.14869	1.18869	1.22987	1.31593	1.40710	1.50363	1.60578	1.71382	1.82804	1.94872
8	1.17166	1.21840	1.26677	1.36857	1.47746	1.59385	1.71819	1.85093	1.99256	2.14359
9	1.19509	1.24886	1.30477	1.42331	1.55133	1.68948	1.83846	1.99900	2.17189	2.35795
10	1.21899	1.28008	1.34392	1.48024	1.62889	1.79085	1.96715	2.15892	2.36736	2.59374
11	1.24337	1.31209	1.38423	1.53945	1.71034	1.89830	2.10485	2.33164	2.58043	2.85312
12	1.26824	1.34489	1.42576	1.60103	1.79586	2.01220	2.25219	2.51817	2.81266	3.13843
13	1.29361	1.37851	1.46853	1.66507	1.88565	2.13293	2.40985	2.71962	3.06580	3.45227
14	1.31948	1.41297	1.51259	1.73168	1.97993	2.26090	2.57853	2.93719	3.34173	3.79750
15	1.34587	1.44830	1.55797	1.80094	2.07893	2.39656	2.75903	3.17217	3.64248	4.17725
16	1.37279	1.48451	1.60471	1.87298	2.18287	2.54035	2.95216	3.42594	3.97031	4.59497
17	1.40024	1.52162	1.65285	1.94790	2.29202	2.69277	3.15882	3.70002	4.32763	5.05447
18	1.42825	1.55966	1.70243	2.02582	2.40662	2.85434	3.37993	3.99602	4.71712	5.55992
19	1.45681	1.59865	1.75351	2.10685	2.52695	3.02560	3.61653	4.31570	5.14166	6.11591
20	1.48595	1.63862	1.80611	2.19112	2.65330	3.20714	3.86968	4.66096	5.60441	6.72750
21	1.51567	1.67958	1.86029	2.27877	2.78596	3.39956	4.14056	5.03383	6.10881	7.40025
22	1.54598	1.72157	1.91610	2.36992	2.92526	3.60354	4.43040	5.43654	6.65860	8.14027
23	1.57690	1.76461	1.97359	2.46472	3.07152	3.81975	4.74053	5.87146	7.25787	8.95430
24	1.60844	1.80873	2.03279	2.56330	3.22510	4.04893	5.07237	6.34118	7.91108	9.84973
25	1.64061	1.85394	2.09378	2.66584	3.38635	4.29187	5.42743	6.84848	8.62308	10.83471

Periods	11%	12%	14%	15%	16%	18%	20%	22%	24%	25%
1	1.11000	1.12000	1.14000	1.15000	1.16000	1.18000	1.20000	1.22000	1.24000	1.25000
2	1.23210	1.25440	1.29960	1.32250	1.34560	1.39240	1.44000	1.48840	1.53760	1.56250
3	1.36763	1.40493	1.48154	1.52088	1.56090	1.64303	1.72800	1.81585	1.90662	1.95313
4	1.51807	1.57352	1.68896	1.74901	1.81064	1.93878	2.07360	2.21533	2.36421	2.44141
5	1.68506	1.76234	1.92541	2.01136	2.10034	2.28776	2.48832	2.70271	2.93163	3.05176
6	1.87041	1.97382	2.19497	2.31306	2.43640	2.69955	2.98598	3.29730	3.63522	3.81470
7	2.07616	2.21068	2.50227	2.66002	2.82622	3.18547	3.58318	4.02271	4.50767	4.76837
8	2.30454	2.47596	2.85259	3.05902	3.27841	3.75886	4.29982	4.90771	5.58951	5.96046
9	2.55804	2.77308	3.25195	3.51788	3.80296	4.43545	5.15978	5.98740	6.93099	7.45058
10	2.83942	3.10585	3.70722	4.04556	4.41144	5.23384	6.19174	7.30463	8.59443	9.31323
11	3.15176	3.47855	4.22623	4.65239	5.11726	6.17593	7.43008	8.91165	10.65709	11.64153
12	3.49845	3.89598	4.81790	5.35025	5.93603	7.28759	8.91610	10.87221	13.21479	14.55192
13	3.88328	4.36349	5.49241	6.15279	6.88579	8.59936	10.69932	13.26410	16.38634	18.18989
14	4.31044	4.88711	6.26135	7.07571	7.98752	10.14724	12.83918	16.18220	20.31906	22.73737
15	4.78459	5.47357	7.13794	8.13706	9.26552	11.97375	15.40702	19.74229	25.19563	28.42171
16	5.31089	6.13039	8.13725	9.35762	10.74800	14.12902	18.48843	24.08559	31.24259	35.52714
17	5.89509	6.86604	9.27646	10.76126	12.46768	16.67225	22.18611	29.38442	38.74081	44.40892
18	6.54355	7.68997	10.57517	12.37545	14.46251	19.67325	26.62333	35.84899	48.03860	55.51115
19	7.26334	8.61276	12.05569	14.23177	16.77652	23.21444	31.94800	43.73577	59.56786	69.38894
20	8.06231	9.64629	13.74349	16.36654	19.46076	27.39303	38.33760	53.35764	73.86415	86.73617
21	8.94917	10.80385	15.66758	18.82152	22.57448	32.32378	46.00512	65.09632	91.59155	108.42022
22	9.93357	12.10031	17.86104	21.64475	26.18640	38.14206	55.20614	79.41751	113.57352	135.52527
23	11.02627	13.55235	20.36158	24.89146	30.37622	45.00763	66.24737	96.88936	140.83116	169.40659
24	12.23916	15.17863	23.21221	28.62518	35.23642	53.10901	79.49685	118.20502	174.63064	211.75824
25	13.58546	17.00006	26.46192	32.91895	40.87424	62.66863	95.39622	144.21013	216.54199	264.69780

TABLE 5–2: Present Value of 1, $p = \frac{1}{(1+i)^n}$

Periods	2%	2½%	3%	4%	5%	6%	7%	8%	9%	10%
1	.98039	.97561	.97087	.96154	.95238	.94340	.93458	.92593	.91743	.90909
2	.96117	.95181	.94260	.92456	.90703	.89000	.87344	.85734	.84168	.82645
3	.94232	.92860	.91514	.88900	.86384	.83962	.81630	.79383	.77218	.75131
4	.92385	.90595	.88849	.85480	.82270	.79209	.76290	.73503	.70843	.68301
5	.90573	.88385	.86261	.82193	.78353	.74726	.71299	.68058	.64993	.62092
6	.88797	.86230	.83748	.79031	.74622	.70496	.66634	.63017	.59627	.56447
7	.87056	.84127	.81309	.75992	.71068	.66506	.62275	.58349	.54703	.51316
8	.85349	.82075	.78941	.73069	.67684	.62741	.58201	.54027	.50187	.46651
9	.83676	.80073	.76642	.70259	.64461	.59190	.54393	.50025	.46043	.42410
10	.82035	.78120	.74409	.67556	.61391	.55839	.50835	.46319	.42241	.38554
11	.80426	.76214	.72242	.64958	.58468	.52679	.47509	.42888	.38753	.35049
12	.78849	.74356	.70138	.62460	.55684	.49697	.44401	.39711	.35553	.31863
13	.77303	.72542	.68095	.60057	.53032	.46884	.41496	.36770	.32618	.28966
14	.75788	.70773	.66112	.57748	.50507	.44230	.38782	.34046	.29925	.26333
15	.74301	.69047	.64186	.55526	.48102	.41727	.36245	.31524	.27454	.23939
16	.72845	.67362	.62317	.53391	.45811	.39365	.33873	.29189	.25187	.21763
17	.71416	.65720	.60502	.51337	.43630	.37136	.31657	.27027	.23107	.19784
18	.70016	.64117	.58739	.49363	.41552	.35034	.29586	.25025	.21199	.17986
19	.68643	.62553	.57029	.47464	.39573	.33051	.27651	.23171	.19449	.16351
20	.67297	.61027	.55368	.45639	.37689	.31180	.25842	.21455	.17843	.14864
21	.65978	.59539	.53755	.43883	.35894	.29416	.24151	.19866	.16370	.13513
22	.64684	.58086	.52189	.42196	.34185	.27751	.22571	.18394	.15018	.12285
23	.63416	.56670	.50669	.40573	.32557	.26180	.21095	.17032	.13778	.11168
24	.62172	.55288	.49193	.39012	.31007	.24698	.19715	.15770	.12640	.10153
25	.60953	.53939	.47761	.37512	.29530	.23300	.18425	.14602	.11597	.09230

Periods	11%	12%	14%	15%	16%	18%	20%	22%	24%	25%
1	.90090	.89286	.87719	.86957	.86207	.84746	.83333	.81967	.80645	.80000
2	.81162	.79719	.76947	.75614	.74316	.71818	.69444	.67186	.65036	.64000
3	.73119	.71178	.67497	.65752	.64066	.60863	.57870	.55071	.52449	.51200
4	.65873	.63552	.59208	.57175	.55229	.51579	.48225	.45140	.42297	.40960
5	.59345	.56743	.51937	.49718	.47611	.43711	.40188	.37000	.34111	.32768
6	.53464	.50663	.45559	.43233	.41044	.37043	.33490	.30328	.27509	.26214
7	.48166	.45235	.39964	.37594	.35383	.31393	.27908	.24859	.22184	.20972
8	.43393	.40388	.35056	.32690	.30503	.26604	.23257	.20376	.17891	.16777
9	.39092	.36061	.30751	.28426	.26295	.22546	.19381	.16702	.14428	.13422
10	.35218	.32197	.26974	.24718	.22668	.19106	.16151	.13690	.11635	.10737
11	.31728	.28748	.23662	.21494	.19542	16192	.13459	.11221	.09383	.08590
12	.28584	.25668	.20756	.18691	.16846	.13722	.11216	.09198	.07567	.06872
13	.25751	.22917	.18207	.16253	.14523	.11629	.09346	.07539	.06103	.05498
14	.23199	.20462	.15971	.14133	.12520	.09855	.07789	.06180	.04921	.04398
15	.20900	.18270	.14010	.12289	.10793	.08352	.06491	.05065	.03969	.03518
16	.18829	.16312	.12289	.10686	.09304	.07078	.05409	.04152	.03201	.02815
17	.16963	.14564	.10780	.09293	.08021	.05998	.04507	.03403	.02581	.02252
18	.15282	.13004	.09456	.08081	.06914	.05083	.03756	.02789	.02082	.01801
19	.13768	.11611	.08295	.07027	.05961	.04308	.03130	.02286	.01679	.01441
20	.12403	.10367	.07276	.06110	.05139	.03651	.02608	.01874	.01354	.01153
21	.11174	.09256	.06383	.05313	.04430	.03094	.02174	.01536	.01092	.00922
22	.10067	.08264	.05599	.04620	.03819	.02622	.01811	.01259	.00880	.00738
23	.09069	.07379	.04911	.04017	.03292	.02222	.01509	.01032	.00710	.00590
24	.08170	.06588	.04308	.03493	.02838	.01883	.01258	.00846	.00573	.00472
25	.07361	.05882	.03779	.03038	.02447	.01596	.01048	.00693	.00462	.00378

TABLE 5–3: Future Value of Annuity of n Rents of 1 Each (ordinary), $F_o = \frac{(1+i)^n - 1}{i}$

Periodic Rents (n)	2%	2½%	3%	4%	5%	6%	7%	8%	9%	10%
1	1.00000	1.00000	1.00000	1.00000	1.00000	1.00000	1.00000	1.00000	1.00000	1.00000
2	2.02000	2.02500	2.03000	2.04000	2.05000	2.06000	2.07000	2.08000	2.09000	2.10000
3	3.06040	3.07563	3.09090	3.12160	3.15250	3.18360	3.21490	3.24640	3.27810	3.31000
4	4.12161	4.15252	4.18363	4.24646	4.31013	4.37462	4.43994	4.50611	4.57313	4.64100
5	5.20404	5.25633	5.30914	5.41632	5.52563	5.63709	5.75074	5.86660	5.98471	6.10510
6	6.30812	6.38774	6.46841	6.63298	6.80191	6.97532	7.15329	7.33593	7.52333	7.71561
7	7.43428	7.54753	7.66246	7.89829	8.14201	8.39384	8.65402	8.92280	9.20043	9.48717
8	8.58297	8.73612	8.89234	9.21423	9.54911	9.89747	10.25980	10.63663	11.02847	11.43589
9	9.75463	9.95452	10.15911	10.58280	11.02656	11.49132	11.97799	12.48756	13.02104	13.57948
10	10.94972	11.20338	11.46388	12.00611	12.57789	13.18079	13.81645	14.48656	15.19293	15.93742
11	12.16872	12.48347	12.80780	13.48635	14.20679	14.97164	15.78360	16.64549	17.56029	18.53117
12	13.41209	13.79555	14.19203	15.02581	15.91713	16.86994	17.88845	18.97713	20.14072	21.38428
13	14.68033	15.14044	15.61779	16.62684	17.71298	18.88214	20.14064	21.49530	22.95338	24.52271
14	15.97394	16.51895	17.08632	18.29191	19.59863	21.01507	22.55049	24.21492	26.01919	27.97498
15	17.29342	17.93193	18.59891	20.02359	21.57856	23.27597	25.12902	27.15211	29.36092	31.77248
16	18.63929	19.38022	20.15688	21.82453	23.65749	25.67253	27.88805	30.32428	33.00340	35.94973
17	20.01207	20.86473	21.76159	23.69751	25.84037	28.21288	30.84022	33.75023	36.97370	40.54470
18	21.41231	22.38635	23.41444	25.64541	28.13238	30.90565	33.99903	37.45024	41.30134	45.59917
19	22.84056	23.94601	25.11687	27.67123	30.53900	33.75999	37.37896	41.44626	46.01846	51.15909
20	24.29737	25.54466	26.87037	29.77808	33.06595	36.78559	40.99549	45.76196	51.16012	57.27500
21	25.78332	27.18327	28.67649	31.96920	35.71925	39.99273	44.86518	50.42292	56.76453	64.00250
22	27.29898	28.86286	30.53678	34.24797	38.50521	43.39229	49.00574	55.45676	62.87334	71.40275
23	28.84496	30.58443	32.45288	36.61789	41.43048	46.99583	53.43614	60.89330	69.53194	79.54302
24	30.42186	32.34904	34.42647	39.08260	44.50200	50.81558	58.17667	66.76476	76.78981	88.49733
25	32.03030	34.15776	36.45926	41.64591	47.72710	54.86451	63.24904	73.10594	84.70090	98.34706

Periodic Rents (n)	11%	12%	14%	15%	16%	18%	20%	22%	24%	25%
1	1.00000	1.00000	1.00000	1.00000	1.00000	1.00000	1.00000	1.00000	1.00000	1.00000
2	2.11000	2.12000	2.14000	2.15000	2.16000	2.18000	2.20000	2.22000	2.24000	2.25000
3	3.34210	3.37440	3.43960	3.47250	3.50560	3.57240	3.64000	3.70840	3.77760	3.81250
4	4.70973	4.77933	4.92114	4.99338	5.06650	5.21543	5.36800	5.52425	5.68422	5.76563
5	6.22780	6.35285	6.61010	6.74238	6.87714	7.15421	7.44160	7.73958	8.04844	8.20703
6	7.91286	8.11519	8.53552	8.75374	8.97748	9.44197	9.92992	10.44229	10.98006	11.25879
7	9.78327	10.08901	10.73049	11.06680	11.41387	12.14152	12.91590	13.73959	14.61528	15.07349
8	11.85943	12.29969	13.23276	13.72682	14.24009	15.32700	16.49908	17.76231	19.12294	19.84186
9	14.16397	14.77566	16.08535	16.78584	17.51851	19.08585	20.79890	22.67001	24.71245	25.80232
10	16.72201	17.54874	19.33730	20.30372	21.32147	23.52131	25.95868	28.65742	31.64344	33.25290
11	19.56143	20.65458	23.04452	24.34928	25.73290	28.75514	32.15042	35.96205	40.23787	42.56613
12	22.71319	24.13313	27.27075	29.00167	30.85017	34.93107	39.58050	44.87370	50.89495	54.20766
13	26.21164	28.02911	32.08865	34.35192	36.78620	42.21866	48.49660	55.74591	64.10974	68.75958
14	30.09492	32.39260	37.58107	40.50471	43.67199	50.81802	59.19592	69.01001	80.49608	86.94947
15	34.40536	37.27971	43.84241	47.58041	51.65951	60.96527	72.03511	85.19221	100.81514	109.68684
16	39.18995	42.75328	50.98035	55.71747	60.92503	72.93901	87.44213	104.93450	126.01077	138.10855
17	44.50084	48.88367	59.11760	65.07509	71.67303	87.06804	105.93056	129.02009	157.25336	173.63568
18	50.39594	55.74971	68.39407	75.83636	84.14072	103.74028	128.11667	158.40451	195.99416	218.04460
19	56.93949	63.43968	78.96923	88.21181	98.60323	123.41353	154.74000	194.25350	244.03276	273.55576
20	64.20283	72.05244	91.02493	102.44358	115.37975	146.62797	186.68800	237.98927	303.60062	342.94470
21	72.26514	81.69874	104.76842	118.81012	134.84051	174.02100	225.02560	291.34691	377.46477	429.68087
22	81.21431	92.50258	120.43600	137.63164	157.41499	206.34479	271.03072	356.44323	469.05632	538.10109
23	91.14788	104.60289	138.29704	159.27638	183.60138	244.48685	326.23686	435.86075	582.62984	673.62636
24	102.17415	118.15524	158.65862	184.16784	213.97761	289.49448	392.48424	532.75011	723.46100	843.03295
25	114.41331	133.33387	181.87083	212.79302	249.21402	342.60349	471.98108	650.95513	898.09164	1054.79118

TABLE 5–4: Present Value of Annuity of *n* Rents of 1 Each (ordinary), $P_o = \dfrac{1 - \dfrac{1}{(1+i)^n}}{i}$

Periodic Rents (n)	2%	2½%	3%	4%	5%	6%	7%	8%	9%	10%
1	.98039	.97561	.97087	.96154	.95238	.94340	.93458	.92593	.91743	.90909
2	1.94156	1.92742	1.91347	1.88609	1.85941	1.83339	1.80802	1.78326	1.75911	1.73554
3	2.88388	2.85602	2.82861	2.77509	2.72325	2.67301	2.62432	2.57710	2.53129	2.48685
4	3.80773	3.76197	3.71710	3.62990	3.54595	3.46511	3.38721	3.31213	3.23972	3.16987
5	4.71346	4.64583	4.57971	4.45182	4.32948	4.21236	4.10020	3.99271	3.88965	3.79079
6	5.60143	5.50813	5.41719	5.24214	5.07569	4.91732	4.76654	4.62288	4.48592	4.35526
7	6.47199	6.34939	6.23028	6.00205	5.78637	5.58238	5.38929	5.20637	5.03295	4.86842
8	7.32548	7.17014	7.01969	6.73274	6.46321	6.20979	5.97130	5.74664	5.53482	5.33493
9	8.16224	7.97087	7.78611	7.43533	7.10782	6.80169	6.51523	6.24689	5.99525	5.75902
10	8.98259	8.75206	8.53020	8.11090	7.72173	7.36009	7.02358	6.71008	6.41766	6.14457
11	9.78685	9.51421	9.25262	8.76048	8.30641	7.88687	7.49867	7.13896	6.80519	6.49506
12	10.57534	10.25776	9.95400	9.38507	8.86325	8.38384	7.94269	7.53608	7.16073	6.81369
13	11.34837	10.98318	10.63496	9.98565	9.39357	8.85268	8.35765	7.90378	7.48690	7.10336
14	12.10625	11.69091	11.29607	10.56312	9.89864	9.29498	8.74547	8.24424	7.78615	7.36669
15	12.84926	12.38138	11.93794	11.11839	10.37966	9.71225	9.10791	8.55948	8.06069	7.60608
16	13.57771	13.05500	12.56110	11.65230	10.83777	10.10590	9.44665	8.85137	8.31256	7.82371
17	14.29187	13.71220	13.16612	12.16567	11.27407	10.47726	9.76322	9.12164	8.54363	8.02155
18	14.99203	14.35336	13.75351	12.65930	11.68959	10.82760	10.05909	9.37189	8.75563	8.20141
19	15.67846	14.97889	14.32380	13.13394	12.08532	11.15812	10.33560	9.60360	8.95011	8.36492
20	16.35143	15.58916	14.87747	13.59033	12.46221	11.46992	10.59401	9.81815	9.12855	8.51356
21	17.01121	16.18455	15.41502	14.02916	12.82115	11.76408	10.83553	10.01680	9.29224	8.64869
22	17.65805	16.76541	15.93692	14.45112	13.16300	12.04158	11.06124	10.20074	9.44243	8.77154
23	18.29220	17.33211	16.44361	14.85684	13.48857	12.30338	11.27219	10.37106	9.58021	8.88322
24	18.91393	17.88499	16.93554	15.24696	13.79864	12.55036	11.46933	10.52876	9.70661	8.98474
25	19.52346	18.42438	17.41315	15.62208	14.09394	12.78336	11.65358	10.67478	9.82258	9.07704

Periodic Rents (n)	11%	12%	14%	15%	16%	18%	20%	22%	24%	25%
1	.90090	.89286	.87719	.86957	.86207	.84746	.83333	.81967	.80645	.80000
2	1.71252	1.69005	1.64666	1.62571	1.60523	1.56564	1.52778	1.49153	1.45682	1.44000
3	2.44371	2.40183	2.32163	2.28323	2.24589	2.17427	2.10648	2.04224	1.98130	1.95200
4	3.10245	3.03735	2.91371	2.85498	2.79818	2.69006	2.58873	2.49364	2.40428	2.36160
5	3.69590	3.60478	3.43308	3.35216	3.27429	3.12717	2.99061	2.86364	2.74538	2.68928
6	4.23054	4.11141	3.88867	3.78448	3.68474	3.49760	3.32551	3.16692	3.02047	2.95142
7	4.71220	4.56376	4.28830	4.16042	4.03857	3.81153	3.60459	3.41551	3.24232	3.16114
8	5.14612	4.96764	4.63886	4.48732	4.34359	4.07757	3.83716	3.61927	3.42122	3.32891
9	5.53705	5.32825	4.94637	4.77158	4.60654	4.30302	4.03097	3.78628	3.56550	3.46313
10	5.88923	5.65022	5.21612	5.01877	4.83323	4.49409	4.19247	3.92318	3.68186	3.57050
11	6.20652	5.93770	5.45273	5.23371	5.02864	4.65601	4.32706	4.03540	3.77569	3.65640
12	6.49236	6.19437	5.66029	5.42062	5.19711	4.79322	4.43922	4.12737	3.85136	3.72512
13	6.74987	6.42355	5.84236	5.58315	5.34233	4.90951	4.53268	4.20277	3.91239	3.78010
14	6.98187	6.62817	6.00207	5.72448	5.46753	5.00806	4.61057	4.26456	3.96160	3.82408
15	7.19087	6.81086	6.14217	5.84737	5.57546	5.09158	4.67547	4.31522	4.00129	3.85926
16	7.37916	6.97399	6.26506	5.95423	5.66850	5.16235	4.72956	4.35673	4.03330	3.88741
17	7.54879	7.11963	6.37286	6.04716	5.74870	5.22233	4.77463	4.39077	4.05911	3.90993
18	7.70162	7.24967	6.46742	6.12797	5.81785	5.27316	4.81219	4.41866	4.07993	3.92794
19	7.83929	7.36578	6.55037	6.19823	5.87746	5.31624	4.84350	4.44152	4.09672	3.94235
20	7.96333	7.46944	6.62313	6.25933	5.92884	5.35275	4.86958	4.46027	4.11026	3.95388
21	8.07507	7.56200	6.68696	6.31246	5.97314	5.38368	4.89132	4.47563	4.12117	3.96311
22	8.17574	7.64465	6.74294	6.35866	6.01133	5.40990	4.90943	4.48822	4.12998	3.97049
23	5.26643	7.71843	6.79206	6.39884	6.04425	5.43212	4.92453	4.49854	4.13708	3.97639
24	8.34814	7.78432	6.83514	6.43377	6.07263	5.45095	4.93710	4.50700	4.14281	3.98111
25	8.42174	7.84314	6.87293	6.46415	6.09709	5.46691	4.94759	4.51393	4.14742	3.98489

QUESTIONS

PART A

1. Explain what is meant by the *time value of money.*
2. What is the fundamental difference between *simple* interest and *compound* interest?
3. Briefly explain each of the following:
   a. Future value of 1.
   b. Present value of 1.
   c. Future value of annuity of *n* rents of 1 each.
   d. Present value of annuity of *n* rents of 1 each.
4. Explain what is meant by the *future value of 1.* Relate it to the present value of 1.
5. If the table value for a future value of 1 is known, how may it be converted to the table value for present value of 1?

PART B

6. Define an *annuity* in general terms. Explain *rents* and relate them to time periods and interest rates.
7. The table for future value of an annuity provides the value 3.09 (rounded) at 3% for three rents; explain the meaning of this table value.
8. What is meant by the *present value* of an annuity? Contrast it with the *future value* of an annuity.
9. Explain the fundamental difference between *(a)* future value of an *ordinary annuity* and *(b)* future value of an *annuity due.*
10. Explain the fundamental difference between *(a)* present value of an *ordinary annuity* and *(b)* present value of an *annuity due.*

EXERCISES (round solutions to nearest dollar)

PART A: EXERCISES 5–1 to 5–10

Exercise 5–1

Lee Company plans to deposit $60,000 today into a special building fund which will be needed at the end of six years. They have found a financial institution (as trustee) that will pay them 12% annual interest on the fund balance.

Required:
How much will the fund total assuming (show computations):

Case A—Annual compounding?

Case B—Semiannual compounding?

Case C—Quarterly compounding?

Exercise 5–2

AKO Company, at the present date, has $40,000 which will be deposited in a savings account until needed. It is anticipated that $111,000 will be needed at the end of nine years to expand some manufacturing facilities. What approximate rate of interest would be required to accumulate the $111,000 assuming compounding on an annual basis? Show computations; no need to interpolate.

Exercise 5–3

Smith Corporation is planning an addition to its office building as soon as adequate funds can be accumulated. The corporation has estimated that the addition will cost approximately $250,000. At the present time $100,000 cash is on hand that will not be needed in the near future. A local savings institution will pay 14% interest (compounded annually). How many periods would be required to accumulate the $250,000? Show computations; no need to interpolate.

Exercise 5–4

West Company has on hand $100,000 cash that will not be needed in the near future. However, the company will expand operations within the next three to five years. The company has decided to establish a savings account locally which will earn 10% interest compounded annually. The interest will be added to the fund each year. Assuming the deposit of $100,000 is made on January 1, 19A, *(a)* compute the balance that will be in the fund at the end of the third year and *(b)* prepare an accumulation schedule for the fund.

Exercise 5–5

Steel Company will need $200,000 cash to renovate an old machine five years from now. Assume a financial institution will increase a fund at 12% annual interest. Compute the amount of cash that must be deposited now to meet the future need assuming (show computations):

Case A—Annual compounding.

Case B—Semiannual compounding.

Case C—Quarterly compounding.

Exercise 5–6

Able Company, on January 1, 1982, has a contract whereby the company is due to receive $50,000 cash on December 31, 1987. The company is short of cash and desires to discount (sell) this claim. Able is willing to accept a 16% annual discount. Under these conditions, how much cash would Able receive on January 1, 1982?

Exercise 5–7

On January 1, 19A, Deer Corporation signed a $200,000 non-interest-bearing note which is due on December 31, 19D. According to the agreement, Deer has the option to pay the $200,000 at maturity date or to pay the obligation in full on January 1, 19A, on a 12% compound interest discount basis. What would be the single amount of cash required on January 1, 19A, to settle the debt in full? Show computations. Assume this debt was incurred to purchase an operational asset. What should be recorded as the cost of the asset? Explain.

Exercise 5–8

Brick Corporation plans a plant expansion which will require approximately $300,000 at December 31, 19C. Since they have some idle cash on hand now, January 1, 19A, they desire to know how much they would have to invest as a lump sum now to accumulate the required amount, assuming 14% annual compound interest is added to the fund each December 31.

Required:

1. Compute the amount that must be invested on January 1, 19A.
2. Prepare an accumulation schedule for the plant expansion fund.

Exercise 5–9

Mellon Company purchased some additional equipment that was needed because of a new contract. The equipment was purchased on January 1, 19A. Because the contract would require two years to complete and Mellon was short of cash, the vendor agreed to accept a down payment of $10,000 and a two-year note for $45,000 (this amount includes all interest charges) due December 31, 19B. Assume a 20% annual rate of interest.

Required:

1. Compute the cost of the equipment. Show computations.
2. Give the entry at date of acquisition of the equipment.
3. Prepare a debt amortization schedule.

Exercise 5–10

B. Ball has a small child. Ball has decided to set up a fund to provide for the child's college education. A local financial institution will handle the fund and increase it each year on a 10% annual compound interest basis. Ball desires to make a single deposit on January 1, 19A, and specifies that the fund must have a $60,000 balance at the end of the 16th year. What amount of cash must be deposited on January 1, 19A? Show computations. Set up an accumulation schedule to cover the first three years.

PART B: EXERCISES 5–11 to 5–20

Exercise 5–11

The Boone family desires to accumulate a fund over the next few years. They will make equal annual contributions to the fund starting on December 31, 19A. The fund will be increased by the trustee by 12% annual interest. What will be the balance in the fund immediately after the last deposit assuming—

1. Five annual contributions of $5,000 each and annual compounding?
2. Ten semiannual contributions of $2,500 each and semiannual compounding?
3. Twenty quarterly contributions of $1,250 each and quarterly compounding?

Exercise 5–12

Chaulk Corporation has decided to accumulate a debt retirement fund by making three equal annual deposits of $22,000 on each December 31, starting at the end of 19A. Assume the fund will accumulate annual compound interest at 14% per year which will be added to the fund balance.

Required:

1. What will be the balance in the fund on December 31, 19C (immediately after the last deposit)?
2. Prepare an accumulation schedule for this fund.
3. Prepare the journal entries for the period January 1, 19A, through December 31, 19C.

Exercise 5–13

Glenn Corporation plans to establish a debt retirement fund, beginning December 31, 19A, to accumulate $90,000. End-of-period contributions of $20,000 will be made to a trustee each December 31, so that the desired amount will be available on December 31, 19D, the date of the last rent. Compute the required interest rate that must be earned by the fund on an annual compound basis to satisfy these requirements. Show your computations.

Exercise 5–14

May Corporation has decided to create a plant expansion fund by making equal annual deposits of $30,000 on each December 31. Interest at 10% compounded annually will be added to the fund balance. The company wants to know how many deposits will be required to build a fund of $953,200 immediately after the last deposit. Show your computations.

Exercise 5–15

Ralph Company desires to accumulate a fund to retire a debt of $100,000. The debt is due on January 1, 1989. Equal annual contributions will be made to the fund by Ralph on each December 31, starting in 1982 and ending in 1988. The fund will be increased each year by 8% annual compound interest. Compute the amount of the equal contributions at each year-end.

Exercise 5–16

Black Company is considering purchasing a used machine that is in excellent mechanical condition. The company plans to keep the machine for 10 years, at which time the residual value will be zero. An analysis of the capacity of the machine and the costs of operating it (including materials used in production) provided an estimate that the machine would increase aftertax net cash inflow by approximately $100,000 per year.

Required:

1. Compute the approximate amount that Black should be willing to pay now for the machine assuming a target earnings rate of 15% per year. Assume also that the revenue is realized at each year-end. Show your computations.
2. What price should be paid assuming a $20,000 residual value?

Exercise 5–17

On January 1, 19A, J. R. Corporation purchased a machine at a cost of $60,000. They paid $35,535 cash and incurred a debt for the difference. This debt is to be paid off in equal annual installments of $6,000 payable each December 31. The interest rate on the unpaid balance each period is 18% per annum. How many equal payments must be made at each year-end? Show your computations.

Exercise 5–18

Complete the following table assuming $n = 7$; $i = 16\%$:

Concept	Symbol	Formula	"Value" Based on $1	Table
1. Future value of 1.	____	____	____	____
2. Present value of 1.	____	____	____	____
3. Future value of ordinary annuity of *n* rents of 1 each.	____	____	____	____
4. Present value of ordinary annuity of *n* rents of 1 each.	____	____	____	____
5. Future value of annuity due of *n* rents of 1 each.	____	____	____	____
6. Present value of annuity due of *n* rents of 1 each.	____	____	____	____

Exercise 5–19

On January 1, 19A, James Company decided to create an expansion fund by making equal annual deposits of $66,000. The fund is required on December 31, 19E. Interest at 12% compounded annually will be added to the fund. Five deposits are planned. Two alternative dates are under consideration, viz:

Alternative A—Make the annual deposits on each December 31 starting in 19A.

Alternative B—Make the annual deposits on each January 1 starting in 19A.

Required:
Complete the following table:

Alternative	Type of Annuity	Balance in the Fund at End of 19E	
		Computations	Amount
A			
B			

Exercise 5–20

High Company agreed on January 1, 19A, to deposit $120,000 cash with a trustee. The trustee will increase the fund on a 10% compound interest basis on the fund balance each successive year. The trustee is required to pay out the fund in 10 equal annual installments to a former employee of High so that the fund is completely exhausted at the end of that time. Two alternative payment dates are under consideration, viz:

Alternative A—Make the annual payments to the former employee each December 31 starting in 19A.

Alternative B—Make the annual payments to the former employee each January 1 starting in 19A.

Required:
Complete the following table:

Alternative	Type of Annuity	Amount of the Equal Annual Payments	
		Computations	Amount
A			
B			

PROBLEMS (round solutions to nearest dollar)

PART A: PROBLEMS 5–1 to 5–7

Problem 5–1

Hines Company plans to deposit $30,000 in a special fund on January 1, 19A, for future use as needed. The fund will accumulate 12% interest per year.

Required:

1. Complete the following table by entering, into each cell, the balance in the fund at the end of the intervals indicated:

Compounding Assumption	Number of Years	
	2	4
Annual		
Semiannual		
Quarterly		

2. Prepare an accumulation schedule based on the first cell (annual only for two years).
3. Give journal entries for the fund based on the first cell (annual only for two years).

Problem 5–2

1. On January 1, 19A, an investor deposited $7,000 into a savings account that would accumulate at 12% annual compound interest for three years. Compute the balance that would be in the savings account at the end of the third year. Prepare an accumulation schedule for this situation.
2. On January 1, 19A, another investor deposited $7,000 into a savings account that would accumulate to $9,317 at the end of three years assuming annual compound interest. Compute the interest rate that would be necessary. Show computations. Prepare an accumulation schedule for this situation.
3. On January 1, 19A, another investor deposited $7,000 into a savings account that would accumulate to $11,108 assuming 8% annual compound interest. Compute the number of periods that would be necessary. Show computations. Prepare an accumulation schedule for this situation.

Problem 5–3

1. An investor planned to deposit $40,000 into a savings account that would accumulate to $43,600 at the end of year 1. Assume the deposit was made at the beginning of year 1. What would be the balance in the fund at the end of the fifth year? The 10th year? The 20th year? Show computations.
2. Another investor planned to deposit $50,000 into a savings account that would accumulate to $141,971 at the end of the 10th year. What rate of annual compound interest would have to be earned on the fund to meet these specifications? Show computations.
3. Another investor planned to deposit $10,000 at annual compound interest. The investor desires to accumulate $25,000 over a 10-year period. What rate of interest would be required to meet these specifications? Show computations. Interpolation is required.

Problem 5–4

Mayor Corporation decided to place $100,000 into a special expansion fund for use in the future as needed. The fund will accumulate at 12% annual compound interest. The fund will be established on March 1, 19A, and the interest will be added to the fund balance on an annual compound interest basis.

Required:

1. Compute the balance that will be in the fund at the end of 3 years, 5 years, and 10 years, respectively.
2. Prepare an accumulation schedule for three years.
3. Give the journal entries for Mayor Corporation for the first three years. Disregard adjusting and closing entries.
4. What adjusting entry would be made on December 31, 19A, assuming this is the end of the accounting period for Mayor Corporation?

Problem 5–5

Easy Company anticipates that it will need $200,000 cash for an expansion in the next few years. Assume an annual interest rate of 14%. The company desires to make a single contribution now, January 1, 19A, so that the $200,000 will be available when needed.

Required:

1. Complete the following table by entering into each cell the amount that must be deposited now to meet the above specifications:

Compounding Assumption	Number of Years	
	2	3
Annual		
Semiannual		

2. Prepare an accumulation schedule based on the first cell.
3. Give journal entries for the fund based on the first cell.

Problem 5–6

Tom's Construction Company has just won a bid on a major contract. The contract will require the purchase of new equipment costing approximately $200,000. The vendor, X Company, requires $50,000 cash down payment and will accept a two-year, $150,000, noninterest-bearing note (assume an interest rate on this type of note to be 20% per annum).

Required:

1. Compute the cost of the equipment on January 1, 19A. Show computations.
2. Give the entry by Tom's on date of purchase to record the equipment and the related financing.
3. Prepare a debt amortization schedule for the note that reflects the annual interest expense and the principal.
4. Give journal entries by Tom's each year while the note is outstanding and for final payment of the note.
5. Assume that Tom's is short of cash on the date of the purchase. To raise cash for the down payment, Tom's is considering the sale (discounting) of a $70,000 noninterest-bearing note receivable which was received from a customer. The note is due on December 31, 19C (i.e., three years hence). Tom's has located an individual that will buy this future claim at an 18% compound annual discount. Compute the amount that Tom's would receive on January 1, 19A, the date of the sale of the note receivable. Show computations.

Problem 5–7

Maybe Company is trying to "clean up" some of its debts. On January 1, 1982, the company has savings accounts as follows:

Date Established	Amount Deposited (a single deposit for each)	Annual Compound Interest Rate
1/1/71	$20,000	8%
1/1/77	30,000	10%

The outstanding debts to be paid off are as follows:

Due Date	Type of Note	Face of Note
12/31/84	Noninterest bearing	$ 60,000
12/31/91	Noninterest bearing	200,000

Required:

1. Compute the amount of cash that can be obtained from the two savings accounts on January 1, 1982.
2. Compute the amount for which the two debts can be settled on January 1, 1982, assuming a going rate of interest of 18%.
3. How much cash, in addition to the cash available from the savings accounts, will be needed to settle the two debts on January 1, 1982?

PART B: PROBLEMS 5–8 to 5–18

Problem 5–8

Ready Corporation is contemplating the accumulation of a special fund to be used for expanding sales activities into the western part of the country. It is January 1, 19A, and the fund will be needed at the beginning of 19D, according to present plans. The fund will earn 12% interest compounded annually. The company is considering two plans for accumulating the fund by December 31, 19C, viz:

Plan A—Make three annual deposits of $50,000 each, starting on December 31, 19A.

Plan B—Make three annual deposits of $50,000 each, starting on January 1, 19A.

Required:

1. What kind of annuity is involved for each plan? Compute the balance that will be in the special fund on December 31, 19C, under each plan. Show computations.
2. Prepare an accumulation schedule for each plan.
3. Tabulate the entries for each plan. Set up a tabulation with the following captions:

Date	Fund, Debit	Cash, Credit	Interest Revenue, Credit

4. Explain why the fund has a different balance under each plan.

Problem 5–9

Lee Corporation desires to establish a special debt retirement fund amounting to $70,000. A trustee has agreed to handle the fund and to increase it on a 10% annual compound interest basis. Lee will make equal annual contributions of $15,083 at the end of each year, starting on December 31, 19A. Assume an ordinary annuity situation.

Required:

1. Determine the number of contributions that Lee must make to meet these specifications. Show computations.
2. Prepare an accumulation schedule for the fund.
3. Prepare the journal entries for the fund over its entire term.

Problem 5–10

Lace Company agreed with its president, J. Smith, to set up a fund with a trustee that will pay Smith $50,000 per year for the three years following retirement. Smith will retire on January 1, 19J, and the equal annual payments are to be made by the trustee each December 31 starting in 19J. The trustee will add to the fund 12% annual compound interest on the fund balance each year-end. The fund is to have a zero balance on December 31, 19L, immediately after the last payment.

Required:

1. Compute the single sum that must be deposited with the trustee on January 1, 19J, to meet these specifications.
2. Prepare a diminution schedule through December 31, 19L. Set up table captions as follows: Date, Cash Payments, Interest Revenue Earned, Fund Decreases, and Fund Balance.

Problem 5–11

Quick Construction Company can purchase a used machine which will be needed on a new job that will continue for approximately three years. It is January 1, 19A, and the machine is needed immediately. Because of a shortage of cash, Quick has asked the vendor for credit terms with no down payment. The vendor charges 20% annual compound interest. The machine can be purchased under these terms by making three payments of $8,000 each on December 31, 19A, 19B, and 19C.

Required:

1. What should be the cash price of the machine on January 1, 19A?
2. Give the entry to record the purchase of the machine on the credit terms.
3. Prepare a debt amortization schedule using the following format:

Date	Cash Payment	Interest Expense	Reduction of Principal	Liability Balance

Problem 5–12

Richie Student is considering the purchase of a Super Sail Boat which has a cash price of $6,500. Terms can be arranged for a $2,000 cash down payment and payment of the remaining $4,500, plus interest at 18% per annum, in three equal annual payments. Assume purchase on January 1, 19A, and payments on each December 31 thereafter.

Required:

1. Compute the amount of each annual payment assuming annual compound interest.
2. What did the boat cost? What was the total interest paid?
3. Prepare a debt amortization schedule using the following format:

Date	Cash Payment	Interest Expense	Reduction of Principal	Liability Balance

Problem 5–13

Lane has an industrious daughter, Lois, who is 15 years old today. For her birthday, Lane invests $20,000 toward her college education. Lane stipulates that Lois may withdraw four equal annual amounts from the fund, the first withdrawal to be made on her 18th birthday. The savings and loan association in which Lane placed the investment will add to the fund annual compound interest at the rate of 14% at the end of each year.

Required:
Compute the amount of each of the four withdrawals by Lois which will completely deplete the fund on the date of the final withdrawal. *Hint:* Diagram the problem situation.

Problem 5–14

RC Company rents a warehouse for an annual rental of $2,000. They have some idle cash and have approached the owner with a proposal to pay three years' rent in advance. The owner has agreed to an annual compound discount rate of 16%.

Required:
1. Assume it is January 1, 19A, and that the three rents are due on January 1, 19A, 19B, and 19C. Compute the amount that RC Company would have to pay as a single sum on January 1, 19A. What kind of an annuity value must be used? Explain.
2. Assume it is January 1, 19A, and that the three rents are due on December 31, 19A, 19B, and 19C. Compute the amount that RC Company would have to pay as a single sum on January 1, 19A. What kind of an annuity value must be used? Explain.
3. Explain why the single sums to be paid as computed under 1 and 2 above are different.

Problem 5–15

On January 1, 19A, Victor Company signed a three-year contract to rent some space that they needed immediately. The lease provided that Victor could pay annual rentals of $17,000 on each January 1, beginning in 19A, or, alternatively, they can pay all of the rent in advance, in one lump sum, at a 12% annual compound discount.

Required:
1. What single sum would have to be paid by Victor on January 1, 19A, for the 19A, 19B, and 19C annual rentals?
2. Assume it is January 1, 19A, and the three rents are due on December 31, 19A, 19B, and 19C. Compute the single sum Victor would have to pay on January 1, 19A.
3. Analyze the difference in the results between 1 and 2 above.

Problem 5–16

On January 1, 19A, Moon Company owes an $80,000 debt which is now due. Since the company is short of cash, they have reached an agreement with the creditor whereby the debt and interest are to be paid in equal annual installments on January 1, 19A, 19B, and 19C. Interest is 18% annual compounding.

Required:
1. What kind of annuity is this? Explain.
2. Compute the amount of the equal annual payments.
3. Prepare a debt amortization schedule, using the following format:

Date	Cash Payment	Interest Expense	Reduction of Principal	Liability Balance
1/1/19A				$80,000

Problem 5–17

East Corporation is negotiating to purchase a plant from another company that will complement East's operations. They have just completed a careful study of the plant and have developed the following estimates:

Expected net cash revenues:	
End of years 1–5 (per year)	$50,000
End of years 6–10 (per year)	40,000
End of year 11	30,000
End of year 12	10,000
Expected net residual value at end of year 12	3,000

Required:
1. Compute the amount that East should be willing to pay for the plant assuming a 16% return on the investment. Assume all amounts are at year-end and are given net of income taxes.
2. Assume the down payment is $150,000. East can pay this, and the bank will lend East the balance at 16% per annum payable in equal annual payments (including interest and principal) over five years. The payments will be at each year-end, starting one year after the date of purchase. Compute the amount of the equal annual payments on the loan. Compute the total interest that will be paid.
3. Give the entries (or entry) to record the purchase in 1 above and the loan in 2 above using the amounts you computed.
4. Give entries at the end of year 1 to record *(a)* net revenue, *(b)* interest expense, and *(c)* the loan payment.

Problem 5–18

In each situation described below, the interest rate is 10% per annum, but interest is compounded semiannually.

Required (round amounts to the nearest dollar):
1. How much will accumulate if an initial deposit of $10,000 is left at interest for three years? Show computations. Support your determination with a schedule covering the entire period.
2. What amount must be paid if $25,000 is borrowed and payment of both principal and interest is to occur as a single lump-sum payment at the end of two years? Show computations.

3. \$20,000 is to be accumulated by the end of four years. How much must be deposited now in a single lump sum? Show computations.
4. \$30,000 is left at interest for two years with no withdrawals. Starting two and one-half years after the deposit, the first of four equal semiannual withdrawals is made. What would be the amount of each withdrawal if: Case A—The final payment completely exhausts the funds? Case B—After four payments, \$10,000 remains on deposit? Prepare a schedule substantiating your determination in Case B.

6

Cash, Short-Term Investments, and Receivables

THIS CHAPTER discusses cash and near-cash items, often called quick (or liquid) assets. The three most liquid assets are cash, short-term investments, and current receivables (including short-term notes receivable). Their interchangeability and other similarities make it convenient to discuss them in the same chapter. Controlling and accounting for this particular group of current assets involve common problems, concepts, and procedures. To facilitate discussion the chapter is divided into three parts as follows:

Part A—Cash
Part B—Short-Term Investments
Part C—Receivables

Part A: Cash

Money is the medium of exchange and is used to express most of the measurements in accounting. Because of its pervasive use by society, the concept of cash is understood by nearly everyone; however, accounting for cash inflows and outflows presents some special problems. This part examines accounting for cash, including its control; reporting cash flows is discussed in Part B of Chapter 23, The Statement of Changes in Financial Position (SCFP), Cash Basis.

COMPOSITION OF CASH

Two primary characteristics of cash are (1) its availability as a medium of exchange and (2) its use as a measurement in accounting for the other items. Although its purchasing power may change, accountants usually make no effort to revalue cash for such changes.[1]

Cash includes coins, currency, and certain types of formal negotiable instruments which are accepted by banks for deposit. Thus, bank drafts, cashier's checks, money orders, certified checks, and ordinary checks constitute cash for accounting purposes. Balances on deposit in commercial banks should be considered cash if subject to immediate use.

[1] This statement applies to cash balances which are already expressed in terms of domestic dollars. Foreign currency balances must be translated to current dollar equivalents; thus, the dollar value of a foreign deposit will fluctuate as international exchange rates vary.

Balances in savings accounts generally should be classified as short-term investments. Cash excludes some items commonly intermingled with cash; postage stamps should be reported as supplies; and IOUs from officers, owners, or employees should be classified as special receivables, not as cash.

A company may agree to maintain **compensating balances** on deposit with a bank that extends credit to the company. Under such arrangements the borrower agrees, in effect, not to withdraw the amount on deposit below a specified limit. The practical effect is to raise interest rates because the sum borrowed cannot be used in its entirety, thus creating a nonspendable portion of a checking account. Existence of such an arrangement must be disclosed; otherwise statement users may assume the entire cash balance is available to meet currently maturing debts and expenses.

Checks which have *not* been mailed or otherwise delivered to the payees by the end of the accounting period should not be deducted from the balance of the Cash account. Entries already made to record such checks should be reversed before preparing the financial statements. An overdraft in a bank account should be shown as a current liability. However, if a depositor has overdrawn one account with Bank A but has positive balances in other accounts in that bank, it is appropriate accounting to offset the negative balance in one account against the positive balance in the other account and report the net asset or liability on the balance sheet because the single bank is in a position to protect both accounts. It is incorrect to offset an overdraft in Bank A against a balance on deposit in Bank B because the positive account is open to withdrawals without knowledge by the other bank. Amounts invested in certificates of deposit (CDs) should be classified as short-term investments.

Petty cash funds (discussed below) and cash held by branches or divisions should be included in cash because such funds ordinarily are used to meet current operating expenses and to liquidate current liabilities.

CONTROL OF CASH

The control of cash is critical in most businesses because cash is *(a)* easy to conceal and transport and *(b)* desired by everyone. The control of cash involves planning cash needs, control of expenditures, recordkeeping to assure that cash is properly accounted for, and short-term cash reports. Thus, adequate control of cash usually requires one or more of the following:

1. A detailed cash budget that specifies planned cash inflows and outflows (not considered in this book).
2. Detailed cash control reports for internal management use as *(a)* assurance that cash is used as planned and *(b)* a basis for revising cash plans.
3. A system of internal control that incorporates the separation of responsibility for *(a)* handling cash and *(b)* the related recordkeeping.
4. Detailed accounting for all cash receipts and cash disbursements to insure against unauthorized uses of cash receipts or improper cash disbursements. Chapter 2, Supplement 2–A, discussed and illustrated the use of control and subsidiary accounts and special journals.
5. Adequate disclosure of cash inflows and outflows in the external financial statements provided to stockholders and others.

Control of Cash Receipts

Cash inflows in most businesses come from numerous sources; therefore, the control procedures vary. However, the following procedures apply in most situations:

1. Separate responsibilities for the cash-handling and cash-recording functions. This separation assures that an individual cannot steal cash and cover the theft by making a fictitious journal entry.
2. Assign cash-handling and cash-recording responsibilities to ensure a continuous and uninterrupted flow of cash from initial receipt to deposit in an authorized bank account. This requires *(a)* immediate counting, *(b)* immediate recording, and *(c)* timely deposit of all cash received.
3. Maintain continuous and close supervision of all cash-handling and cash-recording functions, including daily cash reports for internal use.

Control of Cash Disbursements

The cash outflows in most businesses are for many purposes. Many of the cash defalcations in the disbursements process occur because they are relatively easy to conceal unless there is an effective system to control cash payments. In such situations, one or more of the fundamentals of internal control is missing. Although each control system should be tailored to the situation, several fundamentals are essential; these are:

1. Separate responsibilities for cash disbursement documentation, check writing, check signing, check mailing, and recordkeeping.
2. Make all cash disbursements by check. An exception can be made for small amounts from a petty cash fund.
3. Establish a petty cash fund with tight controls and close supervision.
4. Prepare checks and sign them only when supported by adequate documentation and verification.
5. Supervise all cash disbursement and recordkeeping functions.

Petty Cash. The term **petty cash,** or **imprest cash,** refers to a systematic approach often used for making small expenditures for which the check writing and the related accounting would be too costly. Examples of such payments are for the daily paper delivered to the office, express shipments, local taxi fares, special postage charges on delivery, and minor office supplies. A petty cash system should operate as follows:

1. A reliable employee is designated as the petty cash custodian. This person receives a single amount of cash for specified petty cash purposes, disburses the cash as needed, receives adequate documentation for each disbursement, maintains a running record of the cash on hand, and periodically reports the total amount of cash spent supported by the documentation supporting each disbursement. The record maintained, in addition to the documentation, often is referred to as the petty cash book.
2. When the amount of petty cash runs low, the petty cash custodian issues a formal request for replenishment of the amount spent from the fund, supported by the documentation of the expenditures.
3. The initial cash amount to establish the petty cash fund, and subsequent cash replenishment, are provided by separate checks, made payable to petty cash, and processed in the normal manner.
4. Accounting—the initial check establishing the petty cash fund is recorded as a debit to Petty Cash and a credit to Cash. Checks to replenish the fund are recorded by debiting the expense accounts (or other accounts) for the prior expenditures reported by the custodian and by crediting Cash. Therefore, at all times, the Petty Cash account reflects the same balance.
5. There should be close supervision and surprise audits of petty cash on hand and supporting documentation for expenditures.

To illustrate operation of a petty cash fund, assume one is established in the amount of $300 and employee X is designated as the custodian. At the end of the first week, the custodian requests a replenishment for the $260 spent, supported by documentation that reflected the following: postage, $90; office supplies, $70; taxi fares, $80; and daily paper, $20. The indicated entries would be as follows:

To establish the petty cash fund (at the beginning of the week):

Petty cash	300	
Cash		300

To replenish the fund (at end of the week):

Postage expense	90	
Office supplies expense	70	
Transportation expense	80	
Administrative expense	20	
Cash		260

The effects of the last entry are to (a) to replenish the amount of petty cash held by the custodian to $300, which is the balance maintained in the Petty Cash account, and (b) record expenses incurred from having paid petty cash.

Cash Overage and Shortage

Cash is susceptible to theft, and it is likely that errors will be made in counting cash; therefore, cash overages and shortages are to be expected. Cash overages and shortages should be recorded in an account entitled Cash Over and Short with the offsetting credit or debit to the regular Cash account. A **debit** balance in Cash Over and Short represents an **operating expense,** and a **credit** represents a **miscellaneous revenue.** In the absence of theft, cash overages and shortages tend to balance out to zero over time. In contrast, theft, when discovered, should be recorded as a credit to the regular Cash account and as a debit to *(a)* a receivable if recovery is expected from the individual involved or an insurance or bonding company, or *(b)* a loss account on the presumption that recovery is improbable.

RECONCILIATION OF BANK AND BOOK BALANCES

Upon receipt of the monthly bank statement, the cash balance on deposit reported in the bank statement should be reconciled with the cash balance as reflected in the Cash account in the company books for that bank account. Reconciliation of bank and book balances serves two purposes: (1) it establishes a measure of **control**—that is, it serves to check the accuracy of the records of both the bank and the company; and (2) it facilitates accounting entries because it provides information for entries in the books of the company for items reflected on the bank statement that have not yet been recorded by the company (e.g., a bank service charge).

Reconciliation of the bank balance with the book balance of the Cash account requires an analysis of the **monthly bank statement** and the cash records maintained by the company. Usually the **bank** and **book** cash balances will differ for the following reasons:

A. Items have been recorded as cash receipts in the company books but have not been added to the bank balance on the bank statement.
   Examples:
   1. Deposits in transit—cash deposited in the bank by the company but have not yet been added by the bank to the bank balance.
   2. Cash on hand (i.e., cash not on deposit in the bank).

B. Amounts have been added by the bank to the bank balance but have not yet been recorded as cash receipts in the company books.
   Examples:
   1. Interest earned by the company and added by the bank to the bank balance but has not yet been recorded as a cash receipt in the company books.
   2. Collections of notes receivable by the bank on behalf of the company; these amounts have been added by the bank to the bank balance but have not yet been recorded as cash receipts in the company books.

C. Amounts have been recorded as cash disbursements in the company books but have not yet been deducted by the bank from the bank balance.
   Example:
   Outstanding checks—checks written and recorded as cash disbursements in the company books have not yet cleared through the bank and hence are not yet deducted by the bank from the bank balance.

D. Amounts have been subtracted by the bank from the bank balance but have not yet been recorded as cash disbursements in the company books.
   Examples:
   1. Bank service charge.
   2. Nonsufficient funds (i.e., NSF, or "hot") check received from a customer.

In respect to the NSF check, the company's cash balance includes the amount of the NSF check; however, the bank balance does **not** include this amount of cash. At the time the company deposited the check, the bank increased the company's bank balance on the assumption that the check was good. Later when the check was returned to the bank (marked NSF), the bank decreased the company's bank balance. Therefore, the bank statement totals of "deposits" and "disbursements" both include the amount of the NSF check, with the result that the bank balance does **not** include the amount of the NSF check.

It is possible to reconcile the ending bank and book cash balances by working **from** the bank balance of cash **to** the book balance of cash or to reconcile both the book and bank balances to a common amount known as the correct or **true cash balance.**[2] The true cash balance format is illustrated in Exhibit 6–1, Panel C, based upon the data given in Panel A and the analysis presented in Panel B. Finally, Panel D presents the entries the company would make as a result of the reconciliation.

[2] The "true cash balance" method is convenient in that it separates the reconciliation into two natural subdivisions (i.e., book and bank); the "book" part of the reconciliation provides data for the entries necessary to update the company's Cash account to the true cash balance.

EXHIBIT 6–1: Bank Reconciliation

Panel A—Hypothetical Situation:

Assume X Company began business on July 1, 19A, with a $7,000 deposit in a bank and deposited all its receipts and made all its disbursements by check. During the first month (July), its cash receipts amounted to $11,500 and its cash disbursements by check amounted to $12,300; its ledger account, Cash in Bank, is shown below at July 31.

Company records in July:

Cash in Bank

July 1 balance	7,000	Checks in July	12,300
Deposits in July	11,500		
Total debits	18,500	Total credits	12,300
July 31 balance	6,200		

In addition, assume the following:

a. Only $9,400 of the deposits reached the bank by July 31.
b. Only $12,000 of the checks cleared the bank by July 31.
c. The bank subtracted $40 from X Company's bank balance (and on the bank statement) because a $40 customer check received by X Company late in July and deposited in the bank turned out to be an NSF (i.e., a "hot") check. At the time this check was initially deposited by X Company, the bank credited (i.e., added) $40 to the bank balance of X Company in the customary manner.
d. The bank deducted a service charge of $5 on the bank statement.
e. Prior to receipt of the bank statement from the bank, the company had not known about, and consequently had not recorded, either the $40 NSF item or the $5 service charge.

Panel B—Analysis:

The bank account of X Company would be a liability account (i.e., Deposits Payable) to the bank. At July 31, this account would appear as below:

Bank records in July:

Deposit Payable to X Company

Checks paid in July	12,000	July 1 balance	7,000
NSF check	40	July deposits	9,400*
Service charge	5		
Total debits	12,045	Total credits	16,400
		July 31 balance	4,355

* Includes $40 check which was NSF.

Panel C—Bank Reconciliation:

Because of the differences ([*a*] through [*e*] listed in Panel A) between the book and bank records, X Company should reconcile its $6,200 ending book balance and the $4,355 ending bank balance to the **true cash balance.** The reconciliation is as follows:

Bank Reconciliation (true balance format), July 31, 19A

Bank		**Book**	
Ending balance per bank statement	$4,355	Ending balance per books	$6,200
Add:		Deduct:	
Deposits in transit ($11,500–$9,400)	2,100	NSF check subtracted	(40)
Deduct:		Unrecorded service charge	(5)
Outstanding checks ($12,300–$12,000)	(300)		
True cash balance, ending	$6,155		$6,155

Panel D—Entries:

The reconciling items on the "book" side in Panel C must be recorded in the books of the company by making the journal entry shown below. This entry adjusts the balance per books (i.e., $6,200) to the **true cash balance** (i.e., $6,155).

Expense—bank charges	5	
Account receivable (NSF, customer)†	40	
Cash		45

† If the likelihood of collecting the $40 amount from the NSF customer is low, it would be appropriate to debit Allowance for Doubtful Accounts instead of Accounts Receivable.

Comprehensive Reconciliation

Another format of the bank reconciliation (often referred to as a "comprehensive reconciliation" or a "proof of cash") starts with the bank reconciliation of the preceding period and ties it in with the bank and book records of cash receipts and payments of the current period and ends with the reconciliation for the current period. Its format reconciles all amounts (i.e., beginning balance, cash receipts for the month, cash payments for the month, and the ending balance) per bank and per books to a set of "true" balances (i.e., the amounts which would exist if neither the bank nor the depositor had made any errors and if the reconciliation were complete).

To illustrate the comprehensive reconciliation, the X Company example of Exhibit 6–1 is continued into the next month (i.e., August 19A). Exhibit 6–2, Panel A, presents the hypothetical situation for August, and Panel B presents the comprehensive reconciliation for August.

The mechanical steps in the preparation of the comprehensive reconciliation (Exhibit 6–2, Panel B) are as follows:

1. **First column**—Enter the "bank" and "book" amounts in the first column. These amounts can be taken directly from the last column of the reconciliation for the **preceding period** (July in this example).

2. **Bank section:**
   a. **Bank section, top line**—Enter the total receipts (i.e., $16,270) and the total payments (i.e., $14,978) reported by the bank in August; and in the fourth column, enter the resultant ending balance (i.e., $5,647). These amounts are taken directly from the August bank statement (Panel A).

   b. **Bank section, fourth column**—Enter items recorded by the company but not recorded by the bank. Normally this will consist of deposits in transit (i.e., $1,280) and checks outstanding (i.e., $580) at the end of the current period (i.e., August). The above amounts are determined by comparing the company's cash records with the deposit slips and checks returned with the bank statement. Specifically, during August, X Company recorded $1,280 in cash receipts and $580 in cash payments that were not reported on the August bank statement.

   These amounts also can be determined as follows:

Deposits in transit July 31	$ 2,100
Deposits on books in August	14,400
Total deposits which could clear bank	16,500
Deposits cleared bank in August	15,220
Deposits in transit Aug. 31	$ 1,280
Checks outstanding July 31	$ 300
Checks drawn on books in August	15,250
Total checks which could clear bank	15,550
Checks cleared bank in August	14,970
Checks outstanding Aug. 31	$ 580

   c. **Bank section extensions from first column**—Bring across into the receipts and payments columns the items listed in the first column which were reconciled last month [i.e., for July, $2,100 and $(300)]. Normally these will be subtractions in the receipts and payments columns for the current month (August) because they were recognized by the bank as receipts and payments, respectively, of the current month (August).

   d. **Bank section extensions (leftward) from fourth column**—"Back in" from the fourth column (Aug. 31 Balance) items to be reconciled at the end of the current month (i.e., August—$1,280 and $580). Normally these will be additions in the receipts and payments columns for the current month (August) because they were company receipts and payments during August but were not recognized by the bank as August receipts and payments. Therefore, they must be added to the bank receipts and payments of August (i.e., $16,270 and $14,978) in computing true August receipts and payments (i.e., $15,450 and $15,258).

   e. **Bank section, true cash amounts line**—Complete the bank portion by vertically footing the columns to arrive at true receipts (i.e., $15,450), payments (i.e., $15,258) and the true ending balance (i.e., $6,347). At this point, the "true cash" amounts agree when added both vertically and horizontally.

EXHIBIT 6–2: Comprehensive Bank Reconciliation

Panel A—Hypothetical Situation, X Company, August 31, 19A:

Company records for August:

Cash in Bank

August 1 balance	6,200	Entry to record NSF check and bank charges	45
Deposits in August	14,400	Checks in August	15,250
Total debits	20,600		15,295
August 31 balance	5,305		

Bank records for August:*

Deposit Payable to X Company

Checks in August	14,970	August 1 balance	4,355
Service charge	8	Deposits in August	15,220
		Note collected for X Company	1,050
Total debits	14,978	Total credits	20,625
		August 31 balance	5,647

*Note: In actual practice, X Company would not be provided bank data in this form. It is presented here for instructional convenience. Instead, X Company would receive the bank statement shown below.

Bank Statement for August 19A:

To: X Company
From: Z Bank

Balance carried forward from July		$ 4,355
Deposits:		
Aug. 1 (from X Co. deposit in transit on July 31)	$ 2,100	
Aug. 2–31 (from X Co.)	13,120	
Note collected (on Aug. 31)	1,050	
Total receipts		16,270
Bank charges:		
Checks (drawn by X Co. in July but cleared in August)	300	
Checks (drawn by X Co. in August and cleared in August)	14,670	
Service charge for August	8	
Total disbursements		(14,978)
Balance, Aug. 31		$ 5,647

Panel B—Comprehensive Bank Reconciliation, August 19A

	(1) July 31 Balance	+	(2) August Receipts	−	(3) August Payments	=	(4) Aug. 31 Balance
Bank:							
Bank amounts (unreconciled)	$4,355		$16,270		$14,978		$5,647
Deposits in transit:							
July 31	2,100		(2,100)				
Aug. 31			1,280				1,280
Outstanding checks:							
July 31	(300)				(300)		
Aug. 31					580		(580)
True cash amounts	$6,155		$15,450		$15,258		$6,347
Book:							
Book amounts (unreconciled)	$6,200		$14,400		$15,295		$5,305
Unrecorded service charges:							
July 31	(5)				(5)		
Aug. 31					8		(8)
NSF check returned	(40)				(40)		
Note collected for company			1,050				1,050
True cash amounts	$6,155		$15,450		$15,258		$6,347

3. **Book section:**
   a. **Book section, top line**—Enter total August receipts (i.e., $14,400) and payments (i.e., $15,295) recorded in the company books (Panel A) with the resultant ending book balance (i.e., $5,305) in the fourth column. (This step is the counterpart of 2*a* above.)
   b. **Book section extensions from first column**—Bring across into the receipts and payments columns items listed in the first column which were reconciled last month [i.e., July, $(5) and $(40)] (normally subtracted in the receipts and payments columns because of their recognition by the company as receipts or payments one month late).
   c. **Book section extensions (leftward) from fourth column**—"Back in" from the fourth column (August 31 Balance) items to be reconciled at the end of the current month [i.e., August—$1,050 and $(8)]. Normally these amounts are added in the receipts and payments columns because they were **not** included in the book receipts (i.e., $14,400) and payments (i.e., $15,295); therefore, they must be added to the book receipts and payments of August in computing true August receipts and payments (i.e., $15,450 and $15,258). This step corresponds to 2*d* above.
   d. **Book section, true cash amounts**—Complete the book portion by vertically footing (i.e., adding) the columns to arrive at true receipts (i.e., $15,450) and payments (i.e., $15,258) and the true August 31 balance (i.e., $6,347).

4. **Tests for accuracy:**
   a. The top line of each section when cross-footed should reflect August 31 balances as shown on the bank statement (i.e., $5,647) and in the company's ledger account Cash in Bank (i.e., $5,305).
   b. Total receipts and total payments when footed vertically should reflect agreement between "bank" and "book" amounts (i.e., $15,450 and $15,258).
   c. The bottom line of both sections when added horizontally should reflect the true August 31 balance (i.e., $6,347).

Although the addition or subtraction of items in the inner columns (receipts and payments) is logical, a mechanical rule may assist when one is becoming familiar with this form of reconciliation. All items in the beginning or ending balance columns must be reflected in one of the inner columns. If an item is added in an outer column and appears in an **adjacent** inner column, its sign changes (i.e., it is subtracted in the inner column). On the other hand, if an item in one of the balance columns does not appear in an **adjacent** inner column, it retains the same sign as it had in the balance column.

Returning to the details of Exhibit 6–2, if the company is preparing financial statements as of August 31, it should record the $8 August service charge and the collection of the $1,050 proceeds from the note (assume that $50 is interest) as August transactions so that the cash account in the general ledger and financial statements as of August 31 reflect the true cash balance of $6,347. The entries should be recorded as follows:

Expense—bank charges	8	
Cash		8
Cash	1,050	
Note receivable		1,000
Interest revenue		50

After these entries are posted, the Cash in Bank account of X Company will appear as below (assuming no other entries since August 31):

Cash in Bank

August 31 balance (Exhibit 6–2, Panel A)	5,305	Bank service charge for August	8
Note collection	1,050		
Total debits	6,355	Total credits	8
Balance	6,347		

Usefulness of the Comprehensive Reconciliation. In many entities, it is not practical to separate responsibilities for cash handling and accounting for cash (which includes reconciling bank accounts). This weakness in internal controls provides an opportunity for an employee who *(a)* handles cash and *(b)* reconciles the bank account to steal cash and conceal the theft by manipulating the bank reconciliation. The theft can be concealed easily if (1) the reconciliation is in the standard (i.e., not comprehensive) format and (2) no supervisory employee **com-**

pletely reperforms the reconciliation; mere review of the standard reconciliation will not detect the theft. The comprehensive reconciliation can be performed by supervisory employees as a quick check on the validity of the bank reconciliation.

To illustrate use of the comprehensive reconciliation as a supervisory check, refer to Exhibit 6–2, Panel B, and assume that the standard procedure is to perform the reconciliation only on month-end balances (i.e., July 31 and August 31 in the exhibit). Furthermore, assume that the entity has one employee who receives cash, prepares checks for payment, reconciles the bank account, keeps the books, and manages the office. Also, assume this employee has stolen $50 during July and concealed the theft thus far by writing off as uncollectible the account receivable of a customer who paid $50. The final step in the attempted concealment is to manipulate the July 31 bank reconciliation. This step is necessary because the **bank** balance of cash for the entity at July 31 will be $50 less than it should be. Consequently, it would be necessary to manipulate the July 31 bank reconciliation to conceal this fact. Because *(a)* entities often have a large number of outstanding checks at the time of the bank reconciliation, and *(b)* it is costly for a supervisor to reperform the entire reconciliation, the dishonest employee can merely understate the total amount of outstanding checks (or overstate the deposits in transit) at July 31, and this will conceal the hiatus between bank and book amounts of cash on the standard (i.e., not comprehensive) bank reconciliation format. In this instance, assume the dishonest employee has understated outstanding checks by $50.

To see the usefulness of the comprehensive format for the bank reconciliation, the comprehensive reconciliation below should be compared with the one in Exhibit 6–2, Panel B. Amounts which differ from

Comprehensive Bank Reconciliation

	(1) July 31 Balance	+	(2) August Receipts	−	(3) August Payments	=	(4) Aug. 31 Balance
Bank:							
Bank amounts	**[$4,305]**		$16,270		$14,978		$5,597
Deposits in transit:							
July 31	2,100		(2,100)				
Aug. 31			1,280				1,280
Outstanding checks:							
July 31	**[(250)]**				**(250)**		
Aug. 31					580		(580)
True cash amounts	$6,155		$15,450		$15,308 ←		$6,297 ←
Book:							
Book amounts	$6,200		$14,400		$15,295		$5,305
Unrecorded service charges:							
July 31	(5)				(5)		
Aug. 31					8		(8)
NSF check returned	(40)				(40)		
Note collected for company			1,050				1,050
True cash amounts	$6,155		$15,450		$15,258 ←		$6,347 ←

the corresponding amounts in Exhibit 6–2 are in boldface type. Also, the July 31 **bank** balance (i.e., $4,-305—versus $4,355 in Exhibit 6–2) and the July 31 amount of outstanding checks (i.e., $250—versus $300 in Exhibit 6–2) are bracketed for special emphasis. The July 31 bank balance represents the incentive to manipulate the reconciliation because its amount (i.e., $4,305) is $50 less than it would have been if no theft had occurred. Relatedly, the July 31 amount of outstanding checks (i.e., $250) represents the attempt to conceal the theft. In particular, note that, at July 31, the manipulated reconciliation appears superficially to be intact; true cash is $6,155 for bank and book amounts. This reconciliation would suggest to a supervisor that everything was proper.

However, the supervisor who performs the comprehensive reconciliation for August would begin with the July 31 reconciliation prepared by the dishonest employee. The supervisor would extend all amounts from July 31 across the comprehensive reconciliation in the step-wise progression described earlier in this chapter, enter August reconciling items (i.e., outstanding checks, service charge, etc.), and then foot all columns. The discrepancy between bank and book payments for August (i.e., $15,308 and $15,258) and bank and book balances at August 31 (i.e., $6,297 and $6,347) would alert the supervisor to an "error" in payments. The comprehensive reconciliation does not automatically explain such discrepancies. However, it serves as a means of ascertaining the need for additional inquiry. Moreover, the comprehensive reconciliation requires little time, and low cost to perform.

Part B: Short-Term Investments

Investments usually are classified for balance sheet purposes as either short-term investments (sometimes called marketable or temporary securities) or long-term investments (sometimes simply called investments or permanent investments). This distinction arises because of the nature of the asset held and the intent of management in making the investment. Investment purposes may be outlined as follows:

A. Short-term investments.

Funds invested in marketable securities to produce revenue that would otherwise not be earned on seasonal excesses of cash.

B. Long-term investments (discussed in Chapters 16 and 17).

1. Stocks of other companies (investees) held to achieve control over their operations and policies (i.e., a controlling interest).
2. Securities of other entities (not held for control of the other entity).
3. Advances to (i.e., long-term receivables from) other entities.
4. Funds earmarked for designated purposes such as retirement of a bond issue, plant expansion or replacement, or payment of noncurrent debt.
5. Cash surrender value of life insurance on company executives.
6. Assets other than investment securities held to produce nonoperating revenue or for future use or sale. Such properties are not used currently in regular business operations but may have been so used in the past or may be intended for such use in the future. Alternatively, they are sometimes reported under the caption Other assets if they do not produce current revenue.

SHORT-TERM INVESTMENTS DEFINED

Short-term investments are reported on the balance sheet under the current assets caption. To be classified as a current asset, a short-term investment should meet the following two-fold test:

1. The security must be **readily marketable.** It must be regularly traded on a security exchange or in some other established market.[3]
2. The company's management intention is not to keep the security beyond the current operating cycle or one year, whichever is longer.

In practice, these criteria present problems. First, long-term investments often are readily marketable; thus, this criterion standing alone does not always distinguish short-term from long-term investments. Operationally, the second criterion, **intention of the management,** often is the factor which makes the distinction between a short-term and long-term investment. Intentions *(a)* can be changed often and *(b)* are difficult to "audit." As a consequence, the classification of **readily marketable** securities is beset with some practical problems which can lead to manipulation of reported current assets (and working capital).

VALUATION OF SHORT-TERM INVESTMENTS

Short-term investments are recorded initially at cost in accordance with the cost principle. Subsequent to acquisition and depending upon the nature of the investor entity and the type of investment involved, they may be accounted for at

1. Lower of cost or market (LCM).
2. Cost.
3. Market.

Valuation at Lower of Cost or Market (LCM)

FASB, Statement of Financial Accounting Standards No. 12, "Accounting for Certain Marketable Securities," requires that short-term investments in marketable **equity** securities be valued at each balance sheet date on an LCM basis.[4] Application of this statement to **long-term** investments in marketable equity securities is discussed in Chapter 16; the present chapter focuses on **short-term** investments. **Equity** securities, as used in *FASB Statement 12,* encompass all capital stock (including warrants, rights, and stock options) except preferred stock that, by its terms, must be redeemable either at the option of the issuer or the investor. **Equity securites do not include debt securities** such as bonds and other debt instruments because these securities do not represent ownership shares.

FASB Statement 12 specifies: "The carrying amount of a marketable equity securities portfolio shall be the lower of its aggregate cost or market value, determined at balance sheet date. The amount by which aggregate cost of the portfolio exceeds market value shall be accounted for as the valuation allowance."

To illustrate the application of the LCM concept to short-term investments, suppose the portfolio of short-term securities of Merian Company consists of the three individual securities shown in Exhibit 6–3, as of December 31, 19A, the end of the company's first year of operations. Based upon the data in Exhibit 6–3, two questions arise concerning the valuation of the above short-term investments.

1. How does the LCM rule apply to *(a)* investments in short-term **equity** securities and *(b)* investments in short-term **debt** securities?
2. What valuation represents **market** for comparison with **cost** in applying the LCM rule? That is, in Exhibit 6–3 should the Aggregate Market column total be used or should the Unit LCM column total be used to compare with the Aggregate Cost column total?

The data given in Exhibit 6–3 are used to address these questions.

The answer to the **first question** is that *FASB Statement 12* specifically applies LCM to **equity** securities only. Therefore, for Merian Company in Exhibit 6–3, the *Statement* applies only to the Apex and Caldor shares, and these shares would constitute one portfolio of short-term investments. The Baker bonds

[3] *FASB Interpretation No. 16,* "Clarification of Definitions and Accounting for Marketable Equity Securities that Become Nonmarketable" (Stamford, Conn., February 1977) provides detailed rules pertaining to one aspect of **marketability.**

[4] The provisions of *FASB Statement 12* do not apply to certain industries having specialized practices with respect to marketable securities, including such financial organizations as insurance companies, investment companies, and securities dealers.

EXHIBIT 6–3

MERIAN COMPANY
Short-Term Portfolio of Marketable Securities
December 31, 19A (end of the first year of operations)

Short-Term Marketable Security	December 31, 19A Aggregate Cost*	Aggregate Market†	Unit LCM
Equity securities:			
1. Apex common stock, 50 shares	$ 5,200	$ 4,800	$ 4,800
2. Caldor preferred stock, nonredeemable, par $100, 100 shares	11,000	11,250	11,000
Total portfolio of short-term **equity** securities	16,200	16,050	15,800
Debt securities:			
1. Baker 8% bonds, $10,000 maturity value	9,700	9,600	9,600
Total portfolio of all short-term securities	$25,900	$25,650	$25,400

* Cost includes the basic cost of the securities purchased, plus brokerage fees and transfer fees and taxes paid to acquire the investment shares.

† Market value usually refers to the **closing** price quoted as of the fiscal year-end of the investor company (December 31, 19A, in this example).

would constitute a separate short-term investment portfolio of debt securities. This separation facilitates accounting for the equity security portfolio under the LCM rule and the debt security portfolio **at cost** (rather than at LCM).[5]

The answer to the **second question** is that *FASB Statement 12* specifies **aggregate market.** Thus, for Merian Company, the portfolio of **equity** securities would involve comparison of the aggregate market of $16,050 (not $15,800) with aggregate cost of $16,200. The aggregate market valuation is a better market valuation than the "unit market" valuation because Merian Company would realize the former amount (i.e., $16,050) if the entire short-term portfolio of equity securities were converted to cash as of the statement date.[6] It was probably for this reason that *FASB Statement 12* specified that LCM be applied to the **aggregate** short-term portfolio of equity securities.

[5] Although *FASB Statement 12* limits the application of LCM to short-term investments in marketable **equity** securities, logic and consistency would appear to call for application of LCM to marketable debt securities as well. Any marketable security, equity or debt, is bought for the same purpose: to employ idle cash to earn a short-term return. In the case of bonds classified as short-term investments, it is not likely that they would ever be held to maturity date. Furthermore, the significance of short-term investments is the total amount of cash to be realized from their sale. These factors suggest to the authors that it would be logical to apply LCM to short-term investments in debt securities also.

[6] Some disposal costs may be incurred, but consideration of these is often deferred until they are actually incurred at disposal date of the security.

At December 31, 19A, Merian Company would make the following entry to record the decline in market value below cost of the aggregate short-term portfolio of marketable equity securities:

December 31, 19A—To reduce short-term investment in equity securities to LCM:

Unrealized loss on short-term investments ($16,200 − $16,050)	150	
Allowance to reduce short-term investments to market		150

The above entry ignores the $100 decline in the market value of the investment in Baker bonds, which would be accounted for at cost (i.e., $9,700), as discussed and illustrated under the heading, Valuation of Short-term Investments at Cost.

The Unrealized Loss account is closed to Income Summary and is reported on the income statement as a "financial" item (i.e., in a manner similar to interest expense). The allowance account, as a contra account to short-term investments, should be reported either as a deduction from the cost of short-term investments or as follows:

Current assets:
Short-term investments in marketable equity securities at market value (cost, $16,200) $16,050

Notes to the statements also could be used to disclose the cost amount and the amount of the unrealized loss recognized. The unrealized loss is not a deduction for **income tax purposes:** cost of the securities is used to measure the taxable gain or loss.[7]

In the above entry to record the LCM effect, the debit was to an **unrealized loss** account, and the loss was recognized as a deduction from income of the period in which the market prices dropped.[8] Recoveries in the market value of a portfolio of short-term investments result in an increase in income (as illustrated below). The amount of the market value recovery is credited to an **unrealized gain** account. The amount of "recoveries" (i.e., unrealized gains) recorded cannot exceed the total amount of all cumulative previous unrealized losses recognized on the same portfolio.

Sales of Securities from the Short-Term Portfolio of Investments in Equity Securities. In applying the LCM rule, *FASB Statement 12* distinguishes between realized and unrealized gains and losses. A **realized gain or loss** is the difference between the net proceeds from the sale of a marketable equity security and its cost. When an equity security is sold from the short-term portfolio, any amount of "Allowance to Reduce Short-Term Investments to Market" related to the securities sold is ignored at the time of sale. Instead, the balance in the allowance account is restated at the end of the fiscal year.

To illustrate accounting for a realized loss on sale of short-term investment securities, assume Merian Company, on April 5, 19B, sold the 50 shares of Apex stock for $4,950 and incurred disposal costs of $125. The required entry would be as follows:

April 5, 19B—To record sale of short-term investment:

Cash ($4,950–$125)	4,825	
Loss (realized) on sale of short-term investments	375	
Short-term investments, Apex common stock (original cost) ...		5,200

[7] Any taxable gain or loss ordinarily would be recognized when the security is sold and would be measured by comparing the net sales proceeds with the original cost. Paragraph 22 of *FASB Statement 12* provides that recognition of unrealized gains or losses on marketable securities shall be considered as a timing difference for income tax allocation purposes (see Chapter 10, Part B).

[8] You will find in studying Chapter 16 that "unrealized losses" related to **long-term investments** are not reported in the income statement but rather are reported as a contra account (deduction) to owners' equity. Subsequent recoveries, up to original cost, are recorded as a reduction of the contra account.

Observe that the above entry did not change the December 31, 19A, balance in the allowance account (i.e., $150). At the next fiscal year-end, valuation of the short-term investment portfolio at LCM involves determination of the **balance needed in the allowance account;** this determination requires a new LCM computation for the securities held at the end of that fiscal year.

To illustrate, assume that on September 1, 19B, Merian Company (Exhibit 6–3) purchased (as a short-term investment) 50 shares of Davis common stock, nopar, at $101 per share. In addition, acquisition costs of $50 for brokerage fee and transfer tax were incurred. The entry to record the purchase would be as follows:

September 1, 19B—To record the purchase of a short-term investment:

Short-term investments, Davis common stock, nopar (50 × $101) + $50	5,100	
Cash		5,100

Now assume that there were no additional transactions during 19B that affected the short-term investment portfolio and that the December 31, 19B, market values are: Caldor preferred stock, 106½; and Davis common stock, 107. Based upon these market values and the cost data given above (for the Davis common stock) and in Exhibit 6–3 (for the Caldor preferred stock), the LCM schedule at December 31, 19B, would be as follows:

Short-Term Equity Security	Cost	Market
Caldor preferred stock, nonredeemable, par $100, 100 shares	$11,000	$10,650
Davis common stock, nopar, 50 shares	5,100	5,350
Total aggregate market of short-term investment portfolio	$16,100	$16,000

Aggregate market at the end of 19B is less than aggregate cost by $100 (i.e., $16,100 − $16,000). Therefore, the balance in the allowance account must be decreased from the prior 19A balance of $150 to the required balance of $100 (i.e., a decrease of $50) as reflected in the following T-account:

Allowance to Reduce Short-Term Investments to Market

Debit entry needed	**50**	Bal., 12/31/19A	150
		Bal. needed, 12/31/19B (based on above LCM analysis)	100

The adjusting entry made at December 31, 19B, to bring the balance in the allowance account to its current credit balance of $100 would be as follows:

December 31, 19B—To adjust the balance in the allowance account on the basis of the LCM valuation at the end of the year:

Allowance to reduce short-term investments to market	50	
Unrealized gain on short-term investments*		50

* Some accountants prefer the account title, "Unrealized Loss Recovery on Short-Term Investments," because an "Unrealized Loss" was reported on the income statement of 19A and this credit is in the nature of a "loss recovery" in 19B.

If aggregate market had dropped during 19B to so low a value that the $150 credit balance left over in the allowance account from 19A had been inadequate, the allowance account would have been increased (credited). In contrast, if market had equaled or exceeded cost, the allowance account would have been reduced to a zero balance, and the resulting unrealized gain would have been reported in the income statement in 19B. In no event, however, under the LCM rule, can the total amount of unrealized gains exceed the previously recorded total amount of unrealized losses for the particular portfolio. This is because recognition of a higher total amount of unrealized gains would result in reporting the investments at an amount in excess of cost, which is contrary to the conceptual basis of LCM.

Transfer of Marketable Equity Securities between the Short- and Long-Term Investment Portfolios. *FASB Statement 12* requires that when marketable equity securities are transferred between the short-term and long-term investment portfolios in either direction, the transfer must be effected at their LCM value at the time of the transfer. When market value at the date of transfer is below cost, the lower market value becomes the cost basis for subsequent LCM valuations; the difference between market value and cost on the date of transfer is accounted for as a **realized** loss and included in the determination of income in the period of transfer.

DISCLOSURE OF SHORT-TERM INVESTMENTS IN EQUITY SECURITIES

Disclosure requirements specified by *FASB Statement 12* are the following for short-term investments in equity securities:

a. As of the date of each balance sheet presented, aggregate cost and market value with identification as to which is the carrying amount.

b. As of the date of the latest balance sheet presented, the following:
   - i. Gross unrealized gains representing the excess of market value over cost for all marketable equity securities in the portfolio having such an excess.
   - ii. Gross unrealized losses representing the excess of cost over market value for all marketable equity securities in the portfolio having such an excess.

c. For each period for which an income statement is presented:
   - i. Net realized gain or loss included in the determination of net income.
   - ii. The basis on which cost was determined in computing realized gain or loss (i.e., average cost or other method used).
   - iii. The change in the valuation allowance(s) that has been included in the determination of net income.

The following excerpt from the 1979 annual report of Golden Enterprises, Inc., discloses the information required by *FASB Statement 12:*

	May 31	
	1979	**1978**
Current assets:		
Cash	$1,595,029	$ 867,156
Marketable securities, carried at market (note 1)	4,296,469	3,711,554

Note 1 (in part): Marketable Securities—
To reduce the carrying amount of the marketable equity securities portfolio to market, which was lower than cost, provisions for decline in value of marketable equity securities of $157,834 and $125,296 were charged to income for the years ended May 31, 1979 and 1978, respectively. At May 31, 1979, the valuation allowance of $283,130 consists entirely of unrealized losses.

Marketable securities, other than equity securities, are carried at cost which approximates market value.

Source: *Accounting Trends & Techniques, 1980* (AICPA: New York), p. 130.

VALUATION OF SHORT-TERM INVESTMENTS AT COST

Because *FASB Statement 12* does not apply to **debt securities** held as short-term investments, such securities are accounted for at **cost** rather than at LCM along with short-term investments in equity securities. Short-term investments in debt securities are recorded at cost at acquisition date and are carried at cost unless their market value becomes less than cost (1) by a **substantial amount** and (2) the market value decline is due to a **permanent condition.** When both of these conditions are present, *ARB 43* requires that the short-term investment be written down to market value to recognize the **permanent impairment of asset value.** Subsequent to such a write-down, which would be rare, recoveries in market value are not recognized in the accounts (as is done under the LCM rule) because the reduced carrying value is viewed as "cost" for future accounting purposes. (For income tax purposes, such losses and write-downs are not recognized, and the tax basis of the debt security continues to be its original cost.)

When a **debt security** is acquired as a short-term investment, accrued interest from the last interest date to the date of acquisition must be paid and recognized. To illustrate, assume that on September 1, 19A, Merian Company purchased (as a short-term investment) 10 $1,000 bonds (8 percent annual interest payable each November 30) of Baker Company at 96½ (i.e., $965 per $1,000 bond) plus the nine months' accrued interest, and that acquisition costs of $50 were incurred. The required entry would be the following:

September 1, 19A—To record purchase of bond investment:

Short-term investments, Baker Co. bonds [($10,000 × .965) + $50]	9,700	
Interest Revenue* ($10,000 × 8% × 9/12)	600	
Cash ($9,700 + $600)		10,300

* Alternatively, this debit could be to Interest Receivable; after the subsequent entry is made to record receipt of the interest for the year, the net effect would be the same. If the annual fiscal period ends prior to the next interest date, Interest Receivable should be debited.

At December 31, 19A, and at each subsequent balance sheet date Merian Company holds the Baker bonds, Merian Company will report the short-term bond investment at its cost of $9,700 (unless a permanent, substantial decrease below cost occurs in their market value).

VALUATION OF SHORT-TERM INVESTMENTS AT MARKET

In accounting for short-term investments, the cost method basically retains original cost. The LCM method reduces the original cost valuation to market value (when the latter is lower), and if the market value of the investment recovers, it increases the valuation (but not in excess of original cost). These changes in value result in the reporting of **unrealized** losses and gains. In contrast, the **market value method** revalues the investment portfolio at the end of each period at market value (regardless of cost), which results in the recognition of periodic "holding" gains and losses.

With inflation a continuing phenomenon, significant differences occur in the reported values on cost basis financial statements compared with statements prepared to reflect the effects of price changes. In the case of short-term investments, the differences are likely to be relatively small because of the comparatively short holding period. Nonetheless, many accountants and other business persons advocate market valuation of investment securities, even when market value is **higher** than cost.[9]

Accounting for marketable securities at **market value** poses two problems: (1) determination of the market value of the securities at the end of each period and (2) the method of recognizing the holding gain or loss. Present GAAPs (i.e., the revenue principle) do not permit the recognition of holding gains (except as specified in *FASB Statement 12,* i.e., to the extent of previously recognized holding losses).

To illustrate the issue involved in recognizing holding gains on short-term investments, assume a short-term investment in common stock is acquired at a cost of $10,000 at the beginning of 19A. Assume the market value of the stock at the end of 19A is $11,000. Assuming accounting for short-term investments at market value, the indicated entries would be as follows:

At date of acquisition (record at cost):

Investments, short term	10,000	
Cash		10,000

At end of period (market, $11,000), to record the holding gain:

[9] This position is taken by W. H. Beaver, "Accounting for Marketable Equity Securities," *Journal of Accountancy,* December 1973, pp. 58–64.

Investments, short term	1,000	
Unrealized holding gain on investments (or holding gain on investments; \$11,000–\$10,000)		1,000

Some accountants believe the holding gain of \$1,000 should be reported on the 19A income statement. Others believe the holding gain should be reported on the balance sheet at the end of 19A as an unrealized gain in the owners' equity section of the balance sheet and that a gain should be recognized on the income statement only when the investment is sold. This latter approach reports the investment on the balance sheet at market value but reports net income on the basis of cost—an inconsistent treatment.

To illustrate the two views, assume the investment (recorded above) is sold during 19B for \$11,500. The indicated entry would be as follows:

a. Assuming the holding gain is to be reported on the income statement for 19A:

Cash	11,500	
Investments, short term		11,000
Gain on sale of investments (sale proceeds minus last adjusted market value) (closed to Income Summary)		500

b. Assuming the holding gain is to be reported as a separate element of owners' equity at the end of 19A:

Cash	11,500	
Unrealized holding gain on investments	1,000	
Investments, short term		11,000
Gain on sale of investment (sale proceeds minus cost)		1,500

A balance in the account, Unrealized Holding Gain on Investments, (if used) would be classified as "Unrealized capital" on the balance sheet under Owners' Equity.

The market value method is **not** considered **GAAP** at the present time; however, a special industry exception is made for certain financial institutions such as mutual funds, brokerage firms, and insurance companies. These types of entities use the market value method; however, the issue of how to report the **holding** gains and losses is not settled. Both methods discussed above can be observed in practice.[10]

EVALUATION OF THE METHODS

The LCM method is criticized because it is inconsistent. When market values drop and aggregate market is below aggregate cost, LCM reflects the realizable value of a portfolio of marketable securities; but when aggregate market exceeds aggregate cost, it does not, resulting in an understatement of asset value and income relative to a market value measure. In successive periods, marketable securities may be valued at cost, at market, and then again at cost.[11]

The chief objection to the **cost method** (versus LCM or market value) for short-term investments is that an overstatement of asset values and income results when market value drops below cost. Identical securities are reported at different costs simply because they were acquired at different times. When investments are carried at cost, it is possible to manipulate income by selecting which units are sold if there are two different lots of the same security, which were acquired at different costs. Another opportunity for manipulation exists because securities can be sold just before the close of a period and replaced immediately after the start of the next period, thereby causing a gain or loss to be reported for the period, as desired. Advantages cited for cost are its objectivity, the fact that it parallels the valuation basis used for most other assets, and its conformity with income tax requirements.

The use of the **market value method** is criticized because market values are not always readily determinable. Sometimes the market for a security is "thin," and it is rarely traded.[12] Market value is not viewed by some as relevant for accounting purposes until actual sale of a security because the market value is not realized until an actual sale. On the other hand, the market value method has the advantages that it *(a)* eliminates the inconsistencies cited above against LCM and *(b)* assigns to each period gains or losses that occurred in the value of the investment during the period rather than postponing recognition until the time of sale, as occurs under the cost method. Reporting short-term investments at market value informs statement users of the real value of the asset that management substituted for

[10] Recall that *FASB Statement 12 requires* that LCM unrealized losses and gains *(a)* on short-term investments be reported on the income statement and *(b)* on long-term investments the reporting is different as discussed and illustrated in Chapter 16.

[11] Differences between the cost and the market value of investments (reflected at market value below cost under LCM) are accounted for as timing differences and, hence, give rise to income tax allocation (discussed in Chapter 10, Part B).

[12] In the unlikely event that an investor's holdings of securities were so extensive that liquidation of the entire holdings at once would materially affect the market price, the use of market values is subject to some caution if not criticism.

cash. Finally, it is difficult to manipulate income when securities are valued at market.

Although the market value method is GAAP only for certain financial institutions, many companies report the market values of their short-term (and long-term) investments either parenthetically or in the notes of the financial statements. Thus, both cost and market values often are reported, so that financial statement users can select whichever value they prefer for valuation of security investments. This dual reporting practice fulfills the **reporting principle.**

IDENTIFICATION OF UNITS SOLD

When short-term investments are sold, or otherwise disposed of, a question frequently is posed in respect to identification of unit cost. For example, assume three purchases of stock in XY Corporation as follows: purchase no. 1, 200 shares @ $80; purchase no. 2, 300 shares @ $100; and purchase no. 3, 100 shares @ $110. Now assume 100 shares are sold at $120. What is the cost of the shares sold? For accounting purposes, the decision would appear to be essentially arbitrary, with no generally accepted basis for identifying cost. Most companies identify cost based upon specific identification of the securities sold or a FIFO cost flow assumption because the Internal Revenue Service specifies these methods for tax purposes.[13] Consistency in application from period to period is essential.

INVESTMENT REVENUE ON SHORT-TERM INVESTMENTS

Dividend revenue from short-term investments in **capital stock** of other companies is earned at the time of the declaration of a **cash dividend.** However, when declaration and receipt of the cash dividend occur in the same accounting period, companies usually wait until the cash is received to record dividend revenue. Cash dividends on capital stock (common or preferred) held as an investment are not accrued prior to declaration. **Stock dividends** received on such stock do not represent revenue; rather they serve to reduce the cost per share of the investment.

Bonds purchased at a price above par are acquired at a premium; if acquired below par, at a discount. In the case of short-term investments in bonds, the investment account is debited at cost and premium or discount accounts usually are not used. Premium or discount on a short-term bond investment is not amortized because, by definition, the investment will be converted to cash in the near future instead of being held to maturity. This procedure is in contrast to the accounting for bonds held as a long-term investment, in which case amortization of premium or discount is required (see Chapter 17). Interest receivable on short-term investments in bonds is accrued at the end of the accounting period by means of an adjusting entry.

[13] Use of different methods for *(a)* accounting and *(b)* tax purposes would cause a timing difference, as discussed and illustrated in Chapter 10, Part B.

COMPREHENSIVE ILLUSTRATION OF ACCOUNTING FOR SHORT-TERM INVESTMENTS

This section presents a brief but comprehensive illustration of accounting for short-term investments over a one-year period by a company whose operating cycle extends beyond one year.

As of December 31, 19A, H Company's portfolios of short-term investments in marketable securities were as follows:

Marketable Securities (of H Company)	December 31, 19A		
	Cost	Market	LCM
Equity:			
GHI Corp. common stock (100 shares)	$8,700	$8,475	
Equity portfolio total	$8,700	$8,475	$8,475
Debt:			
DEF Co. bonds, 8%, interest paid Apr. 1 and Oct. 1, $6,000 maturity value	$6,300	$5,900	
Debt portfolio total	$6,300	$5,900	

EXHIBIT 6–4: Accounting for Short-Term Investments—Equity and Debt Securities,* H Company

February 1, 19B—Sold half of the DEF bonds for net proceeds of $3,050. (Accrued interest revenue, $3,000 × .08 × 4/12 = $80; credit to investment account, 1/2 of $6,300 = $3,150).	Cash	3,050	
	Loss on sale of short-term investment	180	
	Investments, short-term (DEF bonds)		3,150
	Interest revenue		80
March 1, 19B—Collected semiannual dividend of $180 on GHI stock (declared earlier during the current period).	Cash	180	
	Dividend revenue		180
April 1, 19B—Collected semiannual interest on DEF bonds ($3,000 × .08 × 6/12 = $120).	Cash	120	
	Interest revenue		120
August 15, 19B—Bought 40 shares of JKL common stock at 87 3/4† plus brokerage fees of $90 for cash [(40 × $87.75) + $90 = $3,600].	Investments, short term (JKL stock)	3,600	
	Cash		3,600
September 1, 19B—Collected semiannual dividend of $180 on GHI stock (declared earlier during the current period).	Cash	180	
	Dividend revenue		180
September 15, 19B—Sold 60 shares of GHI stock at 95 and incurred selling costs of $120 [(60 × $95) − $120 = $5,580; credit to investment account, 6/10 of $8,700 = $5,220].	Cash	5,580	
	Gain on sale of short-term investments		360
	Investments, short term (GHI stock)		5,220
October 1, 19B—Collected semiannual interest on DEF bonds ($3,000 × .08 × 6/12 = $120).	Cash	120	
	Interest revenue		120
November 1, 19B—Paid $7,800 for MNO Company bonds including accrued interest. These 9%, $8,000 par bonds pay interest each February 1 and August 1 ($8,000 × .09 × 3/12 = $180).	Investments, short term (MNO bonds)	7,620	
	Interest receivable‡	180	
	Cash		7,800
November 5, 19B—Collected quarterly dividend of $25 on JKL stock (declared earlier during the current period).	Cash	25	
	Dividend revenue		25
December 31, 19B—Accrued interest on DEF and MNO bonds [($3,000 × .08 × 3/12) + ($8,000 × .09 × 2/12) = $180].	Interest receivable	180	
	Interest revenue		180

* All of the transactions presented relate to **short-term investments**, and specific securities held would be reported on the balance sheet under that caption rather than by the name of the issuer. If the investments are sufficiently numerous, a control account for Short-Term Investments would be established and supported by a subsidiary ledger.

† $87.75 per share.

‡ Interest Receivable, rather than Interest Revenue, is debited because the next interest collection will be February 1, which is in the next fiscal year. Alternatively, Interest Revenue could be debited, in which case, at December 31, 19B, Interest Revenue would be credited for five months' interest (i.e., since August 1, the last cash interest date).

After the reversing entries on January 1, 19B, the company's ledger accounts reflected a $120 (i.e., $6,000 × .08 × 3/12) debit balance in Interest Revenue and a $225 (i.e., $8,700 − $8,475) credit balance in the account, Allowance to Reduce Short-Term Investments to Market Value (no reversing entry for this item). Transactions and related entries for short-term investments during 19B were as shown in Exhibit 6–4.

At December 31, 19B, the cost and market value data on investment securities of H Company are as shown at the top of page 193 (refer to Exhibit 6–4).

Because the cost of the short-term portfolio of equity securities (i.e., $7,080) is less than market value (i.e., $7,160), LCM for the equity portfolio is cost (i.e., $7,080). Therefore, at December 31, 19B, the balance in the Allowance to Reduce Short-Term Investments to Market Value should be $0. At the end of 19A, the credit balance in the allowance account was $225; therefore, the balance in the allowance

Security	Amount Held	Unit Cost	Unit Market	December 31, 19B Cost	Market	LCM
Equity:						
GHI stock	40 shares	$ 87	$ 88	$ 3,480	$3,520	
JKL stock	40 shares	90	91	3,600	3,640	
Equity portfolio total				$ 7,080	$7,160	$7,080
Debt:						
DEF bonds	$3,000	105*	100½	$ 3,150	$3,015	
MNO bonds	$8,000	95¼	94¼	7,620	7,540	
Debt portfolio total				$10,770		

* 105 percent, or 1.05 of maturity value.

account of H Company should be reduced as follows (no such entry is made for the short-term portfolio of debt securities, which are accounted for at cost, $10,770):

December 31, 19B:

Allowance to reduce short-term investments to market ($225 − $0)	225	
Unrealized gain on short-term investments		225

A closing entry by H Company would be required as follows:

Interest revenue*	380	
Dividend revenue	385	
Gain (realized) on sale of short-term investments	360	
Unrealized gain on short-term investments	225	
Loss (realized) on sale of short-term investments		180
Income summary		1,170

* Includes $120 reversal from prior year on DEF bonds.

The financial statements of H Company for 19B would report the following:

Balance sheet:	
Short-term investments:	
Marketable equity securities, at LCM (market value, $7,160)	$ 7,080
Marketable debt securities, at cost (market value, $10,555)	10,770
	$17,850
Income statement:	
Interest revenue	380†
Dividend revenue	385‡
Gain (realized) on sale of short-term investments	360
Loss (realized) on sale of short-term investments	(180)
Unrealized gain on short-term investments	225

† −$120 + $80 + $120 + $120 + $180 = $380.
‡ $180 + $180 + $25 = $385.

Part C: Receivables

This part discusses accounting for receivables. The term **receivables** encompasses an entity's claims for money, goods, or services from other entities. Receivables include amounts due from customers and clients arising from normal operations as well as receivables from other sources. The discussion of receivables is ordered as follows:

1. Trade receivables:
   a. Accounts receivable.
   b. Notes receivable.
2. Special receivables.
3. Use of receivables to secure immediate cash.

TRADE RECEIVABLES

Trade receivables usually mark the first point in the sequence of merchandising and service transactions. The amounts recorded as trade receivables are established by exchange credit transactions. The two principal classes of trade receivables are accounts receivable and notes receivable.

The term **accounts receivable** usually is used to designate trade customers' accounts. Other receivables are separately designated and recorded as special receivables. The title Accounts Receivable is not particularly descriptive because any claim with no written statement of the obligation (i.e., a **note** receivable) is an "account" receivable. Ideally, a more descriptive title, such as Accounts Receivable—Trade Customers could be used for accounts receivable arising from regular sales to customers. This title would convey the true nature of these assets. Ordinarily accounts receivable are classified as current assets on the balance sheet; however, some **special** accounts receivable should not be classified as current assets, as discussed below.

MEASUREMENT OF BAD DEBT LOSSES AND ACCOUNTS RECEIVABLE

When credit is extended on a continuing basis, some bad debt "losses" due to uncollectibility of receivables are inevitable. These bad debt losses are considered a normal expense of business. Measurement of such losses involves the concurrent estimation of *(a)* the amount of **bad debt expense** for the period and *(b)* **valuation of accounts receivable.**[14]

The Accounts Receivable account should reflect the amount billed to customers (net of discounts). A special valuation (i.e., contra asset) account, Allowance for Doubtful Accounts (or Allowance for Bad Debts), is used to report the estimated bad debts included in Accounts Receivable. The residual amount, Accounts Receivable less Allowance for Doubtful Accounts, should be the estimated **net realizable value** of accounts receivable. An adjusting entry is used to record bad debt expense and concurrently to adjust the allowance account; the general form of this adjusting entry is as follows:

Bad debt expense	xx	
Allowance for doubtful accounts		xx

The sales revenue of the period from credit sales is known at the end of the period; however, the specific accounts that ultimately will prove to be uncollectible often will not be known until future periods. The **matching principle** requires that bad debt expense be matched against the sales revenue of a period. Therefore, each period, it is necessary to **estimate** the amount of bad debt expense and record it in an entry similar to the one above before the ultimate determination of whether the individual accounts receivable of the period will be collected.

Two methods are commonly used to estimate the adjustment to the Bad Debt Expense and the Allowance for Doubtful Accounts:

1. Estimation of bad debt expense: Based on experience, the average percentage relationship between actual bad debt losses and **net credit sales** is ascertained. This percentage then is applied to the actual net credit sales of the period to determine both the current expense and concurrent addition to the Allowance for Doubtful Accounts.
2. Estimation of the net realizable value of the current receivables: Age the accounts receivable; from the aging analysis and other available information, estimate the total uncollectible accounts. The balance in the allowance account then is adjusted so that its balance equals the total amount of the estimated uncollectible accounts.

Either of these approaches to estimate bad debts must recognize changes in credit policy, changes in economic conditions, or any other factor which might affect the ability of customers to pay their debts. After a method is selected, it should be continuously reviewed by the accountant and the officers of the company so that rates can be revised to attain reliable results.

The two methods of measuring bad debt expense and the allowance for doubtful accounts outlined above affect the way in which the amount is determined for the adjusting entry to record estimated bad debt expense at the end of the period. In the first approach, the amount calculated on the basis of net credit sales becomes the adjustment amount without regard to any prior balance in the allowance. In contrast, in the second approach, the **allowance** account is adjusted *to* the estimated balance needed;

[14] Receivables arising from sales and services also should be recorded at net of any **trade** discounts. Chapter 7 discusses accounting for discounts on trade receivables.

that is, any existing balance in the allowance is taken into consideration in the computation of the adjustment amount.

To illustrate accounting for bad debt expense and uncollectible receivables, assume the following data for X Company for the year ended December 31, 19J:

January 1, 19J, balances:	
Accounts receivable (debit)	$101,300
Allowance for doubtful accounts (credit)	3,300
Transactions during 19J:	
Credit sales	500,000
Cash sales	700,000
Collections on accounts receivable	420,000
Prior accounts written off as uncollectible during the period	3,800

The indicated entries relating to bad debts are as follows:

To write off the uncollectible accounts:

Allowance for doubtful accounts	3,800	
Accounts receivable (specific accounts)		3,800

After posting this entry, Accounts Receivable will reflect a debit balance of $177,500 (i.e., $101,300 + $500,000 − $420,000 − $3,800). The write-off of individual accounts as uncollectible would occur as a result of a review by the credit department during the period and would precede the end-of-period adjusting entries. In some cases, such as after a large write-off or when currently created receivables are written off before the end of the period, the allowance account may have a temporary *debit* balance prior to the adjusting entry ($500 in this example, i.e., $3,300 − $3,800).

The two different methods for estimating the amount for the adjusting entry for bad debt expense are implemented as follows:

Method 1—Adjustment of the allowance by estimating bad debt expense: Assume experience has indicated that 1.2 percent of credit sales normally will not be collected and that this pattern is expected to continue.

Bad debt expense ($500,000 × .012)	6,000	
Allowance for doubtful accounts		6,000

After posting this entry, the allowance account will reflect a credit balance of $5,500 (i.e., $3,300 − $3,800 + $6,000). It is made without regard to the prior balance in the allowance account.

Method 2—Adjustment of allowance based upon an "aging" of the current receivables: Aging accounts receivable involves an analysis of each individual account to determine the amounts not past due, moderately past due, and considerably past due. Classification of amounts by age (i.e., length of time uncollected) is important because experience indicates that the older an account, the higher the probability of uncollectibility. Aging requires the preparation of an **aging schedule** similar to the illustration in Exhibit 6–5.

Upon completion of the aging schedule, each past-due amount (e.g., Field's account in Exhibit 6–5) is reviewed by credit department personnel to determine its probable collectibility. Another "aging" pro-

EXHIBIT 6–5: Aging Schedule for Accounts Receivable of X Company (at December 31, 19J)

Customer	Receivable Balance Dec. 31, 19J	Not Past Due	Past Due		
			1–30 Days	31–60 Days	Over 60 Days
Davis	$ 500	$ 400	$ 100		
Evans	900	900			
Field	1,650		1,350	$ 300	
Harris	90			30	$ 60
King	800	700	60	40	
Zilch	250	250			
Total	$177,500	$110,000	$31,000	$29,500	$7,000

EXHIBIT 6–6: Estimating Allowance for Doubtful Accounts, Aging Approach for X Company (at December 31, 19J)

Status	Total Balances*	Uncollectible Experience Percentage	Amount Estimated to Be Uncollectible
Not past due	$110,000	.2%	$ 220
1–30 days past due	31,000	1.0	310
31–60 days past due	29,500	8.0	2,360
Over 60 days past due	7,000	40.0	2,800
	$177,500		$5,690

* Amounts agree with amounts on "Total" line in Exhibit 6–5.

cedure is to develop estimated loss percentages for each **age category** based on loss experience of the company. This approach to the aging schedule is shown in Exhibit 6–6.

Based on the computation in Exhibit 6–6, at December 31, 19J, the Allowance for Doubtful Accounts would be adjusted **to** a credit balance of $5,690, as follows:

Bad debt expense	6,190	
Allowance for doubtful accounts		6,190

Computation:
To adjust to the desired credit balance as follows:

Desired balance (see Exhibit 6–6)	$5,690
Debit balance in allowance before adjustment	500
Amount of credit needed	$6,190

In the preceding illustration, the $3,800 write-off of receivables during the current period caused the allowance account to have a debit balance of $500 before the end-of-period adjustment. This does not necessarily indicate that past estimates of bad debt losses were too low. It is possible that the $3,800 write-off includes some receivables created during the same period. If the allowance account were to have a debit balance soon after making the end-of-period adjustment, an inadequate provision for bad debts probably is indicated. When it is determined that bad debt estimates have been too low or too high, current and future rates should be adjusted accordingly. This would be accounted for as a **change in accounting estimate** as prescribed in *APB Opinion No. 20,* "Accounting Changes" (see Chapters 3 and 20).

Evaluation of Methods

Both methods of estimating bad debts are acceptable under GAAP. Each method has certain strengths and weaknesses. The first method discussed, **estimation of bad debt expense** based on credit sales, emphasizes the income statement because of its primary focus on bad debt **expense** and only incidentally measures accounts receivable at net realizable value. The theoretical basis for the estimation of bad debt expense by this method is the **matching principle.**

The second method discussed, **aging the accounts receivable to estimate the net realizable value of present receivables,** suffers from the probability that the bad debt expense reported on the income statement for the period may only incidentally be related to the credit sales of the current period, which would violate the matching principle. It emphasizes the balance sheet because of its primary focus on valuation of **accounts receivable,** and its theoretical basis is the **reporting principle** as applied to balance sheet valuation of accounts receivable.

In practice, both methods often are used together. That is, for interim financial statements, many companies base monthly or quarterly adjusting entries on the estimation of bad debt expense method because of the low cost of applying this method. At the end of the year, however, many companies age their accounts receivable as a check on the reasonableness of the balance in the allowance account.[15]

[15] This procedure is analogous to the year-end physical count of merchandise inventories performed by many companies.

If the balance in the allowance account (before the year-end adjustment) differs materially from the balance implied by the aging schedule, the company must make a judgment as to the appropriate amount to record in the year-end adjusting entry.

In the past, aging the accounts receivable was a costly process because it required credit department personnel to analyze each account receivable individually. The aging method is used more than in the past because widespread use of computer software has lowered the cost of implementing the aging method. Also, the high interest rates of recent years have prompted companies to monitor the analysis and collection of their receivables closely, and aging is the primary way accounts receivable are analyzed.

Bad Debts Collected

When an amount is collected from a customer whose account was previously written off as uncollectible, the customer's account should be debited for the amount actually collected and the allowance account should be credited for the same amount. This entry will cause the debtor's account to reflect a detailed record of the credit and related collections and will correct the allowance account. Such information may be useful in future dealings with the customer. The collection then is recorded as a debit to Cash and a credit to Accounts Receivable.

Customers' Credit Balances

Individual customers' accounts with material credit balances (from prepayments or overpayments) should be reclassified and reported as liabilities. Credit Balance of Customers' Accounts is a suitable liability account title.

Specific Write-off Method

Some small entities use a "specific write-off method" whereby bad debt expense is recorded only when individual customers' accounts prove uncollectible. At that time, Accounts Receivable is credited for the uncollectible balance and Bad Debt Expense is debited. While this procedure has the advantage of greater certainty and is permitted for income tax purposes (as is the allowance method), it is subject to severe criticism on two major counts: (1) Receivables are reported at more than their net realizable value; there is no allowance to deduct even though it is virtually certain that not all receivables will be collected. (2) The period in which the write-off occurs is often later than the period in which the receivable was created; this results in incorrect application of the **matching principle**—the expenses of extending credit should be recognized in the period when the revenue is recognized. For these reasons the specific write-off method is **not** in accordance with GAAP.

OTHER CONSIDERATIONS ABOUT ACCOUNTS RECEIVABLE

This section briefly discusses three accounting aspects of accounts receivable that often are encountered.

1. Accounts Receivable is normally a control account, and detailed records of customer transactions and balances are carried in subsidiary records for each customer.

Chapter 4 indicated that current assets includes all receivables identified with the normal operating cycle. Installment and certain other receivables are current even when not due within 12 months, provided they arise from operating cycle transactions, in which case their classification as current is based upon the expectation of their liquidation within the upcoming operating cycle.

2. When amounts charged to customers on sales contracts include interest amounts which will be earned with the passage of time, such interest amounts should be shown as a deduction from the related receivables in order to report the receivables at present value (i.e., net of interest not yet earned).

3. Special allowance accounts sometimes are provided for discounts expected to be taken by customers, for anticipated sales returns and allowances, for freight charges to be deducted by customers, and the like. Where provided, such accounts have the effect of reducing income for the period in which they are established and of lowering the net reported value of receivables. A good theoretical case can be made for such procedures because they would cause receivables to be reported at their net realizable value. However, because the effects on income and receivables carrying values usually are not material, most entities do not employ such refinements.

NOTES RECEIVABLE

Notes receivable include **trade** notes receivable, which arise from regular operations, and **special** notes receivable. Both kinds of notes are classified either as current or noncurrent assets, depending upon their terms to maturity and their relation to the operating cycle. Trade notes and special notes should be recorded and reported separately.

Notes receivable represent unconditional written promises to pay the payee or holder of the note a specified sum. Ordinarily, the payee will be in possession of the note unless it has been endorsed to a subsequent holder in due course.

Notes may be designated as **(a)** interest bearing or **(b)** noninterest bearing (i.e., discounted). Theoretically, all commercial notes require the payment of interest. Interest-bearing notes require payment of the **face** amount of the note at maturity plus specified interest, and the present value of an interest-bearing note is the same as its maturity amount (i.e., its face value) provided the interest rate specified in the note is realistic.

In contrast, a noninterest-bearing note includes the interest in its face amount and the present value of a noninterest-bearing note is necessarily less than its maturity amount. Notes receivable should be recorded in the accounts and reported at their present value (discussed in Chapter 5). Since an interest-bearing note that specifies a realistic rate of interest will have a present value at date of issuance equal to its face amount, it is recorded at the face amount when received.[16] However, when a note is noninterest bearing or when the specified interest rate on an interest-bearing note is different from the going rate, the present value and the face amount will differ. In these two situations the present value should be computed and reported as discussed and illustrated in Chapter 10 for notes payable.

Notes Receivable Illustrated. For purposes of this chapter a note receivable under two different assumptions (Case A, interest bearing; and Case B, noninterest bearing) will be illustrated.

Assume K Company sold merchandise on April 1, 19A, for $2,000 on credit and received a note receivable due in one year. The going rate of interest is 16 percent, and the accounting period ends on December 31. Assume two different situations, viz:

Case A—Interest-bearing note, face amount $2,000. Payable at maturity, face amount plus interest at 16 percent, $320; total, $2,320.

Case B—Noninterest-bearing (i.e., discounted) note, face amount, $2,320, which includes 16 percent interest on the net amount of the sales price (rather than on the face amount of the note). The amount of the sale is the present value of the note receivable, $2,000 (i.e., $2,320 ÷ 1.16) because the consideration received by the seller (i.e., the note receivable) has a value equal to its **present value** (discussed in Chapter 5). The indicated entries are the same for both cases because the present value of each note is $2,000. The entries would be as follows:[17]

April 1, 19A—To record note and sale:

Notes receivable	2,000	
Sales revenue		2,000

December 31, 19A—Adjusting entry at year-end:

Interest receivable ($2,000 × 16% × 9/12)	240	
Interest revenue		240

March 31, 19B—Collection of note (assuming no reversing entry on January 1, 19B):

Cash	2,320	
Interest receivable		240
Interest revenue		80
Notes receivable		2,000

[16] This can be demonstrated by using the table values of Chapter 5 to discount from maturity to the present *(a)* the maturity amount and *(b)* the interest payments required. These two discounted amounts when summed will always equal the face amount of the interest-bearing note.

[17] An alternative, equivalent sequence of entries for noninterest-bearing notes, which gives the same result, would be as follows:

April 1, 19A:

Notes receivable	2,320	
Discount on notes receivable*		320
Sales revenue		2,000

December 31, 19A:

Discount on notes receivable*	240	
Interest revenue		240

March 31, 19B (assuming no reversing entry on January 1, 19B):

Cash	2,320	
Discount on notes receivable*	80	
Interest revenue		80
Notes receivable		2,320

* Contra account to Notes Receivable.

Provision for Losses on Notes

Provision for uncollectible notes from trade customers usually is included in the credit balance in Allowance for Doubtful Accounts.

DISCOUNTING OF NOTES RECEIVABLE

If a note receivable is sold (and endorsed) to a third party before maturity, the original payee receives cash before maturity but may become **contingently liable** for payment of the note. The sale of a note receivable often is referred to as "discounting" a note receivable, and the existence of a contingent liability depends upon whether the note was endorsed with or without **recourse.** Because one normally is unwilling to purchase a note receivable without recourse,[18] most notes create a contingent liability when discounted.

The **cash** received from discounting a note receivable is computed as follows:

$$\left.\begin{matrix}\text{Cash received}\\ \text{upon}\\ \text{discounting}\end{matrix}\right\} = \left\{\begin{matrix}\text{Maturity}\\ \text{amount}\\ \text{of the note}\\ \text{(face + interest)}\end{matrix}\right\} - \left\{\begin{matrix}\text{Interest charged}\\ \text{by the new}\\ \text{payee}\end{matrix}\right.$$

To illustrate, assume Z Company has a 90-day, 16 percent interest-bearing note receivable, face amount, $3,000. It is discounted at the bank at 18 percent after being held 30 days from issue date. The proceeds and decrease in interest revenue to the seller of the note receivable would be calculated as follows:

Maturity amount:		
Face amount	$3,000.00	
Interest to maturity ($3,000 × 16% × 3/12)	120.00	
Total maturity amount		3,120.00
Interest charged by the new payee ($3,120 × 18% × 2/12)		93.60
Cash received upon discounting		$3,026.40

Z Company, the endorser, would record the discounting transaction as follows:

Cash	3,026.40	
Notes receivable		3,000.00
Interest revenue		26.40

18 If the discount rate is high enough, third parties will be induced to purchase notes receivable without recourse.

Disclosure of Contingent Liability on Discounted Notes Receivable

When a note receivable is discounted, the transfer by endorsement with recourse creates a contingent liability for the original payee (i.e., endorser). Usually, the contingent liability is disclosed by a note, such as the following: "The company is contingently liable for discounted notes receivable amounting to $3,000." Other methods of disclosing the contingent liability are as follows (assuming $10,000 notes receivable held prior to discounting the $3,000 note):

1.	Current assets:		
	Notes receivable (contingent liability for notes receivable discounted, $3,000)		$7,000
2.	Current assets:		
	Notes receivable	$10,000	
	Less: Notes receivable discounted	3,000	$7,000

Contingencies of all types, including contingent liabilities, are discussed in more detail in Chapter 10, Part A.

DISHONORED NOTES RECEIVABLE

When a note receivable is not paid or renewed at maturity, it is said to be dishonored. The accounting procedure for a dishonored note depends on whether the note was discounted. If a discounted note is dishonored, ordinarily it will be necessary for the original payee to pay it (unless the payee sold it without recourse).

To illustrate, assume the $3,000 interest-bearing note discounted by Z Company was defaulted by the maker. Z Company then paid the bank the face amount of the note plus interest and a protest fee of $35. Z Company would record the default as follows:

Special receivable—dishonored note	3,155	
Cash ($3,000 + $120 + 35)		3,155

On the other hand, if this same note had not been discounted, upon dishonor the required entry by Z Company would have been as follows:

Special receivable—dishonored note	3,155	
Notes receivable		3,000
Interest revenue		155
To record dishonored note in the accounts of the maker including accrued interest to maturity date.		

After dishonor, interest accrues on the face amount plus accrued interest and any protest fees at the **legal** rate of interest. However, if the note is uncollectible, the total claim should be written off as a bad debt.

Balance sheet presentation of dishonored notes should list a special receivable with adequate provision for the uncollectibility expectations. Note disclosure is necessary for large notes in default.

SPECIAL RECEIVABLES

Receivables, other than trade receivables, generally are classified as special receivables. Some of the more common types of special receivables are as follows:

1. Deposits made to other parties to cover potential damages, and deposits made to guarantee performance of a contract or payment of an expense.
2. Prepayments to others on contingent purchases and expense contracts.
3. Claims against trade creditors for damaged, lost, or returned goods.
4. Claims against common carriers for lost or damaged goods.
5. Claims against the government for refunds.
6. Advances (i.e., loans) to subsidiaries.
7. Loans to officers and employees.
8. Dividends receivable (cash and property dividends declared but not yet paid by the issuing corporation).
9. Unexpended balances of working funds in the hands of agents.
10. Claims against insurance companies for losses sustained.
11. Claims in litigation.
12. Unpaid stock subscriptions (subscriptions receivable).

Special receivables that are related to the operating cycle or are collectible within one year (whichever is the longer) should be reported as current assets. Other special receivables normally are reported on the balance sheet under a noncurrent caption such as Other assets.[19]

Special receivables should be valued as to collectibility, and a special allowance for doubtful accounts in this category should be established if warranted.

[19] "Advances to subsidiaries" (item 6) normally would be reported under "Investments and funds." Usually most of the receivables listed above are classified as current assets.

USE OF RECEIVABLES TO SECURE IMMEDIATE CASH

Many companies utilize receivables to secure immediate cash prior to their regular collection dates. The common methods of obtaining immediate cash on receivables are: (1) discounting of notes receivable (discussed above), (2) assignment of accounts receivable, (3) factoring of accounts receivable, (4) outright sale of accounts receivable, and (5) pledging accounts receivable. While detailed contractual arrangements vary, the following brief descriptions typify these transactions and their accounting.

Assignment

One use of receivables to secure immediate cash involves the assignment to a financing institution of receivables arising on open-account sales. Frequently, these assignments are made on a "with recourse, nonnotification" basis. "With recourse" means that accounts which become delinquent or uncollectible must be repurchased by the seller or replaced with other accounts receivable of equivalent value. "Nonnotification" means debtors are not informed of the assignment and hence remit to the seller in the usual way. As the seller collects on the receivables assigned, the cash is remitted to the finance company.

The cash advanced by the financing institution may range from 60 percent to 85 percent of the amount in the accounts. Annual interest rates charged may range as high as 20 percent to 30 percent when risks are high, especially when assignment is on a nonrecourse basis, or when a low dollar amount per account causes accounting and collection expenses to be high.

Assignment of receivables with recourse is akin to the discounting of notes receivable, and the accounting procedure is essentially parallel. An illustrative problem is presented to demonstrate the essential accounting for the assignment of accounts receivable.

Assignment Illustrated. W Company assigned $40,000 of its trade receivables to Z Finance Company under a contract, supported by a promissory note, whereby Z Finance Company agreed to advance 75 percent of their amount to W Company and to charge 24 percent interest on the balance outstanding. Debtors remit directly to W since the assignment was "with recourse, nonnotification." The series of transactions and related entries are shown in Exhibit 6–7. The assignment is treated essentially as a sales of the receivables which conforms to a proposed *FASB Statement,* "Accounting and Reporting by Transferors for Transfer of Receivable with Recourse," November 1981.

On January 31 (i.e., after entry *(c)* in Exhibit 6–7), the balance sheet of W Company would report:

W COMPANY

Current assets:		
Accounts receivable (amount assumed)		$150,000
Accounts receivable assigned ($40,000 − $20,500)	$19,500	
Less: Note payable on assigned accounts ($30,000 − $19,700)	10,300	
Equity in accounts receivable assigned		9,200
Total accounts receivable		$159,200

The details of an assignment contract, such as the one illustrated above, will determine the accounting entries.

Factoring

Accounts receivable may be sold on a **without recourse** basis to factors.[20] Customers whose accounts are sold are instructed to pay directly to the factor who assumes the functions of billing, collecting, and so on.

Under a factoring contract, the factor controls the granting of credit by the client. As the latter sells to customers, copies of the sales invoices and supporting documents are sent to the factor. The client usually obtains cash immediately upon transferring the invoices. Gross amounts of the invoices less any sales discounts and allowances and less the factor's commission and a factor's reserve (or margin) to cover expected returns and claims is the measure of cash available. Interest (above the factor's commission) is charged only on cash drawn **prior** to the average due date of the factored invoices. Available money not drawn plus the factor's reserve becomes available without interest cost on the average due date.

[20] Factors are financing organizations which buy trade receivables. Factoring is encountered in many industries but is especially widespread in the textile industry.

EXHIBIT 6–7: Assignment of Accounts Receivable

Transaction	Entries on W Company's Books		
a. Jan. 2: Assigned $40,000 accounts receivable; advance received, 75%; gave note payable.	Accounts receivable assigned	40,000	
	Accounts receivable		40,000
	Cash ($40,000 × 75%)	30,000	
	Notes payable (Z Finance Co.)		30,000
b. Jan. 3–30: Collected $20,000 of assigned accounts less cash discounts $300. In addition, sales returns were $500.	Cash	19,700	
	Sales discounts	300	
	Sales returns	500	
	Accounts receivable assigned		20,500
c. Jan. 31: Remitted collections to finance company plus $600 interest (i.e., $30,000 × .24 × 1/12).	Interest expense	600	
	Notes payable (Z Finance Co.)	19,700	
	Cash		20,300
d. Feb. 1–27: Collected balance of assigned accounts except $200 written off as uncollectible.	Cash	19,300	
	Allowance for doubtful accounts	200	
	Accounts receivable assigned		19,500
e. Feb. 28: Remitted balance due to finance company ($30,000 − $19,700 = $10,300) plus $206 interest (i.e., $10,300 × .24 × 1/12 = $10,506).	Interest expense	206	
	Notes payable (Z Finance Co.)	10,300	
	Cash		10,506

Note: If the collections are remitted directly to the finance company (not deposited by W Company into their own bank account), entries *(b)–(c)* and *(d)–(e)*, respectively, would be combined into two entries.

In addition to interest, factors charge commissions to compensate for their credit and collection services and the credit losses they expect to incur. Since cash needs are often seasonal, proportions of available cash drawn usually will vary throughout the term of the factoring contract.

Outright Sale of Accounts Receivable

Occasionally accounts receivable are sold outright to a third party, usually without recourse. The third party assumes all collection responsibilities and bad debt losses. Outright sale often involves a high discount rate, varying as high as 50 percent, depending upon interest rates and other circumstances. Outright sale occurs most frequently when a business is in serious financial difficulty. No unique accounting problems are involved: Cash is debited, the receivables sold and the related amount of the allowance for doubtful accounts are closed out, and the difference is recorded as interest expense.

Pledging

Loans are sometimes obtained from banks and other lenders by pledging accounts receivable as security. The borrower continues to collect the receivables and usually is required to apply all or a large percent of collections received to reduction of the loan. Also, the borrower absorbs all bad debt losses. This method of lending on receivables sometimes is used because commercial banks may lack express or implied powers to buy accounts receivable. The fact that portions of the receivables have been pledged should be disclosed by balance sheet notes or parenthetical notations. Accounting by the borrower is simlar to that illustrated above for assignment.

QUESTIONS

PART A

1. Define *cash* in the accounting sense.

2. In what circumstances, if any, is it permissible to offset a bank overdraft against a positive balance in another bank account?

3. If you were called upon to establish a petty cash system that would be particularly effective from the standpoint of internal control, what important features would you incorporate into it?

4. Where (if at all) do items *(a)* through *(g)* belong in the following reconciliation?

Balance per bank statement, June 30	\$x,xxx.xx
Additions	
Deductions	
June 30 true balance	\$ 9,600.00
Balance per our ledger, June 30	\$x,xxx.xx
Additions	
Deductions	
June 30 true balance	\$ 9,600.00

a. Note collected by bank for the depositor on June 29; notification was received July 2 when the June 30 bank statement was received.

b. Checks drawn in June which had not cleared bank by June 30.

c. Check of a depositor with a similar name which was returned with checks accompanying June 30 bank statement and which was charged to our account.

d. Bank service charge for which notification was received upon receipt of bank statement.

e. Deposit mailed June 30 which reached bank July 1 (not yet on the bank statement).

f. Notification of charge for imprinting our name on blank checks was received with the June 30 bank statement.

g. Upon refooting cash receipts journal, we discovered that one receipt was omitted in arriving at the total which was posted to the Cash account in the ledger.

5. Briefly describe a "comprehensive" bank reconciliation. What advantage does the comprehensive reconciliation afford over a conventional bank reconciliation which covers a single point in time?

6. Define the following items associated with *cash:*
   a. Compensating balance.
   b. NSF check.
   c. CD.

PART B

7. What criteria must a security meet to qualify as a short-term investment?

8. What is properly included in the cost of short-term investments?

9. In what ways, if any, does the accounting for investments in bonds differ if the securities are held as long-term investments instead of as short-term investments?

10. An investor bought 100 shares of PQ Company stock in January for $6,700 and another 100 shares in March for $7,000. In October, the investor sold 150 of the shares at 77. What is the amount of the gain or loss? Discuss briefly.

11. The account, Allowance to Reduce Short-Term Investments in Equity Securities to Market, may properly be debited or credited. Under what circumstances would this account be credited? Debited? What is the maximum amount it can be debited?

PART C

12. Briefly describe the different methods of estimating bad debt expense and the allowance for doubtful accounts in connection with trade receivables. State which financial statement each method emphasizes. What is the theoretical basis for each emphasis?

13. It sometimes happens that a receivable which has been written off as uncollectible is subsequently collected. Describe the accounting procedures in such an event.

14. How should customer accounts with credit balances be reported in the financial statements?

15. T Company received, from a customer, a $1,000, 15% interest-bearing note which will mature in three months. After holding it two months, the note was discounted by T at the bank at 20%. Compute T's proceeds.

16. How should special receivables be reported on the balance sheet?

17. In relation to accounts receivable, what is the meaning of each of the following terms?
    a. Assignment.
    b. Factoring.
    c. Pledging.

DECISION CASE 6–1

The president of Maryann Company, a fabric retailer, is concerned about valuation of the company's material investment in marketable securities; she wants to value them at closing prices traded on the New York and American Stock Exchanges at year-end. The closing prices were substantially in excess of acquisition cost.

Maryann stated ". . . the thousands of transactions in shares of open-end investment trusts (mutual funds) at prices reflecting current market prices of their portfolios are evidence that most people view these value changes as equivalent to realization. Indeed, the cost of the investment is an incredibly low figure to present."

As Maryann's independent auditor, you explained that some transactions, events, and changes in valuation are not recognized for accounting purposes under generally accepted accounting principles.

Required:

1. List the various types of transactions, events, and changes in valuation that are **not** recognized for accounting purposes under GAAP.
2. *a.* What should be considered in selecting the method of revenue recognition that is most appropriate for a particular situation? Do **not** list methods of revenue recognition.
   b. Discuss the appropriateness of Maryann Company's proposal to recognize as revenue the excess of closing prices listed by the stock exchanges over the cost of the investment. (AICPA adapted)

DECISION CASE 6–2

PART A

FASB Statement 12 generally became effective for financial statements covering annual and interim periods ending on or after December 31, 1975. There were some exceptions as to the effective date, one of which pertained to paragraph 10. Provisions of this paragraph (quoted below) did not apply to transfers of securities between current and noncurrent classifications made as of or before December 31, 1975.

> If there is a change in the classification of a marketable equity security between current and noncurrent, the security shall be transferred between the corresponding portfolios at the lower of its cost or market value at date of transfer. If market value is less than cost, the market value shall become the new cost basis, and the difference shall be accounted for as if it were a realized loss and included in the determination of net income.

The following note to financial statements appeared in the annual report of Norton Simon, Inc., for the fiscal year ended June 30, 1976:

> Marketable equity securities included in short-term investments at June 30, 1975, had a cost of $34,168,000. At June 30, 1975, short-term investments were stated generally at lower of cost or market. Marketable equity securities, with a gross unrealized loss of approximately $10 million at June 30, 1975, were transferred at cost from short-term to long-term investments as of December 31, 1975, in accordance with provisions of *Statement No. 12* of The Financial Accounting Standards Board. Realized losses on marketable equity securities amounted to $400,000 in 1976 and $3,228,000 in 1975. During 1975, the valuation allowance for marketable equity securities was reduced $5,339,000 as a result of realized losses and changes in market value of investments.

Required:

1. Assuming the securities transferred to long-term investments had not changed in value between June 30, 1975, and January 2, 1976, what would have been the differential effect of the December 31, 1975, transfer relative to a January 1976 transfer?
2. Assuming the securities had not been transferred and that their value on June 30, 1976, was the same as at June 30, 1975, how would the note to the financial statements have been modified? Write the modified note.

PART B

Notes to the financial statements relating to marketable securities included in current assets of Stauffer Chemical Company in the annual report for the year ended December 31, 1976, included the following:

Marketable Securities

	($000)	
	1976	**1975**
Marketable securities—at cost	$102,596	$33,370
Approximate gross unrealized losses	(1,309)	(3,296)
Approximate gross unrealized gains	654	12
Valuation allowances	(655)	(3,284)
Marketable securities—at market ..	$101,941	$30,086
Valuation allowance decrease included in income	$ 2,629	$ 882
Realized net loss (specific identification method)	$ 14	$ 223

Required:

Comment on this note and the disclosure it provides.

EXERCISES

PART A: EXERCISES 6–1 to 6–7

Exercise 6–1

What treatment should be accorded the following items held by Jax Company as of December 31?

1. Checks payable to Jax Company in the amount of $900 dated early January of the following year.
2. A customer check payable to Jax Company for $50, included in its December 20 deposit, was returned by the bank stamped "NSF." No entry has yet been made to reflect the return.
3. A $20,000 CD on which interest accrued to December 31 has just been recorded by debiting Interest Receivable and crediting Interest Revenue. The chief accountant proposes to report the $20,000 as "Cash in Bank."
4. Jax operates a $200 petty cash fund. As of December 31 the fund cashier reports expense vouchers covering various expenses in the amount of $167.20 and cash of $31.80.
5. Postage stamps valued at $30 are found in the cash drawer. The chief accountant proposes to report them as cash.
6. A cashier's check in the amount of $200 payable to Jax Company is in the cash drawer; it is dated December 29. The chief accountant proposes to report it as part of cash.
7. Three checks totaling $465 payable to vendors who

have sold merchandise to Jax Company on account dated December 31 are still on hand unmailed after the last mail pickup. They have been entered as payments in the check register and ledger.

8. At December 30, Jax Company had left a note which matures December 31 with its bank for collection. The note is for $2,000 and bears interest at 9%, having run for three months. As yet, Jax has not heard from the bank as to the outcome of its collection efforts but is confident of a favorable outcome because of the extremely high credit rating of the maker of the note.

Exercise 6–2

Indicate the amount (and how derived) at which each of the following independent cases could be properly reported as ordinary cash:

a. Balance in general checking account, Bank H, $6,000; overdraft in special checking account, Bank H, $400; IOU held from company president for $400, received six weeks ago in settlement of advance to the president.

b. Balance in Bank P, $20,000; refundable deposit with state treasurer to guarantee performance of highway contract in progress, $10,000; balance in Banco de Sur America, $9,000 (foreign and restricted).

c. Cash on hand, $800; cash in Bank C, $9,000; cash held by salespersons as advances on expense accounts, $800; postage stamps on hand received from mail-order customers, $50.

d. Balance in checking account, $10,000; demand certificates of deposits, $5,000; deposit with bond sinking fund trustee, $15,000; cash on hand, $1,000.

e. Negotiable instruments in cash drawer on December 31, as shown at the bottom of this page.

Exercise 6–3

As a part of their newly designed internal control system, the Lou Corporation established a petty cash fund. Operations for the first month were as follows:

a. Wrote a check for $500 on August 1 and turned the cash over to the custodian.

b. Summary of the petty cash expenditures:

	Aug. 1–15	Aug. 16–31
Postage	$ 40	$ 58
Supplies used	265	190
Delivery expense	98	178
Miscellaneous expenses	35	40
Totals	$438	$466

c. Fund replenished on August 16.

d. Fund replenished on August 31 and increased by $300.

Required:
Give all entries indicated through August.

Exercise 6–4

Carson Company, as a matter of policy, deposits all receipts and makes all payments by check. The following data were taken from the cash records of the company:

Reconciliation at May 31:

Balance per bank	$5,000
Add: Outstanding deposits	2,200
	7,200
Deduct: Outstanding checks	1,400
Balance per books	$5,800

June Results:

	Per Bank	Per Books
Balance, June 30	$ 3,090	$ 4,200
June deposits	10,600	12,300
June checks	14,500	13,900
June note collected	2,000	—
June bank charges	10	—

Required (for June):

1. Compute the deposits in transit and outstanding checks as of June 30.
2. Reconcile the bank account as of June 30.
3. Give any entries indicated for the books.

(Relates to Exercise 6–2)

From	Date of Check	Other Data	
Customer W	Dec. 29	On past-due account	$500
Customer X	Dec. 30	In payment of $1,000 invoice of Dec. 23	700
Customer Y	Dec. 24	Previously deposited and returned; insufficient funds	300
Customer Z (postdated)	Jan. 2	In full payment of account	400
J. T. Brown	Dec. 29	American Express travelers check	100

Exercise 6–5

Reconciliation of Crabtree Company's bank account at May 31 was as follows:

Balance per bank statement	$10,500
Deposits outstanding	1,500
Checks outstanding	150*
True cash balance	$11,850
Balance per books	$11,864
Unrecorded service charge	14*
True cash balance	$11,850

* Denotes deduction.

June data are as follows:

	Bank	Books
Checks recorded	$11,500	$11,800
Deposits recorded	8,100	9,000
Service charges recorded	12	14
Collection by bank ($800 note plus interest)	820	—
NSF check returned with June 30 statement (will be redeposited; assumed to be good)	50	—
Balances, June 30	7,858	9,050

Required:
1. Compute deposits in transit and checks outstanding at June 30.
2. Prepare a reconciliation for June.
3. Prepare entries needed at June 30.

Exercise 6–6

Babinski Company's cash transactions were made through its accounts at First National Bank. On April 30, the company reconciled its bank and book balances as follows:

Balance per bank statement		$10,900
Deduct outstanding checks:		
No. 698	$ 30	
No. 699	80	
No. 702	25	135
		10,765
Add:		
Deposits in transit	150	
April service charge	3	
Luzinski Co. check charged to our account	40	193
Apr. 30 book balance		$10,958

In summary form, the Cash account on Babinski Company's books for May is as below:

Cash

April 30, balance	10,958	April service charge	3
May collections	14,210	Checks drawn	13,812

At May 31, the following checks were outstanding: no. 702, $25; no. 735, $100; no. 738, $60; and no. 740, $20. The May 31 receipts amounting to $420 were mailed to the bank at the close of business that day. The May service charge of $5 was recorded by the bank only. The $40 item shown on the April 30 reconciliation was corrected by the bank during May. May receipts and payments for Babinski Company's account recorded by the bank were $13,980 and $13,747 respectively. From the foregoing, the correct ending bank balance can be derived.

Required:
Prepare a comprehensive reconciliation for May.

Exercise 6–7

Slippo Company deposits all its receipts in the bank and makes all disbursements by check. Its February 28 bank reconciliation was as follows:

Balance per bank		$7,414
Add:		
Deposits in transit	$170	
Unrecorded bank service charge	6	176
		7,590
Deduct: Outstanding checks		390
Balance per books		$7,200

March data are as follows:

	Per Bank	Per Books
Balance, Mar. 31	$8,024	$5,994
March deposits reflected	4,760	4,900
March checks reflected	6,170*	6,100
Note collected (including $20 interest)	2,020	—
Service charge recorded	—	6

* Erroneously includes a check drawn by Blippo Company for $150.

Required:
1. Determine the apparent deposits in transit and outstanding checks as of March 31.
2. Prepare a comprehensive reconciliation for March.
3. If March 31 were the end of Slippo's fiscal year, what entries would be needed on its books? Draft them.

PART B: EXERCISES 6–8 to 6–12

Exercise 6–8

At January 1, the short-term investments of Temple Company were as follows:

No. Held	Description	Par Value Each	Total Cost
8	Bonds, Day Co., 10% per annum (paid each Apr. 1 and Oct. 1)*	$1,000	$7,800
100	Shares, Knight Co. common stock	50	9,300

* Assume accrued interest reversed January 1.

Market value was in excess of cost at January 1.

The transactions below relate to the above short-term investments and those bought and sold during the year. All transactions are cash.

Feb. 2	Received $150 dividend from Knight Company.
Mar. 1	Sold four (4) Day Company bonds for a total consideration (including accrued interest) of $4,100.
Apr. 1	Collected semiannual interest on Day Company bonds.
May 1	Bought three bonds of King, Ltd. These 12%, $1,000 bonds pay interest each March 1 and September 1. Total consideration paid, $3,050.
June 1	For $4,200 total consideration sold the remaining Day Company bonds.
Aug. 2	Received $150 dividend from Knight Company.
Sept. 1	Collected semiannual interest on King, Ltd., bonds.
Dec. 31	Adjust and close books; recognize all accruals. At January 1, as stated, market value of marketable securities exceeded cost. However, at December 31, market prices on a per security basis were as follows:

	Market Price
Knight Co. common shares	92½
King, Ltd., bonds	102*

* Does not include accrued interest.

Required:
Journalize the foregoing transactions. At year-end make adjusting and closing entries based on GAAP.

Exercise 6–9

Case A—At December 31, 19A, the portfolio of short-term investments of Stutz Company was comprised of the following items:

Description	Quantity	Cost	Unit Market Prices
Hygro Corp. bonds, 14%, $1,000	5	$5,200	101½
Damon common stock ...	50 shares	2,300	40⅝
Martin common stock ...	100 shares	2,100	24

a. At what value should the short-term investments be reported on the December 31, 19A, balance sheet of Stutz Company? Show computations.

b. One year later, the short-term investments of Stutz consisted of the following:

Description	Quantity	Cost	Unit Market Prices
Damon common stock	20 shares	$ 920	37¼
Martin common stock	30 shares	630	23
Dries Corp. bonds, 13%, $1,000	4 bonds	4,040	100½

During 19B, Stutz had sold the 30 Damon shares at a gain of $200 and the 70 Martin shares at a gain of $140. At what value should the short-term investments be reported on the December 31, 19B, balance sheet of Stutz Company? Show computations.

Case B—Brown Company bought, as a short-term investment, seven of the $1,000 bonds of Laczko Corporation on April 1, 19A, at 102 plus accrued interest. These 12% bonds pay interest semiannually each May 1 and November 1. On December 1, 19A, four (4) of the bonds were sold at 101¼ plus accrued interest. Brown Company adjusts and closes books on December 31.

a. Journalize all events (except closing entries) relating to the bonds for 19A assuming the method proscribed by GAAP.

b. If the bonds had been bought as a long-term investment, what added information would have been needed and why?

Exercise 6–10

Prepare journal entries to record the following transactions (use the GAAP method) relating to a short-term investment in the 12% bonds of Moe Corporation. These bonds pay interest each May 1 and November 1.

Aug. 1	Cash of $39,800 is disbursed for $40,000 par value bonds including interest.
Nov. 1	Collected interest.
Dec. 31	Adjust and close books for the year. The market value of the bonds is 96 excluding interest (a "mere temporary" condition).
Jan. 1	Make any desirable reversing entries.
Feb. 1	Sold half of the bonds, receiving a check for $19,600 including accrued interest.
May 1	Collected interest.

Exercise 6–11

In November 19A, Holmes Corporation acquired the following short-term investments in marketable equity securities:

Company X—500 shares common stock (nopar) at $60 per share.
Company Y—300 shares preferred stock (par $10, nonredeemable) at $20 per share.

Additional data:

12/31/19A	Market values: X stock, $52; and Y stock, $24.
3/2/19B	Received cash dividends per share as follows: X stock, $1; and Y stock, 50 cents.
10/1/19B	Sold 100 of the Company Y shares at $25 per share.
12/31/19B	Market values: X stock, $46; and Y stock, $26.

Required:

1. Give all entries indicated for Holmes Corporation for the above short-term investments in marketable equity securities (LCM method) assuming no other short-term investments.
2. Show how the investments and related gains and losses would be reflected on the financial statements of Holmes Corporation for 19A and 19B.

Exercise 6–12

Select the best answer in each of the following; justify your choices.

1. Which of the following transactions would increase a company's positive current ratio?
   a. Sell a short-term investment at a gain.
   b. Borrow money on a short-term note.
   c. Sell a short-term investment at a loss.
   d. Receive a stock dividend on a short-term investment.
2. Green Company owns some shares of stock which its management would like very much to sell. There is, however, serious question about the company's ability to sell the stock quickly at other than a sacrifice price. If the investment is valued at cost, it should be classified as a—
   a. Current asset.
   b. Contra item under capital.
   c. Long-term investment.
   d. Deferred charge.
3. The test of marketability must be met before an investment in securities owned can be properly classified as—
   a. Debentures.
   b. Treasury stock.
   c. Long-term investments.
   d. Current assets.
4. How should the premium or discount on bonds purchased as a short-term investment be reported in published financial statements?
   a. As expense or revenue in the period the bonds are purchased.
   b. As an integral part of the cost of the asset acquired (investment) and amortized over a period of not less than 60 months.
   c. As an integral part of the cost of the asset acquired (investment) until such time as the investment is sold.
   d. As an integral part of the cost of the asset acquired (investment) and amortized over the period the bonds are expected to be held.
5. Marketable securities held to finance future construction of additional plants should be classified on the balance sheet as—
   a. Current assets.
   b. Property, plant, and equipment.
   c. Intangible assets.
   d. Investments and funds.

(all except 1, AICPA adapted)

PART C: EXERCISES 6–13 to 6–21

Exercise 6–13

When examining the accounts of Doon Company, you ascertain that balances relating to both receivables and payables are included in a single controlling account (called Receivables), which has a $46,100 debit balance. An analysis of the details of this account revealed the following:

	Debit	Credit
Accounts receivable—customers	$80,000	
Accounts receivable—officers	4,000	
Debit balances—creditors	900	
Expense advances to salespersons	2,000	
Capital stock subscriptions receivable	9,200	
Accounts payable for merchandise		$38,500
Unpaid salaries		6,600
Credit balances in customer accts.		4,000
Payments received in advance for shipments not yet made		900

Required:

1. Give the entry to reflect correct treatment of the above items and to reclassify items which do not belong in the Receivables account.
2. How should the items be reported on Doon Company's balance sheet?

Exercise 6–14

At January 1, 19B, the credit balance in the Allowance for Doubtful Accounts of the Master Company was $400,000. For 19B, the provision (i.e., expense) for doubtful accounts is based on a percentage of net credit sales. Net credit sales for 19B were $50 million. Based on the latest available facts, the 19B provision (i.e., expense) for doubtful accounts is estimated to be .7% of net credit sales. During 19B, uncollectible receivables amounting to $410,000 were written off against the Allowance for Doubtful Accounts.

Required:
Prepare a schedule to compute the balance in Master's Allowance for Doubtful Accounts at December 31, 19B. Show supporting computations. (AICPA adapted)

Exercise 6–15

An analysis of the Receivables control account (debit balance, $102,900) of Baskin Corporation at December 31 revealed the following:

a.	Accounts from regular sales (current)	$80,000
b.	Accounts known to be uncollectible	2,500
c.	Dishonored notes debited back to customers' accounts	8,000
d.	Credit balances in customer accounts	600
e.	Past-due accounts of customers	6,000
f.	Due from employees	7,000

The Allowance for Doubtful Accounts is adjusted each December 31. Its balance before adjustment on December 31 was a $1,600 debit. It was estimated that losses on receivables at December 31 would average as follows:

Item	Loss Percent
a	2
c	20
e	5

Required:
1. Give journal entries *(a)* to reclassify items which do not belong in the Receivables account and *(b)* to reflect bad debt expense.
2. Indicate proper reporting on Baskin Corporation's December 31 balance sheet. Assume all amounts to be material.

Exercise 6–16

The following data are available concerning a company whose fiscal year is the calendar year:

Sales (of which $80,000 are on credit)	$100,000
Accounts receivable, Jan. 1	60,000
Accounts receivable, Dec. 31	70,000
Allowance for doubtful accts., Jan. 1	2,000 (cr.)
Allowance for doubtful accts., Dec. 31*	1,000 (dr.)

* Before making year-end adjusting entry for bad debt expense.

Required:
1. Assuming there were no recoveries of doubtful accounts which had been previously charged off as uncollectible and no bad debt expense recorded during the year, what was the amount of receivables charged off as uncollectible during the year?
2. What was the amount of cash inflow from receivables during the year?
3. This requirement does **not** use the above data; also, it is independent of 1 and 2 above. Give all entries during the year for bad debts and the related allowance for doubtful accounts based upon the following interrelated data:
   a. Bad debt expense estimated to be 4% of credit sales, which were $80,000 for the year.
   b. Beginning balance in the allowance for doubtful accounts at January 1 was $2,000.
   c. Accounts written off as bad during the year, $5,800.
   d. Bad debts allowance at end of year estimated on basis of aging; the estimate is:
      (1) On receivables less than 60 days old ($20,000), 1%.
      (2) On receivables 60 to 120 days old ($40,000), 3½%.
      (3) On remaining receivables ($10,000), 6%. Assume the year-end adjusting entry is based upon the aging schedule. That is, bad debt expense, in addition to the allowance account, is to be adjusted to attain the net realizable value of accounts receivable called for by the aging schedule.

Exercise 6–17

Churchill Company has been in business three years and is being audited for the first time. Concerning accounts receivable, the auditor ascertained that the company has been charging off receivables as they finally proved uncollectible and treating them as expenses at the time of write-off. (Stated another way, receivables were valued at 100 cents on the dollar.)

It is determined that receivables losses have approximated (and can be expected to continue to approximate) 2% of net sales. Until this first audit, the company's sales and receivable write-off experience was as below:

Year of Sales	Amount of Sales	Accounts Written Off in—		
		19A	19B	19C
19A	$600,000	$5,000	$7,500	$1,000
19B	750,000	—	3,500	6,500
19C	850,000	—	—	4,000

Required:
1. Indicate the amount by which net income was understated or overstated (ignoring income tax effects) each year under the company's policy. Assume for purpose of this requirement that the old policy was also used in arriving at the above amounts for 19C.
2. If Churchill Company were to switch to a more acceptable basis of accounting for bad debts, assuming books were still open for 19C, what entry should be made at year-end, 19C?

Exercise 6–18

Conover Company accepted an interest-bearing note receivable for $4,000 from a customer whose account receivable had become due. In respect to the note, give the indicated journal entry for each of the following independent events; show computations. (Use 30-day months, not days, for interest computations.)

1. Received the note, which matures in four months and bears interest at 12%.
2. Discounted the above note after two months at 15% interest. Make the entry under the two methods of recording.
3. The customer paid the note at maturity.
4. The customer defaulted on the note, and Conover Company paid the holder including a $25 protest fee.

Exercise 6–19

On November 1, 19A, Puch Company received from two customers two notes for merchandise sold to them. Each note was in settlement for a sale of goods for $8,000. Customer A gave a three-month 16% interest-bearing note. Customer B gave a three-month, noninterest-bearing note with an implied interest rate of 16% (i.e., 16% interest on the sales price was included in the face of the note).

Required:

1. Give all entries (including adjusting and closing entries) pertaining to the two notes on Puch Company's books from date of receipt through time of payment assuming the company adjusts and closes its books at December 31, 19A.
2. Show how the notes should be reflected on the December 31, 19A, balance sheet.

Exercise 6–20

Ink, Inc., assigned $60,000 of its receivables to Pen Finance Company. The contract provided that Pen would advance 85% of their gross value. Ink's debtors continued to remit directly to it; the cash, plus finance charges, is then remitted to the finance company.

During the first month, customers owing $41,000 remitted $39,400 to Ink, Inc., thereby taking advantage of $600 cash discounts. Sales returns totaled $1,000. The finance charge paid after the first month was $350.

During the second month, remaining receivables were collected in full except for $400 written off as uncollectible. Final settlement was effected with the finance company, including payment of $150 added interest.

Required:

Give the journal entries needed to record the above assignment of accounts receivable. Omit closing entries.

Exercise 6–21

Determine the best answer to each of the following questions. Write question numbers and answers alongside on the solution you submit.

1. Which of the following methods of determining bad debt expense does not match expense and revenue?
   a. Debiting bad debt expense as accounts are written off as uncollectible.
   b. Debiting bad debt expense in an amount equal to a percentage of sales under the allowance method.
   c. Debiting bad debt expense in an amount equal to a percentage of accounts receivable under the allowance method.
   d. Debiting bad debt expense in an amount equal to an amount derived from aging the accounts receivable under the allowance method.

The following data pertain to questions 2 through 6:

RENNER, INC.
Balance Sheets

	December 31	
Assets	**19B**	**19A**
Current assets:		
Cash	$ 150,000	$100,000
Marketable securities	40,000	
Accounts receivable—net	420,000	260,000
Merchandise inventory	330,000	210,000
Prepaid expenses	50,000	25,000
	990,000	595,000
Land, buildings, and fixtures	565,000	300,000
Less: Accum. depr.	55,000	25,000
	510,000	275,000
	$1,500,000	$870,000
Equities		
Current liabilities:		
Accounts payable	$ 265,000	$220,000
Accrued expense payable	70,000	65,000
Dividends payable	35,000	—
	370,000	285,000
Notes payable—due 19E	250,000	
Stockholders' equity:		
Common stock	600,000	420,000
Retained earnings	280,000	165,000
	880,000	585,000
	$1,500,000	$870,000

RENNER, INC.
Income Statements

	Year Ended December 31	
	19B	19A
Net sales—including service charges	$3,200,000	$2,000,000
Cost of goods sold	2,500,000	1,600,000
Gross profit	700,000	400,000
Expenses—including income tax	500,000	260,000
Net income	$ 200,000	$ 140,000

Additional information available included the following:

Although Renner will report all changes in financial position, management has adopted a format emphasizing the flow of cash.

All accounts receivable and accounts payable relate to trade merchandise. Cash discounts are not allowed to customers, but a service charge is added to an account for late payment. Accounts payable are recorded net and always are paid to take all of the discount allowed. The Allowance for Doubtful Accounts at the end of 19B was the same as at the end of 19A; no receivables were charged against the Allowance during 19B.

The proceeds from the note payable were used to finance a new store building. Capital stock was sold to provide additional working capital.

2. Cash collected during 19B from accounts receivable amounted to—
   a. $3,200,000.
   b. $3,070,000.
   c. $3,040,000.
   d. $2,780,000.
   e. None of the above or not determinable from the above facts.

3. Cash payments during 19B on accounts payable to suppliers amounted to—
   a. $2,335,000.
   b. $2,500,000.
   c. $2,455,000.
   d. $2,575,000.
   e. None of the above or not determinable from the above facts.

4. Cash dividend payments during 19B amounted to—
   a. $120,000.
   b. $115,000.
   c. $85,000.
   d. $35,000.
   e. None of the above or not determinable from the above facts.

5. Cash receipts during 19B which were not provided by operations totaled—
   a. $400,000.
   b. $250,000.
   c. $150,000.
   d. $70,000.
   e. None of the above or not determinable from the above facts.

6. Cash payments for assets during 19B which were not reflected in operations totaled—
   a. $300,000.
   b. $265,000.
   c. $185,000.
   d. $40,000.
   e. None of the above or not determinable from the above facts.

7. The advantage of relating a company's bad debt experience to its accounts receivable is that this approach—
   a. Gives a reasonably correct statement of receivables in the balance sheet.
   b. Relates bad debt expense to the period of sale.
   c. Is the only generally accepted method for valuing accounts receivable.
   d. Makes estimates of uncollectible accounts unnecessary.

8. Kraft, Inc.'s account balances at December 31, 19A, for Accounts Receivable and the related Allowance for Uncollectible Accounts are $600,000 and $4,800, respectively. From an aging of accounts receivable, it is estimated that $7,200 of the December 31 receivables will be uncollectible. The net realizable value of accounts receivable would be—
   a. $600,000.
   b. $592,800.
   c. $592,700.
   d. $591,900.
   e. None of the above.

9. Which of the following statements is **not** valid in determining balance sheet disclosure of accounts receivable?
   a. Accounts receivable should be identified on the balance sheet as "pledged" if they are used as security for a loan even though the loan is shown on the same balance sheet as a liability.
   b. That portion of installment accounts receivable from customers which falls due more than 12 months from the balance sheet date usually would be excluded from the current assets.
   c. Allowances may be deducted from the accounts receivable for discounts, returns, and adjustments

to be made in the future on accounts shown in the current balance sheet.

10. During 19A, Yale Company, which uses the allowance method of accounting for uncollectible accounts, had debits to Doubtful Accounts Expense of $60,000 and wrote off as uncollectible accounts receivable of $55,000. These transactions decreased working capital by—
    a. $0.
    b. $55,000.
    c. $25,000.
    d. $60,000.
    e. None of the above.
11. On a balance sheet, what is the preferable presentation of notes or accounts receivable from officers, employees, or affiliated companies?
    a. As trade notes and accounts receivable if they otherwise qualify as current assets.
    b. As assets but separately from other receivables.
    c. As offsets to capital.
    d. By notes or footnotes. (AICPA adapted)

PROBLEMS

PART A: PROBLEMS 6–1 to 6–7

Problem 6–1

The cash records for Barter Company provided the following data for the month of March:

	Mar. 1	Mar. 31
Balances per bank statement ...	$15,400.09	$14,160.09
Balances per company books ...	14,175.00	13,399.00

Relevant items:

a.	Outstanding checks Mar. 31 (verified as correct)	$1,450
b.	Deposits in transit Mar. 31 (verified as correct)	950
c.	Interest earned on bank balance (reported on bank statement)	18
d.	NSF check (customer check returned with bank statement)	50
e.	Service charge by bank (reported on bank statement)	7
f.	Error in deposit of cash sales (deposit slip showed overage, corrected by bank)	10
g.	Bank error (check for $10.98 cleared at $10.89)	
h.	Note collected by bank for us (including $40 interest)	840
i.	Deduction for church (per signed bank deduction form)	20
j.	Cash on hand	500

Required:

1. Prepare a bank reconciliation in a format to show the correct balance for the March 31 balance sheet. *Hint:* Be alert for a cash overage or shortage.
2. Prepare necessary entries at March 31.

Problem 6–2

The format of a four-column comprehensive bank reconciliation appears below. Items may be added to or subtracted from both "Balances per bank" and "Balances per books" to arrive at "True balances." Additions to the four columns of "Balances per bank" are identified by the letters A through D, while subtractions in these columns from "Balances per bank" are identified by the letters E through H. The last eight letters of the alphabet are used to identify additions to and subtractions from "Balances per books." Thus, S, T, U, and V represent additions while W, X, Y, and Z identify subtractions.

(Relates to Problem 6–2)

	Mar. 1 Balances	March Receipts	March Payments	Mar. 31 Balances
Balances per bank	$X,XXX	$X,XXX	$X,XXX	$X,XXX
Additions	A	B	C	D
Subtractions	E	F	G	H
True balances	$Y,YYY	$Y,YYY	$Y,YYY	$Y,YYY
Balances per books	$Z,ZZZ	$Z,ZZZ	$Z,ZZZ	$Z,ZZZ
Additions	S	T	U	V
Subtractions	W	X	Y	Z
True balances	$Y,YYY	$Y,YYY	$Y,YYY	$Y,YYY

Requirement 1:

Following the format of the first item below, which is answered by way of example, indicate for each numbered item below (by using the letters) what would be added or subtracted and where in the four columns of a comprehensive reconciliation.

C	H	1.	Checks written in March have not cleared bank by March 31.
___	___	2.	All checks written in February which had not cleared by February 28 cleared bank in March.
___	___	3.	A deposit made late in March had not cleared the bank by March 31.
___	___	4.	A service charge levied by the bank against the February 28 balance was recorded on the company books during March.
___	___	5.	A service charge was levied by the bank against the March 31 balance but was not recorded by the company by March 31.
___	___	6.	An NSF customer check deposited in March was returned by the bank late in the month; no entry has yet been made by the company. The check will be redeposited in April.
___	___	7.	The bank collected a note receivable for the company in March. No entry to record the collection had been made on the books by March 31.
___	___	8.	A deposit made by the company in February cleared the bank in March.
___	___	9.	The bank erroneously decreased the company bank balance for a check drawn on another customer's bank account; no correction was made by March 31.

Requirement 2:

Refer to the reconciliation format in Requirement 1. Certain combinations of letters represent valid situations. For example, C and H are a valid representation of checks drawn and recorded by the depositor but not yet cleared at the bank. On the other hand, a combination such as B and H is impossible (in the absence of two counterbalancing errors). For each combination below, if the combination is a valid representation of something that could appear on a comprehensive reconciliation, briefly describe the situation that would fit the combination. On the other hand, if the combination is invalid, simply say so.

1. A and F.
2. A and B.
3. E and G.
4. W and X.
5. Y and Z.
6. U and Z.
7. T and V.
8. W and Y.
9. G and H.

Problem 6–3

The records pertaining to cash for Young Company provided the following data for May:

Bank statement:	
a. Balance, May 31	$34,500
b. Service charges for May	5
c. NSF check returned with May statement; customer gave this check. Young will redeposit next week, assumed to be good	50
d. Note receivable ($5,000) collected for Young by the bank and added to balance	5,200
e. Error from previous month in interest collected on another note receivable; bank credited Young account in May for the amount to correct the error (the May bank statement was first notification of the collection)	100
Books:	
f. Balance, May 31	30,300
g. Cash on hand	400
h. Deposits in transit	3,300
i. Outstanding checks at May 31	2,665

Required:

1. Prepare a bank reconciliation in good form. Assume all amounts provided above are correct. *Hint:* Be alert for a cash overage or shortage.
2. Give required entries for May 31.

Problem 6–4

Meredith Corporation began doing business with Fidelity Bank on October 1. On that date, the true cash balance was $4,000. All cash transactions are cleared through the bank account. Subsequent transactions during October and November relating to the Meredith and Fidelity accounts are summarized below:

	Meredith Co. Books	**Fidelity Bank Books**
October deposits	$7,360	$7,110
October checks	6,290	6,130
October service charge	—	10
October 31 balance	5,070	4,970
November deposits (regular)	8,220	8,280
November checks	9,210	9,220
November service charge	—	15
Note collected by bank (includes $15 interest)		1,015
October service charge (recorded during November)	10	—
November 30 balance	4,070	5,030

Required:

1. On the basis of the foregoing data, prepare a comprehensive bank reconciliation for November.

2. Assuming November 30 is the end of Meredith's fiscal year, give entries that would be required by the bank reconciliation.

Problem 6–5

You are examining the records of a client whose internal control is weak. Part of your work includes reconciliation of cash for December 19A. You have determined that the client's reconciliation as of November 30, 19A, is correct. The following information is available to you:

Client's Reconciliation, November 30, 19A

Cash per general ledger	$2,632
Less: Cash on hand	211
	2,421
Less: Bank service charge for November	9
	2,412
Add: Outstanding checks	991
Balance per bank	$3,403

Cash receipts are summarized weekly; the cash receipts books for December appear below:

Dec. 1	Balance from Nov. 30	$ 2,632
8	Received on accounts	25,775
15	Received on accounts	27,446
22	Received on accounts	4,660
29	Received on accounts	5,887
		$65,300

The cash payments recorded for December were as follows:

Dec. 1	November service charge	$ 9
3	Checks	5,239
5	Checks	3,647
8	Checks	16,395
10	Checks	15,878
12	Checks	4,849
19	Checks	3,123
22	Checks	3,690
31	Checks	7,658
Balance—December 31		4,312
		$65,300

Cash on hand at December 31 amounted to $100. The transactions per the December bank statement, which are correctly recorded by the bank, show that deposits amounted to $62,871; checks paid amounted to $57,952; service charges for the month were $10; and a charge of $100 was made against the account because of the return unpaid of a customer's check (not included in the $57,952). Neither the service charge nor the returned check was recorded on the client's books. The total of outstanding checks as of December 31 was found to be $4,110.

Required:
Prepare a comprehensive bank reconciliation for December. *Hint:* Verify all footings and be alert for errors and/or shortages. (AICPA adapted)

Problem 6–6

In connection with an audit of cash of Wholesalers, Inc., as of December 31, 19A, the following information has been obtained:

a. Balance per bank:

11/30/19A	$ 185,700
12/31/19A	193,674

b. Balance per books:

11/30/19A	154,826
12/31/19A	167,598

c. Receipts for the month of Dec. 19A:

Per bank	1,350,450
Per books	2,335,445

d. Outstanding checks:

11/30/19A	63,524
12/31/19A	75,046

e. Dishonored checks are recorded as a reduction of cash receipts. Dishonored checks which are later redeposited are then recorded as a regular cash receipt. Dishonored checks returned by the bank and recorded by Wholesalers, Inc., amounted to $6,250 during the month of December 19A; according to the books, $5,000 were redeposited. Dishonored checks reported on the bank statement but not in the books until the following months amounted to $250 at November 30, 19A, and $2,300 at December 31, 19A.

f. On December 31, 19A, a $2,323 check written by Ajax Company was charged to Wholesalers, Inc., account by the bank in error.

g. Proceeds of a note of the Karo Company collected by the bank on December 10, 19A, on behalf of Wholesalers, Inc., were not entered on the books:

Principal	$2,000
Interest	20
	2,020
Less: Collection charge	5
	$2,015

h. The company has hypothecated (assigned) its accounts receivable with the bank under an agreement whereby the bank lends the company 80% on the hypothecated accounts receivable. Accounting for and collection of the accounts are performed by the company, and adjustments of the loan are made from daily sales reports and daily deposits.

The bank credits the Wholesalers, Inc., account and increases the amount of the loan for 80% of the reported sales. The loan agreement states specifically that the sales report must be accepted by the bank before the Wholesalers, Inc., bank account is credited. Sales reports are forwarded by Wholesalers, Inc., to the bank on the first day following the date of sales.

The bank allocates each deposit 80% to the payment of the loan and 20% to the Wholesalers, Inc., account. Thus, only 80% of each day's sales and 20% of each collection are entered on the bank statement.

Wholesalers, Inc., accountant records the hypothecation of new accounts receivable (80% of sales) as a debit to Cash and a credit to the bank loan as of the date of sales. One hundred percent of the collections on accounts receivable is recorded as a cash receipt; 80% of the collections is recorded in the cash disbursements book as a payment on the loan.

In connection with the hypothecation, the following facts were determined:

(1) Included in the deposits in transit is cash from the hypothecation of accounts receivable. Sales were $40,500 on November 30, 19A, and $42,250 on December 31, 19A. The balance of the deposit in transit at December 31, 19A, was made up from collections of $32,110 which were entered on the books in the manner indicated above.

(2) Collections on accounts receivable deposited in December, other than deposits in transit, totaled $1,200,000.

(3) Sales for December totaled $1,450,000.

(4) Interest on the bank loan for the month of December, charged by the bank but not recorded on the books, amounted to $6,140.

Required:

1. Prepare bank reconciliations as of November 30, 19A, and December 31, 19A, and reconciliations of cash receipts and disbursements per bank with cash receipts and disbursements per books for the month of December 19A. (Assume that you have satisfied yourself as to the propriety of the above information.) Show computations where applicable.
2. Prepare adjusting journal entries as required to correct the Cash account at December 31, 19A.

(AICPA adapted)

Problem 6–7

Hart Company began doing business with Second Bank on February 1 at which time its true cash balance was $6,000. All the company's cash transactions are cleared through the bank account. Subsequent transactions during February and March relating to Hart Company and its dealings with Second Bank are summarized below:

	Hart Company Books	Second's Bank Books
February deposits	$4,080	$3,770
February checks	4,975	4,810
February service charge	—	5
Feb. 28 balance	5,105	4,955
March deposits (regular)	5,280	5,385
March checks	5,415	5,380
March service charge	—	10
Note collected by bank in Mar. (includes interest of $20)	—	520
February service charge (recorded in March)	5	—
Mar. 31 balance	4,965	5,470

Required:

1. On the basis of the foregoing data, prepare a comprehensive reconciliation for March.
2. Prepare journal entries to bring Hart Company's books up to date as of March 31.

PART B: PROBLEMS 6–8 to 6–14

Problem 6–8

On January 1, 19A, Tofa Company acquired the following short-term investments in marketable equity securities:

Co.	Stock	No. of Shares	Cost per Share
T	Common (nopar)	1,000	$20
U	Common (par $10)	600	15
V	Preferred (par $20, nonconvertible)	400	30

Per share data subsequent to the acquisition are as follows:

12/31/19A	Market values: T stock, $16; U stock, $15; and V stock, $34.
2/10/19B	Cash dividends received: T stock, $1.50; U stock, $1; and V stock, 50 cents.
11/1/19B	Sold the shares of V stock at $38.
12/31/19B	Market values: T stock, $12; U stock, $17; and V stock, $33.

Required:

1. Give all entries indicated for Tofa Company for 19A and 19B. Use GAAP and assume there was no balance in the allowance account on January 1, 19A.
2. Show how the income statement and balance sheet for Tofa Company would reflect the short-term investments for 19A and 19B.

Problem 6–9

The exhibit below purports to set forth the effects of the indicated accounting for investments by Johnston's Store. Where the indicated accounting would make a statement element too high, "+" is used; for too low, "−" is used; if there is no effect (item is correct) "0" is used. There are, however, some mistakes in the exhibit. You are to indicate the number of mistakes on each line and identify the mistakes. Ignore income tax aspects. Each case is independent. Marketable securities are short-term investments for items 2–4.

Problem 6–10

Kinko Company's short-term investment portfolio was recorded at the following costs at December 31, 19A (there was no 19A balance in the allowance account):

	Cost
AB Co., nine 8% bonds (face, $9,000; interest dates Mar. 1 and Sept. 1)	$9,300
BC Corp. common, nopar (50 shares)	1,800
CD Corp., 4% preferred, 150 shares (par, $40)	8,000

Transactions relating to the securities during 19B were as follows:

Jan.	25	Received semiannual dividend check on CD shares.
Mar.	1	Collected semiannual interest on AB bonds.
Apr.	15	Sold 30 shares of BC Corporation stock for $1,020.
May	1	Sold six of the AB bonds for a total consideration (including accrued interest) of $6,350.
June	20	Purchased 50 shares of EF Corporation, common, at 47 plus $30 brokerage fees.
July	25	Received semiannual dividend check on CD shares.
Sept.	1	Collected semiannual interest on AB bonds.
Oct.	1	Purchased a $1,000, 9% bond of DE, Inc., for total consideration of $1,100. Interest payment dates on this bond are February 1 and August 1.
Nov.	17	Sold remaining BC Corporation shares for $700.
Dec.	2	Received $60 dividend check from EF Corporation.
	31	Preparatory to adjusting and closing the books for the year, the following data as to market values of securities held were obtained:

Security	Market
AB bonds (ex-interest)	103
CD preferred	54
DE, Inc., bond (ex-interest)	104
EF common	45

(Relates to Problem 6–9)

	19A Statements			19B Statements		
Items	Current Assets	Net Income	Liabilities	Current Assets	Net Income	Owners' Equity
1. Late in 19A, Johnston's Store issued a note to an officer in exchange for Johnston shares the officer had acquired under option. They are still classified as a short-term investment at year-end 19B.	0	0	+	0	0	0
2. At year-end 19A, accrued interest on bonds (cost method) held as short-term investments was ignored. All investments were sold during 19B.	−	−	0	0	0	−
3. Marketable equity securities were valued at cost ($10,000) at year-end 19A when market was $9,500; and at market ($8,600) when cost was $8,000 at the end of 19B (use LCM).	+	+	0	−	0	+
4. Johnston had bought marketable securities at the end of 19A but had not paid for them, and no entry for their purchase was made until 19B. They were sold for a gain properly recorded during 19B.	−	−	−	0	0	+
5. Shares of stock which had been properly carried as short-term investments (cost method) when initially bought were reclassified to long-term investments during 19B when their market value was below cost. (At end of 19A, cost exceeded market.) The transfer was recorded at cost.	0	0	0	0	0	0

Required:
Journalize the foregoing transactions; adjust and close the books at December 31, 19B. Value the two short-term portfolios of securities (i.e., stocks; bonds) by the methods required by GAAP. *Hint:* Do not overlook reversal of accrued interest adjustment on AB bonds on January 1, 19B.

Problem 6–11

Delco Manufacturing Company has followed the practice of valuing all of its short-term investments in marketable securities as one portfolio at LCM. At December 31, 19B, its account, Short-Term Investment in Marketable Securities, had a balance of $40,000, and the account, Allowance to Reduce Investments from Cost to Market, had a balance of $2,000. Analysis disclosed that on December 31, 19A, the facts relating to the securities were as follows:

Security	Cost	Market	Allowance Required
X Company bonds	$20,000	$19,000	$1,000
Y Company bonds	10,000	9,000	1,000
Z Company bonds	20,000	20,300	–0–
	$50,000		$2,000

During 19B, the Y Company bonds were sold for $9,200; the difference between the $9,200 and the cost of $10,000 was debited to Loss on Sale of Securities. The market price of the bonds on December 31, 19B, was X Company bonds, $19,200; and Z Company bonds, $20,400.

Required:
1. What justification is there for the use of the LCM in valuing short-term investments in marketable securities?
2. Did Delco Company properly apply this rule on December 31, 19A? Explain, including any alternative methods of application.
3. Are there any additional entries necessary for Delco Company at December 31, 19B, to reflect the facts on the balance sheet and income statement in accordance with GAAP? Explain. (AICPA adapted)

Problem 6–12

Coke Corporation bought its first short-term investments in 19A and still held them at December 31 of that year, when they had the following values:

Security	Amount	Cost	Market
AB common stock ..	50 shares	$ 4,000	$ 3,725
CD 8% bonds	$6,000 maturity value	6,400	6,500
		$10,400	$10,225

Cash revenue from these investments was correctly accounted for by the company bookkeeper during 19A and 19B, except that *(a)* no accrual of revenue was reflected at year-end 19A and *(b)* the investments were not accounted for as a single portfolio at LCM, as intended by management.

On July 1, 19B, all of the AB shares were sold for $3,700, and the transaction was recorded by the bookkeeper as follows:

Cash	3,700	
Miscellaneous expense	100	
Loss on sale of securities	200	
AB common stock		4,000

The debit to Miscellaneous Expense represents $100 of selling costs incurred in disposing of the shares.

On August 1, 19B, half of the CD bonds were sold for $3,350, and the transaction was recorded by the bookkeeper as follows:

Cash	3,350	
Miscellaneous expense	50	
Gain on sale of securities		200
CD bonds		3,200

The entry to Miscellaneous Expense reflects selling costs.

The CD bonds regularly pay interest each May 1 and November 1. Quarterly dividends of $40 were collected on the AB common shares on March 15 as well as on June 15. On December 1, 19B, the company bought $5,000 par bonds of EF Corporation for $5,350. These bonds pay 12% interest per annum on February 1 and August 1, and their purchase was recorded as follows:

EF bonds	5,300	
Miscellaneous expense	50	
Cash		5,350

The debit to Miscellaneous Expense represents the expense of buying the bonds. The bookkeeper resigned early in December and had not been replaced by year-end, but there were no securities transactions after the December 1 bond purchase.

Required:
1. Draft entries to correct the accounts as of January 1, 19B, *assuming both equity and debt securities are included in the short-term investment portfolio for LCM purposes* (Note: this is a departure from GAAP, which a company could probably sustain.)
2. Draft entries to correct the errors in the accounts for year 19B. As of December 31, 19B, the CD bonds were quoted at 108 and the EF bonds were quoted at 102.
3. Prepare adjusting and closing entries as of December 31, 19B.

Problem 6–13

Check the best answer in each of the following and provide the basis (including computations where appropriate) to support your choice.

1. Which of the following items should never be included in the current section of the balance sheet?
   a. Premium paid on short-term bond investment.
   b. Receivable from customer not collectible during coming year.
   c. Deferred income taxes resulting from inter-period income tax allocation.
   d. Funded serial bonds.
2. The June bank statement of Lucas Company showed a June 30 ending balance of $187,387. During June, the bank charged back NSF (i.e., insufficient funds) checks totaling $3,056, of which $1,856 had been redeposited by June 30. Deposits in transit on June 30 were $20,400. Outstanding checks on June 30 were $60,645, including a $10,000 check which the bank had certified on June 28. On June 14, the bank charged Lucas's account for a $2,300 item which should have been charged against the account of Luby Company; the bank did not detect the error. During June, the bank collected foreign items for Lucas; the proceeds were $8,684, and bank charges for this service were $19. On June 30, the adjusted cash in bank of Lucas Company is—
   a. $149,442.
   b. $159,442.
   c. $147,142.
   d. $158,242.
   e. None of the above.
3. How is the premium or discount on bonds purchased as a short-term investment generally reported in published financial statements?
   a. As an integral part of the cost of the asset acquired (investment) and amortized over a period of not less than 12 months.
   b. As an integral part of the cost of the asset acquired (investment) until such time as the investment is sold.
   c. As expense or revenue at the time the bonds are purchased.
   d. As an integral part of the cost of the asset acquired (investment) and amortized over the period the bonds are expected to be held.
4. The test of marketability must be met before securities owned can be properly classified as—
   a. Pledged securities.
   b. Common stock.
   c. Bonds payable.
   d. None of the above.
5. George Company maintains two checking accounts. A special checking account is used for the weekly payroll only, and the general checking account is used for all other disbursements. Each week, a check for the aggregate amount of the payrolls is drawn on the general account and deposited in the Payroll account. Individual checks are drawn on the Payroll account. The company maintains a $5,000 minimum balance in the Payroll account. On a monthly bank reconciliation, the Payroll account should—
   a. Show a zero balance per the bank statement.
   b. Show a $5,000 balance per the bank statement.
   c. Reconcile to $5,000.
   d. Be reconciled jointly with the general account in a single reconciliation.
6. Postage stamps and IOUs found in cash drawers should be reported as—
   a. Prepaid expense and receivables.
   b. Cash, because they represent the equivalent of money.
   c. Petty cash.
   d. Investments.
7. Which of the following should not be considered as a current asset?
   a. Installment notes receivable due over 18 months in accordance with normal trade practice.
   b. Prepaid property taxes.
   c. Marketable securities purchased as a short-term investment with cash provided by current operations.
   d. Cash surrender value of a life insurance policy carried by a corporation, the beneficiary, on its president.
8. Which of the following is a current asset?
   a. Cash surrender value of a life insurance policy of which the company is the beneficiary.
   b. Investment in marketable securities for the purpose of continuing control of the issuing company.
   c. Cash designated for the purchase of tangible operational assets.
   d. Trade installment receivables normally collectible in 18 months. (AICPA adapted)

Problem 6–14

This is a *research problem* which requires that certain library materials be consulted. There is no specific, single answer because the answer can differ according to *(a)* the companies selected and *(b)* the date on which it is solved.

Required:

1. Determine the stocks which comprise the Dow Jones Industrial Average and list them in your solution.
2. Select any five of the stocks from 1 above and assume that the company for which you are accounting acquired a portfolio of 100 shares of common stock in each of the five companies selected. Assume that the cost to your company was the per share price as of the close of business on January 2 of the current year. (If January

2 was not a trading day on which the market was open, use the first trading day following January 2.) For each value so determined, assume 1% brokerage and other acquisition costs.

3. As of the date the problem is assigned, ascertain the market value of the portfolio of five stocks. If, for some reason, this date is not feasible, use the next preceding date for which the required information is available.
4. Array the cost and market figures in a schedule and determine the proper balance sheet carrying value of the portfolio based on the assumption the stocks are held as short-term investments.
5. On the assumption that at the close of the preceding period Allowance to Reduce Short-Term Investments to Market had a balance of $800, indicate the required adjusting entry as of the date you ascertain market values in 3 above. For purpose of this requirement assume *(a)* that the securities which accounted for the $800 allowance have been sold, *(b)* that the portfolio now consists only of the five stocks chosen in 2 above, and *(c)* this date is the end of the fiscal year for your company.

PART C: PROBLEMS 6–15 to 6–21

Problem 6–15

Records for Zip Company concerning their receivables and recent sales history provided the following:

Cash sales for the period	$1,200,000
Credit sales for the period	900,000
Balance in trade receivables, start of period	180,000
Balance in trade receivables, end of period	200,000
Balance in allowance for doubtful accts., start of period	3,000 (cr.)
Accounts written off as uncollectible during period	5,000

Recently Zip's management has become concerned about various estimates used in their accounting process, including those relating to receivables and bad debts. The company is reviewing the various alternatives with a view to selecting the most appropriate approach and related estimates.

Assume the following simplified estimates:

1. Bad debt expense approximates ⅜% of credit sales.
2. Bad debt expense approximates ¼% of net sales (cash plus credit sales).
3. Two percent of the uncollected receivables at year-end will be bad at any one time.
4. Aging of the accounts at the end of the period indicated that three fourths of them would incur a 1% loss while the other one fourth would incur a 6% loss.

Required:
For expense recognition and asset valuation, two different approaches are being considered. Identify and briefly explain and give the advantages of each approach. After each explanation, give the entry based on the period data available. Which of these entries would be made during the year? Which of these entries would be made as adjusting entries at the end of the accounting period?

Problem 6–16

From the start of operations in January 19A, Summit Company did not record **estimated** bad debts. Uncollectible receivables were expensed as written off and any recoveries were credited to revenue as collected. On March 1, 19E (after 19D financial statements were issued), the management recognized that Summit's accounting policy for bad debts was incorrect. They concluded that an allowance for doubtful accounts was needed. A policy was established to maintain a year-end balance in the Allowance for Doubtful Accounts equivalent to Summit's historical bad debt loss percentage [i.e., accounts written off (net of recoveries) to credit sales] applied to the year-end balance of Accounts Receivable. The historical bad debt loss percentage is to be recomputed each year based on all available past years up to a maximum of five years.

Information from Summit's records for the five years is as follows:

Year	Credit Sales	Accounts Written Off	Recoveries
19A	$1,500,000	$15,000	$ 0
19B	2,250,000	38,000	2,700
19C	2,950,000	52,000	2,500
19D	3,300,000	65,000	4,800
19E	4,000,000	83,000	5,000

Accounts receivable balances were $1,250,000 and $1,460,000 at December 31, 19D, and December 31, 19E, respectively.

Required:
1. Give the journal entry, with appropriate explanation, to establish the allowance for doubtful accounts as of January 1, 19E. Show supporting computations.
2. Prepare a schedule analyzing the changes in the Allowance for Doubtful Accounts for the year ended December 31, 19E. Show supporting computations.

(AICPA adapted)

Problem 6–17

Pawn Company has been in business for five years but has never had an audit of its financial statements. Engaged to make an audit for 19E, you find that the company's balance sheet carries no allowance for doubtful accounts; instead, uncollectible accounts have been expensed as written off with recoveries credited to income as collected. The company's policy is to write off at December 31 of each year those accounts on which no collections have been received for three months. The installment contracts generally provide for uniform monthly collections over a time span of two years from date of sale.

Upon your recommendation the company agrees to revise its accounts for 19E in order to account for bad debts on the allowance basis. The allowance is to be based on a percentage of sales which is derived from the experience of prior years.

Statistics for the past five years are as follows:

Year	Credit Sales	Accounts Written Off and Year of Sale			Recoveries and Year of Sale
19A	$100,000	(19A) $ 550			
19B	250,000	(19A) 1,500	(19B) $1,000		(19A) $300
19C	300,000	(19A) 500	(19B) 4,000	(19C) $1,300	(19B) 850
19D	325,000	(19B) 1,200	(19C) 4,500	(19D) 1,500	(19C) 500
19E	275,000	(19C) 2,700	(19D) 5,000	(19E) 1,400	(19D) 600

Accounts receivable at December 31, 19E, were as follows:

19D sales	$ 15,000
19E sales	135,000
	$150,000

Required:
Prepare the adjusting journal entry or entries with appropriate explanations to set up the Allowance for Doubtful Accounts. (Support each item with organized computations; income tax implications should be ignored. The books have been adjusted but not closed at December 31, 19E.)

(AICPA adapted)

Problem 6–18

Wingo Company sold a building and the land on which it is located on January 1, 19A, receiving, as its consideration, a $150,000 note receivable maturing in three years without interest. The sale was recorded as follows by Wingo Company:

Note receivable	150,000	
Accumulated depreciation, building ..	100,000	
Building		150,000
Land		60,000
Gain on sale of building		40,000

It has been determined that 12% is a reasonable interest rate to impute to the note. You are recommending adjusting and correcting entries as of December 31, 19A (end of Wingo Company's fiscal year). The books have not been adjusted or closed for 19A.

Required:
1. Give an entry to correct the sale entry and the adjustment for interest as of December 31, 19A. (Round to nearest dollar.)
2. Give entry to recognize interest earned at December 31, 19B.
3. Make entries at end of 19C to *(a)* recognize interest earned and *(b)* record collection of the note.
4. Aside from the correction in 1 above for interest, do you see any other problem in the sale entry as originally made? Explain.

Problem 6–19

Crabb Company has experienced a critical cash flow problem as a result of collection problems with certain customers. Consequently, it has become involved in a number of transactions relating to its notes receivable. The following transactions occurred during a period ending December 31 (end of the accounting period):

May 1 Received an $8,000, 90-day, 9% interest-bearing note from E. M. Smith, a customer, in settlement of an account receivable for that amount.
June 1 Received a $12,000, six-month, 9% interest-bearing note from M. Johnson, a customer, in settlement of an account receivable for that amount.
Aug. 1 Discounted the Johnson note at the bank at 10%.
2 Smith defaulted on the $8,000 note.
Sept. 1 Received a one-year, noninterest-bearing note from D. Karnes, a customer, in settlement of a $5,000 account receivable. The face of the note was $5,400, and the going rate of interest was 8% (on the net amount of the receivable).
Oct. 1 Received a $20,000, 90-day note from R. M. Cates, a customer. The note was in payment for goods Cates purchased and was interest bearing at 15%.
1 Collected the defaulted Smith note plus accrued interest to September 30 (10% per annum on the total amount due for two months).
Dec. 1 Johnson defaulted on the $12,000 note. Crabb Company paid the bank the total amount due plus a $25 protest fee.
30 Collected Cates note in full. Collected from Johnson in full including interest on the full amount at 10% since default date.
31 Accrued interest on outstanding notes.

Required:
1. Give the entry to record each of the above transactions. Show computations.
2. Show how the outstanding notes at December 31 would be reported on the balance sheet.

Problem 6–20

Pratt Company finances some of its current operations by assigning accounts receivable to a finance company. On July 1, 19A, it assigned, with recourse, accounts amounting to $50,000, the finance company advancing 80% of the accounts assigned (20% of the total to be withheld until the finance company has made full recovery), less a commission charge of ½% of the total accounts assigned.

On July 31, Pratt Company received a statement that the finance company had collected $26,000 of these accounts and had made an additional charge of ½% of the total accounts outstanding as of July 31—this charge to be deducted at the time of the first remittance due Pratt Company from the finance company. On August 31, Pratt Company received a second statement from the finance company, together with a check for the amount due. The statement indicated that the finance company had collected an additional $16,000 and had made a further charge of ½% of the balance outstanding as of August 31.

Required (on books of Pratt Company):

1. Give the entry to record the assignment of the accounts on a notification basis (July 1).
2. Give entry to record the data from the first report from the finance company (July 31).
3. Reconstruct the report submitted by the finance company on August 31; show details to explain cash remitted and the uncollected accounts still held by the finance company.
4. Give the entry to record the data in the report of August 31.
5. Explain how the items should be reported on the financial statements of Pratt Company at July 31 and August 31. (AICPA adapted)

Problem 6–21

On January 1, 19A, Lock Company sold property to the Key Company which originally cost Lock $600,000. Key gave Lock a $900,000 note payable in six equal annual installments of $150,000, with the first payment due and paid on January 1, 19A (i.e., an annuity due). There was no established exchange price for the property, and the note has no ready market. The prevailing rate of interest for a note of this type is 12%.

Required:

1. Prepare a schedule to compute the balance in Lock's net receivable from Key at December 31, 19B. Show supporting computations.
2. Prepare a schedule to show the income or loss before income tax for the years ended December 31, 19A, and 19B, that Lock should report. (AICPA adapted)

7

Inventories—General

ACCOUNTING for inventories *(a)* facilitates determination of income by matching appropriate inventory costs with revenues and *(b)* provides an inventory amount for the balance sheet. Such inventory considerations as control, safeguarding, measurement, and cost allocation pose critical problems for accountants because of the materiality of inventories in the typical business. Such factors have caused the accounting profession to give particular attention to inventories. This and the two following chapters present the principal accounting concepts and procedures relating to inventories. This chapter is organized as follows:

Part A—General Issues and Application of the Cost Principle

Part B—Departures from the Cost Principle and Other Issues in Accounting for Inventory

Part A: General Issues and Application of the Cost Principle

THE NATURE OF INVENTORIES

As an accounting category, **inventories** are assets consisting of goods owned by the business at a particular time and held for future sale or for utilization in the manufacture of goods for sale. No other asset includes such an extensive variety of properties under a single heading, for practically all kinds of tangible goods and properties are found in the inventories of one business or another. Machinery and equipment are operational assets of the business using them, but at one time they were part of the inventory of the manufacturer of such equipment. Even a building is an inventory item, a "contract in process," among the assets of the builder.

In many companies, inventories comprise a significant portion of current assets or even total assets. Furthermore, inventories generally represent an active asset because of their constant usage and replacement. Although many inventory items are small, they frequently have considerable value; therefore, the problem of safeguarding inventories is akin to protecting cash. The advisability of adequate stocking of items for sale, coupled with the risk of loss and cost of overstocking, creates critical management planning and control problems. Failure to control inventories and to account for inventory can lead to business failure.[1]

CLASSIFICATION OF INVENTORIES

The major classifications of inventories depend upon the type of business. A trading entity (i.e., wholesale or retail) acquires merchandise for resale, whereas a manufacturing entity acquires raw materials and component parts, manufactures finished products, and then sells them. The flow of inventory costs through these two types of entities may be diagrammed as follows (assuming a perpetual inventory system):

Trading entity:

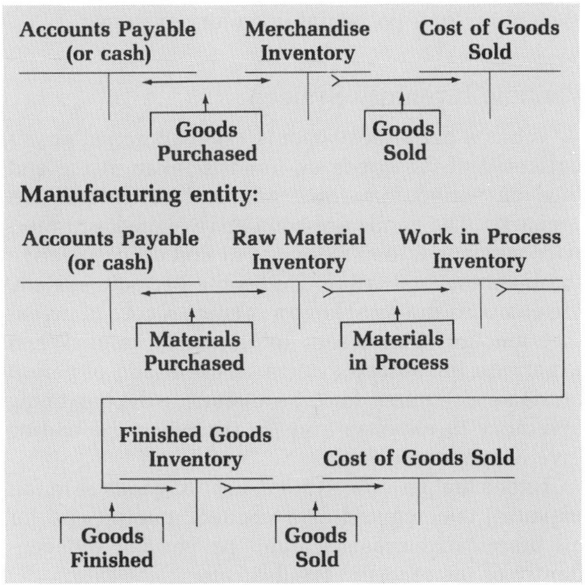

Inventories may be defined as follows:

1. Merchandise inventory—goods on hand purchased by a trading entity for resale. The physical form of the goods is not altered prior to resale.
2. Manufacturing inventory—the combined inventories of a manufacturing entity consisting of—
   a. Raw materials inventory—tangible goods purchased or obtained in other ways (e.g., mining) and on hand for direct use in the manufacture of goods for resale. Parts or subassemblies manufactured prior to use are sometimes classified as raw materials inventory (or **component parts inventory**).
   b. Work in process inventory—goods partly processed and requiring further processing before sale. Work (goods) in process inventory normally is valued at the sum of **direct material, direct labor,** and **allocated manufacturing overhead costs** incurred to date.
   c. Finished goods inventory—manufactured items completed and being held for sale. Finished goods inventory normally is valued at the sum of **direct material, direct labor,** and **allocated manufacturing overhead costs** related to their manufacture.
   d. Manufacturing supplies inventory—items on hand such as lubrication oils for the machinery, cleaning materials, and supply items which comprise an insignificant part of the finished product as, for example, the thread and glue used in binding this book.
3. Miscellaneous inventories—items such as office supplies, janitorial supplies, and shipping supplies. Inventories of this type normally are used in the near future and usually are recorded as selling or general expense when used.

THE DUAL PHASE OF THE INVENTORY PROBLEM

Many inventory accounting problems occur because the amount of goods sold during a fiscal period often differs from the amount of inventory produced or bought during that period. Consequently, the typical situation is one in which physical inventory increases or decreases during the period. This increase or decrease in the physical quantity of inventory necessitates a corresponding **allocation of the total cost of goods available** between *(a)* **expense,** for goods that were sold or used (i.e., cost of goods sold), and *(b)* **assets** for goods that remain on hand (i.e., ending inventory). This allocation involves two distinct phases as follows:

1. Identification and measurement of the **quantity** of physical goods (items and quantities) that should be included in inventory at the end of the period.
2. Measurement of the **accounting values** assigned

[1] For an introductory discussion of accounting for inventories, refer to G. A. Welsch and R. N. Anthony, *Fundamentals of Financial Accounting,* 3d ed. (Homewood, Ill.: Richard D. Irwin, Inc., 1982), chap. 6.

to the physical goods included in inventory at the end of the period. This part of the chapter discusses these two phases and the effect of inventory errors.

IDENTIFICATION OF GOODS (ITEMS) THAT SHOULD BE INCLUDED IN INVENTORY

In identifying the goods that should be included in inventory, accountants apply the general rule that all goods the entity **owns** at inventory date should be included, regardless of their location. Because at the end of an accounting period, a business may *(a)* hold goods which it does not own or *(b)* own goods which it does not hold, care must be exercised in identifying the goods properly includable in inventory.

Goods purchased, though not received, should be included in the inventory of the purchaser provided ownership to such goods has passed. Application of the "passage of ownership" rule generally requires the following: if the goods are shipped **FOB destination,** ownership passes when the purchaser receives the goods from the common carrier; if the goods are shipped **FOB shipping point,** ownership passes when the seller delivers them to the common carrier.

Goods **out** on consignment, those held by agents and those located at branches, should be included in inventory.[2] On the other hand, goods **held** (but owned by someone else) for sale on commission or on consignment and those received from vendors but rejected and awaiting return to vendor for credit should be excluded from inventory.

In identifying items that should be included in inventory, when a question exists as to whether ownership has passed, the accountant must exercise judgment in light of the particular situation. Obviously, legal title should be acknowledged; however, a strict legal determination often is impractical. In such cases, the sales agreement, industry practices, and other evidence of intent should be considered. For example, it is not economical for companies that sell inventory under **FOB destination** terms to keep track of when their sales shipments arrive at the destination (i.e., customer's place of business). In such cases, companies often adopt arbitrary conventions such as "record sales revenue and the consequent decrease in inventory when sales shipments leave the seller's place of business." When conventions such as this are adopted, consistency of application is important.[3]

[2] Consignment is a marketing arrangement whereby the consignor (the owner of the goods) ships merchandise to another party, known as a consignee, who is to act as a sales agent only. The consignee does not purchase the goods but assumes responsibility for their care, and upon sale remits the proceeds (less expenses and a commission) to the consignor. Goods on consignment, since they are owned by the consignor until sold, should be excluded from the inventory of the consignee and included in the inventory of the consignor.

MEASUREMENT OF PHYSICAL QUANTITIES IN INVENTORY

The physical quantities in inventory may be determined by means of *(a)* a **periodic (physical) inventory system** or *(b)* a **perpetual inventory system.**

Periodic Inventory System

When a periodic system is used, an actual physical count of the goods on hand is taken at the end of each period for which financial statements are prepared. The goods are counted, weighed, or otherwise measured, then extended at **unit costs** to derive the inventory valuation. Under the periodic system, the company does **not** keep a running record of inventory amounts purchased, sold, and on hand. When a periodic inventory system is used, end-of-period entries are required for *(a)* transferring the beginning inventory to expense and *(b)* recording the ending inventory as an asset.

Under the periodic system, cost of goods sold (an expense) is computed as a **residual amount** and for all practical purposes cannot be verified independently of the records. To illustrate:

Cost of goods sold:	
Beginning inventory (carried forward from prior period)	$ 50,000
Merchandise purchases (accumulated in Purchases account)	200,000
Total goods available for sale	250,000
Less: Ending inventory (determined by count)	60,000
Cost of goods sold (a residual amount)	$190,000

[3] Strictly, the Inventory account and the detailed inventory record would be decreased at the time of sale only under a perpetual inventory system, which is discussed in the next section.

The accounting entries and external financial reporting under the periodic inventory system were reviewed and illustrated in Chapters 2 and 3.

Perpetual Inventory System

For control purposes, many companies need to keep running totals of inventory on hand. This is especially true for inventory items of high unit value and situations in which it is imperative to have certain quantities of inventory on hand to avoid overstocking and understocking of the various items. When a perpetual system is used, detailed **subsidiary records,** in addition to the usual ledger accounts, are maintained for each inventory item. An **Inventory Control** account is maintained in the general ledger on a current basis. The detailed inventory record for **each** item must provide for recording *(a)* receipts, *(b)* issues, and *(c)* balances on hand, usually in both quantities and dollar amounts. Thus, the physical quantity and valuation of goods on hand at any time are readily available from the accounting records. Consequently, a physical inventory count is unnecessary except to check on the accuracy of the inventory records from time to time. Such checks (physical counts) usually are made at least annually or on a continuous rotation basis.

When a difference is found, the perpetual inventory records are adjusted to the physical count. In such cases, the inventory account is debited or credited as necessary for correction and an inventory adjustment account such as Inventory Shortages (loss) or Overages (gain) is debited or credited. The inventory adjustment account is closed to Income Summary at the end of the period. The balance in the inventory shortage account usually is reported separately on internal financial statements, but it is combined with the cost of goods sold amount on external statements.

A perpetual inventory system also is particularly useful for *(a)* controlling and safeguarding inventory and *(b)* preparing monthly or other interim statements. A perpetual inventory system is one of the essential characteristics of a good **cost** accounting system. The only negative feature of a perpetual system is the cost of implementation; however, advances in computer technology have reduced these costs to levels that allow even small entities to employ perpetual systems. Exhibit 7–1 illustrates a **perpetual inventory record** for item X during 19J.

To illustrate the accounting procedures for the **periodic** and **perpetual** inventory systems, the simplified data of Exhibit 7–2 are used.

Comparative entries for the periodic and perpetual inventory systems are illustrated in Exhibit 7–3, based upon the data given in Exhibit 7–2.

EXHIBIT 7–1: Perpetual Inventory Record

SUBSIDIARY LEDGER

PERPETUAL INVENTORY RECORD

Verification Dates

Article **Item X** Unit **Pounds** Maximum **1,600**

Location **1–15** Bin No. **32** Reorder Level **800**

Date 19J	Ordered		Received or Completed					Issued or Sold				Balance on Hand		
	Order No.	Units	Order No.	Ref.	Units	Unit Cost	Total Cost	Ref.	Units	Unit Cost	Total Cost	Units	Unit Cost	Total Cost
(1)												500	4.00	2,000
(2)			17		1,000	4.00	4,000					1,500	4.00	6,000
(3)									900	4.00	3,600	600	4.00	2,400
(4)	18	700												

EXHIBIT 7–2: Illustrative Inventory Data

Item X	Units	Unit Amt.
Merchandise inventory, beginning (cost)	500	$4
Merchandise purchases during period (cost)	1,000	4
Total goods available for sale	1,500	
Merchandise sold during period (sales price)	900	6
Merchandise inventory, ending	600	

In Exhibit 7–3, two procedural differences between the two inventory systems should be noted, viz:

1. When the **periodic** system is used, only one entry is made to record a sale, that is, at **sales price. No** entry is made at this time to record the related **cost of goods sold** amount.

   When the **perpetual** system is used, two entries are required to record a sale—one for the revenue (at sales price) and one for cost of goods sold (at cost price). Only the perpetual system provides a current accounting for the cost of goods sold amount at the date of each sale.
2. When the **periodic** system is used, purchases of goods during the period are debited to a Purchases account to accumulate total purchases for the period. Also, because no entry is made at the time of sale, the **beginning balance** in the inventory account remains unchanged throughout the period and no detailed record is maintained of the current amount of goods on hand.

   When the **perpetual** system is used, purchases are debited directly to the inventory control account (and concurrently entered into the detailed inventory records as illustrated in Exhibit 7–1), and cost of the current issues (e.g., sales of inventory) are credited to the account as sales are made so that the inventory account carries a perpetual, or continuing, balance of the goods on hand at each date.

MEASUREMENT OF THE ACCOUNTING VALUE OF INVENTORIES

At date of acquisition, inventory items are recorded at cost in harmony with the **cost principle;** subsequently, when sold, their cost is matched with revenue in accordance with the **matching principle.** Inventory items remaining on hand at the end of an accounting period are "valued" on the basis of the cost principle except when their value decreased because of damage, obsolescence, decrease in replacement cost, or similar factors, in which case they are "valued" in accordance with the concept of **conservatism** (for example, lower-of-cost-or-market or net realizable value procedures).

The **accounting value** of inventories represents an allocation of the total cost of goods or materials **available** between that portion used or sold (cost of goods sold) and that portion held as an asset for subsequent use or sale (inventory). The nature of the allocation is indicated in the following diagram (based on the data given in Exhibit 7–2):

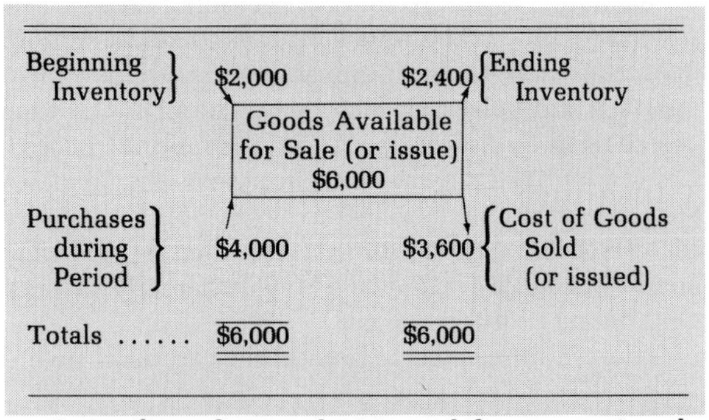

A number of procedures used for measuring the accounting value of inventories satisfy the theoretical requirements. The multiplicity of acceptable procedures suggests the wide variation in inventory characteristics and conditions depending upon the particular situations and purposes. Basically, the accounting values for inventories serve two different purposes. Each purpose implies procedures that may not appear entirely appropriate for the other purpose.

One purpose is to develop a monetary value for the inventory reported on the **balance sheet.** On the balance sheet it is appropriate to report inventory at cost or at its future utility to the business, whichever is lower. The other purpose focuses on the **income statement.** On the income statement it is appropriate to measure the inventory value to attain a proper matching of cost of goods sold against the revenue of the period.

Measurement of acceptable **values** for (1) inventory and (2) cost of goods sold involves two distinct problems, viz:

EXHIBIT 7–3: Comparative Entries under Periodic and Perpetual Inventory Systems (data given in Exhibit 7–2)

Periodic Inventory System			Perpetual Inventory System (assuming no shortage or overage)		
a. Merchandise purchased for resale:					
Purchases (1,000 @ $4)	4,000		Inventory	4,000	
Cash		4,000	Cash		4,000
b. Merchandise sold:					
Cash (900 @ $6)	5,400		Cash	5,400	
Sales revenue		5,400	Sales revenue		5,400
			Cost of goods sold	3,600	
			Inventory (900 @ $4)		3,600
c. Entries at end of the accounting period:					
To close Purchases account:					
Income summary	4,000		None		
Purchases		4,000			
To transfer beginning inventory amount:					
Income summary	2,000		None		
Inventory (beginning)*		2,000			
To record ending inventory amount:					
Inventory (ending)*	2,400		None		
Income summary		2,400			
* These amounts may be closed to Cost of Goods Sold and then to Income Summary with the same results. These amounts were determined by physical count.					
Closing entry:					
None, unless above accounts are first closed to Cost of Goods Sold.			Income summary	3,600	
			Cost of goods sold		3,600
Income statement (partial):					
Sales revenue		$5,400	Sales revenue		$5,400
Cost of goods sold:					
Beginning inventory	$2,000				
Purchases	4,000				
Goods available for sale	6,000				
Ending inventory (by physical count)	2,400				
Cost of goods sold		3,600	Cost of goods sold		3,600
Gross margin		$1,800	Gross margin		$1,800
Balance sheet (partial):					
Current assets:					
Merchandise inventory		$2,400	Merchandise inventory		$2,400

1. Inventory unit cost—selection of an appropriate **unit cost** for valuation of the items in inventory. The principal **inventory valuation methods** are as follows:
   a. Cost basis.
   b. Departure from cost basis:
      1. Lower of cost or market (LCM).
      2. Net realizable value.
      3. Current cost.
      4. Selling price.

2. Inventory flow—selection of an inventory flow method, that is, selection of an **assumed flow** of inventory unit costs. The principal **inventory flow methods** (discussed in Chapter 8) are as follows:
   a. Specific cost.
   b. Average cost.
   c. First-in, first-out (FIFO).
   d. Last-in, first-out (LIFO).

Content of Inventory Cost

The cost principle provides the theoretical foundation for measurement of cost for inventory and cost of goods sold.[4] Inventory cost is measured by the total outlay made to acquire goods and to prepare them for the market. These costs include not only the purchase cost but also those incidental costs such as excise and sales taxes, duties, freight, storage, insurance on the merchandise while in transit or in storage, and all other costs incurred on the goods up to the time they are ready for use or for sale to the customer. Some incidental costs, such as freight-in, frequently can be identified directly with specific goods, while other incidental costs may require an allocation to specific goods.

As a practical matter some incidental costs, although theoretically a cost of goods purchased, often are not included in inventory valuation but are reported as a separate expense; the cost of allocating such costs may not be warranted by the slight increase in accuracy. In such cases, **consistency** in application is particularly important. For example, general administrative and distribution expenses and interest expense are not included in determining inventory costs because they are not directly related to the purchase or manufacture of goods for sale. Theoretically, a part of all such costs could be allocated to inventory; however, any such allocation would be too arbitrary to be meaningful. General and administrative (G&A) expenses often are treated as **period** expenses because they more directly relate to accounting periods than to inventory; consequently, they are deducted on the income statement in the period in which incurred.

[4] *AICPA, Accounting Research Bulletin No. 43,* "Restatement and Revision of Accounting Research Bulletins" (New York, 1961), chap. 4, statement 3.

Freight-In (freight on purchases). In conformity with the cost principle, freight and other incidental costs paid in connection with the purchase of materials for use or merchandise for resale are additions to unit cost. When such costs can be identified with specific goods, they should be added as part of the cost of such goods. However, in some cases identification is impractical. Consequently, such costs often are recorded in a special account such as Freight-In, which is reported as an addition to cost of goods sold in the case of a trading entity and to cost of materials used in a manufacturing entity. However, this practical procedure may overstate cost of goods sold and understate inventory by the amount of such costs that should be allocated to inventory (as opposed to debiting the full amount to cost of goods sold). Theoretically, freight-in should be apportioned to cost of goods sold and to the ending inventory.

Purchase Discounts. Many companies offer cash discounts on credit purchases to encourage early payment. Under the cost principle, the cost of an item is the net cash equivalent paid for the specific item. Payments made for the extension of credit should not be debited to the Inventory account but should be accounted for as interest expense.[5] Theoretically, all cash discounts permitted, whether taken or not, should be omitted from cost. Upon payment of invoices, any discounts not taken constitute interest expense. Since cash discounts are reductions in the cost of specific goods, they reduce both cost of purchases and inventory valuation. Therefore, credit purchases should be recorded **net of discount** to reflect the **correct cost.** Although technically incorrect, purchases sometimes are recorded at the **gross amount** for practical reasons and because the cash discount often is immaterial.

To illustrate recording inventory under the net-of-discount and gross amount approaches, assume merchandise is purchased for $1,000 on credit terms of 2/10, n/30. Assume further that three fourths of the amount is paid within the 10-day discount period. The recording and reporting under these approaches are shown in Exhibit 7–4.

[5] FASB, *Statement of Financial Accounting Standards No. 34,* "Capitalization of Interest Cost" (Stamford, Conn., October 1979), par. 10. An exception to this general rule requires capitalization of interest on one class of inventory as follows: "[a]ssets intended for sale that are constructed or otherwise produced as discrete projects (e.g., ships or real estate developments)" (see par. 96).

EXHIBIT 7–4: Recording and Reporting Inventory at Net and Gross Amounts (perpetual inventory system)

Net of Discount Approach (preferable)			Gross Amount Approach (acceptable)		
Panel A—Recording:					
To record the purchase (perpetual inventory system):					
Merchandise inventory	980		Merchandise inventory	1,000	
Accounts payable (net)		980	Accounts payable (gross)		1,000
To record payment of three fourths of the liability within discount period:					
Accounts payable (net)	735		Accounts payable (gross)	750	
Cash		735	Cash		735
($980 × .75 = $735)			Discount on purchases		15
To record payment of one fourth of the liability after the discount period:					
Accounts payable (net)	245		Accounts payable (gross)	250	
Interest expense*	5		Cash		250
Cash		250			
* Alternative title: Purchase discounts lost.					
To record sale of half the inventory for $1,500 cash:					
Cash	1,500		Cash	1,500	
Sales revenue		1,500	Sales revenue		1,500
Cost of goods sold	490		Cost of goods sold	500	
Merchandise inventory		490	Merchandise inventory		500
($980 × ½ = $490)			($1,000 × ½ = $500)		
Panel B—Reporting:					
Income statement:					
Cost of goods sold		$490	Cost of goods sold ($500 less purchase discount, $15)		$485
Interest expense		5			
Balance sheet:					
Inventory		490	Inventory		500

The net of discount approach correctly reflects the cost of the merchandise in conformity with the cost principle and also correctly states the amount of the liability since most companies take all discounts and pay only the net amount. Note that 2 percent interest saved by paying within 10 days is a significantly higher rate on an annual basis. This method also correctly allocates the discount effect between inventory and cost of goods sold. It follows the cost principle because the true costs of purchases, cost of goods sold, and inventory are recorded and reported. Similarly, accounts payable is recorded and reported at the amount actually payable within the discount period. The net approach reports **purchase discount lost** (a debit) as interest expense rather than reporting **purchase discount** (a credit) as a reduction of cost of goods sold or as "other" revenue.

EFFECT OF INVENTORY ERRORS

Errors in measuring inventory quantities or monetary values are common because of complicating factors such as the sheer size of the inventory, the number of different kinds of items, their physical characteristics, and means of storage. This section demonstrates the effect of inventory errors on the financial statements, using a periodic inventory system for illustrative purposes.

An overstatement of the **ending** inventory overstates pretax income by the same amount, and an understatement of the ending inventory understates pretax income. Conversely, an overstatement of the **beginning** inventory understates pretax income by the same amount, and an understatement of the beginning inventory overstates pretax income. An overstatement of purchases alone overstates cost of goods sold and understates pretax income.

Incorrect inclusion or exclusion of physical units in inventory will cause errors in the financial statements. The following errors are not uncommon.[6]

A. Incorrect **inclusion** of items that should not be in ending inventory because ownership is not present:

1. **Incorrect inclusion of items in the ending inventory, and the credit purchase of these items was recorded**—These two errors result in an overstatement of the ending inventory, purchases, and accounts payable. In this case pretax income will be correctly stated because the errors in inventory and purchases will offset; however, the assets (inventory) and liabilities (accounts payable) on the balance sheet each will be overstated by the same amount.
2. **Incorrect inclusion of items in the ending inventory, but the credit purchase of these items was not recorded**—This error results in an overstatement of the ending inventory; hence, both pretax income and assets are overstated by the same amounts.

B. Incorrect **exclusion** of items that should be admitted to ending inventory because ownership is present:

3. **Incorrect exclusion of items from the ending inventory, but the credit purchase of these items was correctly recorded**—This error results in an understatement of the ending inventory and an understatement of both pretax income and assets by the same amount.
4. **Incorrect exclusion of items from the ending inventory, and the credit purchase of these items was not recorded**—These two errors result in understatement of ending inventory, purchases, and accounts payable. In this case pretax income will be correctly stated because the errors in inventory and purchases will offset; however, the assets (inventory) and liabilities (accounts paya-

[6] Some of the effects of these errors will differ depending upon the inventory flow method used, that is, FIFO, LIFO, etc.

EXHIBIT 7–5: Effects of Inventory Errors (pretax)

		Inventory Error—Incorrectly Included $1,000 in Ending Inventory		Inventory Error—Incorrectly Excluded $1,000 from Ending Inventory	
	Correct Amounts	(1) Purchases in Error (was recorded)	(2) Purchases Are Correct (was not recorded)	(3) Purchases Are Correct (was recorded)	(4) Purchases in Error (was not recorded)
Income statement:					
Sales revenue	$10,000	$10,000	$10,000	$10,000	$10,000
Beginning inventory	3,000	3,000	3,000	3,000	3,000
Purchases	12,000	13,000†	12,000	12,000	11,000*
Total	15,000	16,000	15,000	15,000	14,000
Ending inventory	8,000	9,000†	9,000†	7,000*	7,000*
Cost of goods sold	7,000	7,000	6,000*	8,000†	7,000
Gross margin	3,000	3,000	4,000†	2,000*	3,000
Expenses	1,000	1,000	1,000	1,000	1,000
Income	$ 2,000	$ 2,000	$ 3,000†	$ 1,000*	$ 2,000
Balance sheet:					
Assets (inventory)	$ 8,000	$ 9,000†	$ 9,000†	$ 7,000*	$ 7,000*
Liabilities (payables)	12,000	13,000†	12,000	12,000	11,000*
Retained earnings	20,000	20,000	21,000†	19,000*	20,000

* Under.
† Over.

ble) on the balance sheet each will be understated by the same amount.

The monetary effects of each situation are demonstrated in Exhibit 7–5.

Errors similar to those illustrated above not only cause the financial statements for the current period to be in error but also frequently cause future amounts to be wrong. That is, an error in the ending inventory, if not corrected, will cause a **counterbalancing** error in the next period because the ending and beginning inventories have opposite effects on income amounts of the two periods.

Part B: Departures from the Cost Principle and Other Issues in Accounting for Inventory

Under certain conditions, GAAP requires exceptions to the cost principle in the accounting for inventory. The exceptions may be classified as follows:

1. Lower of cost or market (LCM).
2. Net realizable value.
3. Current cost.
4. Selling price.

LOWER OF COST OR MARKET (LCM)

Under the concept of **conservatism,** losses due to a decrease in the market value (i.e., current replacement cost) of inventory, although not actually incurred in completed transactions, are recognized in the period of occurrence. In contrast, market value gains not evidenced by completed transactions are not recognized until realized. Therefore, under the LCM rule, the unit cost of inventory is identified as the lower of *(a)* original cost when purchased or *(b)* the **current replacement cost** (i.e., the current cost to replace or reproduce the inventory, **not** its current selling price) at the end of the current period. Thus, an item purchased in June 19A for $50 which is still on hand at the end of 19A, at which time it could be purchased for $45, would be reported in the 19A ending inventory at a unit cost of $45. The $5 loss would be reported as an expense on the 19A income statement, and the current cost of $45 becomes the cost for future accounting; hence, $45 would be included in cost of goods sold for the period when the item is sold. The net effect of the LCM application is to shift the $5 loss from 19B (period of sale) to 19A (period the current cost decreased).

The LCM rule was adopted on the basis of *(a)* the matching principle, because the decline in utility of the goods on hand (evidenced by the decrease in current replacement cost) should be recognized as a loss in the period in which the decline in utility took place; and *(b)* the concept of balance sheet conservatism, which holds that the asset inventory should be reported at the lower figure.

In applying the LCM procedure, certain **exceptions** were recognized by the Committee on Accounting Procedure, which issued the definitive pronouncement on LCM. That is, while "market" means current replacement cost (or current reproduction cost, as the case may be),

> (1) Market should not exceed the net realizable value (i.e., estimated selling price in the ordinary course of business less reasonably predictable costs of completion and disposal); and
>
> (2) Market should not be less than net realizable value reduced by an allowance for an approximately normal profit margin.[7]

The concepts of **net realizable value** and **net realizable value less normal profit** may be illustrated as follows for one unit of inventory item A:

Inventory item A, at original cost	$ 70
Inventory item A, at estimated current selling price in **present condition**	$100
Less: Estimated costs of completion and disposal*	40
Net realizable value	60
Less: Allowance for normal profit (10% of sales price)	10
Net realizable value less normal profit	$ 50

* For goods already completed as in a retail company, this becomes "cost of repair to make ready for sale."

The deduction of estimated costs of completion and disposal of the inventory is necessary to prevent inclusion of the inventory at more than its current

[7] *ARB 43,* chap. 4, statement 6.

value. The effect of accounting for inventory at an amount in excess of its net realizable value would be to recognize income prior to actual sale of the inventory.

The exceptions quoted above for net realizable value and net realizable value less normal profit effectively establish a "ceiling" and a "floor" for **market** in the comparison with original **cost** in applying the procedure. Exhibit 7–6 shows how LCM is determined in four different cases for a single unit (the same procedure would apply to an entire inventory).

EXHIBIT 7–6: Exceptions—Determination of Lower of Cost or Market (LCM)

	Case			
	I	II	III	IV
a. Cost (per unit)	$1.00	$1.00	$1.00	$0.45
b. Current replacement cost (per unit)	0.55	0.65	0.45	0.40
c. Ceiling (net realizable value, i.e., estimated sales price less predictable cost of completion and disposal)*	0.60	0.60	0.60	0.60
d. Floor (net realizable value less a normal profit margin)*	0.51	0.51	0.52	0.52
e. Market (selected from [*b*], [*c*], and [*d*] values)	0.55	0.60	0.52	0.52
f. Inventory valuation under LCM rule (selected from [*a*] and [*e*]	0.55	0.60	0.52	0.45

* Additional data to verify ceiling and floor.

	I	II	III	IV
Estimated selling price (later period)	$0.85	$0.90	$0.80	$0.75
Less: Estimated cost to complete and sell	0.25	0.30	0.20	0.15
Net realizable value (ceiling)	$0.60	$0.60	$0.60	$0.60
Less: Estimated normal profit†	0.09	0.09	0.08	0.08
Net realizable value less profit (floor)	$0.51	$0.51	$0.52	$0.52

† 10 percent of sales price; rounded for instructional convenience.

Observe in Exhibit 7–6 that "market" under LCM is never greater than the "ceiling" (net realizable value), nor less than the "floor" (net realizable value less normal profit). The "market" thus derived is compared with cost to determine the appropriate inventory valuation.

The limits (ceiling and floor) are necessary to measure properly the economic utility of the items in inventory. For example, in Case II in Exhibit 7–6, current replacement cost is $0.65 and the net realizable value (ceiling) is $0.60. To carry the $0.65 forward in inventory, which is more than the net realizable value, would result in a deduction from future revenue greater than the economic utility of the goods and a deduction of $0.35 (i.e., $1.00–$0.65) from current income which is less than the anticipated loss of $0.40 (i.e., $1.00–$0.60); hence, the reported income and inventory value of each period would be incorrect.

In Case III, Exhibit 7–6, the net realizable value less normal profit (floor, $0.52) is greater than current replacement cost; therefore, the floor value should be carried forward in inventory. To carry forward a market value of $0.45 (i.e., current replacement cost) would result in an understatement of the inventory because at the floor value of $0.52 a normal profit margin ($0.08) will be earned when the item is sold for $.60. Therefore, if current replacement cost ($0.45) were carried forward in this case, future income on the inventory items would be overstated and current period income understated.[8]

Accounting Problems in Applying Lower of Cost or Market (LCM)

In applying the LCM procedure, two primary accounting problems arise, viz:

1. How should the procedure be applied to determine the overall inventory valuation?
2. How should the resulting inventory valuation be recorded in the accounts and reported on the financial statements?

Determination of Overall Inventory Valuation. In applying the LCM procedure to determine the overall inventory valuation, three approaches are available (*ARB 43,* chap. 4, statement 7): (1) comparison of cost and market separately for each item of inventory, (2) comparison of cost and market separately for each **classification** of inventory, and (3) compari-

[8] The application of LCM to FIFO and average cost (see Chapter 8) causes their results to approximate the LIFO results.

EXHIBIT 7–7: Applying Lower of Cost or Market (LCM)

Commodity	Cost	Market	LCM Applied to: Individual Items	Classification	Total
Classification A:					
Item 1	$10,000	$ 9,500	$ 9,500		
Item 2	8,000	9,000	8,000		
	18,000	18,500		$18,000	
Classification B:					
Item 3	21,000	22,000	21,000		
Item 4	32,000	29,000	29,000		
	53,000	51,000		51,000	
Total	$71,000	$69,500			$69,500
Inventory valuation			$67,500	$69,000	$69,500

son of **total** cost with **total** market for the inventory. Exhibit 7–7 shows the application of each approach.

Generally, the LCM procedure is applied to **individual inventory items.**[9] However, in certain circumstances, application of the procedure to classifications or totals may have greater significance for accounting purposes. For example, in applying the procedure to the raw materials inventory of a manufacturer producing only one major product and using several raw materials having common characteristics, the utility of the total stock of raw material may have more significance than the individual market prices of each raw material. Consistency in application is essential.

A problem arises when different unit costs of a particular commodity must be compared with a single unit **market** price. This situation frequently occurs when first-in, first-out (discussed in Chapter 8) is used. In such cases the aggregate cost for the commodity should be compared with the aggregate market, as shown under "Total" in Exhibit 7–7.

With respect to departures from cost in inventory valuation, once an inventory item has been reduced to a value lower than cost, **subsequent accounting** would consider the reduced value as "cost" for that particular item. Items once reduced for inventory valuation purposes should not be subsequently restored to their original cost.

Recording and Reporting Lower of Cost or Market (LCM). Purchases are recorded at cost; therefore, the introduction of LCM valuation of the inventory each period poses the question of how the **difference** between actual cost and the LCM amount should be recorded and reported. This difference arises because inventory items on hand can now be replaced for less than their original cost; therefore, this difference usually is called an **inventory holding loss.** The basic issue is whether the inventory holding loss should be **separately recorded** in the accounts and **separately reported** on the financial statements or merged into cost of goods sold. Two methods of recording and reporting the effects of the application of LCM found in practice are as follows:

1. Direct inventory reduction method—Under this method the inventory holding loss is **not** separately recorded and reported. Only the LCM amount, rather than the actual cost, of the inventory is recorded and reported each period. **Thus, the inventory holding loss is merged into the ending inventory and cost of goods sold amounts.**
2. Inventory allowance method—Under this method the inventory holding loss is **separately recorded and reported** each period. This separation is accomplished by using a **contra inventory** account, Allowance to Reduce Inventory to LCM. Thus, the inventory and cost of goods sold amounts are *(a)* recorded and reported at actual cost and *(b)* the inventory holding loss is separately recognized. The allowance account is used here in a manner similar to that for investments in short-term equity securities (discussed in Chapter 6).

Both of the above methods derive exactly the same income and total asset amounts; the two methods differ only with respect to the detail in the entries as reflected on the income statement and balance sheet. Both methods are illustrated for study and comparison in Exhibit 7–8. Panel A gives the illustrative data for three consecutive years, Panel B illustrates the related accounting entries under both methods (assuming a periodic inventory system), and Panel C presents the related balance sheet and income statement amounts as they would be reported in the financial statements.

Under the **direct inventory reduction** method, the entries and financial statements are exactly like

[9] *ARB 43,* chap. 4, statement 7.

those previously discussed except that the LCM amount of the ending inventory, rather than the actual inventory cost, is *(a)* recorded directly in the accounts and *(b)* reported on the financial statements. The amount of ending inventory at LCM is carried forward to the next period as the beginning inventory. Thus, **both** of the beginning and ending inventory amounts are **not** reflected at cost, but are reflected at LCM (assuming LCM is lower than cost). These characteristics are evident in Exhibit 7–8, Pan-

EXHIBIT 7–8: Recording and Reporting LCM for Inventory—Periodic Inventory System

Panel A—Illustrative Data ($000):

	19A		19B		19C	
	Beginning	**Ending**	**Beginning**	**Ending**	**Beginning**	**Ending**
A. Cost	–0–	$10	$10	$20	$20	$30
B. Market (replacement)	–0–	11	11	17	17	26
C. LCM (lower of A, B)	–0–	10	10	17	17	26
D. Holding loss (A–C)	–0–	–0–	–0–	3	3	4

Panel B—End-of-Period Inventory Entries:

	Direct Inventory Reduction Method			Inventory Allowance Method		
19A (no holding loss):						
a. Beginning inventory—none						
b. Ending inventory:						
Inventory (ending)	(cost)	10		(cost)	10	
Income summary (cost of goods sold)			10			10
19B (holding loss, ending inventory $3):						
a. Beginning inventory—to close:						
Income summary (cost of goods sold)	(cost)	10		(cost)	10	
Inventory (beginning)			10			10
b. Ending inventory—to record:						
Inventory (ending)	(LCM)	17		(cost)	20	
Income summary (cost of goods sold)			17			20
c. To record holding loss in ending inventory:						
Holding loss					3	
Allowance to reduce to LCM						3
19C (holding losses, beginning inventory, $3; ending inventory, $4):						
a. Beginning inventory—to close:						
Income summary (cost of goods sold)	(LCM)	17		(cost)	20	
Inventory (beginning)			17			20
b. Ending inventory—to record:						
Inventory (ending)	(LCM)	26		(cost)	30	
Income summary (cost of goods sold)			26			30
c. To close allowance account and reverse holding loss on beginning inventory:						
Allowance to reduce to LCM					3	
Holding loss						3
To record holding loss on ending inventory:						
Holding loss					4	
Allowance to reduce to LCM						4

EXHIBIT 7–8 ***(concluded)***

Panel C—Financial Statements—Reporting LCM for Inventory: Direct Inventory Reduction and Inventory Allowance Methods Compared:

REPORTING LCM—DIRECT INVENTORY REDUCTION METHOD
Inventory Holding Loss Merged with Inventory and Cost of Goods Sold

	Year 19A		Year 19B		Year 19C	
Balance sheet:						
Current assets:						
Merchandise Inventory		$10		$17		$26
Income statement:						
Sales revenue (assumed)		$50		$65		$81
Cost of goods sold:						
Beginning inventory (at LCM)	$ 0		$10		$17	
Purchases (assumed)	40		47		61	
Total goods available for sale	40		57		78	
Ending inventory (at LCM)	(10)		(17)		(26)	
Cost of goods sold		30		40*		52*
Gross margin		20		25		29
Expenses (assumed)		(10)		(13)		(16)
Income (pretax)		$10		$12		$13

* The holding loss merged with these amounts is: 19B, $3; and 19C, $1 (i.e., $4 − $3).

REPORTING LCM—INVENTORY ALLOWANCE METHOD
Holding Losses Separately Reported for Inventory and Cost of Goods Sold

	Year 19A		Year 19B		Year 19C	
Balance sheet:						
Current assets:						
Merchandise inventory (at cost)	$10		$20		$30	
Less; Allowance to reduce inventory to LCM	(0)	$10	(3)	$17	(4)	$26
Income statement:						
Sales revenue (assumed)		$50		$65		$81
Cost of goods sold:						
Beginning inventory (at cost)	$ 0		$10		$20	
Purchases (assumed)	40		47		61	
Total goods available for sale	40		57		81	
Ending inventory (at cost)	(10)		(20)		(30)	
Cost of goods sold (at cost)		30		37		51
Gross margin		20		28		30
Expenses (assumed)		(10)		(13)		(16)
Deduct net holding loss effect:						
19A		-0-				
19B				(3)		
19C ($4 − $3)						(1)
Income (pretax)		$10		$12		$13

els B and C, under the heading Direct Inventory Reduction Method.

In contrast, under the **inventory allowance method,** the entries and financial statements *(a)* retain actual costs for inventory and cost of goods sold and *(b)* record and report the holding loss each period in a contra inventory account, Allowance to Reduce Inventory to LCM. At the end of each period, the old balance in this account is closed and the new holding loss (in the ending inventory) is recorded in this allowance account. The net holding loss (i.e., the net effect of the holding losses in the beginning and ending inventories) is reported separately on the income statement. These characteristics are evident in Exhibit 7–8, Panels B and C, under the heading Inventory Allowance Method.

The **direct inventory reduction method** is widely used because *(a)* it is less complex than the allowance method when the periodic system is used, *(b)* the inventory holding loss amount for the period often is not substantial or unusual, and *(c)* disclosure notes can be used to provide the holding loss information. In contrast, the **inventory allowance method** is used because it *(a)* provides full disclosure of the effects of LCM on inventories (the direct inventory reduction method does not), *(b)* is required under certain conditions,[10] *(c)* involves less complexity than does the direct inventory reduction method when the perpetual inventory system is used (perpetual records usually are maintained at cost, not LCM), and *(d)* provides insight into the interperiod effects of LCM.

INVENTORY VALUATION AT CURRENT REPLACEMENT COST AND NET REALIZABLE VALUE

Special inventory categories often contain items that are not in "new condition for resale" (i.e., the items are "used") because they are damaged, shopworn, obsolete, defective, trade-ins, or repossessions. In many of these situations, the business cannot specifically identify the **actual purchase cost** (in their current condition) based upon completed transactions in accordance with the cost principle. Therefore, such an inventory item must be assigned a reliable substitute cost related to its current condition. In such situations, for inventory valuation purposes, **current replacement cost** is used as a substitute if it can be determined reliably in an established "used" market for the item in its current condition.

[10] Ibid., chap. 7, statement 7, par. 14, states: "When substantial and unusual losses result from the application of this rule [LCM], it will frequently be desirable to disclose the amount of the loss **in the income statement as a charge separately identified from . . . . . cost of goods sold,"** (emphasis supplied). The inventory allowance method provides for separate reporting of the holding loss. The direct inventory reduction method merges the holding loss with cost of goods sold automatically; therefore, to some accountants it does not appear compatible with this quotation from *ARB 43* when the difference is substantial in amount and unusual.

When neither the actual purchase cost nor the current replacement cost can be determined reliably, such an item should be valued for inventory purposes at its **estimated net realizable value.**

Current replacement cost is defined for "used" inventory valuation purposes as the price for which the item can be purchased in its present condition. To illustrate a typical situation in which the actual purchase cost is not known but the current replacement cost can be determined reliably, assume X Department Store has on hand a repossessed TV set that cost $650. It was originally sold for $995 and was repossessed when $500 was owed on it by the customer. Also, assume that similar used TV sets could be purchased in the used market for $240. The repossessed item should be recorded as follows:

Inventory—repossessed merchandise	240	
Loss on repossession* (or Allowance for doubtful accounts)	260	
Account receivable		500

* In some situations this may be a gain.

Assume further that during the following year the repossessed TV set was sold for $270 cash. The entry to record the sale could be recorded as follows (assuming a perpetual inventory system):

Cash	270	
Sales revenue—repossessed merchandise		270
Cost of goods sold	240	
Inventory—repossessed merchandise		240

Estimated net realizable value is defined for "used" inventory valuation purposes as the estimated sale price less all costs expected to be incurred in *(a)* preparing it for sale and *(b)* selling it. To illustrate accounting for inventory at **net realizable value** when neither actual cost nor replacement cost can be determined reliably, assume Y Company suffered flood damages to some of its regular inventory. Item W, which originally cost $4,000 (as reflected in the perpetual inventory records), was marked to sell for $7,000. The current replacement cost of item W in its present condition **cannot** be determined reliably because no established used market exists. Therefore, the company will value item W for inventory purposes at its **net realizable value.** Y Company estimated that after cleaning it and making certain repairs, it would sell for $3,000; the estimated cost of the repairs is $200, and estimated sale costs will be $300. Based on these data, the inventory valuation of item W was computed as follows:

Estimated sale price		$3,000
Less: Estimated cost to repair	$200	
Estimated sale costs	300	(500)
Net realizable value for inventory.......		$2,500

Assuming no insurance indemnity, the casualty loss and the inventory would be recorded as follows (assuming a perpetual inventory system):

Inventory—damaged merchandise	2,500	
Casualty loss—flood damage	1,500	
Inventory (regular merchandise)......		4,000

INVENTORIES VALUED ABOVE COST AT SELLING PRICE

Under certain unusual circumstances an inventory item may be valued at selling price. The circumstances, to conform to GAAP, are as follows:

> It is generally recognized that income accrues only at the time of sale, and that gains may not be anticipated by reflecting assets at their current sales prices. For certain articles, however, exceptions are permissible. Inventories of [commodities for which] there is an effective government-controlled market at a fixed monetary value, are ordinarily reflected at selling prices. A similar treatment is not uncommon for inventories representing agricultural, mineral, and other products, units of which are interchangeable and have an immediate marketability at quoted prices and for which appropriate costs may be difficult to obtain. Where such inventories are stated at sales prices, they should of course be reduced by expenditures to be incurred in disposal, and the use of such basis should be fully disclosed in the financial statements.[11]

Under this method, when a decrease occurs in selling price, a holding loss would be reported; conversely, when there is an increase in selling price, a holding gain would be reported. Thus, income would include gross margin and the holding gain or loss for the period. This effect can be attained by valuing the inventory at selling price. To illustrate, assume the following simplified data:

Year	Sales	Purchases at Cost	Ending Inventory at Selling Price	Expenses
19A ...	$ -0-	$1,000	$1,750	$300
19B ...	1,700	-0-	-0-	300

The financial statements with inventory valued at selling price would appear as shown below; the cost basis statement data are shown for comparison.

	Cost Basis		Selling Price Basis	
	19A	19B	19A	19B
Income statement:				
Revenue	$-0-	$1,700	$ 750*	$1,700
Cost of goods sold	-0-	(1,000)	-0-	(1,750)
Expenses	(300)	(300)	(300)	(300)
Gain (loss)	$ (300)	$ 400	$ 450	$ (350)
Balance sheet:				
Inventory	$1,000	-0-	$1,750	-0-

* $1,750 − $1,000 = $750.

Illustrative of several pricing methods, a published financial statement recently reported the following inventory items:

THE RATH PACKING COMPANY

	1979
Current assets:	
Cash	$ 1,083,000
Receivables:	
Trade accounts	13,749,000
Other	2,037,000
	15,786,000
Less—Allowance for doubtful accounts	235,000
	15,551,000
Inventories (Note 1):	
Meat and other products	15,816,000
Materials and supplies	4,141,000
	$19,957,000

Note 1 (in part): Accounting Policies:

A summary of major accounting policies follows:

Inventories: Meat and other products are priced at approximate current market, less allowance for selling and distribution expenses. Materials and supplies are priced at the lower of first-in, first-out cost or market.

Source: AICPA, *Accounting Trends & Techniques, 1980* (New York, 1980), p. 147.

[11] Ibid., chap. 4, statement 9.

RELATIVE SALES VALUE METHOD

The preceding sections on LCM, net realizable value, current cost, and valuation of inventories at selling price represented generally accepted **departures** from cost in specific circumstances. We now return to the use of historical cost in situations in which two or more different kinds of inventory items are purchased for a lump sum and a separate cost for each kind is required for accounting purposes. That is, the total cost must be apportioned to individual kinds. The apportionment of the total cost logically should be related to the economic utility of each kind or group of items. Since the **sales value** of a particular item may be a reasonable indication of its relative utility, apportionment of the joint cost of such "basket purchases" usually is made on the basis of the **relative sales value** of the several items. Also, when joint costs are incurred subsequent to purchase, such costs frequently are allocated on the basis of relative sales value.

To illustrate, assume a packing plant purchased 1,000 bushels of apples (ungraded) for $2,000 and that after purchase the apples were sorted into three grades at a cost of $70 with the following results: grade A, 200 bushels, grade B, 300 bushels; and grade C, 500 bushels. Assume further that sorted apples were selling at the following prices per unit: grade A, $5; grade B, $4; and grade C, $2.50. The cost apportionment may be made as shown in Exhibit 7–9.

EXHIBIT 7–9: Relative Sales Value Method

	Quantity (bushels)	Unit Sales Price	Total Sales Value	Fraction of Total Sales Value	Apportioned Cost
A	200	$5.00	$1,000	$1,000/$3,450	$ 600*
B.....	300	4.00	1,200	1,200/ 3,450	720
C.....	500	2.50	1,250	1,250/ 3,450	750
	1,000		$3,450		$2,070

* ($1,000 ÷ $3,450) × $2,070 = $600. Or alternatively, $3,450 ÷ $2,070 = .60; $1,000 × .60 = 600; $1,200 × .60 = 720; and $1,250 × .60 = $750.

Assuming a perpetual inventory system, the purchase would be recorded as follows:

Inventory—grade A apples	600	
Inventory—grade B apples	720	
Inventory—grade C apples	750	
Cash		2,070

In cost allocations such as illustrated above, quantities lost due to shrinkage or spoilage should be assigned no cost, thereby resulting in a greater unit cost for the remaining units. In the case of real estate developments, improvements such as streets and parks may be apportioned to the cost of the salable areas in the manner illustrated here.

LOSSES ON PURCHASE COMMITMENTS

To "lock in" specific prices for needed items of inventory, companies often contract with a supplier to purchase a specific **quantity** of materials during a specified future **period** at an agreed **unit cost.** Some purchase commitments (contracts) are subject to revision or cancellation before the end of the contract period, whereas others are not subject to revision or cancellation. Each of these situations requires different accounting and reporting procedures.

In the case of purchase contracts **subject to revision or cancellation** where a future loss is **possible** and the amount of the commitment is material, the reporting principle requires note disclosure of the contingency. To illustrate, assume XY Company entered into a purchase contract during October 19J that stated: "During 19K, 50,000 units of material X will be purchased at $5 each. Upon 60 days' notice, this contract is subject to revision or cancellation by either party." A footnote similar to the following should be included in the financial statements for 19J, assuming the current cost of the inventory (contracted for purchase) at the end of 19J was $240,000.

> Note 1. At the end of 19J, a contract was in effect; it will require the Company to pay $250,000 for raw materials during 19K. The purchase contract can be revised or canceled upon 60 days' notice by either party. At the end of 19J, the materials under contract had a current replacement cost of $240,000.

This note should reveal relevant aspects of the contingency; and in most cases, no entry would be required for the $10,000 (i.e., $250,000–$240,000) contingent loss. In this case, the loss is not probable, and note disclosure would be required (contingencies are discussed in Chapter 10).

When purchase contracts are **not subject to revision or cancellation,** and when a loss is probable and the amount can be reasonably estimated, the loss and related liability should be recorded in the accounts and reported in the financial statements.

In the above example, assume the $240,000 market price is measured reasonably and has a high probability of materializing. In *these* circumstances the loss on the purchase commitment should be recorded as follows (assuming a noncancellable contract):

Estimated loss on purchase commitment	10,000	
Estimated liability on noncancellable purchase commitment		10,000

The estimated loss is reported on the 19J income statement, and the liability is reported on the balance sheet. When the goods are received in 19K, Merchandise Inventory (or Purchases) is debited at their market value (i.e., current cost) when purchased; the estimated liability account is debited. To illustrate, assume the above raw materials have a market value at date of delivery of $235,000. The purchase entry would be as follows:

Raw materials (or purchases)	235,000	
Estimated liability on noncancellable purchase commitment	10,000	
Loss on purchase contract	5,000	
Cash		250,000

Even if no loss is probable, FASB, *Statement of Financial Accounting Standards No. 47,* "Disclosure of Long-Term Obligations," March 1981, requires disclosure, either in a note or by way of entries in the accounts, as appropriate, of such items as the *(a)* nature and term of the obligation, *(b)* fixed amount of the obligation, and *(c)* amounts purchased under the obligation.

This treatment records the loss in the period when it actually occurred and is consistent with the provisions of *ARB 43,* chap. 4, statement 10, and FASB, *Statement of Financial Accounting Standards No. 5,* "Accounting for Contingencies" (see Chapter 10).

QUESTIONS

PART A

1. In general, why should the accountant and management be concerned with inventories?

2. List and briefly explain the usual inventory classifications.

3. What general rule is applied by accountants in determining what goods should be included in inventory? How does the location of inventory affect this rule?

4. Assume you are in the process of adjusting and closing the books at the end of the fiscal year (for the purchaser). What treatment for inventory purposes would you accord the following goods in transit? *(a)* invoice received for $10,000, shipped FOB shipping point; *(b)* invoice received for $18,000, shipped FOB destination; and *(c)* invoice received for $6,000, shipped FOB shipping point and delivery refused on the last day of the period because of damaged condition.

5. Complete the following:

	Include in Inventory: Yes	Include in Inventory: No
a. Goods held by our agents for us.	____	____
b. Goods held by us for sale on commission.	____	____
c. Goods held by us but awaiting return to vendor because of damaged condition.	____	____
d. Goods returned to us from buyer, reason unknown to date.	____	____
e. Goods out on consignment.	____	____
f. Goods held on consignment.	____	____
g. Merchandise at our branch for sale.	____	____
h. Merchandise at conventions for display purposes.	____	____

6. Explain the principal aspects of a periodic inventory system.

7. Why is cost of goods sold often characterized as a residual amount? In which inventory system is this characterization more appropriate?

8. Explain the effect of each of the following errors in the ending inventory of a trading business (ignore income taxes):
   a. Incorrectly excluded 300 units of commodity C, valued at $3 per unit, from the ending inventory; the purchase was recorded.
   b. Incorrectly excluded 400 units of commodity D, valued at $4 per unit, from the ending inventory; the purchase was not recorded.
   c. Incorrectly included 100 units of commodity A, valued at $5 per unit, in the ending inventory; the purchase was recorded.
   d. Incorrectly included 200 units of commodity B, valued at $3 per unit, in the ending inventory; the purchase was not recorded.

9. What is meant by the accounting value of inventory? What accounting principles predominate in measuring this value?

10. In determining unit cost for inventory purposes, how should the following items be treated?
    a. Purchase returns.
    b. Purchase (cash) discounts.
    c. Freight on goods and materials purchased.

11. Should purchase discounts be *(a)* deducted in part in the income statement and in part from inventory in the balance sheet or *(b)* deducted in total in the income statement for the period in which the discounts arose? Assume that three fourths of the goods purchased were sold by year-end. Explain.

PART B

12. Cost is the primary basis for inventory valuation. List the four exceptions to cost discussed in the chapter. Under what specified conditions is each generally acceptable?

13. Why is the concept of LCM applied to inventory valuation?

14. What is the rationale underlying the use of the "ceiling" and "floor" values in determining "market" in the application of the LCM concept?

15. How should damaged or obsolete merchandise on hand at the end of the period be valued for inventory purposes?

16. What are the basic assumptions underlying the relative sales value method when used in allocating costs for inventory purposes?

17. Briefly outline the accounting and reporting of losses on purchase commitments when *(a)* the purchase contract is subject to revision or cancellation and *(b)* it is noncancellable and a loss is reasonably probable.

DECISION CASE 7–1

1. Excise taxes and import duties on some products produced or processed by distilleries often exceed the cost of the products themselves. How should such taxes be accounted for? Answer in the context of the accounts to be debited and when the expense should be recognized.

2. Inventories such as grain, flour, and sugar often are accounted for at market value (with the estimated cost of disposal deducted). What is the justification for this valuation procedure? What is the effect on periodic income?

DECISION CASE 7–2

Smith Company has been in operation since 1970 and has experienced satisfactory growth since that time. B. Smith, the organizer, was an experienced and skilled machinist having operated a small custom machine shop for years. In 1970, with the financial assistance of a friend, Smith organized the company to manufacture specially designed trailers for the transportation of horses. Most of the trailers were designed to haul one horse; consequently, they were built to meet the particular desires of each customer. These trailers varied from a standard type to deluxe models in keeping with the horse-show tradition. In 1976, the company started making trailers for boats. Two standard models were developed for sale to sporting goods stores; and, in addition, trailers were made to meet the specifications of individual buyers.

The company recently experienced an unexpected demand for boat trailers which was attributed to their quality, competitive price, and design. Smith is having considerable difficulty keeping up with this demand and hesitates to add capacity, workers, and materials needed, on the basis of expectations, rather than on the basis of firm orders. As a consequence, the firm has lost some business. Customarily a 50% deposit is required on all custom-made trailers.

Smith is particularly interested in the manufacturing side of the business, and he is inclined to ignore the financial and management aspects. As a result of some income tax difficulties, Smith engaged an outside CPA to set up records and help with the financial management of the company. One employee spends part time on the present recordkeeping, which involves minimum records on cash, salaries, receivables, payables, and wages.

The company regularly stocks 23 different items of raw materials and numerous small supplies such as bolts, screws, welding materials, and paint. The company loses about two thirds of the available cash discounts on purchases through oversight. Customarily the company pays freight on the purchases. Finished goods on the lot usually consist of 8 to 15 horse trailers, 20 to 35 boat trailers, plus small quantities of eight other small items manufactured. Frequently, customers leave trailers on the lot a week or more before picking them up. Several kinds of raw material currently on hand are of such a nature that the replacement cost is less than the original cost. The company has always had difficulty with raw materials and supplies; frequently shortages hold up work on jobs for days. Often substitutions of higher cost materials are necessary due to items being out of stock. The raw materials are stored both outside and inside, and individual workers select the material as they need it on a help-yourself basis. Smith feels that the company cannot afford an inventory clerk. Items are reordered from a notebook kept on Smith's desk where individual workers are instructed to write down any items that are low or out of stock. When raw materials are received, they are moved to the storage area and placed wherever space is available. Space is a problem. No inventory records are maintained. No payments are made for raw materials unless the invoice is signed by the employee that checked in the goods. Theft is no problem for the company.

The CPA has decided to install a job order cost system so that costs will be accumulated by job for direct material, direct labor, and manufacturing overhead; and it is recognized that in view of the small size of the company, the overall system must be simple and easy to operate.

The CPA is concerned about the raw material and finished goods inventory situations in particular and has asked you to make recommendations relative to the inventory problem. The CPA has decided to employ FIFO and LCM. Specifically, the CPA wants your suggestions for the company relative to (1) recommendations for better inventory control, (2) determination of quantities in inventory, and (3) the appropriateness of applying LCM to the valuation of the inventory. Sound reasons are expected to support your suggestions.

Required:
Narrate your recommendations to the company giving particular attention to the raw materials and finished goods inventories. Give supporting reasons.

EXERCISES

PART A: EXERCISES 7–1 to 7–10

Exercise 7–1

Listed below for Tolbert Company are items of inventory that are in question. The company stores a substantial portion of the merchandise in a separate warehouse and transfers damaged goods to a special inventory account. The company policy is "satisfied customers."

a.	Items in receiving dept., returned by customer, no communication received from customer	$ 100
b.	Items ordered and in receiving dept., invoice not received from supplier	500
c.	Items counted in whse. by inventory crew	57,000
d.	Invoice received for goods ordered, goods shipped but not received (Tolbert pays freight)	800
e.	Items shipped today, FOB destination, invoice mailed to customer	70
f.	Items currently used for window displays	800
g.	Items on counters for sale per inventory count (not in [*c*])	12,000
h.	Items in shipping dept., invoice not mailed to customer	140
i.	Items in receiving dept., refused by Tolbert because of damage (not in [*c*])	100
j.	Items shipped today, FOB shipping point, invoice mailed to customer	400
k.	Items included in whse. count, damaged, not returnable	200
l.	Items included in whse. count, specifically crated and segregated for shipment to customer in 5 days per sales contract, with return privilege	1,500

Required:
Complete the following tabulation to reflect the correct inventory:

Item	Exclude or Include in Inventory	Amount	Explanation
a. Items counted in whse.	Include	$57,000	Items on hand
b. Etc.			
Total inventory valuation		$	

Exercise 7–2

The records of Bradley Company reflected the following data: sales revenue, $90,000; purchases, $62,000; net income to sales revenue, 8%; beginning inventory, $9,000; and expenses, $22,800.

Required:

1. Reconstruct the income statement. Assume a periodic inventory system.
2. Give entries at the end of the period for the inventories and the other closing entries assuming Case A—a periodic inventory system; and Case B—a perpetual inventory system.

Exercise 7–3

The records for Llano Company at December 31, 19A, reflected the following:

	Units	Unit Price
Sales during period	10,000	$12
Inventory at beginning of period	2,000	6
Merchandise purchased during period (for cash)	18,400	6
Purchase returns during period (cash refund)	100	6
Inventory at end of period	?	6

Total expenses (excl. cost of goods sold), $45,000.

Required:
In parallel columns, give entries for the above transactions, including all entries at the end of the period assuming:

Case A—Periodic inventory system.

Case B—Perpetual inventory system.

Use the following format:

Accounts	Case A	Case B

Exercise 7–4

The independent CPA for Norse Company found the following errors in the records of the company:

a. Incorrect exclusion from the ending inventory of items costing $6,000 for which the purchase was not recorded.

b. Inclusion in the ending inventory of goods costing $2,000, although a purchase was not recorded. The goods in question were being held on consignment from Mason Company.

c. Incorrect exclusion of $4,000 from the inventory count at the end of the period. The goods were in transit (FOB shipping point); the invoice had been received, and the purchase was recorded.

d. Inclusion of items on the receiving dock that were being held for return to the vendor because of damage. In counting the goods in the receiving department, these items were incorrectly included. With respect to these goods, a purchase of $6,000 had been recorded.

The records (uncorrected) showed the following amounts: *(a)* purchases, $180,000; *(b)* pretax income, $20,000; *(c)* accounts payable, $30,000; and *(d)* inventory at the end of the period, $50,000.

Required:
Set up a table to reflect the uncorrected balances, changes occasioned by correction of the errors, and the corrected balances for (1) purchases, (2) pretax income, (3) accounts payable, and (4) ending inventory.

Exercise 7–5

The records of Vaught Company reflected the following:

Sales revenue		$190,000
Cost of goods sold:		
Beginning inventory	$ 10,000	
Purchases	105,000	
Goods available for sale	115,000	
Ending inventory	25,000	90,000
Gross margin		100,000
Expenses		60,000
Net income (pretax)		$ 40,000

The following errors were found that had not been corrected:

a. Accrued expenses not recognized, $6,000.

b. Revenues collected in advance amounting to $4,000 are included in the sales revenue amount.

c. Goods costing $10,000 were incorrectly included in the ending inventory (they were being held on consignment from Banner Company). No purchase was recorded.

d. Goods costing $5,000 were correctly included in the ending inventory; however, no purchase was recorded (assume a credit purchase).

Required:

1. Recast the income statement on a correct basis.
2. What amounts would be incorrect on the balance sheet if the errors are not corrected?

Exercise 7–6

Ellis Company uses a perpetual inventory system. The items on hand are inventoried on a rotation basis throughout the year so that all items are checked twice each year. At the end of the year, the following data relating to goods on hand are available:

Product	Per Perpetual Inventory Units	Unit Cost	Per Physical Count (units)
A	200	$9	180
B	1,500	2	1,520
C	2,000	3	1,900
D	8,000	1	8,000
E	13,000	5	12,800

Required:
Determine the amount of the inventory overage or shortage and give the adjustment to the perpetual inventory records. Give the entry to record the final disposition of any discrepancy that needs to be recorded.

Exercise 7–7

On December 31, 19B, Taft Corporation prepared the annual financial statements and used an ending inventory valuation of $360,000 based on a periodic inventory system. The accounts for 19B have been adjusted and closed. Subsequently, the independent auditor located several discrepancies in the 19B ending inventory. These were discussed with the company accountant who then prepared the following schedule:

a.	Mdse. in store (at 50% above cost)	$360,000
b.	Mdse. out on consignment at sales price (incl. markup of 60% on selling price)	9,600
c.	Goods held on consignment from Brown Electrical Co. at sales price (sales commission, 20% of sales price included)	3,000
d.	Goods purchased, in transit (shipped FOB shipping point; estimated freight, not included, $600), invoice price	5,000
e.	Goods out on approval, sales price, $1,500, cost, $1,000	1,500
	Total inventory as corrected	$379,100

Average income tax rate, 40%.

Required:
1. The auditor did not agree with the "corrected" inventory amount of $379,100. Compute the correct ending inventory amount (show computations) by modifying the "corrected" balance of $379,100.
2. List the items on the income statement and balance sheet for 19B that should be corrected for the above errors and give the amount of the error in the balance of each item affected.
3. Since the accounts have been closed for 19B, a correcting entry in January 19C is needed. Give the required correcting entry.

Exercise 7–8

Starr Hardware Store purchased merchandise on credit for $50,000; terms, 2/15, n/30. Payment for one half of the recorded liability was made during the discount period; the balance was paid after the discount period. The company uses a perpetual inventory system.

Required:
Give entries in parallel columns to record the purchase and payments on the liability assuming:

a. Net of discount approach is used for purchase discounts.
b. Gross amount approach is used for purchase discounts.

Which approach is preferable conceptually? Why?

Exercise 7–9

X Discount Company purchased merchandise on credit for $40,000; terms, 2/10, n/30. Payment was made within the discount period. At the end of the fiscal period, one fourth of this merchandise was unsold. Determine (1) the cost of goods sold that would be reported on the income statement and (2) the ending inventory valuation as regards this particular lot of merchandise assuming:

a. Purchases and accounts payable are recorded at gross, and purchase discounts are deducted in total from purchases on the income statement.
b. Purchases and accounts payable both are recorded at net.
c. Purchases and accounts payable are recorded at gross, and purchase discounts are reported on the income statement as other income.

Evaluate the several approaches. Which approach is preferable conceptually? Why?

Exercise 7–10

Low Buy Stores, Inc. a dealer in radio and television sets, buys large quantities of a television model which costs $600. The contract reads that if 100 or more are purchased during the year, a bonus or rebate of $35 per set will be made. On December 15, the records showed that 150 sets had been purchased and that 10 remained on hand in inventory. A claim for the rebate was made to the vendor, and a check was received on January 20 after the books were closed.

Required:
1. At what valuation should the inventory be shown on December 31? Why?
2. What entry should be made relative to the rebate on December 31? Why?
3. What entry would be made on January 20? Why?

PART B: EXERCISES 7–11 to 7–18

Exercise 7–11

Case A—Topps Company had 1,000 units of product A in inventory at the end of the fiscal period. The unit cost was $60; estimated distribution costs, $3 per unit; and the "normal" profit is $4 per unit. Compute the unit valuation of the inventory under each separate case listed below. Apply the LCM procedure in accordance with the "exceptions" specified by the Committee on Accounting Procedure of the AICPA.

Case	Anticipated Sales Price	Current Replacement Cost
a.	$56	$50
b.	66	57
c.	68	61
d.	50	44
e.	59	57
f.	61	53
g.	73	59
h.	65	61
i.	70	62
j.	60	58

Case B—The management of Topps Company has taken the position that under the LCM procedure the two items listed below should be reported in the ending inventory at $16,600 (total). Do you agree? If not, indicate the correct inventory valuation by item. Show computations.

"Handyman" edgers: 300 on hand; cost, $22 each; replacement cost, $16; estimated sales price, $30; estimated distribution cost, $9 each; and normal profit, 10% of the sales price.

"Handyman" hedge clippers: 200 on hand; cost, $50 each; replacement cost, $36 each; estimated sales price, $90; estimated distribution cost, $28; and normal profit, 20% of sales.

Exercise 7–12

The inventories for the years 19A and 19B are shown below for Caster Wholesalers, Inc.:

Inventory Date	Original Cost	LCM	Difference
1/1/19A	$6,000	$6,000	-0-
12/31/19A	7,000	6,500	$500
12/31/19B	9,000	9,000	-0-

Required:

1. Give in parallel columns the journal entries to apply the LCM procedure to the inventories for 19A and 19B assuming the company utilizes the inventory allowance method where the holding losses in the beginning and ending inventories are separately recognized using periodic inventory procedures.
2. Give in parallel columns the journal entries to apply the LCM procedure to the inventories for 19A and 19B assuming the company uses the direct inventory reduction method (where the holding loss is not separately recognized) using periodic inventory procedures.
3. What are the primary advantages and disadvantages of each method?

Exercise 7–13

Stone Fruit Company purchased 1,910 bushels of ungraded apricots at $2 per bushel. The apricots were sorted as follows: grade one, 600 bushels; grade two, 400 bushels; and grade three, 900 bushels (spoilage 10 bushels). Handling and sorting costs amounted to $180. The current market prices for graded apricots were grade one, $4 per bushel; grade two, $3 per bushel; and grade three, $1 per bushel. The company utilizes a perpetual inventory system. What entry should be made to record the purchase? Show computations of total costs for each grade assuming the relative sales value method of cost allocation is used.

Exercise 7–14

Blackwell Homes, Inc., purchased a tract of land for development purposes. The tract was subdivided as follows: 30 lots to sell at $6,000 per lot and 80 lots to sell at $9,000 per lot. The tract cost $335,000, and an additional $25,000 was spent in general development costs, including streets and alleys. Assuming cost allocation is based on the relative sales value method, give entries for (1) purchase of the tract and payment of the development costs, (2) sale of one $6,000 lot, and (3) sale of one $9,000 lot. Assume a perpetual inventory system.

Exercise 7–15

Acme Land Developers purchased and subdivided a tract of land at a cost of $660,000. The subdivision was divided on the following basis:

10% used for streets, alleys, and parks.

50% divided into 100 lots to sell for $4,000 each.

30% divided into 200 lots to sell for $3,000 each.

10% divided into 50 lots to sell for $2,000 each.

Required:

1. Record the purchase of the lots. Use the relative sales value method to allocate the total cost of $660,000 to the three categories of lots. Assume a perpetual inventory system.

2. During the final month of the year, the paving was completed (included in the $660,000 cost) and sales were made. At the end of the first year, 20, $4,000 lots; 50, $3,000 lots; and 10, $2,000 lots are on hand. Compute the valuation of the inventory at year-end and record the sales and cost of goods sold amounts for each category of lots. Assume the lots are sold for cash.

Exercise 7–16

Tough Nut, Inc. purchased 1,000 bags of orchard-run pecans at a cost of $3,460. In addition, the company incurred $140 for transportation and grading. The pecans graded out as follows:

Grade	Quantity	Current Market Price per Bag
A	300	$7
B	500	6
C	150	5
Waste	50	

Required:
Assuming the relative sales value method is ued to allocate joint costs, give:

1. The entry for purchase assuming a perpetual inventory system (show computations).
2. Valuation of ending inventory assuming the following quantities are on hand: grade A, 100 bags; grade B, 80 bags; and grade C, 20 bags.
3. Sale of 20 bags of the grade A pecans at the above market price for cash.

Exercise 7–17

A fire damaged some of the merchandise held for sale by Tab TV Company. Five television sets and six stereo sets were damaged and not covered by insurance. They will be repaired and sold as used sets. Data are as follows:

	Per Set	
	Television	Stereo
Inventory (at cost)	$300	$200
Estimated cost to repair	40	30
Estimated cost to sell	20	20
Estimated sales price	150	90

Required:
1. Compute the appropriate inventory value for each set.
2. Give the separate entries to record the damaged goods inventory for the television and stereo sets. Assume a perpetual inventory system.
3. Give the entries to record the subsequent repair of the television sets and the stereo sets. (Credit Cash.)
4. Give the entry to record sale for cash of two television sets and one stereo set. (Credit Distribution Costs in the entry to record the sale; thus, it will be necessary to record payment of the distribution costs in a separate entry). Assume the **actual** sales prices equalled the **estimated** sales prices.

Exercise 7–18

G Corporation, during 19B, signed a contract with Black Company to "purchase 20,000 subassemblies at $30 each during 19C."

Required:
1. On December 31, 19B, end of the annual accounting period, the financial statements are to be prepared. Under what additional contractual and economic conditions should disclosure of the contract terms be made only by means of a note in the financial statements? Prepare an appropriate note. Assume the cost is dropping and the estimated current replacement cost is $520,000.
2. What contractual and economic conditions would require accrual of a loss? Give the accrual entry.
3. Assume the subassemblies are received in 19C when their cost was at the estimate you used in 1 above. The contract was paid in full. Give the required entry.

PROBLEMS

PART A: PROBLEMS 7–1 to 7–5

Problem 7–1

Assume you are the independent auditor for the Alford Manufacturing Corporation. The ending inventory for the year ended December 31, 19A, is under consideration. The following problems related to the inventory have arisen, and the company accountant requests your advice on them:

Part A

	Units	
	Product A @ $10	**Product B @ $20**
Finished goods unit inventory data on 12/31/19A— Items counted in whse. (excl. items below)	25,000	12,000
a. Items shipped to customer on 1/1/19B, invoice mailed 12/31/19A (FOB shipping point)		500
b. Items completed by factory, counted in work in process inventory; not transported to whse.	1,000	
c. Items on receiving dock, returned by customer because of major damage, notification from customer received		50
d. Items on trucking company dock, invoice mailed to customer, buyer pays freight	500	
e. Items in damaged condition	20	10
f. Items in shipping department, invoice not mailed to customer	80	
g. Items shipped 12/31/19A (FOB destination), invoice mailed to customer 1/2/19B	100	
h. Items on consignment to Brady Distributing Co.	400	800
i. Items specifically segregated and crated for shipment to Alford Branch No. 10	100	100
j. Items used for display purposes	10	30
k. Items specifically segregated and crated and held for shipment to customer 1/10/19B, per contract of sale for Dec. 19A		500
l. Items on receiving dock, returned by customer, no notification received (not damaged)	20	

Part B

	Units	
	Material X @ $3	**Material Y @ $5**
Raw material unit inventory data on 12/31/19A—Items counted in whse, (excl. items below)	15,000	3,500
a. Purchase invoice received, items not received (FOB shipping point)		300
b. Items set aside for return to vendor next period per agreement 12/20/19A; not up to guaranteed specifications, returned 1/2/19B		100
c. Items issued to factory and returned in damaged condition, not returnable to vendor		50
d. Items from shipment partly damaged when received, returnable to vendor per agreement; shipped 1/3/19B		40
e. Items purchased, on receiving dock, refused because of damage	50	
f. Items purchased, on receiving dock, invoice not received	200	300
g. Items to be returned to vendor per agreement, rejected for incorrect specs	150	
h. Purchase invoice received, items not received (FOB destination)	20	100

Required:
Compute the valuation of the ending inventory of finished goods and raw materials indicating specifically what items you would include and exclude. Give reasons you would present to the company relative to any doubtful items. The following format is recommended:

		Inventory Valuation				
		Product A		Product B		
Item	**Inventory Include/ Exclude**	**Units**	**Amount**	**Units**	**Amount**	**Explanation**

Problem 7–2

Green Corporation's fiscal period ends December 31, 19A. The company uses a periodic inventory system. An independent CPA was engaged after the end of the year to perform an audit. Therefore, the CPA did not observe the taking of the inventory. As a result, an examination was made of the inventory records only.

The financial statements prepared by the company (uncorrected) showed the following: ending inventory, $65,000; accounts receivable, $60,000; accounts payable, $30,000; sales, $400,000; net purchases, $160,000; and pretax income, $45,000.

The following data were found during the audit:

a. Merchandise that cost $18,000 was excluded from the inventory, and the related sale for $23,000 was recorded. The goods had been segregated in the warehouse for shipment; there was no contract for sale but a "tentative order by phone."

b. Merchandise that cost $10,000 was out on consignment to Goode Distributing Company and was excluded from the ending inventory. The merchandise was recorded as a sale of $25,000 when shipped to Goode on December 2, 19A.

c. Merchandise received on January 2, 19B, costing $800 was recorded on December 31, 19A. An invoice on hand showed the shipment was made FOB supplier's warehouse on December 31, 19A. Since the merchandise was not on hand at December 31, 19A, it was not included in the inventory.

d. A sealed packing case containing a product costing $900 was in the Green shipping room when the physical inventory was taken. It was included in the inventory because it was marked *"Hold for customer's shipping instructions."* Investigation revealed that the customer signed a purchase contract dated December 18, 19A, but that the case was shipped and the customer billed on January 10, 19B. A sale was recorded on December 18, 19A.

e. A special item, fabricated to order for a customer, was finished and in the shipping room on December 31, 19A. The customer had inspected it and was satisfied. The customer was billed in full on that date. The item was included in inventory at cost, $1,000, because it was shipped on January 4, 19B.

f. Merchandise costing $700 was received on December 28, 19A. The goods were excluded from inventory, and a purchase was not recorded. You located the related papers in the hands of the purchasing agent; they indicated *"On consignment from Baker Company."*

g. Merchandise costing $2,000 was received on January 8, 19B, and the related purchase invoice recorded January 9. The invoice showed the shipment was made on December 29, 19A, FOB *destination.* The merchandise was excluded from the inventory.

h. Merchandise that cost $11,000 and sold on December 31, 19A, for $16,000 was included in the ending inventory. The sale was recorded. The goods were in transit; however, a clerk failed to note that the goods were shipped FOB shipping point.

i. Merchandise that cost $6,000 was excluded from the ending inventory and not recorded as a sale for $7,500 on December 31, 19A. The goods had been specifically segregated. According to the terms of the contract of sale, ownership will not pass until actual delivery.

j. Merchandise that cost $15,000 was included in the ending inventory. The related purchase has not been recorded. The goods had been shipped by the vendor FOB destination; and the invoice, but not the goods, was received on December 30, 19A.

k. Merchandise in transit that cost $7,000 was excluded from inventory because it was not on hand. The shipment from the vendor was FOB shipping point. The purchase was recorded on December 29, 19A, when the invoice was received.

l. Merchandise in transit that cost $13,000 was excluded from inventory because it had not arrived. Although the invoice had arrived, the related purchase was not recorded by December 31, 19A. The merchandise was shipped by the vendor FOB shipping point.

m. Merchandise that cost $8,000 was included in the ending inventory since it was on hand. The merchandise had been rejected because of incorrect specifications and was being held for return to the vendor. The merchandise was recorded as a purchase on December 26, 19A.

Required:

1. Prepare a schedule with one column for each of the six financial statement items (starting with the uncorrected balances), plus any other columns deemed useful. Show the specific corrections to each balance and the corrected balances. Explain the basis for your decision on all items.
2. Give the entry to correct the accounts assuming the accounts for 19A have been closed.

(AICPA adapted)

Problem 7–3

Spooner Company completed the following selected transactions during 19J for product A:

	Units	Unit Price
Beginning inventory	5,000	$18
Purchases	20,000	18
Purchase returns	1,000	18
Sales	18,000	40
Sales returns	100	40
Ending inventory per physical count	5,800	
Inventory shortage	?	

Expenses (excl. cost of goods sold and income taxes), $340,400.

Required:

1. In parallel columns, give entries for the above transactions including entries at the end of the accounting period, December 31, 19J, for (assume a 40% income tax rate and cash transactions):

   Case A—A periodic inventory system.

   Case B—A perpetual inventory system.
2. Prepare a multiple-step income statement assuming a periodic inventory system and 10,000 shares of common stock outstanding.
3. What amounts, if any, would be different on the income statement assuming a perpetual inventory system is used? Explain.

Problem 7–4

ABC Company has completed the income statement and balance sheet (summarized and uncorrected shown below) at December 31, 19A. Subsequently, during the audit, the following items were discovered:

a. Expenses amounting to $3,000 were not accrued.

b. A conditional sale on credit for $9,000 was recorded on December 31, 19A. The goods, which cost $5,000, were included in the ending inventory because they had not been shipped since the customer's address was not known and the credit had not been approved. Ownership had not passed.

c. Merchandise purchased on December 31, 19A, on credit for $8,000 was included in the ending inventory because the goods were on hand. A purchase was not recorded because the accounting department had not received the invoice from the vendor.

d. The ending inventory was overstated by $10,000 due to an addition error on the inventory sheet.

e. A sale return (on account) on December 31, 19A, was not recorded: sales amount, $15,000; and cost, $8,000. The ending inventory did not include the goods returned.

Required:

Set up a schedule similar to the one at the bottom of this page; make the corrections and derive the corrected amounts. Indicate increases and decreases for each transaction. Explain any assumptions made with respect to doubtful items. Disregard income taxes.

Problem 7–5

Flaten Company purchased merchandise during 19A on credit for $63,000 (includes $3,000 freight charges paid in cash); terms, 3/10, n/30. All of the purchase liability, except $20,000, was paid within the discount period; the remainder was paid within the 30-day term. At the end of the annual accounting period, December 31, 19A, 90% of the merchandise had been sold and 10% remained in inventory. The company uses a perpetual system.

Required:

1. Give entries in parallel columns for the purchase and the two payments on the liability assuming *(a)* purchases and accounts payable are recorded at gross and *(b)* purchases and accounts payable are recorded at net.
2. What amounts would be reported for the ending inventory and cost of goods sold under *(a)* and *(b)* in 1 above. Assume purchase discounts under the gross method are reported as a deduction from cost of goods sold. Explain in general terms why the amounts are different between the two methods.
3. Which method is preferable? Why?

PART B: PROBLEMS 7–6 to 7–12

Problem 7–6

The information shown below relating to the ending inventory was taken from the records of the Print Master Company shown at the top of the next page.

(Relates to Problem 7–4)

	Uncorrected Amounts	Items for Correction (a)	(b)	(c)	(d)	(e)	Corrected Amounts
Income statement:							
Sales revenue	$90,000						
Cost of goods sold	50,000						
Gross margin	40,000						
Expenses	30,000						
Pretax income	$10,000						
Balance sheet:							
Accounts receivable	$32,000						
Inventory	20,000						
Remaining assets	40,000						
Accounts payable	11,000						
Remaining liabilities	6,000						
Common stock	60,000						
Retained earnings	15,000						

Inventory Classification	Quantity	Per Unit Cost	Per Unit Market
Paper:			
Stock X	200	$300	$330
Y	60	250	230
Ink:			
Stock D	20	70	65
E	10	60	62
Toner fluid:			
Stock A	8	75	70
B	4	90	80
C	7	100	110

Required:

1. Determine the valuation of the above inventory at cost and at LCM assuming application by *(a)* individual items, *(b)* classifications, and *(c)* total inventory. The unit costs of the three categories are significantly different; however, within each category the unit costs are similar.
2. Give the entry to record the ending inventory for each approach assuming periodic inventory and the allowance method.
3. Of the three applications computed in 1 above, which one appears preferable in this situation? Explain.

Problem 7–7

The records of Raft Company provide the following data relating to inventories for the years 19J and 19K:

Inventory Date	Original Cost	At LCM
1/1/19J	$40,000	$40,000
12/31/19J	50,000	46,000
12/31/19K	39,000	37,000

Other data available are as follows:

	19J	19K
Sales	$220,000	$245,000
Purchases	135,000	150,000
Adm. and selling expenses	51,000	61,000

The company values inventories on the basis of LCM and uses the periodic inventory system. For problem purposes ignore income taxes.

Required:

1. Give, in parallel columns, for 19J and 19K, the entries to apply the LCM procedure under the allowance method. Set up a format similar to the following:

	Amounts 19J	Amounts 19K
Entries		

2. Prepare an income statement and show the inventory amounts for the balance sheet. Follow the format illustrated in the chapter.

Problem 7–8

Wholesale Grocers Co-op purchased a large quantity of mixed grapefruit for $31,600 which was graded at a cost of $900, as indicated below. Sales (at the sales prices indicated) and losses (frozen, stolen, rotten, etc.) are also listed.

Grade	Baskets Bought	Sales Price per Basket	Baskets Sold	Baskets Lost
A	3,000	$4.00	2,000	50
B	4,000	3.00	3,000	60
C	10,000	1.50	8,000	80
Culls	1,000	.50	900	
Loss	55			

Required:

1. Give entry for purchase assuming a perpetual inventory system. Show computations.
2. Give entries to record the sales and cost of goods sold.
3. Give entry relative to the losses assuming the losses are recorded separately from cost of goods sold.
4. Determine the valuation of the ending inventory.
5. Compute the direct contribution to pretax income for each grade of grapefruit. (Disregard operating, administrative, and selling expenses.)

Problem 7–9

On May 1, 19A, Jones and Smith each invested $90,000 cash in a partnership for the purpose of purchasing and subdividing a tract of land for residential building purposes.

On June 1, they purchased 30 acres comprising the subdivision, at $5,000 per acre, paying $50,000 in cash and giving a one-year, 20% interest-bearing note (with mortgage) for the balance. Development costs amounted to $92,000.

The property was subdivided into 300 lots of equal size, 100 of which were to sell at $3,000 each and the balance at $4,000 each.

During July through December 19A, the following sales were made for half cash and half notes receivable due in six months from date of sale.

	Lots
Group A (sold at $4,000 each)	50
Group B (sold at $3,000 each)	60

Cash collections on the notes receivable up to December 31, 19A, amounted to $49,000 principal plus $1,000 interest. Accrued interest recorded at December 31, 19A, amounted to $1,000.

Operating and selling expenses amounted to $125,000 by the end of December 19A. No payment was made on the note payable.

Required:

1. Journal entries for all of the above transactions. Disregard income taxes.

2. Statement of income for the period May through December of 19A.
3. Compute the inventory of unsold lots on December 31, 19A.

Problem 7–10

Ringo, Inc., completed the following selected (and summarized) transactions during 19A:

a. During the year purchased merchandise for resale, quoted at $150,000, on credit terms, 2/10, n/90; immediately paid 80% of the cash cost.
b. Paid freight charges on purchases amounting to $6,000 cash.
c. Paid 60% of the accounts payable within the discount period. The remaining amount was unpaid at year-end; however, at year-end none was beyond the discount period.
d. Returned merchandise to a vendor because of damage in shipment and received a $1,980 cash refund.
e. During the year sold merchandise for $300,000, of which 10% was on end-of-month credit terms.
f. Repossessed a refrigerator abandoned by a customer who left town. The sales price was $400, of which $300 was unpaid. The refrigerator cost $320. Estimates are that the used refrigerator can be sold for $250, cost of repairs will be $30, and selling costs will be $10.
g. Operating expenses paid in cash, $110,000.
h. Paid $30 to repair the repossessed refrigerator.
i. The purchases amount given in *(a)* included a shipment, on credit, that had a quoted gross cost of $8,000 (terms, 2/10, n/30). The liability has not been paid. The shipment was in transit, FOB destination, at December 31, 19A. The invoice had been received. It was not included in the ending inventory amount.
j. The beginning inventory was $70,000 (at cost, which was the same as LCM).
k. The ending inventory (excluding the repossessed refrigerator) was $78,000 at cost; and at LCM, $75,000.

Accounting policies followed by the company are *(a)* annual accounting period ends December 31; *(b)* purchases and accounts payable are recorded net of cash discounts; *(c)* freight charges are allocated to the merchandise when purchased; *(d)* all cash discounts allowed are taken; *(e)* used and damaged merchandise is carried in a separate inventory account; and *(f)* inventories are reported at LCM, and any holding loss or gain on inventory valued at LCM is separately recognized (i.e., the allowance method).

Required:
1. Give entries for transactions *(a)* through *(i)* assuming periodic inventory system.
2. Give the end of the period entries (adjusting and closing). Assume an income tax rate of 30%.
3. Prepare a multiple-step income statement (19A). Assume 10,000 shares of common stock outstanding.
4. Show how the ending inventory should be reported on the balance sheet at December 31, 19A.

Problem 7–11

Pratt Company completed the following selected (and summarized) transactions during 19A:

a. Merchandise inventory on hand January 1, 19A: $100,000 (at cost, which was the same as LCM).
b. During the year, purchased merchandise for resale at quoted price of $200,000 on credit terms, 2/10, n/30. Immediately paid 85% of the cash cost.
c. Paid freight on merchandise purchased, $9,000 cash.
d. Paid 40% of the accounts payable within the discount period. The remaining payables were unpaid at the end of 19A and were still within the discount period.
e. Merchandise that had a quoted price of $3,000 was returned to a supplier. A cash refund of $2,940 was received because the items were unsatisfactory.
f. During the year, sold merchandise for $370,000, of which 10% was on credit terms, n/30.
g. A television set caught fire and was damaged internally; it was returned by the customer because it was guaranteed. The set was originally sold for $600, of which $400 cash was refunded. The set cost the company $420. Estimates are that the set, when repaired, can be sold for $240. Estimated repair costs are $50, and selling costs are estimated to be $10.
h. Operating expenses (administrative and distribution) paid in cash, $115,000 (includes the $10 in *g*).
i. Excluded from the purchase given in *(b)* and from the ending inventory was a shipment for $7,000 (net of discount). This shipment was in transit, FOB shipping point at December 31, 19A. The invoice was on hand.
j. Paid $50 cash to repair the damaged television set (see [*g*] above).
k. Sold the damaged television set for $245; selling costs allocated, $10.
l. The ending inventory (as counted) was $110,000 at cost, and $107,000 at LCM. Assume an average income tax rate of 40%.

Accounting policies followed by the company are *(a)* annual accounting period ends December 31, *(b)* purchases and accounts payable are recorded net of cash discounts, *(c)* freight charges are allocated to merchandise when purchased, *(d)* all cash discounts are taken, *(e)* used and damaged merchandise is carried in a separate inventory account, and *(f)* inventories are reported at LCM and the allowance method is used.

Required:
1. Give entries for transactions *(b)* through *(k)* assuming periodic inventory system.

2. Give the end of the period entries (adjusting and closing).
3. Prepare a multiple-step income statement (19A). Assume 10,000 shares of common stock outstanding.
4. Show how the ending inventory should be reported on the balance sheet at December 31, 19A.

Problem 7–12

The summarized income statements for the Largo Company are shown below as developed by the company. The inventories given below were valued at cost.

	19C	19D
Sales	$104,000	$97,000
Cost of goods sold:		
Beginning inventory	25,000	20,000
Purchases	75,000	73,000
Total	100,000	93,000
Ending inventory	20,000	15,000
Cost of goods sold	80,000	78,000
Gross margin	24,000	19,000
Less: Operating expenses	14,000	12,000
Pretax income	$ 10,000	$ 7,000

The inventories valued at LCM would have been: at the beginning of 19C, $25,000 (the same as cost); end of 19C, $17,000; and end of 19D, $11,000.

Required:

1. Restate the 19C and 19D income statements applying the LCM rule for each of the following procedures (use a format similar to that illustrated in the text). Disregard income taxes.
   a. Direct inventory reduction method where the inventory holding loss is not reported separately.
   b. Allowance method where the inventory holding losses in both beginning and ending inventories are reported separately.
2. Which procedure is preferable? Why?

8

Inventories—Flow and Matching Procedures

CHAPTER 7 identified two pervasive inventory problems—measurement of inventory **unit cost** and measurement of accounting values. This chapter considers the latter problem, that is, the selection of an assumed inventory cost flow such as average cost, FIFO, or LIFO. To facilitate discussion, this chapter is subdivided as follows:

Part A—Inventory Cost Flow Methods
Part B—Application of LIFO
Supplement 8–A—Miscellaneous Cost Flow Methods
Supplement 8–B—Technological Change in Inventories

Part A: Inventory Cost Flow Methods

The purchase or manufacture of inventory causes an inflow of cost; the sale or issue of inventory causes an outflow of cost. The net difference between these cost flows is the cost remaining in inventory. During an accounting period, items typically are manufactured or purchased at different unit costs. Upon issue or sale of the items, the accountant must select an appropriate unit cost for accounting purposes. Stated differently, the accounting problem with inventory is **costing** the units remaining on hand in inventory and the units sold or used.

A definite policy on the assumed flow of inventory costs is established when a particular inventory flow method is selected. Although inventory flow methods may be consistent with the physical flow of goods in a specific case, the focus is on the flow of **costs** rather than on the flow of physical goods. On this topic *ARB 43* states:

> Cost for inventory purposes may be determined under any one of several assumptions as to the flow of cost factors (such as first-in first-out, average, and last-in first-out); the major objective in selecting a method should be to choose the one which, under the circumstances, most clearly reflects periodic income.[1]

The inventory flow methods discussed in this chapter conform to the **cost principle** and do not involve departures from cost. The central issue is the

[1] AICPA, *Accounting Research Bulletin No. 43,* "Restatement and Revision of Accounting Research Bulletins" (New York, 1961), Chapter 4 statement 4.

EXHIBIT 8–1: Inventory Data

Transactions			Received Units	Received Unit Cost	Units Issued	Units on Hand
Jan.	1	Inventory (@ $1) . . .				200
	9	Purchase	300	$1.10		500
	10	Sale			400	100
	15	Purchase	400	1.16		500
	18	Sale			300	200
	24	Purchase	100	1.26		300

EXHIBIT 8–2: Selection of a Cost Flow Method

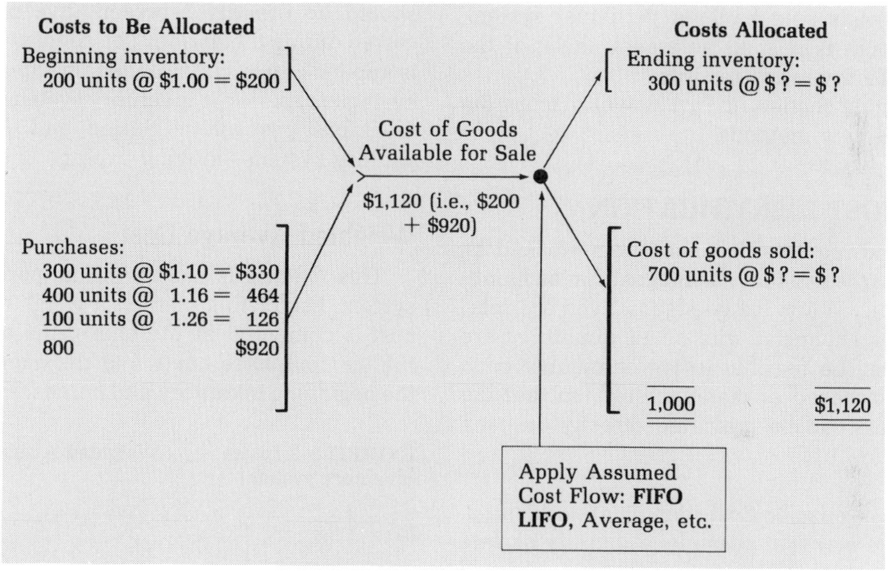

order in which the actual unit costs are assigned to inventory and cost of goods sold. The selection of an inventory flow method determines how the **matching principle** is applied to determine the cost of goods sold amount to be deducted from sales revenue for the period. Under GAAP the method selected should be the one that "most clearly reflects periodic income" in each particular situation. All of the methods will produce the same results if costs do not change; however, this is seldom the case.

The inventory cost flow methods discussed in this chapter are as follows:

1. Specific cost identification.
2. Average cost.
3. First-in, first-out (FIFO) cost.
4. Last-in, first-out (LIFO) cost.
5. Miscellaneous cost flow methods.

For purposes of illustrating the various cost flow methods, the simplified data given in Exhibit 8–1 are used.

Using the data given in Exhibit 8–1, we can illustrate the problem of cost allocation related to a cost flow method for inventory and cost of goods sold purposes as shown in Exhibit 8–2.

The application of some of the inventory cost flow methods will vary depending upon whether **periodic** or **perpetual** inventory procedures are used. The discussions to follow will distinguish between these procedures where they affect the application of the inventory cost flow method.

Under periodic inventory procedures, the quantity of the ending inventory is determined solely by a physical unit count; the unit costs (as defined in Chapter 7) then are applied to derive the inventory valuation by using one of the flow methods discussed in this chapter. Cost of goods sold (or used) is determined by subtracting the ending inventory cost from the cost of **goods available** amount.

In contrast, under perpetual inventory procedures, all receipts and issues of inventory are recorded in the Inventory account to keep an up-to-date inventory balance at all times. As a consequence, the inventory records provide the amounts for inventory and cost of goods sold under a perpetual system. A physical count is needed only as a check of the accuracy of the inventory records.

The remaining section of Part A will discuss the inventory cost flow methods.

SPECIFIC COST IDENTIFICATION

This method requires that each item stocked be specifically marked so that its unit cost can be identified at any time. When the goods involved are relatively large or expensive and small quantities are handled, it may be feasible to tag or number each item when purchased or manufactured, so that the actual unit cost can be indicated directly on each item.

Evaluation of Specific Cost Identification Method. This procedure makes it possible to identify at date of sale the specific **unit cost** of each item sold and each item remaining in inventory. The specific cost identification method relates the **cost flow** with the specific flow of physical goods, and may be used with either periodic or perpetual inventory systems. The specific cost method requires careful identification of each item; consequently, it seldom is used because of the practical limitation created by the detailed records that are required.

One undesirable feature of the method is the possibility of income manipulation by arbitrary selection of items at time of sale. To illustrate, assume three identical stereo sets are available for sale. Their costs are $400, $420, and $426. One is sold for $600. In this instance, reported cost of goods sold (and reported income) would depend upon the particular unit selected for sale. Thus, the specific cost method often lacks objectivity in application. However, this method is essential in situations where individual units have unique characteristics which, by their relative appeal to customers, determine which unit is sold. With automobiles or rare gems, for example, this method should be used because the unique characteristics of such inventories reduces the possibility for income manipulation.

AVERAGE COST

The average cost method is based on the position that the cost of inventory on hand at the end of a period and the cost of goods sold during a period should be broadly representative of the costs incurred during the period. The concept of average cost is applied in two ways, depending upon the inventory system: *(a)* periodic inventory system—weighted-average unit cost for the period; and *(b)* perpetual inventory system—moving average unit cost.

Weighted-Average Cost

This method is used with the periodic inventory system. Under this method a weighted-average unit cost is computed at the end of the period by using the unit purchase costs and the number of units in the beginning inventory and purchases for the period.

EXHIBIT 8–3: Inventory—Weighted-Average Cost (periodic inventory system)

	Units	Unit Price	Total Cost
Goods available:			
Jan. 1 Inventory	200	$1.00	$ 200
9 Purchase	300	1.10	330
15 Purchase	400	1.16	464
24 Purchase	100	1.26	126
Total	1,000	1.12*	1,120
Cost of goods sold at weighted-average cost:			
Jan. 10	400	1.12	448
18	300	1.12	336
	700		784
Ending inventory at weighted-average cost:			
Jan. 31	300	1.12	$ 336

* Weighted-average unit cost ($1,120 ÷ 1,000 = $1.12).

The weighted unit cost is applied to *(a)* the units in the ending inventory and *(b)* the units sold (to derive cost of goods sold). Exhibit 8–3 illustrates application of the weighted-average method using the data given in Exhibit 8–1. In Exhibit 8–3, the weighted-average unit cost is derived by dividing the total cost for goods available for sale by the total number of units available.

Evaluation of the Weighted-Average Cost Method. The weighted-average method is objective, consistent, not subject to manipulation, and relatively easy to apply. The method is appropriate for **periodic** inventory systems because *(a)* the inventory of physical units is not determined (counted) until the end of the period and *(b)* the weighted-average unit cost can be determined only at the end of the period. Thus, the measurements necessary to compute ending inventory and cost of goods sold are determined at the same time, at the end of the accounting period.

Moving Average Cost

When a perpetual inventory system is used, the weighted-average approach cannot be applied because a weighted unit cost cannot be calculated until the end of the period. To overcome this problem, a **moving** weighted-average unit cost is used because the **moving** average provides a new unit cost **after each purchase.** Thus, when goods are sold or issued, the moving average unit cost existing at that time is used. Application of the moving average concept in a **perpetual inventory system** is shown in Exhibit 8–4 (based on data from Exhibit 8–1). Note that the moving average unit cost is computed directly in the inventory record after **each purchase,** thus facilitating the current costing of issues during the period. For example, on January 9, the $1.06 moving average cost was derived by dividing the total cost ($530) by the total units (500), and so forth. The ending inventory of 300 units is costed at the latest moving average unit cost of $1.18 (total $354). Cost of goods sold is the sum of the Issued, Total Cost column, $766 (i.e., $424 + $342).

Evaluation of Moving Average Cost Method. The moving average method is objective, consistent, and not subject to manipulation. It is appropriate for **perpetual** inventory systems because it provides a current average cost on a continuous basis.

Overall Evaluation of the Average Cost Methods

The average cost methods do not match the latest unit cost with sales revenue. Rather, they match the average costs of the period against revenue and value ending inventory at average cost. Therefore, they generally provide inventory and cost of goods sold amounts between the LIFO and FIFO extremes. The amounts on the balance sheet (ending inventory) and on the income statement (cost of goods sold) are consistent as to valuation. Many accountants favor the use of average costs (versus FIFO or LIFO) be-

EXHIBIT 8–4: Inventory—Moving Average Cost (perpetual inventory system)

Date	Received			Issued			Balance		
	Units	Unit Cost	Total Cost	Units	Unit Cost	Total Cost	Units	Unit Cost	Total Cost
Jan. 1							200	$1.00	$200
9	300	$1.10	$330				500	1.06*	530
10				400	$1.06	$424	100	1.06	106
15	400	1.16	464				500	1.14*	570
18				300	1.14	342	200	1.14	228
24	100	1.26	126				300	1.18*	354

* New average computed.

cause extreme values for inventory and cost of goods sold are avoided.

FIRST-IN, FIRST-OUT COST

The first-in, first-out method (FIFO) is based on the position that the first goods purchased or manufactured should be the first units costed out upon sale or issuance. Since the costs are "flowed out" in the same order they flowed in, goods sold (or issued) are costed at the **oldest** unit cost and the goods remaining in inventory are costed at the **newer** unit cost amounts. Application of FIFO requires the identification of **inventory layers** for the different unit costs. FIFO can be used with either periodic or perpetual inventory systems.

Using the data given in Exhibit 8–1 and a physical inventory count at the end of the period, FIFO results would be determined as shown in Exhibit 8–5.

EXHIBIT 8–5: Inventory—FIFO Cost (periodic inventory system)

	Beginning inventory (200 units @ $1)		$ 200
	Add purchases during period (computed above)		920
	Goods available		1,120
Inventory Computation (FIFO)	Deduct ending inventory (300 units per physical inventory count):		
	100 units @ $1.26 (most recent purchase)	$126	
	200 units @ $1.16 (next most recent purchase)	232	
	Total inventory		358
	Cost of goods sold (or issued)		$ 762

The same data are used in Exhibit 8–6 to illustrate the application of FIFO with a perpetual inventory system. Note that the maintenance of inventory layers throughout the period is necessary to assign the appropriate cost to each issue.

When FIFO is used with a **perpetual** inventory system, the issues on the inventory record may be costed out either *(a)* currently throughout the period (i.e., each time there is a withdrawal) or *(b)* all at the end of the period, with the same results. In Exhibit 8–6 issues from inventory on January 10 and 18 (FIFO basis) were costed out as they occurred (i.e., currently). If the costs had not been assigned to issues currently but instead had been assigned at the end of the period, the ending inventory would still have been valued at the same $358; that is, at the costs of obtaining the most recently acquired units (100 @ $1.26 plus 200 @ $1.16). Moreover, FIFO produces the same cost of ending inventory regardless of whether a periodic or a perpetual system is used (compare Exhibits 8–5 and 8–6). In contrast, we shall see in the next section that LIFO usually produces different ending inventory amounts, depending upon whether a periodic or a perpetual system is used.

Evaluation of FIFO Cost Method. FIFO is widely used for inventory costing purposes because *(a)* it is easy to apply, *(b)* it is adaptable to either periodic or perpetual inventory procedures, *(c)* it produces an inventory amount for the balance sheet that approximates current cost, *(d)* the flow of cost **tends** to be consistent with the usual physical flow of goods, *(e)* it is systematic and objective, and *(f)* it is not subject to manipulation. The fundamental weakness of FIFO is that it does not match **current cost** of goods sold with current revenues; rather the oldest unit costs are matched with the current sales revenue. Thus, when costs are rising, reported income under FIFO tends to be higher than under LIFO or average cost.[2] This phenomenon often is referred to as "inventory profits." The measure of the so-called inventory profits is the difference between **actual** cost of goods sold at (actual) FIFO costs and cost of goods sold measured hypothetically at the current cost of goods sold (discussed in Chapter 24). The income tax implications of FIFO also can be serious—when prices are rising, companies that use FIFO report more income than those using LIFO or average cost. Consequently, FIFO users pay more income taxes currently when prices are rising (other things being equal). For example, *The Wall Street Journal* reported that Minnesota Mining and Manufacturing Company, which used FIFO during 1974–78, paid $118 million in income tax that it could have saved during those years by using LIFO. By contrast, its competitor Eastman Kodak used LIFO during

[2] When costs are falling, reported income is lower under FIFO than under LIFO or average.

EXHIBIT 8–6: Inventory—FIFO Cost (perpetual inventory system)

Date	Received			Issued			Balance		
	Units	Unit Cost	Total Cost	Units	Unit Cost	Total Cost	Units	Unit Cost	Total Cost
Jan. 1							200	$1.00	$200
9	300	$1.10	$330				200 300	1.00 1.10	200 330
10				200 200	$1.00 1.10	$200 220	100	1.10	110
15	400	1.16	464				100 400	1.10 1.16	110 464
18				100 200	1.10 1.16	110 232	200	1.16	232
24	100	1.26	126				200 100	1.16 1.26	232} 126} $358

1974–78 and during that period saved $204 million in tax payments.[3]

LAST-IN, FIRST-OUT COST

The last-in, first-out (LIFO) method of inventory costing is based on the position that the latest unit acquisition cost should be matched with current sales revenue. Consequently, under LIFO, the cost **outflows** are the inverse of the cost **inflows** (the opposite of FIFO). The units remaining in ending inventory are costed at the oldest unit costs available; the units in cost of goods sold are costed at the newest unit costs available. LIFO application requires the use of inventory layers for the different unit costs.

Although the LIFO concept is simple, its application is somewhat tedious because of the inverse relationship between the flow of costs into and out of inventory. The detailed recordkeeping is particularly onerous when LIFO is used with a perpetual inventory system and LIFO costs are determined continuously throughout the period (illustrated in Exhibit 8–8).

Finally, one condition for using LIFO for income tax purposes (to obtain the cash flow advantage of LIFO when costs are rising) is that the taxpayer (i.e., entity) also must use LIFO for financial reporting purposes.[4] Therefore, accounting for inventory under LIFO includes complying with tax regulations, which adds complexity.

This section will present the LIFO concept assuming a **single-product** situation, which means separate application of LIFO to each unit cost for each separate product (as opposed to aggregating similar products into inventory "pools").[5] For instructional purposes, a single product is used to illustrate the basic LIFO concepts. Part B discusses and illustrates an aggregation method, called dollar value LIFO, which is how LIFO often is applied in practice.

[3] For details, see G. C. Biddle, "Manager's Journal," *The Wall Street Journal,* January 19, 1981, editorial page. The income tax may be "saved" only temporarily; at some later date (e.g., if the inventory is liquidated) the tax would be paid, other things being equal (see pages 259 & 263).

[4] As recently as July 1979, the Internal Revenue Code precluded companies which used LIFO for income tax purposes from even disclosing **in supplementary form** any earnings measured on a basis other than LIFO. To allow companies to comply with the FASB requirement to disclose income on a current cost basis (discussed in Chapter 24), the Internal Revenue Service (IRS) proposed in July 1979 to amend its LIFO conformity regulation (the proposed amendment would permit companies to disclose inventories and income on a current cost basis even if they used LIFO for tax purposes). Moreover, the IRS announcement said that taxpayers may rely on the proposed regulation in preparing financial statements.

[5] This application is variously called the **quantity, specific goods,** or **unit** LIFO method of applying the LIFO concept.

EXHIBIT 8–7: Inventory—LIFO Cost, Periodic Inventory System (costed at end of period)

	Goods available (see Exhibits 8–1 and 8–2)		$1,120
End-of-Period Inventory Computation	Deduct ending inventory (300 units per physical inventory count):		
	200 units @ $1 (oldest costs available; from Jan. 1 inventory)	$200	
	100 units @ $1.10 (next oldest costs available; from Jan. 9 purchase)	110	
	Ending inventory		310
(LIFO)	Cost of goods sold		$ 810

EXHIBIT 8–8: Perpetual Inventory Record (LIFO cost illustrated—costed currently)

Date	Received			Issued or Sold			Balance		
	Units	Unit Cost	Total Cost	Units	Unit Cost	Total Cost	Units	Unit Cost	Total Cost
Jan. 1							200	$1.00	$200
9	300	$1.10	$330				200 300	1.00 1.10	200 330
10				300 100	$1.10 1.00	$330 100	100	1.00	100
15	400	1.16	464				100 400	1.00 1.16	100 464
18				300	1.16	348	100 100	1.00 1.16	100 116
24	100	1.26	126				100 100 100	1.00 1.16 1.26	100 116 126
Ending inventory →									$342
Cost of goods sold →						$778			

LIFO may be applied with either a periodic or perpetual inventory system. Assuming a **periodic inventory system** and a physical inventory of units at the **end of the period,** LIFO results would be determined as shown in Exhibit 8–7.

When LIFO is applied with a **perpetual inventory system,** the sales (issues) are costed **currently** throughout the period (i.e., each time a sale occurs).[6] Under LIFO, the timing of the costing of sales is important; that is, costing currently usually results in a different inventory valuation and cost of goods sold amount vis-à-vis costing at the end of a period. The **internal** application of LIFO with a **perpetual** inventory system (i.e., costed currently during the period) is shown in Exhibit 8–8. Exhibit 8–8 also illustrates the tedious nature of LIFO inventory computations.

Observe that cost of goods sold and ending inventory each are different between Exhibits 8–7 and 8–8 by $32 (i.e., $342–$310), which is caused by the costing at year-end (periodic system) versus costing during the year (perpetual system). Exhibit 8–9 also is presented along with Exhibits 8–7 and 8–8 to demonstrate why this difference occurs.

The items shown in **bold-face** type in Exhibit 8–9 were entered at the **end** of the period. Note that Exhibit 8–9 (costed at end of period) provides the same inventory valuation ($310) as the **periodic** inventory computation shown in Exhibit 8–7. On the other hand, Exhibit 8–8 (costed currently) provides an inventory valuation of $342. The $32 difference

[6] Throughout this discussion, we used the term **sale** to refer to the event which decreases the balance of inventory on hand. The term **issue** is synonymous with **sale** in this context. Therefore, **cost of goods sold** is synonymous with **cost of issues.**

EXHIBIT 8–9: Perpetual Inventory Record, Hypothetical (LIFO cost illustrated—costed at end of period for demonstration purposes only)

Date	Received			Issued or Sold			Balance		
	Units	Unit Cost	Total Cost	Units	Unit Cost	Total Cost	Units	Unit Cost	Total Cost
Jan. 1							200	$1.00	$200
9	300	$1.10	$330				500		
10				400*			100		
				Detail:					
				100	**$1.26**	**$126**			
				300	**1.16**	**348**			
15	400	1.16	464				500		
18				300			200		
				Detail:					
				100	**1.16**	**116**			
				200	**1.10**	**220**			
24	100	1.26	126				300		
							Detail:		
							200	**1.00**	**200**
							100	**1.10**	**110**
Ending inventory →									**$310**
Cost of goods sold →						$810			

* Since costing of sales is delayed until the end of the period, the first sale (400 units) is costed out of the last purchase (100 units at $1.26), and so on. This is inconsistent with a perpetual inventory system.

(i.e., $342 − $310) occurs because the sales on January 10 and 18 were from different inventory layers in Exhibits 8–8 and 8–9 due to the difference in the timing of costing sales. The difference between the cost of goods sold on the two records is also $32 (i.e., $810 − $778).

During periods of rising prices, LIFO costed at the end of the period will always provide a lower pretax income than will costing currently. Therefore, a company using LIFO for tax purposes would be motivated to cost at the end of the period. Because of this, if a perpetual LIFO system, costed currently, is used for internal purposes, the results usually are restated to an end-of-the-period costing basis for *(a)* income tax and *(b)* external reporting purposes.

LIFO Inventory Liquidation

A serious problem occurs under LIFO procedures when a company fails to maintain the base layer of inventory (i.e., the **beginning** inventory of the period when LIFO was first adopted by the company). To illustrate **LIFO** inventory liquidation, assume the following:

	Units	Unit Cost	Total Cost
Beginning inventory (assumed to be the base layer of LIFO inventory [year 1])	10,000	$1.00	$10,000
Purchases	40,000	1.50	60,000
Total available for sale	50,000		70,000
Sales (44,000 units, costed on LIFO basis) from:			
Purchases	40,000	1.50	60,000
Base layer of inventory	4,000	1.00	4,000
Total	44,000		64,000
Ending inventory	6,000	1.00	$ 6,000

In the above example the company failed to maintain the base year inventory position by 4,000 units. This failure may have been due to:

a. Voluntary inventory liquidation—Management may have decided to reduce normal inventory quantity for some reason, such as a decline in demand, anticipation of a decline in costs, or in anticipation of improvement in the product.[7]
b. Involuntary inventory liquidation—An inventory reduction may have been forced by uncontrollable causes, such as shortages, strikes, delayed delivery dates, or unexpected customer demands.

As a result of the liquidation of part of the base inventory, cost of goods sold includes 4,000 units with an old cost ($1 per unit) matched against current revenue. This liquidation of part of the LIFO base layer distorted reported income relative to income under the normal LIFO relationship of cost and revenue. Assuming the inventory liquidation is temporary, should the 4,000 units be costed out at $1 per unit or at some other cost? The problem is complicated because the 4,000 units will be replaced in the next period at a higher cost, for example, at $1.60 per unit. Should the restoration of the base inventory position be at $1 per unit or at $1.60 per unit? One approach that some companies use involves debiting Cost of Goods Sold with the estimated replacement cost, crediting Inventory at LIFO cost, and crediting the difference to a temporary account as follows (assuming perpetual inventory procedures):

Cost of goods sold (40,000 @ $1.50) + (4,000 @ $1.60)	66,400	
Inventory (40,000 @ $1.50) + (4,000 @ $1)		64,000
Excess of replacement cost of LIFO inventory temporarily liquidated (4,000 @ $0.60)		2,400

When the liquidated inventory is replaced (i.e., the base position restored at $1.60 per unit), the following entry is made:

Inventory (4,000 @ $1)	4,000	
Excess of replacement cost of LIFO inventory temporarily liquidated (4,000 @ $0.60)	2,400	
Accounts payable (4,000 @ $1.60)		6,400

[7] A major criticism of LIFO is that it is subject to income manipulation. For example, year-end purchasing policy can be used to (1) reduce reported income by heavy buying if prices have increased and (2) increase reported income by permitting inventories to decline and "old" low prices to be included in cost of goods sold.

If the replacement cost occurs at a price other than the estimate of $1.60 per unit, the difference represents a change in estimate. *APB Opinion No. 20,* "Accounting Changes," requires that changes in estimates be accounted for prospectively. Therefore, the difference between the actual replacement cost and the estimated replacement cost would be included in cost of goods sold for the year of replacement. Thus, if this were to occur, the last entry given above would include a debit or credit to Cost of Goods Sold.

The credit balance (i.e., $2,400) in the Excess of Replacement Cost of LIFO Inventory Temporarily Liquidated should be reported as a current liability because it represents an amount which will have to be spent to replace inventory.

There is no official pronouncement that specifies how LIFO inventory liquidation should be accounted for when it is due to operational causes, as opposed to attempts to manipulate reported income. Accountants are not in agreement as to the validity of the above procedure. There is general agreement that when an element of manipulation is involved, the above procedure is totally inappropriate. However, when LIFO liquidation occurs for reasons beyond the control of the company, such as strikes affecting suppliers, unavoidable delays in delivery, unusual and unexpected demands, and loss of inventory due to casualty, some accountants believe that it is a reasonable accounting solution to the problem. In such cases they believe it is justified to protect the integrity of the LIFO concept. Other accountants disagree on the basis that it introduces subjective values into the accounts and financial statements. As a practical matter, companies try to avoid liquidating old layers of LIFO inventory during periods of rising prices because it causes their income tax payments to increase significantly.[8]

Recording LIFO in the Accounts

Few companies which report inventory at LIFO cost use LIFO for **internal** accounting and control

[8] Some companies liquidated parts of their LIFO layers of inventory during 1980 in response to high interest rates which increased the cost of acquiring and carrying inventory. For example, General Tire & Rubber Company, which uses LIFO, decreased their inventory level during 1980. One effect of this liquidation was an increase of $6.4 million in their reported income. Another effect was payment of $2.9 million in additional income taxes which could have been avoided by maintaining inventory at beginning levels. See R. E. Winter, "Lifo's Boon of Cash Can Backfire When Companies Reduce Inventories," *The Wall Street Journal,* February 9, 1981, p. 8.

EXHIBIT 8–10: LIFO Cost Compared with FIFO Cost—Prices Rising

Basic Data Assumed

Beginning cash balance	$ 2,000
Beginning inventory balance, 5,000 units @	5 (base inventory)
Purchases during period, 5,000 units @	7
Sales during period, 5,000 units @	18
Expenses (excluding income taxes)	35,000

Income tax rate, 40%.

Comparative Results

	First-In, First-Out Units	@	Amount	Last-In, First-Out Units	@	Amount	Increase (decrease) from FIFO to LIFO
Income statement:							
Sales	5,000	$18	$90,000	5,000	$18	$90,000	-0-
Cost of goods sold	5,000	5	25,000	5,000	7	35,000	$ 10,000
Gross margin			65,000			55,000	(10,000)
Expenses			35,000			35,000	-0-
Pretax income			30,000			20,000	(10,000)
Income taxes (@ 40%)			12,000			8,000	(4,000)*
Net income			$18,000			$12,000	$ (6,000)*
Balance sheet (limited to above transactions):							
Cash (assuming all transactions were cash)			$10,000			$14,000	$ 4,000 *
Inventory			35,000			25,000	(10,000)*
Net difference (same as difference in net income)							$ (6,000)

* Critical differences.

purposes.[9] For internal and control purposes, most companies use either FIFO, average, standard, or variable costing. At the end of the period, these results are converted to LIFO for income tax purposes and for **external financial reporting.** Usually this conversion is external to the accounts. However, in some cases the results of the conversion to LIFO are entered into the accounts as a single amount by using an inventory allowance account (Allowance to Reduce Inventory to LIFO Basis).[10] This allowance is a contra account to the Inventory account. Although the Internal Revenue Code permits a company to use LIFO on the income tax return only if it is also used for its **external financial reports,** this does not require that **LIFO** must be used for internal purposes and entered into the accounts.

Comparison of LIFO with FIFO

The significant effects of LIFO may be emphasized by comparing it with FIFO. As long as unit costs remain constant, the two methods give the same results; when unit costs change materially, the two methods provide different effects on assets (inventories and cash) and net income (expenses, including income taxes). The comparative effects will depend upon the *direction* of the change in unit costs. With **rising** cost, FIFO matches low (older) costs with increased sales revenue (inflated dollars) and provides an inventory valuation approximating higher current cost, whereas LIFO matches high (newer) costs with increased sales revenue and provides an inventory valuation on a low-cost (oldest cost) basis.

Conversely, with **declining** costs, FIFO matches high (older) costs with decreased sales revenue and provides an inventory valuation approximating

[9] When LIFO is used for internal purposes and entered in the accounts, issues usually are costed **currently;** management will not delay interim costing of inventory and cost of goods sold until year-end because these amounts are needed throughout the period for internal reports.

[10] This allowance sometimes is referred to as a "LIFO Reserve." We regard this as a misuse of the term **reserve** because the account is a valuation adjustment to reduce inventory to LIFO cost. No "reserve" exists.

Inventory Flow Methods (based on 600 companies)

Methods	Number of Disclosures*					
	1979	1978	1977	1976	...	1971
First-in, first-out (FIFO)	390	392	392	389	...	333
Last-in, first-out (LIFO)	374	343	332	331	...	144
Average cost	241	224	227	232	...	220
Other	56	52	115	107	...	125
Total inventory method disclosures	1,061	1,011	1,066	1,059	...	822

* Some companies use more than one method.
Source: AICPA, *Accounting Trends & Techniques, 1980* (New York, 1980), table 2–8, p. 139; and *Trends, 1975,* table 2–9, p. 114.

lower current cost. By contrast, LIFO matches low (newer) costs with decreased sales revenue and provides an inventory valuation on a high-cost (older cost) basis.

In summary, FIFO produces a more realistic ending inventory valuation because it approximates current cost. In contrast, LIFO matches the more recent costs with revenue and hence produces a better matching of expense with revenue.

With respect to the **cash flow** effects, when prices are rising, LIFO results in lower pretax income and, consequently, less income tax; therefore, in terms of cash flows, LIFO provides an advantage over FIFO. These effects can be observed in Exhibit 8–10. The data given in that exhibit assume rising prices. Note in particular the impact of LIFO on income taxes, net income, cash, and inventory.

An interesting paradox is evident in Exhibit 8–10. FIFO produces the higher inventory and income amounts, but LIFO produces more cash because it results in less income tax. This paradox provides the basis for a glimpse into the motivations of business managers. If cash flows were the dominant factor, LIFO would be used by most companies during periods of rising prices. If reported income were the dominating factor, most companies would use FIFO. The table presented below indicates that since 1971, there has been a shift toward the use of LIFO; nevertheless, in 1979, more companies used FIFO than LIFO. What could lead so many companies to forego the cash flow advantages of LIFO during an inflationary period such as 1976–79?

Several factors could account for the use of FIFO (or other inventory costing methods than LIFO). One such factor is a debt covenant which specifies that the borrower must *(a)* maintain a certain minimum current ratio (i.e., Current assets ÷ Current liabilities) or *(b)* not exceed a certain **maximum** ratio of long-term debt to owners' equity.[11] Another debt covenant provision limits the amount of dividends a borrower can pay; the limit typically is related to the balance of Retained Earnings. When prices are rising, the use of FIFO (versus LIFO) provides more favorable ratio values (i.e., higher working capital or current ratio, lower debt-equity ratio, and lower ratio of dividends to retained earnings), which provides management with greater flexibility in managing the business. For example, a company with a debt-equity ratio of .60 may be able to obtain lower interest rates on new debt than a company with a debt-equity ratio of .90, other things equal. Similarly, "better ratios" under FIFO may enable the board of directors to declare a higher dividend than would be possible under LIFO.

A second possible factor in the selection of FIFO is a management compensation plan under which executives receive a bonus based upon reported income (cash bonus is discussed in Chapter 10 and executive stock options are discussed in Chapter 14). Because FIFO (versus LIFO) increases reported income, it probably would increase managers' compensation and, thus, motivate managers to use the FIFO method.[12]

A third factor in the selection of FIFO is the desire

[11] More precisely, the debt-equity ratio specified in debt covenants usually is the ratio of long-term debt to net tangible assets (i.e., owners' equity less intangible assets, such as goodwill). *Moody's Industrial Manual* includes summaries of debt covenants under the caption Long-Term Debt.

[12] For a discussion of this motivation, see R. L. Watts and J. L. Zimmerman, "Toward a Positive Theory of the Determination of Accounting Standards," *The Accounting Review* (January 1978), pp. 112–34, esp. p. 116. This motivation was also mentioned in a letter to the editor of *The Wall Street Journal;* see J. Cerepak, "Further Thoughts on FIFO Accounting," *The Wall Street Journal,* January 28, 1981, p. 23.

of management to report higher income in the belief that this will lead to higher prices for the company's stock. Empirical evidence suggests that when companies change **from FIFO to LIFO,** the market bids **up** their stock prices even though this accounting change usually **decreases** reported income during inflation. It is not clear whether investors are reacting to the improved cash flows that result from the tax saving resulting from the change or to other factors.[13] However, the important point is that stock prices did **not** decrease in response to the decrease in reported income caused by the change. These findings suggest that investors look beyond the cosmetic effects of accounting methods and act upon real economic effects, such as cash flow effects. Therefore, it appears unlikely that business managers would select the FIFO method solely in an attempt to manipulate stock prices.

Because of a continuing worldwide inflationary trend and the pervasiveness of income taxes, an increasing number of companies have shifted to LIFO (see the tabulation of Inventory Flow Methods given earlier). In addition to the tax factor discussed above, arguments generally cited for LIFO are (1) it provides a better matching of current costs with current revenue, and (2) it reflects the usual pricing policy of an enterprise—raise selling prices when replacement cost increases even though there are goods still on hand at the old lower cost.

The primary arguments generally cited against LIFO are (1) it understates assets—the inventory on the balance sheet is costed at old, out-of-date unit costs; (2) it does not precisely match replacement cost with revenue; (3) it is subject to manipulation—profits can be manipulated by changing the usual purchasing patterns (e.g., in a period of rapidly rising prices, a company can significantly decrease its reported income by making large purchases at year-end or increase reported income by delaying purchases); (4) it is subject to involuntary inventory liquidation which can cause reported income to exceed "normal" levels significantly; (5) cost flows do not correspond to the physical flow of goods; and (6) it is complex and costly to apply.

The tax advantage of LIFO is transitory when old layers of inventory are liquidated. Because LIFO (like FIFO and average cost methods) is based on **cost,** a company that uses LIFO has the same total pretax income over time as a company that uses FIFO or average cost if all inventory layers are ultimately liquidated. However, to the extent that old layers remain in ending inventory (i.e., are never liquidated), the tax advantage of LIFO remains intact. Therefore, the tax advantage of LIFO involves the timing of the recognition of expense (i.e., cost of goods sold) and, hence, is based on the **time value of money.**

[13] See S. Sunder, "Accounting Changes in Inventory Valuation," *The Accounting Review,* April 1975, pp. 305–15; and A. R. Abdel-Khalik and J. C. McKeown, "Understanding Accounting Changes in an Efficient Market: Evidence of Differential Reaction," *The Accounting Review,* October 1978, pp. 851–68.

MISCELLANEOUS INVENTORY COST FLOW METHODS

Numerous methods for determining the cost of inventory, in addition to those discussed above, have been proposed. Except in a few very unusual situations, none of these has been accepted under GAAP for external financial reporting purposes. However, some of them are used for **internal cost accounting** purposes. As background, these methods are discussed briefly in Supplement 8–A.

Part B: Application of LIFO—Dollar Value LIFO

INVENTORY POOLS

Part A discussed and illustrated LIFO under the quantity of goods approach, in which LIFO is applied to individual units of each separate product. In actual practice, LIFO usually is applied to groups, or **pools,** of similar products rather than to individual products. For example, a building materials company could have different inventory pools for *(a)* wood products, *(b)* masonry products, *(c)* roofing materials, *(d)* hardware, and *(e)* paints (rather than for a long list of individual items). Application of LIFO to pools has two major advantages, which are discussed below.

1. Application of LIFO to pools reduces the probability of liquidating an old LIFO layer of inventory. As discussed in Part A, when ending inven-

tory is less than beginning inventory, this causes older costs from prior periods to be reflected in cost of goods sold. When prices are rising, this inventory liquidation can cause a significant **decrease** in cost of goods sold and **increase** in reported income, relative to normal LIFO results (i.e., in the absence of liquidation). Because the tax consequences of LIFO liquidation can be severe, companies often apply LIFO costing to inventory pools to reduce the probability of liquidation. The logic of the pool concept is that, within an inventory pool, the amounts of some items may increase and the amounts of other items may decrease. If the size of the pool is stable or increasing, liquidation will not occur for the pool.

2. Application of LIFO to pools reduces the accounting cost of applying LIFO. The complexity of applying LIFO to individual units is not apparent in the simplified illustrations of Part A. When applied to hundreds of different types of items, each type of which may be represented by thousands of individual items, the accounting costs may be significant. In contrast, the application of LIFO to pools of similar items reduces accounting costs by reducing the level of detail.

Although the inventory **pool** approach can be applied to the **quantity of goods LIFO** approach (Part A) on a limited basis (i.e., when two or more products are almost identical), the primary method of implementing the inventory pool approach in practice is known as **dollar value LIFO.** "Dollar value" in the title refers to the fact that inventory is accounted for in **pools of dollars** in which individual **units** lose their identities for accounting purposes. The objective of using the dollar value method of LIFO is to *(a)* maximize the LIFO effect, *(b)* reduce the cost of accounting for inventory at LIFO, and *(c)* minimize the chance of unintentional liquidation of LIFO inventory.

Part B of this chapter is organized as follows:

1. Dollar value LIFO method.
   a. Variations in applying dollar value LIFO method.
   b. Inventory liquidation with dollar value LIFO.
   c. Technological changes in LIFO inventories.
   d. Indexing.
2. Initial adoption of LIFO.
3. LIFO allowances.

DOLLAR VALUE LIFO METHOD

Dollar value LIFO, in contrast to the quantity of goods approach, bases the LIFO inventory computations on *(a)* **dollars** of inventory, *(b)* a **specific price index** for each year, and *(c)* broad **inventory pools.** The inventory layers are identified with the price index for the year in which the layer was added. Thus, dollar value LIFO is **not** a distinctly different inventory method; rather it is an approach for computing the LIFO cost of the ending inventory and cost of goods sold each period.

Dollar value LIFO is an approach for **converting** the ending inventory results derived by another method (such as FIFO or average) to a LIFO basis. Typically, a company using dollar value LIFO for income tax and external financial statement purposes will be using another method (usually FIFO or average) in the internal inventory accounts. The problem is to convert the results generated by the internal inventory records to the dollar value LIFO basis.

The dollar value LIFO method can be illustrated by a simple example. Assume the inventory records showed that the FIFO cost of the beginning inventory, stated in beginning-of-period dollars, was $100,000 (i.e., 100,000 units @ $1), and that the FIFO cost of the ending inventory, stated in end-of-period dollars, was $120,000 (i.e., 100,000 units @ $1.20). Because the number of units in inventory remained constant, the $20,000 increase in the FIFO inventory amount resulted solely from an increase in the unit cost of inventory (i.e., from $1 to $1.20). In an actual situation, there may be hundreds or even thousands of different items in the inventory records maintained on a FIFO basis. Assume the company desires to use the **LIFO basis** for external reporting and income tax purposes. The conversion of the hundreds or thousands of FIFO inventory amounts to LIFO amounts would be a formidable task. The dollar value LIFO method is designed to make this conversion without use of the multitude of unit quantity and unit cost data. Rather, it makes the conversion based on *(a)* the beginning and ending **dollar amounts** of inventory cost and *(b)* the change in the **inventory price index** during the period.

Returning to the example given above, the dollar value LIFO **conversion from the FIFO basis to the LIFO basis** would involve the following steps:

1. Obtain the FIFO inventory data in dollars only *(a)* at the beginning of the year ($100,000) and *(b)* at the end of the year ($120,000). Note that no quantity or unit cost data are needed.
2. Compute the inventory price index for the period. The index is $120,000 ÷ $100,000 = 1.2, which indicates that the ratio of ending prices to beginning prices is 1.2 to 1.
3. Restate ending inventory at LIFO cost by dividing the FIFO cost of ending inventory (i.e., $120,000) by the price index for the period (i.e., 1.2). The result, $100,000, represents the **LIFO cost of ending inventory.**

The validity of this procedure can be verified from the following facts:

1. If the quantity of inventory on hand remains unchanged during the period, the LIFO cost also should remain unchanged. If the quantity changes, the LIFO cost also should change.
2. In this example, the increase in FIFO cost (i.e., from $100,000 to $120,000) resulted solely from an increase in the unit cost of inventory, as reflected by the period's price index, 1.2.
3. Because the quantity of inventory did not change during the period, the LIFO cost did not change; it remained at $100,000.

If additional layers of inventory are added in later years, the layers are added at the actual costs incurred in those later years to acquire inventory. The examples which follow illustrate both the addition of inventory layers and the liquidation of older layers.

The discussions and illustrations of dollar value LIFO will be based on the conversion of FIFO inventory results to dollar value LIFO for Tye Company for years 19B and 19C. The FIFO results for each of these years are shown in Exhibit 8–11.[14] In Exhibit 8–11 it is assumed that Tye Company used FIFO for all purposes in 19A. In 19B, the company switched to LIFO for income tax and external reporting purposes but continued using FIFO for internal purposes only. Therefore, the ending 19A inventory, at FIFO cost, becomes the **base layer** of LIFO inventory to start 19B. In practice, the base layer of LIFO inventory would be determined in this way because of the practical impossibility of reconstructing the base layer of inventory at LIFO cost on the date a company began its operations.

Application of the dollar value LIFO method involves the following two distinct phases:

Phase A—computation of a conversion price index for each period. Conversion price indexes are used to convert inventory costs, under whatever inventory method is used for internal purposes (FIFO in this case), to a LIFO basis. Tax regulations and GAAP require that a conversion price index be used that is **specific** to each particular inventory pool within the company as opposed to an external index or a general price index.[15] This requirement means that an internal conversion price index for each inventory pool must be computed each period based upon the change in costs as reflected in the internal inventory and purchase records of the company. The internal conversion price index for an inventory pool must be computed on the basis of actual inventory costs (FIFO basis in this case) as follows:

$$\frac{\text{Ending FIFO inventory for period valued at } \textbf{current year} \text{ actual cost}}{\text{Ending FIFO inventory for period valued at } \textbf{base year} \text{ actual costs}} = \text{Conversion price index for current year}$$

Computation of the internal conversion price index is illustrated for Tye Company in Phase A of Exhibits 8–12 and 8–13 for years 19B and 19C.

Phase B—conversion of the FIFO costs to LIFO costs by using the conversion index numbers computed in Phase A. Conversion requires that each inventory pool be costed at both **base period** costs and **current period** costs. When the total dollar amount of the ending inventory for the current period at base year costs exceeds the dollar total of the beginning inventory for that period, at base year costs, an incremental **inventory layer has been added.** If the difference is less, some inventory **liquidation** has occurred. Any incremental inventory layer, stated at base year cost, then must be converted to current year costs by using the con-

[14] Throughout these discussions we will assume FIFO is used internally; however, other quantity of goods methods, based on cost, could have been assumed. The IRS requires that the internal inventory records be maintained in such manner as to facilitate audits.

[15] An exception to this requirement is explained in a later section, Indexing.

EXHIBIT 8–11: Tye Company—Illustrative Data, FIFO Basis

a. Ending inventory, FIFO basis (per internal inventory accounts; assume two products, A and B, will comprise the inventory pool):

	Product A			Product B			
	Units	Cost	Total	Units	Cost	Total	Total Amount
Year 19A:							
Ending inventory (FIFO)*							
Layer 1	1,000	$1.00	$1,000	2,000	$2.00	$ 4,000	
Layer 2				500	2.20	1,100	
	1,000	$1.00	$1,000	2,500	$2.04	$ 5,100	$6,100
Year 19B:							
Purchases†	3,000	$1.20	$3,600	4,000	$2.50	$10,000	
Sales	(2,800)			(3,500)			
Ending inventory: FIFO	1,200	1.20	1,440	3,000	2.50	7,500	$8,940
Year 19C:							
Purchases†	3,300	1.30	4,290	4,200	2.60	10,920	
Sales	(3,200)			(4,200)			
Ending inventory: FIFO	1,300	1.30	1,690	3,000	2.60	7,800	$9,490

b. FIFO is continued in the internal inventory accounts and for internal management purposes.
c. LIFO was adopted at the start of 19B for (1) income tax purposes and (2) external financial statement purposes.
d. At the end of each year the FIFO results will be converted to dollar value LIFO results.

* Beginning inventory for the year of adoption of LIFO.
† Totals for the year; thus, the unit purchase costs are annual averages.

version price index. Thus, each LIFO inventory layer (in dollars only) is **directly identified** with the conversion price index that was computed for the year in which the layer was added. There is no identification of units or unit costs (as distinguished from quantity of goods LIFO). If the dollar amount of the inventory decreases during the year, the reduction is taken from the most recent layers, that is, in LIFO order.

The FIFO inventory data for Tye Company given in Exhibit 8–11 were used to apply the dollar value LIFO method for year 19B in Exhibit 8–12 and for year 19C in Exhibit 8–13. You should trace the data from Exhibit 8–11 for each year through:

Phase A—Computation of the internal price index; and

Phase B—Conversion of FIFO costs to dollar value LIFO costs.

In both phases of Exhibits 8–12 and 8–13, the ending FIFO inventory is **double costed:** at current year cost and at base year cost. The ratio between these two amounts represents the conversion price index for the current year because it measures the change in inventory costs since the base year. The base year is assigned a **base index** of 1.00, and subsequent changes are measured in terms of that year. Also, observe that the two products are considered to be one inventory pool. In an actual application, a typical inventory pool includes many different products. In Phase B the various inventory layers, identified by year and expressed in base year costs, are restated to actual costs by year of accumulation to derive the dollar value LIFO inventory amount.

The following table compares the results of FIFO with the results of dollar value LIFO for Tye Company for year 19C:

	Year 19C—Cost of Goods Sold Compared for—	
	FIFO—for Internal Purposes (Exhibit 8–11)	Dollar Value LIFO—for External Purposes (Exhibit 8–13)
Beginning inventory	$ 8,940	$ 7,590
Purchases	15,210	15,210
Total	24,150	22,800
Ending inventory	9,490	7,718
Cost of goods sold	$14,660	$15,082

EXHIBIT 8–12: Tye Company—Conversion of FIFO Results to LIFO Basis—Year 19B (dollar value LIFO method)

Phase A—Computation of internal conversion price index (based on FIFO results provided by internal inventory records of Tye Company—per Exhibit 8–11)—19B:

	Inventory at Current Year Cost	÷	Inventory at Base Year Cost	=	Conversion Price Index
Base LIFO inventory (from 19A)	$6,100	÷	$6,100	=	1.00
Ending inventory:					
Product A	1,200 @ $1.20 = $1,440		1,200 @ $1.00 = $1,200		
Product B	3,000 @ 2.50 = 7,500		3,000 @ 2.04 = 6,120		
Totals	$8,940	÷	$7,320	=	1.221

Phase B—Conversion of FIFO costs to dollar value LIFO costs—19B:

	FIFO at Base Year Cost	×	Conversion Price Index	=	LIFO Results
19B ending FIFO inventory per above (current year FIFO cost, $8,940)	$ 7,320				
Base inventory layer	(6,100)	×	1.00	=	$6,100
Difference: 19B additional layer	$ 1,220	×	1.221	=	1,490
19B dollar value LIFO ending inventory					$7,590*

* Report this cost on the 19B balance sheet and use to compute 19B cost of goods sold.

EXHIBIT 8–13: Tye Company—Conversion of FIFO Results to LIFO Basis—Year 19C (dollar value LIFO method)

Phase A—Computation of internal conversion price index (based on FIFO results provided by internal inventory records of Tye Company—per Exhibit 8–11)—19C:

	Inventory at Current Year Cost	÷	Inventory at Base Year Cost	=	Conversion Price Index
Ending inventory:					
Product A	1,300 @ $1.30 = $1,690		1,300 @ $1.00 = $1,300		
Product B	3,000 @ 2.60 = 7,800		3,000 @ 2.04 = 6,120		
Totals	$9,490	÷	$7,420	=	1.279

Phase B—Conversion of FIFO costs to dollar value LIFO costs—19C:

	FIFO at Base Year Cost	×	Conversion Price Index	=	LIFO Results
19C ending FIFO inventory per above (current year FIFO cost, $9,490)	$ 7,420				
Base inventory layer	(6,100)	×	1.00	=	$6,100
19B inventory layer (per above)	(1,220)	×	1.221	=	1,490
Difference: 19C additional layer	$ 100	×	1.279	=	128
19C dollar value LIFO ending inventory					$7,718*

*Report this cost on the 19C balance sheet and use to compute 19C cost of goods sold.

The comparison reflects a lower ending inventory amount for 19C and a higher cost of goods sold amount for dollar value LIFO than for FIFO as would be expected. This difference causes a lower pretax income and lower income tax under LIFO.

Variations in Applying the Dollar Value LIFO Method

There are two variations of the dollar value LIFO method known as (1) double-extension and (2) link-chain approaches.[16] The presentations in Exhibits 8–12 and 8–13 are based on the double-extension approach, which is more common.

The designation **double extension** is based upon the fact that under dollar value LIFO, the ending inventory each period must be double costed (i.e., at base year costs and at current year costs) in both phases of the conversion process.

Dollar value LIFO may be applied on the basis of either:

a. A single pool—A single pool is used for the entire company when (1) the company is a manufacturer or processor and (2) overall operations constitute a "natural business unit." Thus, an automobile manufacturer may use a single pool that would encompass raw materials, component parts, work in process, and finished goods (as if it were one big inventory item).

b. Multiple pools—Each pool encompasses a group of inventory items that are **similar** in respect to raw materials, manufacturing, and distribution. A separate inventory pool is formed for each "natural business" **subunit** of the company. Manufacturers may use either single pool or multiple pools; however, retailers, wholesalers, and jobbers must use multiple pools. For example, a large department store may have separate inventory pools for men's clothing, ladies' clothing, home appliances, and so on.

Because of the higher degree of aggregation and the attendant likelihood of avoiding some liquidation of the base layer, single pool generally is preferred to multiple pools where there is a choice.

[16] The link-chain variation was designed for restrictive situations with which the double-extension variation does not satisfactorily cope (e.g. significant technological changes in the inventory, discussed later). Link chain and double extension are not alternatives for the same set of facts. Because of its limited use and because the computations are similar, the link-chain variation is not discussed and illustrated here.

Inventory Liquidation with Dollar Value LIFO

Frequently, full or partial **liquidation** (or invasion) of one or more of the prior years' dollar value LIFO layers of inventory will occur. Inventory liquidation is taken from the most recent layers in LIFO order. For each layer invaded, the subtraction is based on the conversion price index for the year that the layer was added to inventory. Thus, the dollar value method requires careful accounting for each layer in terms of the index applicable to that layer. **Layers, once liquidated, are never added back.**

To illustrate, assume Tye Company's sales of product A (Exhibit 8–11) for 19C amounted to 3,500 units (instead of 3,200). The 3,500 units would cause the 19C ending inventory to be 1,000 units of product A (instead of 1,300 units). Thus, 200 units of the product A inventory layer added in 19B were liquidated in 19C. The 19C FIFO inventory results would be as follows:

19C ending FIFO inventory:		
Product A	1,000 units @ $1.30 =	$1,300
Product B	3,000 units @ 2.60 =	7,800
Total		$9,100

The conversion computations would be as follows:

Phase A—To compute internal conversion price index for 19C:

	Inventory at Current Year Cost	÷	Inventory at Base Year Cost	=	Conversion Price Index
Product A	1,000 @ $1.30 = $1,300		1,000 @ $1.00 = $1,000		
Product B	3,000 @ 2.60 = 7,800		3,000 @ 2.04 = 6,120		
Total	$9,100	÷	$7,120	=	1.278

Phase B—To convert FIFO results to dollar value LIFO results for 19C:

	FIFO at Base Year Cost	×	Conversion Price Index	=	LIFO Results
19C ending inventory per above (current year FIFO cost $9,100)	$7,120				
Base inventory layer	(6,100)	×	1.00	=	$6,100
19B inventory layer remaining	$1,020*	×	1.221	=	1,245
19C dollar value LIFO ending inventory					$7,345

* There was no 19C layer added, and there was a partial liquidation of the 19B layer of $1,220 − $1,020 = $200 (at base year cost).

Technological Changes in LIFO Inventories

The problem caused by technological changes in LIFO inventories is a special case of inventory liquidation. That is, as technology advances, older products (and product lines) are dropped and new products are added. When LIFO is applied using the quantity of goods approach (Part A) and liquidation of older LIFO layers occurs, the older costs are moved out of inventory to cost of goods sold. The effect of this de facto liquidation is mitigated under dollar value LIFO because of the grouping of inventory into pools. For this reason, dollar value LIFO, and its concept of inventory pools in particular, represents a practical solution to inventory liquidation caused by technological changes in inventories. Supplement 8–B discusses and illustrates how dollar value LIFO mitigates the liquidation problem from technological change in inventories.

Indexing

In the preceding discussions and illustrations of dollar value LIFO, the indexes used were **internal indexes,** computed from the internal inventory data of the company. Computation of an internal index each period required that *(a)* unit cost data and *(b)* physical quantity data for the ending inventory be available for each item in the inventory pool. In complex situations, it may not be cost effective to generate unit quantity and cost data for all items in inventory. In such situations, the index might be derived in another way, viz:

1. Internal index computed on a sampling basis—In situations where determination of detailed unit data for each item in the **entire** inventory pool is impractical (because of technological changes, wide variety of items, or extreme fluctuations in the variety of items), the tax regulations state that an internal index may be computed by using a "representative portion of the inventory pool, or by use of other sound and consistent statistical methods." When this internal sampling approach is used, computation of the internal index is the same as illustrated in Exhibits 8–12 and 8–13, Phase A, except that **sample data** rather than total data are used.
2. External index—In situations where **neither** the entire ending inventory pool nor statistical sampling of the pool is feasible for computing an internal index, an **appropriate external price index** may be used. This situation often is difficult to justify to the IRS. The selection of an external price index avoids the detailed index computations illustrated in Exhibits 8–12 and 8–13, Phase A. Therefore, only Phase B computations are necessary. The use of an **external conversion price index** in the dollar value LIFO approach is referred to as "indexing."

INITIAL ADOPTION OF LIFO

Income tax regulations permit taxpayers to use LIFO for all or part of the total inventory of goods (e.g., for manufacturers—raw materials, work in process, finished goods; for retailers and wholesalers—merchandise for sale). In the typical LIFO situation, the company has changed from some other method to LIFO for **tax** and **external** reporting purposes.

The switch to LIFO involves a change in accounting principle as described in *APB Opinion No. 20,* "Accounting Changes." Paragraph 20 of that *Opinion* requires that the **cumulative** effect of a change in accounting principle be shown between the captions Income before extraordinary items and Net income. However, paragraph 26 of that *Opinion* does not require measurement of the cumulative effect when the cumulative effect is impossible to measure. The specific example given in that paragraph is a change from FIFO to LIFO[17] because it is virtually impossible to reconstruct the exact composition of old inventory cost layers that the company would have reported in prior periods if it had been using LIFO all along (this kind of change is discussed and illustrated in Chapter 20, Part A). The difficulty of computing the cumulative effect of a change to LIFO stems from the arbitrariness of deciding how far back in time to go to identify the base layer of LIFO inventory. Ideally, the company would go all the way back to its origin, but in most cases that is not feasible. Therefore, when a company changes to LIFO, the base year is the year in which the change is made, and the **base year LIFO cost** for the beginning inventory of the year of change (and subsequent years) is the ending inventory for the prior year. The base layer of LIFO inventory must be adjusted to cost regardless of the prior method used (Treas. Reg. §1.472–2). This means that write-downs of the prior year's ending inventory below cost (such as to LCM) must be added back because in this context LCM is not applied to LIFO.[18]

To illustrate a change to LIFO, assume X Company has been using FIFO for all purposes. The company decided to change to LIFO for income tax and external reporting purposes starting in 19D. FIFO will be continued in the internal inventory accounts. The 19D financial statements for X Company provided the following disclosure of the effects of its change from FIFO to LIFO starting in 19D:

FIFO inventory at end of 19C	$1,000,000
FIFO inventory at end of 19D	1,344,000
LIFO inventory at end of 19D	1,224,000
Financial statements for 19D:	
Balance sheet:	
Inventories, at LIFO cost (see Note 4)	1,224,000

Note 4: At the beginning of the current year (19D) the company changed its inventory measurement basis from FIFO to LIFO. Had the FIFO method been continued during 19D, the ending inventory would have been $1,344,000 − $1,224,000 = $120,000 higher than reported in the attached statements. The net effect of the change to LIFO in 19D was to reduce net income (after income taxes) by $120,000 × (1 − .40) = $72,000 (approximately $x.xx per share). Pro forma effects of retroactive application are not realistically determinable.

The management believes that the newly adopted inventory measurement method will attain a better matching of current expenses with current revenues.

LIFO ALLOWANCES

Companies using LIFO for tax and external reporting purposes and some other method, such as FIFO, for internal purposes, sometimes employ a LIFO allowance account (often inappropriately called a LIFO "reserve" account) to reflect the difference between the two inventory amounts.

To illustrate, Allegheny Ludlum Industries, Inc., reported inventories as follows (items boxed are for emphasis):

ALLEGHENY LUDLUM INDUSTRIES, INC. (DEC)

($000)	1979	1978
Current assets:		
Cash	$ 1,680	$ 9,577
Notes and accounts receivable—trade, less allowance for doubtful accounts of $4,133,000 ($5,140,000 at December 31, 1978)	219,361	163,197
Sundry notes and accounts receivable	27,456	47,020
Inventories	243,349	238,439
Prepaid expenses and other current assets	21,562	16,251

NOTES TO CONSOLIDATED FINANCIAL STATEMENTS

Note 1: Summary of accounting policies

Inventories—Inventories are stated at cost, which is not in excess of market. Cost is determined principally by the "last-in, first-out" method or, in the case of certain inventories, by the average cost or "first-in, first-out" methods.

---

[17] When the change is **from** LIFO to another method, the cumulative effect of the change can be measured, and, therefore, under *APB Opinion 20,* it would be disclosed. For example, if the change is from LIFO to FIFO, it is relatively easy, although computationally cumbersome, to reconstruct ending inventory of the prior period at FIFO cost.

[18] This financial accounting "rule" comes from the tax regulations, which have a significant impact on the application of LIFO.

Note 5: Inventories:
The classification of inventories follows:

	($000)	
	12/31/79	12/31/78
Finished goods	$ 48,748	$ 39,468
Work in process	227,564	183,766
Raw materials	97,515	99,640
Supplies	9,131	7,307
	382,958	330,181
Less allowance to reduce carrying value to LIFO basis	139,609	91,742
Net inventories	$243,349	$238,439

At December 31, 1979, and December 31, 1978, the cost of net inventories aggregating approximately $155,000,000 and $146,000,000, respectively, was determined on the "last-in, first-out" (LIFO) method. During 1978, certain inventory quantities were reduced, which resulted in a liquidation of applicable LIFO quantities carried at costs prevailing in prior years. The effect was to increase 1978 earnings from continuing operations by $550,000. Certain inventory quantities were again reduced in 1979 and, as a result, earnings from continuing operations were increased by $5,740,000.

Source: AICPA, *Accounting Trends & Techniques, 1980* (New York, 1980), p. 141.

Of main interest in this actual example are (1) the "allowance to reduce carrying value to LIFO basis, $139,609 and $91,742," (2) disclosure of the extent of application of LIFO, (see Notes 1 and 5), and (3) disclosure of the effects of liquidation of LIFO inventories. These items are bracketed for emphasis in the above disclosures.

SUMMARY

The discussion in Part B explained the primary complexities in applying LIFO. Because *(a)* income can be manipulated under LIFO by altering purchasing patterns near year-end and *(b)* LIFO reduces taxes when prices are rising, LIFO has received much attention from governmental agencies such as the SEC and the IRS. Also, for the same reasons, accounting firms have devoted much research to the study of LIFO. To avoid the specter of income manipulation, accountants insist that LIFO be applied consistently and that the financial statements adequately disclose effects such as *(a)* the impact of LIFO liquidation, *(b)* the extent of usage of LIFO, *(c)* differences between LIFO cost and the cost of another inventory method when inventory methods are changed, and *(d)* the income effects of accounting changes involving inventory. These items were discussed and illustrated above under the captions Initial Adoption of LIFO and LIFO Allowances.

It appears safe to predict that the use of LIFO will become more widespread because of worldwide inflation at high levels and its tax advantage. The table on page 262 indicates that of the companies included in *Accounting Trends & Techniques, 1980,* LIFO and FIFO were used with roughly equal frequency in 1979 (390 uses of FIFO, 374 uses of LIFO). The table indicates that as recently as 1971, FIFO held a much wider margin (333 uses of FIFO; 144 uses of LIFO).

On balance, a shift toward LIFO has occurred and is continuing. From an accounting standpoint, LIFO matches expense (i.e., cost of goods sold) with the revenue of the period better than the other inventory costing methods. With the advent of current cost accounting (discussed in Chapter 24), the argument that LIFO results in an unrealistic (i.e., old) measure of inventory on the balance sheet has lost a great deal of its sting. That is, many of the larger companies are now required to disclose the **current cost** of **inventory** and a **current cost** measure for **cost of goods sold** as supplements to the historical cost financial statements. Therefore, for companies affected by the current cost disclosure requirements of *FASB Statement 33,* users of financial statements now are provided both current cost as well as historical cost measures of inventory and cost of goods sold.

Supplement 8-A: Miscellaneous Cost Flow Methods

This supplement briefly discusses four inventory cost methods used less often than FIFO, LIFO, and average. The four methods discussed are next-in, first-out; base stock; standard costing; and variable, or direct, costing.

NEXT-IN, FIRST-OUT (NIFO) METHOD

NIFO refers to the concept that cost of goods sold should be costed at the unit cost anticipated for the next purchase of a like volume. The concept attempts to measure cost of goods sold as the actual cost of replacing the goods sold. It is maintained that LIFO fails to match precisely replacement cost with current revenues because the method employs the cost of the latest purchase **prior** to the actual sale. NIFO currently is **not** acceptable under GAAP.

BASE STOCK METHOD

The base stock (or normal stock) method is generally viewed as the predecessor of the LIFO method. The method assumes that there is a normal or base stock of goods that should be maintained at all times. The base stock represents a permanent commitment of resources, similar to an operational asset, that is costed at a "normal" price which is viewed as the original cost—usually the lowest cost experienced by the company. Goods must be maintained above the minimum base stock for operational purposes. These goods are viewed as temporary increments and are recorded at cost; issues should be costed out of the increment on a LIFO basis, although FIFO or average sometimes is used for practical reasons. The base stock method is illustrated in Exhibit 8–14.

EXHIBIT 8–14: Base Stock Inventory Method

	Units	Unit Cost	Amount
Base stock	10,000	$0.50	$ 5,000
Extra stock	2,000	1.20	2,400
Total beginning inventory	12,000		7,400
Purchases:			
First	2,000	1.30	2,600
Second	6,000	1.40	8,400
Total available	20,000		18,400
Ending inventory (11,000 units per count):			
Base stock	10,000	0.50	5,000
Extra stock	1,000	1.20	1,200
Total	11,000		6,200
Cost of goods sold	9,000		$12,200

The accounting purpose of using the base stock method is similar to that of last-in, first-out, that is, the matching of current costs with current revenues. The base stock method is not generally used because of the arbitrary nature of both the quantity and unit values of the assumed base stock. Essentially similar results may be obtained under LIFO as revealed in Exhibit 8–14. Like LIFO, the base stock method is subject to manipulation through selective purchasing. Erosion of the **base stock** would be treated in a manner similar to that illustrated on pages 259 and 260 for LIFO liquidation. The base stock method is not permitted for income tax purposes nor is it current GAAP.

STANDARD COST METHOD

In manufacturing entities using a standard cost system, the inventories are valued, recorded, and reported for internal purposes on the basis of a standard unit cost. The standard cost approximates an ideal or expected cost, and its use prevents the overstatement of inventory values because it excludes from inventory those losses and expenses due to inefficiency, waste, and abnormal conditions. Under this method the **differences** between actual cost (which includes losses due to inefficiencies, etc.) and standard cost (which excludes losses due to inefficiencies, etc.) are recorded in separate variance accounts which are written off as a current period "loss" rather than being capitalized in inventory. Standard costing may be applied to raw materials, work in process, and finished goods inventories. Standard costing is used more often in manufacturing situations because of its usefulness for cost control. To illustrate the use of standard costs for raw materials, assume a manufacturing company has just adopted standard cost procedures and that the beginning inventory is zero. During the current period, the company makes two purchases and one issue and records them as follows:

1. To record the purchase of 10,000 units of raw material at $1.10 actual cost; standard cost has been established at $1:

Raw materials (10,000 units @ $1)	10,000	
Raw materials purchase price variance (10,000 units @ $0.10)	1,000	
Accounts payable (10,000 units @ $1.10)		11,000

2. To record issuance of 8,000 units of raw material to the factor for processing:

Material in process	8,000	
Raw materials (8,000 units @ $1) ...		8,000

3. To record the purchase of 2,000 units of raw material at 95 cents:

Raw materials (2,000 units @ $1)	2,000	
Raw materials purchase price variance (2,000 units @ $0.05)		100
Accounts payable (2,000 units @ $0.95)		1,900

Results for the period:

Purchases at actual cost:		
10,000 units @ $1.10	$11,000	
2,000 units @ $0.95	1,900	
Total..........................		$12,900
Issues at standard cost:		
8,000 units @ $1	8,000	
Ending inventory at standard cost:		
4,000 units @ $1	4,000	12,000
Raw materials purchase price variance (debit—charged against current income as a **loss**) ($1,000–$100)		$ 900

Under the procedures illustrated above for raw material, there would be no need to consider inventory flow methods such as LIFO, FIFO, and average, because only one cost—the standard cost—appears in the records. In addition, perpetual inventory records could be maintained in **units only,** because all issues and inventory valuations are at the same standard cost. Standard cost represents a departure from the cost principle as GAAP is currently interpreted. We have included only a brief discussion because for external reporting purposes, standard cost results generally are not used except in special circumstances. Therefore, for external reporting, the standard cost inventory usually is restated by applying one of the generally accepted methods discussed above. Standard costs are widely used for **internal management** planning and control. A detailed discussion of standard cost procedures is beyond the scope of this book and can be found in any complete cost accounting textbook.

VARIABLE, OR DIRECT, COST METHOD

For **internal management** planning and control purposes, the concept of variable, or direct, costing often is used in manufacturing companies. Under this concept, fixed costs (i.e., those that tend to relate to time, such as salaries) and variable costs (i.e., those that vary with productive activities, such as direct material and direct labor) are distinctly segregated. This separation is especially useful for internal management planning and control. One important aspect of this concept is that the cost of goods manufactured is the sum of the variable costs only, that is, direct materials, direct labor, and variable manufacturing overhead. All fixed costs, including fixed manufacturing overhead, are treated as period costs and are deducted from revenues of the period when incurred rather than being capitalized and carried forward in inventory. Hence, fixed costs are not reported as part of cost of inventory or cost of goods sold.

Valuation of inventories at only variable production costs, although highly useful for internal management purposes, is not GAAP for external financial reporting purposes, nor can it be used for tax purposes except in special circumstances. Consequently, for external reporting and tax purposes, companies using variable costing for internal purposes convert the inventory and cost of goods sold to "actual" cost by using other costing methods discussed in this chapter.

Supplement 8-B: Technological Change in Inventories

In the discussions of dollar value LIFO the point was made that it provides a better way of mitigating the effect of LIFO liquidation due to **technological changes** in inventories than did quantity of goods LIFO. With respect to inventories, technological changes are of two kinds: *(a)* dropping and/or adding product lines because of obsolescence, changes in demand, supply availability, competition, and so forth; and *(b)* technological improvements in product lines, such as the move from black and white to color television.

In the quantity of goods LIFO method, the phasing out of an old product would cause the old LIFO inventory costs (usually low relative to current costs) to be moved to cost of goods sold and, when a new product is launched, to be replaced with new inventory costs which usually are much higher.

In contrast, the dollar value LIFO method, in large measure, retains the old LIFO costs when technological changes occur, because it bases the inventory calculation on dollars rather than on specific units. When an old product is replaced in the inventory pool, the base inventory amount is continued. When a new product is added to the inventory pool, a **reconstructed** cost for it is established as the base inventory cost at *(a)* what the item would have cost at the base date (based upon base year price lists, etc.); or *(b)* if the item did not exist at that date, the first cost after the base date that can be reconstructed; or *(c)* if no prior cost can be determined, then the cost at the date that the item was first stocked for use or sale.

The different effects of technological changes on LIFO inventory amounts for the quantity of goods LIFO approach compared with the dollar value LIFO approach may be diagrammed as follows:

	LIFO Inventory Unit Costs				
Product	Base Year	Year 19W	Year 19X	Year 19Y	Year 19Z
A	$1	$ 5	Discontinued		
B	2	8	$ 6	$ 6	Discontinued
C (new)		15	16	16	$17
D (new)			20	21	21

Dollar value LIFO would retain this in the base inventory.

Quantity of goods LIFO would replace base year inventory costs with these current costs.

To illustrate how dollar value LIFO accommodates technological changes in the LIFO inventory, we will adapt the Tye Company data of 19C (Exhibit 8–11). Assume that product A was completely sold and discontinued during 19C and that product C was added to the LIFO inventory pool, resulting in the following 19C ending inventory, FIFO basis:

19C ending inventory FIFO basis:		
Product A—discontinued		
Product B—no change in assumption	3,000 units @ $2.60 =	$ 7,800
Product C—new product*	2,000 units @ 1.10 =	2,200
Total FIFO inventory		$10,000

* Reconstructed base year cost $0.80 per unit.

The dollar value LIFO inventory valuation at the end of 19C would be computed as follows:

Phase A—To compute the internal conversion price index for 19C:

	Inventory at Current Year Cost	÷	Inventory at Base Year Cost	=	Conversion Price Index
Product B . .	3,000 @ $2.60 = $ 7,800		3,000 @ $2.04 = $6,120		
Product C . .	2,000 @ 1.10 = 2,200		2,000 @ 0.80 = 1,600		
Total	$10,000	÷	$7,720	=	1.295

Phase B—To convert the FIFO results to dollar value LIFO results for 19C:

	FIFO at Base Year Cost	×	Conversion Price Index	=	LIFO Results
19C ending inventory (current year FIFO cost $10,000)	$7,720				
Base inventory layer	(6,100)	×	1.00	=	$6,100
19B inventory layer	(1,220)	×	1.221	=	1,490
19C additional inventory layer	$ 400	×	1.295	=	518
19C dollar value LIFO ending inventory					$8,108

Note in the above computations that *(a)* the base layer (and other prior layers) was retained at the old costs (notwithstanding the fact that product A was dropped), and *(b)* the cost of the new product was "reconstructed" at the base year cost (not the cost in 19C when added to the pool, $1.10). These two retentions of old LIFO costs are not possible when the quantity of goods LIFO approach is used. Thus, dollar value LIFO maximizes the LIFO effect, which is considered its primary advantage.

QUESTIONS

PART A

1. What are the primary purposes to be served in selecting a particular inventory cost flow method? Why is the selection particularly important?

2. Briefly explain the differences between periodic and perpetual inventory systems. Under what circumstances is each generally used?

3. Does the adoption of a perpetual inventory system eliminate the need for physical count or measurement of inventories? Explain.

4. Explain the specific identification cost method and when the method is not appropriate.

5. Distinguish between a weighted average and a weighted moving average in determining unit cost. When is each generally used? Explain.

6. Explain the essential features of first-in, first-out (FIFO). What are the primary advantages and disadvantages of FIFO? Explain the difference in the application of FIFO under *(a)* periodic and *(b)* perpetual inventory systems. In contrast with LIFO, how does FIFO affect cash flow?

7. Explain the essential features of last-in, first-out (LIFO). What are the primary advantages and disadvantages of LIFO? Explain the differences in application of LIFO under *(a)* periodic inventory and *(b)* perpetual inventory systems.

8. Explain why LIFO costed currently and LIFO costed at the end of the period may yield different results.

9. What is meant by inventory layers? Why are they significant with respect to the FIFO and LIFO methods?

10. Assuming the LIFO method, what is meant by inventory liquidation? Why is it a serious problem for LIFO but not FIFO?

11. How is LIFO usually applied *(a)* in the accounts, *(b)* on the income tax return, and *(c)* in the external financial statements.

12. Compare the balance sheet and income statement effects of FIFO versus LIFO *(a)* when prices are rising and *(b)* when prices are falling.

PART B

13. What is meant by the quantity of goods LIFO method? What type of entity would be most likely to use quantity of goods (versus dollar value) FIFO?

14. Explain how changes in the item or product mix of LIFO inventories over a period of several years will adversely affect the results of the quantity of goods approach.

15. What are the primary differences and limitations of the LIFO quantity of goods method versus the dollar value method?

16. Why does the change to LIFO present a greater accounting problem than a change from LIFO? How is this problem resolved? What accounting principle governs the extent of disclosure of the effect of the change?

17. What are the basic features of the dollar value LIFO method?

18. What is indexing in the context of applying the dollar value LIFO approach? When can an external rather than an internal price index be used?

DECISION CASE 8–1

Raines Company uses LIFO, unit basis (costed at the end of the period), to cost the ending inventory for income tax and external reporting purposes. Near the end of 19A, the records and related estimates provided the following annual data for one item sold regularly:

	Units	Unit Cost
Beginning inventory (LIFO basis):		
Base inventory (normal min. level)	10,000	$20
Increment no. 1	5,000	30
Purchases (actual)	60,000	37
Sales* (@ $50 per unit)	65,000	

Expenses* (excluding income taxes), $900,000.
Average income tax rate, 30%.

* Including estimates for remainder of 19A.

On December 26, 19A, the company has an opportunity to purchase not less than 30,000 units of the above item at $33 (a special price) with 10-day credit terms. Delivery is immediate, and the offer will expire January 3, 19B. The question has been posed as to whether the purchase (and delivery) should be consummated in 19A or 19B; the management has tentatively decided to make the purchase in 19A.

Required:

1. What is your recommendation as to the purchase date? Support your recommendation with reasons and pro forma (as if) income statement and balance sheet data. Include computations. Assume 40,000 shares of common stock are outstanding.
2. Explain and illustrate why EPS would be changed if the purchase is made in 19A.
3. Would you suspect profit manipulation in this situation if Raines elected to make the purchase in 19A? Explain.

DECISION CASE 8–2

R. Babinski, S. Chasnoff, and T. Doland formed a partnership to import furniture. Their initial partnership agreement provided for equal investments, equal sharing of responsibilities, equal work, equal salaries, and equal shares of the partnership income. After a few years of operation, sales "took off" and the business prospered. On January 1, 19T, they incorporated as BCD, Inc., with each of the former partners owning 33⅓% of the stock of the corporation. The board of directors of BCD, Inc., was comprised of Babinski, Chasnoff, and Doland. The board elected Chasnoff as chairman of the board of directors, Babinski as president of the corporation in charge of operations, and Doland as vice president and controller (Doland was a CPA). Annual compensation of the three officers was set as follows:

Chasnoff	$130,000	plus bonus equal to 2% of annual net income
Babinski	135,000	plus bonus equal to 1% of annual net income
Doland	140,000	plus 5% of annual decrease in income tax payments

The compensation schedule was intended as an incentive device as well as to reflect the relative contributions of the three officers to corporate success. In particular, the bonus plan was intended to motivate Chasnoff and Babinski (who represented the corporation in the business community) to increase sales and to encourage Doland (the accountant) to decrease income tax payments. During 19U, 19V, and 19W, sales and income increased steadily. In the year ended December 31, 19W, net income of the corporation was $500,000, which put the annual earnings of all three officers at $140,000 (this amount cannot be verified). Income tax payments for 19W were $150,000. During 19X, net income, computed on the basis of the FIFO inventory method, which BCD used, increased to $750,000. This increase in corporate income was destined to put Chasnoff's annual earnings at $145,000 and Babinski's at $142,500, but to leave Doland's at $140,000 (neither Babinski nor Chasnoff were aware of this). A major reason for the increase in corporation income was Doland's skill at controlling costs; however, the compensation schedule did not adequately reflect this factor. Doland tried to persuade Chasnoff and Babinski to renegotiate his salary, but they refused because they knew very little about finance and accounting and, therefore, were unable to appreciate Doland's effectiveness at controlling expenses. They were convinced the reason for BCD, Inc.'s success was their superlative sales and management skills.

The cost to BCD, Inc., of its imported furniture was rising rapidly near the end of 19X, but, due to increased competition, the outlook for the company's sales was not bright for 19Y. Doland seized this opportunity to spite Chasnoff and Babinski. Without notifying them, Doland changed inventory methods from FIFO to LIFO, effective January 1, 19X. Also, near year-end 19X, Doland, who controlled all purchases of inventory, stocked up on inventory in response to a pending 20% cost increase announced by BCD's suppliers; the price increase was to become effective in January 19Y. Because of the change to LIFO, income tax payments for 19X decreased to $70,000.

Required:

1. What was the likely effect of the change in inventory method on reported income of BCD for 19X? On the annual bonuses of Babinski and Chasnoff?
2. What was the likely effect of stocking up on inventory on reported income of 19X? On the annual earnings of Babinski and Chasnoff?
3. What was the effect of Doland's actions on his annual bonus?
4. What conclusions can you draw from this situation about accounting income?

EXERCISES

PART A: EXERCISES 8–1 to 8–6

Exercise 8–1

The inventory records of the Ross Company provided the following data for one item of merchandise for sale (assume the transactions in order of the number given):

	Units	Unit Cost	Total Amount
Goods available for sale:			
Beginning inventory	500	$6.00	$ 3,000
Purchases:			
(1)	600	6.10	3,660
(3)	600	6.20	3,720
(5)	400	6.30	2,520
	2,100		$12,900

Sales in units: (2), 900; (4), 500; and (6), 300.

Required:

1. Complete the following (round unit costs to nearest cent and total amounts to nearest dollar).

	Valuation	
Costing Method	Ending Inventory	Cost of Goods Sold
a. FIFO	$______	$______
b. LIFO (unit basis costed at end of period and assume base inventory is 400 units)	$______	$______
c. Weighted average	$______	$______
d. LIFO (same as [*b*] except costed currently)	$______	$______

2. Compute the amount of pretax income and rank the methods in order of the amount of pretax income (highest first) assuming FIFO pretax income is $50,000.
3. Which method is preferable in this instance? Why?

Exercise 8–2

Clara Company was formed on December 1, 19A. The following information is available from the company's inventory records for Product Ply:

	Units	Unit Cost
January 1, 19B (beginning inventory)	800	$ 9.00
Purchases:		
January 5, 19B	1,500	10.00
January 25, 19B	1,200	10.50
February 16, 19B	600	11.00
March 26, 19B	900	11.50

A physical inventory taken on March 31, 19B, showed 1,600 units on hand.

Required:
Prepare schedules to compute the ending inventory at March 31, 19B, under each of the following inventory flow methods: (1) FIFO, (2) LIFO, and (3) weighted average. Show supporting computations. (AICPA adapted)

Exercise 8–3

The raw material records of the Craft Corporation showed the following data relative to inventory item C (assume the transactions occurred in the order given):

	Units	Unit Cost
1. Inventory	300	$2.00
2. Purchase	400	2.10
3. Sale	600	
4. Purchase	500	2.20
5. Sale	500	
6. Purchase	600	2.30

Required:
1. Compute the cost of goods sold for the period and the ending inventory assuming (round unit costs to nearest cent):
   a. Weighted average.
   b. Moving average.
   c. FIFO.
   d. LIFO (unit basis, costed at end, 300 units in base layer).
   e. LIFO (unit basis, costed currently, 300 units in base layer).
2. Under what general circumstances would each be preferable?

Exercise 8–4

The inventory records of Saxton Sales Company showed the following data relative to a particular unit sold regularly (assume transactions in the order given):

	Units	Unit Cost
1. Inventory	2,000	$4.00
2. Purchases	18,000	4.50
3. Sales (@ $13 per unit)	7,000	
4. Purchases	6,000	4.60
5. Sales (@ $13.50 per unit)	16,000	
6. Purchases	3,000	4.70

Required:
1. Complete the following tabulation (round unit costs to nearest cent and total costs of inventory to the nearest $10).

(Relates to Exercise 8–4)

	Ending Inventory	Cost of Goods Sold	Gross Margin
a. FIFO	____	____	____
b. Weighted average	____	____	____
c. LIFO (unit basis costed at end, 2,000 units in base layer)	____	____	____
d. LIFO (unit basis costed currently, 2,000 units in base layer)	____	____	____
e. Moving average (show computations)	____	____	____

2. What method would be preferable? Explain the basis for your choice.

Exercise 8–5

Foster Company uses LIFO (unit basis). The following data were available relative to the primary raw material for 19A:

	Units	Unit Cost
Beginning inventory (base inventory)	5,000	$3.00
Beginning inventory (excess)	1,000	3.10
Purchases	19,000	3.40
Issues	24,000	

The first purchase in period 19B was 10,000 units at $3.70 per unit.

Required:

1. Compute the ending LIFO inventory (costed at end of period) and the cost of issues for 19A.
2. Give the journal entries for purchases and issues; record the 19A inventory invasion in the accounts (debit purchases to Inventory and issues to Work in Process).
3. Give the journal entry for the purchase in 19B.

Exercise 8–6

Uno Company currently uses FIFO for internal and external reporting and tax purposes. The inventory records for 19C reflected the following for one major item sold regularly:

	Units
Beginning inventory (@ $8 cost)	10,000
Purchases during 19C (@ $10 cost)	40,000
Sales during 19C (@ $30)	35,000
Expenses (excl. income taxes)	$ 40,000
Beginning cash balance	$ 20,000
Beginning retained earnings	$500,000
Income tax average rate	30%

The company is considering a change to LIFO (costed at the end) for all purposes. Assume the beginning inventory given above will be the LIFO base inventory.

Required:

1. Assuming all transactions are cash basis, compare LIFO and FIFO results by preparing for each: *(a)* an income statement and *(b)* a partial balance sheet (limited to the above transactions). Include a column for *differences* and show computation of cash balances. Assume 100,000 shares of common stock outstanding.
2. In this situation, based on the data at hand, which inventory method would you recommend? Why?
3. Under what conditions would you recommend the other method?

PART B: EXERCISES 8–7 to 8–12

Exercise 8–7

On January 1, 19K, Larsen Company changed from FIFO to LIFO for income tax and external reporting purposes. The ending inventory for 19J (FIFO basis) was $155,000 (this will be the base inventory amount for LIFO). At the end of 19K the LIFO inventory amount, computed using the dollar value approach, was $160,000; had the company continued using FIFO, this amount would have been $184,000. The average income tax rate is 40%.

Required:

1. Compute the difference in net income for 19K attributable to the change from FIFO to LIFO. Show computations.
2. Prepare an appropriate note to the financial statements for 19K.

Exercise 8–8

Bostic Corporation has been using FIFO since its organization for *(a)* internal management reports and control, *(b)* external reporting to shareholders, and *(c)* income tax purposes. On January 1, 19B, management decided to change from FIFO to LIFO for external reporting and income tax purposes. FIFO will continue in use for internal purposes.

The company has a number of LIFO inventory pools; however, this problem deals with only one of them. The company will apply the dollar value approach for converting the FIFO results to a LIFO basis and will use an internal conversion index computed each year.

The FIFO results for a three-year period, taken directly from the accounts and internal reports for inventory pool no. 1 (composed of five similar items in a "natural business unit"), are shown in the data given in the tabulation at the bottom of this page.

Required:

1. Compute the conversion price indexes needed for the dollar value LIFO application through 19C. Show computations and round conversion ratios to two decimal places.
2. Convert the FIFO results to a LIFO basis for 19B and 19C using the dollar value approach. Show computations.
3. Assuming $8,000 operating expenses, a 40% average tax rate, and 2,000 shares of common stock outstanding,

(Relates to Exercise 8–8)

	Year 19A			Year 19B			Year 19C		
	Units	Unit Cost	Total	Units	Unit Cost	Total	Units	Unit Cost	Total
Sales revenue			$18,200			$24,280			$30,920
Cost of goods sold (FIFO):									
Beginning inventory	800	$2.50	2,000	600	$3.00	1,800	700	$3.60	2,520
Purchases	2,000	3.00	6,000	2,500	3.60	9,000	3,000	4.00	12,000
Ending inventory*	600	3.00	1,800	700	3.60	2,520	900	4.00	3,600
Cost of goods sold	2,200		6,200	2,400		8,280	2,800		10,920

* Deduction.

prepare income statements for 19B and 19C with two headings for each year: *(a)* for internal reports (FIFO basis), and *(b)* for external reports and tax returns (LIFO basis). *Suggestion:* Use one set of side captions and four money columns.

Exercise 8–9

Arlis Company uses LIFO for income tax and external reporting purposes. The LIFO base inventory (at end of 19A) for inventory pool no. 1 amounted to $70,000. The periodic inventory of pool no. 1 taken at the end of 19B, priced at 19B costs on a FIFO basis, amounted to $92,000. Analysis of a statistical sample of the inventory and related computations showed a price index for 19A of 100 and for 19B of 119.

Required:
1. Use the internal indexes already derived to compute the 19B ending LIFO inventory amount assuming the dollar value method.
2. Under what conditions is the sampling index approach appropriate?

Exercise 8–10

On January 1, 19B Academic Associates Company adopted LIFO for income tax and external reporting purposes. The ending inventory for 19A (FIFO basis) amounted to $260,000. The physical inventory taken at the end of 19B, at 19B costs, was valued at $393,600 (FIFO basis). An external price index indicated a 23% increase in prices during 19B. Assume this is a rare situation in which an external price index can be used.

Required:
1. Use the external index to compute the 19B LIFO inventory amount assuming the dollar value approach.
2. Under what special conditions is the external index approach appropriate for converting a FIFO basis inventory to the dollar value LIFO basis?

Exercise 8–11

At the end of the annual accounting period, the inventory records of Scott Company reflected the following:

	19A	19B
Ending inventory at FIFO	$350,000	$390,000
Ending inventory at LIFO	320,000	340,000

The company uses FIFO for internal purposes and LIFO for income tax and external reporting purposes.

Required:
1. Assume the inventory difference is recognized in the accounts. Give the appropriate journal entry for each year.
2. Show how the inventories should be shown on the 19A–19B comparative balance sheet.

Exercise 8–12

Acute Company manufactures a single product. On December 31, 19A, Acute adopted the dollar value LIFO inventory method. The inventory on that date using the dollar value LIFO inventory method was determined to be $300,000. Inventory data for succeeding years are as follows:

Year Ended December 31,	Inventory at Respective Year-End Prices	Relevant Price Index (base year 19A)
19B	$363,000	1.10
19C	420,000	1.20
19D	430,000	1.25

Required:
Compute the inventory amounts at December 31, 19B, 19C, and 19D, using the dollar value LIFO inventory method for each year. (AICPA adapted)

SUPPLEMENT 8–A: EXERCISES 8–13 to 8–14

Exercise 8–13

Thurman Company records standard costs in the accounts. The finished goods inventory records are maintained at standard. When raw material is purchased, the difference between standard cost and actual cost is recorded in a separate variance account and reported as a *loss or gain* for the period in which the goods were purchased. The records relating to one item of raw material for 19A showed the following: standard cost per unit, $8; beginning inventory, 1,000 units; purchases during the period were no. 1—2,000 units at $8.25, no. 2—800 units at $7.90, and no. 3—1,200 units at $8; units issued to work in process (factory), 3,500; expenses paid were $22,500; total cost of goods sold was $40,000; and sales were $70,000.

Required:
1. Give journal entries for the purchases, sales, expenses, and cost of goods sold. Assume no change in the inventory balances in work in process and finished goods. Thurman uses a perpetual inventory system.
2. Prepare an income statement (disregard income taxes). Assume 5,000 shares of common stock outstanding.

Exercise 8–14

WT Manufacturing Company produces in one plant a single product that is distributed nationally. The plant is highly mechanized; therefore, fixed costs are relatively high. Full manufacturing cost and LIFO (unit basis and costed at the end of the period) have been used for internal and external reporting and tax purposes. Because there is only one plant and wide distribution of the product, the controller is considering a variable (direct) costing system for internal purposes. LIFO (unit basis) will continue to be used for income tax purposes. The following year-end amounts were determined on a LIFO (full historical cost) basis:

Sales (8,000 units @ $91)	$728,000
Cost of goods sold (@ $46)	368,000
Gross margin	360,000
Expenses (fixed)	190,000
Pretax income	170,000
Income taxes (@ 40%)	68,000
Net income	$102,000

Beginning inventory, finished goods	None
Manufacturing costs (10,000 units):	
Direct material used	$ 55,000
Direct labor incurred	175,000
Factory overhead, fixed	150,000
Factory overhead, variable	80,000
Ending inventory, finished goods (2,000 units)	(92,000)
Cost of goods sold	$368,000

Required:

1. Recast the above statements for internal purposes on a direct cost basis. Use the beginning inventory as given.
2. Which basis should be used for external reporting purposes? Explain.
3. How is the total fixed expense reported for the period?

PROBLEMS

PART A: PROBLEMS 8–1 to 8–6

Problem 8–1

Bane Company records showed the following transactions, in order of occurrence, relative to raw material Z:

	Units	Unit Cost
1. Inventory	400	$5.00
2. Purchase	600	5.50
3. Issue	700	
4. Purchase	900	5.60
5. Issue	800	
6. Purchase	200	5.95

Required:

Compute the cost of the issues and ending inventory in each of the following completely independent situations (round unit costs to the nearest cent for inventory; show computations):

Assumption	Units and Amount: Ending Inventory	Issues
a. Weighted average.		
b. Moving average.		
c. FIFO.		
d. LIFO costed currently.		
e. LIFO costed at end of period.		

Problem 8–2

The records of Monroe Company showed the following transactions, in the order given, relating to the major inventory item:

	Units	Unit Cost
1. Inventory	3,000	$7.00
2. Purchase	5,000	7.20
3. Sales (@ $15)	4,000	
4. Purchase	7,000	7.50
5. Sales (@ $15)	9,000	
6. Purchase	8,000	7.60
7. Sales (@ $18)	9,000	
8. Purchase	6,000	7.90

Required:

Complete the following tabulation for each independent assumption (round unit costs to the nearest cent for inventory; show computations):

Assumption	Units and Amount: Ending Inventory	Cost of Goods Sold	Gross Margin
a. FIFO.			
b. LIFO costed at end of period (base inventory, 1,000 units).			
c. LIFO costed currently (base inventory, 1,000 units)—support with a perpetual inventory record.			
d. Weighted average.			
e. Moving average—support with a perpetual inventory record.			

Problem 8–3 (Requirement 1*e* relates to Supplement 8–A)

The records of Lee Company showed the following data with respect to one raw material used in the manufacturing process. Assume the transactions occurred in the order given.

	Units	Unit Cost
Inventory	4,000	$7.00
Purchase no. 1	3,000	7.60
Issue no. 1	5,000	
Purchase no. 2	8,000	8.00
Issue no. 2	7,000	
Purchase no. 3	3,000	8.50

Required:

1. Compute cost of materials issued (to work in process) and the valuation of ending inventory for each of the following independent transactions (round unit costs to the nearest cent for inventory; show computations):
   a. FIFO.
   b. LIFO, costed at end of period (base inventory, 4,000 units).
   c. Weighted average.
   d. Moving average.
   e. Standard cost (assuming a standard unit cost of $7.50).
2. In parallel columns, give all entries indicated for FIFO assuming a count of the raw material on hand at the end showed 6,000 units:

   Case A—A perpetual inventory system.

   Case B—A periodic inventory system.

Problem 8–4 (Requirements 1*d* and 2 *Case B* relates to Supplement 8–A)

The records of Byrd Company showed the following data relative to one of the major items being sold. Assume the transactions occurred in the order given.

	Units	Unit Cost
Beginning inventory	7,000	$4.00
Purchase no. 1	6,000	4.20
Sale no. 1 (@ $10)	9,000	
Purchase no. 2	8,000	4.50
Sale no. 2 (@ $13)	4,000	

Required:

1. Compute cost of goods sold, valuation of the ending inventory, and gross margin under each of the following independent assumptions (round unit costs to nearest cent):

(Relates to Problem 8–4)

	Amount		
	Inventory	Cost of Goods Sold	Gross Margin
a. Weighted-average cost with periodic inventory system.			
b. FIFO with perpetual inventory system.			
c. LIFO costed at end of period (base inventory, 7,000 units).			
d. Standard cost, assuming the standard cost is $4 (consider price variance only).			

2. Give all entries indicated by the above data assuming a perpetual inventory system:

   Case A—FIFO ([*b*] above).

   Case B—Standard cost ([*d*] above).

Problem 8–5 (relates to Supplement 8–A)

Knight Manufacturing Company manufactures one main product. Two raw materials are used in the manufacture of this product. The company uses standard costs in the accounts and carries the raw material, work in process, and finished goods inventories at standard. The records of the company showed the following:

(Relates to Problem 8–5)

	Material A		Material B	
Beginning inventory (units)	8,000		5,000	
Standard cost per unit		$2.00		$7.00
Purchases during period:				
No. 1	10,000 @ $2.00		7,000 @ $7.00	
No. 2	20,000 @ 1.90		8,000 @ 7.20	
Issues during period (units)	28,000		16,000	
Ending inventory per physical count (units)	10,000		3,900	

Required:
1. Give all entries indicated relative to raw materials assuming standard costs (assume a perpetual system).
2. Determine the value of the ending inventory and cost of issues for each raw material.
3. Accumulate the amount of the variations from standard for each raw material and explain or illustrate the reporting and accounting disposition of these amounts.

Problem 8–6 (an overview problem)

Green Company maintains perpetual inventory records on a FIFO basis for the three main products distributed by the company. A physical inventory is taken at the end of each six months in order to check the perpetual inventory records.

The following information relating to one of the products, Product A, for the year 19A was taken from the records of the company:

	Units
Beginning inventory	9,000 @ $8.10
Purchases and sales (in order given):	
Purchase no. 11	5,000 @ 8.15
Sale no. 1	10,000
Purchase no. 12	16,000 @ 8.20
Sale no. 2	11,000
Purchase no. 13	4,000 @ 8.30
Purchase no. 14	7,000 @ 8.20
Sale no. 3	14,000
Purchase no. 15	5,000 @ 8.10
Ending inventory (per count)	10,000
Replacement cost (per unit)	$8.00

Required:
1. Reconstruct the perpetual inventory record for Product A.
2. Give all entries indicated by the above data assuming selling price is $21 per unit and that the company employs the inventory allowance method (holding losses separately identified) in recognizing LCM.
3. Prepare the income statement for this product through gross margin.

PART B: PROBLEMS 8–7 to 8–12

Problem 8–7

Midland Company sells three main products. In the past, perpetual inventory procedures have been employed on a FIFO basis. The records of the company showed the following information relating to one of the products:

	Units
Beginning inventory	500 @ $3.00
Purchases and sales (in order given):	
Purchase no. 1	400 @ 3.10
Purchase no. 2	600 @ 3.15
Sale no. 1	1,000
Purchase no. 3	800 @ 3.25
Sale no. 2	700
Sale no. 3	500
Purchase no. 4	700 @ 3.30

In considering a change in inventory policy, the following summary was prepared:

	Illustration (1)	(2)	(3)	(4)
Sales	$15,400	$15,400	$15,400	$15,400
Cost of goods sold	7,110	6,996	6,905	6,930
Gross margin	$ 8,290	$ 8,404	$ 8,495	$ 8,470

Required:
Identify the inventory flow method used for each illustration assuming only the ending inventory was affected. Show computations. (AICPA adapted)

Problem 8–8

Harris Company decided at the beginning of 19A to change from FIFO to LIFO. The records of the company showed the following data for 19A relative to one major inventory item distributed:

	Units	Unit Cost
Beginning inventory (LIFO base inventory layers averaged), 1/1/19A	10,000	$3.00
Purchases and sales (in order given):		
1. Purchase	8,000	3.20
2. Sold (@ $8)	9,000	
3. Sold (@ $8.25)	5,000	
4. Purchase	7,000	3.20
5. Purchase	6,000	3.40
6. Sold (@ $8.75)	8,000	
7. Purchase	3,000	3.50

Expenses (excluding income taxes), $40,000.
Average income tax rate, 35%.

Required:
1. Prepare an income statement for 19A, unit LIFO basis, costed at the end of the period. Assume 10,000 shares of common stock outstanding.
2. Prepare an appropriate footnote, and any other required supporting data, for the change in 19A from FIFO to LIFO.
3. What would be disclosed in 19B relative to the change? Why?

Problem 8–9

Blass, Incorporated, sells two main products regularly. The products form one pool for inventory purposes. The company used FIFO through 19A for all purposes. Starting in

(Relates to Problem 8–9)

	Purchases			Issues			Balance (FIFO)		
19A:									
Ending inventory							400	$1.00	$400
19B:									
Purchases	700	$1.20	$840				400	1.00	400
							700	1.20	840
Sales (@ $3)				400	$1.00	$400			
				100	1.20	120	600	1.20	720
19C:									
Purchases	600	1.35	810				600	1.20	720
							600	1.35	810
Sales (@ $3.40)				600	1.20	720			
				200	1.35	270	400	1.35	540
19D:									
Purchases	500	1.50	750				400	1.35	540
							500	1.50	750
Sales (@ $3.75)				400	1.35	540	500	1.50	750

19B, LIFO was adopted for external reporting and income tax purposes. The inventory pool (the two products combined) records at FIFO reflected the information shown above.

Required:

1. Convert the ending inventory at FIFO to a LIFO basis for 19B, 19C, and 19D assuming the dollar value method is used. Round conversion indexes to two decimal places.
2. Prepare a schedule (that includes inventory, tax, and income) to compare the results for FIFO and LIFO. For analytical purposes, assume *(a)* an average tax rate of 30% and *(b)* a pretax income amount of $300 (FIFO basis) for each year. Which method should be used? Why?
3. Prepare a suitable footnote for the financial statements for 19B assuming LIFO is used for external reporting and income tax purposes.

Problem 8–10

Bone Wholesale Company sells three main products regularly. The products form one pool for inventory purposes. The company used FIFO through 19A for all purposes. After 19A, FIFO was continued for internal management and accounting purposes; however, at the start of 19B, LIFO was adopted for income tax and external reporting purposes. The following data (for the three products combined) were taken from the records for the three years following the adoption of LIFO:

	FIFO Basis per Accounts		
	Units	Cost	Total
19A:			
Ending inventory	2,000	$3.00	$ 6,000
19B:			
Purchases	6,000	3.30	$19,800
Sales (@ $8)	5,000		
Ending inventory	3,000	3.30	9,900
19C:			
Purchases	10,000	3.50	$35,000
Sales (@ $9)	6,000		
Ending inventory	7,000	3.50	24,500
19D:			
Purchases	3,000	4.00	$12,000
Sales (@ $9)	6,000		
Ending inventory:			
Layer 1	1,000	3.50	3,500
Layer 2	3,000	4.00	12,000
Total	4,000		$15,500

Required:

1. Convert the ending inventory at FIFO to a LIFO basis for 19B, 19C, and 19D, assuming the dollar value method is used. Round conversion indexes to two decimal places.
2. Prepare a schedule (which includes inventory, tax, and income) that compares the results of the methods, FIFO and LIFO. For analytical purposes assume *(a)* an average tax rate of 40% and *(b)* a pretax income amount of $5,000 each year under FIFO. Which method should be used? Why?
3. Prepare an appropriate footnote to the financial state-

ments for 19B assuming LIFO is used for external reporting and tax purposes.

Problem 8–11

Cook Company has been using FIFO for all internal and external reporting purposes. At the start of 19B, it adopted LIFO for external financial statement and income tax purposes. The FIFO inventory records reported the following for one inventory pool:

	FIFO Basis
19A ending inventory	$100,000
19B ending inventory	120,000
19C ending inventory	130,000
19D ending inventory	135,000

Internal price index derived: 19A—1.00; 19B—1.10; 19C—1.18; and 19D—1.25

Required:
Convert the ending FIFO inventory amounts to a LIFO basis for 19B, 19C, and 19D, assuming the dollar value method, using the internal price index values given above.

Problem 8–12

Grove Corporation sells two main products. FIFO, with a perpetual inventory system, is used for internal cost accounting and management purposes. On January 1, 19B, the company adopted LIFO for external reporting and income tax purposes; FIFO will continue to be used for internal purposes. The FIFO inventory records are shown below.

Required:
Assume the two products form one pool for inventory purposes. Convert the ending inventory at FIFO to a LIFO basis for 19B, 19C, and 19D, assuming the dollar value method is used. Round conversion indexes to two places.

(Relates to Problem 8–12)

Perpetual Inventory Record

	Purchases*			Issues			FIFO Balance		
	U	UC	TC	U	UC	TC	U	UC	TC
Product X:									
December 31, 19A							200	$100	$20,000
19B:									
Purchases	400	$130	$52,000						
Sales (@ $300)				200	$100	$20,000			
				200	130	26,000			
Balance, 12/31/19B . . .							200	130	26,000
19C:									
Purchases	500	140	70,000						
Sales (@ $300)				200	130	26,000			
Balance, 12/31/19C . . .							500	140	70,000
19D:									
Purchases	100	150	15,000						
Sales (@ $325)				300	140	42,000			
Balance, 12/31/19D . .							200	140	28,000
							100	150	15,000
Product Y:									
December 31, 19A							300	$ 90	$27,000
19B:									
Purchases	400	$ 92	$36,800						
Sales (@ $275)				300	$ 90	$27,000			
Balance, 12/31/19B . . .							400	92	36,800
19C:									
Purchases	100	95	9,500						
Sales (@ $275)				400	92	36,800			
Balance, 12/31/19C . . .							100	95	9,500
19D:									
Purchases	400	96	38,400						
Sales (@ $295)				100	95	9,500			
Balance, 12/31/19D . .				100	96	9,600	300	96	28,800

* U = units, UC = unit cost, and TC = total cost.

9

Inventories—Special Valuation Procedures

NUMEROUS SITUATIONS occur in which accountants must estimate inventory values. Consequently, certain estimating procedures have gained wide acceptance. They are discussed and illustrated in this chapter, which is subdivided as follows:

Part A—Gross Margin Method; Retail Method, FIFO and Average Cost Bases with LCM

Part B—Retail Method, LIFO Cost Basis; Inventories on Long-Term Construction Contracts

Part A: Gross Margin Method; Retail Method, FIFO and Average Cost Bases with LCM

GROSS MARGIN METHOD

The gross margin[1] method is used to approximate the value of an inventory independent of a physical count of the goods, and as a test check on the accuracy of perpetual inventory records. The method is based upon the assumption that the rate of gross margin (gross margin divided by sales), based on recent past performance, will be approximately constant in the short run.

Computation of total goods available for sale is the first step in the gross margin method. This computation is done in the usual manner (i.e., beginning inventory plus purchases), based upon data provided by the accounts. Next, the estimated gross margin is computed by multiplying sales by the estimated rate of gross margin. Then, cost of goods sold is determined by subtracting the estimated gross margin from sales. Finally, subtraction of the estimated cost of goods sold from the cost of goods available for sale gives the ending inventory at estimated cost. The gross margin method is illustrated for X Company in Exhibit 9–1. Panel A presents the illustrative data, and Panel B shows the computation. In Panel B, note the order of computations in the right-hand column. First, gross margin is estimated to be $4,000 (bottom line); second, cost of goods sold is estimated

[1] The gross margin method also is referred to as the gross profit method.

EXHIBIT 9–1: Gross Margin Method of Estimating Ending Inventory—X Company

Panel A—Illustrative Data:

1. Net sales during the period, $10,000.
2. Beginning inventory, $5,000.
3. Purchases during the period, $8,000.
4. Estimated gross margin rate, computed as a percent of sales, 40%.

Panel B—Gross Margin Method Applied:

	Known Data		Computations	Order of Computation Step
Net sales		$10,000*		
Cost of goods sold:				
Beginning inventory	$ 5,000†			
Add: Purchases	8,000*			
Goods available for sale	13,000			
Less: Ending inventory	?		($13,000 − $6,000) = $7,000	3
Cost of goods sold		?	($10,000 − $4,000) = $6,000	2
Gross margin (as % of sales)	40%‡	?	($10,000 × .40) = $4,000	1

* From company records.
† Ending inventory from prior period.
‡ Based on recent past performance.

to be $6,000; and third, ending inventory is estimated to be $7,000.

In some problems relating to the gross margin method, a **cost** percentage (cost of goods sold divided by sales) is given rather than the gross margin percentage (gross margin divided by sales). If either percentage is known, the other can be determined because the two percentages must sum to 100 percent. In the above example, the rate of gross margin is 40 percent of sales; therefore, the cost percentage is 60 percent (100 percent − 40 percent) of sales. The gross margin rate, or markup, was given as a percent of sales (40 percent markup computed on sales), which is the rate needed. However, had the gross margin rate been given as markup computed on cost (i.e., 66⅔ percent), it would have to be converted to a markup percentage on sales. Conversion of markup on cost to markup on sales, or vice versa, may be accomplished algebraically as follows:

Symbols: C = Cost
SP = Selling price
MU = Markup

1. ***MU* on cost known;** .66⅔:
   What is the equivalent *MU* on sales?

   MU on cost ÷ (1 + MU on cost) = MU on sales.
   .66⅔ ÷ (1 + .66⅔) = .40 MU on sales.

2. ***MU* on sales known;** .40:
   What is the equivalent *MU* on cost?

   MU on sales ÷ (1 − MU on sales) = MU on cost.
   .40 ÷ (1 − .40) = .66⅔ MU on cost.

The gross margin method is employed in the following situations:

1. By auditors and others to test the reasonableness of an inventory valuation provided by some other person or determined by some other means, such as a physical inventory count or perpetual inventory records. To illustrate, assume the bookkeeper for X Company in Exhibit 9–1 submitted to the auditor an ending inventory valuation of $10,000. The gross margin method provides an approximation of $7,000 (see Exhibit 9–1, step 3), which suggests that the inventory may be overvalued.
2. To estimate the ending inventory for interim financial reports (monthly or quarterly statements,

for example) prepared during the year where it is impractical to physically count the inventory.

3. To estimate the cost of inventory destroyed by a casualty such as fire or storm. This application would be limited to situations in which the accounting records are not destroyed, because certain data from the accounts are essential. Valuation of inventory lost through casualty is necessary to *(a)* estimate its replacement cost and *(b)* establish a basis for related insurance claims and/or income tax deduction.
4. To develop budget estimates of cost of goods sold, gross margin, and inventory after a sales revenue budget is developed.

Evaluation of the Gross Margin Method

In applying the gross margin method, one must be aware that *(a)* the estimated gross margin rate, based on data from past period(s), may not appropriately reflect changes relating to the present or future periods; and *(b)* the average gross margin rate may include widely varying gross margin rates on different items of inventory. Most companies carry a number of different lines of merchandise, each having a different markup. A change during the period in markup on one or more lines, or a shift in the relative quantities of each line sold, will change the average gross margin rate (markup), thereby affecting the validity of the results derived by the method.

When the gross margin method is applied to broad aggregations of inventory with significantly different markup rates, the computations should be developed for each separate class. Then the estimate for total inventory can be determined by summing the estimates for the separate classes.

The gross margin method accommodates different inventory cost flow assumptions (FIFO, LIFO, average) because the computed gross margin rate is based automatically on the cost method used by the company.

RETAIL INVENTORY METHOD

The retail method of estimating inventory often is used by retail stores, particularly department stores, which sell a wide variety of items. In such situations, perpetual inventory procedures sometimes are impractical, and it is unusual to take a complete physical inventory count more often than once annually.

Several features of department store operation make possible use of the retail inventory method: *(a)* the departments frequently are homogeneous with respect to the markup on items sold within a department and *(b)* articles purchased are immediately priced for resale and the prices are displayed.

The retail inventory method is not a quantity of goods (units) method; rather it is based only on "dollar" amounts. The retail inventory method (1) uses both **retail value** (i.e., selling price) and **actual cost** data provided by the accounts to compute the ratio of cost to retail (referred to hereinafter as the **cost ratio**), (2) calculates the ending inventory at retail value, and (3) converts that retail value to a cost value by using the computed cost ratio.

Application of the retail inventory method requires that **internal records** be kept to provide the following data:

1. Beginning inventory valued at both cost and retail.
2. Purchases during the period valued at both cost and retail.
3. Adjustments to the original marked retail price, such as additional markups, markup cancellations, markdowns, markdown cancellations, and employee discounts.
4. Data relating to other adjustments, such as interdepartmental transfers, returns, breakage, and damaged goods.
5. Sales revenue.

This method is similar to the gross margin method in that the inventory valuation is based on the **ratio of cost to selling price.** The gross margin method uses a projection of the gross margin rate, based upon historical cost, whereas the retail inventory method uses a cost ratio based upon the actual relationship between cost and retail for the **current** period. The cost and retail data required for the retail method are collected on a continuing basis, and because these data are not estimates, the cost ratio is certain. However, because the computed cost ratio is an average (i.e., not specific to each kind of goods sold), the computed inventory amount is an estimate.

The retail inventory method is illustrated in Exhibit 9–2; Panel A presents a simplified set of facts and Panel B illustrates computation of the cost of ending inventory using the retail method.

In Exhibit 9–2, the amounts needed for computation of the cost ratio [i.e., goods available for sale at cost ($210,000) and at retail ($300,000)] are taken from the accounting records. The sales amount (i.e.,

$260,000 at retail) is taken from the Sales Revenue account and is subtracted from goods available for sale at retail (i.e., $300,000). The remainder (i.e., $40,000) is the retail value of ending inventory. It is multiplied by the computed cost ratio, .70 (i.e., $210,000 ÷ $300,000) to estimate ending inventory at cost, $28,000 (i.e., $40,000 × .70).

EXHIBIT 9–2: Retail Method to Compute Ending Inventory—Alpha Corporation

Panel A—Illustrative Data:

1. Beginning inventory (Jan. 1):
   a. At cost, $15,000.
   b. At retail, $25,000.
2. Purchases during January:
   a. At cost, $195,000.
   b. At retail, $275,000.
3. Sales revenue, $260,000.

Panel B—Retail Method Applied:

	At Cost	At Retail
Goods available for sale:		
Beginning inventory (Jan. 1)	$ 15,000*	$ 25,000*
Purchases during January ..	195,000*	275,000*
Total goods available for sale	$210,000	300,000
Cost ratio:		
$210,000 ÷ $300,000 = .70		
Deduct January sales at retail		260,000*
Ending inventory (Jan. 31):		
At retail		$ 40,000
At cost ($40,000 × .70)	$ 28,000	

* Data available from the records.

Markups and Markdowns

The data used in Exhibit 9–2 assumed there were no changes in the **original** marked sales price. The original sales price on some of the merchandise frequently is raised or lowered, particularly at the end of the selling season or when replacement costs are changing. The retail method requires that a careful record be kept of all adjustments to the **original** sales price because these adjustments affect the computation. To apply the retail inventory method, it is important to distinguish among the following terms:

Original sales price—the amount at which the merchandise is **first marked** for sale.

Markup—the **original** or initial amount that merchandise is marked up. Thus, it is the difference between cost and the original sales price. It may be expressed as a dollar amount or a percent of either cost or selling price. It is sometimes referred to as initial markup or markon.

Additional markup—an increase in the sales price **above** the original sales price. Note that the original sales price is the base from which additional markup is measured.

Additional markup cancellations—cancellation of an **additional** markup or a portion of it. Additional markups less additional markup cancellations usually is called net additional markup.

Markdown—a reduction in selling price below the original sales price.

Markdown cancellation—after a reduction in the original selling price (i.e., after a markdown), an increase in the selling price which does not exceed the original sales price (after the original sales price, an increase is an additional markup).

The definitions may be illustrated by assuming an item that cost $8 is originally marked to sell at $10, subsequently marked to sell at $11, then marked down to $10, and finally reduced to sell at $7:

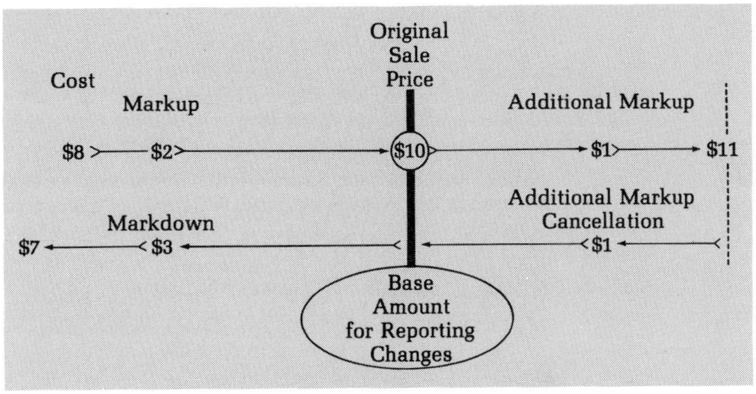

The validity of an inventory amount determined by the retail inventory method depends upon the accuracy with which changes in the original selling price are reported by the merchandising personnel to the accounting department. The importance of the markup/markdown distinction, which may not seem apparent at this point, will be illustrated in the applications which follow.

Application of the Retail Inventory Method

The basic concept and computations underlying the retail inventory method were discussed above and illustrated in Exhibit 9–2. However, the retail method is applied in different ways to estimate the cost of ending inventory under the different inventory cost flow assumptions as outlined in Exhibit 9–3.

FIFO Cost Rationale. To estimate the FIFO cost of ending inventory, the cost and retail amounts of the beginning inventory are excluded from the computation of the cost ratio because under FIFO the cost of the ending inventory necessarily comes from the purchases of the current period, not from beginning inventory.

Average Cost Rationale. To estimate the average cost of ending inventory, the cost ratio is computed on total goods available for sale (i.e., the sum of beginning inventory plus purchases) because the cost of the ending inventory necessarily comes from the total goods available for sale during the period.

LCM Rationale. To estimate the LCM of ending inventory, the cost ratio excludes net markdowns. The rationale is that exclusion of net markdowns from computation of the **retail** value of goods available (markups and markdowns do not affect **cost**) causes the retail value of goods available to be higher than if net markdowns were subtracted from goods available. In turn, this decreases the cost ratio and, thus, produces a conservative (i.e., LCM) estimate of the value of ending inventory. As indicated in Exhibit 9–3, LCM is applied to FIFO and average cost; LCM is not applied to LIFO under the retail method.

To illustrate the FIFO and average cost bases, the data given in Exhibit 9–4 are assumed from the accounting records of KM Company at the end of the accounting period (note that units are not used; only dollars):

EXHIBIT 9–4: Data for Retail Inventory Method, KM Company

	At Cost	At Retail
Inventory at beginning of period	$ 550	$ 900
Purchases during period	6,290	8,900
Additional markups during period		225
Additional markup cancellations during period		25
Markdowns during period		600
Markdown cancellations during period		100
Sales for the period		8,500

Retail Method, FIFO Cost Basis with LCM

When FIFO is used, the ending inventory is costed at the latest unit costs; therefore, the costs in the beginning inventory will be included in cost of goods

EXHIBIT 9–3: Application of the Retail Inventory Method

Basis Desired	Computation of Cost Ratio
1. FIFO cost, LCM.	Exclude beginning inventory from the computation of the cost ratio to implement FIFO cost. To implement LCM, exclude net markdowns from the computation of the cost ratio; include net markdowns in computing ending inventory at **retail** after the cost ratio is computed.
2. Average cost, LCM.	Include beginning inventory in the computation of the cost ratio to implement average cost. To implement LCM, exclude net markdowns from the computation of the cost ratio; include net markdowns in computing ending inventory at **retail** after the cost ratio is computed.
3. LIFO cost.	Must use the LIFO retail method (discussed in Part B).

EXHIBIT 9–5: Retail Method Estimation of Ending Inventory—KM Company (basic data given in Exhibit 9–4)

Panel A—FIFO Cost, LCM

		At Cost	At Retail
Goods available for sale:			
Beginning inventory		$ 550	$ 900
Purchases during period		6,290	8,900
Additional markups during period	$225		
Less: Additional markup cancellations	25		
Net additional markups			200
Total (excluding beginning inventory)		6,290	9,100
Cost ratio: $6,290 ÷ $9,100 = .691 (based on newest costs)			
Total goods available for sale		$6,840	10,000
Deduct:			
Sales			(8,500)
Markdowns	600		
Less: Markdown cancellations	100		
Net markdowns			(500)
Ending inventory:			
At retail			$ 1,000
At approximate FIFO cost, LCM ($1,000 × .691)		$ 691	

Panel B—Average Cost, LCM

		At Cost	At Retail
Goods available for sale:			
Beginning inventory		$ 550	$ 900
Purchases during period		6,290	8,900
Additional markups	$225		
Less: Additional markup cancellations	25		
Net additional markups			200
Total goods available for sale (including beginning inventory)		$6,840	10,000
Cost ratio: $6,840 ÷ $10,000 = .684 (based on average costs)			
Deduct:			
Sales			(8,500)
Remainder			1,500
Markdowns	$600		
Less: Markdown cancellations	100		
Net markdowns			(500)
Ending inventory:			
At retail			$ 1,000
At approximate average cost, LCM ($1,000 × .684)		$ 684	

sold rather than in the ending inventory. To accomplish this effect with the retail method, the beginning inventory is excluded from the computation of the cost ratio. The result will approximate FIFO cost of the ending inventory. Also, to approximate LCM, net markdowns are excluded from the cost ratio. The LCM computations on the FIFO basis for KM Company is shown in Exhibit 9–5, Panel A.

Retail Method, Average Cost Basis with LCM

Under the retail method average inventory cost is derived by dividing total goods available for sale at **cost** by total goods available for sale at **retail;** both totals include the beginning inventory. Therefore, if we calculate the cost ratio on the basis of totals, including the beginning inventory, the retail method derives the approximate average cost. To approximate LCM, net markdowns are excluded from the cost ratio. The LCM computation average cost basis, for KM Company is shown in Exhibit 9–5, Panel B.

The retail inventory methods of estimating the LCM of inventory, illustrated in Exhibit 9–5, implicitly assume **markdowns** occur because the utility of the merchandise has declined. That is, the current purchase price of identical new goods decreased or, stated differently, the goods had a replacement cost which was lower than historical cost. The decrease in replacement cost could result from such factors as obsolescence, spoilage, or excess supply. Therefore, to value the inventory at LCM, the **net markdowns** are omitted from computation of the **cost ratio;** this **lowers** the computed cost ratio (because of a larger denominator). Because the net markdowns are omitted from the retail column (above the cost ratio computation), they must be reflected in the retail column (below the cost ratio) to derive the correct amount for "ending inventory at retail." This effect is accomplished by subtracting the net markdowns along with net sales (i.e., below the cost ratio computation). Observe in Exhibit 9–5 that the inventory amount at retail, $1,000, is the same under FIFO and average. However, the **cost ratios differ** because the numerator and denominator of the cost ratios exclude respectively the cost and retail prices of the beginning inventory under FIFO, and includes these amounts under average cost. The lower of FIFO cost or market is $691 (Panel A), whereas the lower of average cost or market is $684 (Panel B).

Special Items Related to the Retail Inventory Method

Several factors may complicate computation of the ending inventory by the retail inventory method. In resolving these issues it is essential to protect the integrity of *(a)* the computed "normal" cost ratio and *(b)* the amount of ending inventory at retail. Six complicating factors and the way each usually is treated are as follows:

1. Freight-in—This expenditure adds to the **cost** of merchandise; therefore, it should be added to goods available for sale (or directly to purchases) at **cost** but not at retail.
2. Purchase returns—Since purchase returns, as distinguished from allowances, reduce the amount of goods available for sale, they should be deducted from goods available for sale at both **cost** and **retail.**
3. Abnormal casualty losses and missing merchandise arising from unusual or infrequent events (such as a fire or theft) should be deducted from goods available for sale at both **cost** and **retail** because they will not be sold; removal from both cost and retail precludes their effect on the cost ratio as if they had not been purchased in the first place. The damaged merchandise would be set up in a special inventory account at its net realizable value.
4. Sales Returns and Allowances—Since this is a contra account to the Sales Revenue account, Sales Returns and Allowances should be deducted from gross sales. If the returned merchandise is placed back into inventory for resale, no change in the At Cost column is needed because its cost is already properly included in the purchases amount. However, if the merchandise is not returned to inventory (because of damage, for example), then its cost should be deducted in the At Cost column on the sales line after the cost ratio (because net sales has been reduced and the cost also should be reduced).

EXHIBIT 9–6: Special Items, Retail Inventory Method—Average Cost, LCM

				At Cost	At Retail
	Goods available for sale:				
	Beginning inventory			$ 6,050	$ 11,000
	Purchases			57,120	102,000
1.	Freight-in			1,020	
2.	Purchase returns			(560)	(1,000)
	Net additional markups				600
3.	Casualty loss:*				
	At cost			(3,630)	
	At retail				(6,600)
	Total			$60,000	$106,000
	Cost ratio: $60,000 ÷ $106,000 = .566				
	Deduct:				
	Gross sales	$71,200			
4.	Sales returns (merchandise returned to stock)	1,200			
	Net sales				70,000
5.	Discounts to employees				(200)
6.	Normal spoilage				(1,300)
	Net markdowns				(4,500)
	Ending inventory:				
	At retail				$ 30,000
	At average cost, LCM $30,000 × .566 =			$ 16,980	

* The casualty loss could have been recorded as follows per the assumed fact situation:

Cash (from insurance company)	2,000	
Casualty loss (fire damage)	1,630	
Purchases (or cost of goods sold)		3,630

5. Discounts to employees and favored customers—These discounts result from selling merchandise below the "normal" sales price and are not occasioned by market value decreases; therefore, they are different from markdowns. The amount of the discounts is computed as the number of units sold at a discount multiplied by the difference between the marked selling price and the discount price. Such discounts always must be **deducted below the cost ratio,** along with sales, because they are concessions to the recipients and do not reflect general market value decreases. If such discounts were deducted in deriving the cost ratio, the cost ratio would be overstated, which would cause the ending inventory to be overstated.
6. Normal spoilage (including shrinkage and breakage)—This item is measured for retail inventory purposes as the number of units lost multiplied by the marked retail price. This amount must always be **deducted below the cost ratio,** along with sales, because the **expected** cost of normal spoilage implicitly is included in determining the selling price and it does not reflect market value changes. Deduction of normal spoilage in arriving at the cost ratio would overstate the cost ratio and the estimated cost of the ending inventory.

These six special items are illustrated in Exhibit 9–6 and are numbered in the order given above to facilitate study.

The preceding discussion of the retail inventory method presumed that the goods included in a single set of computations are similar in terms of their *(a)* markup percentage and *(b)* relative proportion of the total inventory of the company. In individual departments this is usually the case; however, on a storewide basis it often is not. For example, three fourths of the inventory may have a markup of 80 percent and one fourth a markup of 50 percent. Consequently, the essential data should be accumulated for each sales department and the retail inventory computations then made on a **departmental** basis. The departmental inventories then are summed to derive the total ending inventory.

Part B: Retail Method, LIFO Cost Basis; Inventories on Long-Term Construction Contracts

RETAIL METHOD, LIFO COST BASIS

This section discusses and illustrates the application of LIFO by companies that also use the retail inventory method to estimate their inventory costs. This method is used when LIFO results are desired for an inventory accounted for internally by the FIFO retail method. It is acceptable for interim financial reports, external financial reports, and for income tax purposes (subject to specific constraints in the tax regulations).[2]

The LIFO retail method (often called the dollar value LIFO retail method) requires that *(a)* a distinction be maintained between the base year inventory and subsequent incremental layers and *(b)* the subsequent layers be costed by applying a conversion price index to the results derived from the retail inventory approach. Thus, at the end of each period, the FIFO retail inventory method is used to identify inventory layers;[3] the FIFO results then are converted to a LIFO basis using a conversion price index.

Treasury regulations specify that "variety" stores using the LIFO retail method must use an **internally computed price index.** On the other hand, retailers that qualify as "department" stores (as defined for tax purposes) may use a published external index. In the discussions and illustrations to follow, we will assume a **published price index** is used for conversion purposes.

The **LIFO retail method** is similar to dollar value, LIFO (discussed in Chapter 8, Part B) because it uses an **inventory price index.** However, the LIFO retail method also uses a **computed cost ratio.**

The **LIFO retail method** may be outlined as follows:

a. For each period, first apply the FIFO retail method. However, because FIFO is a **cost** rather

[2] Income tax regulations have a significant impact upon financial accounting for inventory at LIFO cost.

[3] FIFO is used because it, like LIFO, is maintained by inventory layers; average cost is **not** used because it is not maintained by layers.

than an LCM method, the net markdowns must be moved up into the computation of the cost ratio to approximate the FIFO cost of ending inventory, thereby ignoring the adjustment for LCM. The FIFO method, which excludes amounts of the beginning inventory from the cost ratio, must be used; the average cost method, which includes the amounts of the beginning inventory, cannot be used.

b. At the end of each period, the retail inventory FIFO (not LCM) results, **at retail,** are converted to a **LIFO cost** basis by using the dollar value approach. The beginning base year inventory for the year of change to dollar value LIFO is the ending FIFO (not LCM) inventory carried over from the year prior to the change. At the end of each period, conversion of the **FIFO retail** results to a **LIFO cost** basis involves two distinct phases as follows:

Phase A—Computation of an internal conversion price index (for variety stores) for the period similar to the illustration in Exhibit 8–12, Phase A, or selection of an external price index for conversion purposes (by department stores). Phase A will not be illustrated in this chapter because it was illustrated in Chapter 8.

Phase B—Conversion of the ending FIFO (not LCM) inventory results, **at retail,** to a LIFO cost basis by using (1) the conversion price index related to each layer of inventory and (2) the cost ratio of the period to convert ending inventory at retail value to a LIFO cost basis. The LIFO concept is implemented by assuming the last layers of inventory purchased are the first layers sold.

Phase B starts with the ending FIFO inventory, valued at retail and stated in the current year's dollars; this retail amount then is restated to retail in the base year's dollars by dividing it by the current year conversion price index. The result is the total ending inventory for the current year valued at retail but stated in base year dollars. This base year retail value then is identified in terms of the base layer and any additional layers added in years subsequent to the year of the base layer. Each such layer then is converted to LIFO costs by multiplying the base year retail amount by (1) its conversion price index to convert base year retail dollar values into dollars of the year the layer was added and (2) its cost ratio to restate those retail dollar values to cost amounts. The sum of the costs of the various layers, as converted, provides the ending inventory at LIFO cost, which is reported on the balance sheet and used

EXHIBIT 9–7: Data from Company Inventory Records for LIFO Retail Computation—WZ Company

1. The company has been using the retail inventory method (FIFO, not LCM) for *(a)* internal reporting and control purposes, *(b)* external reporting to shareholders, and *(c)* income tax purposes. Starting on January 1, 19B, the company decided to use the LIFO retail method for the latter two purposes.
2. The ending inventory at December 31, 19A, using the retail inventory method, FIFO basis (not LCM), was:
   At retail, $30,000
   At cost ($30,000 × cost ratio .58), $17,400
3. Detailed data subsequent to December 31, 19A (date of the change):*

	19B		19C		19D	
	At Cost	At Retail	At Cost	At Retail	At Cost	At Retail
Purchases	$90,480	$147,000	$101,500	$169,000	$115,800	$186,800
Net additional markups		8,800		9,000		7,000
Net markdowns		5,000		6,000		4,000
Sales		140,000		162,800		197,800
4. Selected external price index (19A = 100)		102		106		110

* A three-year period is used to illustrate initial adoption of LIFO, buildup of additional layers, and subsequent liquidation (in LIFO order) of parts of layers.

5. *Required:*
   a. Compute the ending inventory of WZ Company for 19B, 19C, and 19D using the retail inventory method, FIFO (not LCM) to provide the data for conversion.
   b. Convert the FIFO retail results, computed in 1 above, to LIFO cost.

EXHIBIT 9–8: Application of LIFO Retail—WZ Company, 19B

I. Computation of Ending Inventory at FIFO Cost:

a. Base layer (carried over from 19A): Retail $30,000 × .58 = Cost $17,400.

b. Computation of 19B ending FIFO inventory (not LCM):

	At FIFO Cost		At Retail	Cost Ratio
Goods available for sale:				
Inventory, 1/1/19B (Exhibit 9–7)	$ 17,400		$ 30,000	
Purchases (Exhibit 9–7)	90,480		147,000	
Net additional markups (Exhibit 9–7)			8,800	
Net markdowns (Exhibit 9–7)			(5,000)	
Subtotal (excluding beginning inventory due to FIFO)	90,480	÷	150,800	= .60
Total goods available for sale	$107,880		180,800	
Deduct: Sales			140,000	
Ending 19B inventory: At retail			$ 40,800	
At FIFO cost, $40,800 × .60 =	$ 24,480			

II. Conversion to LIFO Cost:

Phase A—Conversion:

Use external price index for 19B = 1.02

Phase B—Conversion of ending inventory at FIFO retail ($40,800) to LIFO cost:

	At Base Year Retail	Conversion Price Index	Cost Ratio	LIFO Cost
Ending inventory at retail converted to base year retail, $40,800 ÷ 1.02	$40,000			
Comprised of: Base inventory layer	$30,000	× 1.00	× .58 =	$17,400
19B additional inventory layer	$10,000*	× 1.02	× .60 =	6,120
Ending 19B inventory at LIFO cost				$23,520

* Multiplication of this retail amount by the current year conversion price index restated it to current year prices (i.e., $10,000 × 1.02 = $10,200); multiplication of the result by the current year cost ratio restated this 19B layer to 19B cost (i.e., $10,200 × .60 = $6,120).

on the income statement to compute cost of goods sold.

Conversion computations will be illustrated using the data given in Exhibit 9–7. The computations are shown separately for each year in Exhibits 9–8, 9–9, and 9–10. The exhibits should be studied carefully because they are designed to be self-explanatory.

Observe in Phase B (i.e., the bottom part) of Exhibit 9–8 that at the end of 19B, WZ Company had two layers of inventory, with costs of $17,400 and $6,120 (total cost, $23,520). At the end of 19C (see Exhibit 9–9), WZ Company had three layers of inventory, with costs of $17,400, $6,120, and $4,484 (total cost, $28,004). During 19D (see Exhibit 9–10), WZ Company liquidated part of the 19C layer; and at the end of 19D, WZ Company had only two layers, with costs of $17,400 and $5,007 (total cost, $22,407). **Layers (or parts of layers) once liquidated are never restored. New layers are added at their actual cost.**

Based upon the LIFO costs shown in 19D in Exhibit 9–10 (beginning inventory, $28,004; ending inventory, $22,407), WZ Company would make the following entries at the end of 19D (assuming a periodic inventory system and use of LIFO cost):

1. To remove the 19D beginning inventory:

Income summary	28,004	
Inventory (beginning)		28,004

2. To record the 19D ending inventory:

Inventory (ending)	22,407	
Income summary		22,407

EXHIBIT 9–9: Application of LIFO Retail—WZ Company, 19C

I. Computation of Ending Inventory at FIFO Cost:

a. Beginning dollar value LIFO inventory carried over from end of 19B (from Exhibit 9–8):

	At Base Year Retail	Conversion Price Index	Cost Ratio	LIFO Cost
Base inventory layer	$30,000	× 1.00	× .58 =	$17,400
19B additional layer	10,000	× 1.02	× .60 =	6,120
Total	$40,000			$23,520

b. Computation of 19C ending FIFO inventory (not LCM):

	At FIFO Cost		At Retail		Cost Ratio
Goods available for sale:					
Inventory, 1/1/19C (Exhibit 9–8)	$ 24,480		$ 40,800		
Purchases (Exhibit 9–7)	101,500		169,000		
Net additional markups (Exhibit 9–7)			9,000		
Net markdowns (Exhibit 9–7)			(6,000)		
Subtotal (excluding beginning inventory)	101,500	÷	172,000	=	.59
Total goods available for sale	$125,980		212,800		
Deduct: Sales			162,800		
Ending 19C inventory: At retail			$ 50,000		
At FIFO cost, $50,000 × .59 =	$ 29,500				

II. Conversion to LIFO Cost:

Phase A—Conversion price index for 19C = 1.06

Phase B—Conversion of ending inventory at FIFO retail ($50,000) to LIFO cost:

	At Base Year Retail	Conversion Price Index	Cost Ratio	LIFO Cost
Ending inventory at retail converted to base year retail, $50,000 ÷ 1.06	$47,170			
Comprised of: Base inventory layer	$30,000	× 1.00	× .58 =	$17,400
19B inventory layer	10,000	× 1.02	× .60 =	6,120
19C additional inventory layer	7,170	× 1.06	× .59 =	4,484
Ending 19C inventory at LIFO cost				$28,004

If WZ Company used a perpetual inventory system and maintained the Inventory account at FIFO cost throughout 19D, the end-of-period adjusting entry to record the LIFO cost of ending inventory would be as shown below. Note that, prior to the following entry, the Inventory account would reflect FIFO cost (i.e., $25,620; see Exhibit 9–10, Part I).

To convert 19D ending inventory from FIFO to LIFO:

Cost of goods sold	3,213	
Inventory* ($25,620 − $22,407)		3,213

* Many companies use an inventory allowance contra account for this entry; this contra account is discussed in Chapter 8 under the caption LIFO Allowances.

Evaluation of the Retail LIFO Inventory Method

The retail inventory method has been sponsored by the National Retail Merchants Association and approved by the Internal Revenue Service; consequently, it has become an important method of inventory determination. Like the gross margin method, the retail inventory method is an approach for **estimating** the amount of the ending inventory used in computing cost of goods sold on the income statement and for reporting inventory on the balance sheet. It can be used for both financial accounting and income tax purposes.

EXHIBIT 9–10: Application of LIFO Retail—WZ Company, 19D

I. Computation of Ending Inventory at FIFO Cost:

a. Beginning dollar value LIFO inventory carried over from end of 19C (from Exhibit 9–9):

	At Base Year Retail	Conversion Price Index	Cost Ratio	LIFO Cost
Base inventory layer	$30,000	× 1.00	× .58 =	$17,400
19B additional layer	10,000	× 1.02	× .60 =	6,120
19C additional layer	7,170	× 1.06	× .59 =	4,484
Total	$47,170			$28,004

b. Computation of 19D ending FIFO inventory (not LCM):

	At FIFO Cost		At Retail		Cost Ratio
Goods available for sale:					
Inventory, 1/1/19D (Exhibit 9–9)	$ 29,500		$ 50,000		
Purchases (Exhibit 9–7)	115,800		186,800		
Net additional markups (Exhibit 9–7)			7,000		
Net markdowns (Exhibit 9–7)			(4,000)		
Subtotal (excluding beginning inventory)	115,800	÷	189,800	=	.61
Total goods available for sale	$145,300		239,800		
Deduct: Sales			197,800		
Ending 19D inventory: At retail			$ 42,000		
At FIFO cost, $42,000 × .61 =	$ 25,620				

II. Conversion to LIFO Cost:

Phase A—Conversion price index for 19D = 1.10

Phase B—Conversion of ending inventory at FIFO retail ($42,000) to LIFO cost:

	At Base Year Retail	Conversion Price Index	Cost Ratio	LIFO Cost
Ending inventory at retail converted to base year retail, $42,000 ÷ 1.10	$38,182			
Comprised of: Base inventory layer	$30,000	× 1.00	× .58 =	$17,400
19B inventory layer remaining	8,182*	× 1.02	× .60 =	5,007
Ending 19D inventory at LIFO cost				$22,407

* After subtracting the base layer of $30,000, $8,182 remained. Therefore, all of the 19C layer was liquidated and $8,182 of the 19B layer remained. Observe that layers are liquidated in LIFO order and that both the conversion price index and the cost ratio are **always** identified with the layer created at those ratios. **A layer once liquidated is never restored.**

Because the retail inventory method provides only an estimate of the ending inventory, a physical inventory count should be taken at least annually as a check on the accuracy of the computed inventory amounts. Differences between the inventory valuations based on the (1) physical inventory count and (2) retail inventory computation should be carefully analyzed because a difference may indicate *(a)* inventory losses due to breakage, loss, or theft; *(b)* incorrect application of the retail method; *(c)* failure of departmental managers to correctly report markdowns, additional markups, or cancellations; *(d)* errors in the inventory records; *(e)* errors in the physical inventory; or *(f)* inventory manipulation.

The primary uses of the retail inventory method are as follows:

1. To provide estimated inventory valuations for interim periods (e.g., monthly or quarterly) when it is not practical to physically count the inventory and a perpetual inventory system is not used. The method provides estimated inventory valuations needed for interim statements, analyses, and purchasing policy considerations.

2. To provide a means for converting inventory amounts determined by a physical count of inventory, priced at retail, to a cost basis. To eliminate the necessity of marking the cost on the merchandise, or referring to invoices, some retail establishments, after physically counting the inventory, extend the inventory sheets at retail. The retail value then is converted to cost by applying the retail inventory method without reference to the costs of individual items.
3. To provide a basis for **control** of inventory, purchases, theft, markdowns, and additional markups when neither a traditional periodic nor perpetual inventory system is used for these interim purposes.
4. To provide data for external financial reports.
5. To provide data for income tax purposes.
6. To provide a test of the overall reasonableness of a physical inventory costed in the normal manner.

INVENTORIES ON LONG-TERM CONSTRUCTION CONTRACTS

To this point in the chapter we have considered inventories that arise in the conventional manner; that is, inventories that are either purchased from vendors or manufactured over a reasonably short period of time. In those discussions we considered the dual phases of the inventory accounting problem, measuring *(a)* cost of goods sold and *(b)* ending inventory.

In contrast, a unique inventory accounting problem arises in the construction industry. The problem involves measurement of the accounting value of the **construction in process inventory** associated with long-term construction contracts during the extended construction period for items such as buildings, bridges, ships, and dams.

The problem is unique because the construction period often extends over two or more annual accounting periods. Because **inventory valuation** directly affects **income measurement** during the construction period, the two problems of inventory and income measurement are discussed. For example, assume a 2½-year construction period. Should income be recognized as construction progresses (i.e., each period), or should income be recognized only at the end of the 2½ years? The answer to this question affects the accounting value of inventory.

The accounting profession recognizes two distinctly different methods of accounting for inventory and income on long-term construction contracts. The two methods are:

1. The **completed contract method**—All construction costs are accumulated in an inventory account, Construction in Process. Income is recognized only upon completion of the project.
2. The **percentage-of-completion method**—All construction costs **plus** all income recognized during the construction period are accumulated in an inventory account, Construction in Process. Income is recognized each period based upon progress of the construction.

To illustrate the accounting for inventory and income on long-term construction contracts, we will use the following data:

1. Ace Construction Company received a contract to erect a building for $1.5 million. Construction is to start February 1, 19A, and is to be completed 2½ years from that date.
2. Progress billings are to be submitted by the contractor at the end of each month based upon a predetermined schedule which is subject to audit by the purchaser of the building. The progress billings are payable to the contractor within 10 days after the billing.
3. The percentage of completion at the end of each accounting period during construction will be measured by the ratio of total costs incurred to date to estimated total costs to be incurred on the project (costs incurred to date plus estimated costs to complete).
4. Data covering the entire construction period are shown in Exhibit 9–11.

Completed Contract Method

Long-term construction contracts almost always provide for the contractor to bill the purchaser for progress payments (as agreed upon in the contract); such progress billings are debited to Accounts Receivable and credited to Billings on Contracts. The latter is a contra account to Construction in Process Inventory because it represents the purchaser's ownership interest in the asset under construction. If the **net** amount of Construction in Process Inventory (i.e., Construction in Process Inventory, less Billings on Contracts) is a debit, it is reported as a **current asset,** Inventory, because it represents the contractor's ownership interest in the construction inventory. If

EXHIBIT 9–11: Long-Term Construction Contracts—Illustrative Data—Ace Construction Company

	Year 19A	Year 19B	Year 19C	Total
Contract price				$1,500,000
Costs incurred each year	$ 350,000	$550,000	$465,000	1,365,000
Estimated costs to complete (at year-end)	1,000,000	460,000	-0-	-0-
Income on construction				$ 135,000
Progress billings each year	300,000	575,000	625,000	$1,500,000
Collections on billings each year	270,000	555,000	675,000	1,500,000

EXHIBIT 9–12: Apportionment of Estimated Income—Percentage-of-Completion Method—Ace Construction Company

	Year 19A	Year 19B	Year 19C
Contract price	$1,500,000	$1,500,000	$1,500,000*
Less costs:			
Actual cost to date (cumulative)	350,000*	900,000*	1,365,000*
Estimated cost to complete	1,000,000	460,000	
Estimated total costs	1,350,000	1,360,000	1,365,000*
Estimated total income	$ 150,000	$ 140,000	$ 135,000*
Apportionment of total income (based on ratio of costs incurred to date to estimated total construction cost):			
19A:			
($350,000/$1,350,000) × $150,000	$ 38,889		
19B:			
($900,000/$1,360,000) × $140,000		$ 92,647	
Less income recognized to date		38,889	
Income recognized in 19B		$ 53,758	
19C:			
Total income to be recognized (actual)			$ 135,000
Less income recognized to date ($38,889 + $53,758)			92,647
Income recognized in 19C			$ 42,353

* Actual.

the net amount is a credit, it is reported as a **liability** because Billings on Contracts (i.e., the purchaser's ownership) exceeds the Construction in Process Inventory (i.e., the contractor's ownership).

When the contract is completed, the income recognized is the difference between the accumulated credit balance in the Billings on Contracts account and the debit balance in the Construction in Process Inventory account. The accumulated **amount** of Billings on Contracts is essentially the **amount** of sales revenue.[4] The accumulated **amount** of Construction in Process Inventory upon completion of the contract is essentially the **amount** of cost of goods sold. Therefore, it follows that the difference between the two amounts is the pretax income earned on the project.

Under the completed contract method, during the

[4] Billings on Contracts is **not** a revenue account, and Construction in Process is not a cost of goods sold account. Note the emphasis on "amount" in the referenced sentence.

construction period the construction in process inventory is reported on the balance sheet at the total accumulated costs to date, less the total progress billings to date, and income on construction contracts ($135,000 in Exhibit 9–11) is reported only in the year of completion (19C in the example). The entries in the accounts of Ace Construction Company for the completed contract method are illustrated in Exhibit 9–13; the financial statement presentation for each year is shown in Exhibit 9–14.

Percentage-of-Completion Method

Under this method, accounting for a long-term construction contract is the same as the completed contract method explained above except that **income is recognized as earned each accounting period** during construction and added to the account, Construction in Process Inventory. Because the **actual** income on the contract will not be known until completion, an estimate of it must be made each period. The estimated amount of income then is apportioned to each period on the basis of the percentage of the total contract completed (i.e., percentage of completion) during that period.

Percentage of completion usually is determined on the basis of either *(a)* engineering and/or architectural estimates of the work performed to date compared to the total work necessary for the contract or *(b)* the ratio of total costs incurred to date on the contract **to** the total costs which will be incurred on the contract. The estimated amount of income recognized each period is accrued as a debit to Construction in Process Inventory and a credit to Income on Construction. The inventory account is debited for the income recognized because it adds to the contractor's ownership interest in the construction inventory. The income account is closed to Income Summary each period and is reported on the income statement. Computation of the amount of estimated income to be recognized each year by the Ace Construction Company is illustrated in Exhibit 9–12.

Observe in Exhibit 9–12 that the total income on the project is apportioned to each period on the basis of the ratio of costs incurred to date to total costs to be incurred. For example, in 19A, total income of $150,000 was estimated on the project, and $38,889 of that amount was apportioned to 19A. At the end of construction Ace Construction Company earned $135,000 on the project, and the apportionments of income to 19A, 19B, and 19C were as shown in Exhibit 9–12.

The resulting entries in the accounts of Ace Construction Company for each method are reflected in Exhibit 9–13. For each year, entries 1–3 are the same under the completed contract and percentage-of-completion methods. Only entry 4 for recognition of income (boxed for emphasis), differs between the two methods. This difference affects the carrying value of construction in process inventory (see the debit side of entry 4 under the percentage-of-completion method). The financial statement presentation for each period is shown in Exhibit 9–14 for each method.

As Exhibit 9–14 reflects, both methods derive the same results on the balance sheet during the construction period, except for the amount of the ending inventory (i.e., costs in excess of billings) and retained earnings. Under the percentage-of-completion method, the inventory prior to completion of the project is greater in amount by the accumulated pretax income recognized in the current and prior periods. Thus, for Ace Construction Company the ending inventory (i.e., costs in excess of billings) is greater by $38,889 at the end of 19A and by $38,889 + $53,758 = $92,647 at the end of 19B. Recall that the estimated income recognized as earned each year was debited to Construction in Process Inventory in the percentage-of-completion method.

Under either method, when there is a projected loss at any time, it must be recognized in the period in which a loss on the contract appears probable. The loss should be recognized by means of a debit to Loss on Construction and a credit to Construction in Process Inventory. The credit side of the entry removes from the inventory account the amount of costs in excess of expected recovery value. Also, when a loss on the contract is probable, any income previously recognized should be "reversed" and reported as a loss in the period that such determination is made.

For example, assume that at the end of 19B, Ace Construction Company projected a $40,000 loss on the project. Under the **completed contract method,** Ace would make the following entry at the end of 19B (in place of no entry 4 under the completed contract method in Exhibit 9–13):

Loss on Construction	40,000	
Construction in Process Inventory ..		40,000

Under the **percentage-of-completion method,** the entry to recognize the loss would be as follows (in place of entry 4 for 19B under the percentage-of-completion method in Exhibit 9–13):

Loss on Construction ($38,889 from 19A + $40,000)	78,889	
Construction in Process Inventory		78,889

The two entries given above for completed contract and percentage of completion differ by the amount of construction income recognized in 19A under the percentage-of-completion method (i.e., $38,889); this amount must be reversed in the entry to record the loss under the percentage-of-completion method.

After the above entries are posted, the balance in the Construction in Process Inventory account will be $860,000 (i.e., costs incurred to date, $900,000; see Exhibit 9–13, entry 1 for years 19A and 19B) minus the $40,000 loss recognized at the end of 19B. In this situation, Billings on Contracts at the end of 19B (i.e., $875,000; see Exhibit 9–14) exceeds Construction in Process Inventory (i.e., $860,000) by $15,000; this credit balance (i.e., $15,000) would be reported as a liability. In most situations, this liability would be a current liability because Ace Construction Company would reduce progress billings accordingly in the immediate future.

Therefore, whenever a loss appears probable, construction in process inventory would be reported at estimated net realizable value (i.e., $860,000) under either method. Inventory and income amounts reported in prior years would not be retroactively restated in current-year comparative statements. Instead, the change in projections would be accounted for prospectively as a change in estimate, as illustrated above and explained in Chapters 3 and 20.

Evaluation of Long-Term Construction Contract Methods

Both the completed contract and percentage-of-completion methods of accounting for inventory and income on long-term construction contracts are generally accepted. Over the entire construction period, both methods recognize the same total amount of pretax income.

Advocates of the **completed contract** method assert that it is more objective and more conservative because income is not recognized until all of the revenues and expenses for the completed job are known with certainty. However, this method is viewed by some accountants as deficient because income recognition does not reflect performance each accounting period during construction. Although most of the work may be completed prior to the period in which construction is completed, all of the income is reported in the last period. Hence, it results in a poor matching of expense with revenue.

The **percentage-of-completion** method is supported on the basis that, because a contract is in force, the construction company earns revenue as it performs the work on the contract. In this view, it is unreasonable to await completion before recognizing income. However, some accountants consider the percentage-of-completion method as deficient because income during the construction period is measured subjectively and recognized on the basis of **(a) estimates** of work done (percentage of completion) and **(b) estimated** total construction cost.

The accounting profession has sanctioned the use of either method as follows:[5]

> The committee believes that in general when estimates of costs to complete and extent of progress toward completion of long-term contracts are reasonably dependable, the percentage-of-completion method is preferable. When lack of dependable estimates or inherent hazards cause forecasts to be doubtful, the completed-contract method is preferable.

[5] AICPA, *Accounting Research Bulletin No. 45,* "Long-Term Construction-Type Contracts" (New York, 1955).

EXHIBIT 9–13: Long-Term Construction Contracts—Journal Entries for Completed Contract and Percentage-of-Completion Methods Compared, Ace Construction Company

	Method			
	Completed Contract		Percentage of Completion	
Year 19A:				
1. Costs of construction:				
Construction in process inventory	350,000*		350,000	
Cash, payables, etc.		350,000		350,000

* Under the completed contract method this may include a reasonable allocation of general and administrative (G&A) expenses for periods prior to completion.

	Completed Contract		Percentage of Completion	
2. Progress billings:				
Accounts receivable	300,000		300,000	
Billings on contracts		300,000		300,000
3. Collections on billings:				
Cash	270,000		270,000	
Accounts receivable		270,000		270,000
4. Recognition of income:				
Construction in process inventory	(No income recognized		38,889	
Income on construction†	until completion)			38,889
† Closed to Income Summary.				
Year 19B:				
1. Costs of construction:				
Construction in process inventory	550,000		550,000	
Cash, payables, etc.		550,000		550,000
2. Progress billings:				
Accounts receivable	575,000		575,000	
Billings on contracts		575,000		575,000
3. Collections on billings:				
Cash	555,000		555,000	
Accounts receivable		555,000		555,000
4. Recognition of income:				
Construction in process inventory	(No income recognized		53,758	
Income on construction	until completion)			53,758
Year 19C:				
1. Costs of construction:				
Construction in process inventory	465,000		465,000	
Cash, payables, etc.		465,000		465,000
2. Progress billings (final billing):				
Accounts receivable	625,000		625,000	
Billings on contracts		625,000		625,000
3. Collections on billings (in full):				
Cash	675,000		675,000	
Accounts receivable		675,000		675,000

EXHIBIT 9–13 ***(continued)***

	Completed Contract		Percentage of Completion	
4. Recognition of income (and to close the accumulated account balances):				
Construction in process inventory			42,353‡	
Billings on contracts	1,500,000		1,500,000	
Construction in process inventory		1,365,000		1,500,000
Income on construction		135,000		42,353

‡ Alternatively, this entry could be as follows (with the same results):

Billings on contracts	1,500,000	
Construction in process inventory		1,457,647
Income on construction		42,353

EXHIBIT 9–14: Long-Term Construction Contracts—Financial Statements for Completed Contract and Percentage-of-Completion Methods Compared, Ace Construction Company

	Completed Contract			Percentage of Completion		
	19A	19B	19C	19A	19B	19C
Balance sheet:						
Current assets:						
Accounts receivable	$ 30,000	$ 50,000		$ 30,000	$ 50,000	
Inventory:						
Construction in process inventory	350,000	900,000		388,889*	992,647*	
Less: Billings on contracts	300,000	875,000		300,000	875,000	
Costs in excess of billings†	50,000	25,000		88,889*	117,647*	
Income statement:						
Income on construction	-0-	-0-	$135,000	38,889	53,758	$42,353

* These amounts exceed their counterpart amounts under the completed contract method by the amount of income recognized to date.

† Abbreviated titles are used herein for convenience. This account usually is labeled Cost of Uncompleted Contracts in Excess of Billings.

QUESTIONS

PART A

1. What basic assumption is implicit in the *gross margin method?*

2. Approximate the valuation of the ending inventory assuming the following data are available:

Cost of goods available for sale	$170,000
Net sales	150,000
Gross margin rate (on sales)	30%

3. Distinguish between *(a)* gross margin rate on sales, *(b)* gross margin percentage on cost of goods sold, *(c)* cost percentage, *(d)* markup on cost, and *(e)* markup on sales.

4. List four uses of the gross margin method.

5. Why is it frequently desirable to apply the gross margin method by classes of merchandise?

6. Explain the basic approach of the *retail method* of estimating inventories. What data must be accumulated in order to apply the retail method?

7. The ending inventory estimated by the retail inventory method was $90,000. A physical inventory of the merchandise on hand extended at retail showed $75,000. Suggest possible reasons for the discrepancy.

8. What are the primary uses of the retail method of estimating inventories?

9. When are markdowns and markdown cancellations excluded in computing the cost ratio in the retail inventory method?

PART B

10. What are two differences between the retail inventory method under FIFO and average cost versus the LIFO retail method?

11. Explain why the FIFO retail inventory method must be used in combination with LIFO retail to attain LIFO retail results.

12. When LIFO retail is adopted, why must the ending inventory of the period prior to the base year often be recomputed?

13. Explain the essential differences between *(a)* the completed contract method and *(b)* the percentage-of-completion method of accounting for long-term construction contracts.

14. Why is the ending inventory of construction in process larger in amount when the percentage-of-completion method is used compared with the completed contract method? How much larger will the amount be?

EXERCISES

PART A: EXERCISES 9–1 to 9–11

(Unless instructed otherwise, round all markup percentages and cost ratios to two decimal places.)

Exercise 9–1

Assume the following data for Enfield Company for a particular period:

Sales	$120,000
Beginning inventory	16,000
Purchases	80,000

For each of the separate situations below, estimate the ending inventory (round all ratios to three decimal places):

a. Markup is one half on cost.
b. Markup is 60% on sales.
c. Markup is 30% on cost.
d. Markup is 57% on cost.
e. Markup is 40% on sales.

Exercise 9–2

The books of Windsor Company provided the following information:

Inventory, Jan. 1	$ 6,000
Purchases to May 10	80,000
Net sales to May 10	98,000

Before opening for business on May 11, the assets of the company were totally destroyed by fire. The insurance company adjuster found that the average rate of gross margin for the past few years had been 60%.

Required (round all ratios to three decimal places):
What was the approximate value of the inventory destroyed assuming the gross margin percentage given was based on (1) sales and (2) cost of goods sold?

Exercise 9–3

You are engaged in the audit of the records of Marshall Company. A physical inventory has been taken by the company under your observation, to determine the valuation of the inventory; however, the extensions have not been completed. The records of the company provide the following data: sales, $300,000 (gross); return sales, $4,000 (returned to stock); purchases (gross), $155,000; beginning inventory, $50,000; freight-in, $5,000; and purchase returns and allowances, $2,000. The gross margin last period was 34% of net sales; you anticipate that it will be 37% for the year under audit. Estimate the cost of the ending inventory using the gross margin method. Show computations.

Exercise 9–4

The records of Lorie Company provided the following data for January for two products sold:

	Product A	Product B
Beginning inventory, Jan. 1	$ 40,000	$ 60,000
Purchases during January	147,000	186,000
Freight on purchases	3,000	4,000
Sales during January	300,000	400,000

The gross margin rates on sales for the prior year were company overall, 47%; product A, 42%; and product B, 49%.

Required:

1. Estimate the cost of the ending inventory separately and in the aggregate.

2. Under what conditions would one of your responses to 1 above be suspect?

Exercise 9–5

On November 21, 19B, a fire destroyed Charles Company's warehouse where Product Tex was stored. It is estimated that $10,000 can be realized from sale of usable damaged inventory. The accounting records concerning Product Tex reveal:

Inventory at 11/1/19B	$100,000
Purchases from 11/1/19B to 11/21/19B	140,000
Net sales from 11/1/19B to 11/21/19B	220,000

Based on recent history the gross margin has averaged 30% of net sales.

Required:
Prepare a schedule to calculate the estimated loss of inventory based on the gross margin method. Show supporting computations. (AICPA adapted)

Exercise 9–6

Doo-Dad Department Store uses the retail method of inventory. At the end of June, the records of the company reflected the following:

Purchases during June: at cost, $265,000; at retail, $430,000.
Sales during June: $350,000.
Inventory, June 1: at cost, $40,000; at retail, $70,000.

Estimate the ending inventory for June assuming *(a)* FIFO cost basis and *(b)* average cost basis. Show all computations.

Exercise 9–7

Supreme Clothing Store values its inventory using the retail inventory method at the lower of average cost or market. The following data are available for the month of November 19A:

	Cost	Selling Price
Inventory, Nov. 1	$ 53,800	$ 80,000
Markdowns		21,000
Markups		29,000
Markdown cancellations		13,000
Markup cancellations		9,000
Purchases	173,200	223,600
Sales		244,000
Purchase returns and allowances	3,000	3,600
Sales returns and allowances		12,000

Required:
Prepare a schedule to compute the estimated inventory at November 30, 19A, at the lower of average cost or market using the retail inventory method. (AICPA adapted)

Exercise 9–8

Philip Department Store uses the retail inventory method. Information relating to the computation of inventory for 19E is as follows:

	At Cost	At Retail
Beginning inventory	$ 32,000	$ 80,000
Sales		600,000
Purchases	270,000	590,000
Freight on purchases	7,600	
Markups		60,000
Markup cancellations		10,000
Markdowns		25,000
Markdown cancellations		5,000

Estimated normal shrinkage is 2% of sales.

Required:
Calculate the estimated ending inventory for 19E at the lower of average cost or market. Show supporting calculations. (AICPA adapted)

Exercise 9–9

The records of Krebs Department Store showed the following data for Department 20 for January: beginning inventory at cost, $15,000, and $26,000 at selling price; purchases at cost, $150,000, and $297,000 at selling price; gross sales, $310,000; return sales, $6,000 (returned to stock); purchase returns at cost, $4,000, and $7,000 at selling price; and freight-in, $5,960. Determine the approximate valuation of the ending inventory using the retail inventory method *(a)* at average cost and *(b)* at FIFO. Show all computations. Which is lower? What may have accounted for the result? Was LCM applied implicitly by Krebs? If yes, explain.

Exercise 9–10

Use the retail inventory method (LCM basis) to estimate the ending inventory *(a)* at average cost and LCM and *(b)* FIFO cost and LCM for Shivers Retailers based on the following data:

	At Cost	At Retail
Beginnning inventory	$ 91,000	$142,000
Purchases	330,000	561,000
Purchases returned	6,000	10,000
Freight-in	5,000	
Additional markups		12,000
Additional markup cancellations		5,000
Markdowns		9,000
Markdown cancellations		2,000
Sales		540,000
Sales returned (and restored to inventory)		4,000

How is LCM introduced into the computations? Explain the logic of this procedure. Will LCM always produce a lower inventory cost estimate under the retail method than FIFO or average without LCM?

Exercise 9–11

Meadows Retail Store has just completed the annual physical inventory, which involved counting the goods on hand, then pricing them at selling prices. The inventory valuation derived in this manner amounted to $106,000. The records of the company provided the following data: beginning inventory, $80,000 at retail and $52,120 at cost; purchases (including freight-in and returns), $750,000 at retail and $469,920 at cost; additional markups, $20,000; additional markup cancellations, $8,000; gross sales, $733,000; return sales (restored to inventory), $9,000; and markdowns, $6,000.

Required:

1. Estimate the cost of the ending inventory assuming average cost and LCM.
2. Note any discrepancies and give possible reasons for them.

PART B: EXERCISES 9–12 to 9–15

Exercise 9–12

Dorman Retailers uses FIFO retail for internal purposes and the LIFO retail method to convert those results for external reporting and for income tax purposes (starting January 1, 19B).

The following data were provided by the inventory records for the year ended December 31, 19B:

	At Cost	At Retail
1/1/19B, base inventory (carried over from 19A)	$ 6,000	$10,000
Data at end of 19B:		
Sales revenue (net of returns)		70,000
Purchases (net of returns)	54,900	85,000
Net additional markups		7,000
Net markdowns		2,000
Total administrative and selling expenses	10,000	

Assume the conversion index numbers are December 31, 19A, 120; and December 31, 19B, 126. Average income tax rate, 40%.

Required:

1. Compute the FIFO retail inventory results that would be used for internal purposes at the end of 19B.
2. Convert the FIFO retail inventory results to a LIFO basis for external reporting and income tax purposes.
3. Prepare an income statement using the following format:

	Year 19B	
	FIFO Basis	LIFO Basis
Sales revenue	$_____	$_____
Less expenses:		
Cost of goods sold:		
Beginning inventory	_____	_____
Purchases	_____	_____
Total	_____	_____
Ending inventory	_____	_____
Cost of goods sold	_____	_____
Admin. and selling expenses	_____	_____
Total expenses	_____	_____
Pretax income	_____	_____
Income taxes	_____	_____
Net income	_____	_____

Exercise 9–13

Broadway Retail Store had been using the traditional retail inventory method determined on the average cost, LCM basis, for a number of years for all purposes. On January 1, 19M, the company changed to LIFO retail for external reporting and income tax purposes, but retained average cost, LCM for internal purposes.

At the end of 19L and 19M, the retail inventory computations (average, LCM) for internal purposes were as shown at the top of the next page.

Required (round to nearest dollar):

1. Compute the inventory values (at cost and at retail) that should be used as the base inventory and the ending inventory for 19M for conversion purposes. Why are the above inventory values not appropriate for this purpose?
2. Convert the FIFO retail inventory results, computed in 1 above, to the LIFO retail basis for the external reports and income tax use at the end of 19M.
3. Complete the following tabulation for 19M:

	Year 19M		
	Average	FIFO	LIFO
Sales revenue	$_____	$_____	$_____
Cost of goods sold:			
Beginning inventory	_____	_____	_____
Purchases	_____	_____	_____
Total	_____	_____	_____
Ending inventory	_____	_____	_____
Cost of goods sold	_____	_____	_____
Gross margin	_____	_____	_____

(Relates to Exercise 9–13)

	Year 19L			Year 19M		
	At Cost		At Retail	At Cost		At Retail
Beginning inventory, Jan. 1	$ 17,000		$ 30,000	$ 28,000		$ 50,000
Purchases	151,000		268,000	180,000		321,789
Net additional markups			2,000			3,000
Total	$168,000		300,000	$208,000		374,789
Cost ratio ($168,000 ÷ $300,000 = .56)		.56			.55	
Sales			(245,000)			(305,789)
Net markdowns			(5,000)			(9,000)
Inventory, Dec. 31:						
At retail			$ 50,000			$ 60,000
At cost (average, LCM)	$ 28,000			$ 33,000		

Conversion price indexes: 12/31/19L, 150; and 12/31/19M, 168.

Exercise 9–14

Bland Construction Company contracted to build a plant for $500,000. Construction started in January 19A and was completed in November 19B. Data relating to the contract are summarized below:

	19A	19B
Cost incurred during year	$290,000	$115,000
Estimated additional costs to complete	125,000	
Billings during year	230,000	270,000
Cash collections during year	200,000	300,000

Required:
Give the journal entries for Bland, in parallel columns, assuming *(a)* the completed contract method and *(b)* the percentage-of-completion method. Apportion on basis of costs incurred to date to total estimated construction cost.

Exercise 9–15

Use the data given in Exercise 9–14 to complete a tabulation as follows:

	Completed Contract Method	Percentage-of-Completion Method*
Income statement:		
Income:		
19A	$______	$______
19B	______	______
Balance sheet:		
Receivables:		
19A	______	______
19B	______	______
Inventory—construction in process, net of billings:		
19A	______	______
19B	______	______

* Apportion on basis of costs incurred to date to total estimated construction cost.

PROBLEMS

PART A: PROBLEMS 9–1 to 9–7

(Unless instructed otherwise, round all gross margin percentages, markup percentages, and cost ratios to two decimal places.)

Problem 9–1

The records of Yates Corporation provided the following information on August 13, 19A:

Inventory, 1/1/19A	$ 50,000
Purchases, Jan. 1 to Aug. 13	300,000
Sales, Jan. 1 to Aug. 13	400,000
Purchase returns and allowances	3,000
Sales returns (goods returned to stock)	5,000
Freight-in	4,000

A fire completely destroyed the inventory on August 14, 19A, except for goods marked to sell at $6,000 which had an estimated residual value of $4,000, and for goods in transit to which Yates Corp. had ownership; the purchase had been recorded. Invoices recorded on the latter show merchandise cost, $2,000, and freight-in, $100. The average rate of gross margin on sales in recent years has been 35%.

Required:

1. Compute the inventory fire loss.
2. Under what conditions would your response to 1 above be suspect? Explain.

Problem 9–2

Holcomb Stores, Inc. is developing a profit plan. The following planned data were developed for 19C.

a. January 1 planned inventory, $90,000.
b. Planned average rate of gross margin on sales, 30%.

Complete the following profit plan:

Profit Plan Estimates

	Jan.–June	July–Dec.	Total
Sales planned	$160,000	$190,000	$350,000
Cost of goods sold:			
Beginning inventory	?	?	?
Purchases budget	110,000	130,000	240,000
Total goods available	?	?	?
Less: Ending inventory	?	?	?
Cost of goods sold	?	?	?
Gross margin planned	?	?	?

Problem 9–3

Young Retail Store burned on March 19, 19D. The following information (up to the date of the fire) was taken from the records of the company which were stored in a safe: inventory, January 1, $28,000; sales, $140,000; purchases, $90,000; sales returns (restored to stock), $5,000; purchase returns and allowances, $2,000; and freight-in, $4,000. The cost of goods sold and gross margins for the past three years were as follows:

	Cost of Goods Sold	Gross Margin
19A	$469,000	$124,000
19B	435,000	120,000
19C	472,000	127,000

Required:

1. Estimate the cost of the inventory destroyed in the fire.
2. Under what conditions would your response to 1 above be suspect?
3. The insurance company pays indemnity on "market value" at date of the fire. What amount would you recommend that Young submit as an insurance claim? Explain.

Problem 9–4

Fairfield Company in the past valued inventories at cost. At the end of the current period, the inventory was valued at 37½% of selling price as a matter of convenience. However, the cost ratio is not 37½%. The current financial statements have been prepared, and the inventory sheets inadvertently destroyed; consequently, you find it impossible to reconstruct the ending inventory at actual cost per the physical count. Fortunately, the following data are available.

Sales	$300,000
Ending inventory (at 37½% of selling price)	22,500
Purchases (at cost)	182,500
Pretax income	32,000
Beginning inventory (at cost)	20,000

Required:
Prepare a corrected (and detailed) income statement. Show computations and round the cost ratio to four decimal places.

Problem 9–5

The records of Mellon Department Store provided the following data for June:

Sales (gross)	$750,000
Return sales (restored to inventory)	2,000
Additional markups	9,000
Additional markup cancellations	5,000
Markdowns	7,000
Purchases:	
At retail	749,000
At cost	419,540
Purchase returns:	
At retail	4,000
At cost	2,200
Freight on purchases	6,000
Beginning inventory:	
At cost	51,000
At retail	95,000
Employee discounts	1,000
Markdown cancellations	3,000

Required:
Estimate the valuation of the ending inventory assuming (show computations and carry cost ratios to four places and round inventory to nearest dollar):

Case A—Average cost (for illustrative purposes only).

Case B—Average cost, LCM.

Case C—FIFO cost (for illustrative purposes only).

Case D—FIFO cost, LCM.

Problem 9–6

Polson's Department Store uses the retail inventory method. Data for the year ended January 31, 19C, for one department appear below:

Inventory, 1/31/19B:	
Cost	$ 31,850
Sales price	54,000
Purchases for year ended 1/31/19C (gross):	
Cost	137,300
Sales price	275,000
Sales for year (gross)	280,000
Freight on merchandise purchased	6,000
Returns:	
Purchases:	
Cost	1,150
Sales price	2,000
Sales (merchandise restored to inventory)	5,000
Additional markups	4,000
Additional markup cancellations	1,000
Markdowns	12,000
Markdown cancellations	2,000
Employee discounts	500

Required:

1. Estimate the January 31, 19C, inventory valuation using the retail inventory method under each of the following methods (carry cost ratios to three decimal places):
   a. Average cost and LCM.
   b. FIFO cost and LCM.
   c. Average cost (for illustrative purposes only).
   d. FIFO cost (for illustrative purposes only).
2. Since sales returns reenter Polson's inventory after the customer returns the goods, why are sales returns not added back to goods available for sale at cost and at retail?

Problem 9–7

Auditors are examining the accounts of Austin Retailers, Inc. They were present when Austin's personnel physically counted the Austin inventory; however, the auditors made their own tests. The records of Austin Retailers provided the following data for the year:

	At Retail	At Cost
Inventory, Jan. 1	$ 220,000	$145,500
Net purchases	1,473,000	973,500
Freight-in		15,000
Additional markups	16,000	
Additional markup cancellations	9,000	
Markdowns	8,000	
Employee discounts	2,000	
Sales	1,300,000	
Inventory, Dec. 31 (per physical count valued at retail)	395,000	

Required:

1. Compute the ending inventory at average cost and LCM as an audit test of the overall reasonableness of the physical inventory count.
2. Note any discrepancies that are indicated. What factors should the auditors consider in reconciling any difference in results from the analysis?
3. What accounting treatment should be accorded the discrepancy (if any)?

PART B: PROBLEMS 9–8 to 9–17

Problem 9–8

Woods Retailers keeps its internal inventory records on a FIFO (not LCM) basis. At interim reporting dates, Woods' accountants convert the book balances to a LIFO basis for reporting purposes. They use the LIFO retail method for making this conversion. It is now March 31, 19E, and the following data that pertain to the quarter just ended are available from the accounts:

	Quarter Ended 3/31/19E	
	At Cost	At Retail
Base layer from 19C (when LIFO was adopted): index = 100	$ 19,750	$ 38,500
Additional LIFO layer added in 19D; index = 104; cost ratio = .60	30,900	51,500
Beginning inventory, 19E; index = 110	49,500	90,000
Purchases (net)	231,000	400,000
Net additional markups		30,000
Net markdowns		10,000
Return sales		6,000
Sales (gross)		392,000

Price index at end of March 19E = 124.

Required:
Compute the ending inventory at March 31, 19E, at LIFO cost using the retail inventory method. Show all computations in order and round all cost ratios and price index ratios to three places.

Problem 9–9

Rockdale Retailers has used the FIFO retail method, LCM basis, of inventory for all purposes. On January 1, 19F, the company decided to use the LIFO retail method to convert the inventory to the LIFO basis. The results will be used for external reporting and for income tax purposes. The base inventory at the start of 19F was as follows:

(Relates to Problem 9–9)

	19F		19G		19H	
	At Cost	At Retail	At Cost	At Retail	At Cost	At Retail
Sales (net)		$130,000		$140,000		$155,000
Purchases (net)	$100,800	153,000	$112,000	164,000	$121,600	185,000
Net additional markups		7,000		11,000		5,000
Applicable price index (19E = 100)	104		107		111	
Admin. and selling expenses	25,000		27,000		36,000	

	At Cost	At Retail
1/1/19F, base inventory (carried over from 12/31/19E)	$31,000	$50,000

Data from the inventory records for 19F–19H are given above.

Required:

1. Compute the inventory values (at cost and at retail) that should be used as the ending inventories for 19F, 19G, and 19H for conversion purposes.
2. Convert the FIFO inventory results for each year, computed in 1 above, to LIFO retail for use in developing the external financial statements and the income tax return.
3. Complete the following tabulation for 19H:

	Year 19H	
	FIFO Basis	LIFO Basis
Sales revenue	$_____	$_____
Less expenses:		
Cost of goods sold:		
Beginning inventory	_____	_____
Purchases	_____	_____
Total	_____	_____
Ending inventory	_____	_____
Cost of goods sold	_____	_____
Admin. and selling expenses	_____	_____
Total expenses	_____	_____
Pretax income	_____	_____
Income taxes (assume 40% rate)	_____	_____
Net income	_____	_____
Reduction in cash outflows using LIFO	$_____	

Problem 9–10

Harris Department Store has been using the retail inventory method (average, LCM) for a number of years. After extensive consideration the company decided to change to LIFO retail for all purposes. Thus, after the change, instituted on January 1, 19W, FIFO retail cost basis will be computed each period, then these results will be converted to LIFO retail for external reporting and income tax purposes.

The inventory records for the year 19V showed the following computations (i.e., for the year prior to the change):

	At Cost	At Retail
Inventory, 1/1/19V	$ 32,000	$ 54,000
Purchases (net)	493,400	680,000
Net additional markups		6,000
Total	$525,400	740,000
Cost ratio: $525,400 + $740,000 = .71		
Sales (net)		(670,000)
Net markdowns		(10,000)
Inventory, 12/31/19V:		
At retail		$ 60,000
At average cost LCM ($60,000 × .71)	$ 42,600	

Data for the three years 19W–19Y were as shown in the accompanying table.

Required:

1. Compute the inventory value that should be used as the base inventory on January 1, 19W.
2. Compute the inventory values (at cost and at retail) that should be used as the ending inventories for 19W, 19X, and 19Y for conversion purposes (and for internal use).
3. In view of the change from average, LCM, the company decided to adjust the inventory account to the FIFO cost basis for internal purposes. Give the entry to effect this change at the start of 19W.
4. Convert the FIFO inventory results for each year, computed in 2 above, to LIFO retail for use in developing the external financial statements and the income tax return.
5. Complete the tabulation for 19Y shown on the next page.

(Relates to Problem 9–10)

	19W		19X		19Y	
	At Cost	At Retail	At Cost	At Retail	At Cost	At Retail
Purchases (net)	$501,120	$689,000	$497,000	$711,000	$529,250	$722,000
Net additional markups		16,000		10,000		10,000
Net markdowns		9,000		11,000		7,000
Sales (net)		683,900		703,350		732,470
Applicable price index (19V = 200)	208		220		242	
Admin. and selling expenses	45,000		48,000		50,000	

	Year 19Y	
	FIFO Basis	LIFO Basis
Sales revenue	$_____	$_____
Less expenses:		
Cost of goods sold:		
Beginning inventory	_____	_____
Purchases	_____	_____
Total	_____	_____
Ending inventory	_____	_____
Cost of goods sold	_____	_____
Admin. and selling expenses	_____	_____
Total expenses	_____	_____
Pretax income	_____	_____
Income taxes (assume a 40% rate)	_____	_____
Net income	_____	_____
Reduction in cash outflows by using LIFO	$_____	

Problem 9–11

Martin's Store has used the conventional retail inventory method, average (LCM) basis for a number of years for all purposes. The company has decided to use LIFO retail results for external reporting and income tax purposes. The change is to be effective January 1, 19F. Relevant data subject to the change and the next three years follow in the next column.

a. From the internal inventory records—computation of the retail inventory (average, LCM basis) for 19E:

	At Cost	At Retail
Inventory, 1/1/19E	$ 37,000	$ 60,000
Purchases, net	227,000	413,000
Net additional markups		7,000
Total	$264,000	480,000
Cost ratio: $264,000 ÷ $480,000 = .55		
Sales, net		(416,000)
Net markdowns		(14,000)
Inventory, 12/31/19E:		
At retail		$ 50,000
At average cost, LCM ($50,000 × .55)	$ 27,500	

b. Data for 19F–19H are shown at the bottom of this page.

The company will use the retail inventory method, FIFO cost basis for internal purposes starting with 19F.

Required:

1. Compute the inventory value that should be used as the base inventory on January 1, 19F.
2. Compute the inventory values (at cost and retail) that should be used as the ending inventories for 19F, 19G, and 19H for conversion purposes (and for internal use).

(Relates to Problem 9–11)

	19F		19G		19H	
	At Cost	At Retail	At Cost	At Retail	At Cost	At Retail
Purchases (net)	$231,000	$400,000	$262,200	$450,000	$271,600	$470,000
Net additional markups		30,000		17,000		20,000
Net markdowns		10,000		7,000		5,000
Sales (net)		380,000		410,000		485,000
Applicable price index, 19E = 110	116.6		132.0		143.0	
Admin. and selling expenses	70,000		80,000		100,000	

3. In view of the change from average, LCM, the company decided to adjust the inventory account to the FIFO cost basis for internal purposes. Give the entry to effect this change at the start of 19F.
4. Convert the FIFO inventory results for each year, computed in 2 above, to LIFO retail for use in developing the external financial statements and the income tax return.
5. Complete the following tabulation for 19H:

	Year 19H	
	FIFO Basis	LIFO Basis
Sales revenue	$_____	$_____
Less expenses:		
Cost of goods sold:		
Beginning inventory	_____	_____
Purchases	_____	_____
Total	_____	_____
Ending inventory	_____	_____
Cost of goods sold	_____	_____
Admin. and selling expenses	_____	_____
Total expenses	_____	_____
Pretax income	_____	_____
Income taxes (assume 40% rate)	_____	_____
Net income	_____	_____
Reduction in cash outflows by using LIFO	$_____	

Problem 9–12

Super Builders, Incorporated, contracted to construct an office building for the Guinn Company for $900,000. Construction began on January 15, 19A, and was completed on December 7, 19B. Super Builders' fiscal year ends December 31. Transactions by Super Builders relating to the contract are summarized below:

	19A	19B
Cost incurred to date	$500,000	$830,000
Estimated costs to complete	320,000	
Progress billings to date	410,000	900,000
Progress collections to date	375,000	900,000

Required:
1. In parallel columns, give the entries on the contractor's books assuming *(a)* the completed contract method and *(b)* the percentage-of-completion method allocated on the basis of cost. Assume percentage of completion is measured by the ratio of costs incurred to date to total estimated construction costs.
2. For each method, prepare the income statement and balance sheet presentations for this contract by year.
3. What is the nature of the item "Costs in excess of billings" that appears on the balance sheet?
4. Which method would you recommend the contractor use? Why?

Problem 9–13

Quitman Construction Company contracted to build a dam for the city of Lindale for $975,000. The contract provided for progress payments. Quitman Company closes the books each December 31. Work commenced under the contract on July 15, 19A, and was completed on September 30, 19C. Construction activities are summarized below by year:

19A—Construction costs incurred during the year, $180,000; estimated costs to complete, $630,000; progress billings to the city during the year, $153,000; and collections, $130,000.

19B—Construction costs incurred during the year, $450,000; estimated costs to complete, $190,000; progress billings to the city during the year, $382,500; and collections, $380,000.

19C—Construction costs incurred during the year, $195,000. Because the contract was completed, the remaining balance was billed and later collected in full per the contract.

Required:
1. Give the entries on the contractor's books assuming the percentage-of-completion method is used. Show computation of income apportionment on a cost basis assuming percentage of completion is measured by the ratio of costs incurred to date to total estimated construction costs.
2. Prepare income statement and balance sheet presentations for this contract by year (percentage-of-completion basis).
3. Prepare income statement and balance sheet presentations by year assuming completed contract method. For each amount that is different from the corresponding amount in 2 above, explain the reason.
4. Which method would you recommend to this contractor? Why?

Problem 9–14

Dimkoff Construction Company contracted to build a bridge for the city of Saline for $750,000. The contract specified that the city would pay Dimkoff each month the progress billings, less 10%, which was to be held as a "reserve." At the end of the construction, the final payment is to include the reserve. Each billing, less the 10% reserve, must be paid within 10 days after submission of a billing to the city.

Transactions relating to the contract are summarized below:

19A—Construction costs incurred during the year, $200,000; estimated costs to complete, $400,000; progress billings, $190,000; and collections per the contract.

19B—Construction costs incurred during the year, $350,000; estimated costs to complete, $115,000; progress billings, $280,000; and collections per the contract.

19C—Construction costs incurred during the year, $110,000. The remaining billings were submitted by October 1 and final collections completed on November 30.

Required:

1. Complete a tabulation as follows:

Year	Method	Income Recognized	Receivable Ending Balance	Construction in Process Inventory Ending Balance	Costs in Excess of Billings Ending Balance
19A	Completed contract				
	Percentage of completion*				
19B	Completed contract				
	Percentage of completion*				
19C	Completed contract				
	Percentage of completion				

* Apportion on basis of costs incurred to date compared to total estimated construction costs.

2. Explain what causes the ending balance in construction in process to be different for the two methods.
3. Which method would you recommend for this contractor? Why?

Problem 9–15

Jones Contractors, Inc. contracted to construct a building for $300,000. Construction commenced in 19A and was completed in 19C. Data relating to the contract are summarized below:

	19A	19B	19C
Costs incurred during year	$ 80,000	$120,000	$ 50,000
Estimated costs to complete	158,000	39,000	
Billings during year	65,000	130,000	105,000
Collections during year	60,000	128,000	100,000

Required:

Complete a tabulation as follows:

Year	Method	Income Recognized	Receivable Ending Balance	Construction in Process Inventory Ending Balance	Costs in Excess of Billings Ending Balance
19A	Completed contract				
	Percentage of completion*				
19B	Completed contract				
	Percentage of completion				
19C	Completed contract				
	Percentage of completion				

* Apportion on basis of costs incurred to date compared to total estimated construction costs.

Problem 9–16

Swift Construction Company contracted to build a large warehouse for Maybell. Construction began on October 1, 19A, and was completed at the end of the 20th working day in January 19C. Swift had estimated construction costs to be $800,000 and had submitted a bid for $900,000, which was accepted by Maybell officials. The accounting period for Swift ends December 31. The construction contract included the following provisions:

1. Contract price, $900,000; progress payments (based on costs incurred) payable within 10 days of billing.
2. Completion date, December 31, 19B, with a penalty involving reduction of the contract price in the amount of $500 per working day after that date, less the number of days Swift was unable to work because of inclement weather.

Construction activities summarized by year were as follows:

	19A	19B	19C
Costs incurred each year	$200,000	$500,000	$230,000
Estimated cost to complete	600,000	210,000	
Progress billings by year	180,000	505,000	205,000
Progress collections by year	160,000	485,000	245,000*

* Penalty reduction in contract price, 20 days @ $500 = $10,000.

Required:

1. For each year give *(a)* the journal entries and *(b)* the balance sheet and income statement reported by Swift assuming the completed contract method is used. Show computations.
2. For each year give *(a)* the entries and *(b)* the balance sheet and income statement reported by Swift assuming

the percentage-of-completion method is used. Assume the construction income is measured and recognized on the basis of the ratio of costs incurred to date to total estimated completion costs. Show computations.

Problem 9–17

Case A—Curtis Construction Company contracted with Axelrod Associates on July 1, 19A, to erect a four-story building for the latter by December 31, 19C, for $4 million. Curtis chose to account for this contract under the completed contract method. The building was substantially completed on schedule. Estimated percentage of completion, accumulated contract costs incurred, estimated costs to complete the contract, and accumulated billings to Axelrod under the contract were as follows:

	12/31/19A	12/31/19B	12/31/19C
Percentage of completion	10%	60%	100%
Contract costs incurred	$ 350,000	$2,500,000	$4,250,000
Estimated costs to complete contract	3,150,000	1,700,000	—
Billings to Axelrod	720,000	2,160,000	3,600,000

Required (ignore income tax):

1. Prepare schedules to compute the amount that should be reported as "Cost of uncompleted contract in excess of related billings" or "Billings on uncompleted contract in excess of related costs" at the end of 19A, 19B, and 19C.
2. Prepare schedules to compute the income or loss that should be reported as a result of this contract for the years ended December 31, 19A, 19B, and 19C.

Case B—On April 1, 19A, Butler, Inc., contracted with Dalton Company to construct for the latter an electric generator estimated to require two years for completion at a cost of $2,000,000. The contract is on a cost-plus-fixed-fee basis; the fixed fee is stipulated to be $300,000. Butler accounts for the contract on a percentage-of-completion basis. During 19A, Butler incurred costs of $700,000 related to the project, and as of December 31, 19A, the estimate of additional costs to complete the contract is $1,400,000. Dalton was billed $500,000 under the contract.

Required:

Prepare a schedule to compute the amount of construction income that should be reported by Butler for the year ended December 31, 19A. Show supporting computations.

(AICPA adapted)

10

Liabilities and Income Taxes

THIS CHAPTER discusses liabilities of various types and accounting for income tax. To facilitate the discussion, the chapter is subdivided as follows:

Part A—Measuring, Recording, and Reporting Liabilities
Part B—Accounting for Income Taxes
Supplement 10–A—Income Tax Loss Carrybacks and Carryforwards
Supplement 10–B—Changes in Tax Rates
Supplement 10–C—Different Concepts of Income Tax Allocation

Part A: Measuring, Recording, and Reporting Liabilities

CONCEPTS RELATED TO LIABILITIES

FASB Concepts Statement 3 defines liabilities as follows (page xi):

> Liabilities are probable future sacrifices of economic benefits arising from present obligations of a particular entity to transfer assets or provide services to other entities in the future as a result of past transactions or events.

Liabilities are classified as either *(a)* short term (i.e., current) or *(b)* long term because their maturity is important. External users of financial statements have no basis other than these classifications on the balance sheet for assessing the relative currency of liabilities. For this reason, the **classification** of liabilities as current or long-term is important.[1]

Conceptually, a liability should be measured as the **present value** of all future cash (or the cash equivalents of noncash assets or services) to be paid. The transaction that creates the liability provides the basis for measurement of the liability. For example, when an asset is acquired for cash or on credit, the asset and related liability are valued at cost under the cost principle. Sometimes, this correspondence between the "price" of the asset and the valuation of the liability is not so clear-cut. To illustrate, assume a company acquired a machine for which it promised to pay $10,000 at the end of three years

[1] From an **auditing** standpoint, **identification** of existing liabilities is a critical problem because many liabilities are easy to hide or overlook due to the intangible nature of liabilities.

(with no interest payments). Both the liability and the asset are valued at the cost of the asset, which is the present value of the required future cash flow. Assuming a 15 percent rate of interest for this type of debt, measurement of the liability (and the asset) would be as follows:

$$\$10{,}000^{*} \times p_{n=3;i=15\%} = \$10{,}000 \times .65752 \text{ (Table 5–2)} = \$6{,}575$$

* Includes interest.

The present value concept is applicable to all liabilities. However, in accounting for short-term liabilities (particularly those involving accounts payable of one to three months), the interest factor often is ignored because of immateriality and because of the provisions of *APB Opinion 21,* which states (par. 3a) that it does not apply to "receivables and payables arising from transactions with customers or suppliers in the normal course of business which are due in customary trade terms not exceeding approximately one year."

Liabilities usually are recorded and reported at their maturity amount because, for most liabilities, their stated rate of interest (i.e., the interest rate used to compute interest payments) is the same as the market or effective interest rate (i.e., the prevailing marketwide interest rate on liabilities of the same risk and maturity). When the stated rate is the same as the market rate, the present value of that liability is equal to its maturity amount. Aside from the materiality exception noted above for some short-term liabilities, liabilities should be recorded and reported at their present value at date of acquisition.

The present value concept also applies to noninterest-bearing notes (illustrated later) and for bonds or other indebtedness issued above or below par. Bonds payable are reported net of unamortized discount or premium using the interest method. These issues are discussed in the remainder of this chapter and in Chapter 17 (bonds).

Although exchange transactions generally establish the amount and maturity date of a liability, in some situations a definite liability is known to exist, or it is probable that one exists but the exact amount and/or the maturity date are not known precisely. Therefore, one section of this chapter discusses estimated liabilities and loss contingencies.

CURRENT LIABILITIES

Current liabilities for many years were defined as those obligations due within one year of balance sheet date. This definition was related to the older definition of current assets (liquidation within one year). It was recognized that these definitions were unrealistic for many companies. As a consequence, the Committee on Accounting Procedure of the AICPA defined current liabilities as follows:

> The term **current liabilities** is used principally to designate obligations whose liquidation is reasonably expected to require the use of existing resources properly classifiable as current assets, or the creation of other current liabilities.[2]

The committee supplemented the definition of current liabilities as follows:

> As a balance-sheet category, the classification is intended to include obligations for items which have entered into the operating cycle, such as payables incurred in the acquisition of materials and supplies to be used in the production of goods or in providing services to be offered for sale; collections received in advance of the delivery of goods or performance of services; and debts which arise from operations directly related to the operating cycle, such as accruals for wages, salaries, commissions, rentals, royalties, and income and other taxes. Other liabilities [i.e., those arising from transactions that fall outside the "operating cycle"] whose regular and ordinary liquidation is expected to occur within a relatively short period of time, usually 12 months, are also intended for inclusion, such as short-term debts arising from the acquisition of capital assets, serial maturities of long-term obligations, amounts required to be expended within one year under sinking fund provisions, and agency obligations arising from the collection or acceptance of cash or other assets for the account of third persons.
>
> This concept of current liabilities would include estimated or accrued amounts which are expected to be required to cover expenditures within the year for known obligations *(a)* the amount of which can be determined only approximately (as in the case of provisions for accruing bonus payments) or *(b)* where the specific person or persons to whom payment will be made cannot as yet be designated (as in the case of estimated costs to be incurred in connection with guaranteed servicing or repair of products already sold).[3]

The principal types of current liabilities are as follows:

[2] AICPA, *Accounting Research Bulletin No. 43,* "Restatement and Revision of Accounting Research Bulletins" (New York, 1961), chap. 3, par. 7.

[3] Ibid., chap. 3, pars. 7–8.

1. Known liabilities of a definite amount:
   a. Accounts payable.
   b. Short-term notes payable.
   c. Cash dividends payable.
   d. Advances and funds held as short-term deposits.
   e. Accrued liabilities.
   f. Short-term deferred credits (such as revenues collected in advance).
2. Known liabilities, amount dependent on operations:
   g. Taxes (income, sales, and payroll)
   h. Bonus obligations.
   i. Accrued liabilities.
3. Known liabilities, amount estimated.
4. Loss contingencies.

Special accounting problems related to these types of current liabilities are discussed in the following sections.

Accounts Payable

Accounts payable is a designation for recurring **trade** obligations that arise from the acquisition of merchandise, materials, supplies, and services used in the production and/or sale of goods or services. The obligations are directly related to the continuing operations of the entity. Current payables not coming under this definition should be reported separately from accounts payable (e.g., income tax payable and current payments on long-term debt).

Notes Payable

Short-term notes payable are reported as current liabilities. They may be either trade or nontrade notes payable, and each note payable and its terms (e.g., interest rate, term to maturity, collateral, etc.) should be reported separately because the interest rates and other terms reflect upon the credit standing of the borrower. Trade notes payable are defined in the same manner as accounts payable except they involve a promissory note which bears interest. Notes payable may be **secured** by collateral (pledged, or mortgaged, assets), or they may be **unsecured.** For secured notes payable, the company should disclose the nature of the collateral agreement, including the specific assets mortgaged. One approach is to disclose pledged assets in the notes to the financial statement. Another method reports the pledged assets under both the asset and liability captions similar to the following:

Investment:	
Stock of X Corp. at cost (pledged for $3,000 note to Y Bank)	$5,000
Current liabilities:	
Notes payable (secured by stock of X Corp.)	3,000

Interest on Notes Payable

All commercial notes require the borrower to pay interest because of the unavoidable time cost of using money. The commercial world uses two note designations for the interest on notes, viz:

1. **Interest-bearing notes**—those that specify the principal amount as the face amount of the note (excluding interest). Thus, the face amount of the note is paid at maturity date plus a specified interest payment at maturity date or a series of interest payments during the period the note is outstanding. An interest-bearing note also is sometimes called an "ordinary" note.
2. **Noninterest-bearing notes**—those that include both the principal amount and the interest in the face amount of the note. At maturity date, the debtor pays only the face amount (which already includes interest). This type of note also is called a **discounted note** to refer to the fact that the present value of the note is a discounted amount of the face amount.

On all notes, regardless of type, the amount of interest per period should be calculated as

$$\text{Principal amount} \times \text{Effective rate of interest per year} \times \text{Time} = \text{Interest amount}$$

Interest-Bearing (Ordinary) Notes Payable

For an interest-bearing note, the borrower receives cash or equivalent assets or services for the **face amount** of the note, and interest is paid at one or more subsequent dates (in addition to the face of the note which is paid at maturity). Therefore, for an interest-bearing note, the principal amount (face amount) and the cost of the assets received (assuming the stated rate of interest is realistic) are the same; the interest is in addition to these amounts. On an interest-bearing note, the **stated** rate of interest and the **effective** rate of interest are the same (assuming the stated rate is realistic); therefore, its face amount and present value are the same.

To illustrate an interest-bearing note, assume X Company borrowed $10,000 cash and signed a one-year, 12 percent interest-bearing note, dated October 1, 19A. The cash received, principal amount, face amount, and maturity amount would be $10,000 each. At maturity, the face amount of the note plus interest for one year ($1,200), a total of $11,200, would be paid. The borrowing transaction, accrual of interest at the end of the accounting period (December 31, 19A), and payment at maturity (September 30, 19B) would be recorded as follows:

October 1, 19A—To record an interest-bearing note at its present value:

Cash	10,000	
Note payable, short term		10,000

December 31, 19A—Adjusting entry for accrued interest:

Interest expense ($10,000 × 12% × $\frac{3}{12}$)	300	
Interest payable		300

Reporting at December 31, 19A—Interest-bearing note payable:

Income statement:	
Interest expense	$ 300
Balance sheet:	
Current liabilities:	
Note payable, short term	10,000
Interest payable	300

September 30, 19B—Payment of face amount plus interest at maturity (assuming no reversing entry was made on January 1, 19B):

Interest payable	300	
Interest expense ($10,000 × 12% × $\frac{9}{12}$)	900	
Note payable, short term	10,000	
Cash		11,200

Noninterest-Bearing (Discounted) Notes Payable (with no stated interest rate)

For a noninterest-bearing (discounted) note, the borrower receives cash or equivalent assets or services for the face amount of the note **less** the interest amount charged. The face amount of a noninterest-bearing note includes **both** principal and interest amounts; at maturity only the face amount is paid. Because of these features, neither the interest rate nor the amount of interest is stated explicitly in the note. The amount of interest should be computed on the cash (or equivalent assets or services) received because this is the principal amount of the debt. Thus, the principal amount of a noninterest-bearing note is its face amount discounted at the realistic rate of interest for the obligation. To illustrate, assume $10,000 cash is borrowed and a one-year noninterest-bearing note payable dated October 1, 19A, is executed at an agreed rate of interest of 12 percent. The face amount of the note would be:

$$\$10{,}000 + (\$10{,}000 \times 12\%) = \$11{,}200$$

The effective rate of interest would be:

$$\text{Interest paid } (\$11{,}200 - \$10{,}000) \div \text{Cash received } (\$10{,}000) = 12\%$$

Its present value would be:

$$\$11{,}200 \times p_{n=1;\ i=.89286} \text{ (Table 5–2)} = \$10{,}000$$

Entries to account for this noninterest-bearing note (i.e., interest included in the face amount) would be similar to the entries shown above for the interest-bearing (ordinary) note, assuming the Notes Payable account is recorded at its "net" amount (i.e., its present value of $10,000).[4] To account for this noninterest-bearing note, the only modification of the above se-

[4] If the Notes Payable account is entered at its **face** (i.e., gross) amount, i.e., principal plus interest, the recording and reporting of the noninterest-bearing note would be as shown below. Note that the amount of interest expense and the liability balances are the same, regardless of whether the note is recorded at "net" or "gross." Entries at gross would be as follows:

October 1, 19A—To record a noninterest-bearing note payable at its gross (face) amount:

Cash	10,000	
Discount on note payable	1,200	
Note payable, short term		11,200

December 31, 19A—Adjusting entry for accrued interest:

Interest expense ($1,200 × $\frac{3}{12}$)	300	
Discount on note payable		300

Reporting at December 31, 19A—Noninterest-bearing note payable.

Income statement:		
Interest expense		$ 300
Balance sheet:		
Current liabilities:		
Note payable	$11,200	
Less: Unamortized discount	900	10,300

September 30, 19B—Payment of the face amount of the note:

Interest expense ($1,200 × $\frac{9}{12}$)	900	
Note payable, short term	11,200	
Discount on note payable		900
Cash		11,200

quence of entries would be that at December 31, 19A, the adjusting entry for accrued interest would credit Notes Payable instead of Interest Payable. Then, at maturity date, the Notes Payable account will have a credit balance of $11,200 prior to being paid off. The entries and reporting on a **net basis** would be as follows:

October 1, 19A—To record the noninterest-bearing note payable at its net (i.e., present value) amount:

Cash	10,000	
Note payable, short term (noninterest bearing)		10,000

December 31, 19A—To record accrued interest:

Interest expense ($10,000 × .12 × $\frac{3}{12}$)	300	
Note payable, short term		300

Reporting at December 31, 19A:

Income statement:	
Interest expense	$ 300
Balance sheet:	
Current liabilities:	
Note payable, short term ($10,000 + $300)	$10,300

September 30, 19B—To record (a) accrued interest to date and (b) payment of the face amount of the note at maturity:

(a) Interest expense ($10,000 × .12 × $\frac{9}{12}$)	900	
Note payable, short term		900
(b) Note payable ($10,000 + $300 + $900)	11,200	
Cash		11,200

Dividends Payable

Cash (or property) dividends payable (i.e., dividends declared but not yet paid) should be reported as a current liability if there is an intention to pay them within the coming year or operating cycle, whichever is the longer. **Stock dividends** issuable are not current liabilities but are an element of stockholders' equity, as explained in Chapter 15. Cash (and property) dividends payable are reported as a liability between their dates of declaration and dates of payment on the legal basis that declaration is an enforceable contract that the corporation has assumed by virtue of formal declaration.

Liabilities are not recognized for **undeclared** dividends in arrears on preferred stock nor for any other dividends not yet declared formally by the board of directors. Dividends in arrears on cumulative preferred stock should be disclosed in the notes. Scrip dividends payable (liability dividends) are reported as a current liability unless there is no intention to make payment within the near future (see Chapter 15).

Advances and Returnable Deposits

A special type of liability arises when a company receives cash deposits from customers and employees. Deposits may be received from customers as guarantees to cover payment of obligations that may arise in the future or to guarantee performance of a contract or service. For example, when an order is taken, a company may require an advance payment to cover losses that would be incurred should the order be canceled. Such advances create liabilities of the company receiving the cash until the underlying transaction is completed; therefore, they are recorded by debiting Cash and crediting an account such as Liability—Customer Deposits.

Deposits frequently are received from customers as guarantees in the event of noncollection or for possible damage to property left with the customer. For example, deposits taken from customers by gas, water, light, and other public utilities are liabilities of such companies to their customers. Employees may make returnable deposits for the return of keys and other company property, for locker privileges, and for club memberships. Some of these deposits are long term; others are current. Deposits should be reported as current or long-term liabilities, depending upon the time involved between date of deposit and expected termination of the relationships. In cases where the advances or deposits are interest bearing, an adjusting entry is required to accrue interest expense and the related liability.

Accrued Liabilities

Accrued liabilities arise because entities must record expenses they have incurred but not yet paid at the end of the period. Accrued liabilities are recorded in the accounts by making adjusting entries at the end of the accounting period. For example, property taxes for the current year usually are assessed near the end of the calendar year and are payable in the following year. Other examples of accrued liabilities are wages, salaries, warranties, income tax, interest, and bonus. The matching principle requires that such expenses and the related liabilities be estimated (if necessary), recorded in the accounts, and reported on the financial statements on an accrual basis. For liabilities which are recorded on a monthly accrual basis, such as Property Taxes Payable, the amount actually paid and the amount accrued during the year sometimes will differ. Such differences should be accounted for as an adjustment at the end of the period. For clarity in financial reporting, it is important that descriptive account titles be used, such as Wages Payable, Estimated Property Taxes Payable, and Interest Payable.

Deferred Credits

A caption, Deferred credits, positioned after liabilities and before owners' equity, sometimes is shown on balance sheets. Usually this caption includes four types of items, viz:

1. Revenues collected in advance (sometimes called unearned revenue or deferred revenue), such as interest, rent, and advances received for services yet to be rendered.
2. Credits arising through certain external transactions that are difficult to classify. Examples are unearned deposits on royalties and deferred income on installment sales.
3. Credits arising through certain internal transactions. Examples are deferred repairs, allowance for rearrangement costs, and equities of minority interests (on consolidated statements; discussed in Chapter 16).
4. Credits arising from income tax allocation procedures (deferred income taxes; see Part B of this chapter).

Rent collected in advance creates an obligation to render future occupancy (services). Thus, revenues collected in advance are liabilities until the services are provided or until there is a transfer of ownership of goods, as the case may be. For example, subscriptions collected in advance on magazines represent a liability to deliver magazines to the subscriber in the future. As the magazines are delivered, the liability, Subscriptions Collected in Advance, is reduced by transfers to a revenue account, such as Subscription Revenue.

Some of the items listed above (particularly types 2 and 3) are difficult to classify on the balance sheet. This difficulty underlies usage of the vague balance sheet classification, Deferred credits. Reporting this classification below liabilities and above owners' equity is not consistent with the basic accounting model, Assets = Liabilities + Owners' equity, because the model makes no provision for equities that are neither liabilities nor owners' equity. Some of these items clearly are liabilities; others represent valuation adjustments to related items. For these reasons many accountants, including the authors, consider the Deferred credit classification on the balance sheet to be inconsistent with the reporting principle. A sound basis for classification of the various items sometimes reported as deferred credits is as follows:

1. Classify as **current liabilities** *(a)* those short-term items that represent a future claim against current assets whether or not there is an obligation to a specific individual or entity and *(b)* those items that will represent revenue when the current obligations to deliver goods and render services are met.
2. Classify as **long-term liabilities** all items that are consistent with 1 above, except that they are not **current**; that is, extended periods of time are involved.
3. Classify all other items according to their characteristics as asset offsets, owners' equity, or current or long-term liabilities.

On the above basis the following classifications are suggested:

Item	Classification
Interest revenue collected in advance	Current liability
Unearned rent revenue	Current liability
Advances received for services to be rendered in the future	Current liability
Customer deposits, short term	Current liability
Magazine subscriptions collected in advance	Current liability
Deferred repairs	Current liability (represents a "claim" against current assets—may be long-term liability if related to several future periods)
Allowance for rearrangement costs	Current liability

Premium on bonds payable	Long-term liability (add to related bonds payable; see Chapter 17)
Equities of minority interests	Owners' equity (special caption separate from controlling interest; see Chapter 16)
Long-term refundable customer deposits	Long-term liability
Leasehold advances (advances on leases)	Current or long-term liability
Deferred income taxes	Current or long-term liability depending upon the classification of the item that caused the deferred income tax (discussed in Part B)

Funds Collected for Third Parties

Numerous state and federal laws require businesses to collect taxes from customers and employees for remittance to governmental agencies. Taxes collected, but not yet remitted, represent current liabilities. To illustrate, assume a 5 percent sales tax and sales of $400,000; the indicated entries are as follows:

1. At date the tax is assessed (point of sale):

Cash and accounts receivable	420,000	
Sales revenue		400,000
Sales tax payable		20,000

2. At date of remittance to taxing authority:

Sales tax payable	20,000	
Cash		20,000

Payroll Taxes

Companies must pay various payroll taxes in addition to the wages and salaries they pay their employees. Also, it is common for companies to deduct certain amounts from their employees' pay for employees' personal income and social security taxes, union dues, insurance premiums, and the like.

Federal Income Taxes Withheld. Federal income tax laws require employers to withhold from the pay of each employee an amount representing the anticipated income tax payable by the employee. Income taxes so withheld are remitted to the U.S. Treasury through local depositories (banks), and the amounts withheld are current liabilities of the employer until remittance.

FICA Payroll Taxes. Social security laws require that the employer deduct a tax from the pay of each employee under specified conditions. In addition to the tax paid by the employee, the employer must match the contribution of the employee and remit both taxes to the U.S. Treasury. The rates and amount of wages subject to this tax vary. For example, for 1982, employers and employees each pay 6.7 percent of the first $31,800 earned by the employee, for a maximum total tax of $2,131 paid by the employee who earns as much as $31,800 per year; also, an additional tax of $2,131 is paid by the employer. In 1983, these amounts are scheduled to increase to 6.7 percent of the first $33,900 (i.e., maximum total tax of $2,271). These payroll taxes are referred to as FICA taxes because the enabling legislation is the Federal Insurance Contributions Act. The purpose of the tax is to provide retirement pay for retirees and death benefits for the retiree's survivors.

FUTA Payroll Taxes. Another social security tax levied by the federal government finances the cost of administering the federal-state unemployment compensation program. This payroll tax is paid only by the employer (of one or more persons). These payroll taxes usually are called FUTA taxes because the enabling legislation is the Federal Unemployment Tax Act. Recently, the FUTA tax rate has been 3.4 percent on the first $6,000 in wages paid to each employee, with 2.7% payable to the state (of employment) to provide the benefits when paid (if the state laws qualify), and the remaining 0.7 percent payable to the U.S. Treasury.

Accounting for withholding taxes, FICA taxes, and FUTA taxes may be illustrated as follows: Assume salaries of $100,000 for January 1982 and income tax withholding of $20,000.

January 31, 1982—To record salaries and **employee** payroll taxes:

Salary expense	100,000	
Withholding tax payable		20,000
FICA tax payable—employees ($100,000 × 6.70%)*		6,700
Cash		73,300

* This assumes no employee exceeded the maximum wage base (i.e., $31,800 in 1982; $33,900 in 1983; and $36,000 in 1984).

January 31, 1982—To record **employer** payroll taxes:

Expense—payroll taxes	10,100	
FICA tax payable—employer ($100,000 × 6.70%)		6,700
FUTA tax payable—federal ($100,000 × .7%)		700
FUTA tax payable—state ($100,000 × 2.7%)		2,700

At remittance date:

Withholding tax payable	20,000	
FICA tax payable—employees	6,700	
FICA tax payable—employer	6,700	
FUTA tax payable—federal	700	
FUTA tax payable—state	2,700	
Cash		36,800

Between the payroll and remittance dates, the five liabilities recorded would be reported as current liabilities.

Bonus Compensation to Employees

Compensation contracts often provide for the payment of a **bonus** to an officer, branch manager, or other employee of a corporation based upon some indicator of performance such as income of the entity. Such a bonus is a current operating expense and is a current liability until paid. Bonus payments generally are tax deductible under federal tax laws. Bonus contracts relating to income are usually one of two types, viz:

1. The bonus is computed on income after deducting income taxes but before deducting the bonus.
2. The bonus is computed on income after deducting both the bonus and the income taxes.

Because the tax is not determinable before the bonus is computed or vice versa, the computation requires the use of two simultaneous equations because there are two unknowns, bonus *(B)* and tax *(T)*. To illustrate a typical situation, assume Bryan Company reported income of $100,000 before deducting income taxes and before the bonus to the general manager. Assume the tax rate is 40 percent and the bonus rate is 10 percent. Two situations are illustrated.

Situation 1. The bonus is based on income after deducting income taxes but before deducting the bonus.

$$B = .10(\$100{,}000 - T) \quad (1)$$
$$T = .40(\$100{,}000 - B) \quad (2)$$

Substitute the expression for *T*, as given in (2) above, into (1) and solve for *B:*

$$B = .10[\$100{,}000 - .40(\$100{,}000 - B)]$$
$$B = .10[\$100{,}000 - \$40{,}000 + .40B]$$
$$B = \$10{,}000 - \$4{,}000 + .04B$$
$$B - .04B = \$6{,}000$$
$$.96B = \$6{,}000$$
$$B = \underline{\underline{\$6{,}250}}$$

Substitute value of *B* in (2):

$$T = .40(\$100{,}000 - \$6{,}250)$$
$$T = \underline{\underline{\$37{,}500}}$$

Proof of Computations

Computation of tax:	
Income before tax and bonus	$100,000
Deduct bonus (as computed)	6,250
Taxable income	93,750
Multiply by tax rate	.40
Tax	$ 37,500

Situation 2. The bonus is based on income after deducting both income taxes and the bonus.

$$B = .10(\$100{,}000 - B - T) \quad (1)$$
$$T = .40(\$100{,}000 - B) \quad (2)$$

Substitute the expression for *T*, as given in (2) above, into (1) and solve for *B:*

$$B = .10[\$100{,}000 - B - .40(\$100{,}000 - B)]$$
$$B = .10[\$100{,}000 - B - \$40{,}000 + .40B]$$
$$B = \$10{,}000 - .10B - \$4{,}000 + .04B$$
$$B = \$6{,}000 - .06B$$
$$B + .06B = \$6{,}000$$
$$1.06B = \$6{,}000$$
$$B = \underline{\underline{\$5{,}660}}$$

Substitute value of *B* in (2):

$$T = .40(\$100{,}000 - \$5{,}660)$$
$$T = \underline{\underline{\$37{,}736}}$$

Proof of Computations

Computation of tax:	
Income before tax and bonus	$100,000
Deduct bonus (as computed)	5,660
Taxable income	94,340
Multiply by tax rate	.40
Tax	$ 37,736

The entries to record the accrual and payment of the bonus would be as follows for Situation 1:

1. To record bonus:

Employee compensation expense	6,250	
Bonus payable		6,250

2. To record payment of bonus:

Bonus payable	6,250	
Cash		6,250

LONG-TERM LIABILITIES

All liabilities which are not current (as defined in the preceding section) are long-term liabilities. Therefore, bonds payable and long-term notes and mortgages are reported under long-term liabilities.

Long-term liabilities are recorded in the accounts at their present value. The present value of a liability is the sum of the present values of *(a)* the cash maturity amount and *(b)* the cash interest payments to be made, each discounted at the going market rate of interest in effect at inception for that particular type of liability. When the stated rate of interest is realistic (i.e., the market rate) for that particular liability, the present value is equal to the par or principal amount. When the stated interest rate is not realistic, the present value will differ from the principal amount. Two situations often are encountered: (1) debt issued for cash and (2) debt issued for property, goods, or services. *APB Opinion No. 21,* "Interest on Receivables and Payables," provides the guidelines for these two situations.

Debt Issued for Cash

In this situation, *APB Opinion 21* states that the debt "is presumed to have a present value at issuance measured by the cash proceeds exchanged." To illustrate, assume that on January 1, $10,000 cash is borrowed and a note payable for that amount is executed that is due in five years and calls for annual interest payments at 12 percent in addition to the principal of $10,000. The note would be recorded at $10,000, which represents *(a)* the cash proceeds received, *(b)* the principal amount, and *(c)* the present value of the note (assume in this situation the 12 percent is a realistic rate). Entries for the first year would be as follows:

a. Cash	10,000	
Note payable, long term		10,000
b. Interest expense	1,200	
Cash ($10,000 × 12%)		1,200

The present value of this note would be computed as follows:

Maturity amount discounted:	
$\$10{,}000 \times p_{n=5;i=12\%} = \$10{,}000 \times .56743$ (Table 5–2)	$ 5,674
Interest payments discounted:	
$\$1{,}200 \times P_{o_{n=5;i=12\%}} = \$1{,}200 \times 3.60478$ (Table 5–4)	4,326
Present value (same as maturity amount)	$10,000

Debt Issued for Property, Goods, or Services

When a noncash consideration is received for a debt, sometimes (1) interest is **not** stated, or (2) the stated interest **rate** is unreasonable (i.e., it does not reflect the current market rate), or (3) the stated **face amount** of the debt (e.g., a note payable) differs from the market value of the item received or from the market value of the note at the date of the transaction. *APB Opinion 21* specifies that the noncash consideration received should be recorded at its market value or the market value of the debt, whichever is the more clearly determinable. The market value of the debt is its present value based on an appropriate rate of interest at date of issuance. The *Opinion* specifies that if the present value of the debt is different from its face amount, the resulting premium or discount "should be accounted for as an element of interest over the life of the note." Amortization of the discount or premium should be based upon the "interest method" rather than the straight-line method so that the result will be "a constant rate of interest when applied to the amount outstanding at the beginning of any given period."[5]

To illustrate the issuance of a note payable for a noncash consideration, assume a $10,000, five-year note payable that stipulates 9 percent annual interest is issued for a tract of land. The market value of the land cannot be reasonably determined; however, for this kind of transaction, assume the prevailing rate of interest for the issuer is 12 percent. Exhibit 10–1 illustrates the following for the issuer:

Panel A—Computation of the present value of the note to be used as the valuation of the land.

[5] Other methods, such as straight line, may be used "if the interest amounts obtained are not materially different from those that would result from the 'interest' method" (AICPA, *Accounting Principles Board Opinion No. 21,* "Interest on Receivables and Payables" [New York, 1971], par. 14).

EXHIBIT 10–1: Accounting for Note Payable and Noncash Consideration

Panel A—Computation of present value of the note payable ($10,000, 5-year, stated interest rate, 9% payable annually):

Maturity amount discounted:	
$10,000 × $p_{n=5;i=12\%}$ = $10,000 × 5.6743 (Table 5–2)	$5,674
Interest payment (i.e., cash interest to be paid each period) discounted:	
$900 × $P_{o_{n=5;i=12\%}}$ = $900 × 3.60478 (Table 5–4)	3,244
Present value	$8,918

Panel B—Debt and interest amortization schedule (interest method):

At Year-End	Cash Interest Payments	Interest Expense	Amortization of Discount	Balance Sheet Debt Valuation
Start				$ 8,918
1	$900	$8,918 × .12 = $1,070	$1,070 − $900 = $170	9,088
2	900	9,088 × .12 = 1,091	1,091 − 900 = 191	9,279
3	900	9,279 × .12 = 1,113	1,113 − 900 = 213	9,492
4	900	9,492 × .12 = 1,139	1,139 − 900 = 239	9,731
5	900	9,731 × .12 = 1,169†	1,169 − 900 = 269†	10,000*

* At maturity date, i.e., the maturity amount.
† Rounded.

Note: At the end of each year the balance sheet should report the amount shown in the last column above and the income statement should reflect interest expense shown in the third column.

Panel C—Entries (recorded net; the **effective** rate is different from the **stated** rate):‡

a. On transaction date (January 1)

Land	8,918	
Note payable		8,918

b. At end of year 1 (December 31):

Interest expense	1,070	
Note payable		170
Cash		900

Panel D—Balance sheet presentation at the end of year 1:

Long-term liabilities:
Note payable, due in 4 years (maturity amount, $10,000) $9,088*

‡ See footnote 4 for an alternative method (i.e., recorded at gross); both methods produce the same end results.

Panel B—The related debt and interest amortization schedule using the interest method of amortization.

Panel C—Entries to record the transactions for the first year.

Panel D—Balance sheet presentation of the note payable.

Current Maturities of Long-Term Debt

On the balance sheet for the year preceding the payment of all, or a part, of the principal of a long-term debt, the amount to be paid during the upcoming current period, if payable from current assets (reflected on the current balance sheet), should be reported as a current liability (including its "share" of any unamortized premium or discount). FASB, *Statement of Financial Accounting Standards No. 6,* "Classification of Short-Term Obligations Expected to be Refinanced," specifies that this classification should not be used if the payment is to be made from a sinking fund or if the cash is to be derived from other noncurrent sources. The following presentation illustrates the reporting of the current and noncurrent portions of a serial bond payable (i.e., an issue of bonds payable which matures in "serials," or installments, rather than all at a single maturity date). In this illustration, the $100,000 serial reported as a current liability will be paid within one year out of the current assets reported on the current balance sheet. The $400,000 reported as long-term will be paid later than one year from the current date.

Current liabilities:		
Current payment on bond issue ..		$100,000
Long-term liabilities:		
Bonds payable	$500,000	
Less: Current payment	100,000	400,000

Bonds payable are discussed in Chapter 17.

CONTINGENCIES AND ESTIMATED LIABILITIES

Liabilities often must be estimated because (1) a known liability exists but the ultimate amount is uncertain or (2) a loss contingency exists. A contingency is defined in FASB, *Statement of Financial Accounting Standards No. 5,* "Accounting for Contingencies," as "an existing condition, situation, or set of circumstances involving uncertainty as to possible gain (hereinafter a 'gain contingency') or a loss (hereinafter a 'loss contingency') to an enterprise that ultimately will be resolved when one or more future events occur or fail to occur. Resolution of the uncertainty may confirm the acquisition of an asset or the reduction of a liability or the loss or impairment of an asset or the incurrence of a liability."

FASB Statement 5 is the basic pronouncement on contingencies and estimated liabilities and is the basis for this discussion. Therefore, this section is divided into three parts: *(a)* contingent liabilities (loss contingencies) that must be accrued and reported at estimated dollar amounts in the body of the financial statements, *(b)* contingent liabilities which are reported only in the notes to the financial statements, and *(c)* gain contingencies.

FASB Statement 5 delineates contingencies and specifies particular accounting treatments on the basis of whether the contingency is:

a. **Probable.** The future event or events are likely to occur.

b. **Reasonably possible.** The chance of occurrence of the future event or events is more than remote but less than likely.

c. **Remote.** The chance of occurrence of the future event or events is slight.

The provisions of *FASB Statement 5,* relating to contingencies may be summarized as shown in Exhibit 10–2.

Loss Contingencies that Must Be Accrued

FASB Statement 5 requires that a loss contingency must be accrued as a debit to expense or loss and a credit to a liability if **both** of the following conditions are met:

a. Information received prior to the issuance of the financial statements indicates that it is **probable** that an asset has been impaired or a liability has been incurred at the date of the financial statements. Implicit in this condition is that it must be probable that one or more future events will occur confirming the fact of the loss.

b. The amount of the loss can be reasonably estimated.

This situation corresponds to cell 1 in Exhibit 10–2.

FASB Statement 5 identified a number of loss contingencies, including estimated losses on receivables (allowance for doubtful accounts); estimated warranty obligations; litigations, claims, and assessments; and anticipated losses on the disposal of a segment of the business (Chapter 21).

A loss contingency that meets both of the above criteria, in addition to being accrued in the accounts, must be reported *(a)* on the balance sheet as a liability and *(b)* on the income statement as an expense (or loss, as the case may be) in the period in which the loss occurs. Three examples are presented to illustrate the accrual of a loss contingency.

Case A—Product Warranty. Assume R Company sold merchandise for $200,000 cash during the period. Experience has indicated that warranty and guarantee costs will approximate ½ percent of sales.[6] The indicated entries are as follows:

a. In year of sale:

[6] For a recent approach to the estimation of warranty expense, see K. R. Balachandran, R. A. Maschmeyer, and J. L. Livingstone, "Product Warranty Period: A Markovian Approach to Estimation and Analysis of Repair and Replacement Cost," *The Accounting Review,* January 1981, pp. 115–23.

EXHIBIT 10–2: Summary of Accounting for Contingencies

Probabilistic Nature of the Occurrence of the Contingent Event	Amount Can Be Reasonably Estimated	Amount Cannot Be Reasonably Estimated
	Loss Contingency	
Probable	1. Accrue and report in the body of the statements.	2. Do not accrue; report as a **note** in the financial statements.
Reasonably possible	3. Do not accrue; report as a **note** in the financial statements.	4. Do not accrue; report as a **note** in the financial statements.
Remote	5. No accrual or **note** required; however, a note is permitted.	6. No accrual or **note** required; however, a note is permitted.
	Gain Contingency	
Probable	No accrual except in very unusual circumstances. **Note** disclosure required.	**Note** disclosure required; exercise care to avoid misleading inferences.
Reasonably possible	**Note** disclosure required; exercise care to avoid misleading inferences.	**Note** disclosure required; exercise extreme care to avoid misleading inferences.
Remote	Disclosure not recommended.	

Cash	200,000	
Sales revenue		200,000
Estimated warranty expense	1,000	
Estimated warranty liability		1,000

b. Subsequently, during warranty period for actual expenditures:

Estimated warranty liability	987	
Cash (or other resources)		987

c. If the actual expenditure were $1,100, the entry would be:

Estimated warranty liability	1,000	
Estimated warranty expense	100	
Cash (or other resources)		1,100

When warranty expense is immaterial in amount, a company would not accrue it as illustrated above; instead, they would account for it on a cash basis because, for practical reasons, the materiality concept is permitted to override the matching principle.

Case B—Liability from Premiums, Coupons, and Trading Stamps. As a promotional device, many companies offer premiums of one kind or another to customers who turn in coupons, box tops, and so on. At the end of each accounting period, a portion of these coupons or box tops will be outstanding (unredeemed by the customers), some of which ultimately will be turned in for redemption. These outstanding claims for premiums represent an expense and an estimated liability that must be recognized in the period of sale of the merchandise.

To illustrate a typical situation, assume Baker Coffee Company offered to customers a premium—a special coffee cup free of charge (cost to Baker 75 cents each) upon the return of 20 coupons. One coupon is placed in each can of coffee when packed. The company estimated, on the basis of experience, that only 70 percent of the coupons would ever be redeemed. The following additional data for two years are available:

	First Year	Second Year
Number of coffee cups purchased @ $0.75	6,000	4,000
Number of coupons redeemed	40,000	120,000
Number of cans of coffee sold	100,000	200,000

The indicated entries are as follows:

a. To record purchases of cups:

	First Year		Second Year	
Premium inventory	4,500		3,000	
Cash		4,500		3,000

b. To record estimated liability and premium expense on sales:

	First Year		Second Year	
Premium expense*	2,625		5,250	
Estimated premium claims payable		2,625		5,250

* Computations:
Year 1: (100,000 ÷ 20) × $0.75 × .70 = $2,625.
Year 2: (200,000 ÷ 20) × $0.75 × .70 = $5,250.

c. To record redemption of coupons:

	First Year		Second Year	
Estimated premium claims payable	1,500		4,500	
Premium inventory ...		1,500		4,500

* Computations:
Year 1: (40,000 ÷ 20) × $0.75 = $1,500.
Year 2: (120,000 ÷ 20) × $0.75 = $4,500.

Case C—Liability from Litigation. Assume S Company was sued during the last quarter of the current year as a result of an accident involving a vehicle owned and operated by the company. The plaintiff is seeking $100,000 damages. In the opinion of management and company counsel, it is probable that damages will be assessed and a reasonable estimate is $50,000. The indicated entry is:

Estimated loss from pending lawsuit ...	50,000	
Estimated liability from pending lawsuit		50,000

Estimated losses would be classified as ordinary or extraordinary on the income statement in accordance with the provisions of *APB Opinion No. 30,* "Reporting the Results of Operations." Balance sheet classification of the estimated liability would depend upon the expected timing of its settlement.

Estimated liabilities, such as the three illustrated above, ultimately may require expenditures more or less than estimated to satisfy the actual liability. When the estimated liability turns out to be too high or too low, the difference is accounted for as a change in estimate under the provisions of *APB Opinion 20.* That is, there is no correction of prior years' income; the difference is accounted for **prospectively** as a deduction from, or addition to, the previously recorded amount of expense or loss in the income statement of the year of settlement and subsequent years as the case may be.

Occasionally a loss contingency is of such a nature that **note disclosure** is needed, in addition to accrual and reporting in the body of the financial statements in order to meet the requirements of the reporting principle. Published financial reports of companies seldom, if ever, reflect a situation of counsel saying, "We may lose this suit." As an advocate, counsel does everything possible to avoid a **tacit** confession of **guilt** in advance of the final adjudication.

Loss Contingencies Disclosed Only in Notes

The preceding section dealt exclusively with loss contingencies that must be accrued and reported in the body of the financial statements (i.e., cell 1 in Exhibit 10–2). This section discusses **loss contingencies that must be disclosed in notes to the financial statements.**

FASB Statement 5 provides that disclosure of the contingency (in a manner other than accrual of the expense or loss) must be made when there is **at least** a reasonable possibility that a loss or an additional loss may have been incurred. Observe in Exhibit 10–2 that this requirement for note disclosure of the expense or loss appears in **cell 2** on the **probable line** and in **cells 3 and 4** of the **reasonably possible** line. The note must describe the nature of the contingency and give an estimate of the **possible** loss or range of loss, or it must state that a reasonable estimate of the **possible** loss cannot be made.

The accounting treatment of loss contingencies that must be disclosed in notes (but not accrued in the financial statements) does not depend upon the kind of event but rather on the circumstances of probability and reasonability of loss estimates. For example in the case of S Company, given in **Case C** above, since the loss contingency was both probable and the amount could be reasonably estimated, accrual was required. Alternatively, if we assume that management and legal counsel conclude that the plaintiff's case is weak and that it is only **reasonably possible** that damages will be assessed by the court, accrual is not permitted but note disclosure is required (see cells 3 and 4 of Exhibit 10–2). Finally, if we assume instead that the probability of loss is **remote,** accrual is not permitted and note disclosure is not required; however, note disclosure is permitted (see cells 5 and 6 of Exhibit 10–2).

Accounting for the effects of litigation is complicated because of *(a)* legal complexities, *(b)* the time it takes for settlement, and *(c)* the fact that presettlement disclosures may prejudice the outcome of the case. In these situations, *FASB Statement 5,* paragraph 36, suggests that "Among the factors that should be considered [in determining whether it is probable that a loss has occurred] are . . . the opinions or views of legal counsel and other advisors, the experience of the enterprise in similar cases, the experience of other enterprises, and any decision of the enterprise's management as to how the enterprise intends to respond to the lawsuit, claim or assessment." For example, if the enterprise plans to contest the lawsuit forcefully, this is considered good evidence that in their opinion a loss is not probable (no accrual is required) and may not even be reasonably possible (no accrual permitted and note disclosure not required).

GAIN CONTINGENCIES

A gain contingency arises when the characteristics of a contingency are present (as defined earlier), and it may result in an increase in assets or a decrease in liabilities, depending upon one or more future events.

Contingent gains rarely are accrued; however, they are accorded note disclosure, provided the note does not give "misleading implications." The different treatment accorded gain contingencies, compared with loss contingencies, is due to application of the concept of conservatism. *FASB Statement 5* specifies the treatment of gain contingencies as follows:

a. Contingencies that might result in gains are not reflected in the accounts since to do so might be to recognize revenue prior to its realization.
b. Adequate disclosure shall be made of contingencies that might result in gains, but care shall be exercised to avoid misleading implications as to the likelihood of realization.

An example of a gain contingency would be a lawsuit filed by a company against another party for damages. Assuming the case has been decided in favor of the company but is awaiting appeal, and in the opinion of the company counsel and management the appeal will be denied, note disclosure (but not accrual) would be appropriate. Another example would be expropriation (by a foreign government) of the assets of the company, and a concomitant probability that reimbursement will exceed the book value of those assets. In these circumstances the volatile political situation in the foreign country must be recognized. Therefore, note disclosure would be needed (in this situation the final outcome may turn out to be a loss). The note disclosure should be worded carefully to avoid misleading implications about the probability of the gain and its amount. Remote gain contingencies should **not be disclosed.**

ACCRUAL OF GENERAL CONTINGENCY RESERVES AND APPROPRIATIONS OF RETAINED EARNINGS

Prior to *FASB Statement 5,* companies with loss contingencies sometimes accrued the losses by making an entry similar to the following:

Expense (or loss) specified	x,xxx	
Reserve for general contingencies ...		x,xxx

In some cases, the Reserve for General Contingencies account was reported as a liability; in other cases, it was reported as an appropriation of retained earnings.

Accrual of "reserves for general contingencies" is not permitted by *FASB Statement 5.* The *Statement* also provides that in those situations where **appropriations** or "reserves" of retained earnings are recorded, the debit to create them must be to Retained Earnings, not to loss or expense, and the balances in such "reserve" accounts must be reported as an appropriation of retained earnings in the stockholders' equity section of the balance sheet (discussed in Chapter 15).

Part B: Accounting for Income Taxes

Accounting for income taxes is discussed in this chapter because income tax is an important liability of most corporations.[7] This liability merits special attention because accounting for income taxes is subject to specific rules, some of which are controversial. This part of the chapter covers the major com-

[7] Partnerships and sole proprietorships do not pay income taxes; the owners include their shares of company income on their personal income tax returns.

plexities encountered in practice. The discussions are based primarily upon *APB Opinion No. 11,* "Accounting for Income Taxes." Numerous other pronouncements (*APB Opinions 23* and *24, FASB Statement 9,* and *FASB Interpretation 32*) deal with special areas of this topic, but they do not change the general rules specified in *APB Opinion 11.*

APB Opinion 11 establishes the basic requirement that companies should match against the revenue of a period an amount of income tax expense based on the reported pretax **accounting income** of that period regardless of the amount of income tax **payable** (as reflected on the income tax return for the period). Thus, *APB Opinion 11* deals with the amount of income tax **expense** which should be reported on the income statement. The *Opinion* does not specify computation of the amount of income tax **payable** (to the government) because that is determined by the Internal Revenue Code and IRS Tax Regulations.

The complexities in accounting for income tax arise because it is necessary to reconcile the concepts of financial accounting (which govern the amount of income tax expense on the income statement) with the income tax laws (which govern the amount of tax payable, as reflected on the tax return). Fortunately, the two areas adopt the same general notion of income; however, enough differences exist to require special accounting and reporting guidelines.

Preliminary to the substantive discussions to follow, two terms that will be used throughout the remainder of this chapter are defined as follows:

1. **Pretax accounting income**—revenues and gains less expenses and losses (ignoring income tax expense) reported on the income statement in conformity with GAAP. Income tax **expense** reported on the income statement is based on **pretax accounting income.**
2. **Taxable income**—revenues and gains less expenses and losses includable on the tax return in conformity with tax laws and regulations. Income tax **payable** is based on **taxable income.**

This part of the chapter considers the following income tax topics in the order given:

1. **Interperiod** income tax allocation.
2. Income tax effects of prior period adjustments.
3. **Intraperiod** income tax allocation.
4. The investment tax credit.
5. Disclosure of income tax.

Supplement 10–A discusses and illustrates accounting for tax loss carrybacks and carryforwards. Supplement 10–B illustrates the effect of changes in tax rates, and Supplement 10–C discusses different concepts underlying income tax allocation.

INTERPERIOD INCOME TAX ALLOCATION

Interperiod income tax allocation is defined in *APB Opinion 11* as "the process of apportioning income taxes among periods." This definition means that income tax expense reported on the income statement must be based on pretax accounting income rather than on taxable income from the tax return. Any difference between income tax expense and income tax payable for the period that will reverse in one or more future periods must be recognized as **deferred income tax.** Thus, income tax expense results from **allocation** of income tax to the period in which the accounting income which caused the tax is reported. Allocation is necessary to conform to the matching principle as stated in *APB Opinion 11,* paragraph 12:

> Interperiod tax allocation is an integral part of the determination of income tax expense, and income tax expense should include the tax effects of revenue [and gain] and expense [and loss] transactions included in the determination of pretax accounting income.

To illustrate **interperiod** income tax allocation, assume XY Corporation prepared the summarized **pretax** income statements for years 19D and 19E shown in Exhibit 10–3.

Interperiod income tax allocation, based on the **pretax** data given in Exhibit 10–3, is discussed on the next several pages and is illustrated by using four **independent** cases as follows:

Case A—No tax difference; pretax accounting income and taxable income are the **same;** hence, **no** deferred income tax.

Case B—A timing difference; pretax accounting income **less** than taxable income; hence, a deferred income tax **debit.**

Case C—A timing difference; pretax accounting income **more** than taxable income; hence, a deferred income tax **credit.**

Case D—A permanent tax difference; hence **no** deferred income tax.

EXHIBIT 10–3: Illustrative Data for Interperiod Income Tax Allocation

XY CORPORATION
Pretax Income Statements

	19D	19E
Revenues:		
Sales revenue	$100,000	$120,000
Rent revenue	6,000	6,000
Investment revenue	1,000	1,000
Total revenues	107,000	127,000
Expenses:		
Cost of goods sold	65,000	75,000
Depreciation expense (straight line)	10,000	10,000
Interest expense	2,000	2,000
Total expenses	77,000	87,000
Pretax accounting income	$ 30,000	$ 40,000

Assumed average income tax rate, 40%.

Case A—Assume that all revenues and expenses shown in the two income statements in Exhibit 10–3 were properly includable on the income tax returns for the two years. Thus, for both years, **pretax accounting income** and **taxable income** were the same. The entries to record income taxes would be as follows:

19D:

Income tax expense ($30,000 × .40)	12,000	
Income tax payable		12,000

19E:

Income tax expense ($40,000 × .40)	16,000	
Income tax payable		16,000

The income statements would report the respective amounts as expense, and the balance sheets would report the same amounts as a liability (assuming no prepayments on the tax liability). In this case, there is **no deferred income tax** for either year because the amounts for income tax expense and income tax payable were the same for each period.

Case B—Assume that the rent revenue for one full year amounting to $12,000 was collected in full on July 1, 19D, for the following 12 months. Accrual accounting requires XY Corporation to include six months' rent revenue on the income statement for each year. However, for income tax purposes, all of the rent revenue must be included on the income tax return for the period in which collected, 19D. Therefore, for each year pretax accounting income and taxable income were different. Consequently, **deferred income tax must be recognized.** Computation of income tax and the related entry to record income tax for year **19D** would be as follows:

Income tax expense (pretax accounting income, $30,000 × .40)	$12,000
Income tax payable [taxable income, ($30,000 + $6,000) × .40]	14,400
Difference: Deferred income tax (check: $6,000 × .40) (a debit)	$ 2,400

Entry to record income tax for 19D:

Income tax expense	12,000	
Deferred income tax (asset)	2,400	
Income tax payable		14,400

The 19D income statement would report income tax expense of $12,000, and the balance sheet for 19D would report *(a)* income tax payable, $14,400 (assuming no prepayments), and *(b)* a current asset (a debit) for deferred income tax, $2,400. The $2,400 is an asset because it is prepaid income tax expense.

Computation of income tax and the related entry to record income tax for **19E** would be as follows:

Income tax expense (pretax accounting income, $40,000 × .40)	$16,000
Income tax payable [taxable income, ($40,000 − $6,000) × .40]	13,600
Difference: Deferred income tax (check: $6,000 × .40) (a credit)	$ 2,400

Entry to record income tax for 19E:

Income tax expense	16,000	
Income tax payable		13,600
Deferred income tax		2,400

The 19E income statement would report income tax expense of $16,000, and the balance sheet for 19E would report income tax payable of $13,600 (assuming no prepayments). Deferred income tax would not be reported because it has a zero balance—it was debited for $2,400 in 19D and credited for the same amount in 19E. Note that at the end of 19E the deferred income tax amount of $2,400 from 19D reversed or "turned around" because at that time, for this particular transaction, the **total** (for the two years combined) pretax accounting income and **total** taxable income amounts were the same. In summary, the income tax expense was **allocated** to the respective periods in which the related rent revenue was reported for accounting purposes, regardless of when the rent revenue was reported on the tax return.

Case C—We will disregard the assumption in Case B and instead assume that XY Corporation uses straight-line depreciation on the income statement and double-declining-balance (DDB) depreciation on the income tax return for machinery acquired January 1, 19D, that cost $50,000 and had an estimated useful life of five years and no residual value. Depreciation expense each year under each method would be as follows:

Straight-line depreciation:	
$50,000 × 20% (five years)	$10,000
DDB depreciation:	
Year D: $50,000 × 40%	20,000
Year E: ($50,000 − $20,000) × 40%	12,000

In this case the pretax accounting income for each year will be different from the taxable income because of the different amounts of depreciation included in the two income amounts; as a consequence, **deferred income tax must be recognized.** For year **19D,** computation of income tax and the related entry to record income taxes would be as follows:

Income tax expense (pretax accounting income, $30,000 × .40)	$12,000
Income tax payable (taxable income, $20,000* × .40)	8,000
Difference: Deferred income tax (check: $10,000† × .40) (a credit)	$ 4,000

* $30,000 + $10,000 − $20,000 = $20,000.
† $20,000 − $10,000 = $10,000.

Entry to record income tax for 19D:

Income tax expense	12,000	
Income tax payable		8,000
Deferred income tax		4,000

The income statement for 19D would report income tax expense of $12,000, and the balance sheet would report *(a)* a liability for income tax payable of $8,000 (assuming no prepayments) and *(b)* another liability for deferred income tax of $4,000. In this case, deferred income tax is a liability because the tax expense related to it was reported on the income statement and the tax must be paid in later periods when DDB depreciation expense becomes less per period than straight-line depreciation. Thus, the deferred tax (a credit) will completely reverse by the end of the last year (fifth year) of depreciation on the machinery.

Computation of income tax and the related entry to record income tax for **19E** would be as follows:

Income tax expense (pretax accounting income, $40,000 × .40)	$16,000
Income tax payable (taxable income, $38,000* × .40)	15,200
Difference: Deferred income tax (check: $2,000† × .40)	$ 800

* $40,000 + $10,000 − $12,000 = $38,000.
† $12,000 − $10,000 = $2,000.

Entry to record income tax for 19E:

Income tax expense	16,000	
Income tax payable		15,200
Deferred income tax		800

The income statement for 19E would report income tax expense of $16,000, and the balance sheet would report *(a)* a liability for income tax payable of $15,200 (assuming no prepayments) and *(b)* another liability for $4,000 + $800 = $4,800 for deferred income tax payable. During the next three years, this $4,800 credit will be exactly offset by debits because straight-line depreciation expense then will be greater than DDB depreciation (i.e., the deferred tax amounts will completely reverse).

Timing Differences

Two kinds of transactions cause pretax accounting income to differ from taxable income; they are called (1) **timing differences** and (2) **permanent differences.** Cases B–C illustrated timing differences. Case D (to follow) illustrates a permanent difference.

APB Opinion 11, paragraph 13, defines **timing differences** as "differences between the periods in which transactions affect taxable income and the periods in which they enter into the determination of pretax accounting income. Timing differences originate in one period and reverse or 'turn around' in one or more subsequent periods. Some timing differences reduce income taxes that would otherwise be payable currently; others increase income taxes that would otherwise be payable currently." Cases B (rent revenue) and C (depreciation expense) above illustrated timing differences because they caused a difference between pretax accounting income and taxable income that would reverse in one or more subsequent periods. **Timing differences always cause deferred income tax** (either a debit or a credit). Four types of transactions cause timing differences:

1. **Revenues or gains that are included in pretax accounting income before they are included in taxable income.** Examples include **earlier** pretax accounting recognition of:
   a. Gross margin on installment sales (Chapter 22).
   b. Income on construction contracts (Chapter 9).
   c. Unrealized gain on short-term investments in equity securities (Chapter 6).
   d. Investment revenue on investments accounted for by the equity method (Chapter 16).
2. **Expenses or losses that are deducted in determining pretax accounting income before they are deducted in determining taxable income.** Examples include **earlier** pretax accounting recognition of:
   a. Estimated warranty expense (Part A of this chapter).
   b. Estimated loss on disposal of a segment of the business (Chapter 21).
   c. Unrealized loss on short-term investments in equity securities (Chapter 6).
   d. Deferred compensation expense on employees (Chapter 14).

   Each of these items is tax deductible only when decreases in assets occur as a result of completed external transactions.
3. **Revenues or gains that are included in taxable income earlier than they are included in pretax accounting income.** Examples include:
   a. Rent revenue collected in advance, which often is taxed when collected, regardless of when it is earned (Part A of this chapter).
   b. Gain on sale of property leased back (Chapter 19).
4. **Expenses or losses that are deducted in determining taxable income earlier than they are deducted in determining pretax accounting income.** Examples include:
   a. Depreciation expense on an accelerated basis for tax purposes but on a straight-line basis for accounting purposes (Chapter 12).
   b. Costs of organizing a business (e.g., legal fees) which are tax deductible as incurred but which often are capitalized and later amortized as expense in the accounting records.

In summary, timing differences *(a)* relate to items that will be on **both** the income statement and the tax return, but in different reporting periods; *(b)* always cause deferred income tax; and *(c)* reverse in one or more future periods.

Permanent Differences

Permanent differences arise in two situations as follows:

(1) Certain accounting revenues are exempt from taxation and certain accounting expenses are **not deductible** in determining taxable income. Examples include interest revenue on investments in tax-free municipal obligations, insurance expense for premiums paid on officers' life insurance, and amortization expense on goodwill.

(2) Certain taxable revenues and expenses **never** are components of pretax accounting income. Examples include the special deduction ("exclusion" for noncorporate taxpayers) of certain dividends received and the excess of statutory depletion over cost depletion.

Income tax allocation **never** is applied to permanent differences because they do not cause income tax differences that will subsequently reverse. **For a permanent difference, there is no difference between income tax expense and income tax payable.**

Case D—To illustrate a **permanent difference,** return to Exhibit 10–3 for XY Corporation and assume the investment revenue of $1,000 for each year was interest on "tax-free" municipal bonds. Disregarding Case B (rent revenue) and Case C (depreciation expense), income tax expense and income tax payable each year would be the same amount as shown below:

Year	Computation	Income Tax Expense	Income Taxes Payable
19D	($30,000 − $1,000) × .40	$11,600	$11,600
19E	($40,000 − $1,000) × .40	15,600	15,600

Comprehensive Illustration. A worksheet can be used to compute interperiod tax allocation amounts and a single entry in the accounts is made to record the combined effect of all tax differences. To illustrate, we return to Exhibit 10–3 and combine Cases B, C, and D for XY Corporation to show the *(a)* worksheet for the computation of income tax expense and income tax payable and *(b)* presentation of the income tax effects in the financial statements. Exhibit 10–4 presents *(a)* an efficient worksheet format for computing income tax expense, income tax payable, and deferred income tax; and *(b)* disclosure of the income tax effects. Panel A restates the illustrative data (given in Exhibit 10–3 and in respect to Cases B, C, and D, already discussed), Panels B (for 19D) and D (for 19E) illustrate two worksheets and the entries to record income taxes, and Panels C (for

EXHIBIT 10–4: Comprehensive Illustration—Interperiod Income Tax Allocation, XY Corporation

Panel A—Illustrative Data:

1. Pretax income statements (repeated from Exhibit 10–3):

	19D	19E
Revenues:		
Sales revenue	$100,000	$120,000
Rent revenue	6,000	6,000
Investment revenue	1,000	1,000
Total revenues	107,000	127,000
Expenses:		
Cost of goods sold	65,000	75,000
Depreciation expense (straight line)	10,000	10,000
Interest expense	2,000	2,000
Total expenses	77,000	87,000
Pretax accounting income	$ 30,000	$ 40,000

Assumed average income tax rate, 40%.

2. Assumptions:
   Case B—On July 1, 19D, collected $12,000 rent in advance for the following 12 months. This full amount is subject to income tax in the year collected.
   Case C—On January 1, 19D, acquired machinery that cost $50,000; estimated useful life, 5 years, no residual value, straight-line depreciation for financial reporting, and DDB depreciation for tax purposes.
   Case D—Investment revenue of $1,000 was interest earned on tax-free municipal bonds.

Panel B—Income Tax Worksheet and Entry to Record Combined Income Tax Effect, 19D:

Income Tax Expense	Item	Income Tax Payable
$30,000	Pretax accounting income	$ 30,000
(1,000)	Case D—Deduct investment revenue on tax-free municipal bonds (a permanent difference)	(1,000)
	Case B—Add rent revenue taxed in current year ($12,000 − $6,000)	6,000
	Case C—Deduct additional depreciation (DDB) ($10,000 − $20,000)	(10,000)
29,000	Pretax accounting income subject to tax	
	Taxable income	25,000
× .40	Income tax rate	× .40
$11,600	Income tax expense	
	Income tax payable	$ 10,000

Check: Net deferred income tax, $11,600 − $10,000 = $1,600 credit.

Entry to record combined effect of income tax for 19D:

	Debit	Credit
Income tax expense	11,600	
Deferred income tax, short term (rent revenue) ($6,000 × .40)	2,400	
Income tax payable		10,000
Deferred income tax, long-term (depreciation) ($10,000 × .40)		4,000

Exhibit 10–4 ***(continued)***

Panel C—Financial Statements, Including Income Tax, 19D:

Income statement for the year ended December 31, 19D:

Revenues:		
Sales revenue	$100,000	
Rent revenue	6,000	
Investment revenue	1,000	$107,000
Expenses:		
Cost of goods sold	65,000	
Depreciation expense	10,000	
Interest expense	2,000	
Income tax expense	11,600	88,600
Net income		$ 18,400

Balance sheet at December 31, 19D (partial):

Current assets:	
Deferred income tax*	$ 2,400
Current liabilities:	
Income tax payable (assuming no prepayments)	10,000
Long-term liabilities:	
Deferred income tax*	4,000

* These amounts net to $1,600 (credit); see discussion of "Classification of Deferred Income Tax," which follows.

Panel D—Income Tax Worksheet and Entry to Record Combined Income Tax Effect, 19E:

Income Tax Expense	Item	Income Tax Payable
$40,000	Pretax accounting income	$40,000
(1,000)	Case D—Deduct investment revenue on tax-free municipal bonds (a permanent difference)	(1,000)
	Case B—Deduct rent revenue taxed in prior year ($6,000 − $12,000)	(6,000)
	Case C—Deduct additional depreciation (DDB) ($10,000 − $12,000)	(2,000)
39,000	Pretax accounting income subject to tax	
	Taxable income	31,000
× .40	Income tax rate	× .40
$15,600	Income tax expense	
	Income tax payable	$12,400

Check: Net deferred income tax, $15,600 − $12,400 = $3,200 credit.

Entry to record combined effect of income tax for 19E:

Income tax expense	15,600	
Income tax payable		12,400
Deferred income tax, short term (rent revenue) ($6,000 × .40)		2,400
Deferred income tax, long term (depreciation) ($2,000 × .40)		800

EXHIBIT 10–4 ***(concluded)***

Panel E—Financial Statements, Including Income Tax, 19E:

Income statement for the year ended December 31, 19E:

Revenues:		
Sales revenue	$120,000	
Rent revenue	6,000	
Investment revenue	1,000	$127,000
Expenses:		
Cost of goods sold	75,000	
Depreciation expense	10,000	
Interest expense	2,000	
Income tax expense	15,600	102,600
Net income		$ 24,400

Balance sheet at December 31, 19E (partial):

Current liabilities:	
Income tax payable (assuming no prepayments)	$12,400
Long-term liabilities:	
Deferred income tax*	4,800

* Balance in the long-term deferred income tax account, $4,000 + $800 = $4,800; credit; credit balance in the short-term deferred income account, $2,400 − $2,400 = $-0-. See discussion of "Classification of Deferred Income Tax," which follows.

19D) and E (for 19E) present the income tax effects on the two income statements and balance sheets.

Classification of Deferred Income Tax

Deferred income tax is reported on the balance sheet *(a)* as a current or noncurrent asset, if a debit; and *(b)* as a current or long-term liability, if a credit. On this point *APB Opinion 11,* paragraph 57, reads as follows:

> Deferred [tax amounts] should be classified in two categories—one for the net current amount and the other for the net noncurrent amount.

FASB, *Statement of Financial Accounting Standards No. 37,* "Balance Sheet Classification of Deferred Income Taxes," June 1980, paragraph 4, further states that:

> A deferred [tax debit] or credit is related to an asset or liability if reduction of the asset or liability [e.g., reduction of the book value of depreciable assets through depreciation] causes the timing difference to reverse. A deferred [tax debit] or credit that is related to an asset or liability [e.g., depreciable assets] shall be classified as current or noncurrent based on the classification of the related asset or liability. A deferred [tax debit] or credit that is not related to an asset or liability . . . shall be classified [as current or noncurrent] based on the expected reversal date of the specific timing difference.[8]

Therefore, current debits and credits are offset, and noncurrent debits and credits are offset; however, current and noncurrent debits and credits are **not** offset. To illustrate the classification of deferred tax amounts, the classifications shown in Exhibit 10–4 were based on the following analysis of individual items:

[8] Deferred tax amounts that are **not** related to a specific asset or liability are beyond the scope of this book.

	Balance Sheet Classification	
	Current	Noncurrent
Year 19D: Balance in the deferred income tax account, $1,600 credit comprised of:		
Debits:		
Rent revenue collected in advance, a current item because the related liability, Unearned Rent Revenue, is a current liability ($6,000 × .40)	$2,400	
Credits:		
Depreciation of machinery, a noncurrent item because the related asset, Machinery, is a noncurrent asset ($10,000 × .40)		$4,000
Year 19E: Balance in the deferred income tax account, $4,800 credit comprised of:		
Debits:		
None		
Credits:		
Depreciation of machinery, a noncurrent item because the related asset, Machinery, is a noncurrent asset ($10,000 + $2,000) × .40		$4,800

INCOME TAX EFFECTS OF PRIOR PERIOD ADJUSTMENTS

FASB, *Statement of Financial Accounting Standards No. 16,* "Prior Period Adjustments," limits prior period adjustments to two items: *(a)* correction of an error in the financial statements of a prior period and *(b)* adjustments for income tax benefits related to preacquisition operating loss carryforwards of purchased subsidiaries.

If an error caused a misstatement of reported income of a prior period and if the misstated item had an income tax effect, the prior period adjustment would also need to correct for the income tax effect of the error. In such a case, the company most likely would file an amended tax return to claim a refund or to pay additional taxes, as the case may be.

To illustrate, assume TW Corporation inadvertently understated depreciation expense on both the financial statements and the tax return in 19A by $10,000 when the income tax rate was 40 percent. In 19C, the company discovered this error when the income tax rate was 45 percent (there was no error in 19B or 19C). Two entries (or a single combined entry) would correct the error in 19C:

Prior period adjustment (expense correction)	10,000	
Accumulated depreciation		10,000
Receivable for refund of 19A income tax ($10,000 × 40%)	4,000	
Prior period adjustment (tax refund on expense correction)		4,000

Note that the tax rate in effect during the year when the error was made (i.e., 40 percent), rather than the tax rate of the correction year (i.e., 45%) was used in the income tax entry above because the error occurred when the tax rate was 40 percent. Any interest and/or penalties related to the extra income tax, and any interest related to any tax refunds also would affect the net amount of the prior period adjustment.

Changes in tax rates are considered in more detail in Supplement 10–B. The $6,000 debit balance in the Prior Period Adjustment account (i.e., $10,000 − $4,000) would be closed to Retained Earnings and reported on the statement of retained earnings.

INTRAPERIOD INCOME TAX ALLOCATION

APB Opinion 11 specifies two distinctly different types of income tax allocation: *(a)* **interperiod** income tax allocation, caused by timing differences among accounting periods resulting from differences between the income statement and the tax return (discussed above); and *(b)* **intraperiod** income tax allocation, which relates total income tax for the period to the various statement components that caused the tax. It is important to understand that **both** types of income tax allocation must be applied; one is not an alternative to the other.

The concept of intraperiod allocation is to report the income tax (or tax saving) associated with a particular kind of item along with that item in the financial statements (i.e., tax expense must follow the item that caused it). To illustrate intraperiod income tax allocation, assume the following for ABC Corporation:

Pretax income before extraordinary items ...	$40,000
Extraordinary gain (pretax)................	10,000
Total income tax expense, average tax rate 40% [($40,000 + $10,000) × .40]...........	20,000

ABC Corporation would report the results of intraperiod tax allocation of the $20,000 total income tax expense as follows:

Income before income tax and before extraordinary items		$40,000
Less: Income tax expense ($40,000 × .40)		16,000
Income before extraordinary items		24,000
Extraordinary gain (specified).....	$10,000	
Less: Applicable income tax ($10,000 × .40)	4,000	6,000
Net income		$30,000

In this example, as in most of the examples in this textbook, average tax rates are used to illustrate the particular discussion without laborious income tax computations.

Exhibit 10–5 presents five separate cases to illustrate how **total income tax expense** for the period is allocated to the several components of income which caused a tax expense (or a tax saving). Note that in each case the allocations always sum to the total tax amount.

Income tax, with intraperiod tax allocation, would be reported as shown in Exhibit 10–5, Panel B, for five independent cases. Computations are given to show how the allocated amounts were derived. In all five cases, income (loss) before income tax and before extraordinary items is $30,000 and is associated with income tax expense (saving) of $7,000. The following discussion focuses on the application of intraperiod tax allocation to the extraordinary item.

In **Case A,** the extraordinary gain produced tax expense of $4,000, which is computed at the 40 percent tax rate because income for the period has already exceeded the $25,000 layer taxed at 20 percent.

Case B is like Case A, except that the extraordinary gain is taxed at 30 percent because it is a capital gain (assumed tax rate, 30 percent); if the extraordinary item in Case B had been a loss, it would also have been subject to the same 30 percent tax rate.

In **Case C,** the first $30,000 of the extraordinary gain offsets the $30,000 loss before tax and before extraordinary item. The remainder of the extraordinary gain (i.e., $10,000) is taxed at 20 percent.

In **Case D,** the first $5,000 of the extraordinary loss offsets the **last** $5,000 of income before tax and before extraordinary items; the remaining amount of extraordinary loss (i.e., $5,000) offsets income at the 20 percent rate.

In **Case E,** the extraordinary loss (i.e., $40,000) exceeds income before tax and before extraordinary items (i.e., $30,000). The first $30,000 of extraordinary loss offsets all of income before tax and before extraordinary items. The remainder of the extraordinary loss (i.e., $10,000) must be carried back to preceding years or forward to future years under tax loss carryback and carryforward provisions discussed in Supplement 10–A. In this case, we assume a tax loss carryback to preceding years when the applicable tax rate was 20 percent.

Intraperiod income tax allocation involves only the **reporting** phase of accounting and seldom, if ever, the **recording** phase. Therefore, it does not give rise to entries in the accounts and does not modify the entries to record income tax as illustrated in the prior discussion of interperiod income tax allocation.

THE INVESTMENT TAX CREDIT (ITC)

The investment tax credit (ITC) is a provision in the income tax laws designed to encourage investments in new productive assets, such as plant, machinery, and equipment. Currently, the law provides that taxpayers who acquire qualified assets can receive a 10 percent investment tax **credit** as a direct offset to income tax expense and tax payable. This tax credit is important to investors because they can reduce their income tax payable for the year of purchase of the qualified asset by 10 percent of its full cost. The nature of a tax **credit,** as opposed to a tax **deduction,** is that a tax credit causes a direct dollar-for-dollar tax reduction, whereas a tax deduction decreases income tax only by the deduction amount multiplied by the income tax rate. Moreover,

EXHIBIT 10–5: Intraperiod Tax Allocation

Panel A—Illustrative Data:

1. Pretax income:

	Case A	Case B	Case C	Case D	Case E
Income before extraordinary items (loss)	$30,000	$30,000	$(30,000)	$ 30,000	$ 30,000
Extraordinary gain (loss)	10,000	10,000*	40,000	(10,000)	(40,000)
Pretax income (loss)	$40,000	$40,000	$ 10,000	$ 20,000	$(10,000)†
Total income tax expense	$11,000	$10,000	$ 2,000	$ 4,000	$ (2,000)

* Capital gain.
† Involves a tax loss carryback (discussed in Supplement 10–A).

2. Tax rates assumed: 20% on first $25,000 of income or gain; 40% above $25,000; and 30% on capital gains.

Panel B—Application of Intraperiod Tax Allocation to Reporting Income Tax:

Case A:

Income before income tax and before extraordinary gain				$ 30,000
Less: Income tax expense	$25,000 × .20	=	$ 5,000	
	5,000 × .40	=	2,000	7,000
Income before extraordinary gain				23,000
Extraordinary gain (specified)			10,000	
Less: Applicable income tax **expense**	10,000 × .40	=	4,000	6,000
Net income				$ 29,000

Total tax: $7,000 + $4,000 = $11,000 **expense.**

Case B:

Income before income tax and before extraordinary gain				$ 30,000
Less: Income tax expense	$25,000 × .20	=	$ 5,000	
	5,000 × .40	=	2,000	7,000
Income before extraordinary gain				23,000
Extraordinary gain (specified)			10,000	
Less: Applicable income tax **expense** (capital gain)	$10,000 × .30	=	3,000	7,000
Net income				$ 30,000

Total tax: $7,000 + $3,000 = $10,000 **expense.**

Case C:

Income (loss) before income tax and before extraordinary gain				$(30,000)
Less: Income tax saving	$25,000 × .20	=	$ 5,000	
	5,000 × .40	=	2,000	7,000
Income (loss) before extraordinary gain				(23,000)
Extraordinary gain (specified)			40,000	
Less: Applicable income tax **expense**	$25,000 × .20 = 5,000			
	5,000 × .40 = 2,000			
	10,000 × .20 = 2,000		9,000	31,000
Net income				$ 8,000

Total tax: $9,000 − $7,000 = $2,000 **expense.**

Case D:

Income before income tax and before extraordinary loss				$ 30,000
Less: Income tax expense	$25,000 × .20	=	$ 5,000	
	5,000 × .40	=	2,000	7,000
Income before extraordinary loss				$ 23,000
Extraordinary loss (specified)			$10,000	
Less: Applicable income tax **saving**	$ 5,000 × .40 = $2,000			
	5,000 × .20 = 1,000		3,000	7,000
Net income				$ 16,000

Total tax: $7,000 − $3,000 = $4,000 **expense.**

EXHIBIT 10–5 ***(concluded)***

Case E:

Income before income tax and before extraordinary loss			$ 30,000
Less: Income tax expense	$25,000 × .20 =	$ 5,000	
	5,000 × .40 =	$ 2,000	7,000
Income before extraordinary loss			23,000
Extraordinary loss (specified)......		40,000	
Less: Applicable income tax saving	$25,000 × .20 = $5,000		
	5,000 × .40 = 2,000		
	10,000 × .20 = 2,000‡	9,000	(31,000)
Net loss			$ 8,000

Total tax: $7,000 − $9,000 = $2,000 tax **saving.**

‡ Assumes a tax loss carryback to preceding years when applicable tax rate was 20% (discussed in Supplement 10–A).

the taxpayer who utilizes a tax credit is permitted to depreciate the cost of the related asset in full (less any residual value) for income tax purposes, notwithstanding the investment tax credit.[9]

The full amount of the ITC is "received" through a decrease in income tax **payable** in the year in which the qualified asset is purchased; however, it relates to the acquired asset which will contribute to revenue generation over its useful life. Consequently, the question is posed, in terms of the matching principle, whether the income statement effect of the ITC should be *(a)* recorded and reported only in the period of **purchase,** or *(b)* allocated over the **useful life** of the related asset. Unfortunately, at the present time both views are acceptable under current GAAP.

Therefore, two alternative GAAP methods exist for recording and reporting the ITC, viz.:

a. **Flow-Through Method**—Under this method, the full amount of the ITC is recorded and reported as a direct reduction of income tax **expense** of the period in which the related asset is acquired. Thus, the full amount of the ITC "flows through" the **current** income statement and, as a result, increases the reported income of the period of acquisition on a dollar-for-dollar relationship. The primary arguments often given for this method are that *(a)* the ITC is realized in full (through a cash saving) in the period of acquisition; *(b)* the ITC is a tax credit provided by law, and its cash effect is realized exclusively in that period; and *(c)* this method is consistent with the intent of the tax provision to encourage investments in new productive assets by maximizing the overall impact of the ITC in the year of acquisition.

b. **Deferral Method**—Under this method, the total amount of the ITC is recorded as Deferred Investment Tax Credit (a contra account to the related asset account), which then is allocated to each period over the life of the asset as a direct reduction of periodic income tax expense. Thus, the ITC amount is allocated over the estimated useful life of the asset to which it relates. This method relates the ITC to **use** rather than to purchase of the asset. The increase in reported income due to the ITC is spread over the useful life of the related asset rather than being allocated only to the period of acquisition. The primary arguments often given for this method are

[9] The first investment tax credit was provided by the Revenue Act of 1962. Its provisions were revised by the 1964 act, suspended in 1966, and restored in 1967. After yet another suspension, the credit was again restored. The Revenue Act of 1978 sets the credit "permanently" at 10 percent of the cost of qualifying property. It provides for limits on the amount of investment credit usable in a single year. Generally, the first $25,000 of investment credit can be used without limit to offset what would otherwise be the first $25,000 of income tax liability. For 1982, the upper limit on the excess of tax liability over the initial $25,000 which can be offset by the investment tax credit is 90 percent. Thus, if a taxpayer in 1982 initially determines tax liability at $125,000, up to $115,000 of investment tax credit can be used as an offset against the liability. This is computed as below:

		Investment Credit
Initial tax liability......	$125,000	
Deduct first $25,000 (unlimited part) ...	25,000	$ 25,000
Remainder to which limit applies......	100,000	
1982 limit percent	×90%	
Additional investment credit (limited) .		90,000
Total investment credit usable in 1982 .		$115,000

that *(a)* it conforms to the matching principle and, therefore, better measures both periodic income and asset values and *(b)* because a portion of the ITC would be lost if an asset is sold soon after its acquisition, it seems that Congress may have intended for the credit to relate to **use** of the asset giving rise to it.

The characteristics of the ITC and application of the two alternative GAAP approaches are presented in Exhibit 10–6.

Exhibit 10–6 demonstrates the significant differences between the results of the two acceptable alternative methods. **The primary accounting issue is when to reflect the ITC amount in income.** Most companies flow through the ITC on the income statement in the year of acquisition.[10] However, conceptually, the deferral method appears to be preferable.

For the year of acquisition, the flow-through method produces a higher reported income amount and a commensurately higher balance sheet valuation for the asset (see Exhibit 10–6, Panel C). In subsequent years, the deferral method reports a higher income amount but a lower balance sheet valuation (until the end of the useful life of the asset).

Although the deferral method is preferable conceptually, either method may be used under GAAP as specified in *APB Opinions 2* and *4*. This not altogether ideal state of affairs is the result of some early indecision on the part of the APB. To the Board's credit, however, it should be pointed out that in 1971, it issued an Exposure Draft of a proposed *Opinion* which would have allowed only the deferral method. The Board lost the battle in the political arena when the business community pressured Congress to insert a provision in the Revenue Act of 1971 to legally permit choice of either method of accounting for the ITC. Whichever method is adopted must be disclosed and used consistently.

DISCLOSURE OF INCOME TAX

Full disclosure of the components of income tax expense (including deferred income tax) is required. In respect to the income statement, *APB Opinion 11* states that "the components of income tax expense should be disclosed" on the income statement; that is, in addition to **intraperiod** allocation, tax estimated to be payable and the tax effects of timing differences should be reported. The *Opinion* states that these amounts "may be presented as separate items in the income statement or, alternatively, as combined amounts with disclosure of the components parenthetically or in a note to the financial statements." Note disclosures generally are needed to explain the reconciliation of the difference between the income tax expense for the period and the related additions and deductions to income taxes payable (including details of the deferred income tax accounts). Exhibit 10–7 illustrates typical note disclosure. Observe the reconciliation of income tax expense with income tax payable (Note A), disclosure of the effects of **interperiod** tax allocation (Notes A and B), implementation of **intraperiod** tax allocation (separate income tax amounts for income from operations and extraordinary items), and disclosure of the method and the effect of accounting for the investment tax credit (Note C).

Interperiod income tax allocation is complex and has raised much concern among accountants. For instance, many accountants believe current requirements are flawed because deferred income tax amounts are not stated at present value.[11] Given the FASB emphasis on cash flows[12] (discussed in Chapter 1), other accountants favor accounting for income tax entirely without interperiod tax allocation; that is, by debiting income tax expense for the amount of income tax currently payable, which is closer to the cash basis than current practice. Another group points out that deferred income tax amounts often represent a "permanent" deferral of income tax for an entity so long as it is a going concern. On this basis they argue that interperiod tax allocation "muddies the water" of predicting an entity's future cash flows from its accounting income.[13] This brief discussion suggests the controversial nature of interperiod tax allocation and outlines why many accountants believe accounting for income tax should be changed.

---

[10] AICPA, *Accounting Trends & Techniques, 1980* (New York, 1980) (Table 3–13), reported that of the 600 companies surveyed in 1979, 529 companies used the flow-through method and only 67 used the deferral method. Four companies made no reference in their annual reports to accounting for the ITC.

[11] See for example, H. Nurnberg, "Discounting Deferred Tax Liabilities," *The Accounting Review* (October 1972), pp. 655–65.

[12] FASB, *Exposure Draft of Proposed Statement of Financial Accounting Concepts*, "Reporting Income, cash flows, and Financial Position of Business Enterprises" (Stamford, Conn., November 16, 1981).

[13] These arguments are summarized by E. S. Hendriksen, *Accounting Theory*, 3d ed. (Homewood, Ill., Richard D. Irwin, 1977), Chapter 16.

EXHIBIT 10–6: Recording and Reporting the Investment Tax Credit (ITC)

Panel A—Illustrative Data:

January 1, 19A:
Purchased new machinery, cost, $200,000 (10-year life; estimated residual value $30,000).

December 31, 19A:
Pretax income (after $17,000 depreciation on new machine), $60,000.
Income tax expense ($60,000 × 40% tax rate), $24,000.
Investment tax credit ($200,000 × 10%; not included in above amounts), $20,000.

Panel B—Entries for 19A:

Flow-Through Method (ITC as a reduction of income tax expense all in the year of purchase)			Deferral Method (ITC allocated as a reduction of income tax expense over the life of the related asset)		
a. January 1—Purchase qualified machinery:					
Machinery	200,000		Machinery	200,000	
Cash		200,000	Cash		200,000
b. December 31—Record depreciation expense:					
Depreciation expense	17,000		Depreciation expense	17,000	
Accumulated depreciation		17,000	Accumulated depreciation		17,000
c. December 31—Record income tax and ITC:					
Income tax expense	4,000		Income tax expense	24,000	
Income tax payable		4,000	Deferred investment tax credit		20,000
(Income tax expense, $24,000 − ITC, $20,000 = $4,000.)			Income tax payable		4,000
			Deferred investment tax credit	2,000	
			Income tax expense (ITC)		2,000
			($20,000 ÷ 10 years; repeated each year for 10 years, which reduces the deferred amount to zero at the end of 10th year.)		

Panel C—Reporting for 19A:

	Flow-Through			Deferral	
Income statement:					
Depreciation expense		$ 17,000			$ 17,000
Pretax income		$ 60,000			$ 60,000
Income tax expense	$24,000			$24,000	
Investment tax credit	20,000	4,000	(yearly amortization)	2,000	22,000
Net income		$ 56,000			$ 38,000
Balance sheet:					
Machinery (at cost)		$200,000			$200,000
Accumulated depreciation		(17,000)			(17,000)
Deferred investment tax credit		-0-	(unamortized balance $20,000–$2,000)		(18,000)
Carrying value		$183,000			$165,000
Income tax payable		$ 4,000			$ 4,000

EXHIBIT 10–7: Disclosure of Income Tax

B CORPORATION
Income Statement (partial)
For the Year Ended December 31, 19B

Income from operations		$120,000
Less: Income tax expense (Notes A and C)		42,000*
Income before extraordinary items		78,000
Extraordinary items:		
Loss	$30,000	
Less: Applicable tax reduction	12,000	18,000
Net income		$ 60,000

* An average tax rate of 40% is assumed on all items for illustrative purposes ($48,000 – ITC; $6,000 = $42,000).

B CORPORATION
Balance Sheet (partial)
At December 31, 19B

Current liabilities:	
Income tax payable (Notes A and C)......	$29,000
Deferred income tax (Note B)............	11,000
Long-term liabilities:	
Deferred income tax (Note B)............	19,000

Notes to financial statements:

Note A. Income tax payable was computed as follows:

Income tax expense on current operations	$42,000
Add decrease in credit balance of deferred income tax, current	2,000
Deduct increase in credit balance of deferred income tax, long term	(3,000)
Income tax payable on current operations	41,000
Deduct tax saving on extraordinary loss ..	12,000
Income tax currently payable.........	$29,000

Note B. The current portion of deferred income tax (i.e., $11,000) is related to income tax expense on the gross margin on installment sales not yet subject to tax. The noncurrent portion (i.e., $19,000) was for the additional deduction for accelerated depreciation on the tax return over straight-line depreciation reflected on the income statement.

Note C. The corporation accounts for the investment tax credit by the flow-through method, under which income tax expense and income tax payable are reduced by the full amount of the tax credit in the year during which qualifying assets are placed in service. During 19B, the corporation purchased qualifying assets costing $60,000 and accordingly decreased income tax expense of 19B, and income tax payable at December 31, 19B, by $6,000 (i.e., 10 percent of $60,000). Use of the flow-through method causes no timing difference, and, hence, has no effect on interperiod income tax allocation procedures.

Supplement 10-A: Income Tax Loss Carrybacks and Carryforwards

Federal tax laws allow corporations that sustain a loss for the year to **carryback** and/or **carryforward** such losses and thereby to get a cash refund of prior taxes paid or a tax reduction in future years. Under the current law, at the end of the year of loss, the company must make an irrevocable choice of either:

Option (a)—Carryback (in order of year) up to three years of such losses to secure a refund of prior taxes on income of an equivalent amount. If the loss is so large that the carryback provision does not absorb it fully, the remaining loss may become a carryforward (in order of year) until it is absorbed fully, with a limit of fifteen years forward. The carryforward will result in a tax reduction of tax payable for each year forward to which it extends.

Option (b)—Carryforward (in order of years) up to fifteen years.

Assuming year D is the year of loss, the tax provisions may be diagrammed as shown below:

	Carryback			Loss	Carryforward														
Order:	A	B	C	D	E	F	G	H	I	J	K	L	M	N	O	P	Q	R	S
Option *(a)*→	1	2	3		4	5	6	7	8	9	10	11	12	13	14	15	16	17	18
Option *(b)* →					*1*	*2*	*3*	*4*	*5*	*6*	*7*	*8*	*9*	*10*	*11*	*12*	*13*	*14*	*15*

The accounting issue posed by income tax loss carrybacks and carryforwards is the extent to which in the **year of loss** any *(a)* carryback tax refunds and *(b)* potential carryforward tax benefits should be matched against the pretax loss of the period reported on the income statement. To illustrate the accounting for tax loss carrybacks and carryforwards, the situation shown in Exhibit 10–8 will be used, which uses a carryforward period of seven years for instructional convenience.

The choice between the two options, which must be made at the end of the year of loss, is critical because the two options have different cash flow effects. That is, the corporation must weigh the benefit of a certain cash refund (from the carryback) against the likelihood of increases in future tax rates, which would increase the attractiveness of the carryforward option. The carryforward option should be selected only if the corporation expects to earn sufficient income in future years to absorb the loss and is able to do so quickly enough to offset the present value advantage of the carryback option. Therefore, a choice between the two options necessarily involves a projection of future tax rates and future income amounts.

Accounting for Carrybacks and Carryforwards. When an operating loss follows a three-year period of net income sufficient to offset the loss, the resultant loss **carryback** will give rise to a refund of income taxes paid in the prior three periods. Since the refund is virtually certain, the **tax effect** should be recorded in the accounts and reflected in the financial statement for the loss period. On this point *APB Opinion 11* states the following:

> The tax effects of any realizable loss carry**backs** should be recognized in the determination of net income (loss) of the loss periods. The tax loss gives rise to a refund (or claim for refund) of past taxes, which is both measurable and currently realizable; therefore the tax effect of the loss is properly recognizable in the determination of net income (loss) for the loss period.

Carryback—Carryforward Option. To illustrate accounting for a tax loss carry**back** using the data given in Exhibit 10–8, assume X Corporation selected option *(a)*. The carryback would absorb $25,000 of the loss (i.e., $5 + $9 + $11) and result in a receivable for a tax refund of $5,000 ($1 + $1.8 + $2.2). At the end of the year of loss, the following accrual entry would be made by X Corporation:

19D (year of loss):

Receivable for refund of income taxes of prior years (carryback)	5,000	
Gain—Income tax refund from loss carryback (closed to Income Summary)		5,000

The effect of the above entry would cause X Corporation to *(a)* report a $5,000 receivable on its 19D balance sheet and *(b)* reduce the reported loss from $30,000 to $25,000 for 19D. Since the carryback did not fully absorb the $30,000 loss, there is a potential carryforward tax benefit relating to the $5,000 unabsorbed loss (under option [*a*]). Under option *(b)* there never will be a loss carryback.

When there is a carryforward, whether future income amounts will be sufficient to enable the company to realize the full tax benefit of the loss carryforward through a reduction of income tax in future periods is uncertain. One of two accounting approaches must be used for a carryforward, depending upon the degree of uncertainty involved. On this point *APB Opinion 11,* paragraph 45, states:

EXHIBIT 10–8: Carryback and Carryforward—X Corporation Data

	Actual (carryback)			Loss	Estimated (carryforward)						
Year	A	B	C	D	E	F	G	H	I	J	K
Income (loss) —in $000s	$5	$9	$11	$(30)	$5	$5	$50	$55	$60	$75	$100
Tax Rate (%)	20	20	20		20	20	40	40	40	40	45
Tax Paid —in $000s	$1	$1.8	$2.2		$1	$1	$20	$22	$24	$30	$45

Decision: Option *(a)* versus Option *(b)*

> The tax effects of loss carry*forwards* also relate to the determination of net income (loss) of the loss periods. However, a significant question generally exists as to realization of the tax effects of the carry*forwards,* since realization is dependent upon future taxable income. Accordingly, the Board has concluded that the tax benefits of loss carry*forwards* should not be recognized until they are actually realized, except in unusual circumstances when realization is *assured beyond any reasonable doubt* at the time the loss carry*forwards* arise. When the tax benefits of loss carry*forwards* are not recognized until realized in full or in part in subsequent periods, the tax benefits should be reported in the results of those periods [when they are actually realized] as extraordinary items.

To illustrate accounting for a tax loss **carryforward,** assume X Corporation (Exhibit 10–8) applies option *(a).* There are two situations to consider:

Situation 1—The circumstances are **usual;** that is, there is reasonable doubt as to the ultimate realization of the tax benefit of the carryforward, and realization is not assured beyond any reasonable doubt. In this situation, the loss carryforward is **not recognized** (i.e., accrued) in the year of loss. If and when the tax benefit materializes, it is recorded the year in which realization occurs as a debit to tax payable and a credit to an extraordinary gain for the year.

Situation 2—The circumstances are **unusual;** that is, realization of the estimated future amounts of income (and tax benefits) is **assured beyond any reasonable doubt.**[14] In this case, the loss carryforward for 19D (year of loss) should be recorded as follows:[15]

Receivable for estimated future income tax benefit of loss carryforward ($5,000 × .20*)	1,000	
Estimated income tax benefit of loss carryforward (closed to Income Summary)		1,000

* Assumes 19D estimate of future tax rate is 20 percent.

Because of the relatively high level of certainty indicated, the future tax benefit should be recognized in the year of loss since that is the year in which the benefit was considered "earned." This entry would increase the receivable on the 19D balance sheet from $5,000 to $6,000 and reduce the 19D reported loss by an additional $1,000 (see Exhibit 10–9).

EXHIBIT 10–9: Reporting Income Tax Loss Carrybacks and Carryforwards (based on data in Exhibit 10–8—X Corporation)

	Option *(a)*—Carryback Plus Carryforward	
19D Year of Loss	**Situation 1 Carryforward Benefit Not Reasonably Assured**	**Situation 2 Carryforward Benefit Reasonably Assured**
Income statement:		
Net loss before recognition of tax effect	$30,000	$30,000
Deduct tax refund for prior years' tax due to carryback	(5,000)	(5,000)
Deduct estimated tax benefit in future years due to carryforward		1,000
Net loss	$25,000	$24,000
Balance sheet:		
Current assets:		
Receivable for tax benefit of:		
Loss carryback	$ 5,000	$ 5,000
Loss carryforward		1,000

[14] An example of an unusual loss for which realization of the estimated future tax benefits would be assured beyond any reasonable doubt would be a loss that occurred from a single, isolated event that would not be expected to recur; the company has been, and is expected to continue to be, profitable.

[15] In 19E, assuming an actual income of $6,000:

Income tax expense ($6,000 × .20)	1,200	
Receivable for estimated future income tax benefit of loss carryforward ($5,000 × .20)		1,000
Income tax payable		200

Assuming X Corporation elected option *(a)*, the carryback-carryforward option, the income statement and balance sheet at the end of the year of loss would be as shown in Exhibit 10–9 under situations 1 and 2.

Carryforward Option. To compare the accounting for the two options, now assume X Corporation elected option *(b)*, that is, to ignore the carryback option and carryforward the expected future benefits of the 19D loss. Since there is no carryback in this option, the accounting will depend upon the degree of certainty in the projections of future income and income tax rates. Therefore, we will illustrate the same two situations considered under the carryback-carryforward option:

Situation 1—The circumstances are **usual;** that is, realization of the tax benefit of the carryforward is **not** reasonably certain. In this situation, the loss carryforward is not recognized (i.e., accrued) by X Corporation in the year of loss. The tax benefits of the 19D loss are recognized in the future when they occur as reductions in taxes payable of future years. The related entries would be as follows under the assumption that the projected future profits and tax rates given in Exhibit 10–8 were exactly on target:

19D (year of loss)—No entry because there is no carryback and also because future income is uncertain. 19E, 19F, and 19G entries would be as follows (as income subject to tax is earned):

Situation 2—The circumstances are **unusual;** that is, realization of the future tax benefit is assured beyond any reasonable doubt. In this case, X Corporation (Exhibit 10–8) would accrue the estimated future tax benefits as follows in the year of the loss:

Receivable for estimated future income tax benefits of loss carryforward	10,000	
Estimated income tax benefits of loss carryforward (closed to Income summary)		10,000

Computation:

19E	$ 5,000 × .20 =	$1,000	
19F	5,000 × .20 =	1,000	
19G	20,000 × .40 =	8,000	$10,000

Assuming X Corporation elected option *(b)*, the carryforward only, the income statement and balance sheet at the end of the year of loss would be reported as shown in Exhibit 10–10.

In Exhibit 10–10, option *(b)* appears preferable because the cash saved (income tax benefit of the loss) amounted to $10,000 compared to a maximum of $6,000 under option *(a)*. This resulted because the carryforward option took advantage of a 40 percent tax rate in 19G (as opposed to 20 percent under the carryback-carryforward option). This conclusion must be tempered with the element of uncertainty implicit in option *(b)*. For illustrative purposes, the unrealistic assumption was made that the projections were exactly on target. Additionally, in assessing the comparative advantages of the two options when

	19E		19F		19G	
Income tax expense (19E and F, $5,000 × .20; 19G, $50,000 × .40)	1,000		1,000		20,000	
Extraordinary gain, loss carryforward*		1,000†		1,000†		8,000†
Income tax payable [($50,000 − $20,000) × .40]						12,000

* Specified in the quotation above as an extraordinary gain.

† Pretax loss in 19D	$30,000
Absorbed as follows:	
19E .....$ 5,000	
19F 5,000	
19G 20,000	
Total absorbed	$30,000

Extraordinary gain by year:

19E	$ 5,000 × .20 =	$1,000
19F	5,000 × .20 =	1,000
19G	20,000 × .40 =	8,000

EXHIBIT 10–10: Reporting Income Tax Loss Carryforwards (X Corporation)

19D Year of Loss	Option (b)—Carryforward Only: Situation 1 Carryforward Benefit Not Reasonably Assured	Situation 2 Carryforward Benefit Reasonably Assured
Income statement:		
Net loss before recognition of tax effect	$30,000	$30,000
Deduct estimated tax benefit in future years due to loss carryforward	–0–	(10,000)
Net loss	$30,000	$20,000
Balance sheet:		
Current assets:		
Receivable for estimated tax benefit of loss carryforward	–0–	$10,000

the decision must be made (i.e., in the year of loss), the future projections should be discounted to present values because the cash flows under the two options occur at different times.

The Economic Recovery Tax Act of 1981 lengthened the carryforward period from seven to fifteen years. One effect of this law on accounting is a decrease in the uncertainty associated with realization of the tax loss carryforwards. Therefore, companies will be more prone to record, in a loss year, a receivable for the estimated future income tax benefits of loss carryforwards. Other things being equal, they will report smaller losses than before the tax law was changed.

Supplement 10-B: Changes in Tax Rates

Timing differences cause deferred income tax amounts which are computed on the basis of tax rates in effect when the timing difference occurred. Subsequently, the deferred taxes reverse over the cycle of the timing difference. The reversal is based on the tax rates that were used when the deferred tax amount was initially recorded. On this point, APB Opinion 11, paragraph 19, states:

> The deferred taxes are determined on the basis of the tax rates in effect at the time the timing differences originate and are not adjusted for subsequent changes in tax rates or to reflect the imposition of new taxes. (Also see par. 36.)

The fundamental point is that over the cycle of the timing difference for each item, exactly the same amount should be reversed as was recognized as deferred tax initially. When tax rates change during the timing cycle, *(a)* income tax payable must be computed on the basis of the new tax rate (because that is set by law), *(b)* deferred tax amounts are reversed at the rate which was used when they were initially recorded, and *(c)* income tax expense for the period is adjusted to accommodate the difference.

To illustrate accommodation of a change in the tax rates during the timing cycle, assume T Corporation had the following data:

	19A	19B
Pretax accounting income	$20,000	$25,000
Accelerated depreciation (used for tax purposes)	6,000	2,000
Straight-line depreciation (used for financial accounting purposes)	4,000	4,000
Average income tax rate	30%	40%

The entries to record income taxes of 19A and 19B would be as follows:

19A:

Income tax expense ($20,000 × .30)	6,000	
Income tax payable [($20,000 + $4,000 − $6,000) × .30]		5,400
Deferred income tax—19A depreciation [($6,000 − $4,000) × .30]		600

19B:

Income tax expense [($25,000 × .40) + (.40 − .30) ($4,000 − $2,000)]	10,200	
Deferred income tax—19A depreciation [($4,000 − $2,000) × .30] ...	600	
Income tax payable [($25,000 + $4,000 − $2,000) × .40]		10,800

In the above sequence of entries the timing difference which arose in 19A exactly reversed in 19B (but at the 19A tax rate). The tax payable in each year was based on the tax rate then in effect as required by law.

In 19B, income tax expense was based on the 40 percent tax rate then in effect, **adjusted** for the reversal of the deferred tax. The adjustment of $200 was determined by multiplying the change in the tax rates (.40 − .30) times the difference in the two depreciation amounts for 19B ($4,000 − $2,000). Note that the $200 adjustment was **added** to income tax expense for 19B because the deferred tax initially was recorded as a $600 liability at the end of 19A, and the ultimate amount of the liability turned out to be $800 [i.e., ($4,000 − $2,000) × .40]. In contrast, the adjustment of tax expense for the year of reversal would be **subtracted** when the deferred tax initially was recorded as a debit because there would turn out to be an overprovision of deferred tax (assuming the tax rate increased in the later year). If tax rates drop, these relationships reverse.

Supplement 10-C: Different Concepts of Income Tax Allocation

Fundamental Views of Income Tax Expense

There are two fundamentally different views of income tax. One view is that income tax should be accounted for on a current expense basis and the other view is that it should be accounted for on the allocation basis.

Proponents of the **current expense** basis hold that the amount of income tax expense of a period should be measured as the amount of income tax actually payable for that period. They argue that the amount of tax payable **necessarily determines** the tax expense for the period because income tax is determined by law and the legal amount of tax for a period is the amount currently payable. Thus, this basis avoids the difficulties of interperiod allocation of tax which arise from the uncertainty of future income amounts and tax rates. Proponents of this basis also argue that the estimates of deferred tax amounts generally are imprecise because future tax rates change or future income amounts depart from the amounts required to sustain the deferred tax amounts. For these reasons, there are strong advocates of accounting for income tax expense on the current expense basis.

Under **current GAAP**, income tax expense is viewed as a deduction on the income statement similar to cost of goods sold, salary expense, and depreciation expense (and as an offset to an extraordinary item). In this view, income tax expense is measured on the allocation basis and is reported along with all other expenses. This means that income tax expense of a period is based on the pretax accounting income of the period (adjusted for permanent differences), regardless of **when** the income tax will be paid. Thus, it causes the reporting of deferred income tax. Proponents of the current GAAP view of **interperiod income tax allocation** acknowledge the uncertainties involved in the accrual amounts of income tax expense; however, they point out that certain other accounting valuations are inherently uncertain (e.g., depreciation). They believe the accounting model is sufficiently robust to handle the uncertainties involved in interperiod income tax allocation. Moreover, they note that empirically most deferred tax amounts are credit balances (i.e., liabilities). They argue that failure to report deferred income tax and the concomitant higher income tax expense would bias reported amounts of net income upward for the majority of companies (a nonconservative practice).

Different Interpretations of Deferred Income Tax Debits and Credits

Interperiod income tax allocation causes deferred income tax amounts which are reported on the balance sheet. The amounts may be debits or credits. Are such debits assets (i.e., prepaid expenses or deferred charges) and are such credits liabilities, or are they contingencies? Alternatively, are deferred tax debits and credits valuation adjustments (i.e., contra accounts) to the accounts to which they relate? Each of these possible interpretations is discussed below.

Deferred Tax Amounts Viewed as Assets and Liabilities. Deferred tax debits may be viewed as assets because they can be viewed as prepayments of future income tax expense. Such debits arise when the income tax must be paid **before** the related revenue is recognized as earned. To illustrate, return to Case B on page 330. The $2,400 deferred tax debit represents income tax which is payable currently on rent revenue that will be recognized as earned in future periods. Thus, the deferred debit amount can be viewed as an estimated asset.

Deferred tax credits can be viewed as liabilities because such credits arise when the income tax is paid **after** the related expense is recognized as incurred. To illustrate, refer to Case C on page 331. In that entry, the $4,000 deferred tax credit represents an amount of income tax which will become payable during the last half of the life of the asset (assuming for simplicity that income taxes are paid by the year-end date). Viewed this way, the deferred tax credit is an estimated liability.

Deferred Tax Amounts Viewed as Contingencies. Deferred tax amounts can be viewed as contingencies because their ultimate realization depends upon (1) the tax rates during the periods when they reverse; (2) future amounts of reported income; and (3) future changes in tax laws or accounting concepts. FASB, *Statement of Financial Accounting Standards No. 5,* "Accounting for Contingencies," was not in effect in 1967 when interperiod tax allocation was mandated, and it is not currently applied to interperiod income tax allocation. However, if it were applied to interperiod tax allocation, it would provide a conceptual basis for viewing deferred tax amounts as contingencies. That is, the *Statement* requires that if (1) it is probable that a contingent loss (or expense) will occur and (2) the amount of the loss can be reasonably estimated, companies must accrue the loss. These conditions appear to be met for many companies with tax deferrals in the United States. The specifications of *FASB Statement 5* for deferred tax debits also could be applied; however, the results would not be parallel with losses, because of reluctance to recognize contingent assets, and this poses a substantive conceptual issue.

In summary, the *Opinion* leaves the interpretation of tax deferrals open as to whether they are assets and liabilities or contingencies. The APB *Opinions* conform to the accounting model (i.e., Assets = Liabilities + Owners' equity) and from that it follows that deferred tax debits are assets and deferred tax credits are liabilities, even though they are uncertain as to amount at the time they are initially recorded.

Which Tax Rate to Use in Recording Deferred Taxes?

Two different views have been proposed as to what tax rates should be applied in computing deferred income taxes. One view holds that the "beginning" rate should be used (i.e., the deferral method); the other view opts for estimated future tax rates (i.e., the liability method).

Deferral Method. This view is that the current income tax rate when the timing difference originated is the appropriate rate on which to base the tax deferral. Under the deferral method, recorded deferred tax amounts are **not** adjusted for subsequent changes in tax rates. *APB Opinion 11* requires the deferral method because, as stated in paragraph 35 of that *Opinion,* the deferral method "provides the most useful and practical approach to interperiod tax allocation."

Liability Method. This view is that amounts of deferred tax should be based on estimates of the future tax rates which will be in effect when the timing differences reverse. Thus, the liability method provides for adjustment of deferred tax amounts due to changes in tax rates or other factors in periods subsequent to initial recording of the tax deferral. Proponents of this view argue that ultimate realization of the amount of the tax deferral will depend upon the tax rates in effect when the timing differences reverse and thus the amounts to be realized bear no necessary relationship to the tax rates in effect when they originate.

Comprehensive versus Partial Income Tax Allocation

Some accountants favor **comprehensive** allocation of income tax, in which all timing differences are recognized, as described in this chapter. Other accountants favor **partial** allocation under the theory that, in principle, the income tax expense of a period should be the amount of income tax payable for the period.

In contrast to comprehensive allocation, proponents of **partial** allocation base their view on the inherent uncertainty of deferred tax amounts. They also note that many companies indefinitely postpone the payment of deferred tax amounts. This postponement occurs for companies with stable or growing investments in depreciable assets and which use accelerated depreciation for tax purposes and straight-line depreciation for accounting purposes (this is perhaps the most important timing difference). Under partial allocation, indefinite postponement is viewed as virtually synonymous with a permanent difference, to which interperiod tax allocation does not apply. Thus, proponents of partial allocation would not record income tax expense for taxes indefinitely postponed in this way. They would apply interperiod income tax allocation only to **specific short-term timing differences** which would cause material misstatements of reported income if tax allocation were not applied. *APB Opinion 11* requires comprehensive allocation.

Discounting of Deferred Income Tax Amounts

In 1967, when *APB Opinion 11* mandated interperiod income tax allocation, the U.S. inflation rate was approximately 2.7 percent and interest rates were approximately 6 percent. Therefore, **discounted** amounts of deferred income taxes were close to the **undiscounted** amounts. This situation no longer exists because both recent rates of inflation and interest rates have increased.

APB Opinion No. 21, "Interest on Receivables and Payables," August 1971, requires long-term receivables and payables to be accounted for at present value.[16] However, it does not apply to deferred tax amounts (see footnote 3 of *APB Opinion 21*) even though such deferred amounts often are long term. Conceptually, long-term amounts of deferred tax should be discounted to present value similar to other long-term receivables and payables.

If GAAP required deferred tax amounts to be discounted, their present values often would decrease substantially because of (1) high current interest rates and (2) long asset lives that cause many long-term tax deferrals. In the opinions of the authors, deferred taxes should be discounted because their undiscounted amounts are *(a)* not comparable to other similar amounts, *(b)* often highly overstated, and *(c)* potentially misleading to statement users.

[16] The present values of most *current* receivables and payables is approximately the same as their maturity amounts.

QUESTIONS

PART A

1. In evaluating a balance sheet, some bankers say the liability section is one of the most important parts. What are the primary reasons for their position on this point?
2. Some liabilities are reported at their maturity amount. In general, when should liabilities, prior to due date, be reported at less than their maturity amount?
3. How is the *cost principle* involved in accounting for current liabilities?
4. Define *current liabilities.*
5. Differentiate between *secured* and *unsecured* liabilities. Explain the reporting procedures for each.
6. How are cash and stock dividends, declared but not yet paid, classified on the balance sheet? Explain.
7. What are *deferred revenues?* What is the basis for classifying them as current liabilities?
8. Define a *long-term liability.*
9. When goods or services are acquired and a long-term note payable is given that either specifies *(a)* no interest or *(b)* an unrealistically low interest rate, how should the value of the note be measured?
10. What is the accounting definition of a *contingency?* What are the three characteristics of a contingency? Why is the concept important?
11. How does the accountant measure the likelihood of the outcome of a contingency? In general, how does this affect the accounting for and reporting of contingencies?
12. Explain why *loss* contingencies are accounted for and reported differently from *gain* contingencies.

13. Under what circumstances should appropriation of retained earnings with respect to a loss contingency be considered?

14. How would each of the following items usually be reported on the balance sheet? Justify doubtful items.
    a. Cash dividends payable.
    b. Bonds payable.
    c. Accommodation endorsement.
    d. Lawsuit pending.
    e. Stock dividend issuable.
    f. Estimated taxes payable.
    g. Deferred rent revenue.
    h. Unearned interest revenue.
    i. Customer deposits on containers.
    j. Current installment on serial bonds.
    k. Accounts payable.
    l. Loans from officers.
    m. Accrued wages.
    n. Deferred repairs.

PART B

15. Accounting for income taxes under interperiod income tax allocation procedures essentially is accrual accounting for income taxes; otherwise, accounting for income taxes essentially is cash basis accounting. Evaluate this statement.

16. It is common for companies to use an accelerated depreciation method for income tax purposes and straight-line depreciation for financial reporting (book) purposes. Some accountants argue that the deferred income tax liabilities of these companies will never have to be paid so long as they *(a)* continue this depreciation policy, *(b)* expand, and *(c)* continue to replace worn-out depreciable assets with new ones. Evaluate this argument.

17. What is the nature of a permanent difference? Do permanent differences give rise to deferred income taxes? Give three examples of items of permanent difference in accounting for income taxes.

18. What is intraperiod income tax allocation? How does it differ from interperiod income tax allocation?

19. Does the "deferred" caption in deferred income taxes mean that deferred income tax is always a long-term (noncurrent) item? Explain.

SUPPLEMENT 10–A

20. In respect to loss carrybacks and loss carryforwards, which can be recorded with greater certainty of realization of the benefit therefrom? How does this difference in certainty affect the accounting treatment accorded loss carrybacks and carryforwards?

DECISION CASE 10–1

As XYZ Corporation's independent auditor, you are attending the meeting of the board of directors where preparation of the forthcoming annual report is being discussed. One of the directors, known to have a sketchy knowledge of accounting, says, "You accountants were quite ingenuous when you devised income tax allocation. When reported profits are up, you reduce them with an assigned higher income tax expense; when they are down, you do the opposite. Since reported income is going to be embarassingly high this year, I'm thankful for income tax allocation."

Required:
Respond tactfully with an explanation of the rationale underlying income tax allocation.

EXERCISES

PART A: EXERCISES 10–1 to 10–11

Exercise 10–1

On September 1, 19A, Rámon Company borrowed cash on a $4,000 note payable due in one year. Assume the going rate of interest was 12% per year on this type of note for this company. The accounting period ends December 31.

Required:
Complete the tabulation that follows (show computations and round amounts to the nearest dollar):

(Relates to Exercise 10–1)

	Assuming the Note Was—	
	Interest Bearing	Noninterest Bearing (discounted)
a. Cash received	$______	$______
b. Cash paid at due date	$______	$______
c. Total interest paid (cash)	$______	$______
d. Interest expense in 19A	$______	$______
e. Interest expense in 19B	$______	$______
f. Amount of liability to report on balance sheet at 12/31/19A (including any accrued interest)	$______	$______

Exercise 10–2

For each of the following accounts of Dobie Corporation, indicate the balance sheet classification and more preferable title.

a. Sales taxes collected but not yet remitted.
b. Bonds payable, one third paid each year.
c. Advance on rent revenue.
d. Stock dividend declared.
e. Accrued property taxes (estimated).
f. Cash dividend declared but not yet paid.
g. IOU to company president.
h. Accrued interest on note payable.
i. Trade payable.
j. Deposits held from customers—trade.
k. Accrued wage expense.
l. Accommodation endorsement.
m. Reserve for rearrangement costs.
n. Customer payments on orders received (goods not shipped).

Exercise 10–3

The records of the Barnes Corporation provided the following information at December 31, 19A:

a. Notes payable (trade), short-term (includes a $4,000 note given on purchase of equipment that cost $20,000; assets were mortgaged in connection with purchase)	$30,000
b. Bonds payable ($30,000 due each Apr. 1)	90,000
c. Accounts payable (including $3,000 owed to president of the company)	50,000
d. Accrued property taxes (estimated)	1,000
e. Stock dividends issuable on 3/1/19B (at par value)	26,000
f. Cash dividends, payable 3/1/19B	20,000
g. Long-term note payable, maturity amount (unamortized amount, $14,500)	15,000

Required:
Assuming the fiscal year ends December 31, show how each of the above items should be reported on the balance sheet at December 31, 19A.

Exercise 10–4

Pratt Company paid salaries for the month amounting to $80,000. Of this amount, $30,000 was received by employees who had already been paid the $31,800* maximum amount of annual earnings taxable in one year under FICA laws (FICA rate, 6.70%).

Similarly, $14,000 was paid to employees who had already been paid the $6,000* maximum (FUTA rates: 2.7% state and .7% federal). Withholding taxes amounted to $25,000, and $1,200 was withheld for investment in company stock per an agreement with certain employees.

* These amounts refer to 1982 cutoff points for wages subject to FICA and FUTA taxes.

Required:
Give entries to record the *(a)* salary payment and the liabilities for the deductions, *(b)* employer payroll expenses, and *(c)* remittance of the taxes.

Exercise 10–5

Lehigh Company gives the general manager a bonus equal to 20% of income after tax. The bonus is deductible for tax purposes but is not an expense for computing the bonus. Assume an average tax rate of 30%. Income prior to taxes and bonus was $80,000.

Required (round amounts to nearest dollar):
1. Compute the tax and the bonus.
2. Prove your computations.
3. Give entries to record the tax and the bonus.

Exercise 10–6

Bonzo Company has an agreement to pay the president a bonus of 10% of income, after deducting federal income taxes and after deducting an amount equal to 6% on contributed capital (contributed capital is $200,000). Income before deductions for bonus and income taxes was $50,000. The bonus is deductible for tax purposes; assume an average income tax rate of 25%.

Required (round amounts to the nearest dollar):

1. Compute the bonus, tax, and net income after deducting both bonus and tax.
2. Prove the computations.
3. Give the entries to record the tax and the bonus.

Exercise 10–7

On April 1, 19A, Townes, Inc. purchased a heavy machine for use in operations by paying $5,000 cash and signing a $25,000 (face amount) noninterest-bearing note due in two years (on March 31, 19C). The going rate of interest for Townes on this type of note was 16% per year. The company uses straight-line depreciation. The accounting period ends on December 31. Assume a five-year life for the machine and 10% residual value.

Required:

1. Give all entries indicated on April 1, 19A, and December 31, 19A (assume straight-line amortization of the discount). Show computations of the cost of the machine (round amounts to nearest dollar).
2. Complete a tabulation as follows (show computations):

a. Income statement, 19A:
Depreciation expense . . . . $_____
Interest expense . . . . $_____

b. Balance sheet, 19A:
Operational asset—machine . . . . $_____
Accumulated depreciation . . . . $_____
Current liability—interest payable . . . . $_____
Note payable . . . . $_____

3. When should the interest method, rather than the straight-line method, be used to amortize the discount on the note? Compute interest expense for 19A assuming the interest method. Is the difference between the interest method and straight-line amounts of interest expense on the note payable material?

Exercise 10–8

Greenspan Company purchased a small used truck (an operational asset) on April 1, 19A, for $2,000 cash plus a $10,000, two-year note payable. The principal is due on March 31, 19C, and specified 14% interest payable each March 31. Assume the going rate of interest for this type of debt for this company was 18%. The accounting period ends December 31.

Required:

1. Give the entry to record the purchase on April 1, 19A. Show computations (round to nearest dollar).
2. Complete a tabulation as follows; include computations:

a. Amount of cash interest payable each Mar. 31 . . . . $_____
b. Total interest expense for the two-year period . . . . $_____
c. Amount of interest reported on income statement for 19A . . . . $_____
d. Amount of liability reported on balance sheet at 12/31/19A (excluding accrued interest) . . . . $_____
e. Depreciation expense for 19A assuming straight-line (use even months), no residual value, and a four-year life . . . . $_____

Exercise 10–9

Stice, Inc. sells a line of products that carry a three-year warranty against defects. Based on industry experience, the estimated warranty costs related to dollar sales are the first year after sale—1% of sales; second year after sale—3% of sales; and third year after sale—5%. Sales and actual warranty expenditures for the first three-year period were as follows:

	Cash Sales	Actual Warranty Expenditures
19A	$ 80,000	$ 900
19B	110,000	4,100
19C	130,000	9,800

Required:

1. Give entries for the three years for the *(a)* sales, *(b)* estimated warranty expense, and *(c)* the actual expenditures.
2. What amount should be reported as a liability on the balance sheet at the end of each year?

Exercise 10–10

Recliner Furniture Store has initiated a promotion program whereby customers are given coupons redeemable in U.S. savings bonds. One coupon is issued for each dollar of sales. On the surrender of 750 coupons, one $25 savings bond (cost $18.75) is given. It is estimated that 30% of the coupons issued will never be presented for redemption. Sales for the first period were $400,000, and the number of coupons redeemed totaled 225,000. Sales for the second period were $440,000, and the number of coupons redeemed totaled 360,000. The savings bonds are acquired as needed.

Required:
Prepare journal entries (including closing entries) relative to the premium plan for the two periods. Show amounts that should be reported in the balance sheet and income statement for the two periods.

Exercise 10–11

S Company is preparing the annual financial statements at December 31, 19J. A customer fell on the escalator and has filed a lawsuit for $40,000 because of a claimed back injury. The lawyer employed by the company has carefully assessed all of the implications. If the suit is lost, the lawyer's opinion is that the $40,000 will be assessed by the court.

Required:
1. Assume that the conclusion is that it is *reasonably possible* that the company will be liable, and it is reasonably estimated that the amount will be $40,000.
2. Assume instead the lawyer, the independent accountant, and management have reluctantly concluded that it is *probable* that the suit will be successful. Show how this contingency should be reported on the financial statements for 19J. Also, give any entries that should be made in the accounts in 19J.
3. Assume that the conclusion of the legal counsel and management is that it is *remote* that there will be a contingency loss. They believe the suit is without merit. How should this contingency be reported?

PART B: EXERCISES 10–12 to 10–15

Exercise 10–12

Kellogg Corp. would have had identical income before taxes on both its income tax returns and income statements for the years 19A through 19D were it not for the fact that for tax purposes operational assets that cost $120,000 were depreciated by the sum-of-the-years'-digits (SYD) method, whereas for accounting purposes, the straight-line method was used. These operational assets have a four-year estimated life and zero residual value. Excess of revenue over expenses other than depreciation and income taxes for the years concerned were as follows:

	19A	19B	19C	19D
Pretax accounting income (excl. depr.)	$60,000	$80,000	$70,000	$70,000

Assume the average income tax rate for each year was 30%.

Required:
1. Prepare a partial income statement for each year to reflect interperiod tax allocation.
2. Give journal entries at the end of each year to record income taxes.

Exercise 10–13

The pretax income statements for Ajax Corporation for two years (summarized) were as follows:

	19A	19B
Revenues	$180,000	$200,000
Expenses	150,000	165,000
Pretax accounting income	$ 30,000	$ 35,000

For tax purposes, the following differences existed:

a. Expenses on the 19B income statement include goodwill amortization of $10,000 which is not deductible for income tax purposes.
b. Revenues on the 19B income statement include $10,000 rent which is taxable in 19A but was unearned at the end of 19A.
c. Expenses on the 19A income statement include $8,000 of estimated warranty costs which are not deductible for income tax purposes until 19B.

Required:
1. Compute *(a)* income tax expense and *(b)* income taxes payable for each period. Assume an average tax rate of 40%.
2. Give the entry to record income taxes for each period.
3. Recast the above income statements to include income taxes as allocated.

Exercise 10–14

Black Gold Petroleum, Inc., an oil and gas exploration company, earned $75,000 pretax accounting income during 19A and $125,000 during 19B. The records of the corporation showed the following additional data for the two years:

	19A	19B
Straight-line depr. (included in pretax accounting income)	$35,000	$35,000
Accelerated depr. (for income tax purposes)	38,000	32,000
Statutory depletion (for income tax purposes)	65,000	95,000
Cost depletion—an expense (included in pretax accounting income)	44,000	60,000

The assets subject to depreciation were five years old at the end of 19A and are expected to remain in service for an additional five years. The income tax rate is 35% for 19A and 19B.

Required:
1. Identify the item of timing differences given above. Identify the item of permanent difference.

2. Prepare the journal entries to record income taxes for the company for 19A and 19B.
3. Prepare the income statement and balance sheet presentations related to income taxes in the 19A and 19B financial statements.

Exercise 10–15

Stardust Company accounts and related records revealed the following data for the first two years of operations:

	19A	19B
Pretax accounting income	$100,000	$110,000
Rent collections one year in advance	9,000	
Rent revenue allocated (included in pretax accounting income)	6,000	3,000

Stardust Company had no other timing differences, no permanent differences, or other complicating income tax factors in 19A and 19B.

Required:
1. Record income taxes for the company for 19A and 19B assuming the income tax rate for each year was 30%.
2. Record the income taxes for the company for 19A and 19B assuming the income tax rate was 30% for 19A and 40% for 19B. Explain the way you treated the impact of the change in the tax rate from 19A to 19B. (Based upon Supplement 10–B)

SUPPLEMENT 10–A: EXERCISES 10–16 to 10–17

Exercise 10–16

Larson Corporation reported pretax operating income in 19A amounting to $80,000 the first year of operations. In 19B, the corporation experienced a $40,000 pretax operating loss. Assume an average income tax rate of 45%. Future income is highly uncertain.

Required:
1. Compute the income tax consequences for each year.
2. Show how the tax consequences for each year would be reflected in the income statements for each year.
3. Give appropriate entries to record income tax effect for each year.

Exercise 10–17

Wells Corporation experienced a $100,000 pretax operating loss for 19A, the first year of operations. Use an average 40% tax rate.

Required:
1. The 19A loss resulted from an identifiable cause and future taxable income over the next fifteen years is virtually certain to be sufficient to offset the loss.
   a. Give entry and a partial income statement for 19A to reflect appropriate income tax consequences.
   b. Assume it is now the end of 19B and that a pretax operating profit in 19B is reported amounting to $150,000. Give entry and a partial income statement for 19B to reflect appropriate income tax consequences.
2. At the time of the loss there was no realistic basis to conclude that profits in the next fifteen years would be sufficient to absorb the loss.
   a. Give entry and a partial income statement for 19A to reflect appropriate income tax consequences.
   b. Assume pretax operating incomes, following the year of loss, as follows: 19B, break even; 19C, $40,000; and 19D, $80,000. Give entry and a partial income statement for each of these three years to reflect appropriate income tax consequences.

SUPPLEMENTS 10–A AND 10–B: EXERCISE 10–18

Exercise 10–18

Blue Corporation experienced a bad year in 19D. The company reported taxable income (loss) for 19A–19D and had average tax rates as follows:

	19A	19B	19C	19D
Taxable income (loss) ...	$8,000	$32,000	$15,000	$(65,000)
Income tax rate	30%	30%	35%	40%

There were no timing differences or permanent differences in 19A–19D.

Required:
1. Record income taxes for the company assuming:
   a. For 19D, the general provisions of *APB Opinion 11* on tax loss carrybacks and carryforwards apply.
   b. For 19E, the company reported taxable income of $45,000 in 19E and pretax accounting income of $50,000 for 19E (a $5,000 timing difference). The income tax rate for 19E was 45%.
2. Record income taxes for the company assuming:
   a. For 19D, it is virtually certain that taxable income of $10,000 or more will be earned over the next fifteen years.
   b. For 19E, the company reported taxable income of $45,000 in 19E and pretax accounting income for 19E was the same amount (no timing differences). The income tax rate for 19E was 45%.

PROBLEMS

PART A: PROBLEMS 10–1 to 10–11

Problem 10–1

For each of the situations below, indicate (1) correct title, (2) usual balance sheet classification, (3) the amount to report, and (4) explanation of the basis for your classification. (Suggestion: Set up four columns for your response.)

a.	Prepaid rent revenue	$ 3,000
b.	Excess of selling price over par—bonds payable	2,800
c.	Bonds (annual payment $30,000)	90,000
d.	Accrued warranty costs	1,000
e.	Deferred lease revenue	2,000
f.	Reserve for taxes	7,000
g.	Reserve for future contingencies	15,000
h.	Endorsement on note payable	2,000
i.	Trade accounts payable (incl. $2,000 owed to company president)	30,000
j.	Trade notes payable (incl. $9,000 for equipment note)	29,000
k.	Long-term note payable (secured by stock in X Co.)	10,000
l.	Cash dividends (not yet paid)	12,000
m.	Deposits held, from customers	4,000

Problem 10–2

Cadenhead Corp. borrowed cash on August 1, 19A, and signed a $12,000 (face amount), one-year note payable, due on July 31, 19B. The accounting period ends December 31. Assume a going rate of interest of 16% for this company for this type of borrowing.

Required (round amounts to nearest dollar):

1. How much cash should Cadenhead receive on the note assuming *(a)* an interest-bearing note and *(b)* a noninterest-bearing note.
2. Give the following entries for each case:
   a. August 1, 19A, date of the loan.
   b. December 31, 19A, adjusting entry.
   c. July 31, 19B, payment of the note (assuming no reversing entry at December 31, 19A).
3. What liability amounts should be shown in each case on the December 31, 19A, balance sheet?

Problem 10–3

On October 1, 19A, Kimberly Company borrowed cash $36,000 and signed a 12%, one-year note payable, due on September 30, 19B. The accounting period ends on December 31.

Required:

1. Compute the face amount of the note (show computations):
   Case A—An interest-bearing note.
   Case B—A noninterest-bearing note.
2. Complete a tabulation as follows:

		Case A Interest Bearing	Case B Noninterest-bearing
a.	Face amount of note	$______	$______
b.	Total cash received	$______	$______
c.	Total cash paid	$______	$______
d.	Total interest paid	$______	$______
e.	Interest expense in 19A	$______	$______
f.	Interest expense in 19B	$______	$______
g.	Effective rate of interest	______%	______%

3. Give entries indicated for each case at October 1, 19A, December 31, 19A, and September 30, 19B.
4. Show how the liability amounts should be reflected for each case on the balance sheet at December 31, 19A.

Problem 10–4

Kellner Corporation was formed for the purpose of constructing buildings. The first contract involved the construction of an office building. Since the corporation was short of ready cash, an agreement was made with the supervising engineer whereby compensation would be a share of the profits. The agreement provided that the supervising engineer would receive 25% of the profits upon completion of the contract after providing for corporate income tax and after deducting the bonus.

Upon completion of the construction, the records of the corporation showed the following:

Income before tax and before payment to supervising engineer (assume a 40% tax rate)	$450,000
Expenses already deducted from net income, not allowable as deductions in computing income taxes but allowed as a deduction before computing profit to be paid supervising engineer	10,000

Assume the compensation to the supervising engineer is deductible for corporate income tax purposes.

Required:

1. Compute the amounts of *(a)* compensation to the supervising engineer and *(b)* income tax assuming the com-

pensation is an expense in determining the basis for the compensation. Show proof of computations.
2. Give entries to record the compensation and tax expenses.

Problem 10–5

For the purpose of stimulating sales, Toastie Cereal Company places a coupon in each box of cereal sold; the coupons are redeemable in chinaware. Each premium costs the company 90 cents (the cost of printing the coupons is negligible). Ten coupons must be presented by the customers to receive one premium. The following data are available:

Month	Boxes of Cereal Sold	Premiums Purchased	Coupons Redeemed
January	650,000	25,000	220,000
February	500,000	40,000	410,000
March	560,000	35,000	300,000

It is estimated that only 70% of the coupons will be presented for redemption.

Required:
Compute the amount of the premium inventory, liability for premiums outstanding, and premium expense at the end of each month and give the related entries. *Hint:* Set up parallel columns for each period.

Problem 10–6

Chewy Cereal Company gives a premium (costs 75 cents each) for "five box tops sent in plus 25 cents cash to cover premium mailing costs." Actual mailing costs average 20 cents per premium. Data covering two periods are as follows:

	Period	
	First	Second
Premiums purchased	15,000	25,000
Tops redeemed for premiums	50,000	120,000
Boxes of cereal sold @ $2 per box	220,000	250,000

It is estimated that 60% of the tops distributed will never be returned.

Required:
1. Give entries for each period to record sales, premium purchases, premium expenses, redemptions, mailing costs, and closing entries. *Hint:* Set up parallel columns for each period.
2. Indicate how premiums and any related liabilities would be reported on the balance sheet at the end of each period and the amount of premium expense on the income statement for each period.

Problem 10–7

The following selected transactions were completed during the year just ended (December 31, 19A) by Lester Company:

a. Bonds payable dated February 1 with a maturity value of $100,000 were sold at 106 on February 1. The bonds mature in 10 years and bear 12% interest per annum payable on each January 30 (record Bonds Payable at maturity value and any Premium or Discount in a separate account; amortize Premium or Discount by the straight-line method).
b. Merchandise purchased on account amounted to $400,000. Cash payments on account were $340,000; and a $3,000, one-year,16% interest-bearing note, dated September 1, was given to one creditor. Accounts payable carried over from the preceding year were $30,000. Assume periodic inventory system.
c. Cosigned a $5,000 note payable for another party.
d. On June 1, the company borrowed cash and a $23,200, one-year, discounted (i.e., noninterest bearing) note was signed. Assume a going rate of interest of 16%.
e. Payroll records showed the following (assume amounts given are correct):

	Employee			Employer		
Gross Wages	With-holding	FICA	Union Dues	FICA	FUTA State	FUTA Federal
$50,000 ...	$15,000	$3,000	$500	$3,000	$1,350	$350

Remittances were union, $280; withholding taxes, $13,000; FICA, $5,800; FUTA—state, $1,200; and FUTA—federal, $340.
f. The company was sued for $50,000 damages. It appears a judgment against the company of $30,000 is probable. For problem purposes, assume this is an extraordinary item.
g. On November 1, 19A, the company rented some office space in its building to XY Company and collected six months' rent in advance; total, $1,800.
h. Cash dividends declared but not paid, $14,000.
i. On December 31, accrued interest on the bonds (assume straight-line amortization).
j. Accrued interest on the notes at December 31.

Required:
1. Give the entry or entries for each of the above items.
2. Prepare a list (title and amount) of the resulting liabilities at December 31, 19A, assuming it is the end of the period. For each liability, indicate its appropriate classification on the balance sheet. *Hint:* Set up tabulations with three columns: title, amount, and classification.

Problem 10–8

Bubak Hardware, Inc. provides a product warranty for defects on two lines of items sold. Line A carries a two-year warranty for all labor and service (but not parts). The company contracts with a local service establishment to provide the requirements of the warranty. The local service establishment charges a flat fee of $60 per unit payable at date of sale.

Line B carries a three-year warranty for parts and labor on service. Bubak purchases the parts needed under the warranty and has service personnel who perform the work. On the basis of experience, it is estimated that for line B, the three-year warranty costs are 3% of dollar sales for parts and 7% for labor and overhead. Additional data available are as follows:

	Period 1	Period 2	Period 3
Sales in units, line A	700	1,000	
Sales price per unit, line A	$ 610	$ 660	
Sales in units, line B	600	800	
Sales price per unit, line B	$ 700	$ 750	
Actual warranty outlays, line B:			
Parts	$3,000	$ 9,600	$12,000
Labor and overhead	$7,000	$22,000	$30,000

Required:

1. Give entries for period sales and expenses identified by product. *Hint:* Set up parallel columns for the three periods.
2. Complete a tabulation as follows:

	Year-End Amounts		
	Period 1	Period 2	Period 3
a. Warranty expense (on income statement)	$____	$____	$____
b. Estimated warranty liability (on balance sheet)	$____	$____	$____

Problem 10–9

On September 1, 19A, Merrill Company acquired a badly needed machine (an operational asset) by paying $5,000 cash and signing a two-year note with a maturity amount of $15,000 due at the end of the two years; the note did not specify interest. Assume the going rate of interest for this company for this type of loan was 16%. The accounting period ends December 31.

Required (round amounts to nearest dollar):

1. Give the entry to record the purchase of the machine.
2. Complete a tabulation as follows and show computations:

	Straight-Line Method	Interest Method
a. Cash paid at maturity	$____	$____
b. Total interest expense	$____	$____
c. Interest expense on income statement for 19A	$____	$____
d. Amount of the liability (incl. interest) reported on balance sheet at end of 19A	$____	$____
e. Depr. expense for 19A (assume straight line, even months, no residual value, and useful life of 4 years)	$____	$____

3. Should the interest method be used in this situation? Explain.
4. Give the entries to record depreciation and interest expense (both methods) for 19A.
5. Show how the liability should be reflected on the balance sheet at the end of 19A for both methods.

Problem 10–10

On August 1, 19A, Collier Company purchased a large used machine for operations. Payment was made by cash $6,000 and a $30,000 (maturity amount), two-year, noninterest-bearing note payable (due on July 31, 19C). The note did not specify interest; however, for Collier, the going rate for this type of transaction was 18%. Assume straight-line depreciation, a five-year life, and no residual value. The accounting period ends on December 31.

Required (round amounts to nearest dollar):

1. Give the entry to record the purchase of the machine.
2. Complete a tabulation as follows and show computations.

	Interest Amortization	
	Straight-Line Method	Interest Method
a. Face amount of note	$____	$____
b. Cash paid at maturity	$____	$____
c. Total interest expense	$____	$____
d. Interest expense on 19A income statement	$____	$____
e. Amount of liability (including interest) on balance sheet at end of 19A	$____	$____
f. Depr. expense for 19A	$____	$____

(Prepare an amortization schedule for the note that reflects the interest method.)

3. Should the interest method be used in this situation? Explain.
4. Give the entries for 19A to record depreciation and interest expense for both the interest method and the straight-line method of amortizing the discount on the note.

5. Show how the liability should be reflected on the balance sheet at the end of 19A for both methods.
6. Why is the depreciation amount the same regardless of whether the straight-line or interest method is used to compute the interest expense for the period?

Problem 10–11

Fritz Company is preparing the annual financial statements at December 31, 19A, and is concerned about application of *FASB Statement 5.* Four unrelated situations are under consideration, viz:

1. During 19B, a third party (a potential customer) sued the company for $150,000 for a claimed injury that occurred on the premises owned by Fritz. No date for the trial has been set; however, the lawyer employed by Fritz has completed a thorough investigation. Because it can be proven that the third party did fall on the premises, the company lawyer believes it will not be difficult for the plaintiff to prove injury. There is evidence that it was due to negligence by the plaintiff. The attorney believes that it is not probable, but is reasonably possible, that the suit will be successful (for the plaintiff), *but* for a significantly smaller amount.
2. The company had a $10,000, 8%, one-year note receivable from a customer. Fritz discounted the note, with recourse, at the bank to obtain cash before its due date (due on June 1, 19B). If the maker does not pay the bank by due date, Fritz will have to pay it. The customer has an excellent credit rating (having never defaulted on a debt).
3. An outside party has filed a claim against Fritz for $25,000 claiming that certain actions by Fritz caused the party to lose a contract on which the estimated profit was this amount. In the opinion of the attorney hired by Fritz, the probability of the claim being successful is remote. They do not believe it will ever be brought to trial. If necessary, Fritz will defend itself in court.
4. The company owns a small plant in a foreign country that has a book value of $3 million and an estimated market value of $4 million. The foreign government has clearly indicated its intention to expropriate the plant during the coming year and to reimburse Fritz for 50% of the estimated market value.

Required:
For each situation, respond to the following:

a. What accounting recognition (i.e., journal entries), if any, should be accorded each situation at the end of 19A? Explain why.
b. What should be reported on the income statement, balance sheet, and/or by footnote in each situation? Explain why.

PART B: PROBLEMS 10–12 to 10–16

Problem 10–12

American Bridgebuilders, Inc. has contracts for construction of three major projects. The percentage-of-completion method of accounting is used for accounting purposes, while the completed contract method is used for the income tax returns. For purposes of this problem, assume there are no revenues nor expenses other than those included in the total profit figures given.

	Year			Percentage of Completion			
Project	Started	Completed	Total Profit	19A	19B	19C	19D
A	19A	19C	$ 70,000	30%	50%	20%	
B	19B	19C	90,000		20	80	
C	19B	19D	100,000		10	70	20%

Required:
1. For each year, compute *(a)* income tax expense and *(b)* income tax payable; assume an average tax rate of 45%. (If necessary, refer to the section in Chapter 9 entitled Inventories for Long-Term Construction Contracts.)
2. Give the entry to record income tax for each year.
3. Complete a tabulation as follows:

	19A	19B	19C	19D
Income statement:				
Pretax income	$____	$____	$____	$____
Income tax expense ...	$____	$____	$____	$____
Net income	$____	$____	$____	$____
Balance sheet:				
Income tax payable ...	$____	$____	$____	$____
Deferred tax (cr. bal.) .	$____	$____	$____	$____

Problem 10–13

Winters Corporation financial statements for a four-year period reflected the following pretax amounts:

(Relates to Problem 10–13)

	19A	19B	19C	19D
Income statement (summarized):				
Revenues*	$120,000	$130,000	$140,000	$160,000
Expenses†	(80,000)	(92,000)	(95,000)	(128,000)
Depreciation (straight line)	?	?	?	?
Pretax income	$?	$?	$?	$?
Balance sheet (partial):				
Machine (4-year life, no residual value), at cost	$ 40,000	$ 40,000	$ 40,000	$ 40,000
Income tax payable	?	?	?	?
Deferred tax	?	?	?	?

* Includes $10,000 tax-free interest revenue in each of 19A and 19B.
† Includes $4,000 goodwill amortization in each year 19B, 19C, and 19D.

The company has an average tax rate of 40% each year and uses sum-of-the-years'-digits (SYD) depreciation (no residual value) on the income tax return (for problem purposes, assume this method is acceptable for tax purposes in this situation) and straight-line depreciation for accounting purposes.

Required:
1. Complete the above income statements incorporating income tax appropriately allocated.
2. Compute income tax payable for each year.
3. Give the entry for each year to record income tax. Prove the deferred tax amount for each year.
4. Explain why tax allocation provides better financial statement amounts in this situation.
5. Complete the balance sheet presentation of income tax payable and deferred income tax at the end of each year 19A–19D. Assume income tax payable is paid within three months after each fiscal year end.

Problem 10–14

The following data for X Corporation are available for a two-year period:

	19A	19B
Operating income, pretax	$100,000	$120,000
Extraordinary losses, pretax	(15,000)	(17,000)
Prior period adjustment, gain, pretax	7,000	
Timing differences included in above amounts:		
a. Revenue on income statement taxable in following period	5,000	
b. Revenue on income statement, taxable in preceding period		7,000
c. Expense on income statement, tax deductible in following period	8,000	
d. Expense on income statement, tax deductible in subsequent period		6,000
e. Tax deductible portion of the 19A EO loss shown above; tax deductible in 19B only	10,000	
f. Prior period gain on statement of retained earnings, taxable in next period	4,000	
Retained earnings, beginning balance	30,000	55,000

Assume an average income tax rate of 35% on all items, except extraordinary items, to which a 30% tax rate applies. Item *(f)* will require an amended tax return.

Required:
1. Compute income tax expense for each year that should be reported on the income statement. Show operating income, extraordinary items, and prior period adjustments separately.
2. Compute income tax payable for each year that should be reflected on the tax return. Show operating income, extraordinary items, and prior period adjustments separately.
3. Give the entry to record income tax for each year. Do not separate deferred income tax into current and long-term amounts; use one deferred income tax account.
4. Prepare a partial income statement and partial statement of retained earnings for each year to show how income tax expense should be reported. Include both interperiod and intraperiod allocations.

Problem 10–15

Bridges Corporation acquired machinery on July 1, 19C. The list price was $35,000. Bridges paid $15,000 cash and gave a note payable for the remainder with a face amount of $20,000 which included interest at 12% per year (a noninterest-bearing note). The maturity date of the note was July 1, 19E. The machinery had an estimated service life of eight years and no residual value. Bridges uses straight-line depreciation for accounting purposes and double-declining-balance (DDB) depreciation for income tax purposes.

During 19C, Bridges earned $175,000 pretax accounting income. Included in this amount was a deduction of $15,000 for cost depletion of a mineral which the company mines and sells. Income tax regulations provide that taxpayers such as Bridges may deduct for income tax purposes the larger of cost depletion or 6% of the gross revenue from the sale of the extracted minerals. During 19C, Bridges extracted 100,000 pounds of the mineral and sold 90,000 pounds at $3 per pound.

There were no other factors to complicate the company's income tax computations during 19C. The income tax rate during 19C was 20% on the first $25,000 of taxable income and 40% on the excess.

Required:

1. Give the journal entry to record income taxes for 19C. Bridges' fiscal year ends on December 31.
2. What effect did the difference between statutory depletion and cost depletion have on income tax amounts for 19D (the following year)? What type of difference was involved? Explain.

Problem 10–16

El Tango Corporation purchased a machine (which qualified for the 10% investment tax credit) on January 1, 19A, at a cost of $75,000, having an estimated useful life of 12 years and no residual value. The company uses straight-line depreciation and has an average tax rate of 40%. Income (after deducting depreciation expense, but before income tax expense) was 19A, $42,000; and 19B, $50,000.

Required:

1. Give the entries for income taxes and depreciation at December 31, 19A, and December 31, 19B, end of the fiscal period, assuming the—
   a. Flow-through method.
   b. Deferral method.
2. Show the financial statement effects of the above transactions for each year assuming the—
   a. Flow-through method.
   b. Deferral method.

SUPPLEMENT 10–A: PROBLEMS 10–17 to 10–18

Problem 10–17

Coswell, Inc., earned $80,000 pretax accounting income in 19W. During 19W, the following factors complicated the accounting for 19W income taxes:

1. Gross margin on installment sales recognized in accounts during 19W	$270,000
2. Gross margin reportable for income tax purposes—based on cash collections on installment receivables during 19W that arose on installment sales made in—	
19V	120,000
19W	120,000
3. Amortization of goodwill in accounts (not deductible for income tax purposes)	5,000
4. Ultimate disposition of remaining $70,000 of a loss carryforward recorded in 19H; corporation reported at year-end 19V an asset (receivable) of $70,000 × .40 = $28,000, which represented the then-remaining tax benefit (i.e., as yet unrealized) of loss carryforward which was initially recorded in 19H	28,000
5. At the end of 19V balance sheet reported a timing difference that arose from installment sales made in 19V which were accounted for on the sales realization basis and reported for tax purposes on a cash collection basis. Deferred income tax (cr. bal.) from 19V	48,000
6. Income tax rate for all years	40%

Required:

1. Prepare the journal entry to record income tax for 19W. Prepare an income tax worksheet similar to the illustration in the chapter to provide data for the entry.
2. Prepare partial income statements and balance sheets for 19V and 19W to report income tax for the two years in comparative form. Assume that the ending 19V balance in income tax payable was zero and that 19V income tax expense was $30,000.

Problem 10–18

Prince Corporation pretax financial statements for the first two years of operation reflected the following amounts:

	19A	19B
Revenues	$295,000	$330,000
Expenses	320,000	315,000
Pretax income (loss)	$(25,000)	$ 15,000

Assume an average tax rate of 40%.

Required:

1. Assume future income during the next fifteen years is unpredictable (i.e., uncertain):
   a. Restate the above financial statements incorporating the income tax effects appropriately allocated. Show computations.
   b. Give entries to record the income tax effects for each year. Explain the basis for your entries.

2. Assume instead that future income of $10,000 is reasonably certain during the next fifteen years. Complete 1*a* and 1*b* above.

SUPPLEMENTS 10–A AND 10–B: PROBLEM 10–19

Problem 10–19

Oldham Corporation's pretax financial statements for the first four years of operations reflected the following pretax amounts:

	19A	19B	19C	19D
Income statement (summarized):				
Revenue	$125,000	$155,000	$180,000	$230,000
Expenses	120,000	195,000	160,000	200,000
Pretax income (loss)	$ 5,000	$(40,000)	$ 20,000	$ 30,000

Assume an average income tax rate of 30% during 19A and 19B and 40% in 19C and 19D, and that future incomes are uncertain at the end of each year. Management of Oldham Corporation elects to carry the 19B loss back to 19A (and *then* forward) in order to "lock in" the immediate cash refund on the carryback.

Required:

1. Recast the above statements to incorporate the income tax effects. Show computations.
2. Give entries to record the income tax effects for each year.

SUPPLEMENT 10–B: PROBLEM 10–20

Problem 10–20

Difficult Tax Matters, Inc. accounts and related records revealed the following data for the first two years of operations:

	19A	19B
Pretax accounting income	$160,000	$180,000
Income tax differences (all "current"):		
1. Estimated warranty expense (included in pretax accounting income)	15,000	16,000
Cash payments on warranties arising in—		
19A (deductible for tax purposes)	12,000	2,000
19B (deductible for tax purposes)		15,000
		17,000
2. Rent revenue collection one year in advance (taxable in year collected)	6,000	
Rent revenue allocated on accrual basis (included in pretax accounting income)	4,000	2,000
3. Gross margin on installment sales recognized on sales basis (included in pretax accounting income)	175,000	230,000
Gross margin reportable for income tax purposes (on cash collection basis) on installment sales made in—		
19A	65,000	110,000
19B		75,000
		$185,000
Income tax rates	30%	40%

Required:

1. Identify the timing differences and the permanent differences listed above in items 1–3.
2. Using pretax accounting income as the base from which to begin, give the entries to record income taxes for 19A and 19B under each of the following assumptions:
   a. That each item was the only difference that occurred during the year. That is, give the entry for each year for each of the three items as if the other two did not occur.
   b. That all three items occurred during the year. That is, give the combined entry for each year. For this requirement you should prepare an income tax worksheet for each year similar to the one illustrated in the chapter.

11

Operational Assets: Property, Plant, and Equipment—Acquisition and Retirement

THIS CHAPTER and the next two chapters focus on a broad category of assets that may be thought of as operational assets because they are used in the operations of the business and are not held for resale. Operational assets, also referred to as fixed assets, may be classified as follows for accounting purposes:

1. Tangible property, plant, and equipment—Assets in this category have five major characteristics: *(a)* actively used in operations, *(b)* not held as an investment or for resale, *(c)* relatively long lived, *(d)* have physical substance, and *(e)* provide measurable future benefits to the entity. These operational assets are variously described by the terms **property, plant, and equipment; plant assets; capital assets; or tangible fixed assets.** The three classes of this group of assets are:
   a. Those subject to depreciation such as buildings, equipment, tools, and furniture. Depreciation is discussed in Chapter 12.
   b. Those subject to depletion such as mineral deposits and timber tracts. Depletion is discussed in Chapter 12.
   c. Those not subject to depreciation or depletion such as land for plant site, farms, and ranches.
2. Intangibles—Assets in this category are similar to tangible operational assets except that intangibles have no physical substance; their value is represented solely by grants or business rights which confer some operating, financial, or income-producing benefit on the owner. They are amortized over their useful lives. Examples include goodwill, patents, copyrights, and trademarks. Intangible assets are discussed in Chapter 13.

This chapter discusses the acquisition and retirement of property, plant, and equipment. It is subdivided as follows:

Part A—Operational Assets Acquired from Outsiders

Part B—Operational Assets Constructed for Own Use, Capitalization of Interest During Construction, Expenditures Subsequent to Acquisition, and Retirement of Operational Assets

Supplement 11–A—Acquisition Costs of Specific Operational Assets

Part A: Operational Assets Acquired from Outsiders

CAPITAL EXPENDITURES (ASSET) AND REVENUE EXPENDITURES (EXPENSE)

Accounting for expenditures incident to the acquisition and use of operational assets requires that they be classified as either **capital expenditures** (asset) or as **revenue expenditures** (expense).[1] **Capital expenditures** relate to costs which provide benefits to the entity over one or more accounting periods beyond the period of acquisition; hence, such expenditures are recorded in appropriate asset accounts. Capital expenditures made for assets having limited lives are subsequently allocated to the future periods benefited through depreciation, amortization, or depletion. An expenditure that is debited to an asset account or to Accumulated Depreciation is said to have been capitalized.

Revenue expenditures relate to the acquisition of property or other benefits which do **not** extend beyond the current accounting period; hence, they are recorded in appropriate **expense** accounts for the current period. The term **revenue expenditure** refers to the fact that such expenditures are matched against the revenue of the period in which they are incurred. Thus, a more descriptive term would be **expense expenditure.** Correct classification between capital and revenue expenditures is crucial because an incorrect classification may affect reported income for the entire life of an asset (land is an exception).

In cases in which the *(a)* capital expenditure is relatively small, *(b)* future benefit is insignificant, or *(c)* measurement of the future benefit is not reliable, the materiality and conservatism concepts imply that the outlay be accounted for as a revenue expenditure (i.e., expensed). Many companies adopt a realistic accounting policy in this respect such that, for example, expenditures under some limit are expensed as incurred regardless of the future benefit, and expenditures above this limit are capitalized only when the asset acquired has a measurable benefit extending to a future period.

[1] Expenditures incident to acquisition of an operational asset include transactions that require *(a)* payment of cash *(b)* transfer of other assets, or *(c)* incurrence of a liability. See FASB, *Statement of Financial Accounting Standards No. 34,* "Capitalization of Interest Cost" (Stamford, Conn.; 1979), par. 16.

PRINCIPLES UNDERLYING ACCOUNTING FOR PROPERTY, PLANT, AND EQUIPMENT

The accounting for property, plant, and equipment fundamentally rests on the **cost and matching principles.** At date of acquisition, property, plant, and equipment are recorded in the accounts at cost in conformity with the cost principle. The acquisition cost is measured by the cash outlay made to acquire such assets. If a consideration other than cash is given for the asset, the market value of such consideration at the time of the transaction is recorded as the cost of the asset. When the market value of the consideration given cannot be determined reasonably, the asset acquired is recorded at its own market value. When the market values of both items must be estimated, the more reliable estimate is used as the basis for identifying the cost of the asset acquired. All costs incurred to place an asset in service are additions to the cost of the asset.

Subsequent to acquisition, operational assets are carried in the accounts and reported at *(a)* cost (if unlimited life) or *(b)* in the case of a limited life, at cost less accumulated depreciation, amortization, or depletion (reflecting continuing application of the matching principle.)

The following outline identifies the principal topics discussed and illustrated in the remainder of Part A:

1. Acquisition cost of property, plant, and equipment when acquired—
   a. For cash.
   b. On a deferred payment plan.
   c. For stock or other securities.
   d. Through exchanges.
   e. Through lump-sum purchases.
   f. Make-ready costs.
2. Departures from cost:
   a. Donated assets.
   b. Discovery value.
   c. Write-downs due to impairment of use value to the company.

TANGIBLE OPERATIONAL ASSETS ACQUIRED FOR CASH

If a tangible operational asset is purchased for cash, all outlays required to purchase the asset and place it in service, including costs of installation and making ready to use, should be capitalized, in accordance with the cost principle. The capitalizable costs include the invoice price (less discounts), plus incidental costs such as sales tax, insurance during transit, freight, duties, ownership searching, ownership registration, installation, and breaking-in costs. All available discounts, **whether taken or not,** should be deducted from the invoice cost. Discounts not taken should be recorded as discounts lost and treated as interest expense.

TANGIBLE OPERATIONAL ASSETS ACQUIRED ON DEFERRED PAYMENT PLAN

Tangible operational assets acquired on a deferred or long-term payment plan (i.e., on credit) should be recorded at the cash equivalent price, excluding all interest and financing charges. Interest and other finance charges should be debited to Interest Expense and not treated as part of the asset cost (see the Part B section captioned Interest during the Construction Period for an exception).

If the deferred payment contract does not specify interest and financing charges, such amounts should be estimated and subtracted from the **total** amount paid for the asset in determining its cost. If the current cash price for the asset is determinable, the excess to be paid under the deferred payment contract should be treated as interest expense and should be apportioned over the period covered by that contract. If no cash price is determinable for the asset, a realistic amount of interest should be recognized in recording the purchase. These procedures are specified in *APB Opinion 21.*

To illustrate the purchase of an operational asset on a deferred payment contract, assume a machine was purchased under a contract that required payment of $4,600 at the end of each of three years, when the going interest rate was 18 percent per annum on liabilities of this level of risk and time. In particular, note that this deferred payment contract does not separately identify the interest. To record the asset purchased at $13,800 (i.e., $4,600 × 3) would include in the asset cost the interest expense implicit in the contract. Rather, the asset account should be debited for the **present value** of the three payments discounted at 18 percent as follows:

$PV = \text{Annual payment} \times P_{o_{n=3;\, i=18\%}}$ (Table 5–4)
= $4,600 × 2.17427 (present value of an ordinary annuity of 3 rents of 1 each at 18%).
= $10,000 (rounded)

Therefore, the indicated entries are as follows:

a. At date of purchase:[2]

Asset—machinery	10,000	
Installments payable—machinery contract		10,000

b. At payment dates (see the debt payment schedule below for amounts):

	1st Year		2d Year		3d Year	
Interest expense ($10,000 × 18%, etc.) ..	1,800		1,296		704	
Installments payable—machinery contract	2,800		3,304		3,896	
Cash		4,600		4,600		4,600

End of Period	Annual Payment (cash credit)	Interest Expense (debit)		Payment on Principal (debit)	Unpaid Principal
Start......					$10,000
1	$ 4,600	$10,000 × 18%	$1,800	$ 2,800	7,200
2	4,600	7,200 × 18%	1,296	3,304	3,896
3	4,600	3,896 × 18%	704*	3,896	-0-
	$13,800		$3,800	$10,000	

* Rounded $3 to come out even.

[2] Alternatively this entry could be made on a "gross" basis as follows with the same end result in all respects:

Asset—machinery	10,000	
Discount on installment payable*	3,800	
Installments payable—machinery contract ($4,600 × 3)		13,800

* This amount would be shown contra to "Installments Pay-

TANGIBLE OPERATIONAL ASSETS ACQUIRED IN EXCHANGE FOR SECURITIES

The proper valuation of tangible operational assets received in exchange for securities (e.g., debt or equity) of the acquiring company often is difficult to determine because of:

1. The lack of a readily determinable market value for *(a)* the securities (e.g., the common stock of a privately held company) or *(b)* the operational assets involved (e.g., used assets).
2. The absence of an arm's-length bargaining between the parties to the exchange (e.g., operational assets contributed by the organizers in return for the common stock of a newly formed corporation).
3. The nature of the assets involved (e.g., unexplored or unproven mineral deposits, manufacturing rights, patents, chemical formulas, and mining claims).
4. The current market price of the security may be based upon market volume far below the volume of shares involved in the exchange (i.e., a "thin" market).

The **cost principle** holds that assets acquired should be recorded at their then current cash equivalent cost. If this amount is not determinable, the cost of assets acquired through exchange of securities should be measured as follows:

1. Determine the market value of the consideration (i.e., the securities) given. If the securities have an established market price, it should be used as long as the market would absorb at that price the volume of securities involved.
2. If the market value of the securities in the volume exchanged cannot be determined reliably, the market value of the assets acquired should be used if it can be determined reliably. In the absence of an actual cash basis sale of the assets involved in the immediate past, an independent appraisal of them by a professional appraiser may be recorded as the cost of the assets acquired.
3. If a market value for neither the securities given nor the assets received can be determined reliably, values established by the board of directors of the corporation may be used. The law generally allows the directors considerable discretion in establishing values in this situation, except in cases where fraudulent intent on the part of the directors can be shown.

When assets are acquired in exchange for securities, any actual or implied discounts or premiums on the securities should be accounted for in the normal manner. Tangible assets acquired in exchange for bonds payable should be recorded at the current cash value of the bonds, which takes into account any premium or discount on the bonds payable. If there is no currently established market price for the bonds, the cost of the asset can be computed as the **present value** of the bond principal plus the present value of the interest payments, discounted at the going rate of interest on liabilities with this level of risk (present value concepts are discussed in Chapter 5). Operational assets acquired for a combination of cash **and** securities should be capitalized at the sum of the cash, and the market value of securities determined in accordance with the principles discussed above.

TANGIBLE OPERATIONAL ASSETS ACQUIRED IN EXCHANGE FOR ASSETS OTHER THAN SECURITIES

Operational assets often are acquired by trading in another asset in full or as part payment. Some transactions involve an exchange of two or more **nonmonetary** assets; in other cases, an asset is acquired by exchanging another asset plus a payment or receipt of cash (often referred to as "boot"). Prior to *APB Opinion No. 29,* "Accounting for Nonmonetary Transactions," companies accounted for operational assets acquired through **exchanges** of nonmonetary assets in a variety of ways.[3]

APB Opinion 29 specifies the accounting approach for various nonmonetary transactions, including

able—Machinery Contract" on the balance sheet, thus reporting the liability at its present value.

The payment entries would be revised accordingly; the first payment entry would be as follows:

Interest expense ($10,000 × .18)	1,800	
Installments payable—machinery contract	4,600	
Discount on installment payable		1,800
Cash		4,600

[3] Prior to *APB Opinion 29,* exchanges **were** recorded by debiting the asset account for the item acquired at either (1) its quoted list price, or (2) the cash paid plus the book value of the old asset exchanged, or (3) its market value.

those involving the acquisition of tangible operational assets. The **basic principle** established in the *Opinion*, paragraph 18, is:

> Accounting for nonmonetary transactions should be based on the fair values of the assets (or services) involved which is the same as that used in monetary transactions.

Thus, under this basic principle, the **cost** of a tangible operational asset acquired by giving another nonmonetary asset (e.g., a trade-in) is the **market value of the asset surrendered.** A gain or loss on the disposition of the asset surrendered should be recognized in accounting for the exchange. The market value of the asset acquired should be used to measure its cost only if it is more clearly determinable than the market value of the asset surrendered.

The *Opinion* specifies two exceptions to the basic principle as follows: (1) when the market value implicit in the exchange is not "determinable within reasonable limits" (in this situation the carrying value of the asset surrendered usually is retained as the carrying value of the asset received), and (2) when the exchange transaction "is not essentially the culmination of an earning process." The *Opinion* applies to items held for resale (inventory) and productive assets (items used in the operations of the business). This chapter considers **only productive assets.**

Similar Versus Dissimilar Assets

The *Opinion* classifies assets exchanged as similar or dissimilar because the exchange of similar assets seldom indicates the culmination of an earnings process, whereas the exchange of dissimilar assets almost always indicates the culmination of an earnings process. **Similar productive** assets are defined as "assets that are of the same general type, that perform the same function, or that are employed in the same line of business." All other productive assets would be classified as dissimilar. For example, the exchange of an old truck on another truck would involve similar assets; however, the exchange of a tract of speculative land on a truck involves dissimilar assets. The *Opinion* specifies different accounting treatments for the two types of exchanges. In all transactions involving exchanges of nonmonetary assets, the accounting problem is determination of the **cost** that should be recorded for the **asset acquired.**

Accounting Procedures for Exchanges

Dissimilar Assets Exchanged. Both parties record exchanges of **dissimilar** assets on a **market value** basis because such exchanges are considered to **culminate an earnings process.** "Market value" refers to the asset surrendered. That is, the cost of the asset acquired is measured by the market value of the asset surrendered.

When a cash difference is **paid** in an exchange of **dissimilar** assets, the cost of the asset acquired is the **cash paid plus the market value of the asset surrendered.** When a cash difference is **received** the cost of the asset acquired is the **market value of the asset surrendered minus the cash received.** When the market value of the asset surrendered is not reliably determinable, the market value of the asset received is used as the basis for determining its cost.

Similar Assets Exchanged. In contrast to dissimilar assets, when **similar** assets are exchanged and no cash difference (boot) is paid or received, both parties record the exchange on a **book value** basis because it is considered that such exchanges **do not** culminate an earnings process. When a cash difference is paid or received and the assets are similar, the book value basis is altered as illustrated in 2*b* and *c* below. **In no case (involving either similar or dissimilar assets) is the asset received recorded at a cost in excess of its market value if market value is known.**

Accounting for the exchange of assets is illustrated below.

1. **Dissimilar assets**—Use the market value concept; record the asset acquired at the market value of the asset surrendered, plus or minus any cash difference; recognize a gain or loss on disposal of the asset surrendered because the exchange **culminates** an earnings process; that is, the productive function of the asset surrendered is terminated and an asset with a different productive function is acquired.

   Example: Company A has a large crane that cost $50,000; accumulated depreciation to date,

$45,000 (i.e., a carrying value of $5,000). It is exchanged with Company B for a tract of speculative land; cash of $12,000 was paid by Company A. The market value of the crane is determined to be $13,000.

To record the exchange by Company A:

Land ($13,000 + $12,000)	25,000*	
Accumulated depreciation (crane)	45,000	
Machinery (crane)		50,000
Cash		12,000
Gain on disposal of machinery† . . .		8,000

* Cannot exceed market value of the land.

† Market value of the crane recognized, $13,000 less its book value, $5,000, is a gain of $8,000.

2. **Similar assets**—In this situation, *APB Opinion 29* prescribes a **book value** approach because it is assumed that nonmonetary exchanges of similar assets **do not** culminate an earnings process; the asset acquired continues the productive function of the asset surrendered. Recording an exchange of similar assets depends upon whether a cash difference is paid or received. Three possible situations are as follows:

   a. **Similar assets exchanged and no cash difference is paid or received**—The cost of the asset acquired is recorded at the **book value** of the asset surrendered.

   Example: Company A exchanged a large crane that cost $50,000, accumulated depreciation to date, $45,000, for a small crane with a current cash price of $8,000. No cash difference was paid or received. The exchange would be recorded as follows:

Machinery (small crane, at book value of the large crane)	5,000*	
Accumulated depreciation (large crane)	45,000	
Machinery (large crane)		50,000

* Cannot exceed its market value; therefore, a loss, but not a gain, could be recognized in an exchange of this type.

   b. **Similar assets exchanged and a cash difference is paid**—The asset acquired is recorded at the sum of the cash paid plus the book value of the asset surrendered. The asset acquired cannot be recorded at more than its market value. Therefore, no gain can be recorded; however, if the market value of the asset received is less than the sum of the cash paid plus the book value of the asset surrendered, a loss must be recorded.

   Example: Company A exchanged a large crane that cost $50,000, accumulated depreciation, $45,000, for a small crane having a current cash price of $8,000, and **paid** $1,000 cash boot. The transaction would be recorded as follows:

Machinery (small crane, $1,000 + $5,000)	6,000	
Accumulated depreciation (large crane) .	45,000	
Machinery (large crane)		50,000
Cash		1,000

   Had the cash difference been $4,000, the asset acquired would have been recorded at $8,000 and a $1,000 loss recognized.

   c. **Similar assets exchanged and a cash difference (boot) is received**—This transaction is viewed as a sale of **part** of the asset surrendered and an exchange of the remainder of it. In such a transaction, *APB Opinion 29* requires that a gain be recognized on the part of the asset **sold** (i.e., surrendered) if the cash received exceeds the book value of the portion of the asset considered as sold. The cost of the asset acquired is identified as the proportion of the book value of the asset considered to have been **exchanged** (versus sold). Thus, this transaction is treated in part at market value and in part at book value.

   Example: Company A exchanged a large crane that cost $50,000, accumulated depreciation, $45,000, for a small crane with a cash price (i.e., market value) of $8,000, and **received** a cash difference of $2,000. The transaction would be recorded as follows:[4]

[4] The entry to record the exchange can be separated into two component entries, as shown below (see entry on page 368 for computation of the 20 percent–80 percent split of old asset):

a. To record sale of 20 percent of the asset surrendered:		
Cash	2,000	
Accumulated depreciation ($45,000 × .20)	9,000	
Machinery (large crane) ($50,000 × .20) .		10,000
Gain on disposal of machinery		1,000
b. To record exchange of 80% of the large asset for another similar asset (at book value):		
Machinery (small crane)	4,000	
Accumulated depreciation ($45,000 × .80) .	36,000	
Machinery (large crane) ($50,000 × .80)		40,000

Cash	2,000	
Machinery (small crane)*	4,000	
Accumulated depreciation (large crane)	45,000	
Machinery (large crane)		50,000
Gain on disposal of machinery (large crane)†		1,000

Computations:

* Cost of small crane—book value of large crane less the proportion of book value of the large crane sold:

Book value, large crane ($50,000 − $45,000)	$5,000
Proportion of book value of the large crane sold for cash:	

$$\text{Book value of large crane} \times \frac{\text{Cash realized on part sale}}{\text{Cash realized on part sale} + \text{MV of asset acquired on part exchange}}$$

$\$5,000 \times \frac{\$2,000}{\$2,000 + \$8,000}$	1,000
Difference—cost of asset acquired	$4,000

† Gain on disposal of asset surrendered—cash received less portion sold of book value of asset surrendered:

Cash received	$2,000
Proportion of book value of large crane sold (per above)	1,000
Difference—gain on sale of large crane	$1,000

Alternatively, in case of a loss, the *Opinion* requires recognition of the full amount of such loss. To illustrate, assume in the preceding example that the accumulated depreciation was $39,000. The transaction would be recorded as follows:

Cash	2,000	
Accumulated depreciation (large crane)	39,000	
Loss on disposal of machinery (large crane)	1,000	
Machinery (small crane)	8,000*	
Machinery (large crane)		50,000

* Cannot exceed its market value.

Observe that the full amount of the loss is recognized because the asset acquired cannot be recorded in excess of its market value (i.e., $8,000 in this case). Thus, there is no need to calculate the proportionate part of the large crane sold. A loss is reported because the book value of the asset given up (i.e., $11,000) is greater than its market value (i.e., $2,000 + $8,000), as reflected in the exchange transaction.

The *Opinion* does not recognize the list price of an asset acquired as the measure of its cost unless list price is the actual cash equivalent (i.e., market) value of the asset. The list price often is merely a basis for bargaining rather than a genuine cash cost.

To determine market value in exchanges of operational assets, *APB Opinion 29* states that market values should be determined by referring to "quoted market prices, independent appraisals, estimated fair values of assets or services received in exchange, and other available evidence."

If a business successively acquires several generations of **similar** assets by trading the next-to-newest asset as part payment for the newest asset, the effect of accounting for the exchanges at book value under the provisions of *APB Opinion 29* can be to cumulate past errors into the book value of the newest asset. Examples of such errors that can affect this book value include past errors in depreciation and expenditures for repairs. The cycle is broken in the event of a loss on exchange of assets, in which case the new asset is recorded at its market value.

LUMP-SUM PURCHASES OF ASSETS

It is not unusual for a business to acquire several different assets for a lump sum. This type of acquisition, frequently referred to as a basket, group, or lump-sum purchase, poses the problem of apportioning the lump-sum cost to the several different assets acquired. The apportionment is needed to identify the cost of each asset acquired. The apportionment should be based upon some realistic indicator of the relative values of the several assets involved, such as appraised values, tax assessment, cost savings, or the present value of estimated future earnings.

To illustrate, assume $90,000 was paid for property that included land, a building, and some machinery. Assume further that an independent appraisal showed appraised values of the land, $30,000; building, $50,000; and machinery, $20,000. The cost apportionment and entry to record the transaction are shown below:

Cost Apportionment

Asset	Appraised Value	Proportion	Apportioned Cost
Land	$ 30,000	3/10	$27,000
Building	50,000	5/10	45,000
Machinery	20,000	2/10	18,000
Total	$100,000		$90,000

Entry to record the purchase:

Land	27,000	
Building	45,000	
Machinery	18,000	
Cash		90,000

MAKE-READY COSTS

Subsequent to acquisition, but prior to the use of an operational asset, all costs incurred to ready the asset for use should be capitalized as part of the cost of the asset. Prior to operational use, a secondhand asset often requires substantial outlays for repairs, reconditioning, remodeling, and installation, all of which should be capitalized. Reinstallation and rearrangement costs of machinery, rearrangement of building partitions, renovation of buildings, and similar outlays directly related to operational assets purchased new or in a used condition should be capitalized as part of the cost. Overhead items such as insurance, taxes, supervisory salaries, and similar incidental expenditures directly related to a used asset during a period of renovation also should be capitalized. Depreciation should **not** be recorded on such costs prior to the period of use.

DEPARTURES FROM COST IN ACCOUNTING FOR TANGIBLE OPERATIONAL ASSETS

Although accounting for operational assets is based fundamentally upon the cost principle, departure from the cost principle is sanctioned in special circumstances. These departures relate to the following:

1. Donations of assets to the company.
2. High and unexpected discovery value of assets owned by the company.
3. Significant and permanent impairment of use value to the company.
4. Revaluations due to quasi-reorganization of the company (discussed in Supplement 15–A).
5. Capitalization of interest on assets constructed by the company for its own use (discussed in Part B of this chapter).

Donated Assets

Assets occasionally are donated to a corporation by municipalities or other nonprofit organizations, as an inducement to locate a plant or other facility in the area. Often such donations are conditional upon some particular performance by the corporation, such as the employment of a certain number of individuals. Donations of assets to corporations also are made occasionally by the stockholders of the corporation.

Strict adherence to the cost principle would involve recording donated assets at only the amount of incidental costs incurred in acceptance of the asset and in fulfilling the related agreements. Accountability for the resources of the entity and measurement of its earning power require that each operational asset acquired and used by the entity be recorded at its cash equivalent value, regardless of its origin. *APB Opinion 29* states that "a nonmonetary asset received in a **nonreciprocal transfer** should be recorded at the fair market value of the asset received." In the case of a donated asset (donated assets exemplify "nonreciprocal transfers," i.e., transfers in which the donor receives nothing measurable in return), an independent and realistic appraisal of the current market value of the donated asset should be recorded, provided the donation is unconditional. Should the donor impose restrictions, however, any "negative values" arising from such conditions should be deducted from the market value of the asset in determination of the valuation to be recorded. To illustrate, assume a building, including the land on which it is located, is given by a city to XYZ Corporation as an inducement to establish a plant therein. The related transactions may be recorded as follows:

a. To record the market value, per appraisal at date of donation:

Plant building	400,000	
Plant land	100,000	
Contributed capital—donated plant building and land		500,000

b. To record depreciation for first year assuming a 10-year life and no residual value:

Depreciation expense	40,000	
Accumulated depreciation—plant building		40,000

Depreciable assets received by donation should be depreciated in the normal manner on the basis of the market value recorded in the accounts.

If the donation is contingent upon the fulfillment of some contractual obligation by the recipient, the asset should be treated as a contingent asset until the contingent condition has been met. In such a case, FASB, *Statement of Financial Accounting Standards No. 5,* "Accounting for Contingencies," requires that the donated asset be disclosed in the financial statements by note only.

Discovery Value

Property owned by a company may increase in value as a result of the **discovery** thereon of mineral or other natural resources. In such cases the original cost of the property may not provide a reasonable basis for accountability. Nevertheless, the accounting profession is reluctant to recognize accounting values other than cost for natural resources.

The FASB contemplated prescribing discovery value as the basis for accounting for oil and gas **reserves** when it was considering issuance of FASB, *Statement of Financial Accounting Standards No. 19,* "Financial Accounting and Reporting by Oil and Gas Producing Companies." When the final statement was issued in December 1977, however, a majority of the Board members rejected discovery value accounting for oil and gas reserves because

> (a) values that were current when initially recorded quickly become out-of-date and
> (b) the mixture of values of minerals measured at different dates of discovery lacks both the verifiability of historical costs and the relevance of current values.[5]

In its deliberations to develop *FASB Statement 19,* the FASB also considered other approaches for measuring and reporting the oil and gas reserves. Two methods given primary consideration are known as the (1) successful efforts method and (2) full cost method.[6] *FASB Statement 19* prescribed the successful efforts method. The Securities and Exchange Commission (SEC) did not agree with this conclusion; therefore, in 1978 the SEC issued its *Accounting Series Release (ASR) 253,* which *(a)* permitted listed companies to continue use of either the successful efforts or the full cost method and *(b)* specified that, as supplementary information, oil and gas companies experiment with a form of discovery value, which the SEC designated as Reserve Recognition Accounting (RRA), to account for their proved reserves.[7] The SEC expected that the RRA approach eventually would be required as the basic method of accounting for oil and gas reserves. In 1981 the SEC abandoned the plan to ultimately require RRA as the basic method. A special supplementary disclosure is required for the oil and gas reserves of the company. Currently, accounting for oil and gas producing companies is in accordance with *FASB Statement 19,* as amended and interpreted.

The controversy, briefly reviewed above, surrounding the historical cost (HC) and discovery value (RRA) approaches brought the FASB and the SEC into conflict and involved the U.S. Congress as well. This controversy provides an interesting glimpse of the political factors that often influence standard setting in accounting.

Write-down of Operational Assets due to Impairment of Use Value

As a general principle, operational assets should not be carried at a book value in excess of their economic value in use, or, if not in use, they should not be carried in excess of their net realizable value.

If an operational asset suffers **permanent impairment of its operational value by a material amount,** it should be written down or written off as the circumstances warrant. For example, a plant may become idle due to factors such as continuing decline in demand, obsolescence of its products, or inadequate transportation facilities, so that it has little or no resale value and its decreased value, if any, can only be realized as salvage. In such cases, GAAP **requires** an immediate write-down to net realizable value and recognition of the **impairment loss** for the period. Normally the write-down should be accomplished through a credit to the accumulated depreciation account (in recognition of obsolescence) and a debit to a nonrecurring loss.

---

[5] FASB, *Statement of Financial Accounting Standards No. 19,* "Financial Accounting and Reporting by Oil and Gas Producing Companies" (Stamford, Conn., 1977), par. 138.

[6] See Chapter 13 section captioned Exploration Costs for a discussion of these two methods.

[7] **Proved reserves** is a technical term used in the oil and gas industry to refer to quantities of oil and gas that appear with reasonable certainty to be economically recoverable from known oil and gas reserves. In this context, **reserve** means an actual inventory of assets in the ground.

Part B: Operational Assets Constructed for Own Use, Capitalization of Interest during Construction, Expenditures Subsequent to Acquisition, and Retirement of Operational Assets

The following outline identifies the principal topics discussed in Part B:

1. Assets constructed for own use.
2. Capitalization of interest during the construction period.
3. Expenditures subsequent to acquisition:
   a. Repairs and maintenance.
   b. Extraordinary repairs and renewals.
   c. Replacements and betterments.
   d. Additions.
   e. Rearrangements of assets.
4. Retirement of operational assets.

ASSETS CONSTRUCTED FOR OWN USE

Some companies construct portions of their operational assets; for example, a utility may use its own work crews to extend transmission facilities and construct pipelines. Other companies which normally would not build their own facilities may do so when their personnel and properties otherwise would be idle. All labor and material costs directly identified with such construction should be capitalized as a cost of the new assets. Determining the amount of **overhead** cost which should be allocated to the construction is more controversial. Two accounting problems arise in this context: (1) What overhead costs can be directly identified with the new construction? (2) Should the normal company overhead be allocated to self-constructed assets on the same basis as to regular production for inventory? Alternatively, should only the **incremental** overhead caused by the construction be allocated to self-constructed assets?

Identification of specific overhead costs with specific construction projects can become complex. Some overhead elements, such as permits and licenses, can be directly associated with the construction. Also, when machinery is depreciated on a machine-hours or output basis, and that machinery is used on a self-construction project, it is easy to relate that depreciation to the project. On the other hand, when the machinery is depreciated on a time basis (i.e., the straight-line, sum-of-the-years'-digits [SYD], or declining-balance method), allocation of depreciation is likely to be more arbitrary. Other elements of overhead, such as insurance, taxes, and utilities, also are difficult to identify with particular self-construction projects.

Some accountants believe the only sound basis of allocating overhead costs is to assign to self-constructed assets only the incremental overhead cost directly caused by the project. In contrast, other accountants believe self-construction projects should bear the same proportion of overhead costs as would regular production. In their view, for example, if overhead is allocated on the basis of labor-hours, and 8 percent of labor-hours are associated with self-construction, the 8 percent of **total** overhead (i.e., regular plus incremental) should be debited to the self-constructed assets. Those favoring allocating overhead on this basis maintain that self-constructed assets should be accounted for on the same basis as inventory and that unless the same basis is followed, special favors are granted to self-constructed assets. In particular, not allocating some portion of the total overhead to self-construction would result in an undervaluation of self-constructed assets and an overstatement of inventory and cost of goods sold. The counterargument by those who favor allocating only the **incremental** overhead to self-constructed assets is that allocation of overhead to self-constructed assets when idle capacity exists does not affect normal production; in this view, capitalization of overhead other than that directly caused by the self-construction results in overstatement of the cost of self-constructed assets and understatement of inventory and cost of goods sold.

This dispute has not been resolved. The AICPA's *Accounting Research Monograph No. 1* says the central question is whether the overhead costs in question have "discernible future benefits." A useful criterion in answering that question is

> . . . that, in the absence of compelling evidence to the contrary, overhead costs considered to have "discernible future benefits" for the purpose of determining the cost of inventory should be presumed to have "discernible future benefits" for the purpose of determining the cost of a self-constructed depreciable asset.[8]

Under this criterion it would appear that both **normal** and **incremental** overhead costs would be debited to self-constructed assets; it should be remembered, however, that this *monograph* is not binding on accountants.

Excess Costs of Construction

The actual cost of self-constructed assets may differ from their cost if acquired from outsiders. When a company determines that its cost of self-constructed properties exceeds the prospective cost of acquiring similar properties of equal capacity and quality from outsiders, it should debit the excess cost to expenses (or loss) of the period in which the self-construction is completed. Failure to do so carries forward cost elements which have no future benefit. On the other hand, when the cost of self-constructed facilities is less than their prospective cost if acquired from outsiders, the assets should be recorded at actual cost. Writing them up to the prospective cost and recognition of the cost saving as revenue or gain of the current period is not permitted under GAAP.

CAPITALIZATION OF INTEREST DURING THE CONSTRUCTION PERIOD

Whether assets are being self-constructed or acquired from outsiders, there is often a lengthy waiting period between the authorization and start of a project and its completion. A controversial question concerns whether to capitalize (i.e., debit the asset for) interest cost during the construction period, or to account for it as interest expense. There is general agreement that time-related costs, such as taxes and insurance, during construction should be debited to the asset under construction rather than being treated as current expenses. Consistent logic would support capitalization of interest during the construction period (interest costs incurred after construction is completed always should be expensed). However, capitalization of interest causes complications. For example, unless the funds were borrowed specifically to finance the construction, it is difficult to determine the proper amount of interest to capitalize. If no funds were borrowed specifically to finance the construction, assignment of interest to the constructed assets requires imputation of an interest rate to the construction project.

Public utilities often have capitalized interest during construction. Instead of matching interest on funds borrowed to finance construction with current revenue (i.e., as interest expense), they have capitalized it as a cost of the assets built. Utility customers are charged regulated rates designed to *(a)* give utility company stockholders a "fair" rate of return on their investment and *(b)* provide equitable utility rates for present and future utility customers. If the interest were recognized as current expense, present customers would have to pay increased utility rates to cover the added expense and would, in effect, be financing facilities which will benefit future customers. By including the interest in the cost of the constructed assets (thereby raising future depreciation amounts on them), the future customers who benefit from the assets pay for the interest that helped make the assets and the related utility service a reality.

Capitalization of interest during construction traditionally has not been widespread, but the practice grew in the early 1970s. Consequently, in 1979, the FASB issued *Statement of Financial Accounting Standards No. 34,* "Capitalization of Interest Cost," which governs the capitalization of interest (as revised by *FASB Statement 42,* November 1980). *Statements 34* and *42,* provide the following basic guidelines (par. citations to follow are from *FASB Statement 34*):

1. **Underlying concept** (par. 6)—The historical cost of acquiring an asset includes the costs necessarily incurred to bring it to the condition and location necessary for its **intended use** (i.e., for operational assets, readiness for use, and for inventory, readiness for sale.)
2. **Qualifying assets** (par. 9)—Interest shall be capitalized for the following types of assets:
   a. Assets that are constructed or otherwise produced for an enterprise's **own use** (including

[8] C. W. Lamden, D. L. Gerboth, and T. W. McRae, *Accounting for Depreciable Assets* (New York: AICPA, 1975), p. 57.

assets constructed or produced for the enterprise by others for which deposits or progress payments have been made).

b. Assets intended for **sale or lease** that are constructed or otherwise produced as **discrete** projects (e.g., ships or real estate developments).

3. **Interest not capitalized** (par. 10)—Interest shall not be capitalized for the following:
   a. Inventories that are routinely manufactured or otherwise produced in large quantities on a **repetitive** basis.
   b. Assets that already are **in use or are ready for their intended use** in the earning activities of the enterprise.
   c. Assets that are **not being used** in the earning activities of the enterprise and that are not undergoing the activities necessary to get them ready for use.
   d. Land that is **not undergoing activities** necessary to get it ready for its intended use (e.g., operational assets for own use, or inventory for resale) is not a qualifying asset (par. 11).
4. **Interest capitalization period** (pars. 17 and 18)—The beginning and end of the capitalization period is as follows:
   a. The capitalization period shall **begin** when all of three conditions are present (par. 17):
   (1) Qualifying expenditures (defined below) for the qualifying asset actually have been made.
   (2) Activities that are necessary to get the asset ready for its intended use actually are in progress.
   (3) Interest cost actually is being incurred.
   b. Interest capitalization shall **continue** only so long as these three conditions are present.
   c. The capitalization period shall **end** when the asset is substantially complete and ready for its intended use (par. 18).

Amount of Interest Capitalized

The amount of interest to be capitalized **theoretically** is the interest which could have been avoided if the expenditures for the assets had not been made. Application of this theoretical concept necessitates definition of the *(a)* interest rate for capitalization and *(b)* qualifying asset expenditures. *FASB Statement 34* defines these factors as follows:

a. **Interest rate for capitalization** (i.e., the capitalization rate) (par. 13)—The amount of interest to be capitalized may be determined by applying the appropriate capitalization rate(s) to the average accumulated expenditures for the qualifying asset(s). The **average capitalization rate** may be:
(1) Based upon the average rate(s) applicable to the borrowings (i.e., debt) outstanding of the entity during the period, or
(2) If the enterprise has new borrowing(s) directly associated with the qualifying asset, it may use *(a)* the average capitalization rate specified in (1) above, or *(b)* the specific rate(s) on the new borrowing(s), and use the average capitalization rate for all expenditures not covered by the specific new borrowings.[9]

b. **Average accumulated qualifying expenditures** (pars. 13 and 16)—The appropriate capitalization rate(s) is applied to the **average accumulated expenditures on the qualifying asset during the period. Expenditures** are defined as those for the qualifying asset that "have required the payment of cash, the transfer of other assets, or the incurring of a liability on which interest is recognized (in contrast to liabilities, such as trade payables, accruals, and retained earnings on which interest is not recognized). However, reasonable approximations of net capitalized expenditures may be used."

c. **Limit on interest capitalized** (par. 15)—A "cap" is specified for the total amount of interest that can be capitalized **each accounting period** as follows: "The total amount of interest cost capitalized in an accounting period shall not exceed the total amount of interest cost incurred by the enterprise in that period." This "cap" precludes the capitalization of interest on owners' equity.

FASB Statement 34 does not provide specific guidelines for computation of the *(a)* average capitalization rate related to the borrowings outstanding during the period or *(b)* average accumulated expenditures during the period. Most applications observed to date compute both of these averages monthly or quarterly, although some companies compute them semiannually or annually. The appropriate period to use for this purpose depends upon the sta-

[9] *FASB Statement 34*, par. 52.

EXHIBIT 11–1: Capitalization of Interest—X Corporation

Panel A—Illustrative Data:

1. On January 1, 19C, X Corporation acquired a tract of land as a building site at cost of $30,000; payment was cash $10,000, plus a $20,000, three-year note, 15 percent interest payable each December 31; total expenditure .... $ 30,000
2. During 19C, building construction involved the following expenditures for design, subcontractors, supervision, and other construction costs: March 31, $90,000; June 30, $89,000; September 30, $58,000; and December 31, $45,000; total expenditures* $282,000

* Quarterly payments, at the end of each quarter, are assumed to simplify the illustration.

3. Company X owed the following liabilities at December 31, 19C:

a. Note payable on the land, 1 above	$ 20,000
b. Note payable to finance the building construction, dated 7/1/19C; principal and 16% interest payable in equal annual installments of $31,035† each June 30, over 10 years	150,000
c. Long-term note payable, 10 percent interest payable each December 31, dated 1/1/19A, maturity 12/31/19E (not related to the building construction)	50,000
d. Accounts payable, short term; no interest recognized (not related to the building construction)	15,000

† $150,000 ÷ $P_{o_{n=10;\ i=16\%}}$ (4.83323; Table 5–4) = $31,035.

4. On December 31, 19C, the building essentially was completed and ready for use.
5. The company decided to use the **average quarterly** interest rates on **all** borrowings for capitalization.

Panel B—Entries to Record the Transactions for the Year 19C (given above) Including Capitalization of Interest During Construction of the Building:

1. January 1, 19C, purchase of the land:

Land	30,000	
Cash		10,000
Note payable, land, 15%		20,000

2. During 19C, expenditures on construction of building (total $282,000):

	March 31		June 30		September 30		December 31	
Building	90,000		89,000		58,000		45,000	
Cash		90,000		89,000		58,000		45,000

3. July 1, 19C, borrowed $150,000 to finance building construction:

Cash	150,000	
Note payable, building, 16%		150,000

4. December 31, 19C, to record all interest during 19C:

Building (interest capitalized; see Exhibit 11–2 for computation)	18,466	
Interest expense ($3,000 + $5,000 + $12,000 − $18,466)	1,534	
Cash, land note ($20,000 × 15%)		3,000
Cash, long-term note ($50,000 × 10%)		5,000
Interest payable, building note ($150,000 × 16% × 6/12)		12,000

bility of the amounts and timing throughout the annual accounting period. If the amounts occur evenly (both as to amount and timing) **annual** computation of the two averages would be appropriate; alternatively, if the periodic amounts vary greatly, **monthly** or **quarterly** computations of the two averages would be necessary. In the illustrations to follow, we use quarterly averages to reduce the computational details.

Disclosures required in **each accounting period,** either in the tabular portion of the financial statements or the notes include *(a)* the total amount of interest cost incurred and *(b)* any amount thereof that was capitalized. Exhibit 11–1, Panel A, presents data for X Corporation used to illustrate capitalization of interest, and Panel B gives the entries to record the costs of acquiring land and constructing a building, which includes capitalized interest.

EXHIBIT 11–2: Computation of Interest to be Capitalized—X Corporation

Panel A—Capitalization Period—The interest capitalization period started on January 1, 19C, because *(a)* expenditures were being made, *(b)* activities had started to get the asset ready for its intended use, and *(c)* interest cost was being incurred. The capitalization period continued through 19C and ended December 31, 19C, because the building was essentially completed and ready for use on that date.

Panel B—Computation of Interest to be Capitalized:

1. Interest on the land note is capitalized as a cost of the building because it was acquired as the building site.
2. Steps each quarter to compute (1) average accumulated expenditures; (2) average capitalization rate; and (3) interest to be capitalized (limited to actual interest incurred):

First Quarter 19C:

Step 1—Computation of average accumulated expenditures:

	Expenditures	Months	Dollar-Months	Average Accumulated Expenditures
January 1 land	$ 30,000	× 3	$ 90,000	
March 31 construction	90,000	× 0	-0-	
Accumulated	$120,000		$ 90,000	$90,000 ÷ 3 = $30,000*

Step 2—Computation of average capitalization rate:

	Principal		
Land note, 15%	$20,000	× 15% × 3/12 = $ 750	
Long-term note, 10%	50,000	× 10% × 3/12 = 1,250	
Total	$70,000	$2,000	$2,000 ÷ $70,000 = 2.86%

Step 3—Interest potentially capitalizable ($30,000 × 2.86%)	$ 858	
Maximum capitalizable (cap), actual interest (per above)	2,000	
Capitalize lower amount		$858

Second Quarter 19C:

Step 1—Computation of average accumulated expenditures:

From 1st quarter	$120,000	× 3	$360,000	
June 30 construction	89,000	× 0	-0-	
Accumulated	$209,000		$360,000	$360,000 ÷ 3 = $120,000*

Step 2—Computation of average capitalization rate; no change from 1st quarter		2.86%
Step 3—Interest potentially capitalizable ($120,000 × 2.86%)	$3,432	
Maximum capitalizable (cap), actual interest; same as 1st quarter	2,000	
Capitalize lower amount		$2,000

Third Quarter 19C:

Step 1—Computation of average accumulated expenditures:

From 2d quarter	$209,000	× 3	$627,000	
September 30 construction	58,000	× 0	-0-	
Accumulated	$267,000		$627,000	$627,000 ÷ 3 = $209,000*

Step 2—Computation of average capitalization rate:

Land note, 15%	$ 20,000	× 15% × 3/12 = $ 750	
Long-term note, 10%	50,000	× 10% × 3/12 = 1,250	
Construction note, 16%	150,000	× 16% × 3/12 = 6,000	
Total	$220,000	$8,000	$8,000 ÷ $220,000 = 3.64%

Step 3—Interest potentially capitalizable ($209,000 × 3.64%)	$7,608	
Maximum capitalizable (cap), actual interest (per above)	8,000	
Capitalize lower amount		$7,608

Fourth Quarter 19C:

Step 1—Computation of average accumulated expenditures:

From 3d quarter	$267,000	× 3	$801,000	
December 31 construction	45,000	× 0	-0-	
Accumulated	$312,000		$801,000	$801,000 ÷ 3 = $267,000*

Step 2—Computation of average capitalization rate; no change from 3d quarter		3.64%
Step 3—Interest potentially capitalizable ($267,000 × 3.64%)	$9,719	
Maximum capitalizable (cap), actual interest (per above)	8,000	
Capitalize lower amount		$8,000

Panel C—Summary for Year 19C (computed above by quarter):

Total actual interest cost ($2,000 + $2,000 + $8,000 + $8,000) = $20,000
Total interest capitalized ($858 + $2,000 + $7,608 + $8,000) = 18,466
Difference—interest expense reported on income statement = $ 1,534

* These amounts are the same as the beginning quarterly amounts only because of the simplifying assumption in this illustration that all expenditures are made at the end of each quarter.

In Exhibit 11–1, Panel B, entries 1 through 3 would be made at the time each transaction occurred and entry 4 would be made at the end of the accounting period to capitalize the appropriate amount of interest on the construction project. Cash is credited for interest ($3,000) on the land note and on the long-term note ($5,000) because their terms require interest payments each December 31. The building note requires interest payment on June 30; therefore, interest for six months ($12,000) must be accrued. Observe that in entry 4, $18,466 of interest is capitalized and $1,534 of interest is expensed, as discussed below.

Exhibit 11–2 presents the computation of **interest to be capitalized on the construction project** during 19C. Panel A indicates that X Corporation met the three conditions required for capitalization, and Panel B indicates that the interest on the land note should be capitalized as part of the cost of the **building** (not the land) because the land was acquired specifically as a building site.[10]

Panel B of Exhibit 11–2 presents the computation of the interest cost to be capitalized by X Corporation during 19C, and Panel C presents a summary of the results. For capitalization purposes, X Corporation decided to use the average quarterly rates on **all borrowings outstanding.** This computation involves three separate steps for each quarter, viz:

Step 1—Computation of the average accumulated expenditures.[11]

Step 2—Computation of the weighted-average capitalization rate.

Step 3—Computation of the *(a)* interest potentially capitalizable (based upon expenditures), and *(b)* maximum interest capitalizable (the "cap," actual interest incurred) and selection of the lower of these two amounts as the amount of **interest to be capitalized.**

Note that in computing the average accumulated expenditures (step 1) that interest capitalized at the end of the prior quarters is included in the cumulative expenditure amount.

Because X Corporation accumulates construction costs by quarters (see Exhibit 11–1), the capitalizable interest is computed for each quarter. Exhibit 11–2, Panel B, indicates that, for the first quarter of 19C, the average accumulated expenditures on which interest should be capitalized was $30,000. The weighted-average interest rate for the first quarter was 2.86 percent, and the interest potentially capitalizable for the first quarter was $858 (i.e., $30,000 × 2.86 percent). The total interest cost for the first quarter was $2,000. Because total interest (i.e., $2,000) exceeds the interest potentially capitalizable (i.e., $858), the amount of interest to be capitalized for the first quarter is $858. If total interest for the first quarter had been less than capitalizable interest (say $500), only $500 of interest cost would have been capitalized as part of the cost of the building. For the year, interest of $18,466 is capitalized and interest of $1,534 is expensed, as shown in the summary at the bottom of Exhibit 11–2.

Exhibit 11–3 presents the effects of the above transactions on the financial statements of X Corporation for 19C.

In Exhibits 11–2 and 11–3, the capitalization rates each quarter were computed as the **average interest rate on all borrowings** during the period. An alternate procedure permitted by *FASB Statement 34,* pars. 13 and 50–52 relates the specific amounts of interest on the land and building notes to the construction project and uses an average rate based on other (i.e., non-construction) borrowings which would be applied to the remaining construction expenditures during the period. Either procedure is acceptable.

EXPENDITURES SUBSEQUENT TO ACQUISITION

Repairs and Maintenance

After acquisition, numerous costs are incurred related to the **use** of operational assets. Examples include repairs, maintenance, betterments, and replacements. What outlays should be debited to the asset account, to the accumulated depreciation account, to expense, or to some combination of these

[10] Land not undergoing activity to ready it for use does not qualify for interest capitalization. Land being developed as land for sale (for example, developed lots) qualifies, and interest should be capitalized as part of the cost of the land. Otherwise, any interest capitalized on debt related to land should be debited to a building account or other account for the structure being built thereon (see *FASB Statement 34,* par. 11).

[11] Some accountants would include in the average accumulated expenditures the amount of interest capitalized in prior periods (e.g., Exhibit 11–2, Second Quarter, 19C, $120,000 + $858 = $120,858, instead of the $120,000). If such interest is included, the effect would be to compound interest quarterly rather than annually as specified for the quarterly borrowings (see Exhibit 11–1, Panel A).

EXHIBIT 11–3: Capitalization of Interest on Financial Statements (partial) for 19C—X Corporation

(For basic data, see Exhibit 11–1, Panels A and B, and Exhibit 11–2, Panel C.)

Balance sheet, at 12/31/19C:		
Operational assets:		
Land, plant site		$ 30,000
Plant ($90,000 + $89,000 + $58,000 + $45,000 + $18,466)	$300,466	
Less: Accumulated depreciation	-0-	300,466
Liabilities:		
Accounts payable		15,000
Interest payable		12,000
Long-term note payable		50,000
Land note payable		20,000
Plant note payable		150,000
Income Statement, for the year ended 12/31/19C:		
Interest expense (See note)		1,534

Notes to the financial statements:
During 19C, total interest cost was $20,000, of which $18,466 was capitalized.

accounts? The problem is important because of the difficulty distinguishing between the different types of outlays, such as ordinary repairs as opposed to extraordinary repairs, and because each type of outlay requires different treatment in the accounts and financial reports.

Maintenance and Ordinary Repairs. **Maintenance costs** are those costs, such as lubrication, cleaning, adjustment, and painting, which are incurred on a continuous basis to keep operational assets in usable condition. **Ordinary repairs** (as distinguished from major repairs) are outlays for parts, labor, and related supplies which are necessary to keep the asset in operating condition but neither *(a)* add materially to the use value of the asset, nor *(b)* prolong its life appreciably. Ordinary repairs are recurring and usually involve relatively small expenditures. Examples of ordinary repairs are repairing a broken chain or electrical circuit and replacing spark plugs. Because maintenance costs and ordinary repairs are similar, they usually are combined for accounting purposes.

Ordinary repair and maintenance expense may be accounted for using either of two approaches:

1. **As incurred approach**—Expense is debited for each outlay as incurred. Since use of the asset precedes repairs, sometimes it is argued that the matching principle is not adequately implemented. However, immateriality of the amount of any difference in the amount of expense recorded under the incurred approach versus the allocation approach (see below) and the short time between use and recurring repairs mitigate the violation of strict theory.

2. **Allocation approach**—In the case of a new asset, repairs and maintenance initially will be low, increasing in amount as the asset is utilized. Repair costs also follow use and tend to vary during the year. Rather than debiting operating expense as the repairs are incurred, sometimes it is preferable to use the allocation approach. The allocation approach requires an estimate of the total cost of repairs and maintenance during *(a)* the life of the asset or *(b)* during the year, depending upon the period over which allocation is desired. The amount of estimated repairs is allocated to each interim period on the basis of time (e.g., an equal amount each month or year, as the case may be) or on the basis of production or output. Repair and Maintenance Expense is debited each period, and a liability account is credited for the estimated amount. Actual expenditures for ordinary repairs and maintenance then are debited to the liability account when incurred. To illustrate the allocation approach, assume ordinary repairs and maintenance for the year have been estimated at $18,000 and that this amount is to be allocated on a time basis (an equal amount

each month). Assume that the actual repairs and maintenance costs incurred for the first month amounted to $1,100. The entries would be as follows:

a. To record the estimated ordinary repair and maintenance expense and the related liability for the month:

Repair and maintenance expense ($18,000 ÷ 12)	1,500	
Estimated liability for repairs and maintenance		1,500

b. To record actual outlays for the month for ordinary repairs and maintenance:

Estimated liability for repairs and maintenance	1,100	
Cash or payables		1,100

The income statement would report repair and maintenance expense of $1,500 for the month. The $400 credit balance in the liability account would be reported on the interim balance sheet as a current liability because it reflects a future demand on current assets. In this example, at the end of the year any credit balance in the liability account would be debited; the offsetting credit would be transferred to the related expense account. That is, repair and maintenance expense would be adjusted to the actual cost of repairs for the period.

The allocation approach for ordinary repairs and maintenance has been accorded general acceptability by the accounting profession. In seasonal businesses, every possible repair item often is deferred to the end of the busy season at which time there is a repair "catchup." In such circumstances, matching is served better under allocation than on an as-incurred basis. However, in some situations the allocation method may be used inappropriately to manipulate income.

Extraordinary Repairs and Renewals

Extraordinary or major repairs involve relatively large amounts, are not recurring in nature, and usually increase the **use value** (efficiency and use utility) or the service life of the asset beyond what it was before the repair. There are two acceptable **alternative** approaches to accounting for extraordinary repairs:

1. **Increase the asset account**—If the expenditure serves primarily to increase the use value (utility), the cost is debited to the related asset account.
2. **Reduce the accumulated depreciation account**—If the expenditure serves primarily to increase the service life of the asset (and perhaps the residual value), the cost is debited to the related accumulated depreciation account.

In either case, the revised book value (cost minus accumulated depreciation) is the **same.** The revised book value, taking residual value into consideration, is depreciated over the estimated remaining life. Examples of extraordinary repairs are major overhauls, major improvements in the electrical system, and strengthening the foundation of a building.

Because of the difficulty of making a realistic distinction between increase in utility and increase in useful life as a result of extraordinary repairs, and because the two approaches give the same net results (with the same set of facts), both are widely used. Often the depreciation rate must be revised.

Replacements and Betterments

Replacement involves the removal of a major part or component of plant or equipment and the substitution of a new part or component of essentially the **same type and performance capabilities.** Replacement may involve specific subunits or a number of major items similar in many respects to an extraordinary repair. In fact, the line between replacements and extraordinary repairs often is difficult to draw.

In contrast to a replacement, a **betterment,** or improvement, constitutes the removal of a major part or component of plant or equipment and the substitution of a different part or component having significantly **improved and superior** performance capabilities. The result of the improved substitute is to increase the overall efficiency of the asset and also to increase the **useful life** of the primary asset. The replacement of an old shingle roof with a modern fireproof tile roof, installing a more powerful engine in a shrimp boat, and replacement with an improved electrical system in a building are examples of betterments.

Because of the different circumstances in which **replacements and betterments** are made, three different accounting approaches are used, viz:

1. **Substitution**—Conceptually this method assumes a disposal of the old unit and acquisition of a new unit. Therefore, these two separate events are recorded as follows:
   a. The cost of the old unit replaced is removed from the asset account, the accumulated depreciation on the old unit is removed, and a loss on disposal is recognized.
   b. The new replacement unit is debited to the asset account.

   To illustrate, assume the old shingle roof on Building A, original cost $20,000, 80 percent depreciated, is replaced by a fireproof tile roof that cost $60,000. The two entries (which could be combined) are as follows:

   a. To remove old roof from the accounts:

Accumulated depreciation		
(old roof, $20,000 × 80%)	16,000	
Loss on disposal of plant assets	4,000	
Building (old roof)		20,000

   b. To record acquisition of new roof:

Building (new roof)	60,000	
Cash		60,000

   Theoretically, this method is sound; however, it can be applied only when the cost of the old subunit and the related accumulated depreciation are known or can be reliably estimated.
2. **Capitalize**—This approach is used when the old costs and related accumulated depreciation amounts are not known, and when the primary effect is to increase efficiency (i.e., a betterment), rather than to lengthen the economic life of the basic asset. The cost of the betterment is debited to the primary asset in conformity with the cost principle. In this approach, the cost and accumulated depreciation on the unit replaced are not removed from the accounts because they cannot be determined reliably. Often the depreciation rate must be revised.
3. **Reduce accumulated depreciation**—This approach is recommended when the primary effect is to lengthen the remaining life of the related asset (a replacement); however, it is used as a full-fledged alternative to capitalization in the asset account. The cost of the replacement is debited to the related accumulated depreciation account on the basis that it is a recovery of past depreciation and that the life of the primary asset is lengthened. The cost and accumulated depreciation on the unit replaced are not removed from the accounts. Often the depreciation rate must be revised.

In their 1979 annual reports, Borden, Inc.; FMC Corporation; and Getty Oil Company disclosed that they capitalize the cost of extraordinary repairs, renewals, and betterments, and they expense the cost of ordinary repairs and maintenance.[12]

Additions

Additions are extensions, enlargements, or expansions made to an existing asset. Examples are an extra wing or room added to a building and the addition of a production unit to an existing machine. An addition represents a capital expenditure and should be recorded in the operational asset accounts at acquisition cost. Work done on the existing structure, such as shoring up the foundation to accommodate the addition or the cutting of an entranceway through an existing wall, should be regarded as a part of the cost of the addition and capitalized. The cost of an addition, less any estimated residual value, normally should be depreciated over its own service life or the remaining life of the original asset of which it is a part, whichever period is the shorter if it is an integral part of the older asset. If not an integral part, it should be depreciated over its own useful life.

Pollution control devices have been added by many entities to comply with laws and court or administrative orders. Sometimes, either because the original assets (which are the source of the pollution) were acquired when prices were low or because of stringency of the control regulations, the antipollution devices are quite costly in relation to the original assets. The devices themselves are capitalizable as plant additions.

A question arises as to the accounting classification of fines, damages, or penalties assessed for earlier pollution. Some people have argued that such costs should be expensed in the current period; others contend the costs should be capitalized and depreciated over future periods. The authors prefer the first alternative.

---

[12] For details, see the "Disclosure of Accounting Policies" in each company's annual report.

Rearrangement of Assets

The cost of reinstallation, rerouting, or rearrangement of factory machinery to increase efficiency should be capitalized if the benefits of the rearrangement will extend beyond the current accounting period. Such costs should be capitalized as a deferred charge and amortized over the ensuing periods benefiting from the rearrangement. If no measurable future benefit is to be derived from such outlays, or if the periods benefited cannot be estimated reliably, such expenditures should be expensed as incurred.

RETIREMENT OF OPERATIONAL ASSETS

Operational assets may be retired voluntarily by sale, trade, or abandonment—or involuntarily lost as a result of casualty, such as fire or storm. If the asset is subject to depreciation, it should be depreciated to the date of retirement. Likewise, taxes, insurance premium costs, and similar costs should be accrued up to the date of retirement. At the date of retirement, the cost of the asset and its related accumulated depreciation should be removed from the accounts. To illustrate, assume a truck costing $32,000 on February 1, 19A, is sold on July 1, 19E, for $6,500. Straight-line depreciation has been recorded on the basis of an estimated service life of five years and an estimated residual value of $2,000. The company closes its books on December 31 of each year. The entries at date of sale would be as follows:

1. Depreciation expense	3,000	
Accumulated depreciation—equipment		3,000

To record 6 months' depreciation for 19E at $500 per month computed as follows:

Amount to be depreciated ($32,000 − $2,000)	$30,000
Service life—5 years or 60 months.	
Depreciation, $30,000 × 6/60	3,000

2. Cash	6,500	
Accumulated depreciation—equipment ($30,000 × 53/60)	26,500	
Delivery equipment		32,000
Gain on sale of equipment*		1,000

To record retirement of old truck by sale:

* Sales price			$6,500
Less book value of asset sold:			
Original cost		$32,000	
Accumulated depreciation:			
19A—11 months	$5,500		
19B—12 months	6,000		
19C—12 months	6,000		
19D—12 months	6,000		
19E—6 months	3,000	26,500	5,500
Gain on sale			$1,000

The accounting entries for an exchange were discussed and illustrated earlier in the chapter. If an operational asset is abandoned or disposed of because it has no value, the cost and accumulated depreciation amounts should be removed from the accounts and any loss on abandonment, including costs of disposal, recognized.

Outlays made to restore and repair uninsured assets damaged through fire, storm, or other casualty should be recorded as losses and closed to the Income Summary account.[13] Outlays made to improve properties beyond their approximate operating condition prior to the casualty should be apportioned between losses and the asset. Damaged assets not restored should be reduced to a carrying value consistent with the decrease in going-concern utility. Accounting for **insured** casualty losses is discussed in Chapter 13.

[13] When the casualty loss is both *(a)* unusual and *(b)* occurs infrequently, as defined in *APB Opinion 30*, it must be reported as an extraordinary item.

Supplement 11-A: Acquisition Costs of Specific Operational Assets

In determining the acquisition cost of an operational asset, the general principles discussed heretofore are applicable; however, certain items of property give rise to special problems in applying the general principles. These special problems are considered below.

Land

The acquisition cost of land should be recorded in an account captioned Land or Real Estate. Some of the specific elements of land cost include the following:

1. Original contract price.
2. Broker's commission.
3. Legal fees for examining and recording ownership.
4. Cost of ownership guarantee insurance policies.
5. Cost of real estate surveys.
6. Cost of an option when it is exercised.
7. Cost of razing an old building (net of any salvage).
8. Cost of canceling an unexpired lease.
9. Payment by the purchaser of accrued or unpaid taxes on the land to date of purchase.

On the other hand, the cost of land does not include fees for surveying, ownership searches, geological options, legal and other expert services on land **not** purchased; nor does it include expenditures in connection with disposal of refuse, costs of easements or rights-of-way which are limited as to time, assessments for repairs to roads and sidewalks, or repairs to other improvements.

Land improvements, such as paving, fencing, and lighting, should be set up in separate asset accounts and depreciated. Unlike the land itself, these items have finite lives. Some costs incurred to improve the usefulness of land confer such lasting or permanent benefits that they can be legitimately debited to the Land account. Examples include costs associated with draining, clearing, landscaping, landfilling, grading, and installing of sewers.

Companies sometimes acquire rights to use land for long periods. These include leases and easements (i.e., rights to use the land for facilities such as tracks, building sites, and parking lots).

Lease accounting is discussed in Chapter 19. Where amounts are paid over a specific period, it is necessary to amortize any advanced down payment (in excess of the periodic rents) over the term of the contract. Periodic rentals are expensed as incurred.

A special problem arises concerning the treatment of taxes and carrying charges in respect to real estate held for investment or for future use. From a conservative point of view, such charges should be recorded as current expenses. However, accounting theory tends to hold the view that since the asset is not producing revenue against which the charges may be offset, the carrying charges should be capitalized, particularly when the market value of the property is increasing. If the real estate is producing revenue through rent, for example, or is declining in value, there are sound reasons for treating the carrying costs as a current expense. Such charges may be either capitalized or expensed for income tax purposes.

Buildings

Specific cost elements of buildings include the following:

1. Original contract price or cost of construction.
2. Expenses incurred in remodeling, reconditioning, or altering a purchased building to make it suitable for the purpose for which it was acquired.
3. Cost of excavation or grading or filling of land for the specific building.
4. Expenses incurred for the preparation of plans, specifications, blueprints, and so on.
5. Cost of building permits.
6. Payment by the purchaser of unpaid or accrued taxes on the building to date of purchase.
7. Architects' and engineers' fees for design and supervision.
8. Other costs such as temporary buildings used during the construction period.
9. Unanticipated expenditures such as rock blasting, piling, or relocation of the channel of an underground stream.

The cost of a building should include neither extraordinary costs incidental to the erection of the building, such as those due to a strike, flood, fire, or other casualty, nor the cost of abandoned construction.

Removable building equipment may have a shorter life than the building and may be subject to replacement without impairment of the integrity of the building, in which case it should be separately recorded as building equipment and separately depreciated. Razing costs of a building that has been used by an entity should be identified with the retirement of the old building.

Machinery, Furniture, Fixtures, and Equipment

Specific cost elements of machinery, furniture, fixtures, and equipment include the following:

1. Original contract or invoice cost.
2. Freight-in, import duties, handling and storage costs.

3. Specific in-transit insurance costs.
4. Sales, use, and other taxes imposed on the acquisition.
5. Costs of preparation of foundations, protective apparatus, and other costs in connection with making a proper site for the asset.
6. Installation costs, including company overhead on the same basis as it is debited to inventory.
7. Costs of testing and preparation for use.
8. Costs of reconditioning used items when purchased.

Because machine and hand tools are relatively low in cost per unit, are frequently lost or broken, and thus have a short service life, they normally are not accorded the same treatment as other tangible operational assets; rather they are accounted for in one of three ways, viz:

1. Capitalized at date of purchase, periodically inventoried, and the asset account adjusted to their inventory value in present condition, thereby debiting the losses due to wear and tear, breakage, theft, and disappearance to current expense.
2. Capitalized as an asset at a conservative valuation for the ordinary or normal stock; all subsequent tool purchases are then debited to current expense.
3. Expensed as acquired (see Chapter 12).

Patterns and Dies

Patterns and dies are used in the fabrication of many manufactured items such as automobile bodies and firearms. Patterns and dies used for regular production over a period of time should be recorded in an operational asset account, Patterns and Dies, and depreciated over their estimated service lives. Patterns and dies that are purchased or constructed for a particular job or order should be debited directly to the cost of that job.

Leasehold Improvements

Improvements on **leased** property, such as buildings, walks, landscaping, and certain types of permanent equipment (generally referred to as fixtures), unless specifically exempted in the lease agreement, revert to the owner of the property upon termination of the lease. Improvements on leased property of this nature are referred to as **leasehold improvements.** The cost of such improvements should be capitalized by the lessee in a tangible operational asset account entitled Leasehold Improvements (considered by some to be an intangible asset). The cost of the leasehold improvements should be depreciated over the term of the lease or the service life of the improvement, whichever is the shorter. Renewal provisions in the lease agreement normally are disregarded in depreciating leasehold improvements.

QUESTIONS

PART A

1. Operational assets used in day-to-day business operations can be classified as tangible or intangible; distinguish between the two, giving examples. Under what balance sheet caption are tangible operational assets reported? Give at least one synonym for whatever title you specify.

2. Distinguish between *capital* and *revenue* expenditures. What accounting implications are involved?

3. Relate the *cost principle* to the acquisition of operational assets. Relate the *matching principle* to operational asset accounting.

4. How is asset acquisition cost determined when the consideration given is securities?

5. In determining the cost of an operational asset, how should the following items be treated: *(a)* invoice price, *(b)* freight, *(c)* discounts, *(d)* title verification costs, *(e)* installation costs, *(f)* breaking-in costs, and *(g)* cost of major overhaul before operational use?

6. A machine is purchased on the following terms: cash, $40,000, plus 10 semiannual payments of $5,000 each. How should the acquisition cost of the machine be recorded? Explain.

7. Basically, how are assets recorded when they are acquired by exchanging another asset?

8. When several assets are bought for a single lump-sum consideration, a cost apportionment procedure is usually employed. Explain the procedure. Why is apportionment necessary?

9. Should donated assets be reflected in the accounts? If so, how should they be recorded and at what value?

10. What is discovery value? If discovery value is reflected in the accounts, what is the effect on subsequent expense amounts?

PART B

11. Some businesses self-construct plant assets. What costs should be capitalized? In connection with self-construction of assets, explain what to do with *(a)* general company overhead and *(b)* any excess costs incurred.

12. Capitalization of interest during the period operational assets were under construction has been a widespread practice in one industry. Identify the industry; explain why interest capitalization was practiced in that industry.

13. Basically, what amount of interest is capitalized as a part of the cost of an asset?

14. For what types of assets requiring a substantial completion or processing time is interest capitalization inappropriate?

15. Where interest is properly being capitalized on an asset requiring a substantial completion period, when must interest capitalization cease?

16. What types of debt do *not* give rise to capitalized interest?

17. XYZ Company borrowed $2 million at 12% to finance construction of a new loading pier which turned out to cost $3 million aside from capitalized interest. XYZ owes other debt. To what extent, if any, can interest in excess of $240,000 be capitalized in any full year the pier is under construction. As to the other debt, how is the rate determined for capitalization purposes?

18. Distinguish between maintenance, ordinary repairs, and extraordinary repairs.

19. Explain the accounting for *(a)* extraordinary repairs, *(b)* replacements, and *(c)* betterments.

20. The XY Corporation added a new wing at a cost of $300,000, plus $10,000 spent in making passageways through the walls of an old structure to the existing plant. The plant was 10 years old and was being depreciated by an equal amount each year over a 30-year life. Over what period should the new wing be depreciated?

21. What are *leasehold improvements?* How should they be accounted for?

22. Outline the accounting steps related to the disposition of an operational asset assuming it is not traded in on another asset.

DECISION CASE 11–1

One of your clients, a savings bank with several local branches, recently acquired ownership to a lot and building located in a historical part of the city. The building was in a dilapidated condition, unsuitable for human habitation. The bank thought at the time that it was acquiring a site for a new branch. Although a firm of architects recommended demolition, the city council, in whose discretion such activity rests, refused consent to demolish the building in view of its historical and architectural value.

In order to comply with safety requirements and to make the building suitable for use as a branch location, the bank spent $250,000 restoring and altering the old building. It had paid $90,000 for the building and lot, and had contemplated spending $200,000 on a new building after demolishing the old structure. Somewhat similar old buildings in less run-down condition could have been bought in the same area for about the same $90,000 price. It is possible, even likely, that some of these which were not so old could have been demolished without governmental intervention, and the bank could have carried out its original plan.

Now that the restoration has been completed and the bank is making final plans to open its newest branch in the restored building, the bank has been informed by the State Historical Commission that the building qualifies for and will receive a plaque designating it as a historical site. This designation will be of some value in attracting traffic to the site, will probably result in the building being pointed out when tours of the city visit the area, and so on. Under present laws, receipt of the designation may well mean that the bank can never demolish the structure and is obligated to preserve it, even if the property is later vacated.

Required:

1. Discuss the pros and cons of capitalizing the entire $250,000 spent on restoration of the building.
2. How should the $90,000 original expenditure be treated?

What would have been the cost of the land if the bank had been able to carry out its original plans?

3. Sooner or later, your client is likely to seek advice as to proper accounting for subsequent costs—repairs, depreciation, possible improvements, and so on. What advice would you give?

DECISION CASE 11–2

A corporation which does not have a subsidiary ledger for plant recorded the construction of a new factory building by the following entry:

Factory building	xx	
Cash		xx

After reviewing contracts and cost data, the corporation's public accountant recommended that the company use the following classifications in future accounting for the building:

Building foundation	$xx
Framing and sheathing	xx
Outside finish	xx
Roof	xx
Interior finish	xx
Partitions	xx
Acoustical ceiling	xx
Electric wiring	xx
Electric fixtures	xx
Furnace	xx
Boiler	xx
Plumbing system	xx

What might be the advantages (or disadvantages) of following the recommendation? Discuss fully from the standpoint of the effect of the recommendation on maintenance, depreciation, and retirement.

(AICPA adapted)

DECISION CASE 11–3

The invoice price of a machine is $10,000. Various other costs relating to the acquisition and installation of the machine amount to $4,000 and include such things as transportation, electrical wiring, special base, and so forth. The machine has an estimated life of 10 years and no residual value.

The owner of the business suggests that the incidental costs of $4,000 be debited to expense immediately for three reasons: (1) if the machine should be sold, these costs cannot be recovered in the sales price; (2) the inclusion of the $4,000 in the machinery account will not necessarily result in a closer approximation of the market price of this asset over the years because of the possibility of changing price levels; and (3) debiting the $4,000 to expense immediately will reduce federal income taxes.

Required:

Discuss each of the points raised by the owner of the business.

(AICPA adapted)

DECISION CASE 11–4

ABC Smelting Company, which operates in the southwest, agreed in a court settlement to:

a. Install pollution control equipment on its smelters at an estimated cost of $23 million.

b. Pay specified medical expenses for children living near its facilities who were suffering from lead poisoning; tentatively estimated cost of $2 million to be paid as families incur expenses.

c. Pay the city and state a civil penalty of $250,000 over a four-year term in equal $62,500 installments.

Required:

1. For each item above, discuss the propriety of capitalizing versus expensing the cost.
2. What amount should be ascribed to each item immediately after the settlement (before any payments are made)?

EXERCISES

PART A: EXERCISES 11–1 to 11–10

Exercise 11–1

When examining the accounts of a new corporate client, you encounter the following items at year-end:

	Identity	Description or Added Data	Valuation Data
a.	Franchise	Just acquired as perpetual franchise.	Cost, $60,000
b.	Land	Purchased last year for future plant site.	Cost, $160,000
c.	Building	Purchased 12 years ago for whse. (depreciated over 45-year life by straight-line method; no residual value).	Cost, $450,000
d.	Patent	Purchased three years ago (half of useful life has elapsed and is reflected by amortization recorded).	Cost, $58,000
e.	Fixtures	Purchased at start of current year (straight line, 20-year life, no residual value).	Cost, $30,000
f.	Returnable containers	Bought three years ago (depreciated on basis of 10-year life by straight-line method; 20% are expected not to be returned).	Cost, $30,000
g.	Goodwill	Arose when business acquired a division in 19B which has since been merged in as integral part of client corporation.	Remaining unamortized balance, $64,000
h.	Land	Bought for speculative purposes last year.	Cost, $92,000
i.	Hand tools	Bought at various times.	Remaining balance is value at date of examination, $8,000

Required:
Indicate the balance sheet classification and amount for each of the foregoing items.

Exercise 11–2

What is the proper cost to use for recording the land in each of the following independent cases? Give reasons in support of your answer.

Case A—At the middle of the current year gave a check for $31,000 for the land and assumed the liability for unpaid taxes: taxes in arrears last year, $900; assessed for current year, $200.

Case B—Issued 1,000 shares of capital stock for the land. The par value of the stock was $50 per share; the market value (stock sells daily with an average daily volume of 5,000 shares) was $63 per share at time of purchase of land. Vendor offered to sell the land for $62,000 cash. Competent appraisers valued the land at $64,000.

Case C—Issued 14,000 shares (par value per share of $1) par value capital stock with a "market value" of $6 per share (based upon a recent sale of ten shares) for the land. The land was recently appraised at $80,000 by competent appraisers.

Case D—Rejected an offer two years ago by the vendor to sell the land for $7,500 cash. Issued 1,000 shares of capital stock for the land (market value of the stock based on several recent large transactions, $7.20 with normal weekly stock trading volume).

Exercise 11–3

a. Delivery equipment was purchased having a list price of $24,000; terms were 2/10, n/30. Payment was made within the discount period.

b. Delivery equipment was purchased having a list price of $18,000; terms were 2/10, n/30. Payment was made after the discount period.

c. Delivery equipment listed at $10,000 was purchased and invoiced at 2/10, n/30. In order to take advantage of the discount, the company borrowed $8,000 of the purchase price by issuance of a 60-day, 18% note which was paid with interest at maturity.

Required:
Give entries in each separate situation for costs, borrowing, and any expenses involved.

Exercise 11–4

Baines Company purchased a machine, having an estimated 10-year useful life, on a time payment plan. The list price of the machine was $62,500. Terms were $14,000 cash down payment plus three equal annual payments of $20,000 each to include interest on the unpaid balance at 16% per annum.

Required (round to nearest dollar):

a. Give entry to record the purchase.

b. Give entry for depreciation at the end of one year assuming straight-line depreciation and no residual value.

c. Give entry to record the last $20,000 payment.

Exercise 11–5

For each of the following numbered items, indicate, by using one of the five lettered choices listed below, which accounting treatment is correct. Explain questionable items and assumptions you make. Each cost, identified as a numbered item, was incurred by a corporation incident to acquisition of a new machine.

Lettered Choices:

a. Increases or decreases Machinery account.
b. Debit an expense account for current period.
c. Debit Prepaid Expense or Deferred Charge and amortize separately from machinery.
d. Debit Plant, Property, and Equipment account (other than machinery).
e. An accounting treatment other than the four choices above. Explain.

Items Affecting Cost:

1. Invoice price of the machinery, before discount.
2. Cash discount for prompt payment of foregoing invoice, not taken.
3. Cost of moving machinery into place.
4. Cost of installing sound insulation so new machine will not disturb those who work near it.
5. Cost of removing old machine which this machinery replaced.
6. Sales tax based on purchase price of new machinery.
7. Special electrical wiring required to connect new machine.
8. Enlargement of electrical system of plant to accommodate new machine and provide for some expected future needs.
9. Service contract paid in full covering first two years' operation of the machine.
10. Cost of materials used while testing new machine.
11. Payment to technicians who assisted with break-in of new machine.
12. Cost of training three of our employees who will operate machine.
13. Debit to machine which was offest by credit to Miscellaneous Revenue amounting to anticipated first year's savings from use of new machine.
14. Insurance premium paid covering first year of protection of new machine against hazards to which it will be exposed.
15. Repair incurred during first year of operations.

Exercise 11–6

Williams Company purchased a tract of land on which were located a warehouse and an office building. The cash purchase price was $154,000 plus $9,000 fees in connection with the purchase. The following data were collected concerning the property:

	Tax Assessment	Vendor's Book Value	Original Cost
Land	$20,000	$10,000	$10,000
Warehouse	40,000	15,000	50,000
Office building	60,000	25,000	80,000

Required:
Journalize the purchase; show computations.

Exercise 11–7

Katz Company bought a machine on a time payment plan. The cash purchase price was $22,789. Terms were $6,000 cash down payment plus four equal annual payments of $6,000 which includes interest on the unpaid balance at 16% per annum.

Required:

1. Give entry to record the purchase. Show computations (round to nearest dollar).
2. Give entry to record depreciation at the end of the first full year assuming straight-line depreciation, an eight-year life, and no residual value.
3. Prepare a schedule to reflect the accounting entries for each of the four installment payments. Round amounts in schedule to nearest dollar.

Exercise 11–8

Select the best answer for each of the following. Briefly justify your choice for each item.

1. If a corporation purchased a lot and building and subsequently demolished the building and now uses the property as a parking lot, the accounting treatment of the cost of the building at acquisition would depend on—
   a. The significance of the cost allocated to the building in relation to the combined cost of the lot and building.
   b. The length of time for which the building was held prior to its demolition.
   c. The contemplated future use of the parking lot.
   d. The intention of management for the property when the building was acquired.
2. Property, plant, and equipment may properly include
   a. Cash paid on machinery purchased but not yet received.
   b. Idle equipment awaiting sale.
   c. Property held for investment purposes.
   d. Land held for possible future plant site.
   e. None of the above.
3. If the present value of a note issued in exchange for a plant asset is less than its face amount, the difference should be:
   a. Included in the cost of the asset.
   b. Amortized as interest expense over the life of the note.
   c. Amortized as interest expense over the life of the asset.
   d. Included in interest expense in the year of issuance.
4. When a closely held corporation issues preferred stock for land, the land should be recorded at the
   a. Total par value of the stock issued.
   b. Total book value of the stock issued.

c. Appraised value of the land.
d. Total liquidating value of the stock issued.

5. The debit for a sales tax levied and paid on the purchase of machinery preferably would be to—
   a. The Machinery account.
   b. A separate Deferred Charge account.
   c. Miscellaneous Tax Expense (which includes all taxes other than those on income).
   d. Accumulated Depreciation, Machinery.
6. The Wise Corporation purchased a new machine on October 31, 19A. A $250 down payment was made, and three monthly installments of $800 each are to be made beginning on November 30, 19A. The cash price would have been $2,500. Wise paid no installation charges under the monthly payment plan, but a $50 installation charge would have been incurred with a cash purchase. The amount to be capitalized as the cost of the machine during 19A would be—
   a. $2,700.
   b. $2,650.
   c. $2,550.
   d. $1,850.
   e. None of the above.

(AICPA adapted)

Exercise 11–9

Grant Company has some old equipment that cost $57,500; accumulated depreciation is $34,000. This equipment was traded in on a new machine that had a list price of $70,000; however, the new machine could be purchased without a trade-in for $65,000 cash. The difference is to be paid as cash.

Required:
Give the entry to record the acquisition of the new machine under each of the following independent cases:

Case A—The new machine was purchased for cash with no trade-in.

Case B—The equipment and the machine are dissimilar. The old machine is traded in, and $45,000 cash is paid.

Case C—Same as Case B except that the equipment and the machine are similar.

Exercise 11–10

When construction was in progress on what later became a notable skyscraper and landmark in one of the nation's largest cities, construction had advanced to the point that the basement and two above-ground stories of steelwork were completed. It was then noticed that parts of the structure were sinking. This development made it necessary to remove the partial structure, reexcavate for the foundation, install pilings to prevent future sinking, and then to replicate the prior work.

Required:

1. Assume the owner of the building (i.e., not the contractor) will absorb the additional costs because the building is being erected under a cost-plus contract. Should the added costs be capitalized by the owner, or should only the costs originally incurred be capitalized as the cost of the building and the additional costs recorded and reported in some other way? If the latter, explain why and how.
2. Assume instead that the contractor, not the building owner, was required to absorb the additional costs. Should the contractor capitalize the additional costs or account for them in some other way? Explain.

PART B: EXERCISES 11–11 to 11–18

Exercise 11–11

Kelsey Company manufactured a new machine for its own use. The ledger account below reflects related debits and credits made during the year to the Machinery account. The machinery was ready for use at the end of the year.

Machinery (new)

Cost of dismantling old machine replaced	1,900	Cash proceeds from sale of old machine	1,500
Labor costs	22,000		
Raw materials used	24,000		
Installation costs	3,000		
Materials spoiled	800		
Profit on construction	5,000		
Spare parts	4,500		
Auxiliary tools	3,000		

Your investigation revealed the following additional facts:

1. The old machine that was removed had originally cost $30,000; accumulated depreciation was $29,000.
2. The manufacturing overhead account balance is $200,000; you determine that 94% of this relates to ordinary manufacture and the remainder to the self-construction.
3. Cash discounts average 2% on all raw material purchases; the entire amount of discounts taken was recorded as Purchase Discounts.
4. The installation costs represent a payment to outsiders for technical assistance during the break-in period of the machine.
5. Materials spoiled represent the cost of materials used during the testing and break-in period.
6. Profit on construction was credited to an account with

that title. Kelsey Company estimates it saved at least $5,000 by self-constructing the machinery instead of purchasing it.

7. The debit for spare parts represents the cost of parts purchased and set aside to cover breakdowns and maintenance during the first two years of normal use of the machinery.
8. Auxiliary tools are items used in conjunction with the machine which have an estimated useful life of five years. The machine is expected to last from 10 to 12 years.

Required:
Prepare journal entries to correct the machinery account and other accounts of Kelsey Company. Insofar as possible, key your entries to the numbers identifying data above.

Exercise 11–12

A governmental agency acquired, by foreclosure, an unprofitable coal mine which had an underground fire smoldering in it. Not wanting to be in the coal mining business, the agency offered the mine for sale. XYZ Mining Company estimated the mine market value at $1 million and estimated that it would cost $100,000 to extinguish the fire and clear the mine of accumulated smoke and residue of the fire. XYZ offered the government agency a gross price of $850,000 for the mine, but specified that $100,000 would be taken off the gross price to allow for extinguishing the fire and clearing the residue. The agency accepted the offer and at the end of 30 days received the $750,000. Receipt occurred in the next fiscal year of XYZ.

Required:
1. Give the entries that should be made on XYZ's books to record:
   a. The purchase agreement.
   b. Payment of the $750,000.
   c. Incurrence of $120,000 actual costs to extinguish the fire and perform clean-up work.
2. In view of the fact the company bought the mine at what appears to be a bargain price, discuss the propriety of recognizing the saving as "discovery value."

Exercise 11–13

Sharp Company is constructing a building for its own use and has been capitalizing interest on average expenditures on a monthly basis since development on the project began. The following data apply to March:

March 1, accumulated expenditures	4,000,000*
March 2–31, accumulated expenditures	5,000,000†

* $400,000 relates to accounts payable on which no interest is paid.

† $600,000 relates to accounts payable on which no interest is paid.

Sharp Company is obligated on the following debts:

12% note payable incurred specifically to finance the construction	$1,600,000
15% short-term note payable	2,000,000
8% mortgage note payable	1,200,000
Capitalized lease (on which March interest amounted to $3,000)	228,570

Required:
1. Determine *(a)* total interest cost to be expensed during March and *(b)* interest cost to be capitalized during March as part of the building cost.
2. Describe what effect, if any, costs of land on which the building is being erected would have on the amount of interest properly capitalizable.

Exercise 11–14

Pointer Company operates two separate plants. In plant A, the accounting policy is to consider all ordinary (minor) repairs as expense when cash outlays are made for repairs. In contrast, in plant B, the accounting policy is to use the accrual approach that debits repair and maintenance expense equally each period. Pointer Company has little seasonality in its production. Selected data for 19A are as follows:

	Plant A	**Plant B**
Estimated repair costs budgeted for year	3,000	$3,000
Actual repair costs incurred and paid:		
First quarter	600	400
Second quarter	800	700
Third quarter	1,000	1,100
Fourth quarter	700	1,000

Required:
1. Give the entries in parallel columns for each plant for each of the four quarters.
2. Would you recommend any changes in the accounting policies? Explain and justify your response.

Exercise 11–15

In this exercise all items of property concerned are operational assets, not inventory, unless specified to the contrary. "List prices" are not necessarily market values.

Required:
Give journal entries where specified to record the following transactions:

1. Land carried on the books of P Company at $20,000 is exchanged for a computer carried on the books of Q Corporation at $30,000 (cost, $35,000; accumulated depreciation, $5,000). Market value of both assets is $36,000. Journalize on books of both P and Q. The land and the computer are used in different lines of business.

2. Land carried on the books of P Company at $90,000 is exchanged for land carried on the books of Q Corporation at $78,000. Market value of each tract is $100,000. Journalize on Q's books.
3. A truck which cost P Company $6,000, on which $3,000 depreciation has been accumulated, has a market value of $3,400. It is traded to a dealer along with cash of $5,600 for a new truck which has a $12,400 list price. Journalize on P's books.
4. A truck which cost P Company $6,000, on which $5,000 depreciation has been accumulated, is traded to a dealer along with $6,300 cash boot. The new truck would have cost $7,000 if only cash had been paid; its list price is $7,500. Journalize on P's books.
5. Fixtures which cost P Company $15,000, on which $9,000 depreciation is recorded, and for which the market value is $8,000, are traded to Q Corporation along with $500 cash boot. In exchange, P received fixtures from Q carried on Q's books at cost of $13,000 less $6,000 accumulated depreciation. Journalize on books of both P and Q; if necessary, round amounts to the nearest dollar.

Exercise 11–16

Select the best choice for each of the following. Briefly justify your choice for each item.

1. The debit for a sales tax properly levied and paid on the purchase of machinery preferably would be a charge to—
   a. A separate deferred charge account.
   b. Miscellaneous tax expense (which includes all taxes other than those on income).
   c. Accumulated Depreciation, Machinery.
   d. The machinery account.
2. Hardy, Inc. purchased certain plant assets under a deferred payment contract. Hardy agreed to pay $10,000 per year for five years. The plant assets should be valued at—
   a. $50,000.
   b. $50,000 plus a "going" interest charge.
   c. Present value of a $10,000 annuity for five years at the "going" interest rate.
   d. Present value of a $10,000 annuity for five years discounted at the bank prime interest rate.
3. When a closely held corporation issues preferred stock for land, the land should be recorded at the
   a. Total par value of the stock issued.
   b. Total book value of the stock issued.
   c. Appraised value of the land.
   d. Total liquidating value of the stock issued.

Items 4, 5, and 6 are based on the following information:

Two independent companies, Beam and Wall, are in the home building business. Each owns a tract of land, being held for development, but each company would prefer to build on the other's land. Accordingly, they agree to exchange their land.

An appraiser was hired, and from his report and the companies' records, the following information was obtained:

	Beam Co.'s Land	**Wall Co.'s Land**
Cost and book value	$ 80,000	$50,000
Market value based upon appraisal	100,000	90,000

The exchange of land was made, and based on the difference in appraised values, Wall paid $10,000 cash to Beam.

4. For financial reporting purposes, Beam would recognize a pretax gain on this exchange in the amount of—
   a. $2,000.
   b. $6,000.
   c. $10,000.
   d. $20,000.
5. For financial reporting purposes, Wall would recognize a pretax gain on this exchange in the amount of—
   a. $0.
   b. $10,000.
   c. $30,000.
   d. $40,000.
6. After the exchange, Beam would record its newly acquired land on its books at—
   a. $70,000.
   b. $72,000.
   c. $80,000.
   d. $92,000.
7. The Maddox Corporation acquired land, buildings, and equipment from a bankrupt company at a lump-sum price of $90,000. At the time of acquisition, Maddox paid $6,000 to have the assets appraised. The appraisal disclosed the following values:

Land	$60,000
Building	40,000
Equipment	20,000

   What cost should be assigned to the land, buildings, and equipment, respectively?
   a. $30,000, $30,000, and $30,000.
   b. $32,000, $32,000, and $32,000.
   c. $45,000, $30,000, and $15,000.
   d. $48,000, $32,000, and $16,000.
8. An improvement made to a machine increased its market value and its production capacity by 25% without extending the machine's useful life. The cost of the improvement should be—
   a. Expensed.
   b. Debited to accumulated depreciation.

c. Capitalized in the machine account.
d. Allocated between accumulated depreciation and the machine account. (AICPA adapted)

Exercise 11–17

Select the best choice for each of the following. Briefly justify your choice for each item.

1. Property, plant, and equipment are conventionally presented in the balance sheet at—
   a. Replacement cost less accumulated depreciation.
   b. Historical cost less residual value.
   c. Original cost adjusted for general price-level changes.
   d. Acquisition cost less depreciated portion thereof.
2. In those rare instances where appraisal increments in the value of plant and equipment have been recorded, depreciation on the appraisal increments should be—
   a. Ignored because the increments have not been paid for and should not be matched with revenue.
   b. Debited to retained earnings.
   c. Debited to expense.
   d. Debited to an appropriation of retained earnings.
3. Kelly Company exchanged inventory items that cost $8,000 and normally sold for $12,000 for a new delivery truck with a list price of $13,000. The delivery truck should be recorded on Kelly's books at—
   a. $8,000.
   b. $8,667.
   c. $12,000.
   d. $13,000.
4. Good Deal Company received $20,000 in cash and a used computer with a market value of $180,000 from Harvest Corporation for Good Deal's existing computer having a market value of $200,000 and an undepreciated cost of $160,000 recorded on its books. How much gain should Good Deal recognize on this exchange, and at what amount should the acquired computer be recorded, respectively?
   a. Zero and $140,000.
   b. $4,000 and $144,000.
   c. $20,000 and $160,000.
   d. $40,000 and $180,000.
5. The Ackley Company exchanged 100 shares of Burke Company common stock, which Ackley was holding as an investment, for a piece of equipment from the Flynn Company. The Burke Company common stock, which had been purchased by Ackley for $30 per share, had a quoted market price of $34 per share at the date of exchange. The piece of equipment had a recorded amount on Flynn's books of $3,100. What journal entry should Ackley have made to record this exchange?

		Debit	Credit
a.	Equipment	3,000	
	Investment in Burke Co. common stock		3,000
b.	Equipment	3,100	
	Investment in Burke Co. common stock		3,000
	Gain		100
c.	Equipment	3,100	
	Other expense	300	
	Investment in Burke Co. common stock		3,400
d.	Equipment	3,400	
	Investment in Burke Co. common stock		3,000
	Gain		400

6. Blacker Company exchanged a business machine for a new machine. The old machine had an original cost of $3,500, an undepreciated cost of $1,600, and a market value of $2,000 when exchanged. In addition, Blacker paid $2,200 cash for the new machine. The list price of the new machine was $4,300. At what amount should the new machine be recorded for financial accounting purposes?
   a. $3,500.
   b. $3,800.
   c. $4,200.
   d. $4,300.
7. Branch Theatre Corporation recently purchased the Bergstrom Theatre and the land on which it is located. Branch plans to raze the building immediately and to build a new modern theater on the site. The cost of the Bergstrom Theatre should be
   a. Written off as an extraordinary loss in the year the theater is razed.
   b. Capitalized as part of the cost of the land.
   c. Depreciated over the period from the date of acquisition to the date that the theater is to be razed.
   d. Capitalized as part of the cost of the new theater.

(AICPA adapted)

Exercise 11–18

The plant building of Milton Company is old (estimated remaining useful life, 10 years) and demands continuous maintenance and repairs. The company's books show that the building cost $200,000, and that accumulated depreciation was $150,000 at the beginning of the current year. During the current year, the following expenditures relating to the plant building were made:

a.	Added a new storage shed attached to building, estimated useful life of eight years	$64,000

b. Removed original roof; original cost, $16,000; replaced it with guaranteed, modern roof	30,000
c. Unusual and infrequent repairs due to damage from flood in desert; repairs did not increase the use value or the economic life of the asset	4,000
d. Continuing, frequent, and low cost repairs	22,000
e. Complete overhaul of the plumbing system (old costs not known)	12,000

Required:
Give the journal entry to record each of the above items. Explain the basis for your treatment of each item.

PROBLEMS

PART A: PROBLEMS 11–1 to 11–7

Problem 11–1

An examination of the property, plant, and equipment accounts of Roebuck Company disclosed the following transactions:

a. Purchased a new machine having a list price of $20,000. Failed to take a 1% cash discount available upon full payment of the invoice within 10 days. Shipping costs paid by the vendor amounted to $100. Installation costs amounted to $250, including $100 which represented 10% of the monthly salary of the factory superintendent (installation period, two days). A wall was torn out and replaced (moved two feet) at a cost of $500 to make room for the machine.

b. Purchased an automatic counter to be attached to a machine in use. The counter cost $630. The estimated useful life of the counter was 7 years, whereas the estimated life of the machine was 10 years.

c. During the first month of operations the machine (see [a] above) became inoperative due to a defect in manufacture. The vendor repaired the machine at no cost; however, the specially trained operator was idle during the two weeks the machine was inoperative. The operator was paid the regular wages ($540) during the period, although the only work performed was to observe the repair by the factory representative.

d. After one year of use, exchanged the electric motor on a machine for a heavier motor at an exchange cash cost of $400. The new motor had a list price of $1,250. The parts list indicated a list price for the original motor of $900 (estimated life, 10 years).

e. Bought fixtures for which the list price was $4,500; paid cash $1,500 and gave a one-year, noninterest-bearing note payable for the balance. The current interest rate for this type of note was 15%. Round to nearest dollar.

f. Contracted for a building at a price of $400,000. Settlement was effected with the contractor by transferring $400,000 face value of 20-year 12% company bonds payable, at which time financial consultants advised that the bonds would sell at 94.

Required:

1. Prepare entries to record each of the above transactions. Explain and justify your decision on questionable items.
2. Record depreciation at the end of the year in which the foregoing transactions took place. Assume that all of the transactions affecting depreciation, except *(d)* and *(f)*, occurred early enough in the year to warrant recording a full year's depreciation and that *(f)* occurred at a time that would warrant depreciation for one-half year. Roebuck Company uses straight-line depreciation. None of the assets is expected to have a residual value except the fixtures (for which the residual value is $400). Estimated useful lives: fixtures, 6 years; machinery, 10 years; and building, 40 years. Make three separate entries—one for the fixtures, one for the building, and one for the machinery and related items. Transaction *(b)* took place in the year following the year for which you are to record depreciation.

Problem 11–2

Exquisite Trash Company contracted to buy a Dempster Loader, agreeing to make an equal annual payment of $9,800 at the end of each of the next three years. The Dempster Loader has a list price of $21,308, which also is the cash price, an estimated service life of five years, and estimated residual value of $1,000.

Required (round to nearest dollar):

1. Determine the approximate interest rate implicit in the contract and then record the purchase of the loader in accordance with GAAP.
2. Assuming Exquisite's fiscal year coincides with the payment dates, record the first payment and record depreciation at the end of the first year.
3. Give similar entries at the end of the third year.

Problem 11–3

Machinery with a market value of $10,000 is acquired in a noncash exchange. Below are listed seven independent assumptions as to the consideration *given* in the noncash exchange:

a. Bonds held as a long-term investment, which originally cost $19,000 and had been written down 50% because of a perceived permanent loss of their value.
b. Common stock held as a long-term investment, which originally cost $11,200 and with a book value of $9,700 (LCM) on the most recent balance sheet date.
c. Common stock held as a short-term investment, which originally cost $9,400, was included in the short-term portfolio of similar investments. The stock had a market value of $10,300 on the latest balance sheet date, at which time the Allowance for Decline in Value of Short-Term Investments reflected a balance of $1,000.
d. Inventory valued at $6,700 on the most recent balance sheet as part of a perpetual inventory carried at LCM. When originally acquired the goods had cost $7,100.
e. Similar used machinery with a book value of $3,000 and a market value of $3,400 plus cash boot of $6,600. When new, the used machinery surrendered cost $8,800.
f. Land with a book value of $7,500 and a market value of $10,000.
g. A noninterest-bearing note for $11,200 maturing in one year. Similar notes required 12% interest at the date of the exchange.

Required:
1. Give the journal entry required for each of the above independent assumptions.
2. Identify by letter those transactions which might require additional entries at end of the fiscal year in which the new machinery was acquired. Give a brief statement to support each such selection. This requirement does not apply to year-end depreciation of new or old machinery.

Problem 11–4

Bliss Company bought equipment on July 1, 19A, for which its entries throughout the 1½ years of ownership were as below:

July 1, 19A:

Equipment	25,000	
Installment note payable		25,000

December 31, 19A:

Depreciation expense (½ year)	1,250	
Accumulated depreciation		1,250

July 1, 19B:

Installment note payable	8,333	
Cash		8,333

December 31, 19B:

Depreciation expense	2,500	
Accumulated depreciation		2,500

As can be inferred from the foregoing, the equipment is being depreciated on a straight-line basis with an assumed 10-year life and zero residual value. The $25,000 installment note is payable in three equal annual installments which include interest. Assume 18% is a reasonable interest rate on debts with the risk characteristics of this installment note.

Required (round amounts to nearest dollar):
1. Prepare a schedule to reflect the entries for the note.
2. Give the journal entry or entries to correct Bliss Company's books as of December 31, 19B, on the basis that the books are still open as of that date.

Problem 11–5

Hart Company acquired a machine by trading in another machine and paying $35,000 cash. The machine traded in originally cost $40,000 and had accumulated depreciation at the date of exchange of $30,000. The market value of the machine traded in at date of exchange was $9,000. Hart is considering recording this transaction by one of the two following methods:

	Method 1		Method 2	
Machinery	44,000		45,000	
Accumulated depreciation (traded in)	30,000		30,000	
Loss on disposal of machinery	1,000			
Cash		35,000		35,000
Machinery (traded in)		40,000		40,000

Required:
1. Identify and discuss the reasons and assumptions needed for recording the above transaction using method 1.
2. Identify and discuss the reasons and assumptions needed for recording the above transaction using method 2.
3. Suppose the market value of the machine traded in was $15,000 at the time of the exchange. How would the exchange be recorded in accordance with GAAP? (Assume the same amount of cash boot as above, $35,000.)

(AICPA adapted)

Problem 11–6

Assume that the market value of equipment acquired by Roberson Company in a noncash transaction is not determinable by reference to a cash purchase.

Required:

1. Explain how Roberson Company should determine the capitalizable cost of equipment purchased by exchanging for it each of the following:
   a. Bonds which have an established market price.
   b. Common stock which does not have an established market price.
   c. Similar equipment which has a determinable market price.
2. Assume that the equipment was acquired and had been used by Roberson Company for three years. Expenditures related to the equipment must be made. Identify the various types of expenditures that might be involved and explain the appropriate accounting for each.

(AICPA adapted)

Problem 11–7

At December 31, 19A, certain accounts included in the property, plant, and equipment section of the Townsand Company's balance sheet had the following balances:

Land	$100,000
Buildings	800,000
Leasehold improvements	500,000
Machinery and equipment	700,000

During 19B, the following transactions occurred:

a. Land site number 621 was acquired for $1 million. Additionally, to acquire the land, Townsand paid a $60,000 commission to a real estate agent. Costs of $15,000 were incurred to clear the land. During the course of clearing the land, timber and gravel were recovered and sold for $5,000.

b. A second tract of land (site number 622) with a building was acquired for $300,000. The closing statement indicated that the land value was $200,000 and the building value was $100,000. Shortly after acquisition, the building was demolished at a cost of $30,000. A new building was constructed for $150,000 plus the following costs:

Excavation fees	$11,000
Architectural design fees	8,000
Building permit fee	1,000

The building was completed and occupied on September 30, 19B.

c. A third tract of land (site number 623) was acquired for $600,000 and was put on the market for resale.

d. Extensive work was done to a building occupied by Townsand under a lease agreement that expires on December 31, 19K. The total cost of the work was $125,000, which consisted of the following:

Item	Cost	Estimated Useful Life—Years
Painting of ceilings	$ 10,000	1
Electrical work	35,000	10
Construction of extension to current working area	80,000	30
	$125,000	

The lessor paid half the costs incurred in connection with the extension to the current working area.

e. During December 19B, costs of $65,000 were incurred to improve leased office space. The related lease will terminate on December 31, 19D, and is not expected to be renewed.

f. A group of new machines was purchased under a royalty agreement which provides for payment of royalties based on units of production for the machines. The invoice price of the machines was $75,000, freight costs were $2,000, unloading costs were $1,500, and royalty payments for 19B were $13,000.

Required:

1. Prepare a detailed analysis of the changes in each of the following balance sheet accounts for 19B:
   a. Land.
   b. Buildings.
   c. Leasehold improvements.
   d. Machinery and equipment.

   Disregard the related accumulated depreciation accounts.
2. List the items in the fact situation which were not used to determine the answer to 1 above, and indicate *where, or if,* these items should be included in Townsand's financial statements.

(AICPA adapted)

PART B: PROBLEMS 11–8 to 11–19

Problem 11–8

Acme Company utilized its own facilities to construct a small addition to its office building. Construction began on March 1 and was completed on June 30 of the same year. Prior to the decision to construct the asset with its own facilities, the company accepted bids from outside contractors; the lowest bid was $240,000. Detailed costs accumulated during the construction period are summarized as follows:

Materials used (incl. $120,000 for normal production)	$180,000

Direct labor (incl. $300,000 for normal production)	450,000
General supplies used on construction	8,000
Rent paid on construction machinery	3,000
Insurance premiums on construction	1,700
Supervisory salary on construction	5,000
Total gen. admin. overhead for year	115,000
Total factory overhead for year:	
Fixed ($10,000 due to construction)	100,000
Variable	60,000
Direct labor-hours (incl. 100,000 hours for normal production)	120,000

The company allocates factory overhead to normal production on the basis of direct labor hours.

Required:
Compute the amounts that might be capitalized:

a. Assuming the plant capacity to be 120,000 direct labor-hours and that the construction displaced production for sale to the extent indicated.
b. Assuming the plant capacity to be 200,000 direct labor-hours and that idle capacity was utilized for the construction.

Hint: Use overhead rates for factory overhead.

Problem 11–9

Milholland Company began construction of a new building on January 1, 19B. The company's only debt is an unrelated long-term $3 million note bearing interest at 12% per annum. The company capitalizes interest on the building on the basis of *average* quarterly cumulative expenditures. As of the end of each quarter of the six-month construction period, *cumulative* construction expenditures (not including interest) were as below; however, expenditures are made evenly during the quarter. Millholland's fiscal year ends on December 31. Interest is paid quarterly.

Quarter during 19B	Construction Expenditures
First quarter	$2,700,000
Second quarter	5,800,000

Required:
1. Determine the amount of interest cost to be capitalized and expensed each quarter.
2. Make all journal entries related to the construction and interest cost.

Problem 11–10

Prepare journal entries to record the following transactions related to the acquisition of operational assets. Justify your position on doubtful items.

a. Purchased a tract of land for $29,000; assumed taxes already assessed amounting to $180. Paid title fees, $50, and attorney fees of $300 in connection with the purchase. Payments were in cash.
b. Purchased property which included land and buildings for $78,900 cash. The purchase price included an offset of $900 for unpaid taxes. Purchaser borrowed $30,000 at 15% interest (principal and interest due one year from date) from the bank to help make the cash payment. The property was appraised for taxes as follows: land, $22,000; and building, $44,000.
c. Prior to use of the property purchased in *(b)* above, the following expenditures were made:

Repair and renovation of building	$12,000
Installation of 220-volt electrical wiring	4,000
Removal of separate shed of no use (sold scrap lumber for $50)	300
Construction of new driveway	1,000
Repair of existing driveways	600
Deposits with utilities for connections	50
Painting company name on two sides of building	400
Installation of wire fence around property	2,500

d. The land purchased in *(a)* above was leveled and two retaining walls were built to stop erosion that had created two rather large gulleys across the property. Total cash cost of the work was $4,500. The property is being held as a future plant site.
e. Purchased a used machine at a cash cost of $12,500. Subsequent to purchase the following expenditures were made:

General overhaul prior to use	$1,500
Installation of machine	500
Cost of moving machine	150
Cost of removing two small machines to make way for larger machine purchased	100
Cost of reinforcing floor prior to installation	140
Testing costs prior to operation	60
Cost of tool kit (new) essential to adjustment of machine for various types of work	170

Problem 11–11

This problem deals with the effects of accounting errors on financial statements of a manufacturing company whose fiscal year is the calendar year. The company has a six-month inventory turnover; most of its depreciable assets are depreciated over an eight-year life by the straight-line method, with zero estimated residual value. If an error makes a statement element too high, "+" should be used; if it causes the element to be too low, "−"; if the error has no effect or is completely counterbalanced, "0." There are, however, in the exhibit that follows, certain mistakes in reflecting the effects of the errors. You are to indicate for each line the number of mistakes and to identify which items are wrong and why. Answer each question independently of the others. *Hint:* Remember that depreciation of factory machinery is an element of factory overhead.

(Relates to Problem 11–11)

	Statement for 19A			Statements for 19B		
Transactions	**Net Operational Assets (book value)**	**Selling or General Expense**	**Cost of Goods Sold**	**Total Assets on Balance Sheet**	**Net Income**	**Owners' Equity**
1. The company completed self-construction of an annex to the Office Building on April 1, 19A, and failed to debit any overhead to the project.	0	0	+	0	+	0
2. Replacement of a major component of Factory Machinery early in 19A was charged to Factory Overhead. The component cost twice as much as the one replaced (the latter was 60% depreciated).	–	0	+	–	+	–
3. Cost of rearranging Factory Machinery late in 19A was not recorded at all that year. When the invoice was received early in 19B, payment was debited to Factory Overhead.	–	0	–	0	–	–
4. Deposits paid to electric utilities early in 19A for added meters installed in the factory were debited to Factory Machinery.	+	0	+	–	–	–
5. Early in 19A, the company paid legal fees of $1,500 in connection with title search for a site bought for employee parking. The fee was debited to Legal Fees (a general expense).	–	0	0	–	0	–
6. In midyear 19A, the company paid $2,000 for engineering services related to testing new factory machinery. Factory Overhead was debited.	–	0	+	–	0	+
7. Repairs which kept office fixtures in normal operating condition were made June 30, 19A, and debited to Office Fixtures.	+	+	0	+	0	+

Problem 11–12

Two *dissimilar* operational assets were exchanged when the accounts of the two companies involved reflected the following:

Account	Company A (designate as asset A)	Company B (designate as asset B)
Operational asset	$5,000	$8,000
Accumulated depreciation . . .	3,000	5,300

The market value of asset A was realistically determined to be $3,400; no realistic estimate of market value could be made for asset B.

Required:

1. Give the exchange entry for each company assuming no cash difference was involved.
2. Give the exchange entry for both companies assuming a cash difference of $800 was paid by Company A to Company B.

Problem 11–13

Part 1

Company J had an old machine that originally cost $12,000 and had accumulated depreciation to date of $7,500. The old machine was exchanged for a *similar* machine that had a cash price of $6,500. Two independent cases are assumed:

Case A—There was a direct exchange (no cash difference was paid or received).

Case B—Company J exchanged the old machine for the other machine and paid a cash difference of $2,000.

Part 2

Company K had an old machine that originally cost $12,000 and had accumulated depreciation to date of $9,000. The old machine was exchanged for a *similar* machine that had a firm cash price of $3,400. Two independent cases are assumed:

Case C—There was a direct exchange (no cash difference was paid or received).

Case D—Company K exchanged the old machine for the other machine and received a cash difference of $500.

Required (round amounts to nearest dollar):

1. Give the entries to record the exchange of similar assets in Cases A, B, C, and D.
2. Give the entries for each case assuming the assets were dissimilar.

Problem 11–14

Two *similar* operational assets were exchanged when the accounts of the two companies involved reflected the following:

Account	Company X (designate as asset X)	Company Y (designate as asset Y)
Operational asset	$5,000	$8,000
Accumulated depreciation	3,000	5,300

The market value of asset X was realistically determined to be $2,200; no realistic estimate could be made for asset Y.

Required (round amounts to nearest dollar):

1. Give the exchange entry for each company assuming no cash difference is involved.
2. Give the exchange entry for each company assuming a cash difference of $500 was paid by Company X to Company Y.

Problem 11–15

Brand Company, a manufacturer, operates three plants in different locations. This problem focuses on plant no. 1. The plant asset records reflected the following at the beginning of the current year, January 1, 19A:

Plant building (residual value, $20,000; estimated useful life, 30 years)	$120,000
Accumulated depreciation	80,000
Machinery (residual value, $35,000; estimated useful life, 15 years)	200,000
Accumulated depreciation	115,500

During the current year ending December 31, 19A, the following transactions (summarized) relating to the above accounts were completed:

a. Expenditures for nonrecurring, relatively large repairs that tend to increase economic utility but not economic lives of assets:

Plant building	$62,000
Machinery	21,000

b. Replacement of original electrical wiring system of plant building (original cost, $21,000) 39,000

c. Additions:

Plant building—added small wing to plant building to accommodate new equipment acquired; wing has useful life of 15 years and no residual value	45,000
Machinery—added special protection devices to 10 machines; devices are attached to machines and will have to be replaced every five years (no residual value)	7,000

d. Outlays for maintenance parts, labor, etc. to keep assets in normal working condition:

Quarter	Plant Building	Machinery
1	$1,400	$ 2,000
2	1,800	6,000
3	1,800	1,000
4	2,000	10,000

Required:

1. Give appropriate entries to record transactions *(a)* through *(c)*. Explain the basis underlying your decisions.
2. Give appropriate entries by quarter, in parallel columns, for transaction *(d)* assuming the accounting policy is (1) to record all ordinary repairs as expense when cash outlays are made and (2) to use the accrual approach. The annual budgeted amounts for repair and maintenance expense were plant building, $7,200; and machinery, $17,000.
3. Which approach used in 2 above do you prefer? Explain.

Problem 11–16

The books of Cooper Manufacturing Company had never been audited prior to 19C. In auditing the books for the year ended December 31, 19F, the auditor found the following account for the plant:

Plant and Equipment

19C:		19C:	
Plant purchased	90,000	Sale of scrap	300
Repairs	5,300	Depreciation (6%)	6,000
Legal	600	19D:	
Title fees	50	Depreciation (6%)	8,040
Insurance	3,000	19E:	
Taxes	1,200	Cash proceeds from old machine	1,150
19D:		Depreciation (6%)	8,160
Addition to plant	15,000	19F:	
Write-up	20,000	Depreciation (6.4%)	8,520
Interest cost related to the plant addition	1,500		
Repairs	500		
Machinery for new addition	2,000		
19E:			
New machine	3,000		
Installation	600		
19F:			
Machinery overhaul	1,350		
Replaced roof	900		
Fence	2,000		

(Balance, $114,830)

Additional data relating to plant and equipment developed during the audit follow:

a. The plant was purchased during January 19C. At that time the tax assessment listed the plant as follows: plant site at $10,000, the building at $20,000, and the machinery therein at $30,000. The estimated life of the plant and machinery was 20 years.

b. During the first six months of 19C, the company expended the amounts listed in the account for the year in getting the plant ready for operation; operations began July 1. The repairs pertain to both the building and machinery. No breakdown was available. The legal fees were incurred in connection with the plant purchase and applied to all components of it. The $3,000 insurance premium represented a one-year policy on the plant and equipment, dated January 1, 19C ($1,000 of the premium applied to the machinery). The property tax rate for the year was 2%. The scrap was accumulated during the "repair period."

c. In 19D, a plant addition was completed costing $15,000, at which time the company was paying 10% on some borrowed funds. The addition was under construction for four months. During the year, $1,500 was spent for ordinary repairs, of which one third was capitalized. Machinery costing $2,000 was purchased. The asset account was written up by $20,000 to bring it in line with the bank's security allowance on loans (Contributed Capital was credited).

d. During 19E, a new machine was purchased (July 1) for $3,000 plus installation costs of $600; an old machine costing an estimated $2,100 was sold for $1,150. The old machine was acquired when the plant was acquired.

e. During 19F, several items of equipment were completely reconditioned at a cost of $1,350. Minor repairs were debited to expense during the year. The roof was replaced on one wing of the plant. A fence was constructed around the plant to keep unauthorized personnel out; it is estimated that the fence will have 10 years of remaining life.

Required:

1. Set up a worksheet to compute the correct balances for the following accounts (suggested columnar captions): Land, Buildings, Machinery, Land Improvements, and Accumulated Depreciation (the company follows a policy of recording 6% straight-line depreciation on ending balances except for Land Improvements. Disregard residual value and round amounts to nearest dollar). Suggested line captions: list each item by year. Justify any assumptions that you make.
2. Give one compound entry to correct the accounts assuming the books have already been closed for 19F.

Problem 11–17

(This problem is an appropriate assignment where class members are reasonably well grounded in cost accounting. It is perhaps inadvisable to assign the problem where the cost accounting foundation is marginal).

Braxton Corporation received a $400,000 low bid from a reputable manufacturer for the construction of special production equipment needed by Braxton in an expansion program. Because the company's own plant was not operating at capacity, Braxton decided to construct the equipment itself and the company accountant recorded the following production costs related to the construction:

Services of consulting engineer	$ 10,000
Work subcontracted	20,000
Materials	200,000
Plant labor normally assigned to production	65,000
Plant labor normally assigned to maintenance*	100,000
Total	$395,000

* Included in manufacturing overhead.

Management prefers to record the cost of the equipment under the incremental cost method. Approximately 40% of the corporation activities are devoted to government supply contracts, which are all based in some way on cost. The contracts require that any self-constructed equipment be allocated its full share of all costs related to the construction.

The following information is also available:

a. The above production labor was for partial fabrication of the equipment in the plant. Skilled personnel were required and were assigned from other projects. The maintenance labor would have been idle time of non-production plant employees who would have been retained on the payroll whether or not their services were utilized.

b. Payroll taxes and employee fringe benefits are approximately 30% of labor cost and are included in manufacturing overhead cost. Total manufacturing overhead for the year was $5,630,000.

c. Manufacturing overhead is approximately 60% variable and is applied on the basis of production labor cost. Production labor cost for the corporation's normal products totaled $6,810,000.

d. G&A expenses include $22,500 of executive salary cost and $10,500 of postage, telephone, supplies, and miscellaneous expenses identifiable with this equipment construction.

Required:

1. Prepare a schedule computing the amount which should be reported as the full cost of the constructed equipment to meet the requirements of the government contracts. Any supporting computations should be in good form.
2. Prepare a schedule computing the incremental cost of the constructed equipment.
3. What is the greatest amount that should be capitalized as the cost of the equipment? Why? (AICPA adapted)

Problem 11–18

Summers Manufacturing Company was incorporated on January 2, 19A, but was unable to begin manufacturing activities until July 1, 19A, because new factory facilities were not completed until that date.

The Land and Building account at December 31, 19A, was as follows:

Date		Item	Amount
19A			
Jan.	31	Land and building	$ 91,000
Feb.	28	Cost of removal of building	1,500
May	1	Partial payment of new constr.	35,000
	1	Legal fees paid	2,000
June	1	2d payment on new constr.	30,000
	1	Insurance premium	1,800
	1	Special tax assessment	2,500
	30	General expenses	12,000
July	1	Final payment on new constr.	35,000
Dec.	31	Asset write-up	12,500
			223,300
	31	Depreciation—19A at 1%	2,233
		Account balance	$221,067

The following additional information is to be considered:

a. To acquire land and building the company paid $41,000 cash and 500 shares of its 5% cumulative preferred stock, par value $100 per share.

b. Cost of removal of old buildings amounted to $1,500 with the demolition company retaining all materials of the building.

c. Legal fees covered the following:

Cost of organization	$ 500
Examination of title covering purchase of land	1,000
Legal work in connection with constr. work	500
	$2,000

d. Insurance premium covered premiums for three-year term beginning May 1, 19A.

e. The special tax assessment covered street improvements.

f. General expenses covered the following for the period from January 2, 19A, to June 30, 19A:

President's salary	$ 6,000
Plant superintendent covering supervision on new building	5,000
Office salaries	1,000
	$12,000

g. Because of a general increase in construction costs after entering into the building contract, the board of directors increased the value of the building $12,500, believing such increase was justified to reflect market value at the time the building was completed. Retained Earnings was credited for this amount.

h. Estimated life of building—50 years. Write-off for 19A—1% of asset value (1% of $223,300 = $2,233).

Required:

1. Prepare entries to reflect correct land, building, and accumulated depreciation accounts at December 31, 19A.
2. Show the proper presentation of land, building, and accumulated depreciation on the balance sheet at December 31, 19A. (AICPA adapted)

Problem 11–19

Equipment which cost $12,800 on January 1, 19A, was sold for $7,000 on June 30, 19F. It had been depreciated over a 10-year life by the straight-line method on the assumption its residual value would be $800.

A warehouse that cost $225,000, residual value $15,000, was being depreciated over 35 years by the straight-line method. When the structure was 20 years old, an additional wing was constructed at a cost of $76,000. The estimated life of the wing considered separately was 25 years, and its residual value is $10,000. The accounting period ends December 31.

Required:

1. Give entries (and show computations) to record
   a. The sale of the equipment. Include current depreciation in the sale entry.
   b. The addition; cash was paid.
   c. Depreciation for the warehouse and its addition after the latter has been in use for one year.
2. Show how the building and attached wing would be reported on a balance sheet prepared immediately after entry *(c)* in 1 above.

12

Property, Plant, and Equipment—Depreciation and Depletion

THE PRECEDING CHAPTER delineated the primary characteristics of operational assets. The attribute common to all operational assets is that they are acquired and utilized because of their revenue-generating **potential** in use rather than for resale. They can be viewed by the enterprise as comprising a store of economic service values that will expire as they are used in the revenue-generating process. Therefore, as operational assets are used to generate revenue, the cost "used up" must be matched with the revenues generated during each period of use to fulfill the requirements of the **matching principle** for income measurement. The matching process is applied to most operational assets (land is an exception). This process deals exclusively with the measurement of periodic expense and only incidentally with valuation of the related asset.

To facilitate discussion, this chapter is subdivided as follows:

Part A—Basic Concepts and Methods of Depreciation

Part B—Additional Depreciation Issues and Depletion

Supplement 12–A—Annuity and Sinking Fund Methods of Depreciation

Part A: Basic Concepts and Methods of Depreciation

TERMINOLOGY AND BASIC CONCEPTS

The costs of three distinct classes of operational assets are matched with revenue over the useful lives of the assets. The accounting terminology for these different types of expense is as follows:

1. **Depreciation**—the accounting process of allocating against periodic revenue the periodic expiration of the cost of **tangible** property, plant, and equipment.
2. **Depletion**—the accounting process of allocating against periodic revenue the periodic expiration of the cost of an asset represented by a **natural resource,** such as mineral deposits and timber stands.
3. **Amortization**—the accounting process of allocating against periodic revenue the periodic expiration of the cost of **intangible assets** represented

by **special rights** or benefits, such as prepaid insurance, patents, copyrights, and leaseholds. Sometimes "amortization" is used as a general term to include all types of periodic apportionments.

This chapter discusses depreciation and depletion. Chapter 13 considers the amortization of intangibles.

Conceptually, the cost of property, plant, and equipment represents a long-term prepayment of expense; the expense is prepaid in advance of utilization of the asset and hence is recorded as an asset. As the economic service life of the asset expires, the cost of the asset is systematically allocated to operations as an expense.

Accounting Terminology Bulletin 1, paragraph 56, defines depreciation accounting as follows:

> **Depreciation accounting** is a system of accounting which aims to distribute the cost or other basic value of tangible capital assets, less salvage value (if any), over the estimated useful life of the unit in a systematic and rational manner. It is a process of allocation, not of valuation.

In accounting for operational assets, the underlying principles are *(a)* at acquisition, the assets are recorded at cost on the basis of the **cost principle;** *(b)* subsequent to acquisition, those assets with a determinable limited life are reported at cost less the accumulated portions of such costs that have expired (depreciation, depletion and amortization); and *(c)* "used up" portions of cost are recognized as current expense in conformity with the **matching principle.**

DEPRECIATION

To understand the nature of depreciation accounting, it is necessary to examine its effects on *(a)* the income statement, *(b)* dividends, *(c)* cash flow, *(d)* the balance sheet, and *(e)* the statement of changes in financial position (SCFP) (discussed in Chapter 23).

Depreciation is recognized on the income statement as selling, administrative, or manufacturing expense (i.e., in cost of goods sold), depending upon the nature and use of the assets involved. Depreciation may affect the income statement in two ways. One way is a direct debit to expense. For instance, depreciation on company automobiles used by salespersons would be classified as a selling expense. On the other hand, depreciation on machinery used in the factory would be recorded as a part of the cost of inventory; when the inventory is sold, the cost of the inventory (including an element of depreciation) is debited to Cost of Goods Sold. But, that portion of depreciation remaining in the cost of inventory on hand at the end of the period is reported as an **asset** (inventory) until the inventory is sold. It follows that income of a given period is reduced by depreciation initially included in the cost of inventory only to the extent that such goods are sold during that period.

Depreciation and Dividends

Because depreciation expense reduces reported pretax income, the amount of retained earnings likewise is reduced. This effect reduces income tax payments and the reported amount of retained earnings available for dividends; consequently, over the life of an operational asset, an amount equivalent to the cost of the tangible operational asset (less any residual value) is "held back" from retained earnings and dividend availability. Thus, depreciation accounting tends to prevent the impairment of monetary capital through dividends based upon overstated earnings. Failure to recognize depreciation expense causes overstatement of income with an attendant possible dissipation of capital through liquidating dividends. As discussed in Chapter 24, it is possible for capital to be dissipated also as a result of recording depreciation on the historical cost (HC) basis in accordance with GAAP—when inflation occurs and compensating adjustments are not made to pricing and dividend policies. The following section explores this same notion in the context of depreciation and cash flow.

Depreciation and Cash Flow

Depreciation accounting measures an expense and matches it with revenue. When revenue is sufficient, depreciation, like other expenses, is recovered. It should be apparent, however, that recording depreciation has no effect upon the amount of assets coming into the business through sales of product. But if a business can sell its product for enough to cover all operating expenses including depreciation, the assets received from customers (cash and receivables) will exceed total expense outlays by at least the amount of the depreciation. Because dividends usually are declared out of net income, net assets equal to the amount of depreciation expense will be retained in a business which operates at a profit or merely at break-even.[1]

It is important to realize that although the depreciation provision will result in holding back assets from dividends equivalent to the provision, it does not specificially provide or "hold back" cash. The relationship between depreciation and cash flow is that although most expenses require cash when incurred, depreciation is a noncash expense; the cash was disbursed when the operational asset was acquired. Therefore, the **cash inflow from net income may be more** than reported net income because of the noncash expenses (e.g., depreciation and amortization) reported on the income statement. The fact that depreciation has been recognized on certain assets does not mean that cash (or even other assets) necessarily will be available to replace those assets when their service lives expire. The assets retained as a result of deducting depreciation from income are not automatically segregated into a fund for replacements. In fact, the retained funds probably will be used to pay off liabilities and to purchase new and different types of assets which also can be used to generate cash. Therefore, while such funds are not automatically segregated for asset replacement, the revenue-generating process of most companies is intended to produce the cash for replacement of old assets.

Depreciation Is an Estimate

The importance of depreciation varies with the nature of the business and the extent of its holdings of operational assets. Significantly, reported income is no more accurate than the estimate of the periodic depreciation expense.

With the possible exception of inventories, no single area of accounting offers as much potential variety of practice or choice as does depreciation accounting. About the only "constant" is the starting point, which usually is historical acquisition cost; there are not many variables in measuring cost, though such matters as determining market values in nonmonetary exchanges and treatment of overhead on self-construction afford examples of how identical assets acquired at the same time can begin with different costs.

In depreciation accounting, uncertain elements about an asset must be estimated such as its useful life (in years, productive output, or hours of use) and residual value. Sometimes it is necessary to anticipate the cost of dismantling or restoration incident to retirement of a plant asset. Because different companies estimate such costs differently, it is not surprising that different depreciation methods characterize depreciation accounting.

Under current GAAP, the depreciation policies of a company do not have to be based upon the characteristics and uses of the company's operational assets. Thus, the selection from among the various depreciation methods (discussed in subsequent sections of this chapter) is a "free" choice. For this reason, it is desirable for companies to disclose as much information as reasonably possible about why a particular depreciation method was selected.

CAUSES OF DEPRECIATION

The causes of depreciation may be classified as follows:

Physical Factors	Functional Factors
1. Wear and tear from operation.	1. Inadequacy.
2. Action of time and other elements.	2. Obsolescence, including supersession.
3. Deterioration and decay.	

Significantly, a **change in the market value** of an operational asset is not recognized as one of the causes of depreciation under GAAP.[2] The three physical factors, as they affect the service life of a tangible

[1] Different methods of depreciation have different effects on cash flow, which is reflected on the SCFP. For example, accelerated depreciation in the early years will give a higher depreciation expense amount than will straight line; consequently, income taxes would be lower. This would result in a saving of cash paid for income taxes during the early periods.

[2] Under current GAAP, depreciation is not caused by changes in the market value of an operational asset; however, when the book value of an asset is significantly above its use value to the entity, in terms of market value (e.g., an idle plant), the asset must be written down to reflect any permanent and significant **impairment** of value. The effect of such a write-down is not recorded as depreciation expense.

operational asset, are self-explanatory. The two functional factors are less obvious. Inadequacy is brought about by the expansion of a business which results in the operational asset being unequal to the increased service required, even though it still may be in good condition and capable of the service originally expected of it. Obsolescence may arise from inadequacy, supersession, and other causes such as the outmoding of the product being produced or the service being rendered. Supersession occurs when new assets can render improved service. In such cases it may be desirable to discard the old assets.

Depreciation accounting considers all predictable factors that tend to limit the economic usefulness of operational assets to the enterprise. The periodic apportionment of cost through depreciation must be based upon both the physical and functional causes of depreciation. Generally those factors that operate more or less continuously are given recognition in depreciation accounting, whereas sudden and unexpected factors such as storms, floods, sudden change in demand, and radical outmoding of assets must be accorded special treatment. One of these special treatments might be applied to account for a fire and result in the immediate removal of an asset from the accounts and the recording of a related casualty loss.

The useful life of operational assets also is influenced by the repair and maintenance policies of the firm. Inadequate maintenance and repair may reduce expense temporarily; however, the useful life of assets will be shortened, thereby increasing the periodic depreciation expense.

In the case of facilities temporarily idle or being held pending future use, depreciation should continue because the physical and functional causes, which tend to reduce the ultimate economic usefulness of the asset to the firm, continue. Operational assets that will not be returned to service should be reduced to their estimated net realizable value in anticipation of disposal. Special asset accounts normally should be established to account for idle facilities.

FACTORS IN DETERMINING DEPRECIATION EXPENSE

Periodic depreciation expense should represent allocation of the original cost (less the estimated residual value) of the asset to operations in proportion to the economic benefit received each period from use of the asset. The variables which must be considered in computing periodic depreciation expense are as follows:

1. Actual cost (as defined in the preceding chapter).
2. Estimated residual (scrap or salvage) value.
3. Estimated service life.

Thus, computation of depreciation is based on one "actual" and two "estimated" factors. The residual value is the estimated amount which may be recovered through sale, trade-in allowance, or by other means when the asset finally is retired from service. In estimating the residual value, allowance must be made for the costs of dismantling and disposing of the retired asset. For example, assume it is estimated that upon retirement the asset can be sold for $2,500 and that the costs of dismantling and selling are estimated at $500. In this case the residual value would be $2,000.

In practice, residual value often is ignored entirely—a procedure which is acceptable when the recovery and disposal amounts may offset (in which case residual value is zero), when the amounts involved are immaterial, or when the estimates involve a wide margin of error. Moreover, because residual value is estimated years in advance, theoretically, it should be discounted to present value for depreciation computations. Often the present value of estimated future residual value is negligible.

In estimating the service life of an asset for accounting purposes, it is important to realize that service life implies *(a)* use of the asset by the present owner, *(b)* use of the asset for the purpose for which acquired, and *(c)* a specific repair and maintenance policy over the life of the asset. The periodic amount of depreciation on an asset should be representative of the expiration of the "economic service potentials" of the asset to the enterprise. Thus, the service life should be determined on a basis which is integrally linked with the expiration of such values. For example, service life may be measured in terms of *(a)* definite time periods such as months or years, *(b)* units of output, or *(c)* hours of operating time. Selection of a measure of service life conceptually should depend upon the nature of the asset involved and the primary causes of its depreciation.

RECORDING DEPRECIATION

Periodic depreciation is recorded as a debit to an expense account or a cost of manufacturing account (factory overhead) and a credit to a contra asset account entitled Accumulated Depreciation. Rather than a direct credit to the related asset account, this special contra account traditionally has been credited to maintain a separation of the original cost and the amount of that cost expired through depreciation. The contra account should not be labeled "reserve" for depreciation because depreciation provides no such "reserve." Depreciation is recorded in the general ledger accounts as well as in subsidiary records which detail the various depreciable assets.

METHODS OF DEPRECIATION

Methods of depreciation focus on computation of the amount of depreciation expense to be recorded each period. A number of methods have been developed, each of which provides a different pattern of depreciation expense over the life of the asset. The depreciation methods may be classified as follows:

a. Based on time:
 (1) Straight line.
b. Based on output:
 (2) Service hours.
 (3) Units of output.
c. Reducing depreciation charge:
 (4) Sum-of-the-years' digits (SYD).
 (5) Double-declining balance (DDB).
d. Based on investment and interest concepts (discussed in Supplement 12–A):
 (6) Annuity.
 (7) Sinking fund.

To illustrate these methods, Exhibit 12–1 presents the basic data used throughout this chapter.

Straight-Line Method

The straight-line method is used widely because of its simplicity. This method relates depreciation directly to the passage of time rather than to specific use of the asset. It is called straight line because it recognizes an equal amount of depreciation expense in each of the periods of the service life of the asset; thus, when graphed against time, periodic depreciation expense, accumulated depreciation, and asset book value are all indicated by straight lines. The use of the formula for computing periodic depreciation expense (annual in this case) is illustrated below.

$$D = \frac{C - R}{n}$$

or

$$D = \frac{\$100 - \$10}{3} = \$30 \text{ per period}$$

Depreciation frequently is expressed as a **rate.** For the illustrative amounts, the periodic (annual) rate r may be expressed as either *(a)* 33⅓ percent on net depreciable value (i.e., $30 ÷ $90 = 33⅓%) or *(b)* 30 percent on cost (i.e., $30 ÷ $100 = 30%).

Exhibit 12–2 illustrates application of straight-line depreciation over the life of the illustrative asset.

The straight-line method is simple. It meets the criterion of being "systematic and rational" (*ARB 44,* revised, par. 2). It is appropriate when the following conditions prevail:

EXHIBIT 12–1: Simplified Data Used to Illustrate Depreciation

Item	Symbol	Illustrative Amount
Acquisition cost	*C*	$ 100
Residual value	*R*	10
Estimated service life	*n*	
Years		3
Service hours		6,000
Productive output in units		9,000
Depreciation rate (per year, per service hour, or per unit of productive output)	*r*	
Dollar amount of depreciation per period	*D*	

EXHIBIT 12–2: Depreciation Table and Entries, Straight-Line Method (life, three years)

Year	Depreciation Expense (debit)	Accumulated Depreciation (credit)	Balance Accumulated Depreciation	Undepreciated Asset Balance (book value)
0				$100
1	$30	$30	$30	70
2	30	30	60	40
3	30	30	90	10 (residual value)
	$90	$90		

1. The decline in economic service potential of the asset is approximately the same each period.
2. The decline in economic service potential of the asset is related to the passage of time rather than to use.
3. Use of the asset is consistent from period to period.
4. Repairs and maintenance are essentially the same each period.

Straight-line depreciation is deficient in that *(a)* depreciation is computed as a function of time rather than a function of use, which often is not the case; *(b)* it may not satisfactorily match expense with revenue; and *(c)* it causes a distortion, relative to a pure rate-of-return concept, in certain rate-of-return computations. This distortion results because under the straight-line method, depreciation expense is a constant amount each period, and as a result, the effect of depreciation on income is also by a constant periodic amount. As the asset is depreciated over time, its book value (and also the book value of total assets) decreases. When net income is divided by total assets to compute the rate of return on total assets, the computed periodic rate of return increases each period and gives the appearance of an increasing rate of return on the asset. In reality, the **rate of return** probably is constant, even though computed rate of return indicates otherwise.

Service Hours Method

The service hours method is based upon the assumption that the decrease in service life of the operational asset is conditioned primarily by the actual running time of the asset rather than by the mere passage of time. Rather than equal periodic amounts of depreciation expense, this method results in a periodic expense which correlates with the amount of time the asset is operated. If a machine is operated twice as much in the current period as in the prior period, the depreciation for the current period will be twice as much as that of the last period. In utilizing this method, the service life of the asset must be estimated in terms of total probable service or working hours prior to retirement; then a rate per service hour is computed.

Assuming a 6,000-hour estimated useful life, the formula for the depreciation rate would be as follows:

$$r = \frac{C - R}{n}$$

or

$$r = \frac{\$100 - \$10}{6{,}000} = \$0.015 \text{ per service hour}$$

Assuming 2,000 actual hours of running time the first year, depreciation expense would be as follows:

$$D = r \times \text{Service hours, current period}$$

or

$$D = \$0.015 \times 2{,}000 = \$30$$

Exhibit 12–3 illustrates application of the service hours method over the life of the illustrative asset.

The service hours method accords with the GAAP criterion of "rational and systematic" and produces a logical matching of expense and revenue if the asset loses service potential on the basis of running time. Under this method, the amount of depreciation varies with the productive output of the asset. However, to the extent that running time occurred without productive output, this relationship would not hold. When obsolescence is not a primary factor in depreciation and the economic service potential of the asset is used up primarily by running time, the service hours method appears appropriate. Also, wide variations in use from period to period suggests application of the service hours method. For many assets, such as buildings, furniture, and typewriters, it would be impracticable, if not impossible, to apply the service hours method. In contrast, it would be appropriate for assets such as delivery equipment and oil drilling equipment.

EXHIBIT 12–3: Depreciation Table and Entries, Service Hours Method (life, 6,000 hours)

Year	Service Hours Worked*	Depreciation Expense (debit)		Accumulated Depreciation (credit)	Balance Accumulated Depreciation	Undepreciated Asset Balance (book value)
0						$100
1	2,000	(2,000 × $0.015)	$30	$30	$30	70
2	3,000	(3,000 × $0.015)	45	45	75	25
3	1,000	(1,000 × $0.015)	15	15	90	10 (residual value)
	6,000		$90	$90		

* It is assumed that the asset was actually used in this manner and that the original estimate of useful life was confirmed.

Productive Output Method

Under this method, the service life of the asset is estimated in terms of the number of **units** of output. A proportionate part of the total cost to be depreciated (cost less residual value) is allocated to each unit of output as a cost of production; consequently, depreciation amounts fluctuate with changes in the volume of output. Each unit of output includes a constant amount of depreciation, in contrast to the straight-line method where each unit of output is allocated a different amount of depreciation if output varies from period to period.

The cost to be depreciated over the life of the asset is divided by the estimated service life in units to derive a depreciation rate per unit of output; multiplication of this rate by the output for the period gives the periodic depreciation amount. Thus computation of the rate, assuming an estimated productive life of 9,000 units of output, would be as follows:

$$r = \frac{C - R}{n}$$

or

$$r = \frac{\$100 - \$10}{9{,}000} = \$0.01 \text{ per unit of output}$$

Assuming 4,000 units of actual output during the first year, depreciation expense would be computed as follows:

$$D = r \times \text{Units of output, current period}$$

or

$$D = \$0.01 \times 4{,}000 = \$40$$

Exhibit 12–4 illustrates an application of the productive output method over the life of the illustrative asset.

The productive output method and the service hours method both reflect the fact that some assets, such as trucks and machinery, usually depreciate in direct proportion to usage. These methods usually more closely relate the benefit derived from the use of the asset to the physical use of the asset than do the other methods. The productive output method is particularly appropriate where *(a)* obsolescence is not a major factor, *(b)* actual output can be realistically measured, and *(c)* the service life in units of output can be estimated reliably.

The differences between the periodic depreciation under the service hours method (Exhibit 12–3) and the productive output method (Exhibit 12–4) are due to a change in the efficiency of operations—the asset was used more efficiently in some periods than in others. This observation would lead to the conclusion that in situations where either method could be applied, the productive output method generally would be preferable.

Comparison of Straight-Line and Output Methods. It is important to recognize the effect of the different depreciation methods on **total** cost of products and on **unit** product cost when depreciable assets are used in manufacturing. The straight-line method reports depreciation as a **fixed amount per period** but as a **variable amount per unit** of output. In contrast, the service hours method and the productive output method report depreciation as a **variable amount per period** but as a **fixed amount per**

EXHIBIT 12–4: Depreciation Table and Entries, Productive Output Method (life, 9,000 units)

Year	Units of Output*	Depreciation Expense (debit)		Accumulated Depreciation (credit)	Balance Accumulated Depreciation	Undepreciated Asset Balance (book value)
0						$100
1	4,000	(4,000 × $0.01)	$40	$40	$40	60
2	3,000	(3,000 × $0.01)	30	30	70	30
3	2,000	(2,000 × $0.01)	20	20	90	10 (residual value)
	9,000		$90	$90		

* It is assumed that the asset was actually used in this manner and that the original estimate of useful life was confirmed.

unit of output. To illustrate, assume an asset that cost $600 (no residual value) with an estimated life of five years or 500 units of output. Assume further that output was year 1—90; year 2—100; year 3—110; year 4—120; and year 5—80. The comparative depreciation amounts and unit costs for the straight-line and output methods are compared below:

		Output Depreciation		Straight-Line Depreciation	
Year	Units of Output	Amount	Unit Cost	Amount	Unit Cost
1	90	$108	$1.20	$120	$1.33
2	100	120	1.20	120	1.20
3	110	132	1.20	120	1.09
4	120	144	1.20	120	1.00
5	80	96	1.20	120	1.50
	500	$600		$600	

These distinctions are important in cost analyses used for pricing, control, and other decision-making purposes.

Accelerated Depreciation Methods

The accelerated methods are designed to allocate the cost to be depreciated so that periodic depreciation amounts are higher in the early years and lower in the later years of the life of the operational asset. The accelerated methods are based upon the assumption that new assets are more efficient than old assets; therefore, the economic service potentials rendered by the asset are greater during the early life of the asset. If the cost of these greater values being consumed through utilization of the asset is to be matched with the resulting revenue, some form of accelerated depreciation theoretically is desirable. The accelerated methods also are defended on the ground that the annual depreciation amount should decrease as repair expenses on the asset increase, thus resulting in a smooth pattern of total expense (i.e., depreciation plus repairs) for the use of the operational asset.

Numerous procedures have been proposed for computing accelerated depreciation expense; however, the principal methods currently being used are the following:

1. Sum-of-the-years' digits (SYD).
2. Double-declining balance (DDB).

Sum-of-the-Years'-Digits (SYD) Method. This method (abbreviated as SYD) applies a decreasing fraction each succeeding period to the cost to be depreciated. The fractions are determined by using as the denominator the sum-of-the-years' digits for the life of the asset. The numerator, which changes each period, is the years' digits in reverse order. For example, the illustrative asset, with an estimated service life of three years, would be depreciated as follows:

Denominator:
  Sum-of-the-years' digits (SYD): 1 + 2 + 3 = 6.
Numerators:
  Digits in reverse order: 3, 2, and 1.
Fractions:
  First period, $\frac{3}{6}$.
  Second period, $\frac{2}{6}$.
  Third period, $\frac{1}{6}$.

EXHIBIT 12–5: Depreciation Table and Entries, Sum-of-the-Years'-Digits (SYD) Method (life, three years)

Year		Depreciation Expense (debit)	Accumulated Depreciation (credit)	Balance Accumulated Depreciation	Undepreciated Asset Balance (book value)
0 . . .					$100
1 . . .	($\frac{3}{6}$ × $90)	$45	$45	$45	55
2 . . .	($\frac{2}{6}$ × $90)	30	30	75	25
3 . . .	($\frac{1}{6}$ × $90)	15	15	90	10 (residual value)
		$90	$90		

Exhibit 12–5 illustrates application of the SYD method for the illustrative asset.

Note that the reducing fraction is multiplied by the cost to be depreciated (cost less residual value) in each period. When the life of the asset is relatively long, it is convenient to compute the denominator (sum of the digits) using the following formula:

$$\text{SYD} = n\left[\frac{n+1}{2}\right]$$

Therefore, for an asset with a 25-year life,

$$\text{SYD} = 25\left[\frac{25+1}{2}\right] = 325$$

Double-Declining Balance (DDB) Method. Accelerated depreciation methods are acceptable for federal income tax purposes; however, the tax regulations have provided that the amount of depreciation must not be more than double the amount that would result under the straight-line method **when the residual value is ignored.** This provision gave rise to the double-declining-balance (DDB) method. Under this method the periodic depreciation rate is double the straight-line rate; residual value is ignored. Each year this rate is multiplied by the declining book value. Based on the illustrative data given in Exhibit 12–1, the DDB rate would be 67 percent (i.e., 33⅓% × 2). The depreciation would be computed as shown in Exhibit 12–6.[3]

The accelerated methods discussed above are acceptable under GAAP. The SYD and DDB methods are the accelerated methods used most widely.[4] The important theoretical criterion for a depreciation method to satisfy is an acceptable matching of periodic depreciation expense with periodic revenue.

[3] Income tax regulations impose numerous restrictions on the methods of computing depreciation for income tax purposes.

[4] A third accelerated depreciation method is the fixed-percentage-on-declining-base method. To apply this method the book value of the asset (undepreciated asset balance) is multiplied by a constant percentage rate. Because a constant rate is applied to a **declining base,** each successive periodic depreciation amount will be less than the amount for the preceding period. The rate is computed taking into account the cost, estimated life, and residual value; consequently, the rate will automatically provide for the residual value at the end of the service life of the asset. The depreciation rate (the fixed percentage) and its application are illustrated below for the basic data of Exhibit 12–1:

$$r = 1 - \sqrt[n]{\frac{R}{C}}$$

or

$$r = 1 - \sqrt[3]{\frac{\$10}{\$100}} = .536, \text{ or } 53.6\%$$

Calculation of $\sqrt[n]{\frac{R}{C}}$ can be done by use of logarithms or hand calculators.

Depreciation Table and Entries, Fixed-Percentage-on-Declining-Base Method (life, three years)

Year		Depreciation Expense (debit)	Accumulated Depreciation (credit)	Balance Accumulated Depreciation	Undepreciated Asset Balance (book value)
0					$100.00
1	(53.6% × $100)	$53.60*	$53.60	$53.60	46.40
2	(53.6% × $46.40)	24.87	24.87	78.47	21.53
3	(53.6% × $21.53)	11.53	11.53	90.00	10.00 (residual value)
		$90.00	$90.00		

* Carried to nearest cent to demonstrate that the correct residual value remains.

EXHIBIT 12–6: Depreciation Table and Entries, Double-Declining-Balance (DDB) Method (life, three years)

Year	Annual Rate	Depreciation Expense (debit)	Accumulated Depreciation (credit)	Balance Accumulated Depreciation	Undepreciated Asset Balance (book value)
0					$100
1	67%	67% × $100 = $67	$67	$67	33
2	67%	67% × $ 33 = 22	22	89	11
3	67%	1*	1*	90	10 (residual value)

* Remaining amount needed for total depreciation of $90 and residual value of $10.

Part B: Additional Depreciation Issues and Depletion

DEPRECIATION BASED ON INVESTMENT CONCEPTS

The preceding paragraphs discussed depreciation methods that provide (1) a **constant** depreciation amount per period (straight line), (2) a **decreasing** depreciation amount per period (SYD and DDB), or (3) **varying** depreciation amounts per period (output methods). The **compound interest methods** represent a distinctly different approach; they provide an **increasing** amount of depreciation per period. The other approaches to depreciation have been criticized because they ignore the investment characteristics of the ownership of operational assets. Depreciation based on investment concepts views an operational asset as an investment, and the return on that investment, in the same manner as an annuity investment. Implicit is the concept that the periodic returns on the investment in the operational asset over its useful life comprise both principal and interest. Therefore, the depreciation amount each period is construed to include two elements: (1) the recovery of the investment (i.e., principal), which is credited to accumulated depreciation and (2) the remainder, which is credited to an account for **imputed interest revenue** on the investment in the operational asset. Over the life of the asset, as the economic utility of the asset declines, its book value decreases accordingly. Therefore, the imputed interest revenue also decreases, and the amount of periodic depreciation expense increases. The effect of the depreciation entry each period is an increasing amount of periodic depreciation expense and a decreasing amount of net income. The two methods—annuity and sinking fund—give the same net effect on income; they are illustrated in Supplement 12–A to this chapter.

SPECIAL DEPRECIATION SYSTEMS

Unique features of certain kinds of depreciable assets have caused practical adaptations of the depreciation methods discussed above. The most common adaptations, generally referred to as **systems,** are discussed in this section under the following captions:

1. Inventory (or appraisal) system.
2. Retirement and replacement systems.
3. Group and composite life systems.

Each of these methods is considered to be appropriate under GAAP if applied properly, and only in the unique situation that each one accommodates. As practical cost-benefit applications, they generally attain an acceptable level of reliability, especially when materiality is considered.

Inventory (or Appraisal) System

Under the inventory depreciation system, purchases of depreciable assets are debited to an operational asset account in the usual manner, and depreciation usually is credited to the same account, not to an accumulated depreciation account. The amount recorded as depreciation for the period is determined by estimating the "value" of the assets on hand in their present condition; the asset account then is reduced to this amount, and depreciation expense is debited in the amount of the difference between prior book value and the new estimated value. Residual recoveries on occasional disposal of some of the assets are recorded as a reduction of depreciation expense for the period. The value of the asset on hand (in its present condition) is determined by inventory procedures and an estimate of its **acquisition cost** taking into account its present condition. As implied by its name, the inventory system is similar in some respects to the procedures used in a periodic system of accounting for merchandise inventory (discussed in Chapter 7).

To illustrate, assume the Hand Tools account showed an ending balance of $880; an inventory of the tools on hand at the end of the period, valued at **acquisition cost** and adjusted for present condition, indicated a value of $560. Broken and obsolete tools were sold for $70. The entry to record the periodic depreciation is as follows:

Cash	70	
Depreciation expense—hand tools ($320 − $70)	250	
Hand tools ($880 − $560)		320

The inventory system is appropriate for situations in which the asset account represents **numerous asset items with low unit cost,** such as hand tools, machine tools, patterns and dies, and dishes, flatware, and so forth, in a restaurant.

In particular, care must be exercised to exclude changes in value due to changes in the price level or other market fluctuations; otherwise the depreciation amount will include noncost elements such as unrealized (holding) market gains and losses. A conventional matching of depreciation expense and periodic revenues requires that the items be valued at original cost adjusted for present condition. Also, much of the depreciation amount may represent items stolen or lost.

Retirement and Replacement Systems

The retirement and replacement systems of depreciation frequently are used by public utilities because of the peculiar problems of accounting for certain assets such as poles and other line items. Also, they are used in accounting for low-cost items such as hand tools. Under retirement and replacement systems, no periodic entry is made for depreciation in the normal manner; instead depreciation is recognized only at the **time of replacement** of the asset.

The basic distinction between the retirement and replacement systems is that under the **retirement** system, the cost of the **old** asset (less its residual value) is debited to depreciation expense when it is replaced (i.e., a FIFO assumption), whereas under the **replacement** system the cost of the **new** asset (less residual value of the **old** asset) is debited to depreciation expense when it replaces the old asset (i.e., a LIFO assumption). In applying either method, any residual recovery is recorded as a reduction of depreciation expense. To illustrate both systems, assume the Hi-Power Utility Company replaced 10 old utility poles with 10 new poles that cost $300 each. The old poles replaced originally cost $100 each and have a residual value (i.e., net realizable value) of $20 each. Thus, the entries related to the poles were:

Basic entries common to both systems:

1. Acquisition of old poles initially:

Pole inventory ($100 × 10)	1,000	
Cash		1,000

2. Installation of old poles initially:

Transmission line ($100 × 10)	1,000	
Pole inventory		1,000

3. Purchase of new replacement poles:

Pole inventory ($300 × 10)	3,000	
Cash		3,000

Depreciation entries are different:

A. Retirement system (FIFO):

4. To record depreciation expense:

Depreciation expense [10 × ($100 − $20)]	800	
Salvage inventory (net realizable value, old poles, 10 × $20)	200	
Transmission line (cost of old poles) (10 × $100)		1,000

5. To record installation of the new poles:

Transmission line (cost of new poles, $300 × 10)	3,000	
Pole inventory (cost of new poles)		3,000

B. Replacement system (LIFO):

4. To record depreciation expense:

Depreciation expense [10 × ($300 − $20)] ..	2,800	
Salvage inventory (net realizable value, old poles, 10 × $20)	200	
Pole inventory (cost of new poles)		3,000

5. To record installation of the new poles: Entry not needed because of LIFO assumption

This example illustrates that the **retirement** system represents a FIFO approach, whereas the **replacement** system represents a LIFO system in allocating the asset cost to depreciation. The retirement system provides depreciation amounts based on older costs and reports the operational asset at newer costs, whereas the replacement system provides depreciation amounts based on newer costs and reports the operational asset at the older cost.

Neither system is designed specifically to match expense with revenue, inasmuch as depreciation is recognized only when assets are being replaced. Once the company has reached a relatively stable level of growth and replacement, however, the periodic depreciation amount may approximate the amounts that would be computed under one of the usual methods (such as straight line). These systems have been used by utility companies because of the practical difficulty in depreciating large numbers of relatively low-cost items such as poles, cross-members, brackets, and conduits at many locations. In such situations the distinction between ordinary repairs and capitalizable replacements is difficult to establish and apply to individual assets. Although lacking in theoretical justification, the retirement system has some appeal from a practical standpoint, especially where retirement system depreciation closely approximates depreciation expense under one of the usual methods.

Group and Composite Life Systems

In actual practice, many companies group certain operational assets for depreciation purposes. For example, all of the one-ton trucks may be grouped for depreciation purposes, or an entire operating assembly, such as a plant or a refinery, may be depreciated as a single unit. In such cases an **average depreciation** rate is applied to the group or assembly.

Where an average rate of depreciation is applied to a number of **homogeneous** assets (as characterized by similar characteristics and service lives), such as the trucks mentioned above, the procedure is referred to as **group depreciation.** Where an average or composite rate of depreciation is applied to a number of **heterogeneous** assets having dissimilar characteristics and service lives, such as the plant or the refinery mentioned above, the procedure is referred to as **composite depreciation.** The two methods are similar in mechanical application of an average rate and in the resulting journal entries; the main difference between them is the groups of assets to which they are applied (**homogenous** assets-**group** depreciation; **heterogeneous** assets-**composite** depreciation).[5]

Under the two systems, all of the assets in the group are recorded in one asset control account, and one accumulated depreciation account is established for the entire group. Consequently, the book value as reflected in these two accounts applies to the entire group and not to individual assets. Subsequent acquisitions of items belonging to the group are debited to the group asset account at cost. Depreciation is computed by multiplying an **average depreciation rate** by the balance in the group asset account regardless of the age of each individual asset represented therein. The rate may be computed and applied to cost or to cost less residual value, as desired. The depreciation entry is made by debiting Depreciation Expense and crediting Accumulated Depreciation for the periodic amount of depreciation thus computed.

Upon retirement of an asset from the group, the group asset account is credited for the **original cost** of the item and the Accumulated Depreciation account is debited for the **same amount less any residual recovery.** The systems, therefore, do not recognize "losses or gains" on retirement of single assets in the group.[6]

Group System. To illustrate the **group system** (i.e., homogeneous items), assume Robertson Wholesale Corporation purchased 10 forklift trucks for warehousing purposes, at a cost of $4,800 each. Each truck has an estimated residual value of $800 at the end of the estimated service life of five years. The company depreciates the trucks on a group basis. Assuming depreciation is recognized on the **ending**

[5] For a full discussion of depreciation of multiple asset accounts (group and composite), see J. D. Coughlan and W. K. Strand, *Depreciation: Accounting, Taxes and Business Decisions* (New York: Ronald Press, 1969), chap. 5. Group depreciation can utilize the straight-line or double-declining-balance formulas but cannot be based on SYD or output formulas.

[6] Ibid.

balance in the asset account, typical entries under the **group system** are indicated below:

1. To record the initial purchase of 10 forklift trucks at $4,800 each:

Trucks	48,000	
Cash		48,000

2. To record group depreciation at the end of the first year:

Depreciation expense ($48,000 × 16⅔%)	8,000	
Accumulated depreciation		8,000

Computation:

Cost	$48,000
Estimated residual value	8,000
To be depreciated over 5 years	$40,000
Depreciation per year ($40,000 ÷ 5)	$ 8,000
Depreciation rate on asset balance ($8,000 ÷ $48,000)	16⅔%

3. To record retirement of one truck at the end of the second year due to damage; amount received from insurance, $3,000:

Cash	3,000	
Accumulated depreciation (cost less residual recovery)	1,800	
Trucks		4,800

4. To record purchase of two additional forklift trucks at $5,000 each:

Trucks	10,000	
Cash		10,000

5. To record the retirement of a truck that has been used for 5½ years, and then sold to a salvage yard for $300, original cost, $4,800:

Cash	300	
Accumulated depreciation	4,500	
Trucks		4,800

In applying the group system it may be necessary to compute the **book value** of a specific asset in the group. For example, when a unit is transferred from one group account to another group account, as might be done when the asset is moved from one organizational division of the company to another, it is desirable that the original acquisition cost and accumulated depreciation to date be transferred in the accounts. In such cases the accumulated depreciation for a specific asset may be computed as follows:

$$\frac{\text{Present age}}{\text{Service life}} \times \left(\text{Acquisition cost} - \text{Residual value}\right)$$

To illustrate, assume a truck is being transferred from division A to division B; the truck originally cost $4,800 and has been in operation two years. Its estimated service life is five years, and the estimated residual value, $800. The truck has been depreciated on a group basis; the **average** group rate being used is 16⅔ percent per year. The entry to record the transfer might be as follows:

Truck—division B	4,800	
Accumulated depreciation, division A*	1,600	
Truck—division A		4,800
Accumulated depreciation, division B*		1,600

* Computation: (2 yrs. ÷ 5 yrs.) × ($4,800 − $800) = $1,600.

EXHIBIT 12–7: Computation of Composite Depreciation Rate under Composite Depreciation—Operating Assembly XY

Component Item	Original Cost	Residual Value	Amount to Be Depreciated	Estimated Service Life (years)	Annual Depreciation
A	$50,000	$5,000	$45,000	15	$3,000
B	20,000	4,000	16,000	10	1,600
C	7,000	600	6,400	8	800
D	3,000	-0-	3,000	3	1,000
	$80,000	$9,600	$70,400		$6,400*

* Composite life: $70,400 ÷ $6,400 = 11 years.
Composite depreciation rate on cost: $6,400 ÷ $80,000 = 8%

Depreciation first period:

Depreciation expense ($80,000 × 8%)	6,400	
Accumulated depreciation		6,400

Composite System. Under the composite system the individual assets in the group may have a wide range of service lives. Because of this condition, composite life depreciation is subject to theoretical objections. In establishing the average rate under composite depreciation, a **composite rate** usually is computed. Composite life is the weighted-average life of the various units in the composite group, and the composite depreciation rate is the ratio of the periodic depreciation to the acquisition cost of all components of the operating unit, as illustrated in Exhibit 12–7, on p. 412.

If there are no changes in the asset account illustrated in Exhibit 12–7, the assembly will be depreciated to the residual value at the end of the 11th year. Additions and disposals of parts of the composite unit are recorded as illustrated above for the group system. The rationale underlying group and composite depreciation systems recognizes that depreciation estimates are based on averages. Under both systems, additions and disposals that have significantly different lives, residual values, or costs may necessitate a change in the group or composite depreciation rate. Moreover, an implicit assumption underlying their use is that gains or losses on disposition of single assets are of minor significance.

The main objection to the group and composite systems is that it is possible for them to conceal faulty estimates of useful life and residual value for long periods and through their failure to recognize gains or losses, not correct for changes in asset usage or for other errors. Also, in case individual assets become idle, depreciation on these idle assets can be computed more precisely under unit (versus group and composite) methods. In such situations the assets involved should be **removed** from the group and accounted for separately.

FRACTIONAL YEAR DEPRECIATION

Implicit in the preceding illustrations has been the assumption that the asset year and the company's fiscal year coincide; however, assets seldom are purchased on the first day of a fiscal period and are seldom retired at the end of the fiscal year. Therefore, depreciation often must be computed for fractional parts of the year. An accounting policy generally is established so that consistent amounts of depreciation are recorded for fractional parts of the year.

Policies widely used are as follows:[7]

1. Depreciate from the first of the month all assets **acquired** on or before the 15th of the month; if **acquired** after the 15th, do not depreciate for the partial month. Assets **disposed of** on or before the 15th of the month are not depreciated for the partial month; if **disposed of** after the 15th, record a full month's depreciation.
2. To determine the monthly depreciation amount, divide the annual amount by 12 regardless of the method of depreciation used.
3. For methods other than straight-line depreciation, when the asset year and the fiscal year do not coincide, compute partial depreciation on the basis of the months for each of the partial years of the asset life and sum the results.

To illustrate implementation of the third policy, assume the asset used in Exhibit 12–5 was acquired on May 1, year 1, and was retired on April 30, year 4. The fiscal year ends on December 31. Using SYD depreciation, as given in Exhibit 12–5, the computations and results would be as follows:

Year	Annual Depreciation (Exhibit 12–5)	Months	Computation	Depreciation Expense
1	$45	8	($45 × 8/12)	$30
2	30	12	($45 × 4/12) + ($30 × 8/12)	35
3	15	12	($30 × 4/12) + ($15 × 8/12)	20
4		4	($15 × 4/12)	5
	$90	36		$90

[7] Alternatives, in addition to the three listed, include (1) depreciation computed on the balance in the asset account at the beginning of the year; (2) depreciation computed on the balance in the asset account at the end of the year; and (3) depreciation computed only on assets acquired during the first half of the year, and no depreciation on assets disposed of during the first half of the year. If these short-cut alternatives produce results that are not materially different from more precise application, they qualify under GAAP.

DEPRECIATION POLICY

Accounting Trends & Techniques, 1980, the AICPA annual survey of practices of 600 selected industrial corporations, indicates that in 1979 annual reports, the straight-line method is used more than all other methods combined, comprising 72 percent of total usage. Accelerated depreciation methods account for over 21 percent of the total, while unit-of-production methods account for over 5 percent. Details from the 1980 survey are presented in Exhibit 12–8.

The same study indicates that approximately 78 percent of the companies had material differences between depreciation reported on published financial statements and depreciation reported for income tax purposes;[8] this requires income tax allocation. For the most part, accelerated methods were used for tax purposes while straight line was used for financial reporting.

Companies use accelerated depreciation methods for tax purposes because of the cash flow advantage afforded by the faster tax write-offs. Differences between depreciation amounts for tax purposes and depreciation amounts for financial reporting purposes cause **timing** tax differences, as discussed in Chapter 10. Therefore, the tax advantage of accelerated depreciation methods **reverse** in later years of asset use. Nonetheless, the **time value of money** makes the accelerated methods attractive from a cash flow standpoint.

[8] AICPA, *Accounting Trends & Techniques, 1980* (New York, 1980), table 3–12, p. 282.

DEPRECIATION DISCLOSURES

Because of the significant effects of the depreciation methods used, on both financial position and the results of operations, the APB in *Opinion 12* reaffirmed an earlier *ARB* that the following disclosures should be made in the financial statements or accompanying notes:

a. Depreciation expense for the period.
b. Balances of major classes of depreciable assets, by nature or function, at the balance sheet date.
c. Accumulated depreciation, either by major classes of depreciable assets or in total, at the balance sheet date.
d. A general description of the methods used in computing depreciation on major classes of depreciable assets.

This was augmented in *APB Opinion No. 22,* "Disclosure of Accounting Policies," which cited depreciation methods and amortization policies as examples of required disclosures.

DEPLETION

Nature of Depletion

In accounting, **depletion** is the allocation of the cost of a natural resource (wasting asset) against revenue as it is exploited and sold. Examples of such resources are ore, oil, coal, timber, and gravel. In accounting for such assets, the original cost is recorded in accordance with the **cost principle** and subsequently amortized over the total production available, in harmony with the **matching principle.**

EXHIBIT 12–8: Depreciation Methods*

	Number of Companies			
	1979	**1978**	**1977**	**1976**
Straight line	556	560	559	567
Declining balance	63	67	67	66
Sum-of-the-years' digits	34	35	34	37
Accelerated method—not specified	71	67	60	71
Unit of production	46	44	40	41

* AICPA, *Accounting Trends & Techniques, 1980* (New York, 1980), table 3–10, p. 278. The columns sum to more than 600 because some companies use different depreciation methods for different classes of depreciable assets.

Accounting for Depletion

Allocation of the **cost** of the natural resource to units of inventory usually is accomplished by dividing *(a)* the cost of the asset (less any residual value) by *(b)* the estimated number of units that can be withdrawn economically. Essentially, this is the technique used in the production (output) depreciation method. The **unit depletion rate,** thus computed, is multiplied by the actual units withdrawn during the period to determine the depletion amount for the period. As with other tangible assets, three factors are involved: (1) actual cost, including all development costs related to the resource; (2) estimated production over the life of the resource; and (3) estimated residual value of the property upon exhaustion of the natural resource.

The depletion amount for a period first is debited to the Inventory account for the natural resource (e.g., oil, coal, or gravel) and credited to the related asset account. Then, as the inventory items are sold, the inventory cost, including depletion, is expensed as cost of goods sold in the normal manner. Therefore, at the end of the accounting period, part of the periodic depletion amount is included in the Inventory account, to the extent that units of the natural resource were withdrawn but not sold during the period.

To illustrate accounting for depletion, assume it is estimated by reserve geologists that a given mineral lease has a potential production of 100,000 units, and that the total cost of the lease, including development costs, is $460,000 with no residual value. The estimated depletion rate per unit of mineral and its application would be computed as follows, assuming 10,000 units were extracted during the period:

Estimated depletion rate:
$460,000 ÷ 100,000 units = $4.60 per unit
Actual production for period:
10,000 units
Depletion amount for period:
10,000 × $4.60 = $46,000

If 8,000 units were sold during the period and 2,000 were on hand at the end of the period, the mineral inventory account would include depletion of $9,200 (i.e., 2,000 × $4.60) and cost of goods sold reported on the income statement would include depletion of $36,800 (i.e., 8,000 × $4.60).

Acquisition costs and development costs, and tangible property costs associated with a natural resource should be set up in separate asset accounts. If any of the resulting facilities, such as buildings, are likely to have a shorter life than the natural resource, their acquisition cost, less any estimated residual value, should be depreciated over the shorter period.

In view of the difficulties in estimating underground deposits of minerals, the evaluation of additional information derived through further developmental work and the additional costs incident thereto, the depletion rate must be changed from time to time. The new rate is determined by dividing the unamortized cost plus any additional development costs by the **remaining** estimated reserves. Past depletion amounts are **not** revised. Instead, the change in depletion rate is accounted for prospectively as a change in accounting estimate in the manner described above, in accordance with the provisions of *APB Opinion No. 20,* "Accounting Changes" (discussed in Chapter 20).

Depletion and Income Taxes

The depletion procedures described above are used for financial and cost accounting purposes. For federal income tax purposes, other depletion methods may be employed in accordance with the Internal Revenue Code. For example, the Code permits taxpayers to use **statutory or percentage depletion** rather than cost depletion illustrated above. Under statutory depletion, a stated percentage of gross **income** derived from the sale of the natural resource asset may be taken as the depletion deduction on the tax return. The percentage varies from 5 percent on some deposits to 22 percent on others. Some of the more common depletion percentages are listed below:

Sulphur and uranium; if from deposits in the United States, asbestos, lead, zinc, nickel, and certain others	22%
Oil and gas*	20%
Gold, silver, copper, iron ore, and oil shale (from U.S. deposits)	15
Coal and sodium chloride	10
Clay and shale used for certain purposes	7½
Other clay	5
Certain other minerals and metallic ores	14

* For many years the percentage rate on oil and gas was 27½ percent; in 1969 it was reduced to 22 percent, and in 1981, it was reduced to 20 percent; by 1984, the rate is scheduled to be 15 percent. Recently it was eliminated for larger oil producers but still has limited applicability.

Under the Code, the sum of the statutory depletion charges allowed may (and in practice frequently does) exceed the original cost of the resource. The use of cost depletion for financial reporting purposes and statutory depletion for income tax purposes gives rise to a **permanent tax difference,** as discussed in Chapter 10.

Depletion and Liquidating Dividends

Dividends sometimes are paid by small natural resource companies in an amount equivalent to accumulated income plus the accumulated amount of depletion. State laws often permit such dividends. This practice is common when the company has no plans to replace the natural resource in kind and operations are to cease upon exhaustion of the deposit. In such cases, the stockholders should be informed of the portion of each dividend that represents a return of capital (i.e., the depletion amount). To illustrate, assume the Tex Oil Company accounts showed the following (summarized):

Assets	$1,000,000
Accumulated depreciation	(200,000)
Accumulated depletion	(100,000)
	$ 700,000
Liabilities	$ 150,000
Capital stock	500,000
Retained earnings	50,000
	$ 700,000

The board of directors could declare a dividend of $150,000 which would be recorded as follows:

Retained earnings	50,000	
Return of capital to stockholders	100,000	
Cash		150,000

The return of capital ($100,000) to stockholders would be reported as a deduction in the owners' equity section of the balance sheet.

CHANGES AND CORRECTION OF DEPRECIATION AND DEPLETION

Occasionally a business will change the method of depreciation used, change estimates of service life or residual value, or locate errors. *APB Opinion No. 20,* "Accounting Changes," specifies how each of these three different situations should be accounted for and reported. The provisions of the *Opinion* are discussed and illustrated in Chapter 20. As they relate to depreciation and depletion, they may be summarized briefly as follows (using the term **depreciation** to refer to depletion and amortization as well):

1. **Change in accounting principle**—a change from one generally accepted method to another generally accepted method (such as from SYD to straight line). Changes of this type require an adjustment for the differences in accumulated depreciation to date between the old and new methods. This difference is recorded as a "depreciation adjustment" which is reported on the income statement for the period of change between the captions Income before extraordinary items and Net income.
2. **Change in estimate**—a change in the estimated useful life and/or the residual value. Changes of this type are made **prospectively.** This means that the undepreciated balance is apportioned to the new remaining life taking into account the new estimated life and/or new residual value.
3. **Accounting error**—Errors in depreciation made in prior years should be corrected when found. If the error affected the current period only, the incorrect entry can be reversed and the correct entry made, all during the current period. However, if the error affected one or more prior periods, the correcting entry involves making a **prior period adjustment** (reported on the statement of retained earnings) for the net effect of the error up to the **beginning** of the year during which the error is corrected. To illustrate, assume that a machine that cost $10,000, estimated service life of five years, no residual value, was incorrectly debited to expense when acquired. The error was discovered during the third year after acquisition. The correcting entry and the depreciation entry for the third year follow:

   a. Correcting entry:

Machine	10,000	
Accumulated depreciation ($10,000 × ⅖)		4,000
Prior period adjustment—error correction		6,000

   b. Adjusting entry for depreciation expense, end of third year:

Depreciation expense ($10,000 ÷ 5)	2,000	
Accumulated depreciation		2,000

Supplement 12-A: Annuity and Sinking Fund Methods of Depreciation

The annuity and sinking fund methods of depreciation are based on the same concepts that underlie an annuity investment. In this situation an investment is made and subsequently returns are received, usually each period. Each periodic return includes two separate elements: *(a)* a return of principal and *(b)* investment revenue. Over time, the periodic return of principal is larger (this represents depreciation) and the periodic interest element is smaller as the asset diminishes in value with use. The annuity and sinking fund methods yield the same overall effect on the income statement and balance sheet; their differences relate to the **reporting** of depreciation expense and imputed interest revenue on the income statement.

To illustrate the annuity and sinking fund methods of depreciation, assume the following simplified data:

Investment in plant item at cost at beginning of year 1	$100
Estimated useful life of plant item	3 years
Residual or scrap value estimated at end of year 3	$ 10
Average cost of capital	10%
Present value of 1 for 3 periods at 10% (Table 5–2)	.75131
Present value of ordinary annuity of 3 rents at 10% (Table 5–4)	2.48685

ANNUITY METHOD OF DEPRECIATION

To apply this method, the annual depreciation amount is computed on an annuity basis. The amount of the estimated annual earnings from the investment (e.g., $37.19 in the example below) is assumed to represent depreciation expense; accumulated depreciation is credited for the portion that represents return of principal (e.g., col. *c* below), and the difference is credited to **imputed** interest revenue (e.g., col. *b* below).

To illustrate, the periodic amount of depreciation expense would be computed as follows:

$$\text{Depreciation expense} = \frac{C - (R \times p)}{P_o} = \frac{\$100 - (\$10 \times .75131)}{2.48685} = \$37.19$$

where C refers to cost, R refers to residual value, p refers to the present value of 1, and P_o refers to the present value of an ordinary annuity.

With this value we can construct a depreciation schedule reflecting the entries for depreciation and the periodic book value of the asset from acquisition to retirement. The schedule would be as shown at the bottom of this page.

Observe that the above schedule is identical with an annuity amortization schedule (Chapter 5) except for the column captions. Also observe the following characteristics of the annuity method, as revealed by the entries in the above schedule, viz:

1. Depreciation Expense is debited each period for a **constant** amount, and total depreciation expense exceeds the cost to be depreciated ($90

Depreciation Schedule and Journal Entries—Annuity Method

Year	*(a)* Depreciation Expense Dr.	*(b)* Interest Revenue Cr.	*(c)* Accumulated Depreciation Cr.	*(d)* Unamortized Asset Balance
0	—	—	—	$100.00
1	$ 37.19	$10.00	$27.19	72.81
2	37.19	7.28	29.91	42.90
3	37.19	4.29	32.90	10.00
	$111.57	$21.57	$90.00	

(a) Constant amount from formula as computed above.
(b) Previous unamortized asset balance multiplied by .10.
(c) *(a)–(b)*.
(d) Previous balance minus current amount in *(c)*.

in the example) because depreciation expense **includes** the imputed interest.

2. Accumulated Depreciation is credited for an **increasing** amount each period, and in total it is the same as the amount to be depreciated.
3. Interest Revenue (this is imputed interest) is credited for a **decreasing** amount each period to reflect the constant rate of return on a declining investment.
4. Because of the net effect of Depreciation Expense and Interest Revenue, there is an **increasing net expense** effect on the income statement. It is the same as the credit to accumulated depreciation each period.
5. The carrying value of the asset decreases each period by a continuously increasing amount.

SINKING FUND METHOD OF DEPRECIATION

The sinking fund method is similar to the annuity method. The main difference is that under the sinking fund method, imputed interest is not separately recorded and reported, while under the annuity method imputed interest is accorded separate recognition. It should be pointed out that while a sinking fund to replace the asset being depreciated might be maintained, most companies would prefer to invest in other productive assets and that formal sinking funds (asset replacement funds) are quite rare. The journal entries, assuming depreciation only and no actual sinking fund, for the two methods are as follows:

Observe in the illustration that the sum of the three annual amounts **credited to accumulated** depreciation under both methods is $90 (enough to replace the asset if its replacement cost does not rise and if the $10 estimated residual value is realized). Also observe that if a series of three payments of $27.19 [i.e., $90 ÷ 3.31 ($Fo_{n=3,\,i=10\%}$; Table 5–3)] were made to a sinking fund earning 10 percent, $90 would accumulate at the end of three years.

To summarize, the above entries reveal that the only difference between the two methods is the treatment of **imputed** interest: Both credit the same periodic amounts to accumulated depreciation; both produce the same periodic income; however, the annuity method produces a **higher** periodic depreciation expense, which is reduced by the credit to imputed interest.

The compound interest methods have been criticized on the grounds that they are not "rational" since an increasing amount of periodic depreciation over the life of the asset is inconsistent with the fact that ownership costs based on value tend to decrease in later years. Also, a part of the periodic depreciation amount under the **annuity method** is for imputed or theoretical interest; the offsetting credit for this element is made to Interest Revenue; therefore, it affects the reported income or loss of the period in which the depreciation is recorded.

For a combination of reasons, the compound interest methods have been used relatively little in practice. Many entities, for reasons already cited, prefer to adopt depreciation methods which result in a somewhat opposite pattern of depreciation expense

Annuity and Sinking Fund Depreciation Methods Compared

	Annuity Method		Sinking Fund Method	
Year 1:				
Depreciation expense	37.19		27.19	
Accumulated depreciation		27.19		27.19
Interest revenue		10.00		
Year 2:				
Depreciation expense	37.19		29.91	
Accumulated depreciation		29.91		29.91
Interest revenue		7.28		
Year 3:				
Depreciation expense	37.19		32.90	
Accumulated depreciation		32.90		32.90
Interest revenue		4.29		

(i.e., more depreciation in earlier years and less depreciation in later years).

The limited extent to which these methods have been used seems to be confined largely to public utilities. There is some theoretical justification for their use by regulated businesses where a precalculated rate of return on investment virtually is assured by the rate-setting process and revenues wherein the rates are set on the basis of a regulated rate of return on invested capital. Generally, it can be said that they do not conform to current GAAP.

QUESTIONS

PART A

1. Distinguish among amortization, depletion, and depreciation.
2. Explain the effects of depreciation on *(a)* the income statement and *(b)* the balance sheet.
3. Explain the relationship of depreciation to *(a)* cash flow and *(b)* assets.
4. What is the relationship between depreciation and replacement of the assets being depreciated?
5. What are the primary causes of depreciation? What effect do changes in the market value of the asset being depreciated have on the depreciation estimates?
6. List and briefly explain the three factors which must be considered in allocating the cost of an operational asset.
7. What is meant by *accelerated methods of depreciation?* Under what circumstances would these methods generally be appropriate?
8. As between the SYD and DDB depreciation methods, which method will always produce the larger amount of depreciation in the first year of use of an asset?

PART B

9. What accounting policy problems arise when the entity's fiscal year and the asset year do not coincide? Consider the case of a company that closes its books on June 30 but has bought a depreciable asset on January 1.
10. Briefly explain the inventory system of depreciation. Under what circumstances is such a system appropriate?
11. Compare the retirement and replacement depreciation systems.
12. How are composite life depreciation and group depreciation similar?
13. There are three categories in respect to change and correction of depreciation. Briefly explain each and outline the accounting involved as specified in *APB Opinion 20.*
14. Define *depletion.* How is depletion generally computed for financial and cost accounting purposes?
15. What depreciation methods are based on compound interest principles? How are the methods similar? Dissimilar?

DECISION CASE 12–1

Some of the major car rental companies account for the gain or loss on disposal of their used cars as an adjustment of depreciation expense of the period of disposal rather than reporting gains or losses on disposal.

Required:

On what grounds, if any, can such a procedure be justifiable? Would your answer be different if the procedure were used by relatively few (versus most) companies in the industry?

DECISION CASE 12–2

A friend of yours recently inherited capital stock in Major Mining Corporation. The friend recently received the first annual financial report from the company since the inheritance. One aspect of the report in particular troubles your friend; consequently, you have been asked for an explanation of what the company seems to be saying. The excerpt reads:

> Depletion of mines is computed on the basis of an overall unit rate applied to the pounds of principal products sold from mine production. The corporation makes no representation that the annual amount represents the depletion actually sustained or the decline, if any, in mine values attributable to the year's operations, or that it represents anything other than a general provision for the amortization of the remaining book value of mines.

Specifically, your friend asks: (1) Is the depletion amount reported on the income statement meaningless? (2) Are the company's mines becoming more or less valuable? (3) What is the significance of the book value of the company's mines?

Required:
Respond to your friend's questions. Identify each element of your response with the three questions your friend has asked.

DECISION CASE 12–3

In situations where depreciable properties are treated as units rather than being part of a group of assets depreciated on a composite or group basis, the question sometimes arises as to just what constitutes a property unit for accounting purposes. For example, a building as a single entity may be designated as the basic property unit. Alternatively the elevators, escalators, heating and air-conditioning system, other mechanical equipment, plumbing, electrical system, and the basic building structure could be accounted for as separate property units.

Required:

a. What accounting problems arise if what could be accounted for as a single property unit is instead accounted for as a number of separate asset units?

b. Identify and explain some advantages of accounting separately for smaller property units as opposed to aggregation as a single property unit.

DECISION CASE 12–4

1. A new client has certain fully depreciated tangible operational assets which are still used in the business.
   (a) Discuss the possible reasons why this could happen.
   (b) Comment on the significance of the continued use of these fully depreciated assets.
2. In the past these fully depreciated assets and their accumulated depreciation have been merged with other operational assets and related depreciation on the balance sheet. Discuss the propriety of this accounting treatment, including a discussion of other possible treatments and the circumstances in which they would be appropriate. (AICPA adapted)

DECISION CASE 12–5

Nice Homes Corporation sells and erects shell houses. These are frame structures that are completely finished on the outside but are unfinished on the inside except for flooring, partition studding, and ceiling joists. Shell houses are sold chiefly to customers who are handy with tools and who have time to do the interior wiring, plumbing, wall completion, finishing, and other work necessary to make the shell houses livable dwellings.

Nice Homes buys shell houses from a manufacturer in unassembled packages consisting of all lumber, roofing, doors, windows, and similar materials necessary to complete a shell house. Upon commencing operations in a new area, Nice Homes buys or leases land as a site for its local warehouse, field office, and display houses. Sample display houses are erected at a total cost of from $35,000 to $40,000, including the cost of the unassembled packages. The chief element of cost of the display houses is the unassembled packages, since erection is a short-term, low-cost operation. Old sample models are torn down or altered into new models every three to seven years. Sample display houses have little salvage value because dismantling and moving costs amount to nearly as much as the salvage value of an unassembled package.

Required:

1. A choice must be made between (1) expensing the costs of sample display houses in the period in which the expenditure is made and (2) spreading the costs over more than one period. Discuss the relative merits of each method.
2. Would it be preferable to depreciate the cost of display houses on the basis of *(a)* the passage of time or *(b)* the number of shell houses sold? Explain.

(AICPA adapted)

EXERCISES

PART A: EXERCISES 12–1 to 12–7

Exercise 12–1

To demonstrate the mechanical computations involved in several methods of depreciation, the following simplified situation is presented:

Acquisition cost	$ 8,600
Residual value	$ 600
Estimated service life:	
Years	5
Service hours	10,000
Productive output	32,000

Required:

Compute the annual depreciation under each of the following situations (show computations and round to the nearest dollar):

1. Straight-line depreciation; compute the depreciation amount and rate for each year.
2. Service hours method; compute the depreciation rate and amount for the first year assuming 2,200 service hours of actual operation.
3. Productive output method of depreciation; compute the depreciation rate and amount for the first year assuming 3,800 units of output. Is all of the depreciation amount (computed in your answer) expensed during the current period?
4. SYD method; compute the depreciation amount for each year.
5. DDB method; compute the depreciation amount for each year.

Exercise 12–2

Equipment which cost Marcus Company $15,000 will be depreciated on the assumption it will last eight years and have a $1,000 residual value. Several possible methods of depreciation are under consideration.

Required:

1. Prepare a schedule which shows annual depreciation expense, accumulated depreciation, and book values for the *first two* years assuming (show computations and round to nearest dollar):
   a. SYD method.
   b. Productive output method. Estimated output is a total of 84,000 units, of which 9,000 will be produced the first year; 12,000 for each of the next two years; 15,000 the fourth year; 10,000 the fifth, sixth, and seventh years; and 6,000 the final year.
2. What criteria would you consider important in selecting a method?

Exercise 12–3

Friday Company acquired a depreciable asset at a cost of $9,600 which is estimated to have a useful life of four years and residual value of $1,600.

Required:

1. Prepare a depreciation table for the entire life of the asset reflecting use of the following methods (show computations and round to nearest dollar):
   a. Straight-line method.
   b. SYD method.
   c. DDB method.
2. What criteria should be considered in selecting a method?

Exercise 12–4

James Company bought a machine for $10,000 which has an estimated service life of four years and a residual value of $750.

Required:

1. Prepare a depreciation table covering the life of the asset reflecting use of the following methods (show computations and round to nearest dollar):
   a. SYD method.
   b. Productive output method. Total output is estimated at 36,000 units. Assume actual output for the four years was sequentially: 11,000; 8,000; 6,000; and

11,000 units. Round the rate to four decimal places.

c. DDB method.

2. Assume same facts as in 1c above except that in the third year, after 10 months, the machine was sold for $1,600 cash. Journalize the depreciation and the sale.

Exercise 12–5

Kraft Company bought equipment on January 1, 19A, for $22,000 for which the expected life is 10 years and residual value is $2,000. Under three acceptable depreciation methods, the annual depreciation expense and cumulative balance of accumulated depreciation at the end of 19A and 19B are shown below.

(Relates to Exercise 12–5)

	Method A		Method B		Method C	
Year	Annual Expense	Accumulated Amount	Annual Expense	Accumulated Amount	Annual Expense	Accumulated Amount
19A	$3,636	$3,636	$4,400	$4,400	$2,000	$2,000
19B	3,272	6,908	3,520	7,920	2,000	4,000

Required:

1. Identify the depreciation method used in each instance.
2. Project continued use of the same method through years 19C and 19D and determine the annual depreciation expense and accumulated depreciation amount for each year under each method.

Exercise 12–6 (Also Reviews Chapter 10, Part B)

From time to time, Congress considers enactment of income tax provisions designed to furnish incentives for various types of businesses. Assume that the tax laws are modified to provide that these periods can be used to depreciate major classes of assets fully:

Asset Class	Life (in years)
Factory buildings, stores, warehouses	10
Machinery and equipment	5
Light trucks and automobiles	3

Required:

1. If the new provision applies only to assets bought after the effective date of the law, what would be the immediate accounting impact? What would be the accounting impact in future years?
2. Assume that, if the law provides that when the remaining life of a depreciable asset exceeds the life specified above, the life specified in the law must be used as the interval over which the remaining book value can be depreciated. Z Company owns the following depreciable properties which are being depreciated using the straight-line method over the useful lives shown above; none of the assets has a residual value.

Asset	Cost	Years Already Used	Expected Life (years)
Building A	$100,000	12	30
Building B	200,000	8	40
Machinery	330,000	9	15
Office equipment	100,000	10	12
Light trucks	60,000	2	6

Prepare a columnar schedule which shows, for each asset listed, book value, depreciation for income tax purposes the first year the law is effective, and depreciation for financial accounting purposes for that year.

3. If Z Company's income is taxed at the rate of 40%, give the entries to record depreciation and income tax allocation the first year the new provisions are applied.

Exercise 12–7

Butler Stores, Inc., depreciates its display cases on a straight-line basis. Transactions relative to display cases in store A were as follows:

a. January 2, 19A: Bought six display cases for an aggregate price of $16,500, paying cash.

b. December 31, 19A: On the assumption the residual value of the cases would total 10% of original cost and the cases have a useful life of five years, recorded depreciation at year-end.

c. Recorded depreciation at year-end, December 31, 19B.

d. January 2, 19C: One display case was sold for $1,250 cash.

e. Two additional display cases were bought January 10, 19C, at the same unit price as the original cases.

f. Recorded depreciation at December 31, 19C, for full year for all cases.

g. Transferred one of the original display cases to Store C on January 2, 19D.

Required:
Give entries for each transaction; show computations; closing entries are not required. Use a Fixtures account for the display cases and identify fixtures by store (e.g., store A, store C).

PART B: EXERCISES 12–8 to 12–17

Exercise 12–8

Electric Utility Company purchased 500 poles at $120 per pole, the debit being to the Inventory—Poles P-1 account. Subsequent to the purchase, 100 of the new poles were used to replace an equal number of old poles (Poles M-1) which were carried in the tangible operational asset account, Poles—M-1. The old poles originally cost $30 each and had an estimated residual value of $10 per pole.

Required:
1. Give all indicated entries *(a)* assuming the replacement system is employed and *(b)* assuming the retirement system is used.
2. Compare the effect on the periodic depreciation expense and the asset accounts as between the two systems.

Exercise 12–9

Madison Company owned a power plant which consisted of the following, all acquired on January 1, 19C:

	Cost	Estimated Residual Value	Estimated Life (years)
Building	$600,000	None	30
Machinery, etc.	180,000	$18,000	10
Other equipment	150,000	10,000	5

Required (carry decimals to two places):
1. Compute the total straight-line depreciation for 19D on all items combined.
2. Compute the composite depreciation rate on the plant.
3. Determine the composite life of the plant.

Exercise 12–10

Smithson Company owned the following machines, all acquired at the same time:

Machine	Cost	Estimated Residual Value	Estimated Life (years)
A	$12,000	None	3
B	20,000	$2,400	8
C	30,000	2,000	10
D	38,000	2,000	12

Required:
1. Calculate total depreciation if machines are depreciated on a unit basis by the straight-line method.
2. Determine the composite depreciation rate if the machines are depreciated as a group.
3. Determine the group life of the machines.

Exercise 12–11

Alpha Company's records show the following property acquisitions and retirements during the first two years of operations:

Year	Cost of Property Acquired	Estimated Useful Life (years)	Retirements: Year of Acquisition	Retirements: Amount
19A ..	$50,000	10	—	—
19B ...	20,000	10	19A	$7,000

Property is depreciated for one-half year in the year of acquisition. Retired property is to be depreciated for one-half year in its year of retirement. Assume zero residual values for depreciation computations and that asset retirements result in losses (that is, no residual or sale proceeds from retirement).

Required:
Determine depreciation expense for 19A and for 19B and the balances of the Property and related Accumulated Depreciation accounts at the end of each year under the following depreciation methods (show computations and round to the nearest dollar):

a. Straight-line method.
b. SYD method. (AICPA adapted)

Exercise 12–12

Bower Company owned 10 warehouses of a similar type except for varying size. The group system is applied to the 10 warehouses, the rate being 8% per year on cost. At the end of the 10th year, the asset account Warehouses showed a balance of $5,300,000 (residual value $300,000) and the Accumulated Depreciation account showed a balance of $2,400,000. Shortly after the end of the 10th year, warehouse no. 8, costing $400,000, was retired and demolished. Materials salvaged from the demolition were sold for $53,000, and $15,000 was spent on demolition.

Required:
Give entries to record *(a)* depreciation for the 10th year, *(b)* retirement of the warehouse, and *(c)* depreciation for the 11th year.

Exercise 12–13

Jackson Company's investment in a gravel quarry amounted to $4,000,000, of which $400,000 could be ascribed to land value after the gravel has been removed. Geologists who were engaged to estimate the removable gravel reported originally that six million cubic yards (units) could be extracted. In the first year, 900,000 units were extracted and 820,000 units were sold. In the second year, 800,000 units were extracted and sales were 850,000 units.

At the start of the third year, management of Jackson had the quarry examined again, at which time it was determined the remaining removable gravel was 3 million units. Production and sales for the third year amounted to 300,000 units. In the fourth year, production was 750,000 units while sales amounted to 600,000 units.

Required:

1. Calculate depletion expense to be reported on Jackson's income statement for each of the four years. Show supporting computations.
2. Show how the gravel inventory (FIFO basis) and the gravel deposit would be reported on Jackson's balance sheet at the end of the fourth year. Assume an accumulated depletion account is used.

Exercise 12–14

Jones Minerals, Inc., paid $1,700,000 for property with removable ore estimated at 2 million pounds. The property has an estimated value of $100,000 after the ore has been extracted. Before any ore could be removed it was necessary to incur $400,000 of developmental costs. In the first year, 200,000 pounds were removed and 175,000 pounds of ore were sold; in the second year, 300,000 pounds were removed and 325,000 pounds were sold. In the course of the second year's production, discoveries were made which indicated that if an added $1,470,000 is spent on developmental costs during the third year, future removable ore will total 2.7 million pounds. After incurring these added costs, production for the third year amounts to 540,000 pounds, and sales, 531,000 pounds.

Required:

1. Calculate depletion expense that Jones should report on its income statement for each of the three years. Show supporting computations and round unit costs to three decimal places.
2. Show how the resource and the inventory should be reported by Jones on its balance sheet at the end of the third year (FIFO basis). Assume an accumulated depletion account is used.
3. Give the journal entry to record depletion expense at the end of the three years.

Exercise 12–15

There are both similarities and differences to be found in the accounting treatments of depreciation and depletion.

Required:

1. Describe cost depletion and statutory depletion. Under what conditions, if any, is statutory depletion permitted?
2. List *(a)* the similarities and *(b)* the differences in accounting treatments of depreciation and cost depletion.
3. Operational assets donated to corporations are placed on the books, and their depreciation or depletion is recorded. Discuss the accounting justification for recording on the books *(a)* operational assets received as a gift and *(b)* their depreciation or depletion.

(AICPA adapted)

Exercise 12–16

Select the best choice for each of the following. Briefly justify your selection of each item.

1. Exploitation Company acquired a tract of land containing an extractable natural resource. Exploitation Company is required by its purchase contract to restore the land to a condition suitable for recreational use after it extracts the natural resource. Geological surveys estimate the recoverable natural resource will be 3 million tons, and that the land will have a value of $600,000 after restoration. Relevant cost information follows:

Land	$6,000,000
Restoration	900,000
Geological surveys	300,000

   If Exploitation Company maintains no inventories of extracted material, what should be the debit to depletion expense per ton of material extracted?
   a. $1.80.
   b. $1.90.
   c. $2.00.
   d. $2.20.
2. As generally used in accounting, what is depreciation?
   a. It is a process of asset valuation for balance sheet purposes.
   b. It applies only to long-lived intangible assets.
   c. It is used to indicate a decline in market value of a long-lived asset.
   d. It is an accounting process which allocates long-lived asset cost to accounting periods.
3. Property, plant, and equipment should be reported as valued at cost less accumulated depreciation on a balance sheet dated December 31, 19x9, unless
   a. Some obsolescence is known to have occurred.
   b. An appraisal made during 19x9 disclosed a higher value.

c. The amount of insurance carried on the property is well in excess of its book value.
d. Some of the property still on hand was written down in 19x5 due to permanent impairment of its use value.

4. Which of the following statements is the assumption on which straight-line depreciation is based?
   a. The operating efficiency of the asset decreases in later years.
   b. Service value declines as a function of time rather than use.
   c. Service value declines as a function of obsolescence rather than time.
   d. Physical wear and tear are more important than economic obsolescence.
5. Upon purchase of certain depreciable assets utilized in its production process, a company expects to be able to replace these assets by adopting a policy of never declaring dividends in amounts larger than net income (after deducting depreciation). If a net income is earned each year, recording depreciation will coincidentally result in sufficient assets being retained within the enterprise which, if in liquid form, could be used to replace those fully depreciated assets if—
   a. Prices remain reasonably constant during the life of the property.
   b. Prices rise throughout the life of the property.
   c. The retirement depreciation method is used.
   d. Obsolescence was an unexpected factor in bringing about retirement of the assets replaced.
6. In 19x1, Anton Company purchased a tract of land as a possible future plant site. In January 19x9, valuable sulphur deposits were discovered on adjoining property and Anton Company immediately began explorations on its property. In December 19x9, after incurring $100,000 exploration costs, which were accumulated in an asset account, the company discovered sulphur deposits appraised at $1 million more than the value of the land. To record the discovery value the company should debit—
   a. $100,000 to an expense account.
   b. $100,000 to an asset account.
   c. $1,000,000 to an asset account and $100,000 to an expense account.
   d. $1,000,000 to an asset account. (AICPA adapted)

Exercise 12–17 (questions 9 and 10 based on Supplement 12–A)

Select the best choice for each of the following. Briefly justify your selection of each item.

1. Odell Corporation quarries limestone at two locations, crushes it, and sells it to be used in road building. The Internal Revenue Code provides for 5% depletion on such limestone. Quarry no. 1 is leased on a year-to-year basis with the company paying a royalty of 1 cent per ton of limestone quarried. Quarry no. 2 is owned, the company having paid $100,000 for the site; the company estimates that the property can be sold for $30,000 after production ceases. Other data follow:

	Quarry No. 1	Quarry No. 2
Est. total reserves, tons ...	30,000,000	100,000,000
Tons quarried through 12/31/x1	2,000,000	40,000,000
Tons quarried, 19x2	800,000	1,380,000
Sales, 19x2	$600,000	$1,000,000

   19x2 depletion of quarry no. 1 for financial reporting purposes is—
   a. $3,000.
   b. $8,000.
   c. $30,000.
   d. $29,600.
   e. None of the above.
2. Assume the same facts as in question 1. 19x2 depletion of quarry no. 2 for financial reporting purposes is—
   a. $0.
   b. $1,380.
   c. $966.
   d. $50,000.
   e. None of the above.
3. Assume the same facts as in question 1, except that a new engineering study performed early in 19x2 indicated that as of January 1, 19x2, 75 million tons of limestone were available in quarry no. 2. 19x2 depletion of quarry no. 2 for financial reporting purposes is—
   a. $772.80.
   b. $840.
   c. $0.
   d. $50,000.
   e. None of the above.
4. Which of the following reasons provides the best theoretical support for accelerated depreciation?
   a. Assets are more efficient in early years and initially generate more revenue.
   b. Expenses should be allocated in a manner that "smooths" earnings.
   c. Repairs and maintenance costs will probably increase in later periods, so depreciation should decline.
   d. Accelerated depreciation provides easier replacement because of the time value of money.
5. A principal objection to the straight-line method of depreciation is that it—
   a. Provides for the declining productivity of an aging asset.
   b. Ignores variations in the rate of asset use.

c. Tends to result in a constant rate of return on a diminishing investment base.
d. Gives smaller periodic write-offs than decreasing charge methods.

6. Lay Corporation, which has a calendar year accounting period, purchased a new machine for $10,000 on April 1, 19x1. At that time Lay expected to use the machine for nine years and then sell it for $1,000. The machine was sold for $5,000 on September 30, 19x7. Assuming straight-line depreciation, no depreciation in year of acquisition, and a full year of depreciation in the year of retirement, the gain to be recognized at the time of the sale would be—
   a. $1,000.
   b. $500.
   c. $445.
   d. $0.
   e. None of the above.
7. A graph is set up with "depreciation expense" on the vertical axis and "time" on the horizontal axis. Assuming linear relationships, how would the graphs for straight-line and SYD depreciation, respectively, be drawn?
   a. Vertically and sloping down to the right.
   b. Vertically and sloping up to the right.
   c. Horizontally and sloping down to the right.
   d. Horizontally and sloping up to the right.
8. On July 1, 19x1, Gusto Corporation purchased equipment at a cost of $22,000. The equipment has an estimated residual value of $3,000 and is being depreciated over an estimated life of eight years under the DDB method of depreciation. For the six months ended December 31, 19x1, Gusto recorded one-half year's depreciation. What should be the amount of depreciation (rounded to the nearest dollar) on this equipment for the year ended December 31, 19x2?
   a. $4,158.
   b. $4,750.
   c. $4,813.
   d. $5,500.
9. The depreciation method that does not result in decreasing charges is—
   a. DDB.
   b. Fixed-percentage-on-book value.
   c. Sinking fund.
   d. SYD.
10. Use of the annuity method of calculating depreciation over an asset's life results in—
   a. Constant amounts of depreciation expense.
   b. Decreasing amounts of depreciation expense.
   c. Increasing credits to interest revenue.
   d. Constant credits to interest revenue.

SUPPLEMENT 12–A: EXERCISE 12–18

Exercise 12–18

Equipment costing $50,000 and an estimated life of three years with a residual value of $8,000 is to be depreciated by compound-interest methods.

Required (round to nearest dollar):
Using a 15% rate prepare a depreciation table covering the entire life of the asset assuming—

1. Annuity method.
2. Sinking fund method (round latter to nearest dollar).

PROBLEMS

PART A: PROBLEMS 12–1 to 12–11

Problem 12–1

Depreciation continues to be one of the more important problem areas in accounting.

Required:
1. *a.* Explain the factors that should be considered when applying the conventional concept of depreciation to the determination of how the value of a newly acquired computer system should be assigned to expense for financial reporting purposes. (Ignore income tax considerations.)
   b. What depreciation methods might be used for the computer system?
2. *a.* Explain the conventional accounting concept of depreciation accounting.
   b. Discuss its conceptual merit with respect to *(i)* the value of the asset, *(ii)* periodic amounts of expense, and *(iii)* the discretion of management in selecting the method. (AICPA adapted)

Problem 12–2

Vaught Company purchased a special machine at a cost of $91,000. It was estimated that the machine would have a net resale value at the end of its useful life of $7,000. Statistics relating to the machine over its service life were as follows:

Estimated service life:

Years	5
Output, units	6,000

Actual operations:

Year	Units of Output
1	1,400
2	1,300
3	1,000
4	1,100
5	1,200

Required:
Prepare a depreciation table for each assumption below indicating entries for the asset over the useful life under the following methods: *(a)* straight line, *(b)* output, *(c)* SYD, and *(d)* DDB. Show computations and round to nearest dollar.

Problem 12–3

Akers Company purchased a piece of special factory equipment on January 1, 19A, costing $63,750. In view of pending technological developments it is estimated that the machine will have a resale value upon disposal in four years of $15,500 and that disposal cost will be $1,750.

Data relating to the equipment follow:

Estimated service life:

Years	4
Service hours	20,000

Actual operations:

Calendar Year	Service Hours
19A	5,500
19B	5,000
19C	4,800
19D	4,600

Required (round to nearest dollar and show computations):
1. Prepare a depreciation table for the service hours method assuming the books are closed each December 31.
2. Compute depreciation expense for the first and second years assuming *(a)* straight line, *(b)* SYD, and *(c)* DDB.

Problem 12–4

Machinery which cost Hayes Corporation $10,000 is expected to last 10 years and have a $500 residual value. Several depreciation methods in common use were applied to these data. The results in terms of annual depreciation amounts covering year 2 and year 3 are set out below:

Year	Method A	Method B	Method C
1	?	?	?
2	$1,600	$1,555	$950
3	1,280	1,382	950

Required (round to nearest dollar):
1. What is the book value of the asset at the end of year 3 for each of the three methods used to compute year 2 and year 3 depreciation given in the table above?
2. In connection with methods B and C, suppose that after the completion of year 3, it is determined the total remaining life of the machinery is five instead of seven years. Determine the annual depreciation amount and the balance of Accumulated Depreciation at the end of year 4 and year 5.

Problem 12–5

On January 1, 19A, Barth Company, a small machine-tool manufacturer, acquired for $1 million a piece of new industrial equipment. The new equipment was eligible for the investment tax credit, and Barth took full advantage of the credit and accounted for the amount using the flow-through method. The new equipment had a useful life of five years, and the residual value was estimated to be $100,000. Barth estimates that the new equipment can produce 10,000 machine tools in its first year. Production is then estimated to decline by 1,000 units per year over the remaining useful life of the equipment.

The following depreciation methods may be used:

a. DDB.
b. Straight line.
c. SYD.
d. Units of output.

Required:
1. Which depreciation method would result in the maximization of income for financial statement reporting for the *three*-year period ending December 31, 19C? Prepare a schedule showing the amount of accumulated depreciation at December 31, 19C, under the method selected. Show supporting computations in good form. *Ignore present value, income tax, and deferred income tax considerations in your answer.*
2. Which depreciation method would result in the minimization of income tax reporting for the *three*-year period ending December 31, 19C? Prepare a schedule showing the amount of accumulated depreciation at December 31, 19C, under the method selected. Show supporting computations in good form. *Ignore present value considerations in your answer.* (AICPA adapted)

Problem 12–6

Selected accounts included in the property, plant, and equipment section of the Kingston Corporation's balance sheet at December 31, 19x8, had the following balances (at original cost):

Land	$175,000
Land improvements	90,000
Buildings	900,000
Machinery and equipment (acquired 1/1/x1)	850,000

During 19x9 the following transactions occurred:

a. A tract of land was acquired for $125,000 as a potential future building site.

b. A plant facility consisting of land and building was acquired from Nostrand Company in exchange for 10,000 shares of Kingston's common stock. On the acquisition date, Kingston's stock had a closing market price of $45 per share on a national stock exchange. The plant facility was carried on Nostrand's books at $89,000 for land and $130,000 for the building at the exchange date. Current appraised values for the land and building, respectively, are $120,000 and $240,000.

c. Machinery was purchased at a total cost of $300,000. Additional costs were incurred as follows:

Freight and unloading	$ 5,000
Sales and use taxes	12,000
Installation	25,000

d. Expenditures totaling $75,000 were made for new parking lots, streets, and sidewalks at the corporation's various plant locations. These improvements had an estimated useful life of 15 years.

e. A machine costing $50,000 on January 1, 19x1, was scrapped on June 30, 19x9. DDB depreciation has been recorded on the basis of a 10-year life.

f. A machine was sold for $20,000 on July 1, 19x9. Original cost of the machine was $36,000 at January 1, 19x6, and it was depreciated on the straight-line basis over an estimated useful life of seven years and a residual value of $1,000.

Required:

1. Prepare a detailed analysis of the changes in each of the following balance sheet accounts for 19x9 (disregard accumulated depreciation):
   a. Land.
   b. Land improvements.
   c. Buildings.
   d. Machinery and equipment.
2. List the items in the fact situation which were not used to determine the answer to 1 above, showing the pertinent amounts and supporting computations for each item. In addition, indicate where, or if, these items should be included in Kingston's financial statements.

(AICPA adapted)

Problem 12–7

The accounts for Trucks and Accumulated Depreciation on the books of Nye Delivery Company are as shown at the bottom of this page:

Required:

1. Prepare a depreciation schedule showing correct account balances and depreciation by year, assuming the estimated lives of trucks no. 3 and no. 4 were changed from three to four years (other trucks have estimated service lives of three years and no estimated residual value) on January 1, 19E. Suggested captions: Date Acquired, Truck No., Trucks (debit-credit*), Correct Depreciation by Year (five columns), and Accumulated Depreciation (debit-credit*).

(Relates to Problem 12–7)

Trucks

1/1/19A	Trucks no. 1 and 2 (cost, $3,600 each)	7,200	1/1/19C	Truck no. 1 scrapped	3,600
1/1/19C	Truck no. 3	3,780	1/1/19D	Truck no. 2 scrapped	3,600
1/1/19D	Truck no. 4	3,840			
7/1/19D	New tires truck no. 3	600			

Accumulated Depreciation

1/1/19C	Truck no. 1 scrapped ($700 received as salvage)	2,400	12/31/19A	Depreciation	2,400
1/1/19D	Truck no. 2 scrapped ($300 received as salvage)	3,300	12/31/19B	Depreciation	2,400
			12/31/19C	Depreciation	2,460
			12/31/19D	Depreciation	2,460
			12/31/19E	Depreciation	1,905

2. Prepare journal entry or entries to correct the books as of December 31, 19E, assuming they were not yet closed for 19E. The schedule prepared for 1 above should provide the data needed.

Problem 12–8

As of December 31, 19F, the Machinery account on the books of Keener Company was as below:

(Relates to Problem 12–8)

Machinery

1/1/A	Purchase	$50,000	12/31/A	Depreciation	$5,000
7/1/B	Purchase	10,000	9/1/B	Machinery sold	1,000
11/1/C	Purchase	36,000	12/31/C	Depreciation	6,300
			12/31/D	Depreciation	7,800
			7/1/E	Machinery sold	1,000
			12/31/E	Depreciation	7,800
			12/31/F	Depreciation	9,300

Additional data:

Machinery sold September 1, 19B, cost $3,600 on January 1, 19A; machinery sold July 1, 19E, cost $2,500 on January 1, 19A. Machinery costing $2,000, which was purchased on July 1, 19B, was destroyed on July 1, 19F, and was a total loss. Assume the debits in the machinery account are correct.

Required:

1. Prepare a depreciation schedule showing *correct annual depreciation* and *account balances.* Assume 10-year life on all items, straight-line depreciation, and no residual value. Suggested captions: Date Acquired, Machinery (debit-credit*), Correct Depreciation by Year (six columns), and Accumulated Depreciation (debit-credit*).
2. Prepare journal entry or entries to correct the books on December 31, 19F, assuming the books are not closed for 19F.

Problem 12–9 (requirement *e* based on Supplement 12–A)

Garret Company bought a new machine for $30,000. It is expected to have a six-year useful life and a residual value of $6,000 at the end of that time. You have been requested to draw up schedules which will show annual depreciation for the machine each year under each of several different depreciation methods and assumptions as to how the machine will be used throughout its productive life (round to the nearest dollar).

The independent methods for which you are to supply depreciation data are as follows:

a. Use of the straight-line method. After using the method four years, at the start of the fifth year the residual value is revised downward to an estimated $3,000.

b. Use of SYD depreciation with no revision in life estimate or residual value.

c. Use of units of production depreciation on the assumption the machinery can produce 96,000 units, and production throughout the six years of use will occur as follows: year 1, 18,000 units; year 2, 17,000; year 3, 17,000; year 4, 16,000; year 5, 13,000; and year 6, 15,000.

d. Use of units-of-production depreciation with the same starting assumption as in *(c)* and the same production in the first three years. In the fourth year, however, the total production estimate over the entire service life of the machine was revised to 107,000 units, and production for years 4, 5, and 6 were, respectively, 24,000 units; 14,000 units; and 17,000 units.

e. Use of the sinking fund method. An 18% interest rate should be assumed.

Problem 12–10 (requirement *e* based on Supplement 12–A)

Management of a company which has just acquired an operational asset at a cost of $50,000 that is to be depreciated over five years to a residual value of $8,000 has asked you to develop alternate depreciation schedules based on various depreciation methods and assumptions as to usage.

a. The straight-line method will be used. After recording depreciation three years in accordance with the original assumptions, the residual value is changed to $10,000.

b. Show depreciation under the productive output method if scheduled production using the asset will be year 1, 200,000 units; year 2, 160,000 units; year 3, 140,000 units; year 4, 100,000 units; and year 5, 72,000 units.

c. Instead, the productive output method will be used as in *(b)* and through the first two years the total expectation and planned production are the same. However, at the start of year 3 the total production estimate over the service life of the asset is revised to 750,000 units, and scheduled production in years 3, 4, and 5 will be 200,000 units; 90,000 units; and 100,000 units, respectively.

d. The SYD method will be used.

e. The annuity method will be used in conjunction with a 15% annual interest rate.

Required:
Prepare depreciation schedules which show depreciation expense for each year together with accumulated depreciation and book value for each situation and method described above.

Problem 12–11 (based in part on Supplement 12–A)

Equipment which cost $50,000 and has a five-year estimated life and residual value of $8,000 will depreciate various amounts in its second full year under various depreciation methods and formulas.

Third-year depreciation under the methods listed (but not in the same order) amounted to (1) $8,400; (2) $7,200; (3) $8,400; (4) $10,625; and (5) $14,871. The depreciation methods used were *(a)* annuity, *(b)* DDB, *(c)* productive output, *(d)* straight line, and *(e)* SYD.

In connection with the annuity method, an 18% interest rate was used. The productive output method assumed 672,000 units could be produced; in the first three years actual output was 200,000 units, 180,000 units, and 170,000 units, respectively.

Required:
Alongside the letters identifying the five methods, write the number associated with the amounts of third-year depreciation. Support each answer with calculations.

PART B: PROBLEMS 12–12 to 12–18

Problem 12–12

Operational assets being depreciated on a composite basis by a manufacturer are set out in the schedule below:

Component	Cost	Estimated Residual Value	Estimated Life (years)
A	$44,700	$2,700	10
B	14,000	0	7
C	38,000	8,000	15
D	6,200	200	5

Required:
1. Calculate the composite life and annual composite depreciation rate for the group of assets listed above. Record depreciation after one full year of use. Round the depreciation rate to three decimal places.
2. During the second year, it became necessary to replace component B, which was sold for $8,000. The replacement component cost $16,000 and has an estimated residual value of $2,600 at the end of its estimated six-year useful life. Record the retirement and substitution, which was a cash acquisition.
3. Record depreciation at the end of the second full year.

Problem 12–13

Wealthy Minerals Company bought mineral-bearing land for $135,000 which engineers say will yield 200,000 pounds of economically removable ore; the land will have a value of $30,000 after the ore is removed.

To work the property, the company built structures and sheds on the site which cost $30,000; these will last 12 years, and because their use is confined to mining and it would be expensive to dismantle and move them, they will have no residual value. Machinery which cost $30,000 was installed at the mine, and added cost for installation was $6,000. This machinery should last 15 years; like the structures, usefulness of the machinery is confined to these mining operations. Dismantling and removal costs when the property has been fully worked will approximately equal the value of the machinery at that time; therefore, Wealthy does not plan to use the structures or the machinery after the minerals have been removed.

In the first year, Wealthy removed only 10,000 pounds of ore; however, production was doubled in the second year. It is expected that all of the removable ore will be extracted within eight years from the start of operations.

Required:
1. Prepare a schedule showing unit and total depletion and depreciation and book value of the operational assets for the first and second year of operation.
2. On the assumption that in the first year 80% of production was sold, and in the second year, the inventory carried over from the first year plus 80% of the second year's production was sold, give entries to record accumulated depreciation and depletion. To show the effect of these costs, make the offsetting debits to cost of goods sold and inventory. Use "accumulated" accounts.

Problem 12–14

Goode Corporation, a manufacturer of steel products, began operations on October 1, 19A. The accounting department of Goode has started the operational asset and depreciation schedule accompanying this problem. You have been asked to assist in completing this schedule. In addition to ascertaining that the data already on the schedule are correct, you have obtained the following information from the company's records and personnel:

a. Depreciation is computed from the first of the month of acquisition to the first of the month of disposition.
b. Land A and building A were acquired from a predecessor corporation. Goode paid $812,500 for the land and building together. At the time of acquisition, the land had an appraised value of $72,000 and the building had an appraised value of $828,000.

c. Land B was acquired on October 2, 19A, in exchange for 3,000 newly issued shares of Goode's common stock. At the date of acquisition, the stock had a par value of $5 per share and a market value of $40 per share. During October 19A, Goode paid $10,400 to demolish an existing building on this land so it could construct a new building.

d. Construction of building B on the newly acquired land began on October 1, 19B. By September 30, 19C, Goode had paid $210,000 of the estimated total construction costs of $300,000. Estimated completion and occupancy date is July 19D.

e. Certain equipment was donated to the corporation by a local university. An independent appraisal of the equipment when donated placed the market value at $40,000 and the residual value at $2,000.

f. Machinery A's total cost of $110,000 includes installation expense of $550 and normal repairs and maintenance of $11,000. Residual value is estimated at $5,500. Machinery A was sold on February 1, 19C.

g. On October 1, 19B, machinery B was acquired with a down payment of $4,000 and the remaining payments to be made in 10 annual installments of $4,000 each beginning October 1, 19C. The prevailing interest rate was 18% on debts with risk characteristics similar to this debt.

Required:

Number your answer sheet from 1 to 14. For each numbered item on the schedule accompanying this problem, supply the correct amount next to the corresponding number on your answer sheet. Round each answer to the nearest dollar. *Do not recopy the schedule.* Show supporting computations in good form. (AICPA adapted)

Problem 12–15

Liverpool Company utilizes a number of small machine tools in its operations. Although there are numerous variations in the tools, they cost approximately the same and have similar useful lives. The company carries a Machine Tools account in the records; the account showed a balance of $1,600 (200 tools) at the end of 19A. Acquisitions, retirements, and other data for a period of two years are given below:

	19B	19C
Acquisitions	100 @ $7.50	120 @ $7.75
Retirements:		
Number	150	80
Salvage proceeds	$90	$100
Ending inventory	150 @ $5.00	190 @ $5.50

Required:

1. Give entries for each of the two years assuming (round to even dollars and show computations):
   a. The inventory system is used.
   b. The retirement system is used.
   c. The replacement system is used.
2. Prepare a tabulation covering the two years to present the annual depreciation amount and the balance in the Machine Tools account under each system.

Problem 12–16

Lieb Company utilizes a large number of identical small tools in operations. On January 1, 19A, the first year of operations, 1,000 of these tools were purchased at a cost of $3 each. On December 31, 19A, 200 of the tools were

(Relates to Problem 12–14)

GOODE CORPORATION
Operational Asset and Depreciation Schedule
For Fiscal Years Ended September 30, 19B, and September 30, 19C

Assets	Acquisition Date	Cost	Residual Value	Depreciation Method	Estimated Life in Years	Depreciation Expense Year Ended September 30: 19B	19C
Land A	10/1/19A	$ (1)	n.a.	n.a.	n.a.	n.a.	n.a.
Building A	10/1/19A	(2)	$47,500	Straight line	(3)	$14,000	$ (4)
Land B	10/2/19A	(5)	n.a.	n.a.	n.a.	n.a.	n.a.
Building B	Under construction	210,000 to date	—	Straight line	30	—	(6)
Donated equipment	10/2/19A	(7)	2,000	150% declining balance	10	(8)	(9)
Machinery A	10/2/19A	(10)	5,500	SYD	10	(11)	(12)
Machinery B	10/1/19B	(13)	—	Straight line	10	—	(14)

n.a.—Not applicable.

sold or scrapped for $100, the estimated residual value being $100 (50 cents each). During the year the 200 were replaced at a cost of $4.20 each. On December 31, 19B, 300 of the tools were sold or scrapped for $75; they had an estimated residual value of 25 cents each and were replaced at a cost of $4.50 each. On December 31, 19C, 140 of the tools were sold or scrapped for $35 (residual value, 25 cents each), each being replaced at a cost of $3.60.

Required:

1. Give entries to record all indicated transactions, assuming the company employed the *(a)* retirement system and *(b)* replacement system.
2. Compare the results under the two systems by showing periodic depreciation for each year and the balance in the Tools account at each December 31, 19A–19C.

Problem 12–17 (reviews Chapter 10, Part B and Chapter 12)

River Rocks, Inc., mines and processes rock and gravel. It started in business on January 1, 19A, when it purchased the assets of another company. You have examined its financial statements at December 31, 19A, and have been requested to assist in planning and projecting operations for 19B. The company also wants to know the maximum amount by which notes payable to officers can be reduced at December 31, 19B.

The adjusted trial balance on December 31, 19A, was as follows:

Cash	$ 23,000	
Accounts receivable	24,000	
Mining properties	60,000	
Accumulated depletion		$ 3,000
Equipment	150,000	
Accumulated depreciation		10,000
Organization cost	5,000	
Accumulated amortization		1,000
Accounts payable		12,000
Federal income tax payable		22,000
Notes payable to officers		40,000
Capital stock		100,000
Contrib. capital in excess of par		34,000
Sales		306,000
Production costs (including depreciation and depletion)	184,000	
Administrative expense (including amortization and interest)	60,000	
Federal income tax expense	22,000	
	$528,000	$528,000

You are able to develop the following information:

1. The total yards of material sold is expected to increase 10% in 19B, and the average sales price per cubic yard will be increased from $1.50 to $1.60.
2. The estimated recoverable reserves of rock and gravel were 4 million cubic yards when the properties were purchased.
3. Production costs include direct labor of $110,000 of which $10,000 was attributed to inefficiencies in the early stages of operation. The union contract calls for 5% increases in hourly rates effective January 1, 19B. Production costs, other than depreciation, depletion, and direct labor, will increase 4% in 19B.
4. Administrative expense, other than amortization and interest, will increase $8,000 in 19B.
5. The company has contracted for additional movable equipment costing $60,000 to be in production on July 1, 19B. This equipment will result in a direct labor-hour savings of 8% as compared with the last half of 19A. The new equipment will have a life of 20 years. All depreciation is computed on the straight-line method. The old equipment will continue in use.
6. The new equipment will be financed by a 20% down payment and a 10% three-year chattel mortgage. Interest and principal payments are due semiannually on June 30 and December 31, beginning December 31, 19B. The notes payable to officers are demand notes dated January 1, 19A, on which 9% interest is provided for and was paid on December 31, 19A.
7. Accounts receivable will increase in proportion to sales. No bad debts are anticipated. Accounts payable will remain substantially the same.
8. Percentage depletion allowable on rock and gravel is to be computed at 5% of gross income and is limited to 50% of taxable income before depletion.
9. It is customary in the rock and gravel business not to place any value on stockpiles of processed material which are awaiting sale.
10. Assume an income tax rate of 40%.
11. The company has decided to maintain a minimum cash balance of $15,000.
12. The client understands that the ethical considerations involved in preparing the following statements will be taken care of by your letter accompanying the statements. (Do not prepare the letter.)

Required:

1. Prepare a statement showing the net income projection for 19B. Note: Round all amounts to the nearest $100. If the amount to be rounded is exactly $50, round to the next higher $100. Round all percentages to the nearest percent.
2. Prepare a statement which will show cash flow projection for 19B and will indicate the amount that notes payable to officers can be reduced at December 31, 19B.

(AICPA adapted)

Problem 12–18 (reviews Chapters 11 and 12)

For each of the following situations, *(a)* select the best response from those given and *(b)* explain the basis for your choice, showing computations where appropriate.

1. Gorch Company sold an item of plant equipment. Gorch received a noninterest-bearing note to be paid $1,000 per year for 10 years. The going rate of interest for this transaction is 15%. What discount from the face amount of the note (i.e., $10,000) should Gorch reflect on this transaction?
   a. Zero.
   b. $3,290.
   c. $4,981.
   d. $6,710.
2. Blacker Company exchanged a business car for a new car. The old car had an original cost of $7,500, an undepreciated cost of $1,600, and a market value of $2,000 when exchanged. In addition, Blacker paid $6,200 cash for the new car. The list price of the new car was $8,300. At what amount should the new car be recorded for financial accounting purposes?
   a. $7,500.
   b. $7,800.
   c. $8,200.
   d. $8,300.

Items 3 and 4 are based on the following information: On January 2, 19A, Kirk Manufacturing Company acquired some equipment from Quarter Corporation. The sale contract requires Kirk to make 12 annual payments of $10,800 at the end of each year. The first payment was made on December 31, 19A, and no deposit was required. The equipment has an estimated useful life of 20 years with no anticipated residual value. The prevailing interest rate for Kirk in similar financing arrangements is 18%.

3. At what amount should Kirk have capitalized this equipment?
   a. $51,767.
   b. $81,390.
   c. $103,720.
   d. $106,040.
4. How much interest expense should Kirk have recorded in 19A?
   a. Zero.
   b. $6,507.
   c. $7,200.
   d. $9,318.

The following data pertain to questions 5 and 6 only. On July 1, 19A, Miller Mining, a calendar-year corporation, purchased the rights to a copper mine. Of the total purchase price, $2.8 million was allocable to the copper. Estimated reserves were 800,000 tons of copper. Miller expects to extract and sell 10,000 tons of copper each month. Production began immediately. The selling price is $25 per ton. Miller uses percentage depletion (15%) for tax purposes. To aid production, Miller also purchased some new equipment on July 1, 19A. The equipment cost $76,000 and had an estimated useful life of eight years. However, after all the copper is removed from this mine, the equipment will be of no use to Miller and will be sold for an estimated $4,000. Use straight-line depreciation.

5. If sales and production conform to expectations, what is Miller's depletion expense on this mine for financial accounting purposes for the calendar year 19A?
   a. $105,000.
   b. $210,000.
   c. $225,000.
   d. $420,000.
6. If sales and production conform to expectations, what is Miller's depreciation expense on the new equipment for financial accounting purposes for the calendar year 19A?
   a. $4,500.
   b. $5,400.
   c. $9,000.
   d. $10,800.
7. Willard, Inc., purchased some equipment on January 2, 19A, for $24,000 (no residual value). Willard used straight-line depreciation based on a 10-year estimated life. During 19D, Willard decided that this equipment would be used only three more years and then replaced with a technologically superior model. What entry, if any, should Willard make as of January 1, 19D, to reflect this change?
   a. No entry.
   b. Debit an extraordinary item for $4,800, and credit accumulated depreciation for $4,800.
   c. Debit a prior period adjustment for $4,800, and credit accumulated depreciation for $4,800.
   d. Debit depreciation expense for $4,800, and credit accumulated depreciation for $4,800.

(AICPA adapted)

SUPPLEMENT 12A: PROBLEMS 12–19 to 12–20

Problem 12–19

Equipment costing $100,000 has an estimated three-year life and $20,000 residual value.

Required (round to nearest dollar):
Using a 16% annual earnings rate on the equipment, prepare a depreciation table covering the entire life of the equipment assuming:

1. Annuity method.
2. Sinking fund method.

Problem 12–20

Machinery with an estimated life of 10 years and a residual value of 15% was acquired for $10,000. If the company can earn 18% annually on the machinery, what depreciation entries would be made at the end of each of the first two years assuming the *(a)* annuity method and *(b)* sinking fund method. Also, *(c)* derive the formula for annual depreciation under the annuity method. *Hint:* The formula is a rearrangement of the basic present value equation expressing the theoretical cost of an asset.

13

Intangible Assets

ASSETS such as inventories and property, plant, and equipment provide utility to their owner because of their physical substance. Certain other assets are inherently intangible and provide utility because they confer rights which are not dependent upon their having physical substance. The following list briefly summarizes the intangible assets discussed in preceding chapters and the utility they provide for their owner:

Asset	Utility
1. Cash (Chapter 6).	1. Exchange value.
2. Accounts receivable, notes receivable, and short-term investments in bonds (Chapter 6; for long-term investments in bonds, see Chapter 17).	2. Cash inflow.
3. Short-term investments in stocks (Chapter 6; for long-term investments in stocks, see Chapter 16).	3. Participation in *(a)* selection of management by voting shares, *(b)* dividends, *(c)* asset distributions in liquidation, and *(d)* capital appreciation.
4. Prepaid expenses (Chapter 4).	4. Use of goods or services already paid for such as office supplies, rent, and insurance.

This chapter discusses other types of intangible assets, deferred charges, and other issues related to intangibles. These topics are discussed and illustrated in this chapter as follows:

Part A—Basic Concepts, Intangible Assets, and Deferred Charges

Part B—Development Stage Enterprises, Insurance, and Disposal and Reporting of Intangibles

Part A: Basic Concepts, Intangible Assets, and Deferred Charges

The long-term intangibles used in operating a business generally are classified for accounting purposes as **intangible** assets; other titles used are intangible operational assets, intangible fixed assets, or, simply, intangibles. This classification includes intangible long-lived assets such as patents, copyrights, franchises, trademarks, trade names, secret processes, and goodwill. The primary characteristics of these intangible assets are *(a)* they have no physical substance, *(b)* their ownership confers some exclusive rights, *(c)* they provide future benefits to operations, and *(d)* they are relatively long-lived. For example, a company that owns a patent which is used in the manufacture or sale of its products has a valuable intangible asset.

Intangible assets may be classified on the basis of—

1. **Identifiability:**
   a. **Identifiable**—Most intangibles have separate identities and can be sold individually; examples include patents, copyrights, and trademarks.
   b. **Unidentifiable**—Other intangibles are inseparable from the entity itself and cannot be realized without selling the enterprise; the principal example is goodwill.
2. **Manner of acquisition:**
   a. **Acquired externally**—Intangibles may be acquired from external sources by purchase; a typical example is a franchise.
   b. **Developed internally**—Intangible assets may be developed by the company itself in the course of its operations; examples are trademarks and patents.

ACCOUNTING FOR INTANGIBLE ASSETS

Accounting for intangible assets involves essentially the same accounting principles and procedures as for tangible property, plant, and equipment (discussed in Chapters 11 and 12), that is:

1. At acquisition—measuring and recording acquisition cost in conformity with the **cost principle.**
2. During period of use—measuring, recording, and reporting expiration of the service potential over the period of benefit in conformity with the **matching principle.** This process of allocating the acquisition cost of intangibles to expense is usually referred to as **amortization.**
3. At disposition—recording and reporting disposal at date of sale, exchange, or end of the economic useful life of the intangible asset.

Accounting for intangible assets acquired after October 1970 is prescribed by *APB Opinion No. 17,* "Intangible Assets." Accounting for intangible assets acquired on or before October 31, 1970, may be accounted for in accordance with *APB Opinion 17* or *ARB 43,* chapter 5 (otherwise this *ARB* was superseded by the *Opinion*).

Prior to *APB Opinion 17* intangible assets were accounted for on the basis of **life expectancy.** Intangible assets having limited lives were amortized over their estimated period of future use. Intangible assets having indeterminate lives were not amortized until a realistic determination of useful life could be made. Often this determination was never made; hence, the cost of such intangibles were never amortized. *Opinion 17,* among other things, stopped this practice (for assets acquired after October 1970) by providing (para. 27 and 29) that

> . . . the value of intangible assets at any one date eventually disappears and . . . the recorded costs of intangible assets should be amortized by systematic [debits] to income over the periods estimated to be benefited. . . . The cost of each type of intangible should be amortized on the basis of the estimated life of that specific asset. . . . The period of amortization should not, however, exceed 40 years.

MEASURING AND RECORDING THE COST OF INTANGIBLE ASSETS

Intangible assets should be recorded at acquisition at their current cash equivalent cost in conformity with the cost principle. When an intangible asset is acquired for some consideration other than cash, cost is determined by the market value of the consideration given or, if that cannot be determined reliably, by the market value of the right acquired.[1] for

[1] If neither the market value of the consideration given or the intangible asset acquired can be determined with sufficient reliability, the board of directors may have to assign a value to the intangible asset.

example, if a patent is acquired by the issuance of capital stock, the cost of the patent should be measured as the market value of the shares of stock issued; if the shares issued do not have an established market value consistent with the volume issued for the patent, then evidence of the market value of the patent should be sought as the measurement of cost in the transaction.

IDENTIFIABLE INTANGIBLE ASSETS

Identifiable intangible assets are so designated because they can be specifically and separately identified apart from the enterprise itself. Thus, they can be sold separately. Examples are patents, copyrights, franchises, and trademarks (but not goodwill). They may be *(a)* acquired externally by purchase or *(b)* developed internally. In either instance, they are recorded initially at cost, in conformity with the cost principle, and their cost is expensed subsequently as the economic service value of the asset declines, in conformity with the matching principle.

Because of the wide variety of intangible assets, the procedures tend to vary somewhat in applying the foregoing principles and guidelines. In the next few paragraphs, we will discuss the specifically identifiable intangible assets commonly encountered in business.

Patents

A patent is an exclusive right recognized by law and registered with the U.S. Patent Office. A patent enables the holder to use, manufacture, sell, and control the patent without interference or infringement by others. In reality, the registration of the patent with the Patent Office is no guarantee of protection. Therefore, the patent is not conclusive until it has been successfully defended in court. For this reason there is general agreement that the cost of **successful** court tests should be capitalized as part of the cost of the patent.

The cost of a patent acquired by purchase is determined according to the **cost principle;** that is, cost of a purchased patent is measured as the market value of the consideration given or, if that cannot be determined reliably, as the market value of the patent received.[2] internally developed patents resulting from the company's own research and development (R&D) activities must be accounted for as specified by *FASB Statement 2* as discussed under a subsequent heading Research and Development (R&D) Costs. This *Statement* specifies that laboratory costs leading to the development of the patent must be expensed as incurred. The only costs of an internally developed patent that can be capitalized are legal fees and other costs associated with registration of the patent, such as models and drawings required for the registration.

Patents have a legal life of 17 years. The useful life of most patents is shorter because technological progress, substitute products, and other improvements cause the product or process covered by the patents to lose its competitive advantage before 17 years elapse. Patent costs should be amortized over the useful life or legal life, whichever is shorter.

Copyrights

A copyright is a form of protection given by law to the authors of literary, musical, artistic, and similar works. Owners of copyrights are granted certain exclusive rights such as *(a)* to print, reprint, and copy the work; *(b)* to sell or distribute copies; and *(c)* to perform and record the work.

A new copyright law became effective in January 1978. Under its provisions, copyrighted works already protected by law retain the then-existing copyright term of 28 years, renewable under some conditions for an additional period of protection of 47 years. For works created after January 1978, the new law provides a term lasting for the author's life plus an added 50 years. Copyrights can be transferred, and many business entities owning copyrights have received them by transfer. Under the new law, authors or certain of their heirs can terminate transfers of copyrights after 35 years under certain conditions.

As a practical matter, few copyrights have economic value for nearly so long a period as their legal lives or the terms for which transfers are effective. Costs of copyrights should be amortized over the period the copyrighted items are expected to produce revenue. In no case is it permissible to amortize a copyright acquired after October 1970 over a period exceeding 40 years.

Franchises

A common type of franchise is a grant by a governmental unit for use of public properties or to furnish public-utility-type services. Costs of obtaining a fran-

[2] See footnote 1.

chise should be recorded in a Franchise account and should be amortized over the term of the franchise or 40 years, whichever is shorter.

Another common type of franchise involves the granting of a right by one entity to another entity to use a specific designation (such as Kentucky Fried Chicken) subject to certain obligations agreed to by the contracting parties. Again, accounting for the franchise by the franchisee (i.e., the purchaser) involves initial capitalization of the cost of the asset (the right under franchise) and its subsequent amortization over the shorter useful life or 40 years. Annual payments by the franchisee to the franchisor for services such as assistance with promotional campaigns, accounting, and organizational matters should be expensed by the franchisee as incurred because they do not create a measurable future benefit for the franchisee.

Trademarks

Trademarks can be registered with the federal patent office to help substantiate ownership. Thus, names, symbols, or other devices providing distinctive identity for a product are afforded a degree of legal protection. Amounts paid or incurred directly for the acquisition, development (if there is a directly related and reliably measurable future benefit), protection, expansion, registration, or defense of a trademark or trade name should be capitalized. Such capitalized balances should be amortized over the useful life of the trademark or 40 years, whichever is shorter.

UNIDENTIFIABLE INTANGIBLE ASSETS (GOODWILL)

Unidentifiable intangible assets are so designated because they result from a number of concurrent economic factors, they cannot be related to specific assets (e.g., identifiable assets such as machines, buildings, patents, and franchises), and they cannot be identified separately from the total business. The primary example of an unidentifiable intangible asset is goodwill. In accounting, goodwill is recorded only when it is purchased, usually in conjunction with the acquisition of an entity; its cost is measured as the excess of the price paid for the entity over the sum of the **market values of the identifiable net assets** (i.e., identifiable assets minus liabilities assumed) of that entity.

Basic Concepts

Conceptually, goodwill is an economic advantage which exists when the total value of a business is more than the value of all of its identifiable **net** assets. This economic advantage arises because the expected earnings of the business exceed the level of earnings on only its identifiable **net** assets (i.e., its assets minus its liabilities). Goodwill arises as the result of numerous factors such as customer acceptance, service to customers, efficient operations, reputation for dependability, and location.

Goodwill may be either *(a)* created internally or *(b)* purchased. In the normal process of building a business over time, an element of goodwill often is developed. This **internally** developed goodwill is **not recorded** in the accounts **nor reported** on the financial statements for two basic reasons: (1) there have been no direct and identifiable disbursements for it (which was not the case for the identifiable assets); and (2) to the extent that expenses (such as cost of goods sold associated with superior products and advertising) may have contributed to goodwill. Such expenses were recognized on past income statements and any attempt to separate out of them an element of goodwill would be so arbitrary that the reliability principle would not be fulfilled.[3]

In contrast, **purchased goodwill** should be recorded. Purchased goodwill is recorded in the accounts only when a business is purchased and the total price paid exceeds the then **market value** of all of the identifiable tangible and intangible assets purchased, minus any liabilities assumed. Therefore, accounting for goodwill involves three distinct phases as follows:

[3] Another unidentifiable intangible asset, almost never encountered in practice, is known as **going value.** A business that is established and operating but with only average profits is more valuable than a collection of similar assets and liabilities about to be launched as a business. This difference, the "more valuable" aspect, is the essence of going value (sometimes called **going-concern value**). Thus, going value is akin to goodwill but different from it. Goodwill relates to above-average profitability; going value does not. Goodwill often is reported on financial statements. Going value is seldom reported on financial statements. In acquisition transactions in which goodwill is properly recognized, a portion of the payment may actually represent a payment for going value, but separation of the two is almost never attempted. Any going value in such a case usually is subsumed under goodwill.

1. Estimation of the value of goodwill **prior** to purchasing a business. This estimate is used as a basis for negotiations between the buyer and seller of the business.
2. Measurement, **after** purchase, of the actual cost of goodwill as reflected in the price actually paid to acquire the business.
3. Amortization of goodwill subsequent to its purchase.

Estimation of goodwill and measurement of the cost of goodwill are discussed immediately below. Amortization of goodwill is discussed under the heading, Amortization of the Cost of Intangible Assets.

Estimating and Recording the Value of Goodwill

In negotiations relating to the purchase or sale of a business, the accountant may be requested to assist in estimating the value of goodwill. Computations based upon an analysis of asset values and income potential frequently are useful in such negotiations because the value of an entity's goodwill is directly related to its asset values and income potential. Other aspects of the negotiations involve the collectibility of the entity's receivables; salability of its inventories; market value of its property, plant, and equipment; and the liabilities of the entity to be assumed in the purchase.

If the business actually is purchased (i.e., if the deal is consummated), the actual price paid for any goodwill is included in the total price of the business. The **actual** price paid for goodwill may differ significantly from the estimated value used as a basis for negotiations.

In the process of developing an estimate of the value of an entity's goodwill to be used in negotiating the purchase of an entity, the past earnings of the entity, properly adjusted, may provide a sound basis for estimating its future earning potential. In estimating future earnings, the earnings history of the firm usually is studied. As a basis for estimating future earnings, the following steps may be suggested (these steps will vary depending upon the specific situation):

1. Select for study a series of past years' earnings which appear to be most likely to be good predictors of future earnings. The period of years should be long enough to reveal the pattern of earnings fluctuations experienced by the company and short enough to provide data relevant to the prediction. Some companies may use a 3-year time period; others may use 5 years, or even 10, depending on the specific situation.
2. Adjust these past earnings for:
   a. Unusual and/or nonrecurring gains and losses.
   b. Earnings effects of changes in accounting estimates and principles.
   c. Changes which are expected to occur in expenses and revenues in the future.
3. Analyze the trend and uniformity of past earnings. Even though past earnings may have been above normal, any observed downward trend in the immediate past may indicate the disappearance of above-normal earning capacity. Such a downward trend may indicate dissipation of goodwill value.
4. On the basis of the above analysis, project the future earnings. Econometric methods are available for this estimation process.

To illustrate the above steps and the negotiations between the buyer and the seller, assume Company B (the buyer) was interested in purchasing the net assets (including any goodwill) of Company S. Prior to the negotiations, Company B obtained extensive historical data from Company S. Based on these and other data, Company B developed an estimated price which they would be willing to pay; this price included an amount for goodwill because they believed Company S had excellent earnings potential. This estimated price represented a "ball park amount"; however, it was not divulged to Company S. After extended negotiations, the two companies agreed upon an actual cash price for the total assets of Company S, less the liabilities assumed. This entire process is illustrated in Exhibit 13–1 as follows:

Panel A—Summary of the historical financial data of Company S that was provided to Company B.

Panel B—Summary of the related projections made by Company B, on the basis of which they computed the estimated *(a)* purchase price including *(b)* value of the goodwill of Company S.

Panel C—Computation of the estimated offering price and value of the goodwill of Company S.

Panel D—Entry by Company B to record the acquisition of Company S.

EXHIBIT 13–1: Valuing and Recording Goodwill When a Business Is Purchased

Panel A—Historical Data Used for Estimating Offering Price and Goodwill:

Data on Company S (seller)

Year	Earnings (adjusted for nonrecurring and/or unusual items)	Book Values Used as the Starting Point for Estimating Market Values: Total Assets	Liabilities	Owners' Equity
19A	$18,000	$162,000	$ 82,000	$ 80,000
19B	17,000	172,000	90,000	82,000
19C	19,000	190,000	105,000	85,000
19D	19,000	197,000	110,000	87,000
19E	21,000	210,000	120,000	90,000
Total	$94,000	$931,000	$507,000	$424,000
Five-year average	$18,800	$186,200	$101,400	$ 84,800

Panel B—Related Projections Made by Purchaser (Company B):

1. Estimated average annual earnings for each of the next 10 years, $25,000.
2. Estimated current market value of the net assets (exclusive of goodwill) of Company S (assets $220,000, less liabilities to be assumed, $120,000), $100,000.
3. Expected annual rate of return on the total investment (i.e., the purchase price), 15 percent.

Panel C—Estimation of the *(a)* Purchase Price and *(b)* Valuation of Goodwill:

a. Estimated purchase price (i.e., present value of the expected annual earnings) $25,000 × $P_{o_{n=10;\ i=15\%}}$ (5.01877, Table 5–4)		$125,000*
Less: Net assets purchased (exclusive of goodwill), at current market value:		
Assets	$220,000	
Liabilities to be assumed	120,000	100,000
b. Estimated value of goodwill		$ 25,000

* Rounded to nearest $1,000.

Panel D—Entry by Company B to Record Acquisition of Company S at an Actual Negotiated Cash Price of $122,000 (assumed):

Identifiable assets, detailed (Panel B)	220,000	
Goodwill [$122,000 − ($220,000 − $120,000)]	22,000	
Liabilities (Panel B)		120,000
Cash		122,000

In Exhibit 13–1, Panel A, the financial data for the past five years and other data (including future plans) formed the basis for Company B to estimate average annual earnings of $25,000 (Panel B, item 1), which is significantly higher than the $18,800 average for the prior five years. Also, Company B estimated the current market value of the identifiable assets which would be acquired ($220,000 given in Panel B, item 2). Estimates of the various identifiable assets were derived by the use of price lists, market values for used assets, appraisals, and specific price indexes. Moreover, Company B, after considering all of the potentials of Company S and the risks associated with the investment, decided it must earn a 15 percent annual rate of return on the investment (ROI) in Company S for it to be worthwhile.

Exhibit 13–1, Panel C, illustrates how Company B used the estimates derived in Panel B to develop the estimated purchase price which they kept in mind during the negotiations with the owners of Company S. An important product of this computation was the estimated amount to be paid for goodwill (i.e., the amount to be paid in excess of the market value of the identifiable **net** assets acquired). Panel C reflects an estimated purchase price of $125,000 for the entity, and as a result, a price of $25,000 for the goodwill. However, Panel D indicates that the negotiations resulted in an actual cash price of $122,000, which reduced the price actually paid for goodwill from the $25,000 estimate to an actual valuation of $22,000. Panel D presents the entry made by Company B to record the actual results of the completed negotiations. Consistent with the **cost principle,** Company B recorded the assets purchased at their market values at date of acquisition and recorded the liabilities assumed at their net present value. In this example, the present value and the book value of the liabilities of Company S were the same, $120,000. It is important to note that the actual cost of goodwill is determined when the actual purchase price is contractually agreed upon by the buyer and the seller. Subsequent to acquisition of Company S, the amount of goodwill must be amortized over a period not in excess of 40 years; the straight-line method usually is used.

The above illustration assumed that Company B purchased Company S outright rather than purchasing a **controlling interest** of its outstanding voting shares. The latter situation is discussed and illustrated in Chapter 16.

The acquisition of another business and the recognition of goodwill is fairly common. For example, in 1979, American Broadcasting Companies, Inc., reported intangible assets (i.e., goodwill, as explained in Note A of its 1979 annual report) of $80.5 million, which was 6.3 percent of its total assets of $1.274 billion. A more acquisition-oriented company in the same industry, Harte-Hanks Communications, Inc., reported goodwill of $167.3 million, which was 54.2 percent of total assets of $308.9 million in 1979. In contrast, Atlantic Richfield Company reported no intangibles in its 1979 annual report, even though it had acquired Anaconda Company several years earlier. However, in 1979, Atlantic Richfield reported deferred charges of $96.7 million (i.e., .7 percent of total assets of $13.8 billion), which may have included the cost of goodwill.

AMORTIZATION OF THE COST OF INTANGIBLE ASSETS

The cost of intangible assets should be **amortized** by systematic debits to expense over the estimated periods of useful life, just as the cost of tangible assets having a limited period of usefulness is depreciated. It is not desirable from the standpoint of income measurement (i.e., in applying the matching principle) to accelerate the amortization process and write off the cost of intangibles substantially before the end of their usefulness. Intangible assets often are (because of precedent) amortized by a direct credit to the asset account rather than to an allowance (contra) account (and a related debit to expense).

In estimating the future useful life of an intangible asset, the following factors should be considered:[4]

a. Legal, regulatory, or contractual provisions that may limit the maximum useful life.
b. Provisions for renewal or extension that may alter a specified limit on useful life.
c. Effects of obsolescence, demand, and other economic factors that may reduce useful life.
d. Useful life that may parallel the service life expectancies of individuals or groups of employees.
e. Expected actions of competitors and others that may restrict present competitive advantages.
f. An apparently unlimited useful life that may in fact be indefinite, and benefits that cannot be reasonably projected.
g. An intangible asset that may be a composite of many individual factors with varying effective useful lives.

APB Opinion 17 states that "the straight-line method of amortization—equal annual amounts—should be applied unless a company demonstrates that another systematic method is more appropriate." The *Opinion* also states that changes in amortization rates should be accounted for **prospectively** as a change in estimate; that is, the remaining unamortized cost should be amortized over the remaining life. Under GAAP, the total amortization period cannot exceed 40 years. Intangibles very rarely have a residual value.

[4] AICPA, *APB Opinion No. 17,* "Intangible Assets" (New York, 1970), par. 27.

DEFERRED CHARGES

A deferred charge is an expenditure for a service which will contribute to the generation of revenues in the future; it is a **long-term prepaid expense.**[5] Deferred charges are classified on the balance sheet as noncurrent assets because their effect on revenues extends beyond the period for current assets. Deferred charges have no physical substance and can rarely be realized through their sale. Examples of deferred charges include organization costs, machinery rearrangement costs, long-term prepaid insurance premiums, prepaid leasehold costs, and long-term debit balances arising from interperiod income tax allocation.

Under the definition of assets given in FASB, *Statement of Financial Accounting Concepts No. 3,* "Elements of Financial Statements of Business Enterprises," December 1980, **debt issue cost** does not qualify as an asset (see pars. 159–61). However, *APB Opinion 21* (par. 16) specifies that debt issue cost be reported as a deferred charge. This practice continues because *FASB Concepts Statement 3,* page xiii, states that the definitions therein "neither require nor presage upheavals in present practice, although they may in due time lead to some evolutionary changes in practice."

Deferred charges are amortized over the future periods during which they will contribute to the generation of revenues. The 40-year maximum useful life for amortization of intangible assets specified in *APB Opinion 17* appears to apply to deferred charges; however, deferred charges seldom have lives that long.[6]

In the next few paragraphs we discuss the deferred charges usually encountered in practice, viz:

1. Organization costs.
2. Leasehold costs.
3. Research and development (R&D) costs.

[5] The term **charge** often is used by accountants as a synonym for **debit.**

[6] *APB Opinion 17,* par. 6, states: "The provisions of this Opinion apply to costs of developing identifiable assets that a company defers and records as assets. Certain costs, for example, research and development costs and preoperating costs, present problems which need to be studied separately." Specific mention in *Opinion 17* of research and development (R&D) costs and preoperating (i.e., organization) costs, both of which usually are classified as deferred charges, implies that *Opinion 17* applies to deferred charges except those two which were specifically singled out for further study.

Organization Costs

Expenditures are incurred as an integral part of organization and initial promotion of a business. Costs such as legal fees, state incorporation fees, stock certificate costs, stamp taxes, underwriting costs, and office expenses incident to organizing the company are capitalized as **organization costs** on the basis that such costs benefit the operations of future years. To expense the total amount in the first year of operation would result in an incorrect matching of expense with revenue.

Because the life of a business generally is indefinite, the length of the period which will receive the benefits of this cost usually is indeterminate. For this reason, and because the recognition of organization costs as an asset depends upon intangible values presumably attached to the particular business, organization costs usually are amortized over an arbitrarily selected short period of time. This practice is encouraged by the tax rules, which permit the business to amortize most organization costs ratably over any period not less than five years.

Stock Issue Costs

A troublesome amortization problem for a corporation arises in accounting for **stock issue costs,** such as, the costs of printing stock certificates, attorney fees related to the issue of stock, commissions paid for sale of the stock, accountants' fees, and the cost of filing a prospectus (i.e., a selling circular) with the SEC. Two main approaches to accounting for stock issue costs are found in practice:

1. **Debit all stock issue costs to a deferred charge asset account, Organization Costs, and amortize under the "40-year" rule applicable to intangible assets.** Although this practice is fairly common, many accountants believe it is conceptually deficient because *(a)* the cost relationship to future revenues is tenuous, and *(b)* such costs theoretically should be amortized over the indefinite life of the corporation.
2. **Offset stock issue costs against the sales price of the stock.** Under this practice such costs would be included in the determination of stock premium or discount. In this alternative such costs would not be recognized separately nor amortized against future revenues. A troublesome problem arises when the stock is issued at par

(or stated) value. In such a case, the cash received by the corporation is less than the par (or stated) value of the stock, and the corporation must record a discount on the stock.[7] This approach appears to be the most widely used primarily because stock issue costs often are not material and this method avoids incurring the accounting cost of amortizing immaterial amounts.

Leaseholds

Often a business leases property from its owner under an operating lease and makes prepayments which cover the term of the lease (such as a "lease bonus" payment to secure the lease).[8] The prepayment is debited to an asset account often entitled Leasehold or Prepaid Rent Expense. The cost of this asset is amortized over the period benefited (which is usually the lease term), and the periodic amortization is usually accorded the same accounting treatment as periodic rental payments under the lease. The cost of leasehold improvements, such as modifications of the leased property, sometimes is debited to the Leasehold account and sometimes is set up in a separate Leasehold Improvements account. Leasehold Improvements should be amortized over the term of the lease or the life of the improvements, whichever is shorter. Accounting for leaseholds is illustrated in Chapter 19.

Research and Development (R&D) Costs

Research and development costs, commonly called R&D, are among the most important expenditures made by modern industrial companies. The tabulation in Exhibit 13–2 indicates the significance of R&D.

EXHIBIT 13–2: Significance of R&D

Industry	R&D Costs as Percent of Sales	R&D Costs as Percent of Profits
Aerospace	4.2	102.1
Automotive	3.2	124.0
Chemicals	2.3	36.5
Containers	0.8	22.3
Drugs	4.8	49.1

Source: *Business Week*, July 7, 1980.

At one time, unamortized R&D costs were a significant balance sheet asset and were reported as a deferred charge. Accounting practice for R&D costs was quite varied; some companies recorded R&D costs as expense in the period they were incurred; others deferred varying portions of their R&D expenditures as assets, and practice as to amortization of the deferred portion was far from uniform.

This variety of practice as to accounting for such important expenditures received the attention of the FASB and resulted in the issuance of FASB, *Statement of Financial Accounting Standards No. 2,* "Accounting for Research and Development Costs," in 1974. This *Statement* specifies accounting practices for R&D costs.

Among other things, *FASB Statement 2* provides that:

1. All R&D costs covered by the *Statement* shall be debited to expense when incurred. Stated another way, R&D expenditures (except for item 3 below) must not be capitalized.
2. Financial statements must disclose **total** R&D costs debited to expense in each period for which an income statement is presented.
3. Item 1 above does not apply to R&D costs where work is done for others under contract. Also, exceptions were made for certain government-regulated entities. In these areas, R&D costs can be debited to an asset account when incurred and subsequently amortized.

As specified in *FASB Statement 2,* R&D costs encompass those costs of materials, equipment and facilities, personnel, intangibles purchased from others, contract services, and allocated indirect costs specifically related to R&D. These would include the following:

a. Laboratory research aimed at discovery of new knowledge.
b. Searching for applications of new research findings or other knowledge.

[7] In most jurisdictions, it is illegal to issue stock at a discount.

[8] A lease which does **not** effectively transfer most of the rewards and risks of ownership to the lessee is referred to as an operating lease. A lease which transfers such rewards and risks of ownership is referred to as a capital lease. Leases are discussed in Chapter 19.

c. Conceptual formulation and design of possible product or process alternatives.
d. Testing in search for or evaluation of product or process alternatives.
e. Modification of the formulation or design of a product or process.
f. Design, construction, and testing of preproduction prototypes and models.
g. Design of tools, molds, and dies involving new technology.
h. Design, construction, and operation of a pilot plant that is not of a scale economically feasible to the enterprise for commercial production.
i. Engineering activity required to advance the design of a product to the point that it meets specific functional and economic requirements and is ready for manufacture.

It can be argued that *FASB Statement 2* represents a practical solution to what had been a serious problem. Study had indicated it was difficult to establish criteria for identifying R&D costs which would have future benefit and, as noted above, there was considerable diversity of practice in accounting for R&D. One of the chief aims of standard-setting bodies such as the FASB is to reduce diversity of accounting practice.

Critics of *FASB Statement 2* argue that while expensing R&D costs when incurred might yield approximately the same periodic expense as capitalization and amortization of R&D, the balance sheet consequences of *Statement 2* are hard to defend. In essence, the standard requires companies to report that their R&D expenditures have no future benefit because no intangible or deferred charge related to R&D can appear on the balance sheet.[9] Successful companies operating in industries in which R&D amounts are significant actually have almost priceless assets as a result of their R&D efforts, but no amount related to R&D costs appears on their balance sheets. Regardless of which side of the argument has more appeal to you, the standard has had strong support in accounting practice and has eliminated a major area of diversity.

As noted in the earlier discussion of patents, companies can no longer apportion a part of their R&D expenditures to the cost of an internally developed patent. Patent costs can include cost of **securing** the patent but not expenditures which led to developing the patent.

EXPLORATION COSTS

Oil and gas producing companies have, for many years, used either of two basic accounting methods to account for costs incurred in searching for and developing oil and gas reserves. Many smaller companies have used the **full cost** method under which they capitalized the costs associated with the discovery and development of both producing wells and those which were unsuccessful (dry holes). The full cost method is based largely on the theoretical argument that the cost of drilling dry holes is as much a part of exploration activities as is the cost of drilling successful wells. Stated differently, "You have to drill some dry holes to find oil and gas." In this view, such dry hole costs should be capitalized because such dry hole costs were incurred to generate future revenues.

Most larger oil companies use the **successful efforts** method under which they capitalize only the costs of searching for and developing successful wells; they debit to expense the costs associated with most dry holes (as soon as they are sure of the outcome) on the theory that dry hole costs produce no oil and provide no benefit for future periods.

In February 1978, the FASB attempted to eliminate this dichotomy when it issued *FASB, Statement of Financial Accounting Standards No. 19,* "Financial Accounting and Reporting by Oil and Gas Producing Companies." This *Statement* rejected the full cost method on the grounds that dry hole costs have no future benefit, and required all oil and gas producing companies to use the successful efforts method. In articulating its position, the FASB asserted that similar activities should be accounted for similarly and that they found no basis for allowing different methods of accounting for the same type of event to produce different asset values and income amounts.

Accounting requirements of *FASB Statement 19* included the following controversial provisions:

1. Oil and gas companies were required to use a version of the "successful efforts" method of accounting for costs of searching for and developing oil and gas reserves. In essence, this means that

[9] A company owning a laboratory facility in which R&D activities are conducted and which has alternative future uses (in R&D projects or otherwise) should account for the facility as an operational asset. Depreciation and other costs related to such facilities should be accounted for as R&D expenses.

usually only the costs of **successful** wells could be capitalized and subsequently amortized. Costs of **unsuccessful** exploratory wells (dry holes) were required to be debited to expense as soon as the wells were determined to be unsuccessful. Full costing (a procedure which would capitalize costs of both successful and unsuccessful wells with subsequent amortization of the capitalized costs) was prohibited.

2. All exploration costs except the costs of drilling **exploratory** wells were recorded as expense when incurred.

In a move which many perceived as a severe setback to the private sector's efforts to determine accounting principles the SEC, in August 1978, determined that traditional accounting methods—successful efforts and full cost—failed to provide sufficient useful information on the financial position and operating results of oil and gas producers. It added that requiring either method as a uniform basis of accounting and reporting would be unwarranted.

The SEC then undertook a major effort to develop "Reserve Recognition Accounting" (RRA), a form of discovery value accounting (see Chapter 11 discussion under heading, Discovery Value). The SEC planned to develop RRA sufficiently so that by 1981 RRA would replace the two traditional methods. Meanwhile, the SEC continued to accept financial statements prepared under the successful efforts method as prescribed in *FASB Statement 19* or the full cost method under rules the SEC promulgated.

Because of the developments described above, in 1979, the FASB issued *Statement of Financial Accounting Standards No. 25,* "Suspension of Certain Accounting Requirements for Oil and Gas Producing Companies." *Statement 25* suspended the effective date of applying *FASB Statement 19* related to the successful efforts method. Then, early in 1981, the SEC announced abandonment of the program to develop RRA as the primary method of accounting by oil and gas companies. However, the SEC retained the requirement that RRA disclosures be made on a supplementary basis (i.e., not in the primary financial statements) until the FASB could develop a set of "value-based" (versus "cost-based") disclosure requirements for oil and gas companies. The FASB immediately placed the oil and gas accounting issue on its agenda.

Part B: Development Stage Enterprises, Insurance, and Disposal and Reporting of Intangibles

DEVELOPMENT STAGE ENTERPRISES

The subject of accounting for enterprises in the development stage is closely akin to deferred charges because in the past companies in the development stage have capitalized a wide range of costs which would have been expensed under normal operating conditions. This was done because, during the development stage, they incur high start-up costs and usually have little or no revenues against which they can be matched.

Because of the lack of guidelines and the wide variety of practices, the FASB issued *Statement of Financial Accounting Standards No. 7,* "Accounting and Reporting by Development Stage Enterprises." The *Statement* defines development stage enterprises essentially as follows (pars. 8–9):

> An enterprise shall be considered to be in the development stage if it is devoting substantially all of its efforts to establishing a new business and either of the following conditions exists: (a) planned principal operations have not commenced or (b) planned principal operations have commenced but there has been no significant revenue therefrom. A development stage enterprise will typically be devoting most of its efforts to activities such as financial planning; raising capital; exploring for natural resources; developing natural resources; research and development; establishing sources of supply; acquiring property, plant, or other operating assets, such as mineral rights; recruiting and training personnel; developing markets; and starting up production.

FASB Statement 7 requires development stage enterprises to present financial statements prepared on the same basis as other businesses; special reporting formats are unacceptable. Capitalization of costs is subject to the same assessment of future benefit and recoverability applicable to established businesses. Thus, the *Statement* specifies that a development stage enterprise is required to present (par. 11):

a. A balance sheet, including any cumulative net losses reported with a descriptive caption such as "deficit accumulated during the development stage" in the owners' equity section.
b. An income statement, showing amounts of revenue and expenses for each period covered by the income statement and, in addition, cumulative amounts from the enterprise's inception.
c. A statement of changes in financial position, showing the sources and uses of financial resources for each period for which an income statement is presented and, in addition, cumulative amounts from the enterprise's inception.
d. A statement of stockholders' equity, showing from the enterprise's inception for each stock issuance:
    1. Date and number of shares issued for cash or other consideration.
    2. Dollar amounts (per share or other equity unit) assigned to consideration received for securities.
    3. The nature of any noncash consideration received for stock issued and the basis for determining the value of the noncash consideration.

The *Statement* also requires that the financial statements be **specifically identified** as those of a development stage enterprise and must include a description of the nature of the development stage in which the enterprise is engaged.

INSURANCE

Practically all businesses carry one or more kinds of insurance. Insurance requires prepayment of the premiums, at which time an asset with intangible characteristics is created. Depending on the type of insurance and time covered, the prepaid premiums may be *(a)* a current asset (i.e., short-term prepayments), *(b)* a long-term investment (i.e., cash surrender value of life insurance policies), or *(c)* a deferred charge (i.e., long-term prepayments).

Although there are many different kinds of insurance, the usual kinds carried by businesses include *(a)* liability insurance, *(b)* casualty insurance, and *(c)* life insurance on key executives.

Liability Insurance

Liability insurance involves a contract whereby the insurance company, in consideration for a stated premium, is contractually obligated for certain liabilities to third parties that arise from specified events such as damages sought by a customer for injuries in an accident on company premises. The premium typically is paid in advance for periods of one to five years. Prepaid premiums represent a type of intangible asset. To illustrate, assume that on January 1, 19A, Company B paid a $2,500 five-year premium for a liability insurance policy. The accounting and reporting for 19A could be as follows:

Entries:

January 1, 19A—insurance premium paid:

Prepaid insurance	2,500	
Cash		2,500

December 31, 19A—adjusting entry:

Insurance expense ($2,500 ÷ 5)	500	
Prepaid insurance		500

Reporting at December 31, 19A

Income statement:	
Insurance expense	$ 500
Balance sheet:	
Current assets:	
Prepaid insurance	500
Deferred charges:	
Prepaid insurance, long term	1,500

Casualty Insurance

Casualty insurance involves a contract whereby the insurance company in consideration for a premium payment assumes an obligation under certain circumstances to reimburse the policyholder an amount not exceeding the **replacement cost** of the property (in its present condition) lost due to storm, fire, and so forth, as specified in the policy. The indemnity in no case exceeds the **lower** of **replacement cost** or the amount stipulated in the contract, that is, the **face amount** of the policy (if the latter is lower).

Many casualty insurance policies carry a **coinsurance clause** which provides that if the property is insured for less than a stated percentage (often 80 percent) of its **replacement cost** at the time of a loss, the insured is a **coinsurer** with the insurance company.[10] As a coinsurer, the insured must bear a share of losses. The share of a loss borne by an insured party when there is a coinsurance clause is determined by application of the policy provision that the insurance company will pay the **lowest** of the three following amounts:

1. Face of the policy.
2. Replacement cost of the property lost.
3. Coinsurance indemnity (determined by formula).

To illustrate the effect of a coinsurance clause, assume the following for Company C:

1. Policy on casualties—face, $7,000; coinsurance clause, 80 percent.
2. Casualty—fire; replacement cost of the property lost at date of fire (there was a partial loss of the property), $5,680.
3. Total replacement cost of the insured property immediately prior to the fire, $10,000.

Computation of the coinsurance indemnity (by formula):

$$\left\{\frac{\text{Face of policy}}{.80 \times \text{Total replacement cost of insured property at date of casualty}}\right\} \times \left\{\begin{matrix}\text{Replacement}\\ \text{cost of the property lost}\end{matrix}\right\} = \left\{\begin{matrix}\text{Coinsurance}\\ \text{indemnity}\end{matrix}\right\}$$

$$\frac{\$7{,}000}{.80 \times \$10{,}000} \times \$5{,}680 = \underline{\underline{\$4{,}970}}$$

Thus, the insurance company would reimburse the insured party for $4,970 because it is lower than either the face of the policy ($7,000) or the replacement cost of the property ($5,680).

Blanket Policy. When a company takes out a casualty insurance policy covering several items of property (often called a blanket policy), the policy usually includes a so-called average clause, which provides that the protection will pertain to each item of property based upon the proportion of the replacement cost of each insured property to the total replacement cost of the property insured. For example, assume that a blanket policy for $180,000, with an 80 percent coinsurance clause, insured two buildings—Building A with replacement cost of $200,000 and Building B with replacement cost of $100,000 at the date of fire. The face of the policy would be allocated as $120,000 (i.e., $200,000 ÷ $300,000 = ⅔ of $180,000) on Building A and $60,000 (i.e., $100,000 ÷ $300,000 = ⅓ of $180,000) on Building B. If a fire loss of $40,000 occurred in Building B, the maximum coinsurance indemnity would be as follows:

$$\frac{\$60{,}000}{.80 \times \$100{,}000} \times \$40{,}000 = \$30{,}000$$

Because $30,000 (i.e., the formula amount) is less than either the replacement cost of the property lost ($40,000) or the effective face of the policy on Building B ($60,000), the actual indemnity would be $30,000, the amount set by the formula.

Indemnity under Several Policies. Where more than one insurance policy covers the same property and the policies have different coinsurance clauses, losses are prorated to policies based upon the face amounts of the various policies. The indemnity under each policy is computed by applying the basic coinsurance formula. To illustrate, assume Acme Company has two insurance policies covering an asset with replacement cost of $100,000. On the date that a fire destroys 40 percent of the asset, the face amounts of the two policies are $20,000 and $60,000, as shown in Exhibit 13–3, column (2). If the coinsurance clauses of the two policies are 75 percent and 90 percent, respectively (see Exhibit 13–3, column [1]), the indemnity under each policy would be as shown in column (5).

If the two policies shown in Exhibit 13–3 had specified no coinsurance, the indemnities paid under the policies would have been $10,000 and $30,000, respectively, as shown in column (3). In contrast, assume the policies had the same coinsurance clauses (say,

[10] The effect of coinsurance is to encourage insured parties to carry adequate insurance. In the absence of a coinsurance clause, small losses will be fully indemnified when a small amount of insurance is carried. However, if policies contain a coinsurance clause, such losses will be shared by the insured and the insurance company.

EXHIBIT 13–3: Indemnity under Two Policies with Variable Coinsurance Clauses

Policy	(1) Coinsurance	(2) Face of Policy	(3) Loss Proration*	(4) Coinsurance Indemnity†	(5) Indemnity (lowest)
1	75%	$20,000	$10,000	$10,667	$10,000
2	90	60,000	30,000	26,667	26,667
		$80,000	$40,000		$36,667

* ($20,000 ÷ $80,000) × $40,000 = $10,000.
($60,000 ÷ $80,000) × $40,000 = $30,000.

† $\frac{\$20{,}000}{.75\ (\$100{,}000)} \times \$40{,}000 = \$10{,}667.$

$\frac{\$60{,}000}{.90\ (\$100{,}000)} \times \$40{,}000 = \$26{,}667.$

75 percent); in this case, the computations would be as shown in Exhibit 13–3, except that the indemnity under policy 2 would be modified to include the 75 percent coinsurance clause instead of the 90 percent illustrated.

ACCOUNTING FOR A CASUALTY AND RELATED INSURANCE

Sometimes assets are lost due to what is termed a **casualty.** A casualty may result from an event such as a fire, flood, or storm. Accounting for a casualty involves *(a)* removing from the accounting records the asset lost, *(b)* recording any collection of indemnity from the insurance company, *(c)* adjusting any prepaid insurance affected by the loss, and *(d)* closing the net amount of the casualty gain or loss to Income Summary (**gains** can result when insurance indemnities at replacement cost exceed book values). In accounting for a casualty, certain procedures should be followed, viz:

1. Determine to what extent the accounting records have been damaged or destroyed. Supplement damaged records or reconstruct them if they have been destroyed.
2. Adjust the accounts for assets lost in the casualty to the date of the casualty. For example, make all necessary adjusting entries for depreciation, amortization, accrued and prepaid expense, and revenue items affected from the date of the last year-end to the date of the casualty.
3. Determine the **book value** (after the adjustments in 2 above) of all assets destroyed by the casualty, as of the date of the casualty.
4. Open a Casualty Loss account in the general ledger. Debit Casualty Loss for:
   a. Book value of assets destroyed.
   b. Expenses incurred in connection with the casualty.
   c. Prepaid insurance (after adjustment in 2 above) for the portion of the policy absorbed by the insurance indemnity.
5. Determine the amounts recoverable under the policies in force. Credit Casualty Loss for any *(a)* insurance indemnity plus *(b)* salvage recovery from the sale of damaged assets whose cost previously has been debited to Casualty Loss.[11]
6. Close the net balance of Casualty Loss to Income Summary.

If a perpetual inventory system is used, and if the records are not destroyed, the amount of the inventory on hand at the time of the fire can be determined from the inventory records. In the absence of such records, the amount of the inventory may be estimated by the gross margin method as described in Chapter 9.

Accounting for a Casualty Illustrated

Assume the Fire Alarm Company suffered a fire loss on July 1 of the current year; the relevant data are given in Exhibit 13–4. The entries to adjust the books to the date of the fire, to record the fire loss, and to record the settlement with the insurance company, with explanations and computations, are given in Exhibit 13–5.

[11] Salvage recovery from sale of damaged assets may, instead, go to the insurance company under terms of the settlement.

The two adjusting entries given in Exhibit 13–5 (i.e., entry 1 for depreciation and entry 2 for insurance) are exactly like those at year-end, except they were recorded as of July 1, the date of the fire. Entries 3 and 4 record the casualty losses on the building and inventory (perpetual system), respectively; they are based on the respective book values on the date of the fire.[12] Entry 5 records the insurance settlement in the amount of $200,000. Entry 6 is needed to record the amount of prepaid insurance at July 1, which is "absorbed" by the insurance indemnity (i.e., $3,840). This amount of prepaid insurance (i.e., the unexpired premium) is liquidated and included implicitly in the insurance indemnity of $200,000 (entry 5). Therefore, it is "lost" insofar as future insurance protection under the present policy is concerned, and consequently, it is debited to Casualty Loss (or alternatively, Casualty Clearing Account).

For the insured assets, the Casualty Loss account reflects a credit balance (i.e., a gain) of $28,160 (before closing), because the indemnity was based on replacement cost, which was more than the book value of the assets on the date they were destroyed. This result (i.e., a casualty "gain") would be the usual outcome because the replacement cost of many assets exceeds their book value. The Casualty Loss account is closed to Income Summary as shown in entry 7.

LIFE INSURANCE

Life insurance companies sell insurance policies that call for a stipulated payment to the beneficiary of the policy (indemnity) in case of death of the insured. In an **ordinary life** policy, the premiums are paid until the death of the insured, at which time the stipulated benefit is paid to the beneficiary. During the period the policy is in force, it has both a cash surrender value and a loan value. In a **limited payment** policy, the premiums are paid for a stated number of periods or until the death of the insured (if prior to the end of the stipulated period) and the benefit is paid at death. As with the ordinary life policy, a limited payment policy also has a cash surrender value and a loan value. In **term insurance,** the premium payments are made for a stated number of periods or until death (if prior to the end of the stipulated period); the benefit is paid only if death occurs within the stated number of periods. Term insurance has no cash surrender or loan value, and the policy must be renewed at the end of the stipulated period; otherwise it lapses. At renewal, a new premium scale is effective based on the increased age. Because there are no complexities in accounting for term insurance, the discussion to follow will be limited to ordinary life policies.[13]

Companies have an insurable interest in certain of their **executives.** Thus, it is common for companies to insure the lives of certain key executives; the proceeds from the policy upon the death of the insured executive are payable to the company to compensate for the loss incurred in replacing a deceased executive. In accounting for a life insurance policy of this type, premiums paid (cash paid less any dividends earned on the policy) and the related cash surrender value of the policy must be recorded and reported.[14]

Cash Surrender and Loan Values

The cash surrender value of a policy is the sum payable upon the cancellation of the policy at the request of the insured. The loan value of a policy is the amount the insurance company will loan on a policy maintained in force. The cash surrender value is computed as of the **end** of the year; the loan value is computed as of the **beginning** of the year (thus, it is less by interest for one year). Each policy contains a schedule which indicates the cash surrender value and the loan value for each policy year. Since the policy can be canceled and a portion of the premiums which have been paid may be returned in the form of the cash surrender value, not all of the premiums paid constitute expense. Thus, periodic

[12] If a periodic inventory system is used, the following entries would be made on July 1 to record the historical cost (HC) of the inventory lost:

1. Adjusting entries:

Income summary	80,000	
Inventory (beginning)		80,000
Inventory (on date of fire)	90,000*	
Income summary		90,000

* Estimated using some technique such as the gross margin method (see Chapter 9).

2. Entry to record loss on inventory destroyed:

Casualty loss	90,000	
Inventory (on date of fire)		90,000

[13] Accounting for a limited payment policy would be similar to accounting for an ordinary life policy.

[14] Ordinary life insurance policies issued by **mutual** insurance companies usually pay dividends to policyholders because the policyholders are the "owners" of mutual insurance companies.

EXHIBIT 13–4: Illustrative Data for Casualty Loss—Fire Alarm Company

Basic Data to Date of Fire Loss (July 1):	
a. **Account balances January 1 of current year:**	
Prepaid insurance	$ 6,400
Inventory (at cost), perpetual	80,000
Building (at cost)	180,000
Accum. depr., building (depr. rate, 3⅓% per year on cost)	60,000
b. **Replacement cost at date of fire (July 1):**	
Inventory (same as historical cost), perpetual system, 100% loss	$ 90,000
Building—total replacement cost, net of accum. depr.	300,000
Building—amount of loss at replacement cost, net of accum. depr., two-thirds loss ($300,000 × ⅔)	200,000
c. **Insurance coverage:**	
Inventory	None
Building, insured—face of policy (policy includes an 80% coinsurance clause)	$250,000
Unexpired insurance on January 1 of current year (24 months unexpired)	6,400

expense is only the excess of the periodic premium paid over the periodic increase in the cash surrender value.

The diagram at the top of page 452 illustrates that in the early years of an ordinary life policy, substantially all of each periodic premium is for insurance protection. Cash surrender value customarily starts accumulating in the third year or later. As time passes, an increasing portion of each premium payment adds to the cash surrender value. This is a general pattern; individual policies differ widely with respect to accumulation of cash values.

Once a policy begins to accumulate a cash surrender value, that part of each premium payment which increases the cash surrender value represents the acquisition of an asset. Cash surrender value is reported on the balance sheet under **Investments and Funds.**

To illustrate one sequence of entries, assume the following data were taken from an insurance policy with a face amount of $25,000:

Year	Premium (beginning of year)	Cash Surrender Value (end of year)
1	$720	-0-
2	720	-0-
3	720	$210
4	720	290
5		(Etc., as specified in the policy)

Based on the above data, the indicated entries would be as follows:

Year 1:

On premium payment date:

Life insurance expense	720	
Cash		720

At year end:

Cash surrender value of life insurance	70*	
Life insurance expense		70

* $210 ÷ 3 years = $70. Recognition of this addition to cash surrender value anticipates that the policy will be kept in force at least through the third policy year when the cash surrender value actually arises. An alternative (and more conservative) treatment would recognize the $210 in the third year and reduce insurance expense for that year by the same amount.

Year 2:
Same as year 1.

Year 3:
Same as year 1.

Year 4:

On premium payment date:

Life insurance expense	720	
Cash		720

At year-end:

Cash surrender value of life insurance ($290 − $210)	80	
Life insurance expense (current)		80

EXHIBIT 13–5: Entries to Record a Casualty Loss—Fire Alarm Company (based on Exhibit 13–4)

July 1—To adjust asset accounts to date of fire (no entry needed for perpetual inventory system (see footnote 12 for periodic inventory system):

1. Depreciation expense, building	3,000	
Accumulated depreciation, building		3,000

January 1 to July 1: $\$180,000 \times 3\frac{1}{3}\% \times \frac{6}{12} = \$3,000$.

2. Insurance expense	1,600	
Prepaid insurance		1,600

Expired January 1 to July 1: $\$6,400 \times \frac{6}{24} = \$1,600$.

July 1—To remove book value of assets destroyed:

3. Casualty loss (building)	78,000	
Accumulated depreciation, building [($60,000 + $3,000) × ⅔]	42,000	
Building ($180,000 × ⅔)		120,000
4. Casualty loss (inventory)	90,000	
Inventory (perpetual)		90,000

During July—To record indemnity received from the insurance company:

5. Cash	200,000	
Casualty loss		200,000

Computation:

Face of policy	$250,000
Replacement cost of portion of building lost	200,000
Formula: [$250,000 ÷ (.80 × $300,000)] × $200,000	208,333

Use lower amount, $200,000. Note that in this example, the coinsurance clause would not come into play because the building was insured for more than 80 percent of its replacement cost.

6. To adjust the balance in the Prepaid Insurance account:

Casualty loss (insurance)	3,840	
Prepaid insurance		3,840

Analysis of prepaid insurance:

Unexpired January 1	$6,400
Amortized to July 1	1,600
Unexpired July 1 (date of fire)	$4,800

Amount of unexpired insurance on July 1 absorbed by indemnity:
Indemnity ÷ Face of policy ($200,000 ÷ $250,000) × $4,800 .... $3,840

December 31—To close the casualty loss account:

7. Casualty loss	28,160	
Income summary		28,160

Analysis of the casualty loss account (entry numbers keyed to entries above):

Casualty Loss

3. Building	78,000	5. Indemnity	200,000
4. Inventory	90,000		
6. Absorbed insurance	3,840		
7. Closed to Income Summary	28,160		
	200,000		200,000

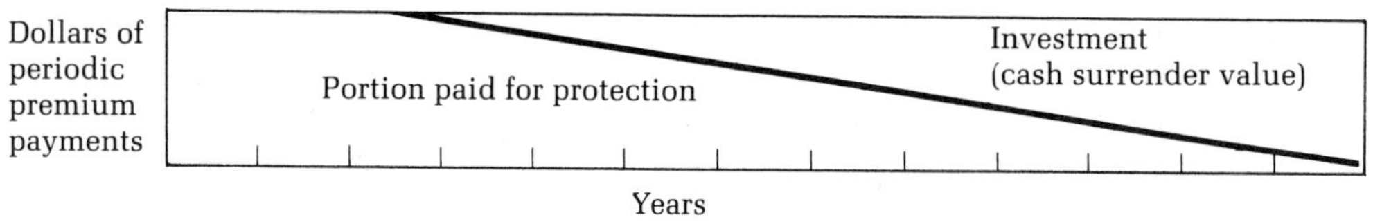

A balance in the account, Cash Surrender Value of Life Insurance, is reported on the balance sheet under the caption, Investments and Funds. Each year thereafter the Cash Surrender Value of Life Insurance account would be debited for the increase in the cash surrender value as shown by the table in the policy. The above example was simplified by assuming the policy year and the accounting year coincided. If they do not coincide, as in the normal case, an adjusting entry at the end of each accounting period would be required for the prepaid amount of insurance expense.

The following entry would be made when the face of the policy is paid at the death of the executive whose life was insured by the company, assuming the cash surrender value of the policy at date of death was $3,500 and that three months' premium is to be refunded in accordance with the policy provision that premiums paid beyond date of death are refunded.

Cash [$25,000 + ($\frac{3}{12}$ × $720)]	25,180	
Life insurance expense ($\frac{3}{12}$ × $720)		180
Cash surrender value of life insurance		3,500
Gain on settlement of life insurance indemnity...............		21,500

The gain normally would be extraordinary.

DISPOSAL AND IMPAIRMENT OF VALUE OF INTANGIBLE ASSETS

Disposal

When an intangible asset is sold, exchanged, or otherwise disposed of, the unamortized cost (or cost and accumulated amortization if separately recorded) must be removed from the accounts and a gain or loss on disposal recorded.

Because financial analysts often view intangibles as being of questionable value and because of overconservatism, accounting practice in the past tended to encourage their arbitrary write-down to a nominal amount, either by lump sum in one period or over an unrealistically short estimated life.[15] Contemporary accounting principles do not permit this practice because, from an accounting standpoint, it biases income and financial position downward. On this point, *APB Opinion 17* (par. 28) states that intangible assets "should not be written off in the period of acquisition" and "analysis of all factors should result in a reasonable estimate of the useful life. . . ."

Impairment of Value

During the period of use of an intangible asset or a deferred charge, an estimate of the value of future benefit associated with the asset may indicate that its book value exceeds its economic utility (i.e., use value) to the enterprise. In such situations the unamortized cost should be written down, and a loss recognized, to reflect the **impairment** of value. The revised value should be amortized over the estimated remaining useful life, not to exceed 40 years from date of acquisition (*APB Opinion 17,* par. 31). When a write-down occurs due to such an impairment of value, disclosure is required in notes to the financial statements (*APB Opinion 17,* par. 31).

REPORTING INTANGIBLES

Noncurrent assets classified as intangibles are variously reported under balance sheet headings

[15] Evidence that financial analysts and other investors do not share the accounting viewpoint that the costs of assets reported as intangibles (principally goodwill) represent assets is provided by the provisions of debt covenants (i.e., the contract between borrower and lender). Debt covenants often require the debtor company to maintain its ratio of long-term debt to **net tangible assets** below a specified maximum. In such situations, computation of this ratio requires the subtraction of intangibles from owners' equity as though the intangible assets have no real value. The purpose of such debt covenant provisions is to protect creditors in the event the debtor company fails; therefore, for creditors, it is logical to consider intangible assets such as goodwill as not being assets because they have no separate sales value in the forced liquidation of a company. However, for accounting purposes, goodwill and all other recorded intangible assets have future service potential. Otherwise, a rational purchaser would not expend assets to purchase them.

such as **Intangibles, Deferred charges,** and **Other assets.** Although reasonably precise definitions have been provided in this chapter and are desirable, in practice comparable distinctions often are not made among these three captions. Therefore, considerable variation among companies can be observed in their balance sheet reporting of intangibles. Often each major intangible asset reported on the balance sheet is described in detail in the financial statement notes. For example, Hershey Foods Corporation reported in Note 2 of its 1979 annual report that it paid $39.8 million for goodwill as part of the $164 million purchase price of Friendly Ice Cream Corporation. In Note 1 of the report, Hershey disclosed that the company amortizes the cost of goodwill purchased after October 31, 1970 (the effective date of *APB Opinion 17*) over 40 years; for goodwill purchased prior to that date, Hershey carries it "at cost until such time as there may be evidence of diminution" of value. The practice of not amortizing the cost of goodwill purchased prior to October 31, 1970, is common, and it is consistent with the provisions of *APB Opinion 17.*

QUESTIONS

PART A

1. What distinguishes intangible assets from the remaining assets traditionally reported outside the current asset category? How are intangible assets reported on the balance sheet?
2. What outlays are properly considered part of the cost of an intangible asset?
3. Cite the factors that should determine whether or not an intangible asset is amortized and, if so, over what period of time.
4. What is an *identifiable intangible asset?* Give some examples of such assets.
5. What is the nature of a *franchise?* Of a *trademark?*
6. Explain the conceptual nature of *goodwill* and the basis on which goodwill is amortized.
7. What is the role of the accountant in valuation of goodwill?
8. Briefly describe *going value.* How can it be distinguished from goodwill?
9. Define a *deferred charge.* Is it an intangible?
10. How are deferred charges distinguished from prepaid expenses? Give examples of each.
11. What items are properly debited to organization costs? Should organization costs be amortized? Explain.
12. What are the basic provisions of the *FASB Statement* on accounting for research and development (R&D) costs?
13. Succinctly describe the full cost and successful efforts methods of accounting for exploration and development costs in the oil and gas industry.
14. The 1980 edition of *Accounting Trends & Techniques,* an annual survey of reporting practices of 600 industrial companies, indicates that in 1979 there were 156 instances of goodwill not being amortized. Does this mean that *APB Opinion 17* is being widely ignored or is there a better explanation? If so, what is the better explanation?
15. What is the maximum number of years over which a patent should be amortized? What determines this maximum? Under what circumstances, if any, should a shorter amortization term be used?
16. Distinguish *trademarks* from *copyrights.* Wherein are they similar? Dissimilar?
17. Give examples of situations in which the accounting carrying value of an intangible asset can increase. Does the accounting value of an intangible necessarily bear a close relationship to its economic value?

PART B

18. What is a *development stage company?* Are development stage companies subject to the same or different accounting rules than other companies? Explain briefly.
19. Some casualty policies have *coinsurance clauses.* What is the purpose of such a clause? How does its presence in a policy affect the indemnity which the insured party can collect if the insured property is totally destroyed?
20. When a casualty occurs for which insurance is in force, certain accounting steps should be taken. Basically, what are these accounting steps?

21. What is the relationship between *cash surrender* value and *loan* value of a life insurance policy? Which one affects accounting entries? How?

22. For what reasons do some companies insure the lives of executives and name the companies as beneficiaries?

DECISION CASE 13–1

In the broadcast industry (radio, TV, and cable) when one entity is acquired by another, the consideration paid by the buyer often is considerably in excess of the market value of the tangible net assets of the seller. The buyer pays the excess price because the station has a license protecting its right to continue broadcasting in a location and on an assigned frequency, or the cable company has a franchise to do business in a territory and/or already has an established network of customers.

The excess consideration paid in these transactions often is ascribed to goodwill. Under current GAAP, goodwill is reported separately and must be amortized over a reasonable period not to exceed 40 years. Some accountants contend that the goodwill in these cases is a perpetual asset and therefore should not be subject to amortization. Others have taken an opposite position that the goodwill is not an asset but rather should be reported as a contra balance in the owners' equity section of the acquirer's balance sheet.

Required:
GAAP notwithstanding, give logical arguments in support of, and against, each of these contrasting positions? What arguments support the current GAAP rules?

DECISION CASE 13–2

The National Broadcasting Company (NBC) was reported to have incurred costs of $750,000 in the development of its "N" logo shown at intervals in its TV broadcasts. Shortly after the N was announced and first used by NBC, it was discovered that an educational TV network in Nebraska had already been using a similar logo. To obtain exclusive rights to its already costly N, NBC agreed, in an out-of-court settlement, to pay $55,000 cash to the Nebraska network and to furnish it with various new and used color TV equipment without cost. The equipment to be transferred was conservatively valued at $500,000. A spokesman for the Nebraska network said the equipment to be provided by NBC would have cost $750,000 if bought new and that for the two years preceding the settlement, efforts to get a $750,000 appropriation from the Nebraska legislature to buy such equipment had been unsuccessful. Terms of the settlement provided that $2,500 of the cash settlement was to be paid to William Korbus. He had designed the Nebraska network's N at a cost of $100. Delivery of the equipment to the Nebraska network was to begin approximately three months after the announced settlement and was to occur over a four-month interval.

Required:
1. How should NBC account for its original costs of $750,000 related to the logo? How should it account for the settlement with the Nebraska network and Korbus?
2. Assuming that accounting principles for not-for-profit organizations such as the Nebraska network were similar to those for a commercial entity, how should the Nebraska network account for the settlement?
3. What are the accounting implications of the fact that two different networks could spend such different sums for items that were almost identical?

DECISION CASE 13–3

Exxon Corporation and two partners, Mobil Oil and Champlin Petroleum Company, paid cash bonuses of $632 million for rights to drill for oil and gas on six different offshore tracts in the Gulf of Mexico near Florida.

Required:
1. Between the date of the bonus payment and the time drilling begins, how should the $632 million expenditure be accounted for? What about other costs?
2. After spending an added $15 million to drill seven wells

on the acreage, the venturers unfortunately found no oil or gas in commercial quantities and announced there were no plans for additional drilling on the tracts. Assuming the rights to drill do not expire for another 10 years, what accounting is indicated?

DECISION CASE 13–4

The time lapse between the date a new product is conceived and the date it is available for sale to customers often is lengthy. The following listing of commonplace products and the number of years it took to make them marketable realities is indicative.

Antibiotics	30
Automatic transmission	16
Cellophane	12
Dry soup mixes	19
Fluorescent lights	33
Frozen foods	15
Instant coffee	22
Instant rice	18
Nylon	12
Photography	56
Radio	24
Television	63
Zippers	30

On the other hand, instant cameras and filter cigarettes made it to the stores in two years, and long-playing records took only three.

In the light of the foregoing, if you were a member of a standards-setting body such as the FASB, what would be your basic position as to proper accounting for R&D costs? Cite the considerations that caused you to reach your basic conclusions.

DECISION CASE 13–5

Under provisions of *FASB Statement 2,* R&D costs must be expensed in the period in which they are incurred except for costs of R&D activities conducted for others under contract and indirect costs that are specifically reimbursable under terms of a contract.

How should these exception-type costs be accounted for and reported? Support whatever conclusions you reach.

EXERCISES

PART A: EXERCISES 13–1 to 13–11

Exercise 13–1

On January 1, 19A, Pitt Company sold a patent to Chatham, Inc.; the patent had a net carrying value on Pitt's books of $10,000. Chatham gave Pitt an $80,000 discounted note payable in five equal annual installments of $16,000, with the first payment payable on January 1, 19B. There was no established exchange price for the patent, and the note has no ready market value. The prevailing rate of interest for a note of this type at January 1, 19A, was 12%.

Required:
Compute the income or loss before income taxes that Pitt should record for the years ended December 31, 19A, and 19B, as a result of the above facts. (AICPA adapted)

Exercise 13–2

The data below pertain to two separate intangible assets:

	Asset X	Asset Y
Cost	$12,000	$14,000
Estimated economic life	Indefinite	14 years

Required (assume straight-line amortization):
1. Give annual entry for amortization, if any, for each asset. (Assume both were acquired after 1970.)
2. Assume asset Y has been in use for eight full years and it is determined at the start of the ninth year that its remaining life will be four years. Give the appropriate amortization entry for asset Y at the end of its ninth year.

Exercise 13–3

Check the best answer in each of the following and indicate the basis for your choice.

1. A deferred charge should be—
   a. Expensed as incurred.

b. Capitalized and not amortized until it clearly has no value.
c. Capitalized and amortized over the estimated period benefited.
d. Capitalized and amortized over the estimated period benefited but not exceeding 40 years.

2. R&D costs incurred after *FASB Statement 2* should be—
   a. Capitalized on a selective basis and not amortized.
   b. Capitalized, then amortized over 40 years.
   c. Expensed in the year in which they are incurred.
   d. Debited directly to retained earnings.
3. Goodwill is most closely akin to—
   a. Going value.
   b. Franchises.
   c. Trademarks.
   d. Copyrights.
4. On January 15, 19A, a corporation was granted a patent on a product. On January 2, 19J, to protect its patent, the corporation purchased a patent on a competing product that originally was issued on January 10, 19F. Because of its unique plant, the corporation does not feel the competing patent can be used in producing a product. The cost of the competing patent should be—
   a. Amortized over a maximum period of 17 years.
   b. Amortized over a maximum period of 13 years.
   c. Amortized over a maximum period of 8 years.
   d. Expensed in 19J.
5. Goodwill should be written off—
   a. As soon as possible against retained earnings.
   b. As soon as possible as an extraordinary item.
   c. By systematic debits against retained earnings over the period benefited, but not more than 40 years.
   d. By systematic debits to expense over the period benefited, but not more than 40 years.
6. A large publicly held company has developed and registered a trademark during 19A. How should the cost of developing and registering the trademark be accounted for?
   a. Debited to an asset account that should not be amortized.
   b. Expensed as incurred.
   c. Amortized over 25 years if in accordance with management's evaluation.
   d. Amortized over its useful life or 17 years, whichever is shorter. (Items 3–6, AICPA adapted)

Exercise 13–4

For the past five years, the total assets of Atwood Company have averaged $400,000 while average liabilities amounted to $280,000. Cumulative total earnings for the five-year period have been $255,000. Included in the latter figure are extraordinary gains of $45,000 and nonrecurring losses of $30,000. In calculating goodwill where a transfer of the business to new interests is contemplated, the parties agree that annual earnings for a five-year period should be capitalized at 20%.

Required:
In light of the foregoing, calculate the implied value of the goodwill of Atwood Company, if any, agreed upon by the purchaser and seller of the company. Show computations.

Exercise 13–5

Hotstrike Mining Company, which is available for purchase can be expected to produce for the next three years; its minerals likely are to be exhausted at that time and have a zero residual value due to restoration cost obligations. Best estimates place its net receipts at $40,000 for the first year; thereafter, annual net receipts will decrease by $10,000.

Required:
Using an assumed 18% return rate and assuming net receipts occur at year-end, calculate the goodwill purchased if Hotstrike is purchased for $75,000. Round calculations to nearest dollar.

Exercise 13–6

After considerable analysis the following projections were derived as a basis for estimating the potential value of goodwill in anticipation of negotiations for the sale of Walton, Inc.:

Average annual earnings projected	$ 84,000
Market value of identifiable net assets of Walton	240,000

Rate of return expected on investments by prospective purchaser, 18%. Expected recovery period for investment, five years.

Estimate the value of the goodwill of Walton, Inc.

Exercise 13–7

Parson Corporation is negotiating with Feder Company with a view to purchasing the entire assets and liabilities of the latter. You have been asked to help evaluate the "goodwill on the basis of the latest concepts." Accordingly, you decide to utilize the present value approach. The following data have been assembled on Feder Company:

	Market Value	Book Value
Total identifiable assets (exclusive of goodwill)	$2,500,000	$2,400,000
Liabilities	1,000,000	1,000,000
Average annual earnings expected (next five years)	520,000	

Required (round to nearest dollar):

1. Estimate the value of the goodwill of Feder Company assuming a 16% earnings rate is required by Parson on its investments.
2. Assume the deal is consummated on January 1. Parson's offer, as accepted, was cash equal to the market value of the net identifiable assets plus the goodwill computed in 1 above. Give entry on Parson's books to record the transaction.
3. Give entry for amortization of goodwill on December 31, the end of Parson's fiscal year. Assume goodwill is amortized over 40 years.

Exercise 13–8 (Note: This method of computing goodwill was not illustrated in the chapter.)

Black Company is contemplating the acquisition of White Company. Black estimates that White can earn $20,000 per year over the indefinite future. Black also believes that an appropriate normal earnings rate for White is 14% on (Black's estimate of) the market value of White's average owners' equity (over the indefinite future) of $120,000. Finally, Black customarily requires a 20% return on excess earnings of companies it purchases to compensate for the greater risk associated with excess earnings.

Required (round amounts to nearest dollar):

1. Compute the purchase price (including goodwill) which Black Company should be willing to pay for the investment in White Company assuming Black is willing to pay for 10 years of excess earnings.
2. Compute the annual amount of goodwill amortization assuming Black Company amortizes goodwill using the straight-line method over its expected useful life.

Exercise 13–9

Barb Company provided information on its intangible assets as follows:

a. A patent was purchased from the Lou Company for $1,500,000 on January 1, 19x1. Barb estimated the remaining useful life of the patent to be 10 years. On January 1, 19x1, the patent was carried in Lou's accounting records at a net book value of $1,250,000.

b. During 19x2, a franchise was purchased from the Rink Company for $500,000. In addition, 5% of revenue from the franchise must be paid to Rink. Revenue from the franchise for 19x2 was $2,000,000. Barb estimates the useful life of the franchise to be 10 years and records a full year's amortization (straight line) in the year of purchase.

c. Barb incurred R&D costs in 19x2 as follows:

Materials and equipment	$120,000
Personnel	140,000
Indirect costs	60,000
	$320,000

Barb estimates that these costs will be recouped by December 31, 19x5.

d. On January 1, 19x2, Barb, based on new events that have occurred in the field, estimates that the remaining life of the patent purchased on January 1, 19x1, is only five years from January 1, 19x2.

Required:

1. Prepare a schedule showing the intangibles section of Barb's balance sheet at December 31, 19x2. Show supporting computations.
2. Prepare a schedule showing the income statement effect for the year ended December 31, 19x2, as a result of the above facts. Show supporting computations.

(AICPA adapted)

Exercise 13–10

Select the best answer in each of the following. Briefly justify your choices.

1. If a company constructs a laboratory building to be used as an R&D facility, the cost of the building is matched against earnings as—
   a. R&D expense in the period(s) of construction.
   b. Depreciation deducted as part of R&D costs.
   c. Depreciation or immediate write-off depending on company policy.
   d. An expense at such time as productive research and development has been obtained from the facility.
2. Why are certain costs of doing business capitalized when incurred and then depreciated or amortized over subsequent accounting cycles?
   a. To reduce the federal income tax liability.
   b. To aid management in the decision-making process.
   c. To match the costs of production with revenues as earned.
   d. To adhere to the accounting concept of conservatism.
3. In January 19B, the Idea Company purchased a patent for a new consumer product for $170,000. At the time of purchase the patent was valid for 17 years. Due to the competitve nature of the product, the patent was estimated to have a useful life of 10 years. During 19F, the product was removed from the market under governmental order because of a potential health hazard present in the product. What amount should Idea debit to expense during 19F assuming amortization is recorded at the end of each year?
   a. $10,000.

b. $17,000.
c. $102,000.
d. $130,000.

4. In accordance with GAAP, which of the following methods of amortization is normally recommended for intangible assets?
   a. Sum-of-the-years'-digits (SYD).
   b. Straight line.
   c. Units of production.
   d. Double-declining balance (DDB)
5. On December 31 of the current year (last day of the corporation's fiscal year), M Corporation sold for $15,000 a patent for which M had paid $50,000 and which had a book value of $6,000 at the time. The terms of sale were as follows:

   $5,000 down payment.
   $5,000 payable on Dec. 31 of each of next two years.

   The sale agreement made no mention of interest; however, 10% would be a reasonable rate for this type of transaction. What should be the amount of the notes receivable net of any unamortized discount on December 31 of the year of sale (rounded to the nearest dollar)?
   a. $8,678.
   b. $9,091.
   c. $10,000.
   d. $11,000. (AICPA adapted)

Exercise 13–11

Select the best answer in each of the following. Briefly justify your choice.

1. A copyright granted to a composer in 1982 has a legal life of—
   a. 17 years.
   b. 28 years.
   c. The life of the composer plus 50 years.
   d. 40 years.
2. Which of the following is not properly classified as an intangible asset?
   a. A copyright acquired by transfer.
   b. Goodwill.
   c. A patent acquired as an outgrowth of the owner's R&D activities.
   d. Losses incurred by a development stage company.
3. P Corporation acquired Company A in 1968 and Company B in 1982. In both instances the acquired companies were dissolved and their assets and operations merged with other assets and activities of P. In both instances P paid more than book value for its acquisitions and most of the difference was attributable to goodwill. In accounting for the goodwill—
   a. P must amortize the goodwill of each company over a similar time period.
   b. P need not amortize the goodwill of either company.
   c. P need not amortize the goodwill associated with A but must amortize the goodwill associated with B.
   d. P need not amortize the goodwill associated with B but must amortize the goodwill associated with A.
4. Patents and copyrights have definite legal lives and should be amortized over—
   a. Their legal lives.
   b. Their useful lives.
   c. Their legal or useful life, whichever is shorter.
   d. A period not to exceed 40 years.
5. X company incurred $50,000 of costs in R&D activities. These costs need not be expensed if—
   a. They give promise of a successful outcome.
   b. The projects are completed and have culminated in a profitable patent for X.
   c. X is doing contract research for another company, and the costs relate to the contract which is still in progress.
   d. The projects were begun before the issuance of *FASB Statement 2.*
6. Organization costs—
   a. Are not covered by *APB Opinion 17* and need not be amortized.
   b. Must be amortized over a period not to exceed 40 years.
   c. Should be reported as a contra item under Owners' Equity.
   d. Should be expensed as soon as they are incurred.
7. Some intangibles are characterized as specifically identifiable, while others lack the property of specific identifiability. An example of the latter is—
   a. A trademark.
   b. A perpetual franchise.
   c. A franchise for a limited term.
   d. Goodwill.
8. The legal life of a patent is—
   a. 28 years.
   b. 17 years.
   c. The life of the holder of the patent (if a natural person).
   d. 40 years.

PART B: EXERCISES 13–12 to 13–19

Exercise 13–12

Grife Company operates retail branches in various cities. Branches in four cities are served out of warehouse no. 16, which sustained fire damage on April 10.

Between January 1 and April 10 recorded shipments from warehouse no. 16 to its four stores were as below:

Branch	Shipments
W	$80,500
X	92,000
Y	69,000
Z	23,000

Shipments to branches are marked up 15% above cost, and sales prices are reflected in the foregoing amounts. The January 1 inventory at warehouse no. 16 was $48,100; purchases between January 1 and April 10 totaled $224,600; freight-in was $2,300; and purchase returns totaled $9,200.

To arrive at the April 10 inventory for insurance settlement purposes it was agreed to deduct 10% for goods shopworn and damaged prior to the fire.

A compromise agreement between the insurance adjuster and Grife Company management set the current replacement cost of inventory lost in the fire at $21,480.

Required:

1. Estimate the amount of inventory in the warehouse at April 10.
2. Determine the indemnity claim if the warehouse contents were insured by a single $20,000 policy having a 65% coinsurance clause. Calculate to nearest dollar.

Exercise 13–13

Select the best answer in each of the following and indicate the basis for your choice (show computations if appropriate).

1. Where the policy has an 80% coinsurance clause, if the market value of the property is $10,000, the amount of loss is $8,500, and insurance carried is $7,000, the indemnity collectible would be—
   a. $10,000.
   b. $8,500.
   c. $8,000.
   d. $7,000.
   e. None of the foregoing.
2. Suppose the facts are as in 1 above except that the amount of the loss is $7,000; then the indemnity collectible would be—
   a. $10,000.
   b. $8,000.
   c. $7,000.
   d. $6,000.
   e. None of the foregoing.
3. Which of the following is not properly reported as a deferred charge?
   a. Stock issue costs.
   b. Discount on bonds payable.
   c. Organization costs.
   d. Deferred income taxes.
4. Prepaid expenses and deferred charges are alike in that they are both—
   a. Reported as current assets on a classified balance sheet.
   b. Destined to be debited to expense in some subsequent period in harmony with the matching principle.
   c. Reported as other assets.
   d. Applicable to the fiscal period immediately following the balance sheet on which they appear.
5. Inger Company bought a patent in January 19A for $6,800. For the first four years, it was amortized on the assumption that the total useful life would be eight years. At the start of the fifth year, it was determined six years would be the probable total life. Amortization at the end of the fifth year should be—
   a. $1,133.
   b. $1,700.
   c. $850.
   d. None of the foregoing.
6. XY Company has a lease on a site which does not expire for 25 years. With the landowner's permission, XY erected on the site a building which will last 50 years. XY should recognize expense in connection with the building's cost—
   a. One fortieth each year.
   b. One twenty-fifth each year.
   c. In totality as soon as it is completed.
   d. One fiftieth each year.
7. Where there is an 80% coinsurance clause, the market value of the insured property is $30,000, and the amount of loss and of the face of the policy are, respectively, $15,000 and $12,000, indemnity collectible would be—
   a. $7,500.
   b. $12,000.
   c. $15,000.
   d. $30,000.

Exercise 13–14

Assuming that all policies contain an 80% coinsurance clause, show what the insurance company would pay under each of the following cases:

	Case A	Case B	Case C
Total replacement cost of insured property	$30,000	$12,000	$18,000
Replacement cost of property lost	21,000	3,840	3,600
Face of policy	27,000	6,000	15,000

Exercise 13–15

On January 1, Carson's Store had $360 unexpired premiums on an 80% coinsurance fire policy, which ran one year, for $15,000 on its merchandise. On January 1, the inventory was $20,000. January purchases were $44,000, and January sales were $60,000. A fire on February 1 destroyed the entire stock on hand.

Required:
Give journal entries to record the estimated inventory and the fire loss assuming a 30% gross margin rate on sales.

Exercise 13–16

Hoover Company sustained a casualty (fire) loss on February 28. The following data were available (fiscal year ends December 31):

a. Sixty percent of the inventory burned; historical cost (HC) and replacement cost of inventory lost were both $1,800. Assume periodic inventory procedures and that beginning inventory ($1,500) has not yet been removed from the inventory account.
b. Furniture and fixtures: depreciation $20 per month; replacement cost of the item burned, $3,600 (original cost, $3,000; accumulated depreciation to January 1, $480).
c. Insurance premium $96 per year paid on last January 1 for one year; payment of the indemnity absorbed a prorata portion of the unexpired (i.e., prepaid) premium, as illustrated in the chapter. No insurance expense has been recorded for January or February.
d. Settled with insurance company; face of policy, $5,000, 90% coinsurance clause; replacement cost of property insured, $7,500. Close Casualty Loss account.

Required:
Give indicated journal entries.

Exercise 13–17

Assuming that each policy contains an 80% coinsurance clause, indicate what each insurance company would pay under the following cases:

	Case A	Case B	Case C
Total replacement cost of insured property	$15,000	$10,000	$25,000
Replacement cost of property lost	4,000	3,200	24,000
Face of policies:			
X Insurance Company	6,000	4,000	10,000
Y Insurance Company	6,000	3,500	12,500

Exercise 13–18

Ajax Hardware Company carried casualty insurance on its furniture and fixtures with three different insurance companies. Determine the liability of each insurance company under policies for the amounts indicated and with the coinsurance clauses shown. At the date of the fire the insured property had a current total replacement cost of $120,000, and the current replacement cost of the assets lost in the fire was $15,000.

Company	Coinsurance Clause	Face of Policy
A	100%	$30,000
B	70	30,000
C	None	20,000

Exercise 13–19

On January 1, Garfield Company purchased a $100,000 ordinary life insurance policy on its president. The following data relate to the first five years:

Year	Annual Advance Premium	Cash Surrender Value (year-end)	
		Increase	Cumulative
1	$2,000	-0-	-0-
2	2,000	-0-	-0-
3	2,000	$2,100	$2,100
4	2,000	1,080	3,180
5	2,000	1,125	4,305
6	Etc.	Etc.	Etc.

Required:
1. Give all entries indicated up to death of the president on July 2 of the fifth year.
2. Give entry to record insurance settlement upon death of the president. The premium unexpired was refunded. Assume the policy year and accounting year coincide.

PROBLEMS

PART A: PROBLEMS 13–1 to 13–8

Problem 13–1

Case A—One of your corporate clients bought all of the assets of another company whose operations were compatible with those of the client and continued to operate the business of the acquired entity as a separate division. The purchase price paid included an excess consideration for such items as customer lists, going-concern value, and goodwill, aside from what was paid for identifiable tangibles and intangibles. Under terms of the original contract, if the division (i.e., the acquired unit) proves sufficiently profitable, an added payment will become due. This added payment is almost certain to materialize and will approximately equal what was already paid for customer lists, going-concern value, and goodwill. These intangibles have been amortized since acquisition over a more or less arbitrary eight-year total life. The client has inquired whether the added payment, which is clearly related, can be amortized over 12 years from the date the payment is to be made. If this were to be done, vestiges of the balance related to the new payment would remain on the books as much as seven years after the last of the first payment had been fully amortized.

Case B—Another corporate client is in a regulated industry and has franchise rights granted by a federal commission. The rights are worth considerably more than the cost of obtaining them; they can be transferred with the permission of the commission (which usually is not difficult to obtain). The rights do not lapse as long as the client is a going concern, although they could be revoked. Revocation of such rights has rarely occurred. The client's management contends there is no need to amortize the franchise rights over 40 years, much less a shorter period. Indeed, some of the managers feel they should be written up in value.

Required:
Draft memoranda setting forth your recommendations concerning the above situations. Support whatever positions you take.

Problem 13–2

Blass Corporation, a retail farm implements dealer, has increased its annual sales volume to a level three times greater than the annual sales of a dealer purchased eight years ago in order to begin operations.

The board of directors of Blass Corporation recently received an offer to negotiate the sale of Blass Corporation to a larger competitor. As a result, the majority of the board wants to increase the stated value of goodwill on the balance sheet to reflect the larger sales volume developed through intensive promotion and the current market prices of the company's products. However, a few of the company's board members would prefer to eliminate goodwill altogether from the balance sheet in order to prevent "possible misinterpretations." Goodwill was properly recorded when the business was acquired eight years ago.

Required:

1. *a.* Discuss the meaning of the term *goodwill.* Do not discuss goodwill arising from consolidated statements or the conditions under which goodwill is recorded.
   b. What technique is commonly used to estimate the value of goodwill in negotiations to purchase a going concern.
2. Why are the book and market values of the goodwill of Blass Corporation different?
3. Discuss the propriety of—
   a. Increasing the stated value of goodwill prior to the negotiations.
   b. Eliminating goodwill completely from the balance sheet prior to negotiations. (AICPA adapted)

Problem 13–3

Transactions during the first year of the newly organized Rosen Corporation included the following:

Jan. 2	Paid $4,000 attorney's fees for assistance in securing the corporate charter, drafting bylaws, and advising on operating in other states (which the company intends).
31	Paid $700 for television commercials advertising the grand opening. In addition, during the grand opening the company gave premiums taken from inventory to customers and visitors which cost $8,000.
Feb. 1	Paid invoice received from financial institution which underwrote and sold the company's $400,000 par value stock at a 10% premium. Per agreement, the underwriter charged 1% of the gross proceeds from the stock sale.
Mar. 1	Paid $29,000 to a franchisor for the right to open in the company premises a Tastee Food lunch counter. The initial franchise runs 10 years from March 1 and can be renewed upon payment of a second amount negotiated on the basis of sales under the initial franchise.
May 1	Acquired for $10,200 a newly issued patent to be held to produce royalty income.
July 1	Paid consultants $6,000 for services in securing a trademark enabling the company to market under the now-protected name Rosen's Recipe.
Oct. 1	Obtained a license from the city to conduct operations in a newly opened department. The license, which cost $600, runs for one year from date and is renewable.
Nov. 1	Acquired another business and paid (among other amounts) $12,000 for its goodwill. The payment represents an amount based on purchase of five years' expected above-normal profits.
Dec. 31	Amortized those assets subject to amortization over their indicated lives. Where no life is specified, amortized over the longest term possible. Amortization is on a monthly basis; in other words, acquisition of an intangible in July would call for a half year's amortization.

Required:

1. Journalize the foregoing transactions.
2. Present the Intangibles assets section of Rosen's balance sheet as of December 31.

Problem 13–4

On June 30, 19A, your client, Brown Corporation, was granted two patents covering plastic cartons that it has been producing and marketing profitably for the past three years. One patent covers the manufacturing process, and the other covers the related products.

Brown executives tell you that these patents represent the most significant breakthrough in the industry in the past 30 years. The products have been marketed under the registered trademarks Safetainer, Duratainer, and Sealrite. Licenses under the patents have already been granted by your client to other manufacturers in the United States and abroad and are producing substantial royalties.

On July 1, Brown commenced patent infringement actions against several companies whose names you recognize as those of substantial and prominent competitors. Brown's management is optimistic that these suits will result in a permanent injunction against the manufacture and sale of the infringing products and collection of damages for loss of profits caused by the alleged infringement.

The financial vice president has suggested that the patents be recorded at the discounted value of expected net royalty receipts.

Required:

1. What is an intangible asset? Explain.
2. *a.* What is the meaning of "discounted value of expected net receipts"? Explain.
   b. How would such a value be calculated for net royalty receipts?
3. What basis of valuation for Brown's patents would be generally accepted in accounting? Give supporting reasons for this basis. (AICPA adapted)

Problem 13–5

Your new client, Laser Company, is being audited for the first time. In the course of your examination, you encounter in the ledger an account titled Intangibles which is presented below:

Intangibles

6/30/19A Goodwill	9,000	12/31/19B Amortization	480
12/31/19A R&D	10,700	12/31/19C Amortization	1,200
4/1/19B Goodwill	14,600		
6/30/19B Patent	9,600		
12/31/19B R&D	13,900		
6/1/19C Goodwill	12,900		
7/1/19C Bond discount	4,800		
12/31/19C R&D	17,100		

By tracing entries to the journal and other supporting documents, you ascertain the following facts:

a. The June 30, 19A, entry was made when, somewhat surprisingly, the first six months' operations were profitable; a loss had been anticipated. At the direction of the company president, and with the approval of the board of directors, an entry was made debiting Intangibles and crediting Retained Earnings for $9,000.

b. All debit entries dated December 31 pertaining to R&D arise from the fact that the company has continuously engaged in an extensive R&D program to keep its products competitive and to develop new products. The debits represent half of the costs of the R&D program for each year and were transferred at year-end from the R&D expense account.

c. The April 1, 19B, entry was made after an extensive advertising campaign had seemingly proved particularly successful. Sales rose 8% after the campaign and never dropped again to less than a 4% increase over their former level. The debit represents the cost of the campaign.

d. The $9,600 debit on June 30, 19B, represents the purchase price of a patent bought because the company feared if it fell into other hands, it would damage the company's products competitively.

e. The June 1, 19C, debit was made after Laser acquired a division of another profitable company. The price represented an excess payment of $12,900 over the market values of identifiable net assets acquired and was based on an expectation of continued high profitability. This cost of goodwill should properly be carried in an Investment in Affiliate account (covered in Chapter 16).

f. The July 1, 19C, debit for $4,800 represents discount on a 10-year $100,000 bond issue marketed by the company on that date. (Since the amount is relatively immaterial, use of straight-line amortization need not be changed.)

g. The credits to the Intangibles account represent an attempt by the company bookkeeper to amortize the year-end balances 10% each year (subject to the policy described below). When you question the bookkeeper and company officials, you learn the company's policy is to amortize those intangibles it regards as having limited lives over 10 years. For this purpose, acquisitions and retirements are accounted for in terms of the most proximate quarter in which they entered or were removed from the books. All items are regarded as amortizable except R&D and goodwill. You concur with the judgment as to the 10-year life of those intangibles properly subject to amortization.

Required:

Make journal entries to correct Laser's books as of December 31, 19C, on the assumption the books have been adjusted but not closed for the year as of that date. (Although years such as 19A and 19B have not been specifically identified as particular calendar years, for purposes of your solution, assume all events of the problem have occurred recently and that the current pronouncements of authoritative bodies reflected in the text apply to the various items.)

It is suggested that you key your entries to the letter, identifying the items in the problem. Explain each correcting entry. For the most part, compound entries should be avoided unless elements of the entry are closely related.

Problem 13–6

In 19B, White Research Associates signed a long-term contract which it accounts for under the code name Starfare. The purpose of the Starfare project is to develop advanced radar gear for a government agency.

To facilitate its work, White purchased a five-year-old patent from Jupiter Technologies, Ltd. It expects to apply the technology covered by this patent over the estimated three-year life of the Starfare project, and subsequently, to apply it to other company work and/or projects for a total of eight years. White's fiscal year is the calendar year.

In February 19C, after the books of White were adjusted and closed for 19B, your examination of debits to the Starfare project account reveals the following:

Date		Item	Debit
19B:			
July	1	Cost of patent bought from Jupiter Technologies	$ 62,000
	15	Legal fees related to acquisition of Jupiter patent	2,000
Jan.–Dec.		Direct labor applicable to Starfare project	40,000
		Direct materials applicable to Starfare project	23,800
Dec.	31	Amortization of R&D Costs applicable to Starfare	2,500
	31	Income earned on Starfare project	8,824
		Total debits in 19B..........................	$139,124
19C:			
Jan.	3	Legal fees incurred in successful defense of Jupiter patent..............................	$ 15,000

Further investigation reveals the following:

1. There were no credits to the Starfare Project account. The $139,124 balance was reported as Inventory—Re-

(Relates to Problem 13–7)

Transactions	Debit to Retained Earnings	Debit to Current Expenses	Capitalize as an Intangible	None of the Foregoing
1. Acting on recommendations of High Technology, Inc., Y spends $60,000 rearranging its machinery. Benefits are expected to last six years.				
2. Y paid High Technology $90,000 for R&D work the latter has done under contract for Y. The results are expected to increase Y's profits over the next seven years.				
3. D Corporation incurs legal costs of $500,000 successfully defending one of its patents in an infringement suit. The patent runs six more years.				
4. Assume D's suit in 3 above had turned out adversely and that D was forced to write off its patent carried at $80,000. How should the write-off be treated?				
5. Jay Company paid Zippy Corporation $50,000 for the exclusive right to repair auto transmissions in the city of Erehwon, using the Zippy name and logo in signs, ads, and the like. The franchise runs for as long as Jay is in business but cannot be transferred.				
6. P Company spend $400,000 developing a new manufacturing process on which it will apply for a patent.				
7. P incurs $50,000 legal and registration costs related to securing a patent on the process described in 6 above.				
8. In 19G, Uno Company paid an author $40,000 for the copyright to the author's novel and for rights to produce a movie based on it. The copyright was issued in 19F, and the author is elderly.				
9. As a result of an out-of-court settlement, X Company paid $14 million to another corporation because it had infinged on the payee's patent. Most of the agreed payment relates to sales made by X in prior years, the remainder to current sales.				
10. X incurred legal costs of $750,000 in connection with the litigation described in 9 above.				

search in Progress on the December 31 balance sheet.

2. White has accumulated all R&D costs in a deferred charge account which it amortizes at year-end. Actual R&D applicable to Starfare for 19B was $8,500.
3. The Starfare project contract provides that White is entitled to—
   a. Apply overhead at 40% of direct labor costs to the project; overhead does not include R&D costs or patent amortization. Analysis reveals that in 19B, 90% of overhead was allocated to cost of goods sold and 10% to inventory.
   b. Accrue income at 8% of its costs subject to subsequent audit and approval by government auditors.
   c. Bill the government agency which let the contract for 96% of its accumulated costs (including accrued profits) at three-month intervals. (No billing was made until December 31, 19B, at which time White debited $114,359 to a Due from U.S. Government account and credited Progress Billings.)

Required:
Give journal entries as of February 19C to correct White's accounts. Ignore income tax and round amounts to nearest dollar.

Problem 13–7

By means of a check mark in the appropriate column, indicate how each of the expenditures listed in the table on p. 463 should be accounted for at the time it is incurred. If the amount should be split, check more than a single column. Assume that each expenditure occurred late in the current fiscal year of the **entity making payment.** Give reasons for each answer.

Problem 13–8

Brannen Corporation was incorporated on January 3, 19A. The corporation's financial statements for its first year's operations were not examined by a CPA. You have been engaged to examine the financial statements for the year ended December 31, 19B, and your examination is substantially completed. The corporation's trial balance appears below.

BRANNEN CORPORATION
Trial Balance
December 31, 19B

	Debit	Credit
Cash	$ 11,000	
Accounts receivable	68,500	
Allowance for doubtful accts.		$ 500
Inventories	38,500	
Machinery	75,000	
Equipment	29,000	
Accumulated depreciation		10,000
Patents	102,000	
Prepaid expenses	10,500	
Organization costs	29,000	
Goodwill	24,000	
Licensing agreement no. 1	50,000	
Licensing agreement no. 2	49,000	
Accounts payable		147,500
Unearned revenue		12,500
Capital stock		317,000
Retained earnings, 1/1/19B	27,000	
Sales		668,500
Cost of goods sold	454,000	
Selling and general expenses	173,000	
Interest expense	3,500	
Extraordinary losses	12,000	
Totals	$1,156,000	$1,156,000

The following information relates to accounts that may yet require adjustment:

1. Patents for Brannen's manufacturing process were acquired January 2, 19B, at a cost of $68,000. An additional $34,000 was spent in December 19B to improve machinery covered by the patents and was charged to the Patents account. Depreciation on operational assets has been properly recorded for 19B in accordance with Brannen's practice, which provides a full year's depreciation for property on hand June 30 and no depreciation otherwise. Brannen uses the straight-line method for all depreciation and amortization.
2. The balance in the Organization Costs account properly includes costs incurred during the organization period. Brannen has exercised its option to amortize Organization Costs over a five-year period beginning January 19A for federal income tax purposes and wishes to amortize these costs for accounting purposes in the same manner. No amortization has yet been recorded.
3. On January 3, 19A, Brannen purchased licensing agreement no. 1, which was believed to have an unlimited useful life. The balance in the Licensing Agreement No. 1 account includes its purchase price of $48,000 and expenses of $2,000 related to the acquisition. On January 1, 19B, Brannen bought licensing agreement no. 2, which has a life expectancy of 10 years. The balance in the Licensing Agreement No. 2 account includes its $48,000 purchase price and $2,000 in acquisition expenses, but it has been reduced by a credit of $1,000 for the advance collection of 19C revenue from the agreement.

   In late December 19A an explosion caused a permanent 60% reduction in the expected revenue producing value of licensing agreement no. 1, and in January 19C a flood caused additional damage that rendered the agreement worthless.
4. The balance in the Goodwill account includes *(a)* $8,000

paid December 30, 19A, for an advertising program it is estimated will assist in increasing Brannen's sales over a period of four years following the disbursement and *(b)* legal expenses of $16,000 incurred for Brannen's incorporation on January 3, 19A.

5. No amortization has yet been recorded for 19B.

Required:
Prepare journal entries as of December 31, 19B, as required by the information given. Note: Prior to the explosion, licensing agreement no. 1 should have been amortized in accordance with provisions of *APB Opinion 17.*

(AICPA adapted)

PART B: PROBLEMS 13–9 to 13–16

Problem 13–9

Nye Company suffered a fire loss on July 1. Between January 1 and July 1 the company had made sales of $60,000 and inventory purchases of $44,000. January 1 beginning inventory was $6,400. The costs of both beginning inventory and purchases were evenly divided between inventory items that had different markup percentages. Nye Company made half its sales at a 50% markup on cost and the other half at a markup that represented 25% of the sales price.

The fire destroyed 60% of Nye Company's July 1 inventory (stated in dollars rather than units), but fortunately the inventory was insured for market value (i.e., replacement cost) of $10,000 with an 80% coinsurance clause. Nye Company determines that the replacement cost of its inventory at July 1 exceeds its cost by 10%. Prepaid insurance is not a consideration in this problem.

Required:
1. Compute the historical cost of Nye Company's inventory destroyed by the fire.
2. Compute the amount of the insurance recovery on the fire loss.
3. Prepare journal entries to record the fire loss and insurance recovery. Nye Company uses a perpetual inventory system.

Problem 13–10

The Dolfo Corporation is a small manufacturing company producing a highly flammable cleaning fluid. On May 31, 19G, the company had a fire which completely destroyed the processing building and the in-process inventory; some of the equipment was saved.

The cost of the operational assets destroyed and their related accumulated depreciation at January 1, 19G, were as follows:

	Cost	Accumulated Depreciation
Building	$40,000	$24,667
Machinery and equipment	15,000	4,375

At present prices the cost to replace the destroyed property would be building, $80,000; and machinery and equipment, $37,500. At the time of the fire it was determined that the destroyed building was 62.5% depreciated and the destroyed machinery and equipment was 33.3% depreciated. The insurable value (i.e., replacement cost) of all the building and machinery and equipment was determined to be $75,000, but insurance premiums were structured in such a way as to only provide indemnification equal to the market value (i.e., current replacement cost) of the *undepreciated portion* of the building and the machinery and equipment.

After the fire a physical inventory was taken. The raw materials were valued at $30,000, the finished goods at $60,000, and supplies at $5,000.

The inventories on January 1, 19G, consisted of—

Raw materials	$ 15,000
Work in process	50,000
Finished goods	70,000
Supplies	2,000
Total	$137,000

A review of the accounts showed that the sales and gross margin for the last five years were as follows:

	Sales	Gross Margin
19B	$300,000	$ 86,200
19C	320,000	102,400
19D	330,000	108,900
19E	250,000	62,500
19F	280,000	84,000

Dolfo Corporation uses the FIFO inventory method. As a result, the historical cost (HC) of the inventory closely approximates its current replacement cost, which is the insurable value of the inventory under the insurance policy.

The sales for the first five months of 19G were $165,000. Raw material purchases were $50,000. Freight on purchases was $5,000. Direct labor for the five months was $40,000; for the past five years manufacturing overhead was 50% of direct labor.

Insurance on the property and inventory was carried with three companies. Each policy included an 80% coinsurance clause. The amount of insurance carried with the various companies was as follows:

	Building, Machinery, and Equipment	Inventories
Company A	$30,000	$38,000
Company B	20,000	35,000
Company C	15,000	35,000

The cost of cleaning up the debris was $7,000. The value of the scrap salvaged from the fire was $600.

Required:

1. Compute the value of inventory lost.
2. Compute the expected recovery from each insurance company. (AICPA adapted)

Problem 13–11

The records of Bridges Company showed at date of fire (all merchandise destroyed): sales, $240,000; beginning inventory, $15,000; purchases, $205,000; insurance (one-year policy for $14,000 with 70% coinsurance clause) premium, $200; salespersons' salaries, $15,000; and general expense, $13,000. The fire occurred six months after the premium was paid. It was agreed that the gross margin percentage based on sales was $16\frac{2}{3}$% and that the insurable value of inventory was its historical cost because the company uses FIFO. Therefore, the historical cost of ending inventory approximates its replacement cost.

Required:

1. Compute the indemnity to be received from the insurance company.
2. Give entries relating to the casualty loss.
3. Prepare a classified income statement for the period ending on a date immediately following the fire. Ignore income taxes.

Problem 13–12

Estimate the amount (to the nearest dollar) of insurance collectible by Safety Company on each of the following assets assuming the policies include a 70% coinsurance clause:

Asset	Replacement Cost	Loss Suffered	Insurance Carried
Buildings	$80,000	$42,000	$65,000
Furniture	20,000	18,000	15,000
Delivery equipment	9,000	4,000	5,000
Merchandise	?	60%	10,000

To find the value of the merchandise destroyed, the following facts are submitted from which to select the significant data:

The gross margin averages 30% of sales.
The replacement cost of inventory is the same as its historical cost.

Purchases for the period	$65,000
Beginning inventory	19,400
Return purchases	2,000
Salespersons' commissions and advertising	8,000
Interest revenue	200
Postage and stationery	1,000
Sales	84,000
Credit department expense	700
Sales returns	2,000

Problem 13–13

South Company operates in a leased building; it adjusts and closes books each December 31. On April 30, a fire seriously damaged its inventory and fixtures. Inventory was totally destroyed; fixtures were two-thirds destroyed. Different insurance policies cover the assets, but both have a common feature under which they are canceled for future or remaining coverage to whatever extent a portion of the total potential indemnity is collected by the insured.

The company uses a periodic inventory system, and the accounting records were saved; these reveal that in the past three years gross margin has averaged 38% of sales price. The January 1 inventory was $73,280. Between January 1 and April 30 purchases and sales were, respectively, $116,320 and $206,500. Inventory was insured by a $65,000 policy with no coinsurance clause. The latest premium payment covering a one-year period from September 1 of last year amounted to $720 on this policy.

When the books were closed last December 31, the fixtures were 2½ years old. Accounts related to the fixtures and their insurance policy are set forth below.

Fixtures

Debit	Credit
Balance 20,000	

Accumulated Depreciation

Debit	Credit
	Year 1 900
	Year 2 1,800
	Year 3 1,800

Prepaid Insurance

Debit	Credit
Policy A 42	
Policy B 480	

Policy A expired February 28 of the current year. Policy B was immediately put in force to replace it and covers a two-year period. It is for $10,000 maximum coverage, provides for indemnity on the basis of replacement cost of any loss, and has an 80% coinsurance clause. It is determined that the replacement cost of the fixtures when the fire occurred was $15,000 and that the damage amounted to a loss of two-thirds of their replacement cost.

Required (round amounts to nearest dollar):

1. Adjust the books to April 30 and reflect the inventory as of that date.
2. Open a Casualty Loss account; set up the indemnities collectible as a receivable due from the insurance company.
3. Transfer the net balance in Casualty Loss to Income Summary.

Problem 13–14

On April 1, 19A, Cox Company insured the life of its president, Clara Cox, for $100,000, naming itself as beneficiary. Annual premiums paid each April 1 are $3,600. As a result of the third premium payment and at the end of the third policy year, the policy has a cash surrender value of $1,800. One year later this will increase to $2,430. Allocate the third-year cash surrender value equally to each of the first three years.

Cox Company adjusts and closes its books on December 31 and debits premium payments to Prepaid Insurance. All premiums are paid when due. Ms. Cox died on April 3, 19D. No refund of unexpired premiums as of date of death is provided for in the policy.

Required:
Make all entries related to the policy through April 3, 19D, including adjusting and closing entries at the end of each year the policy is in force.

Problem 13–15

Brentwood Company, one of your corporate clients, is somewhat "insurance minded" and maintains in force, several life insurance policies which have a cash surrender value feature on which the corporation is beneficiary. Several questions have arisen concerning the accounting presentation or treatment of these policies and their cash surrender value aspects.

a. One policy is on the life of the company president (who is not a stockholder). A substantially high proportion of what could be borrowed against this policy has been borrowed; the loan amounts to 73% of the cash surrender value at balance sheet date. One reason for borrowing this way is that the interest rate is about half the rate at which other loans could be obtained. You are asked for advice as to how to report the loan on the company's balance sheet and whether the fact that there may be a current liability against the policy changes the classification of cash surrender value.

b. Looking to the future and possible repayment of the loan on the policy mentioned, especially if interest rates should fall, a hypothetical question is posed. Assuming the loan is repaid, would it be mandatory to report cash surrender value on this policy since the insurance is carried to cover the loss it is anticipated would be sustained as the result of the death of a key official?

c. Most of the stock of the corporation is held by a few large stockholders. To retain control within a limited group, your client has bought policies on the lives of these principal stockholders which will provide for repurchase of their stock in the event of a stockholder's death. The cash surrender value of these policies has been reported on the balance sheet. You are asked whether further disclosure is necessary.

d. For a time, another officer of the corporation (who also is not a stockholder) personally "owned" and paid premiums on a substantial life insurance policy on which his wife was beneficiary. For business reasons, your client bought the policy from him at a price equal to his past premium payments ($80,000). The corporation became beneficiary of the policy and beneficial owner of its cash surrender value ($45,000); the latter amount was recorded in the accounts as an asset. The $35,000 difference is being amortized over the life expectancy of the insured as disclosed in a mortality table. You are asked for your concurrence or disagreement with this accounting treatment.

Required:
Draft a reply responding to the above questions. Give reasons to support whatever positions you take.

Problem 13–16

Select the best answer in each of the following. Briefly justify your choice.

1. Which of the following cost items would be matched with current revenues on a basis other than association of cause and effect?
   a. Goodwill.
   b. Sales commissions.
   c. Cost of goods sold.
   d. Purchases on account.
2. If four separate carriers have written fire insurance policies totaling $60,000 on a single property with a replacement cost of $100,000, what fraction of a $20,000 loss would be collectible from a carrier whose $30,000 policy contains a 90% coinsurance clause?
   a. 60/90.
   b. 30/90.
   c. 30/60.
   d. 20/100.
3. Four separate carriers have written fire insurance policies totaling $160,000 on a single property valued at $200,000. The fraction of a partial loss of $40,000 that will be collectible from a carrier whose $60,000 policy contains a 90% coinsurance clause would be—
   a. 9/10.
   b. 4/5.
   c. 2/3.
   d. 1/5.
   e. None of the above.
4. How should R&D costs be accounted for according to *FASB Statement 2?*
   a. Must be capitalized when incurred and then amortized over their estimated useful lives.

b. Must be expensed in the period incurred unless contractually reimbursable.
c. May be either capitalized or expensed when incurred, depending upon the facts of the situation.
d. Must be expensed in the period incurred unless it can be clearly demonstrated that the expenditure will have significant future benefits.

5. Cash surrender value of life insurance policies on corporate executives should be shown in the balance sheet as—
a. Cash.
b. Short-term investment.
c. Prepaid expense.
d. Long-term investment.

6. H Company incurred R&D costs in 19C as follows:

Materials used in R&D projects	$ 400,000
Equipment acquired that will have alternate future uses in future R&D projects	2,000,000
Depreciation for 19C on above equipment	500,000
Personnel costs of persons involved in R&D projects	1,000,000
Consulting fees paid to outsiders for R&D projects	100,000
Indirect costs reasonably allocable to R&D projects	200,000
	$4,200,000

The amount of R&D costs debited to H's 19C income statement should be—
a. $1,500,000.
b. $1,700,000.
c. $2,200,000.
d. $3,500,000.

7. P Company is planning to invest $40,000 in a royalty-producing copyright. P's expected rate of return from the three-year project is 20%. The cash flow, net of income taxes, will be $15,000 for the first year and $18,000 for the second year. Assuming the rate of return is exactly 20%, what would be the cash flow, net of income taxes, for the third year?
a. $8,681.
b. $11,000.
c. $11,497.
d. $25,920.

(AICPA adapted)

14

Corporations—Formation and Contributed Capital

THE CORPORATE FORM of business organization has become a dominant one in the United States. This particular form gained widespread use primarily as a result of the legal foundations upon which it is built. A corporation is, in the eyes of the law, an entity separate and apart from its owners. Limited liability of corporate owners, easy transfer of ownership, and the corporation's facility for capital accumulation are three advantages contributing to the growth of the corporate form of business. In view of the unique features of the corporate form, accountants have devoted much attention to the special accounting problems of accounting for corporations. This chapter and the next chapter consider these special accounting problems.

This chapter discusses the contributed capital of corporations, including stock rights and options. It is subdivided as follows:

Part A—Contributed Capital at Formation
Part B—Stock Rights and Options
Supplement 14–A—Incorporation of a Going Business

Part A: Contributed Capital at Formation

FUNDAMENTAL CONCEPTS

Corporations, like proprietorships and partnerships, use assets and incur liabilities. The residual interest in the entity's assets (i.e., its assets minus its liabilities) is the stockholders' (or shareholders') equity of the entity. *FASB Concepts Statement 3* (par. 43) defines owners' equity as ". . . the residual interest in the assets of an entity that remains after deducting its liabilities. In a business enterprise, the [owners'] equity is the ownership interest."

In a proprietorship, owner's equity usually is represented by a single owner's equity account, and in a partnership, by a separate owner's equity account for each partner. In contrast, accounting for a corporation generally requires a number of owners' equity accounts. As a result, unique problems are encountered in accounting for the owners' equity of a corporation. In other respects, accounting for transactions and events is largely unaffected by the form of business organization.

Accounting for corporate owners' equity distinguishes among different **sources of capital** primarily to comply with legal requirements of the various states. Thus, the sources of the capital used in the enterprise should be clearly segregated in the accounts. The primary sources of corporate capital are *(a)* contributions by the owners and *(b)* earnings retained in the business. Traditionally, the term **capital** has been used to refer to owners' equity. It includes contributions by owners plus retained earnings. In recent years, owners' equity in a corporation has been more often called stockholders' or shareholders' equity, or simply, owners' equity. The accountant should be familiar with the following classes of equities and capital:

1. **Total equities**[1]—Total equities represents the total asset interests of all creditors and owners of a particular corporation; it is the sum of the creditors' equity and the owners' equity.
2. **Owners' equity**[2]—Owners' equity is the residual interest in the assets of an entity that remains after deducting the entity's liabilities; it is the total of contributed capital and all subsequent accretions in the form of additional contributions, retained earnings, and any unrealized capital recognized to date.
3. **Contributed capital**—Contributed capital is the investment made by the owners; in a corporation it is the total amount **paid in** by all parties other than creditors, plus stock issued in stock dividends. It does not include appropriated or unappropriated retained earnings.
4. **Legal or stated capital**—Legal capital is that portion of corporate capital that is required by statute to be retained in the business for the protection of creditors.

CLASSIFICATIONS OF CORPORATIONS

State, rather than federal, laws provide for the formation and operation of corporations. Although state laws relating to corporations vary in many respects, they are similar in their basic provisions. The statutes of all states provide for the existence of a separate entity and for the basic unit of ownership (i.e., capital stock).[3] Corporations are brought into legal existence by submitting an application (called articles of incorporation) for a **charter** to the secretary of state for approval. An approved charter specifies the conditions under which the corporation may operate, such as what business activities are permitted, the types and amount of capital stock that may be issued, and the method of electing officers. The charter is supplemented with bylaws which are adopted by the stockholders.

Corporations may be classified as follows:

By ownership:

1. Public corporations, when they relate to governmental units or business operations owned by governmental units. Examples are the Tennessee Valley Authority, the Port of New York Authority, and the many municipal transit systems.
2. Private corporations, when they are privately owned. Such corporations may be nonstock (nonprofit organizations such as colleges and churches) or stock usually organized for profit making, such as General Motors, Xerox, and Johnson & Johnson.

By state of incorporation and operation:

3. Domestic corporations, when operating in the state in which incorporated.
4. Foreign corporations, when operating in states other than the one in which incorporated.

By availability of ownership interests:

5. Open, or publicly held, corporations, when the capital stock is available for purchase. The shares of open corporations often are "listed" by one of the stock exchanges, such as the New York, American, or one of the regional stock exchanges.
6. Closed, or closely held, corporations, when the

---

[1] FASB *Statement of Financial Accounting Concepts No. 3*, "Elements of Financial Statements of Business Enterprises" (Stamford, Conn., December 1980), uses the term **equity** to refer to owners' equity. This terminology also is used in finance. In this book, for clarity, we use the term **equities** to refer to the total of liabilities and owners' equity, and the term **owners' equity** to refer to the **owners'** interest in the assets of the business.

[2] Ibid.

[3] The formation and operation of corporations (particularly with respect to shareholders' equity) are subject to the laws of the various states. These laws vary significantly in many respects. Some years ago the American Bar Association (specifically its Committee on Corporate Laws) developed a recommendation called the Model Business Corporation Act. The various states have adopted many of the recommendations in the Model Act. Nevertheless, differences among state statutes continue to prevail.

capital stock is not available for purchase and usually is held by only a few shareholders.

NATURE OF CAPITAL STOCK

Shares of capital stock, represented by stock certificates, evidence ownership in a corporation. Shares may be transferred freely by shareholders unless there is an enforceable agreement not to do so. Ownership of shares entitles the holder to certain basic rights. These rights are as follows:

1. The right to participate in the **management** of the corporation through participating and voting in stockholder meetings.
2. The right to participate in the **profits** of the corporation through dividends declared by the board of directors.
3. The right to share in the distribution of **assets** of the corporation at liquidation or through liquidating dividends.
4. The right to purchase shares of the capital stock of the corporation on a pro rata basis when new issues are offered for sale. This **preemptive** right is designed to give each shareholder the opportunity to maintain his or her proportional ownership in the corporation. Some corporations have withheld this preemptive right because of the difficulty it creates when the corporation issues new stock.

These basic rights are shared proportionately by all stockholders unless the charter or bylaws (and as noted on the stock certificates) specifically provide otherwise. In the case of one class of stock, all holders enjoy the basic rights; in the case of two or more classes of stock, the holders of one class of stock may have rights that have been withheld contractually from the others.

To account for owners' equity, the accountant should understand the following terms:

1. Authorized capital stock—the number of shares of stock that can be issued legally, as specified in the charter.
2. Issued capital stock—the number of shares of authorized capital stock that have been issued to date.
3. Unissued capital stock—the number of shares of authorized capital stock that have not been issued.
4. Outstanding capital stock—the number of shares of capital stock that have been issued and are being held by shareholders.
5. Treasury stock—those shares once issued and later reacquired and held by the corporation, that is, the difference between issued shares and outstanding shares.
6. Subscribed stock—unissued shares of stock set aside to meet subscription contracts. Subscribed stock usually is not issued until the subscription price is paid in full.

In accounting for owners' equity, the following terminology appears to represent current trends:

1. Contributed capital (sometimes referred to as paid-in capital):
   a. Capital stock:
      (1) Preferred stock.
      (2) Common stock.
   b. Other contributed capital or additional paid-in capital (an obsolete term, capital surplus, sometimes is used):
      (1) From owners:
      Contributed capital in excess of par or stated value (sometimes called premium on capital stock) and contributed capital from treasury stock and stock retirement transactions.
      (2) From outsiders:
      Contributed capital from donation of assets.
2. Retained earnings (an obsolete term, earned surplus, sometimes is used):
   a. Appropriated (also referred to as reserves).
   b. Unappropriated.
3. Unrealized capital increment or decrement.

Exhibit 14–1 illustrates the stockholders' equity section of a balance sheet. Observe in the exhibit that owners' equity is reported by source, that is, contributed capital, retained earnings, and unrealized loss on long-term investments in the capital stock of other corporations.

Classes of Capital Stock

Corporations tend to use several different types of capital stock which give the respective sharehold-

EXHIBIT 14–1: Stockholders' Equity Section of a Balance Sheet

Stockholders' Equity

Contributed capital:		
Capital stock:		
Preferred stock, 6%, par $10, cumulative and nonparticipating, 20,000 shares authorized; 15,000 issued and outstanding	$150,000	
Preferred stock subscribed, 100 shares	1,000	
Total preferred stock outstanding and subscribed	151,000	
Common stock, nopar value, 10,000 shares authorized; 8,000 shares issued and outstanding, stated value $5	40,000	$191,000
Other contributed capital:		
In excess of par value, preferred stock	12,000	
In excess of stated value, common stock	3,000	
Donation of plant site	5,000	20,000
Total contributed capital		211,000
Retained earnings:		
Appropriated for bond sinking fund	50,000	
Unappropriated	70,000	
Total retained earnings		120,000
Unrealized loss on long-term investments in marketable equity securities		(6,000)
Total stockholders' equity		$325,000

ers specific privileges, restrictions, and responsibilities. Some of these restrictions may result from provisions of state statutes, the charter, or the bylaws of the corporation, and are made operative by contract between the corporation and the shareholders. The two primary classifications of capital stock are *(a)* par value and nopar value stock and *(b)* common and preferred stock.

Par Value Stock. The laws of each state permit the issuance of par value stock, that is, shares of stock with a designated dollar "value" per share as provided for in the articles of incorporation and as printed on the face of the stock certificates. Par value stock may be either common or preferred. In the early history of corporations in the United States, only par value stock was authorized. Because the owners of a corporation under earlier laws were not personally liable to the corporation's creditors, those statutes were intended to afford some measure of protection to creditors. In this respect the courts tended to hold that shareholders who had paid **less** than par value for their stock could be assessed an additional amount equal to the discount to satisfy creditors' claims. Par value stock sold initially at less than par is said to have been issued at a discount, whereas par value stock sold above par is said to have been issued at a premium. Today, the issuance of par value stock at a discount is illegal in most states.[4]

Par value has no particular relationship to market value. However, par value has significance in most states in that (1) it represents the minimum amount that must be paid in at initial sale of the stock; (2) in the case of insolvency, if the par value of all outstanding shares was fully paid in (or an equivalent amount of retained earnings was capitalized as in a stock dividend), the shareholders cannot be held personally liable; (3) it establishes the minimum amount of owners' equity the law requires to be maintained; and (4) it is the basis on which preferred dividends are declared. To avoid a real or implied discount, many corporations use a very low par value, such as $1, and offer the stock at a much higher price.

Nopar Stock. True nopar stock does not carry a designated or assigned value per share—nor is such provided for in the articles of incorporation. However, the laws of some states authorize the issuance

[4] Despite laws that forbid issuance of par value stock at a discount, it sometimes happens de facto when promoters and others receive shares of stock in exchange for noncash assets or services which are overvalued.

of nopar stock with a **stated** or **assigned** value. The stated or assigned value is established by the corporate directors or the bylaws of the corporation.

The use of an assigned or stated value places the nopar stock on essentially the same basis as par value stock for accounting purposes. Both common and preferred stock may be represented by nopar shares. Nopar stock was first permitted by statute in New York in 1912; since then, the authorization of stock without par value has become so widespread that today practically all states permit its issuance. The chief advantages **claimed** for this type of stock are (1) it avoids a contingent liability of stockholders for stock discount, and (2) in some jurisdictions there is less tax on nopar shares. The chief disadvantage of nopar stock is that some jurisdictions levy higher franchise and other taxes on nopar stock.

Legal Capital

Accounting principles for assets and liabilities are determined by standard-setting bodies such as the FASB and SEC. In contrast, the reporting of sources of stockholders' equity is determined principally by the statues of the state in which the company is chartered. Therefore, any discussion of accounting for stockholders' equity must generalize because of differences among state laws.

The concept of **legal capital** arose because the stockholders of a corporation have limited personal liability for the debts of the corporation. Generally, the maximum amount the stockholders can lose in a corporation is limited to the amount of their investment, whereas partners and sole proprietors can lose their entire investment and their personal assets may be subject to claims of business creditors if business assets are insufficient to satisfy those claims. In other words, the liability of partners and proprietors is said to be unlimited. The need to protect corporate creditors in exchange for the limited liability of the stockholders caused the development of the concept of legal capital. Legal capital generally is that part of stockholders' equity which cannot be impaired by a voluntary action of the stockholders (or board of directors). Transfers of assets to shareholders via dividend payments or buying back their stock (treasury stock) are prohibited if such transfers would impair legal capital because such transfers could jeopardize the claims of the corporate creditors.

In most states the par or stated value of shares issued to stockholders is the starting amount of legal capital. For this reason, shares issued to stockholders by the corporation for an amount less than par carried a contingent discount liability for the stockholders before state laws began outlawing issuances of stock at a discount. Such laws meant that stockholders were subject to an assessment equal to any discount; in other words, their liability was not limited to their original investment, but extended also to the amount of the discount. Under the so-called trust fund doctrine the par or stated value of shares is maintained in trust for the protection of corporate creditors.[5]

Maintenance of legal capital generally means that a corporation must refrain from paying dividends when their effect would be to impair the contributed capital (at least to the extent of par) and that treasury stock cannot be bought by the company when such cumulative expenditures would exceed the cumulative amount of Retained Earnings. Legal capital can be impaired as a result of operating losses, but such losses involve involuntary actions on the part of stockholders. Whether legal capital at a specific date is based on shares issued or shares outstanding depends upon the laws of the state of incorporation.

Common Stock. Common stock represents the basic issue of shares and normally carries all of the basic rights listed in a preceding paragraph. When there is only one class of stock, all of the shares are common stock.

The common shareholders are the residual owners of the corporation. As such, their position is more risky than the positions of *(a)* creditors, to whom the corporation owes legally enforceable principal and interest amounts on specified dates, and *(b)* preferred shareholders, whose shares usually specify fixed dividend and liquidation amounts per share. Consequently, the common shareholders are exposed to all the risks and enjoy the benefits of corporate success, or failure, after creditor and preferred shareholder claims are met.

[5] See Committee on Corporate Laws (Section of Corporation, Banking and Business Law), American Bar Association, *The Model Business Corporation Act* (as amended to January 1, 1980); and T. J. Fiflis and H. Kripke, *Accounting for Business Lawyers* (St. Paul, Minn.: West Publishing Co., 1977), Chapter X.

Preferred Stock. Preferred stock is so designated because it confers certain preferences or privileges over the common stock. The preferences may relate to the following:

1. Dividends.
   a. Cumulative or noncumulative.
   b. Nonparticipating, partially participating, or fully participating with common stockholders in dividends in excess of the stated preferred dividend.
2. Assets in liquidation.
3. Redemption at a specified date.
4. Convertibility to other securities.

Because the right to vote is a basic right, preferred shareholders have full voting rights unless specifically prohibited in the charter. Likewise, all the other basic rights of stock ownership apply to preferred stock unless specifically withheld in the charter.

Preferred stock usually is par value stock, in which case the dividend preference is expressed as a percentage of par. For example, 6 percent preferred stock carries a dividend preference of 6 percent of the **par value** of each share, which means that when the corporation declares a dividend, preferred shareholders must get their 6 percent preferred dividend before common shareholders receive any dividends. In the case of nopar preferred stock, the dividend preference necessarily is expressed as a specific dollar **amount** per share.

To identify specifically the preferences relating to preferred stock, corporations must indicate on the stock certificate the exact nature of the preferences; that is, whether the stock is cumulative, participating, callable, or convertible.[6]

Cumulative Dividend Preferences on Preferred Stock. **Noncumulative** preferred stock provides that dividends not declared (i.e., dividends "passed") for any prior year or years are lost permanently as far as the preferred shareholders are concerned. As a result, the noncumulative restriction is an undesirable feature for investors.

Cumulative preferred stock provides that dividends in **arrears** (i.e., not declared) from prior years accumulate, at the **preference rate,** and must be paid in full to the preferred shareholders when dividends are declared, before the common stockholders may receive a dividend. If only a part of the preference is met for any year, then the balance of the cumulative preference remains in arrears. Cumulative preferred stock carries the right, in liquidation of the corporation, to dividends in arrears to the extent the corporation has retained earnings. However, express provisions may be made in the charter and bylaws concerning dividends in arrears in such situations. When the charter is silent as to the cumulative feature, most courts have ruled that preferred stock is cumulative.[7] Therefore, in this book, we assume preferred stock is cumulative unless stated otherwise. *APB Opinion 9* (par. 35) states: "When cumulative preferred dividends are in arrears, the per share and aggregate amounts thereof should be disclosed."

Participating Dividend Preferences on Preferred Stock. Preferred stock is **nonparticipating** when the dividends on such stock for any one year are limited in the charter to a specified preference rate (plus any cumulative preferences). **Partially participating** preferred stock provides that the shareholders thereof participate above the preferential rate on a prorata basis with the common stockholders, but only up to an additional rate which is specified in the charter and on the stock certificate. For example, a corporation may issue 6 percent preferred stock, with participation up to a total of 8 percent, in which case participation privileges with the common shareholders would be limited to an additional 2 percent. Preferred stock is fully participating when the preferred shareholders are entitled to dividends (in addition to the basic preference rate) on a prorata basis (based on par or stated value) with the holders of common stock.

Because accountants are called upon to advise management on dividend decisions, it is important that computation of dividends be understood. Dividend computations for par value stock are illustrated in Exhibit 14–2. In that exhibit, Illustrations 2, 3, and 4 show that the "Common, current (to match preferred 5 percent)" does not mean that the common stock also carries a stated annual dividend rate of 5 percent; no such provision attaches to the common. However, before paying "participation" dividends to preferred shareholders, the common shareholders must be given a "match" equal to the preferred rate; otherwise, the common would suffer another disad-

[6] Frequently preferred stock is specified as nonvoting. In many cases the distinction between common and preferred stock represents restrictive or negative features. For example, noncumulative, nonparticipating, and nonvoting are negative features.

[7] R. A. Howell, J. R. Allison, and N. T. Henley, *Business Law: Text and Cases,* 2d ed. (Hinsdale, Ill.: Dryden Press, 1981), p. 656.

vantage. The percent rate on the preferred gives it a preference only when dividends are inadequate to accord each class of stock proportionate (i.e., 5% in Exhibit 14–2) treatment. The allocation of dividends among the various classes of stock may be affected by state laws.

If the common stock is **nopar** and the preferred stock has participating privileges, a specified dollar amount per common share must be established in the charter for the participation matching computations. Exhibit 14–3 illustrates dividend computations for nopar stock.

Asset Preference. Preferred stock which is **preferred as to assets** (i.e., which has a liquidation preference) provides that the preferred shareholders, in case of corporate dissolution, have a priority up to par value or other stated amount per share over common shareholders. Once this liquidation preference is satisfied, the remainder of the assets is distributed to the common shareholders. *APB Opinion 10* (par. 10) requires that "the liquidation preference of the preferred stock be disclosed in the equity section of the balance sheet in the aggregate . . . rather than on a per share basis or by disclosure in notes."

Redemption Preference. Preferred stock having a **redemption** privilege (i.e., redeemable stock) provides that the preferred **shareholder** has the option, under the conditions specified, of turning in the shares owned to the corporation for a specified price per share. Redeemable preferred stock, with specified redemption dates and amounts, and a cumulative dividend preference, is very much like debt. For instance, B. F. Goodrich Company; Reichhold Chemicals, Inc.; and Schering-Plough Corporation have issued redeemable preferred stock requiring these companies to redeem a specified number of their preferred shares on specified dates and prices. Consequently, some accountants believe that such preferred stock should be reported as a liability and that the related dividends should be accounted for as interest expense. Redemption privileges and the specified conditions should be disclosed by the issuing corporation in its financial statements (tabular portion or notes).

Convertibility Privilege. Preferred stock may carry a **convertibility** provision, which means that at the option of the preferred **shareholder,** the preferred shares owned may be exchanged for (converted) other securities such as common stock. Because the conversion privilege offers the preferred shareholder the option of holding the original preferred stock or converting it to another specified security, convertible preferred stock is favored by investors. Convertibility privileges should be disclosed by the issuing corporation in its financial statements (tabular portion or notes).

Callable Preferred Stock. Preferred stock may be **callable;** that is, the **corporation** may, at its option, call the preferred stock (purchase it for cancellation) under specified conditions of time and price. *APB Opinion 10* (par. 11) states that the corporation should disclose, "on the face of the balance sheet or in notes pertaining thereto: the aggregate or per share amounts at which preferred shares may be called. . . ."

ACCOUNTING FOR ISSUANCE OF PAR VALUE STOCK

Accounting for stockholders' equity emphasizes **source;** accordingly, if a corporation has more than one class of stock, separate accounts should be maintained for each class. In case there is only one class of stock, an account titled Capital Stock usually is employed. In cases where there are two or more classes of stock, account titles such as Common Stock; Preferred Stock, 5 percent; and Common Stock, Nopar are appropriate. The sequence of transactions related to issuance of stock is *(a)* authorization of shares, *(b)* subscriptions (i.e., the issuance of shares on credit), if used by the corporation, *(c)* collections on subscriptions (when subscriptions are used), and *(d)* issuance of the shares.

Authorization

The authorization in the charter to issue a specified number of shares may be recorded in the journal and in the ledger account by notation as follows:[8]

Notation:

Common Stock—Par Value $100 per Share
(authorized 5,000 shares)

[8] An alternative way of recording the authorization of capital stock is by a journal entry as follows:

Unissued common stock	500,000	
Common stock authorized, par $100 (5,000 shares)		500,000
To record authorization of 5,000 shares of common stock, par value $100 per share.		

Observe the two accounts, Unissued Common Stock and Common Stock. The Unissued Common Stock account is credited when the shares are issued.

EXHIBIT 14–2: Dividend Computations for Par Value Stock

Panel A—Illustrative Data:

Preferred stock, 5%, $100 par value, 1,000 shares outstanding	$100,000
Common stock, $50 par value, 4,000 shares outstanding	200,000

Panel B—Dividend Computations:

	Preferred	Common
Illustration No. 1: Preferred stock is cumulative, nonparticipating; dividends two years in arrears; dividends declared, $28,000:		
Step 1—Preferred in arrears (5% × $100,000 × 2)	$10,000	
Step 2—Preferred, current (5% × $100,000)	5,000	
Step 3—Common (balance)		$13,000
	$15,000	$13,000
Illustration No. 2: Preferred stock is cumulative, fully participating; dividends two years in arrears; dividends declared, $28,000:		
Step 1—Preferred in arrears (5% × $100,000 × 2)	$10,000	
Step 2—Preferred, current (5% × $100,000)	5,000	
Step 3—Common, current (to match preferred 5%; 5% × $200,000)		$10,000
Step 4—Balance (ratably based on par values; ⅓ to pref.; ⅔ to com.)	1,000	2,000
	$16,000	$12,000
Illustration No. 3: Preferred stock is noncumulative, partially participating up to an additional 2%; dividends declared, $28,000:		
Step 1—Preferred, current (5% × $100,000)	$ 5,000	
Step 2—Common, current (to match preferred 5%; 5% × $200,000)		$10,000
Step 3—Preferred, partial participation, additional 2% (2% × $100,000)	2,000	
Step 4—Common, current (to match preferred 2%; 2% × $200,000)		4,000*
Step 5—Common (balance)		7,000
	$ 7,000	$21,000

* For step 4 to be completed as shown, this amount must be enough to provide $4,000 (i.e., 2 percent of par value) for common. Otherwise, the amount in step 3 would have to be recomputed (see illustration no. 4 below for an example of this situation).

	Preferred	Common
Illustration No. 4: Preferred stock is noncumulative, partially participating up to an additional 2%; dividends declared, $16,000:		
Step 1—Preferred, current (5% × $100,000)	$ 5,000	
Step 2—Common, current (to match preferred 5%; 5% × $200,000)		$10,000
Step 3—{ Preferred, partial participation (⅓ × $1,000)	333†	
{ Common (ratably with preferred based on par values; ⅔ × $1,000)		667
	$ 5,333	$10,667

† Cannot exceed $2,000 (i.e., $100,000 × 2%).

Stock Issued for Cash

In most situations capital stock is sold and issued for cash rather than on a subscription basis. The issuance of 1,000 shares of common stock (par $100) for cash of $102 per share would be recorded as follows:

Cash	102,000	
Common stock, par $100 (1,000 shares)		100,000
Contributed capital in excess of par, common stock		2,000

The capital stock account is credited for the par value of the stock issued, and the excess over par is credited to a descriptively named contributed capital account to record **source** in detail.

EXHIBIT 14–3: Dividend Computations for Nopar Stock

Panel A—Illustrative Data:

a. Preferred stock, 5 percent, par $100, cumulative and fully participating, 1,000 shares outstanding.
b. Common stock, nopar, 15,000 shares outstanding; participation matching amount specified on the stock certificates, $1 per share.
c. Total dividends to be paid in 19C, $48,000; no dividends were declared or paid in 19A or 19B.

Panel B—Dividend Computations:

	Preferred	Common
Preferred, in arrears (5% × $100,000 × 2)	$10,000	
Preferred, current (5% × $100,000)	5,000	
Common, to match (15,000 shares × $1)		$15,000
Participation:*		
Preferred	4,500	
Common		13,500
Total	$19,500	$28,500

* Computations:

Preferred: $\frac{(1{,}000 \text{ shares} \times \$100 \times 5\% = \$5{,}000)}{(\$5{,}000 + \$15{,}000)} \times \$18{,}000\dagger$ $4,500

Common: $\frac{(15{,}000 \text{ shares} \times \$1 = \$15{,}000)}{(\$5{,}000 + \$15{,}000)} \times \$18{,}000$ 13,500

Total: † $48,000 − $10,000 − $5,000 − $15,000 .... $18,000.

ACCOUNTING FOR ISSUANCE OF NOPAR STOCK

Because the statutes in many states permit two types of nopar stock, **true** nopar stock and **stated value** nopar stock, there is some variation in accounting. Nopar stock with a stated value is accounted for as discussed above for par value stock because the stated value places the nopar stock on essentially the same basis as par value stock. Amounts received in excess of stated value should be credited to an account with a descriptive title such as Contributed Capital in Excess of Stated Value, Nopar Common Stock.

Authorization of nopar stock may be recorded by notation as shown for par value stock under the above heading, "Authorization." With respect to nopar stock, most states require that the total number of shares **authorized** be shown on each stock certificate, in addition to the customary imprint of the number of shares represented by that particular stock certificate.

The entries to record **true nopar stock** should indicate the **number of shares** as well as the dollar amounts. In the case of true nopar stock, the accounting treatment should follow the applicable legal requirements. Thus, if the statutes provide that all proceeds represent legal capital, then the capital stock account should be credited for the full amount received. If the statutes establish a minimum amount per share, then at least this amount should be credited to the capital stock account. In the absence of legal requirements, the total amount received should be credited to the nopar capital stock account.

STOCK SUBSCRIPTIONS

Often in conjunction with the organization of a corporation, prospective stockholders may sign a contract to purchase a specified number of shares on credit with payment to be made at one or more specified dates in the future. Such an agreement is known as a **stock subscription.** Because a legal contract is involved, accounting recognition must be given to this transaction. The purchase price is debited to Stock Subscriptions Receivable; Capital Stock Subscribed is credited for the par, stated, or assigned amount per share; and the difference is credited to Contributed Capital in Excess of Par (or stated value) as though the subscriber had paid for the subscribed shares in full.

To illustrate, assume 100 shares of preferred stock, par $10, are subscribed for at $12; the entry would be as follows:

Stock subscriptions receivable—preferred stock	1,200	
Preferred stock subscribed, par $10 (100 shares)		1,000
Contributed capital in excess of par, preferred stock		200

Observe that the premium is recorded when the subscription is recorded rather than later when all of the cash is collected because of the legal claim (i.e., the stock subscription receivable) the corporation has on the subscriber.

The credit balance in Capital Stock Subscribed reflects the corporation's obligation to issue the 100 shares upon fulfillment of the terms of the agreement by the subscribers. This account is reported on the balance sheet in a manner similar to the related capital stock account (see Exhibit 14–1). Stock subscriptions receivable is classified as a current asset if the corporation expects current collection; otherwise, it is classified as an "other" asset. If there are **no plans for collection,** subscriptions receivable cannot be considered an asset and, therefore, should be offset against capital stock subscribed in the stockholders' equity section of the balance sheet.

In some cases, subscription contracts call for installment payments. In such cases, separate "call" accounts may be set up for each installment. If the corporation has a number of subscriptions, usually it is desirable to maintain a **subscribers' ledger** as a subsidiary record to the stock subscriptions receivable account in a manner similar to that maintained for trade accounts receivable.

Collections on stock subscriptions receivable may be in cash, property, or services. The appropriate account is debited, and subscriptions receivable is credited. If a noncash asset or a service is received, the **amount** recorded would be based on the market value of those assets or services.

Stock certificates usually are not issued until the subscription price is paid in full. Therefore, the last collection often requires two entries. To illustrate, assume the last collection on the above subscription (for $1,200) was $400; the entries would be as follows:

To record the last collection:

Cash	400	
Stock subscriptions receivable—preferred stock		400

To record issuance of the stock:

Preferred stock subscribed	1,000	
Preferred stock, par $10 (100 shares)		1,000

Accounting for stock subscriptions of **nopar stock** is illustrated in Exhibit 14–4.

When stock is issued, a **stock certificate,** specifying the number of shares represented, is prepared for each shareholder. An entry to reflect the number of shares held by each shareholder is made in the **stockholder ledger,** which is a subsidiary ledger to the capital stock account.

Subscriptions—Default on Subscriptions Receivable

When a subscriber **defaults** after fulfilling a part of the subscription contract, certain complexities arise. In case of default, the corporation may decide to (1) return to the subscriber all payments made or (2) issue shares equivalent to the number paid for in full, rather than the total number contracted. These two options obviously involve no disadvantage to the subscriber, although the corporation may incur a later economic loss if the stock prices drop. The laws of most states cover the contingency where the corporation does not elect either of these alternatives. Such laws vary considerably; two contrasting provisions are as follows:

a. The subscribed stock is **forfeited** and all payments made by the defaulting subscriber are forfeited by the subscriber; hence, the forfeited amount is credited to the contributed capital of the corporation. Further, the corporation is free to sell the shares again. Provisions of this type favor the corporation.

b. The stock is forfeited, and the corporation must resell the stock under a **lien,** whereby the original subscriber must be reimbursed for the amount that the **net receipts** for the stock (i.e., the total cash collected from both the first and second sales, less the costs incurred by the corporation in making the second sale) exceed the **original subscription price.** To avoid an incentive to default, the refund to the defaulting subscriber cannot exceed the amount paid to the date of default less resale costs—Exhibit 14–5 illustrates the accounting for this provision.

EXHIBIT 14–4: Entries for Subscriptions of Nopar Stock

	Stated Value Stock*		True Nopar Value Stock	
1. To record authorization of 10,000 shares of nopar stock:				
Notation—10,000 shares of nopar common stock authorized	Stated value, $5		No stated value	
2. To record cash sale and issuance of 5,000 shares @ $6:				
Cash	30,000		30,000	
Common stock, nopar, stated value $5		25,000		
Common stock, nopar				30,000
Contributed capital in excess of stated value, nopar common stock		5,000		
3. To record subscription taken for 5,000 shares @ $6; 20 percent collected in cash:				
Cash (5,000 × $6 × .20)	6,000		6,000	
Stock subscriptions receivable, nopar common stock	24,000		24,000	
Nopar common stock subscribed (5,000 shares)		25,000		30,000
Contributed capital in excess of stated value, nopar common stock		5,000		
4. To record collection of subscription receivable and issuance of all of the subscribed shares:				
Cash	24,000		24,000	
Stock subscriptions receivable, nopar common stock		24,000		24,000
Nopar common stock subscribed	25,000		30,000	
Common stock, nopar, stated value $5 (5,000 shares)		25,000		
Common stock, nopar (5,000 shares)				30,000

* Entries for par value stock would be similar.

ACCOUNTING FOR STOCK PREMIUM AND DISCOUNT

The preceding discussions explained that amounts received in excess of par value are credited to an appropriately designated stock "premium" account. Similarly, amounts received less than par are debited to an appropriately titled stock "discount" account. Stock premium constitutes an increase in total stockholders' equity, whereas stock discount serves to reduce total owners' equity. Accountants seldom encounter stock discount.

Contributed capital in excess of par value is classified as contributed capital and should remain in the accounts until retirement of the stock. Upon retirement of the stock, the related premium should be removed from the accounts. Some states allow such contributed capital to be debited (i.e., "used") for stock dividends, and a few states permit debits to such accounts for cash dividends as well. When such a dividend is paid, the shareholders receiving the dividend should be informed that it represents a return of original investment (i.e., a liquidating dividend) rather than a distribution of earnings.

Separate premium accounts should be established for each class of stock as needed. Any discount recorded should not be offset against a premium. Discount can be eliminated by additional collections (stock assessments) from shareholders, capitalization of retained earnings, or through retirement of the related stock. If a discount is recorded, it should be reported on the balance sheet as a negative item directly under the class of stock to which it relates.

SPECIAL SALES OF STOCK

A corporation may sell and issue each class of stock separately as assumed in the preceding discussions. In some situations shares of two or more classes of securities may be sold for one lump sum.

EXHIBIT 14–5: Default on Stock Subscriptions—Shares Sold under Lien

1. Corporation H receives from Subscriber S a subscription for 100 shares of preferred stock, par $10, at $12 per share.

Stock subscription receivable, preferred stock	1,200	
Preferred stock subscribed, par $10 (100 shares)		1,000
Contributed capital in excess of par, preferred stock		200

2. Corporation H receives a $400 installment on the subscription from Subscriber S:

Cash	400	
Stock subscription receivable, preferred stock		400

3. Subscriber S defaults on the subscription. Corporation H records default under provision *(b)*:

Preferred stock subscribed, par $10 (100 shares)	1,000	
Contributed capital in excess of par, preferred stock	200	
Stock subscription receivable, preferred stock ($1,200 − $400)		800
Payable to Subscriber S (pending resale of formerly subscribed shares)		400

4. Corporation H resells the formerly subscribed shares for $15 per share. Corporation H paid the cost of resale, $50, and debited this amount to the Payable to Subscriber S account.

Resale of shares:		
Cash [(100 × $15) − $50]	1,450	
Payable to Subscriber S (resale costs)	50	
Preferred stock, par $10 (100 shares)		1,000
Contributed capital in excess of par, preferred stock ($1,500 − $1,000)		500

5. Corporation H pays stipulated amount to Subscriber S:

Payable to Subscriber S	350	
Cash		350

Computation:

Amount to be paid to Subscriber S based on lien provision:		
Net receipts for the stock:		
Cash collected from Subscriber S	$ 400	
Cash collected from resale of shares	1,500	
Less: Cost of resale	(50)	
Net receipts		$1,850
Original subscription price		1,200
Remainder payable to Subscriber S, subject to limitation		$ 650
Limitation—total actual payments made by Subscriber S, less resale costs (i.e., $400 − $50)		$ 350
Therefore, pay $350 to Subscriber S.		
Contributed capital from subscription and sale:		
Net receipts for stock	$1,850	
Less refund to Subscriber S	350	
Contributed capital	$1,500	

Also, a corporation may issue stock for services or noncash assets rather than for cash. Each of these situations creates a special accounting problem.

When two or more classes of securities are sold and issued for a single lump sum, the total proceeds must be allocated among the several classes of securities on some logical basis. Two methods available for such situations are *(a)* the proportional method, in which the lump sum received is allocated proportionally among the classes of stock on the basis of the relative market value of each security; and *(b)* the incremental method, in which the market value of one security is used as a basis for that security and the remainder of the lump sum is allocated to the other class of security. Allocation among the classes of stock should depend upon the information available. To illustrate three typical situations, assume 100 shares of common stock (par value $100 per share) and 50 shares of preferred stock (par value $80 per share) are sold for a lump sum of $15,000.

Situation 1: The common stock is selling at $104 and the preferred stock at $101—apportionment on basis of relative market values (proportional method):

Cash	15,000	
Common stock, par $100 (100 shares)		10,000
Preferred stock, par $80 (50 shares)		4,000
Contributed capital in excess of par, common stock		97
Contributed capital in excess of par, preferred stock		903

Computations (rounded):

Common:

$$\frac{(100 \times \$104 = \$10{,}400)}{(\$10{,}400 + \$5{,}050)} \times \$15{,}000 = \$10{,}097: \$10{,}097 - \$10{,}000 = \$\ 97$$

Preferred:

$$\frac{(50 \times \$101 = \$5{,}050)}{(\$10{,}400 + \$5{,}050)} \times \$15{,}000 = \ \ 4{,}903: \$\ 4{,}903 - \$\ 4{,}000 = \$903$$

Total proceeds $15,000

Situation 2: The common stock is selling at $104; no market has been established for the preferred stock—apportionment on basis of market value of one class of shares (incremental method):

Cash	15,000	
Common stock, par $100 (100 shares)		10,000
Preferred stock, par $80 (50 shares)		4,000
Contributed capital in excess of par, common stock ($4 per share)		400
Contributed capital in excess of par, preferred stock ($1,000 − $400)		600

Situation 3: No market value is determinable for either class of stock. In this case an arbitrary allocation is the only alternative. In the absence of any other logical basis, a **temporary** allocation may be made on the basis of relative par values. Should a market value be established for one of the securities in the relatively near future, a correcting entry based on such value would be appropriate. The entry to record the arbitrary allocation on the basis of relative par values would be similar to that shown above for situation 1, except that the apportionment of the $15,000 received would be based on the relative par values of the two securities (i.e., $\frac{\$10{,}000}{\$14{,}000} \times \$15{,}000 = \$10{,}714$ allocated to the common, and $\frac{\$4{,}000}{\$14{,}000} \times \$15{,}000 = \$4{,}286$ allocated to the preferred).

Noncash Sale and Issuance of Stock

When a corporation issues stock as payment for noncash assets or services, the question of stock valuation for accounting purposes arises. The values to apply in this situation, in determination of the proceeds, are as follows, in order of preference.[9]

1. Current market value of the stock issued or the current market value of the noncash assets or services received, whichever can be measured more reliably.
2. Appraised value of the assets or services received.
3. Valuation of the assets or services established by the board of directors.

The exchange of noncash assets for stock has given rise to many abuses over the years through improper valuation of the assets received. Overvalued assets create an overstatement of stockholders' equity—a condition referred to as **watered stock.** On the other hand, undervaluation of assets creates an understatement of stockholders' equity giving rise to what is frequently referred to as **secret reserves.** Secret reserves also may be created by depreciating or amortizing assets over a period substantially less than their useful lives.

ASSESSMENTS ON SHAREHOLDERS

Some states permit the issuance of **assessable stock,** providing the charter includes such a provision. Also in some states, under certain conditions, the board of directors may assess the stockholders a certain amount per share, although the stock is not identified as assessable stock. A stock assessment involves the collection of cash from the stockholders in proportion to the shares held without the issuance of additional stock. Stock assessments may be used when a corporation is in dire need of cash,

[9] AICPA, *APB Opinion No. 29,* "Accounting for Nonmonetary Transactions" (New York, May 1973), par. 4, specifically states that it does not apply to the "c. Acquisition of nonmonetary assets or services on issuance of the capital stock of an enterprise. . . ." Nevertheless, preference 1 is consistent with the spirit of the *Opinion.*

facing probable bankruptcy, or when the stock originally was issued at a discount. If the stock originally was issued at a discount, the assessment (up to the amount of the discount) is credited to the discount account. If no stock discount is carried in the accounts, the credit is to a contributed capital account with an appropriate title such as Contributed Capital, Stock Assessments.

UNREALIZED CAPITAL INCREMENT

Unrealized capital **increment,** as a category of stockholders' equity, is not widely used in practice. It arises when assets are written up from cost; thus, it violates the cost principle. Because of adherence to the cost principle and the concept of conservatism, assets rarely are written up from cost to market value. An example of such a write-up might involve the **discovery value** of natural resources. Other examples are to be found in financial companies. Typically, in insurance and investment companies, the investment portfolio is adjusted to market value periodically because it is current GAAP in these industries to account for their investments at market value. An upward adjustment of the asset account requires an offsetting credit to either revenue or unrealized capital increment.

There are a number of unsettled issues such as *(a)* measurement of the market value of the assets and *(b)* classification of the credit as revenue or unrealized capital. As the profession moves toward "value accounting," these issues necessarily will come into sharper focus and demand definitive solutions.

The write-up of operational (fixed) assets to appraisal (i.e., estimated market) value was discussed briefly in Chapter 11 with respect to discovery value of natural resources. Except for certain farm products and natural resources, investments of financial institutions, and perhaps other assets, current GAAP does not permit the write-up of assets to market value. However, if such a write-up were to be credited to the account, **Unrealized Capital Increment,** the account would be reported as a separate, positive item of owners' equity, rather than as part of income.

UNREALIZED CAPITAL DECREMENT

Unrealized capital **decrement** (i.e., a debit balance) is a contra, or negative, amount in stockholders' equity. It arises when assets are written down under special circumstances. For example, FASB, *Statement of Financial Accounting Standards No. 12,* "Accounting for Certain Marketable Securities," requires the recording of an "unrealized loss on long-term investments in equity securities." This unrealized capital decrement on **long-term** investments must be reported as a contra item in stockholders' equity as discussed in Chapter 16, Part A.

Part B: Stock Rights and Options

STOCK RIGHTS

Corporations often issue **stock rights** that provide the holder with an option to acquire a specified number of shares of capital stock in the corporation under prescribed conditions and within a stated future time period. When rights are issued to **current stockholders,** the corporation issues **one stock right for each share of stock owned;** however, it may take more than one right to acquire an additional share of stock.

Evidence of ownership of stock rights is a certificate commonly known as a **stock warrant,**[10] which specifies *(a)* the option price per share of the specified stock (there may be no price), *(b)* the number of rights required to obtain a share of the stock, *(c)* the number of rights represented by the warrant, *(d)* the expiration date of the rights, and *(e)* instructions for exercising the rights. When more than one right is required to obtain one share of stock in the future, such rights represent fractional shares and they often are referred to as **fractional share** rights.

Stock rights usually have value and, as a consequence, are bought and sold in the capital markets. Three dates are important with respect to the valuation of stock rights: (1) date of announcement, (2) date of issuance of the rights, and (3) date of expiration. Between the date of announcement and the date of issuance of the rights, the stock to which they relate will sell **rights on;** that is, the price of the stock will be incremented by the value of the rights because the stock and the rights are not separable during that period of time. After the rights are issued and until the rights expire, the shares and rights sell

[10] Stock rights sometimes are referred to as stock warrants.

separately; consequently, the shares sell **ex rights** during this period of time and the rights have a separate price.

Situations in which stock rights often are issued include the following:

1. To give existing shareholders the first opportunity to buy additional shares when the corporation decides to raise additional equity capital by selling **unissued** shares to current shareholders.
2. As compensation to outsiders (such as underwriters, promoters, and professionals) for services rendered to the corporation.
3. As compensation to officers and other employees of the corporation; these are often referred to as **stock options.**
4. To represent fractional shares when a stock dividend is declared and issued (discussed and illustrated in Chapter 15).
5. To enhance the marketability of other securities issued by the corporation, such as giving common stock rights with convertible bonds payable (discussed and illustrated in Chapter 17).

The issuance of stock rights poses accounting problems for both the recipient (i.e., the investor) and the issuing corporation. Accounting for stock rights received by an **investor** is discussed in Chapter 16.

In respect to the **issuing corporation,** at least a memorandum entry must be made at date of issuance of stock rights because the balance sheet, or notes to the statements, must disclose the number of stock rights outstanding by class of stock. However, accounting entries usually are made in the accounts for most of the situations listed above. Since situations 4 and 5 are discussed in other chapters, the following discussion will focus on the first three situations listed above.

Situation 1: The issuance of stock rights related to the issuance of additional shares to current shareholders may be illustrated as follows:

	Amount
Balances of X Corporation prior to decision to issue rights:	
Common stock, par $10 authorized 100,000 shares, issued and outstanding 30,000 shares	$300,000
Contributed capital in excess of par, common stock	150,000
Retained earnings	70,000

Decision of X Corporation:
To increase the outstanding shares by 50% (i.e., issue 15,000 additional shares).
Issue price per share to current stockholders—$30 plus two stock rights.
Announcement date: January 1, 19J.
Issue date for rights: March 1, 19J.
Expiration date for rights: September 1, 19J.

Market prices:
Rights—between announcement and issue dates, average $1 per right.
Stock—At announcement date, $30 per share.
—At expiration date, $34 per share.

The indicated entries by X Corporation are:

January 1, 19J—date of announcement: None.

March 1, 19J—date of issuance: Memorandum only:

Issued 30,000 stock rights to current shareholders for 15,000 shares of stock to be sold. Each share will be sold for $30 cash plus the receipt of two stock rights. After September 1, 19J, all outstanding rights will expire and the remaining shares will be sold on the market at the then current market price.

July 1, 19J—date of exercise of 1,000 stock rights by one shareholder:

Cash (1,000 rights ÷ 2 = 500 shares) × $30	15,000	
Common stock, par $10 (500 shares)		5,000
Contributed capital in excess of par, common stock		10,000

(Remaining rights outstanding, 29,000 for 14,500 shares of common stock.)

Situation 2: A corporation sometimes needs to conserve cash during the early part of its life and, as a consequence, to issue its own shares for professional services rendered. In some instances, stock rights rather than shares are issued. To illustrate, assume that at the end of 19A, its first year of operations, Jones Corporation issued 600 stock rights to an attorney for legal services when the rights were selling at $2 each. The rights specify that for each three rights tendered, one share of common stock, par $50, will be issued for $60 cash at any time up to the end of the fifth year of the life of the corporation. The indicated entries on the books of the issuing corporation would be as follows:

Year 19A—date of issuance of stock rights:

Expense—legal services (600 rights @ $2)*	1,200	
Stock rights outstanding (600 rights for 200 shares of common stock)		1,200

* Observe that the rights are valued at their current market price.

Year 19D—The 600 stock rights are tendered by the attorney and 200 shares (i.e., 600 ÷ 3 = 200) are issued:

Cash (200 shares @ $60)	12,000	
Stock rights outstanding (600 rights)	1,200	
Common stock, par $50 (200 shares)		10,000
Contributed capital in excess of par		3,200

During the period the stock rights are outstanding, the item "Stock rights outstanding (for 200 shares), $1,200" should be **reported under stockholders' equity along with the capital stock account to which it relates.**

STOCK OPTIONS GRANTED TO EMPLOYEES (SITUATION 3)

This section discusses and illustrates accounting for the third situation in which stock rights are issued by corporations, to represent stock options for employees (see list on page 483).

Corporations often establish plans whereby shares of stock in the company are issued to employees. During 1979, for example, 523 of the 600 companies surveyed by *Accounting Trends & Techniques* disclosed stock option plans. The purposes of stock option plans are varied, such as to encourage ownership in the company by employees, to raise capital, or to provide additional compensation to employees.

Often **stock** options (represented by stock rights) are granted to a particular group of employees as a form of compensation. In this situation the stock rights usually are specified as **nontransferable;** however, the shares received through exercise of the rights are **transferable.**

Plans for the issuance of stock to employees are designated with a variety of terms, none of which has been accorded standard usage. For instance, Hewlett-Packard Company refers to its plan simply as a "stock option plan," whereas Fairchild Industries, Inc., refers to its plan as a "stock incentive plan" and Interlake, Inc., has a "stock incentive program" consisting of a "stock appreciation rights plan," a "stock awards plan," and a restricted "stock purchase plan." In stock option plans, the issuing corporation is designated as the **grantor,** and the employee recipient is designated as the **grantee.**

The most important characteristic of a stock option plan from an accounting perspective is whether the plan causes **additional cost to the company.** Thus, for accounting purposes, the key distinction is between the following two categories of stock option plans.

1. **Noncompensatory plans**—These plans specify the issuance of company stock to employees at a price that is not significantly less than **market price;** thus, there is *(a)* **no** additional cost to the company and *(b)* **no** additional compensation to the employee. An example of a noncompensatory plan is the employee stock purchase plan of Digital Equipment Corporation. In its 1979 annual report, Digital stated that the plan resulted in no expenses in connection with the plan other than incidental expenses of issuing the shares; hence, the plan is noncompensatory. Many noncompensatory plans are implemented through voluntary employee payroll deductions.
2. **Compensatory plans**—These plans involve both *(a)* **cost** to the grantor and *(b)* **compensation** to the grantee. Such plans specify the issuance of company stock to employees at a set price per share (to be paid by the employee), which is significantly less than the current market price of the stock.[11] In some cases, the employee receives the stock under specified conditions at no cost. For instance, in 1979, Fairchild Industries, Inc., recognized $1.352 million of expense in connection with its compensatory stock incentive plan.

Accounting for stock options is governed by *Accounting Research Bulletin (ARB) No. 43* (chap. 13B), as amended and supplemented by *APB Opinion No. 25,* "Accounting for Stock Issued to Employees." The discussions to follow are based on these two pronouncements.

ACCOUNTING FOR NONCOMPENSATORY PLANS

Because **noncompensatory** stock options involve no expense to the company and no compensation

[11] By contrast, in noncompensatory plans, the discount (of market price minus option price) is "no greater than would be reasonable in an offer of stock to stockholders or others" (AICPA, *APB Opinion No. 25,* "Accounting for Stock Issued to Employees" [New York, October 1972], par. 7).

to the employees, they cause no unique accounting problems. To illustrate accounting for noncompensatory stock options, assume Company Y has a stock purchase plan whereby employees may acquire stock from the company at a discount of 4% from the market price through payroll deductions. Typical entries for a noncompensatory plan, including $7,200 of voluntary payroll deductions for employee stock purchases, would be (amounts assumed):

1. To record the monthly payroll and related deductions:

Salary and wage expense	90,000	
Withholding income tax payable		18,400
Payroll taxes payable		6,500
Liability—employee stock purchase plan*		7,200
Cash (or salary and wages payable)		57,900

* Per payroll deductions authorized by employees.

2. To record issuance of the requisite number of shares to employees (market price, $18.75):

Liability—employee stock purchase plan	7,200	
Capital stock, par $15 (400 shares*)		6,000
Contributed capital in excess of par		1,200

* $7,200 ÷ ($18.75 × .96) = 400 shares.

ACCOUNTING FOR COMPENSATORY PLANS

The basic issues in accounting for **compensatory** stock options involve *(a)* measurement of the **amount** of compensation expense to the company (in addition to regular salary) and *(b)* **timing** of the periodic expense recognition. These issues can be pinpointed by illustration. For this purpose, Exhibit 14–6, Panel A, provides the specifications of a typical compensatory plan and gives the illustrative data for the stock option transactions of one executive employee of the grantor corporation; Panel B of the exhibit details the questions which must be answered to account for the stock options granted under the plan.

Theoretical Considerations

The **theoretical** responses to the questions posed in Exhibit 14–6, Panel B, are not complicated; they may be summarized as follows:

1. The issuance of options to employees that involve *(a)* compensation expense to the company and *(b)* compensation to the employee consti-

EXHIBIT 14–6: Compensatory Stock Option Plan—AB Corporation

Panel A—Plan Specifications and Actual Data for Stock Option Transactions of Executive Z:

1. AB Corporation—plan specifications—executive stock options:
   - *a.* Options approved for **each** of 10 designated executives.
   - *b.* 5,000 shares of common stock, par $5, for each executive.
   - *c.* Nontransferable, exercisable three years after grant and prior to expiration date, which is five years from date of grant; exercise of option requires continuing employment during the option exercise period.
   - *d.* Option price, $20 per share.
2. On January 1, 19B, executive Z was granted an option for 5,000 shares:
   - *a.* For services to be performed 19B through 19F (approximately equal services each year).
   - *b.* At January 1, 19B, the quoted market price was $30 per share.
   - *c.* The option was exercised by executive Z in December 19F when the quoted market price per share was $40 (a steady increase during 19B through 19F).

Panel B—Questions Which Must Be Answered to Account for AB Corporation's Stock Option Plan:

The fundamental task for the accountant is to measure and report the annual amounts of compensation expense during the period 19B through 19F. To do this, the following questions must be answered:

1. Is the plan compensatory?
   - *a.* If no, there are no unique accounting problems (see caption "Accounting for Noncompensatory Plans").
   - *b.* If yes, then—
2. When should the compensation be measured?
3. What is the total amount of the compensation?
4. To what accounting periods should the compensation cost, as measured, be assigned as expense?
5. What entries should be made in the accounts?
6. How should the effects be reported on the financial statements?

tutes a **compensatory** plan; all other plans are noncompensatory.

2. The compensation cost should be measured when the grantor corporation foregoes alternative uses (such as sale) of the shares. This usually is identified as the date on which the option is granted to a specific individual, that is, the **date of grant.**
3. The total amount of the compensation cost should be measured as the **market value** of the **stock rights** (not the shares themselves) at the date of the grant to the specific individual.
4. The total amount of compensation cost, thus measured, should be assigned as **expense** of the accounting periods in which the **services are rendered.** This serves to match the compensation expense with the related revenues in conformity with the **matching principle.**

Practical Considerations

The accounting profession has found it difficult to promulgate accounting rules for compensatory stock options. The primary problem is one of **measurement.** Let's review the practical guidelines provided by *ARB 43* and *APB Opinion 25.* This review is cast in the framework of the six questions listed in Exhibit 14–6, Panel B.

Question 1: **Is the Plan Compensatory?** Because this decision is fundamental to the accounting, *APB Opinion 25* (par. 7) defines a **noncompensatory** plan as one that meets four criteria, as follows:

> . . . at least four characteristics are essential in a noncompensatory plan: *(a)* substantially all full-time employees meeting limited employment qualifications may participate, . . . *(b)* stock is offered to eligible employees equally or based on a uniform percentage of salary or wages, . . . *(c)* the time permitted for exercise of an option or purchase right is limited to a reasonable period, and *(d)* the discount from the market price of the stock is no greater than would be reasonable in an offer of stock to stockholders or others.

All other plans are classified as **compensatory.**

The stock option plan of AB Corporation (Exhibit 14–6, Panel A) is compensatory because it does not meet all four of the criteria for a **non**compensatory plan; that is, *(a)* it is limited to only 10 executives (not substantially all full-time employees), and *(b)* the discount from the market price of the stock is 33⅓ percent [i.e., ($30 − $20) ÷ $30]; discounts associated with noncompensatory plans range as high as 15 percent. Either factor makes the plan compensatory.

Question 2: **When Should the Compensation Be Measured?** In a compensatory plan, the amount of compensation theoretically should be measured on the date of grant to an individual employee because that is when the grantor corporation foregoes alternative uses of the shares by giving the options to a specific employee. However, the amount of compensation in some plans cannot be measured reliably on the date of grant because either the number of optioned shares or the option price is not known at that time. To resolve this problem, *APB Opinion 25* specifies that compensation should be measured at a **measurement date** defined in paragraph 10 of the *Opinion* as follows:

> The **measurement date** for determining compensation cost in stock option . . . plans is the first date on which are known both (1) the number of shares that an individual employee is entitled to receive and (2) the option . . . price, if any.

Thus, depending on the specifications of the particular option plan, the **measurement date** may be either: *(a)* the date of grant, or *(b)* a date subsequent to the date of grant. This latter situation occurs, for example, when either the number of shares or their option price depends upon the future performance of the company, such as net income. In respect to AB Corporation (Exhibit 14–6, Panel A), the measurement date is the date of grant because in this case both the *(a)* number of optioned shares (5,000 for executive Z) and *(b)* option price ($20) are known at the date of grant.

Question 3: **What Is the Total Amount of the Compensation?** The difference between the quoted market price of the stock at the measurement date and the option price, multiplied by the number of optioned shares determines the total amount of the compensation.[12] *APB Opinion 25* states that "if the

[12] The valuation of stock options has received considerable attention in finance, primarily due to increased trading in options on the Chicago Board Options Exchange. Option valuation is complex because the option price depends on *(a)* the time to maturity of the option, *(b)* the risk-free interest rate, and *(c)* the variance of the stock price—in addition to the stock price and the option price of the stock. GAAP uses the last two factors, stock price and option price, in **approximating** the value of an option. For a discussion of the option pricing model, see C. W. Smith, "Option Pricing: A Review," *Journal of Financial Economics,* September 1976, pp. 3–51.

quoted market price is unavailable, the best estimate of the market value of the stock should be used to measure compensation." For the stock option plan of AB Corporation (Exhibit 14–6, Panel A) total additional compensation of executive Z is $50,000 [i.e., ($30 − $20) × 5,000 shares].

When the measurement date is subsequent to the date of grant, the number of shares, the option price, and the market price must be **estimated** for the measurement of the compensation expense of the grantor corporation because accruals of **estimated** annual compensation expense must be recorded for each period between the date of grant and the measurement date. Total **actual** compensation cost then is measured and recorded as a **deferred expense** on the measurement date. Thereafter, annual compensation expense is the amortized portion of such deferred expense as earned by the employee.

Question 4: **To What Accounting Periods Should the Measured Compensation Be Assigned as Expense?** The total amount of compensation expense should be allocated to the periods in which the services are performed so that compensation expense is matched with the related revenues. This allocation usually requires accrual, and/or deferral, of the compensation expense.

With respect to AB Corporation, the total compensation cost of $50,000 should be assigned as expense equally to each year of the five-year period 19B–19F because executive Z will work full time for the company during that period, which is the period "covered" by the option grant.

Questions 5 and 6: **What Entries Should Be Made, and How Should the Effects of the Stock Options Be Reported?** The answers to these questions are presented in Exhibits 14–7 and 14–8. Exhibit 14–7 illustrates the case of AB Corporation (see Exhibit 14–6, Panel A), in which the measurement date is the date of grant. Exhibit 14–8 illustrates a situation in which the measurement date is subsequent to the date of grant. In each exhibit, Panel A describes the illustrative data, Panel B gives the entries, and Panel C presents the reporting on the financial statements.

Exhibit 14–8, Panel A, item 2, illustrates the estimation of future option and market prices of optioned stock for a case in which the **measurement date is subsequent to the date of grant.** As shown in the exhibit, the grantor corporation would use the **actual** market price of its stock at the end of each year as the estimate of the future market price on the measurement date.[13] When the market price of the stock changes from year to year, the grantor's entry to record compensation expense involves a change in accounting estimate (discussed in Chapter 20).

In Exhibits 14–7 and 14–8, Panel C reports Unamortized Deferred Compensation Expense as a contra account to Executive Stock Options Outstanding. This treatment is used because the stock options are outstanding (they have been issued to the employee); however, the employee has not yet earned all of the stock options, consequently, no owners' equity has been created for the unearned stock options.[14]

Employee stock options outstanding may be allowed to lapse because of:

a. Failure of an employee to fulfill the option obligations due to severance, disability, or death. Such situations should be accounted for as a change in accounting estimate in conformity with *APB Opinion 20.* The **credit** balance relating to the particular lapsed option carried in the stock options outstanding account, and any related **debit** balance carried in the deferred compensation expense account, should be removed, and the "net credit difference" should be accounted for as a reduction of **compensation expense** for the current and any future relevant periods as a change in estimate.

b. Failure to exercise because the option price of the stock is higher than the quoted market price of the stock (i.e., it would not be rational to exercise the options). In this situation, there is no **future** compensation expense related to options because they have already been "earned." Therefore, *FASB Interpretation 28* (par. 5)[15] requires that **compensation expense** of the period

[13] Stock prices have been shown to follow a random walk, which means that it is very difficult to predict future stock prices from past stock prices. Therefore, often the best estimate of a future stock price is the current stock price. See E. F. Fama, *Foundations of Finance* (New York: Basic Books, 1976), chap. 5. *APB Opinion 25,* par. 13, requires use of the end-of-period stock price as the estimate of future stock price.

[14] *APB Opinion 25,* par. 14, also states, "If stock is issued in a plan before some or all of the services are performed, part of the consideration recorded for the stock issued is unearned compensation and should be shown as a **separate reduction of stockholders' equity.** The unearned compensation should be accounted for as expense of the period or periods in which the employee performs service."

[15] FASB, *Interpretation No. 28,* "Accounting for Stock Appreciation Rights and Other Variable Stock Option or Award Plans" (Stamford, Conn., December 1978).

EXHIBIT 14–7: Accounting for Compensatory Stock Options of AB Corporation—Measurement Date Is Date of Grant

Panel A—Illustrative Data (measurement date is date of grant):

1. AB Corporation—executive stock option plan:
   Options approved for **each** of 10 designated executives under the following terms:
   a. 5,000 shares of common stock, par $5.
   b. Nontransferable, exercisable three years after grant and prior to expiration date, which is five years from date of grant; exercise of options requires continuing employment during the option exercise period.
   c. Option price, $20 per share.
2. On January 1, 19B, executive Z was granted an option for 5,000 shares:
   a. For services to be performed 19B through 19F (approximately equal each year).
   b. At January 1, 19B, the quoted market price was $30 per share.
   c. The option was exercised by executive Z in December 19F when the quoted market price per share was $40 (a steady increase during 19B–19F).

Panel B—Entries of AB Corporation for Stock Option Transactions of Executive Z:

1. January 1, 19B—date of grant; to record total deferred compensation expense and the issuance of stock options to executive Z:

Deferred compensation expense	50,000	
Executive stock options outstanding (for 5,000 shares of common stock)		50,000

($30 − $20) × 5,000 shares = $50,000.

2. December 31, 19B, through 19F—to record the annual apportionment of compensation expense to compensation expense (equal amount for each of the five years):

Compensation expense	10,000	
Deferred compensation expense		10,000

$50,000 ÷ 5 years = $10,000 per year.

3. December 31, 19F—exercise date, to record the stock rights tendered by executive Z and issuance of the 5,000 shares:

Cash (5,000 shares @ $20 option price)	100,000	
Executive stock options outstanding (for 5,000 shares)	50,000	
Common stock, par $5 (5,000 shares)		25,000
Contributed capital in excess of par, common stock		125,000

Panel C—Reporting on the Financial Statements of 19B:

Income statement:

Compensation expense	10,000

Balance sheet:

Stockholders' Equity

Contributed capital:		
Common stock, par $5, authorized 500,000 shares, issued and outstanding 200,000 shares (assumed)		$1,000,000
Executive stock options outstanding (for 5,000 shares of common stock)	$50,000	
Less: Unamortized Deferred compensation expense	40,000	10,000
Other contributed capital (etc.)	(not illustrated)	

Note: For additional disclosures required, see the last section of the chapter.

of forfeiture be **credited** up to the amount of any related compensation expense previously recorded; Executive Stock Options Outstanding would be debited. This treatment effectively accounts for the lapse of the stock options as a change in accounting estimate (actually, a realization that differs from a previously estimated amount).

During the 1970s, a new type of compensation instrument, known as **stock appreciation rights,** emerged. Under such arrangements, the grantee can receive cash in the amount of the difference between a stipulated price and the market value of the grantor corporation's stock on a specified measurement date. Some plans offer grantees the option of taking cash or exercising stock options, as discussed above. The

EXHIBIT 14–8: Accounting for Compensatory Stock Options of AB Corporation—Measurement Date Subsequent to Date of Grant

Panel A—Illustrative Data (measurement date is subsequent to date of grant):

1. Date of grant to executive K—January 1, 19B:
   a. A stock option for 5,000 shares of common stock, par $5, is granted to executive K, exercisable after three years from date of grant and within five years from date of grant.
   b. Option price—to be established on December 31, 19D, by reducing the basic option price of $20 by the percentage increase in net income for 19B through 19D (a three-year period).
   c. Additional compensation will be for services to be rendered from January 1, 19B, to December 31, 19F, assuming approximately equal services each year.
   d. Market price per share of stock on date of grant, $20.
2. **Estimates** made on December 31, 19B, and December 31, 19C, of amounts for December 31, 19D, measurement date:
   a. Percentage increase in net income for 19B through December 31, 19D: 15 percent.
   b. Resulting estimated option price on December 31, 19D, measurement date: $20 × (1 − .15) = $17 per share.
   c. Market price estimated for December 31, 19D, measurement date: For 19B, use the actual market price on December 31, 19B—$22 per share; for 19C, use the actual market price on December 31, 19C—$24 per share.
3. **Actual** amounts on December 31, 19D, the measurement date:
   a. Percentage increase in net income for 19B through December 31, 19D: 10 percent.
   b. Resulting actual option price: $20 × (1 − .10) = $18 per share.
   c. Market price per share of stock quoted on December 31, 19D: $28.
4. December 19F—Executive K exercised the option during December 19F when the quoted price per share was $40.

Panel B—Entries of AB Corporation for Stock Option Transactions of Executive K:

1. January 1, 19B (date of grant to executive K):
   No entry—measurement and recording of compensation expense will begin on December 31, 19B, and will be based on estimated amounts until the measurement date.
2. December 31, 19B—end of period; to record stock options and compensation earned by executive K during 19B—based on estimated future market price (use actual current market price, $22) and estimated future option price (i.e., $17).

Deferred compensation expense	25,000	
Executive stock options outstanding [($22 − $17) × 5,000]		25,000
Compensation expense ($25,000 ÷ 5)	5,000	
Deferred compensation expense		5,000

3. December 31, 19C—end of period; to record stock options and compensation earned by executive K during 19C—based on estimated future market price (use actual current market price, $24) and estimated future option price (i.e., $17).

Deferred compensation expense	10,000	
Executive stock options outstanding {[($24 − $17) × 5,000] − $25,000}		10,000
Compensation expense {[($24 − $17) × 5,000] − $5,000} ÷ 4	7,500	
Deferred compensation expense		7,500

EXHIBIT 14–8 *(concluded)*

Panel B *(concluded)*:

4. December 31, 19D—measurement date; to record stock options and compensation earned by executive K, during 19D—based on actual current market price (i.e., $28) and actual option price (i.e., $18) on the measurement date:

Deferred compensation expense	15,000	
Executive stock options outstanding {[($28 − $18) × 5,000] − ($25,000 + $10,000)}		15,000
Compensation expense {[($28 − $18) × 5,000 − ($5,000 + $7,500)] ÷ 3}	12,500	
Deferred compensation expense		12,500

5. December 31, 19E, and 19F—end of period; to record compensation earned by executive K during 19E and 19F:

Compensation expense (same as 19D)	12,500	
Deferred compensation expense		12,500

6. December, 19F—exercise date; to record the stock rights tendered by executive K and the issuance of the 5,000 shares:

Cash ($18 × 5,000 shares)	90,000	
Executive stock options outstanding (for 5,000 shares)	50,000	
Common stock, par $5 (5,000 shares)		25,000
Contributed capital in excess of par		115,000

Panel C—Reporting on Financial Statements of 19C–19D:

	19C		19D	
Income statement:				
Compensation expense		$7,500		$12,500
Balance sheet:				
Contributed capital:				
Common stock, par $5, authorized 500,000 shares; issued and outstanding 80,000 shares (assumed)		$400,000		$400,000
Executive stock options outstanding (for 5,000 shares); see Note X	$ 35,000*		$50,000‡	
Less: Unamortized Deferred compensation expense	(22,500)†	12,500	25,000§	25,000
Other contributed capital, etc. (not illustrated here)				

* $25,000 + $10,000 = $35,000.
† ($25,000 − $5,000) + ($10,000 − $7,500) = $22,500.
‡ $35,000 + $15,000 = $50,000.
§ $22,500 (from 19C) + $15,000 − $12,500 = $25,000.
Note X: For additional disclosures required, see the last section of the chapter.

accounting for stock appreciation rights is similar to that for stock options, except that a liability (instead of stock options) is recorded as compensation expense is accrued.[16]

ADDITIONAL DISCLOSURES REQUIRED FOR STOCK OPTION PLANS (NONCOMPENSATORY AND COMPENSATORY)

ARB 43 (chap. 13B, par. 15) requires grantor companies to disclose certain information about their stock option plans. The purpose of these disclosures is to alert existing and potential investors and creditors of the company's obligation to make such shares available to employees under existing option plans. This information would be important, for example, to an investor contemplating purchases of a controlling interest in the company. Based upon the reporting principle, the required disclosures are as follows:

a. The status of the option plan at the end of the period.
b. The number of shares under option.
c. The option price.
d. The number of shares into which options are exercisable.

[16] Ibid.

e. The number of shares exercised during the period and the option price thereof.

Exhibit 14–9 summarizes the decisions and sequence of entries for:

1. Noncompensatory plans.
2. Compensatory plans:
   a. Measurement date on date of grant.
   b. Measurement date subsequent to date of grant.

EXHIBIT 14–9: Stock Issued to Employees—Summarized

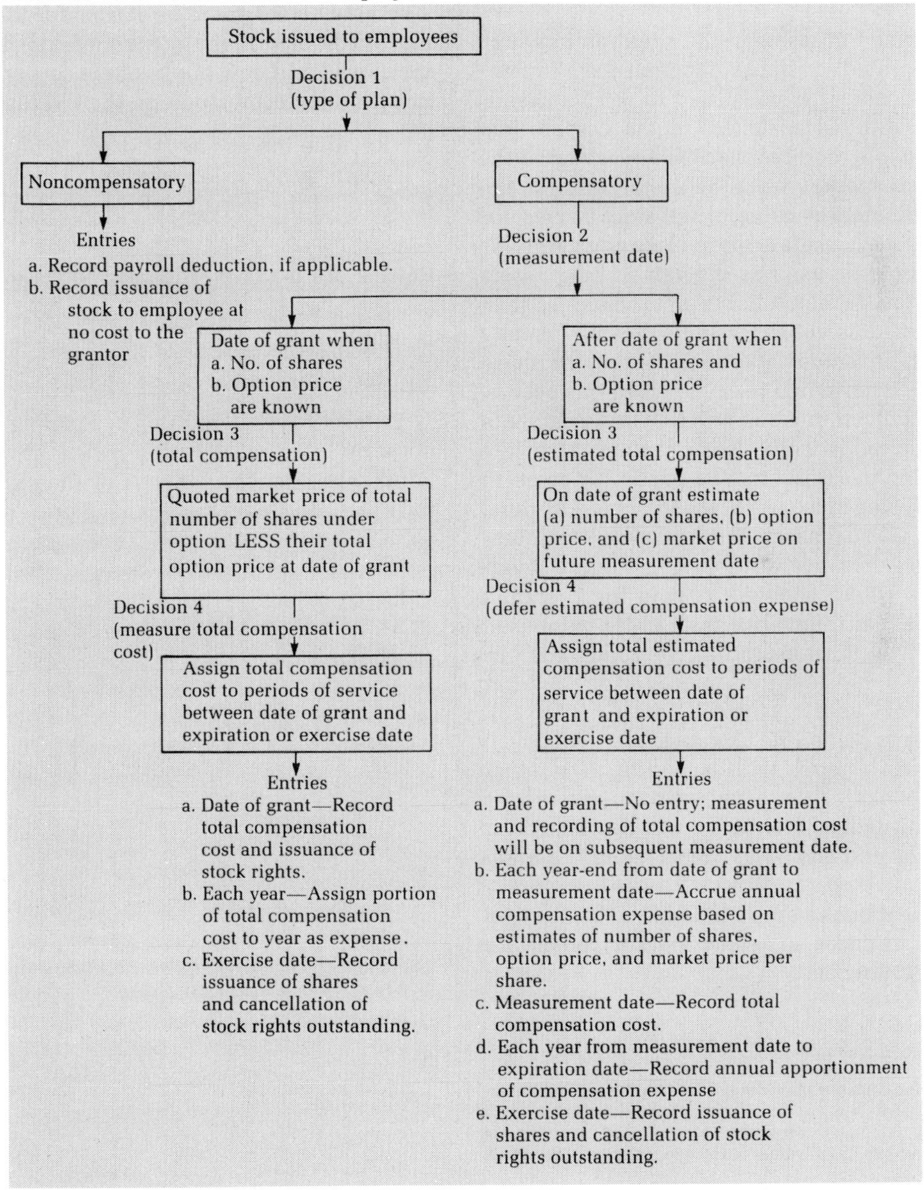

Supplement 14-A: Incorporation of a Going Business

The owner(s) of a proprietorship or partnership may decide to incorporate. In such situations, an accounting problem arises with respect to the values to be placed on the assets received for shares of stock.

In accounting for assets in the situation in which an unincorporated business incorporates, for accounting purposes, it is construed to sell its assets, net of any liabilities assumed, to the corporation. The cost principle requires that the buyer record the assets at their market value as of the date of the exchange. The market value of the stock issued for the **net** assets (i.e., assets acquired less any liabilities assumed) should be used as the value of the assets acquired; if this is not reliably determinable, then the assets should be valued by other means—usually by appraisal. In some situations neither of these values can be determined reliably; when this occurs, the parties involved must be relied upon to estimate market values realistically. It is not unusual, in the case of a going business, for the parties to agree to an exchange value in excess of the total market value of the identifiable net assets (both tangible and intangible) acquired because of the recognition of **goodwill.** In cases where goodwill is paid for, it should be recorded as an intangible asset at its purchased price.[17] Goodwill is measured as the difference between the total consideration paid and the **market value** of the **net** assets acquired (see Chapter 13).

The entries to record the exchange of a going business for shares of stock will depend upon whether the original books of the acquired business will be continued or whether new books will be opened for the corporation and any adjustments made to market values.

If the **original books** are retained, two basic steps are required in cases in which **market values** are recorded, as follows:

1. Entries are made to revalue the assets (and any other items agreed upon) in accordance with the cost principle. The accounting measure of the cost of the assets acquired and liabilities assumed is their respective market values on the date of the exchange.
2. Entries are made to close out the old owners' equity accounts and to replace them with corporate capital accounts.

If **new books** are to be started for the corporation, the old books of the proprietorship or partnership are closed and new books of the corporation opened. Entries should be made on the **old books** to—

1. Revalue the assets (and any other items agreed upon) in accordance with the cost principle.
2. Record the transfer of the assets.
3. Record receipt of the stock and its distribution.

Entries are made on the **new books** to—

1. Record the stock authorization.
2. Record the receipt of the assets.
3. Record issuance of the stock.

Exhibit 14–10 illustrates accounting for the incorporation of a partnership when new corporation books are opened. Panel A of the exhibit presents the illustrative data, and Panel B presents the entries.

[17] In some situations the only change is in the form of organization; that is, the ownership and management continue unchanged, as when a partnership is incorporated. Here a case can be made for carrying forward the book values with no recognition of goodwill.

EXHIBIT 14–10: Incorporation of AB Partnership; XYZ Corporation Opens New Books

Panel A—Illustrative Data:

1. Balance sheet of AB Partnership prior to incorporation:

Debit		Credit	
Cash	$ 2,000	Accounts payable	$ 5,000
Accounts receivable	10,000	Notes payable	2,000
Allowance for doubtful accounts	(1,000)	A, capital	32,000
Inventory	21,000	B, capital	18,000
Operational assets	40,000		$57,000
Accumulated depreciation	(15,000)		
	$ 57,000		

Note: Partners A and B had divided profits and losses: 60 percent for A and 40 percent for B.

2. Incorporation terms and related facts:
   a. XYZ Corporation is formed with 20,000 shares of common stock authorized (par value, $5 per share); 12,000 of the shares are issued in exchange for the assets, except the cash; the liabilities are assumed by the corporation.
   b. It was agreed that the inventory should be written down to $16,000 and that the accumulated depreciation should be $14,000. The book value of the remaining assets represented market value at the time of transfer to XYZ Corporation.
   c. The 12,000 shares and the $2,000 cash are to be divided between A and B according to their capital balances after the above adjustments. The remaining 8,000 shares were sold to the public at $5.10 per share. This transaction establishes the market value of the common stock of XYZ Corporation.

Panel B—Entries:

Entries on (New) Books of XYZ Corporation	Entries on (Old) Books of AB Partnership		
1. To record authorization of capital stock:			
Notation: Common stock, par $5; authorized 20,000 shares.	No entry.		
2. To record adjustments of asset values to current market value (i.e., cost to XYZ Corporation):			
No entry.	Accumulated depreciation	1,000	
	Adjustment account	4,000	
	Inventory		5,000
3. To record goodwill purchased by XYZ Corporation from AB Partnership:			
No entry.	Goodwill*	17,200	
	Adjustment account		17,200

* Computation:

Market value of shares exchanged (12,000 at $5.10)	$61,200
Market value of net assets (after adjustment and excluding cash)	44,000†
Goodwill	$17,200

† Book value of net assets (i.e., owners' equity)

before adjustments ($32,000 + $18,000)	$50,000
Less: Adjustment	(4,000)
Cash to owners A and B	(2,000)
Market value of net assets transferred to XYZ Corporation	$44,000

EXHIBIT 14–10 ***(concluded)***

Panel B ***(concluded):***

4. To close Adjustment Account to partners' capital accounts and to divide the gain based upon their profit and loss sharing percentages:					
No entry.			Adjustment account	13,200	
			A, capital ($13,200 × .60)		7,920
			B, capital ($13,200 × .40)		5,280
5. To record transfer of assets and liabilities as adjusted:					
Accounts receivable	10,000		Allowance for doubtful accounts	1,000	
Inventory	16,000		Accumulated depreciation	14,000	
Operational assets	40,000		Accounts payable	5,000	
Goodwill	17,200		Notes payable	2,000	
Allowance for doubtful accounts		1,000	A, capital	39,920	
Accumulated depreciation		14,000	B, capital	23,280	
Accounts payable		5,000	Cash		2,000
Notes payable		2,000	Accounts receivable		10,000
Common stock		60,000	Inventory		16,000
Contributed capital in excess of par, common stock		1,200	Operational assets		40,000
			Goodwill		17,200
6. To record sale of 8,000 shares at $5.10 per share:					
Cash	40,800		No entry.		
Common stock		40,000			
Contributed capital in excess of par, common stock		800			

QUESTIONS

PART A

1. Explain the meaning of each of the following: total equity, contributed capital, owners' equity, and legal capital.

2. Define public, private, domestic, foreign, open, and closed corporations.

3. What are the four basic rights of shareholders? How may one or more of these rights be withheld from the shareholder?

4. Explain each of the following: authorized capital stock; issued capital stock; unissued capital stock; outstanding capital stock; subscribed stock; and treasury stock.

5. In accounting for corporate capital, why is *source* particularly important?

6. Distinguish between *par* and *nopar* stock.

7. Distinguish between *common* and *preferred* stock.

8. Explain the difference between *cumulative* and *noncumulative* preferred stock.

9. Explain the difference between *nonparticipating, partially participating,* and *fully participating preferred stock.*

10. Under what circumstances should stock subscriptions receivable be reported *(a)* as a current asset, *(b)* as a noncurrent asset, and *(c)* as a deduction in the stockholders' equity section of the balance sheet?

11. What is a *liquidating dividend?* Why is it important that a liquidating dividend be identified separately?

12. Explain and illustrate *secret reserves* and *watered stock.*

13. How should premium and discount on capital stock be accounted for and reported?

14. How are assets valued when shares of stock are given in payment thereof?

15. What is the difference between unrealized capital *increment* and unrealized capital *decrement?*

16. What is a *stock assessment?*

PART B

17. What are *stock rights?*
18. In what situations are stock rights frequently issued?
19. Distinguish between a *compensatory* and a *noncompensatory* stock option plan.
20. What is the *measurement date* for a stock option plan? Why is it sometimes later than the date of grant?
21. What is the amount of total compensation in a stock option plan?
22. Why are estimates necessary when the measurement date is later than the date of grant of a stock option that is compensatory?

DECISION CASE 14–1

CPZ Corporation acquired a tract of land for long-term use as a future plant site in exchange for $50,000 cash plus a noninterest-bearing note whose aggregate maturity value totals $100,000. The note matures serially in $20,000 annual amounts; the first $20,000 is due one year from the date of the land transfer; the last $20,000 is due at the end of five years. However, instead of being payable in cash, each $20,000 maturity amount is to be settled by issuance of $20,000 par value common stock of CPZ Corporation to the holder of the note. On the date land was acquired and stock was issued, the market value of the stock issued by CPZ Corporation was $180,000.

Required:

1. Discuss how the transaction should be recorded at time of the land transfer and what disclosures would be appropriate if financial statements were prepared immediately thereafter.
2. Suppose financial statements are being prepared three years after the land transfer. How would the amount and classification of the land reported by CPZ differ from your answer to 1 above?
3. How, if at all, would your answer to 2 above differ if CPZ Corporation were a realty company and the land had been acquired to be resold in parcels?

DECISION CASE 14–2

Unless restricted or withheld, corporate stockholders have four basic rights. In the case of stockholders of large, publicly held companies, at least three of the four rights are almost meaningless.

Required:

Which of these rights often lack practical significance for stockholders of large, publicly held companies and why?

DECISION CASE 14–3

C. Banfield, an engineer, developed a special device to be installed in backyard swimming pools that would set off an alarm should anything fall into the water. Over a two-year period Banfield's spare time was spent developing and testing the device. After receiving a patent, three of Banfield's friends, including a lawyer, considered plans to market the device. Accordingly, a charter was obtained which authorized 25,000 shares of $10 par value stock. Each of the four organizers contributed $2,000, and each received in return 200 shares of stock. They also agreed that each would receive 500 additional shares. The remaining shares were to be held as unissued stock. Each organizer made a proposal as to how the additional 500 shares would be paid for. These individual proposals were made independently; then the group considered them as a package. The four proposals were as follows:

Banfield: The patent would be turned over to the corporation as payment for the 500 shares.

Lawyer: One hundred shares would be received for legal services already rendered during organization, 100 shares would be received as advance payment for legal retainer fees for the next three years, and the balance would be paid for in cash at par.

Friend no. 2: A small building, suitable for operations, would be given to the corporation for the 500 shares of stock. It was estimated that $2,000 would be needed for renovation. The owner estimates that the market value of the building is $75,000 and there is a $58,000 loan on it to be assumed by the corporation.

Friend no. 3: To pay $1,000 cash on the stock and to give an interest-bearing note for $4,000 (subscriptions receivable) to be paid out of dividends over the next five years.

Required:
You have been engaged as an independent CPA to advise the group. Specifically, you have been asked the following questions:

1. How would the above proposals be recorded in the accounts? Evaluate the valuation basis for each.
2. What are your recommendations for an agreement that would be equitable to each organizer? Explain the basis for such recommendations.

DECISION CASE 14–4

[*Note to professor:* Requirement 2 of this case can be made a research (library) assignment. In addition to affording students an opportunity to become familiar with *Accounting Trends & Techniques,* they can also learn about corporate annual reports first hand if they are directed to find one company with redeemable preferred stock and to report on its disclosures concerning that stock.]

APB Opinion 10, effective in 1966, and *SEC Accounting Series Release 268,* effective in 1979, represent two minor milestones in the development of accounting principles for preferred stock. *FASB Statement 47,* effective in 1981, extended somewhat the disclosure requirements for redeemable preferred stock.

APB Opinion 10 recommends that a liquidation preference (excess of involuntary liquidation value over par or stated value) be disclosed in the owners' equity section of the balance sheet in the aggregate.

SEC *ASR 268* requires that preferred stock with mandatory redemption requirements *not* be shown as owners' equity. A supplemental SEC staff bulletin states that preferred stock with mandatory redemption requirements be stated on the balance sheet at an amount not less than the mandatory redemption price.

Required:

1. From the standpoint of an investor who reads financial statements, what is the significance, if any, of the procedure required by *APB Opinion 10?*
2. What is your surmise as to the effect of *ASR 268* on the way SEC-regulated companies reported their owners' equity in their 1979 annual reports? This matter can be researched by consulting the 1980 edition of *Accounting Trends & Techniques.*
3. What is the proper reporting procedure of a company that has *callable* preferred stock outstanding?

EXERCISES

PART A: EXERCISES 14–1 to 14–11

Exercise 14–1

Allen Corporation received a charter authorizing 100,000 shares of $10 par value stock. During the first year, 40,000 shares were sold at $15 per share. Five hundred additional shares were issued in payment for legal fees. At the end of the first year, reported net income was $20,000. Dividends of $8,000 were paid on the last day of the year. Liabilities at the year-end amounted to $40,000.

Required:
Complete the following tabulation (show calculations):

Item	Amount	Assumptions
a. Total equities	$	
b. Owners' equity	$	
c. Contributed capital	$	
d. Issued capital stock	$	
e. Outstanding capital stock	$	
f. Unissued capital stock	$	
g. Treasury stock	$	

Exercise 14–2

Bell Corporation's charter authorized 60,000 shares of nopar common stock and 20,000 shares of 6%, cumulative and nonparticipating preferred stock, par value $10 per share. Stock issued to date: 40,000 shares of common sold at $200,000 and 10,000 shares of preferred stock sold at $18 per share. In addition, subscriptions for 2,000 shares of preferred have been taken, and 30% of the purchase price of $18 has been collected. The stock will be issued upon collection in full. The Retained Earnings balance is $82,000. At year-end there was a $6,000 unrealized loss on long-term investments in equity securities.

Required:
Prepare the stockholders' equity section of the balance sheet in good form.

Exercise 14–3

Prepare, in good form, the stockholders' equity section of the balance sheet for Clampet Manufacturing Company.

Retained earnings	$ 91,000
Premium on common stock	40,000
Preferred stock subscribed (2,000 shares)	20,000
Preferred stock, 6%, par $10, authorized 25,000 shares (14,000 shares issued)	140,000
Common stock, par $20, authorized 50,000 shares (10,000 shares issued)	200,000
Stock subscriptions receivable, preferred	4,000
Donation of plant site	10,000
Premium on preferred stock	30,000
Unrealized loss on long-term investment in equity securities	5,000

Exercise 14–4

The following data were provided by the accounts of Drake Corporation at December 31, 19C:

Subscriptions receivable (noncurrent)	$ 5,000
Retained earnings, 1/1/19C	150,000
Capital stock, par ?, authorized 100,000 shares	600,000
Future site for office (donated to Drake)	15,000
Capital stock subscribed, 1,000 shares (to be issued upon collection in full)	10,000
Premium on capital stock	300,000
Subscriptions receivable, capital stock (due in three months)	2,000
Bonds payable	100,000
Net income for 19C (not included in retained earnings above)	93,000
Dividends declared and paid during 19C	40,000

Required:

1. Respond to the following (state any assumptions made):

a. Total retained earnings at end of 19C is . . $______
b. Retained earnings on 1/1/19C was . . . . . . $______
c. Number of shares outstanding is . . . . ______
d. Legal capital is . . . . $______
e. Total stockholders' equity is . . . . $______
f. Number of shares issued is . . . . ______
g. Average selling price per share including any shares subscribed was . . . . $______
h. Number of shares sold including any shares subscribed was . . . . ______
i. Par value per share is . . . . $______

2. Prepare the stockholders' equity section of the balance sheet at December 31, 19C. Use good form, complete with respect to details.

Exercise 14–5

Babcock Corporation has the following stock outstanding:

Common, $50 par value—6,000 shares.
Preferred, 6%, $100 par value—1,000 shares.

Required:
Compute the amount of dividends payable in total and per share on the common and preferred for each separate case:

Case A—Preferred is noncumulative and nonparticipating; dividends declared, $20,000.

Case B—Preferred is cumulative and nonparticipating; two years in arrears; dividends declared, $34,000.

Case C—Preferred is noncumulative and fully participating; dividends declared, $24,000.

Case D—Preferred is noncumulative and fully participating; dividends declared, $40,000.

Case E—Preferred is cumulative and participating up to an additional 3%; three years in arrears; dividends declared, $60,000.

Case F—Preferred is cumulative and fully participating; three years in arrears; dividends declared, $50,000.

Exercise 14–6

Garner Corporation reported net income during four successive years as follows: $1,000; $2,000; $1,000; and $23,000.

The capital stock outstanding consisted of $70,000 common (par $20 per share) and $30,000 of 5% preferred (par $10 per share).

Required:
If net income in full were declared and paid as dividends each year, determine the amount to be paid on each class of stock for each of the four years assuming:

Case A—Preferred is noncumulative and nonparticipating.
Case B—Preferred is cumulative and nonparticipating.
Case C—Preferred is noncumulative and fully participating.
Case D—Preferred is cumulative and fully participating.

Exercise 14–7

MOE Corporation received a charter authorizing the issuance of 200,000 shares of common stock. Give the journal entries in parallel columns for the following transactions during the first year assuming Case A—true nopar stock; and Case B—par value of $5 per share.

a. To record authorization (memorandum).
b. Sold 100,000 shares at $7; collected in full and issued the shares.
c. Received subscriptions for 10,000 shares at $7 per share; collected 60% of the subscription price. The stock will not be issued until collection is in full.
d. Issued 200 shares to an attorney in payment for legal fees.
e. Issued 10,000 shares and paid cash $190,000 in payment for a building.
f. Collected balance on subscriptions receivable in *(c)*.

State and justify any assumptions you made. Assume all transactions occurred within a short time span.

Exercise 14–8

Pope Manufacturing Company's charter authorized the issuance of 400,000 shares of nopar common stock. Give journal entries for the following transactions assuming Case A—the board of directors set a stated value of $1 per share; and Case B—the stock is true nopar. Set up two pairs of columns so that Case A is to the left and Case B is to the right. Explain and justify any assumptions you make. Assume all transactions occurred within a short time span.

a. Authorization recognized (memorandum).
b. Sold 120,000 shares at $5 and collected in full; the shares were issued.
c. Received subscriptions for 10,000 shares at $5 per share; collected 40% of the subscription price. The shares will be issued upon collection in full.
d. Issued 500 shares for legal services.
e. Issued 2,000 shares and paid $75,000 cash for some used machinery.
f. Collected balance of subscriptions in *(c)*.

Exercise 14–9

Leslie Corporation charter authorized 100,000 shares of $10 par value stock. A. B. Cook subscribed for 500 shares at $25 per share, paying $2,500 down, the balance to be paid $1,000 per month. The stock will not be issued until collection in full. After paying for three months, Cook defaulted. One month later, the corporation sold the stock for $33 per share.

Required:

1. Give all entries relative to the 500 shares originally subscribed for by Cook asssuming Leslie refunded all collections made to date of default.
2. Give the entry for the default assuming shares equivalent to the collections were issued to Cook (at $25 per share). Also give the entry for the sale of the remaining shares at $33.

Exercise 14–10

The charter for Bower Manufacturing Company authorized 100,000 shares of common stock ($10 par value) and 10,000 shares of preferred stock ($50 par value). The company issued 500 shares of common and 200 shares of preferred stock for used machinery.

Required:
For each separate situation, give the entry to record the purchase of the machinery assuming Case A—the common stock currently is selling at $70 and the preferred at $80; Case B—the common stock has been selling at $70, and there have been no recent sales of the preferred stock; and Case C—there is no current market price for either class of stock (however, the machinery has been appraised at $48,000).

State and justify any assumptions made.

Exercise 14–11

The charter of VET Company authorized 10,000 shares of common stock, par $20, and 10,000 shares of preferred stock, par $10. The following transactions were completed. Assume each is completely independent.

a. Sold 200 shares of common and 100 shares of preferred for a lump sum amounting to $6,150. The common had been selling during the current week at $25, and the preferred at $12.
b. Issued 90 shares of preferred stock for some used equipment. The equipment had been appraised at $1,200; the book value shown by the seller was $600.
c. A 10% assessment on par was voted on both the common and preferred when 6,000 shares of common and 4,000 shares of preferred were outstanding. The assessment was collected in full.
d. Sold 300 shares of common and 200 shares of preferred to one person for a total cash price of $10,000. The common recently had been selling at $26; there were no recent sales of the preferred.

Required:
Give the journal entry for each transaction. State and justify any assumptions you made.

EXERCISES

PART B: EXERCISES 14–12 to 14–14

Exercise 14–12

Lambert Corporation has outstanding 50,000 shares of common stock, par $5. The company has decided to sell an additional 25,000 shares of unissued common stock at $12 per share and to give the current stockholders first chance to buy shares proportionally equivalent to the number now held. To facilitate this plan each shareholder was issued one right for each share currently held. Two rights must be submitted to acquire one additional share for $12. Rights not exercised lapse on April 9, 19A.

Required:
Give any entry or memorandum that should be made in the accounts of Lambert Corporation on each of the following dates:

January 15, 19A, the date of the announcement that the rights will be issued on March 1, 19A.

March 1, 19A, issuance of all the rights. At this date the stock of Lambert Corporation was quoted on the market at $12.50 per share.

March 27, 19A, exercise by current shareholders of 98% of the rights issued.

April 9, 19A, the remaining rights outstanding lapsed because of the deadline.

Exercise 14–13

Fisk Company has a stock purchase plan with the following provisions:

> Each full-time employee, with a minimum of one year's service, may acquire common stock, par $10, in the company through payroll deductions at 4% below the market price on the date selected by the employee for stock purchase, up until the day before the second year of service begins.

Employee Barrett signed a payroll deduction form on January 1, 19C, for $40 per month. At that date, the market price of the stock was $27. Assume a monthly salary of $1,000 and total payroll deductions in the aggregate of 22%. At the end of 19C, Barrett requested that stock be purchased equal to the amount accumulated to his credit. At that date, the market price of the stock was $25.

Required:
1. Is this a compensatory plan? Explain.
2. What is the total additional compensation to Barrett? Explain.
3. How many shares is Barrett entitled to? Show computations.
4. Give entries to record *(a)* one monthly payroll and *(b)* issuance of the shares assuming unissued shares are used.

Exercise 14–14

Deere Corporation is authorized to issue 300,000 shares of common stock, par $1; to date 140,000 shares have been issued. The corporation initiated a stock bonus plan during 19x1 for designated managers. Each manager will receive stock options to purchase 1,000 shares of common stock, if still employed by the company, any time after two years from date of grant, January 1, 19x1. The rights are nontransferable and expire after December 31, 19x5. The option price is $15 per share; the market price on date of grant was $18. The services will be rendered approximately equally over the five-year period ending December 31, 19x5.

Required:
1. Is this a noncompensatory plan? Explain.
2. What is the measurement date? Explain.
3. What is the amount of total compensation for each manager?
4. Over what period should this compensation expense (for one manager) be assigned? How much should be assigned to 19x1? to 19x2? Explain.
5. What entry should be made on the date of grant (for one manager)?
6. What entry should be made on December 31, 19x1 (for one manager)?
7. Give the entry to record the exercise of the option by one manager on December 31, 19x5, when the market price of the common stock was $37 per share.

SUPPLEMENT 14-A: EXERCISE 14–15

Exercise 14–15

Nowlin Corporation was incorporated with 500 shares of capital stock, par $100; 400 of the shares were issued for the equity in the Allen and Baker Partnership. The remaining 100 shares were sold at $102. The balances in the accounts of the partnership were as follows:

Cash	$ 1,000
Notes receivable	8,000
Accounts receivable	17,000
Inventory	6,000
Operational assets	15,000
	$47,000
Accounts payable	$10,000
Allowance for doubtful accounts	1,000
Accumulated depreciation	2,000
Allen, capital	20,000
Baker, capital	14,000
	$47,000

The following adjustments were to be made prior to the exchange: decrease inventory to $4,000 and increase accumulated depreciation to $9,000. The partners shared profits and losses as follows: Allen, 55%; Baker, 45%.

Required:
Give entries to record the changes to the corporate form assuming the old books are to be continued (compute goodwill assuming the market value of the stock issued was $102 per share).

PROBLEMS

PART A: PROBLEMS 14–1 to 14–10

Problem 14–1

Using appropriate data from the information given below, prepare, in good form, the stockholders' equity section of a balance sheet for Reo Corporation.

Stock subscriptions receivable, preferred stock	$ 8,000
Reserve for bond sinking fund	43,000
Unrealized capital increment per appraisal of natural resources (discovery value)	45,000
Preferred stock, 6%, authorized 1,000 shares, par $100 per share, cumulative and fully participating	70,000
Bonds payable, 7%	125,000
Common stock, nopar, 5,000 shares authorized and outstanding	260,000
Donation of future plant site (to Reo)	6,000
Premium on preferred stock	14,000
Discount on bonds payable	1,000
Retained earnings, unappropriated	50,000
Preferred stock subscribed (to be issued upon collection in full)	10,000
Unrealized loss on long-term investments in equity securities	5,000

Problem 14–2

Vaught Corporation was granted a charter authorizing 10,000 shares of 6% preferred stock, par value $10 per share, and 50,000 shares of common stock, nopar value. No stated or assigned value was identified with the common stock. During the first year, the following transactions occurred:

a. 20,000 shares of common stock were sold for cash at $10 per share.
b. 1,000 shares of preferred stock were sold for cash at $25 per share.
c. Subscriptions were received for 1,000 shares of preferred stock at $25 per share; 20% was received as a down payment, and the balance was payable in two equal installments. The shares will be issued upon collection in full.
d. 5,000 shares of common stock, 500 shares of preferred stock, and $15,500 cash were given as payment for a small plant that the company needed. This plant originally cost $40,000 and had a depreciated value on the books of the selling company of $20,000. Assume the prior market price per share did not change.
e. The first installment on the preferred subscriptions was collected.

Required:
1. Give journal entries to record the above transactions. State and justify any assumptions you made.
2. Prepare the stockholders' equity section of the balance sheet at year-end. Retained earnings at the end of the

year amounted to $8,000. There was an $11,000 balance in the account, Unrealized Loss on Long-Term Investments in Equity Securities.

Problem 14–3

Waters Corporation's charter authorized 500,000 shares of $5 par value stock. B. Smith subscribed for 10,000 shares at $20 per share and paid a 40% cash down payment. The remaining 60% was payable in three equal semiannual amounts. After paying the first semiannual amount, Smith defaulted. The stock is issuable at date of full payment.

Required:

1. Give the entries to record *(a)* the subscription and *(b)* collection of the first semiannual amount.
2. Assumption A—Give the entries to record *(a)* the default by Smith and the issuance to Smith of shares equivalent to the cash paid by Smith, and *(b)* sale one month later of the remaining subscribed shares to another party for cash at $22 per share (the cost of reselling was 40 cents per share).
3. Assumption B—Give the entries to record *(a)* the default by Smith and *(b)* resale one month later under lien of all of the subscribed shares to another party for cash at $22 per share (the cost of reselling was 40 cents per share) including any cash refunded to Smith.

Problem 14–4

The charter for Stanton Corporation, to conduct a manufacturing business, authorized 300,000 shares of common stock, nopar value, and 50,000 shares of 6% preferred stock which is cumulative and nonparticipating with par value per share of $10. During the early part of the first year, the following transactions occurred:

a. Each of the six incorporators subscribed to 1,000 shares of the common at $15 per share and 500 shares of the preferred at $12 per share. Half the subscription price was paid, and half the subscribed shares issued.
b. Another individual purchased 500 shares of common and 100 shares of preferred stock paying $9,280 cash.
c. One of the incorporators purchased a used machine for $40,000 and immediately transferred it to the corporation for 2,000 shares of common stock, 200 shares of preferred stock, and a one-year, 15% interest-bearing note for $8,000.
d. The investors paid the subscriptions, and the remaining stock was issued.

Required:

1. Give all entries indicated for the Stanton Corporation.
2. Prepare the stockholders' equity section of the balance sheet. Assume retained earnings of $61,000 at year-end.

Problem 14–5

Union Corporation received a charter that authorized 100,000 shares of common stock. During the first year, the following transactions affecting stockholders' equity were completed:

a. Immediately after incorporation sold 60,000 shares at $25 per share for cash.
b. Near year-end received a subscription for 1,000 shares at $25 per share, collected 60% in cash, balance due in two equal installments within one year. The stock will be issued upon collection in full.
c. Near year-end issued 500 shares for a used machine that would be used in operations. The machine had cost $20,000 new and was carried by the seller at a book value of $11,000. It was appraised at $13,000 six months previously by a reputable independent appraiser.
d. Collected half of the unpaid subscriptions in *(b)*.

Required:

1. Give entries for each of the above transactions assuming: Case A—the stock has a par value of $10 per share; Case B—the stock is true nopar value; and Case C—the stock is nopar (however, it is assigned a stated value of $5 per share). Set up parallel amount columns for each case. State and justify any assumptions you make.
2. Prepare the stockholders' equity section of the balance sheet at the end of the first year for each case. Assume a balance in Retained Earnings of $135,000 at year-end.

Problem 14–6

The charter for Elam Corporation authorized 500,000 shares of common stock. During the first year of operations, the following transactions affected stockholders' equity:

a. Immediately after incorporation sold 400,000 shares of capital stock at $10 per share; collected cash.
b. Immediately after incorporation received a subscription for 10,000 shares of capital stock from one individual at $10 per share. Collected 40% of the subscription, and the balance is due at the end of one year. The shares will be issued upon collection in full.
c. Near year-end exchanged 6,000 shares of capital stock for a plant site. The site was carried on the books of the seller at $25,000, and it had been appraised within the past month at $65,000. The market value of the stock is $10 per share.
d. Collected $12,000 on the subscription in *(b)*.

Required:

1. Give entries for the above transactions assuming:

Case A—Par value stock; $2 par value per share.

Case B—True nopar value stock.

Case C—Nopar value stock with a stated value of $1 per share.

Set up parallel amount columns for each case. State and justify any assumptions you make.

2. Prepare the stockholders' equity section of the balance sheet at the end of the first year for each case. Assume a $93,000 ending balance in the Unappropriated Retained Earnings account, a reserve for bond sinking fund of $27,000, and unrealized loss on long-term equity investments of $11,000.

Problem 14–7

The charter of Holden Corporation authorized the issuance of 20,000 shares of 6% cumulative, nonparticipating preferred stock, par $10 per share, and 100,000 shares of common stock, nopar value. During the first year of operations, the following transactions affecting stockholders' equity were completed:

a. The promoters sold 9,000 shares of the preferred stock at $25 cash; the stock was issued.
b. Subscriptions were received for an additional 1,000 shares of preferred stock at $25 per share; 20% was collected, the balance is to be paid in four equal installments; the stock will be issued upon collection in full.
c. Each of the three promoters was issued 1,000 shares of common stock (only the common stock carried voting privileges) at $20 per share; each paid one fifth in cash. The remainder was considered to be reimbursement for promotional activities; the shares were issued. Debit Organization Expense.
d. An individual purchased 100 shares of preferred and 100 shares of common stock and paid a single sum of $4,400. The stock was issued. Assume a current market price of $25 for the preferred stock and that no current market value for the common was firmly established.
e. Collected cash from the subscribers ([*b*] above) for the first installment.
f. Issued 5,000 shares of common stock for a used plant. The plant had been appraised during the past month at $110,000 and was carried by the seller at a book value of $60,000.

Required:
1. Prepare journal entries to record the foregoing transactions. State and justify any assumptions you make.
2. Prepare the stockholders' equity section of the balance sheet assuming retained earnings at year-end of $22,000 and unrealized loss on long-term investment in equity securities of $6,200.

Problem 14–8

The stockholders' equity section of the balance sheet for the Star Corporation at the end of its first fiscal year was reported as follows:

Contributed capital:		
Capital stock:		
Preferred, 6%, cumulative, nonparticipating, $100 par value, redeemable at $125 per share, authorized 5,000 shares; issued and outstanding 4,185 shares	$ 418,500	
Preferred stock subscribed, 465 shares	46,500	$ 465,000
Common stock, stated value $8 per share authorized 1,500,000 shares; issued and outstanding 954,000 shares	7,632,000	
Common stock subscribed, 106,000 shares	848,000	8,480,000
Other contributed capital:		
In excess of par, pref.	15,000	
In excess of stated value, com.	21,200	36,200
Retained earnings		110,000
Total stockholders' equity.............		$9,091,200

Required:
Prepare journal entries during the first year as indicated by the above report. Use the memorandum approach to record the authorization and assume that all stock was purchased through subscriptions under terms of 30% cash down payment and 70% payable six months later. Also assume that of the 70%, all but 10% of the subscribers had paid in full by year-end. Shares are not issued until collection in full from the subscriber.

Problem 14–9

Zapata Corporation reported net income during five successive years as follows: $20,000; $30,000; $9,000; $5,000; and $480,000. The capital stock consisted of $300,000, $20 par value common, and $200,000, $10 par value 6% preferred.

Required:
For each separate case, prepare a tabulation showing the amount (and computations) each class of stock would receive in dividends (1) if the entire net income were distributed each year and (2) if 60% of each year's earnings were distributed that year.

Case A—Preferred stock is noncumulative and nonparticipating.

Case B—Preferred stock is cumulative and nonparticipating.

Case C—Preferred stock is cumulative and fully participating.

Problem 14–10

The charter for Ace Corporation authorized 5,000 shares of 6% preferred stock, par value $20 per share, and 8,000 shares of common stock, par value $50 per share. All of the authorized shares have been issued. In a five-year period, annual dividends paid were $4,000; $40,000; $32,000; $5,000; and $36,000, respectively.

Required:
Prepare a tabulation (including computations) of the amount of dividends that would be paid to each class of stock for each year under the following separate cases:

Case A—Preferred stock is noncumulative and nonparticipating.
Case B—Preferred stock is cumulative and nonparticipating.
Case C—Preferred stock is noncumulative and fully participating.
Case D—Preferred stock is cumulative and fully participating.
Case E—Preferred stock is cumulative and partially participating up to an additional 2%; assume the dividend for year 5 was $42,000 instead of $36,000.

PART B: PROBLEMS 14–11 to 14–15

Problem 14–11

Roll Corporation is authorized to issue 100,000 shares of common stock, par $25, of which 60,000 are outstanding. During 19x1, the company initiated a stock bonus plan for certain executives. The plan provides for each qualified executive to receive an option for 1,000 shares of the common stock. Subject to continued employment, the option is exercisable at any time after three years and prior to expiration, which is five years from the date of grant. The option is nontransferable, and the specified option price is $60 per share. The option is considered to be additional compensation, prorated equally, for the year of the grant and the following four years. On January 1, 19x1, J. Doe, the company president, was granted an option under the plan when the market price of the stock was $71. Assume Doe exercised the grant during the latter part of 19x5 when the market price of the stock was $90 per share.

Required:
1. Is this a compensatory plan? Explain.
2. What is the measurement date? Explain.
3. What is the amount of the total compensation to Doe?
4. Over what period should Doe's compensation be assigned as expense? How much should be assigned to 19x1? to 19x2? Explain.
5. Give appropriate entries on the following dates for Doe's option (if none, explain why):
   a. Date of grant.
   b. Measurement date.
   c. End of each year, starting on December 31, 19x1.
   d. Exercise date.
6. Illustrate how Doe's option would affect the income statements and balance sheets at the end of 19x1 and 19x2.

Problem 14–12

Jackson Corporation has a stock option plan for the top managers that includes the following provisions:

a. Each manager that qualifies will receive an option to acquire 10,000 shares of Jackson common stock, par $2, at an option price of $12 per share.
b. The option is nontransferable and, if not exercised, expires after five years from date of grant.
c. The option cannot be exercised prior to the end of two years from date of grant and requires continued employment in the company.
d. The stock option is for additional compensation for the year of the grant and the following four years; approximately equal each year.

An option was granted to the president on January 1, 19x1, at which time the common stock was selling at $17 per share. Assume the option is exercised on December 31, 19x5, when the stock is quoted at $35 per share.

At January 1, 19x1, common stock, par $2 (authorized 200,000 shares), 90,000 were outstanding.

Required:
1. Is this a compensatory plan? Explain.
2. What is the measurement date? Explain.
3. Compute the total compensation expense for one grantee.
4. Over what period of time should this total compensation be assigned as expense? Explain.
5. For one grantee, give appropriate entries for the following dates (if none, explain why):
   a. Date of grant.
   b. Measurement date.
   c. End of each year, starting on December 31, 19x1.
   d. Exercise date.
6. For one grantee, illustrate how the option would affect the income statements and balance sheets at the end of 19x1 and 19x2.

Problem 14–13

Manford Corporation has 100,000 shares of common stock, par $20, authorized, of which 40,000 shares are outstanding. The company has a stock option plan that provides the following:

a. Each qualified manager shall receive on January 1, a computed number of shares of common stock at a computed option price per share. The computation of each amount shall be made three years after the option is granted and will be related to the increase in net income over the three-year period. The plan provides additional compensation for qualified managers for services to be performed approximately equally during the years 19x1–x5.
b. The options are nontransferable and must be exercised

not earlier than three years and not later than five years from date of grant. Affiliation with the company is required through the exercise date.

On January 1, 19x1, an option was granted to J. Dean, the controller. At that date, the common stock was quoted on the market at $50 per share. Assume Dean exercised the option near the end of 19x5.

	Estimates Made 12/31/x1 of What Amount Would Be 12/31/x3*	Actual Amount on 12/31/x3
Number of shares optioned	500	510
Option price	$60	$62
Market price per share	$67†	$71

* Estimate at 12/31/x2 same as estimate at 12/31/x1.
† Estimate of future market price based on actual current market price on 12/31/x1.

Required:
1. Is this a compensatory plan? Explain.
2. When is the measurement date? Explain.
3. Over what period should total compensation expense for Dean be assigned?
4. Give appropriate entries (related to Dean) for the following dates (if none, explain why):
   a. Date of grant.
   b. End of 19x1 and 19x2.
   c. Measurement date.
   d. End of 19x3, 19x4, and 19x5.
   e. Exercise date.
5. Show how Dean's option would affect the income statements and balance sheets for 19x2 and 19x3.

Problem 14–14

Huber Corporation is authorized to issue 200,000 shares of common stock, par $10; to date, 75,000 shares have been issued. On January 1, 19x2, the corporation initiated a stock option plan for the three top managers. The plan provides that each manager will receive an option to purchase, no later than December 31, 19x6, 2,000 shares of the common stock at a base option price of $48, adjusted for changes in earnings per share (EPS), and providing continued employment. The option price is to be established on December 31, 19x4, and will be based on changes in EPS. EPS for 19x1 was $2. The option price will be established at the end of 19x4 as follows:

> The option price per share will be the basic option price of $48 adjusted proportionately upward or downward in inverse relationship to changes in EPS from December 31, 19x1, through 19x4.

The options are nontransferable and expire on December 31, 19x6. The stock was quoted at $45 per share on the market on January 1, 19x2. On December 31, 19x2, the management has made what they consider to be realistic estimates that EPS would increase steadily to $3.20 at December 31, 19x4, and that the stock price would be $46 per share on that date; this latter estimate was based upon the actual market price of the stock on December 31, 19x2, which was $46. These estimates were not revised in 19x3 because the actual market price of the stock was $46 on December 31, 19x3, and EPS expectations remained the same. EPS on December 31, 19x4, actually turned out to be $3, and the actual market price of the stock was $47.

The president received the options with the option price unknown at January 1, 19x2. Assume the president exercised the option, the last day possible, on December 31, 19x6.

Required:
1. Is this a compensatory plan? Explain.
2. What is the measurement date? Explain.
3. Over what period should total compensation expense for the president be assigned?
4. Give appropriate entries (related to the president) on the following dates (if none, explain why):
   a. Date of grant.
   b. End of 19x2 and 19x3.
   c. Measurement date.
   d. End of 19x4, 19x5, and 19x6.
   e. Exercise date.
5. Show how the president's option would affect the income statements and balance sheets for 19x3 and 19x4.

Problem 14–15

On January 1, 19A, the board of directors of Mini Motors, Inc., approved two stock purchase plans with respect to its common stock, par $10. The specifications of each plan were as follows:

Plan	Employees Eligible	Discount from Market Price	Date Number of Shares and Option Price Determined	Exercise Period
No. 1 . .	Executives	20%—minimum option price of $28.	12/31/19B	On Jan. 2 and June 2 of 19E
No. 2 . .	All hourly employees	4%	Jan. 2 of each year 19A–19E	Jan. 2 of each year 19A–19E

Under plan no. 1 employees will earn the options evenly over 19A–19D. Plan no. 1 options expire on June 3, 19E.

During the years 19A–19E, Mini Motors Company completed the following transactions relating to the two plans (the accounting fiscal year ends December 31):

January 2, 19A:
 Plan no. 1—granted an option for 1,000 shares to each of five executives.

Plan no. 2—granted an option for 50 shares to each of the 150 employees.
Quoted price of the stock, $30 per share.

December 31, 19A:
Quoted price of the stock, $37 per share.
Estimated market price expected to be $37 per share on December 31, 19B.

December 31, 19B:
Quoted market price, $40 per share.

January 2, 19C:
Plan no. 2—issued 7,500 shares based on the quoted market price of $40 per share.

January 2, 19E:
Plan no. 1—issued 1,500 shares.
Quoted market price of the stock, $44 per share.

June 2, 19E:
Plan no. 1—issued 3,400 shares.
Quoted market price of the stock, $45 per share.

June 3, 19E:
All plan no. 1 outstanding options lapse.

Required:

1. Is each plan compensatory or noncompensatory? Explain. When is the measurement date?
2. Give the required journal entries to record all transactions listed for—
   a. Plan no. 1.
   b. Plan no. 2.

SUPPLEMENT 14-A: PROBLEMS 14–16 to 14–17

Problem 14–16

BC Corporation was authorized 5,000 shares of capital stock, par $50 per share. The shares were issued as follows:

a. 4,000 shares sold for cash at $105 per share.
b. 1,000 shares for the owners' equity of the BC Partnership, which reported the following balance sheet at "appraised market value."

Accounts receivable (net)	$ 13,000
Inventory	20,000
Operational assets (net)	67,000
	$100,000
Notes payable	$ 20,000
B, capital	40,000
C, capital	40,000
	$100,000

Required:

1. Give the required entries on the books of BC Partnership to reflect the recognition of goodwill (based on $105 per share) and to close out the partnership books. Assume the partners shared profits equally.
2. Give all entries required on the books of BC Corporation from organization through acquisition of BC Partnership.
3. Prepare an unclassified balance sheet for BC Corporation immediately after recording the acquisition of BC Partnership.

Problem 14–17

Consolidated Corporation was organized to take over the partnership of L and M. The charter authorized 10,000 shares of capital stock, par value $100 per share. The balance sheet as of June 30, 19X, for L and M was as follows (at book value):

L AND M PARTNERSHIP
Assets

Cash	$ 10,000
Accounts receivable	13,000
Allowance for doubtful accounts	(1,000)
Prepaid expenses	1,000
Buildings	90,000
Accumulated depreciation	(20,000)
Equipment	60,000
Accumulated depreciation	(30,000)
Land	10,000
	$133,000

Liabilities and Owners' Equity

Accounts payable	$ 29,000
Accrued expenses payable	4,000
L, capital	60,000
M, capital	40,000
	$133,000

The partnership profits and losses were divided 65% to L and 35% to M. Incorporators were L, M, N, O, and P. The latter three purchased 2,000 shares each at $102. According to the agreement, 1,500 shares will be issued to L and M in the ratio of their capital balances at the end in payment for the business (including the liabilities). Prior to dissolution, the $10,000 cash on hand will be distributed to L and M based on their capital ratios prior to adjustment. The following adjustments, based on appraised market values prior to the exchange, were agreed upon:

Allowance for doubtful accounts increased to $3,000.

Accumulated depreciation, buildings decreased to $7,000.
Land revalued to $20,000.

Goodwill recognition based on the "appraised market values" and $102 per share for the capital stock.

Required:

1. Prepare entries for Consolidated Corporation assuming the old partnership books are to be continued and used by the corporation. The partnership will go out of existence.
2. Prepare an unclassified balance sheet immediately after the above entries.

15

Corporations—Retained Earnings and Changes in Stockholders' Equity after Formation

CHAPTER 14 identified the three major categories of corporate capital: contributed capital; retained earnings; and unrealized capital. Contributed capital and unrealized capital were discussed in Chapter 14. This chapter discusses **retained earnings**, dividends, and contraction and expansion of corporate capital after formation. It is subdivided as follows:

Part A—Retained Earnings and Dividends

Part B—Contraction and Expansion of Corporate Capital after Formation

Supplement 15–A—Quasi-Reorganizations

Part A: Retained Earnings and Dividends

CHARACTERISTICS OF RETAINED EARNINGS

Retained earnings represent accumulated net income (or net loss), gains and losses, and prior period adjustments of a corporation, less its cash and property dividends, and stock dividends. If the accumulated losses and distributions of retained earnings exceed the accumulated gains, there will be a **deficit** (i.e., a debit balance) in retained earnings.

Some variation in terminology with respect to retained earnings exists in practice. The term **earned surplus** once was commonly used to denote what was defined above as retained earnings. More descriptive terminology is needed to provide statement users with a clear description of the nature of each item reported. Also, the older term is a misnomer because no "surplus" exists. As explained in Chapter 14, a distinction is maintained between contributed capital and retained earnings to delineate the sources of a corporation's capital.

Total retained earnings may include two categories: appropriated retained earnings and unappropriated retained earnings. The Retained Earnings account (if not designated otherwise) represents the **unappropriated** portion of retained earnings (i.e., it has not been set aside or appropriated for specific purposes). The second category, **appropriated** retained earnings, may include specially designated amounts, which may be reflected in separate accounts, such as Retained Earnings Appropriated for Bond Sinking Fund and Retained Earnings Appropriated for the Cost of Treasury Stock. This category is discussed in a subsequent section.

The **usual** debits and credits to the Retained Earnings account are as follows:

Retained Earnings

Debits	Credits
Net loss (incl. extraordinary gains and losses)	Net income (incl. extraordinary gains and losses)
Prior period adjustments	Prior period adjustments
Cash dividends	
Stock dividends	

Observe that no **credits** occur as a result of the sale, issuance, purchase, or exchange of the corporation's own capital stock. Such credits are accounted for as elements of contributed capital. In certain circumstances, **debits** to Retained Earnings may occur as a result of treasury stock and stock retirement transactions, as discussed in Part B.

EFFECT OF DIVIDENDS ON THE CORPORATION

Dividends consist of distributions to the corporation's stockholders in proportion to the number of shares of stock held. The term **dividends** used alone usually refers to cash dividends. When dividends are in a form other than cash, they should be labeled according to what is distributed. The following types of dividends are encountered with some frequency:

1. Cash dividends.
2. Property dividends.
3. Liability (scrip) dividends.
4. Liquidating dividends.
5. Stock dividends.

Distributions to stockholders may involve—

1. The distribution of corporate **assets** and a decrease in **total** owners' equity, as in the case of cash, property, or liquidating dividends.
2. The creation of a **liability** and a decrease in **total** owners' equity, as in the case of liability dividends or a cash dividend declared but not yet paid.
3. No change in assets, liabilities, or **total** owners' equity, but only a change in the **internal categories of owners' equity**, as in the case of a stock dividend.

A question arises on the "use" of retained earnings for dividends. Dividends are not **paid** with retained earnings but with cash or some other asset (except in the case of a stock dividend). More specifically, dividends generally reduce **both** retained earnings and assets. Cash or property dividends cannot be paid without this dual effect.

Elements of corporate capital other than retained earnings may be decreased by a dividend declaration. The laws of all states allow retained earnings to be used as a basis for all dividends, although some states place restrictions even here, such as a provision that dividends in any one year may not exceed the earnings of the preceding year. Some states permit debits to certain contributed capital accounts, such as contributed capital in excess of par, as a basis for cash dividends, providing creditor interests are not jeopardized.[1] Generally, statutes are more liberal with respect to stock dividends because no assets are distributed in this case. The statutes of the particular state are controlling; however, in the absence of any statement or information to the contrary, one should assume a debit to Retained Earnings when dividends are recorded.

Relevant Dates in Accounting for Dividends

Four dates are important in accounting for dividends: (1) date of declaration, (2) date of record, (3) ex-dividend date, and (4) date of payment. Prior to payment, dividends must be formally **declared** by the board of directors of the corporation. Stockholders normally cannot force a dividend declaration; the courts consistently have held that dividend declaration is a matter of discretion of the duly elected board of directors. In deciding whether to declare a dividend (and of what type), the board of directors should consider the financial impact of the dividend on the company, the adequacy of cash and retained earnings, expectations for the future, and corporate growth and expansion needs.

On the **date of declaration,** the board formally announces the dividend declaration. In the case of a cash or property dividend, the declaration is recorded on this date as a debit to Retained Earnings

[1] A liquidating dividend may be involved; see subsequent section on liquidating dividends.

and a credit to Dividends Payable. In the absence of fraud or illegality, the courts have held that formal declaration of a cash, property, or liability dividend constitutes an enforceable contract between the corporation and the shareholders. In view of the irrevocability of this action, on dividend declaration date such dividends are recorded and a liability (i.e., dividends payable) is recognized. In the case of **stock dividends,** no corporate assets are involved, directly or indirectly; therefore, the courts generally have held that a stock dividend declaration is revocable up to the date of issuance. Consequently, no entry is required on declaration date; however, many accountants prefer to make an entry on declaration date to recognize the intention to issue additional stock (i.e., credit Stock Dividends Issuable, which is reported as an item under stockholders' equity).[2]

The **date of record** is selected by the board and stated in the declaration; usually it follows the declaration date by two to three weeks. The date of record is the date on which the list of **stockholders of record** is prepared. Individuals holding stock at this date, as shown in the corporate stockholders' record, receive the dividend, regardless of sales or purchases of stock after this date. No dividend entry is made in the accounts on this date.

Technically, the **ex-dividend date** is the day after the date of record. However, to provide time for transfer of the stock, the stock exchanges advance the effective ex-dividend date by three or four days. Thus, one who holds the stock on the day prior to the stipulated ex-dividend date receives the **dividend.** Between the declaration date and the ex-dividend date, the **market price** of the stock includes the dividend. On the stipulated ex-dividend date, the price of the stock drops because the recipient of the dividend already has been identified, and succeeding owners of the stock will not receive that particular dividend. Thus, dividend revenue is earned on the **declaration date** and not on the date of record, the ex-dividend date, or the date of payment.

The **date of payment** also is determined by the board of directors, and usually is stated in the declaration; the date of payment usually follows the declaration by four to six weeks. At the date of payment of cash or property dividends, the liability recorded at date of declaration is debited and the appropriate asset account is credited. A stock dividend distribution usually is recorded only on the date of its issuance as illustrated in a subsequent section.

Dividends on par value stock may be stated as a certain percent of the par value, but dividends on nopar stock must be stated as a dollar amount per share.

[2] See subsequent section on stock dividends. Also, in the case of cash dividends, if the declaration date and payment date are in the same accounting period, there would be no compelling reason to make an entry in the accounts on the declaration date.

TYPES OF DIVIDENDS

Cash Dividends

Cash dividends are the usual form of distributions to stockholders. The declaration must meet the preferences of the preferred stock and then may extend to the common stock (as discussed and illustrated in Chapter 14).

To illustrate a cash dividend, assume the following announcement is made: The board of directors of Bass Company, at their meeting on January 20, 19A, declared a dividend of 50 cents per share, payable March 20, 19A, to shareholders of record on March 1, 19A. Assume further that 10,000 shares of nopar capital stock are outstanding.

At date of declaration (January 20, 19A):

Retained earnings (10,000 shares × $0.50) .	5,000	
Cash dividends payable		5,000

At date of record (March 1, 19A):

No entry. The list of dividend recipients is prepared.

At date of payment (March 20, 19A):

Cash dividends payable	5,000	
Cash		5,000

Cash Dividends Payable is reported on the balance sheet as a current liability if the duration of the dividend liability is short term.

Property Dividends

Corporations occasionally pay dividends in assets other than cash. Such dividends are known as **property dividends.** The property may be securities of other companies held by the corporation, real estate, merchandise, or any other asset designated by the board of directors. Noncash assets transferred as a property dividend are valued at their market value for recording the dividend. The market value at the declaration date is used because, as in the case of a cash dividend, on the declaration date the corporation gives up (i.e., foregoes by implicit contract) all alternative uses of the assets to be distributed. Subsequent market price changes (upward or downward) accrue to the shareholder (recipient of the asset), and hence are ignored by the corporation.

A property dividend should be recorded at the current market value of the assets transferred according to *APB Opinion No. 29,* "Accounting for Nonmonetary Transactions." Therefore, when the corporation's book value of the property to be distributed in the dividend is different from its market value on the declaration date, the corporation should recognize a gain or loss on disposal of the asset as of the declaration date. Most property dividends are paid with the securities of other companies which the dividend issuing corporation has held as an investment. Among other advantages, this kind of "property" avoids the problem of indivisibility of units that would occur with most assets other than cash.

The following excerpt from *The Wall Street Journal* (May 18, 1981, p. 28) illustrates a property dividend:

> Oakwood Petroleums Ltd. has set a date of June 1 to pay holders of record May 22 a previously proposed special dividend in the form of shares of its affiliate American Oakwood Energy Ltd. As previously reported, common shareholders will receive one share of American Oakwood for each five shares of Oakwood Petroleums.

Assuming Oakwood Petroleums *(a)* had 5,000 shares of its own common shares outstanding, *(b)* had paid $100 for each share of American Oakwood Energy it held as an investment (1,000 shares), *(c)* carried the investment shares at cost (i.e., $100,000), and *(d)* the market value of each American Oakwood Energy share was $150 on declaration date, the dividend transactions of Oakwood Petroleums would be recorded as follows:

At declaration date:

Investment in stock of American Oakwood Energy [1,000 shares × ($150 − $100)]	50,000	
Gain on disposal of investment		50,000
Retained earnings (1,000 shares × $150)	150,000	
Property dividend payable		150,000

At payment date:

Property dividend payable	150,000	
Investment in stock of American Oakwood Energy		150,000

Liability Dividends

Strictly speaking, any dividend involving the distribution of assets is a liability dividend **between** the declaration date and the date of payment. Nevertheless, a **liability** or **scrip dividend** is a special category of dividend which refers to instances in which the board of directors declares a dividend and issues promissory notes, bonds, or scrip (similar to a note payable) to the stockholders. In essence, this type of declaration means that a comparatively long time will lapse between the declaration and payment dates. In most cases, scrip dividends are declared when a corporation has sufficient retained earnings to serve as a basis for dividends but is short of cash. A stockholder may hold the scrip until due date and collect the dividend, or in some cases a stockholder may be able to discount the scrip to obtain immediate cash. When notes are involved, the due date and rate of interest are specified. Scrip often is interest bearing and usually is payable at a specified future date. The immediate effect of a scrip or liability dividend is a debit to Retained Earnings and a credit to a liability account such as Scrip Dividends Payable or Notes Payable to Stockholders. Upon payment, Cash is credited and the liability account debited. Because interest paid on a liability dividend is not a part of the dividend, any interest payments should be debited to Interest Expense rather than directly to Retained Earnings as a part of the dividend. In other respects, accounting for a liability dividend is like that for a cash dividend.

Liquidating Dividends

Distributions that constitute a **return of contributed capital** rather than earnings are known as liquidating dividends, and owners' equity accounts other than Retained Earnings are debited. Liquidating dividends may be either intentional or unintentional. **Intentional** liquidating dividends occur when the board of directors knowingly declares dividends which will, in effect, represent a return of investment to the shareholders, as in the case when a corporation is reducing permanent capital.

Mining companies sometimes pay dividends on the basis of earnings computed prior to deduction of depletion, which would be an intentional liquidating dividend equal to the amount of depletion. A mining company might pay such a liquidating dividend when it is exploiting a nonreplaceable asset which becomes terminal when exhausted. Stockholders should be informed of the portion of any dividend that represents a return of capital. Such dividends are not income and, hence, usually are not taxable to shareholders as income but serve to reduce the cost basis of their stock investment.

In accounting for liquidating dividends, Contributed Capital rather than Retained Earnings is debited because a portion of contributed capital is returned. Rather than debiting the capital stock accounts, as would be done if shares were being retired, other contributed capital accounts such as the "in excess of par" accounts may be debited. In some cases it may be desirable to set up a special account, Capital Repayment, which would be treated as a deduction (contra account) in the contributed capital section of the balance sheet.

Unintentional liquidating dividends may occur when income, and, hence, retained earnings, are overstated because of errors or inappropriate accounting. For example, any error that overstated revenue or understated expense would cause retained earnings to be overstated. In such cases, if reported retained earnings (prior to correction) were used in full for dividends, part of the dividend would be a liquidating dividend. Unintentional liquidating dividends also occur when corporations pay cash (or property) dividends in excess of their income adjusted for **price changes.** This occurs when historical cost amounts for expenses are matched against current revenue. The resultant historical cost income exceeds **current cost basis income,** in which expenses are based upon the current cost of assets used up in the revenue process. Companies seldom pay dividends in excess of their **historical cost** (HC) income, but it is not uncommon for a company's dividends to exceed its current cost basis income.[3] This topic is discussed in Chapter 24.

[3] For discussion of actual situations in which such liquidating dividends have occurred, see "Living Off Capital," *Forbes*, November 10, 1980, pp. 230–36. On the other hand, Modigliani and Cohen argue that this effect is mitigated by the purchasing power gains of companies with liabilities during periods of inflation. See F. Modigliani and R. A. Cohen, "Inflation, Rational Valuation, and the Market," *Financial Analysts Journal*, March/April 1979, pp. 24–44.

Stock Dividends

A stock dividend is a distribution to stockholders of **additional shares of stock** of the corporation. A common stock dividend does not change the assets, liabilities, or total stockholders' equity of the issuing corporation, nor does it change the proportionate ownership of any common stockholder. Rather, it causes the transfer of an amount from Retained Earnings to the permanent capital accounts (i.e., capital stock and contributed capital in excess of par); therefore, it only changes the "internal content" of stockholders' equity between contributed capital and retained earnings.[4]

A stock dividend may be issued from treasury stock or unissued stock, and common or preferred shares may be issued. When the stock dividend is of the same class as that held by the recipients, it is called an **ordinary** stock dividend. When a different class of stock is issued, it is called a **special** stock dividend (e.g., preferred shares issued to the common shareholders). It was noted in a preceding section that state laws vary as to the availability of various classes of stockholders' equity for stock dividends. Some states permit the use of certain **contributed** capital accounts, such as Contributed Capital in Excess of Par and even Unrealized Capital. All states permit retained earnings to be used as a basis for stock dividends.

In the absence of information to the contrary, it should be assumed that the debit is to Retained Earnings. The credit always is to the respective contributed capital accounts for the particular shares issued.

Numerous reasons exist for a company to issue a stock dividend, such as the following:

1. To permanently retain income in the business by **capitalizing** a portion of the retained earnings. The effect of a stock dividend, through a debit to Retained Earnings and offsetting credits to permanent capital accounts, is to raise the contributed (and legal) capital and thereby "shelter" the new legal capital from declaration of cash or property dividends.
2. To continue dividends without distributing assets (usually cash), that may be needed for operations. This action may be motivated by a desire to pacify stockholders; they may be willing to

[4] When Contributed Capital (instead of Retained Earnings) is debited for a stock dividend, this effect would not occur.

accept a stock dividend representing accumulated earnings because the additional shares received can be sold for cash. Ordinary stock dividends are not subject to income tax to shareholders; they serve instead to reduce the investment cost per share to the investor.

3. To increase the number of shares outstanding, which reduces the market price per share and which in turn is reputed to increase trading of the shares in the market.

Stock Dividend and Stock Split Compared. From an accounting perspective, it is important to distinguish between a stock dividend and a stock split. Both *(a)* increase total shares outstanding and *(b)* do not change total stockholders' equity. In contrast, their basic difference is that they produce different amounts of contributed capital and retained earnings.

A **stock dividend** does not involve the distribution of assets or the creation of a liability. It does not change **total** corporate capital. Usually, the only effect of a stock dividend on the issuing corporation's balance sheet is a transfer of part of the retained earnings to contributed capital and an increase in the number of shares outstanding. A stock dividend does not affect the par value per share, nor does it affect the assets, liabilities, or total capital. Instead a stock dividend only affects the **internal** content of stockholders' equity. The following excerpt from *The Wall Street Journal* (May 22, 1981, p. 17) illustrates the announcement of a stock dividend:

> Sonesta International Hotels Corp. declared a . . . stock dividend of two additional shares of common for every share issued and outstanding. The new shares will carry the same 80 cents a share par value as existing stock. [The] dividends are payable July 6 to stock of record June 15.

In contrast to a stock dividend, a **stock split** increases the number of shares and at the same time it involves a **pro rata reduction in the par value per share.** A stock split is accomplished by replacing the old shares with a greater number of new shares having a lower par value per share; total par value outstanding remains the same after a stock split. A stock split does not cause a transfer of retained earnings to contributed capital; thus, neither contributed capital nor retained earnings is changed. A **reverse** stock split decreases the number of shares and involves a pro rata increase in par value per share. In the case of a stock split, the number of shares, but not the dollar amount of **contributed capital,** is changed. In contrast, in a stock dividend, the dollar amount of contributed capital is changed. The following announcement from *The Wall Street Journal* (May 21, 1981, p. 32) illustrates a stock split:

> Superior Oil Co. holders approved an amendment in the charter to effect a five-for-one stock split, payable July 10 to stock of record June 19.[5]

To illustrate the different effects of a stock dividend and a stock split, assume X Corporation is authorized to issue 40,000 shares of common stock, par $100, of which 10,000 shares were issued initially at par, and retained earnings has a current balance of $1,600,000. The different effects of a 100 percent stock dividend and a two-for-one stock split may be contrasted as shown below:

[5] Presumably, Superior Oil Company reduced the par value of each share of its stock to one fifth of the prior par value.

X Corporation

	Prior to Dividend or Split	After: Stock Dividend	After: Stock Split
Stock outstanding:			
10,000 shares, par $100	$1,000,000		
20,000 shares, par $100		$2,000,000	
20,000 shares, par $50			$1,000,000
Retained earnings	1,600,000	600,000	1,600,000
Total stockholders' equity	$2,600,000	$2,600,000	$2,600,000

Amount of Retained Earnings Capitalized for a Stock Dividend. Because a stock dividend capitalizes retained earnings, the question arises as to the amount of retained earnings to capitalize (i.e., transfer to contributed capital) for the additional shares issued. The **statutory minimum** in most states is par or stated value.[6] In the case of preferred stock it may be either par value or the liquidating value. However, the amount transferred from retained earnings to contributed capital need not be limited to the statutory minimum. GAAP reflects a definite position on this issue. Two distinct situations affecting the amount to be capitalized are as follows:

Situation 1—A small stock dividend: When the proportion of the additional shares issued is **small** in relation to the total shares **previously outstanding,** the **current market value** of the additional shares should be capitalized. The Committee on Accounting Procedure of the AICPA stated:

> . . . many recipients of stock dividends look upon them as distributions of corporate earnings and usually in an amount equivalent to the [market] value of the additional shares received. Furthermore, it is to be presumed that such views of recipients are materially strengthened in those instances, which are by far the most numerous, where the issuances are so small in comparison with the shares previously outstanding that they do not have any apparent effect upon the share market price and, consequently, the market value of the shares previously held remains substantially unchanged. The committee therefore believes that where these circumstances exist the corporation should in the public interest account for the transaction by transferring from [retained earnings] to the category of permanent capitalization . . . an amount equal to the [market] value of the additional shares issued [i.e., the market value immediately after issuance].[7]

Use of **market value immediately after issuance** is further buttressed by the fact that the market price per share, in the case of a small stock dividend, may not drop proportionately to the increased number of shares outstanding after the dividend. When market price per share does not drop proportionately, the shareholders receive a real value increase in their holdings.

Situation 2—A large stock dividend:[8] When the proportion of the additional shares issued is **large** in relation to the total shares previously outstanding, no less than the legal minimum (generally par value) should be capitalized, as the Committee stated:

> Where the number of additional shares issued as a stock dividend is so great that it has, or may reasonably be expected to have, the effect of materially reducing the share market value, the committee believes that the implications and possible constructions discussed in the [above quotation] are not likely to exist. . . . Consequently, the committee considers that under such circumstances there is no need to capitalize [retained earnings], other than to the extent occasioned by legal requirements.[9]

The dividing line between the two situations described above (a small versus a large stock dividend) is very difficult to draw. The economic basis for the distinction between small and large stock dividends is the behavior of the per share stock price rather than the proportion of new to old shares. The market price per share will depend upon a number of factors, such as the economic characteristics of the company and the condition of the economy in general. In this setting, stock dividends can serve as "signals" about the economic characteristics of companies issuing stock dividends. For instance, a stock dividend effectively is an increase in the cash dividend rate if the issuing corporation regularly pays cash dividends and does not decrease the per share cash dividend concurrently with the stock dividend. The following announcement in *The Wall Street Journal* (May 13, 1981, p. 33) is an example of such a stock dividend:

> Avnet Inc. declared a 10% stock dividend and the usual quarterly of 25 cents on stock prior to the

[6] In the case of **true** nopar stock, usually the amount capitalized is the current market value.

[7] AICPA, *Accounting Research Bulletin No. 43,* "Restatement and Revision of Accounting Research Bulletins" (New York, 1961), chap. 7, sec. B, par. 10.

[8] The financial press, as well as *ARB 43,* often refers to "large" stock dividends as stock "splits," or "split-ups," and to "small" stock dividends simply as stock dividends. Their distinction between these two categories concerns the perceived effect of the issuance of new shares on the market price of the stock. From an accounting perspective, the essential difference between stock dividends and stock splits is whether the issuing corporation makes an entry to capitalize retained earnings. This capitalization occurs for stock dividends, but not for stock splits, as we use these terms in this book. For this reason, we distinguish between the two categories on the accounting basis.

[9] *ARB 43,* chap. 7, sec. B, par. 10.

stock dividend. Both are payable July 1 to stock of record June 5.

Increases in the cash dividend rate are believed to be "good signals" about corporations because they evidence the willingness of management to commit the corporation to a higher dividend payout (companies are reluctant to decrease their cash dividend rates).[10]

Apparently, the Committee on Accounting Procedures believed good "signals" (i.e., those signals which keep stock prices from adjusting down proportionately for the number of new shares issued) occur more often with **small** stock dividends than with **large** stock dividends. In considering this problem, the Committee identified "small" stock dividends as those stock dividends involving less than 20 percent or 25 percent of the number of shares previously outstanding.[11]

In the case of **special** stock dividends, such as a stock dividend in preferred stock issued to common shareholders, the market value of the dividend (i.e., the preferred) shares should be capitalized by the issuing corporation because issuance of the dividend shares usually would not be expected to have much impact on the market value of the other (i.e., the common) stock. In this instance, shareholders would appear to receive a dividend equal to the market value of the dividend shares received.

[10] This issue was examined by E. F. Fama, L. Fisher, M. C. Jemsen, and R. Roll, "The Adjustment of Stock Prices to New Information," *International Economic Review,* February 1969, pp. 1–21. For an extended discussion of corporate signaling, see N. J. Gonedes, "Corporate Signaling, External Accounting and Capital Market Equilibrium: Evidence on Dividends, Income, and Extraordinary Items," *Journal of Accounting Research,* Spring 1978, pp. 26–79.

[11] A counter-example is provided by the 33⅓ percent stock dividend of Service Corporation International, in which the company announced its intention to maintain the quarterly cash dividend rate of 11 cents per share after the stock dividend (see *The Wall Street Journal,* May 18, 1981, p. 28). This "large" stock dividend could be expected to provide "good news" to investors inasmuch as it effectively increased the cash dividend rate by 33⅓ percent. Hence, the stock price could be expected to react to this "large" stock dividend as though it were a "small" stock dividend.

Empirical research has been conducted to determine whether stock prices decrease proportionately for "large," but not for "small," stock dividends. Chottiner and Young found that stock "prices on the ex [dividend] date fully adjusted [downward] in the case of distributions of 4–20 percent, and did not fully adjust for distributions of 0–3 percent and 25–200 percent." They concluded that the evidence was not consistent with the 20–25 percent guideline of GAAP. See S. Chottiner and A. Young, "A Test of the AICPA Differentiation between Stock Dividends and Stock Splits," *Journal of Accounting Research,* Autumn 1971, pp. 367–74.

DIVIDEND DECLARATION AND PAYMENT ILLUSTRATED

Exhibit 15–1 illustrates accounting for four situations involving stock dividends. Panel A of the exhibit presents the illustrative data, and Panel B presents the entry to record issuance of the dividend shares. No entry is required at date of declaration because the declaration of a stock dividend is revocable, and it makes no claim on assets (hence, does not create a liability).[12]

When a balance sheet is prepared between the dates of declaration and distribution of a stock dividend, the dividend may be reported in a note in the financial statements.[13] For example, in their 1979 annual report, Crown Central Petroleum Corporation disclosed the following in Note H to their December 31, 1979, balance sheet:

> [Six percent] stock dividends were declared on the Class A and Class B Common Stocks payable on February 7, 1980, to holders of record on January 25, 1980, pursuant to which 242,094 shares of Class A Common Stock and 60,642 shares of Class B Common Stock were issued.

To conclude the discussion of **stock dividends,** we reemphasize that an important aspect of such dividends is that a part of the retained earnings often is transferred to **permanent** capital (i.e., "capitalized"). This transfer reflects that the company has "grown through earnings" by permanently removing such earnings from dividend availability. For many corporations a significant amount of their contributed

[12] Some accountants make an entry on declaration date and another entry on issue date by using a temporary contributed capital account entitled Stock Dividend Distributable. The two entries would be as follows:

Declaration date:

Retained earnings	xx	
Stock dividends distributable (at par value, an element of stockholders' equity)		xx
Contributed capital in excess of par, common stock		xx

Issuance date:

Stock dividends distributable	xx	
Common stock		xx

[13] Alternatively, if the company makes a journal entry at declaration date, debiting Retained Earnings and crediting Stock Dividends Distributable, as shown in footnote 12, the stock dividend is reported via the Stock Dividend Distributable account in the stockholders' equity section of the balance sheet rather than as a liability. This event may be supplemented by a note.

EXHIBIT 15–1: Stock Dividend Entries—Z Corporation

Panel A—Illustrative Data Prior to the Dividend:

Preferred stock, par value $20, 10,000 shares authorized, 5,000 shares outstanding		$100,000
Common stock, par value $10, 20,000 shares authorized, 10,000 shares outstanding		100,000
Contributed capital in excess of par, preferred stock		10,000
Contributed capital in excess of par, common stock		15,000
Retained earnings		150,000
Total stockholders' equity		$375,000
Market price per share immediately before issuance of dividend shares:		
Preferred	$25	
Common	24	

Panel B—Stock Dividend Entry at Date of Issuance of Dividend Shares:

Situation 1—A small stock dividend: A 10 percent common stock dividend (i.e., one additional share is issued for each 10 shares held) is declared on the common stock. The market price remains $24 per share.

Retained earnings (1,000 shares at market, $24)	24,000	
Common stock, par $10 (1,000 shares)		10,000
Contributed capital in excess of par, common stock		14,000

Situation 2—A large stock dividend: A 50 percent common stock dividend (i.e., one additional share for each two shares held) is declared on the common stock. The market value per share drops immediately to $16.

Retained earnings (5,000 shares at par, $10)	50,000	
Common stock, par $10 (5,000 shares)		50,000

Situation 3—A large stock dividend: A 50 percent common stock dividend is declared on the common stock. The market value drops immediately to $16 per share. Management decides to capitalize on the basis of the average paid in.

Retained earnings (5,000 shares at $11.50*)	57,500	
Common stock, par $10 (5,000 shares)		50,000
Contributed capital in excess of par, common stock		7,500

* Computation: ($100,000 + $15,000) ÷ 10,000 shares = $11.50.

Situation 4—A special stock dividend: A 20 percent common stock dividend (i.e., one additional share for each five shares held) is issued to **both common and preferred shareholders.** The market price per share does not change appreciably after issuance from $24.

Retained earnings (3,000 shares* at $24)	72,000	
Common stock, par $10 (3,000 shares)		30,000
Contributed capital in excess of par, common stock		42,000

* Computation: (10,000 + 5,000) × .20 = 3,000 shares

capital came from this source. For this reason, the reported retained earnings of many companies is less than their accumulated earnings, minus cash or property dividends paid, over the life of the corporation.

DIVIDENDS IN ARREARS ON PREFERRED STOCK

Dividends not yet declared on cumulative preferred stock are called **dividends in arrears.** Dividends in arrears on cumulative preferred stock, prior to declaration of such dividends, do not constitute a liability to the corporation.[14] However, the **report-**

[14] In the case of cumulative preferred stock which is redeemable at the discretion of the stockholder, a case can be made for reporting cumulative dividends in arrears as a liability. GAAP does not require accrual of such dividends. However, FASB, *Statement of Financial Accounting Standards No. 47,* "Disclosure of Long-Term Obligations" (Stamford, Conn., March 1981), par. 10c, requires **disclosure** of redemption requirements for redeemable stock (redemption requirements include payment at redemption of any dividends in arrears).

ing principle requires that cumulative dividends in arrears be reported. A note to the financial statements may report the number of years and amounts of dividends in arrears. An alternative method is to report the amount of dividends in arrears as an **appropriation of retained earnings.** For example, retained earnings of $30,000 may be reported as shown in the next column.

Retained earnings:		
Unappropriated	$20,000	
Appropriated for preferred dividends in arrears (not declared)	10,000	$30,000

FRACTIONAL SHARE RIGHTS

Often fractional share rights must be issued with a stock dividend when the stock dividend is not on

EXHIBIT 15–2: Fractional Share Rights in a Stock Dividend—Z Corporation

Panel A—Illustrative Data:

1. Z Corporation declared a 20 percent (i.e., one for five) stock dividend on the 10,000 shares outstanding of its common stock, par $10 (i.e., a stock dividend of 2,000 common shares).
2. The market value of the common shares was $24.
3. Of the 2,000 dividend shares, 1,730 full shares were issued, in addition to 1,350 fractional share rights calling for the remaining 270 shares. Each fractional share right represented one fifth of a share of stock (i.e., 1,350 fractional share rights × 1/5 share each = 270 shares). These fractional share rights were issued to shareholders that held numbers of shares not evenly divisible by 5 (e.g., a holder of nine shares would receive one additional share plus four fractional share rights of 1/5 share each); thus, to obtain one common share, five such rights must be presented to Z Corporation.

Panel B—Stock Dividend Entries:

1. Date of issuance of dividend shares, including fractional share rights (dividend assumed to be "small"; hence, market value capitalized):

Retained earnings (2,000 shares at market, $24)	48,000	
Common stock, par $10 (1,730 shares × $10)		17,300
Common stock rights outstanding (1,350 rights for 270 shares of par $10)		2,700
Contributed capital in excess of par, common stock (2,000 shares × $14*)		28,000

* Market value, $24—Par value, $10 = Premium, $14.

2. Date of disposition of fractional share rights under four different cases:

Case A—All fractional share rights are turned in to Z Corporation, and the 270 shares are issued.

Common stock rights outstanding	2,700	
Common stock, par $10 (270 shares)		2,700

Case B—Only 90 percent of the rights are turned in for 243 shares (i.e., 270 × 90%), and the remainder lapse.

Common stock rights outstanding	2,700	
Common stock, par $10 (243 shares)		2,430
Contributed capital, lapse of stock rights (135 rights for 27 shares, par $10)†		270

† A credit to Contributed Capital leaves the full amount of Retained Earnings (i.e., $48,000) capitalized. Some accountants prefer to credit Retained Earnings here because $270 (i.e., 10 percent) of the fractional share rights were not exercised.

Case C—Assume the fractional share rights specified that *(a)* five such rights could be turned in for one share of stock at no cost or *(b)* each right could be turned in for its market value of $4.80 cash (i.e., $24 ÷ 5). Cash was disbursed for 350 rights, and the remaining 1,000 rights were turned in for the requisite number of shares.

Common stock rights outstanding	2,700	
Contributed capital in excess of par, (350 rights ÷ 5 × $14; entry 1)‡	980	
Common stock, par $10 (1,000 rights ÷ 5 = 200 shares)		2,000
Cash (350 rights × $4.80)		1,680

‡ Contributed Capital in Excess of Par is debited because the payment of cash in effect, liquidated contributed capital credited in the issuance entry (entry 1).

EXHIBIT 15–2 ***(concluded)***

Panel B ***(concluded):***

Case D—Assume Z Corporation did not issue fractional share rights (entry 1). Instead, it paid shareholders the market value of $4.80 (i.e., $24 ÷ 5) for each fractional share right. The **issuance** of the **stock dividend** would be recorded as follows (in place of entry 1).

Retained earnings (2,000 shares at market, $24)	48,000	
Common stock, par $10 (1,730 shares × $10)		17,300
Contributed capital in excess of par, common stock (1,730 shares × $14)		24,220
Cash (1,350 fractional share rights × $4.80)		6,480

Panel C—Financial Statement Presentation of Effects of Stock Dividend—including fractional share rights, between date of issuance (entry 1 above) and date of disposition of fractional share rights (entry 2); for basic data, see Exhibit 15–1, Panel A:

Z Corporation
Stockholders' Equity

Contributed capital:		
Capital stock:		
Preferred stock, $20 par value, 10,000 shares authorized, 5,000 shares outstanding		$100,000
Common stock, $10 par value, 20,000 shares authorized, 11,730 shares outstanding	$117,300	
Common stock fractional share rights outstanding (for 270 shares)	2,700	120,000
Total capital stock		220,000
Other contributed capital:		
Contributed capital in excess of par, preferred stock	10,000	
Contributed capital in excess of par, common stock [$15,000 (Exhibit 15–1) + $28,000 (entry 1 above)]	43,000	53,000
Total contributed capital		273,000
Retained earnings:		
Unappropriated [$150,000 (Exhibit 15–1) − $48,000 (entry 1 above)]		102,000
Total stockholders' equity		$375,000

a one-for-one basis. For example, if a corporation had a stockholder who owned 150 shares of its common stock and the corporation issued a 15 percent stock dividend, the corporation would issue 22 full shares and one fractional share **right** for one half of a share of common stock (i.e., 150 shares × 15% = 22.5 shares). Soon after issuance, stock rights usually are traded on the market. To illustrate the accounting for fractional share rights related to a stock dividend, Exhibit 15–2 extends the stock dividend situation of Z Corporation given in Exhibit 15–1. Panel A restates the illustrative data; Panel B gives the entries to record the stock dividend, including fractional share rights, under varying specifications; and Panel C presents the effects on the financial statements.

In Exhibit 15–2, Panel C, observe that stock rights outstanding are reported along with the related stock account, which reports that the sum of all fractional share rights represents full shares (270 shares in this instance).

DIVIDENDS AND TREASURY STOCK

Dividends are not paid on treasury stock. However, treasury stock occasionally is used for the issuance of a stock dividend. If treasury stock is used for this purpose, the stock dividend should be recorded by a debit to Retained Earnings (or other appropriate account) for the **market value** of the treasury stock issued and a credit to Treasury Stock for the **book value** of the treasury stock issued, and any credit difference is credited to Contributed Capital. A debit difference would be to Contributed Capital or Retained Earnings, as outlined under the Part B heading, Recording and Reporting Treasury Stock Transactions.

In respect to treasury stock, a stock dividend usually is not deemed to increase the number of shares of treasury stock held. However, should the opposite view prevail, the amount of retained earnings that should be capitalized is a critical issue.

LEGALITY OF DIVIDENDS

The availability of retained earnings and certain elements of contributed capital as a basis for dividends was mentioned in the first section of this chapter. Precise identification of the elements of stockholders' equity that are available for cash, property, and stock dividends, respectively, would require study of the laws of each state; such a study is beyond the scope of this text. Nevertheless at least two provisions appear uniform: (1) dividends may not be paid from **legal capital** (usually represented by the capital **stock** accounts); and (2) unappropriated retained earnings are available for dividends. Between these two boundaries, numerous variations exist, depending upon the respective state statutes and the type of dividend, such as the following:

1. All contributed capital, other than legal capital, is available for dividends.
2. Specified items of contributed capital, other than legal capital, are available for dividends.
3. Contributed capital, other than legal capital, is available for dividends on preferred stock but not on common stock.
4. Unrealized capital is not available for any kind of dividends.
5. Unrealized capital is available for stock dividends only.
6. Debits in the contributed capital accounts and a deficit in Retained Earnings must be restored before payment of any dividends.
7. Dividends from retained earnings must not reduce the Retained Earnings balance below the cost of treasury stock held.

The accountant has a responsibility when the legality or accounting treatment of dividends are at issue to *(a)* ensure that such matters are referred to an attorney and *(b)* ascertain that the financial statements report all material facts concerning such dividends.

APPROPRIATIONS (INCLUDING RESTRICTIONS) OF RETAINED EARNINGS

From time to time, retained earnings may be **appropriated** as a result of management action, a contract, or a law. An appropriation of retained earnings constitutes a **restriction** on a specified portion of accumulated earnings for a specific purpose. Such specific appropriations nevertheless represent a part of **total** retained earnings. Thus, retained earnings is comprised of two subcategories: (1) appropriated retained earnings and (2) unappropriated retained earnings.

Retained earnings are appropriated primarily to protect the **cash position** of the corporation by reducing the amount of cash dividends that otherwise might be paid. Appropriations arise in the following situations:

1. To fulfill a **legal requirement**, as in the case of a restriction on retained earnings equivalent to the cost of treasury stock held as required by state law.
2. To fulfill a **contractual agreement**, as in the case of a debt covenant that stipulates a restriction on the use of retained earnings for dividends.
3. To report a discretionary action by the board of directors to restrict a portion of retained earnings as an aspect of **financial planning.**
4. To report a discretionary action by the board of directors to restrict a portion of retained earnings in anticipation of **possible future losses.**

Item 1 in the above list is discussed in Part B of this chapter; the remaining items are discussed below. Preliminary to the discussions to follow, observe that appropriations of retained earnings have no direct effect upon assets. An appropriation is a "clerical" identification and does not set aside specific assets such as cash; this effect would occur only if, as a separate action, cash is set aside in a separate fund, such as a Bond Sinking Fund.

Appropriations of retained earnings may be accounted for by either of two approaches, viz:

1. **Make no entries in the accounts.** Report the appropriations or restrictions either parenthetically on the balance sheet (or statement of retained earnings) or in a note to the statements.
2. **Make entries in the accounts.** Report the restrictions as appropriated retained earnings in the balance sheet.

In recent years the first approach has been used increasingly; the following excerpt from the 1979 financial statements of Ethyl Corporation illustrates note disclosure of a retained earnings appropriation:

> *Note 9: Retained Earnings Restriction*—The Company's articles of incorporation and note agreements

> contain restrictions, among others, against the payment of cash dividends and purchases of the Company's stock. At December 31, 1979, $107,998,000 of retained earnings was free of such restrictions under the agreement presently most restrictive.

Many companies disclose retained earnings restrictions in notes labeled Long-Term Debt or Credit Arrangements. For example, Motorola, Inc., recently disclosed that their "revolving credit agreement restricts retained earnings available for payment of cash dividends. At December 31, 1979, approximately $45 million . . . of retained earnings was not restricted for dividend payments" (on that date, total retained earnings was $751.3 million).

When the "entry" approach is used, the restriction is recorded in the accounts as a debit to the Retained Earnings account (i.e., unappropriated retained earnings) and as a credit to a descriptively designated appropriated account.[15] Under this approach, the basic principle is that an appropriation account **never** is debited for **any** reason, except to return the balance to the original source, that is, to the unappropriated Retained Earnings account. Thus, a retained earnings appropriation never is debited for a loss. Typical entries under the second approach would be as follows:

1. To record appropriation of $100,000 for a designated purpose:

Retained earnings	100,000	
Retained earnings appropriated (designated)		100,000

2. To remove appropriation and return appropriated amount to unappropriated retained earnings:

Retained earnings appropriated (designated)	100,000	
Retained earnings		100,000

The above entries apply to all types of retained earnings appropriations.

When the need for an appropriation ceases or management decides to remove the appropriation, the appropriation is no longer reported. If the second approach (i.e., formal appropriation entries) is used, any prior entries made to record the appropriation are reversed so that the appropriated amount is returned to unappropriated retained earnings.

Different Types of Appropriations

Appropriation Related to a Contractual Agreement. To offer security to lenders, credit agreements often include various provisions restricting payment of cash and property dividends, as illustrated above for Ethyl Corporation and Motorola. Another common provision, referred to as a bond sinking (or redemption) **fund**, calls for the periodic deposit of a specific amount of cash in a fund, held by a trustee, to be used to retire the bonds at maturity. A third type of provision calls for the periodic **appropriation** of a specific amount of retained earnings. The entries to record such an appropriation and its removal at the end of the contract period would be made as shown above.

Appropriation as an Aspect of Financial Planning. Many corporations that began with a small initial capital investment have grown by retaining a large portion of the earnings in the business. In such circumstances it may be desirable to capitalize a portion of accumulated earnings by issuing stock dividends. Alternatively, the board of directors may disclose their intention not to use a specific amount of retained earnings for cash or property dividends through an appropriation account such as the following:

Retained Earnings Appropriated for Investment in Plant

Retained Earnings Appropriated for Working Capital

Appropriation for Possible Future Losses. In anticipation of possible future losses, the board of directors sometimes will direct that a portion of retained earnings be appropriated and specifically identified with titles such as the following:

Retained Earnings Appropriated for Possible Future Inventory Cost Declines[16]

---

[15] Recall the discussion of *reserves* in Chapter 4. The term **reserve** should be limited in usage to appropriations of retained earnings according to AICPA, *Accounting Terminology Bulletin No. 1,* "Review and Resumé" (New York, 1961), pars. 57–64.

[16] An appropriation for possible future inventory cost decline is not the same account discussed in Chapter 7 with respect to the valuation of inventory at LCM (Allowance to Reduce Inventory to Lower of Cost or Market). That account was related to a cost decline that had **already** materialized, whereas the appropriation account relates to a **possible** cost decline in the **future.**

Retained Earnings Appropriated for Possible Loss in Pending Lawsuit

Retained Earnings Appropriated for Self-Insurance

Even if the anticipated event does materialize, any actual loss arising therefrom should be recorded as an ordinary, unusual or infrequent, or extraordinary item, as would be done when there is no related appropriation account; such losses should **not** be debited to the appropriation account. After the loss is recognized as a deduction to derive net income, the appropriation should be returned to unappropriated retained earnings. Thus, the effect of having reported the appropriation prior to the loss was to report unappropriated retained earnings at its balance that will exist after the loss occurs (if the anticipated amount of the loss equals the actual amount).

REPORTING RETAINED EARNINGS

Under GAAP, the statement of retained earnings may include the following:

1. Beginning balance.
2. Restatement of beginning balance for prior period adjustments.
3. Restatement of beginning balance for retroactive-type accounting changes.
4. Net income or loss for the period.
5. Dividends.
6. Appropriations of retained earnings.
7. Adjustments made pursuant to a quasi-reorganization.
8. Ending balance.

Of the items in the above list, net income or loss, dividends, and appropriations of retained earnings have been discussed, and quasi-reorganizations are discussed and illustrated in Supplement 15–A. Prior period adjustments and restatements of retained earnings for retroactive-type accounting changes are reported similarly in single-period statements—by adjusting the beginning balance of retained earnings for the year during which the related event occurred.

EXHIBIT 15–3: Reporting Prior Period Adjustment on Statement of Retained Earnings in Single-Period Statements

Panel A—Illustrative Data (RST Corporation):

1. For the year ended December 31, 19K, RST Corporation reported the following:
   a. Retained earnings balance December 31, 19J, $158,000.
   b. Net income, $52,000.
   c. Dividends declared and paid, $30,000.
2. During 19K, it was discovered that 19J depreciation expense was understated by $20,000 (the applicable tax rate during 19J was 30 percent). An amended tax return was submitted for 19J.

Panel B—Reporting Retained Earnings:

RST CORPORATION
Statement of Retained Earnings
For Year Ended December 31, 19K

Balance in retained earnings, 1/1/19K	$158,000
Adjustments applicable to prior periods (a debit):	
Correction of accounting error in 19J, net of $6,000 income tax saving (see Note 4)	(14,000)
Balance in retained earnings, 1/1/19K, as adjusted	144,000
Add: Net income for 19K	52,000
	196,000
Deduct: Dividends for 19K	(30,000)
Balance in retained earnings, 12/31/19K	$166,000

Note 4: During 19J, the company inadvertently understated depreciation expense by $20,000. This accounting error caused an overstatement of the reported income of 19J, and of the balance in retained earnings at December 31, 19J (January 1, 19K), by $14,000, which reflects the $6,000 tax effect of the error. The error was detected and corrected during 19K by debiting Retained Earnings for a Prior Period Adjustment in the aftertax amount of $14,000. To correct other affected accounts, Income Tax Payable was debited for the $6,000 tax saving, and Accumulated Depreciation was credited for $20,000.

Reporting of these two items is discussed and illustrated below.

Prior Period Adjustments

FASB Statement 16 identifies the following two categories of events as prior period adjustments:

a. Correction of an error in the financial statements of a prior period, and
b. Adjustments that result from realization of income tax benefits of preacquisition operating loss carry-forwards of purchased subsidiaries.

Reporting of a prior period adjustment for an error correction in **single-period statements** is illustrated in Exhibit 15–3 for RST Corporation.

Retroactive-Type Accounting Change

The types of accounting changes for which the prior balance in retained earnings is restated to reflect the new accounting method include *(a)* change from LIFO to another inventory costing method, *(b)* change in method of accounting for long-term construction contracts (discussed in Chapter 9), and *(c)* change to or from the full-cost method, which is used in the extractive industries (discussed in Chapter 13). Chapter 20 discusses and illustrates retroactive-type accounting changes.

Part B: Contraction and Expansion of Stockholders' Equity after Formation

INSTITUTIONAL FACTORS AND BASIC PRINCIPLES

Once the corporate charter is granted and the bylaws are approved, provisions governing corporate capital (i.e., stockholders' equity) are established; however, this does not mean that such provisions may not be changed. Aside from the sale of unissued shares already authorized and issuance of stock dividends, a corporation may obtain authorization for **additional** classes of stock, **expansion** of the number of shares of currently authorized stock, or **change** of the par or stated values. Also, it may **contract and expand** corporate capital by purchasing and selling its own shares in the marketplace. Callable and redeemable shares may be acquired and retired and convertible shares may be exchanged. The corporation may undergo a corporate reorganization involving a significant change in the entire capital structure; or it may combine with other entities. These changes are controlled in various manners: by state laws, by charter and bylaw provisions, or by the shareholders themselves. Upon approval of the shareholders, the bylaws may be changed and even a new or amended charter obtained.

In accounting for such changes in corporate capital, other than as a result of earning income (or loss), and other than the result of reorganizations (see quasi-reorganization, discussed in Supplement 15–A), four basic principles have general applicability, viz:

1. Different sources of stockholders' equity should be recorded and reported separately.
2. Information should be accumulated and reported to meet the requirements of GAAP and the prevailing laws.
3. A corporation cannot recognize, as income or as increases in retained earnings, gains that result from capital stock transactions between itself and its owners, including treasury stock transactions. Accounting recognition of **increases** of net assets resulting from transactions relating to the corporation's own stock are recorded as changes in contributed capital rather than as gains. However, **decreases** of net assets can be debited to retained earnings because their effect is similar to that of a cash or property dividend.
4. Increases in authorized shares, authorized legal capital, changes in par or stated values, or exchanges of its own equity shares (such as its own preferred shares for its own common shares) do not create gains, losses, or credits to retained earnings. Debits to retained earnings from such capital transactions are viewed as similar to dividends.

TREASURY STOCK

Expansion and contraction of contributed capital after formation frequently arise from treasury stock transactions. The statutes of most states permit a corporation to purchase its own stock subject to certain limitations. **Treasury stock** is a corporation's own stock (preferred or common) that *(a)* has been issued, *(b)* subsequently is reacquired by the issuing corporation, and *(c)* after acquisition has not been resold or formally retired. Thus, the purchase of treasury stock does not reduce the number of **issued** shares but does reduce the number of **outstanding** shares. Treasury shares subsequently may be resold and again are classified as outstanding shares.

Companies exercise extreme care in transactions involving their own stock (including treasury stock) because of the corporation's opportunity to use insider information to the detriment of a shareholder from whom the corporation is acquiring, or to whom the corporation is selling, its own stock. For example, an oil company with inside knowledge of a profitable oil discovery could withhold the "good" news and acquire treasury stock at an artificially low market price. Alternatively, a company could withhold "bad" news and sell its own stock (including treasury stock) at an artificially high market price. This latter action would unfairly deprive the purchasing shareholder of the excess cash paid for the stock. For these reasons, the securities laws (particularly Rules 10b–5 and 10b–6 of the Securities and Exchange Act of 1934) prohibit corporations from engaging in detrimental acts, including those related to transactions involving their own stock.[17]

Shareholders may view the acquisition of treasury shares by a corporation as an alternative to cash dividends because, like dividends, it provides cash flow to the selling shareholders. Moreover, it provides a tax advantage to the selling shareholders for whom any long-term gain on sale of the shares to the corporation often is taxed at lower rates, whereas cash and property dividends are taxed as ordinary income.

The purchase of treasury stock decreases both assets and stockholders' equity, whereas a sale of treasury stock increases both assets and stockholders' equity. Treasury stock may be obtained by purchase, by settlement of an obligation, or through donation. Treasury stock does not carry voting, dividend, or liquidation privileges. Although the acquisition of treasury stock involves the disbursement of assets, treasury stock is not an asset because a corporation cannot own itself.[18] In this respect, treasury stock has the same effect as unissued stock, which is not an asset.

Treasury stock may be acquired for the following reasons:

1. The corporation has excess cash, and the stock is considered to be underpriced; hence, the corporation attempts to augment its net assets (but not its income) by buying the shares "low" and later selling them "high." Also, the acquisition and holding of treasury stock may reduce future dividends.
2. To use for employee stock options, bonus plans, and direct sale to employees (when there are no unissued shares).
3. To use in exchange for other securities or assets.
4. To use for a stock dividend.
5. To increase earnings per share.
6. To buy out one or more particular stockholders.

RECORDING AND REPORTING TREASURY STOCK TRANSACTIONS

Different views exist as to the approach that should be used in accounting for treasury stock. These views may be grouped broadly under two methods, viz:

1. Cost method (one-transaction concept).
2. Par value method (dual-transaction concept).

Both of these methods are generally accepted; however, they yield different results for certain individual items within the stockholders' equity section of the balance sheet. For the same situation, the **total** amount of stockholders' equity is the same under both methods.

Cost Method

The cost method sometimes is referred to as the one-transaction concept because the **purchase and subsequent sale** of the treasury stock are viewed as one extended transaction. At acquisition, the **cost** of the treasury stock is debited to a "holding" ac-

[17] D. S. Ruder, "Dangers in a Corporation's Purchases of Its Own Shares," *The Practical Lawyer,* May 1967, pp. 75–91.

[18] Nevertheless, in 1979, 6 of the 417 companies surveyed by *Accounting Trends & Techniques* which reported treasury stock, classified it as an asset (see AICPA, *Accounting Trends & Techniques, 1980* [New York, 1980], table 2–36).

count called Treasury Stock. At date of subsequent resale, the Treasury Stock account is credited for the **cost** of the treasury stock, and any difference between selling price and cost is recorded as a change in one or more stockholders' equity accounts as illustrated in Exhibit 15–4.

Separate treasury stock accounts should be established for each class of stock. When treasury stock is acquired at different costs, specific shares should be identified; otherwise a FIFO or average cost per share must be used to determine the credit to the Treasury Stock account (at cost) at resale date.

Under the cost method, the balance in the Treasury Stock account at the end of the accounting period is **reported** as an **unallocated reduction** of the total amount of stockholders' equity, as shown in Exhibit 15–4, Panel C.

Par Value Method

The par value method sometimes is referred to as the dual-transaction concept because it views the purchase and sale of treasury stock as two completely independent and unrelated transactions. Thus, two objectives of the par value method are as follows:

a. At date of acquisition of treasury stock—to make a final accounting with the retiring stockholder and to adjust the capital accounts on a "stock retirement" basis.
b. At date of sale of treasury stock—to record the reissuance essentially in the same manner as for the sale and issuance of unissued stock.

To accomplish these two purposes, the Treasury Stock account is carried at the par or stated value per share, hence, the designation par value method. Under the **par value method,** the accounting for treasury stock at each transaction date is as follows:

a. **Date of acquisition**—The final accounting with the retiring stockholder is recorded as a credit to Cash for the price paid and a debit to Treasury Stock for the par value (in the case of par value stock), stated value (in the case of nopar stock with a stated value), or average amount credited to the capital stock account (in case of true nopar stock). When the par value method is used, a **debit or credit difference** between the price paid for the treasury stock and the amount recorded in the Treasury Stock account often requires a **step allocation.**

In case of a **debit difference** between the price paid for the treasury stock and the amount recorded in the Treasury Stock account, the step allocation, subject to account balances, is made as follows:

Step 1—debit Contributed Capital in Excess of Par (or stated value, or average paid in) on the stock for the **proportionate part** applicable to the number of treasury shares acquired (as would be done if the shares were retired, which reflects the nature of the par value method).

Step 2—debit Contributed Capital from Treasury Stock Transactions (to the extent needed, but not in excess of any credit balance in that account from the same class of stock).

Step 3—allocate any remainder to the Retained Earnings account.

Alternatively, in lieu of the above step allocation, *APB Opinion 6* (par. 12a) states, "the excess [debit difference] may be [debited] entirely to retained earnings in recognition of the fact that a corporation can always capitalize or allocate retained earnings for such purposes."

In the case of a **credit difference** between the price paid for the treasury stock and the amount recorded in the Treasury Stock account, the step allocation, subject to account balances, is made as follows:

Step 1—debit Contributed Capital in Excess of Par on the stock for the **proportionate part** applicable to the number of treasury shares acquired.

Step 2—The sum of the proportionate part of Contributed Capital in Excess of Par debited (step 1), **plus** the credit difference, is credited in full to Contributed Capital from Treasury Stock Transactions.

b. **Date of resale**—under the par value method, the entry for resale of treasury stock is essentially the same as the entry for original sale: Cash is debited for the amount of cash received, and Treasury Stock is credited for par value, stated value, or average paid in (the case of true nopar stock). At date of resale, any **credit difference** between sale price received and the amount credited to Treasury Stock (i.e., par value, stated value, or average paid in) is credited in full to Contributed Capital from Treasury Stock Transactions. A **debit difference** is debited to Contributed Capital from Treasury Stock Transactions (to the extent that account has a credit balance), and any remainder is debited to Retained Earnings.

Exhibit 15–4 illustrates accounting for treasury stock by the cost and par value methods. Panel A of the exhibit presents the illustrative situation, Panel B gives the entries to record the treasury stock transactions, and Panel C presents the financial statement disclosure of the effects.

The basic difference between the cost and par value methods is depicted in Exhibit 15–4, Panel C; it reveals the different ways the two methods **report** treasury stock. The **par value method** maintains a

EXHIBIT 15–4: Recording and Reporting Treasury Stock—Cost and Par Value Methods

Panel A—Illustrative Situation (initial sale of stock):

To record the initial sale and issuance of 10,000 shares of common stock, par $25, at $26 per share:

Cash (10,000 shares @ $26)	260,000	
Common stock, par $25 (10,000 shares)		250,000
Contributed capital in excess of par, common stock (10,000 shares × $1)		10,000

Panel B—Entries to Record Treasury Stock Transactions:

1. To record the acquisition of 2,000 shares of treasury common stock at $28 per share:

Cost Method

Treasury stock, common stock (2,000 shares @ $28)	56,000	
Cash		56,000

Par Value Method

Treasury stock, common stock (2,000 shares @ par, $25)	50,000	
Contributed capital in excess of par, common stock @ $1)	2,000	
Contributed capital from treasury stock transactions, common stock	–0–*	
Retained earnings	4,000	
Cash		56,000

* No available credit balance to absorb a debit. Alternatively, had the 2,000 shares been acquired for $46,000, Contributed Capital from Treasury Stock Transactions would be credited for $6,000.

2. To record sale of 500 shares of the treasury stock at $30 per share (above cost and above par):

Cost Method

Cash (500 shares @ $30)	15,000	
Treasury stock, common stock (500 shares @ cost, $28)		14,000
Contributed capital from treasury stock transactions, common stock*		1,000

* Had this sale been at cost ($28 per share), no entry would have been made to Contributed Capital from Treasury Stock Transactions, Common Stock.

Par Value Method

Cash (500 shares @ $30)	15,000	
Treasury stock, common stock (500 shares @ par, $25)		12,500
Contributed capital from treasury stock transactions, common stock		2,500†

† Had this sale been at cost ($28 per share), sale proceeds would have been $14,000 and a credit of $1,500 (i.e., $14,000 − $12,500) would have been made to Contributed Capital from Treasury Stock Transactions, Common Stock).

3. To record the sale of another 500 shares of the treasury stock at $19 per share (below cost and below par, which would be an unusual occurrence):

Cost Method

Cash (500 shares @ $19)	9,500	
Contributed capital from treasury stock transactions, common stock‡	1,000	
Retained earnings	3,500	
Treasury stock, common stock (500 shares @ cost, $28)		14,000

‡ Debit limited to the credit balance in this account (entry 3); any remainder is debited to Retained Earnings.

Par Value Method

Cash (500 shares @ $19)	9,500	
Contributed capital from treasury stock transactions, common stock§	2,500	
Retained earnings	500	
Treasury stock, common stock (500 shares @ par, $25)		12,500

§ Debit limited to the credit balance in this account (entry 3); any remainder is debited to Retained Earnings.

EXHIBIT 15–4 *(continued)*

Panel C—Financial Statement Reporting (Stockholders' Equity)

Cost Method

Contributed capital:	
Common stock, par $25, authorized 50,000 shares, issued 10,000 shares, of which 1,000 are held as treasury stock	$250,000
Contributed capital in excess of par, common stock	10,000
Contributed capital from treasury stock transactions, common stock	-0-
Total contributed capital	260,000
Retained earnings ($40,000*–$3,500)	36,500
Total contributed capital and retained earnings	296,500
Less: Treasury stock, 1,000 shares at cost, $28	28,000
Total stockholders' equity	$268,500

* Balance assumed.

Par Value Method

Contributed capital:	
Common stock, par $25, authorized 50,000 shares, issued 10,000 shares	$250,000
Less: Treasury stock, 1,000 shares at par, $25	(25,000)
Total common stock outstanding, 9,000 shares	225,000
Contributed capital in excess of par, common stock ($10,000–$2,000)	8,000
Contributed capital from treasury stock transactions, common stock	-0-
Total contributed capital	233,000
Retained earnings ($40,000*–$4,000–$500)	35,500
Total stockholders' equity	$268,500

"source of capital" reporting, wherein treasury stock is reported as a **negative** element of contributed capital; by contrast, under the **cost method** treasury stock is reported as an **unallocated negative** element of total stockholders' equity. For this reason, the par value method theoretically is preferable. Nevertheless, probably due to its relative simplicity, the cost method is used more often. For example, in 1979, of the 600 companies reported in *Accounting Trends & Techniques, 1980,* 379 companies used the cost method, and only 44 companies used the par value method. However, 39 of the 379 companies using the cost method **reported** the cost of the treasury stock as a deduction from issued stock of the same class, a type of hybrid approach (AICPA, *Accounting Trends & Techniques, 1980,* table 2–36).

ACCOUNTING FOR NOPAR TREASURY STOCK

Nopar stock having a **stated** or **assigned** value per share is accounted for in the same manner as illustrated above for par value stock under each of the two methods. The stated or assigned value per share is treated as if it were par.

In the case of **true nopar stock,** the cost method almost always is used because it can be applied exactly the same as for par value stock (as discussed above). When the par value method is used with true nopar stock, the **average amount per share** reflected in the nopar capital stock account (i.e., the average amount paid in) usually is used as the "basic value" in the place of par or stated value. Other than the fact that with true nopar stock, there is no account for Contributed Capital in Excess of Par (or Stated Value), the accounting for true nopar stock under the par value method would be similar to that illustrated in Exhibit 15–4.

TREASURY STOCK RECEIVED BY DONATION

Shareholders occasionally donate shares of a corporation's stock back to the corporation. Such donations may *(a)* be made to raise needed working capital through resale of the donated stock or *(b)* constitute return of the stock in recognition of an overvaluation of assets originally given in exchange for the stock. Stock received by donation is classified as **treasury stock** unless it is formally retired. Neither **total assets nor total equity** is changed by the donation of treasury stock. Three methods have been employed in recording the receipt of donated treasury stock, viz:

1. **Cost method**—When the donated stock is re-

ceived, debit the Treasury Stock account for the current market value of the stock and credit Contributed Capital, Donated Treasury Stock for the same amount. Upon subsequent sale, any net asset increases or decreases that result from selling the treasury stock for amounts in excess of its carrying value would be accounted for as illustrated in Exhibit 15–4, Panel B, for the cost method.

2. **Par value method**—When the donated stock is received, debit the Treasury Stock account for the par or stated value (or in the case of true nopar stock, average paid in), debit the account which originally was credited for the premium, and credit an appropriately designated contributed capital account. Subsequent sales would be recorded as illustrated in Exhibit 15–4, Panel B, for the par value method.
3. **Memo method**—When donated stock is received, a memorandum entry is made on the basis that there was no cost. Subsequent sales would require a credit to contributed capital for the full sale price.

FORMAL RETIREMENT OF TREASURY STOCK

A corporation may decide to **constructively** retire treasury shares (by amending the charter) and have them revert to an unauthorized (i.e., not subject to resale or reissuance) status. When treasury stock is retired in this manner, all capital account balances **related to the treasury shares** (including **contributed capital from treasury stock transactions**) are reduced on a **proportional basis,** and any net debit difference is debited to Retained Earnings. A net credit difference is credited to Contributed Capital from Stock Retirement.

To illustrate, we will continue the Exhibit 15–4 example assuming par value stock. Recall that the capital balances, after the illustrative entries, reflected the following (refer to Exhibit 15–4, Panel C):

	Cost Method	Par Value Method
Common stock, par $25, 10,000 shares issued	$250,000	$250,000
Contributed capital in excess of par, common stock	10,000	8,000
Treasury stock (1,000 shares):		
At cost	(28,000)	
At par value		(25,000)
Retained earnings	36,500	35,500
Total stockholders' equity	$268,500	$268,500

The entry to record formal retirement of all of the 1,000 shares of treasury stock would be as follows:

	Cost Method		Par Value Method	
Common stock, par $25	25,000		25,000	
Contributed capital in excess of par, common stock [($10,000 ÷ 10,000 shares = $1 per share of original premium) × 1,000 shares]	1,000			
Retained earnings	2,000			
Treasury stock:				
At cost		28,000		
At par				25,000

Had there been a credit balance in Contributed Capital from Treasury Stock Transactions, Common

Stock,[19] it would have been debited and the difference, if a debit, debited to Retained Earnings and, if a credit, credited to Contributed Capital from Retirement of Common Stock. In the highly unlikely event that fewer than all of the treasury shares are retired, the various debits and credits would be proportionately less.

RESTRICTION OF RETAINED EARNINGS FOR TREASURY STOCK

In Chapter 14 legal capital was discussed and the point was made that state laws historically were designed to protect creditor interests through the maintenance of **legal capital** and restriction of cash and property dividends. When treasury stock is purchased, assets of the corporation are disbursed to the owners of the shares purchased. Should a corporation have a completely free hand in this matter, it is not difficult to perceive how creditor interests (or the interests of another class of shareholders) may be jeopardized through the distribution of corporate assets via treasury stock purchases, even though legal capital may be reported correctly. To prevent this situation, many states have laws limiting the cost of treasury stock that may be held at any one time to some amount such as the total retained earnings. This provision has the effect of *(a)* requiring restriction of retained earnings equivalent to the cost of treasury stock held and *(b)* reducing the amount of retained earnings that may be used for dividends until the treasury shares are resold.[20] Moreover, debt covenants often limit the amount of treasury stock a corporation may purchase. For instance, Brunswick Corporation, Grumman Corporation, and Amerada Hess Corporation have been restricted by their debt covenants as to the amounts of their own stock they may purchase.

Retained earnings restrictions related to treasury stock may be reported by note disclosures in the financial statements or by formal appropriation entries, as outlined under the Part A heading, Appropriations (Including Restrictions) of Retained Earnings.

[19] A debit balance would not arise in this account because such debits would be made to Retained Earnings.

[20] In some states the restriction applies to retained earnings; on the other hand, some states permit the purchase of treasury stock equivalent in cost to other capital items such as contributed capital in excess of par.

FORMAL RETIREMENT OF CALLABLE AND REDEEMABLE STOCK

Corporations frequently issue **callable** preferred stock which provides that the corporation, **at its option** after a certain date, can call in the shares at a specified price for formal retirement. In contrast, **redeemable** stock provides that **at the option of the stockholder,** and under certain conditions, the shares tendered by the shareholders will be retired at a specified price per share. "Redemption" usually signifies both acquisition and formal retirement of the stock by the issuing corporation. The call or redemption price is at or above par and usually is above the original issue price.[21] Shares called, or redeemed, are not classified as treasury stock.

When callable or redeemable stock is acquired and formally retired, all capital balances relating to the specific shares are removed from the accounts; any net debit is debited to Retained Earnings as a de facto dividend, and any net credit is credited to a contributed capital account such as Contributed Capital from Retirement of Stock. If the stock is cumulative preferred and there are dividends in arrears, such dividends are paid and debited to Retained Earnings.

To illustrate several typical situations, assume a corporation had 2,500 shares of callable preferred stock (par value $100) outstanding, $250,000; contributed capital in excess of par, preferred stock, $10,000; and retained earnings, $45,000. Now assume the corporation called and formally retired 1,000 shares of the preferred stock. Three different assumptions as to the **call and retirement** are illustrated below:

Assumption 1: The preferred stock is noncumulative and callable at the original issue price of $104 per share.

[21] *APB Opinion 10,* par. 10, recommends that "any liquidation preference of the stock be disclosed in the equity section of the balance sheet in the aggregate, either parenthetically or 'in short' rather than on a per share basis or by disclosure in notes." Amounts of arrearages on cumulative preferred dividends also should be disclosed. Also, *FASB Statement No. 47,* par. 10, states that the balance sheet should disclose "The amount of redemption requirements for all issues of capital stock that are redeemable at fixed or determinable prices on fixed or determinable dates, separately by issue or combined."

Preferred stock (1,000 shares at par, $100)	100,000	
Contributed capital in excess of par, preferred stock ($4 per share)	4,000	
Cash (1,000 shares @ $104)		104,000

Assumption 2: The preferred stock is noncumulative and callable at $110 per share—$6 per share above the original issue price of $104.

Preferred stock (1,000 shares at par, $100)	100,000	
Contributed capital in excess of par, preferred stock ($4 per share)	4,000	
Retained earnings	6,000	
Cash (1,000 shares @ $110)		110,000

Assumption 3: The preferred stock is 5 percent cumulative; three years' dividends are in arrears. The stock is callable at $101 plus the dividends in arrears, which must be paid.

Retained earnings ($100,000 × 5% × 3 years)	15,000	
Cash		15,000

Note: Dividends on the remaining preferred shares (i.e., those not being called for retirement at this time) are not considered in this entry; cumulative dividends on them also would have to be paid and recorded at this time.

Preferred stock (1,000 shares at par, $100)	100,000	
Contributed capital in excess of par, preferred stock ($4 per share)	4,000	
Contributed capital from retirement of preferred stock		3,000
Cash (1,000 shares @ $101)		101,000

If true nopar stock is formally retired, the average price per share originally credited to the stock account is removed from the capital stock account, Cash is credited, and any net debit or credit is accounted for as illustrated above. If nopar stock with a stated or assigned value is retired, the procedures illustrated above for par value stock are followed.

CONVERTIBLE STOCK

Corporations sometimes issue **convertible** preferred stock which gives the shareholder an option, within a specified time period, to exchange the convertible preferred shares currently held for other classes of capital stock (or bonds) at a specified rate. The converted shares usually are formally retired when received by the corporation. Conversion privileges require the issuing corporation to set aside a sufficient number of units of the other security to fulfill the conversion privilege until they are exercised, or expire. If the preferred stock is cumulative, any dividends in arrears at date of conversion must be paid.

At date of conversion, all account balances related to the converted shares are removed and the new shares issued are recorded at their par or stated value. Any difference, if a credit, is recorded in an appropriately designated contributed capital account; if a debit, Retained Earnings is reduced. To illustrate three typical situations, assume the following data and that the converted stock is formally retired:

Preferred stock, noncumulative, par $2, shares outstanding, 100,000	$200,000
Contributed capital in excess of par, preferred stock	20,000
Common stock, par $1, shares authorized, 500,000; shares outstanding, 150,000	150,000
Contributed capital in excess of par, common stock	50,000

Situation 1: The conversion privilege specifies the issuance of one share of common stock for each share of preferred stock turned in for conversion. Shareholders turn in 10,000 shares of preferred stock for conversion.

Preferred stock (10,000 shares at par, $2)	20,000	
Contributed capital in excess of par, preferred stock ($0.20 per share)	2,000	
Common stock (10,000 shares at par, $1)		10,000
Contributed capital from conversion of preferred stock		12,000

Situation 2: The conversion privilege specifies the issuance of two shares of common stock for each share of preferred stock converted. Shareholders turn in 10,000 shares of preferred stock for conversion.

Preferred stock (10,000 shares at par, $2)	20,000	
Contributed capital in excess of par, preferred stock ($0.20 per share)	2,000	
Common stock (20,000 shares at par, $1)		20,000
Contributed capital from conversion of preferred stock		2,000

Situation 3: The conversion privilege specifies the issuance of three shares of common stock for each share of preferred stock converted. Shareholders turn in 10,000 shares of preferred stock for conversion.

Preferred stock (10,000 shares at par, $2)	20,000	
Contributed capital in excess of par, preferred stock ($0.20 per share)	2,000	
Retained earnings	8,000	
Common stock (30,000 shares at par, $1)		30,000

Conversion of bonds for capital stock is discussed in Chapter 17.

CHANGING PAR VALUE

A corporation, if it conforms with the applicable state laws, may amend the charter and bylaws to change the par value (and/or the number of authorized shares) of one or more classes of authorized stock. Par value stock may be called in, formally retired, and replaced with nopar stock or stock of a different par value; conversely, nopar stock may be replaced with par value stock.[22]

To record changes in par value, all capital account balances pertaining to the old stock retired are removed from the accounts and the new stock issued is recorded. If an additional credit is needed, an appropriately designated contributed capital account is credited; if an additional debit is needed, Retained Earnings is debited. The entries are similar to those illustrated above for recording the conversion of convertible preferred stock.

[22] In a stock split the par value is reduced and the number of shares outstanding is increased proportionately; therefore, the balance in the capital stock account is unchanged. Only a memorandum entry in the original stock account is needed to reflect the new par value per share and the number of shares outstanding after the split.

Supplement 15-A: Quasi-Reorganizations

If a corporation has sustained heavy losses over an extended period of time which causes a significant **deficit** in Retained Earnings and there are unrealistic carrying values for the assets, a quasi-reorganization may be desirable from the management and accounting points of view.

Quasi-reorganization refers to a procedure whereby a corporation, without **formal** court proceedings of dissolution, can establish a new basis for accounting for assets and stockholders' equity. In effect, a quasi-reorganization is an accounting reorganization in which a "fresh start" is effected in the accounts with respect to certain assets, liabilities, legal capital, and retained earnings.

The Committee on Accounting Procedure of the AICPA recognized the procedure, provided it is properly safeguarded.[23] The Securities and Exchange Commission also recognized quasi-reorganization and listed certain safeguards or conditions with respect to it. These conditions are summarized below:

1. Retained earnings immediately after the quasi-reorganization must be zero.
2. Upon completion of the quasi-reorganization no deficit shall remain in any corporate capital account.
3. The effects of the whole procedure shall be made known to all stockholders entitled to vote and appropriate approval in advance obtained from them.
4. A fair and conservative balance sheet shall be presented as of the date of the reorganization and the readjustment of values should be reasonably complete, in order to obviate as far as possible future readjustments of like nature.[24]

The accounting guidelines to record a quasi-reorganization are *(a)* the recorded values relating to appropriately selected assets are restated; *(b)* the capital accounts are restated, and the Retained Earnings account is restated to a zero balance; and *(c)* the corporate entity is unchanged.[25] Subsequent to a quasi-reorganization there must be full disclosure on the financial statements of the year of reorganization of (1) the reorganization procedure and (2) its effects. Also, the retained earnings amount is "dated" for a period of 3 to 10 years following the reorganization as illustrated below.

Under the conditions presented in Exhibit 15–5,

[23] *ARB 43,* chap. 7, sec. A.

[24] Securities and Exchange Commission, *Accounting Series Release No. 25.*

[25] For a detailed treatment of quasi-reorganization, see J. S. Schindler, *Quasi-Reorganization* (Michigan Business Studies, vol. 13, no. 5) (Ann Arbor: Bureau of Business Research, University of Michigan, 1958).

EXHIBIT 15–5: Accounting for a Quasi-Reorganization (January 1, 19J)

Panel A—Hypothetical Situation:

1. Balance sheet at January 1, 19J, immediately prior to quasi-reorganization:

Current assets	$ 200,000
Operational assets	1,300,000
	$1,500,000
Liabilities	$ 300,000
Capital stock	1,500,000
Contributed capital in excess of par	100,000
Retained earnings	(400,000)
	$1,500,000

2. The inventories are overvalued by $50,000, and the carrying value of the operational assets should be reduced by $350,000.

Panel B—Entries and Balances:

Accounts	Balances before Quasi-Reorganization	Entries to Record Quasi-Reorganization		Balances after Quasi-Reorganization
Current assets	$ 200,000		*(a)* $ 50,000	$ 150,000
Operational assets	1,300,000		*(b)* 350,000	950,000
Total assets	$1,500,000			$1,100,000
Liabilities	$ 300,000			$ 300,000
Capital stock	1,500,000	*(d)* $700,000		800,000
Contributed capital in excess of par	100,000	*(c)* 100,000		-0-
Retained earnings	(400,000)	*(a)* 50,000 *(b)* 350,000	*(c)* 100,000 *(d)* 700,000	(Note 1)
Total liabilities and stockholders' equity	$1,500,000			$1,100,000

Note 1 (on balance sheet). Retained earnings represents accumulations since January 1, 19J, at which time a $400,000 deficit was eliminated as a result of a quasi-reorganization.

Explanation of entries:

(a) To write down a current asset (inventory) by $50,000.
(b) To write down an operational asset by $350,000.
(c) To write off contributed capital in excess of par as a partial offset to the deficit in retained earnings, $100,000.
(d) To change retained earnings to a zero balance and to restate legal capital by the same amount (i.e., $400,000 + $50,000 + $350,000 − $100,000 = $700,000). This leaves legal capital at $800,000, the amount necessary to reconcile the basic accounting model after quasi-reorganization. Legal capital can be restated by (1) reducing par value per share (requires a charter change) or (2) reducing the shares outstanding (no charter change required).

Panel A (note the $400,000 debit balance in Retained Earnings), the company could consider two alternatives. First, the corporation could be dissolved, pay creditors, and then form a new corporation. The new corporation would receive the remaining assets and report their total amount as the stockholders' equity of the new corporation.

Alternatively, the corporation may undergo a quasi-reorganization (without dissolution) which would be less cumbersome and less expensive than legal reorganization. By complying with the conditions set forth above, including creditor and stockholder approval, the quasi-reorganization may be effected without paying off the creditors at this time. The entries needed are reflected in Exhibit 15–5, Panel B. That exhibit also shows the restated balance sheet amounts immediately after the quasi-reorganization. The quasi-reorganization restatements of specific account balances are reflected in retained earnings, which is then restated to a zero balance and legal capital is reduced accordingly.

In general, a quasi-reorganization is justified when *(a)* a large deficit from operations exists, *(b)* it is approved by the stockholders, *(c)* the cost basis of accounting for operational assets becomes unrealistic in terms of going-concern values,[26] *(d)* a break in continuity of the historical cost basis clearly is needed so that realistic financial reporting is possible, *(e)* the Retained Earnings balance is totally inadequate to absorb an obvious decrease in going-concern asset values, and *(f)* a "fresh start," in the accounting sense, appears to be desirable or advantageous to all parties who are concerned with the corporation. A quasi-reorganization, by approval of the creditors and shareholders, usually is supervised by a court to assure adequate protection of the interests of both parties. Because legal capital, as measured in the accounts, is reduced in a quasi-reorganization, all concerned parties seek equity through court supervision to avoid future litigation.

[26] The AICPA *Technical Aids* (CCH, sec. 4220.01) state: "Thus, the official statements of the SEC and the APB can be interpreted as indicating that a quasi-reorganization, if otherwise appropriate, could result in a write-up as well as a write-down of assets." *APB Opinion 6*, par. 17, states: "The Board is of the opinion that property, plant and equipment should not be written up by an entity to reflect appraisal, market or current values which are above cost. This statement is not intended to change the accounting practice followed in connection with quasi-reorganizations or reorganizations."

Also, restructure of debt that sometimes occurs in a quasi-reorganization does not come under the provisions of *APB Opinion 26* or *FASB Statement 15* (debt restructure is discussed in chap. 17, Part C).

QUESTIONS

PART A

1. What are the principal sources and dispositions of retained earnings?
2. Differentiate between total retained earnings and the balance of the Retained Earnings account.
3. What is the position of the accounting profession on use of the word *surplus?* What is the basis for this position?
4. What are the four important dates relative to dividends? Explain the significance of each.
5. Distinguish between cash dividends, property dividends, and liability dividends.
6. What is a *liquidating dividend?* What are the responsibilities of the accountant with respect to such dividends?
7. Explain the difference between intentional and unintentional liquidating dividends.
8. Basically what is the difference between a cash or property dividend and a stock dividend?
9. Distinguish between a stock *dividend* and a stock *split.*
10. What are the reasons for appropriations of retained earnings?
11. Explain the distinction between *(a)* a bond sinking fund and *(b)* an appropriation of retained earnings for bond sinking fund.
12. What items are properly reported on the statement of retained earnings?
13. Is the following statement correct? "Retained earnings was reduced by $10,000 appropriated for plant expansion." Explain.

PART B

14. Define *treasury stock.*
15. Explain the theoretical difference between the *one-transaction* concept and the *dual-transaction* concept in accounting for treasury stock.
16. In comparing the recording of treasury stock at cost with recording at par, "total capital is unaffected; however, subdivisions thereof are affected." Explain this statement.
17. Why have many states limited purchases of treasury stock to the amount reported as retained earnings? How may the restriction on retained earnings be removed?
18. In recording treasury stock transactions why are "gains" recorded in a contributed capital account whereas "losses" may involve a debit to Retained Earnings?
19. How is treasury stock reported on the balance sheet *(a)* under the cost method and *(b)* under the par value method?
20. How is the restriction on retained earnings, equal to the cost of treasury stock held, reported on the balance sheet?
21. How is stock donated back to the corporation recorded?

SUPPLEMENT 15–A

22. What is a quasi-reorganization? Under what conditions is it acceptable?

DECISION CASE 15–1

As XYZ Corporation's independent auditor, you are attending the meeting of the board of directors where preparation of the forthcoming annual report is being discussed. One of the directors, known to have a sketchy knowledge of accounting, says, "You accountants were quite ingenuous when you devised income tax allocation. When reported profits are up, you reduce them with an assigned higher income tax expense; when they are down, you do the opposite. Since reported income is going to be embarassingly high this year, I'm thankful for income tax allocation."

At the meeting, this director, obviously concerned over the huge increase in reported earnings, suggests relief by an appropriation of retained earnings.

Required:

Explain the consequences of an appropriation of retained earnings. To what "relief" is this director referring?

DECISION CASE 15–2

Drake Company was started in 1975 to manufacture a wide range of plastic products from three basic components. The company was originally owned by 23 shareholders; however, five years after formation, the capital structure was expanded considerably, at which time preferred stock was issued. The preferred is nonvoting, cumulative, nonparticipating, 6% stock. The company has experienced a substantial growth in business over the years. This growth was due to two principal factors: *(a)* the dynamic management and *(b)* geographic location. The firm served a rapidly expanding area with relatively few regionally situated competitors.

The last audited balance sheet showed the following (summarized):

Balance Sheet
December 31, 1982

Cash	$ 11,000
Other current assets	76,000
Investment in K Co. stock (at cost)	30,000
Plant and equipment (net)	310,000
Intangible assets	15,000
Other assets	8,000
	$450,000
Current liabilities	$ 38,000
Long-term notes payable	60,000
Preferred stock, par value $100 (500 shares)*	50,000
Common stock, $15 par value (10,000 shares)*	150,000
Premium on preferred stock	2,000
Retained earnings	25,000
Profits invested in plant	125,000
	$450,000

* Authorized shares—preferred, 2,000; common, 20,000.

The board of directors has not declared a dividend since organization; instead, the profits are used to expand the company. This decision was based on the facts that the original capital was small and there was a decision to limit the number of shareholders. At the present time, the common stock is held by slightly fewer than 50 individuals. Each of these individuals also owns preferred shares; their total holdings approximate 46% of the outstanding preferred. The preferred was issued at the time of the expansion of capital.

The board of directors has been planning to declare a dividend during the early part of 1983, payable June 30. However, the cash position as shown by the balance sheet has raised serious doubts as to the advisability of a dividend in 1983. The president has explained that most of the cash was temporarily tied up in inventory and plant.

The company has a chief accountant but no controller. The board relies on an outside CPA for advice concerning financial management. The CPA was asked to advise about the contemplated dividend declaration. Four of the seven members of the board felt very strongly that some kind of dividend must be declared and paid and that all shareholders "should get something."

Required:

You have been asked to analyze the situation and make whatever dividend proposals that appear to be worthy of consideration by the board. Present amounts to support your recommendations in a form suitable for consideration by the board in reaching a decision. Provide the basis for your proposals and indicate any preferences that you may have.

DECISION CASE 15–3

Ellis Corporation purchased equipment with a cash price of $144,000, for $107,000 cash and a promise to deliver an indeterminate number of shares of its $5 par common stock, with a market value of $15,000 on January 1 of each year for the next four years. Hence, $60,000 in "market value" of shares will be required to discharge the $37,000 balance due on the equipment.

The corporation then acquired 5,000 shares of its own stock (which became treasury shares) in the expectation that the market value of the stock would increase substantially before the delivery dates.

Required:

1. Discuss the propriety of recording the equipment at—
   a. $107,000 (the cash payment).
   b. $144,000 (the cash price of the equipment).
   c. $167,000 (the $107,000 cash payment + the $60,000 market value of treasury stock that must be transferred to the vendor in order to settle the obligation according to the terms of the agreement). Assume an ordinary annuity.
2. Discuss the arguments *for* treating the balance due as—
   a. A liability.
   b. Treasury stock subscribed.
3. Assuming that legal requirements do not affect the decision, discuss the arguments *for* treating the corporation's treasury shares as—
   a. An asset awaiting ultimate disposition.
   b. A capital element awaiting ultimate disposition.

(AICPA adapted)

EXERCISES

PART A: EXERCISES 15–1 to 15–10

Exercise 15–1

Furness Corporation's books on January 1 showed the following balances (summarized):

Cash	$ 35,000
Other current assets	25,000
Operational assets (net)	235,000
Other assets	55,000
	$350,000
Current liabilities	$ 30,000
Long-term liabilities	60,000
Capital stock, 2,000 shares	200,000
Contributed capital in excess of par	10,000
Retained earnings	50,000
	$350,000

The board of directors is considering a cash dividend, and you have been requested to provide certain assistance as the independent CPA. The following matters have been referred to you:

1. What is the maximum amount of cash dividends that can be paid at January 1? Explain.
2. Approximately what amount of dividends would you recommend based upon the data from the accounts? Explain.
3. What entries would be made assuming a $26,000 cash dividend is declared with the following dates specified: *(a)* declaration date, *(b)* date of record, and *(c)* date of payment.
4. Assuming a balance sheet is prepared between declaration date and payment date, how would the dividend declaration be reported?

Exercise 15–2

On June 1, 19G, Grant Corporation had outstanding 10,000 shares of capital stock, par value $10 per share. The shares were held by 10 stockholders, each having an equal number of shares. The Retained Earnings account showed a credit balance of $60,000, although the company was short of cash. The company owned 20,000 shares of stock in AB Company that had been purchased for $20,000. The current market value is $1.25 per share. On June 1, 19G, the board of directors of Grant Corporation declared a dividend of $3 per share "to be paid with AB stock within 30 days after declaration date and scrip to be issued for the difference. The scrip will be payable at the end of 12 months from declaration date and will earn 12% interest per annum." The accounting period ends December 31.

Required:

1. Give all entries related to dividends through date of payment of the scrip.
2. Report all items related to the dividend declaration as they should be reported on *(a)* the balance sheet and *(b)* the income statement at the end of 19G, including any notes needed for full disclosure (i.e., write the notes as they should appear in the statements).

Exercise 15–3

The records of Holden, Inc., showed the following at the end of 19C:

Preferred stock, 6% cumulative, nonparticipating, par $20	$200,000
Common stock, nopar value (50,000 shares issued)	240,000
Contrib. capital in excess of par, pref. stock	30,000
Retained earnings	125,000
Investment in stock of X Corp. (500 shares at cost)	10,000

The preferred stock has dividends in arrears for 19A and 19B. On January 15, 19C, the board of directors passed the following resolution: "The 19C dividend shall be 6% on the preferred stock and 95 cents per share on the common stock; the dividends in arrears are to be paid on March 1, 19C, by issuing a property dividend using the requisite amount of X Corporation stock. All dividends for 19C are to be paid in cash on March 1, 19C." On January 15, 19C, the stock of X Corporation was selling at $60 per share and at $62 on March 1, 19C.

Required:

1. Compute the amount of the dividends to be paid to each class of shareholders, including the number of shares of X Corporation stock and the amount of cash required by the declaration. Assume that divisibility of the shares of X Corporation poses no problem.
2. Give journal entries to record all aspects of the dividend declaration and the subsequent payment.

Exercise 15–4

On December 1, 19B, the board of directors of Jax Mining Company declared a maximum dividend permitted by the state law. The company never had declared a dividend prior to this time. There were 100 stockholders, each holding 200 shares of stock with a par value of $5 per share. The laws of the state provide that "dividends may be paid equal to all accumulated profits prior to the depletion amount." Retained Earnings showed a balance of $60,000; depletion for the year amounted to $12,000 (accumulated depletion was $20,000). The dividend was payable 60 days after declaration date.

Required:

1. Give all entries related to the dividend through the payment date.
2. What special notification, if any, should be given the shareholders?
3. What items related to the dividend declaration would be reported on a balance sheet dated December 31, 19B, assuming net income for 19B of $15,000 (included in the $60,000 balance of retained earnings given above)? Write any note that may be needed to fully disclose the dividend.

Exercise 15–5

The records of Nourse Corporation showed the following balances on November 1, 19A:

Capital stock, par $10	$275,000
Contributed capital in excess of par	110,000
Retained earnings	195,000

On November 5, 19A, the board of directors declared a stock dividend of one additional share for each five shares outstanding; issue date, January 10, 19B. The market value of the stock immediately after the declaration was $18 per share.

Required:

1. Give entries in parallel columns for the stock dividend assuming, for problem purposes, *(a)* market value is capitalized, *(b)* par value is capitalized, and *(c)* average paid in is capitalized. Assume the company records the dividend on declaration and credits an account titled, Stock Dividends Distributable (not a liability).
2. Explain when each value should be used.
3. What should be reported on the balance sheet at December 31, 19A, assuming no intervening transactions?

Exercise 15–6

The accounts of Olivera Corporation provide the following data at December 31, 19C:

Capital stock, par $5, authorized shares 100,000; issued and outstanding 20,000 shares	$100,000
Contributed capital in excess of par	60,000
Retained earnings	120,000

On May 1, 19D, the board of directors of Olivera Corporation declared a 50% stock dividend (i.e., for each two shares outstanding one additional share is to be issued) to be issued on June 1, 19D. The stock dividend is to be capitalized at the average of contributed capital per share at December 31, 19C.

On June 1, 19D, all of the required shares were issued for the stock dividend except for those required by 1,300 fractional share rights (representing 650 full shares) issued.

On December 1, 19D, the company honored 900 of the fractional share rights by issuing the requisite number of shares. The remaining fractional share rights were still outstanding at the end of 19D.

Required:

1. Give the required entries by Olivera Corporation at each of the following dates:
   a. May 1, 19D.
   b. June 1, 19D.
   c. December 1, 19D.
2. Prepare the stockholders' equity section of the balance sheet at December 31, 19D, assuming net income for 19D was $30,000.
3. Assume instead that the fractional share rights specified that *(a)* two such rights could be turned in for one share of stock without cost or *(b)* each right could be turned in for $2.50 cash. As a result, 900 rights were turned in for shares, 200 rights for cash, and the remainder lapsed. Give the entry to record the ultimate disposition of all the fractional share rights.

Exercise 15–7

Strake, Inc., made the following entry to record the ultimate disposition of all fractional share rights issued in connection with a "small" stock dividend:

Fractional share rights outstanding	3,750	
Common stock, par $10		2,000
Additional contributed capital		1,250
Cash		500

Required:

1. What dispositions were made of the total of the fractional share rights, as evidenced by the above entry? State specifically what the stockholders did with their fractional share rights to dispose of them.
2. On what date would Strake, Inc., have known the number of fractional share rights it would have to issue as a part of the stock dividend distribution?
3. How would the above entry be altered if the stock dividend had been "large" instead of "small"?
4. How may the dollar amount of the debit to the Fractional Share Rights Outstanding account exceed the amount credited to the Common Stock account?

Exercise 15–8

Hayba Manufacturing Company's books carried an account entitled Reserve for Profits Invested in Fixed (operational) Assets, $425,000. Capital stock outstanding, par value $20, amounted to $400,000.

The company also had bonds outstanding of $200,000. The following accounts also were carried: Bond Sinking Fund, $90,000; and Bond Sinking Fund Reserve, $90,000.

The board of directors voted a 10% stock dividend and directed that the market value of the stock, $150 per share, be capitalized using as a basis "the general reserves" to the extent possible.

Required:

Give entries for the following using preferable titles:

a. To originally establish the reserve related to fixed (operational) assets.
b. To record the issuance of the stock dividend.
c. To originally establish the bond sinking fund.
d. To originally establish the reserve for bond sinking fund.
e. To record payment of the bonds assuming the bond sinking fund and the reserve each have a $160,000 balance at retirement date.

Exercise 15–9

Using the simplified data below for the year ended December 31, 19X, construct (1) a single-step income statement and (2) a statement of retained earnings. Assume all amounts are material and annual data. Disregard EPS.

Current items	
a. Sales revenue	$400,000
b. Cost of goods sold	160,000
c. Expenses	120,000
d. Extraordinary loss (pretax)	20,000
e. Prior period adjustment—correction of error in recording income taxes of a prior year (a debit)	2,100
f. Appropriation to reserve for bond sinking fund	10,000
g. Dividends declared and paid	30,000
Balances—beginning of period:	
h. Retained earnings	130,000
i. Reserve for bond sinking fund	60,000

Income taxes—assume a 40% average rate.

Exercise 15–10

Using the simplified data below, construct comparative statements of (1) income (single step) and (2) retained earnings for 19A and 19B. Assume all amounts are material, annual data, and an average tax rate of 40% on all items. Disregard EPS.

Current items:	**19A**	**19B**
a. Sales	$110,000	$120,000
b. Cost of goods sold	45,000	50,000
c. Expenses	25,000	29,000
d. Extraordinary gain	3,000	
e. Extraordinary loss		6,000
f. Dividends declared and paid .	12,000	10,000
g. Appropriation for profits invested in operational assets ..	40,000	

h. Prior period adjustment—correction of accounting error made in prior period; no tax effect (a debit)	2,200	
Beginning balances:		
Unappropriated retained earnings	$130,000	?
Appropriation for profits invested in operational assets	-0-	?

PART B: EXERCISES 15–11 to 15–20

Exercise 15–11 (A review exercise)

Each numbered item in the accompanying table changes the *amount* of owners' equity. Some affect retained earnings directly and appear on the retained earnings statement; others affect retained earnings indirectly because they are reported on the income statement; others are not reported on either statement.

(Relates to Exercise 15–11)

Item	Directly on Retained Earnings Statement	On Income Statement	On Neither Statement
1. Extraordinary casualty loss.			
2. Purchase of treasury stock (cost method).			
3. Declaration of cash dividend payable next period.			
4. Correction of prior year's income.			
5. Sale of additional common stock of the enterprise.			
6. Write off receivable from largest customer who is bankrupt.			
7. Recognize dividends from stock investment.			
8. Recognize loss on disposal of segment of business.			
9. Amortize discount on bonds payable.			
10. Change from straight-line depreciation in second year to sum-of-years' digits.			
11. Exchange stock for land.			
12. Investors tender their convertible preferred stock for the common stock of the enterprise.			

Required:
Indicate with a check mark where each of the numbered items should be reported.

Exercise 15–12

Tidwell Company issued 5,000 shares of $20 par value common stock, which was sold originally at $50 per share. On January 15, Tidwell purchased 20 shares of its own stock at $55 per share. On March 1, 16 of the treasury shares were sold at $58. The balance in Retained Earnings was $25,000 prior to these transactions.

Required:
1. Give all entries indicated in parallel columns assuming for treasury stock *(a)* the cost method and *(b)* the par value method.
2. What would be the resulting balance in each stockholders' equity account for each method?

Exercise 15–13

Minnesota Corporation had the following stock outstanding:

Common stock, nopar, 20,000 shares (sold at $15)	$300,000
Preferred stock, par $10, 5,000 shares (sold at $25)	50,000

The following treasury stock transactions were completed:

a. Purchased 50 shares of the common stock at $17 per share.
b. Purchased 20 shares of the preferred stock at $27.
c. Sold 30 shares of the common stock at $14.
d. Sold 10 shares of the preferred stock at $36.

Required:
1. Give entries for all of the above stock transactions assuming the par value method is used for treasury stock.
2. Give resulting balances in each stockholders' equity account; assume a beginning balance in Retained Earnings of $23,000.

Exercise 15–14

Quillen Corporation had outstanding 10,000 shares of preferred stock, par value $10 and 10,000 shares of nopar common stock sold initially for $20 per share. Contributed capital in excess of par on the preferred stock amounted to $40,000; the Retained Earnings balance is $31,600. The corporation purchased 200 shares of its preferred at $22 per share and 300 shares of its common at $25 per share. Subsequently, 100 shares of the common treasury stock were sold for $20 per share.

Required:
1. Give entries to record the treasury stock transactions assuming the cost method is used.
2. Prepare the resulting stockholders' equity section of the balance sheet.

Exercise 15–15

At January 1, 19A, the records of Unser Company showed the following:

Capital stock, par $10, 50,000 shares outstanding	$500,000
Contributed capital in excess of par	250,000
Retained earnings	160,000

During the year, the following transactions affecting stockholders' equity were recorded:

a. Purchased 500 shares of treasury stock at $20 per share.
b. Purchased 500 shares of treasury stock at $22 per share.
c. Sold 600 shares of treasury stock at $25.
d. Net income for 19A was $42,000.

The state law places a restriction on retained earnings equal to the cost of treasury stock held.

Required:
1. Give entries for the initial issuance and for each of the above transactions, in parallel columns, assuming *(a)* the cost method and *(b)* the par value method. Assume FIFO flow for treasury stock. Set up an account for the appropriation of retained earnings.
2. Give the resulting balances in each capital account. Include any required disclosure related to the treasury stock.

Exercise 15–16

During year 19B, Veech Corporation had several changes in stockholders' equity. The comparative balance sheets for 19A and 19B reflected the following amounts in stockholders' equity:

	Balances December 31	
	19A	19B
Capital stock, par $10, issued	$600,000*	$700,000†
Contrib. capital in excess of par	180,000	230,000
Contrib. capital, sale of treasury stock		1,000
Retained earnings	120,000	146,000
Treasury stock	18,000	1,400

* Includes 1,000 shares of treasury stock.

† Includes 100 shares of treasury stock (the 1,000 shares were sold and 100 shares were bought).

Required:
1. What method was used to account for treasury stock? Explain the basis for your conclusion.
2. Give the required entry for each transaction that affected stockholders' equity during 19B. Explain how you determined the amounts used in each entry.

Exercise 15–17

The records for Pincoff Corporation at December 31, 19A, showed the following, assuming the cost method was used for treasury stock:

Assets	$139,000
Liabilities	32,000
Stockholders' equity:	
Capital stock, par $10, 7,000 shares	70,000
Treasury stock, 1,000 shares (at cost)	17,000
Contributed capital in excess of par	14,000
Retained earnings	40,000

Required:
Prepare balance sheets for the corporation with special emphasis on the stockholders' equity section if the state law places a restriction on retained earnings equal to the cost of treasury stock held and if the corporation sets up a special appropriated account for this requirement. Also assume the following:

1. The cost method is used.
2. The par value method is used. *Hint:* Certain of the above account balances must be modified.

Exercise 15–18

Monet Corporation had 30,000 shares of $10 par value capital stock authorized, of which 20,000 shares were issued three years ago at $15 per share. During the current year, the corporation received 500 shares of the capital stock as a bequest from a deceased shareholder; in addition (at approximately the same date), 1,000 shares were purchased at $14 per share. State law places a restriction on retained earnings equal to the cost of treasury stock held. At the end of the year, a cash dividend of 85 cents per share was paid; prior to the dividend; retained earnings amounted to $40,000.

Required:
1. Prepare entries to record all of the transactions assuming the cost method for recording treasury stock is used. Record the donated stock at its market value.
2. Prepare the stockholders' equity section of the balance sheet at year-end and include all required disclosures related to the treasury stock.

Exercise 15–19

The records for Maryville, Inc., reflected the following data on stockholders' equity:

a. Preferred stock, par $50, issued 2,000 shares.
b. Preferred treasury stock, 200 shares (cost $54 per share).
c. Premium on preferred stock at original issue, $2 per share.
d. Common stock, par $100, issued 3,000 shares.
e. Common treasury stock, 300 shares (cost $98 per share).
f. Premium on common stock at original issue was $3 per share.
g. Retained earnings, unappropriated, $110,000.
h. Retained earnings appropriated for cost of treasury stock held, $40,200. The state law places a restriction on retained earnings equal to the cost of treasury stock held.

The shareholders voted to retire all of the treasury stock forthwith and to purchase for retirement another 400 shares of common stock that could be purchased immediately at $125 per share.

Required:
Give entries in parallel columns for the following transactions, assuming the (1) cost method and (2) par value method:

a. Purchase of the 400 shares of outstanding common stock and their immediate retirement. This transaction does not affect treasury stock.
b. Retirement of all of the treasury shares. Give separate entries for the preferred and common.

Exercise 15–20

The records of Lawrence Corporation reflected the following:

Preferred stock, 1,000 shares outstanding, par $100	$100,000
Common stock, 1,000 shares outstanding, par $50	50,000
Contrib. capital in excess of par, pref. stock	5,000
Contrib. capital in excess of par, common stock	2,000
Retained earnings	50,000

The preferred stock is convertible into common stock. Give entry, or entries, required in each of the following cases:

Case A—The preferred shares are converted to common share for share.

Case B—The preferred shares are converted to common stock on a one-for-three basis; that is, three shares of common are issued for each share of preferred.

Case C—The preferred shares are converted, on a share-for-share basis, for a new class of stock known as Common Class B, nopar.

Case D—The preferred shares are converted to common stock on a one-for-five basis (i.e., five shares of common are issued for each share of preferred) plus a cash payment by the holders of the preferred in the amount of $35 per share of common received.

Case E—The preferred shares are converted to common stock on a par-for-par basis; that is, two shares of common are issued for each share of preferred.

SUPPLEMENT 15–A

Exercise 15–21

Martinez Company had experienced a net loss for a number of years. Recently a new president was hired. The board of directors agreed to a quasi-reorganization and to restate certain items in the accounts as outlined by the new president, subject to stockholder and creditor approval. Prior to the restatement, the balance sheet reported the following (summarized at June 30, 19A):

Cash	$ 5,000
Receivables	16,000
Inventories	210,000
Operational assets (net)	560,000
Other assets	44,000
	$835,000

Current liabilities	$ 65,000
Long-term liabilities	85,000
Capital stock (8,000 shares)	800,000
Contributed capital in excess of par	40,000
Retained earnings	(165,000)
Reserve for contingencies	10,000
	$835,000

The stockholders approved the quasi-reorganization effective July 1, 19A, which carried the following provisions:

a. The inventories to be reduced to a LCM value of $140,000.
b. Receivables of $3,000 to be written off as worthless.
c. The operational assets to be reduced to a net carrying value of $400,000.
d. The capital structure to be adjusted so that the deficit will be eliminated and the capital reduced (including a reduction in shares outstanding if needed) by the net adjustment made to assets.

Required:

1. Give entries to record the quasi-reorganization as approved by the stockholders.
2. Prepare an unclassified balance sheet after the quasi-reorganization, including an explanatory note to fully disclose the effect of the quasi-reorganization.

PROBLEMS

PART A: PROBLEMS 15–1 to 15–10

Problem 15–1

Tomasco, Inc., began operations in January 19x1 and had the following reported net income or loss for each of its five years of operations:

19x1	$ 150,000	loss
19x2	130,000	loss
19x3	120,000	loss
19x4	250,000	income
19x5	1,000,000	income

At December 31, 19x5, the Tomasco capital accounts were as follows:

Common stock, par value $10 per share; authorized 100,000 shares; issued and outstanding 50,000 shares	$ 500,000
4% nonparticipating noncumulative preferred stock, par value $100 per share; authorized, issued and outstanding 1,000 shares	100,000
8% fully participating cumulative preferred stock, par value $100 per share; authorized, issued and outstanding 10,000 shares	1,000,000

Tomasco has never paid a cash or stock dividend. There has been no change in the capital accounts since Tomasco began operations. The appropriate state law permits dividends only from retained earnings.

Required:

Prepare a worksheet showing the *maximum* amount available for cash dividends on December 31, 19x5, and how it would be distributable to the holders of the common shares and each of the preferred shares. Show supporting computations. (AICPA adapted)

Problem 15–2

The balance sheet at December 31, 19D, for Belk Retailing Company is shown below in summary:

Cash	$ 28,000
Receivables	36,000
Inventory	110,000
Investments—4,000 shares of Taylor stock at cost	6,000
Operational assets (net)	80,000
Other assets	10,000
	$270,000
Current liabilities	$ 26,000
Bonds payable	50,000
Preferred stock	20,000
Common stock, nopar (5,000 shares)	100,000
Contributed capital in excess of par, preferred	5,000
Retained earnings	69,000
	$270,000

The preferred stock is 6%, $100 par value, and cumulative. Dividends are three years in arrears (excluding the current year, 19E).

The investment in stock of Taylor Company has been held for a number of years; that stock is now selling for $5 per share.

On November 1, 19E, the board of directors of Belk declared dividends as follows:

a. Preferred stock, all dividends in arrears plus current year dividend; payment to be made by transferring the requisite number of shares of Taylor stock at $5 per share.

b. Common stock, $4 per share for the current year, payment to be made by transferring the remainder of the Taylor stock and issuing a scrip dividend for the balance. The scrip will earn 12% annual interest and will be paid at the end of six months from date of declaration.

Required:

1. Compute the amount of dividends payable to each class of shareholder and indicate the amount of the scrip dividend.
2. Give entries to record the transfer of the Taylor stock and the issuance of the scrip dividend (assume declaration and payment dates are the same). Make separate entries for the common and preferred stock.
3. Give the adjusting entry at December 31, 19E, for the interest on the scrip dividend.
4. Give the entry to record payment of the scrip dividend and interest on April 30, 19F.
5. Prepare the stockholders' equity section of the balance sheet as of December 31, 19E. Assume reported net income of $26,000 for 19E (including the interest on the scrip dividend and gain on disposal of Taylor stock).

Problem 15–3

On November 5, 19A, the board of directors of McMurray Corporation declared *(a)* a stock dividend whereby each holder of common stock is to receive two shares of common for each five shares held (i.e., 40%) and *(b)* a cash dividend on the preferred stock for the one year in arrears and for the current year. The board of directors specified that the average originally paid in per share of common will be capitalized for the stock dividend. Assume the declaration and issue (or payment) dates are the same. At November 1, 19A, the records of the corporation showed:

Stockholders' Equity

Preferred stock, 6%, $10 par value, authorized 20,000 shares, issued 10,000 shares	$100,000
Common stock, nopar, stated value $5, authorized 50,000, issued 15,000 shares	75,000
Contrib. capital in excess of par, preferred	20,000
Contrib. capital in excess of stated value, common	30,000
Retained earnings	160,000

Upon issuance of the stock dividend, 5,000 fractional share rights (for 2,000 shares) were distributed to stockholders. On December 30, 19A, 4,500 fractional share rights were exercised for the 1,800 shares. The remaining rights are outstanding to date.

Required:

1. Give entries to record *(a)* issuance of the stock dividend, *(b)* payment of the cash dividend, and *(c)* exercise of the rights.
2. Prepare the stockholders' equity section of the balance sheet after giving effect to the entries in 1 above assuming net income for 19A was $18,000.
3. Give the entry to record the lapse of the remaining rights on October 30, 19B.

Problem 15–4

On December 31, 19A, the accounts for Maire Corporation showed the following balances:

Stockholders' Equity

Preferred stock, 6%, par value $25, authorized 10,000 shares, outstanding 8,000 shares	$200,000
Common stock, nopar, stated value $10, authorized 20,000 shares, outstanding 12,000 shares	120,000
Contrib. capital in excess of par, preferred	15,000
Contrib. capital in excess of stated value, common	30,000
Retained earnings	175,000

During 19B, the following sequential transactions were recorded relating to the capital accounts:

a. Apr. 1 A stock dividend was issued whereby (1) each holder of 10 preferred shares received 1 share of common stock and (2) each holder of 6 shares of common stock received 1 share of common. The market price of the common stock was $15 per share immediately after issuance of the stock dividend. In issuing the stock dividend, 2,700 shares of common stock and 1,000 fractional share rights were issued. Each functional share right represents one tenth of a share of stock.

b. Nov. 1 All of the rights were redeemed except 100 which remained outstanding.

c. Dec. 15 A 6% cash dividend on the preferred shares and a 75 cents per share dividend on the common shares were declared and paid.

d. Dec. 31 Reported net income was $66,093.

Required:

1. Prepare journal entries for each of the above transactions during 19B.
2. Prepare the stockholders' equity section of the balance sheet at December 31, 19B.
3. Now assume that Maire had paid cash to the shareholders in lieu of issuing fractional share warrants. The cash distribution was based on the market value of $15 per share. Give the entry on April 1, 19B, to record the dividend transaction. What would be the total stockholders' equity of Maire Corporation on December 31, 19B, in this situation if all other factors remain as they were given above?

Problem 15–5

The records of Baker Company showed the following balances at the end of 19A:

Current assets	$ 165,000
Operational assets (net)	960,000
Other assets	300,000
Investment in X Corp. stock (5,000 shares at cost)	5,000
	$1,430,000
Current liabilities	$ 60,000
Long-term liabilities	100,000
Preferred stock, 6%, par $100	300,000
Common stock, no par, 100,000 shares outstanding	800,000
Contrib. capital in excess of par, preferred	12,000
Retained earnings	158,000
	$1,430,000

To date, 3,000 shares of the preferred stock (6%, $100 par value, cumulative, nonparticipating) have been issued. Authorized shares were: common, 200,000; and preferred, 3,000. No dividends were declared or paid for 19A. During the subsequent two years, the following transactions affected stockholders' equity:

Year 19B:

a. Feb. 1 Declared and immediately issued one share of X Corporation stock for each share of preferred stock as a property dividend. The current market value of X stock was $3.50 per share. In addition, a cash dividend was paid to complete payment of the dividends in arrears.

b. Oct. 1 Declared and immediately issued scrip dividends amounting to 6% on the preferred and 80 cents per share on the common stock. Interest on the scrip is 7% per year.

c. Dec. 31 Reported net income was $150,000 including any effects of the above transactions.

Year 19C:

d. Sept. 30 Paid the scrip dividends including 7% per annum interest for 12 months.

e. Nov. 1 Declared and issued a stock dividend, payable in common stock to holders of both preferred and common stock. The preferred holders to receive "value" equivalent to 6%, and the common holders to receive one share for each five shares held. The "value" and the amount to be capitalized per share as a debit to Retained Earnings is the market value. The current price per share of the common stock is $1.50.

Issued the stock dividend in full to the preferred. Fractional share rights for 500 shares (i.e., 2,500 rights) were issued to common stockholders.

f. Dec. 1 The fractional share rights specified that five such rights could be turned in for one share of common stock. On this basis, 1,800 of the outstanding fractional share rights were turned in. The remaining 700 rights are outstanding.

g. Dec. 31 Reported net income was $91,000, including any effects of the above transactions.

Required:

1. Prepare journal entries for each of the foregoing transactions (round amounts to nearest dollar).
2. Prepare the stockholders' equity section of the balance sheet at December 31, 19C, after giving recognition to the foregoing transactions.

Problem 15–6

Harrel & Company was organized with an authorization for 50,000 shares of $10 par value stock. During the first five years of operations, the following transactions affected stockholders' equity. Assume they occurred in the order given.

Year 19A:

a. Received subscriptions for 20,000 shares of stock at $15 per share; 50% was collected from each subscriber as a down payment; the stock is not issued until fully paid.

b. Balance was collected on all but 1,500 shares.

c. Reported net income was $5,000.

Year 19B:

d. The balance was collected on 1,400 of the subscribed shares. Subscriptions for the other 100 shares were defaulted. The subscriber was refunded the amount paid in less 20% of the purchase price per agreement. Issued the 1,400 shares.

e. Reported net income was $7,000.

Year 19C:

f. Declared and paid a cash dividend amounting to 50 cents per share on the shares outstanding.

g. Reported net income was $18,000.

Year 19D:

h. Sold 5,000 shares of stock at $18; collected cash and issued stock.

i. Reported net income, $20,000.

Year 19E:

j. Declared a 10% stock dividend on the shares outstanding. The board of directors voted that the "average paid in to date per share" be capitalized (exclude the default recovery). Immediately issued the stock dividend and fractional share rights for 200 of the shares.

k. Rights for 190 shares received and stock issued; the balance lapsed.

l. Declared and paid a 20 cents per share dividend—half payable in cash, balance in scrip payable in six months with interest at 14% per annum.

m. Accrued two months' interest on the scrip dividends.

n. Reported net income $18,000 (includes the interest on the scrip).

Required (round amounts to nearest dollar):

1. Prepare entries for each of the foregoing transactions.
2. Prepare the stockholders' equity section of the balance sheet at the end of 19E, after giving effect to the foregoing transactions.

Problem 15–7

The following annual data were taken from the records of Gray Company at December 31, 19X (assume all amounts are material; the items in parentheses are credit balances):

Current items:	
a. Sales	$(402,000)
b. Cost of goods sold	230,000
c. Expenses	85,000
d. Extraordinary loss	20,000
e. Stock dividend issued	50,000
f. Cash dividend declared and paid	19,000
g. Correction of accounting error involving income taxes from prior period (debit)	8,000
h. Current appropriation to reserve for bond sinking fund	10,000
i. Current appropriation to reserve for plant expansion	40,000

Income taxes:

Assume an average tax rate of 40% on all items except the prior period adjustment.

Balances, January 1, 19X:	
j. Unappropriated retained earnings	$(120,000)
k. Reserve for bond sinking fund	(20,000)
l. Reserve for plant expansion	(60,000)

Required:

1. Prepare a single-step income statement for the year ended December 31, 19X. Disregard EPS.
2. Prepare a statement of retained earnings for the year ended December 31, 19X.

Problem 15–8

Griswold Corporation records provided the following annual data at December 31, 19A, and 19B (assume all amounts are material):

	19A	19B
Current items:		
a. Sales	$240,000	$260,000
b. Cost of goods sold	134,000	143,000
c. Expenses	71,000	77,000
d. Extraordinary loss	7,000	2,000
e. Cash dividend declared and paid	20,000	
f. Stock dividend issued		30,000
g. Appropriation to reserve for bond sinking fund	10,000	10,000
h. Increase in bond sinking fund	10,000	10,000
i. Prior period adjustment—error correction (debit)	6,000	
j. Income taxes—assume an average rate of 46% on all items including extraordinary items and prior period adjustments.		
Balances, January 1, 19A:		
k. Reserve for bond sinking fund	70,000	?
l. Unappropriated retained earnings	160,000	?
m. Reserve for plant expansion	65,000	?
n. Bond sinking fund	70,000	?
o. Bonds payable	100,000	?

Required:

1. Prepare a single-step comparative income statement for years 19A and 19B. Disregard EPS.

2. Prepare a comparative statement of retained earnings for the years 19A and 19B.

Problem 15–9

Myers Corporation records provided the following unclassified data at December 31, 19X.

a. Appropriation during the year of retained earnings for reserve for bond sinking fund, $15,000; the prior balance in this reserve account was $65,000.
b. Balance in Retained Earnings, Unappropriated account per books at end of prior year, $100,000.
c. Cash dividends declared on preferred stock December 31 of the year just ended, payable the following January 15 amounting to $10,000.
d. Declared and issued a small stock dividend on common stock July 1, 19X; par $20,000; and market value, $30,000.
e. Preferred stock sold during 19X: 200 shares, par $100; and market, $130.
f. Income statement data for 19X: sales, $350,000; cost of goods sold, $160,000; and expenses, $80,000.
g. Correction of accounting error from a prior period (a debit), $8,000.

Income taxes—assume an average rate of 40% on all items including extraordinary items and the correction (item [*g*]).

Required:
1. Prepare a single-step income statement. Disregard EPS.
2. Prepare a statement of retained earnings.

Problem 15–10

Perkins Corporation is undergoing an audit. The books show an account entitled Surplus which is reproduced below covering a five-year period, January 1, 19B, to December 31, 19F.

Credits

19B–19E	Net income carried to surplus ...	$ 800,000
19B	By debit to goodwill—authorized by management	50,000
12/31/19C	Contrib. capital in excess of par	6,000
1/1/19D	Correction of prior accounting error†	2,000
1/1/19D	Donation to company—operational asset	5,000
3/31/19D	Refund of prior years' income taxes†	9,000
7/1/19E	Reduction in capital stock from par value, $100, to par value, $50, with no change in number of shares outstanding (10,000); approved by shareholders	500,000
12/31/19F	Net income, 19F	170,000
		$1,542,000

† Not included in net income 19B–19E.

Debits

19B–19E	Cash dividends declared	$ 520,000
12/31/19B	To reserve for bond sinking fund (required annually 19A–19E)	20,000
12/31/19D	Reserve for bond sinking fund ...	20,000
12/31/19E	Reserve for bond sinking fund ...	20,000
9/1/19F	Fifty percent stock dividend	250,000
		$ 830,000

Required:
1. The above account is to be closed and replaced with appropriate accounts. Complete a worksheet analysis of the above account to reflect the correct account balances and the corrections needed. It is suggested that the worksheet carry the following columns: *(a)* surplus account per books; *(b)* net income, 19F; *(c)* corrected unappropriated retained earnings, December 31, 19F; and *(d)* columns for debits and credits to any other specific accounts needed.
2. Give the entry or entries to close this account as of December 31, 19F, and to set up appropriate accounts in its place. (AICPA adapted)

PART B: PROBLEMS 15–11 to 15–16

Problem 15–11 (a review problem)

During May 19A, Gilroy, Inc., was organized with 3,000,000 authorized shares of $10 par value common stock, and 300,000 shares of its common stock were issued for $3,300,000. Net income through December 31, 19A, was $125,000.

On July 3, 19B, Gilroy issued 500,000 shares of its common stock for $6,250,000. A 5% stock dividend was declared on October 2, 19B, and issued on November 6, 19B, to stockholders of record on October 23. The market value of the common stock was $11 immediately after issuance of the dividend shares. Gilroy's net income for 19B was $350,000.

During 19C, Gilroy had the following transactions:

a. In February, Gilroy reacquired 30,000 shares of its common stock for $9 per share. Gilroy uses the cost method to account for treasury stock.
b. In June, Gilroy sold 15,000 shares of its treasury stock for $12 per share.

c. In September, each stockholder was issued (for each share held) one stock right to purchase two additional common shares of common stock for $13 per share. The rights expire on December 31, 19C.
d. In October, 250,000 stock rights were exercised when the market value per share of common stock was $14.
e. In November, 400,000 stock rights were exercised when the market value of the common stock was $15 per share.
f. On December 15, 19C, Gilroy declared its first cash dividend to stockholders of $0.20 per share, payable on January 10, 19D, to stockholders of record on December 31, 19C.
g. On December 21, 19C, in accordance with applicable state law, Gilroy formally retired 10,000 shares of its treasury stock. The market value of the common stock was $16 per share on this date.
h. Net income for 19C was $750,000.

Required:
Prepare a schedule of all transactions affecting the capital stock (shares and dollar amounts), additional paid-in capital (including contributed capital in excess of par, etc), retained earnings, treasury stock (shares and dollar amounts), and the amounts that would be reported on Gilroy's balance sheet at December 31, 19A, 19B, and 19C, as a result of the above facts. Show supporting computations.

(AICPA adapted)

Problem 15–12

Reed Corporation reported the following summarized data prior to the transactions given below:

Assets	$660,000
Less: Liabilities	100,000
	$560,000
Stockholders' equity:	
Preferred stock, $10 par	$300,000
Common stock, $5 par	150,000
Contrib. capital in excess of par, pref. stock	30,000
Retained earnings	80,000
	$560,000

The state law places a restriction on the retained earnings equal to the cost of treasury stock held, and Reed sets up an appropriation of retained earnings to meet this requirement.

The following transactions affecting stockholders' equity were recorded:

a. Purchased preferred treasury stock, 500 shares at $15.
b. Purchased common treasury stock, 1,000 shares at $20.
c. Sold preferred treasury stock, 100 shares at $17.
d. Sold common treasury stock, 400 shares at $14.

Required:
1. Give entries in parallel columns for the treasury stock transactions *(a)* through *(d)*, assuming (1) the cost method and (2) the par value method is used.
2. Prepare the resulting balance sheet (unclassified) for each method.

Problem 15–13

For each question given below, select the best answer from among those given. Explain the basis for your choice.

1. When preferred stock is purchased and retired by the issuing corporation for less than its original issue price, proper accounting for the retirement
   A. Increases the amount of dividends available to common shareholders.
   B. Increases the contributed capital.
   C. Increases reported income for the period.
   D. Increases the treasury stock held by the corporation.
   E. None of the above.
2. The spread between the cost of treasury stock and a subsequent higher selling price of the treasury stock should be credited to—
   A. Contributed capital.
   B. Capital stock.
   C. Retained earnings.
   D. "Other" income.
3. Hillside Corporation has 80,000 shares of $50 par value common stock authorized, issued and outstanding. The 80,000 shares were issued at $55 each. Retained earnings of the company is $160,000. If 1,000 shares of Hillside common stock were reacquired at $62 and the par value method of accounting for treasury stock were used, the balance in the Common Stock account would decrease by—
   A. $62,000.
   B. $55,000.
   C. $50,000.
   D. None of the above.
4. Company G originally issued 100,000 shares of its $20 par common stock at $40 per share. Over its first 10 years of operations, the company earned $75,000 and declared no dividends. In the 11th year of operations, Company G purchased 500 shares of its own stock (as treasury stock) at a cost of $65 per share. One year later, Company G formally retired the treasury stock. If Company G uses the cost method of accounting for treasury stock, it should record the retirement of the treasury stock as follows:

A.	Common stock	30,000	
	Treasury stock		20,000
	Contributed capital from treasury stock transactions		10,000

B.

Common stock	30,000	
Contributed capital from treasury stock transactions	2,500	
Treasury stock		32,500

C.

Common stock	20,000	
Contributed capital in excess of par, common stock	12,500	
Treasury stock		32,500

D.

Common stock	10,000	
Retained earnings	22,500	
Treasury stock		32,500

E. If none of the above, give the correct entry.

5. Which of the following statements is true in respect to the differences and similarities between the cost and par value methods of accounting for treasury stock?
   A. Company A paid $26,000 cash for treasury stock that the company had originally issued for $15,000 (which was $10,000 above par). If Company A uses the par value method of accounting for treasury stock, it will report more contributed capital and less retained earnings than under the cost method at any time the company currently holds treasury stock.
   B. The cost method results in a larger total owners' equity than the par value method.
   C. Under the par value method, the balances in the contributed capital accounts are more realistically reported than under the cost method.
   D. The balance in Retained Earnings is the same under the two methods for a given set of facts; however, the total contributed capital is different under the two methods.
   E. All of the above statements are true.

Problem 15–14

Bonanza Corporation had authorized and outstanding 5,000 shares of capital stock, par value $50 per share. The stockholders approved the exchange of two new shares for each share of the old stock.

Required:
Prepare entries to record the change under each of the following separate cases (assume a sufficient balance in retained earnings):

Case A—The old stock was sold at par, and the new stock was nopar value stock with no stated or assigned value.

Case B—The old stock was sold at a premium of $4 per share, and the new stock was nopar value stock with a stated value of $20 per share.

Case C—The old stock was sold at a premium of $5 per share, and the new stock was nopar value stock with a stated value of $30 per share.

Case D—The old stock was sold at par, and the new stock was nopar value stock with a stated value of $27.50 per share.

Case E—The old stock originally was sold at a premium of $2 per share, and the new stock was $25 par value.

Case F—The old stock was sold at a premium of $3 per share, and the new stock was nopar value stock with no stated or assigned value.

Case G—The old stock was sold at a premium of $1 per share, and the new stock was nopar value stock with no stated or assigned value.

Problem 15–15

At the end of 19B the comparative balance sheets for Sandford Corporation reported the following stockholders' equity amounts:

	Balances December 31	
	19A	**19B**
Preferred stock, par $10, shares authorized 20,000	$150,000	$200,000
Common stock, nopar, shares authorized 100,000; issued near the end of 19A, 30,000; 19B, 31,000	210,000	218,000
Contributed capital in excess of par, preferred stock	74,000	154,000
Contributed capital, sale of preferred treasury stock		1,600
Treasury stock, preferred stock ...	2,000	1,000
Treasury stock, common stock	2,100	3,500*
Retained earnings appropriated for treasury stock:		
Preferred (at cost)	5,124	2,462
Common (at cost)	1,950	3,550
Retained earnings unappropriated†	53,000	91,962

* Increased for 200 shares.
† No dividends were declared during 19B.

Required:
1. At the end of 19A, what had been the average selling price per share (by the corporation) of the *(a)* preferred and *(b)* common shares?
2. What method is being used to account for treasury stock? Explain.
3. Complete the following tabulation for the treasury stock held at December 31, 19A (show computations):

	Number of Treasury Shares Held	Average Cost per Share
Preferred	________	________
Common	________	________

4. How many shares were outstanding at December 31, 19A, for *(a)* preferred and *(b)* common?
5. What was the total amount of shareholders' equity at December 31, 19A?
6. Give the required entry for each transaction that affected stockholders' equity during 19B.

Problem 15–16 (a review problem)

Howard Corporation is a publicly owned company whose shares are traded on a national stock exchange. At December 31, 19B, Howard had 25,000,000 shares of $10 par value common stock authorized, of which 15,000,000 shares were issued and 14,000,000 shares were outstanding.

The stockholders' equity accounts at December 31, 19B, had the following balances:

Common stock	$150,000,000
Additional paid-in capital	80,000,000
Retained earnings	50,000,000
Treasury stock	18,000,000

During 19C, Howard had the following transactions:

a. On February 1, 19C, a secondary distribution of 2,000,000 shares of $10 par value common stock was completed. The stock was sold to the public at $18 per share, net of offering costs.

b. On February 15, 19C, Howard issued at $110 per share, 100,000 shares of $100 par value, 8% cumulative preferred stock with 100,000 detachable warrants. Each warrant contained one right which with $20 could be exchanged for one share of $10 par value common stock. On February 15, 19C, the market price for one stock right was $1.

c. On March 1, 19C, Howard reacquired 20,000 shares of its common stock for $18.50 per share. Howard uses the cost method to account for treasury stock.

d. On March 15, 19C, when the common stock was trading for $21 per share, a major stockholder donated 10,000 shares which are appropriately recorded as treasury stock.

e. On March 31, 19C. Howard declared a semiannual cash dividend on common stock of 10 cents per share, payable on April 30, 19C, to stockholders of record on April 10, 19C. The appropriate state law prohibits cash dividends on treasury stock.

f. On April 15, 19C, when the market price of the stock rights was $2 each and the market price of the common stock was $22 per share, 30,000 stock rights were exercised. Howard issued new shares to settle the transaction.

g. On April 30, 19C, employees exercised 100,000 options that were granted in 19A under a noncompensatory stock option plan. When the options were granted, each option had a preemptive right and entitled the employee to purchase one share of common stock for $20 per share. On April 30, 19C, the market price of the common stock was $23 per share. Howard issued new shares to settle the transaction.

h. On May 31, 19C, when the market price of the common stock was $23 per share, Howard declared a 5% stock dividend distributable on July 1, 19C, to stockholders of record on June 1, 19C. The appropriate state law prohibits stock dividends on treasury stock. On July 1, 19C, immediately after issuance of the dividend shares, the market price of the common stock was $20.

i. On June 30, 19C, Howard sold the 20,000 treasury shares reacquired on March 1, 19C, and an additional 280,000 treasury shares costing $5,600,000 that were on hand at the beginning of the year. The selling price was $25 per share.

j. On September 30, 19C, Howard declared a semiannual cash dividend on common stock of 10 cents per share and the yearly dividend on preferred stock, both payable on October 30, 19C, to stockholders of record on October 10, 19C. The appropriate state law prohibits cash dividends on treasury stock.

k. On December 31, 19C, the remaining outstanding rights expired.

l. Net income for 19C was $25,000,000.

Required:

Prepare a worksheet to be used to summarize, for each transaction, the changes in Howard's stockholders' equity accounts for 19C. The columns on this worksheet should have the following headings:

Date of transaction (or beginning date)
Common stock—number of shares
Common stock—amount
Preferred stock—number of shares
Preferred stock—amount
Common stock warrants—number of rights
Common stock warrants—amount
Additional paid-in capital (including contributed capital in excess of par, etc.)
Retained earnings
Treasury stock—number of shares
Treasury stock—amount

Show supporting computations. (AICPA Adapted)

SUPPLEMENT 15–A: PROBLEMS 15–17 to 15–19

Problem 15–17

The following account balances were shown on the books of Overton Corporation at December 31:

Noncumulative preferred stock, par $100, 5%, 2,000 shares	$200,000
Common stock, par $50, 5,000 shares	250,000
Retained earnings (deficit)	(45,000)

At a stockholders' meeting (including holders of preferred shares) the following actions related to the quasi-reorganization were decided upon:

a. That an amendment to the charter be obtained authorizing a total issue of 5,000 shares of cumulative, 6% preferred, par $100 per share, and 40,000 shares of nopar common stock.

b. That all outstanding stock be returned in exchange for new stock as follows:

(1) For each share of old preferred, one share of new preferred. Purchased for cash at par 20 shares of old preferred stock from a dissatisfied stockholder and the remainder exchanged.

(2) For each share of old common, two shares of new common; the credit to the nopar stock account shall be at an amount which creates a credit balance in contributed capital from conversion sufficient to exactly eliminate the deficit in retained earnings. All of the old shares were exchanged.

c. That the past operating deficit be written off against the credit created by the conversion of the common stock.

During the ensuing year the following transactions were effected:

d. Sold 200 shares of the new preferred stock at $112 per share.

e. The company issued 1,200 shares of nopar common in payment for a patent tentatively valued by the seller at $20,000. (The current market value of a share was $15.)

f. The company sold 50 shares of nopar common at $19 per share, receiving cash. Also issued 100, $1,000 bonds at 102; one share of common stock, as a bonus, was given with each bond.

g. At the end of the year, the board of directors met and was informed that the net income before deductions for bonuses to officers was $100,000. The directors took the following actions:

(1) Ordered that 500 shares of nopar common stock (from authorized but unissued shares) be issued to officers as a bonus. The market price of a nopar common share on this date was $16.

(2) Declared and paid dividends (for one year) on the preferred stock outstanding.

Required:

1. Prepare journal entries to record the above transactions.
2. Prepare the stockholders' equity section of the balance sheet after giving effect to the above transactions.

Problem 15–18

During the last five years, Norwood Corporation has experienced severe losses. A new president has been tentatively employed who is confident the company can be saved from bankruptcy (and dissolution). Working with an independent CPA, the new president has proposed a quasi-reorganization with the constraints that *(a)* the capital structure must be changed to eliminate the deficit in retained earnings and *(b)* it must be approved by the stockholders and creditors. The board approved the proposal and submitted it to a vote of the stockholders and creditors.

Prior to quasi-reorganization, the balance sheet (summarized) reflected the following:

Cash	$ 20,000
Accounts receivable	94,000
Allowance for doubtful accounts	(4,000)
Inventory	150,000
Operational assets	800,000
Accumulated depreciation	(300,000)
Deferred charges	40,000
	$ 800,000
Current liabilities	$ 150,000
Long-term liabilities	240,000
Common stock, par $50	500,000
Preferred stock, par $100	100,000
Contrib. capital in excess of par on pref. stock	30,000
Retained earnings, deficit	(220,000)
	$ 800,000

The quasi-reorganization proposal, as approved by the stockholders and creditors, provided the following:

a. To provide adequately for probable losses on accounts receivable, increase the allowance to $6,000.

b. Write down the inventory to $100,000 because of obsolete and damaged goods.

c. Reduce the book value of the operational assets to $400,000 by increasing accumulated depreciation.

d. By agreement of the creditors, reduce all liabilities by 5%.

e. Reduce the par value of the preferred shares to $60.

f. Close out the contributed capital in excess of par on the preferred stock.

g. Call in the old common stock and issue a new common stock, nopar. Set up a new nopar common stock account with the balance needed to reduce retained earnings to zero.

Required:

1. Give a separate entry for each of the above changes.
2. Prepare an unclassified balance sheet immediately after the quasi-reorganization.

Problem 15–19

Marks Corporation, a medium-sized manufacturer, has experienced losses for the past five years. Although operations for the year ended resulted in a loss, several important changes resulted in a profitable fourth quarter; as a result, future operations of the company are expected to be profitable.

The treasurer suggested a quasi-reorganization to *(a)* eliminate the accumulated deficit of $325,000 in retained earnings, *(b)* write up the $600,000 cost of operating land and buildings to their market value, and *(c)* set up an asset of $175,000 representing the estimated future tax benefit of the losses accumulated to date.

Required:

1. What are the characteristics of a quasi-reorganization? That is, of what does it consist?
2. List the conditions under which a quasi-reorganization generally would be justified.
3. Discuss the propriety of the treasurer's proposals to—
   a. Eliminate the deficit of $325,000.
   b. Write up the value of the operating land and buildings of $600,000 to their market value.
   c. Set up an asset of $175,000 representing the future tax benefit of the losses accumulated to date.

(AICPA adapted)

16

Long-Term Investments in Equity Securities

A COMPANY may invest in another company by acquiring either *(a)* debt securities (i.e., notes, mortgages, and bonds) or *(b)* equity securities (i.e., common and preferred stock).[1] Investments may be acquired with the intention of holding them on a short-term or long-term basis. Short-term investments were discussed in Chapter 6.

Investments are classified as current assets when they meet the dual test of (1) ready **marketability** and (2) a clear **intention by management to convert them to cash during the upcoming year or normal operating cycle,** whichever is the longer. All investments that do not meet both of these criteria are classified as long-term investments and reported on the balance sheet under the heading Investments and Funds (see Chapter 4). Long-term investments include debt and equity securities and other assets held for investment purposes. They may or may not meet the test of ready marketability; however, the **intention** of management should be to retain them beyond the time span for current assets.

The purpose of this chapter is to discuss accounting for **long-term investments in equity securities.**[2] The chapter is subdivided as follows:

Part A—Investments in Equity Securities
Part B—Consolidated Financial Statements

Part A: Investments in Equity Securities

RECORDING LONG-TERM INVESTMENTS AT DATE OF ACQUISITION

At date of acquisition of a long-term investment, an appropriately designated investment account is debited for the full cost of the investment in accordance with the **cost principle.** Cost includes the basic cost of the security plus brokerage fees, excise taxes, and any other transfer costs incurred by the purchaser. Stock may be purchased for cash, on margin, or on a subscription basis. When stock is purchased on margin, only part of the purchase price is paid initially and the balance is borrowed. The stock should be recorded at its full cost, including the por-

[1] Equity securities, as used in *FASB Statement 12,* encompasses all capital stock (including stock rights, options, and warrants) except preferred stock that by its terms either must be redeemed by the issuing enterprise or is redeemable at the option of the investor.

[2] Chapter 17 discusses investments in **debt** securities.

tion financed with borrowed funds. A stock subscription to buy the stock of another corporation creates an asset represented by the stock investment and a liability for the amount to be paid. Interest paid on a subscription contract, or on funds borrowed to purchase the investment, should be recorded as interest expense and **not** capitalized as part of the cost of the investment.

When **noncash considerations** (property or services) are given for long-term investments, the cost assigned to the securities should be measured by the market value of the consideration given. However, if that cannot be determined reliably, cost may be measured by the market value of the securities acquired. Inability to determine either value in an exchange of unlisted or closely held securities for property for which no established market value exists may require the use of appraisals or estimates.

Securities frequently are purchased between regular interest or dividend dates. Under GAAP, interest is recorded as it accrues on debt securities but **dividends are not accrued** on equity securities. In the case of a purchase of **cumulative** preferred stock on which the issuing corporation has been regularly paying dividends, the correct treatment is debatable. The authors would not accrue dividends (even in this case) because dividends legally do not accrue.[3]

To illustrate the purchase of a stock investment between regular dividend dates, assume that on October 1, 19A, X Corporation purchased 500 shares of the common stock of Y Corporation, par $5, at $20 per share. Dividends are paid regularly around July 1 of each year; the last dividend was 50 cents per share. The investment in **equity securities** would be recorded at acquisition date as follows:

Long-term investment, Y Corporation common stock (500 shares)	10,000	
Cash		10,000

(Note: Dividends are **not** accrued.)

Alternatively, assume that on October 1, 19A, X Corporation purchased a $10,000, 12 percent bond (interest payable each July 1) of Y Corporation for $10,000 plus accrued interest. The acquisition of this long-term investment in **debt securities** would be recorded as follows:

Long-term investment, Y Corporation bond (at cost)	10,000	
Investment revenue ($\$10,000 \times .12 \times 3/12$)	300	
Cash		10,300

(Note: Interest is accrued to date of purchase as discussed in Chapter 17.)

Special Cost Problems

A purchase of two or more classes of securities for a single lump sum (sometimes called a lump-sum or basket purchase) necessitates allocation of the total cost to each class of securities based upon their relative market values. For example, if a block of security A purchased separately would cost $1,000 and a block of security B purchased separately would cost $2,000, one third of the total lump-sum cost would be allocated to A and two thirds to B whether the combined cost was $3,000 or some other amount. In case one class of securities has a known market value and the other does not, the known market value is used for that class and the remainder of the lump-sum price is allocated to the other. If neither has a known market value, defer any apportionment until evidence of at least one market value is established.

Securities sometimes are acquired in exchange for other securities. The securities acquired should be recorded at the market value of those given up or, if that cannot be determined reliably, at their own market value at the time of the exchange. To illustrate an **exchange of securities,** assume that each holder of a share of $100 par value preferred stock in AB Corporation becomes entitled to receive in exchange five shares of nopar common stock of the company. An investor who had paid $6,000 for 50 shares of preferred stock makes the exchange. At the time of the exchange, the nopar common stock was selling at $27. The exchange would be recorded as follows:[4]

[3] Theoretically, dividends should be recognized when stock is purchased between the declaration date and record date (ex-dividend date) because the corporation incurred a liability at the declaration date. The price of a listed stock (especially preferred) tends to rise as the regular dividend date approaches and to decline by approximately the amount of the dividend as soon as the stock goes "ex-dividends." Prices of stocks are subject to many variables which may obscure these price movements, even though they are present.

[4] A more extended discussion of the exchange of securities is presented in Chapter 17; there an alternate treatment in which no gain or loss is recognized also is presented. The authors are of the opinion that the treatment illustrated here is preferable.

Long-term investment in nopar common stock of AB Corporation ($27 × 250 shares)	6,750	
Long-term investment in preferred stock of AB Corporation		6,000
Gain on exchange of stock investment		750

In accounting for investments, usually it is necessary to maintain an identification of each security acquired, which can be done by using the stock or bond certificate number. In effect, this requires the maintenance of inventory records with respect to securities so they may be properly "costed out" upon disposition. For example, if 10 shares of X Corporation stock are purchased at $150 per share and later an additional 30 shares are purchased at $200 per share, the subsequent sale of 5 shares at $180 per share would pose a cost identification problem. If the five shares can be identified by certificate number as a part of the first purchase, a **gain** of $30 per share should be recognized. Alternatively, if they are identified with the second purchase, a **loss** of $20 per share should be recognized. If an averaging procedure were applied, the result would be a loss of $7.50 per share computed as follows:

First purchase	10 shares @ $150	= $1,500
Second purchase	30 shares @ 200	= 6,000
Total	40	$7,500
Average cost per share $7,500 ÷ 40 shares		= $187.50
Sale price per share		= 180.00
Loss per share		= $ 7.50

Usually identification of shares sold is not difficult. However, where blocks of shares have been transferred through an estate, or where the issuing corporation has exchanged substitute securities for those originally purchased, an identification problem can arise. Federal tax laws require use of "first-in, first-out" where specific identification cannot be made. Use of either FIFO or an average cost procedure is acceptable for financial accounting purposes; however, most companies use the same approach for tax and accounting purposes to avoid having to record deferred income taxes.

ACCOUNTING FOR STOCK INVESTMENTS SUBSEQUENT TO ACQUISITION

In accounting for long-term investments, in stock subsequent to acquisition date, two important factors are *(a)* the distinction between **voting** stock and **nonvoting** stock, such as nonvoting preferred stock; and *(b)* the **proportion** of voting shares owned to the total of such shares outstanding (i.e., the level of ownership of the voting shares).[5]

There are three different methods of accounting for stock investments, viz: (1) cost, (2) equity, and (3) market value. Each of these methods is used under certain specified conditions. In addition, when one company owns a **controlling interest** in the voting stock of another company, the controlling company usually must prepare **consolidated financial statements** (discussed in Part B of this chapter).

The distinction between **voting stock** and **nonvoting stock** is important because the former permits the owner to exercise some influence or control through voting on the operating and financing policies of the other company. The degree of influence or control depends upon the **proportion of outstanding voting shares owned** as an investment (usually the common stock) to the total of such shares outstanding. Therefore, in accounting for long-term investments in the voting capital stock of another company, *APB Opinion No. 18,* "Equity Method for Investments in Common Stock," defined two important concepts, "significant influence" and "control," essentially as follows:

1. **Significant influence**—This is the ability of the investor company to affect, in an important degree, the operating and financing policies of another company through ownership of a sufficient portion of its voting stock. Ability to exercise significant influence also may be indicated in several other ways, such as representation on the board of directors, interchange of managerial personnel, material intercompany transactions, or technological dependency. To achieve a reasonable degree of uniformity, the APB provided

[5] Level of ownership refers to the proportion of voting shares owned to the total voting shares outstanding. To illustrate, assume Company X purchased 20,000 shares of common stock of Company Y when Y had 100,000 total shares outstanding. The level of ownership by X in Y would be 20,000 ÷ 100,000 = 20%.

EXHIBIT 16–1: Accounting for Long-Term Equity Investments

Investment Characteristics	Level of Ownership	Reporting Method
A. No significant influence or control:		
1. Nonvoting stock owned.	All levels	Cost
2. Voting stock owned.	All levels less than 20%	Cost
B. Significant influence but not control:		
3. Voting stock owned.	20% through 50%	Equity
C. Controlling interest:		
4. Voting stock owned, but for special reasons not appropriate to consolidate.	Over 50%	Equity
5. Voting stock owned, appropriate to consolidate.	Over 50%	Consolidated statement basis

an operational rule that an investment of **20 percent or more of the outstanding voting stock** should lead to the presumption that, in the absence of evidence to the contrary, an investor has the ability to exercise **significant influence** over the other company.[6]

2. **Controlling interest**—A controlling interest exists when the investor company owns enough of the voting stock of the other company to effectively control its operating and financing policies. Ownership of **over 50 percent** of the outstanding voting stock usually would assure **control;** however, in some situations this may not be the case (discussed in Part B). In still other situations, ownership of less than 50 percent may create a controlling interest. Factors such as the number of shareholders and the extent of shareholder participation in voting bear on the point at which a controlling interest is attained. Operationally, the presumption is that a controlling interest is represented by over 50 percent of the voting stock.

Accounting for long-term investments in stock may be outlined as shown in Exhibit 16–1. The cost, equity, and market value methods are discussed immediately below. Consolidated statements are discussed in Part B. Based upon its survey of 600 companies, *Accounting Trends & Techniques, 1980,* Table 2–15, reported that in 1979, 332 investor companies accounted for their investments by the equity method, whereas 149 companies used the cost method. Consolidated statements may be based upon either the cost or the equity method with the same end results as discussed in Part B.

COST METHOD

Under the cost method, long-term investments in **equity securities** are recorded in the accounts at **cost.** Subsequently, they are accounted for at lower of cost or market (LCM). On this point, *FASB Statement 12* (pars. 8–9) states:

> The carrying value of a marketable equity securities portfolio shall be the lower of its aggregate cost or market value, determined at the balance sheet date. The amount by which aggregate cost of the portfolio exceeds market value shall be accounted for as the valuation allowance.

[6] An investor may be **unable** to exercise significant influence over the investee's policies when:

a. Opposition by the investee, such as litigation or complaints to governmental regulatory authorities, challenges the investor's ability to exercise significant influence.
b. The investor and investee sign an agreement under which the investor surrenders significant rights as a shareholder.
c. Majority ownership of the investee is concentrated among a small group of shareholders who operate the investee without regard to the views of the investor.
d. The investor tries and fails to obtain representation on the investee's board of directors.

The above list, from FASB, *Interpretation No. 35,* "Criteria for Applying the Equity Method of Accounting for Investments in Common Stock" (Stamford, Conn., May 1981), is intended to be illustrative and not all-inclusive.

> Marketable equity securities owned by an entity shall . . . be grouped into separate portfolios according to the current or noncurrent classification of the securities for the purpose of comparing aggregate cost and market value to determine carrying amount.

Realized and Unrealized Gains and Losses

Statement 12 makes a careful distinction between realized and unrealized gains and losses on marketable equity securities. A **realized** gain or loss represents the difference between the net proceeds received and the investment cost of an equity security at date of sale. In contrast, an **unrealized** gain or loss on marketable equity securities represents the difference between the aggregate market value and aggregate cost of the long-term investment portfolio on a given date.

A **realized** gain or loss on an investment in a marketable equity security is recognized when the security is sold. A **realized** loss is recognized when an investment security is *(a)* written down because of a **permanent** decline in its market value or *(b)* transferred between the short-term and long-term portfolios when its market value is below its cost. **Unrealized** gains and losses are recognized only at the end of the accounting period, when an adjusting entry is made to apply the LCM concept to the investment portfolio.

Application of Lower of Cost or Market (LCM) to Investments in Equity Securities

To apply the LCM concept, *FASB Statement 12* defines cost **after acquisition** as the original cost of the equity security, except for the following situations, which establish a new (i.e., lower) cost basis for the individual equity security:

a. Transfer of an individual equity security between the short-term and long-term investment portfolios, when its market value is below its cost.

b. Write-down of an individual equity security (rather than the portfolio) to a market value which is below cost to reflect a **permanent,** as opposed to a temporary, decline in market value.

In the adjusting entry made at the end of the period to **apply LCM,** an **allowance** account (a contra asset account) is used to record the difference between aggregate (portfolio) cost and aggregate (portfolio) market, and an unrealized loss (or loss recovery) account is used for the other side of the entry. On the balance sheet, the allowance account balance is subtracted from the cost of the portfolio and the accumulated unrealized loss amount is reported under the owners' equity caption as unrealized capital.[7] Under no circumstances can the cumulative unrealized gains (i.e., loss recovery) recorded exceed the cumulative unrealized losses on the long-term portfolio of equity securities because this would result in the investments being written up above cost.

Under the cost method, cash dividends received are recorded as investment revenue. A cash dividend should be recorded as a receivable on declaration date; however, if the dividend declaration and payment dates both occur during the same period, the same effect is attained by a single entry on the payment date as follows:

Cash (amount assumed)	7,500	
Investment revenue		7,500

Occasionally, an investor receives a dividend that is entirely, or in part, a **liquidating dividend** (see Chapter 15). Dividends received in excess of earnings accumulated since the acquisition date of the investment are considered liquidating dividends. In such instances, the investor should reduce the investment account for the amount of the liquidating dividend. Dividends received in noncash assets should be recorded at the market value of the assets received.

Exhibit 16–2 illustrates application of the cost method for long-term investments in equity securities. In Exhibit 16–2, Panel B, observe the following:

1. On December 31, 19A and 19B (entries 2 and 5), LCM is applied to the aggregate long-term investment portfolio, **not** to individual securities.
2. The April 14, 19B, realized loss due to the **permanent** decline in the market value of Y Corporation stock ($25,000) and the August 10, 19B, realized gain on the sale of Z Corporation stock ($4,000) both are closed to Income Summary and reported on the income statement, as shown in Panel C.
3. On August 10, 19B, when 1,000 shares of Z Corporation stock were sold, a realized gain was recognized for the difference between the selling price and the original cost. Also, a proportionate part

[7] In contrast, recall from Chapter 6 that for short-term equity investments classified as current assets, **both** the realized and unrealized gains and losses are reported on the current income statement.

EXHIBIT 16–2: Cost Method for Long-Term Equity Investments—ABC Company Is Investor

Panel A—Illustrative Data:

1. January 5, 19A—ABC Company purchased the following equity securities as a long-term investment (less than 20 percent of the outstanding voting shares in each case):
   Y Corporation, common stock, par $5, 5,000 shares at $12.
   Z Corporation, preferred stock, par $10, 4,000 shares at $20.
2. December 31, 19A—Market values: Y stock, $10; and Z stock, $21.
3. April 14, 19B—Market value of Y Corporation stock decreased to $7; for purposes of this illustration, the decrease was considered to be permanent.
4. August 10, 19B—Unexpectedly sold 1,000 shares of the Z Corporation stock for cash, $24.
5. December 31, 19B—Market values: Y stock, $5.50; and Z stock, $22 (any increase or decrease from previous market values is considered to be temporary).

Panel B—Entries:

1. January 5, 19A:

Long-term investments in equity securities	140,000	
Cash [(5,000 × $12) + (4,000 × $20)]		140,000

2. December 31, 19A—Adjusting entry to LCM:

Unrealized loss on long-term investments in equity securities	6,000	
Allowance to reduce long-term investments in equity securities to market		6,000

Computation:

Security	Shares	Cost	Market	Unrealized Gain (Loss)
Y	5,000	@ $12 = $ 60,000	@ $10 = $ 50,000	$(10,000)
Z	4,000	@ 20 = 80,000	@ 21 = 84,000	4,000
Total		$140,000	$134,000	$ (6,000)

3. April 14, 19B—Permanent decrease in value of Y Corporation stock.

Realized loss in market value of long-term investments [5,000 × ($12 − $7)]	25,000	
Long-term investments in equity securities		25,000

4. August 10, 19B—Unexpected sale of 1,000 shares of Z Corporation stock:

Cash (1,000 × $24)	24,000	
Long-term investments in equity securities (1,000 × $20)		20,000
Realized gain on sale of long-term investments		4,000

5. December 31, 19B—Adjusting entry to LCM:

Allowance to reduce long-term investments in equity securities to market	4,500	
Unrealized loss on long-term investments in equity securities		4,500

Computation:

Security	Shares	Cost	Market	Unrealized Gain (Loss)
Y	5,000	@ $ 7 = $35,000	@ $ 5.50 = $27,500	$(7,500)
Z	3,000	@ 20 = 60,000	@ 22.00 = 66,000	6,000
Total		$95,000	$93,500	$(1,500)

Credit balance in allowance account (before December 31, 19B, adjustment)	$6,000
Credit balance needed in allowance account	1,500
Adjustment needed (debit)	$4,500

EXHIBIT 16–2 ***(concluded)***

Panel C—Financial Statements of ABC Company:

Income statement:	19A		19B	
Realized loss in market value of long-term investments		—		$25,000
Realized gain on sale of long-term investments		—		4,000
Balance sheet:				
Investments and funds:				
Investments in equity securities, at cost	$140,000		$95,000	
Less: Allowance to reduce equity investments to market	(6,000)		(1,500)	
Investment portfolio at LCM		$134,000		$93,500
Stockholders' equity:				
Unrealized capital:				
Unrealized loss on long-term investments in equity securities		(6,000)		(1,500)

of the balance in Allowance to Reduce Long-Term Investments in Equity Securities to Market **was not removed** for the securities sold. Instead, the allowance account for the entire portfolio is adjusted only at the end of the period.

4. On December 31, 19B, the $4,500 **credit** to Unrealized Loss on Long-Term Investments in Equity Securities is in the nature of a loss recovery because it represents a recovery of the prior write-down of the aggregate portfolio to its market value (i.e., $6,000 − $1,500 = $4,500).

Exhibit 16–2 does **not** illustrate accounting for a change in **classification** of an individual equity security arising from its transfer between the short-term and long-term investment portfolios. When such a transfer occurs, the security must be transferred at the LCM value at date of transfer. This value then becomes **cost** for subsequent periods. If market is below cost, the difference must be accounted for as a realized loss and reported on the current income statement in the manner shown for the realized losses reported in Exhibit 16–2, Panel C.

EQUITY METHOD

The equity method is different conceptually from the cost method. It is based on the presumption that the investor owns a sufficient number of the outstanding voting shares of another company (usually called the investee company) to exercise significant influence (although not control) over the operating and financing policies of the other company. An important element is influence over the **dividend policy** of the investee. This presumption radically changes the basis for recognition of **investment revenue** from that used in the cost method.

APB Opinion 18 states that investors should use the equity method in accounting for investments in common stock of unconsolidated subsidiaries (foreign as well as domestic) and also for investments in common stock where the "investment in voting stock gives it the ability to exercise significant influence over operating and financial policies of an investee even though the investor holds 50 percent or less of the voting stock." The *Opinion* also states that "an investment (direct or indirect) of 20 percent or more of the voting stock of an investee should lead to a presumption that in the absence of evidence to the contrary, an investor has the ability to exercise significant influence over an investee."[8] *Opinion 18* sets forth procedures for applying the equity method. Among them are the following:

a. Intercompany profits and losses should be eliminated.

b. A difference between the cost of an investment and the amount of underlying equity in net assets of an investee (i.e., goodwill) should be accounted for as if the investee were a consolidated subsidiary.

c. The investment in common stock should be shown in the balance sheet of the investor as a single amount, and the investor's share of the

[8] See footnote 6 for examples of situations in which an investor that owns 20 percent or more of the investee's voting stock may not be able to exercise sufficient influence over the investee to warrant use of the equity method.

investee's earnings or losses should be shown in the income statement of the investor as a single amount except for the extraordinary items as specified in *(d)* below.

d. The investor's share of the investee's extraordinary items and prior period adjustments should be reported by the investor in accordance with *APB Opinion 30* and *FASB Statement 16*, respectively; that is, the investor should classify such items in a manner similar to its own extraordinary items and prior period adjustments.

e. Sales of stock of the investee by the investor should be accounted for as gains or losses equal to the difference at the time of sale between selling price and carrying amount of the stock sold.

Thus, under the equity method the **cost** of the investment at acquisition date is recorded as a debit to the **investment account.** Subsequently, each period, the investment account is (1) increased for the investor's proportionate share of the investee's earnings, or decreased for losses, and (2) decreased by all dividends received from the investee. Entries then are made to adjust the investee's income recognized by the investor *(i)* to eliminate any intercompany gains and losses ([*a*] above) and *(ii)* for any differences in the measurements of the investee's expenses (e.g., depreciation) by the investee and the investor; such differences often result because the investee company measures its expenses, and, hence, its income, at historical cost, whereas the investor measures the investee's expenses based upon the market values of the investee's assets at the acquisition date of the investment ([*b*] above). These latter entries are necessary because the investor must account for such expenses on the basis of the investor's cost, which is the market value of the related assets at acquisition date of the investment. When an investee reports extraordinary gains or losses, the investor must report its share separately as extraordinary ([*d*] above).

Therefore, subsequent to acquisition, each period the investor makes the following six types of entries:

1. **Records** the proportionate share of the investee's reported income by debiting the investment account and crediting the Investment Revenue account. In case of a loss, the investment account is credited and Investment Loss is debited. If the investee reports extraordinary items, they must be separately recorded in this entry. Thus, the investor's investment account increases and decreases with the gains and losses of the investee company. When the investee earns income, the investor is presumed to **earn** a proportionate part of that income, with a consequent increase in asset value (and vice versa for losses).
2. **Records** dividends received as a debit to the Cash account and a credit to the investment account. In effect, dividends paid by the investee company to the investor are viewed as a conversion of part of the investment account balance to Cash, and thus a liquidation of that part of the investment.
3. **Records** the proportionate share of additional expense if the investor's cost (i.e., market value of the investee's assets on date of acquisition) was in excess of the investee's book value at that date.

Examples of additional expenses that must be recorded are as follows:

a. **Depreciation expense.** Assume Investor Company acquired 20 percent of the outstanding voting shares (i.e., a 20 percent interest in the net assets) of Investee Company. Assume further that at date of acquisition, depreciable assets owned by Investee Company were carried at $500,000, but the market value (cost to the investor) was $700,000 (a difference of $200,000). Assuming straight-line depreciation, a 10-year remaining life, and no residual value, Investor Company would recognize additional annual depreciation of $4,000 [i.e., ($200,000 × .20) ÷ 10 years]. Otherwise, the investment revenue recognized by Investor Company and the investment account on the books of Investor Company would be overstated. The additional depreciation amount is debited to the Investment Revenue account and credited to the investment account. It would not be appropriate for Investor Company to record this additional depreciation by debiting Depreciation Expense and crediting Accumulated Depreciation, because Investor Company reports the market value of depreciable assets of Investee Company as an implicit part of the cost in the investment account rather than in a separate operational asset account. A similar example would be the amortization of patents (or other intangibles) owned by Investee Company.

b. **Inventory and short-term investments.** Assets such as inventory and short-term investments held by the Investee Company at date of acquisition may necessitate recognition of additional expense similar to depreciation expense as discussed above. For example, if at date of acquisition of the investment, the Investee's carrying value for inventory or short-term investments is less than their market value (cost to the Investor), additional expense would have to be recognized as a credit to the investment account and a debit to the Investment Revenue account when the item is sold. This entry usually is made in the year following acquisition because the disposal of current assets usually will occur during the next period.[9] Likewise, when a long-term asset is disposed of subsequent to acquisition date of the investment, any gain or loss reported by the Investee Company must be adjusted for any "accounting differences" between the carrying value of the Investee and the market value purchased and recorded by the Investor. It is important to recall that all such adjustments to the investment account and the revenue account must be related to the Investor's **proportionate ownership.**

4. **Records** amortization each year of any purchased **goodwill** resulting from the acquisition transaction. As explained in Chapter 13, goodwill is measured as the excess of the cost of the investment to the investor over the market value of the identifiable **net** assets of the investee. Identifiable assets exclude goodwill because it is not physically identifiable or separately recorded in the accounts of the investee company in any form. For example, if goodwill purchased is computed to be $56,000 at acquisition date and if a 40-year amortization period is used, additional expense of $1,400 (i.e., $56,000 ÷ 40) would be recognized each year by the investor as a debit to Investment Revenue and a credit to the investment account. Goodwill is amortized against Investment Revenue in the manner described in (3) immediately above for additional depreciation and cost of goods sold, because it reduces investment revenue (or increases investment loss); this amortization amount is credited to the investment account because the cost of goodwill is included in the investment account as an implicit element of acquisition cost.
5. **Records** gain or loss on the sale of all or a part of the investment equal to the difference between the sale price and the then carrying value of the investment (as reflected in the investment account).
6. **Eliminates** intercompany gains and losses (discussed in Part B).

[9] For Investee's inventory costed by the LIFO method, the difference between book value and market value of a LIFO base layer would not be adjusted in the manner described above as long as the LIFO base layer is not liquidated.

Exhibit 16–3 illustrates application of the equity method. Panel A presents the illustrative data and computation of Investor's purchased goodwill and excess cost (over Investee's cost) of Investee's assets. Panel B gives the entries and T-accounts of Investor, and Panel C illustrates the financial statements of Investor.

In Exhibit 16–3, the ending balance in the investment account represents the adjusted 20 percent ownership interest of Investor Company in the net assets of Investee Company. The $305,600 ending balance is reported on the balance sheet of Investor Company, as shown in Panel C. The revenue and gain accounts represent the proportionate share of the income (as adjusted) of Investee Company that is recognized in the accounts of Investor Company, as shown in Panel C.

For the investor, the equity method differs from the cost method because the two methods are based upon different concepts of (1) investment valuation and (2) income recognition. The conceptual difference is that the equity method effectively treats the Investor and Investee companies as one entity for investment valuation and income recognition purposes. In contrast, the cost method is used for investments in which this close relationship between the Investor and Investee does not exist.

To illustrate the differences between the cost and equity methods, note that if Investor Company had not been able to exercise significant influence over the operating and financing policies of Investee Company, Investor would have accounted for the investment by the cost method. Under the cost method, Investor Company would have reported the investment at $300,000 (i.e., cost), which is $5,600 (i.e., $305,600 − $300,000) less than under the equity method. Also, under the cost method, Investor would have reported investment revenue of $10,000, the amount of dividends received from Investee Company. This amount of investment revenue is also $5,600 (i.e., $15,600 − $10,000) less than the amount of investment revenue reported under the equity method. The two differences (i.e., $5,600) are the same because under the equity method the investment account is adjusted from the cost basis in the amount of the investor's share of the investee's income, less dividends received. Similarly, investment revenue is different between the cost and equity methods by the investor's proportionate share of the

EXHIBIT 16–3: Accounting for Long-Term Investments by the Equity Method—Investor Company

Panel A—Illustrative Data:

1. On January 1, 19A, Investor Company purchased 1,800 shares (representing 20 percent) of the outstanding voting common stock of Investee Company for $300,000 cash. Investor Company can exercise significant influence over Investee Company's operating and financing policies. Therefore, Investor Company applies the equity method.
2. Data on Investee Company at January 1, 19A:

		Book Value	Market Value
Assets not subject to depreciation:			
Inventory (FIFO basis)		$ 400,000	$ 405,000
Land		150,000	165,000
Total		550,000	570,000
Assets subject to depreciation (net of accum. deprec.; remaining life, 10 years)		500,000	700,000
Total assets		$1,050,000	$1,270,000
Liabilities		$ 50,000	$ 50,000
Common stock (9,000 shares, par $100)	$900,000		
Retained earnings	100,000	1,000,000	1,220,000
Total liabilities and shareholders' equity		$1,050,000	$1,270,000

3. Computation of goodwill purchased by Investor Company:

Purchase price for 20 percent interest in Investee Company		$ 300,000
Market value of identifiable **net** assets purchased:		
Total market value of assets of Investee Company	$1,270,000	
Less total liabilities of Investee Company	(50,000)	
Market value of identifiable **net** assets of Investee Company	1,220,000	
Proportionate part purchased by Investor Company	× .20	
Market value of identifiable **net** assets purchased		244,000
Goodwill purchased		$ 56,000*

* Amortization of goodwill over 40 years (assumed): $56,000 ÷ 40 = $1,400 per year.

4. Computation of Investee's asset values purchased by Investor (proportionate part of each asset of Investee Company adjusted to market value on January 1, 19A):

	Market Value		Book Value	Proportionate Part of Market Value over Book Value
Inventory	$405,000	−	$400,000	(×20%) = $ 1,000†
Land	165,000	−	150,000	(×20%) = 3,000
Depreciable assets	700,000	−	500,000	(×20%) = 40,000‡

† Additional cost of goods sold in 19A based on the assumption that the beginning inventory is sold during 19A: $1,000.
‡ Additional depreciation over 10 years (assumed no residual value): $40,000 ÷ 10 = $4,000 per year.

5. On December 31, 19A, Investee Company reported the following data for the year ended on that date:

a. Income before extraordinary items	$ 80,000
Extraordinary gain (net of tax)	30,000
Net income	$110,000
b. Total cash dividends declared and paid during 19A	$ 50,000

EXHIBIT 16–3 ***(concluded)***

Panel B—Investor Company's Entries and Related T-Accounts:

1. January 1, 19A—To record acquisition of investment:

Investment, Investee Company common stock (1,800 shares)	300,000	
Cash		300,000

2. December 31, 19A—To recognize investment revenue and an increase in the investment account, based on the proportionate share of income reported by Investee Company (Panel A, item 5):

Investment, Investee Company common stock ($110,000 × .20)	22,000	
Investment revenue ($80,000 × .20)		16,000
Extraordinary gain (appropriately described) ($30,000 × .20)		6,000

3. December 31, 19A—To record cash dividend received on Investee Company shares (Panel A, item 5b):

Cash ($50,000 × .20)	10,000	
Investment, Investee Company common stock		10,000

4. December 31, 19A—To record depreciation on the $40,000 **increase** in depreciable assets implicit in the purchase price paid for the investment (Panel A, item 4):

Investment revenue ($40,000 ÷ 10 years)	4,000	
Investment, Investee Company common stock		4,000

5. December 31, 19A—To record periodic amortization of the $56,000 goodwill purchased (Panel A, item 3):

Investment revenue ($56,000 ÷ 40 years)	1,400	
Investment, Investee Company common stock		1,400

6. December 31, 19A—To record additional cost of goods sold associated with excess of market value over book value of inventory of Investee Company (Panel A, item 4), assuming the goods were sold during 19A:

Investment revenue [($405,000 − $400,000) × .20]	1,000	
Investment, Investee Company common stock		1,000

7. Investor's T-accounts (entry references are for entry numbers above):

Investment, Investee Company Common Stock (1,800 shares; 20 percent)

1. Acquisition (cost)	300,000	3. Dividends received	10,000
2. Proportionate share of net income of investee	22,000	4. Additional depreciation	4,000
		5. Amortization of goodwill	1,400
		6. Additional cost of goods sold	1,000
Balance	305,600		

Investment Revenue (ordinary)

4. Additional depreciation	4,000	2. Reported income	16,000
5. Amortization of goodwill	1,400		
6. Additional cost of goods sold	1,000		
		Balance	9,600

Extraordinary Gain (appropriately described)

		2. Reported gain	6,000
		Balance	6,000

Panel C—Investor Company's Financial Statement Presentation, December 31, 19A:

Balance sheet:	
Investment, Investee Company common stock, at equity	$305,600
Income statement:	
Investment revenue on investment accounted for by the equity method	9,600
Extraordinary gain (appropriately described)	6,000

income of the investee, less dividends received from the investee. The equity method gives the same net results on the financial statements as would consolidation procedures discussed in Part B; as a consequence it is frequently referred to as "one-line consolidation."

The following excerpt from the 1979 annual report of The Mead Corporation is typical for reporting investments accounted for by the equity method. In this disclosure, Mead uses the term **jointly owned companies** to refer to companies in which its investment is sufficient to warrant application of the equity method. Also, Mead combines "investments in" and "advances to" (i.e., receivables from) jointly owned companies, which is a common practice.

THE MEAD CORPORATION
Balance Sheet
($ millions)

	December 31	
	1979	**1978**
Investments and other assets:		
Investments in and advances to jointly owned companies (Note C)	$285.8	$238.3

Note C (partial): Mead's investments in nonconsolidated jointly owned companies are stated at cost plus equity in undistributed earnings, which approximates the portion of shareholders' equity applicable to Mead's investment. The composition of Mead's total investments in these companies is:

($ millions)

	December 31	
	1979	**1978**
Investments at cost	$ 55.8	$ 54.4
Equity in undistributed earnings	228.2	181.8
Mead's investments in jointly owned companies	284.0	236.2
Advances	1.8	2.1
Total investments in and advances to jointly owned companies	$285.8	$238.3

Instead of the term "jointly owned companies," the term "affiliated companies" often is used. Also, investment revenue under the equity method often is referred to as "equity in earnings of affiliated companies."

MARKET VALUE METHOD

The market value method of accounting for long-term investments is fundamentally different from the other methods. The market value method is based upon the concept of **current market value accounting;** that is, each individual investment is revalued at each balance sheet date to the then current market price of the securities held. Thus, **investment valuation** is at current market value and **investment revenue** for the period is comprised of dividends received (i.e., declared by the investee) plus or minus the change in the market value of the securities held during the period.[10]

Many accountants believe that all marketable securities, whether short term or long term, should be accounted for using the market value method because market value data *(a)* report the economic consequences of holding the investment, *(b)* are more useful to decision makers than cost or equity data in projecting future cash flows, and *(c)* often are objectively determinable for many stocks.[11]

At the present time, the market value method is **not** in accordance with GAAP except in a few special circumstances. The market value method is widely used by insurance companies, pension funds, and mutual funds in accounting for their investment portfolios. The method is applied in those situations only to securities which are readily marketable; the cost method is used for "nonmarketable" securities. The market value method may be outlined as follows:

1. At date of acquisition, investments are recorded at cost in accordance with the cost principle.
2. Subsequent to acquisition, each individual investment account periodically is adjusted to the then current market value of the securities held. The adjusted amount then becomes the "carrying value" for subsequent accounting.
3. Revenue recognized each period includes:
   a. All cash or property dividends received (i.e., declared by the investee) during the period.
   b. The increase (or decrease) in the market value of the portfolio during the period (see footnote 10). This amount often is referred to as the **market** or **holding gain** or **loss.**
4. At disposition of the investment, the difference

[10] Under an alternative procedure, investment revenue is the amount of dividends earned; the change in the market value of investment securities is reported as unrealized capital in the owners' equity section of the balance sheet, rather than as investment revenue.

[11] Variants of this view are presented by W. J. Morris and B. A. Coda, "Valuation of Equity Securities," *Journal of Accountancy,* January 1973, pp. 48–54; and W. H. Beaver, "Accounting for Marketable Equity Securities," *Journal of Accountancy,* December 1973, pp. 58–64.

between carrying value and sale price is recognized as a gain or loss.

Numerous arguments have been advanced in respect to the valuation of marketable securities at market value. The principal arguments cited against this are *(a)* it violates the cost principle and places on the balance sheet values that may not be objectively determined and may be temporary; *(b)* it violates the traditional realization principle since revenue is recognized on market changes rather than on sale; and *(c)* because of the volatility of some stock prices, it introduces a possible yo-yo effect on net income. In contrast, the proponents argue that *(a)* valuation at market value is more relevant information for decision making than costs which might have been incurred in the distant past; *(b)* it avoids "managed" earnings through the sale of selected investments acquired at a low original cost and a high current market value; and *(c)* it avoids the LCM inconsistency.

Chapter 6, Part B, illustrates accounting for short-term investments by the market value method, which is applied to long-term investments in the same manner as illustrated there. We suggest that you refer to that earlier discussion and illustration.

SOME SPECIAL PROBLEMS IN ACCOUNTING FOR STOCK INVESTMENTS

Several special problems relating to the acquisition, holding, and sale of stock investments are discussed below under the following headings:

1. Stock dividends received on investment shares.
2. Stock split of investment shares.
3. Stock rights on investment shares.
4. Investments in convertible securities.
5. Special-purpose funds.

Stock Dividends Received on Investment Shares

To conserve cash and yet make a distribution to shareholders, a corporation may issue a stock dividend. When a stock dividend is issued, the distributing corporation debits Retained Earnings and credits the appropriate capital stock accounts (discussed in Chapter 15). The effect of a stock dividend as far as the issuing corporation is concerned is to "capitalize" a part of retained earnings; significantly, a stock dividend does not decrease the assets of the issuing corporation.

From the **investor's** point of view, the nature of a stock dividend is suggested by the effect on the issuing corporation. The investor neither receives assets from the corporation nor owns more of the issuing corporation; the investor merely has more shares to represent the same prior proportional ownership. Thus, the receipt of a stock dividend in the same class of stock as already owned results, from the investor's viewpoint, in more shares but no increase in the cost (carrying value) of the holdings.

The investor should make no entry for revenue nor change the investment account other than to record a memorandum entry for the number of shares received. In case of a sale of any of the shares, a new cost per share is computed by adding the new shares to the old and dividing this sum into the carrying value. Exhibit 16–4 illustrates how an investor would determine the amounts needed to account for *(a)* receipt of dividend shares in a stock dividend in the same class of stock and *(b)* subsequent sale of the stock. The procedures illustrated in the exhibit would be followed for the cost, equity, and market value methods; the only difference in application would be the total carrying value (i.e., cost, market, or equity amount). For all three methods, the appropriate total carrying value would be divided by the new total number of shares owned to determine the carrying value per share after the dividend.

If the stock dividend is of a different class of stock than that on which the dividend was declared, such as preferred stock received as a dividend on common stock, or vice versa, three methods of accounting for the dividend have been suggested:

1. Record the new stock at an amount determined by apportioning the carrying value of the old stock between the new stock and the old stock on the basis of the relative market values of the different classes of stock **after** issuance of the dividend.
2. Record the new stock in terms of shares only, and when it is sold, recognize the total sale price as a gain.
3. Do not change the carrying value of the old stock but record the new stock at its market value upon receipt with an offsetting credit to dividend revenue. This method is predicated on the assumption that stock of a different class received as a dividend is no different from a property dividend.

EXHIBIT 16–4: Investor Accounting for a Stock Dividend in the Same Class of Stock—Investor X

Panel A—Illustrative Data:

Investor X purchased 100 shares of stock of ABC Corporation at $90 and subsequently received a 50 percent dividend payable in identical stock, and later sold 20 shares at $85.

Panel B—Effects on Investor X:

	Shares	Cost per Share	Total Cost	Sales Proceeds	Gain (Loss)
Purchase	100	$90	$9,000		
Stock dividend	50		-0-		-0-
Total	150	60*	9,000		
Sold	20	60	1,200	$1,700†	$500
Ending balance	130	60	$7,800		

* $9,000 ÷ 150 shares = $60.
† $85 × 20 shares = $1,700.

Of these three methods, the first is the most consistent with GAAP, and the second is the most conservative; the third appears to be seldom used.

Exhibit 16–5 illustrates application of the first method to apportionment of cost to the old and new stocks. The apportionment procedure illustrated would be followed for the cost, equity, and market value methods, with the appropriate carrying value apportioned as illustrated.

Stock Split of Investment Shares

A stock split is effected when a corporation issues new or additional shares without "capitalizing" (debiting) retained earnings or otherwise adding to the dollar amount of **legal capital.** In a stock split the number of shares outstanding is increased, accompanied by a proportionate decrease in the par or stated value per share of stock (discussed in Chapter 15). Although a stock split is basically different from a stock dividend from the point of vew of the **issuer,** the two are virtually identical from the point of view of the **investor.** In both cases the investor has more shares than before the split or dividend, but with the same total cost as before.[12] To the **investor,** the accounting for a stock split is the same as for a stock dividend of the same class as already owned; that is, a memorandum entry is made to record the number of new shares received and the revised cost per share.

[12] In a reverse split, such as a two-for-three split, the number of outstanding shares is reduced rather than increased. Reverse stock splits are rare.

Stock Rights on Investment Shares

The privilege accorded stockholders (investors) of purchasing additional shares of stock from the issuing corporation at a specific price and by a specified future date commonly is known as a **stock right.** The certificate evidencing one or more rights often is referred to as a stock **warrant.** For instance, in its 1979 annual report, American Broadcasting Companies, Inc., reported "Warrants: At December 31, 1979, warrants to purchase 534,945 shares of the Company's common stock were outstanding. The warrants are exercisable at $16 per share and expire January 2, 1982."

The term **stock right** usually is interpreted to mean **one right for each share of old stock.** For example, a holder of two shares of stock who receives the rights to subscribe for one new share is said to own two stock rights rather than one; that is, there is one right per old share regardless of the "new" share arrangement. Rights have value when the holder can buy additional shares through **exercise** of the rights at a lower price per share than on the open market without rights. As the spread between the privileged price and the market price changes subsequent to issuance of the rights, the value of the rights will change.

EXHIBIT 16–5: Investor Accounting for a Stock Dividend in a Different Class of Stock—Investor X

Panel A—Illustrative Data:

1. Investor X purchased 50 shares of JKL Company common stock for $7,500 cash.
2. When the market value of the common stock was $10,000, Investor X received a stock dividend of 20 shares of JKL preferred stock with a market value of $2,500. Using the relative sales value method, the cost may be apportioned as follows:

$$\text{Apportioned cost to common} = \$7{,}500 \times \frac{\$10{,}000}{\$12{,}500} = \$6{,}000$$

$$\text{Apportioned cost to preferred} = \$7{,}500 \times \frac{\$2{,}500}{\$12{,}500} = \underline{1{,}500}$$

$$\underline{\underline{\$7{,}500}}$$

Panel B—Indicated Entry to Record Receipt of Stock Dividend by Investor X:

Investment in preferred stock of JKL Company	1,500	
Investment in common stock of JKL Company		1,500

When the intention to issue stock rights is declared, the stock will start selling in the market "rights on"; that is, the market price of the share sold "rights on" includes the value of a share and the value of a right. After the rights are issued, the shares will sell in the market "ex rights." After issuance, rights usually have a separate market from that of the related stock and thus will be separately quoted at a specific market price. After rights are received, the investor has shares of stock and stock rights, both arising out of the single original cost.

To determine the gain or loss on the sale of either the stock or the rights, it is necessary to apportion the total cost of the investment between the stock and the rights. This apportionment usually is done by the use of the relative sales value method; that is, the total cost of the old shares is divided between the old stock and the rights in proportion to their relative market values at the time the rights are issued.

Exhibit 16–6 illustrates accounting for stock rights by the investor under two independent cases.

Investments in Convertible Securities

An enterprise may invest in preferred stock or bonds that are convertible into common stock under specified conditions. An accounting measurement problem arises at the time of conversion because the cost or book value of the convertible securities generally is different from the market value of the common stock received at the time of conversion. Two alternative views are held on this point:

1. At date of conversion, record the book value of the convertible security given up as the cost of the new security received; thus no gain or loss on conversion would be recognized. This position is supported by the argument that the original transaction established the value of both securities (the original as well as the potential) because the investor purchased the convertible security with full knowledge of the conversion option. In this view, prearranged conversion does not constitute a distinct exchange transaction.
2. At date of conversion, record the new security received at its market value and recognize a gain or loss on conversion. This position is supported by the argument that a distinct and separate exchange transaction has occurred at conversion. In this view, the very fact of conversion points to a shift in value in favor of the new security.

The former view tends to prevail in practice, although the latter accords more closely with economic reality. This topic also is discussed in Chapter 17 in respect to the accounting treatment of convertible bonds payable.

SPECIAL-PURPOSE FUNDS

Companies often set aside cash, and sometimes other assets, in special funds to be used in the future

EXHIBIT 16–6: Accounting for Stock Rights by the Investor—AB Company

Panel A—Illustrative Data:

1. AB Company purchased 500 shares of stock in XY Corporation at $93 per share.
2. At a later date, AB Company received 500 stock rights entitling AB Company to subscribe to 100 additional shares at $100 per share. Thus, each stock right represents one-fifth of a full share of AB stock.
3. Upon receipt of the rights, each share of stock on which the rights were issued had a market value of $120 (ex rights), and the rights had a market value of $4 each at the time they were received.

Panel B—Entries:

Case A—Assume that instead of subscribing for the additional shares, the investor later sold the rights at $4.50 each. The investor's entries are:

1. To record acquisition of stock investment:

Investment—stock of XY Corporation (500 shares @ $93)	46,500	
Cash		46,500

2. To record receipt of 500 rights on XY Corporation stock investment:

Investment—stock rights of XY Corporation*	1,500	
Investment—stock of XY Corporation		1,500

* Allocation of investment cost to stock rights on basis of relative market values:

Shares: $\frac{\$120}{\$124} \times \$46{,}500 = \$45{,}000$ (i.e., $90 per share)

Rights: $\frac{\$4}{\$124} \times \$46{,}500 = \quad 1{,}500$ (i.e., $3 per right)

Total cost $46,500

3. To record sale of the 500 stock rights of XY Corporation at $4.50 each:

Cash (500 rights @ $4.50)	2,250	
Investment—stock rights of XY Corporation (500 rights @ $3)		1,500
Gain on sale of stock rights		750

Case B—Assume the investor exercised the rights to subscribe to the additional shares and later sold one of the **new** shares for $140. The investor's entries are:

1. To record acquisition of stock investment—Same as entry 1 above.
2. To record receipt of stock rights—Same as entry 2 above.
3. To record exercise of the 500 rights and receipt of 100 new shares of stock of XY Corporation:

Investment—stock of XY Corporation [100 shares @ $115 (i.e., $100 cash + 5 rights @ $3)]	11,500	
Investment—stock rights of XY Corporation (500 rights @ $3)		1,500
Cash (100 shares @ $100)		10,000

4. To record sale of one of the new shares for $140 cash:

Cash (1 share @ $140)	140	
Investment—stock of XY Corporation (1 share @ $115)		115
Gain on sale of stock investment		25

If the rights are not sold or exercised, they will lapse. In this situation, theoretically, a loss equivalent to the allocated cost of the rights should be recognized by the investor. However, as a practical matter, the allocation entry (entry 2 in both cases above) usually is reversed for the portion that lapses.

for a specific purpose. Funds may be set aside by contract, as in the case of a bond sinking fund; by law, as in the case of rent deposits; or voluntarily, as in the case of a plant expansion fund.

Special-purpose funds may be either a current asset, as in the case of short-term savings accounts, or a noncurrent asset, when they are not directly related to current operations. The latter are classified under the heading Investments and Funds (Chapter 4). Typical long-term funds are as follows:

1. Funds set aside to retire a specific long-term liability, such as bonds payable, mortgages payable, long-term notes payable (Chapter 10).
2. Funds set aside to retire preferred stock (Chapter 14).
3. Funds set aside to purchase major assets, such as land, buildings, and plant (Chapter 11).

Typically, special-purpose funds are deposited with an independent **trustee,** such as a financial institution. In this situation, arrangements often are agreed upon whereby a specific rate of interest will be earned each period on the balance in the fund. Usually, the return earned on the fund each period is added to the fund balance.

Part B: Consolidated Financial Statements

The purpose of Part B is to present the fundamental concepts underlying consolidated financial statements. The numerous complexities involved are deferred to advanced texts that devote primary attention to the topic.

CONCEPT OF A CONTROLLING INTEREST

When an investor company owns over 50 percent of the outstanding voting stock of another company, in the absence of overriding constraints, a controlling interest is deemed to exist. The investor company is called the **parent** company, and the other company is known as a **subsidiary.** In a parent-subsidiary relationship, both corporations continue as separate legal entities; consequently, they are separate accounting entities (refer to separate entity assumption, Chapter 1). As separate entities, they have separate accounting systems and separate financial statements. Because of the ownership relationship, the **parent company** (but not the subsidiary) is required to prepare **consolidated financial statements** which view the parent and the subsidiary (or subsidiaries) as a single economic entity. To prepare consolidated financial statements, the **separate** financial statements of the parent and the subsidiary are combined each period by the parent company into one overall set of financial statements as if they were one single entity. The income statement, balance sheet, and statement of changes in financial position (SCFP) are consolidated in this manner.

Consolidated financial statements are not always prepared when over 50 percent of the stock of another corporation is owned because certain constraints may preclude the exercise of a controlling interest. To qualify for consolidation as a single economic entity, two basic elements must be present (*ARB 51,* pars. 2 and 3):

1. **Control of voting rights**—This is presumed to exist when over 50 percent of the outstanding **voting** stock of another entity is owned by the investor. Nonvoting stock is excluded because it does not provide an avenue for control by vote. However, control may not exist even though over 50 percent of the voting stock is owned, as in the case of a foreign subsidiary over which restrictions are imposed by the foreign country such that effective control cannot be exercised by the parent company. In such situations, the subsidiary would not qualify for consolidation. These are commonly called **unconsolidated subsidiaries** and are accounted for under either the cost method or the equity method (see Part A of this chapter). For instance, in its 1979 annual report, Harnischfeger Corporation reported that, ". . . a wholly owned Brazilian subsidiary . . . is carried at cost due to economic uncertainty." In this case, "economic uncertainty" precluded the parent company from exercising the influence necessary to apply either the equity method or consolidation procedures.
2. **Most meaningful financial presentation**—This element means that the statement user must be

given financial statements that best present the operating circumstances. In some situations "unconsolidated subsidiaries" may result because they are in different lines of business which are sufficiently incompatible that meaningful consolidation is not possible. A common example is a finance subsidiary owned by a parent company which is engaged primarily in manufacturing or retailing. Such was the case for another subsidiary of Harnischfeger Corporation, for which it reported in its 1979 Summary of Significant Accounting Policies, "The consolidated financial statements include the accounts of all majority-owned subsidiaries, except a wholly owned domestic finance subsidiary, which is accounted for under the equity method."

Although each company (parent and subsidiaries) keeps separate accounts and prepares separate financial statements, these individualized statements do not present a comprehensive report of the **economic unit** as a whole. Because the entire economic unit effectively is under the management (and stockholders) of the parent company, the parent's financial statements must incorporate the financial statements of the subsidiary companies. When a subsidiary is less than 100 percent owned, there is a group of minority shareholders, that is, a **minority interest,** that must be recognized in the consolidated financial statements.

ACQUIRING A CONTROLLING INTEREST

A company may acquire a controlling interest in the voting stock of another company in two basic ways, viz:

1. **Pooling of interests**—The voting stock of an existing corporation is acquired by the parent by exchanging shares of its own capital stock for the acquired shares of the subsidiary. In this situation, the parent disburses no cash or other assets and incurs no liabilities for the acquisition. For example, *The Wall Street Journal* (June 10, 1981, p. 28) reported that Mercantile Texas Corporation, a bank holding company, ". . . agreed in principle to acquire Merchants & Planters National Bank of Sherman, Texas, by exchanging 575,000 of its common shares for all 200,000 Merchants & Planters common shares outstanding," a transaction valued at $19.8 million.
2. **Purchase**—The voting stock of an existing corporation is acquired by the parent by paying cash, transferring noncash assets, or incurring debt. In this situation, the parent disburses a significant amount of resources.

ACCOUNTING AND REPORTING PROBLEMS

GAAP requires that each subsidiary prepare its own financial statements in the usual manner. However, the parent company is required to prepare **consolidated** financial statements which include all subsidiaries, except those designated as **unconsolidated** subsidiaries, as described above. We emphasize that the **parent company,** not the subsidiary company, prepares consolidated statements. Consolidated financial statements include an item-by-item combination (aggregation) of the parent and subsidiary statements. For example, the amount of cash shown on a consolidated statement would be the sum of the amounts of cash shown on the separate statements of the parent and the subsidiaries.

The emphasis in accounting for a controlling interest is on the consolidated financial statements. Either the cost or equity method may be used by the parent company in its accounts; the cost method is used in the illustrations of this chapter primarily for instructional convenience. However, the resulting consolidated financial statements must be the same regardless of the accounting method used in the accounts.[13]

This part of the chapter will focus on the **preparation** of consolidated financial statements. In prepar-

[13] In the case of a controlling interest, the investment account may be carried on either the cost or equity basis by the parent company. The cost basis is often used because the parent company does not desire to formally enter into its accounts the income, dividend offset, additional depreciation, amortization of goodwill, and so on, required by the equity method. Also, the accounting periods of the parent and the subsidiary may be different, and changes in percentage of ownership complicate the formal approach. Not infrequently, a company, when it moves from the equity approach range (i.e., 20 percent–50 percent) to a controlling interest range (over 50 percent), will adjust the accounts from the equity basis to the cost basis for these reasons. Because consolidation is a **reporting** approach, as opposed to an accounts approach, a worksheet is used, and the accounts of the parent are unaffected by the consolidation procedures. Under either method, the consolidation procedures are adapted on the worksheet so that the consolidated results are precisely the same whether the cost or equity method is used in the accounts of the parent company.

ing consolidated financial statements, the **method of acquisition—pooling of interests** versus **purchase**—has a significant impact both on the parent company and the consolidated statements.

Consolidated financial statements are prepared by means of a worksheet. There is no need to make separate consolidation entries in the accounts. In practically all situations, a special worksheet approach is essential. The essential steps in preparation of the worksheet by the parent company can be summarized as follows:[14]

1. The assets and liabilities of tne subsidiary are substituted for the investment account reflected on the books of the parent. This substitution is accomplished by "eliminating" the owners' equity accounts of the subsidiary against the investment account of the parent.
2. Elimination of intercompany receivables and payables.
3. Elimination of intercompany revenues, expenses, gains, and losses.
4. Elimination of other intercompany items.
5. Adjustments on the worksheet are made to reflect certain acquisition effects that differ from the book values, such as goodwill purchased by the parent as part of the cost of the investment in the subsidiary.
6. The remaining revenues and expenses of the parent and subsidiary are combined to derive a consolidated income statement.
7. The assets and liabilities of the parent and subsidiary are combined to derive a consolidated balance sheet.
8. The resource inflows and outflows of the parent and subsidiary are combined to derive a consolidated statement of changes in financial position (SCFP).

Consolidated financial statements commonly are prepared *(a)* at the date of acquisition of a controlling interest (balance sheet only) and *(b)* for each accounting period subsequent to acquisition (income statement, balance sheet, and SCFP). Consolidation results are influenced significantly by the way the stock of the subsidiary was acquired, that is, by *(a)* pooling of interests or *(b)* purchase.

[14] It is important to realize that these steps refer to worksheet entries and to the resultant financial statements and not to the journals and ledgers of the separate legal entities involved.

COMBINATION BY POOLING OF INTERESTS

The acquisition of a controlling interest by the parent company in the stock of a subsidiary company by an exchange of shares of stock often occurs because the combination can be effected without the disbursement of cash or other resources by the parent company. The exchange of shares is viewed as the **uniting of ownership interests** (and not as a purchase/sale transaction) between the parent company and the shareholders of the subsidiary company. Therefore, the recorded assets, liabilities, revenues, expenses, and so forth, for both entities are combined for consolidated statement purposes at their **recorded** book values. The incomes of the parent and its subsidiaries are combined and restated as consolidated income. Because a purchase/sale transaction is not presumed for the exchange of shares, market values of the assets of the subsidiary are not considered in consolidation.

APB Opinion No. 16, "Business Combinations" (par. 47), states, "the combining of existing voting common stock interests by the exchange of stock is the essence of . . . [a] pooling of interests." However, the *Opinion* specifies 12 conditions that must be met in order for the pooling of interests method to be appropriate; and if they are met, the pooling of interests method **must be used.** All combinations not meeting all 12 specifications **must** use the purchase method. Not all stock exchanges will meet the criteria for pooling of interests.

The **general** characteristics of the **pooling of interests** method of preparing consolidated statements may be summarized as follows:

1. The parent company must own 90 percent or more of the voting shares of the subsidiary.
2. The assets and liabilities of the combining companies are reported at the previously established **book values** of each company. Although adjustments may be made to reflect consistent applications of accounting principles, the **current market values** of the assets of the subsidiary at the time of the combination are **not used** as a substitute for their book values at that date.
3. No goodwill results from the combination.
4. The Retained Earnings balances of the combining companies are added to determine the Retained Earnings balance of the combined companies at date of acquisition.

5. After combination, financial statements which pertain to precombination periods must be restated on the combined basis "as if" the companies were combined throughout those periods.

As stated above, at date of acquisition a consolidated balance sheet usually is prepared by the parent company; at the end of each subsequent period, a consolidated income statement, balance sheet, and SCFP are prepared.

Consolidated Balance Sheet Immediately after Acquisition, Pooling of Interests Method

Exhibit 16–7 illustrates preparation of a consolidated balance sheet immediately after acquisition by a parent company of a 90 percent interest by a pooling of interests. Panel A of the exhibit presents the illustrative data, Panel B gives the entry of the parent company to record the acquisition, and Panel C illustrates the worksheet used to prepare a consolidated balance sheet immediately after the combination.

In Exhibit 16–7, Panel C, the worksheet is started by entering the two separate balance sheets, using **book values** for each company immediately **after** the acquisition entry. Note that two account balances on the Company P balance sheet (i.e., the investment and parent common stock accounts) were changed to reflect the above acquisition entry. The worksheet is designed to provide an orderly procedure for com-

EXHIBIT 16–7: Consolidated Balance Sheet, Company P (parent) and Company S (subsidiary), Pooling of Interests Method, Immediately after Acquisition of a 90 Percent Interest by Company P

Panel A—Illustrative Data:

1. Company P (parent) acquired 90 percent of the outstanding voting stock of Company S (subsidiary); therefore, minority shareholders own the remaining 10 percent.
2. Company P issued 900 shares of its $100 par common stock to the shareholders of Company S for 900 shares of the outstanding $100 par common stock of Company S. This is an exchange of shares (a continuity of the previously existing ownership), and we will assume that it meets the 12 conditions (specified in *APB Opinion 16*) for pooling of interests (including the criterion which requires at least 90 percent ownership). Company S will continue as a separate legal entity and as a 90 percent subsidiary of Company P.
3. Immediately prior to the exchange, their respective balance sheets reflected the following:

	Company P Book Value	Company S Book Value	Company S Market Value
Cash	$610,000	$ 20,000	$ 20,000
Accounts receivable (net)	10,000*	40,000	40,000
Inventories	20,000	30,000	25,000
Plant and equipment (net)	200,000	110,000	151,000
Patents (net)	20,000	10,000	14,000
	$860,000	$210,000	$250,000
Current liabilities	$ 10,000	$ 20,000*	
Long-term liabilities	50,000	40,000	
Common stock (par $100)	600,000	100,000	
Retained earnings	200,000	50,000	
	$860,000	$210,000	

* At date of acquisition, Company S owed Company P $5,000 accounts payable. Carrying and market value are assumed to be the same for receivables and payables.

Panel B—Entry by Parent Company P at Date of Acquisition†:

Investment in Company S common stock (90 percent ownership)	90,000	
Common stock (900 shares at $100 par)		90,000

† Because the acquisition under the pooling of interests concept is not viewed as a purchase/sale transaction, it usually is recorded at par value of the stock issued or the proportionate share acquired of the subsidiary's contributed capital. Some accountants prefer to use average contributed capital per share. This is an unsettled issue; however, in any case, the elimination entry is adapted to attain the pooling of interests results.

EXHIBIT 16–7 *(concluded)*

Panel C—Worksheet to Develop Consolidated Balance Sheet, Pooling of Interests Method:

COMPANY P AND ITS SUBSIDIARY, COMPANY S (90 PERCENT OWNERSHIP)
Pooling of Interests Method
Immediately after Acquisition

Account	Balance Sheet per Books		Eliminations		Consolidated Balance Sheet
	Company P	Company S	Debit	Credit	
Cash	610,000	20,000			630,000
Accounts receivable (net)	10,000	40,000		*(b)* 5,000	45,000
Inventories	20,000	30,000			50,000
Investment in Company S	90,000			*(a)* 90,000	
Plant and equipment (net)	200,000	110,000			310,000
Patents (net)	20,000	10,000			30,000
	950,000	210,000			1,065,000
Current liabilities	10,000	20,000	*(b)* 5,000		25,000
Long-term liabilities	50,000	40,000			90,000
Common stock (par $100):					
Company P	690,000*				690,000
Company S		100,000	*(a)* 90,000		10,000M
Retained earnings:					
Company P	200,000				200,000
Company S		50,000			45,000
					5,000M
	950,000	210,000			1,065,000

M—minority shareholders' 10 percent interest in Company S.
* Includes effect of acquisition entry (i.e., $600,000 + $90,000 = $690,000).
Eliminations:
(a) To eliminate the investment account balance against the stockholders' equity (90 percent) of the subsidiary.
(b) To eliminate the intercompany debt of $5,000.

bining the two separate balance sheets into a consolidated statement (the last column). The pair of columns for **eliminations** is used to prevent double counting of **reciprocal items** (i.e., items that are strictly between the two companies). In this instance, two such items must be eliminated, viz:

a. The investment account balance reflected on the balance sheet of Company P ($90,000) must be eliminated because in its place the various assets and liabilities of Company S will be added to those of the parent. Similarly, 90 percent of the common stock reported by Company S must be offset because it is owned now by the parent. Thus, elimination entry *(a)* on the worksheet offsets the investment account balance on the balance sheet of the parent against the stock account reflected on the balance sheet of the subsidiary.

b. Intercompany debt—Included in current liabilities of Company S is $5,000 accounts payable owed to Company P; therefore, accounts receivable on the balance sheet of Company P also includes this amount. When the two balance sheets are combined, this intercompany debt must be eliminated, because it is not a payable or receivable involving the combined entity and outsiders. Elimination entry *(b)* on the worksheet effects this elimination.

After the elimination entries for all intercompany items are reflected on the worksheet, the two balance sheets are aggregated horizontally line by line. The 10 percent interest of the **minority shareholders** of Company S represented by their proportionate share of the stockholders' equity is set out separately (denoted as M). The last column of the worksheet provides all the data needed to prepare a formal consolidated balance sheet. Note that the **book values** of Company S are added to the **book values** of Company P; the **market values given in the data above do not affect the accounting for a combination by pooling of interests.**

COMBINATION BY PURCHASE

The acquisition of a controlling interest by purchase occurs when the combination does not meet all of the 12 conditions for a pooling of interests. Typically, an acquisition by purchase occurs when the parent company acquires a controlling interest in the subsidiary company by purchasing the voting stock from the subsidiary's stockholders with cash or other resources. This situation is viewed as a purchase/sale transaction, and the **market values** related to the **subsidiary** must be introduced into the consolidation procedures in accordance with the cost principle. *APB Opinion 16* (par. 66) states: "Accounting for a business combination by the purchase method follows the principles normally applicable under historical cost accounting to recording acquisitions of assets and issuances of stock and to accounting for assets and liabilities after acquisition." This citation means that the parent company must debit the investment account for the **market value** of the shares of the subsidiary acquired, on the presumption that the parent paid market value for the investment. The significant implication of this requirement

EXHIBIT 16–8: Consolidated Balance Sheet, Company P (parent) and Company S (subsidiary), Purchase Method, Immediately after Acquisition of a Controlling Interest by Company P

Panel A—Illustrative Data:

1. Company P purchased, in the open market, 90 percent of the 1,000 shares of outstanding voting stock of Company S for $211,000 cash.
2. Balance sheets of Company P and Company S immediately prior to the combination were as shown in Exhibit 16–7, Panel A, item 3.
3. Computation of goodwill purchased by Company P:

Purchase price for 90% interest in Company S		$211,000
Market value of identifiable **net** assets purchased:		
Total market value of identifiable assets of Company S (Exhibit 16–7, Panel A, item 3)	$250,000	
Less total liabilities of Company S	(60,000)	
Market value of identifiable **net** assets of Company S	190,000	
Proportional part purchased by Company P	×.90	
Market value of identifiable **net** assets purchased		171,000
Goodwill purchased		$ 40,000

4. Proportionate part of each asset of Company S adjusted to market value (i.e., parent's cost) as of date of combination:

	Parent's Cost (Market Value)		Subsidiary's Book Value	Proportionate Part of Excess of Cost (Market) over Book Value
Inventory	$ 25,000	−	$ 30,000	(×.90) = $ (4,500)†
Plant and equipment	151,000	−	110,000	(×.90) = 36,900
Patents	14,000	−	10,000	(×.90) = 3,600
Goodwill (per above)	40,000		-0-	40,000
Total (see worksheet entry [*a*])				$76,000

† Parent's cost (i.e., market value) is less than subsidiary's book value.

Note: If total purchase cost is less than the summed market values of individual assets less liabilities, the difference is applied to reduce the valuations of the identifiable tangible and intangible assets. This is, negative goodwill is not recognized.

Panel B—Entry by Parent Company P at Date of Acquisition:

Investment in Company S common stock (90% ownership)	211,000	
Cash		211,000

EXHIBIT 16–8 ***(concluded)***

Panel C—Worksheet to Develop Consolidated Balance Sheet, Purchase Method:

COMPANY P AND ITS SUBSIDIARY, COMPANY S (90 PERCENT OWNERSHIP)
Purchase Method
Immediately after Acquisition

Account	Balance Sheet per Books		Eliminations and Adjustments		Consolidated Balance Sheet
	Company P	Company S	Debit	Credit	
Cash	399,000*	20,000			419,000
Accounts receivable (net)	10,000	40,000		*(c)* 5,000	45,000
Inventories	20,000	30,000		*(a)* 4,500	45,500
Investment in Company S	211,000*			*(a)* 76,000 *(b)* 135,000	
Plant and equipment (net)	200,000	110,000	*(a)* 36,900		346,900
Patents (net)	20,000	10,000	*(a)* 3,600		33,600
Goodwill			*(a)* 40,000		40,000
	860,000	210,000			930,000
Current liabilities	10,000	20,000	*(c)* 5,000		25,000
Long-term liabilities	50,000	40,000			90,000
Common stock:					
Company P	600,000				600,000
Company S		100,000	*(b)* 90,000		10,000M
Retained earnings:					
Company P	200,000				200,000
Company S		50,000	*(b)* 45,000		5,000M
	860,000	210,000			930,000

M—minority shareholders' 10 percent interest in Company S.
* Includes effects of the acquisition entry ($610,000 − $211,000 = $399,000).
Eliminations and adjustments:
(a) To record the adjustment of assets to market value and to eliminate the net effect from the investment account (Panel A, item 4).
(b) To eliminate the proportionate part of the stockholders' equity of the subsidiary (90 percent) and to eliminate an equal amount from the investment account (which now must be zero).
(Note: Entries [*a*] and [*b*] may be combined.)
(c) To eliminate the intercompany payable/receivable of $5,000.

is that in preparing consolidated statements, the assets of the **subsidiary** (including any purchased goodwill) must be valued at their **market values at date of acquisition** before being aggregated with the **book values** of the assets of the parent company.[15]

Although there are numerous additional complexities in application of the **purchase** method, the **general** characteristics may be outlined as follows:

1. On the consolidated balance sheet, the assets and liabilities of the subsidiary are reported by the parent company at their date of acquisition cost in conformity with the cost principle. **Cost** (i.e., the cash equivalent) is the price paid for the stock of the subsidiary and is the **market value of the stock acquired at that date.**
2. Individual assets of the subsidiary are reported at their individual market values as of the date of acquisition. These include all identifiable tangible and intangible assets (receivables, inventory, land, equipment, patents, etc.). Liabilities of the subsidiary usually are reported at their book values (because these usually are their equivalent market values).

[15] Recall that in a pooling of interests, book values rather than market values of the subsidiary are used in consolidation.

3. The difference between the total purchase cost and the market value of the **identifiable** assets acquired (less the liabilities assumed) is reported as "goodwill from acquisition." Goodwill from acquisition subsequently is amortized as an expense on the parent's consolidated income statements.
4. At date of combination, the Retained Earnings balance of the combined entity is defined as the Retained Earnings balance of the parent company; thus, the Retained Earnings balance of the subsidiary is eliminated and not reported in the consolidated balance sheet.
5. After the combination, financial statements of precombination periods must report the data of the parent company only.

Consolidated Balance Sheet Immediately after Acquisition, Purchase Method

Exhibit 16–8 illustrates preparation of a consolidated balance sheet on the **purchase basis** immediately after acquisition. This purchase illustration is based partially upon the data given for Company P and Company S in Exhibit 16–7, Panel A.

In preparing the worksheet shown in Exhibit 16–8, the first step is to determine the amount of **goodwill purchased** by consideration of the market values of the subsidiary, Company S, and to identify the assets of the subsidiary that have a market value different from their book value as shown in Panel A, items 3 and 4, respectively.

The worksheet shown in Exhibit 16–8, Panel C, is started by entering the two balance sheets, using amounts immediately after the acquisition entry. Observe that two accounts (i.e., Cash and Investments) on Company P balance sheets have been changed to reflect the acquisition entry. Also, the middle pair of columns are headed Eliminations and Adjustments because *(a)* adjusting entries must be made to adjust the assets of Company S from book value for the proportionate part of the market value purchased by Company P (entry [*a*] on the worksheet) and *(b)* elimination entries must be made for intercompany items (entries [*b*] and [*c*] on the worksheet). The computations of these amounts are given in Exhibit 16–8, Panel A, items 3 and 4, and indicate that inventories must be reduced by $4,500; plant and equipment increased by $36,900; patents increased by $3,600; and goodwill recorded in the amount of $40,000 to reflect the proportionate part of the excess of market value over book value of each of these items acquired by Company P. The net offset for these amounts is recorded in the investment account as an elimination because that account was debited at acquisition for the market value of the net assets acquired (90 percent).

The worksheet is completed by extending each item horizontally, taking into consideration the eliminations and adjustments. The last column provides all of the data needed to prepare a formal consolidated balance sheet on the purchase basis.

In summary, a comparison of Exhibit 16–7 with Exhibit 16–8 reflects the following underlying conceptual difference: in pooling of interests the book values of the subsidiary are added to the book values of the parent, whereas in a purchase the market values of the subsidiary at acquisition are added to the book values of the parent. No goodwill is recognized in a pooling of interests; in contrast, goodwill usually is recognized in a purchase. In the illustrations of consolidation to follow, these basic differences will be maintained in the combined statements of all subsequent periods.

PREPARING CONSOLIDATED STATEMENTS SUBSEQUENT TO ACQUISITION

At the end of each accounting period subsequent to acquisition of a controlling interest in another company, the parent company (but not the subsidiary companies) will prepare a consolidated balance sheet, consolidated income statement, and consolidated SCFP. The worksheets illustrated in Exhibits 16–7 and 16–8 can be expanded to develop both a consolidated balance sheet and income statement. A separate worksheet usually is needed to develop a consolidated SCFP. That statement is discussed in Chapter 23.

In this section, an expanded worksheet to develop a consolidated balance sheet and income statement subsequent to acquisition will be be illustrated assuming *(a)* pooling of interests and *(b)* purchase. The same data will be used for both illustrations. The section will conclude with an illustration of the formal consolidated statements on a purchase basis.

Consolidated Statements Subsequent to Acquisition, Pooling of Interests Method

Exhibit 16–9 illustrates the preparation of a consolidated balance sheet and income statement one year after acquisition, using the illustration of Companies P and S given in Exhibit 16–7. Panel A of Exhibit 16–9 presents the separate financial statements for Companies P and S one year after the January 1, 19A, acquisition by **pooling of interests** (illustrated in Exhibit 16–7), and Panel B presents the worksheet to consolidate their financial statements for the year ended December 31, 19A. (See page 574.)

The expanded consolidation worksheet shown in Exhibit 16–9 for the **pooling of interests method** is the same type as the worksheet shown in Exhibit 16–7 (consolidated balance sheet at acquisition) with the income statement added. The reported amounts from the separate statements are entered directly on the worksheet. For worksheet convenience, and to facilitate understanding, common stock, retained earnings at date of acquisition, and income since acquisition are set out separately. The expanded worksheet involves only one item not previously discussed—the $7,000 intercompany sales. During the year, Company S transferred to Company P goods with a cost of $7,000. Company S recorded this as a sale, and Company P recorded it as a purchase (cost of goods sold). This transaction is an intercompany item that must be eliminated to prevent double counting of sales and cost of goods sold; when Company P sold the goods to outsiders, a sale was recorded at that time.[16] The eliminations are explained at the bottom of the worksheet. Because the consolidated statements are prepared on a pooling of interests basis, the **book values** of the two companies are aggregated item by item. Note that consolidated income is the sum of the net income amounts reported by the companies separately; the same is true with respect to consolidated retained earnings.

Consolidated Statements Subsequent to Acquisition, Purchase Method

Exhibit 16–10 illustrates preparation of a consolidated balance sheet and income statement by the **purchase method** one year after acquisition. The financial statements for Companies P and S given in Exhibit 16–9, Panel A, will be used. However, because that information assumes pooling of interests, it must be adapted to reflect a combination by **purchase.** Exhibit 16–10, Panel A, presents the illustrative data for the consolidation by the purchase method, and Panel B presents the consolidation worksheet.

The expanded consolidation worksheet shown in Exhibit 16–10 on the purchase method follows the format shown in Exhibit 16–8 (consolidated balance sheet at date of acquisition) with the addition of the income statement. Recall that the worksheet at acquisition date in Exhibit 16–8 reflected *(a)* adjustments of the assets of Company S to market value, including goodwill; *(b)* elimination of the parent's investment account against subsidiary owners' equity; and *(c)* elimination of intercompany debt. Exhibit 16–10 includes one additional concept not previously discussed; that is, the write-up of Company S assets, including goodwill, necessitates **adjustments for additional expenses** for depreciation, patent amortization, and amortization of goodwill for the period (adjustment [*d*]). The eliminations and adjustments are explained below the worksheet.

The consolidated income statement and balance sheet (purchase method) for Company P are shown in Exhibit 16–11. Note the manner of presenting the minority interest and the more descriptive caption for goodwill, "Cost of investment in excess of market value of identifiable net assets of subsidiary" (these items are boxed for emphasis).

Alternatively, the minority interest reported in Exhibit 16–11 often is reported along the following lines:

Stockholder's Equity		
Common stock, par $100, 6,000 shares outstanding		$600,000
Retained earnings		235,750
Total interest of parent company		835,750
Interest of minority stockholders in subsidiary:		
Common stock	$10,000	
Retained earnings	6,200	16,200
Total stockholders' interest, incl. interest of minority stockholders		$851,950

In summary, the results of the *(a)* pooling of interests and *(b)* purchase methods are compared in Exhibit 16–12.

The comparison shown in Exhibit 16–12 reveals that net income is lower (by $5,050) under the pur-

[16] The elimination of intercompany sales of $7,000 assumed the goods were transferred at cost. If *(a)* the transfer price included an element of profit for the selling entity and *(b)* the goods were still held by the purchasing entity, the profit residue (unrealized intercompany inventory profit) would be eliminated by debiting Sales for the sales price, crediting Cost of Goods Sold for the cost price, and crediting Ending Inventory for the seller's markup.

chase method because that approach requires *(a)* adjustment of the subsidiary's assets to market value and *(b)* recognition of goodwill, each of which must be allocated on an annual basis to **expense** ($3,690 + $360 + $1,000 = $5,050). Cash and capital stock are lower under the purchase method because, at acquisition, cash rather than capital stock was used to acquire the controlling interest. The purchase method requires recognition of market values (for subsidiary assets) and purchased goodwill, which caused the goodwill of $39,000 to be reported under the purchase method. Retained earnings is higher under pooling of interests because it is the sum of the parent and subsidiary amounts; in contrast, when the purchase method is used, retained earnings of the subsidiary at acquisition is eliminated along with the subsidiary's other owners' equity accounts because they represent the parent company's investment. The minority interest in net income and retained earnings is the same under both methods.

Principally because of *(a)* the effect on cash and *(b)* the accounting effects on net income and retained earnings, companies usually prefer pooling of interests. Also, because the pooling of interests method retains the book value basis of accounting for subsidiary assets, pooling provides the parent company with the opportunity to report later gains on the sale of subsidiary assets with market values in excess

EXHIBIT 16–9: Consolidated Financial Statements, Company P (parent) and Company S (subsidiary), 90 Percent Ownership, Pooling of Interests Method

Panel A—Illustrative Data:

Reported amounts at end of 19A—pooling of interests method:

	At December 31, 19A	
	Company P	**Company S**
Income statement:		
Sales revenue	$520,000	$105,000*
Cost of goods sold	300,000*	53,000
Depreciation expense	20,000	4,000
Patent amortization expense	2,000	1,000
Other expenses	138,000	35,000
Total expenses	460,000	93,000
Net income	$ 60,000	$ 12,000
Balance sheet:		
Cash	$639,000	$ 24,000
Accounts receivable (net)	15,000†	45,000
Inventories	30,000	29,000
Investment in Company S (pooling basis)	90,000‡	
Plant and equipment (net)	180,000	106,000
Patents (net)	18,000	9,000
Total assets	$972,000	$213,000
Current liabilities	$ 12,000	$ 21,000†
Long-term liabilities	40,000	30,000
Common stock (par $100)	690,000	100,000
Retained earnings	230,000§	62,000
Total equities	$972,000	$213,000

* Includes intercompany sales of $7,000; transferred at cost.
† Includes intercompany debt of $3,000.
‡ Carried forward at amount recorded at date of acquisition.
§ During 19A, Company P declared and paid a $30,000 cash dividend.

EXHIBIT 16–9 *(concluded)*

Panel B—Worksheet to Develop Consolidated Income Statement and Balance Sheet, Pooling of Interests Method:

COMPANY P AND ITS SUBSIDIARY, COMPANY S (90 PERCENT OWNERSHIP)
At December 31, 19A
Pooling of Interests Method

Items	Reported Amounts		Eliminations		Consolidated Statements
	Company P	Company S	Debit	Credit	
Income statement:					
Sales revenue	520,000	105,000	*(c)* 7,000		618,000
Cost of goods sold	300,000	53,000		*(c)* 7,000	346,000
Depreciation expense	20,000	4,000			24,000
Patent amortization expense	2,000	1,000			3,000
Other expenses	138,000	35,000			173,000
	460,000	93,000			546,000
Income (to balance sheet)	60,000	12,000			72,000
Apportioned for consolidation:					
Minority interest (10% × $12,000)					1,200M
Parent interest					70,800
Balance sheet:					
Cash	639,000	24,000			663,000
Accounts receivable (net)	15,000	45,000		*(b)* 3,000	57,000
Inventories	30,000	29,000			59,000
Investment in Company S	90,000			*(a)* 90,000	-0-
Plant and equipment (net)	180,000	106,000			286,000
Patents (net)	18,000	9,000			27,000
	972,000	213,000			1,092,000
Current liabilities	12,000	21,000	*(b)* 3,000		30,000
Long-term liabilities	40,000	30,000			70,000
Common stock:					
Company P	690,000*				690,000
Company S		100,000	*(a)* 90,000		10,000M
Retained earnings (at acquisition):					
Company P ($200,000 − $30,000)	170,000				170,000
Company S		50,000			45,000
					5,000M
Income (from income statement)	60,000	12,000			70,800
					1,200M
	972,000	213,000			1,092,000

M—Minority shareholders' interest of 10 percent in Company S.
* Includes effects of the acquisition entry (i.e., $600,000 + $90,000 = $690,000; see Exhibit 16–7).
Eliminations:
(a) To eliminate investment account balance against stockholders' equity (90 percent ownership) of the subsidiary.
(b) To eliminate intercompany debt of $3,000.
(c) To eliminate intercompany sales of $7,000 (at cost).

of cost. This opportunity is not likely under the purchase method because the assets of the subsidiary are recorded at market value when they are acquired by the parent. Another reason why companies may prefer pooling of interests is that the parent company will report a higher rate of return under pooling of interests than under purchase because the reported net asset value base is lower and the reported income is higher under pooling of interests. Pooling transactions were fairly common during the mid-1960s, prior to the issuance of *APB Opinion 16.*

On the other hand, the stockholders of the acquired company often prefer to receive cash rather than stock of the parent company. In respect to the accounting aspects and the opportunity to manipulate reported earnings, *APB Opinion 16* placed severe restrictions on use of the pooling of interests approach, as evidenced by the requirement that a business combination satisfy all of 12 criteria for it to be accounted for as a pooling of interests.

Finally, we emphasize that **none** of the entries reflected on a consolidated worksheet (e.g., Exhibit 16–10) are recorded in the accounts of the parent or subsidiary companies. They are merely worksheet entries used to derive the consolidated financial statements reported by the parent company.

EXHIBIT 16–10: Consolidated Financial Statements, Company P (parent) and Company S (subsidiary), 90 Percent Ownership, Purchase Method.

Panel A—Illustrative Data:

1. Reported amounts at end of 19A—purchase method:

	At December 31, 19A	
	Company P	**Company S**
Income statement:		
Sales revenue	$520,000	$105,000*
Cost of goods sold	300,000*	53,000
Depreciation expense	20,000	4,000
Patent amortization expense	2,000	1,000
Other expenses	138,000	35,000
Total expenses	460,000	93,000
Net income	$ 60,000	$ 12,000
Balance sheet:		
Cash	$428,000	$ 24,000
Accounts receivable (net)	15,000†	45,000
Inventories	30,000	29,000
Investment in Company S (purchase method)	211,000‡	
Plant and equipment (net)	180,000	106,000
Patents (net)	18,000	9,000
Total assets	$882,000	$213,000
Current liabilities	$ 12,000	$ 21,000†
Long-term liabilities	40,000	30,000
Common stock (par $100)	600,000	100,000
Retained earnings	230,000§	62,000
Total equities	$882,000	$213,000

* Includes intercompany sales of $7,000; transferred at cost.
† Includes intercompany debt of $3,000.
‡ Carried forward at amount recorded (cost) at date of acquisition.
§ During 19A, Company P declared and paid a $30,000 cash dividend.

2. The goodwill and related asset values computed at date of acquisition (Exhibit 16–8, Panel A, items 3 and 4) are used **without change** for consolidation purposes in subsequent years. Recall the following amounts: goodwill, $40,000; inventory decrease, $4,500; plant and equipment increase, $36,900; and patents increase, $3,600.

EXHIBIT 16–10 ***(concluded)***

Panel B—Worksheet to Develop Consolidated Income Statement and Balance Sheet, Purchase Method:

COMPANY P AND ITS SUBSIDIARY, COMPANY S (90 PERCENT OWNERSHIP)
At December 31, 19A
Purchase Method

Items	Reported Amounts		Eliminations and Adjustments		Consolidated Statements
	Company P	Company S	Debit	Credit	
Income statement:					
Sales revenue	520,000	105,000	*(e)* 7,000		618,000
Cost of goods sold	300,000	53,000		*(e)* 7,000	346,000
Depreciation expense	20,000	4,000	*(d)* 3,690		27,690
Patent amortization expense	2,000	1,000	*(d)* 360		3,360
Goodwill amortization expense			*(d)* 1,000		1,000
Other expenses	138,000	35,000			173,000
	460,000	93,000			551,050
Income (to balance sheet)	60,000	12,000			66,950
Apportioned for consolidation:					
Minority interest (10% × $12,000)					1,200M
Parent interest					65,750
Balance sheet:					
Cash	428,000*	24,000			452,000
Accounts receivable (net)	15,000	45,000		*(c)* 3,000	57,000
Inventories	30,000	29,000		*(a)* 4,500†	54,500
Investment in Company S	211,000*			*(a)* 76,000	
				(b) 135,000	-0-
Plant and equipment (net)	180,000	106,000	*(a)* 36,900	*(d)* 3,690	319,210
Patents (net)	18,000	9,000	*(a)* 3,600	*(d)* 360	30,240
Goodwill (net)			*(a)* 40,000	*(d)* 1,000	39,000
	882,000	213,000			951,950
Current liabilities	12,000	21,000	*(c)* 3,000		30,000
Long-term liabilities	40,000	30,000			70,000
Common stock:					
Company P	600,000				600,000
Company S		100,000	*(b)* 90,000		10,000M
Retained earnings (at acquisition):					
Company P ($200,000 − $30,000)	170,000				170,000
Company S		50,000	*(b)* 45,000		5,000M
Income (from income statement)	60,000	12,000			65,750
					1,200M
	882,000	213,000			951,950

M—Minority shareholders' 10 percent interest in Company S.

* Includes effects of the acquisition entry.

† LIFO assumed. When this cost flows out of inventory, this credit would be to cost of goods sold; subsequently it would be credited to Company P retained earnings.

Adjustments and eliminations:

(a) To adjust the assets of Company S to market and to eliminate the net effect from the investment account (per goodwill computations Exhibit 16–8, Panel A, items 3 and 4).

(b) To eliminate the proportionate part of stockholders' equity of the subsidiary owned by the parent (90 percent) and to eliminate an equal amount from the investment account (which now must be zero).

(c) To eliminate the intercompany debt, $3,000.

(d) To recognize additional market value expenses: depreciation, $36,900 ÷ 10 years = $3,690; patent amortization, $3,600 ÷ 10 years = $360; and goodwill amortization, $40,000 ÷ 40 years = $1,000.

(e) To eliminate intercompany sales, $7,000 (at cost).

EXHIBIT 16–11

COMPANY P AND SUBSIDIARY, COMPANY S
Consolidated Income Statement (purchase method)
For the Year Ended December 31, 19A

Sales revenue		$618,000
Expenses:		
Cost of goods sold	$346,000	
Depreciation expense	27,690	
Patent amortization expense	3,360	
Goodwill amortization expense	1,000	
Other expenses	173,000	551,050
Consolidated net income including minority interest		66,950
Minority interest in net income of subsidiary (10%)		1,200
Consolidated net income		$ 65,750

Consolidated Balance Sheet (purchase method)
At December 31, 19A

Assets

Cash		$452,000
Accounts receivable (net)		57,000
Inventories		54,500
Plant and equipment (net)		319,210
Patents (net)		30,240
Cost of investment in excess of market value of identifiable net assets of subsidiary		39,000
Total assets		$951,950
Liabilities		
Current liabilities	$ 30,000	
Long-term liabilities	70,000	$100,000
Interest of Minority Stockholders in Subsidiary		
Common stock	10,000	
Retained earnings	6,200	16,200
Stockholders' Equity		
Common stock, par $100, 6,000 shares outstanding	600,000	
Retained earnings ($170,000 + $65,750)	235,750	835,750
Total liabilities and stockholders' equity		$951,950

EXHIBIT 16–12: Comparison of Pooling of Interests and Purchase Methods (based upon Exhibits 16–9 and 16–10); for year ended 12/31/19A

	Method		
	Pooling (Exhibit 16–9)	Purchase (Exhibit 16–10)	Difference—Pooling over Purchase
Net income:			
Parent interest	$ 70,800	$ 65,750	$ 5,050
Minority interest	1,200	1,200	-0-
Cash	663,000	452,000	211,000
Investment in Company S	-0-	-0-	-0-
Plant and equipment (net)	286,000	319,210	(33,210)
Goodwill	-0-	39,000	(39,000)
Liabilities	100,000	100,000	-0-
Capital stock, Company P	690,000	600,000	90,000
Retained earnings:			
Parent interest	285,800	235,750	50,050
Minority interest	6,200	6,200	-0-

QUESTIONS

PART A

1. Distinguish between debt and equity securities; also between short-term and long-term investments.

2. What accounting principle is applied in recording the acquisition of an investment? Explain its application in cash and noncash acquisitions.

3. Explain why *interest revenue* is accrued on investments but *dividend revenue* is not accrued.

4. Under the cost method, no distinction is made between voting and nonvoting stock, but the distinction is important with respect to the equity and consolidation methods. Explain why.

5. Explain when the cost method of accounting for equity investments is applicable.

6. Explain how the LCM concept is applied to long-term investments in equity securities. How is "cost" determined when an investment is reclassified from short-term to long-term or vice versa?

7. Explain the basic features of the equity method of accounting for long-term investments. When is the equity method applicable? To what other method is it most closely related? Explain.

8. Assume Company R acquired, as a long-term investment, 30% of the outstanding voting common stock of Company S at a cash cost of $100,000. At date of acquisition, the balance sheet of Company S showed total shareholders' equity of $250,000. The market value of the assets of Company S was $20,000 greater than their book value at date of acquisition. Compute goodwill purchased. What accounting method should be used. Explain why.

9. Assume the same facts as given in Question 8, with the additional data that the net assets have a remaining estimated life of 10 years and goodwill will be amortized over 20 years (assume no residual values and straight-line depreciation). How much additional depreciation and amortization expense should be reported by the investor, Company R, each year in accounting for this long-term investment? Give the entries to record additional depreciation and amortization of goodwill.

10. The *equity method* of accounting for a long-term investment usually will reflect a larger amount of investment revenue than would the cost method in the same circumstances. Explain why.

11. Explain the basic features of the *market value method* of accounting for investments. Is it a generally accepted method? Explain.

12. How would the market value method of accounting for investments, in contrast to the cost method, tend to prevent "managed" earnings?

13. Fundamentally, the investor accounts for an ordinary stock dividend and a stock split in the same way. Briefly, explain the accounting that should be followed by the investor in these situations.

14. What is a convertible security? Assume an investor has a convertible security with a book value of $200,000 which is turned in to the issuer for conversion. The investor receives, in conformance with the conversion, common stock with a current market value of $225,000. Explain how the investor should account for the conversion of this long-term investment.

15. What is a stock right (or warrant)? If stock rights have a market value, how would the investor account for the receipt of stock rights?

PART B

16. Outline the characteristics of an acquisition transaction of a long-term investment that would be accounted for as a *(a)* pooling of interests and *(b)* purchase.

17. Contrast the primary effects on the balance sheet and income statement of a pooling of interests versus a purchase. Why are the effects different?

18. Explain why market values are used in the purchase method but not in the pooling of interests method.

19. Explain why goodwill is recognized in a purchase but not in a pooling of interests.

20. What are intercompany items? Why must they be eliminated in preparing consolidated financial statements?

21. What is meant by *minority interest* in consolidated statements? How is this interest reported on *(a)* the income statement and *(b)* the balance sheet?

22. Explain the basic reasons why many companies, other things being equal, would prefer the pooling of interests method over the purchase method of accounting for parent/subsidiary relationships.

DECISION CASE 16–1

Lee Corporation is currently negotiating a combination with Rudd Corporation, a successful enterprise that would complement the operations of Lee. An important factor in the negotiations has been the potential effects of the merger on Lee's financial statements. Accordingly, Lee management has requested that pro forma (i.e., "as if") financial statements be prepared under two assumptions.

The balance sheets for the two corporations for the year just ended (prior to combination) are shown in the following table:

	Lee Corporation	Rudd Corporation Book Value	Rudd Corporation Appraised Value
Balance sheet:			
Cash	$ 485,000	$ 15,000	$ 15,000
Receivables (net)	30,000	65,000	50,000
Inventories	85,000	70,000	70,000
Land	50,000		
Plant (net)	600,000	100,000	230,000
Patents (net)	10,000	30,000	40,000
	$1,260,000	$ 280,000	
Current liabilities	$ 40,000	$ 15,000	
Long-term liabilities	110,000	25,000	
Common stock (par $100)	1,000,000	200,000	
Retained earnings	110,000	40,000	
	$1,260,000	$ 280,000	
Income statement:			
Sales	$6,000,000	$1,000,000	
Costs and expenses (excl. depr. and amortization)	5,754,000	967,000	
Depreciation	65,000	10,000	
Amortization of patents	1,000	3,000	
Income	$ 180,000	$ 20,000	

At year-end, Rudd Corporation owed a $10,000 current liability to Lee Corporation. For case purposes, assume that all depreciable assets and intangible assets have a remaining useful life of 10 years from date of combination.

Required:

1. Assume that Lee will purchase all of the outstanding stock of Rudd for a cash consideration of $460,000.
   a. Give the pro forma entry for the investment.
   b. Prepare a pro forma balance sheet on a purchase basis (or if you prefer, present a pro forma consolidation worksheet).
2. Assume instead that Lee will acquire all of the outstanding shares of Rudd by exchanging stock on a share-for-share basis.
   a. Give the pro forma entry for the exchange.
   b. Prepare a pro forma balance sheet (or worksheet) on a pooling of interests basis.
3. Identify the amounts on the two pro forma consolidated balance sheets that will be different between (1) and (2) above and explain the reasons for each. Identify and explain the amounts that would be different on the income statements for the next period as between (1) and (2).

EXERCISES

PART A: EXERCISES 16–1 to 16–12

Exercise 16–1

During 19A, Marshall Company purchased shares in two corporations, as indicated below, with the intention of holding them as long-term investments. Transactions were in the following order:

a. Purchased 100 shares of the 10,000 shares outstanding of common stock of M Corporation at $31 per share plus a 5% brokerage fee and a transfer cost of $45.
b. Purchased 200 shares of preferred stock (nonvoting) of N Corporation at $78 per share plus a 3% brokerage fee and a transfer cost of $42.
c. Purchased 20 shares of common stock of M Corporation at $35 per share plus a 5% brokerage fee and a transfer cost of $5.
d. Received $4 per share cash dividend on the N Corporation stock (from earnings since acquisition).

Required:

1. Give the indicated entries in the accounts of Marshall Company for transactions *(a)*, *(b)*, *(c)*, and *(d)*. Assume the cost method is appropriate and that these are the only long-term equity investments held.
2. The market values of the shares held at the end of 19A were M stock, $34; and N stock, $75. Give the appropriate adjusting entry for Marshall Company; show computations and assume the decline is temporary.
3. The market values of the shares held at the end of 19B were M stock, $36; and N stock, $77. Give the appropriate adjusting entry with computations. Assume the decline is temporary.
4. Show how the income statement and balance sheet for Marshall Company would report the long-term investments for 19A and 19B.

Exercise 16–2

Ray Company purchased common stock (par value $50) of the Sams Corporation as a long-term investment. Transactions related to this investment were as follows and in the order given.

a. Purchased 500 shares of the common stock at $90 per share (designated as lot no. 1).
b. Purchased 2,000 shares of the common stock at $95 per share (designated as lot no. 2).
c. At the end of the first year, Sams Corporation reported net income of $52,000.
d. Sams Corporation paid a cash dividend of $2 per share on the common stock.
e. After reporting net income of $5,000 for the second year, Sams Corporation issued a stock dividend whereby each stockholder received one additional share for each two shares owned. At the time of the stock dividend the stock was selling at $85.
f. Sams Corporation revised its charter to provide for a stock split. The par value was reduced to $25. The "old" common stock was turned in, and the holders received in exchange two shares of the new stock for each old share owned.

Required:
Give the entries for each transaction as they should be made in the accounts of Ray Company. Show computations. Assume the cost method and less than 20% ownership throughout.

Exercise 16–3

On January 1, 19A, Johns Company purchased 300 of the 1,000 outstanding shares of common stock of Rankin Corporation for $23,200. At that date, the balance sheet of Rankin showed the following book values:

Assets not subject to depreciation	$40,000
Assets subject to depreciation (net)	26,000*
Liabilities	6,000
Common stock (par $50)	50,000
Retained earnings	10,000

* Market value, $30,000; the assets have a 10-year remaining life (straight-line depreciation).

Required:
1. Assuming the equity method is appropriate, give the entry by Johns to record the acquisition at a cost of $23,200. Assume a long-term investment.
2. Show the computation of goodwill purchased at acquisition.
3. Assume at December 31, 19A (end of the accounting period), Rankin Corporation reported a net income of $12,000. Assume goodwill amortization over a 10-year period. Give all entries indicated on the records of Johns Company.
4. In February 19B, Rankin Corporation declared and paid a $2 per share cash dividend. Give the necessary entry by Johns.

Exercise 16–4

On January 1, 19A, Brand Corporation purchased 2,000 of the 8,000 outstanding shares of common stock of Low Corporation for $20,000 cash. At that date, Low's balance sheet reflected the following book values:

Assets not subject to depreciation	$25,000
Assets subject to depreciation (net)	30,000*
Liabilities	5,000
Common stock (par $5)	40,000
Retained earnings	10,000

* Market value, $38,000; estimated remaining life of 10 years (straight-line depreciation).

Required:
1. If goodwill is relevant to this investment, show the computation of goodwill purchased at acquisition.
2. At the end of 19A, Low reported income before extraordinary items, $19,000, extraordinary loss, $2,000, and net income, $17,000. In December 19A, Low Corporation paid a $1 per share cash dividend. Reconstruct the following accounts (use T-account format) for Brand Corporation: Cash, Investment in Low Corporation Stock, Investment Revenue—Ordinary, and Investment Revenue—Extraordinary. Apply the appropriate method and assume straight-line amortization of any goodwill is over ten years. Date and identify all amounts entered in the accounts.

Exercise 16–5

On January 3, 19A, Breen Company purchased 2,000 shares of the 10,000 outstanding shares of common stock of Kokomo Corporation for $14,600 cash. At that date, the balance sheet of Kokomo reflected total shareholders' equity of $60,000. In addition, the market value of the assets, subject to depreciation, was $3,000 in excess of their book value reported on the Kokomo balance sheet. Assume a 10-year remaining life (straight-line depreciation) and amortization of goodwill over 10 years.

Required:
Set up captions as follows and enter the indicated information (show computations):

(Relates to Exercise 16–5)

Information— Breen Accounts	Assuming Cost Method Appropriate	Assuming Equity Method Appropriate
a. Entry at date of acquisition.		
b. Goodwill purchased—computation only.		
c. Entry on 12/31/19A to record $15,000 net income reported by Kokomo.		
d. Entry on 12/31/19A for additional depreciation expense.		
e. Entry on 12/31/19A for amortization of goodwill.		
f. Entry on 12/31/19A to recognize decrease in market value of Kokomo stock, quoted market price, $7 per share. Assume this is the only long-term equity investment held.		
g. Entry on 3/31/19B for a cash dividend of $1 per share declared and paid by Kokomo.		

Exercise 16–6

On January 10, 19A, Bliss Company purchased as a long-term investment 12% of the 10,000 shares of the outstanding common stock of Company Y (par value $40 per share) at $50 per share. During 19A, 19B, and 19C, the following additional data were available:

	19A	19B
Reported net income by Co. Y at year-end	$30,000	$35,000
Cash dividends by Co. Y at year-end	$10,000	$15,000
Quoted market price per share of Co. Y stock at year-end	57	55

On January 2, 19C, Bliss Company sold 100 shares of the Company Y shares at $56 per share.

Required:

1. Assuming the market value method is used, give all entries indicated in the accounts of Bliss Company assuming market changes are reported on the income statement.
2. Prepare a tabulation to show the investment revenue of Bliss Company and the balance in the investment account at year-end 19A, 19B, and 19C. Assume no cash dividends were paid by Company Y during 19C and that the quoted market price of Company Y common stock was $56 per share at December 31, 19C.

Exercise 16–7

On January 1, 19A, Taft Company purchased, as a long-term investment, 6% of the 50,000 (par $10) shares of the outstanding common stock of Company S at $11 per share. During the years 19A, 19B, and 19C, the following additional data were available:

	Company S
End of 19A:	
Reported net income	$30,000
Cash dividends declared and paid	20,000
Market value per share	15
End of 19B:	
Reported net income	25,000
Cash dividends declared and paid	15,000
Market value per share	14

January 10, 19C:
Taft Company sold 200 shares of the Company S stock at $17.50 per share.

Required:

1. Assuming the market value method is used, give all entries related to the investment for Taft Company assuming—
   a. Market changes are reported on the income statement.
   b. Market changes are reported on the balance sheet as a separate element of owners' equity.
2. In parallel columns for each assumption, show at the end of 19A, 19B, and on January 10, 19C (after sale of the 200 shares), the following:
   a. Balance of the investment account.
   b. Balance in the unrealized owners' equity each year-end.
   c. Revenue from the investment for each period.

   For this requirement assume there were no additional investment transactions during 19C and the market value of Company S stock was $17.50 per share on December 31, 19C.

Exercise 16–8

During January 19A, Union Company purchased 20% of the 5,000 shares of outstanding common stock of Company B at $20 per share. At that date, the following data were available:

	Company B	
	At Book Value	Market Value per Appraisal
Assets not subject to depr.	$ 60,000	$63,000*
Assets subject to depr. (10-year remaining life)	40,000	45,000
	$100,000	
Liabilities	$ 20,000	20,000
Common stock (par value $10)	50,000	
Retained earnings	30,000	
	$100,000	

* Difference due to inventory (FIFO).

At the end of 19A, Company B reported net income of $15,000 and paid cash dividends of $5,000. At the end of 19A, Company B common stock was quoted on the market at $22 per share.

In January 19B, Union Company sold 100 shares of the Company B common stock at $23 per share.

Required:
In parallel columns prepare entries for the accounts of Union Company from the date of the purchase of the long-term investment through date of sale of the 100 shares assuming: Case A—the cost method is used; Case B—the equity method is used; and Case C—the market value method is used (market value changes are reported as revenue on the income statement). Assume goodwill is amortized over a 20-year period and the Company B stock is the only long-term equity investment held. Use straight-line depreciation and amortization.

Exercise 16–9

Gray Company purchased, for a lump sum of $104,070, the three different stocks listed below:

Company and Stock	Number of Shares
X Corporation, common stock, par $10	200
Y Corporation, preferred stock, par $100	400
Z Corporation, common stock, nopar	500

In addition, Gray paid transfer fees and other costs related to the acquisition amounting to $790. At the time of purchase, the stocks were quoted on the local market at the following prices per share: X common, $70; Y preferred, $120; and Z common, $90.

Required:
Give entry to record the purchase of these long-term investments and payment of the transfer fees. Show computations. Record each stock in a separate account.

Exercise 16–10

Each of the following situations is completely independent; however, both relate to the receipt of a stock dividend by an investor.

Case A—Corporation K had 20,000 shares of $50 par value stock outstanding when the board of directors voted to issue a 25% stock dividend (i.e., one additional share for each four [4] shares owned).

Required:
Mason Company owns 2,000 shares of the Corporation K stock (a long-term investment) acquired at a cost of $65 per share. After receiving the stock dividend, Mason Company sold 200 shares of the additional stock for $70 per share. Give the entries for Mason Company to record (1) acquisition of the 2,000 shares, (2) receipt of the stock dividend, and (3) sale of the 200 shares. Assume the cost method.

Case B—During the course of an audit, you find accounts as follows:

Investments in Stocks of Company A ($100 par value)

	Debits	
Jan. 1	Cost of 100 shares	$17,500
Feb. 1	50 shares received as a stock dividend (at par $100)	5,000
	Credits	
July 1	25 shares of dividend stock sold at $125	3,125

Income Summary

	Credits	
Feb. 1	Stock dividend on Company A stock ..	$ 5,000
Aug. 1	Cash dividend on Company A stock ...	3,000

Required:
Assuming the cost method, restate these accounts on a correct basis. Give reasons for each change.

Exercise 16–11

Corporation M issued one stock right for each share of common stock owned by investors. The rights provided that for each six rights held, a share of preferred stock could be purchased for $80 cash (par of the preferred was $80 per share). When the rights were issued, they had a market value of $7 each and the common stock was selling at $142 per share (ex rights). Taylor Company owned 300 shares of Corporation M common stock, acquired as a long-term investment at a cost of $22,350. Assume the cost method.

Required:

1. How many rights did Taylor Company receive?
2. Determine the cost of the stock rights to Taylor Company and give any entry that should be made upon receipt of the rights.
3. Assume Taylor Company exercised the rights when the market value of the preferred stock of Corporation M was $130. Determine the cost of the new stock and give the entry to record the exercise of the rights.
4. Assume instead that Taylor Company sold its rights for $7.40 each. Give entry to record the sale.

Exercise 16–12

Give entries in the accounts of Cisco Corporation under the cost method for the following transactions which occurred over a period of time and in the chronological order shown:

a. Cisco Corporation purchased 100 shares of Bell Corporation common stock at $99 per share as a long-term investment.

b. Bell Corporation issued a 10% stock dividend in additional common shares.

c. Bell Corporation issued rights to present common stockholders entitling each holder of five old shares to buy one additional share of new common stock at $96. At the time, the rights sold for $4 per right and the shares outstanding sold for $116 each (ex rights). Make an allocation to the rights.

d. Cisco Corporation exercised its rights and bought new shares.

e. Cisco Corporation sold 120 shares of Bell stock for $12,000, failing to identify the specific shares disposed of. (Use FIFO procedures.)

PART B: EXERCISES 16–13 to 16–18

Exercise 16–13

On January 1, 19A, Company A acquired all of the outstanding shares of Company B common stock by exchanging, on a share-for-share basis, 4,000 shares of its own stock. The balance sheets reflected the following summarized data immediately before acquisition:

	Company A	Company B
Assets not subject to depr.	$180,000	$40,000*
Assets subject to depr. (net and 10-year remaining life)	120,000	25,000
	$300,000	$65,000
Liabilities	$ 20,000*	$ 5,000
Common stock (par $10)	200,000	40,000
Retained earnings	80,000	20,000
	$300,000	$65,000

* Includes a $4,000 debt owed by Company A to Company B.

Required:

1. Give entry in the accounts of Company A for the acquisition of this long-term investment by the pooling of interests method.
2. Prepare a consolidation worksheet immediately after acquisition. Assume the pooling of interests method.

Exercise 16–14

Refer to the balance sheets immediately before acquisition for Companies A and B as given in Exercise 16–13.

Assume the same requirements and facts except that Company A exchanged, on a share-for-share basis, 3,600 shares of its own stock for a 90% interest in Company B.

Exercise 16–15

In January 19A, Company P purchased, for $149,000 cash, all of the 10,000 outstanding voting shares of the common stock of Company S. Immediately before acquisition the following additional summarized data were available:

(Relates to Exercise 16–15)

	Company P Book Value	Company S Book Value	Company S Market Value (appraised)
Assets not subject to depr.	$410,000	$ 80,000*	$ 85,000†
Assets subject to depr. (net)	200,000	60,000	67,000‡
Total	$610,000	$140,000	$152,000
Liabilities	$ 40,000*	$ 10,000	
Common stock (par $10)	500,000	100,000	
Retained earnings	70,000	30,000	
Total	$610,000	$140,000	

* Includes a $12,000 debt owed by Company P to Company S.
† Market value excess over cost is all on short-term investments.
‡ Estimated remaining life, 10 years (straight-line depreciation).

Required:

1. Give entry in the accounts of Company P to record acquisition of this long-term investment assuming the purchase method.
2. Compute the amount of goodwill purchased.
3. Prepare a consolidation worksheet immediately after acquisition using the purchase method.
4. How much additional expense (assume a 40-year amortization period for goodwill) will be reflected on the consolidated income statement each year after the acquisition?

Exercise 16–16

Refer to the balance sheets immediately before acquisition for Companies P and S given in Exercise 16–15. Assume the same facts except that Company P purchased 60% of the outstanding shares of Company S for $96,200 cash.

Required:

1. Give entry in the accounts of Company P to record acquisition of this long-term investment assuming the purchase method.
2. Compute the amount of goodwill purchased.
3. Prepare a consolidated worksheet immediately after acquisition using the purchase method.
4. How much additional depreciation expense and goodwill amortization (assume a 40-year amortization period) will be reflected on the consolidated income statement each year after the acquisition?

Exercise 16–17

On January 1, 19A, Company J purchased an 80% interest in Company K for $116,400. At acquisition, the goodwill purchased was computed as follows:

Purchase price for 80% interest in Company K		$116,400
Market value of identifiable assets	$153,000*	
Less liabilities	20,000	
Market value of identifiable net assets	133,000	
Proportion purchased	×.80	
Market value of identifiable net assets purchased		106,400
Goodwill purchased		$ 10,000

* Includes $5,000 excess over book value of operational assets.

At the end of 19A, the financial statements reflected the following (summarized):

	Reported at End of Year 19A	
	Company J	Company K
Income statement:		
Sales revenue	$360,000	$ 80,000
Interest revenue		400
	360,000	80,400
Cost of goods sold	150,000	42,000
Other operating expenses	109,600	26,300
Interest expense	400	100
	260,000	68,400
Net income	$100,000	$ 12,000
Balance sheet:		
Current assets	$172,000	$ 80,000
Investment in Company K	116,400	
Operational assets (net)	400,000	90,000
	$688,400	$170,000
Current liabilities	$ 50,000	$ 30,000
Common stock	500,000	100,000
Retained earnings	138,400	40,000*
	$688,400	$170,000

* At acquisition, the balance was $28,000.

Intercompany items at year-end were as follows:

a. Company J sold Company K inventory (goods at cost) during the year amounting to $5,000.
b. Company J paid Company K $400 interest during the year. The related liability was created and paid off during 19A.
c. Company J owed Company K $3,000 at the end of the year.

Required:
Prepare a worksheet to develop a consolidated income statement and balance sheet at the end of 19A assuming the purchase method. Assume straight-line depreciation is used, the operational assets have a 10-year remaining life, and goodwill will be amortized over 20 years.

Exercise 16–18

On January 1, 19A, X Company purchased 80% of the outstanding common stock of Y Company at a cost of $137,200. At acquisition, the goodwill purchased was computed as follows:

Purchase price for 80% interest in Y Co.		$137,200
Market value of identifiable assets	$191,500*	
Less liabilities	25,000	
Market value of identifiable net assets	166,500	
Proportion purchased	×.80	
Market value of identifiable net assets purchased		133,200
Goodwill		$ 4,000

* Includes excess over book value of inventory, $1,250; and operational assets, $6,250.

After one year of operations, each company prepared a balance sheet and income statement as follows (summarized):

	Reported at End of Year 19A	
	X Company	Y Company
Income statement:		
Sales revenue	$340,000	$ 90,000
Cost of goods sold	190,000	46,000
Depreciation expense	32,000	15,000
Other operating expenses	72,000	17,000
Interest expense	2,000	1,000
	296,000	79,000
Net income	$ 44,000	$ 11,000
Balance sheet:		
Current assets	$170,800	$ 40,000
Investment in Y Company	137,200	
Operational assets (net)	330,000	160,000
	$638,000	$200,000
Liabilities	$138,000	$ 30,000
Common stock	400,000	150,000
Retained earnings	100,000	20,000*
	$638,000	$200,000

* Balance at date of acquisition, $9,000.

Additional data:

a. Sales of X Company to Y Company during the year were $15,000 (at cost).

b. Depreciation on operational assets—assume a 10-year remaining life and straight-line method.

c. Amortization of any goodwill—assume a 20-year amortization period.

Required:

Prepare a worksheet to develop a consolidated income statement and balance sheet at the end of 19A assuming the purchase method.

PROBLEMS

PART A: PROBLEMS 16–1 to 16–6

Problem 16–1

On January 1, 19A, Glenn Company purchased 4,000 shares of the 20,000 shares outstanding of common stock (par $10) of Dean Corporation for $64,000 cash and 3,000 shares of the 100,000 shares outstanding of common stock (nopar) of Childres Corporation for $21,000 cash as a long-term investment. These are the only long-term equity investments held. The accounting periods for the companies end on December 31.

Subsequent information was as follows:

	Dean	Childres
December 31, 19A:		
Income reported for 19A	$40,000	$20,000
Cash dividend per share declared and paid during 19A	1.50	None
Market price per share of stock	12	8
October 20, 19B:		
Sold 1,000 shares of Childres stock at $10 per share.		
December 31, 19B:		
Income reported for 19B	50,000	26,000
Cash dividend per share declared and paid during 19B	1.00	.50
Market price per share of stock	14	11
Reclassified Childres stock as a current asset (short-term investment).		

Required:

1. Assuming the cost method, give all entries indicated for Glenn Company for 19A and 19B.
2. Show how the long-term investments in equity securities and the related investment revenue would be reported on the financial statements of Glenn Company at the end of each year.

Required:

1. Set up captions and enter the indicated information (show computations) as shown below.
2. Reconstruct the investment account for each assumption; also reconstruct the "allowance" and "unrealized capital" accounts.
3. Explain why the investment account balance is different between the cost and equity methods.

(Relates to Problem 16–2)

Information (James's accounts)	Assuming Cost Method Is Appropriate	Assuming Equity Method Is Appropriate
a. Entry at date of acquisition		
b. Amount of goodwill purchased.		
c. Entries at 12/31/19B:		
(1) Investment revenue and dividends.		
(2) Additional depreciation expense.		
(3) Amortization of goodwill.		
(4) Additional expense associated with short-term investments (held by Clay) for which market value (i.e., purchase price to James) exceeded book value.		
(5) Recognition of change in market value of Clay stock.		
d. Entries at 12/31/19C:		
(1) Investment revenue and dividends.		
(2) Additional depreciation expense.		
(3) Amortization of goodwill.		
(4) Recognition of change in market value of Clay stock.		

Problem 16–2

On January 1, 19B, James Company purchased 3,000 of the 15,000 outstanding shares of common stock of Clay Corporation for $80,000 cash as a long-term investment (the only long-term equity investment held). At that date, the balance sheet of Clay Corporation showed the following book values (summarized):

Assets not subject to depreciation	$140,000*
Assets subject to depreciation (net)	100,000†
Liabilities	40,000
Common stock (par $10)	150,000
Retained earnings	50,000

* Market value, $150,000; difference relates to short-term investments.

† Market value, $140,000, estimated remaining life, 10 years. Assume straight-line depreciation and amortization of goodwill over 20 years.

Additional subsequent data on Clay Corporation:

	19B	19C
Income before extraordinary items	$25,000	$26,000
Extraordinary item—gain		5,000
Cash dividends declared and paid	10,000	12,000
Market value per share	25	26

Problem 16–3

During January 19A, Jack Company purchased 1,000 shares of the 10,000 outstanding shares of common stock (par $20) of Williams Corporation for $36,000 cash as a long-term investment (the only long-term equity investment held). During 19A, 19B, and 19C, the following additional data were available:

	19A	19B
Net income reported by Williams at year-end	$15,000	$20,000
Cash dividends declared and paid by Williams during the year	10,000	12,000
Market price per share (Williams stock)	40	37

On January 2, 19C, Jack sold 100 shares of the Williams stock at $38 per share.

Required:
(Suggestion—Set up a three-column tabulation for Requirements 1–3.)

1. Give all entries indicated in the accounts of Jack Company assuming the cost method is used.
2. Give all entries indicated in the accounts of Jack Com-

pany assuming the market value method is used and that market value changes are reported on the income statement.

3. Give all entries indicated in the accounts of Jack Company assuming the market value is used and that market value changes are reported as unrealized capital on the balance sheet.
4. Explain why the investment account balance is different between 1 and 2 above.

Problem 16–4

In January 19A, Jay Company purchased 10% of the 100,000 outstanding common shares of Barlow Company at $6 per share as a long-term investment (the only long-term equity investment held). During the years 19A and 19B, the following additional data were available:

	Barlow Company
End 19A:	
Reported net income	$30,000
Cash dividends declared and paid	15,000
Market value per share	9
End 19B:	
Reported net income	(4,000) loss
Cash dividends declared and paid	10,000
Market value per share	7

Required:

(Suggestion: Set up a three-column tabulation for Requirements 1–3.)

1. Give all entries indicated in the accounts of Jay Company assuming the cost method is used.
2. Give all entries indicated assuming that the market value method is used and that market value changes are reported on the income statement.
3. Give all entries indicated assuming that the market value method is used and that market value changes are reported as unrealized capital on the balance sheet.
4. Prepare a tabulation to reflect at each year-end, for each of the above requirements the following: *(a)* the balance in the investment account at each year-end, *(b)* the balance in any unrealized capital accounts, and *(c)* investment revenue for Jay Company.
5. Give the entry assuming 1,000 shares of Barlow Company were sold by Jay early in 19C at $8 per share.

Problem 16–5

During January 19A, Perry Company purchased 20% of the 30,000 outstanding common shares of McDonald Company at $16 per share as a long-term investment (the only long-term equity investment held). At date of acquisition of the shares, the following data in respect to McDonald Company had been assembled by Perry Company:

	McDonald Company At Book Value	McDonald Company At Market Value
Assets not subject to depr.	$250,000	$260,000*
Assets subject to depr., net (10-year remaining life; straight line)	200,000	220,000
	$450,000	
Liabilities	$ 50,000	$ 50,000
Common stock (par $10)	300,000	
Retained earnings	100,000	
	$450,000	

* Difference due to inventory (FIFO).

Selected data available at year-end:

	19A	19B
Reported net income, McDonald Company:		
Income before extraordinary items	$20,000	$(10,000) loss
Extraordinary gain	10,000	
Cash dividends declared and paid:		
McDonald Company	8,000	5,000
Quoted market price per share, McDonald Company stock	21	15

Required:

1. In parallel columns, prepare all entries for Perry Company in respect to the investment assuming *(a)* the cost method is appropriate, *(b)* the equity method is appropriate (amortize any goodwill over 20 years using the straight-line method), and *(c)* the market value method is used and market value changes are reported on the income statement.
2. Prepare a tabulation for each assumption in 1 above to reflect *(a)* the balance in the investment account at each year-end, *(b)* investment revenue—ordinary for each period, *(c)* investment gain—extraordinary for each period and *(d)* the balance in the allowance account.

Problem 16–6

Foster Corporation completed the following transactions, in the order given, relative to the portfolio of stocks held as long-term investments:

a. Purchased 200 shares of common stock (par value $50) of M Corporation at $70 per share plus a brokerage commission of 4% and transfer costs of $20.

b. Purchased, for a lump sum of $96,000, the following stocks of N Corporation:

Stocks	Number of Shares	Market Price at Date of Purchase
Class A, common, par value $100	200	$ 50
Preferred, par value $50	300	100
Class B, nopar common stock (stated value $100)	400	150

c. Purchased 300 shares common stock of M Corporation at $80 per share plus a brokerage commission of 4% and transfer costs of $60.

d. Received a stock dividend on the M Corporation stock; for each share held, an additional share was received.

e. Sold 100 shares of M Corporation stock at $45 per share (from lot 1).

f. Received a two-for-one stock split on the class A common stock of N Corporation (the number of shares doubled).

g. Received cash dividends as follows (all declared during period of receipt):

M Corporation common stock—$5 per share.
N, class A, common stock—$3 per share.
N preferred—6%.
N, class B, nopar common stock—$1.50 per share.

Required:

1. Give entries for Foster Corporation for the above transactions assuming the cost method is appropriate. Show calculations and assume FIFO order when shares are sold.
2. Prepare an inventory of the long-term investment portfolio; include number of shares and balance sheet valuations after giving effect to the above transactions.

PART B: PROBLEMS 16–7 to 16–11

Problem 16–7

In January 19A, Harold Company acquired, as a long-term investment, 9,000 of the 10,000 outstanding common stock shares of Stanley Company (par $20) by issuing 18,000 shares of its own common stock (par $10). Immediately prior to acquisition, the balance sheets reflected the following (summarized):

	Harold Co. Book Value	Stanley Co. Book Value	Stanley Co. Market Value
Cash	$290,000	$ 70,000	$ 70,000
Receivables (net)	63,000†	36,000	33,000
Inventories	237,000	170,000	160,000
Operational assets (net)	260,000	100,000	150,000*
Patents (net)		14,000	10,000*
Total	$850,000	$390,000	$423,000
Current liabilities	$ 60,000	$ 10,000†	
Long-term liabilities	150,000	140,000	
Common stock	514,000	200,000	
Retained earnings	126,000	40,000	
Total	$850,000	$390,000	

* Estimated useful life; operational assets, 10 years; patent, 5 years. Assume purchased goodwill recognized will be amortized over 20 years.

† Includes a $4,000 debt owed by Stanley Company to Harold Company.

Required:

1. Assume the acquisition meets all of the criteria for the pooling of interests method.
   a. Give the entry to record the stock exchange in the accounts of Harold Company at date of acquisition.
   b. Prepare a consolidation worksheet for the balance sheet immediately after acquisition.
2. Assume the same facts as above except that instead of the exchange of shares, Harold Company paid $286,700 cash for 9,000 shares of Stanley Company common stock. Also assume the acquisition qualifies as a purchase.
   a. Give the entry to record the acquisition in the accounts of Harold Company.
   b. Compute the amount of goodwill purchased (show computations).
   c. Prepare a consolidation worksheet for the balance sheet immediately after acquisition.
3. To compare the two methods, pooling of interests versus purchase, complete the tabulation as follows:

Item (consolidated)	Consolidated Amounts the Same or Different?	Explanation of Reasons
1. Current assets.		
2. Investment account balance.		
3. Liabilities.		
4. Common stock balance.		
5. Retained earnings balance.		
6. Minority interest amount.		
7. Future net income.		

Problem 16–8

On January 1, 19A, Company A acquired 90% of the common stock of Company B by issuing 13,500 shares of its own common stock to the shareholders of Company B for an equal number of Company A shares. After one year of operations, each company prepared an income statement and balance sheet as follows (summarized):

	Reported at End of Year 19A	
	Company A	Company B
Income statement:		
Sales revenue	$620,000	$140,000
Interest revenue	700	
	620,700	140,000
Cost of goods sold	370,000	75,000
Depreciation expense	40,000	15,000
Other operating expenses	132,700	36,300
Interest expense	1,000	700
	543,700	127,000
Net income	$ 77,000	$ 13,000
Balance sheet:		
Current assets	$335,000	$101,000
Investment in Company B	135,000	
Operational assets (net—remaining life, 10 years)	330,000	149,000
	$800,000	$250,000
Liabilities	$ 80,000	$ 40,000
Common stock (par $10)	600,000	150,000
Retained earnings	120,000	60,000*
	$800,000	$250,000

* Balance at acquisition date, $47,000.

Intercompany items and adjustments for 19A:

a. Company B sold $17,000 worth of goods (at cost) to Company A during the year.
b. Company B paid Company A $700 interest during the year.
c. At the end of 19A, Company B owed Company A $20,000.

Required:

1. Prepare a worksheet for 19A to develop a consolidated income statement and balance sheet. Use the pooling of interests basis. Assume straight-line depreciation.
2. Prepare a consolidated income statement and balance sheet clearly identifying the minority interest.

Problem 16–9

Refer to the balance sheets for Companies A and B given in Problem 16–8. Assume the same facts except that Company A purchased 13,500 shares (90%) of the common stock of Company B at a cash cost of $226,000. At date of acquisition, the depreciable operational assets, at market value, were $43,000 above book value.

The purchase method changes the trial balance for Company A given in Problem 16–8 as follows (new balances):

Current assets	$109,000
Investment account (at cost)	226,000
Common stock (par $10)	465,000

Required:

1. Compute the purchased goodwill at date of acquisition. Show computations.
2. Prepare a worksheet for 19A to develop a consolidated income statement and balance sheet. Use the purchase basis. Use straight-line depreciation and amortize goodwill over 20 years.

Problem 16–10

On January 1, 19A, Company A purchased for cash, in the open market, 80% of the outstanding common stock of Company B at a cost of $188,000. At date of acquisition, based upon an appraisal of Company B assets for consolidation purposes, the depreciable operational assets had a market value of $10,000 above their book value and the current assets had a market value of $7,500 less than their book value.

After one year of operations, each company prepared an income statement and balance sheet as follows (summarized):

	Reported at End of Year 19A	
	Company A	Company B
Income statement:		
Sales revenue	$630,000	$180,000
Interest revenue	1,000	
	631,000	180,000
Cost of goods sold	370,000	98,000
Depreciation expense	37,000	16,000
Other operating expenses	140,000	45,000
Interest expense	4,000	1,000
	551,000	160,000
Net income	$ 80,000	$ 20,000
Balance sheet:		
Current assets	$372,000	$110,000
Investment in Co. B (at cost)	188,000	
Operational assets (net)	360,000	160,000
Total	$920,000	$270,000
Current liabilities	$ 70,000	$ 30,000
Common stock (par $10)	760,000	200,000
Retained earnings	90,000	40,000*
Total	$920,000	$270,000

* Balance at date of acquisition, $20,000.

Data relating to 19A eliminations and adjustments:

a. During the year, Company A sold merchandise to Company B for $35,000 (at cost).
b. During 19A, Company B paid Company A $1,000 interest on loans.
c. At the end of 19A, Company B owed Company A $20,000.
d. The depreciable assets of Company B have an estimated remaining life of 10 years (no residual value, straight-line depreciation).
e. Goodwill is to be amortized over a 20-year life.

Required:

1. Compute the goodwill purchased at date of acquisition; show computations.
2. Prepare a worksheet to develop a consolidated income statement and balance sheet on the purchase basis.

Problem 16–11

Refer to the balance sheets for Companies A and B given in Problem 16–10. Assume the same facts except that Company A acquired a 90% interest in Company B by exchanging 18,000 shares of its own common stock for an equal number of shares in Company B.

The pooling of interests method changes the trial balance given for Company A in Problem 16–10 as follows (new balances):

Current assets	$560,000
Investment account	180,000
Common stock (par $10)	940,000

Required:

1. Prepare a worksheet for 19A to develop a consolidated income statement and balance sheet. Use the pooling of interest basis.
2. Prepare a consolidated income statement and balance sheet clearly identifying the minority interest.

17

Accounting for Bonds as Long-Term Liabilities and Investments, and Debt Restructure

COMPANIES seeking long-term financing usually consider either issuing shares of capital stock (common or preferred) or issuing long-term debt. The long-term effects of issuing long-term debt are quite different from issuing shares of voting capital stock (discussed in Chapter 14). In contrast to capital stock (equity securities), the issuance of long-term debt commits the company to fixed interest payments each period, regardless of the periodic income or loss, and to payment of the principal at a stated maturity date. Also, the issuance of debt securities does not affect the ownership interests of the company. The interest paid on debt is deductible for income tax purposes, which reduces the cost of borrowing. For example, a stated or coupon rate of interest of 15 percent and a 40 percent average income tax rate results in an aftertax interest rate of 9 percent (see the discussion of financial leverage in Chapter 21). Primarily because of this income tax difference, usually it is believed that debt financing is less costly than equity financing.

Long-term liabilities include obligations such as long-term notes payable, mortgages payable (i.e., a long-term note secured by a mortgage on specified assets), pension obligations (Chapter 18), lease obligations (Chapter 19), and bonds payable. This chapter analyzes bonds from the viewpoints of *(a)* the issuer (i.e., the borrower) and *(b)* the investor (i.e., the lender). This dual approach is logical because the accounting and reporting concepts and procedures for the issuer and the investor are essentially the same; that is, there is "accounting symmetry" between the debtor and creditor. Bonds represent a long-term liability for the issuer and usually a long-term investment for the investor.[1] This chapter is subdivided as follows:

Part A—Fundamentals of Accounting for Bonds by the Issuer and Investor

Part B—Special Problems in Accounting for Bonds

Part C—Changes in Obligations Prior to Maturity Date

Supplement 17–A—Serial Bonds

Supplement 17–B—Economic Analysis of Bond Refunding Transactions

Supplement 17–C—Troubled Debt Restructure—Computation of New Effective Interest Rate

---

[1] Bonds sometimes are held as short-term investments, in which case they are accounted for in the manner discussed in Chapter 6. They are recorded at cost. Any premium or discount usually is not amortized in view of the short holding period. In contrast, this chapter focuses on long-term investments in bonds.

Part A: Fundamentals of Accounting for Bonds by the Issuer and Investor

NATURE OF BONDS

Bonds are accompanied by a relatively high degree of formality. The issuer prepares a formal bond agreement, often called the **bond indenture,** which specifies the terms of the bonds, including all **restrictions or covenants** designed to protect the interests of the bondholders (lenders). The bond indenture specifies such items as authorized amount for issuance, periodic interest (including dates), maturity date, conversion and call privileges (if any), sinking fund requirements, restrictions of retained earnings (discussed in Chapter 15), dividend restrictions, maximum debt-to-equity ratio permitted for the borrower, and the responsibilities of a trustee designated to protect the interests of the lenders.

The investors receive bond certificates, which are contractual representations that a debt is owed by one party, the issuer, to one or more other parties, the investors. A bond certificate indicates the principal amount, specified interest dates (usually semiannual), the stated rate of interest based upon the principal amount, and any other special agreements. Thus, a bond may be defined as a formal (i.e., written) promise to pay a specified principal at a designated date in the future and, in addition, periodic interest on the principal at a specified rate per period.

Bonds are used to borrow large amounts from the capital markets, including individuals, by dividing the total long-term debt into a number of small units, usually in denominations of $10,000 and $1,000. The total amount to be borrowed, evidenced by the bond certificates, usually is referred to as the **bond issue.**

CLASSIFICATION OF BONDS

Bonds may be classified in various ways as follows:

1. Character of the issuing corporation—The borrower may be a private corporation issuing **industrial** bonds or a public entity issuing **municipal** or other **government** bonds.

2. Character of the security—**Secured** bonds are supported by a lien, or mortgage, on specific assets, whereas **unsecured** bonds have no such support. Unsecured bonds are frequently called **debenture bonds. Guaranty security bonds** are those which in case of default will be paid as to principal and interest by a third party designated as the guarantor. For example, a parent corporation may guarantee payment of bonds issued by one or more of its subsidiary companies. **Lien security bonds** are secured by a lien on particular kinds of property, such as securities (collateral trust bonds), rolling stock (car trust and equipment bonds), or on realty (real estate bonds).

3. Purpose of issue—**Purchase money bonds** are issued in full or part payment for property. **Refunding bonds** are issued to retire existing obligations and may have the same security as the retired debt. **Consolidated bonds** replace several prior issues with a single issue and consolidate the securities for the retired issues. These types are comparatively rare.

4. Payment of interest—**Income bonds** differ from **ordinary** bonds in that the payment of interest each period on income bonds depends on the earning of income by the issuer. **Participating bonds** have a specified minimum stated rate of interest plus a stated participation in the income of the issuer; they may have a specified limited participation or an unlimited participation.

Registered bonds are recorded in the name of the investor, and the periodic interest payments are sent only to that person; therefore, a sale or transfer by the investor must be reported to the issuer, trustee, or other party designated for this purpose. In contrast, **coupon bonds** have a coupon attached for each periodic interest payment. At each coupon due date, the holder of the bond simply detaches the appropriate coupon, signs it, and cashes it as if it were a check. Sale of a coupon bond does not require registration of title transfer.

5. Maturity of principal—Bonds maturing at a specified date are called **straight** (or ordinary) **bonds;** that is, the entire bond issue matures at a single date. Bonds maturing at a series of stated installment dates, say one fifth each year, are called **serial bonds** (discussed in Supplement 17–A). **Callable bonds** give the **issuer** the option to retire them at a stated price before the obligatory maturity date. **Redeemable bonds** give the **investor** the option to turn them in for a stated redemption price prior to maturity. **Convertible bonds** give the **investor** the option to turn

them in and to receive, in exchange, other specified securities of the borrower (usually common stock).

FINANCIAL MARKET CONDITIONS

In going to the financial (i.e., money) market, a borrower needing a large sum of money must make the fundamental decision whether to employ debt or capital stock, or a combination. This decision depends on a number of factors, some peculiar to the company and some based on the nature of the financial market.

Bonds may be marketed initially by the borrower in several ways. Typically, an entire bond issue is sold to investment bankers who **underwrite** the bond issue at a specified price and then market the bonds at a higher price to individual investors, thus realizing underwriter's compensation. Underwriting a bond issue means that the investment institution promises the issuer a specified amount of cash for the issue and handles the formal arrangements of a bond issue. This specified amount usually is recorded as the selling price by the issuer. Alternatively, the investment banker may agree to act as a selling agent for the borrower for an agreed commission; the selling price less the costs of selling is remitted to the issuer. Increasingly, issuers are selling their bonds privately to financial institutions and individual investors.

In considering an investment decision, the investor should weigh the **guaranteed** fixed interest rate and the bond maturity specifications against the **potential** for dividends. Thus, bonds generally are less risky as investments than stock. Consequently, investors demand a higher rate of return on stock investments than on bond investments. Both interest revenue (except for tax-free municipal bonds) and dividend revenue (there are certain limited exceptions) are subject to income tax to the investor.

ILLUSTRATIVE DATA FOR BONDS

For illustration of bonds in Part A, a common set of facts will be used. Typically, bonds specify a long term from date of issuance to date of maturity (e.g., 10, 20, or more years), fractional interest rates, and semiannual interest payments. However, to simplify and shorten the illustrations at the outset, we will use a five-year term, even interest rates, and annual rather than semiannual interest. These simplifications will not affect the basic concepts and accounting procedures.[2] The common set of facts used in this section are as shown in Exhibit 17–1, Panel A.

To facilitate study, analysis, and problem solving, it is often helpful to prepare a **time scale** for the bond issue (or investment) that details important data such as issue date, interest dates, maturity date, period outstanding, and interest rates. A time scale for the above bond issue would appear as shown in Panel B of Exhibit 17–1.

BOND INTEREST AND PRICES

Bonds have fixed maturity amounts, definite maturity dates, and specified interest payments. The market price of bonds fluctuates inversely with changes in the market interest rate. When the market interest rate rises, the market price of outstanding bonds falls; when the market interest rate falls, the market price of bonds rises. Although the market price of bonds tends to move with the interest market, the price also is influenced by changes in the issuer's financial standing and the approach of maturity (at which time the market value and maturity amount normally will coincide).

The bond indenture and the face of each bond certificate always specify a **stated** interest rate which is applied to the principal amount of the bond to determine the amount of **cash interest** that will be paid each period.[3] For example, each bond certificate of X Corporation (see Exhibit 17–1) will specify a stated rate of 7 percent per year. Thus, each of the $10,000 bonds will always pay $700 cash interest each annual interest period (payable on December 31), and a $1,000 denomination bond will always pay $70 cash, regardless of its issue or market price. In the case of semiannual interest payments, the bonds of X Corporation would pay 3.5 percent stated interest each six months.

In contrast to the stated rate of interest, the **yield** or **effective** rate is the true rate of interest incurred by the issuer and earned by the investor after taking into account the issue (or purchase) price of the bond.[4] Because the financial market may establish

[2] After the introductory illustrations, semiannual interest payments are assumed in the chapter.

[3] The stated rate also is referred to as the contract, nominal, or coupon rate of interest. The principal also often is referred to as the face, maturity, or par amount.

[4] The yield rate is also called the effective, true, or market rate.

EXHIBIT 17–1: Illustrative Data for Bonds—Issuer, X Corporation; Investor, Y Corporation

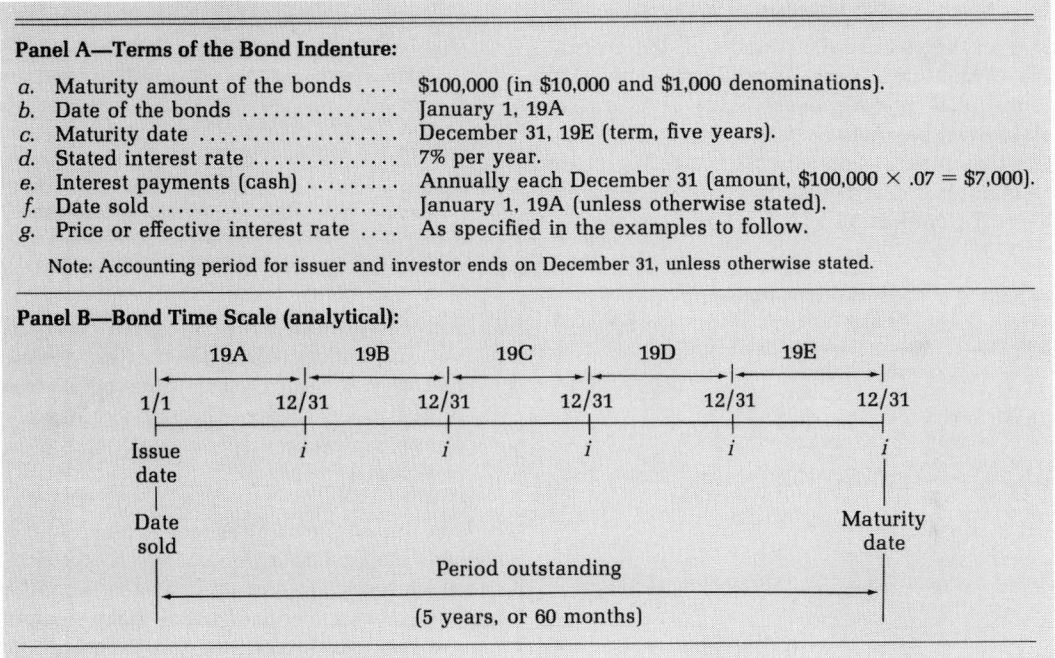

Panel A—Terms of the Bond Indenture:

a.	Maturity amount of the bonds	$100,000 (in $10,000 and $1,000 denominations).
b.	Date of the bonds	January 1, 19A
c.	Maturity date	December 31, 19E (term, five years).
d.	Stated interest rate	7% per year.
e.	Interest payments (cash)	Annually each December 31 (amount, $100,000 × .07 = $7,000).
f.	Date sold	January 1, 19A (unless otherwise stated).
g.	Price or effective interest rate	As specified in the examples to follow.

Note: Accounting period for issuer and investor ends on December 31, unless otherwise stated.

Panel B—Bond Time Scale (analytical):

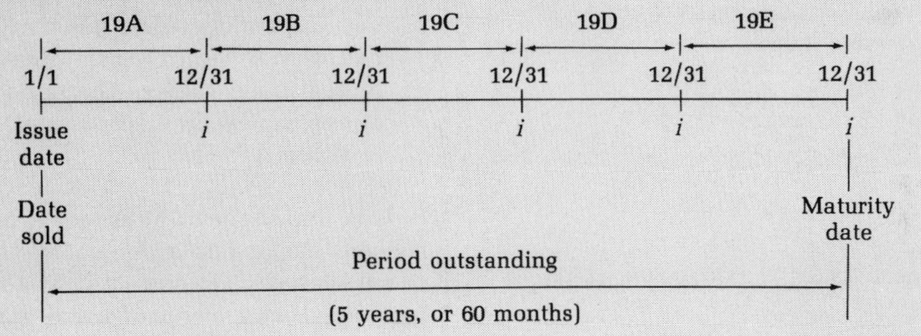

a rate of interest on the bonds different from the stated rate, bonds may sell at more or less than their face or par amount.

A bond sold at **par** will incur interest expense for the issuer at the stated rate of interest and will earn interest revenue for the investor at the same rate of interest. Only in this situation will *(a)* the stated and yield rates of interest be the same and *(b)* the bond be sold at its face, or maturity, amount. A bond sold at a **discount** (less than par) will incur interest expense for the issuer at a yield rate higher than the stated rate, and it will earn for the investor the higher yield rate. Conversely, a bond sold at a **premium** (more than par) will incur interest expense for the issuer at a yield rate which is lower than the stated rate and likewise will earn interest revenue for the investor at the lower yield rate.[5]

Investment firms often quote bonds on a yield basis. A 7 percent bond quoted at 7–50 can be bought at a price that will yield 7.5 percent on the price of the bond each year from date of sale to maturity date. Thus, a $1,000 bond with a stated rate of 7 percent, payable 3.5 percent semiannually, sold on a 7.50 percent (yield rate) basis five years before maturity would have a price of $979.47 (see Exhibit 17–2, Table C). The $20.53 discount is an adjustment of the stated interest rate to the higher yield rate. Bonds may be quoted in relation to their par or maturity amount. For example, a $1,000 bond quoted at 100 is selling for $1,000 (i.e., at par); if quoted at 97, it is selling at $970 (i.e., at a discount of $30); and if quoted at 103, it is selling at $1,030 (i.e., at a premium of $30).

[5] This discussion assumes that the issuer sells the bonds directly to the investors with no bond issue costs. Bond issue costs will be discussed in a later section.

Determination of Bond Prices

The price of a bond is the present value of all of its expected net future cash inflows discounted at the market (as opposed to the stated) rate of interest. Thus, the present value of a bond is the sum of two present value amounts: *(a)* the present value of its maturity amount plus *(b)* the present value of the series of future interest payments. Computation of the price of a bond (its present value) is shown below because it is an especially important aspect of this chapter.

The **bond price** may be computed by either of

two ways, each of which use tables that incorporate the same present value determinations, viz:

1. Based on the yield rate, compute *(a)* the present value of the future **cash principal** (i.e., the face amount) plus *(b)* the present value of the future **cash interest payments.**

   To illustrate, assume the $100,000, 7 percent (annual interest payments), five-year bonds were sold by X Corporation to Y Corporation (see Exhibit 17–1) as follows:

Case A—Sold at a Yield Rate of 8 Percent

Computation of the bond price:
Present value of future principal:
$100,000 × $p_{n=5;\,i=8\%}$ (Table 5–2)
= $100,000 × .68058 .... $68,058
Present value of future annual interest payments:
$7,000 × $P_{o_{n=5;\,i=8\%}}$ (Table 5–4)
= $7,000 × 3.99271 27,949
Bond price at 8% yield rate $96,007

Amount of discount; $96,007 − $100,000 = $3,993, because the yield rate (8 percent) was higher than the stated rate (7 percent).

Case B—Sold at a Yield Rate of 6 Percent

Computation of the bond price:
$100,000 × $p_{n=5;\,i=6\%}$ (Table 5–2)
= $100,000 × .74726 .... $ 74,726
$7,000 × $P_{o_{n=5;\,i=6\%}}$ (Table 5–4)
= $7,000 × 4.21236 29,486
Bond price at 6% yield rate $104,212

Amount of premium: $104,212 − $100,000 = $4,212, because the yield rate (6 percent) was lower than the stated rate (7 percent).

2. Refer to a **bond table** that gives bond prices for various stated rates, yield rates, and times to maturity. Exhibit 17–2 shows excerpts from three typical bond tables. The bond prices computed above can be verified by referring to Exhibit 17–2, Table A.

It is important to note that a bond sold (or purchased) at par has a present value **identical** to the par or maturity amount. In contrast, a bond sold (or purchased) at a discount has a present value at the time of issuance **lower** than par or maturity amount

EXHIBIT 17–2: Excerpts from Five Typical Bond Tables

Table A—Face of Bond, $100,000; Stated Interest, 7 Percent Payable Annually

	Time to Maturity		
Yield	3 Years	4 Years	5 Years
6.00	102,673.01	103,465.11	104,212.37
6.50	101,324.24	101,712.90	102,077.84
7.00	100,000.00	100,000.00	100,000.00
7.50	98,699.74	98,325.33	97,977.05
8.00	97,422.90	96,687.88	96,007.29

Table B—Face of Bond, $100,000; Stated Interest, 10 Percent Payable Annually

	Time to Maturity		
Yield	5 Years	6 Years	7 Years
8.00	107,985.42	109,245.76	110,412.74
8.50	105,910.96	106,830.38	107,677.78
9.00	103,889.65	104,485.92	105,032.95
9.50	101,919.86	102,209.91	102,474.80
10.00	100,000.00	100,000.00	100,000.00
10.50	98,128.57	97,853.91	97,605.35
11.00	96,304.10	95,769.46	95,287.80
11.50	94,525.18	93,744.56	93,044.45
12.00	92,790.45	91,777.18	90,872.49

EXHIBIT 17–2: *(concluded)*

Table C—Face of Bond, $100,000; Stated Interest, 7 Percent Payable Semiannually

	Time to Maturity				
Yield	**3 Years**	**3½ Years**	**4 Years**	**4½ Years**	**5 Years**
6.00	102,708.60	103,115.14	103,509.84	103,893.05	104,265.10
6.50	101,343.14	101,543.00	101,736.56	101,924.03	102,105.60
7.00	100,000.00	100,000.00	100,000.00	100,000.00	100,000.00
7.50	98,678.73	98,485.52	98,299.30	98,119.80	97,946.81
8.00	97,378.93	96,998.97	96,633.63	96,282.33	95,944.56

Table D—Face of Bond, $100,000; Stated Interest, 8 Percent Payable Semiannually

	Time to Maturity				
Yield	**2 Years**	**2½ Years**	**3 Years**	**3½ Years**	**4 Years**
6.00	103,717.09	104,579.71	105,417.20	106,230.28	107,019.69
6.50	102,771.24	103,410.40	104,029.44	104,629.00	105,209.69
7.00	101,836.54	102,257.53	102,664.27	103,057.28	103,436.98
7.50	100,912.85	101,120.82	101,321.27	101,514.47	101,700.70
8.00	100,000.00	100,000.00	100,000.00	100,000.00	100,000.00
8.50	99,097.85	98,894.82	98,700.07	98,513.25	98,334.06
9.00	98,206.23	97,805.01	97,421.06	97,053.65	96,702.05
	4½ Years	**5 Years**	**6 Years**	**10 Years**	**15 Years**
6.00	107,786.11	108,530.20	109,954.01	114,877.48	119,600.45
6.50	105,772.09	106,316.80	107,355.31	110,904.51	114,236.44
7.00	103,803.85	104,158.30	104,831.67	107,106.20	109,196.02
7.50	101,880.19	102,053.20	102,380.68	103,474.05	104,457.31
8.00	100,000.00	100,000.00	100,000.00	100,000.00	100,000.00
8.50	98,162.16	97,997.28	97,687.40	96,676.41	95,805.25
9.00	96,365.60	96,043.64	95,440.71	93,496.04	91,855.55

Table E—Face of Bond, $100,000; Stated Interest, 10 Percent Payable Semiannually

	Time to Maturity				
Yield	**4 Years**	**4½ Years**	**5 Years**	**5½ Years**	**6 Years**
8.00	106,732.74	107,435.33	108,110.90	108,760.47	109,385.07
8.50	104,997.84	105,513.51	106,008.17	106,482.65	106,937.79
9.00	103,297.94	103,634.37	103,956.36	104,264.45	104,559.29
9.50	101,632.26	101,796.91	101,954.10	102,104.15	102,247.39
10.00	100,000.00	100,000.00	100,000.00	100,000.00	100,000.00
10.50	98,400.40	98,242.66	98,092.79	97,950.43	97,815.10
11.00	96,832.72	96,523.91	96,231.19	95,953.73	95,691.74
11.50	95,296.22	94,842.76	94,413.96	94,008.48	93,625.04
12.00	93,790.21	93,198.31	92,639.93	92,113.12	91,616.16

(by the amount of the discount); a bond sold (or purchased) at a premium has a present value at the time of issuance **higher** than par or maturity amount (by the amount of the premium).

In the bond market *(a)* bonds are priced via present value computations and usually *(b)* the virtual **certainty** of the future cash flows (principal and interest payments) removes much of the guesswork from the application. Therefore, bond valuation is a clear-cut "market" application of present value concepts.

ACCOUNTING FOR AND REPORTING BONDS (ISSUER AND INVESTOR)

In accounting for bonds, the **issuer** records the cash amount received for a bond as the value of the liability (i.e., the maturity amount minus any discount or plus any premium). Similarly, the **investor** records the cash amount paid for a bond as the cost (present value) of the bond investment.

The data given in Exhibit 17–1 for X and Y Corporations and the computation of bond prices in Cases A and B under the heading Determination of Bond Prices are used to illustrate the entries to record *(a)* the issuance of bonds at different prices and *(b)* the periodic interest and amortization of any discount or premium. We assume the entire issue, $100,000, was sold by X Corporation to Y Corporation on January 1, 19A (date of the bonds) under three different cases—at par, at a discount, and at a premium. Exhibit 17–3, Panel A, restates illustrative data; Panel B presents issuance/purchase and interest entries.

Amortization of Bond Discount and Premium

Bond discount and premium affect the **reported** amounts of interest expense for the issuer and interest revenue for the investor. For example, the interest effects in each of the three cases illustrated in Exhibit 17–3 can be summarized as follows:

	Case A (sold at par)	Case B (sold at discount)	Case C (sold at premium)
Price of the bonds (cash received)	$ 100,000	$ 96,007	$ 104,212
Payment of principal at maturity (cash paid)	(100,000)	(100,000)	(100,000)
Payment of periodic interest ($7,000 × 5, cash paid)	(35,000)	(35,000)	(35,000)
Difference—total interest expense	$ 35,000	$ 38,993	$ 30,788
Average interest expense under straight-line amortization (÷5)	$ 7,000	$ 7,799	$ 6,158

When sold at par, in Case A above, the total interest expense of $35,000 reflects both a stated and yield rate of 7 percent. In contrast, the total interest in Case B is $38,993, which is greater than $35,000 by the amount of the discount ($3,993), because the bond price of $96,007 reflects a yield rate of 8 percent. In Case C, the total interest is $30,788, which is less than $35,000 by the amount of the premium ($4,212), because the bond price reflects a yield rate of 6 percent. Thus, we see that bond discount and premium affect *(a)* investment or liability amounts on the balance sheet and *(b)* interest revenue or expense amounts on the income statement. To record and report these effects in accordance with the matching principle, bond discount and premium must be **amortized** as interest over the **period the bond is outstanding, that is, the period from date of sale to maturity date.** The two amortization methods used are (1) the **straight-line** method and (2) the **interest** method.

Straight-Line Method of Amortization. Under this method, an **equal dollar amount** of the discount or premium is amortized each period over the period the bonds are outstanding. To illustrate for Cases B and C above, the amortization each period for the five-year life of the bonds would be recorded as shown in Exhibit 17–3, Panel B.

The straight-line method of amortization produces a **stable dollar amount** of interest each period rather than a constant rate of interest each period. It can be used under GAAP **only** when the interest amounts obtained are not materially different from the **interest method** results (*APB Opinion 21,* par. 15). Straight-line amortization is simple, but it is not theoretically sound, as explained in the next section.

Interest Method of Amortization. The interest method sometimes is called present value amortization. Exhibit 17–4 illustrates the accounting when the interest method is used. As explained in the preceding paragraph, the interest method is required by *APB Opinion 21* (unless the interest amounts computed using another method are not materially different). The interest method is based upon the concept of an annuity (discussed in Chapter 5) because *(a)* the stable dollar amount of cash interest each period is viewed as a "rent" and *(b)* periodic interest amount (i.e., the effective interest amount) is computed by applying a **constant rate** to the periodic book value or carrying amount of the bonds. The constant rate is the yield rate of interest as illustrated in Exhibit 17–4 (Case B, 8 percent, and Case C, 6 percent). Case B involves a **discount;** therefore, the effective interest amount **increases** each period (as shown in the second amount column) because the carrying value (as shown in the last amount column) is increasing. In contrast, Case C involves a **premium;** therefore, the effective interest amount **decreases** each period because the carrying value is decreasing.

When the interest method is used, it is convenient to prepare an **amortization schedule** such as those illustrated in Panel B of Exhibit 17–4. The entries for the issuer and investor, as illustrated in Exhibit 17–4, Panel C, for the periodic interest and amortization of premium or discount, can be taken directly from the amortization schedule.

REPORTING BONDS ON THE FINANCIAL STATEMENTS

Reporting by the Issuer

Bonds payable should be reported at their carrying value under the balance sheet heading, Long-term Liabilities (except for bonds to be paid during the next current period). The issuer should deduct unamortized bond discount (a debit balance) from the face amount of the related bonds payable, whereas unamortized bond premium (a credit balance) should be added to the face amount of the bonds. *APB Opinion 21* specifically states that bond discount or premium "should not be classified as a deferred charge or deferred credit." To assure full disclosure, the *Opinion* indicates that the face of a note (or bond) payable and the yield rate of interest should be disclosed in the financial statements or in the notes to the statements.[6] To illustrate, the long-term liability for bonds payable should be reported essentially as follows (refer to Exhibit 17–4, Case B):

X CORPORATION—ISSUER
Balance Sheet (partial)
At December 31, 19A

Long-term liabilities:		
Bonds payable, maturity amount (due 12/31/19E, 7% interest, payable annually)	$100,000	
Less unamortized discount (based on 8% effective interest)	3,312	
Bonds payable less unamortized discount		$96,688

Reporting by the Investor

Long-term investments in bonds should be reported under the balance sheet heading, Investments and Funds. The amount reported as the carrying value should be the face amount of the bonds, plus or minus any unamortized premium or discount. In addition, the current market value, if determinable and materially different from the carrying value, and the yield rate of interest used for amortization purposes should be reported to assure full disclosure. For example, the long-term investment analyzed in Exhibit 17–4, Case B, usually is reported as follows:

Y CORPORATION—INVESTOR
Balance Sheet (partial)
At December 31, 19A

Investments and funds:	
Investment in 7% bonds of X Corp. (amortized cost based on 8% effective interest, due 12/31/19E)	$96,688

For the investor, the maturity amount ($100,000), the unamortized discount ($3,312), and the difference ($96,688) could be shown separately in a manner similar to that illustrated above for the issuer.

ACCOUNTING FOR SEMIANNUAL INTEREST PAYMENTS

Most bonds specify interest as an annual rate but require semiannual interest payments. In this situation, the semiannual rate used is half the annual rate and the number of interest periods is double the number of years to maturity (see Chapter 5).

[6] AICPA, *APB Opinion No. 21,* "Interest on Receivables and Payables" (New York, August 1971) par. 16, and appendix, par. 20.

EXHIBIT 17–3: Recording Bond Issuance and Periodic Interest—Issuer and Investor

Panel A—Illustrative Data:

1. Basic data for issuer, X Corporation, and investor, Y Corporation—see Exhibit 17–1, Panel A.
2. Bond issue price (see the preceding heading, Determination of Bond Prices):
   Case A—maturity value (at par).
   Case B—$96,007 (at a discount).
   Case C—$104,212 (at a premium).

Panel B—Entries for Issuer and Investor:

At issuance date (January 1, 19A):

Case A—The bond issue was sold (and purchased) at par, $100,000 on January 1, 19A:

Issuer's Books—X Corporation			Investor's Books—Y Corporation		
Cash	100,000		Bond investment	100,000	
Bonds payable		100,000	Cash		100,000

Case B—The bond issue was sold (and purchased) at a discount, $96,007 (recorded gross of discount):

Issuer's Books—X Corporation			Investor's Books—Y Corporation		
Cash	96,007		Bond investment	100,000	
Discount on bonds payable	3,993		Discount on bond investment		3,993
Bonds payable		100,000	Cash		96,007

Case C—The bond issue was sold (and purchased) at a premium, $104,212 (recorded gross of premium):

Issuer's Books—X Corporation			Investor's Books—Y Corporation		
Cash	104,212		Bond investment	100,000	
Premium on bonds payable		4,212	Premium on bond investment	4,212	
Bonds payable		100,000	Cash		104,212

Alternative entries—recorded **net** of any discount or premium:

Case B—

Issuer			Investor		
Cash	96,007		Bond investment	96,007	
Bonds payable		96,007	Cash		96,007

Case C—

Issuer			Investor		
Cash	104,212		Bond investment	104,212	
Bonds payable		104,212	Cash		104,212

The net approach records the liability and the investment at the net amount that would be reported on the balance sheet. It also simplifies the amortization of premium and discount since the periodic amortization entries are made directly to the liability and investment accounts, so that at maturity date they both reflect the maturity amount. The "gross" and "net" approaches derive precisely the same results on the periodic financial statements. Either approach is acceptable.

At interest date (December 31, 19A):

December 31, annual interest and amortization (each year for five years):

Case B—bonds sold at a discount (straight-line amortization):

Issuer's Books—X Corporation			Investor's Books—Y Corporation		
Interest expense	7,799		Cash	7,000†	
Discount on bonds payable		799*	Discount on bond investment	799*	
Cash		7,000†	Interest revenue		7,799

Note: To simplify, it is assumed that the investor receives the cash on the same date that the issuer disburses the cash and that this is the end of the fiscal year.

Case C—bonds sold at a premium (straight-line amortization):

Issuer's Books—X Corporation			Investor's Books—Y Corporation		
Interest expense	6,158		Cash	7,000	
Premium on bonds payable	842‡		Premium on bond investment		842‡
Cash		7,000	Interest revenue		6,158

* Amortization: $3,993 ÷ 5 years = $799.
† Cash: $100,000 × .07 = $7,000.
‡ Amortization: $4,212 ÷ 5 years = $842.

EXHIBIT 17–4: Amortization of Bond Discount and Premium—Interest Method

Panel A—Illustrative Data:

1. Basic data—Exhibit 17–1.
2. Issue price of bonds:
   Case B—$96,007 (at a discount).
   Case C—$104,212 (at a premium).

Panel B—Amortization Schedules, Interest Method:

Case B—Bonds sold at a discount (@ $96,007):

Date	Cash Interest (7 percent annual)	Effective Interest (8 percent annual)	Discount Amortization	Balance Unamortized Discount	Carrying Amount of Bonds
1/1/19A starting date				3,993	96,007
12/31/19A	7,000[a]	7,681[b]	681[c]	3,312[d]	96,688[e]
12/31/19B	7,000	7,735	735	2,577	97,423
12/31/19C	7,000	7,794	794	1,783	98,217
12/31/19D	7,000	7,857	857	926	99,074
12/31/19E	7,000	7,926	926	–0–	100,000

[a] $100,000 × .07 = $7,000 (based on stated rate).
[b] $96,007 × .08 = $7,681 (based on yield rate of interest).
[c] $7,681 − $7,000 = $681.
[d] $3,993 − $681 = $3,312.
[e] $96,007 + $681 = $96,688 (or $100,000 − $3,312 = $96,688).

Case C—Bonds sold at a premium (@ $104,212):

Date	Cash Interest (7 percent annual)	Effective Interest (6 percent annual)	Premium Amortization	Balance Unamortized Premium	Carrying Amount of Bonds
1/1/19A starting date				4,212	104,212
12/31/19A	7,000[a]	6,253[b]	747[c]	3,465[d]	103,465[e]
12/31/19B	7,000	6,208	792	2,673	102,673
12/31/19C	7,000	6,160	840	1,833	101,833
12/31/19D	7,000	6,110	890	943	100,943
12/31/19E	7,000	6,057	943	–0–	100,000

[a] $100,000 × .07 = $7,000 (based on stated rate).
[b] $104,212 × .06 = $6,253 (based on yield rate of interest).
[c] $7,000 − $6,253 = $747.
[d] $4,212 − $747 = $3,465.
[e] $104,212 − $747 = $103,465 (or $100,000 + $3,465 = $103,465).

Panel C—Entries at Interest Dates:

December 31, 19A, annual interest and amortization:*

Case B—Bonds sold at a discount (interest method amortization):

Issuer's Books—X Corporation	Debit	Credit	Investor's Books—Y Corporation	Debit	Credit
Interest expense	7,681		Cash	7,000	
Discount on bonds payable		681	Discount on bond investment	681	
Cash		7,000	Interest revenue		7,681

Computations: Case B above.

Case C—Bonds sold at a premium (interest method amortization):

Issuer's Books—X Corporation	Debit	Credit	Investor's Books—Y Corporation	Debit	Credit
Interest expense	6,253		Cash	7,000	
Premium on bonds payable	747		Premium on bond investment		747
Cash		7,000	Interest revenue		6,253

Computations: Case C above.

* If separate accounts are not used to record discount or premium, the amortization entry would be made directly to the respective liability or investment accounts.

To illustrate the accounting process when interest is paid semiannually, assume the bonds issued on January 1, 19A, by X Corporation (Exhibit 17–1) specified semiannual interest payments on June 30 and December 31. The stated semiannual interest rate would be 3.5 percent, and the number of semiannual **interest periods** would be 10; if sold at an annual yield rate of 8 percent, the semiannual **effective rate** would be 4 percent. The price of this bond issue on January 1, 19A, would be computed as shown in Exhibit 17–5, Panel A.

The bond amortization schedule for this situation is presented in Exhibit 17–5, Panel B. The entries for the issuer and the investor for this example are the same as illustrated in Exhibit 17–4 except that *(a)* an interest entry (including amortization for six months) must be made at each semiannual interest date and *(b)* the amounts of cash, interest, and discount amortization will be as reflected in Exhibit 17–5, Panel B.

EXHIBIT 17–5: Bonds with Semiannual Interest Payments

Panel A—Illustrative Data:

1. Basic data—Exhibit 17–1 is adapted as follows:
   a. Interest: Stated rate 7 percent, payable semiannually (i.e., 3.5 percent each semiannual period) on each June 30 and December 31. Yield rate of interest, 8 percent per year.
   b. Issue price of the bonds, $95,944, computed as follows:

Present value of future principal:	
$100,000 × $p_{n=10;\ i=4\%}$ (Table 5–2) = $100,000 × .67556	$67,556
Present value of future semiannual interest payments:	
$3,500 × $P_{o_{n=10;\ i=4\%}}$ (Table 5–4) = $3,500 × 8.11090	28,388
Bond price (semiannual interest payments)	$95,944

Panel B—Amortization Schedule, Interest Method (semiannual):

Date	Cash Interest (3½ percent semiannual)	Yield Interest (4 percent semiannual)	Discount Amortization	Balance Unamortized Discount	Carrying Amount of Bonds
1/1/19A starting date				4,056	95,944
6/30/19A	3,500[(a)]	3,838[(b)]	338[(c)]	3,718[(d)]	96,282[(e)]
12/31/19A	3,500	3,851	351	3,367	96,633
6/30/19B	3,500	3,865	365	3,002	96,998
12/31/19B	3,500	3,880	380	2,622	97,378
6/30/19C	3,500	3,895	395	2,227	97,773
12/31/19C	3,500	3,911	411	1,816	98,184
6/30/19D	3,500	3,927	427	1,389	98,611
12/31/19D	3,500	3,944	444	945	99,055
6/30/19E	3,500	3,962	462	483	99,517
12/31/19E	3,500	3,983*	483	-0-	100,000

* Rounded to come out even.
(a) $100,000 × .035 = $3,500 (based on stated interest rate).
(b) $95,944 × .04 = $3,838 (based on yield rate).
(c) $3,838 − $3,500 = $338.
(d) $4,056 − $338 = $3,718.
(e) $95,944 + $338 = $96,282 (or $100,000 − $3,718 = $96,282).
Note: Interest entries for Issuer and Investor follow the pattern illustrated in Exhibit 17–4, Panel C.

Part B: Special Problems in Accounting for Bonds

Part B of this chapter considers six additional issues related to bonds as follows:

1. Bonds sold and purchased between interest dates.
2. Accounting for bonds when interest periods and fiscal periods do not coincide.
3. Bond issue costs.
4. Nonconvertible bonds with detachable stock warrants.
5. Convertible bonds.
6. Some innovative debt securities.

For illustrative purposes, in this part of the chapter, a different fact situation will be used to specify semiannual interest payments. For instructional convenience, early maturity and even interest rates will be used to shorten the illustrations. The fact situation is given in Exhibit 17–6, Panel A; Panel B presents the related amortization schedule.

BONDS SOLD AND PURCHASED BETWEEN INTEREST DATES

Bonds rarely are traded on interest dates. This situation necessitates recognition in the accounts of accrued interest from the **last interest date** to the date of the transaction. When bonds are sold between interest dates, the amount of cash paid to the seller by the purchaser is increased by the amount of the accrued interest for the same period. Accrued interest arises because of a particular characteristic of bonds. That is, the **full amount** of the periodic **stated** interest on a bond will be paid in cash on each interest date after sale, regardless of its sale date. Therefore, when a bond is purchased between interest dates, the amount paid for the bond by the investor will be *(a)* the price of the bond plus *(b)* any accrued interest from the last interest date.

EXHIBIT 17–6: Illustrative Data for Bonds in Part B: Issuer, Cox Corporation; Investor, Day Corporation

Panel A—Terms of the Bond Indenture:

a. Maturity amount of the bonds	$100,000 ($10,000 and $1,000 denominations).
b. Date of the bonds	January 1, 19A.
c. Maturity date	December 31, 19C (3 years).
d. Stated interest rate	8%, payable 4% semiannually.
e. Interest payments (cash)	$4,000 each June 30 and December 31.
f. Date sold	As specified in each example to follow.
g. Yield interest rate and bond price	7% (3½% semiannually); price, $102,664 (Exhibit 17–2, Table D).

Panel B—Amortization Schedule, Interest Method—assuming sale and issuance on January 1, 19A:

Date	Cash Interest (4 percent semiannual)	Yield Interest (3½ percent semiannual)	Premium Amortization	Balance Unamortized Premium	Carrying Amount of Bonds
1/1/19A starting date				2,664	102,664
6/30/19A	4,000[a]	3,593[b]	407[c]	2,257[d]	102,257[e]
12/31/19A	4,000	3,579	421	1,836	101,836
6/30/19B	4,000	3,564	436	1,400	101,400
12/31/19B	4,000	3,549	451	949	100,949
6/30/19C	4,000	3,533	467	482	100,482
12/31/19C	4,000	3,518*	482	-0-	100,000

* Rounded to come out even.
[a] $100,000 × 4% = $4,000 (based on stated interest rate).
[b] $102,664 × 3½% = $3,593 (based on yield rate).
[c] $4,000 − $3,593 = $407.
[d] $2,664 − $407 = $2,257.
[e] $100,000 + $2,257 = $102,257 (or $102,664 − $407 = $102,257).

Otherwise, the seller would have no way of collecting the interest earned since the last interest date. For example, practically every issue of *The Wall Street Journal* will carry notices of bond offerings, and a typical quotation is "$100,000,000, 9% bonds, due December 31, 1990, to yield 9.25%. Interest accrued from June 30, 1981, to be added."

Bonds Sold between Interest Dates at Par

To illustrate the accounting for bonds sold at par between interest dates, assume that, on November 1, 19A, Cox Corporation (Exhibit 17–6) sold to Day Corporation $100,000 of its 8 percent (semiannual interest) bonds, originally dated January 1, 19A. The last interest date was June 30, 19A. The sale price to Day Corporation was at par plus the four months' accrued interest (July 1 through November 1, 19A). This situation is diagrammed on a time scale in Exhibit 17–7, Panel A, and the related entries for the issuer and investor are presented in Panel B. The amount of cash flowing from the investor to the issuer can be computed as is demonstrated in the following example:

EXHIBIT 17–7: Bonds Issued between Interest Dates

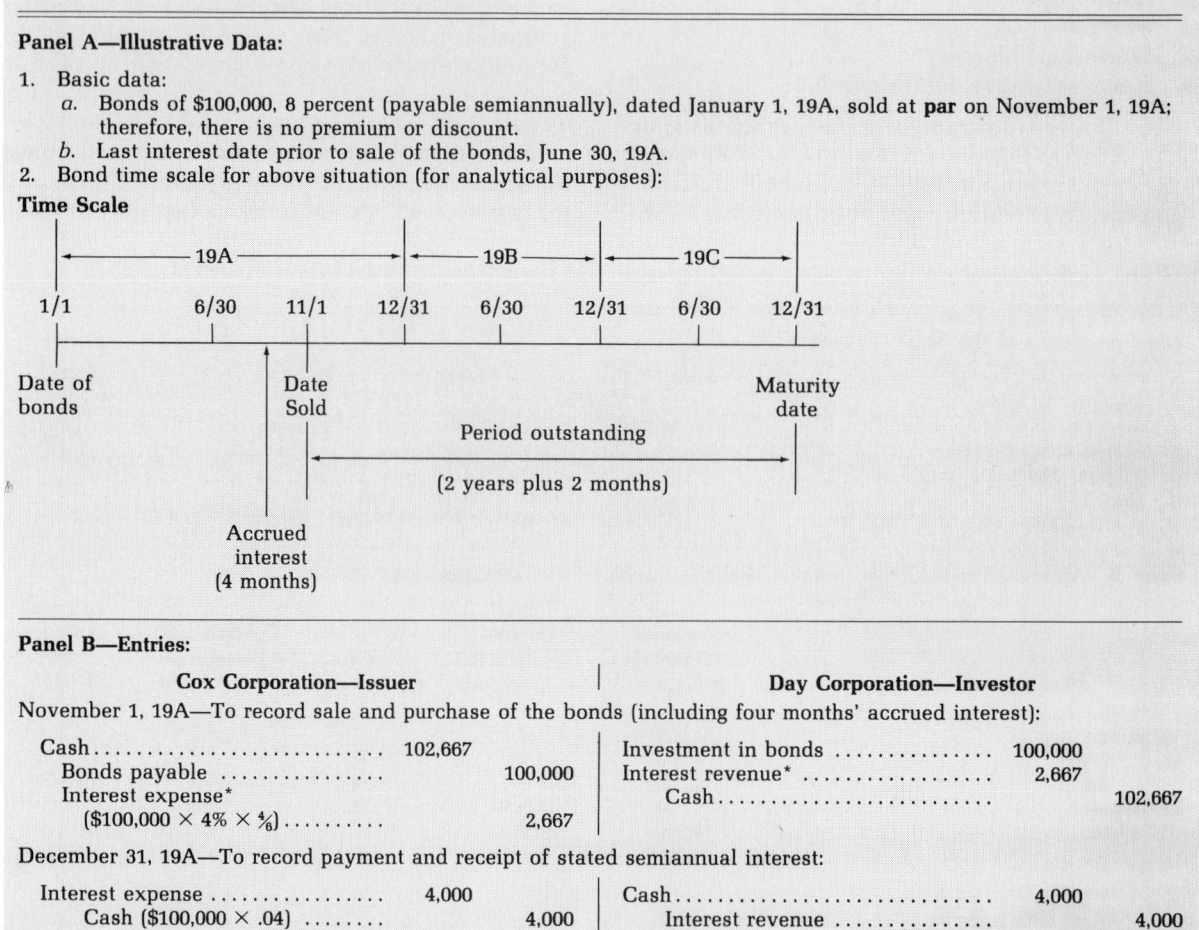

Panel A—Illustrative Data:

1. Basic data:
   a. Bonds of $100,000, 8 percent (payable semiannually), dated January 1, 19A, sold at **par** on November 1, 19A; therefore, there is no premium or discount.
   b. Last interest date prior to sale of the bonds, June 30, 19A.
2. Bond time scale for above situation (for analytical purposes):

Time Scale

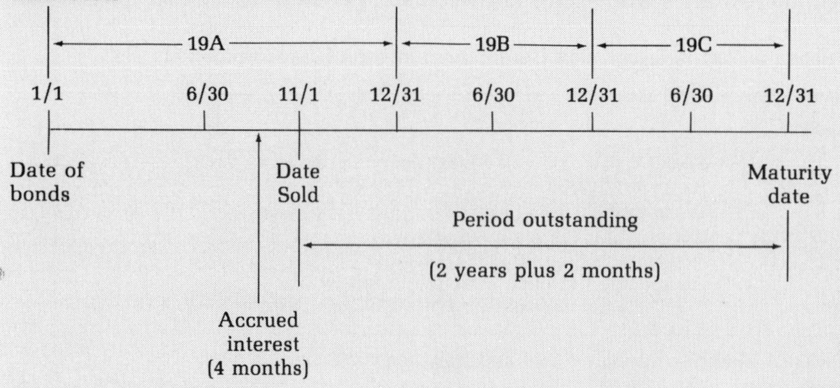

Panel B—Entries:

Cox Corporation—Issuer			**Day Corporation—Investor**		
November 1, 19A—To record sale and purchase of the bonds (including four months' accrued interest):					
Cash	102,667		Investment in bonds	100,000	
Bonds payable		100,000	Interest revenue*	2,667	
Interest expense* ($100,000 × 4% × 4/6)		2,667	Cash		102,667
December 31, 19A—To record payment and receipt of stated semiannual interest:					
Interest expense	4,000		Cash	4,000	
Cash ($100,000 × .04)		4,000	Interest revenue		4,000

* If the purchase/sale transaction date is in one accounting period and the next interest date is in the following accounting period, most accountants use interest payable and interest receivable, respectively, in these two entries. Both approaches derive the same ultimate net effect because the adjusting entries can be made to accord with the prior entry.

Sale price of the bond issue on 11/1/19A (at par)	$100,000
Add: Accrued interest since last interest date (June 30 to Nov. 1—$100,000 × .04 × $\frac{4}{6}$)	2,667
Total cash paid on date of sale/purchase transaction	$102,667

The issuer and the investor would make the entries in 19A shown in Exhibit 17–7, Panel B. After posting both entries, the respective interest expense and interest revenue accounts will stand at $1,333 (i.e., $4,000 − $2,667), which represents interest for the two months outstanding ($100,000 × .04 × $\frac{2}{6}$ = $1,333). Similarly, bond transactions between **individual investors** when not on an interest date require recognition of accrued interest by both parties.

Bonds Sold between Interest Dates at a Discount or Premium

When a bond is traded between interest dates at a **discount** or **premium,** the accounting illustrated in Exhibit 17–7, Panel B, is followed except that the discount or premium must be recorded and then amortized over the **period outstanding,** that is, the period from the date of sale (not the date of the bond) to the maturity date.

To illustrate, assume Cox Corporation sold $100,000 of the 8 percent bond issue, reflected on the time scale shown in Exhibit 17–7, Panel A, at a 7 percent yield rate on November 1, 19A. Recall that the bonds were dated January 1, 19A, and mature on December 31, 19C; thus they are sold two years plus two months before maturity. The bond price on November 1, 19A, to yield 7 percent, and the cash flow would be computed as shown in Exhibit 17–8, Panel A.

In Exhibit 17–8, Panel B, the bond premium ($1,977) must be amortized over the total period outstanding (26 months). Assume straight-line amortization can be used because the amounts of periodic interest computed using the straight-line amortization method would not be materially different from interest method amounts. On the next interest date, the cash interest for the full six months and amortization of premium for the two months since date of sale would be recorded as shown in Exhibit 17–8, Panel B.

After these two entries are posted to the accounts, the respective interest expense and revenue accounts will reflect net interest amounts (of $3,848 − $2,667 = $1,181) for two months, the period outstanding since the date of sale.[7]

Alternatively, amortization based on the **interest method** would be as illustrated in Exhibit 17–9, Panel B. When the bond transaction is between interest dates, as in this illustration (two months before the next interest date), the amortization amount at the first interest date after acquisition must be **uniquely** determined. It is computed as the difference between the sale price at transaction date (November 1, 19A, in the example) and the sale price at the next interest date (i.e., December 31, 19A) as shown in Exhibit 17–9, Panel B. Entries to record the semiannual interest and premium amortization also are shown in Exhibit 17–9, Panel C. This is an important example because typically bonds are bought and sold between interest dates, at a discount or premium, and often the interest method must be used.

ACCOUNTING FOR BONDS WHEN INTEREST PERIODS AND FISCAL PERIODS DO NOT COINCIDE

Typically, the end of the accounting period does not coincide with the interest date on bonds. In this situation, an issuer must **accrue** interest on a bond from the last interest date to the end of the accounting period. In such a situation, the investor also must accrue interest revenue on a bond investment.

In respect to bonds with a discount or premium, the discount or premium must be amortized for the period between the last amortization date and the year-end date; otherwise, interest for the period is misstated by the omitted amount of amortization.

To illustrate, assume (for this example only) that the accounting periods for Cox Corporation and Day Corporation end on March 31 and that the bonds were sold on January 1, 19A, as assumed in the amortization schedule shown in Exhibit 17–6, Panel B.

[7] These entries assume amortization on interest dates; amortization often is delayed until the end of the accounting period. These entries also assume discount and premium are recorded separately (i.e., at gross). If the alternative (i.e., **net**) approach shown in the tabulation of entries in the middle of Exhibit 17–3, Panel B, is followed, the amount amortized would be recorded directly in the liability and investment accounts, respectively.

EXHIBIT 17–8: Bonds Sold at a Premium between Interest Dates—Straight-Line Amortization

Panel A—Illustrative Data:

1. Basic data, see Exhibit 17–6, Panel A.
2. Additional data:
   a. Bond of $100,000, 8 percent (payable semiannually), dated January 1, 19A, sold on November 1, 19A, to yield 7 percent per year.
   b. Bond time scale for analytical purposes; same as shown in Exhibit 17–7, Panel A.
3. Computation of *(a)* sale price of bond and *(b)* total cash flow on date of sale:
   a. Bond price computed ($100,000, 8 percent semiannually, sold to yield 7 percent, two years plus two months before maturity date; see Exhibit 17–2, Table D):

Bond price if sold on prior interest date, 6/30/19A (2½ yrs. to maturity)	$102,258
Bond price if sold on next interest date, 12/31/19A (2 yrs. to maturity)	101,837
Difference	$ 421

Interpolation for bond price on 11/1/19A:*

$101,837 + ($421 × 2/6) = $101,837 + $140 =	$101,977

b. Total cash flow at date of sale (11/1/19A):

$101,977 + accrued interest ($100,000 × .04 × 4/6 = $2,667) =	$104,644

* Straight-line interpolation was used for simplicity. In practice, bond prices between interest dates usually are computed on a daily interest rate discounting basis using the number of days between the date of sale and the maturity date.

Panel B—Entries:

November 1, 19A—to record sale/purchase of bond issue:

Issuer			Investor		
Cash	104,644		Bond investment	100,000	
Interest expense		2,667	Interest revenue	2,667	
Premium on bonds payable		1,977	Premium on bond investment	1,977	
Bonds payable		100,000	Cash		104,644

December 31, 19A—to record semiannual interest payment and amortization of bond premium using **straight-line** amortization:

Issuer			Investor		
Interest expense	3,848		Cash	4,000	
Premium on bonds payable	152†		Premium on bond investment		152†
Cash ($100,000 × .04)		4,000	Interest revenue		3,848

† Amortization: $1,977 ÷ 26 (total months outstanding) = $76 per month.
$76 × 2 (months outstanding this period) = $152.

At the end of the accounting period, the following adjusting entries would be made:[8]

March 31, 19A—Adjusting entry for accrued interest and premium amortization for the three months, January–March 19A (computations based on data from the amortization schedule shown in Exhibit 17–6, Panel B).

Issuer—Cox Corporation:

Interest expense ($3,593 × 3/6)	1,797	
Premium on bonds payable ($407 × 3/6)	203*	
Interest payable ($100,000 × .04 × 3/6)		2,000

* Assuming straight-line amortization, this amount would be $2,664 × 3/36 = $222, and interest expense would be $2,000 − $222 = $1,778.

Investor—Day Corporation:

Interest receivable	2,000	
Premium on bond investment		203
Interest revenue		1,797

BOND ISSUE COSTS

Typically a number of costs are incurred in preparing and selling a bond issue. Bond issue costs

[8] These entries assume amortization on interest dates; amortization may be delayed until the end of the accounting period.

EXHIBIT 17–9: Bonds Sold at a Premium between Interest Dates—Interest Method Amortization

Panel A—Illustrative Data: Same as in Exhibit 17–8, Panel A.

Panel B—Bond Interest and Premium Amortization between Interest Dates, Interest Method (semiannual interest payments):

Date	Cash Interest (4 percent semiannual)	Effective Interest (3½ percent semiannual)	Premium Amortization	Balance Unamortized Premium	Carrying Amount of Bonds
11/1/19A starting date				1,977	101,977[a]
12/31/19A	4,000[b]	3,860[b]	140[c]	1,837	101,837
6/30/19B	4,000	3,564[d]	436[e]	1,401[f]	101,401[f]
12/31/19B	4,000	3,549	451	950	100,950
6/30/19C	4,000	3,533	467	483	100,483
12/31/19C	4,000	3,517	483	-0-	100,000

Computations:

[a] Per bond price computation in Exhibit 17–8, Panel A.
[b] $100,000 × .04 = $4,000, and $4,000 − $140 = $3,860.
[c] Amortization to December 31, 19A:

Bond price on date of sale, November 1, 19A	$101,977
Bond price on **next** interest date, December 31, 19A (per above)	101,837
Amortization for 2 months	$ 140

Sequential computations:

[d] $101,837 × .035 = $3,564, etc.
[e] $4,000 − $3,564 = $436, etc.
[f] $1,837 − $436 = $1,401; $101,837 − $436 = $101,401, etc.

Panel C—Entries:

2. December 31, 19A—To record semiannual interest payment and amortization of bond premium using **interest method** amortization:

Issuer			Investor		
Interest expense	3,860		Cash	4,000	
Premium on bonds payable	140		Premium on bond investment		140
Cash ($100,000 × .04)		4,000	Interest revenue		3,860

include legal, accounting, underwriting, and other fees, commissions, engraving, printing, registration, and promotion costs. GAAP classifies these expenditures collectively as a **deferred charge** (i.e., Unamortized Bond Issue Cost) rather than as an element of bond discount or premium.[9] Bond issue costs should be accounted for separately from bond premium and bond discount. Bond issue costs should be amortized over the period the bonds will be outstanding (between the sale date and the maturity date) because it is assumed that related future revenue benefits will flow from the proceeds of the financing. Theoretically, bond issue costs should be amortized using the interest method; however, the straight-line method generally is used because of immateriality.

To illustrate accounting for bond issue costs, assume Cox Corporation sold the $100,000 bonds for $102,664 (see Exhibit 17–6) on January 1, 19A (also date of the bonds). Bond issue costs were $1,000.

a. January 1, 19A—to record sale and issuance:

Cash ($102,664 − $1,000)	101,664	
Unamortized bond issue cost	1,000	
Premium on bonds payable		2,664
Bonds payable		100,000

b. June 30, 19A—To record amortization on bond issue costs using straight-line basis:

Interest expense (or bond issue expense)	167	
Unamortized bond issue cost ($1,000 ÷ 6)		167

[9] *APB Opinion 21,* par. 16.

NONCONVERTIBLE BONDS WITH DETACHABLE STOCK WARRANTS

Debt securities, usually bonds, sometimes are issued with **stock warrants** (i.e., stock rights) attached. A stock warrant gives the holder an option to purchase from the issuer, within a stated time period, a specified number of shares of common stock at a specified price per share. Detachable stock warrants are often "attached" to bonds to enhance the marketability of the bonds. Bonds with detachable stock warrants usually carry a lower interest rate than otherwise and tend to sell for a higher price than ordinary bonds.

Detachable stock warrants can be separated from the bonds and traded on the market; that is, they are **equity securities** that are **separable** from the debt security. Because of this separability, *APB Opinion No. 14,* "Accounting for Convertible Debt and Debt Issued with Stock Purchase Warrants," states that "the portion of the proceeds of debt securities issued with detachable stock purchase warrants which is allocable to the warrants should be accounted for as paid-in capital. The allocation should be based on the relative [market] values of the two securities at time of issuance." When the market value of one security (i.e., the bond or the detachable stock warrant) cannot be determined, the market value of the other should be subtracted from the total consideration to determine the value of the other security.

In contrast, if stock warrants are **not** detachable, there will be no separate market for them. In this case, *APB Opinion 14* stipulates that the full amount of the proceeds be recognized in the bond accounts and that the stock warrants **not** be recorded as owners' equity (i.e., not as stock warrants outstanding). Thus, there is no separate accounting on issue date for warrants that are not detachable.

To illustrate accounting for nonconvertible bonds with detachable stock warrants, assume AB Corporation issued $100,000, 8 percent, 10-year, **nonconvertible bonds with detachable stock warrants.** Each $1,000 bond carried 10 detachable warrants; each warrant was for one share of common stock, par $10, at the specified option price of $15 per share. The bonds, including the warrants, sold at $105,000, and shortly after issuance, the warrants were quoted on the market for $4 each. Because no market value could be determined for the bonds under these conditions, the *(a)* bond issuance and *(b)* subsequent tender of the detachable stock warrants would be recorded as follows by the issuer and investor:

a. To record issuance of bonds with detachable stock warrants:

Issuer:		
Cash	105,000	
Bonds payable, 8% (with detachable stock warrants)		100,000
Premium on bonds payable		1,000
Detachable stock warrants outstanding (1,000 warrants @ $4)		4,000
Investor:		
Bond investment	100,000	
Premium on bond investment	1,000	
Investment—detachable stock warrants (1,000 warrants @ $4)	4,000	
Cash		105,000

b. To record subsequent tender, by the investor, of the 1,000 detachable stock warrants for common stock:

Issuer:		
Cash (1,000 × $15)	15,000	
Detachable stock warrants outstanding	4,000	
Common stock, 1,000 shares, par $10		10,000
Contributed capital in excess of par, common stock		9,000
Investor:		
Investment in common stock, 1,000 shares	19,000	
Investment—detachable stock warrants		4,000
Cash (1,000 × $15)		15,000

Because of the contractual option price, the market value of the stock at the date the warrants are tendered is not recognized.

CONVERTIBLE BONDS

A **convertible bond** is a debt security which may be converted under specified conditions (often must be on an interest date) to capital stock (usually common stock) of the issuer, at the **option of the investor.** Typically, convertible bonds also are **callable** (usually on an interest date) at a specified redemption or call price at the **option of the issuer** and are subordinated to nonconvertible debt. Subordinated means a lower class; that is, the convertible debt ranks below nonconvertible debt as a claim against assets in case of insolvency. Generally, convertible bonds can be sold at an interest rate lower than for nonconvertible bonds because investors impute a value to the conversion privilege.

Convertible bonds also have a conversion ratio or a conversion price specified in the bond indenture. The **conversion ratio** is the number of shares of common stock the holder of a convertible bond will receive when it is tendered for conversion. In contrast, the **conversion price** of the stock into which the bond may be converted is the face amount of the convertible bond divided by the number of shares of common stock (per bond) to be received upon conversion.

To illustrate the conversion ratio and conversion price of convertible bonds, assume AB Corporation issued $1,000 convertible bonds, each of which could be converted, at the option of the holder at any interest date after the second year from issuance, to 10 shares of AB Corporation common stock. The conversion ratio for each bond would be 10 (shares of stock) to 1 (bond). Or, stated differently, the conversion price of the stock would be $1,000 ÷ 10 shares = $100.

Convertible bonds generally offer certain advantages to both the issuer and the investor. The primary advantages to the issuer are *(a)* a lower rate of interest and *(b)* a means of securing equity (stockholder) financing in the long run (after conversion, this is the net effect since the debt is not paid in cash). The call option can be used by the issuer to force conversion when the aggregate price of the stock to be issued on conversion is greater than the call price of the bonds; in this case, a rational investor would take the stock in lieu of the cash.

The primary advantages of convertible bonds to the investor are *(a)* an option to receive either the face of the bond at maturity or to convert to common stock of the issuer, *(b)* a guaranteed rate of interest to conversion date or maturity, and *(c)* the opportunity to realize the benefits of appreciation in the price of the common stock of the issuer.

Accounting for the Issuance of Convertible Bonds

Convertible bonds specify a lower rate of interest than would nonconvertible debt with similar debt characteristics because they can be converted to common stock. The basic valuation question upon issuance is: What portion of the sales price should relate to **debt** and what portion should be allocated to **stockholders' equity?** The problem is similar to that illustrated for detachable stock warrants under the preceding heading, Nonconvertible Bonds with Detachable Stock Warrants. Because of the inseparability of the debt and the conversion option, *APB Opinion 14* specifies that the issuance should be recorded as debt and that "no portion of the proceeds from the issuance should be accounted for as attributable to the conversion feature."

To illustrate accounting for the issuance of convertible bonds, assume AB Corporation sold $100,000, 8 percent, **convertible** bonds for $106,000. The conversion feature specified that at the option of the **investor,** each $1,000 bond was convertible to 10 shares of AB Corporation common stock, par $75, on any interest date after the end of the second year from date of issuance. The issuer and investor would record the transaction as follows:

Issuer:		
Cash	106,000	
Premium on bonds payable		6,000
Bonds payable, 8%, convertible		100,000
Investor:		
Bond investment (AB Corporation, convertible bonds)	100,000	
Premium on bond investment	6,000	
Cash		106,000

Accounting for Conversion

When convertible bonds are tendered by the **investor** for conversion, the issuer and investor must *(a)* update all related account balances to a current status as of the date of the conversion (this updating includes recording interest accruals and discount or premium amortization) and *(b)* remove the resulting bond carrying values from the accounts. When conversion is on an interest date, all related account balances already are current.

Recording the conversion transaction poses a question as to the correct **valuation** to record for the new security issued. Two methods currently are acceptable under GAAP, viz:

1. **Book value method**—record the new security issued at the carrying value of the old security.

2. **Market value method**—record the new security issued at either its current market value or the current market value of the old security converted, whichever is the more reliably determinable.

To illustrate accounting for conversion, assume AB Corporation has $100,000 of 8 percent convertible bonds outstanding which were initially sold for $106,000. These bonds are tendered by the investors for conversion on an interest date, to 1,000 shares of common stock, when the unamortized bond premium amounted to $3,000 (carrying value of bonds was $103,000) and the common stock (par $75) had a current market price of $110 per share. The entries under each method would be as follows:

Issuer—AB Corporation:	Book Value Method		Market Value Method	
Bonds payable, convertible	100,000		100,000	
Premium on bonds payable	3,000		3,000	
Loss on conversion of convertible bonds			7,000	
Common stock (1,000 shares @ $75)		75,000		75,000
Contributed capital in excess of par*		28,000		35,000

* $103,000 − $75,000 = $28,000; 1,000 shares × ($110 − $75) = $35,000.

Investor:	Book Value Method		Market Value Method	
Investment in stock, AB Corp.	103,000		110,000	
Investment in bonds, AB Corp.		100,000		100,000
Premium on bond investment		3,000		3,000
Gain on conversion of bond investment				7,000

The book value method appears to be used widely because the conversion transaction is viewed by many accountants as the culmination of a single transaction which started when the convertible bonds were issued. However, to the authors the book value method appears deficient conceptually because the book value method ignores the market values of the debt and equity securities involved in the conversion; consequently, it does **not** recognize a gain or loss on the settlement of a debt security nor on the issuance of a stock split or a stock dividend.[10]

[10] *APB Opinion No. 29,* "Accounting for Nonmonetary Transactions" (New York, May 1973), does not apply to a stock split or a stock dividend.

Convertible bonds that are reacquired by exercise of a call provision (i.e., at the option of the issuer), rather than by conversion by the investor, are accounted for under the provisions of *APB Opinion No. 26,* "Early Extinguishment of Debt," and FASB, *Statement of Financial Accounting Standards No. 4,* "Reporting Gains and Losses from Early Extinguishment of Debt," as discussed in Part C of this chapter.

SOME INNOVATIVE DEBT SECURITIES

Persistent double-digit inflation, high and fluctuating interest rates, and a shortage of long-term lendable funds have caused the recent development of some innovative debt securities. One innovation has been the issuance of long-term debt instruments with variable stated interest rates. For example, most large lending institutions now offer loans on which the interest rate will be adjusted periodically with reference to the then-existing prime interest rate. This innovation is an attempt to "protect" each party to the loan against some of the uncertainties of inflation. It does not pose any substantive accounting problems.

Another innovation is called participation loans. In this type of long-term loan, the lender will charge a relatively low interest rate and, in return, obtain an "ownership" in the project for which the loan is made. For example, a recent participation loan specified an 11 percent annual interest rate when the "going" incremental borrowing rate was 20 percent and provided for the lender a 50 percent participation (i.e., ownership interest) in a large office building to be constructed. This arrangement, which was in response to the very high interest rate of 20 percent, resolved a serious cash flow problem facing the borrower during the first several years after completion of the project. The cash flow problem was imminent because at the 20 percent interest rate, the annual cash expenses (including interest) exceeded annual cash revenues. Innovative debt arrangements, such as this one, pose substantive accounting problems such as: What rate of interest should be recognized in the accounting process? How should each party measure and record the amount of the receivable/payable? How should the "participation" agreement be measured and recorded in the accounts? Is the "participation" a sale/purchase transaction? The accounting profession will have to address these issues.

As a final example, a particularly innovative bond issue, dubbed "Silver-Lined Bonds," was announced by the Sunshine Mining Company during 1980.[11] The announcement described a bond issue of $25 million 8½ percent, due April 15, 1995. The bonds were indexed to silver; that is, each $1,000 redeemable (i.e., at the option of the investor) bond is payable at maturity (or redemption) in cash of $1,000 or the market price of 50 ounces of silver, whichever is the higher at that time. These bonds were designed primarily to provide a hedge against inflation. Substantive accounting questions are posed by this bond issue, such as: Does the issuance of such bonds constitute only long-term financing, a sale of silver, or convertible debt (i.e., into silver)? How should the issuer and the investor record the payable and receivable, respectively *(a)* at issuance, *(b)* during the time to maturity (or redemption), and *(c)* at maturity (or redemption)? Also, the problem is posed as to how each party should measure the timing and amount of the related revenues and expenses.[12] In this instance, Sunshine recorded bonds payable at their principal (i.e., face) amount and accrues interest at the stated rate. Also, the company has dedicated (i.e., agreed to set aside) future silver production sufficient to retire the bonds.

[11] *The Wall Street Journal,* April 14, 1980.

[12] For a discussion of the accounting implications of this particular example, see R, J. Swieringa, "The Silver-Lined Bonds of Sunshine Mining," *The Accounting Review,* January 1981, pp. 166–75.

Part C: Changes in Obligations Prior to Maturity Date

In recent years there has been a significant increase in situations in which debtors (borrowers) have been unable to meet specific debt obligations because of financial difficulties. Also, for a number of reasons there have been an increasing number of early extinguishments of debt including bond refunding transactions. This part of the chapter discusses three topics that focus on changes in debt obligations prior to maturity date; they are as follows:

Topic	Basic Reference
1. Early extinguishment of debt.	*APB Opinion No. 26,* "Early Extinguishment of Debt." FASB, *Statement of Financial Accounting Standards No. 4,* "Reporting Gains and Losses from Extinguishment of Debt."
2. Classification of short-term obligations expected to be refinanced.	FASB, *Statement of Financial Accounting Standards No. 6,* "Classification of Short-Term Obligations Expected to Be Refinanced."
3. Troubled debt restructuring.	FASB, *Statement of Financial Accounting Standards No. 15,* "Accounting by Debtors and Creditors for Troubled Debt Restructurings."

EARLY EXTINGUISHMENT OF DEBT

APB Opinion 26 defines early extinguishment as "the reacquisition of any form of debt security or instrument before its scheduled maturity **except through conversion by the holder,** regardless of whether the debt is viewed as terminated or is held as so-called 'treasury bonds.' All open-market or mandatory reacquisitions of debt securities to meet sinking fund requirements are early extinguishments" (emphasis supplied).

APB Opinion 26 specifies the appropriate accounting for early extinguishment of debt. The *Opinion* is based upon the fundamental concept that "all extinguishments of debt before scheduled maturities are fundamentally alike. The accounting for such transactions should be the same regardless of the means used to achieve the extinguishment."

FASB Statement 4 specifies that "gains and losses from extinguishment of debt that are included in the determination of net income shall be aggregated and, if material, classified as an extraordinary item, net of related income tax effect. That conclusion shall apply whether an extinguishment is early or at a scheduled maturity date or later."[13]

Early extinguishment of debt may be by *(a)* exercise of a call privilege by the issuer, *(b)* purchase in the open market by the issuer, or *(c)* retirement of old debt by issuing new debt (called refunding). Each of these extinguishments will be discussed and illustrated immediately below.

Exercise of Call Privilege by Issuer

Bonds and certain other debt instruments frequently carry a **call provision** stating that at the option of the **issuer,** the debt may be called for payment prior to its maturity. Call time limits and call reacquisition price are specified in the bond indenture and are printed on each bond certificate. Early extinguishment by call almost always is required to be on an interest date, in which case the amortization of any discount or premium and bond issue costs will be up to date and there will be no accrued interest. At call date all of the related debt accounts are reduced to zero and an **extraordinary** gain or loss is recognized in the amount of the difference between the call price and the carrying value of the bond accounts.

To illustrate the exercise of a call privilege, assume that on January 1, 19A, Corporation A issued 10-year, $100,000, 10 percent (payable semiannually on June 30 and December 31), callable bonds. The bonds can be called by the issuer at 101 at any time after December 31, 19C. At issuance date the bonds sold for $106,504 based on a 9 percent yield rate.

On July 1, 19D, Corporation A called in all of the bonds and retired them. For simplicity, assume the company used the straight-line method of amortizing bond premium.

The indicated entries at issuance and recall are as follows:

January 1, 19A—issuance:

Cash	106,504	
Bonds payable, 10%, callable at 101		100,000
Premium on bonds payable		6,504

July 1, 19D—recall at 101:

Bonds payable, 10%, callable at 101	100,000	
Premium on bonds payable (unamortized, $6,504 × 13/20)	4,228	
Cash		101,000
Extraordinary gain, early extinguishment of debt		3,228

Purchase in the Open Market by Issuer

Borrowers sometimes extinguish indebtedness by purchasing their own debt securities in the open market. Such open-market purchases may or may not be on an interest date. If not on an interest date, the amortization of any discount, premium, bond issue cost, and accrued interest must be recorded from the last interest date to the date of purchase prior to recording the early extinguishment. Any material gain or loss, measured as the difference between the carrying amount of the debt and the cost of retiring it, is reported as an extraordinary item under the provisions of FASB *Statement 4.* It is believed that the FASB required classification of the gain or loss as extraordinary because some companies were "manufacturing book gains" by acquiring their debt securities at depressed prices.

To illustrate purchase in the open market, assume that on January 1, 19A, Corporation B issued 10-year, $100,000, 8 percent (payable semiannually on June 30 and December 31) bonds. At issuance date the bonds sold for $87,538 (i.e., at a yield rate of 10 percent), and bond issue costs were $1,000; therefore, net proceeds of the issuance were $86,538 (i.e., $87,538 − $1,000).

On January 1, 19D, Corporation B purchased all of the bonds in the open market at $85,000. On this date, unamortized bond issue costs were $700. For simplicity, assume the company used straight-line amortization of bond discount.

[13] FASB *Statement No. 15* specifies the accounting for troubled debt restructions. It states (par. 10) that the provisions of APB No. 26 (as amended by FASB Statement No. 4) do not apply to accounting for troubled debt restructuring.

The indicated entries at issuance and reacquisition are as follows:

January 1, 19A—issuance:

Cash	86,538	
Discount on bonds payable	12,462	
Unamortized bond issue cost	1,000	
Bonds payable, 8%		100,000

January 1, 19D—reacquisition:

Bonds payable, 8%	100,000	
Discount on bonds payable (unamortized, $12,462 × 14/20)		8,723
Unamortized bond issue cost		700
Extraordinary gain, early extinguishment of debt		5,577
Cash		85,000

Refunding Bonds Payable

Early extinguishment of an outstanding issue of old bonds by the issuance of new bonds is called **refunding.** The refunding transaction may involve one of the following situations:

1. Direct exchange of the new bonds for the old bonds held by the current bondholders. In this case the old bondholders become the new bondholders.
2. Issuance of new bonds to obtain cash to purchase the old bonds in the bond market. In this case a new group of bondholders replaces the old group.
3. Issuance of new bonds to obtain cash to **call** the old callable bonds, if they contain a call provision.

APB Opinion 26 specifies that the accounting for all three situations shall be essentially the same regardless of the means used to achieve the extinguishment. An illustration of refunding is presented in Exhibit 17–10 for the three situations listed above.

In refunding transactions, two different viewpoints are very important. One is the **accounting result;** more specifically this refers to the gain or loss that is recognized in the accounts and reported on the income statement for the year of refunding. The other viewpoint is the **economic result;** more specifically, this refers to the economic gain or loss incurred by the refunding entity, which is not reported in the income statement.

Exhibit 17–10 presents **only** the accounting result for each of the three refunding situations listed above. Panel C of Exhibit 17–10 presents a comparison of the accounting gains and losses (historical cost [HC] basis) with the economic gains and losses (present value basis). The latter computations are presented in Supplement 17–B.

In summary, the **decision** on early extinguishment of debt should be based on a present value analysis (i.e., an economic analysis similar to the analysis presented in Supplement 17–B) of the respective future cash flows, although under current GAAP the **accounting** must be based on the historical amounts (carrying value) of the debt extinguished.

Because of the significance of early extinguishment of debt, *FASB Statement 4* requires, in addition to classification of the accounting gain or loss as extraordinary, disclosure in the notes to the financial statements of the following:

a. A description of the extinguishment transactions, including the sources of any funds used to extinguish debt if it is practicable to identify the sources.
b. The income tax effect in the period of extinguishment.
c. The per share amount of the aggregate gain or loss net of related income tax effect.

CLASSIFICATION OF SHORT-TERM OBLIGATIONS EXPECTED TO BE REFINANCED

Occasionally, a short-term obligation (i.e., a current liability) is expected to be refinanced on a long-term basis, thereby avoiding the use of current assets during the ensuing fiscal year (or operating cycle, if longer). Examples are construction loans and currently maturing portions of long-term debt that will be refunded. Prior to the issuance of *FASB Statement 6,* May 1975, such obligations were variously reported as *(a)* current liabilities, *(b)* long-term liabilities, and *(c)* special noncurrent liabilities (such as "other" liabilities).

To attain uniformity in reporting, *Statement 6* (par. 11) reaffirmed the definition of current liabilities (see Chapter 4) and stated that a short-term obligation shall be **excluded** from current liabilities **only** if either:

EXHIBIT 17–10: Refunding Bonds Payable Illustrated

Panel A—Hypothetical Situation:

1. On January 1, 19A, Corporation C issued $100,000, 5 percent (payable semiannually each June 30 and December 31), 10-year bonds, callable at 101; the bonds initially were issued at par. It is January 1, 19E (i.e., four years after issuance), and they are quoted on the market at 86 (i.e., $86,000), which reflects a current interest rate of 8 percent.
2. On January 1, 19E, Corporation C decided to refund by issuing new, six-year bonds with interest payable semiannually on June 30 and December 31. The new bonds will sell at par (because they bear interest that is the same as the current market rate) and mature on December 31, 19J.
3. Corporation C is considering three alternative refunding situations: (1) an **exchange** of new bonds for the old bonds, (2) sale of the new bonds to **purchase** the old bonds in the open market, and (3) sale of the new bonds to **call** the old bonds.

Panel B—Entries for Each of the Three Alternative (and independent) Refunding Situations:

Situation 1—On January 1, 19E, $90,000 of new 8 percent bonds to be issued to the investors for return of the $100,000 of old 5 percent bonds.

Bonds payable, 5% (at carrying value)	100,000	
Bonds payable, 8% (at face amount)		90,000
Extraordinary gain, early extinguishment of debt		10,000

Situation 2—On January 1, 19E, when the current market interest rate is 8 percent, new 8 percent bonds to be sold in the open market to obtain the cash needed to purchase the old bonds in the market at 86 (i.e., $86,000). The new 8 percent bonds will sell at par; therefore, $86,000 of bonds would be issued at par.

a. To record sale and issuance of the 8 percent bonds at the market price of 100 (par):

Cash	86,000	
Bonds payable, 8%		86,000

b. To record purchase (retirement) of the old 5 percent bonds at the market price of 86:

Bonds payable, 5% (at carrying value)	100,000	
Cash (at market value)		86,000
Extraordinary gain, early extinguishment of debt		14,000

Situation 3—On January 1, 19E, when the current market interest rate is 4 percent, new 4 percent bonds to be sold and issued to obtain the cash needed to call the old bonds at 101 (i.e., $101,000). The old bonds could be purchased in the market for $105,300. The new 4 percent bonds will sell at par; therefore, $101,000 of new bonds would be issued at par.*

a. To record sale and issuance of the 4 percent bonds at the market price of 100 (par):

Cash	101,000	
Bonds payable, 4%		101,000

b. To record call of the old bonds at the call price of 101:

Bonds payable, 5% (at carrying value)	100,000	
Extraordinary loss, early extinguishment of debt	1,000	
Cash		101,000

* Unrealistic interest rate used for illustrative purposes only.

Panel C—Accounting and Economic Gains and Losses Compared (pretax):

	Accounting Gains and Losses (see Panel B above)†	Economic Gains and Losses (see Supplement 17-B)
Situation 1	$10,000 gain	$4,000 loss
Situation 2	14,000 gain	–0–
Situation 3	1,000 loss	4,300 gain

† Reported on income statement as an extraordinary item.

> (a) After the date of an enterprise's balance sheet but before that balance sheet is issued, a long-term obligation or equity securities have been issued for the purpose of refinancing the short-term obligation on a long-term basis; or (b) Before the balance sheet is issued, the enterprise has entered into a financing agreement that clearly permits the enterprise to refinance the short-term obligation on a long-term basis on terms that are readily determinable. . . .

Thus, liabilities that meet these conditions must be reported as long-term liabilities and the disclosure in notes to the statements must include "a general description of the financing agreement and the terms of any new obligation incurred or expected to be incurred or equity securities issued or expected to be issued as a result of a refinancing."[14]

TROUBLED DEBT RESTRUCTURING

When interest rates rise sharply and economic conditions become depressed, debtors sometimes experience severe financial strains and even bankruptcy. Foreclosures, repossessions, reorganizations, and a relaxing of contractual interest and principal payments on existing debt often occur. Generally, creditors are inclined to agree to restructure debt to make it possible for the debtor to continue in business rather than going into bankruptcy. Because of an increasing number of troubled debt restructurings, the FASB issued *Statement 15,* which specifies precise accounting and reporting guidelines for both the debtor (borrower) and the creditor (lender). This section discusses and illustrates the accounting for troubled debt restructuring.

Troubled debt restructuring is defined as a situation "when the creditor for economic or legal reasons related to the debtor's financial difficulties grants a **concession** to the debtor that it would not otherwise consider. That concession stems from an agreement between the creditor and the debtor or is imposed by law or a court"[15] (emphasis added).

Troubled debt restructurings may occur before, at, or after the stated maturity of the debt. The date of **consummation** is the date of the restructuring (i.e., the date for accounting recognition).[16] Fundamentally, there are two types of restructuring arrangements:

1. Transfer of assets or equity interest from the debtor to the creditor to satisfy a debt fully or partially.
2. Modification of terms of the debt with respect to *(a)* interest payments and/or *(b)* face amount. This type may involve amounts only, timing only, or both. There are two important subsets to this type:
   i. The restructured total of future cash payments (face plus interest) is equal to, or **more** than, the prerestructure carrying (book) amount of the debt. In this situation, **no** entry is made on date of restructure. Effectively, this means that subsequent to the restructure date, a new future interest rate (based on the carrying amount of the debt) must be computed and used.
   ii. The restructured total of future cash payments (face plus interest) is **less** than the prerestructure carrying (book) amount of the debt. In this situation, an entry to recognize a **gain by the debtor** and a **loss by the creditor** must be made on date of restructure. Effectively, this means that subsequent to the restructure date, **no** new future interest rate (based on the carrying amount of the debt) will be computed or used.

Each of these restructuring arrangements is discussed and illustrated in the paragraphs to follow. In those illustrations observe the "accounting symmetry" between the debtor and creditor except for the **classification** of certain gains and losses (*FASB Statement 15,* par. 173).

In all situations, a **troubled debt restructure** is distinguished from other debt-related transactions because of a **concession by the creditor to the debtor.** A concession occurs when the creditor agrees to a satisfaction of the debt with less (and/or delayed) economic resources than were called for by the original debt agreement. Common examples are payment of the obligation with noncash assets or the debtor's stock with a market value which is less than the

[14] FASB, *Statement of Financial Accounting Standards No. 6,* "Classification of Short-Term Obligations Expected to be Refinanced" (Stamford, Conn., May 1975), par. 15.

[15] A debt restructuring is not necessarily a troubled debt restructuring for purposes of the *Statement,* even if the debtor is experiencing some financial difficulties. Instead, the critical issue in a **troubled** debt restructuring is the granting of **concessions** to the debtor.

[16] *FASB Statement 15* amends AICPA, *APB Opinion No. 26,* "Early Extinguishment of Debt" (New York, October 1972), to the extent needed to exclude from that *Opinion's* scope early extinguishment of debt through troubled debt restructurings.

obligation; reduction and/or deferral of interest payments; and reduction and/or deferral of principal.

Transfer of Assets or Equity Interest to Satisfy Debt

The basic concept underlying the transfer of assets or an equity interest by the debtor to the creditor in troubled debt restructuring is that the item transferred should be recorded by both parties at its **current market value** (i.e., cash equivalent value) at the time of restructuring, and the carrying amount of the debt should be removed from the records.[17]

Transfer of Assets. In this situation the asset transferred has a market value which is less than the carrying amount of the debt satisfied; this is a concession by the creditor. Thus, the debtor will realize a gain and the creditor will incur a loss on the restructure.

For the **debtor,** this situation requires recognition of **two** different "gains or losses": (1) the difference between the carrying (book) amount of the asset and its market value must be recorded as a gain or loss on **disposal,** and (2) the excess of the carrying (book) amount of the debt settled over the market value of the assets transferred must be recorded as a gain by the debtor on **restructuring.** *Statement 15* specifies that the gain or loss on **disposal** shall be classified as ordinary, unusual or infrequent, or extraordinary in accordance with the provisions of *APB Opinion 30.*[18] In contrast, the gain on **restructuring** recognized by the debtor must be reported as an **extraordinary item** net of related income tax effect (*FASB Statement 15,* par. 21).

At date of restructure the **creditor** must recognize the loss on receivable restructuring, which is the excess of the carrying (book) value of the receivable settled over the current market amount of the assets (or other considerations) received. This loss is classified as ordinary, unusual or infrequent, or extraordinary in accordance with the provisions of *APB Opinion 30.*

The transfer of assets to satisfy a debt is shown in Exhibit 17–11, p. 618, Panel B, as Situation 1.

Transfer of Equity Interest. In this situation the debtor transfers its own capital stock to the creditor to satisfy a debt; the market value of the stock transferred is less than the obligation satisfied. This agreement is a **concession by the creditor to the debtor,** which means that the debtor realizes a gain and the creditor incurs a loss on the restructure.

For the **debtor,** this situation requires that the stock issued be recorded at market value in the normal manner with the difference between par or stated value and the market value of the stock recorded as contributed capital in excess of par. The excess of the prerestructure carrying amount of the debt over the market value of the stock issued is recorded as an **extraordinary gain.** The stock must be recorded by the creditor at its market value. A loss on receivable restructure equal to excess of the carrying (book) amount of the receivable over the **market value** of the stock received is recorded. The transfer of an equity interest to satisfy a debt is illustrated in Exhibit 17–11, Panel B, as Situation 2.

Modification of Terms of Debt

Modification of terms of debt in a troubled debt restructure may involve one or more of the following changes: *(a)* reduction in the interest rate, *(b)* extension of the payment date for interest, *(c)* reduction of the face amount, *(d)* extension of the payment date of the face amount, and *(e)* reduction in any accrued interest (i.e., interest accrued before the restructure date). In these modifications of terms, no assets or equity interests are transferred from the debtor to the creditor on the restructure date.

Modification of the terms of a debt requires consideration of a **new** *(a)* effective interest rate and *(b)* carrying amount of the payable settled. Accounting on the date of restructure and subsequently depends upon whether the restructured total future **cash** payments are more, or less, than the **carrying** (book) amount of the debt, which is defined as "the face amount increased or decreased by applicable accrued interest and applicable unamortized pre-

[17] Market value of assets is measured by their market price if an active market for them exists. If no active market exists for the assets transferred but exists for similar assets, the selling prices in that market may be helpful in estimating the market value of the assets transferred. If no market price is available, a forecast of expected cash flows may aid in estimating the market value of assets transferred, provided the expected cash flows are discounted at a rate commensurate with the risk involved.

[18] If the asset transferred is a receivable from a third party, *FASB Statement 15* states that recognition must be given to estimated uncollectible accounts included in the receivables.

mium, discount, or issue costs."[19] Two situations are discussed and illustrated as follows:

Situation 1—When the total of the **future cash payments is equal to, or more than, the prerestructure carrying amount of the debt,** the accounting is as follows:

At date of restructure: No entry is made in the accounts of either the debtor or creditor because the total future cash payments is sufficient to pay the principal, and any cash above that amount is construed to be payment of interest. A new effective interest rate must be computed.

Subsequent to restructure date: *FASB Statement 15* (par. 16), requires that each periodic cash payment subsequent to the restructure be recorded by the debtor and creditor as part interest and part principal using the interest method (as prescribed in *APB Opinion 21,* par. 16). To apply the interest method the **new effective interest rate must be computed at restructure date** and used throughout the remaining restructured term of the debt. The **new** effective interest rate is the one that equates the present value of the future cash payments specified in the restructure agreement with the prerestructure carrying amount of the debt. In some situations the new effective rate can be computed directly (as illustrated in Exhibit 17–12) using selected values from present value tables (Tables 5–2 and 5–4).

Exhibit 17–12, Situation 1, illustrates a restructure which *(a)* defers the remaining five periodic interest payments ($100 each) to maturity date, and *(b)* reduces the principal amount from $1,000 to $800. In this situation the **total future cash payments of $1,300** [i.e., (5 × $100) + $800] **is more than the prerestructure carrying amount of the debt** of $1,000. Therefore, **no entry** is made to decrease the carrying amount by either party on restructure date. Subsequent to restructure date, each party must make an entry to record annual interest even though no cash is paid on interest dates in this situation. These entries are based on the interest method; using the **new** effective interest rate, as illustrated in Exhibit 17–12, Panel B, under Situation 1. Because the total cash payment on maturity date is $1,300 and no cash payments are made during the interim restructure periods, the balances in the *(a)* debtor's liability account and *(b)* creditor's receivable account are increased by periodic accrual entries from $1,000 to $1,300 as shown in the tabular entries of Panel B.

Situation 2—When the total **future cash payments are less than the prerestructure carrying amount of the debt,** the accounting is as follows:

At date of restructure: On the restructure date each party records a reduction in the carrying amount of the debt to the total amount of cash scheduled to be paid under the restructure agreement. To the creditor, a loss is recognized and to the debtor a gain is recognized. In this situation, a new effective interest rate is **not computed or used** because the **total** of the future cash payments after restructure is not sufficient to pay any interest after the date of restructure (i.e., the interest rate, if computed, would be negative). Therefore, the entries by the debtor and creditor, respectively, must **decrease the carrying amount** of the debtor's liability and the creditor's receivable, to the **total** of the future cash payments subsequent to restructure date. This decrease in the carrying amount of the debt results in recording an **extraordinary** gain by the debtor and an **ordinary** loss by the creditor.

Subsequent to restructure date: Each party records all of the cash paid by the debtor to the creditor as a decrease of the new carrying amounts because in this situation **no interest** is recognized after restructure date.

Exhibit 17–12, situation 2, illustrates a situation which *(a)* reduces the interest payments from $100 to $60 and *(b)* reduces the principal amount from $1,000 to $600. In this situation, the total **future cash payments of** $900 [i.e., ($60 × 5) + $600] **is less than the prerestructure carrying amount of the debt of $1,000.** Therefore, on restructure date, the debtor must recognize a $100 extraordinary gain, along with the concurrent reduction of the liability balance, and the creditor must recognize a $100 ordinary loss, along with the concurrent reduction of the receivable balance. After the last entry (end of fifth year), both the debtor's liability account balance and the creditor's receivable balance will be zero.

Many accountants do not agree with the accounting treatment of modification of terms of debt man-

[19] FASB, *Statement of Financial Accounting Standards No. 15,* "Accounting by Debtors and Creditors for Troubled Debt Restructurings" (Stamford, Conn., June 1977), par. 13.

EXHIBIT 17–11: Troubled Debt Restructure—Settlement of Debt by Transfer of Assets or Equity Interest

Panel A—Hypothetical Situation:

1. At date of restructure: Debtor Company owes Creditor Company *(a)* an overdue $1,000, five-year, 10 percent (payable annually) note plus *(b)* accrued interest of $50 on the note.
2. At date of restructure: Creditor Company, because of the weak financial position of the debtor, has agreed to a concession, which involves the transfer of noncash items with a market value less than the amount of the past-due debt.
3. Two different situations are illustrated below for this debt restructure.

Panel B—Entries at Date of Restructure for Two Different Restructure Situations:

Situation 1, Transfer of Assets—At date of restructure, Debtor Company has asset X, which has a carrying (book) amount of $500 and a market value of $700. Creditor Company has agreed to accept this asset in full settlement of the debt principal and the accrued interest (this settlement represents a concession).

a. To recognize the gain on disposal of asset X:

Debtor Company			Creditor Company		
Asset X ($700 − $500)	200				
Gain on disposal of asset X		200*			

b. To record settlement of the debt by transfer of asset X:

Debtor Company			Creditor Company		
Note payable	1,000		Asset X (market value)	700	
Interest payable	50		Loss on receivable restructure	350‡	
Asset X		700	Note receivable		1,000
Extraordinary gain on debt restructure ($1,050 − $700)		350†	Interest receivable		50

Situation 2, Transfer of Equity Interest—At date of restructure, Debtor Company has 600 shares of its unissued common stock (par $1), which has a market value of $1.50 per share. Creditor Company has agreed to accept this stock in full settlement of the debt principal and the accrued interest.

To record settlement of the debt by transfer of the unissued common stock:

Debtor Company			Creditor Company		
Note payable	1,000		Investment, common stock of Debtor Company (600 shares × $1.50)	900	
Interest payable	50		Loss on receivable restructure	150‡	
Common stock, par $1 (600 shares)		600	Note receivable		1,000
Contributed capital in excess of par 600 × ($1.50 − $1.00)		300	Interest receivable		50
Extraordinary gain on debt restructure ($1,050 − $900)		150†			

* This gain must be reported separately from the gain on restructure (see entry *b*). It must be classified in accordance with the provisions of *APB Opinion 30* as ordinary, unusual or infrequent, or extraordinary depending on the circumstances.

† Debtor must report gains on restructure as extraordinary (*FASB Statement 15*, par. 21). The reason for restructure (i.e., a concession to the debtor) effectively precludes a loss to the debtor.

‡ Creditor must classify these losses in accordance with the provisions of *APB Opinion 30*, as ordinary, unusual or infrequent, or extraordinary, depending on the circumstances. The reason for restructure (i.e., a concession by the creditor) effectively precludes a gain to the creditor.

dated by *FASB Statement 15* (as illustrated in Exhibit 17–12, situations 1 and 2). They believe that the gain to the debtor and the loss to the creditor should include both the *(a)* amount of the principal concession and *(b)* the interest concession. That is, the gain (loss) on modification of terms should be the difference between the *(a)* prerestructure carrying amount of the debt, and *(b)* the present value of the cash payments (i.e., principal and interest) after restructure. This treatment is consistent with the conceptual approach to valuation of receivables and payables as mandated in *APB Opinion No. 21*, "Interest on Receivables and Payables" because it measures the true economic gain or loss of each party.

In contrast, *FASB Statement 15* mandates that the loss (gain) on modification of terms shall be mea-

EXHIBIT 17–12: Troubled Debt Restructure—Modification of Terms (principal and interest)

Panel A—Hypothetical Situation:

1. At date of restructure: Debtor Company owes Creditor Company a $1,000 ten-year, 10 percent (payable annually) note; maturity date is five years from date of restructure.
2. At date of restructure, Creditor Company, because of a critical cash flow problem of the debtor, agreed to a concession which *(a)* defers the interest payments and *(b)* reduces the principal amount of the debt.
3. Two different situations are illustrated below.

Panel B—Entries at Date of Restructure and Subsequently:

Situation 1, Total Cash More than Debt Carrying Amount—At date of restructure, Creditor Company agreed to *(a)* defer the five annual interest payments of $100 each to maturity date and *(b)* reduce the principal from $1,000 to $800; thus, no cash will be paid until maturity date, at which time $1,300 will be paid.

a. Date of restructure: No entry is made by either party because the total restructured cash payments [($100 × 5) + $800 = $1,300] is **more** than the prerestructured carrying amount of the debt ($1,000). The new effective interest rate is 5.4 percent.*

b. Annual entries subsequent to restructure (1) to recognize interest at the new effective rate, and (2) to amortize the principal from $1,000 down to $800. Tabulation of the annual entries of Debtor Company and Creditor Company:

Date	Debtor: Debit—Interest Expense Creditor: Credit—Interest Revenue	Credit—Payable Debit—Receivable	Payable Balance Receivable Balance
Start			$1,000
End year 1	$1,000 × 5.4% = $ 54	$ 54	1,054
End year 2	1,054 × 5.4% = 57	57	1,111
End year 3	1,111 × 5.4% = 60	60	1,171
End year 4	1,171 × 5.4% = 63	63	1,234
End year 5	1,234 × 5.4% = 66 (rounded)	66	1,300
	$300	$300	

c. Entry at maturity for full payment of the debt (including interest):

Debtor			Creditor		
Note payable	1,300		Cash	1,300	
Cash		1,300	Note receivable		1,300

Situation 2, Total Cash Less than Debt Carrying Amount—At date of restructure Creditor Company agreed to *(a)* reduce the annual interest payments from $100 to $60 and *(b)* reduce the principal from $1,000 to $600; thus, the total cash to be paid is $900 [i.e., ($60 × 5) + $600], which is less than the carrying amount of the debt (i.e., $1,000). In this situation, *(a)* the debtor will record a $100 extraordinary gain, and the creditor will record a $100 loss; and *(b)* all cash paid subsequent to restructure date will be recorded as reductions of the principal.

a. Date of restructure: Each party must make an entry because the total restructured future cash payments [($60 × 5) + $600 = $900] is **less** than the prerestructured carrying amount of the debt ($1,000). The entry reduces the carrying amount of the debt to the total cash to be paid ($900) and recognizes a gain (loss).

Debtor Company			Creditor Company		
Note payable	100		Loss on receivable restructure	100	
Extraordinary gain on debt restructure		100	Note receivable		100

b. At each interest date (years 1–5); all cash applied to principal:

Note payable	60		Cash	60	
Cash		60	Note receivable		60

c. At maturity date:

Note payable	600		Cash	600	
Cash		600	Note receivable		600

Note—After the last entry (on maturity date) the balance in the note payable and note receivable accounts, respectively, will be zero.

* Computation of new effective interest rate after restructure:
$1,000 ÷ $1,300 = .76923, value for $p_{n=5;\, i=?}$ Reference to Table 5–2, for $n = 5$, indicates an approximate rate of 5.4% (straight-line interpolation; see Chapter 5). By calculator: $\$1,300 = \$1,000\,(1 + i)^5$; $1.3 = (1 + i)^5$; $(1.3)^{.2} = 1 + i$; $1.05387 = 1 + i$; $i = 5.4\%$

sured as the difference between the *(a)* prerestructure carrying amount of the debt and *(b)* total future cash payments required after restructure, a procedure which ignores the present value of the restructured cash flows based on a realistic current interest rate.

These two opposing views can be compared by referring to Exhibit 17–12, situation 2. The comparative results are as follows, assuming the going market interest rate on debts, such as the one being restructured, is 20 percent:

	FASB Viewpoint		Conceptual Viewpoint
Carrying amount of debt on restructure date	$1,000		$1,000
Total cash payments after restructure ($60 × 5) + $600	900		
Present value of cash payments after restructure:			
Principal: $600 × $p_{n=5;i=20\%}$(.40188, Table 5–2)		$241	
Interest: $60 × $P_{o_{n=5;i=20\%}}$(2.99061, Table 5–4)		179	420
Gain (loss) on debt restructure by the creditor	$ (100)		$ (580)

Financial institutions (i.e., creditors) appear to strongly prefer the FASB approach because under the FASB approach they do not report what, in fact, is an **economic loss.**

DISCLOSURE REQUIREMENTS

FASB Statement 15 (pars. 164–72) prescribes detailed disclosure requirements for both the debtor and creditor.

In substance, disclosure by the **debtor** must include *(a)* a description of the major changes for each restructuring; *(b)* the aggregate gain on restructuring and the related income tax effect; *(c)* aggregate loss or gain on transfers of assets; *(d)* the per share amount of the aggregate gain on restructuring of payables, net of related income tax effect; and *(e)* information on any related contingent payments.

Disclosure by the **creditor** must include, for outstanding receivables that have been restructured, by major category: *(a)* the aggregate recorded investment, *(b)* gross interest revenue that would have been recorded without restructure, *(c)* the amount of interest revenue on those receivables that was included in net income for the period, and *(d)* the amount of commitments to lend additional funds to debtors whose terms have been modified in troubled debt restructurings.

Supplement 17-A: Serial Bonds

An issue of bonds with provision for repayment of principal in a series of **installments** is called a serial bond issue. Serial bonds are well adapted for use by school districts and other taxing authorities which borrow money upon agreement that a special tax will be levied to pay off the obligation. As the taxes are collected, the cash usually is used to pay off the indebtedness.

DETERMINING SELLING PRICE OF SERIAL BONDS

The selling price of serial bonds may be derived by computing the selling price for each serial separately in the same way that an ordinary bond issue is valued, and then totaling the prices of the various serials. For example, assume that serial bonds carrying 7 percent interest payable 3½ percent semiannually are sold to yield 5 percent per annum with the following maturity dates: $10,000 at end of 12 months, $20,000 at end of 18 months, and $30,000 at end of 24 months. The selling price of each serial, as well as that of the whole issue, may be *(a)* derived from a bond table (similar to Exhibit 17–2) or *(b)* computed as follows:[20]

[20] Although not realistic, a short time span is used to simplify the computations.

	Bond Price	Premium
Serial no. 1 (due in 12 months—2 interest periods):		
Principal: $10,000 × .95181*	$ 9,518	
Interest payments:		
$350 × 1.92742†	675	
	10,193	$ 193
Serial no. 2 (due in 18 months—3 interest periods):		
Principal: $20,000 × .92860	18,572	
Interest payments:		
$700 × 2.85602	1,999	
	20,571	571
Serial no. 3 (due in 24 months—4 interest periods):		
Principal: $30,000 × .90595	27,179	
Interest payments:		
$1,050 × 3.76197	3,950	
	31,129	1,129
Total price of all serials	$61,893	
Total premium on all serials		$1,893

* Table 5–2—$p_{n=2;i=2\ 1/2\%}$.
† Table 5–4—$P_{o_{n=2;i=2\ 1/2\%}}$.

AMORTIZATION OF PREMIUM AND DISCOUNT ON SERIAL BONDS

Amortization of premium or discount on serial bonds is identical to that on ordinary bonds; however, the computations involve more arithmetic. When the results are **not** materially different from the interest method, the straight-line method may be used; otherwise, the interest method must be used. In both methods, the amount of periodic amortization must be related to the amount of bonds **outstanding** during the period. Therefore, the amount of periodic amortization of premium or discount will decrease as each serial is paid off at its maturity date.

Straight-line amortization of the $1,893 premium from the above example is computed for each period in Exhibit 17–13. Observe that the premium on each serial is apportioned to the number of periods each serial is outstanding.[21]

[21] Occasionally problems are given that fail to specify a basis for determining the amount of premium or discount applicable to each serial. In this situation, an approximation known as dollar-periods or "bonds outstanding" allocation is used. The method inherently is straight line and should not be used when the interest method is mandated. To illustrate, the $1,893 total premium could be allocated as follows:

Serial	Par	Periods Outstanding (semiannual)	Dollar Periods	Allocation Fraction		Allocation to Serials
1	$10,000	2	$ 20,000	20/200	×	$1,893 = $ 189
2	20,000	3	60,000	60/200	×	$1,893 = 568
3	30,000	4	120,000	120/200	×	$1,893 = 1,136
			$200,000			$1,893

The amounts in the last column are then allocated to each period on a straight-line basis, as illustrated in Exhibit 17–13.

EXHIBIT 17–13: Amortization of Premium on Serial Bonds—Straight—Line Method

Serial No.	Total Premium to Be Amortized	Amortization of Premium—Straight—Line Method			
		At End of 6 Months	At End of 12 Months	At End of 18 Months	At End of 24 Months
1	$ 193	$ 96	$ 97		
2	571	190	190	$191	
3	1,129	282	282	282	$283
	$1,893	$568	$569	$473	$283

The entries for the foregoing example are given below, with the added assumption that $5,000 par of the serial no. 3 bonds, which were to mature at the end of 24 months, were purchased for $5,100 and retired (early extinguishment) at the end of 12 months.

1. To record sale of the bonds:

Cash	61,893	
Premium on bonds payable		1,893
Bonds payable		60,000

2. To record payment of interest and straight-line amortization of premium at the end of six months:

Interest expense	1,532	
Premium on bonds payable (Exhibit 17–13)	568	
Cash ($60,000 × .035)		2,100

3. To record payment of interest and amortization of premium at end of 12 months:

Interest expense	1,531	
Premium on bonds payable	569	
Cash ($60,000 × .035)		2,100

4. To record payment of serial no. 1 bonds at the end of 12 months:

Bonds payable (serial no. 1)	10,000	
Cash		10,000

5. To record retirement of $5,000 of serial no. 3 bonds at end of 12 months for $5,100 cash:

Bonds payable	5,000	
Bond premium	94*	
Extraordinary loss, early extinguishment of debt	6	
Cash		5,100

* ($5,000/$30,000) × ($282 + $283) = $94.

6. To pay interest, amortize premium, and pay off serial no. 2 bonds at end of 18 months:

Interest expense	1,149	
Bond premium [$191 + (5/6 × $282)]	426	
Cash ($45,000 × .035)		1,575
Bonds payable	20,000	
Cash		20,000

7. To pay interest, amortize premium, and pay off serial no. 3 bonds at end of 24 months:

Interest expense	639	
Bond premium (5/6 × $283)	236	
Cash ($25,000 × .035)		875
Bonds payable	25,000	
Cash		25,000

Interest method amortization requires knowledge of the yield rate of interest and the selling price. When serial bonds are involved, an amortization schedule should be prepared in the same manner as the amortization schedule for ordinary (nonserial) bonds except that the maturity values of each installment must be deducted from the "carrying value" amounts when the installments are paid. An amortization schedule showing present value amortization of the premium and payment of the three serial installments on the serial bond issue illustrated in the preceding section is given in Exhibit 17–14. In the example, recall that the sale price was $61,893 and the yield rate was 2½ percent semiannually. In Exhibit 17–14, observe that the computations are identical to those previously illustrated for ordinary bonds (Exhibit 17–9), except for the payments on principal as each serial matures.

When the interest method is used and some portion of a serial is retired before maturity, the carrying

EXHIBIT 17–14: Serial Bond Entries Tabulated—Interest Method Amortization

Date	Cash Cr.	Interest Expense Dr.	Bond Premium Dr.	Bonds Payable Dr.	Carrying Amount
At issue	—	—	—	—	61,893
End 6 months	2,100	1,547*	553	—	61,340
End 12 months	2,100	1,534	566	—	60,774
End 12 months	10,000	—	—	10,000	50,774
End 18 months	1,750	1,269	481	—	50,293
End 18 months	20,000	—	—	20,000	30,293
End 24 months	1,050	757	293	—	30,000
End 24 months	30,000	—	—	30,000	—
	67,000	5,107	1,893	60,000	

* $61,893 × .025 = $1,547.

EXHIBIT 17–15: Serial Bond Entries Tabulated—Interest Method Amortization (effect of early extinguishment)

Date	Cash Cr.	Interest Expense Dr.	Bond Premium Dr.	Bonds Payable Dr.	Extraordinary Loss on Early Extinguishment Dr.	Carrying Amount
Balance, end 12 months	—	—	—	—	—	50,774*
End 12 months	5,100	—	96	5,000	4	45,678†
End 18 months	1,575	1,142	433	—	—	45,245
End 18 months	20,000	—	—	20,000	—	25,245
End 24 months	875	630‡	245	—	—	25,000
End 24 months	25,000	—	—	25,000	—	—

* From Exhibit 17–14, line 4.
† $50,774 − $96 − $5,000 = $45,678.
‡ Rounded to come out even.

amount at the date of early extinguishment must be reduced for the portion retired. To illustrate, assume $5,000 par of serial no. 3 bonds are purchased for retirement at the end of 12 months (i.e., two interest periods before maturity date); the reduction in carrying amount would be as follows:

Principal: $5,000 × .95181 (i.e., $p_{n=2;i=2\ 1/2\%}$ Table 5–2)	$4,759
Interest payments: $175 × 1.92742 (i.e., $P_{o\ n=2;i=2\ 1/2\%}$ Table 5–4)	337
Carrying amount retired (including premium retired, $96)	$5,096

The retirement, using the present value computed above, is reflected in Exhibit 17–15, which is a continuation of Exhibit 17–14, starting with line 4. Observe that the first line of Exhibit 17–15 reflects the entry for early extinguishment. The loss, if material in amount, would be reported as an extraordinary item in conformance with FASB, *Statement of Financial Accounting Standards No. 4,* "Reporting Gains and Losses from Extinguishment of Debt."

Supplement 17-B: Economic Analysis of Bond Refunding Transactions

Part C of this chapter discussed and illustrated accounting for three different bond **refunding** situations—situation 1, a direct **exchange** of new bonds for old bonds; situation 2, sale of new bonds in the market to obtain cash to **purchase** the old bonds in the open market; and situation 3, sale of new bonds in the market to obtain cash to **call** the old bonds at the stipulated call price.

The purpose of this supplement is to analyze refunding transactions from the **economic point of view,** that is, in terms of the discounted cash flows of the old and new bonds involved in refunding transactions. The discussions will emphasize the fact that GAAP accounting for refunding gives results which differ significantly from the economic effects of refunding.

Prior to studying this supplement you should be familiar with the discussions in the chapter and Exhibit 17–10. Each of the three situations listed above will be discussed in order. The amounts used in these discussions will be those provided in Exhibit 17–10, p. 614.

Situation 1 (direct exchange of **new** bonds, $90,000, 8 percent payable semiannually, with six years to maturity for **old** bonds, $100,000, 5 percent payable semiannually, with six years to maturity) may be analyzed from the economic point of view and compared with the accounting results. In this situation the exchange was favorable to the bondholders because the **present value** of the old bonds at the current 8 percent going rate of interest was as follows:

Principal: $100,000 × $p_{n=12;i=4\%}$ (Table 5–2)	
$100,000 × .62460	$62,460
Interest: $100,000 × .025 × $P_{o_{n=12;i=4\%}}$	
(Table 5–4) $2,500 × 9.38507	23,540*
Total present value (theoretical market price)	$86,000

* Rounded for instructional convenience; total market value, $86,000.

Receiving bonds worth more than $86,000 would provide an incentive for exchange by the bondholders, and any value below that amount would provide a disincentive. In this refunding decision, new bonds of $90,000 were issued to extinguish the old bonds which had a market value of $86,000. Thus, Corporation C incurred an **economic loss** of $4,000, although it reported an **accounting gain** of $10,000 (see Exhibit 17–10, Panel C). The accounting gain of $10,000 represents the accumulated reduction of $14,000 in the market value of the old bonds since issuance (i.e., $100,000 − $86,000), less the $4,000 excess of market value of new bonds given to the bondholders, over the market value of the old bonds (i.e., $90,000 − $86,000).

Situation 2 (issuance of new bonds [$86,000] to obtain cash to purchase the old bonds at their market value [$86,000]) may be analyzed from the economic view and compared with the accounting results. In this situation, the issuing company would report a $14,000 **accounting gain,** although the company actually would incur an **economic loss** (pretax) in the amount of any bond issue costs on the new issue. If there had been no bond issue costs, the **economic gain** (or loss) would be exactly zero because the present value of **each** new bond issued at the market interest rate of 8 percent at date of refunding was $86,000, viz:

	Old 5 Percent Bonds	New 8 Percent Bonds
PV of principal (face amount):		
Old: $100,000 × $p_{n=12;i=4\%}$ (.62460)	$62,460	
New: $86,000 × $p_{n=12;i=4\%}$ (.62460)		$53,716
PV of interest payments:*		
Old: $2,500 × $P_{o_{n=12;i=4\%}}$ (9.38507)	23,540	
New: $3,440 × $P_{o_{n=12;i=4\%}}$ (9.38507)........		32,284
Total present value (theoretical market) ...	$86,000	$86,000

* Rounded for instructional convenience.

The **economic gain** (or loss) of **zero** is compared with the **accounting gain** of **$14,000** in Exhibit 17–10, Panel C.

Situation 3 (issuance of new bonds [$101,000] to obtain cash to call the old bonds at the stipulated call price of 101) involves a change in the fact situation used in situations 1 and 2 (both of those situations involved an **accounting gain**). Situation 3 is changed to derive an **accounting loss** and an **economic gain.** For this purpose, retain the basic facts of situations 1 and 2, except as follows: Assume the current market rate of interest is 4 percent, rather than 8 percent as in situations 1 and 2.[22] In this case, the **theoretical** price of the outstanding 5 percent bonds **would be** $105,300. However, because Corporation C can call the bonds at 101, the actual bond price will not rise above $101,000 (because investors would be aware of the call privilege at 101). Under these conditions, Corporation C can issue new 4 percent bonds with a face value of $101,000, at par, to obtain the cash needed to retire the old 5 percent bonds. Thus, the company will earn an **economic gain** of $4,300 (i.e., $105,300 − $101,000) on refunding. However, the accounting entries for the refunding would record an **accounting loss** of $1,000.

In situation 3, as well as in situations 1 and 2, the difference between the **accounting** results and the **economic** results of refunding are due to the fact that under historical cost (HC) accounting, changes in the market value of outstanding bonds payable are **not** recognized as they occur. Instead, market value changes are recognized only when a completed transaction occurs. The accounting result obtained in this situation is germane to the HC model; how-

[22] These same assumptions were made in Exhibit 17–10.

ever, the paradoxical nature of the results are depicted clearly in the case of bond refunding.

A substantive reason for a company to refund its outstanding debt, and in particular, for it to refund old, low-interest debt with a lower face amount of new, high-interest debt, is to decrease the amount of its outstanding debt. Such a decision could be needed to conform to existing debt covenants. Another reason is to reduce tax payments by increasing interest expense deductions. For example, in situation 2 immediately above, interest expense was increased from $2,500 to $3,440. Therefore, a refunding may appear from the economic perspective to be unwarranted, but when all facts are considered, it may turn out to be a "wise" decision.

Supplement 17-C: Troubled Debt Restructure—Computation of New Effective Interest Rate

Exhibit 17–16 illustrates a debt restructure in which the total future cash payments by the debtor to the creditor is **more** than the prerestructure carrying amount of the debt; for this reason, neither the debtor nor the creditor recognizes a gain or loss at date of restructure. Instead, each party must compute the new interest rate which is implicit in the restructure agreement. This new rate is the interest rate which discounts the total future cash payments under the restructure agreement to the carrying amount of the **prerestructured** debt.

The focal point of Exhibit 17–16 is Panel B, which illustrates computation of the new implicit interest rate by an iterative (i.e., trial-and-error) process. Iteration is necessary in this situation because the restructured debt involves both periodic interest payments by the debtor to the creditor (i.e., an annuity) and a principal payment at maturity. Panel C of the exhibit presents the related journal entries by both the debtor and the creditor.

EXHIBIT 17–16: Troubled Debt Restructure (iteration to compute new effective interest rate)

Panel A—Hypothetical Situation:

1. Debt to be restructured: principal, $5,000,000; annual interest rate, 20 percent, payable at each year-end, $1,000,000. Time to maturity, five years.
2. Restructure agreement: Reduce principal to $4,000,000 and reduce annual interest payments to $477,500.

Panel B—Analysis of Restructure:

1. Type of modification of terms:

Total future cash payments ($477,500 × 5) + $4,000,000	$6,387,500
Prerestructure carrying amount of the debt	5,000,000

Total cash payments **more** than carrying amount; therefore, no entry required at restructure date.

2. Computation of new effective rate of interest (by iteration):
Objective: To find interest rate which equates *(a)* present value of future cash flows, after restructure (principal, $4,000,000 and interest, $477,500) with *(b)* prerestructure carrying amount of the debt ($5,000,000).

	Trial @ 10 Percent	Trial @ 7 Percent	Trial @ 6 Percent
Principal, $4,000,000 (Table 5–2):			
1st trial at 10% (× table value, .62092)	$2,483,680		
2d trial at 7% (× table value, .71299)		$2,851,960	
3d trial at 6% (× table value, .74726)			$2,989,040
Interest, $477,500 (Table 5–4):			
1st trial at 10% (× table value, 3.79079)	1,810,102		
2d trial at 7% (× table value, 4.10020)		1,957,846	
3d trial at 6% (× table value, 4.21236)			2,011,402
Total present value of future cash flows (to be compared with $5,000,000 carrying amount of the debt)	$4,293,782 (too low)	$4,809,806 (too low)	$5,000,442 (close enough use 6%)

Panel C—Accounting Entries (none at date of restructure):

a. Annual entries subsequent to restructure tabulated:

Date	D*—Credit Cash C*—Debit Cash	D—Debit Interest Expense C—Credit Interest Revenue	D—Debit Payable C—Credit Receivable	D—Payable Balance C—Receivable Balance
Start				$5,000,000
End year 1	$477,500	$5,000,000 × .06 = $300,000	$177,500	4,822,500
End year 2	477,500	4,822,500 × .06 = 289,350	188,150	4,634,350
End year 3	477,500	4,634,350 × .06 = 278,061	199,439	4,434,911
End year 4	477,500	4,434,911 × .06 = 266,095	211,405	4,223,506
End year 5	477,500	4,223,506 × .06 = 253,994†	223,506	4,000,000

* Explanations: D—Debtor; C—Creditor. † Rounded to come out even.

b. Entry at maturity date:

Debtor			Creditor		
Payable	4,000,000		Cash	4,000,000	
Cash		4,000,000	Receivable		4,000,000

QUESTIONS

PART A

1. What are the primary characteristics of a *bond?* What distinguishes it from *capital stock?*

2. Contrast the following classes of bonds: *(a)* industrial versus governmental, *(b)* secured versus unsecured, *(c)* ordinary versus income, *(d)* ordinary versus serial, *(e)* callable versus convertible, and *(f)* registered versus coupon.

3. What are the principal advantages and disadvantages of bonds versus common stock for *(a)* the issuer and *(b)* the investor?

4. Explain the stated and yield rates of *interest* on a bond. Describe their relationship to the market price of a bond.

5. Distinguish between the face amount and the price of a bond. When are they the same? When different? Explain.

6. Explain the significance of bond discount and bond premium to *(a)* the issuer and *(b)* the investor.

7. Assume a $1,000, 6% (payable semiannually), 10-year bond is sold at an effective rate of 8%. Explain two ways to determine the sale price of this bond.

8. Explain why and how bond *discount* and bond *premium* affect *(a)* the balance sheet and *(b)* the income statement of the investor.

9. What is the conceptual difference between the *straight-line* and *interest* methods of amortizing bond discount and premium?

10. Under GAAP, when is it appropriate to use *(a)* straight-line and *(b)* interest method amortization for bond discount or premium?

PART B

11. When the end of the accounting period of the investor is not on a bond interest date, adjusting entries must be made for *(a)* accrued interest and *(b)* discount or premium amortization. Explain in general terms what each adjustment amount represents.

12. When bonds are sold (or purchased) between interest dates, accrued interest must be recognized. Explain why.

13. What are *convertible bonds?* What are the primary reasons for their use?

14. Why is the accounting different for convertible bonds with detachable stock warrants and those without detachable stock warrants?

PART C

15. What is meant by early extinguishment of debt? How should any resultant gain or loss be reported?

16. What is meant by *refunding?* When would it generally be advantageous to the issuer?

17. What is meant by *troubled debt restructuring?* What are some of the features of typical restructuring arrangements?

EXERCISES

PART A: EXERCISES 17–1 to 17–7

Exercise 17–1

Rowe Corporation authorized $600,000, 8% (payable 4% semiannually), 10-year bonds payable. The bonds were dated January 1, 19A; interest dates are June 30 and December 31.

Assume four different cases with respect to the sale of the bonds:

Case A—Sold on January 1, 19A, at par.

Case B—Sold on January 1, 19A, at 102.

Case C—Sold on January 1, 19A, at 98.

Case D—Sold on March 1, 19A, at par.

Required:

1. For each case, what amount of cash interest will be paid on the first interest date, June 30, 19A?
2. In what cases is the stated rate of interest not 4% each semiannual period?
3. In what cases will the yield rate of interest be *(a)* the same, *(b)* higher, or *(c)* lower than the stated rate?
4. After sale of the bonds, in what cases will the carrying or book value of the bonds (as reported on the balance sheet) be *(a)* the same, *(b)* higher, or *(c)* lower than the maturity or face amount?
5. After the sale of the bonds, in Cases A, B, and C, which case will report interest expense (as reported on the income statement) *(a)* the same, *(b)* higher, or *(c)* lower than the amount of cash interest paid each period?

Exercise 17–2

A $10,000 bond, 8% (payable 4% semiannually), 10-year (remaining period outstanding), was sold by A to B, on an interest date, at an effective rate of 10%. The bond price was computed as follows: $3,769 + $4,985 = $8,754.

Required:
Explain in detail, using values for "i" and "n" how each of the two dollar amounts was computed. Explain why the computation derives the bond price.

Exercise 17–3

Compute the bond price for each of the following situations (show computations and round to nearest dollar):

a. A 10-year $1,000 bond; annual interest at 7% (payable 3½% semiannually) purchased to yield 6% interest.
b. An eight-year, $1,000 bond; annual interest at 6% (payable annually) purchased to yield 7% interest.
c. A 10-year, $1,000 bond; annual interest at 6% (payable semiannually) purchased to yield 8% interest.
d. An eight-year, $1,000 bond; annual interest at 6% (payable annually) purchased to yield 6% interest.

Exercise 17–4

Y Corporation issued to Z Corporation a $30,000, 8% (payable 4% semiannually on June 30 and December 31), 10-year bond dated and sold on January 1, 19A. Assumptions: Case A—sold at par; Case B—sold at 103; and Case C—sold at 97.

Required:
In parallel columns for the issuer and the investor (assume a long-term investment), give the appropriate journal entries for each case on (1) January 1, 19A, and (2) June 30, 19A. Assume the difference between amortization amounts is not material; therefore, use straight-line amortization.

Exercise 17–5

New Corporation sold to Old Corporation a $10,000, 9% (payable 4½% semiannually on June 30 and December 31),

(Relates to Exercise 17–7)

Item	Balance Sheet	Income Statement	Statement of Retained Earnings
1. Appropriation of retained earnings is increased.			
2. Stock dividend is declared and issued.			
3. Bondholders turn in their convertible bonds for common stock of the enterprise (book value method).			
4. Land is bought for cash.			
5. Annual depreciation is recorded.			
6. Cash dividend is declared.			
7. Bonds payable (issued at par) are paid at maturity.			
8. Accrued wages are recognized at end of year.			
9. Common stock is issued at a premium to acquire land.			
10. Cash is invested in bonds as a long-term investment.			
11. Overstatement of income of last year is corrected.			
12. Cash in bank is transferred to petty cash fund.			
13. Interest-bearing note payable and interest are paid at maturity.			

10-year bond, dated and sold on January 1, 19A. The bond was sold at an 8% yield rate (4% semiannually). Round to nearest dollar.

Required:
1. Compute the price of the bond.
2. In parallel columns for the issuer and the investor (assume a long-term investment), give the appropriate journal entries on *(a)* January 1, 19A, and *(b)* June 30, 19A. Assume the difference between the amortization amounts is material; therefore, use the interest method.

Exercise 17–6

Red Corporation sold to White Corporation a $10,000 bond, 7% interest (payable annually on December 31). The bond was sold on January 1, 19A, matures December 31, 19D, and the yield rate was 8%.

Required (round to nearest dollar):
1. Determine the selling price of the bond by reference to Exhibit 17–2. Prove your answer by computing the present value of each of the future cash flows. Show computations.
2. Prepare a bond amortization schedule using the interest method.
3. In parallel columns give entries for the issuer and the investor (a long-term investment) for the following assuming the interest method of amortization: *(a)* sale of the bond, *(b)* first interest payment, and *(c)* all entries on the maturity date, December 31, 19D.
4. Show how the bond should be reported on the balance sheets of the issuer and the investor at December 31, 19A.

Exercise 17–7 (a review exercise)

Each numbered item (p. 628) affects one or more financial statements—balance sheet, income statement, and/or statement of retained earnings. For each statement **directly** or **indirectly** affected, place an X in the appropriate column.

PART B: EXERCISES 17–8 to 17–13

Exercise 17–8

On September 1, 19A, Newman Company sold Youngblood Company $30,000, five-year, 9% (payable semiannually) bonds for $32,320 plus accrued interest. The bonds were dated July 1, 19A, and interest is payable each June 30 and December 31. The accounting period for each company ends on December 31.

Required:
In parallel columns, give entries on the books of the borrower and investor (a long-term investment) for the following dates: September 1, 19A; December 31, 19A; January 1, 19B; and June 30, 19B. Assume the difference between the amortization amounts is not material; therefore, use straight-line amortization.

Exercise 17–9

Ryan Corporation issued $150,000, three-year, 8% (payable semiannually) bonds payable for $156,400 plus accrued interest. Interest is payable each February 28 and August 31. The bonds were dated March 1, 19A, and were sold on July 1, 19A. The accounting period ends on December 31.

Required:
1. How much accrued interest should be recognized at date of sale?
2. How long is the amortization period?
3. Give entries for Ryan Corporation through February 19B (including reversing entries). Use straight-line amortization.
4. Would the above amounts also be recorded by the investor? Explain.

Exercise 17–10

Koy Corporation sold and issued to Lott Corporation (as a long-term investment) $50,000, four-year, 11% bonds on September 1, 19A. Interest is payable semiannually on February 28 and August 31 . The bonds mature on August 31, 19E, and were sold to yield 10% interest. The accounting period for both companies ends on December 31.

Required:
1. Compute the price of the bond (show computations and round to nearest dollar).
2. In parallel columns, give all entries required through February 19B (including reversing entries) in the accounts of the borrower and the investor. Assume the difference between the amortization amounts is not material; therefore, use straight-line amortization.

Exercise 17–11

Radian Company issued to Seivers Company $30,000, four-year, 8% bonds dated June 1, 19A. Interest is payable semiannually on May 31 and November 30. The bonds were issued on March 1, 19B, for $29,171 plus accrued interest. The accounting period ends December 31 for both companies. The yield interest rate was 9%.

Required (round to nearest dollar):
1. Verify the bond price by using values from Exhibit 17–2. Use straight-line interpolation.
2. Prepare a bond amortization schedule starting on March

1, 19B, and continuing to maturity, May 31, 19E. Use the interest method.
3. In parallel columns, give entries for the issuer and the investor (as a long-term investment) for the following dates: March 1, 19B, and May 31, 19B. Use interest-method amortization.

Exercise 17–12

Hardware Corporation issued $150,000, 6%, 10-year bonds with detachable stock warrants. Each $1,000 bond carried 20 detachable warrants, each of which was for one share of Hardware common stock, par $20, with a specified option price of $60. The bonds sold at 102 including the warrants (no bond price exwarrants was available), and, immediately after date of issuance, the detachable stock warrants were selling at $4 each.

The entire issue was acquired by Software Company as a long-term investment.

Required:
1. Give entries for the issuer and the investor at date of acquisition of the bonds.
2. Give entry for the investor assuming subsequent sale of all the warrants to another investor at $5.50 each.
3. Give entries for the issuer and investor assuming subsequent tender of all of the warrants by the investor for exercise at the specified option price. At this date the stock was selling at $75 per share.

Exercise 17–13

Stonewall Corporation issued $40,000, 5%, 10-year convertible bonds. Each $1,000 bond was convertible to 10 shares of common stock (par $50) of Stonewall Corporation at any interest date after three years from issuance. The bonds were sold at 105 to Mason Corporation as a long-term investment.

Required:
1. Give entry for the issuer and investor at the date of issuance.
2. Give entries for the issuer and investor assuming that the conversion privilege is subsequently exercised by Mason Corporation immediately after the end of the third year. Assume 30% of any premium or discount has been amortized and that, at date of conversion, the common stock was selling at $125 per share.

PART C: EXERCISES 17–14 to 17–20

Exercise 17–14

On January 1, 19A, Vue Company issued $100,000 face value bonds payable with a stated interest rate of 12%, payable annually each December 31. The bonds mature in 25 years and have a call price of 103, exercisable by Vue Company after the fifth year. The bonds originally sold at par.

On January 1 of the 11th year the company contemplated calling the bonds at 103. At that time the bonds were quoted on the market at a price to yield 10%.

Required:
1. Give the issuance entry required on January 1, 19A.
2. Give the entry for extinguishment of the bonds by calling them on January 1 of the 11th year.
3. Was exercise of the call economically favorable for the issuer? Show computations. *(Based on Supplement 17–B)*

Exercise 17–15

On January 1, 19A, Wolf Company issued $200,000 face value bonds payable with a stated rate of interest of 5%, payable annually each December 31. The bonds mature in 25 years and are callable after the 5th year at 101. The bonds originally sold on January 1, 19A, at par.

On January 1 of the 11th year, the bonds *(a)* could be called at 101 or *(b)* acquired in the open market for $148,643 (a yield rate of 8%).

Required:
1. Give the issuance entry on January 1, 19A.
2. Give the entry on January 1 of the 11th year for early extinguishment assuming *(a)* the call privilege is exercised and *(b)* the bonds are acquired in the open market.
3. Was the early extinguishment economically favorable to the issuer *(a)* if the call privilege is exercised and *(b)* if the bonds are acquired in the open market? Show computations. *(Based on Supplement 17–B)*

Exercise 17–16

Down Company owed Super Bank a $50,000, one-year, 10% (payable on December 31) note payable dated January 1, 19A. During 19A, Down Company experienced unusual difficulties and was unable to pay the note and interest. On January 1, 19B, the bank agreed to settle the debt and interest (for 19A) for $2,000 cash plus some land that had a current market value of $30,000. At December 31, 19A, the records of Down Company reflected the acquisition cost of the land to be $20,000.

Required:
Give all entries required on January 1, 19B, to record this debt restructure *(a)* for Down Company and *(b)* for Super Bank.

Exercise 17–17

Slow Company owed Quick Finance Company a $100,000, 10% (payable annually each December 31) note payable dated January 1, 19A. At December 31, 19C, Slow was experiencing serious financial problems and could not pay the principal and interest (for 19C). Since this was the maturity date for the note, an agreement was reached whereby Quick would settle the debt and interest in full for $12,000 cash plus a tract of land (Slow's acquisition cost was $7,000) plus 1,000 shares of Slow common stock (par $10 per share) that had a current market price of $35 per share. The current market value of the land on January 1, 19D, was $20,000. The agreement was accepted by both parties, and settlement was effected on January 1, 19D.

Required:
Give all entries required to record the debt restructure for *(a)* Slow Company and *(b)* Quick Finance Company. Show details and computations.

Exercise 17–18

Depaw Company owed Crow Company a $20,000, 10% (annual interest payable each December 31), four-year note payable dated January 1, 19A. Depaw Company faced extreme financial difficulties. Neither company had accrued interest for the year 19B. On January 2, 19C, an agreement was reached that the interest for 19B would be paid; also, the interest amount for the remainder of the term of the note would be reduced to $1,218 in total, payable on December 31, 19D (maturity date).

Required:
1. Compute the new effective rate of interest. Show computations.
2. Give all entries required on date of restructure (January 2, 19C) for each company.
3. Give all entries required on December 31, 19C, and 19D, for each company.

Exercise 17–19

Brown Company owed City Bank a $50,000, 10% (payable each December 31), four-year note payable dated January 1, 19A. Early in 19B, it became clear that Brown Company would experience difficulty in making the annual interest payment. Due to expected continuing difficulties, the company may default on the note (as well as other obligations). On January 2, 19C, the two parties agreed to restructure the debt by *(a)* reducing the remaining annual interest payments to $2,240 each and *(b)* reducing the principal amount (maturity amount) to $48,000. Brown paid the interest for the year 19B.

Required:
1. Compute the new effective rate of interest. Show computations.
2. Give all entries required on date of restructure (January 2, 19C) for each company. If no entry is required, explain the reason.
3. Give all entries required at December 31, 19C, and 19D, for each company.

Exercise 17–20

Stine Company owed National Bank a $60,000, 10% (payable each December 31), four-year note payable dated January 1, 19A. Stine Company has experienced severe financial difficulties and is likely to default on the note and interest during 19C unless some concessions are made. Consequently, on January 2, 19C, the parties agreed to restructure the debt as follows: *(a)* interest payments each year to be reduced to $1,000 per year for 19C and 19D, and *(b)* reduce the principal amount to $30,000. On December 31, 19B, Stine paid $6,000 interest for 19B.

Required:
1. Does this restructure change the effective interest rate? Explain. Is the new effective rate of interest needed for accounting purposes in this situation? Explain.
2. Give all entries required for each party on the date of restructure, January 2, 19C.
3. Give all entries required for each party on December 31, 19C, and 19D.

PROBLEMS

PART A: PROBLEMS 17–1 to 17–3

Problem 17–1

BD Corporation sold EF Corporation (as a long-term investment) a $20,000, 7%, 10-year bond. The bond was dated January 1, 19A, and interest is payable annually each December 31. Assume the accounting periods end December 31. Assume three different cases in respect to the sale of the bond:

Case A—sold on January 1, 19A, at 7% yield.

Case B—sold on January 1, 19A, at 6% yield.

Case C—sold on January 1, 19A, at 8% yield.

Required:
1. For each case, compute the amount of interest that will be paid (i.e., cash) on the first interest date, December 31, 19A.
2. Identify which cases sold at *(a)* par, *(b)* a discount, and *(c)* a premium.
3. For each case, indicate *(a)* the stated interest rate and *(b)* the yield rate of interest.

4. Identify those cases where the amount of cash paid and received for the bond was *(a)* the same as par, *(b)* greater than par, and *(c)* less than par.
5. Subsequent to the transaction, in which cases will the respective balance sheets report the bonds at *(a)* par, *(b)* more than par, and *(c)* less than par?
6. Subsequent to the transaction, what cases will report interest expense and interest revenue (on the respective income statements) at more or less than the periodic amount of interest paid in cash?
7. Identify those cases where the maturity value of the bond liability (or bond investment) will be *(a)* the same as, *(b)* higher, or *(c)* lower than the book value.
8. Can straight-line amortization be used in each case? Explain.
9. What is the effect of periodic amortization of bond premium and discount on *(a)* interest expense (as reported on the income statement) and *(b)* bond carrying value (as reported on the balance sheet).

Problem 17–2

Alpha Corporation sold Beta Corporation $200,000, 8% (payable semiannually on June 30 and December 31), three-year bonds. The bonds were dated and sold on January 1, 19A, at a yield rate of 10%. The accounting period for each company ends on December 31.

Required:
1. Compute the price of the bonds (round to nearest dollar).
2. Prepare an amortization schedule for the life of the bonds (use the interest method and round to the nearest dollar).
3. Prepare in parallel columns, entries for the issuer and the investor (as a long-term investment) through December 31, 19A.
4. Show how the issuer and the investor would report the bonds on their respective balance sheets at December 31, 19A.
5. What would be reported on the income statement for each party for the year ended December 31, 19A?

Problem 17–3

Howe Corporation sold to Luck Company, $40,000, 7% (payable semiannually on June 30 and December 31), four-year bonds dated January 1, 19A. The bonds were sold on January 1, 19A, at a yield rate of 6%.

Required (round to nearest dollar):
1. Compute the price of the bonds.
2. Prepare an amortization schedule over the life of the bonds assuming the interest method of amortization.
3. In parallel columns for the issuer and investor (as a long-term investment) give all journal entries from issuance through fiscal year-end 19A. Assume the accounting period for Howe ends on December 31 and for Luck, on November 30.
4. Show how the issuer and the investor should report the bonds on their respective balance sheets on December 31, 19A, and November 30, 19A, respectively.
5. What would be reported on the income statement for each party for the year ended December 31, 19A, and November 30, 19A, respectively?

PART B: PROBLEMS 17–4 to 17–10

Problem 17–4

Foyt Corporation sold Mears Corporation $50,000 bonds on June 1, 19A, for $51,320 plus any accrued interest. The bond indenture provided the following information:

Maturity amount	$50,000
Date of bonds	April 1, 19A
Maturity date	March 31, 19C (2 years)
Stated interest rate	6½%, payable semiannually
Interest payments	March 31 and September 30

Required:
1. In parallel columns, give entries for the issuer and investor (as a long-term investment) from date of sale to maturity. Assume the difference between the amortization amounts is not material; therefore, use straight-line amortization. Also assume the accounting periods end December 31.
2. Show how the bonds would be reported on the balance sheet of each company at December 31, 19A.
3. What would be reported on the income statement for each party for the year ended December 31, 19A?

Problem 17–5

Jones Corporation issued bonds, face amount $100,000, three-year, 8% (payable semiannually on June 30 and December 31). The bonds were dated January 1, 19A, and were sold on November 1, 19A, to yield 9% interest. The bonds mature on December 31, 19C. The bonds were purchased as a long-term investment by Smith Corporation. Refer to Exhibit 17–2 for appropriate table values.

Required (round to nearest dollar):
1. Construct a time scale that depicts the important dates for this bond issue.
2. Determine *(a)* the price of the bond issue on the date of sale and *(b)* the total cash paid by Smith Corporation.
3. In parallel columns, give the entries at November 1, 19A, for the issuer and the investor.
4. Prepare a bond amortization schedule from date of sale to maturity date using the interest method.

5. In parallel columns, give the entries for interest and amortization at the interest date, December 31, 19A.
6. Determine and verify the balance in the interest accounts of the two parties to the transaction immediately after 5 above.
7. Assume the accounting period for each party ends on February 28. In parallel columns, give the adjusting entries for each party on February 28, 19B. Assume the interest method of amortization.
8. Compute the amount of amortization per month for each party assuming straight-line amortization is appropriate (i.e., the difference between the amortization amounts is not material).

Problem 17–6

Randy Corporation issued $200,000, 8% (payable each February 28 and August 31), four-year bonds. The bonds were dated March 1, 19A, and mature on February 28, 19E. They were sold on August 1, 19A, to yield 8½% interest. The bonds were purchased by Voss Corporation as a long-term investment. The accounting period for each company ends on December 31. Refer to Exhibit 17–2 for appropriate table values.

Required (round to nearest dollar):
1. Diagram a time scale depicting the important dates for this bond issue.
2. Determine *(a)* the price of the bond issue on the date of sale and *(b)* the total cash paid by Voss Corporation.
3. Prepare an amortization schedule from date of sale to maturity using the interest method of amortization.
4. In parallel columns, give entries for the borrower and the investor from date of sale through February 28, 19B. Base amortization on 3 above.
5. Compute the amount of amortization per month for each party assuming the straight-line method is appropriate (i.e., the difference between the amortization amounts is not material).

Problem 17–7

Case A

On January 1, 19A, when its $30 par value common stock was selling for $80 per share, a corporation issued $10,000,000 of 4% convertible debentures due in 10 years. The conversion option allowed the holder of each $1,000 bond to convert the bond into five shares of the corporation's $30 par value common stock. The debentures were issued for $11,000,000. The present value of the bond payments at the time of issuance was $8,500,000, and the corporation believes the difference between the present value and the amount paid is attributable to the conversion feature. On January 1, 19B, the corporation's $30 par value common stock was split 3 for 1. On January 1, 19C, when the corporation's $10 par value common stock was selling for $90 per share, holders of 40% of the convertible debentures exercised their conversion options. For convenience, assume the corporation uses the straight-line method for amortizing any bond discount or premium.

Required:
1. Prepare the entry to record the original issuance of the convertible debentures.
2. Prepare the entry to record the exercise of the conversion option, using the book value method. Show supporting computations.

Case B

On July 1, 19C, Salem Corporation issued $2,000,000 of 7% bonds payable in 10 years. The bonds pay interest semiannually. The bonds include detachable warrants giving the bondholder the right to purchase for $30, one share of $1 par value common stock at any time during the next 10 years. The bonds were sold for $2,000,000. The value of the warrants at the time of issuance was $100,000.

Required:
Prepare the entry to record the issuance of the bonds.
(AICPA adapted)

Problem 17–8

Friendly Corporation issued $500,000, 6%, nonconvertible bonds with detachable stock warrants. Each $1,000 bond carried 20 detachable stock warrants, each of which called for one share of Friendly common stock, par $50, at a specified option price of $60 per share. The bonds sold at 106, and the warrants were immediately quoted at $1 each on the market.

Goode Company purchased the entire issue as a long-term investment.

Required:
1. Give the following entries for Friendly Corporation (the borrower):
   a. To record the issuance of the bonds.
   b. To record the subsequent exercise by Goode of the 10,000 stock warrants.
2. Give the following entries for Goode Company (the investor):
   a. Acquisition of the bonds (including the warrants).
   b. Subsequent sale to another investor of half of the stock warrants at $1.50 each.
   c. Subsequent exercise of the remaining half of the stock warrants (by tendering them to Friendly Corporation.) The market value of the stock was $62 per share.

Problem 17–9

On January 1, 19A, Hillside Corporation issued $50,000, 5%, five-year convertible bonds with the provision that the holder of each $1,000 bond could tender it for conversion to 15 shares of Hillside common stock, par $50, at any time after 19B. The company estimated that nonconvertible bonds would have to carry an interest rate of 7½% to sell at par. The bonds were sold for $54,000. On July 1, 19C, the stock was selling at $75 per share. Assume straight-line amortization.

Required:

1. Give entries for Hillside at—
   a. Date of issuance—January 1, 19A.
   b. Date of conversion—July 1, 19C, assuming all bonds were turned in for conversion.
2. Assume Valley Corporation acquired all of the bonds. Give entries by Valley at—
   a. Date of acquisition.
   b. Date of conversion.

Problem 17–10

Assume the same situation given in Problem 17–9 except that instead of being convertible, each $1,000 bond had 15 detachable stock warrants. Each warrant was for one share of common stock at a specified price of $60 per share. Immediately upon issuance of the bonds on January 1, 19A, the warrants sold on the market at $2.

Required:

1. Give entry by Hillside Corporation at date of issuance, January 1, 19A.
2. Give entries for Valley Corporation at date of acquisition (as a long-term investment) on January 1, 19A.
3. Explain the basis for the values recognized in 1 and 2 above.
4. Assume 100 of the detachable stock warrants are tendered on July 1, 19C. At that date the stock was selling at $70 per share. Give entry for *(a)* Hillside Corporation and *(b)* Valley Corporation.

PART C: PROBLEMS 17–11 to 17–16

Problem 17–11

On July 1, 19A, Wonder Corporation issued $500,000, 5% (payable each June 30 and December 31), 10-year bonds payable. The bonds were callable at the option of the issuer at 102 at any time after the third year. The bonds were issued at 97, and issue costs of $1,400 were paid. Assume straight-line amortization of discount and bond issue costs. Disregard income tax effects.

Due to an increase in interest rates, these bonds were selling in the market at the end of June 19D at a yield rate of 8%. Because the company had available cash, $100,000 (face amount) of the bonds were purchased in the market on July 1, 19D, for $84,156. The accounting periods end December 31.

Required:

1. Give entry by Wonder Corporation to record issuance of the bonds on July 1, 19A.
2. Give entry to record retirement of the bonds ($100,000) on July 1, 19D. How should the gain or loss be reported on the 19D financial statements of Wonder?
3. Was the early extinguishment favorable to Wonder? *(Based on Supplement 17–B)*

Problem 17–12

This problem consists of three unrelated parts. Parts A and B relate to Parts A and B, respectively, of the chapter.

Part A

On January 1, 1982, the Hopewell Company sold its 8% bonds that had a face value of $1,000,000. Interest is payable at December 31, each year. The bonds mature on January 1, 1992. The bonds were sold to yield a rate of 10%.

Required:
Prepare a schedule to compute the total amount received from the sale of the bonds. Show supporting computations.

Part B

On September 1, 19A, the Junction Company sold at 104 (plus accrued interest), 4,000 of its 9%, 10-year, $1,000 face value, nonconvertible bonds with detachable stock warrants. Each bond carried two detachable warrants; each warrant was for one share of common stock, at a specified option price of $15 per share. Shortly after issuance, the warrants were quoted on the market for $3 each. No market value can be determined for the bonds above. Interest is payable on December 1, and June 1. Bond issue costs of $40,000 were incurred.

Required:
Prepare the entry to record the issuance of the bonds. Show supporting computations.

Part C

On December 1, 19x1, The Cone Company issued its 7%, $2,000,000 face value bonds for $2,200,000, plus accrued interest. Interest is payable on May 1 and November 1. On December 31, 19x3, the book value of the bonds, inclusive of the unamortized premium, was $2,100,000. On July 1, 19x4, Cone reacquired the bonds at 98, plus accrued interest. Cone appropriately uses the straight-line method for the amortization of bond premium because the results do not materially differ from using the interest method.

Required:
Prepare a schedule to compute the gain or loss on this early extinguishment of debt. Show supporting computations.

(AICPA adapted)

Problem 17–13

Adler Corporation issued $200,000, 4½% (payable each December 31), 10-year bonds on January 1, 19A. The issuer could call them at any time after 19D at 104. The bonds sold on January 1, 19A, at 98. Straight-line amortization is used.

Due to a large increase in interest rates, the bonds were being sold in the market at the end of 19E at 86 (i.e., at a yield rate of 8%). In view of this situation, Adler decided to issue a new series of bonds (a refunding issue) in the amount of $150,000 (8% payable annually, five-year term) on January 1, 19F; the new issue was sold at par. Adler has cash on hand sufficient for the remaining cost of retirement of the old bonds. Disregard income tax effects.

Required:
1. Give entry to record issuance of the bonds on January 1, 19A.
2. Assume the refunding issue is sold at par; give the required entry for Adler.
3. Assume all of the old bonds are purchased in the open market at 86 on January 2, 19F. Give the required entry for Adler. How should the gain or loss be reported on the financial statements?
4. Was the refunding transaction favorable to Adler Corporation?

Problem 17–14

On January 1, 19x1, Grand Corporation issued $100,000, 9% (payable each June 30 and December 31), 10-year bonds payable (convertible and callable) at a 10% yield rate of interest. Each $1,000 bond is convertible, at the option of the holder, into Grand common stock (par $10) as follows: first five years—25 shares for each bond tendered; second five years—20 shares for each bond. The bonds can be called, at the option of Grand, after the fifth year at 101.

On July 1, 19x7, the market interest rate on comparable bonds is 8%, and the common stock is quoted on the market at $52 per share.

Required (round to nearest dollar):
1. Record issuance of bonds on January 1, 19x1. Show computation of the bond issue price.
2. Give entry to record payment of bond interest and the amortization of bond premium or discount on June 30, 19x1. Assume interest method amortization.
3. Prepare the journal entries at July 1, 19x7, to record each of the following separate assumptions (use straight-line amortization):

   Assumption A—All of the bondholders turned in their bonds for conversion to common stock. Use the market value method to record the conversion.

   Assumption B—Grand called all of the bonds at the stipulated call price.

   Assumption C—Grand refunded all of the outstanding 9% bonds by purchasing them in the open market at the current yield rate of interest. Cash for the refunding was obtained by issuing new 8% bonds (interest payable semiannually) at par; cash proceeds were $103,000 (face amount of bonds sold).
4. Which of the three above alternative means of retiring the old 9% bonds payable was most likely to occur? Why?

Problem 17–15

On January 1, 19A, Overdue Corporation sold to Liquid Corporation $100,000, 7% (payable annually on December 31), 10-year bonds payable to yield 8% interest. After paying interest for 19A and 19B, Overdue Corporation encountered severe financial difficulties which made it apparent that Liquid Corporation would have to make some concessions as to debt terms. Therefore, a debt restructure was agreed to on January 1, 19C, that provided *(a)* the remaining term to maturity would be 20 years from January 1, 19C, and *(b)* interest would be reduced so that the same amount of total dollar interest would be paid over the new term to maturity (20 years) as would have been paid over the old term to the old maturity date (8 years). Assume straight-line amortization of bond premium or discount.

Required (round to nearest dollar):
1. Give entry by each party to record issuance of the bonds payable on January 1, 19A. Show computations of the original bond issuance price.
2. Compute the carrying amount of the bonds by the debtor and creditor on January 1, 19C.
3. Compute the new effective rate of interest (round to the nearest percent; then use straight-line interpolation to compute approximate interest rate to two decimal places).
4. Give all entries for both the debtor and the creditor on the date of restructure, January 1, 19C. If no entry is required, explain why. Use the approximate interpolated interest rate computed in 3 above and then round to the nearest dollar.
5. Give all entries for both the debtor and the creditor on two interest dates, December 31, 19C, and 19D.

Problem 17–16

On January 1, 19F, Day Corporation owed a $65,000 note payable to Cox Corporation that required the payment of 10% interest on each December 31; the note was due on December 31, 19F. Because of continuing serious financial difficulties, Day informed Cox that default (and discontinuance of the business) was probable unless some concessions on terms could be negotiated. Day has paid interest through December 31, 19E. Therefore, on January 1, 19F, Cox agreed to the following restructure of the debt:

a. Day will transfer immediately $15,000 of its accounts receivable to the creditor in settlement of $14,000 of the debt. The accounts of Day reflected $1,000 in the allowance for doubtful accounts that related to these receivables; thus, the current net realizable value of the receivables was reasonably stated at $14,000.
b. Day will transfer immediately its long-term investment in 800 shares of common stock (par $10) of Tye Corporation in partial settlement of the debt. Day accounts reflected a carrying value of $30,000 for the Tye stock, and its current market value was $32,000.
c. Day will pay $10,000 cash at the end of five years from January 1, 19F (date of restructure) to settle the remaining $19,000 of the principal. That is, the restructured maturity date is December 31, 19J.
d. Day will pay $5,000 total interest over the five-year period from January 1, 19F (i.e., $1,000 cash interest per year).

Required:
1. Give any required entry of the debtor and the creditor on date of restructure, January 1, 19F. Explain how you made the decision as to *(a)* whether entries are required and *(b)* the basis for the "values" used. How would other "agreed values" produce a biased measure of restructure gain or loss?
2. Give the required entries for the debtor and the creditor on the next interest date, December 31, 19F, and on the restructured maturity date, December 31, 19J.

SUPPLEMENT 17–A: PROBLEMS 17–17 to 17–18

Problem 17–17

A serial issue of $700,000 of bonds dated April 1, 19A, was sold on that date for $707,600. The interest rate is 8%, payable semiannually on March 31 and September 30. Scheduled maturities are as follows:

Serial	Date Due	Amount
B	March 31, 19B	$100,000
C	March 31, 19C	200,000
D	March 31, 19D	200,000
E	March 31, 19E	200,000

Required:
1. Prepare an amortization schedule for the issuer; use straight-line amortization and dollar-period allocation.
2. Give all entries for the issuer relating to the bonds including reversing entries through March 31, 19B. The issuing company adjusts and closes its books each December 31. Use straight-line amortization.

Problem 17–18

On January 1, 19x1, Tobin Corporation sold serial bonds (dated January 1, 19x1) due as follows: serial A, $10,000, December 31, 19x5; serial B, $15,000, December 31, 19x6; and serial C, $25,000, December 31, 19x7. The bonds carried a 3% coupon (stated) interest rate per semiannual period (each June 30 and December 31) and were sold to yield 4% interest per semiannual period.

Required (round to nearest dollar):
1. Compute the selling price of the bond issue.
2. Prepare an amortization schedule for Tobin for the life of the bond issue assuming the interest method is used.
3. Give Tobin's entry to record retirement of half of serial C at 99½ on June 30, 19x7. Assume the accounting period ends December 31.

SUPPLEMENT 17–C: PROBLEM 17–19

Problem 17–19

Bonds of $2,000,000 maturity value, originally sold at par, 10% stated interest rate payable at each year-end, with six remaining years to maturity, are the subject of proposed debt restructure agreements.

Required (round to the nearest dollar):
Calculate the new rate of interest by the iterative method illustrated in Exhibit 17–16 under each of the following independent proposed restructuring agreements:

1. The same amount of principal is payable at maturity, but annual interest payments are to be reduced to $140,000.
2. The same amount of interest is to be paid annually but the principal payment at maturity is to be $1,320,000.
3. Annual interest payments are to be reduced to $180,000 and the principal payment at maturity is to be $1,850,000.

SUPPLEMENTS 17–A, 17–B, and 17–C: PROBLEM 17–20

Problem 17–20

XYZ Company is indebted on a serial bond issue, sold at par, which calls for payment of annual interest at 10% on the debt outstanding at each year-end. Three serials of $300,000 each remain to be paid and one serial is at each of the next three year-ends. In other words, at the next year-end, $300,000 of principal and $90,000 of interest is payable; after another year, another $300,000 of principal and $60,000 of interest is payable; and at the end of the last year, $300,000 of principal and $30,000 of interest is payable.

Required (round to the nearest dollar):

CASE A—If, under a restructuring agreement, each principal amount is to be reduced to $250,000 and the interest is to be paid at 10% on the restructured amount of the principal, bondholders would sustain both an economic loss and an accounting loss to be reported under provisions of FASB *Statement No. 15.* The market rate of interest at the time of the restructuring agreement is 8%.

1. What amount of *economic* loss will the bondholders sustain?
2. What aggregate amount of *accounting* loss would bondholders report?

CASE B—Suppose the restructuring agreement reduces the principal of each serial by 2% and reduces the annual interest per serial to $21,000.

1. Determine the new, reduced rate of interest using the iterative method illustrated in Exhibit 17–16.
2. What aggregate amount of *accounting* loss would the bondholders report?

18

Accounting for Pensions by the Employer

PENSION PLANS sponsored by private employers in the United States are large and important. The assets controlled by pension plans now account for a staggering dollar amount; between 1950 and 1980, the number of persons covered by private pension and deferred profit-sharing plans rose from fewer than 10 million to more than 35.5 million.[1] Total assets of private, noninsured pension plans amounted to more than $236 billion in 1980 (up from $33 billion in 1960).[2] Of the 600 companies included in the annual survey by *Accounting Trends & Techniques, 1980,* 536 disclosed pension expense.[3] For example, IBM's cost of its retirement plans for 1980 was $1.109 billion, 4.8 percent of total expenses and 31.1 percent of net income.[4] This chapter focuses on accounting for the costs incurred by companies for the pension plans covering their employees. The chapter is subdivided as follows:

Part A—Accounting for Pensions—Fundamentals
Part B—Accounting for Pensions—Additional Issues
Supplement 18–A—Descriptions of Acceptable Actuarial Cost Methods under *APB Opinion 8*

Part A: Accounting for Pensions—Fundamentals

PENSION PLAN FUNDAMENTALS

The primary purpose of pension plans is to provide retirement income to employees. Companies often establish **defined-benefit** plans which state the amount of benefits to be received by employees after retirement. Often the benefit is a specified amount per month, based on years of credited service. Other types of plans do not define specific benefits; rather, they specify that the retired employees will receive whatever benefits can be paid from the pension fund accumulation and its earnings. In this latter type of plan, referred to as **defined-contribution** plans, the amount of the pension benefits is uncertain; only the

---

[1] *Social Security Bulletin,* February 1981 (Washington, D.C.: U.S. Social Security Administration), p. 2.

[2] *SEC Monthly Statistical Review,* October 1980 (Washington, D.C.: U.S. Securities and Exchange Commission), p. 8.

[3] AICPA, *Accounting Trends & Techniques, 1980* (New York, 1980), p. 267.

[4] *Annual Report, 1980,* International Business Machines Corporation, pp. 21, 26.

contributions to the pension fund are specified for certain.

Most pension plans are established by the employer through a formal retirement plan that meets Internal Revenue Code qualifications so that:

1. Contributions paid by the employer into the pension plan are deductible for income tax purposes when paid.
2. Earnings of the pension fund are not subject to income tax.
3. Employer contributions on behalf of employees are not taxable to employees when the contributions are made.
4. Retirement benefits are taxable to retirees; this defers the tax, which is favorable to employees because in retirement they are usually in lower income tax brackets than when they were employed.

Accounting for pensions involves two separate considerations: (1) accounting for the employer whose employees are covered by a pension plan, and (2) accounting for the funding agency (i.e., trustee). Accounting for the employer involves the recognition of pension expense and the payment of cash into a pension fund administered by the funding agency, which is the topic of this chapter.

In contrast, accounting for the funding agency involves investment of the pension fund assets and making the required pension payments to retirees. FASB, *Statement of Financial Accounting Standards No. 35,* "Accounting and Reporting by Defined Benefit Plans," March 1980, addresses financial reporting by "pension plans" as separate entities. It is not concerned with issues relating to disclosures in the financial statements of employers about the plans they initiate (which is the topic of this chapter). Reporting by pension plans *per se* is beyond the scope of this book.

The accounting and reporting approaches presented in this chapter are based primarily on *APB Opinion No. 8,* "Accounting for the Cost of Pension Plans," interpretations of that *Opinion,* and FASB, *Statement of Financial Accounting Standards No. 36,* "Disclosure of Pension Information," May 1980. The FASB has had the topic of pension accounting (along with other aspects of employee benefits) under consideration for some time, but at the publication date of this book, no new pronouncement materially affects accounting for pension plans beyond the provisions of the aforementioned pronouncements.

Federal legislation, entitled The Employee Retirement Income Security Act of 1974 (ERISA, and also known as the Pension Reform Act of 1974), has had substantial impact on the **administration** of pension plans. Also, it has affected some phases of accounting for pension plans. For example, prior to ERISA, employers with **defined benefit plans** had the option of funding or not funding (i.e., setting aside cash into a pension fund) certain pension costs. ERISA had the effect of legally requiring companies to fund a higher proportion of their total pension costs than previously.

The discussions and illustrations in this chapter focus on accounting, funding, and reporting for defined benefit pension plans by the employer. This topic involves four primary phases as follows:

1. Estimating the pension benefits that will be paid to each employee after retirement.
2. Estimating the amount of the employer's cash contributions to the pension fund, which will be used to pay the retirement benefits to retired employees, and allocating the employer's cash contributions to employee service periods prior to their retirement.
3. Allocating the employer's pension expense, in a rational and systematic manner, to the accounting periods during which the employee "earns" the pension benefits, which will be paid later.
4. Monitoring and adjusting cash contributions and pension expense for changes in expectations in respect to the pension plan and the factors which affect it, such as earnings on the pension fund, changes in pension benefits, and revisions of mortality rates.

PENSION ACCOUNTING DEFINITIONS

1. **Actuarial factors**—Actuarial factors are the probabilistic data used to determine the amounts of pension funding and pension cost. Actuarial determinations and estimates are an integral part of accounting for pension costs because pension costs are inherently future oriented; therefore, measures of pension costs are uncertain. Pension related events with uncertain outcomes, which pension actuaries must estimate, include retirement age, mortality (the life expectancies of em-

ployees both before and after retirement), employee turnover, interest rates and gains and losses on pension plan investments, administrative requirements, future salary levels, pension benefits, and vesting provisions (defined below).

2. **Funding**—Funding refers to the employer's cash contributions into a pension fund for the payment of pension benefits to retired employees. Most pension plans are **noncontributory,** which means that the employer provides **all** of the funding. Usually, an independent funding agency such as an insurance company administers the funding plan.[5] Under such an arrangement, the employer disburses cash to the funding agency. The funding agency invests the funds in securities and other assets; receives revenue from pension plan investments and, upon retirement of employees, disburses cash (i.e., pension benefits) to retirees; and deducts an administrative fee. Funding may be handled in three ways:
   a. Cash is set aside by the company into a pension fund administered internally by the company.
   b. Cash is paid to an independent pension funding agency which administers the plan.
   c. Cash is paid to an insurance company to purchase retirement annuities for the retirees. The insurance company assumes full responsibility for paying the defined benefits to the retirees.
3. **Vesting**—Vesting (or **vested benefits**) refers to an employee's right to receive a pension benefit even though that person does not remain an employee of the company until retirement.
4. **Normal pension cost**—Normal pension cost is the annual pension cost assigned each year subsequent to the inception of a pension plan for the pension credits earned during the current period by all employees covered by the pension plan. Normal pension cost is measured each year as the actuarially determined **present value** of providing future benefits to employees as specified by the pension plan. The annual amount is recorded as pension expense and is reported on the current income statement; therefore, a more descriptive title would be normal pension **expense.** Other pension costs are designated as past service costs, prior service costs, and actuarial gains and losses.
5. **Past service cost**—Past service cost is the pension cost for employee services rendered prior to inception of a pension plan but specified by the plan as qualifying for pension benefits. Past service cost is measured as the actuarially determined present value of providing those retirement benefits. Thus, past service cost is a one-time "catch-up" cost, which is in addition to normal pension cost, and it must be expensed (amortized) over the current and future periods.[6]
6. **Prior service cost**—Prior service cost is pension cost assigned, under the actuarial method in use, to years **prior to the date of a particular actuarial revaluation;** it arises primarily from *(a)* **amendments** to the pension plan subsequent to initiation date of the plan and *(b)* **actuarial revaluations** of the plan. Thus, prior service cost usually occurs frequently. At initiation of a pension plan, **past** service cost is measured (see definition above); subsequent to the initiation of a pension plan, actuarial revaluations of the plan and its operation must be made from time to time by an actuary because conditions change. Such acturial revaluations often necessitate a change in certain pension costs and cash funding requirements. Because prior service cost relates to years prior to the date of the actuarial revaluation or plan amendment, it is a "catch-up cost;" therefore, **conceptually** it is similar to past service cost except that past service cost is caused by the inception of the pension plan, whereas prior service cost is the result of an actuarial revaluation or plan amendment. An actuarial revaluation usually results in a change in the amounts of normal service cost of future periods as well.[7]
7. **Actuarial gains and losses**—Actuarial gains and

[5] An FASB *Discussion Memorandum,* "Employer's Accounting for Pensions and Other Postemployment Benefits" (Stamford, Conn., February 1981), p. 105, refers to the independent organization that administers the pension plan as the **funding agency.**

[6] In some instances past service cost also may arise after the inception of a pension plan. For example, it is common for a plan to specify that new employees become eligible under the pension plan only after, say, three years of service, and when they become eligible, they get credit for the prior three years—a past service cost.

[7] Pension plan terminology varies considerably among actuaries, companies, accountants, and statutory provisions (e.g., ERISA). For example, prior service cost often is used in a general sense to refer to all costs prior to an actuarial revaluation; it also is used in a more specific sense. For instructional purposes, in this chapter it is used in a specific sense as defined above and in Part B under the heading, Amortization of Prior Service Cost.

losses are the effects on actuarially calculated pension costs (i.e., normal, past, and prior service costs) of *(a)* deviations **between** actual prior experience and the actuarial assumptions used or *(b)* changes in actuarial assumptions as to future events. Actuarial gains and losses are measured each year, and their amounts must be expensed (i.e., amortized) over the current and future periods (discussed in Part B). Actuarial gains and losses are not the same as normal, past, or prior service costs.

For instructional purposes, in this chapter we keep the four elements of pension expense (i.e., normal service cost, past service cost, prior service cost, and actuarial gains and losses) separate. In actual practice, these distinctions often are not so clear-cut, depending upon the **actuarial cost method** used (discussed in Supplement 18–A). The separate amounts can be aggregated to determine total pension expense for the period.

CONCEPTS WHICH UNDERLIE PENSION ACCOUNTING

A pension plan often defines the pension **benefit** which the plan extends to each employee upon retirement; the amount of the benefit usually is determined by a formula related to such factors as length of service, earnings, and other actuarial factors. The plan also specifies how the employer company intends to provide sufficient funds, during the employment period, to meet the specified benefits. Typically, each year of the employment period, the employer pays cash into a pension fund which usually is administered by an outside funding agency. The funding agency has the responsibility to *(a)* invest the funds in accordance with a specific agreement and *(b)* upon retirement of the employee, to disburse the funds in accordance with the periodic benefits specified in the pension plan. Because the pension fund will earn a rate of return on the assets of the fund, the employer will disburse less cash than is paid out ultimately to the retirees. Over the life of a company, its total **pension expense** is measured as the **total cash** disbursed by the company into the pension fund.

Fundamentally, accounting for a pension plan by the **employer** (not the funding agency) involves two distinct phases during the employment period:

1. Determination of the amount of pension **expense** which must be recorded each year and reported on the current income statement.
2. Determination of the amount of **cash** that will be paid into the pension fund each year.

These two amounts may be the same in a given year (i.e., when the expense amount is fully funded during the year), or different (i.e., when the expense amount is either underfunded or overfunded during the year).

These two phases require the application of future value and present value concepts and accrual accounting. To illustrate application of these basic concepts in accounting by the employer for pension costs during the employment period, a hypothetical and highly simplified situation is presented in Exhibit 18–1. Panel A outlines the hypothetical situation; Panel B illustrates computation of the periodic cash funding and pension expense amounts (normal pension expense, as defined above, is assumed); and Panel C illustrates the basic entries for *(a)* the employer during the employment period and *(b)* the funding agency during the employment and retirement periods.

Panel B of Exhibit 18–1 shows a two-step future value/present value computation needed to determine (1) the pension fund amount which will be required at retirement date, based on a defined pension benefit of $10,000 at each year-end for 12 years of retirement; and (2) the annual cash payment that must be made into the pension fund by the employer over the assumed 15-year employment period to provide that amount. Because the pension expense is assumed in the illustration to be fully funded each year, the amounts for *(a)* pension expense and *(b)* cash funding are the same.

Exhibit 18–2 extends the hypothetical pension situation of Happy Hart Company. In Exhibit 18–1, the focus was on a single employee, J. Doe. Exhibit 18–2 relates to the overall company for several years; it presents three panels: A, a description of Happy Hart's hypothetical pension situation; B, a diagram of the pension events and costs defined earlier under the heading Pension Accounting Definitions; and C, the basic entry of the employer for pension expense and funding. The diagram depicts normal pension cost, past service cost, prior service cost, and actuarial gains and losses in terms of the periods to which they relate. The primary purpose of the diagram is to illustrate the technical definitions of these terms.

EXHIBIT 18–1: Pension Fund Accumulation and Disbursement (Hypothetical)

Panel A—Hypothetical Situation:

Happy Hart Company adopted a pension plan on January 1, 19C, which covered all employees. Under the plan, J. Doe, an employee since January 1, 19C, is to receive pension benefits. The plan specifies that at the end of 15 years, Doe will retire; upon retirement Doe will receive retirement benefits of $10,000, at each year-end, for a period of 12 years.

Assume the fund will earn a net 8 percent interest rate during the accumulation (funding) period, and 9 percent during the disbursement (retirement) period.

Question: For normal pension cost, and assuming full funding (i.e., cash payments into a pension fund) each year by Happy Hart Company, how much must be deposited with the funding agency for each of the 15 years of employment by J. Doe?

Panel B—Response Diagrammed and Computed for One Employee, J. Doe:

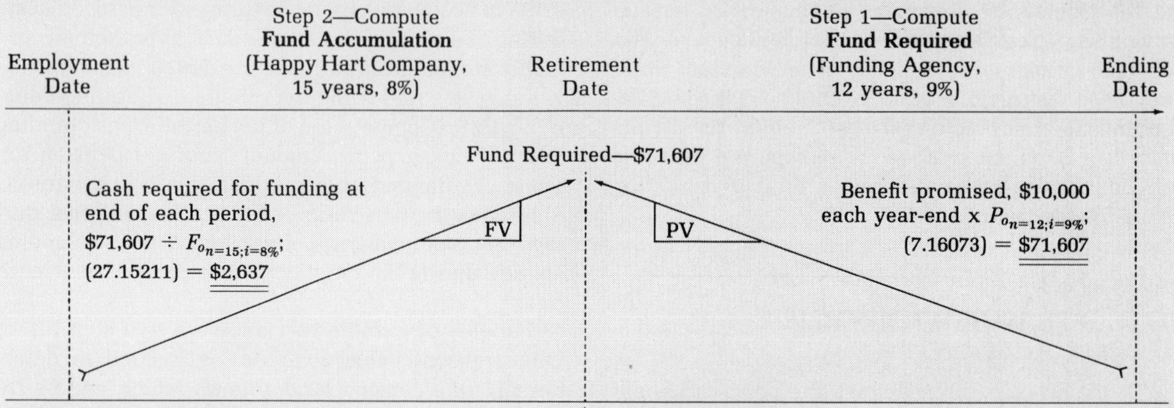

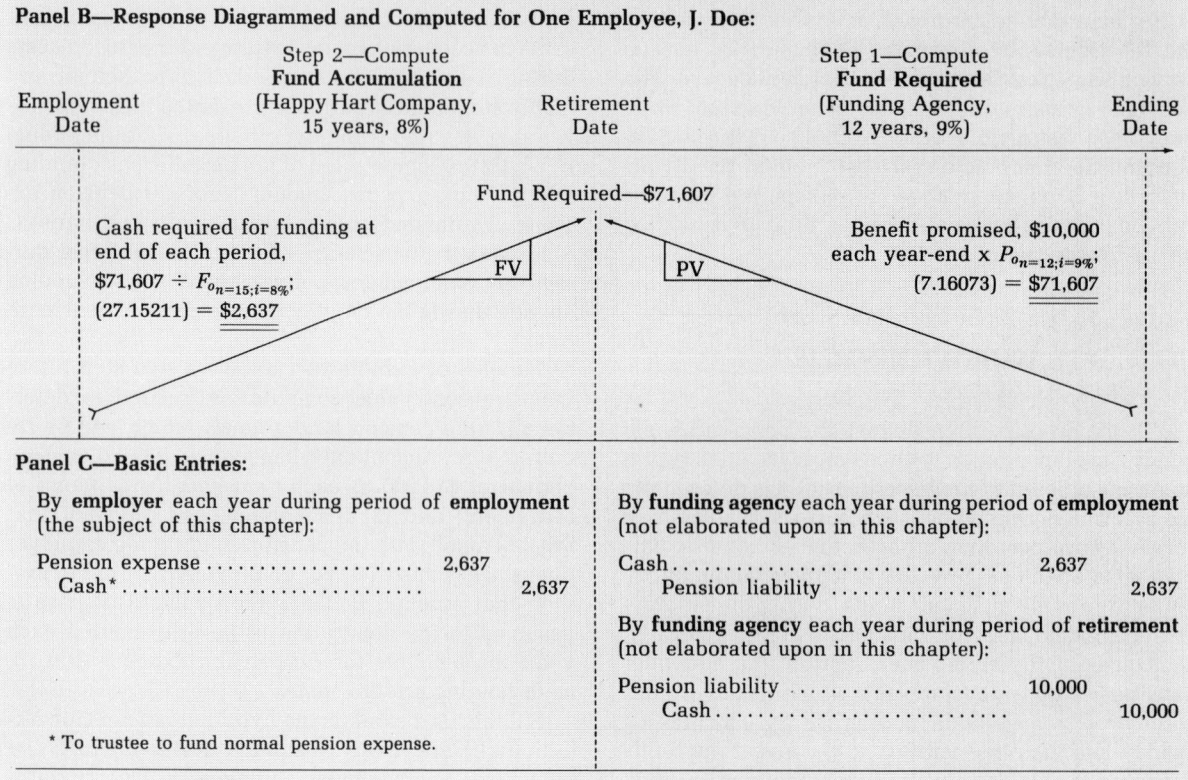

Panel C—Basic Entries:

By **employer** each year during period of **employment** (the subject of this chapter):

Pension expense	2,637	
Cash*		2,637

By **funding agency** each year during period of **employment** (not elaborated upon in this chapter):

Cash	2,637	
Pension liability		2,637

By **funding agency** each year during period of **retirement** (not elaborated upon in this chapter):

Pension liability	10,000	
Cash		10,000

* To trustee to fund normal pension expense.

Specifically, **normal pension cost** is measured and recorded currently as incurred (as opposed to being amortized). In contrast, **past service cost** relates to 19A and 19B because the pension plan was initiated on January 1, 19C, and covered employee service during 19A and 19B. Because past service cost is a one-time cost, it is measured at the plan initiation date, then amortized as expense over the current and future periods benefited by adoption of the plan. **Prior service cost,** in the example, relates to 19A–19I because of the plan amendment on January 1, 19J, which increased the pension benefits of covered employees for all employee services during 19A–19I. This example illustrates that prior service cost also can include some past service cost. This occurs in the illustration because the increase in pension benefits from the plan amendment in 19J applied to all prior service, including "past service" during 19A–19B.

Exhibit 18–2 focuses on pension plan **definitions;** it does not address the **accounting** problem of allocating normal service cost, past service cost, prior ser-

EXHIBIT 18–2: Diagram of Pension Events and Costs

Panel A—Hypothetical Situation:

Happy Hart Company was organized on January 1, 19A, and immediately employed 10 people. On January 1, 19C, the company initiated a noncontributory pension plan (50 employees at that time). The plan provided the following:

1. Pension credit for all employee service performed for the company during 19A and 19B (past pension credit).
2. Vesting for each employee is on the first day of the second year of employment.
3. Annual funding of normal pension credits as earned (required by ERISA).
4. Funding of past service cost over a 15-year period, starting at the end of 19C.
5. Funding agency—Third Municipal Bank.
6. Actuary—True-Risk Actuary Associates. The actuary reviews the pension plan at each year-end and recommends the pension cost revaluations and funding requirements.
7. The actuarial revaluations at the ends of 19C–19I indicated no actuarial gains or losses.
8. On January 1, 19J, the pension plan was amended to increase the amount of the monthly pension benefit for all employees upon retirement. This caused a prior period pension cost.
9. Near the end of 19K, the funding agency reported a significant and unexpected loss on the sale of some pension plan investments. The actuary revaluated the actuarial assumptions and reported an actuarial loss on December 31, 19K.

Panel B—Diagram of Pension Events and Costs (assuming no changes after initiation):

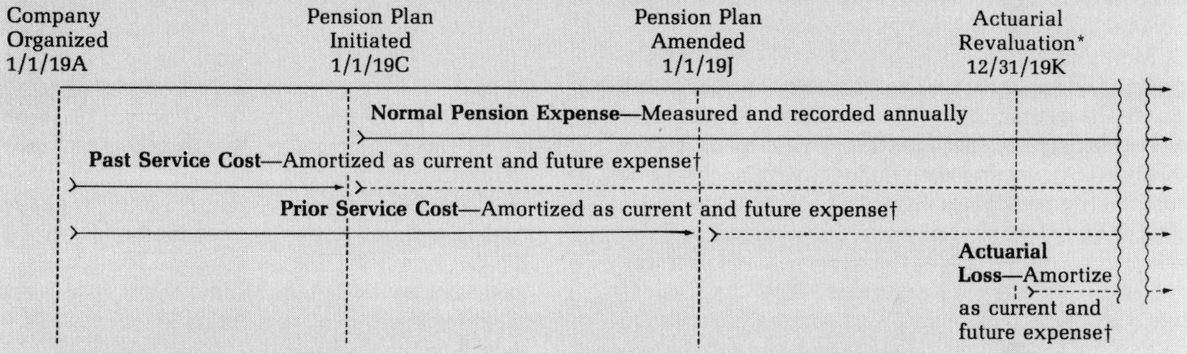

* Actuarial revaluation is at each year-end—the hypothetical situation assumes no actuarial gain or loss until 19K.
† Allocation period varies as discussed later for each of these three costs.
Note: This diagram assumes each of the four costs are identified separately (see later section, Actuarial Cost Methods).

Panel C—Employer's Basic Accounting Entry Each Year for Pensions:

Pension expense‡	xx,xxx	
Cash§		xx,xxx

‡ Includes (1) normal pension expense, (2) amortized past service cost, (3) amortized prior service cost, and (4) amortized actuarial gains (losses).
§ Funding—this may be more or less than pension expense, in which case a deferred charge or liability, respectively is recorded as discussed later.

vice cost, and actuarial gains and losses to **expense.** Because actuaries generally provide the amounts of pension cost, we assume throughout this chapter that those amounts are given. However, the **timing of the recognition of pension expense** (i.e., allocation of pension cost to future periods as expense) remains one of the critical accounting issues for pensions. Accordingly, most of this chapter is devoted to this allocation problem.

APPLICATION OF THE MATCHING PRINCIPLE TO PENSIONS

APB Opinion 8 (par. 11) specifies that pension expense should be determined on the **accrual basis.** Therefore, the amount of periodic pension expense is governed by the **matching principle.** For **normal** pension cost (i.e., expense), the matching principle is applied by recording the actuarially determined present value of future pension benefits to be paid to employees for their services rendered during the current period. Because the actuary provides this amount, it presents no particular accounting problem.

Past service cost, prior service cost, and actuarial gains and losses present a theoretical problem because these elements of pension expense are "catch-up" costs of the **past.** Therefore, in one view, it may appear logical for past and prior service cost to be debited directly to retained earnings rather than matched against revenue on the income statements of the current and future periods. This treatment is **not** permitted by GAAP, however, because *(a)* employees on whom past service benefits are bestowed are considered to be more efficient in the future as a result of the longer experience, *(b)* it is difficult to measure the past services and to relate them to past revenues, and *(c)* accountants are reluctant to debit any form of expense (or credit any form of revenue) directly to retained earnings.[8]

Moreover, the practice of making direct debits to retained earnings for past service pension cost would ignore the current and future benefit to the employer of the decision to institute the pension plan. Under this line of reasoning, the employer with past service cost had no pension expense to recognize before inception of the plan, and it would be illogical to debit retained earnings for (past service) pension cost that did not exist in those prior years.[9] Therefore, under this view past (and also prior) service cost should be debited to expense in the current and future periods that will be affected by the decision to institute the plan. *APB Opinion 8* adopted this view, as outlined in the next section (see item 3).

Another theoretical problem in application of the matching principle occurs when the period over which past and prior service costs are funded differs from the period over which they are expensed (i.e., "amortized"). This unique problem involves the recognition of interest on any difference between expense and funding amounts; it is discussed and illustrated in Part B.

APB OPINION 8 AND PENSION ACCOUNTING

Issuance of *APB Opinion No. 8,* "Accounting for the Cost of Pension Plans," in 1966, marked the first significant effort by the accounting profession to standardize pension plan accounting. The *Opinion* recognized different perceptions of the computation of pension costs as valid; thus, while it specified certain standards, it did not aim for total uniformity. Two companies having almost identical pension plans, adopted at the same time, can be in compliance with the *Opinion* and yet have different patterns of reported pension expense.

The principal provisions of the *Opinion* are as follows:

1. Pension costs (including related administrative expense) should be accounted for on the **accrual basis.**
2. Annual pension costs recorded should be based on an accounting method that uses an acceptable **actuarial cost method** and results in a pension cost that falls between a determinable maximum and minimum. Actuarial cost methods are discussed briefly in the next section (they are discussed in more detail in Supplement 18–A), and maximum and minimum limits are discussed in Part B of the chapter.
3. Past service costs and prior service costs should be recognized over **current and future periods** as affected by the related funding plan. They do not constitute corrections of prior period earnings; hence, they are **not** debited directly to retained earnings.
4. Actuarial gains and losses (except for single occurrences as discussed later) should be allocated over **current and future periods** in a manner similar to changes in accounting estimates.
5. The amount of pension expense recognized in a period is **not** necessarily the amount of cash paid to the funding agency. Funding is a **financing** consideration, and expensing is an **accounting** consideration. However, funding of a plan may affect the periodic pension expense.
6. Certain **disclosures** in the body of financial statements and in the notes are required (see Part B).

[8] Prior period adjustments are limited to (1) error corrections and (2) realizations of income tax benefits of preacquisition operating loss carryforwards of purchased subsidiaries (FASB, *Statement of Financial Accounting Standards No. 16,* "Prior Period Adjustments" [Stamford, Conn., June 1977], par. 11, discussed in Chapter 15).

[9] The reasoning and effect are the same for prior service cost; the only difference is that the event that causes prior service cost is a revaluation or amendment of the plan, whereas the event that causes past service cost is inception of the plan.

ACTUARIAL COST METHODS

Actuarial cost methods were developed by actuaries primarily as **funding** techniques, that is, as a way to compute the amounts needed for the periodic **cash** funding payments. Because determination of the cash funding requirements requires estimating the underlying pension costs, the actuarial cost methods also are useful in determining **pension costs for accounting purposes.** *APB Opinion 8* (par. 24) and Supplement 18–A identified five actuarial cost methods as acceptable, viz:

1. Accrued benefit (i.e., unit credit) method.
2. Entry age normal method.
3. Attained age normal method.
4. Aggregate method.
5. Individual level premium method.

APB Opinion 8 also cites two methods as unacceptable for accounting purposes because they are cash-basis methods and defer recognition of pension expense until the employee retires. One method, **terminal funding,** defers all funding and expensing until the employee retires. Another method, referred to as **pay as you go,** disburses cash and recognizes expense as retirement benefits are paid. The deficiency of these methods is that they do not **accrue** pension expense during the period of employment; hence, they violate the **matching principle.**

Although the various acceptable actuarial methods use present value concepts and rely on actuarial assumptions, they differ in a number of ways, including: *(a)* whether they include past service cost in the determination of normal pension cost or determine the two separately, *(b)* how they relate actuarial gains and losses to pension cost, and *(c)* how they identify pension cost with particular periods of employee service. In short, the various acceptable actuarial cost methods result in different configurations of pension expense over time. These differences may be likened to the differences in depreciation expense that result from use of the different generally accepted depreciation methods. Exhibit 18–3 presents graphs of annual cost patterns under the five acceptable methods. Supplement 18–A describes these five actuarial cost methods in more detail.

EXHIBIT 18–3: Annual Cost Patterns of Pension Cost under Acceptable Actuarial Cost Methods

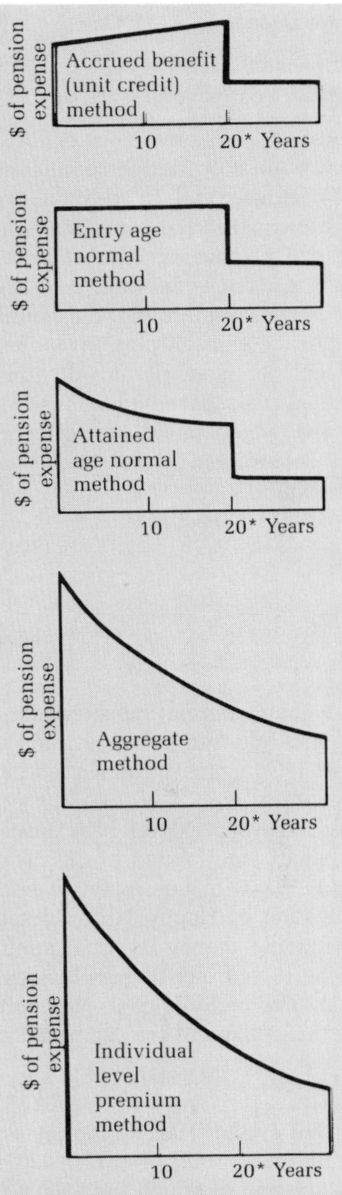

* Maturity date of the pension plan. A population of employees and former employees receiving pension benefit is "mature" when their age distribution is stable and is expected to be duplicated year after year through new employees, deaths, and withdrawals. See FASB, *Discussion Memorandum,* "Employer's Accounting for Pensions and Other Postemployment Benefits" (Stamford, Conn., February 1981), p. 106.

Source: W. A. Dreher, "Alternatives Available under *APB Opinion No. 8:* An Actuary's View," *Journal of Accountancy,* September 1967, p. 41.

PENSION ACCOUNTING ILLUSTRATED

To illustrate accounting for pension costs, refer to Exhibit 18–2 and assume the following amounts were provided for Happy Hart Company by True-Risk Actuaries at the end of the first year of the pension plan, December 31, 19C:

1. Normal pension expense for 19C, $40,000.
2. Past service cost at January 1, 19C, $350,000.

In accordance with the provisions of ERISA, Happy Hart Company will fully fund the annual **normal pension cost** at each year end. In addition, the company has decided to expense (i.e., amortize) and fund the present value of the **past service cost** of $350,000 over a 15-year period at each year-end. True-Risk Actuary Associates, in consultation with the funding agency, estimated that the pension plan investments should earn 8 percent per year, net of all administrative fees and related costs. Based upon these data, Happy Hart Company would make the following entries:

December 31, 19C:

1. Pension expense (normal pension cost)	40,000	
Cash		40,000
2. Pension expense (past service cost)	40,890	
Cash		40,890

In entry 1 above, normal pension cost of $40,000 is expensed and fully funded in 19C and will be reported on the 19C income statement as part of total pension expense.

In contrast, the $350,000 of past service cost is partially expensed and funded in 19C. The past service cost of $350,000 in this example constitutes a funding obligation of Happy Hart Company to be paid to the funding agency in equal annual installments over the 15-year period plus interest at 8 percent per year. The periodic cash payments at each year-end on this obligation are computed as follows:

$$\$350{,}000 \div P_{o_{n=15;\ i=8\%}} \text{ (8.55948, Table 5–4)} = \underline{\underline{\$40{,}890}}$$

Observe that Happy Hart Company will pay to the funding agency a total of $613,350 (i.e., $40,890 per year × 15 years) of which the $350,000 (present value) will be principal and $263,350 (i.e., $613,350 − $350,000) will be interest to compensate the funding agency for earnings on the pension fund that would have been earned had the full $350,000 been funded at the start. Should Happy Hart Company decide to fund the full $350,000 at January 1, 19C, it would pay the funding agency only the principal of $350,000.

Now, we address the question of the amount that should be recorded as pension expense for **past service cost** in the second entry. The amount that should be expensed may be the same as the funding amount (i.e., $40,890); however, the expense and funding amounts may differ. *APB Opinion 8* (par. 17) specifically prohibits **expensing** of the total amount of all of the past service cost in the first period only, because it would violate the **matching principle.**[10] Instead, the *Opinion* specifies that the past service cost must be **amortized** as expense over a future period of not less than 10 years nor more than 40 years. In contrast to expensing, for **funding** ERISA permits a 40-year period for plans which were initiated on or before January 1, 1974. For plans initiated after that date, the maximum funding period is 30 years. Happy Hart Company elected both to fund and amortize the past service cost over the 15-year period.

For Happy Hart Company the past service cost of $350,000 represents the January 1, 19C, **present value** of an ordinary annuity of 15 annual rents (because it is being amortized annually over 15 years) of $40,890 each, at 8 percent per year. Therefore, the amount of each rent constitutes the amount of pension expense for each year 19C–19Q for past service cost. Note that the total amount of past service pension expense recognized will be $613,350 (i.e., $40,890 × 15), rather than $350,000, because of the inclusion of interest. The interest arises from the fact that past service cost was not fully funded at the plan's inception, at which time the plan granted to employees future benefits with a present value of $350,000.

In entry 2 above, the amount of the credit to Cash is the same as the debit to Pension Expense because the past service cost is amortized and funded over the same period (i.e., 15 years).[11] The interest rate used to compute funding amounts also is used to compute the periodic expense amounts because *APB Opinion 8* directly ties the amortization and funding together. In respect to the pension expense in entry 2 above, it is difficult to understand what is being

[10] The *Opinion* sets maximum and minimum limits on the amount of pension expense (including normal, past, and prior service cost) to recognize in any one year; the maximum limit precludes immediate expensing of all of the past service cost at inception of the plan, even if past service cost is fully funded at inception (a rare occurrence). Part B discusses maximum and minimum limits.

[11] Part B considers cases in which the expense amortization period and cash funding period for past service cost are different.

amortized in this entry because Happy Hart Company recorded no asset (nor the offsetting liability) for past service cost. Therefore, "amortization" applies to an **unrecorded** deferred charge; unfortunately, use of the term **amortization** potentially is misleading in this context.

Part B: Accounting for Pensions—Additional Issues

Part B of this chapter considers six additional issues in accounting for pensions, as follows:

1. Effect of funding on pension expense.
2. Amortization of past service cost.
   a. Funding period longer than amortization period.
   b. Funding period shorter than amortization period.
3. Amortization of prior service cost.
4. Amortization of actuarial gains and losses.
5. Vested benefits.
6. Minimum and maximum limits on annual pension expense.
7. Pension plan disclosures by:
   a. Employer
   b. Funding agency (pension fund).

EFFECT OF FUNDING ON PENSION EXPENSE

In Part A, funding was defined as paying cash into a pension fund from which future pension benefits will be paid to retired employees. Also, Part A explained that pension costs must be accounted for on the **accrual basis.** The funding and amortization amount is the same when the funding period and the amortization period are the same (as illustrated in Part A). This section considers those situations in which the funding and amortization periods are different; this causes the pension funding and expense amounts to differ.

Under *APB Opinion 8,* the amount of periodic pension expense is affected by the amount of periodic pension funding. When past or prior service costs exist, their amounts usually are significant, and often they are funded over a lengthy period. As a result, companies sometimes amortize past (and prior) service cost over different periods than their funding periods. When such a difference occurs, an **interest** equivalent must be computed on the amount of the **cumulative difference** between the debit to Pension Expense and the credit to Cash. If the funding period is longer than the amortization period (i.e., funding is slower), the interest equivalent on the cumulative difference is added (i.e., debited) to Pension Expense and credited to a liability entitled, Liability—Pension Expense in Excess of Funding.[12] On the other hand, if the funding period is shorter than the amortization period (i.e., funding is faster), the interest equivalent on the cumulative difference is deducted (i.e., credited) to Pension Expense and debited to a deferred charge entitled, Deferred Charge—Funding in Excess of Pension Expense.[13] These two situations are illustrated, for past service cost, in the following section; two worksheets are illustrated, which facilitate the *(a)* discussions and *(b)* preparation of the related pension expense and funding entries.

AMORTIZATION OF PAST SERVICE COST

Funding Period Longer than Amortization Period

Exhibit 18–4 illustrates the accounting for **past service cost** when the funding period is longer than the related amortization period. Exhibit 18–4, Panel A, summarizes the hypothetical situation, Panel B presents the amortization and funding schedule, and Panel C gives the entries that would be made by Employer Company for selected years. For instructional convenience, in Exhibits 18–4 and 18–5 we make two simplifying assumptions, *(a)* the past service service cost and the related funding are not changed throughout the 15–year period, and *(b)* the minimum and maximum limits prescribed by *APB Opinion 8* are ignored temporarily. The minimum and maximum rule is discussed and illustrated in a subsequent section of this chapter.

The worksheet presented in Exhibit 18–4 includes two different **present value** schedules—one for amor-

[12] Rather than being reported as interest expense, this interest is included with, and reported as part of, pension expense.

[13] Ibid.

EXHIBIT 18–4: Scheduled Amortization of Past Service Cost and Related Funding—Funding Period Longer than Amortization Period

Panel A—Hypothetical Situation:

1. Employer Company adopted a pension plan on January 1, 1982; as of that date the actuary estimated the total present value of past service cost to be $350,000.
2. Management decided to amortize the past service cost over 13 years and to fund it over 15 years.
3. The funding agency estimated that the pension fund will earn a net return of 8 percent per year.
4. The actuary estimated normal pension expense for 1982 of $40,000, which is funded fully for the year.
5. No additional changes in past service cost or funding.

Panel B—Amortization and Funding Schedule Prepared by Employer Company Accountant (amortization and funding at year-end):

Year	Amortization of Past Service Cost—13 Years			Funding 15 Years	Balance Sheet—Liability	
	(a) 13-Year Cost Amortization Factor	*(b)* Addition for Interest	*(c)* Past Service Pension Expense Dr.*	*(d)* Cash Cr.	*(e)* Credit (Debit)	*(f)* Account Balance
1982	$ 44,283	—	$ 44,283	$ 40,890	$ 3,393	$ 3,393
1983	44,283	$ 271	44,554	40,890	3,664	7,057
1984	44,283	565	44,848	40,890	3,958	11,015
1985	44,283	881	45,164	40,890	4,274	15,289
1986	44,283	1,223	45,506	40,890	4,616	19,905
1987	44,283	1,592	45,875	40,890	4,985	24,890
1988	44,283	1,991	46,274	40,890	5,384	30,274
1989	44,283	2,422	46,705	40,890	5,815	36,089
1990	44,283	2,887	47,170	40,890	6,280	42,369
1991	44,283	3,390	47,673	40,890	6,783	49,152
1992	44,283	3,932	48,215	40,890	7,325	56,477
1993	44,283	4,518	48,801	40,890	7,911	64,388
1994	44,283	5,151	49,434	40,890	8,544	72,932
1995	—	5,835	5,835	40,890	(35,055)	37,877
1996	—	3,013†	3,013	40,890	(37,877)	—
	$575,679	$37,671	$613,350	$613,350	-0-	-0-

* Subject to maximum and minimum limits; see subsequent discussion of this topic.
† Rounded to come out even.
(a) Periodic amortization = $350,000 ÷ 7.90378 (Table 5–4, $P_{o_{n=13;\ i=8\%}}$) = $44,283 to column *(a)*.
(b) Eight percent of preceding balance of column *(f)*.
(c) Column *(a)* + *(b)*.
(d) Periodic funding = $350,000 ÷ 8.55948 (Table 5–4, $P_{o_{n=15;\ i=8\%}}$) = $40,890.
(e) Column *(c)* − *(d)*.
(f) Preceding balance in *(f)*, plus or minus column *(e)*.

Panel C—Scheduled Entries at Selected Year Ends:

	1984		1994		1996	
Pension expense (past service cost)	44,848		49,434		3,013	
Cash		40,890		40,890		40,890
Liability—pension expense in excess of funding		3,958		8,544	37,877	
Pension expense (normal)	40,000		xx,xxx		xx,xxx	
Cash		40,000		xx,xxx		xx,xxx

EXHIBIT 18–5: Scheduled Amortization of Past Service Cost and Related Funding—Funding Period Shorter than Amortization Period

Panel A—Hypothetical Situation:

1. Employer Company adopted a pension plan on January 1, 1982; as of that date the actuary estimated the total present value of past service cost to be $350,000.
2. Management decided to amortize the past service cost over 17 years and to fund it over 15 years.
3. The funding agency estimated that the pension fund will earn a net return of 8 percent per year.
4. The actuary estimated normal pension expense for 1982 of $40,000, which is funded fully for the year.
5. No additional changes in past service cost or funding.

Panel B—Amortization and Funding Schedule Prepared by Employer Company Accountant (amortization and funding at year-end):

	Amortization of Past Service Cost—17 Years			Funding 15 Years	Balance Sheet—Deferred Charge	
Year	*(a)* 17-Year Cost Amortization Factor	*(b)* Reduction for Interest	*(c)* Past Service Pension Expense Dr.*	*(d)* Cash Cr.	*(e)* Debit (Credit)	*(f)* Account Balance
1982	$ 38,370	—	$ 38,370	$ 40,890	$ 2,520	$ 2,520
1983	38,370	$ 202	38,168	40,890	2,722	5,242
1984	38,370	419	37,951	40,890	2,939	8,181
1985	38,370	654	37,716	40,890	3,174	11,355
1986	38,370	908	37,462	40,890	3,428	14,783
1987	38,370	1,183	37,187	40,890	3,703	18,486
1988	38,370	1,479	36,891	40,890	3,999	22,485
1989	38,370	1,799	36,571	40,890	4,319	26,804
1990	38,370	2,144	36,226	40,890	4,664	31,468
1991	38,370	2,517	35,853	40,890	5,037	36,505
1992	38,370	2,920	35,450	40,890	5,440	41,945
1993	38,370	3,356	35,014	40,890	5,876	47,821
1994	38,370	3,826	34,544	40,890	6,346	54,167
1995	38,370	4,333	34,037	40,890	6,853	61,020
1996	38,370	4,882	33,488	40,890	7,402	68,422
1997	38,370	5,474	32,896	—	(32,896)	35,526
1998	38,370	2,844†	35,526	—	(35,526)	—
	$652,290	$38,940	$613,350	$613,350	-0-	-0-

* Subject to maximum and minimum limits; see subsequent discussion of this topic.
† Rounded to come out even.
(a) Periodic amortization: $350,000 ÷ 9.12164 (Table 5–4, $P_{o_{n=17;\ i=8\%}}$) = $38,370.
(b) Eight percent of preceding balance of column *(f)*.
(c) Column *(a)* − *(b)*.
(d) Periodic funding = $350,000 ÷ 8.55948 (Table 5–4, $P_{o_{n=15;\ i=8\%}}$) = $40,890.
(e) Column *(d)* − *(c)*.
(f) Preceding balance in *(f)*, plus or minus column *(e)*.

Panel C—Scheduled Entries at Selected Year-Ends:

	1984		1996		1998	
Pension expense (past service cost)	37,951		33,488		35,526	
Deferred charge—pension funding in excess of expense	2,939		7,402			35,526
Cash		40,890		40,890		
Pension expense (normal)	40,000		xx,xxx		xx,xxx	
Cash		40,000		xx,xxx		xx,xxx

tization of past service cost (column [*a*]) and one for cash funding (column [*d*]). When these two PV schedules are different, as they are in Exhibit 18–4 (i.e., because pension expense amortization is 13 periods, and cash funding is 15 periods), they can be **reconciled** only by computing an **interest equivalent** each period on their cumulative difference (*APB Opinion 8,* par. 23) and by including that interest as a **part of pension expense** (rather than interest expense or interest revenue). In Exhibit 18–4, because the amortization of past service cost is faster (i.e., over a shorter period) than the cash funding, this timing difference creates a liability (column [*f*]). Interest accrues on this liability, and the "interest equivalent" must be **added** to the cost amortization factor (column [*a*]) to derive pension expense (i.e., column [*c*]). Thus, the interest equivalent amount is included in determining the balance in the liability account at the end of each period.

To illustrate the effects of different timing schedules for amortization and funding of past service cost and the resultant interest equivalent, we will trace the computations presented in Exhibit 18–4 for the year 1984 because that year demonstrates the full cycle (underscored for instructional purposes). First, the interest equivalent, at 8 percent, on the cumulative difference for 1984, reflected in column *(b),* is $565 (i.e., the preceding liability balance, $7,057 × 8%). Next, that interest amount ($565) is **added** to the computed 13-year amortization factor (column [*a*]) of $44,283 to give the past service pension expense for 1984 of $44,848 (column [*c*]). For 1984, the liability was increased by $3,958 (columns [*e*] and [*f*]) from $7,057 to $11,015. This increase of $3,958 is the sum of two amounts: (1) the $3,393 difference between the 13-year pension cost amortization factor ($44,283) and the 15-year funding amount ($40,890) and (2) the interest equivalent of $565. Thus, the interest equivalent is added to derive pension expense for the year and the liability balance at year-end. During 1995 and 1996, the full annual funding payments (column [*d*]) continue (after past service pension cost has been amortized completely); therefore, during these two periods (1) the cumulative amounts of pension expense (column [*c*]) and cash funding (column [*d*]) are brought into agreement and (2) the cumulative interest equivalent is paid fully. In Exhibit 18–4, Panel C, the entry at the end of 1996 includes a debit to the liability account (which reduces it to a zero balance), a credit to Cash for the last funding payment, and a debit to Pension Expense for the interest equivalent only (because the basic component of past service pension expense was amortized completely by the end of the 13th year (i.e., 1994). In summary, at the end of 1996 pension expense and cash payments must **total** to the same amount (i.e., $613,350).

Funding Period Shorter than Amortization Period

Exhibit 18–5 illustrates the accounting for **past service cost** when the funding period is shorter than the related amortization period, which causes the pension expense and funding amounts to be different. Exhibit 18–5, Panel A, summarizes the hypothetical situation (identical to Panel A of Exhibit 18–4, except for the 17-year amortization period versus 13 years in Exhibit 18–4), Panel B presents the amortization and funding schedule, and Panel C gives the entries that would be made by Employer Company for selected years. This illustration continues the two simplifying assumptions of *(a)* no changes in amortization and funding and *(b)* no effect of the minimum-maximum limits.

In Exhibit 18–5, Panel B, the annual amortization factor (17 years) is $38,370 (column [*a*]) and the annual funding amount (15 years) is $40,890; the annual cash funding factor is more because the expense amortization is **slower** than the cash funding (i.e., 17 years versus 15 years). In contrast to the situation illustrated in Exhibit 18–4 (amortization 13 years and funding 15 years), in Exhibit 18–5 the **interest equivalent** on the cumulative difference between the debit to Pension Expense and the credit to Cash is (1) **subtracted** each period to compute past service pension expense and (2) added to the deferred charge balance (column [*f*]). In Exhibit 18–5, the rationale for the interest equivalent is the same as given above for Exhibit 18–4 except that the relationships essentially are inverse in that (1) there is a deferred charge (rather than a liability) and (2) the interest equivalent is in the nature of interest revenue on the deferred charge; consequently, the interest is **deducted** in computing past service pension expense.

To illustrate, we will trace the computations presented in Exhibit 18–5 for 1984 (ruled for instructional purposes). First, the interest equivalent, at 8 percent, for 1984 is $419 (i.e., $5,242 × 8%). Next, the interest equivalent ($419) is **deducted** from the computed 17-

year amortization factor (column [*a*]) of $38,370 to give the **past service expense** for 1984 of $37,951 (column [*c*]). For 1984, the deferred charge was **increased** by $2,939 (columns [*e*] and [*f*]) from $5,242 to $8,181. This increase of $2,939 is the **sum** of two amounts: (1) the $2,520 difference between the 15-year funding amount ($40,890) and the 17-year pension cost amortization factor ($38,370) and (2) the interest equivalent of $419. Thus, the interest equivalent is **deducted** to compute annual past service pension expense but effectively **added** to compute the deferred charge balance at the end of each period. In Exhibit 18–5, the amounts of pension expense for 1997 and 1998 are large (compared to the last two years in Exhibit 18–4) because the amortization continued through those two years, although the funding did not.

AMORTIZATION OF PRIOR SERVICE COST

Accounting for prior service cost, as defined on page 640, is the same as accounting for past service cost because the two types of pension cost conceptually are the same. That is, both refer to employee service that (1) occurred prior to the event causing it and (2) is given credit for pension benefit purposes. The difference between past service cost as illustrated in Exhibits 18–4 and 18–5 and prior service cost is that the former arises from adoption of a pension plan, which provides for past service credits, whereas prior service cost arises from (1) actuarial revaluations of the pension plan and (2) amendments to the plan. Therefore, past service cost occurs only **once** (i.e., when the pension plan is initiated), whereas prior service cost occurs **each time** an existing pension plan is revalued or amended. In some cases **prior** service (i.e., service prior to a plan amendment) includes **past** service (i.e., service before inception of the plan) because the amendment may occur before past service cost is fully amortized and funded. This situation could change the actuarially determined amount of prior service cost from what its amount would have been if past service cost had already been amortized and funded. Regardless of whether or not prior service cost includes past service cost, the preceding illustrations of accounting for past service cost also would apply to prior service cost. Refer to Part A of the chapter for the situation in which the amortization and funding period is the same; also refer to the two illustrations in Exhibits 18–4 and 18–5 in which the amortization and funding periods differ.

AMORTIZATION OF ACTUARIAL GAINS AND LOSSES

The previous discussions have considered normal pension cost, past service cost, and prior service cost. This section discusses an additional pension cost—actuarial gains and losses. Actuarial gains and losses usually occur each year, but their annual amounts often vary significantly in amount; therefore, an averaging procedure is used. The average amount of the actuarial gain or loss for the year usually is deducted from, or added to, normal pension expense.

APB Opinion 8 defines actuarial gains and losses as "the effects on actuarially calculated pension cost of (1) deviations between actual prior experience and the actuarial assumptions used or (2) changes in actuarial assumptions as to future events." Actuarial assumptions used in estimating pension funding and expenses are based on **estimates of future events.** As time passes, the actual events usually do not coincide with the prior estimates. As actual conditions change, assumptions about the future events must be revised. Thus, from time to time, it is necessary to reflect actual experience that differs from assumed amounts and to revise assumptions to be used in the future. For example, events that can cause an actuarial gain or loss include interest or dividend rates on the pension fund investments that differ from prior assumptions; unexpected changes in employee turnover; and **realized,** as well as **unrealized,** gains and losses in the market value of pension fund investments. Such events cause actuarial gains or losses, which must be reflected in the accounting entries because they change both pension expense and cash funding.

APB Opinion 8 (par. 31) recognizes two kinds of actuarial gains and losses, viz:

1. Actuarial gains and losses that *(a)* "arise from a **single occurrence** not directly related to operation of the pension plan" and *(b)* are **"not in the ordinary course** of the employer's business." An example of such an occurrence is a plant closing, in which case any resulting actuarial gain or loss should be treated as an adjustment of the gain or loss from **that occurrence,** and **not** as an adjustment of pension expense for the year. Another

example is a merger or acquisition accounted for as a purchase, in which case any resulting actuarial gain or loss should be treated as an adjustment of the purchase price of the subsidiary.

2. Actuarial gains and losses that are *(a)* **directly** related to the operation of the pension plan and *(b)* in the **ordinary course** of the employer's business, that is, actuarial gains and losses other than those specified in *(1)* immediately above *(par. 31)*. For instructional convenience we refer to these as the **usual** actuarial gains and losses.

APB Opinion 8 (par. 30) specifies that the **usual** actuarial gains and losses should be allocated to the current and future periods (in a manner similar to changes in accounting estimates) to reflect the long-range nature of pension cost. Accounting for **unrealized** (i.e., market value changes) increases or decreases in the value of pension fund investments is particularly troublesome. *APB Opinion 8* specifies that such unrealized changes should be accounted for as actuarial gains or losses, but states that undue weight should not be given to short-term fluctuations in the market prices of securities held in the pension fund, and that in the case of **debt** securities, it would ordinarily not be advisable to recognize changes in their market value if it is anticipated that they will be held to maturity.

Two methods commonly used for **amortizing** the **usual actuarial gains and losses** are referred to as **spreading** and **averaging.**[14] Exhibit 18–6 illustrates the **spreading** method used for the **usual** actuarial gains and losses. In that exhibit, the usual actuarial gains and losses are applied to decrease (or increase) **normal pension expense.** For each year, normal pension expense is assumed to be $40,000 prior to recog-

[14] The two methods are similar. The principal differences between them are (1) under **spreading,** actuarial gains and losses usually are recognized over a period of 10–20 years, whereas under **averaging,** actuarial gains and losses often are recognized over a five-year period (see *APB Opinion 8,* pars. 29–30); and (2) under **spreading,** "net [actuarial] gains or losses are applied to current and future [expense], either through the normal cost or through the past service cost (or prior service cost)," whereas under **averaging,** "an average of annual net [actuarial] gains and losses, developed from those that occurred in the past with consideration of those expected to occur in the future, is applied to the normal cost" (see par. 26).

EXHIBIT 18–6: Allocation of Actuarial Gains and Losses—Spreading Method (five-year* straight-line basis)—Normal Pension Expense Assumed per Year, $40,000

	Actuarial Gains and Losses		
Year	Actual Actuarial Gain (Loss)	Applied to Decrease Pension Expense if a Gain (Increase if a Loss)	Normal Pension Expense (Including Actuarial Gain or Loss)
1	$ 5,000	$1,000[(a)]	$39,000[(b)]
2	2,000	1,400[(c)]	38,600
3	6,000	2,600	37,400
4	(1,000)	2,400	37,600
5	7,000	3,800	36,200
6	3,000	3,400[(d)]	36,600
7	(8,000)†	3,000[(e)]	37,000
8	1,000	2,000[(f)]	38,000
9	(12,000)	(200)	40,200
10	(4,000)	(2,400)	42,400

* Five years used instead of 10 to 20 to illustrate a completed cycle.
† Due to plant closing; recognized immediately as part of gain or loss from plant closing; **not** amortized as part of pension expense; no other actuarial gain or loss this year.
(a) $5,000 ÷ 5 = $1,000.
(b) $40,000 − $1,000 = $39,000.
(c) ($5,000 + $2,000) ÷ 5 = $1,400.
(d) ($2,000 + $6,000 − $1,000 + $7,000 + $3,000) ÷ 5 = $3,400.
(e) ($6,000 − $1,000 + $7,000 + $3,000 + $0) ÷ 5 = $3,000.
(f) (−$1,000 + $7,000 + $3,000 + $0 + $1,000) ÷ 5 = $2,000.

nition of the allocated amount of actuarial gain or loss.

In Exhibit 18–6, the **usual** actuarial gain or loss for each year is spread over a five-year period. For example, the $5,000 gain for year 1 is applied to decrease **normal** pension expense by $1,000 (i.e., $5,000 ÷ 5 years) each year during years 1–5. Therefore, for year 1, normal pension expense is $39,000 (i.e., $40,000 − $1,000). For year 2, normal pension expense is $38,600 {i.e., $40,000 − [($5,000 + $2,000) ÷ 5]}. By the end of year 5, all of the year 1 gain has been spread, and in year 6, the amount of actuarial gain or loss applied to pension expense is comprised of the gains and losses during years 2–6 (i.e., $2,000 + $6,000 − $1,000 + $7,000 + $3,000 = $17,000). As a result, normal pension expense for year 6 is $36,600 [i.e., $40,000 − ($17,000 ÷ 5)].

The loss in year 7 occurred from a plant closing, a single occurrence, which was not related to the operation of the pension plan or fund; therefore, it is recognized immediately as part of the gain or loss on the plant closing and not as pension expense. There were no other actuarial gains or losses in year 7; therefore, the amount of **net** actuarial loss applied to pension expense in year 7 is $3,000 (i.e., the net actuarial **gains** from the five years (including zero for year 7) spread over years 3–7, (i.e., $6,000 − $1,000 + $7,000 + $3,000 + $0 = $15,000) ÷ 5]. Normal pension expense for year 7 is $37,000 (i.e., $40,000 − $3,000).

The amount allocated to the year, if a loss (i.e., a debit), is recorded as an increase in **normal** pension expense; if it is a gain (i.e., a credit), it is recorded as a decrease in normal pension expense for the year. To illustrate, refer to Exhibit 18–6. In year 1, a $1,000 actuarial gain was recognized, with $4,000 (i.e., $5,000 − $1,000) of the actual actuarial gain deferred to future periods. Assuming Employer Company has *(a)* normal pension expense of $40,000 each year and *(b)* funds the actuarial losses (gains) each year along with the normal pension expense, pension expense and funding would be in accordance with the last column of Exhibit 18–6. For example, the entries for two selected years would be as follows:

Year 1:		
Pension expense (normal)	39,000	
Cash		39,000
Year 10:		
Pension expense (normal)	42,400	
Cash		42,400

VESTED BENEFITS

Benefits are **vested** when they belong to the employee even though the employee does not continue employment with the entity in whose service the benefits were earned (see page 640). Thus, Vested benefits apply to three groups: (1) former employees who have already retired and are receiving defined benefits; (2) former employees who have left the company prior to retirement, but are eligible under the pension plan for defined benefits; and (3) current employees with vested benefits. Vested benefits can be viewed as guaranteed pension benefits already earned.[15]

MINIMUM AND MAXIMUM LIMITS ON ANNUAL PENSION EXPENSE

APB Opinion 8 recognizes that different actuarial cost methods result in different amounts of annual pension expense. While the *Opinion* was deliberately flexible to accommodate different actuarial cost methods and different views concerning the timing of pension expense recognition, it set minimum and maximum limits for the amounts recorded as **annual pension expense.**

The "Amortization and Funding" schedules presented in Panel B of Exhibits 18–4 and 18–5 were developed, for instructional convenience, independent of the APB specification which applies minimum and maximum limits to the computed pension expense for each year. In this section, we will extend those discussions to consider *(a)* computation of the minimum and maximum limits each year and *(b)* one application of those limits to pension accounting.

Exhibit 18–7 summarizes computation of the minimum and maximum limits for total annual pension expense as specified in *APB Opinion 8*. The primary differences between the defined minimum and maximum limits arise from their different treatments of past service costs, prior service costs, and vested benefits. Past and prior service costs are included in the **minimum** only as interest on the **unfunded** portion of such costs and are included in the **maximum** as 10 percent of the total estimate of these

[15] ERISA imposed stringent safeguards in behalf of employees' vesting rights. An employee now must be at least 25 percent vested in benefits derived from employer contributions after five years of covered service. By the time an employee has 15 years of covered service, the vesting must have risen (according to a table in the law) to 100 percent. Under another provision an employee with five years of covered service must be at least 50 percent vested in the accrued benefit from employer contributions when the sum of the employee's age and years of covered service totals 45.

EXHIBIT 18–7: Minimum and Maximum Limits for Annual Pension Expense

Element of Annual Amount of Pension Expense	Minimum Annual Pension Expense	Maximum Annual Pension Expense
1. Normal cost.	Recognize full amount as expense.	Recognize full amount as expense.
2. Past service cost.	Recognize only interest on unfunded portion.	Recognize 10% until fully amortized.
3. Prior service cost (resulting from actuarial revaluations and amendments of pension plan).	Recognize only interest on unfunded portion.	Recognize 10% until fully amortized.
4. Vested benefits.	Recognize actuarially computed value of vested benefits in excess of the market value of the pension fund as determined by a special formula.*	Not applicable because vested benefits usually are included implicitly in the sum of the above three amounts.†
5. Interest on the difference between amounts of past and prior service cost amortized and funded.	Not applicable because this interest is included in the provision for vested benefits.‡	Include (or deduct).§

* In the above phraseology, **pension fund** includes *(a)* an addition for any balance sheet pension liabilities which have accrued to the benefit of covered employees and *(b)* a subtraction for any balance sheet deferred charges for pension amounts prepaid by the employer and, hence, claimed as an asset by the employer, rather than by the pension fund (i.e., the employees). See *APB Opinion 8*, par. 17.

† *Interpretation of APB Opinion 8*, pars. 9 and 10.

‡ *APB Opinion 8*, par. 17.

§ *APB Opinion 8*, pars. 42 and 43.

costs (i.e., in effect a minimum 10–year amortization period). As related to **vested benefits,** the minimum amount of annual pension expense is derived by applying a special formula to the actuarial value of all vested benefits in excess of the pension fund. The formula and its applications are not illustrated herein; for details refer to *APB Opinion 8*, par. 17, and *Interpretation of APB Opinion 8*, pars. 9 and 10. In contrast, the maximum amount of annual pension expense needs no separate addition for vested benefits because the maximum usually includes vested benefits automatically.

Exhibit 18–8 illustrates a simplified application of the minimum and maximum limits on pension expense. Panel A presents the hypothetical situation; Panel B illustrates computation of the minimum and maximum limits; Panel C presents the determination of the appropriate amount of pension expense for 1983; and Panel D presents the entry for 1983. Exhibit 18–8 is important because it extends the situation presented in Exhibit 18–5 (and the related discussions). In that exhibit we temporarily disregarded the GAAP rule on minimum and maximum limits. In Exhibit 18–8 we present the effects of the minimum and maximum limits on the accounting for pension costs.

The GAAP minimum and maximum limits on periodic pension expense, as specified in *APB Opinion 8*, are not based on any obvious theoretical concepts; this GAAP rule is strictly a practical one, which the *Opinion* justified as required to narrow the wide diversity in practice.[16]

[16] *APB Opinion 8* was issued in 1966 when interest and inflation rates were much lower than in the late 1970's and early 1980's. The formula prescribed in 1966 to compute minimum and maximum pension expense appeared realistic at that time. Given the 10-year amortization period specified for past and prior service cost as components of the maximum, the limit will operate for any combination of interest rates and years for which the present value of an annuity is less than 10. At the present time it is **not** realistic. Because of the current high interest rates, this maximum limit will be operable, usually for the first 10 years, unless the term over which past and prior service costs are amortized is long, viz:

Interest rate	Required years before PV of annuity exceeds 10
2%	12
4%	14
6%	16
8%	21
9%	27
10%	Infinity

Exhibit 18–8, Panel B, illustrates computation of the minimum and maximum limits in accordance with the formula specified in *APB Opinion 8.* **Normal pension** cost (including the **usual** actuarial gains and losses illustrated previously) is the same for both the minimum and the maximum. In contrast, past service cost and prior service cost are quite different between the minimum and maximum—the minimum is **interest** (at the pension fund interest rate) on the **unfunded** portion of those costs, and the **maximum** is 10 percent of the total of such costs. The minimum amount of past service cost for interest on the unfunded portion is computed by multiplying the present value of the **unfunded balance** at the end of the preceding period by the estimated interest rate applicable to the pension fund. Computation of the *(a)* unfunded balance of past service cost and *(b)* interest on that unfunded balance is illustrated for the first two years (1982 and 1983) in Exhibit 18–8, Panel B. Each year the unfunded balance of the prior year is **decreased** by the amount of the funding of the current year and is **increased** by the current year's interest on the unfunded balance and any pension benefits paid; this computation gives the ending unfunded balance of the current year. Pension benefits, when paid during the year, must be **added** in the computation because their payment reduces the pension fund which, in turn, **increases** the year-end **unfunded balance.** This computation is continued each year. Total **vested benefits** (the amount is computed using a special formula) in **excess** of the total value of the pension fund is added to compute the minimum limit. The amount shown in Exhibit 18–8, Panel B, is assumed to be $1,000.[17]

The last item illustrated in Exhibit 18–8, Panel B, is **interest** on the **difference** between the amounts of past and prior service costs *(a)* **amortized** and *(b)* **funded.** This 1983 interest amount was $202 because the funding of past service cost was $40,890 (see Exhibit 18–5) while the amount amortized was $38,370 (see Exhibit 18–5); the difference of $2,520, multiplied by the pension fund interest rate of 8 percent, produces the $202 (see Exhibit 18–5).

[17] This situation, in which vested benefits exceed the pension fund, is not uncommon, especially in the early years after a plan is adopted or amended and funding occurs more slowly than amortization. For example, at December 31, 1979, the vested benefits of the pension plan of National Can Corporation exceeded the pension fund investments by $30.7 million (see Note A of the corporation's 1979 annual report).

In overall perspective, let us consider why we used two separate amortization and funding schedules (in Exhibits 18–5 and 18–8) for the same situation. The primary reason was for instructional convenience, in order to discuss **separately** the basic theoretical concepts of pension accounting (Exhibit 18–5) and application of an accounting rule which is based solely on practical considerations (e.g., the minimum-maximum rule in Exhibit 18–8). However, another important reason—a strictly practical one—is occasioned by the dynamics of most pension plans. Some or all of the many variables in a pension plan may change over time, such as changes in the *(a)* annual amount of normal cost, *(b)* actuary's estimates of past service cost, prior service cost, and vested benefits, *(c)* funding and amortization periods, and *(d)* interest rate on the pension fund. Such changes, assuming material effects, may require a change in the amortization and funding schedule for one or more periods. As a result, this schedule is changed often (sometimes every year). Such changes require information about the previously **scheduled** amortization and funding amounts (as in Exhibit 18–5, Panel B) and all revisions to date. The manner in which one such change is made was illustrated in Exhibit 18–8. For illustrative purposes we used the minimum-maximum constraint as explained above. The illustration was simplified by assuming no prior service costs because they are accounted for in the same manner as past service costs.

There is widespread criticism of the extreme arbitrariness involved in accounting for pension costs as specified in *APB Opinion 8;* the minimum-maximum rule often is cited as the prime example. During periods of high interest rates, the minimum limit can exceed the maximum limit because an interest rate in excess of 10 percent can cause the interest amount included in the minimum to exceed the 10 percent amount of past service cost included in the maximum amount. For this and other reasons, the FASB is restudying this important topic.

PENSION PLAN DISCLOSURES

APB Opinion 8 requires that the amount of pension expense be reported in the tabular portion of

EXHIBIT 18–8: Application of Minimum and Maximum Limits on Pension Expense

Panel A—Hypothetical Situation of Employer Company:

1. Normal pension cost each year, provided by actuary, $40,000.
2. Basic data on **past service cost** as given in Exhibit 18–5, Panels A and B:
   a. January 1, 1982, actuary estimated present value of past service cost of $350,000.
   b. Past service cost is amortized over 17 years, at year-end.
   c. Past service cost is funded over 15 years at $40,890 each year-end (8 percent interest rate).
3. Prior service cost provided by actuary, none.
4. Vested benefits in excess of pension fund balance, determined by special formula, at year-end 1983, $1,000.

Panel B—Computation of Minimum and Maximum Limits on Pension Expense, Year-End, 1983:

Elements of Pension Expense	Minimum Annual Pension Expense		Maximum Annual Pension Expense	
1. Normal pension expense	Given	$40,000	Given	$40,000
2. Past service cost	Interest on unfunded portion	26,969*	Ten percent of total ($350,000 × .10)	35,000
3. Prior service cost	Interest on unfunded portion, none assumed	—	Ten percent of total, none assumed	—
4. Vested benefits	In excess of pension fund investments	1,000	Not applicable	—
5. Interest on difference between amounts of past and prior service cost funded and **amortized** in previous years (ignoring the interest addition or deduction—Exhibit 18–5, col. 2)	Not applicable	—	(Funding, 1982, $40,890 − Past service expense, 1982, $38,370**) × .08	(202)
Total pension expense limits	**Minimum**	$67,969	**Maximum**	$74,798

* Computation of interest on unfunded past service cost:
** Some accountants would use $35,000 for this computation. We use $38,370 because it is actuarially sound.

Date	Funding of Past Service Cost	Interest on Unfunded Balance at 8%	Add Pension Benefits Paid to Retirees	Unfunded Balance Past Service Cost
1/1/82				$350,000
12/31/82	$40,890	$350,000 × .08 = $28,000	$-0-	337,110†
12/31/83	40,890	337,110 × .08 = 26,969	-0-	323,189
Etc.				

† $350,000 − $40,890 + $28,000 + $-0- = $337,110, etc.

Panel C—Application of Minimum-Maximum Limits to Determine the Appropriate Amount of Pension Expense for 1983:

Considerations	Total Pension Expense
1. Computed Amount of Total Pension Expense, ignoring minimum and maximum limits (Exhibit 18–5; $40,000 + $38,168)	$78,168
2. Minimum pension expense, computed in Panel B above	67,969
3. Maximum pension expense, computed in Panel B above	74,798
4. Total pension expense for 1983—Maximum limit is used because the computed amount (1 above) exceeds the maximum limit	$74,798

EXHIBIT 18–8 ***(concluded)***

Panel D—Actual Entry for 1983:

	1983	
Pension expense	74,798	
Deferred charge—pension funding in excess of expense	6,092	
Cash		80,890

the income statement or in the related notes.[18] Also, when the periods for amortizing and funding past or prior service cost differ, the deferred charge or liability balance which results must be reported on the balance sheet. When employees have **vested** pension rights, any excess of the actuarial value of such rights over the amounts funded or accrued should be reported as a long-term liability. The debit side of the entry in which such a liability is recognized would be to a deferred charge account entitled Deferred Pension Cost or some similar title.

In addition to disclosure of the amount of the annual pension expense, notes to the financial statements also should contain the following:[19]

1. A brief statement that a pension plan exists, identifying or describing the employee groups covered.
2. A statement of the company's accounting and funding policies.
3. A statement of the nature and effect of significant matters affecting comparability for all periods for which statements are presented. This statement should disclose changes in accounting methods (actuarial cost method, amortization of past or prior service cost, treatment of actuarial gains and losses, etc.), changes in actuarial assumptions or other circumstances, and any plan adoptions or amendments.
4. Actuarial present value of **vested** benefits and actuarial present value of **nonvested** accumulated benefits.
5. Net assets available for benefits.
6. Assumed rates of return used in determining the accumulated plan benefits.
7. Date on which the information on the benefits was determined.

In February 1981, the FASB issued a *Discussion Memorandum,* entitled "Employers' Accounting for Pensions and Other Postemployment Benefits." It is the FASB's first step in a comprehensive review of the subject of this chapter. This project is expected to result in significant changes to existing GAAP as set forth in *APB Opinion 8.* The project is being undertaken by the FASB because of *(a)* changes in the pension environment since 1966 when *Opinion 8* was issued, *(b)* the concern about unfunded pension obligations, and *(c)* the flexibility permitted under current GAAP for pension accounting.[20]

A significant issue in accounting for pensions involves the earnings rate used by actuaries in the present value discounting to compute the periodic pension expense and funding amounts. It appears that in practice the actual (or in some cases the expected future) earnings rate on the pension fund assets is used. Many actuaries use low earnings rates to be conservative; nevertheless, because pension funds usually include common stock investments, the

---

[18] Although the 1974 ERISA legislation affected the **administration** of pension plans and aimed at making employee benefits plans more secure for employees, it had relatively little impact on the employer's financial accounting for pension plans.

[19] Items 1–3 in the list are required by *APB Opinion No. 8.* Items 4–7 are required by FASB, *Statement of Financial Accounting Standards No. 36,* "Disclosure of Pension Information" (Stamford, Conn., May 1980).

[20] For differing viewpoints on the seriousness of the problem of unfunded pension obligations, see A. F. Ehrbar, "Those Pension Plans Are Even Weaker than You Think," *Fortune,* November 1977, pp. 104–14; P. A. Gervirty and R. C. Phillips, "Unfunded Pension Liabilities . . . THE NEW MYTH," *Financial Executive,* August 1978, pp. 18–24; and D. D. Ezra, "How Actuaries Determine the Unfunded Pension Liability," *Financial Analysts Journal,* July/August 1980, pp. 43–50.

earnings rates reflect the risk inherent in those investments. Under normal conditions, the use by actuaries of a "risky" earnings rate to compute pension expense and funding amounts would be a reasonable actuarial approach because the pension fund could be expected to earn that "risky" rate on the pension fund assets; and those earnings would decrease the amount of funding required of the employer. However, if the economy were to experience a sudden depression that decreased security values throughout the entire economy, it is not clear who would suffer the losses experienced by the pension fund. If the ultimate loss were absorbed by the employees and retirees (through lower pension benefits), then use by actuaries of the "risky" earnings rate may be justified. However, if the ultimate loss were absorbed by the corporation (through additional funding amounts to shore up the depleted pension fund), then it would seen that actuaries should be using a lower earnings rate in their present value discounting; one candidate for this lower earnings rate is the so-called "risk-free" rate, which often is interpreted to mean the interest rate on government Treasury Bills. Use of this lower rate in the discounting would result in higher periodic expense and funding amounts. At first glance, this appears to be an actuarial, rather than an accounting, problem; however, the accountant is responsible for the amounts of pension expense and liability reported. For this reason, the accountant should be concerned about the earnings rate used to discount future pension amounts to present values.[21]

Exhibit 18–9 presents some highlights of the pension reporting practices of the 600 companies included in the 1980 survey by *Accounting Trends & Techniques.*

[21] Professor William H. Beaver brought this issue to our attention.

EXHIBIT 18–9: Pension Reporting by Employers

Item Reported	Number of Companies
On income statement:	
Normal cost and amortization of prior service cost*	469
Normal cost—no reference to prior service cost*	42
Normal cost—no unfunded prior service cost*	21
Companies disclosing amount of pension plan expense	536
On balance sheet:	
Noncurrent assets:	
Employee benefits prepaid	8
Current liabilities:	
Pension or retirement plan contributions payable	55
Noncurrent liabilities:	
Pension or retirement plan contributions payable	62

* "Prior" service cost includes "past" service cost in this tabulation.

Source: AICPA, *Accounting Trends & Techniques, 1980* (New York, 1980), tables 2–18, 2–21, 2–28, 3–8.

Supplement 18-A: Descriptions of Acceptable Actuarial Cost Methods under APB Opinion No. 8

1. **Accrued benefit (unit credit) method.** Future service benefits are funded as they accrue. Thus, the normal cost under this method for a particular year is the present value of the units of future benefit credited to employees for service in that year. Prior [including past] service cost under the unit credit method is the present value at the valuation date of the units of future benefit credited to employees for service prior to the valuation date. As to an individual employee, the annual normal cost for an equal unit of benefit each year increases because the period to the employee's retirement continually shortens and the probability of reaching retirement increases [see Exhibit 18–3; note the rise in the graph during years 1–20]. As to the employees collectively, however, the step-up effect is masked, since older employees generating the highest annual cost are continually replaced by new employees generating the lowest. For a mature employee group, the

normal cost would tend to be the same each year [see Exhibit 18–3; note that the graph is flat during the period from year 20 and following].

2. **Entry age normal method.** Under the entry age normal method, the normal costs are computed on the assumptions (1) that every employee entered the plan at the earliest time he would have been eligible had the plan always been in existence and (2) that contributions have been made on this basis from the entry age to the date of the actuarial valuation. Normal cost under this method is the level amount (or level percentage of compensation) to be contributed for each year. Prior [including past] service cost under this method is the amount of the fund that would have been accumulated had annual contributions equal to the normal cost been made in prior years and all actuarial assumptions been precisely accurate [see Exhibit 18–3; note that the graph is flat over its full range].
3. **Attained age normal method.** The attained age normal method is a variant of the accrued benefit method and the aggregate method (see 4 below), but in it past service cost is recognized separately. The cost of each employee's benefits assigned to years after the inception of the plan is spread over the employee's future service life. Normal cost contributions under the attained age normal method, usually determined as a percentage of payroll, tend to decline but less markedly than under the aggregate method [see Exhibit 18–3; note the gradual decline in annual cost during years 1–20, similar to the aggregate method; also note that the graph is flat from year 20 and following, similar to the accrued benefit method].
4. **Aggregate method.** The aggregate method applies on a collective basis the principle followed for individuals in the individual level premium method [see 5 below]. That is, the entire unfunded cost of future pension benefits (including benefits to be paid to employees who have retired as of the date of the valuation) is spread over the average future service lives of employees who are active as of the date of the valuation. In most cases this is done by the use of a percentage of payroll. The aggregate method does not deal separately with past service cost (but includes such cost in normal cost). Annual contributions under the aggregate method decrease and ultimately approach those under the entry age normal method, but the rate of decrease is less extreme than under the individual level premium method [see Exhibit 18–3].
5. **Individual level premium method.** The individual level premium method assigns the cost of each employee's pension in level annual amounts, or as a level percentage of the employee's compensation, over the period from the inception date of a plan (or the date of his entry into the plan, if later) to his retirement date. Thus, past service cost is not determined separately but is included in normal cost. The individual level premium method generates annual costs which are initially very high, but ultimately drop to the level of the normal cost determined under the entry age normal method. The high initial costs arise because the past service cost (although not separately identified) for employees near retirement when the plan is adopted is in effect amortized over a short period [see Exhibit 18–3].

QUESTIONS

PART A

1. What are some of the uncertainties with which actuaries must deal when they estimate the cost of future benefits under a pension plan?
2. What is *vesting?*
3. How does past service cost arise? What is the relationship of past service cost to prior service cost?
4. What is an *actuarial cost method?* Do the acceptable actuarial cost methods produce similar or dissimilar periodic expense patterns over the term of a pension plan? Explain.
5. What is *normal pension cost?* How is normal pension cost accounted for?

PART B

6. The Gambel Company has a contributory pension plan for all of its employees. In 19A, a total of $100,000 was withheld from employees' salaries and deposited

into a pension fund administered by an outside trustee. In addition, Gambel deposited $280,000 of its own money into the fund in 19A. Based on the report of Gambel's outside actuaries which was received in December 19A, the 19A actuarial cost of the pension plan was $450,000. As a result of this report, Gambel deposited $70,000 of its own money into the fund on January 12, 19B. How much should be reported as pension expense in Gambel's 19A income statement?

a. $350,000.
b. $380,000.
c. $420,000.
d. $450,000.

Briefly support your answer choice.

(AICPA adapted)

7. If pension expense for past service cost exceeds funding payments for a period, what kind of account arises, and how should it be reported in the financial statements? Suppose the reverse is true; that is, pension funding payments exceed pension expense. What then?
8. What guidelines as to the *minimum* and *maximum* annual pension expense are set out in *APB Opinion 8?*
9. What are *actuarial gains* and *losses?* How should they be accounted for?
10. What financial statement disclosures of pension-related information are required under GAAP?
11. What does the acronym ERISA stand for? Thus far, has financial accounting been greatly affected by it?

DECISION CASE 18–1

The corporation where you are employed as controller has not had a pension plan, but its directors are seriously considering adopting one. You have been called in to explain several matters to the board of directors from an accounting standpoint and to comment on them.

Item 1: A substantial number of the employees have worked for the corporation for many years. From an accounting and financial standpoint what would happen if the company does not adopt a pension plan now but does adopt one at a future date?

Item 2: The directors are concerned about recognition of the company's liability for past service cost. One of them, who has some familiarity with accounting, asked "If we book the liability for past service cost, what account or accounts will we debit?" Respond in terms of GAAP. Consider also what the company might do if it were not required to conform to GAAP.

Item 3: What are the effects in the accounts of a fast amortization of past service cost (compared with the rate of funding)? What are the arguments favoring slow amortization of past service cost (compared with the rate of funding)?

EXERCISES

PART A: EXERCISES 18–1 to 18–4

Exercise 18–1

The independent actuary engaged by Roose Company determined that should it adopt the type of pension plan contemplated, its unfunded past service cost would amount to $171,190.

Required (disregard maximum-minimum limits and round to the nearest dollar):

1. Compute the annual amounts for funding and amortization of the past service cost over a 15-year period, based on the assumption that the pension fund investments can earn 8% annually.
2. Assume the actuary determined the normal pension cost to be $120,000 for year 1 and $132,000 for year 2. Record pension expense for both years.
3. Indicate what would be reported on Roose Company's income statement and balance sheet for each of the two years. Ignore note disclosures.

Exercise 18–2

Snider Company initiated a pension plan on a funded basis several years after the company began operations. Its consulting actuary determined that at inception of the plan the past service cost amounted to $79,427.

Required (disregard maximum-minimum limits and round to the nearest dollar):

1. Using a 7% interest rate, compute the annual amounts for *(a)* funding and *(b)* amortization of the past service

cost over a 12-year period and funding over a 12-year period.

2. Give journal entries relating to the pension plan covering its first two years of operation based upon funding in accordance with the amounts computed for 1 above and on the assumptions that the plan year and the fiscal year coincided and normal pension expense for the first two years were $50,000 for year 1 and $53,000 for year 2.

Exercise 18–3

Select the best answer in each of the following. Briefly justify each selection.

1. When a company adopts a pension plan for accounting purposes, past service cost should be—
   a. Treated as a prior period adjustment because no future periods are benefited.
   b. Amortized under accrual accounting to current and future periods.
   c. Amortized in accordance with procedures used for income tax purposes.
   d. Treated as an expense of the period during which the funding occurs.
2. When pension expense is presented in a statement of income, past and current service costs—
   a. Must be shown separately in computing income before extraordinary items.
   b. Must be separated so that past service cost can be treated as a prior period adjustment.
   c. Must be separated so that past service cost can be treated as an extraordinary item.
   d. May be either combined or shown separately in computing income before extraordinary items.
3. The terminal funding method and pay-as-you-go method of accounting for pension plans are not generally accepted accounting methods because—
   a. They do not require the funding of past service cost.
   b. They are not actuarially sound.
   c. They do not recognize pension costs prior to the retirement of employees.
   d. They are not acceptable methods for federal income tax purposes.
4. What is the difference between the terms past service cost and prior service cost?
   a. Past service cost refers to cost applicable to periods prior to a particular date of actuarial valuation, and prior service cost refers to costs applicable to employee service prior to inception of a pension plan.
   b. Past service cost refers to costs applicable to employee service prior to inception of a pension plan, and prior service cost refers to costs applicable to periods prior to a particular date of actuarial valuation.
   c. Past service cost refers to costs applicable to a pension plan for an employee who enters the plan after inception of the plan in order to bring the employee's benefits into line with the other participants in the plan, and prior service cost refers to changes in prior period pension cost that are caused by a change in actuarial valuation.
   d. There is no difference between the two terms, and they may be used interchangeably.

(AICPA adapted)

Exercise 18–4

Plans are being made to fund the prospective pension benefits of a group of employees of Gilliam Company due to retire in nine years and to be paid amounts from one to five years after retirement as below:

End of year 1	$ 70,000
End of year 2	50,000
End of year 3	30,000
End of year 4	15,000
End of year 5	5,000
Thereafter	-0-
Total of pension payments	$170,000

Funds deposited with the pension fund trustee will earn 6% per annum. The pension plan contract calls for deposit of an amount sufficient to fund all of the expected payments from the fund by the date the employees retire.

Required (round amounts to nearest dollar and disregard maximum-minimum limits):

1. *(a)* Compute the amount required by the trustee on the employees' retirement date assuming the first pension payment is one year after retirement, and *(b)* prepare a schedule reflecting the 6% earnings on unused funds and pension payout by the trustee, to retirees scheduled over the five-year period.
2. Using the funding amount computed in 1 above, compute the amount of each of eight equal annual payments required to fully fund the pensions assuming a 6% interest rate. The payments into the pension fund will be made the last eight years of employment preceding retirement, and the last payment into the fund will coincide with the retirement date of the employees. Hint—a diagram may be helpful.

PART B: EXERCISES 18–5 to 18–13

Exercise 18–5

Set forth below is an amortization schedule of a company which adopted a pension plan at a time when its past service cost amounted to $1,000,000. This past service cost is being funded in a lesser number of years than it is being amortized.

(Relates to Exercise 18–5)

(a)	(b)	(c)	(d)	(e)	(f)	(g)
1	$149,030		$149,030	$174,015	$ 24,985	$ 24,985
2	149,030	$ 1,999	147,031	174,015	26,984	51,969
3	149,030	4,158	144,872	174,015	29,143	81,112
4	149,030	6,489	142,541	174,015	31,474	112,586
5	149,030	9,007	140,023	174,015	33,992	146,578
6	149,030	11,726	137,304	174,015	36,711	183,289
7	149,030	14,663	134,367	174,015	39,648	222,937
8	149,030	17,835	131,195	174,015	42,820	265,757
9	149,030	21,261	127,769	—	(127,769)	137,988
10	149,030	11,042*	137,988	—	(137,988)	—

* Reflects rounding.

Required (disregard maximum-minimum limits):

1. What interest rate was assumed in making the amortization and funding calculations? Show how you arrived at your results.
2. Supply appropriate titles for columns *(a)* through *(g)* of the schedule.
3. If the normal costs in years 1 and 2 were, respectively, $90,000 and $110,000, what were *(a)* total disbursements for pensions for these two years and *(b)* total pension expense for these two years?
4. What balance sheet amounts would be shown by this company in respect to its pension plan at the end of years 8 and 9, and what is the nature of the account under which the amounts would be reported?

Exercise 18–6

Richards Company initiated a funded pension plan and gave employees credit for past service. The actuary estimated the past service cost at inception of the plan at $50,000.

Required (round amounts to nearest dollar and disregard maximum-minimum limits):

1. Using a 5% annual rate, calculate the periodic amortization factor and periodic funding payments assuming (short amortization periods are assumed for computational ease):

   Case A—Funding and amortization are over three years.

   Case B—Funding is over four years; amortization is over three.

   Case C—Funding is over two years; amortization is over three.

2. Prepare an amortization and funding schedule for the past service cost for Case C.
3. Give entries for four years for Case C. Normal costs for the years are, respectively, $64,000, $71,000, $77,000, and $80,000.
4. Indicate what would be reported on the income statement and the balance sheet under Case C for the four years. If note disclosure is required, write the note for the financial statements at the end of year 1. Net assets available for benefits are $90,890 at the end of year 1. Vested benefits on that date are $80,000.

Exercise 18–7

Select the best answer in each of the following and explain the basis for your choice.

1. The Thoughtful Corporation adopted an employee pension plan on January 1, 19A, for all of its eligible employees. Thoughtful has agreed to make annual payments to a designated trustee at the end of each year. Data relating to the plan follow:

Normal cost	$100,000
Past service cost, 1/1/19A (unfunded)	600,000

   Funds held by trustee are expected to earn a 7% annual return.

   In accordance with *APB Opinion 8*, what is the maximum pension expense that Thoughtful can record for 19A?

   a. $105,000.
   b. $160,000.
   c. $165,000.
   d. $175,000.

2. The amount of cost, on an accrual basis, that should be assigned each period to the pension plan for current services is known as—

   a. Past service cost.
   b. Prior service cost.
   c. Normal cost.
   d. Vesting cost.

3. In accounting for a pension plan, any difference be-

tween the pension cost debited to expense and payments into the fund should be reported as—
a. An offset to the liability for past service cost.
b. Accrued or prepaid pension cost.
c. An operating expense in this period.
d. An accrued actuarial liability.

4. When accounting for pension cost, a company—
a. Allocates total pension costs systematically and rationally.
b. Records fluctuating gains and losses on pension fund investments as they occur.
c. Gives immediate recognition to all pension costs for which legal liability exists.
d. Establishes a positive relationship between contributions to the fund and the recorded pension expense.

5. Benefits under a pension plan that are not contingent upon an employee's continuing service are—
a. Granted under a plan of defined contribution.
b. Based upon terminal funding.
c. Actuarially unsound.
d. Vested.

6. The account Deferred Pension Expense would arise when—
a. The rate of funding and amortization are the same.
b. Funding is accomplished in a shorter period than amortization of past service cost.
c. Amortization of past service cost and funding are ignored.
d. Amortization of past service cost is over a shorter period than funding. (1,3–5 AICPA adapted)

Exercise 18–8

The following tabulation was prepared for a company which had $70,000 past service cost and decided 7% was an appropriate interest rate to use. Funding payments for past service cost are made at the end of each year.

Required (disregard maximum-minimum limits):
1. Indicate how the value marked † was calculated.
2. Indicate how the value marked ‡ was calculated.
3. Show how the amounts in columns *(b)*, *(c)*, *(e)*, and *(f)* were computed.
4. Give the company's entry to record pension expense at the end of 19J if, in addition to the amount paid to the sinking fund trustee for past service cost, $10,000 was paid for 19J normal pension cost.
5. Give entry to record pension expense at the end of 19K if, in addition to the amount paid for past service cost, $9,000 was paid for 19K normal cost.

(Relates to Exercise 18–8)
Schedule of Past Service Pension Cost and Related Funding (amortization period 10 years; funding period 12 years)

	Amortization of Past Service Cost—10 Years			Funding—12 Years	Balance Sheet—Liability	
	(a)	*(b)*	*(c)*	*(d)*	*(e)*	*(f)*
Year	10-Year Amortization Factor	Addition for Interest	Past Service Pension Expense Dr.	Cash Cr.	Credit (Debit)	Account Balance
19A	$9,966†		$ 9,966	$8,813‡	$ 1,153	$ 1,153
19B	9,966	$ 81	10,047	8,813	1,234	2,387
19C	9,966	167	10,133	8,813	1,320	3,707
19D	9,966	259	10,225	8,813	1,412	5,119
19E	9,966	358	10,324	8,813	1,511	6,630
19F	9,966	464	10,430	8,813	1,617	8,247
19G	9,966	577	10,543	8,813	1,730	9,977
19H	9,966	698	10,664	8,813	1,851	11,828
19I	9,966	828	10,794	8,813	1,981	13,809
19J	9,966	967	10,933	8,813	2,120	15,929
19K	—	1,115	1,115	8,813	(7,698)	8,231
19L	—	582*	582	8,813	(8,231)	—

* Rounded.

Exercise 18–9

Indicate the best answer in each of the following and briefly explain the basis of your choices.

1. Which of the following disclosures of pension plan information is not required by *APB Opinion 8* to be included in the financial statements?
   a. The estimated pension expense for the period.
   b. The amount paid from the pension fund to retirees during the period.
   c. A statement of the company's accounting and funding policies for the pension plan.
   d. The nature and effect of significant pension plan matters affecting comparability for all periods presented.
2. The terms *accrued benefit, entry-age normal, attained age normal, aggregate cost,* and *individual level premium*—
   a. Are synonymous in meaning.
   b. Relate to vesting.
   c. Identify actuarial cost methods.
   d. Are unacceptable for use in modern pension accounting.
3. Following the guides set by the Accounting Principles Board, the minimum amount of expense permitted in accounting for pension plan expense is—
   a. Normal cost.
   b. Normal cost, plus a prescribed percentage of prior (or past) service cost.
   c. Normal cost, plus interest on unfunded prior (or past) service cost, plus a prescribed percentage of any increase in prior service costs arising from amendments to the plan.
   d. Normal cost, plus interest on unfunded prior (or past) service cost, plus a possible provision for vested benefits.
4. A pension fund actuarial gain or loss that is caused by a plant closing should—
   a. Be recognized immediately as a gain or loss.
   b. Be spread over the current year and future years.
   c. Be debited or credited to the current pension expense.
   d. Be recognized as a prior period adjustment.
5. Which of the following actuarial cost methods is not an acceptable method for determining pension cost?
   a. Unit credit.
   b. Individual level premium.
   c. Terminal funding.
   d. Entry age normal.
6. In March 19A, Musso Company adopted a pension plan for its eligible employees. Unfunded past service cost was determined to be $7,000,000, and this amount will be paid in 10 annual installments of $1,000,000 to an outside funding agency administering the plan.

   Additional information:

Past service cost will be amortized over 20 years.	
Normal cost for 19A (remitted to funding agency in 19A)	$560,000
Amortization of past service cost for 19A	650,000

   What is the deferred pension cost for 19A?
   a. $350,000.
   b. $440,000.
   c. $500,000.
   d. $560,000.

(All except no. 2, AICPA adapted)

Exercise 18–10

Bliss Company has its pension plan actuarially evaluated annually with the result that it evaluates the actuarial gains or losses on an annual basis. The history of its actuarial gains and losses appears below.

Year	Gain (Loss)	Year	Gain (Loss)
19A	$ 6,000	19G	$(4,000)
19B	3,000	19H	6,000
19C	7,000*	19I	3,000
19D	4,000	19J	4,000
19E	(2,000)	19K	2,000
19F	5,000	19L	3,000

* Due to closing of plant in which no employee benefits had vested.

Required:
Prepare a schedule showing for each year the amount that would be applied to reduce Bliss Company's normal pension expense if the actuarial gains and losses are amortized on a 10-year spreading basis.

Exercise 18–11

1. Unfunded past service cost of Kraft Company was $400,000 at January 1, 19A, and unfunded prior service cost (in addition to any past service cost), due to plan amendments, was $100,000. Normal cost was $55,000 for 19A and 19B and funded fully each year-end. No benefits vested during the year. The past and prior service costs (due to amendment of the plan) will be amortized over 25 years from January 1, 19A. Calculate the minimum-maximum pension expense limits for the company for 19B assuming a 7% interest rate and that Kraft recognizes pension expense at year-end.
2. Unfunded prior service cost (including past service cost) of Largo Company on January 1, 19A, amounted to $550,000. This amount will be amortized over 15 years from January 1, 19A. Normal cost for 19B of $92,000 was recognized at year-end. Payment to the pension fund at year-end amounted to $132,000. No benefits vested during the year. Calculate the minimum and maximum pension expense limits for the company for 19B (assuming a 6% return on pension fund assets).

Exercise 18–12

An actuary computed the present value of the past service cost for Louis Company as $700,000. Assume normal pension cost of $105,000 each year. Round all required computations to nearest dollar.

1. Assume the past service cost is both fully funded and amortized over 13 years by an annual amount of $83,756 each year-end. What interest rate is being used? What amount of total annual pension expense should be recognized until something changes either the normal cost or past or prior service cost? Consider the limits on pension expense specified in *APB Opinion 8.*
2. Assume the past service cost is amortized as in 1 above, and funding is over 12 years. What would be the annual funding payments? Assuming no other change through the second year, what is the annual pension expense for the first and second years?

Exercise 18–13

Expected annual pension benefits to be received by a group of Liston Company's employees due to retire in eight years and to be paid one year to four years after retirement are as follows:

End of year 1	$40,000
End of year 2	25,000
End of year 3	13,000
End of year 4	8,000
Thereafter	-0-
Total pension payments	$86,000

Funds deposited with the pension fund trustee are expected to earn 7% per annum. The contract states that a sum sufficient to fund all of the prospective payments must be on deposit by the date the employees plan to retire, assuming the first pension payment is made one year after retirement date.

Required (round amounts to nearest dollar):

1. *(a)* Compute the amount that must be on deposit as of the employees' retirement date, which is one year before the first retirement payment. *(b)* Prove the correctness of your calculation by preparing a schedule which reflects earnings and the payout over the four-year period.
2. Using the funding amount computed in 1 above, determine the equal annual contributions to the pension fund trustee which will fully fund the pension payout requirements. Assume the accumulation is to occur over the last eight years the employees are on the payroll, and that the last deposit is made on retirement date, which is one year before the first payout.
3. Suppose (instead of as in 2 above) that the pension plan was adopted six years before the employees would retire and that they were to be given credit for the two years of employment preceding adoption of the plan. Determine *(a)* the amount of past service cost as of the date of inception of the plan and *(b)* how much must be contributed in equal annual payments over the six-year period in order to fully fund the pension arrangement.

PROBLEMS

PART A: PROBLEMS 18–1 to 18–3

Problem 18–1

Pension plans have developed in an environment characterized by a complex interaction of social concepts, legal considerations, actuarial techniques, income tax laws, and accounting practices. *APB Opinion 8* delineates acceptable accounting practices for the cost of pension plans.

Required:
The following terms are relevant to accounting for the cost of pension plans. Define or explain briefly each of the following:

a. Normal cost.
b. Past service cost.
c. Prior service cost.
d. Funded plan.
e. Vested benefits.
f. Actuarial gains and losses.
g. Interest.

(AICPA adapted)

Problem 18–2

Annual pension payments of $150,000 are to be paid to retired employees of Ellis Company at the start of each year based on past service credits already earned by employees. The payments are expected to continue seven years beyond the initial payment. An interest rate of 6% is considered appropriate.

Required (round amounts to nearest dollar):

1. Calculate the present value of the past service benefits.
2. Assuming a fund equal to the amount calculated in 1 above is held by the pension fund trustee at the time

the pension payments to the retirees are to begin, prepare a schedule to show how the payments will deplete the fund over the term of the payments. Suggested headings: Start of Year; Interest at 6%; Pension Payment; Reduction of Fund; and Fund Balance.

3. Describe how the present value of the past service benefits would be calculated if the first payment of $150,000 was paid immediately and later payments were made at one-year intervals thereafter; the second payment was $135,000, and the third payment was $109,000.

Problem 18–3

Pension benefits of $150,000 per year are to be paid to a group of employees who are scheduled to retire in 15 years. It is expected the benefits will be paid for eight years, then cease. The first benefit payment is to occur one year after retirement. Money on deposit to fund the pensions is expected to earn 6% per year.

Required (round amounts to nearest dollar):

1. Calculate *(a)* the amount that would have to be deposited in a single lump sum on the date the employees retire and *(b)* instead, the amount of each annual payment required to a pension fund trustee if 15 funding payments are to be made, the last of which is on the retirement date.
2. Assume the same level of benefits based on 15 years' service but the plan was not adopted until five years later. Thus, 10 equal annual payments, the last of which is on the employees' retirement date, are to be paid to the pension fund trustee. Calculate the amount of each annual funding payment under this modification.
3. Assume that pension payments are to be made at the start of each year for eight years; in other words, the first payment is to occur on the date the employees retire.
   a. Calculate the amount of each equal annual payment to the pension fund if there are 15 payments and the last payment to the sinking fund trustee is on the same date as the first payment to the pensioners.
   b. Prove the accuracy of your results with a table reflecting the trustee's payouts and interest revenue over the eight-year period. Suggested column headings: Year; Payments; Interest; Reduction of Principal; and Balance of Principal.

PART B: PROBLEMS 18–4 to 18–15

Problem 18–4

The actuary for Alpha Company determined that the past service cost under the pension plan about to be adopted will be $70,000 and that pension fund investments can be expected to earn 8%. Management accepts the actuary's recommendations and has decided to fund the past service cost over an 8-year period but to amortize it over a 10-year period.

Required (disregard maximum-minimum limits and round to the nearest dollar):

1. Prepare a schedule of past service pension costs and related funding if the first payment and first amortization are to be made at the end of 19A. The plan was adopted early in January 19A.
2. Based on amounts derived in the schedule, give the entries at the end of 19D to record the 19D funding payment on the past service cost amount plus $8,000 paid for normal pension costs for 19D.
3. Based on amounts derived in the schedule, give the entries at the end of 19I to record the funding payment on the past service cost amount plus $9,000 paid for normal pension cost for 19I.

Problem 18–5

Pratt Company initiated a funded, noncontributory pension plan effective January 1, 19A. This was several years after the company began operations. There was a past service cost of $30,000. Because the company had excess cash, it decided to fund the past service cost fully as of year-end 19A, and to amortize the past service cost over four years. In connection with the latter, the pension fund trustee estimated that the pension fund investments will earn 7% over the foreseeable future. The funding payments will be made to the pension fund trustee.

Required (disregard maximum-minimum limits and round amounts to nearest dollar):

1. Prepare a schedule of amortization and funding of the past service cost. Round all amounts to the nearest dollar.
2. Assuming that normal pension costs are 19A, $16,000; 19B, $18,400; 19C, $24,000; and 19D, $31,500, give the entries related to pension expense and cash payments for each year.
3. Suppose the first eligible employee retired late in 19C and was paid first benefits amounting to $500 late that year. Give any entries indicated for Pratt. Explain.
4. Indicate amounts that would be reported on the income statement and balance sheet for 19A, 19B, 19C, and 19D.

Problem 18–6

After having been in business a number of years without a pension plan, Corso Corporation adopted a funded noncontributory pension plan. For simplicity, the number of periods will be limited and the first year of the pension plan will be designated as 19A. Past service cost as of January 1, 19A, amounted to $60,000. Normal pension costs for 19A were $12,000; in the four succeeding years they were $13,500, $16,000, $18,400, and $19,900.

Required (round amounts to nearest dollar and disregard maximum-minimum limits):

1. Using an 8% interest rate and assuming year-end funding, prepare schedules of amortization and funding for each of the following sets of assumptions as to years over which amortization and funding of past service cost is to occur:

	Periods	
	Amortization	**Funding**
Case A	4	4
Case B	3	4
Case C	4	3
Case D	4	1

2. For each case, give the entries related to pension expense and cash payments for 19A, 19D, and 19E (round all computations to nearest dollar).
3. For each case, indicate amounts concerning the pension plan that would be reported on the income statement and balance sheet for 19A, 19D, and 19E.

Problem 18–7

Set forth below is an amortization and funding schedule for a company whose past service cost was determined to be $1,000,000 when its pension plan was adopted. If the company were to amortize this amount of past service cost over a 10-year period and to fund it over a 12-year period, and if the expected earnings rate on pension fund investments were 6%, the schedule presented below would apply.

Required (round amounts to nearest dollar):

1. If the company's normal pension cost for years 1 and 2, respectively, amounted to $260,000 and $309,000, and management had decided initially to postpone funding of the past service cost, what is the *minimum* pension expense the company could report under provisions of *APB Opinion 8?* Show computations. (Assume there are no vesting requirements.)
2. If the company instead decided to implement the funding and amortization as reflected on the schedule, what is the *maximum* pension expense the company could report for years 1 and 2 if normal pension costs are the same as given in 1 above?
3. Again assume the normal pension costs for the first two years are the same as given in 1 above. In this instance management decided to amortize the $1,000,000 past service cost over 10 years but to fund it over 8 years and to use a 7% annual rate in connection with past service cost. Calculate the 10-year amortization factor and the 8-year funding factor; prepare a partial schedule (through the first two years) and indicate the *maximum* allowed pension expense for years 1 and 2 under provisions of *APB Opinion 8.* Round to nearest dollar.

Problem 18–8

Santos Corporation has been in business for approximately 25 years. Recently management made a decision to institute

(Relates to Problem 18–7)

Schedule of Amortization of Past Service Cost and Related Funding

	Amortization of Past Service Pension Cost—10 Years				Balance Sheet—Liability	
Year	**10-Year Amortization Factor**	**Addition for 6 Percent Interest**	**Past Service Pension Expense**	**12-Year Funding**	**Credit (Debit)**	**Account Balance**
1	$135,867.96	—	$135,867.96	$119,277.03	$ 16,590.93	$ 16,590.93
2	135,867.96	$ 995.46	136,863.42	119,277.03	17,586.39	34,177.32
3	135,867.96	2,050.64	137,918.60	119,277.03	18,641.57	52,818.89
4	135,867.96	3,169.13	139,037.09	119,277.03	19,760.06	72,578.95
5	135,867.96	4,354.74	140,222.70	119,277.03	20,945.67	93,524.62
6	135,867.96	5,611.48	141,479.44	119,277.03	22,202.41	115,727.03
7	135,867.96	6,943.62	142,811.58	119,277.03	23,534.55	139,261.58
8	135,867.96	8,355.69	144,223.65	119,277.03	24,946.62	164,208.20
9	135,867.96	9,852.49	145,720.45	119,277.03	26,443.42	190,651.62
10	135,867.96	11,439.10	147,307.06	119,277.03	28,030.03	218,681.65
11	—	13,120.90	13,120.90	119,277.03	(106,156.13)	112,525.52
12	—	6,751.51	6,751.51	119,277.03	(112,525.52)	—

a funded, noncontributory pension plan. An independent trustee has been selected to receive and disburse the pension funds in accordance with the plan. To shorten this problem the amounts are relatively small and the number of periods limited. Assume the pension plan started on January 1, 19B, and that estimates through 19F made by the actuary were as follows:

1. Past service cost at the beginning of 19B, $60,000.
2. Normal pension costs are 19B, $12,000; 19C, $14,000; 19D, $17,000; 19E, $18,500; and 19F, $19,800.
3. Interest rate, 5%.

In respect to amortization of past service costs and their funding, there are four separate cases:

	Periods	
Case	**Amortization**	**Funding**
A..............	4	4
B..............	3	4
C..............	4	3
D..............	4	1

Required (for each case, show computations and round amounts to nearest dollar; disregard maximum-minimum limits):

1. Prepare a schedule of amortization and funding (assume funding at year-end).
2. Give the entries for years 19B, 19E, and 19F.
3. Give the balances to be reported on the financial statements of Santos Corporation for 19B, 19E, and 19F.

Problem 18–9

An actuary determined that the past service cost of Davis Company was $67,100 and recommended that an 8% interest rate be used in its funding and amortization calculations.

Required (round all amounts to the nearest dollar and disregard maximum-minimum limits; payments are at year-end):

Prepare a schedule to reflect past service pension costs for the company under the terms indicated.

1. Management of Davis Company has determined that the past service cost is to be funded over a 10-year period and to be amortized over 12 years.
2. Instead, assume the decision is to amortize the past service cost over 8 years but (as above) to fund it over 10 years.
3. In conjunction with the schedule prepared for 1 above, assume that in addition to the year-end payment for past service cost funding, Davis also pays $17,000 normal costs at the end of each year (10 and 11). Give journal entries to record pension expense and the payments at the end of the 10th and 11th years.

Problem 18–10

Blass Company was organized in 1970. The decision was made to iniate a funded, noncontributory pension plan starting January 1, 1982. The First State Bank will be the independent funding agency. The actuary determined the past service cost at date of inception of the plan (as of January 1, 1982) to be $30,000 and the normal pension cost for the year 1982 to be $9,300. Since the company had excess cash, it decided to completely fund the past service cost at the end of 1982. Past service cost will be amortized over four years; a 6% rate of interest can be earned on pension fund investments.

Required (round amounts to nearest dollar and disregard maximum-minimum limits):

1. Prepare a schedule of funding and amortization of past service costs.
2. Give all entries indicated for 1982.
3. Give entries for 1983–87 assuming the following normal pension costs: 1983, $14,000; 1984, $16,000; 1985, $18,000; 1986, $20,000; and 1987, $22,000.
4. Assume a long-time employee retired during 1987 and was paid a first monthly pension benefit of $300. Give any entries that Blass should make. Explain.
5. What would be reported on the income statement and balance sheet for each period 1982–87 inclusive?

Problem 18–11

Brand Company began operations a number of years ago. Recently its management decided to add pensions as a fringe benefit for the employees. The actuary employed determined that as of the year the pension plan was to begin, past service costs amounted to $800,000. A decision was made to amortize these costs over eight years and to fund them over six years. Star Trust Company will serve as the independent trustee of the noncontributory pension plan; a 7% interest rate can be earned on pension fund investments.

Required (disregard maximum-minimum limits and round to the nearest dollar):

1. Prepare a schedule of amortization and funding for the past service cost.
2. Give journal entries for years, 1, 3, 6, and 7 if normal pension costs paid for these years are, respectively, $59,000, $68,000, $75,000, and $84,000, and other payments are in accordance with the schedule developed in 1 above.
3. Give any necessary entry to record payments in year 6 to long-time employee Ramona who retired in that year and who drew pension benefits that year amounting to $1,800. Explain.

4. What would be reported on the income statement and balance sheet of Brand Company for years 1, 3, 6, and 7 in respect to its pension plan?

Problem 18–12

Ross Corporation was organized more than a decade ago. Four years ago the company established a formal pension plan to provide retirement benefits for all employees. The plan is noncontributory and funded through an independent trustee, Second Bank, which pays all pension benefits as they become due. Past service cost of $121,930 is being amortized over 15 years and funded over 10 years. Ross also funds an amount equal to current normal cost net of any actuarial gains and losses. There have been no plan amendments since inception. Portions of the independent actuary's report covering the latest year appear below.

I. Current year's funding and pension cost:		
Normal cost (before adjustment for actuarial gains) computed under entry age normal method		$34,150
Actuarial gains:		
Investment gains (losses):		
Excess of expected dividend revenue over actual dividend revenue		(350)
Gain on sale of investments		4,050
Gains in actuarial assumptions for:		
Mortality		3,400
Employee turnover		5,050
Reduction in pension cost from closing of plant		8,000
Net actuarial gains		20,150
Normal cost (funded currently)	$ 14,000	14,000
Past service costs:		
Funding	18,171	
Amortization		14,245
Total funded	$ 32,171	
Total pension expense for financial statement purposes		$28,245
II. Fund assets:		
Cash	$ 4,200	
Dividends receivable	1,525	
Investment in common stocks, at cost (market value, $177,800)	162,750	
Total fund assets	$168,475	

Required:

1. Comment on *(a)* treatment of actuarial gains and losses and *(b)* computation of pension expense for financial statement purposes relative to GAAP requirements for accounting for pension plan costs.
2. What interest rate is being used in connection with the past service cost amortization and funding? Support your findings. (AICPA adapted)

Problem 18–13

Liberty, Inc., a calendar-year corporation, adopted a company pension plan at the beginning of 19B. This plan is to be funded and noncontributory. Liberty used an appropriate actuarial cost method to determine its normal annual pension expense for 19B and 19C as $80,000 and $91,000, respectively, which is paid in the same year.

Liberty's actuarially determined past service cost was funded on December 31, 19B, at an amount properly computed as $106,000. This past service cost is to be amortized at the maximum amount permitted by generally accepted accounting principles. The interest factor assumed by the actuary is 6%.

Required:
Prepare entries to record the funding of past service cost on December 31, 19B, and the pension expenses for the years 19B and 19C. Under each journal entry give the reasoning to support your entry. Round to the nearest dollar. (AICPA adapted)

Problem 18–14

A partial schedule reflecting amortization and funding of past service cost appears below. Amounts are rounded to the nearest dollar.

Year	*(a)*	*(b)*	*(c)*	*(d)*	*(e)*	*(f)*
1 . . .	$17,686	—	$17,686	$20,000	$2,314	$ 2,314
2 . . .	17,686	$162	17,524	20,000	2,476	4,790
3 . . .	17,686	335	17,351	20,000	2,649	7,439
4 . . .	17,686	521	17,165	20,000	2,835	10,274

Required (round amounts to nearest dollar and disregard maximum-minimum limits):

1. What interest rate is being used?
2. Based on the funding amounts in column *(d)*, which are to continue through the end of the 10th year, what amount of past service cost is being funded? (Answer to the nearest dollar.)
3. What is the length of the amortization period? Show computations.
4. Assign appropriate captions to columns *(a)* through *(f)* and complete the schedule for the funding and amortization. (A slight rounding error is expected.)
5. Record pension expense and the pension funding payments for the 10th and 11th years if, in addition to the year-end funding, payment of $41,000 is made for normal pension cost for each of these years.

Problem 18–15

On January 1, 19A, Brand Corporation instituted a pension plan. On that date actuaries determined the past service cost to be $5,400,000. During 19A, and again in 19B, Brand employees earned $3,150,000 in present value of future pension benefits (recognized at year-end). Brand appointed Low-Risk Insurance Company as the funding agency of the plan and makes all funding payments to Low-Risk at the end of each year. Interest on the unfunded pension liability accrues at 7% per year. Brand funds an amount each year equal to the pension expense recognized for the year. Brand's fiscal year ends on December 31. No plan amendments or revaluations, vesting, or benefit payments occurred in 19A or 19B.

Required:

1. Present the journal entries that Brand would make on December 31, 19A, and 19B, to recognize pension expense of the corporation assuming past service cost is amortized over 10 years under the following assumptions:
   a. The minimum-maximum rule is ignored (for illustrative purposes only).
   b. The minimum-maximum rule is applied according to GAAP.
2. What amount of unfunded pension liability would Brand report in the tabular portion of its balance sheet at December 31, 19A? 19B? Give the reason for your answer.
3. What amount of unfunded pension liability would Brand report in the notes to its financial statements for the year ended December 31, 19A? 19B?
4. What is the basic reason for the difference between the answers to 2 and 3 above?

19

Accounting for Leases

A lease contract involves two parties at a minimum, a lessor and a lessee, and an asset which is leased. The lessor owns the leased asset and receives periodic rents from the lessee in exchange for allowing its use. The lessee has an obligation to pay periodic rents and the contractual right to use the lessor's asset.

Leasing is very common in the United States, accounting for an estimated $150 billion of volume in 1979.[1] That same year, 537 of the 600 companies surveyed in *Accounting Trends & Techniques* leased some of their operational assets.[2] Because of increasing use of leasing to finance the acquisition of the use of assets, the accounting profession has promulgated extensive accounting guidelines for leases. This chapter discusses and illustrates these guidelines; it is subdivided as follows:

Part A—Fundamentals of Accounting for Leases by Lessors and Lessees
Part B—Additional Issues in Accounting for Leases
Supplement 19–A—Leveraged Leases

Part A: Fundamentals of Accounting for Leases by Lessors and Lessees

HISTORICAL BACKGROUND OF ACCOUNTING FOR LEASES

Standards of financial accounting and reporting for leases have been evolving since 1949 when *ARB 38* was issued. The latest of the accounting profession's major efforts to set standards for lease accounting is FASB, *Statement of Financial Accounting Standards No. 13,* "Accounting for Leases," May 1980, as amended and interpreted.[3] Many of the amendments and interpretations deal with specific issues which are beyond the scope of this book. Nevertheless, *FASB Statement 13,* as amended and

[1] S. R. Rose, "Leasing: The Creative Force of Asset Financing," *Fortune,* August 27, 1979, pp. 55–79.

[2] AICPA, *Accounting Trends & Techniques 1980* (New York: AICPA, 1980), table 2–27.

[3] In May 1980, the FASB combined *FASB Statements 17, 22, 23, and 26–29,* and *FASB Interpretations 19, 21, 23, 24, 26* and *27,* in a revised version of FASB, *Statement of Financial Accounting Standards No. 13,* "Accounting for Leases" (Stamford, Conn., May 1980).

interpreted, is the primary source for this chapter.

Leasing became popular after World War II, increased significantly during the 1960s and 1970s, and continues to be important in the 1980s. At the outset lease agreements were fairly standard; however, in recent years they have become quite complex, which is due to an important degree to the opportunities to maximize income tax advantages. Today leases vary considerably from operating leases (such as the short-term rental of a truck for one or a number of days) to leveraged capital leases (such as the long-term rental of a large computer). Lessors usually are leasing companies, individual investors, or manufacturers. Lessees are from practically all industries and may be large, medium, or small businesses. The primary advantages attributed to leasing include the following:

1. Leasing may provide an important avenue to a manufacturer for increasing sales of its products (i.e., on lease/buy contracts as a secondary means of selling products).
2. Leasing may resolve a critical cash problem for the lessee by making available 100 percent financing for the leased asset.[4]
3. In the case of an operating-type lease, the lessee's debt-to-equity ratio is not increased.
4. Leasing makes immediately available, to the lessee, needed equipment that is not obsolete and is in new or good condition.
5. Leasing often helps the lessee to avoid the risk and cost of idle equipment.
6. Leasing may provide significant income tax advantages to the parties to the lease agreement. These tax advantages stem from the investment tax credit, accelerated depreciation, and tax deductibility of the full amount of the lease payments. Lease agreements often are drawn to shift the tax advantages to the party that is in the higher tax bracket (see Supplement 19–A).

BASIC ACCOUNTING FOR LEASES

FASB Statement 13, par. 1, defines a lease as "an agreement conveying the right to use property, plant, or equipment (land and/or depreciable assets) usually for a stated period of time."[5]

For accounting purposes, leases are classified broadly as *(a)* **operating** leases and *(b)* **capital** leases. The specific provisions of the lease agreement between the lessor and lessee (i.e., the lease contract), rather than the characteristics of the leased asset, determine the lease classification. An **operating lease does not transfer a material ownership interest from the lessor to the lessee.** In contrast, **a capital lease specifies the transfer of a material ownership interest** in the leased asset from the lessor to the lessee.[6] An example of a **lease provision** that evidences the transfer of a material ownership interest in the leased asset is the transfer of title to the leased asset from the lessor to the lessee at the end of the lease term.

To illustrate the features of an **operating**-type lease (versus a **capital**-type lease), assume Lessor Company leased a computer to Lessee Company on a monthly basis, and Lessor Company is responsible for all maintenance, property taxes, and insurance. In this lease the lessee incurred one risk—the payment of the rentals—and obtained one benefit—temporary use of the asset; thus, no material ownership interest was transferred. In contrast, to illustrate a **capital**-type lease, assume Lessor Company leased an identical computer to Lessee Company on a long-term, noncancellable lease, and the lease specified that, at the end of the lease term, Lessee Company could retain the leased asset with no additional payments. In this case the **lessee** assumed practically all of the risks and rewards of ownership from the date of the lease agreement.

Operating leases pose no significant accounting problems. In contrast, capital leases pose difficult accounting issues because they effectively transfer a **material ownership interest** (i.e., most of the risks

[4] An important issue to the lessee is determination of whether to lease or buy the needed asset. Certain finance texts consider this issue in greater detail.

[5] This definition does not include [*a*] "agreements that are contracts for services that do not transfer the right to use property, plant, or equipment from one contracting party to the other . . . , [*b*] lease agreements concerning the rights to explore for or to exploit natural resources such as oil, gas, minerals, and timber . . . , nor [*c*] licensing agreements for items such as motion picture films, plays, manuscripts, patents, and copyrights."

[6] The transfer of a **material ownership interest** often is described as a transfer of "most of the risks and rewards of ownership" of the leased asset. Risks involve such disadvantages as casualty loss, wear and tear, obsolescence, and maintenance. Rewards often involve such benefits as the right to use, collect periodic rents, benefit from increase in the value of the leased asset, and may include transfer of ownership of the leased asset at the end of the lease term.

and rewards of ownership) from lessor to lessee without a formal transfer of ownership of the leased asset. This transfer of a material ownership interest strongly suggests that the *(a)* lessor should record a sale and *(b)* lessee should record a purchase of the leased asset when the lease is initiated. However, lessees, in accounting for leases, often are motivated to avoid reporting the lease liability (and capitalizing the leased asset) because recording the lease liability increases their debt-to-equity ratio. Therefore, a basic thrust of *FASB Statement 13* is to provide guidelines for deciding when lessees should recognize a capital-type lease and, as a consequence, record the leased item as an asset and record the related lease liability.[7]

This thrust is consistent with the **reporting principle,** which requires that an entity report all of its assets and liabilities. In respect to income measurement, the **matching principle** governs the amount of expense to be reported for leases, and the **cost principle** governs the determination of the cost of any leased assets capitalized; in turn, asset cost affects the future amount of expense recognized.

Lessors often are motivated to record a lease as a sale of the leased asset and to recognize revenue on the sale at the date the lease is initiated. Therefore, the basic accounting issue for lessors is the recognition of revenue. Consequently, a basic thrust of *FASB Statement 13* is to provide guidelines for the recognition of lease revenue by the lessor. The **revenue principle** is of primary importance to the lessor, and the **reporting principle** governs the disclosures of lease revenue and any lease receivables created by the lease.

In view of these issues, *FASB Statement 13* basically provides the following accounting and reporting guidelines:

[7] *APB Opinion 5* (1964) contained similar guidelines which proved ineffective in requiring lessees to capitalize leased assets with lease provisions which are similar to installment purchases (i.e., capital leases).

Summary of Accounting Guidelines for Lessees

Lessor			Lessee		
Operating Leases					
No recognition of a sale at inception of the lease.			No capitalization of cost of leased asset at inception of the lease.		
Recognize periodic collection as rent revenue:			Recognize period payment as rent expense:		
Debit: Cash	xx		Debit: Rent expense	xx	
Credit: Rent revenue		xx	Credit: Cash		xx
Recognizes depreciation expense.					
Capital Leases					
Recognize transfer (similar to a sale) of the leased asset at inception of the lease:			Recognize acquisition (similar to a purchase) of the leased asset at inception of the lease:		
Debit: Lease receivable	xx		Debit: Leased asset	xx	
Credit: Asset leased*		xx	Credit: Lease liability		xx
* See Exhibit 19–5 for a sales-type lease.					
Recognize periodic collection part as interest revenue and part as reduction of principal of the receivable:			Recognize periodic payment part as interest expense and part as reduction of principal of the liability:		
Debit: Cash	xx		Debit: Interest expense	xx	
Credit: Interest revenue		xx	Debit: Lease liability	xx	
Credit: Lease receivable		xx	Credit: Cash		xx
			Recognize depreciation expense.		

Because each lease involves both a lessor and a lessee, an "accounting symmetry" exists theoretically; that is, the two parties usually record opposite and symmetrical entries. This symmetry is evident in the above summary. Such symmetry is prevalent in many kinds of transactions, such as a credit sale (i.e., between the seller and buyer) and bonds (i.e., between the borrower and lender). In Part A of this chapter this symmetry is maintained for instructional purposes.[8]

LEASE ACCOUNTING TERMINOLOGY

FASB Statement 13 (par. 5) provides definitions for the following terms (emphasis added):[9]

1. **Fair [market] value of the leased property** is "the price for which the property could be sold in an arm's-length transaction between unrelated parties."
2. A **bargain purchase option** is a "provision allowing the lessee, at his option, to purchase the leased property for a price which is sufficiently lower than the expected fair [market] value of the property at the date the option becomes exercisable, that exercise of the option appears, at the inception of the lease, to be reasonably assured."
3. A **bargain renewal option** is a "provision allowing the lessee, at his option, to renew the lease for a rental sufficiently lower than the fair rental of the property at the date the option becomes exercisable, that exercise of the option appears, at the inception of the lease, to be reasonably assured."
4. The **lease term** is "the fixed noncancelable term of the lease plus [*a*] all periods, if any, covered by bargain renewal options . . . and [*b*] all periods, if any, covered by ordinary renewal options preceding the date as of which a bargain purchase option . . . is exercisable; . . . however, in no case shall the lease term extend beyond the date a bargain purchase option becomes exercisable."
5. The **estimated residual value** of the leased asset is "the estimated fair [market] value of the leased [asset] at the end of the lease term." Depending upon the provisions of the lease agreement, estimated residual value may **not** be guaranteed; or it may be guaranteed in full or in part by the lessee or by a third-party guarantor. If it is **not** guaranteed in full, the **unguaranteed residual value** is "the estimated residual value exclusive of any portion guaranteed."
6. **Minimum lease payments** (emphasis added):
   [*a*] "From the standpoint of the **lessee:** The payments that the lessee is obligated to make or can be required to make in connection with the leased property, [excluding] . . . the lessee's obligation to pay . . . executory costs such as insurance, maintenance, and taxes in connection with the leased property. . . . If the lease contains a bargain purchase option, only the minimum rental payments over the lease term . . . and the payment called for by the bargain purchase option shall be included in the minimum lease payments. [If the lease does **not** contain a bargain purchase option], minimum lease payments include the following:
      [i] The minimum rental payments called for by the lease over the lease term.
      [ii] Any guarantee by the lessee of the residual value at expiration of the lease term, whether or not payment of the guarantee constitutes a purchase of the leased property.
      [iii] Any payment that the lessee must make or can be required to make upon failure to renew or extend the lease at the expiration of the lease term, whether or not the payment would constitute a purchase of the leased property."[10]

   [*b*] "From the standpoint of the **lessor:** The payments described in [*a*] above plus any guarantee of the residual value . . . by a third party unrelated to either the lessee

[8] However, in some cases a lease may be classified differently (i.e., as an operating-type or as a capital-type) by the lessor and lessee. In such cases the "accounting symmetry" does not exist.

[9] The definitions presented here are adapted from *FASB Statement 13* to capture their essence without excessive detail. They are presented together to consolidate the definitions in one place even though some of the definitions are used only in Part B. Therefore, you should refer to these definitions throughout the chapter.

[10] Because these so-called penalty payments would be accounted for in a manner similar to a guarantee of residual value by the lessee, they are not discussed separately in this chapter. Instead, the related discussions and illustrations focus (in Part B) on guaranteed residual value.

or the lessor." [Note: When there is a bargain purchase option, residual value is of no future concern to the lessor because the leased asset will be retained by the lessee at the end of the lease term.]

7. Lessor's **gross investment in the lease** [only for direct financing and sales-type leases] is the minimum lease payments, net of executory costs, plus the unguaranteed residual value retained by the lessor.
8. Lessor's **net investment in the lease** [only for direct financing and sales-type leases] is the gross investment less unearned interest revenue included therein.
9. The **interest rate implicit in the lease** is "the discount rate that, when applied to [*a*] the minimum lease payments . . . excluding that portion of the payments representing executory costs to be paid by the lessor, together with any profit thereon, and [*b*] the **unguaranteed** residual value . . . accruing to the benefit of the lessor, causes the aggregate present value at the beginning of the lease term to be equal to the fair [i.e., market] value of the leased property . . . at the inception of the lease, minus any investment tax credit retained by the lessor and expected to be realized by him."[11] [This definition applies to both the lessor and the lessee.]
10. The **lessee's incremental borrowing rate** is "the rate that, at the inception of the lease, the lessee would have incurred to borrow over a similar term the funds necessary to purchase the leased asset."

CLASSIFICATION OF LEASES

In the preceding section the two basic classifications of leases—operating and capital—were discussed briefly. *FASB Statement 13* provides subclassifications of leases for the lessor and lessee as follows:

Standpoint of lessor:

1. Capital leases—broadly defined as a lease that transfers a material ownership interest in the leased asset (i.e., most of the risks and rewards of ownership) from the lessor to the lessee, or includes a "bargain purchase option." The following subclassifications are used:
   a. Direct financing leases.
   b. Sales-type leases.
   c. Leveraged leases.
2. Operating leases—all other leases.

Standpoint of lessee:

1. Capital leases—defined as above (with no subclassifications).
2. Operating leases—all other leases.

The next several sections discuss and illustrate accounting by the lessor and lessee for the above lease classifications (leveraged leases are discussed in Supplement 19–A). Operating leases are discussed first because they pose **no** new substantive accounting issues.

ACCOUNTING FOR OPERATING LEASES BY LESSOR AND LESSEE

An operating lease does not transfer a material ownership interest in the leased asset from the lessor to the lessee. It does not meet the criteria (discussed below) for classification as a capital lease. An example of an operating lease situation is presented in Exhibit 19–1: Panel A describes the hypothetical situation illustrated and Panel B gives the illustrative entries.

---

[11] Because of the highly technical nature of this definition, it is illustrated as follows:

1. Minimum lease payments—five annual rentals of $13,743 each, payable at December 31 of each year. Lease term begins on January 1, 19A; lease contains no guarantee of residual value nor a bargain purchase option.
2. Executory costs (maintenance, taxes, insurance) included in each lease payment—$600.
3. Unguaranteed residual value of leased asset accruing to benefit of lessor at end of lease term—$20,000.
4. Fair (i.e., market) value of leased property at inception of lease—$60,000.
5. Investment tax credit retained and realized by lessor—$6,000 (i.e., 10 percent of $60,000).

Computation of interest rate implicit in the lease:

Fair value − Investment tax credit = PV of minimum lease payments excluding executory costs + PV of unguaranteed residual value retained by lessor

$$\$60{,}000 - \$6{,}000 = (\$13{,}743 - \$600) \times P_{o_{n=5;i=?}} + (\$20{,}000 \times p_{n=5;i=?})$$
$$\$54{,}000 = \$13{,}143 \times 3.35216^* \text{ (Table 5–4, } i = 15\%)^* + \$20{,}000 \times .49718^* \text{ (Table 5–2, } i = 15\%)$$
$$\$54{,}000 = \$54{,}000^*$$

* Trial and error selection of rates until a rate is identified which "balances" the above equation. In this example the interest rate implicit in the lease is 15 percent per year.

EXHIBIT 19–1: Operating Lease—Accounting by Lessor and Lessee

Panel A—Hypothetical Situation:

1. Lessor rents an office to Lessee for an annual rental of $4,800, payable in advance each March 1.
2. The fiscal years of each party end on December 31.

Panel B—Entries:

Lessor			Lessee		
March 1, 19A: To record annual rental:					
Cash	4,800		Rent expense	4,800	
Rent revenue		4,800	Cash		4,800
December 10, 19A: To record payment of property taxes on the entire building:					
Expense	6,000		No entry.		
Cash		6,000			
December 31, 19A (etc.): To record payment of monthly telephone bill incurred by the lessee:					
No entry.			Expense	65	
			Cash		65
December 31, 19A (end of accounting year): To record adjusting entry (two months' rent unearned by lessor and prepaid by lessee):					
Rent revenue ($4,800 × 2/12)	800		Prepaid rent expense	800	
Unearned rent revenue		800	Rent expense		800

Rent Paid in Advance on Operating Leases

An operating lease becomes slightly more complex when, in addition to the periodic rent, a nonrefundable down payment is made in advance. In this situation, the down payment is debited to Cash and credited to Unearned Rent Revenue by the **lessor.** The **lessee** debits an asset account called Leasehold (sometimes called Prepaid Rent Expense) and credits Cash. Each party must amortize the prepayment over the life of the lease on a systematic and rational basis. Alternative amortization methods commonly used by the lessor (for Unearned Rent Revenue) and the lessee (for Leaseholds) are as follows:

1. **Straight-line method**—A **constant-dollar amount** of the prepayment is allocated as expense to each period covered by the lease.
2. **Interest (present value) method**—A constant **rate** of expense allocation is used per period, as determined by application of the annuity concept to the prepayment. This method uses the present value of an annuity concept (Table 5–4).

Recording by the lessor and lessee for this type of situation, including the alternative methods of amortization of the prepayment, is presented in Exhibit 19–2. Panel A presents the hypothetical situation and Panel B gives the entries.

In Exhibit 19–2, Case A (i.e., the straight-line method), each party amortizes $2,000 of the prepayment per year. In contrast, under Case B (i.e., the interest method), the annual amortization increases (from $1,778 in 19A to $2,231 in 19C; see column [3]), because of the decreasing annual interest amount (column [2]) on the declining unamortized balance of the advance rental (column [4]). In the authors' opinion, the **interest method** theoretically is preferable because it gives effect to the interest element of the advance rental; that is, the lessor receives cash in advance and "incurs" interest expense on the unearned rent revenue (a liability), and the lessee pays cash in advance and "earns" interest revenue on the asset, leasehold (see the alternative set of entries given at the bottom of Exhibit 19–2). Nevertheless, the straight-line method frequently is used because *(a)* it is less complex, *(b)* the amortization amounts produced by the two methods often are not materially different, and *(c)* many accountants interpret *FASB Statement 13* to specify straight line for most situations.

BASIS FOR RECOGNIZING CAPITAL LEASES

Prior to the issuance of *FASB Statement 13,* most lessees accounted for leases using the operating lease procedures described in the preceding section. Many accounting theorists contended that this approach was improper. In their view, a lease that transfers a material ownership interest in the leased property creates an asset for the **lessee** that is more than a temporary right to use the leased property. They contended that this interest should be recognized by the lessee by capitalizing the lease rentals at their present value. Further, they reasoned that such a lease creates a liability equal to the present value of the future rents, which also should be recognized by the lessee. Similar reasoning led to the conclusion that the **lessor** should recognize a sale of the asset, in which case the lessor would record a receivable and remove the cost of the asset from the lessor's records. Following this line of reasoning, the material ownership interest should be **depreciated** by the lessee (rather than by the lessor). Moreover, the lease rental payments should be accounted for by both parties in the same manner as periodic payments on a long-term liability, that is, as a combination of interest and reduction of debt.

Proponents of lease capitalization also pointed out that recognition of an asset and a liability on lessees' financial statements would make their statements more comparable with those of entities which purchased their operating properties and financed the purchase price with long-term debt. They argued that a lessee company which leased properties under long-term leases and a company that owned similar properties financed by long-term debt were in essentially the same economic position. Both companies were committed to a series of regular payments over a long term; lessees paid "rents," while owners paid interest and principal on the debt. Both had exclusive rights to use similar assets over most or all of the useful lives of the assets. For many long-term lease contracts, both were committed to pay repairs and maintenance, taxes and insurance, and similar **executory costs** associated with assets over their useful lives. If lessees could avoid recognition of assets and liabilities while owners could not, their financial statements would not be comparable even though they were in similar economic and, to some extent, similar legal positions.

Opposition to the capitalization of lease rentals centered mainly around reluctance of lessees to recognize a liability. They pointed out that various other long-term executory contracts are not recognized under GAAP, and that leases should not be singled out for different treatment.[12] Lessees noted that sudden recognition of large, previously unrecorded long-term lease liabilities would cause many lessees to be in technical default on some of their debt covenants because when they incurred other long-term debt, they often agreed concurrently to limit their indebtedness to a certain amount or to maintain a certain ratio of assets to debt. Also, for many lessees, a switch from operating lease accounting to lease capitalization would reduce earnings for periods shortly after the change, but would not change aggregate long-term earnings.

Criteria for Capital Leases—Lessors and Lessees

FASB Statement 13 specifies detailed criteria for a lease contract to qualify as a capital lease. Four of the criteria apply to both lessors and lessees; if **any one** of these four criteria is met by the lessee, the lease qualifies as a capital lease for the lessee. In contrast, lessors must meet any one of the four criteria plus two additional criteria (which do not apply to lessees). Exhibit 19–3 presents the specified criteria and their application to the lessor and lessee. Because of these two additional criteria for the lessor, not all leases that qualify as capital leases to the lessee qualify as capital leases to the lessor.

[12] Employment contracts whereby employers agree to pay certain salaries for future services, purchase commitments which do not involve probable losses, and pensions are but a few of the types of executory contracts for which an asset and corresponding liability are not recognized under GAAP.

Thus, a capital lease to the lessee could be an operating lease to the lessor.

ACCOUNTING FOR CAPITAL LEASES

The classification of leases given under the preceding heading, Classification of Leases, indicated that for the **lessor**, capital leases are subdivided as follows:

a. Direct financing leases—At inception of the lease, the lessor does not recognize a "manufacturer's or dealer's profit (loss)." That is, the lessor determines the rental payments based upon the **cost** to the lessor of the leased asset plus interest at the implicit rate charged by the lessor. In such leases, the cost (or carrying amount, if different) and the market value of the leased property are assumed to be the same. This assumption means that the rentals are based upon the lessor's cost or carrying amount and that interest revenue is the **only** revenue recognized on the lease by the lessor.

b. Sales-type leases—At inception of the lease, the lessor recognizes a "manufacturer's or dealer's

EXHIBIT 19–2: Operating Lease with Amortization of Advance Rental—Accounting by Lessor and Lessee

Panel A—Hypothetical Situation:
Lessor rents an office to Lessee under the following lease terms:

a. Lease term, three years, beginning January 1, 19A.
b. Annual rental, $4,800 payable in advance each January 1.
c. Advance rental (i.e., a down payment in addition to annual rentals), $6,000, payable January 1, 19A.
d. Interest rate applicable to the advance rental, 12 percent.
e. Fiscal years of each party end on December 31.

Panel B—Entries:

Lessor			**Lessee**		
January 1, 19A:					
To record advance rental:					
Cash	6,000		Leasehold (prepaid rent expense)	6,000	
Unearned rent revenue		6,000	Cash		6,000
To record annual rental:					
Cash	4,800		Rent expense	4,800	
Rent revenue		4,800	Cash		4,800
December 31, 19A (end of the accounting period): To record amortization of advance rental (for 12 months):					
***Case A*—straight-line method:**					
Unearned rent revenue	2,000		Rent expense	2,000	
Rent revenue		2,000	Leasehold		2,000
Computation: $6,000 × 12/36 = $2,000.					
Closing entry (Case A):					
Rent revenue ($4,800 + $2,000)	6,800				
Income summary		6,800			
***Case B*—interest method** (from column 3 of the table below):*					
Unearned rent revenue	1,778		Rent expense	1,778	
Rent revenue		1,778	Leasehold		1,778
Closing entry (Case B):					
Rent revenue ($4,800 + $1,778)	6,578		Income summary	6,578	
Income summary		6,578	Rent expense		6,578

EXHIBIT 19–2 ***(concluded)***

Computations: Schedule of Amortization of Advance Rental Payment—Interest Method

Period	(1) Periodic Rent	(2) Interest (12 Percent)	(3) Amortization of Advance Rental	(4) Unamortized Balance of Advance Rental
1/1/19A				$6,000
12/31/19A	$2,498[(a)]	$ 720[(b)]	$1,778[(c)]	4,222[(d)]
12/31/19B	2,498	507	1,991	2,231
12/31/19C	2,498	267*	2,231	-0-
	$7,494	$1,494	$6,000	

* Rounded to come out even.

[(a)] Implied annual rent = $6,000 ÷ $P_{o_{n=3;i=12\%}}$.
= $6,000 ÷ 2.40183 (Table 5–4)
= $2,498

[(b)] $6,000 × .12 = $720.

[(c)] $2,498 − $720 = $1,778.

[(d)] $6,000 − $1,778 = $4,222.

Note: An **ordinary annuity** is assumed, that is, that the advance payment represents the present value of three equal year-end amounts of $2,498 each. Alternatively, an **annuity due** could have been assumed, that is, that the three payments would be at the **beginning** of each period.

* An alternate set of entries could be made to recognize **separately** the interest on the advance rental, as follows:

Lessor			Lessee		
Unearned rent revenue	1,778		Rent expense	2,498	
Interest expense	720		Interest revenue		720
Rent revenue		2,498	Leasehold		1,778

profit (loss)" and, in addition, determines the rental payments based upon *(a)* the **selling price** of the leased asset and *(b)* interest at the implicit interest rate charged by the lessor. In such leases, the market value of the leased asset usually is its normal sale price, and this sale price usually exceeds cost (or carrying amount, if different). In such leases the lessor recognizes both *(a)* a profit (loss) on the sale of the leased asset and *(b)* interest revenue on the lease receivable.

c. Leveraged leases—discussed in Supplement 19–A.

In contrast to the two types of capital leases for the lessor, for the **lessee,** both direct financing leases and sales-type leases usually qualify as capital leases.[13] For all capital leases, the lessee records *(a)* the leased asset at its cost, *(b)* periodic interest expense on the related lease liability, *(c)* periodic depreciation expense based on the recorded cost of the leased asset, and *(d)* executory costs such as taxes, insurance, and maintenance.

Termination of Lease Agreements

A capital lease agreement may terminate due to *(a)* a change of provisions in the lease, *(b)* renewal or extension of the original lease, or *(c)* expiration of the lease term. *FASB Statement 13* specifies the accounting for termination by the lessee and lessor as follows:

By lessee: "A termination of a capital lease shall be accounted for by removing the asset and obligation, with gain or loss recognized for the difference" (par. 14c).

By lessor: "A termination of the lease shall be accounted for by removing the net investment [i.e., carrying value of the lease receivable] from the accounts, recording the leased asset at the lower of its original cost, present fair value, or present carrying amount, and the net adjustment shall be [debited] to income of the period" (par. 17, f,iii).

The remainder of this part of the chapter will focus on accounting for capital leases by the lessor and

[13] Because the lessor must apply the same lease capitalization criteria as the lessee, plus two additional criteria, capital-type leases to the lessor usually would be capital leases to the lessee. However, this is not always the case because it is possible for the lease agreement to satisfy criterion 4 (Exhibit 19–3) for the lessor, but not for the lessee. This situation can result from *(a)* use of different interest rates in the present value discounting by the lessor and lessee or *(b)* guarantee of residual value by a third-party guarantor. These topics are discussed in Part B of this chapter.

EXHIBIT 19–3: Criteria for Capital Leases—Lessor and Lessee

For Lessor	For Lessee
Must meet any one of the following four criteria:*	Must meet any one of the following four criteria:*
1. The lease transfers ownership of the leased asset to the lessee by the end of the lease term.	1. Same.
2. The lease contains a bargain purchase option.	2. Same.
3. The lease term is equal to 75 percent or more of the total estimated economic life of the leased asset.	3. Same.
4. The present value of the minimum lease payments at the inception of the lease is at least 90 percent of the fair (i.e., market) value of the leased asset at that time.	4. Same.
Must meet both of the following additional criteria:	
5. Collectibility of the minimum lease payments is reasonably assured.	5. Not applicable.
6. No important uncertainties surround the amount of unreimbursable costs yet to be incurred by the lessor under the lease.†	6. Not applicable.

* Criteria 3 and 4 do not apply if *(a)* the beginning of the lease term falls within the last 25 percent of the total economic life of the leased asset, *(b)* land is the only asset leased, or *(c)* the lease involves both land and building(s). For leases that involve both land and buildings see *FASB Statement 13*, par. 26.

† Important uncertainties might include commitments by the lessor to guarantee performance of the leased asset in a manner more extensive than the typical product warranty or to protect the lessee from obsolescence of the leased asset. However, the necessity of estimating executory costs such as insurance, maintenance, and taxes to be paid by the lessor does not by itself constitute an important uncertainty under this provision.

lessee. First, we will discuss and illustrate a direct financing lease and next a sales-type lease. For each situation, we will use a common illustration and present symmetrical entries for the lessor and lessee.

Exhibit 19–4 illustrates the accounting for a **direct** financing lease to the lessor and for a **capital** lease to the lessee. Panel A presents a hypothetical lease situation that qualifies as a capital lease to both parties. Panel B gives the entries for both the lessor and the lessee, and Panel C illustrates the lease amounts that would be reported on the 19A income statements and balance sheets of the lessor and the lessee. The next two sections discuss the detailed accounting procedures for capital leases by the lessee and lessor, respectively.

Lessee Accounting for Capital Leases

The lessee records a capital lease, at date of inception, by debiting an asset account, with a title such as Leased Property, and crediting Lease Liability for the **present value** of all future rents required (i.e., minimum lease payments as discussed in a subsequent section). Thus, the **lessee's basic approach** to lease valuation can be expressed as follows:

$$\begin{array}{l}\text{Valuation of}\\ \text{leased asset}\\ \text{and related}\\ \text{liability*}\end{array} = \begin{array}{c}\text{Periodic}\\ \text{lease}\\ \text{payments}\end{array} \times \begin{array}{l}\text{Present value}\\ \text{of annuity of}\\ n \text{ rents at } i \text{ rate}\\ \text{of interest}\end{array}$$

* Part B discusses bargain purchase option and residual value; they will affect this computation. For instructional purposes we assume in Part A that these two factors are zero.

In Exhibit 19–4, the lessee's computation of the valuation of the leased asset and the related lease liability is:

$$= \$20{,}000 \times 3.78448 \text{ (Table 5–4, } P_{o_{n=6;i=15\%}}) $$
$$= \underline{\underline{\$75{,}690}}$$

Determination of the appropriate rate of interest to use in the present value discounting is important because it directly affects the valuation of the leased asset and the related lease liability recorded by the lessee. The higher the interest rate used, the lower will be the amount capitalized for the asset and the amount recorded for the liability, and vice versa.

The candidates for the interest rate to be used by the lessee are the *(a)* interest rate **implicit in the lease** (i.e., the rate used by the lessor) and *(b)* lessee's incremental borrowing rate (see definitions under the heading, Lease Accounting Terminology.) In Part A, we assume both parties use the interest rate implicit in the lease. Part B discusses the use of different rates by the lessor and lessee under the heading, Use of Different Interest Rates by Lessor and Lessee.[14]

[14] *FASB Statement 13* constrains the value of the leased asset thus computed; that is, if the present value of the lease payments exceeds the fair (i.e., market) value of the leased asset at inception of the lease, the asset and liability must be recorded at the fair (i.e., market) value of the leased asset.

EXHIBIT 19–4: Accounting for a Capital Lease—Direct Financing; Lessor and Lessee Accounting

Panel A—Hypothetical Situation (simplified by assuming no bargain purchase option and zero residual value):

1. On January 1, 19A, lessor and lessee signed a six-year lease; the estimated useful life of the leased property is six years (there are no collection or cost uncertainties, and the present value of the rentals equals the cost of the leased asset, $75,690). Thus, the lease qualifies as a direct financing lease.
2. Lessor retains ownership of the leased asset, and the estimated residual value is zero.
3. The lease requires six annual rentals of $20,000 each, payable each December 31. Lessor had a 15 percent target rate of return (i.e., implicit rate of interest) on the cost of the asset; therefore, the lessor computed the periodic rentals as follows: $75,690 ÷ $P_{o_{n=6;i=15\%}}$ (3.78448, Table 5–4) = $20,000.
4. The fiscal year of each party ends on December 31.

Panel B—Entries:

Lessor			Lessee		
January 1, 19A (inception of lease):					
Lease receivable	75,690		Leased property*	75,690	
Asset (on direct financing lease)		75,690	Lease liability (on capital lease)		75,690
December 31, 19A (first rental):					
Cash (see amortization schedule below)	20,000		Lease liability	8,647	
Lease receivable		8,647	Interest expense	11,353	
Interest revenue		11,353	Cash		20,000
December 31, 19A (end of accounting period):					
To record depreciation expense for one year		Not applicable	Depreciation expense ($75,690 × 1/6)	12,615	
			Accumulated depreciation		12,615

* Lessee's computation of his cost of leased asset: $20,000 × $P_{o_{n=6;i=15\%}}$ (3.78448, Table 5–4) = $75,690.

Lease Amortization Schedule (ordinary annuity basis):

Date	Annual Lease Payments	Annual Interest at 15 Percent	Reduction of Lease Receivable/Liability	Lease Receivable/Liability Balance
1/1/19A	Initial value			$75,690[(a)]
12/31/19A	$ 20,000	$11,353[(b)]	$ 8,647[(c)]	67,043[(d)]
12/31/19B	20,000	10,056	9,944	57,099
12/31/19C	20,000	8,565	11,435	45,664
12/31/19D	20,000	6,850	13,150	32,514
12/31/19E	20,000	4,877	15,123	17,391
12/31/19F	20,000	2,609	17,391	-0-
	$120,000	$44,310	$75,690	

[(a)] Known by lessor; computed as shown above by lessee (see note * above).
[(b)] $75,690 × .15 = $11,353.
[(c)] $20,000 − $11,353 = $8,647.
[(d)] $75,690 − $8,647 = $67,043.

Panel C—Financial Statements, 19A:

Income statement, lessor: Interest revenue, $11,353.
Income statement, lessee: Interest expense, $11,353; and depreciation expense, $12,615.
Balance sheet, lessor: Lease receivable, $67,043 (from lease amortization schedule above).
Balance sheet, lessee: Leased property (cost $75,690 less accumulated depreciation, $12,615, from Panel B entries for Lessee), $63,075.
Lease liability, $67,043 (from lease amortization schedule above).
(Detailed disclosures are given in Part B of this chapter under Lease Disclosure.)

FASB Statement 13 specifies that the **lessee** shall depreciate the asset cost ($75,690 in Exhibit 19–4) in a manner consistent with the lessee's normal depreciation policy. The period of depreciation must be the lease term rather than the life of the leased property.[15] In respect to **residual value,** when ownership of the leased asset is **retained by the lessor** at the end of the lease term, the **lessee** must ignore residual value if no residual value is guaranteed by the lessee. If the lessee **does** guarantee a residual value amount, that guaranteed amount **must** be used by the lessee as the residual value.

However, if ownership of the leased asset **transfers from the lessor to the lessee** at the end of the lease term, the **lessee** should depreciate the capitalized cost over the **total** useful life of the leased asset to the lessee (rather than over the term of the lease). In this case, the lessee should use the estimated residual value as of the end of the useful life of the asset (rather than as of the end of the lease term). The longer useful life and lower residual value are used in such situations because it is assumed that the lessee will retain the asset permanently after the end of the lease term. This assumption is required by *FASB Statement 13* when the lease *(a)* contains a bargain purchase option or *(b)* transfers ownership of the leased asset from the lessor to the lessee at the end of the lease term. Bargain purchase options and residual value are discussed in more detail in Part B.

The account titles used in Exhibit 19–4 may vary; for example, instead of using an accumulated depreciation (or amortization) account, credits in the depreciation entries could be made directly to the asset account (which parallels the procedures outlined in *FASB Statement 13*). The "depreciation" can be viewed as the amortization of an intangible (i.e., a right to use the leased property). Also, the debit could be to Expense—Amortization of Leased Property Rights, instead of Depreciation Expense.

Accounting Trends & Techniques, 1980, pp 211–18, shows that some lessee companies report their leased assets as a part of property, plant, and equipment, and designate the related expense as "depreciation," while a few other lessee companies report their leased assets separately as intangible operational assets and designate the related expense as "amortization."

[15] Residual value is discussed in more detail in Part B of this chapter under the heading "Residual Value in Capital Leases."

The lessee's entries given in Exhibit 19–4, Panel B, essentially parallel those that would be recorded for an actual purchase on an installment basis, that is, the purchase of an asset on credit, payment of the liability and interest thereon, and depreciation of the asset.[16]

Lessor Accounting for Capital Leases—Direct Financing Lease

Exhibit 19–4 illustrates accounting by the lessor and lessee for one type of capital lease—direct financing. **Lessor** accounting (but not lessee accounting) for capital type leases is somewhat different for *(a)* **direct financing leases** versus *(b)* **sales-type leases.** This section discusses lessor accounting for **direct** financing leases.

The lessor classifies the lease as a **direct financing** lease if there is no "manufacturer's or dealer's profit

[16] In Exhibit 19–4, Panel B, the entry at date of inception of the lease was recorded at "net"; alternatively, it could have been recorded at "gross" as follows, which gives the same results for each party:

Lessor

January 1, 19A (inception of lease):		
Lease receivable	120,000	
Asset (on lease)		75,690
Unearned interest revenue		44,310
December 31, 19A (1st rental):		
Cash	20,000	
Unearned interest revenue	11,353	
Lease receivable		20,000
Interest revenue		11,353

Lessee

January 1, 19A (inception of lease):		
Leased property	75,690	
Discount on lease liability	44,310	
Lease liability		120,000
December 31, 19A (1st rental):		
Lease liability	20,000	
Interest expense	11,353	
Cash		20,000
Discount on lease liability		11,353

FASB Statement 13 (pars. 17 and 18) implies to some people that the lessor, but not the lessee, **must** record a capital-type lease at "gross." However, because either approach can be adapted easily to conform the company's financial statement disclosures to *Statement 13,* either approach can be used for the **recording** phase of accounting for leases, as indicated by inquiry of the FASB. Moreover, this general principle holds: **The FASB is concerned with the information a company discloses and only incidentally with the specific journal entries it makes.**

(loss)," in which case the lessor's cost (or carrying amount, if different) of the leased asset is assumed to equal its fair (i.e., market) value at the inception date (see prior heading, Accounting for Capital Leases). Typically, leasing companies (as opposed to manufacturers and dealers) have only direct financing leases, rather than sales-type leases, because they purchase property for lease and not for resale; thus, they usually emphasize lease rentals rather than selling prices. The lessor's profit objective is to set the periodic rentals at a level sufficiently high to yield the target (expected) rate of return on the lessor's investment in the leased asset. Expressed as a formula, the **lessor's basic approach** to computation of the amount of each periodic rent is as follows:

$$\text{Periodic rental}^* = \frac{\text{Lessor's investment (i.e., cost or carrying amount, if different) in leased asset}}{\text{Present value of annuity of } n \text{ rents at } i \text{ rate of interest}}$$

* Part B discusses bargain purchase option and residual value; they will affect this computation. For instructional purposes we assume in this Part that these two factors are zero.

In Exhibit 19–4, the lessor's computation of the periodic rent is:

$$\text{Rent} = \$75{,}690 \div 3.78448 \text{ (Table 5–4; } P_{o_{n=6;i=15\%}}) = \$20{,}000.$$

The implicit interest rate used by the lessor as the discount rate in the above present value computation is the lessor's target rate of return on the investment.

In Exhibit 19–4, Panel B, the entries illustrate basic accounting symmetry between the lessor and lessee. In respect to this symmetry, observe that the lessor's equation given above is a rearrangement of the **lessee's** formula (see preceding heading, Lessee Accounting for Capital Leases) when the lessor's investment in the leased asset is the same as the lessee's valuation of the leased asset and related liability.

Lessor Accounting for Capital Leases—Sales Type

Sales-type leases were defined under the heading, Accounting for Capital Leases. **The basic distinction between direct financing leases and sales-type leases is that in a sales-type lease, a gross margin (i.e., "manufacturer's or dealer's profit or loss") is recognized by the lessor at inception of the lease.** Operationally, this means that in a sales-type lease the fair (i.e., market) value of the leased asset at the inception of the lease is greater or less than the lessor's cost (or carrying amount, if different).

Sales-type leases typically arise when a manufacturer or dealer, in addition to offering its products on a cash or normal short-term credit basis, will use a leasing arrangement as a secondary means of marketing its products. However, a lessor need not be a manufacturer or dealer to realize a "profit or loss" at inception of the lease if the market value of the leased asset is greater (or less) than its cost or carrying amount. The profit objective of a company that will either sell or lease its products is to earn a profit on the sale of a leased asset and also to earn interest on the related lease receivable. Thus, for a sales-type lease, two distinctly different "profits" are recognized during the lease term:

1. **Manufacturer's or dealer's profit** (more precisely, gross margin or gross profit) is recognized in full **at date of inception** of the lease, which is computed as follows:

$$\left\{\begin{matrix}\text{Normal sales price}\\ \text{(market value)}\\ \text{of the leased asset}\end{matrix}\right\} - \left\{\begin{matrix}\text{Cost (or carrying}\\ \text{amount, if different)}\\ \text{of the leased asset}\end{matrix}\right\}$$

2. **Interest revenue** on the lease receivable is recognized **over the term of the lease;** the total amount of interest is computed as follows:

$$\left\{\begin{matrix}\text{Gross lease}\\ \text{receivable (includes}\\ \text{the interest charge)}\end{matrix}\right\} - \left\{\begin{matrix}\text{Normal sales price}\\ \text{(market value)}\\ \text{of the leased asset}\end{matrix}\right\}$$

Exhibit 19–5 illustrates accounting for a sales-type lease by Lessor X and Lessee Y. Panel A presents the hypothetical situation, Panel B gives the lessor's and lessee's entries, and Panel C illustrates the amounts reported on the income statements and balance sheets for the first year. The lessee's entries are presented to illustrate that they are not affected by whether the lease is direct financing or sales type to the lessor. It is important to emphasize that for a **sales-type** lease the **lessee** capitalizes the leased asset on the basis of its normal **selling price** rather than on the lessor's cost because in a sales-type lease the lessor computes the periodic rental based on the selling price of the asset rather than on cost.

In Exhibit 19–5, the lessor's entry at inception of

EXHIBIT 19–5: Accounting for a Capital Lease—Sales Type; Lessor and Lessee Accounting

Panel A—Hypothetical Situation (simplified by assuming no bargain purchase option and zero residual value):

1. On January 1, 19A, Lessor X and Lessee Y signed a six-year lease, which qualified as a capital lease to both parties. The annual rental is payable each December 31.
2. The leased asset had a cash-equivalent sales price (i.e., market value) of $95,000 and cost Lessor X, $75,690, which indicates a gross margin of $19,310. The asset had an estimated useful life of six years and a zero estimated residual value.
3. Lessor X retains title to the leased asset and, based upon a 15 percent target (expected) return on the receivable, computed the annual rentals, which are payable each December 31, as: $95,000 ÷ $P_{o_{n=6;i=15\%}}$ (3.78448, Table 5–4) = $25,103.
4. The fiscal year ends on December 31 for both parties.

Panel B—Entries:

Lessor

January 1, 19A (inception of lease):

Lease receivable	95,000	
Cost of goods sold	75,690	
Sales revenue		95,000
Asset (on sales-type lease)		75,690

December 31, 19A (first rental; see schedule below):

Cash	25,103	
Lease receivable		10,853
Interest revenue		14,250

December 31, 19A (end of accounting period):

To record depreciation expense for one year.	Not Applicable

Lessee

Leased property	95,000	
Lease liability		95,000

Lessee's computation:
$25,103 × 3.78448 = $95,000.

Lease liability	10,853	
Interest expense	14,250	
Cash		25,103

Depreciation expense ($95,000 × 1/6)	15,833	
Accumulated depreciation		15,833

Lease Amortization Schedule (ordinary annuity basis):

Date	Annual Lease Payments	Annual Interest at 15 Percent	Reduction of Lease Receivable/Liability	Lease Receivable/Liability Balance
1/1/19A	Initial value			$95,000[a]
12/31/19A	$ 25,103	$14,250[b]	$10,853[c]	84,147[d]
12/31/19B	25,103	12,622	12,481	71,666
12/31/19C	25,103	10,750	14,353	57,313
12/31/19D	25,103	8,597	16,506	40,807
12/31/19E	25,103	6,121	18,982	21,825
12/31/19F	25,103	3,278*	21,825	–0–
	$150,618	$55,618	$95,000	

* Rounded to come out even.
[a] Known by lessor; computed by lessee as shown above.
[b] $95,000 × .15 = $14,250.
[c] $25,103 − $14,250 = $10,853.
[d] $95,000 − $10,853 = $84,147.

Panel C—Financial Statements, 19A:

Income statement, lessor: Sales revenue, $95,000; cost of goods sold, $75,690; and interest revenue, $14,250.
Income statement, lessee: Interest expense, $14,250; and depreciation expense, $15,833.
Balance sheet, lessor: Lease receivable, $84,147 (from lease amortization schedule above).
Balance sheet, lessee: Leased property (cost $95,000 less accumulated depreciation, $15,833 from Panel B entries for Lessee), $79,167.
Lease liability $84,147 (from lease amortization schedule above).
(Detailed disclosures are given in Part B of this chapter under Lease Disclosures.)

a sales-type lease records the lease as though it were a normal sale of the leased asset. That is, the lessor debits the lease receivable and credits sales revenue for the sale price of the leased asset, which in the hypothetical situation of the exhibit, is the same as the present value of the rents to be received. Concurrently, the lessor debits cost of goods sold and credits the leased asset for its cost or carrying amount, $75,690. The difference of $19,310 (i.e., $95,000 − $75,690) measures the lessor's gross margin (i.e., manufacturer's or dealer's profit) on the "sale." The subsequent entries by the lessor to record collections of periodic rent, interest revenue, and reduction of the lease receivable are similar to the lessor's entries under a direct financing lease (Exhibit 19–4).[17]

Lease Amortization—Annuity Due Basis. The lease agreements in Exhibit 19–4 and 19–5 specified year-end rental payments, which means an **ordinary** annuity. Alternatively, the lease agreements could have specified rental payments at the **start** of each period (which is the usual situation). In this case, each situation would involve an **annuity due.**

To illustrate an **annuity due** situation, we will refer to Exhibit 19–4. In that situation the lessor would compute the annual rentals as $75,690 ÷ (3.78448, Table 5–4, × 1.15) = $17,391 (rounded). Similarly, the lessee would compute the amount that should be capitalized at the inception of the lease as $17,391 × (3.78448 × 1.15) = $75,690 (rounded). The **annuity due** amortization schedule would be as shown in Exhibit 19–6. The **pattern of entries** in this modification of the example would be similar to that illustrated in Exhibit 19–4, except that the amounts of interest and depreciation each period would differ. Interest at each year-end would be **accrued** because the cash flow is on January 1 of each year. Exhibit 19–7, Part B, presents a comprehensive example of an **annuity due situation.**

[17] If the lease agreement had specified the periodic rents at the beginning of the period, the present value of the lease receivable and the related amount of sales revenue would involve an **annuity due,** similar to the computations and amortization schedule given in Exhibit 19–6. Only the **amounts** in Exhibits 19–4 and 19–5 **(ordinary annuity)** would be altered for an annuity due; the **account titles** would remain the same as in Exhibits 19–4 and 19–5.

EXHIBIT 19–6: Capital Lease—Amortization Schedule; Annuity Due Basis (basic data given in Exhibit 19–4, Panel A; annual lease payments, $17,391)

Date	Annual Lease Payments	Annual Interest at 15 Percent	Lease Receivable/ Liability Balance
1/1/19A . . .	Initial value		$75,690[b]
1/1/19A . . .	$17,391[a]		58,299[c]
12/31/19A . . .		$8,745[d]	67,044[e]
1/1/19B . . .	17,391		49,653
12/31/19B . . .		7,448	57,101
1/1/19C . . .	17,391		39,710
12/31/19C . . .		5,957	45,667
1/1/19D . . .	17,391		28,276
12/31/19D . . .		4,241	32,517
1/1/19E . . .	17,391		15,126
12/31/19E . . .		2,269	17,395
1/1/19F . . .	17,395*		-0-

* Rounded to come out even.
[a] Lessor: $75,690 ÷ (3.78448, Table 5–4, × 1.15) = $17,391.
[b] Lessee: $17,391 × (3.78448 × 1.15) = $75,690.
[c] $75,690 − $17,391 = $58,299.
[d] $58,299 × .15 = $8,745.
[e] $58,299 + $8,745 = $67,044.

Part B: Additional Issues in Accounting for Leases

Part A discussed and illustrated the fundamentals of accounting for leases by lessees and lessors. Part B considers the following additional issues in accounting for leases:

1. Bargain purchase options in capital leases.
2. Residual value in capital leases.
3. Executory and initial direct costs (lessor).
4. Sale-and-leaseback arrangements.
5. Use of different interest rates by lessor and lessee—the interest rate implicit in the lease versus the lessee's incremental borrowing rate.
6. Classification of lease receivables and payables.
7. Lease disclosure requirements.

BARGAIN PURCHASE OPTIONS IN CAPITAL LEASES

The definition of a bargain purchase option (BPO) is given in Part A under the heading, Lease Accounting Terminology. You should read that definition before proceeding. A BPO permits the lessee to purchase the leased property, during a specified period of the lease term, at a "bargain" price which is sufficiently low to make it reasonably assured that the lessee will take advantage of the "bargain." In effect, a BPO is the sale of the "residual value" of the leased property by the lessor to the lessee at the specified "bargain" price.

The inclusion of a BPO in a capital lease contract creates **two** cash flows to the lessor from the lessee: one is from the periodic rentals and the other is from the BPO price. Thus, a BPO affects *(a)* the amount of the annual rentals required to meet the lessor's target rate of return and *(b)* the lessee's capitalizable cost of the leased asset. Relative to the Part A situations, which assumed zero residual value of the leased asset and no BPO, the annual rental in a lease with a BPO is **less** than otherwise because the lessor recovers part of the investment in the leased asset through the BPO price; this recovery reduces the amount that must be received from the periodic rentals. The lessor includes the BPO amount in computing the amount of each annual rental, and the lessee includes the BPO in computing the cost of the leased asset to be capitalized (i.e., the present value of minimum lease payments).

Exhibit 19–7 illustrates lessor and lessee accounting for a BPO situation. The situation, given initially in Exhibit 19–4, is adapted in two ways: *(a)* the lease agreement includes a BPO of $10,000 exercisable at the end of the six-year lease term and *(b)* the lease payments are on January 1 of each year; therefore, the situation also involves an **annuity due.**

Exhibit 19–7, Panel A, describes a BPO situation in the context of a **direct financing** lease to the lessor and a **capital lease** to the lessee. Panel B presents representative entries of the lessor and lessee.

Exhibit 19–7, Panel A, presents the **lessor's** inclusion of the assumed BPO amount of $10,000 in the computation of the annual rentals. Observe that the lessor must include the two different cash inflows: *(a)* one when the BPO is exercised, which involves a present value of lump-sum computation (Table 5–2); and *(b)* another from the annual rentals, which involves present value of annuity computation (Table 5–4). This two-stage computation by the lessor is based upon the *(a)* lease specifications; *(b)* lessor's recorded cost (or carrying value, if different) of the leased asset because the lease is a direct financing lease; and *(c)* lessor's target rate of return (i.e., the implicit interest rate) on the investment.

The **lessee** has knowledge of the lease specifications (which include the annual rental amount of $16,398) and the BPO (at end of sixth year, $10,000). We assume that the lessee has been informed by the lessor that the implicit rate of interest in the lease is 15 percent.[18] With these data, the lessee computes the capitalizable cost of the leased asset, which includes the present value of **both** the periodic rentals and the BPO. Details of the lessee's computations are given in Exhibit 19–7, Panel B.

Exhibit 19–7, Panel B, presents representative entries for the lessor and lessee. At inception date of the lease, January 1, 19A, the first lease payment of $16,398 is recorded because this is an annuity **due** situation. Therefore, the **lessor** credits the leased asset account for its balance ($75,690); debits Cash for the first rental ($16,398) and debits the remaining lease receivable amount of $59,292 (i.e., $75,690 − $16,398).[19] The **lessee** records the computed capitalizable cost of the asset, payment of the first rental, and the amount of the remaining liability in a symmetric entry.

On December 31, 19A, each party must **accrue** interest for one year because the second rental payment of cash will not be made, nor recorded, until the next day, January 1, 19B. On January 1, 19B, all of the $16,398 cash rental will be recorded as a reduction of the lease receivable and lease liability accounts, respectively.

Only the **lessee** records **depreciation** expense on the leased asset because under a capital lease a purchase of the leased asset is assumed. When there is a BPO, the lessee depreciates the leased assets over its **total** expected useful life (less any estimated residual value at the end of that time) rather than the lease term of six years, because it is assumed that the BPO will be exercised, in which case the lessee will continue "ownership" of the leased asset beyond the lease term. That is, the lessee depreciates the asset just as if the lessee actually owned the asset.

If on December 31, 19F (the BPO date), the lessee let the bargain purchase option lapse, the lessor and the lessee would remove from their respective ac-

[18] Assumed to be less than the incremental borrowing rate of the lessee.

[19] These data could be recorded as two entries, one at $75,690 and the other at $16,398.

EXHIBIT 19–7: Accounting for Direct Financing Lease with Bargain Purchase Option (annuity due basis)

Panel A—Hypothetical Situation (adapted from Exhibits 19–4 and 19–5):

1. On January 1, 19A, lessor and lessee signed a six-year lease which qualifies as a direct financing lease to the lessor and a capital lease to the lessee. The leased asset cost the lessor $75,690; the estimated total life of the asset is eight years, and the estimated residual value at that time is zero.
2. The lessee has an option to purchase the asset for $10,000 on December 31, 19F; at that date (i.e., end of the sixth year), the estimated residual value is $15,000.
3. The lease requires six annual rentals of $16,398, payable each January 1. Lessor had a target rate (i.e., the implicit interest rate) of 15 percent on the cost of the asset; therefore, the lessor computed the periodic rentals as follows:

Cost (or carrying value, if different) of leased asset	$75,690
Deduct: *PV* of BPO; $10,000 × $p_{n=6;i=15\%}$ (.43233, Table 5–2)	4,323
Net cost to recover through rentals	$71,367
Annual rental: $71,367 ÷ $P_{d_{n=6;i=15\%}}$ (3.78448, Table 5–4, × 1.15 = 4.35215)	$16,398

4. The fiscal year of each party ends on December 31.

Panel B—Entries:

Lessor			Lessee		
January 1, 19A (inception of lease):					
Cash	16,398		Leased property†	75,690	
Lease receivable*	59,292		Lease liability		59,292
Asset		75,690	Cash		16,398
December 31, 19A (adjusting entries):					
Lease receivable	8,894		Interest expense*	8,894	
Interest revenue*		8,894	Lease liability		8,894
* Computation: See schedule below.			Depreciation expense	9,461	
			Accumulated depreciation		9,461
			($75,690 ÷ 8 years = $9,461).		
December 31, 19F (exercise of BPO):					
Cash	10,000		Lease liability	10,000	
Lease receivable		10,000	Cash		10,000

† Lessee's computation of cost of leased asset (the lessee capitalizes the BPO):

PV of rentals: $16,398 × $P_{d_{n=6;i=15\%}}$ (3.78448, Table 5–4, × 1.15 = 4.35215)	$71,367
PV of BPO: $10,000 × $p_{n=6;i=15\%}$ (.43233, Table 5–2)	4,323
Valuation of leased asset to be capitalized (rentals plus BPO)	$75,690

Lease Amortization Schedule with Bargain Purchase Option (annuity due basis):

Date	Annual Lease Payments	Annual Interest at 15 Percent	Lease Liability/Receivable Balance
1/1/19A	Initial value		$75,690[a]
1/1/19A	$16,398		59,292[b]
12/31/19A		$8,894[c]	68,186[d]
1/1/19B	16,398		51,788
12/31/19B		7,768	59,556
1/1/19C	16,398		43,158
12/31/19C		6,474	49,632
1/1/19D	16,398		33,234
12/31/19D		4,985	38,219
1/1/19E	16,398		21,821
12/31/19E		3,273	25,094
1/1/19F	16,398		8,696
12/31/19F		1,304	10,000
12/31/19F (BPO price)	10,000		-0-

[a] Computed above. [b] $75,690 − $16,398 = $59,292.
[c] $59,292 × .15 = $8,894. [d] $59,292 + $8,894 = $68,186.

counts all remaining balances related to the lease contract and recognize a loss. If that had occurred (assuming the December 31, 19F, accrual entry has been made), the **lessor's** and the **lessee's** December 31, 19F, entries to record lapse of the bargain purchase option would be as follows, assuming the *new* estimate of residual value of the leased asset on that date was $8,000 (instead of the original estimate of $15,000) and that the lease was not renewed:[20]

Lessor:

Asset (new residual value)	8,000	
Loss on lapse of lease purchase option	2,000	
Lease receivable (Exhibit 19–7, Panel B)		10,000

Lessee:

Lease liability (Exhibit 19–7, Panel B)	10,000	
Loss on lapse of lease purchase option	8,923	
Accumulated depreciation ($9,461.25 × 6)	56,767	
Leased property		75,690

RESIDUAL VALUE IN CAPITAL LEASES

Residual value often exists at the termination date of a capital lease, especially when the lease term is less than the total estimated economic life of the leased property. In such cases, two different estimated residual values may have to be considered; one is the estimated residual value at the end of the lease term, and the other is the estimated residual value at the end of the total estimated useful life of the leased property. For example, in Exhibit 19–7, Panel A, item 2, the **estimated** residual value at the end of the six-year lease term was $15,000, and at the end of the asset's eight-year total estimated life, the estimate was zero.

[20] The **lessor** has a loss of $2,000 because the estimated $8,000 residual value on the BPO date, December 31, 19F, was less than the balance in the Lease Receivable account of $10,000. Had there been no change in the original estimate of residual value of $15,000, the lessor would record a gain of $5,000. Alternate computation of the **lessee's** loss:

Cash disbursed from 1/1/19A through 12/31/19F ($16,398 × 6)		$98,388
Expenses recognized through 12/31/19F:		
Interest (Exhibit 19–7, 2nd col.)	$32,698	
Depreciation ($75,690 × 6/8)	56,767	
Total expenses recognized		89,465
Excess of payments over amounts debited for the lease (i.e., the loss)		$ 8,923

Because an estimated residual value at the end of the lease term has **economic value,** that residual value must be incorporated in the accounting for the lease. Therefore, it is necessary to determine which party (i.e., lessor or lessee) the lease agreement specifies shall own the residual value (i.e., own the leased asset) at the end of the lease term.

The accounting impact of an estimated residual value (at the end of the lease term) in a capital lease may be summarized as follows:[21]

Lessee gets the residual value:

1. The leased property and its residual value at the end of the lease term belong to the **lessee** at no additional cost (above the annual lease rentals). In this situation, the residual value does not affect *(a)* the **lessor's** computation of the periodic lease payments nor the lessor's accounting or *(b)* the **lessee's** cost to be capitalized. However, the **lessee** should depreciate the asset over its **total** useful life less any estimated residual value at the end of that total life.
2. The estimated residual value at the end of the lease term is "purchased" by the lessee through a BPO. In this situation the BPO amount is included in the lease accounting by **both** the **lessor** and **lessee** as illustrated in Exhibit 19–7. In a BPO situation the **lessee** should depreciate the capitalized cost leased asset over its total useful life (rather than the lease term) less any estimated residual value as of the end of that total life because it is assumed that the lessee will exercise the BPO.

Lessor retains the residual value:

3. The estimated residual value retained by the lessor, at the end of the lease term, may be *(a)* **unguaranteed** by the lessee or *(b)* **guaranteed,** in full or in part, by the lessee or *(c)* guaranteed by a third party, depending upon the provisions of the lease agreement. The first two situations are discussed below.

[21] If the estimated residual value at the end of the lease term is zero, the accounting and related lease computations are as illustrated in Part A of this chapter because a zero residual value was assumed throughout those discussions. The provisions of *FASB Statement 13* relating to residual value in capital leases are complex and difficult to understand (e.g., refer to the definition of **guaranteed** and **unguaranteed** residual values in Part A, Lease Accounting Terminology).

Unguaranteed Residual Value Retained by Lessor

When the lease agreement provides that the **lessor** shall retain the leased asset at the end of the lease term, any residual value is owned by the **lessor.** When that residual value is **unguaranteed** by the lessee, the **lessor** should compute the periodic rentals by subtracting the present value of the estimated residual value from the total amount to be recovered under the lease agreement. Similarly, the **lessee** will capitalize only the lease payments, which would exclude any amount for residual value. This means that the **lessee does not** capitalize the unguaranteed residual value retained by the lessor.[22]

To illustrate a capital lease with an **unguaranteed** residual value, Exhibit 19–4 (ordinary annuity basis) is adapted; Exhibit 19–8 presents the adapted situation. Panel A restates that situation to incorporate an unguaranteed residual value of $20,000 at the end of the lease term. The lessor's computation of the annual rentals also is shown in Panel A. Observe that subtraction of the residual value in the lessor's computation causes the annual rental to decrease from $20,000 to $17,715. Panel B presents selected entries for the lessor and lessee and the lessee's computation of the cost of the leased asset to be capitalized (which does not include the unguaranteed residual value). The entries (and the amortization schedules) are different between the lessor and lessee (even if they used the same implicit interest rate) because the estimated unguaranteed residual value is retained in the lessor's accounts, but is not capitalized in the lessee's accounts. The lessor's entry on January 1, 19A, date of inception of the lease, removes the cost of the leased asset and records the receivable (including the $20,000 residual value). The **last entry,** made at the termination of the lease removes the residual value ($20,000) from the receivable and returns it to its original asset account.[23]

The **lessee** records the value of the leased asset and the lease liability at the present value of the minimum lease payments, which excludes the unguaranteed residual value (see footnote 22). In computing depreciation expense over the lease term, the lessee disregards all unguaranteed residual values.

The separate amortization schedules for the lessor and lessee given in Exhibit 19–8 should be examined carefully because they are different. In particular, the **lessor's** amortization schedule, as illustrated, is designed to leave an asset balance of $20,000 (i.e., the residual value) in the lessor's Lease Receivable account. The initial value for the lessor is the lessor's cost of the leased asset ($75,690) because the lease is a direct financing lease to the lessor. In contrast, the **lessee's** amortization schedule starts with the lease liability amount ($67,043).

At the end of the lease term the residual value of the leased asset, which in this situation is retained by the lessor, is transferred by the **lessor** from the Lease Receivable account to the original asset account (see December 31, 19F entry); in contrast, all of the **lessee's** lease account balances will be zero at that time.

Residual Value Guaranteed by Lessee and Retained by Lessor

In this situation, the lessor retains the residual value of the leased asset, and the lease agreement requires the lessee to **guarantee a specified minimum residual value** at the end of the lease term. For example, assume that the lease agreement specified that the lessee must guarantee $15,000 of the total estimated residual value of $20,000. Any guaranteed residual value usually is negotiated between the parties when the lease terms are agreed upon. Under this particular lease provision, the lessee must pay the lessor for any excess of the guaranteed amount over the "actual" residual value, which is determined (usually by an external independent party) at the end of the lease term. To continue the example of Exhibit 19–8, assume the actual residual value at the end of the lease term determined in accordance with the lease contract turns out to be $14,000, rather than the previously estimated $20,000. Assuming a $15,000 guarantee of residual value, the lessee will pay the lessor $1,000 cash.

A residual value guarantee by the lessee, when included in a capital lease (either direct financing

---

[22] If the **direct-financing** lease agreement requires a partial guarantee of residual value, the lessee would capitalize the present value of the guaranteed amount, as discussed in the next section. For a **sales type lease,** it means that the **lessor does not** include in sales revenue or cost of goods sold the present value of the residual value retained by the lessor.

[23] Some accountants prefer to leave the residual value in its original asset account during the lease term because it will not be "collected for" during that term. Both approaches produce the same end results. *FASB Statement 13,* par 18a, states that "the unguaranteed residual value accruing to the benefit of the lessor" should be "recorded as [included in] the gross investment in the lease." This specification relates more fundamentally to computation of the lease payments by the lessor and not to the details of a specific journal entry (see last sentence of footnote 16).

EXHIBIT 19–8: Accounting for Capital Lease (direct financing) with Unguaranteed Residual Value

Panel A—Hypothetical Situation (adapted from Exhibit 19–4):

1. On January 1, 19A, lessor and lessee signed a six-year direct financing lease. Lessor's cost (or carrying value, if different) was $75,690.
2. Lessor retains ownership of the leased asset at the termination of the lease term. At that time the estimated residual value (RV) is $20,000, which is **unguaranteed** by the lessee because the contract did not impose a residual value guarantee on the lessee.
3. The lease requires six annual rentals of $17,715, payable each December 31. The lessor's target rate of return is 15 percent; therefore, lessor computed the periodic rentals, on **ordinary** annuity basis, as follows:

Cost of the leased asset	$75,690
Deduct: PV of the estimated RV, $20,000 × $p_{n=6;i=15\%}$ (.43233, Table 5–2)	8,647
Net asset cost to be recovered through rentals	$67,043

Annual rental: $67,043 ÷ $P_{o_{n=6;\ i=15\%}}$ (3.78448, Table 5–4) = $17,715

4. The fiscal year of each party ends on December 31.

Panel B—Entries:

Lessor

January 1, 19A (inception of lease):

Lease receivable	75,690*	
Asset		75,690

* This entry records the $20,000 RV in the lease receivable account. The entry could have been made to record the RV in an asset account, Leased Property.

December 31, 19A (first rental):

Cash	17,715	
Lease receivable		6,361
Interest revenue		11,354

See lessor's amortization schedule below.

Lessee

January 1, 19A:

Leased property†	67,043	
Lease liability		67,043

December 31, 19A:

Lease liability	7,659	
Interest expense	10,056	
Cash		17,715

See lessee's amortization schedule below.

Depreciation expense	11,174	
Accumulated depreciation		11,174

$67,043 ÷ 6 years = $11,174.

December 31, 19F (end of lease term—to remove the RV from the Lease Receivable account):

Lessor:

Asset	20,000	
Lease receivable		20,000

Lessee: No entry.

† Lessee's computation of cost of leased asset (the unguaranteed residual value is not capitalized by the lessee): $17,715 × $P_{o_{n=6;i=15\%}}$ (3.78448, Table 5–4) = $67,043.

Lease Amortization Schedules (ordinary annuity basis):

		Lessor			Lessee		
Date	Lease Payments	Interest at 15 Percent	Receivable Reduction	Receivable Balance	Interest at 15 Percent	Liability Reduction	Liability Balance
1/1/19A	Initial value			$75,690			$67,043
12/31/19A	$ 17,715	$11,354	$ 6,361	69,329	$10,056	$ 7,659	59,384
12/31/19B	17,715	10,399	7,316	62,013	8,908	8,807	50,577
12/31/19C	17,715	9,302	8,413	53,600	7,587	10,128	40,449
12/31/19D	17,715	8,040	9,675	43,925	6,067	11,648	28,801
12/31/19E	17,715	6,589	11,126	32,799	4,320	13,395	15,406
12/31/19F	17,715	4,916‡	12,799	20,000(RV)	2,309‡	15,406	-0-
	$106,290	$50,600	$55,690		$39,243	$67,043	

‡ Rounded to come out even.

EXHIBIT 19–9: Accounting for a Capital Lease (direct financing) with Guaranteed Residual Value

Panel A—Hypothetical Situation (adapted from Exhibit 19–4):

1. On January 1, 19A, lessor A and lessee B signed a six-year direct financing lease. Lessor's cost (or carrying value, if different) was $75,690. The lease terms qualify the lease as direct financing.
2. Lessor retains ownership of the leased asset at termination of the lease; on January 1, 19A, lessor and lessee estimated a residual value of $15,000. Also, the terms of the lease agreement specify that the lessee will **guarantee** a minimum residual value of $15,000. If the actual residual value determined at the end of the lease term is less than $15,000, the lessee must pay the difference in cash at lease termination date.
3. The lease requires six annual rentals of $18,287, payable each December 31. The lessor's target rate of return is 15 percent; therefore, the lessor computed the periodic rentals, on **ordinary** annuity basis, as follows:

Cost of the leased asset	$75,690
Deduct the PV of the guaranteed residual value:	
$15,000 × $p_{n=6;i=15\%}$ (.43233, Table 5–2)	6,485
Net asset cost to be recovered through rentals	$69,205
Annual rental: $69,205 ÷ $P_{o_{n=6;i=15\%}}$ (3.78448, Table 5–4)	$18,287

4. The actual residual value at December 31, 19F, was determined independently to be $14,000.
5. The fiscal year of each party ends December 31.

Panel B—Entries:

January 1, 19A (inception of lease):

Lessor	Debit	Credit	Lessee	Debit	Credit
Lease receivable	75,690		Leased property*	75,690	
Asset		75,690	Lease liability		75,690

December 31, 19A (first rental):

Lessor	Debit	Credit	Lessee	Debit	Credit
Cash	18,287		Lease liability	6,933	
Interest receivable		6,933	Interest expense	11,354	
Interest revenue		11,354	Cash		18,287
			Depreciation expense	10,115	
			Accumulated depreciation		10,115
			($75,690 − $15,000) ÷ 6 years = $10,115.		

December 31, 19F (lease termination; assuming an actual residual value of $14,000):

Lessor	Debit	Credit	Lessee	Debit	Credit
Asset	14,000		Lease liability	15,000	
Cash ($15,000 − $14,000)	1,000		Loss on lease contract	1,000	
Lease receivable		15,000	Leased property		15,000
			Cash		1,000

* Lessee's computation of cost of leased asset (the guaranteed residual value is capitalized):

Lease payments: $18,287 × $P_{o_{n=6;\ i=15\%}}$ (3.78448, Table 5–4)	$69,205
Guaranteed RV: $15,000 × $p_{n=6;\ i=15\%}$ (.43233, Table 5–2)	6,485
Total cost of leased asset to be capitalized	$75,690

Lease Amortization Schedule (ordinary annuity basis):

Date	Annual Lease Payments	Annual Interest at 15 Percent	Decrease in Receivable/Liability	Lease Receivable/Liability Balance
1/1/19A	Initial value			$75,690
12/31/19A	$18,287	$11,354	$ 6,933	68,757
12/31/19B	18,287	10,314	7,973	60,784
12/31/19C	18,287	9,118	9,169	51,615
12/31/19D	18,287	7,742	10,545	41,070
12/31/19E	18,287	6,161	12,126	28,944
12/31/19F	18,287	4,343*	13,944	15,000 (guaranteed RV)

* Rounded to come out even.

or sales type), is intended to accomplish one or more purposes, such as to *(a)* protect the lessor against loss on the residual value and *(b)* encourage the lessee to exercise diligence in the use and maintenance of the leased asset during the lease term.

To compute the periodic lease payments, the **lessor** will subtract the present value of the residual value (including both guaranteed and unguaranteed portions) from the total amount to be recovered under the lease agreement because at the inception of the lease the lessor would expect to realize the full amount of the residual value (partially in cash and/or the unguaranteed residual value of the leased asset) at the end of the lease term.

To illustrate a capital lease with a **residual value fully guaranteed** by the lessee and retained by the lessor, Exhibit 19–4 again is adapted. Exhibit 19–9 presents the adapted situation. Panel A restates the situation to incorporate a **guaranteed residual value of $15,000** and illustrates how the lessor incorporates the guaranteed residual value to compute the periodic rentals. Observe that this lease provision causes the annual rentals to decrease from $20,000 (Exhibit 19–4) to $18,287. Also, note that the **lessee** capitalizes $75,690 (i.e., the same amount recognized by the lessor), which is the "net cost to be recovered through rentals" of $69,205 (as computed in Panel A, 3) **plus** the present value of the guaranteed residual value of $6,485. The **lessee** capitalizes the sum of these two amounts (i.e., $75,690) because that is the total present value to be paid by the lessee (see Panel B, Lease Amortization Schedule, last column).

At the termination of the lease on December 31, 19F, the **actual** residual value is determined (independently as specified in the lease agreement) and compared with the guaranteed amount to derive any deficiency owed by the lessee to the lessor. In Exhibit 19–9, it is assumed that the "actual" residual value at the end of 19F was determined independently to be $14,000. Therefore, the lessee is obligated to pay the lessor $1,000 cash (i.e., $15,000 − $14,000). If the guaranteed value had been **less** than the **actual** value, the lessor would have no obligation to make a refund to the lessee.

Estimated residual values on capital leases should be evaluated periodically to determine whether they are realistic. If such estimates are revised by a material amount, a change in estimate should be recognized and the subsequent lease entries (and schedules) revised accordingly (see FASB Statement 13, par. 17d).

You should compare Exhibits 19–8 (**unguaranteed** residual value situation) and 19–9 (**guaranteed** residual value situation). These two exhibits are similar; however, there are important differences between them which may be summarized as follows:

1. When the residual value is **unguaranteed** (Exhibit 19–8), the **lessor** computes the lease payments based on the estimated residual value and the **lessee** computes the amount to capitalize by omitting the residual value. Thus, the lessor and lessee must use different amortization schedules (see Exhibit 19–8, Panel B).
2. When the residual value is **fully guaranteed** by the lessee (Exhibit 19–9) both the lessor and lessee incorporate the guaranteed amount in their respective computations. Thus, they may use the same amortization schedule, assuming they use the same interest rate for discounting (see Exhibit 19–9, Panel B).

When the **lessee guarantees only a portion of the estimated residual value** of the leased asset, the **lessor** bases the computation of the periodic lease payments (and the related amortization schedule) on the estimated residual value (similar to Exhibit 19–8). Then, for the **lessee,** given the computed periodic lease payments, the lessee's entries (and the related amortization schedule) would be based on the **guaranteed residual value.** As a result, the amounts recorded by the lessor and lessee would not be the same (i.e., not symmetrical as to amounts).

EXECUTORY AND INITIAL DIRECT COSTS (LESSOR)

Two kinds of lease costs incurred by the **lessor** are accorded special accounting treatment; they are *(a)* executory costs and *(b)* initial direct costs.

Executory Costs

Executory costs of ownership and use include insurance, property taxes, and maintenance. In the case of an **operating** lease, the executory costs typically are paid by the lessor and are recovered by the lessor in the periodic lease rentals. In contrast, in the case of a **capital** lease, a major part, if not all, of the executory costs usually are shifted to the lessee for payment, in which case they are not imbedded in the periodic rentals. However, to the extent that the executory costs are paid by the lessor, they should be excluded by the **lessee** in computing the present value of the periodic rentals for capitalization purposes. If such executory costs are not known by the lessee, they should be estimated.

Initial Direct Costs (Lessor)

Initial direct costs are incremental costs incurred by the **lessor** in negotiating and consummating a lease agreement; they include legal fees, cost of credit and other investigations, commissions and employees' compensation directly related to initiating the lease, and clerical costs of preparing and processing the lease documents.

In the case of an operating lease, the initial direct costs should be apportioned over the lease term on a reasonable basis (usually straight line). In the case of a **direct financing lease,** such costs should be **allocated** by the lessor, against lease revenue in the ratio of earned lease revenue to unearned lease revenue. In the case of a **sales-type lease,** the initial direct costs should be **expensed** in the year in which the lease is incurred (i.e., as an offset to manufacturer's or dealer's profit).

SALE-AND-LEASEBACK ARRANGEMENTS

When the owner of an asset sells it and immediately leases it back from the buyer, the transaction is identified as **sale-and-leaseback** and becomes subject to the provisions of paragraphs 32–34 of *FASB Statement 13,* as amended by *FASB Statement 28.* The characteristics of a typical sale-and-leaseback arrangement may be diagrammed for the seller-lessee and the buyer-lessor as follows:

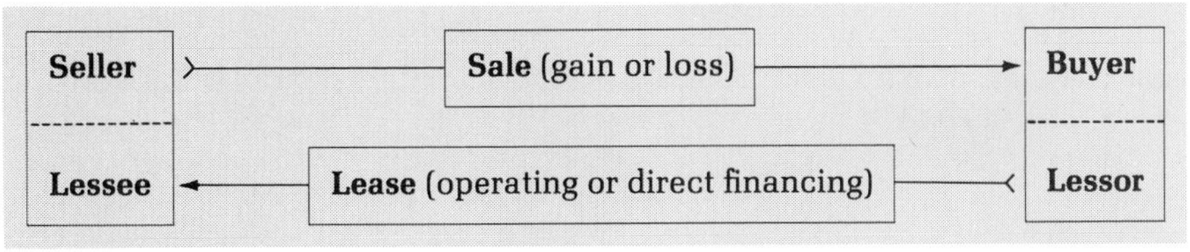

The primary advantage offered by a sale-and-leaseback arrangement is similar to that in other leases; that is, it allows the lessee to take a tax deduction for lease payments on leased assets. The inducements to lessors also are tax related, principally due to the investment tax credit and early tax deductions for accelerated depreciation and interest expense on any debt used to finance the purchase of the asset for leasing.

Under the provisions of *FASB Statements 13* and *28,* the lessor and lessee in a sale-and-leaseback arrangement identify the lease as an operating or capital lease by applying the criteria listed under the Part A heading, Criteria for Capital Leases, with the exception that the **buyer-lessor's** options for classifying the lease are limited to operating leases and direct financing leases. Beyond the lease classification, sale-and-leaseback arrangements pose a problem for the **seller-lessee** (they pose no special problem for the buyer-lessor) in accounting for any gain or loss on the sale of the asset to the buyer-lessor. A sale-and-leaseback arrangement poses a problem for the seller-lessee because of the high probability that the sale-and-leaseback transactions are not independent of each other. Without constraints, for instance, the seller-lessee could sell the asset to the buyer-lessor for an unrealistically high (or low) price purposely to report a gain (or loss) on the sale and then lease the asset back under an agreement with a present value equal to the sale price of the asset. In such a case, after both transactions the seller-lessee would be in essentially the same economic position as if neither the sale nor the leaseback had occurred, but would have reported a "phantom" gain or loss on the sale. Because of such possibilities for manipulation, the FASB specified detailed guidelines for seller-lessees.

In general, *FASB Statement 13* treats sale-and-leaseback arrangements as though the two transactions were a single financing transaction in which any gain or loss on the sale is deferred and amortized by the seller-lessee.[24] In this regard, *Statement 13* (par. 33) as amended by *Statement 28* (par. 3.c.) states:

> Any profit or loss on the sale shall be deferred and amortized [by the lessee] in proportion to the amortization of the leased asset, if a capital lease, or in proportion to the related gross rental [debited]

[24] *FASB Statement of Financial Accounting Standards No. 28,* "Accounting for Sales with Leasebacks, an Amendment of FASB Statement No. 13" (Stamford, Conn., May 1979) provides accounting guidelines for exceptions to the more general situation covered by *Statement 13.*

to expense over the lease term, if an operating lease, unless. . . .

c. The fair [market] value of the property at the time of the transaction is less than its undepreciated cost, in which case a loss shall be recognized immediately up to the amount of the difference between undepreciated cost and fair [market] value.

Exhibit 19–10 illustrates the seller-lessee's accounting for a sale-and-leaseback arrangement under three different cases. Panel A describes the hypothet-

EXHIBIT 19–10: Seller-Lessee Accounting for a Sale-and-Leaseback

Panel A—Hypothetical Situation:

1. Seller-lessee owned an asset with an estimated four-year useful life, no estimated residual value, and fair (i.e., market) value of $46,000.
2. On January 2, 19A, Seller-Lessee sold the asset to Buyer-Lessor for cash, $46,000.
3. On January 3, 19A, the two parties signed a four-year lease effective immediately, with annual lease payments of $16,439, payable each December 31.
4. At 16 percent the present value of lease payments on the asset was $46,000 (i.e., $16,439 × $P_{o_{n=4;i=16\%}}$, 2.79818, Table 5–4).
5. Alternative cases, which require different entries:
   I. Capital lease—Seller-Lessee's asset cost (i.e., carrying value), $43,000.
   II. Capital lease—Seller-Lessee's asset cost (i.e., carrying value), $50,000.
   III. Operating lease—Seller-Lessee's asset cost (i.e., carrying value), $43,000.

Panel B—Seller-Lessee's entries:

Case I—Capital Lease	Case II—Capital Lease	Case III—Operating Lease
January 2, 19A—To record sale of asset:		
Cash . . . . 46,000 Asset . . . . 43,000 Unearned gain on sale-and-leaseback 3,000	Cash . . . . 46,000 Loss on sale of asset . . . . 4,000* Asset . . . . 50,000 * Closed to Income Summary.	Cash . . . . 46,000 Asset . . . . 43,000 Unearned gain on sale-and-leaseback 3,000
January 3, 19A—To record inception of lease:		
Leased asset . . . . . 46,000 Lease liability 46,000	Same entry as in Case I.	No entry.
December 31, 19A—To record lease payment and end-of-period adjustments:		
Interest expense ($46,000 × .16) . . . . 7,360 Lease liability ($16,439 − $7,360) . 9,079 Cash 16,439	Same entry as in Case I.	Rent expense . . . . . 16,439 Cash 16,439
Depreciation expense ($46,000 ÷ 4) . . . . . 11,500 Accumulated depreciation . . 11,500	Same entry as in Case I.	No entry.
Unearned gain on sale-and-leaseback ($3,000 ÷ 4) . . . . . . 750 Depreciation expense 750	No entry.	Unearned gain on sale-and-leaseback ($3,000 ÷ 4) . 750 Rent expense . 750

ical situation, including the three cases, and Panel B gives the seller-lessee's entries.

Under Cases I and III of Exhibit 19–10, the Seller-Lessee must defer recognition of the $3,000 gain on sale of the asset. The gain is amortized at year-end as an adjusting entry. Under Case I (the capital lease), Seller-Lessee would credit Depreciation Expense for the amortized portion of the gain (i.e., $750); under Case III (the operating lease), Seller-Lessee credits Rent Expense. The credits to these accounts (instead of a gain account) is consistent with the FASB's view that the sale-and-leaseback transactions essentially comprise a single financing transaction. Thus, recognition of the gain is viewed as an adjustment of the Seller-Lessee's expense associated with the leased asset, rather than as a gain from a separate transaction.

Under Case II, the Seller-Lessee must recognize the loss (i.e., $4,000) on the date of sale. In this case, the loss is recognized immediately because the fair (i.e., market) value of the leased asset was less than the seller-lessee's carrying value, which is considered compelling evidence that the Seller-Lessee sustained a loss in value.

USE OF DIFFERENT INTEREST RATES BY LESSOR AND LESSEE

In the prior lease illustrations in this chapter, we assumed that the **lessee** used the interest rate implicit in the lease for discounting the minimum lease payments to their present value. The implicit rate in the lease agreement is the rate the **lessor** used to compute the periodic lease payments. In respect to the appropriate interest rate to use for the discounting, *FASB Statement 13* (par. 7d) states:

> A lessor shall compute the present value of the minimum lease payments using the interest rate implicit in the lease. . . .
>
> A lessee shall compute the present value of the minimum lease payments using his incremental borrowing rate . . . unless (i) it is practicable for him to learn the implicit rate computed by the lessor and (ii) the implicit rate computed by the lessor is less than the lessee's incremental borrowing rate. If both of those conditions are met, the lessee shall use the implicit rate.

Therefore, in some cases, for accounting purposes, the **lessee** will use his own incremental borrowing rate; in other cases, the **lessee** will use the interest rate implicit in the lease. In all cases, the **lessor** is required, for accounting purposes, to use the interest rate implicit in the lease. The essential accounting for leases by lessees and lessors, as illustrated in this chapter, is the same regardless of whether the two parties use the same interest rate. Use of different interest rates causes asymmetry in the recorded amounts; however, the symmetry in the account titles usually remains intact. Note that the choice of a specific interest rate by the **lessee** does not affect total expenses (i.e., interest expense plus depreciation expense); what is affected is the timing of the recognition of each of these two expenses.

CLASSIFICATION OF LEASE RECEIVABLES AND PAYABLES

When a lessor has lease receivables (and the lessee has lease payables) extending beyond one year (or the operating cycle of the business, whichever is longer), a problem arises in classifying the balances as **current** or **noncurrent.** The lessor's lease receivable, as well as the lessee's payable, should be reported net of any interest included in the lease payment amounts, or stated differently, at present value using the interest rate applied to the lease.

To illustrate the classification of lease receivables (payables) for reporting purposes, refer to the amortization schedule in Exhibit 19–5, Panel B. We shall illustrate the lease classification from the perspective of the lessor's lease receivable; the same conclusions also apply to classification of the lessee's lease payable.

At December 31, 19A, and assuming the operating cycle is one year or less, the lessor would classify the next upcoming lease receivable of $25,103 (collectible on December 31, 19B) as a **current asset** and the four remaining receivables of $25,103 each which are payable after that date as **noncurrent assets.** These amounts must be reduced by the **unearned interest** included therein. Although at the time the December 31, 19B, receivable will be collected, the lessor will recognize $12,622 of interest revenue, the lease receivable payable at that time does not have a present value of $12,481 (i.e., $25,103 − $12,622). Rather, its present value at the 15 percent interest rate being used is $21,825 (i.e., $25,103 × $p_{n=1;i=15\%}$ = $25,103 × .86957, Table 5–2, rounded to come out even). Similarly, the receivable due on December 31, 19C, has a present value at December 31, 19A, of $18,982 (which can be read from the amortization schedule in Exhibit 19–5 on the third line from the bottom). If this seems confusing, perhaps it will help to recall that the interest earned relates to the entire amount of the **unrecovered investment** (shown in the last column), not to any one year's lease receipt (shown in the first amount column). The other three uncollected payments of $25,103 each will not be collected until after more than one year from the December 31, 19A, balance sheet date; therefore, they are subject to larger discounts because of the time value of money. Thus, a partial balance sheet of the lessor at December 31, 19A, would show the following:

Current assets:		
Lease receivable	$ 25,103	
Less: Unearned interest....	(3,278)	$21,825
Noncurrent assets:		
Lease receivable ($25,103 × 4)....................	100,412	
Less: Unearned interest ($6,121 + $8,597 + $10,750 + $12,622)	(38,090)	62,322
Total lease receivable		$84,147*

* See Exhibit 19–5, Panel B, amortization schedule, last column.

LEASE DISCLOSURE REQUIREMENTS

FASB Statement 13 requires disclosure of many details concerning leasing arrangements in the financial statements or their accompanying notes. The primary lease disclosures may be summarized as follows:

Lessee disclosures:

1. For capital leases, disclose:
   a. The gross amount of assets recorded under capital leases presented by major classes according to nature or function.
   b. Future minimum lease payments in the aggregate and for each of the five succeeding fiscal years, with separate deductions from the total for *(a)* executory costs (including any profit thereon) included in the minimum lease payments and *(b)* the amount of the imputed interest necessary to reduce the net minimum lease payments to present value.
   c. The total of minimum sublease rentals to be received in the future under noncancelable subleases.
   d. Total contingent rentals (rentals on which the amounts are dependent on some factor other than the passage of time) actually incurred.
2. For operating leases having initial or remaining noncancelable lease terms in excess of one year, disclose:
   a. Future minimum rental payments required in the aggregate and for each of the five succeeding fiscal years.
   b. The total of minimum rentals to be received in the future under noncancelable subleases.
3. For all operating leases, disclose rental expense, with separate amounts for minimum rentals, contingent rentals, and sublease rentals.
4. Provide a general description of the lessee's leasing arrangements including, but not limited to, the following:
   a. The basis on which contingent rental payments are determined.
   b. The existence and terms of renewal or purchase options and escalation clauses.
   c. Restrictions imposed by lease agreements, such as those concerning dividends, additional debt, and further leasing.

Lessor disclosures:

1. For sales-type and direct financing leases, disclose:
   a. The components of the net investment in sales-type and direct financing leases:
      (1) Future minimum lease payments to be received, with separate deductions for *(i)* amounts representing executory costs (including any profit thereon) included in the minimum lease payments and *(ii)* the accumulated allowance for **uncollectible** minimum lease payments receivable.
      (2) The unguaranteed residual values accruing to the benefit of the lessor.
      (3) Unearned interest revenue.
   b. Future minimum lease payments to be received for each of the five succeeding fiscal years.
   c. Total contingent rentals included in income.
2. For operating leases, disclose:

a. The cost and carrying amount, if different, of property on lease or held for leasing by major classes of property according to nature or function, and the amount of accumulated depreciation in total.

b. Minimum future rentals on noncancelable leases in the aggregate and for each of the five succeeding fiscal years.

c. Total contingent rentals included in income.

3. Provide a general description of the lessor's leasing arrangements.

The following excerpt from the 1979 annual report of Jantzen, Inc., illustrates typical lease disclosures of a **lessee.** You should trace the 1979 amounts of current and long-term lease obligations (i.e., liabilities of $174,163 and $2,197,452, respectively) from the tabular presentation of the balance sheet to the detailed amounts given in Note 4.

JANTZEN, INC.

	August 1979	August 1978
Current liabilities (in part):		
Current portion of capitalized lease obligations *(Note 4)*	174,163	302,714
Long-term debt	10,226,977	10,838,669
Capitalized lease obligations *(Note 4)*	2,197,452	2,371,615

Notes to financial statements:

Note 1 (in part): Operations and Significant Accounting Policies: Plant, equipment, and depreciation—The amortization of assets recorded under capital leases is included with depreciation.

Note 4: Capitalized lease obligations—Leases that meet the criteria of capital leases have been capitalized and the related assets are included in plant and equipment in the following amounts at August 25, 1979 and August 26, 1978:

	1979	1978
Land	$ 257,800	$ 257,800
Buildings and improvements	2,068,000	2,068,000
Machinery and equipment	1,276,200	1,276,200
	3,602,000	3,602,000
Less accumulated depreciation	1,205,000	1,035,000
	$2,397,000	$2,567,000

Minimum future obligations on capitalized lease obligations in effect at August 25, 1979, are as follows:

1980	$ 334,353
1981	275,148
1982	269,229
1983	267,191
1984	265,705
Thereafter through 1994	2,316,726
Total minimum lease payments	3,728,352
Less amount representing interest	1,356,737
Present value of net minimum lease payments	2,371,615
Less current portion	174,163
Long-term obligation at August 25, 1979	$2,197,452

The interest rates for capitalized leases vary from 5.65% to 7.46%.

Source: AICPA, *Accounting Trends & Techniques, 1980* (New York: AICPA, 1980), p. 213.

SUMMARY OF LEASE ACCOUNTING ISSUES

Accounting for leases is controversial. Lessees often desire to avoid recognition of lease liabilities and capitalization of the related assets. In contrast, lessors often desire to classify leases as sales-type so they can recognize a manufacturer's or dealer's profit at the date of inception of the lease. These opposite motivations have spawned some "creative" lease agreements, which are structured to satisfy these motivations through lease specifications which qualify the lease as a capital lease to the lessor but as an operating lease to the lessee.

From the criteria for capital leases (Exhibit 19–3), it would appear that a capital lease to a lessor must qualify as a capital lease to the lessee because the lessor must satisfy two additional criteria not applicable to the lessee. Avoiding this accounting symmetry requires creativity. For example, the lease agreement can easily avoid satisfying criteria 1 through 3 for a capital lease (Exhibit 19–3), while criterion 4 can be satisfied by the lessor but not by the lessee. This effect can be accomplished by including in the lease agreement a residual value guarantee which causes the present value of the minimum lease payments to be more than 90 percent of the fair (i.e., market) value of the leased asset. Thus, the lease qualifies as a capital lease (i.e., direct financing or sales-type) to the lessor. The lessee can avoid satisfying criterion 4 by engaging, for a fee, a third party guarantor to guarantee the residual value demanded by the lessor. Thus, the lease is classified an operating lease to the lessee. Another way for the lessee to avoid satisfying criterion 4 is to use a higher incremental borrowing rate in the present value discounting while carefully avoiding learning of the lower implicit rate used by the lessor.

Another controversial lease accounting topic emerged in 1981 with passage of the Economic Recovery Tax Act. That Act allowed the transfer through leases of certain tax benefits; for example, investment tax credits (discussed in Chapter 10) and depreciation deductions under the newly enacted Accelerated Cost Recovery System. In October 1981, the FASB issued an exposure draft of a proposed statement entitled "Accounting for the Sale or Purchase of Tax Benefits through Tax Leases." The provisions of that exposure draft are beyond the scope of this book; but they, along with the preceding paragraphs of this summary, illustrate the challenge of accounting for leases.

Supplement 19-A: Leveraged Leases

FUNDAMENTAL CHARACTERISTICS

A **leveraged lease** is a complex form of a capital lease which involves one or more parties in addition to a lessor and lessee. Debt is a key element of a leveraged lease arrangement; the lender (loan participant) is an added party. Instead of providing 100 percent of the cost of **depreciable** property to be leased, the lessor usually provides from 20 percent to 40 percent and the lender furnishes the remaining needed funds with a nonrecourse loan. Nonrecourse in this context means that the lender cannot take assets other than the leased property in the event the lessor fails to pay the amount owed to the lender.

A lessor with taxable income from other sources is in a position to benefit from leveraged leasing because, for **tax** purposes, the lessor can deduct from taxable income depreciation expense on the leased property and use the investment tax credit to reduce income taxes further—even though the lease would qualify otherwise as a capital lease for **financial accounting** purposes. Although the lessor may put up only 20 percent of the cost of depreciable property to be leased, 100 percent of the investment tax credit and depreciation can be used by the lessor to reduce income taxes.

The lender's loan is secured by a first lien on the leased property, by assignment of the lease, and assignment of the lease rentals. This means that the lender has first priority on the leased property and the lease receivables under the lease agreement in the event the leveraged lessor fails to pay the lender the amount owed on the debt incurred to purchase the leased property. Creditworthiness of the lessee is important. Title to the leased property is vested in an **owner trustee** who issues trust certificates evidencing each participant's equity interest. An **indenture trustee** holds the security interest in the leased property for the benefit of the lender and receives rental payments from the lessee which then are distributed to the lender and to the lessor through the owner trustee.

Because the contractual arrangements are complex and costly, it is seldom feasible to apply leveraged leasing to low-cost assets. It would cost as much to arrange a leveraged lease on a $50,000 asset as on a $1,000,000 one, and since the "front-end" costs are high, rentals from the less costly asset would not justify the "front-end" expenses.

CASH FLOWS UNDER LEVERAGED LEASES

In a typical leveraged lease the **lessor** experiences a net cash inflow during the early years of the lease, a net cash outflow in the later years, and a terminal receipt of cash if the leased asset has a residual value and is sold after the lease terminates. Early tax-deductible expenses are relatively high because interest on the unpaid debt is high in the early years and because of accelerated depreciation. This combination, plus investment tax credit, causes tax benefits in the early years of the lease which create net cash inflows because of the reduction of tax that otherwise would be paid on income **from other sources.** In the later years, a reverse effect is experienced: lower interest and depreciation amounts cause taxable income to rise and tax payments to increase. However, due to the time value of money, the early cash inflows create a distinct advantage in favor of leveraged leasing.

To illustrate a leveraged lease, Exhibit 19–11 is

based on the assumptions that the lessor acquired an asset for $1,000,000 on which a down payment of $200,000 was paid, leaving $800,000 to be paid in equal annual installments over the next five years. If the interest rate agreed to between the lessor and the lender was 12 percent and five equal annual payments are to be made at the **end** of each year, annual payments of $221,928 will fully pay the debt and related interest.[25] The payments are reflected in columns *(c)* and *(d)* of Exhibit 19–11. The first year's interest is $96,000 (i.e., 12 percent × $800,000), and the remainder of the payment, $125,928 (i.e., $221,928 − $96,000 = $125,928), reduces the principal.

Assume the lessor depreciates the $1,000,000 cost of the asset down to $100,000 using the double-declining-balance (DDB) method. The asset is assumed to have a residual value of $100,000 at the end of the five-year lease term. Thus, depreciation for the first year amounts to $400,000 (i.e., $1,000,000 × 40%) and the second year it is $240,000 (i.e., [$1,000,000 − $400,000] × 40%). Annual depreciation is reflected in column *(b)*. The lessor leases the asset for five annual **year-end** rents of $295,000 reported in column *(a)*. The lessor's expenses are added and the total is reflected in column *(e)*. Subtraction of column *(e)* from the rents in column *(a)* yields taxable income in column *(f)*. The income or loss in column *(f)* is combined with the lessor's other income (not shown) and taxed at 40 percent. Thus, when the result in column *(f)* is a loss, insofar as the leveraged lease is concerned, the lessor experiences a tax saving of 40 percent of the amount of the loss because losses on the leveraged lease activities reduce income that otherwise would be taxable at 40 percent. Whenever the result in column *(f)* reflects income before tax, the lessor must pay 40 percent of that amount as income tax.

The lessor's annual cash flow is shown in column *(h)*, and the cumulative cash flow is shown in column *(i)*. Many elements of the cash flow are fixed; the debt payments cause a periodic outflow of $221,928 and the rents cause a periodic inflow of $295,000. Were it not for income tax savings (treated as an inflow) or income tax expense (treated as an outflow), the net inflow each year would be $73,072 (i.e., $295,000 − $221,928).

Two other inflows and outflows warrant brief attention. Recall that the lessor's down payment is $200,000; this would cause an outflow, before regular operations begin, of that amount were it not for the fact that the investor receives a 10 percent investment credit of $100,000 (i.e., $1,000,000 × 10%). The difference between the $200,000 down payment and the $100,000 investment credit is reflected as a $100,000 net outflow on line 1*a*. Line 1*b* reflects regular first-year leasing activities.

One other special inflow needs to be mentioned. Recall that the asset has a residual value of $100,000 after five years. It is assumed that this amount is realized by cash sale of the asset at book value after the fifth year and that inflow is reflected on the line captioned "Residual."

From above note that the net cash inflow each year would be $73,072 were it not for income taxes. For the first year's operations reported on line 1*b*, we see that the result is a tax saving of $80,400; this, added to the regular net inflow of $73,072 gives the $153,472 reflected in line 1*b* in column *(h)*. When this amount is combined with $100,000 outflow on line 1*a*, we arrive at the cumulative net cash inflow of $53,472 shown in column *(i)* on line 1*b*.

A proof of cash flows and of income appears in the bottom portion of Exhibit 19–11. The most revealing aspect of Exhibit 19–11 is column *(h)* which shows the timing of the cash flows, because this is the distinguishing characteristic of leveraged leases. Observe in particular that the flows are positive in years 1–4 and negative during year 5. As indicated above, the time value of money helps make leveraged leases advantageous to the lessor.

This example has shown that the lessor would be $259,217 better off at the conclusion of the five-year lease term. However, under *FASB Statement 13*, annual income of the lessor from a leveraged lease is measured in such a way that annual income would differ from aftertax income [i.e., column *(f)* minus column *(g)*]. *Statement 13* requires leveraged lessors to recognize lease revenue in years when the lessor's net investment in leased property is positive,

[25] Debt payment amounts were computed by dividing $800,000 by the present value of an ordinary annuity of five rents at 12% [i.e., $800,000 ÷ 3.60478 (Table 5–4) = $221,928]. Columns *(c)* and *(d)* in Exhibit 19–11 were based on these values; for example, the first two years' data are as follows:

Year	Payment	Interest	Reduction of Principal	Unamortized Principal
1*a*...........				$800,000
1*b*...........	$221,928	$800,000 × .12 = $96,000	$125,928	674,072
2............	221,928	$674,072 × .12 = $80,889	141,039	533,033
Etc.				

EXHIBIT 19–11: Schedule of Cash Flows—Leveraged Lease

Year	(a) Annual Rentals	(b) Annual Depre-ciation	(c) Annual Interest at 12 Percent	(d) Principal Reduc-tion	(e) Total Expense (b) + (c)	(f) Taxable Income (Loss) (a) − (e)	(g) Tax Saving (Expense) 40 Percent of (f)	(h) Annual Cash Flow (a) + (g) −[(c) + (d)]	(i) Cumulative Cash Flow
1*a*								$(100,000)	$(100,000)
1*b*	$ 295,000	$400,000	$ 96,000	$125,928	$ 496,000	$(201,000)	$ 80,400	153,472	53,472
2	295,000	240,000	80,889	141,039	320,889	(25,889)	10,356	83,428	136,900
3	295,000	144,000	63,964	157,964	207,964	87,036	(34,814)	38,258	175,158
4	295,000	86,000*	45,008	176,920	131,008	163,992	(65,597)	7,475	182,633
5	295,000	30,000*	23,779	198,149	53,779	241,221	(96,488)	(23,416)	159,217
Residual								100,000	259,217
Totals	$1,475,000	$900,000	$309,640	$800,000	$1,209,640	$ 265,360	$(106,143)	$ 259,217	$ 259,217

Proof of Cash Flows and Proof of Income

Cash inflows:	
Rents (5 × $295,000)	$1,475,000
Investment credit	100,000
Residual value	100,000
Total inflows	$1,675,000
Cash outflows:	
Down payment	$ 200,000
Payments (5 × $221,928)	1,109,640
Income taxes	106,143
Total outflows	1,415,783
Cumulative flow	$ 259,217

Revenue:	
Rents	$1,475,000
Expenses:	
Depreciation	900,000
Interest	309,640
Total expenses	1,209,640
Income before taxes	265,360
Taxes	(106,143)
Income	159,217
Add: Investment tax credit	100,000
Net income	$ 259,217

* Rounded to nearest $1,000.

but to recognize no loss for years when the net investment is negative.[26]

[26] Net investment of a leveraged lessor in leased property is defined in *FASB Statement 13* as (1) rentals receivable under the leveraged lease, plus (2) any receivable for investment tax credit to be realized, plus (3) any residual value of the leased property, minus (4) lessor's nonrecourse debt on borrowing to acquire the leased property, minus (5) unearned lease revenue, minus (6) any investment tax credit deferred for recognition in future periods.

The FASB income formula is complex, and the results for any particular leveraged lease can be obtained only by calculation of a yield rate for the lessor for that particular lease. This determination is difficult without a computer because of the large number of iterative attempts that ordinarily would be necessary to derive the yield rate. Details of the FASB approach are presented in Appendix E of *FASB Statement 13*.

QUESTIONS

Part A

1. Match the lettered items immediately below with the statements numbered (in parens) that follow.

   A. Lessor; B. Capital lease; C. Operating lease; D. Lessee.
   (1) Contract in which lessor finances property leased.
   (2) Lender in a lease contract transaction.
   (3) Tenant in a lease contract transaction.
   (4) Type of lease which requires capitalization.
   (5) Type of lease which does not require capitalization.
   (6) Property owner in a lease contract transaction.

   Questions 2 and 3 below are based on the following information: Briefly explain your choices.

   The Marne Company purchased a machine on January 1, 19A, for $900,000 for the express purpose of leasing it. The machine is expected to have a five-year life, no residual value, and to be depreciated on a straight-line basis. On March 1, 19A, Marne leased the machine to the Dal Company for $390,000 a year for a four-year period ending February 28, 19E. During the year ended December 31, 19A, Marne incurred total maintenance and other related expenses of $15,000 under the provisions of the lease. Dal paid $390,000 to Marne on March 1, 19A.

2. Under the operating method, what should be the income before income taxes derived by Marne from this lease for the year ended December 31, 19A?
   a. $55,000.
   b. $70,000.
   c. $115,000.
   d. $160,000.

3. What should be the amount of rent expense incurred by Dal from this lease for the year ended December 31, 19A?
   a. $70,000.
   b. $120,000.
   c. $250,000.
   d. $325,000. (2 and 3, AICPA adapted)

4. Give highlights of the operating method for leases by lessors and lessees.

5. Often advance rental payments are received under operating lease contracts that extend well beyond a single fiscal year. Outline possible accounting procedures to be followed in respect to such advance rentals.

6. What is meant by *capitalization* of leases?

7. From a lessee standpoint, leases are classified as capital or operating leases. By what criteria can a capital lease be identified?

8. From a lessor standpoint, a lease that is a capital lease to a lessee corresponds conceptually to two types. Identify the types and distinguish between them.

Part B and Supplement 19–A

9. How does a lessee determine what interest rate is appropriate for capitalization of a lease?

10. What are executory costs?

11. What distinguishes leveraged leases from other leases? What pattern of cash flows can normally be expected in a leveraged lease?

DECISION CASE 19–1

Pertinent provisions of *FASB Statement 13* concerning the interest rate to be used in capitalizing leases are cited below:

"A lessor shall compute the present value of the minimum lease payments using the *interest rate implicit in the lease. . . .* A lessee shall compute the present value of the minimum lease payments using his incremental borrowing rate . . . unless *(i)* it is practicable for him to learn the implicit rate computed by the lessor, and (ii) the implicit rate computed by the lessor is less than the lessee's incremental borrowing rate. If both of these conditions are met, the lessee shall use the implicit rate."

Interest rate implicit in the lease is defined as the discount rate which, when applied to the minimum lease payments (excluding executory costs) and to the unguaranteed residual value of the property to the lessor, causes the present value at the start of the lease term to equal the [market] value of the property to the lessor at the inception of the lease.*

APB Opinion 21, which deals with the imputation of interest to receivables and payables, indicates that the choice of an interest rate "may be affected by the credit standing of the issuer, restrictive covenants, the collateral, payment and other terms pertaining to the debt, and, if appropriate, the tax consequences to the buyer and seller."

* There are some qualifications to this abstracted definition, but they are not important for present purposes. Italics supplied in the first quotation.

Required:

Evaluate the foregoing criteria in light of the following assertions:

1. Asking a lessor what interest rate is inherent in a lease transaction would be similar to asking a farmer what rate is implicit in the price the farmer can expect *now* for next fall's corn crop. There are varying degrees of risk in any operation having a distant future; the higher the farmer's future risks are thought to be, the higher the farmer will set his or her rate and, likewise, on the lessor.
2. The assumption that a lease has an implicit interest rate, in many cases, represents circular reasoning in that the market value of the leased asset itself (i.e., the benchmark value used in determining the implicit rate) is determined by market forces. The value of the property stems from the rentals it will command rather than the rentals stemming from the value of the property.
3. One determinant of the implicit interest rate in a lease is the residual value of the property to be leased. This is a subjective judgment which, depending on the property, can be substantially in error. Lessors will not disclose what this guess is.

DECISION CASE 19–2

The corporation where you are employed as controller is contemplating leasing (as a lessee) a greater proportion of its operational assets than in the past. As assets become fully depreciated and/or are retired, many of them would be replaced by leased assets. You have been asked by the board of directors to advise about certain specific financial accounting issues.

Item 1: The company is heavily in debt, and one director is concerned about becoming a lessee under a capital lease because we "do not want all that debt on the balance sheet." Can you offer any comments that might assuage these anxieties?

Item 2: Having learned that interest must be recognized in connection with lease obligations and that within modest limits there may be some discretion as to interest rates chosen, some board members want to use the lowest possible rate while others want to use the highest rate. Specifically, you are asked what would be the difference insofar as the financial statements are concerned between the two alternatives.

Item 3: If some of the lease contracts contemplated could be drawn so as to avoid the lease capitalization requirements of *FASB Statement 13,* what would be the effect on the financial statements of using such lease contracts?

EXERCISES

PART A: EXERCISES 19–1 to 19–6

Exercise 19–1

Radner Company signed an operating lease contract effective for 10 years from January 1, 19A. Radner is to pay $60,000 at the start of the lease plus $8,000 monthly rentals throughout the lease term. Prior to occupancy, Radner spent $20,000 renovating the property to be leased and also built an addition to the leased property with the lessor's consent at a cost of $120,000. The estimated life of the addition is 15 years, and its residual value is zero. The lease contract does not contain a renewal option.

Required:
Give all entries on Radner's books to reflect the preoccupancy outlays, leasehold, and rental payments for 19A and entries at the end of 19A assuming Radner's fiscal year is the calendar year. Straight-line amortization is to be used.

Exercise 19–2

In lieu of paying three annual $7,000 rentals, with each payment due in advance, a lessor and lessee agree upon a single lump-sum advance payment of $18,830, which covers the entire lease period. This reflects recognition of interest at an annual rate of 12% over the lease term.

Required:
1. Show how the lump-sum amount was calculated, and prepare an amortization schedule on an annuity due basis covering the three-year lease term.
2. Give the entry by the lessee to record the initial payment under this operating lease and entries at end of the first year assuming the lease year and the lessee's fiscal year coincide.

Exercise 19–3

Vermeil Company paid $5,000 on January 1, 19A, to Dexter Properties as a lease bonus to secure a three-year lease on premises it will occupy starting from that date. Additionally, $6,000 will be paid as rent on each December 31 throughout the term of the lease. The lease contains no specific renewal agreement. Vermeil adjusts and closes its books each December 31. Dexter will maintain the property, pay taxes and other ownership costs.

Required (round to the nearest dollar):
1. What type of lease contract is involved?
2. What are Vermeil's alternatives as to treatment of the $5,000? Develop an interest method amortization schedule using a 14% rate.
3. What is Vermeil's total occupancy cost for 19A under each alternative given in your response to 2 above?
4. What lease-related items should Vermeil's financial statements report as of December 31, 19A, if the amortization schedule developed in 2 above is used?

Exercise 19–4

Part A

Capital leases and operating leases are the two classifications of leases described in FASB pronouncements, from the standpoint of the lessee.

Required:
1. Describe how a capital lease would be accounted for by the lessee both at the inception of the lease and during the first year of the lease, assuming the lease transfers ownership of the property to the lessee by the end of the lease term.
2. Describe how an operating lease would be accounted for by the lessee both at the inception of the lease and during the first year of the lease, assuming equal monthly payments are made by the lessee at the beginning of each month of the lease.

   Do *not* discuss the criteria for distinguishing between capital leases and operating leases.

Part B

Sales-type leases and direct financing leases are two of the classifications of leases described in FASB pronouncements, from the standpoint of the lessor.

Required:
Compare and contrast a sales-type lease with a direct financing lease as follows:
1. Net investment in the lease.
2. Recognition of interest revenue.
3. Manufacturer's or dealer's profit.

Do *not* discuss the criteria for distinguishing between the leases described above and operating leases.

(AICPA adapted)

Exercise 19–5

Carnes Leasing Company agreed with White Corporation to provide the latter with equipment under lease for a four-year period. The equipment cost Carnes $18,500 and will have no residual value when the lease term ends. Carnes expects to collect all rentals from White and has no material cost uncertainties. The market value of the equipment was $18,500 at the inception of the lease. The four equal annual rents (amount to be determined by the student) are to be paid in advance starting January 1, 19A, at which time the equipment was delivered. White has agreed to pay taxes, maintenance, and insurance throughout the lease term as well as any other "ownership" costs. Carnes expects a 12% return. White's incremental borrowing rate is 15%, but management of White Corporation is aware of Carnes rate of return. The fiscal year of both companies ends December 31.

Required (round to the nearest dollar):

1. What kind of lease is this to White? To Carnes? What interest rate should White use?
2. Prepare an amortization schedule reflecting the interest and principal elements of White's payments over the four-year term of the lease. Give all journal entries relating to the lease for White Corporation for 19A including year-end adjusting and closing entries.
3. Give all journal entries for Carnes Leasing Company relating to the lease for 19A including year-end adjusting and closing entries.

Exercise 19–6

Grand Company uses leases as a means of selling its products. The company contracted with May Corporation to lease the latter a product to be used by May as an operational asset. The market value of the asset at the inception of the lease is $40,000; it cost Grand $30,000 and is carried in its inventory at that value. Payments of $7,384 are to be made by May at the end of each of the six quarters following inception of the lease. Grand's implicit interest rate is 3% per quarter.

Required (round to the nearest dollar):

1. Prepare an amortization schedule for use by Grand covering the six-quarter term of the lease.
2. Give Grand's journal entries at the inception of the lease and upon receipt of the first payment. Assume the first receipt coincides with the end of Grand's fiscal year. Record its closing entries insofar as the lease transactions are concerned.

PART B: EXERCISES 19–7 to 19–10

Exercise 19–7

Select the best answer in each of the following. Briefly justify each choice.

1. On the first day of its fiscal year, Lessor, Inc., leased certain property at an annual rental of $100,000 receivable at the beginning of each year for 10 years. The first payment was received immediately. The leased property which is new had cost $450,000 and has an estimated useful life of 12 years and no residual value. Lessor's implicit rate is 18%. Lessor had no other costs associated with this lease. Lessor should have accounted for this lease as a sales-type lease but it mistakenly treated the lease as an operating lease. What was the effect on net earnings during the first year of the lease by having treated this lease as an operating lease rather than as a sales-type lease?
   a. No effect.
   b. Overstated.
   c. Understated.
   d. The effect depends on the method selected for income tax purposes.
2. The appropriate valuation of leased assets under an operating lease on the statement of financial position of a lessee is as follows:
   a. Zero.
   b. The absolute sum of the lease payments.
   c. The sum of the present values of the lease payments discounted at an appropriate rate.
   d. The market value of the asset at the date of the inception of the lease.
3. What are the three types of expenses that a lessee experiences with capital leases?
   a. Lease expense, interest expense, amortization expense.
   b. Interest expense, amortization expense, executory costs.
   c. Amortization expense, executory costs, lease expense.
   d. Executory costs, interest expense, lease expense.
4. When measuring the present value of future rentals to be capitalized in connection with a lease, identifiable payments to cover taxes, insurance and maintenance should be accounted for as follows:
   a. Included with the future rentals to be capitalized.
   b. Excluded from future rentals to be capitalized.
   c. Capitalized, but at a different rate and recorded in a different account than future rentals.
   d. Capitalized, but at a different rate and during a different period from the rate and period used for the future rental payments.
5. GAAP requires that certain lease agreements be accounted for as purchases. The theoretical basis for this treatment is that a lease of this type:
   a. Effectively conveys all of the benefits and risks incident to the ownership of property.
   b. Is an example of form over substance.
   c. Provides the use of the leased asset to the lessee for a limited period of time.
   d. Must be recorded in accordance with the concept of cause and effect.
6. Your client constructed an office building at a cost of $500,000. He sold this building to Jones at a material

gain and then leased it back from Jones for a stipulated annual rental. How should this gain be treated?

a. Recognized in full as an ordinary item in the year of the transaction.

b. Recognized in full as an extraordinary item in the year of the transaction.

c. Amortized as an adjustment of the rental cost, an ordinary item, over the life of the lease.

d. Amortized as an extraordinary item over the life of the lease.

(AICPA adapted)

Exercise 19–8

The present value to a lessor of a lease on which the lessee is obligated to make a $20,000 payment at the end of each of the next three years and on which there is an unguaranteed residual value of $4,000 at the end of the lease term is $49,133 if the lessor's implicit interest rate is 14%.

Required (round amounts to the nearest dollar):

1. Prepare an amortization schedule for the lessor covering the three years of the foregoing lease.
2. Determine the present value of a similar lease assuming the lessor's implicit rate is 12% and prepare an amortization schedule similar to the one required in 1 above.
3. Assume instead that each of the three $20,000 annual payments is paid at the beginning of each year, in advance, and that the $4,000 residual value is expected at end of the lease term of three years. What is the present value of the minimum lease payments at 14%? Prepare the lessor's amortization schedule for such a lease.

Exercise 19–9

Flier Company (as a lessee) leased a computer under a capital lease for a period of six years, contracting to pay $9,600 rent in advance at the start of the lease term and five like amounts of rent annually thereafter. The lease was negotiated July 1, 19A, at which time the first payment was made. Flier's fiscal year is the calendar year. Straight-line depreciation is used by Flier. Assume the annual effective interest rate implicit in the lease is 15%.

An incomplete amortization schedule related to the lease follows:

Date	Payment	Interest	Balance
7/1/19A			$41,781
7/1/19A 1st pmt.	$9,600		32,181
6/30/19B		$4,827	37,008
7/1/19B 2d pmt.	9,600		27,408
6/30/19C		4,111	31,519
7/1/19C 3d pmt.	9,600		21,919

Required:

1. Prepare appropriate headings and complete the above amortization schedule through the final payment.
2. Prepare the entry Flier Company should make at the inception of the lease.
3. Prepare Flier's adjusting and closing entries at December 31, 19A.
4. Indicate what would be reported on Flier's December 31, 19A, balance sheet in respect to the lease. Assume Flier's operating cycle is one year.
5. If Flier has the right to buy the computer for $5,000 on the day of the last lease payment, this "bargain purchase option" should, in effect, be discounted on July 1, 19A, for five periods at 15% ($5,000 × .49718 = $2,486), which adds $2,486 to the initial valuation. Thus, the amortization schedule becomes the following:

Date	Payment	Interest	Balance
7/1/19A			$44,267
7/1/19A 1st pmt.	$9,600		34,667
6/30/19B		$5,200	39,867
7/1/19B 2d pmt.	9,600		30,267
6/30/19C		4,540	34,807
7/1/19C 3d pmt.	9,600		25,207

a. Show what would appear on the last two lines of the amortization schedule.

b. Record the sixth payment and the exercise of the "bargain purchase option."

c. Assume instead that the computer is not purchased and that the lease is canceled by mutual agreement on July 1, 19F, when the sixth payment became due. The balance of the liability prior to the sixth payment was $14,600, and the computer had been depreciated on the assumption of a seven-year life with zero residual value at the end of seven years.

Exercise 19–10

Lessor J and Lessee K contract for the lease of a machine for six rentals of $6,000. The first $6,000 rental is to be paid at the inception of the lease, and $6,000 is to be paid at the start of each of five quarters thereafter. They also agree that at the time of the sixth payment, for an added $6,930 payment, K can buy the property. The interest rate is 2.5% per quarter.

Required (round to nearest dollar):

1. Calculate the present value of the minimum lease payments and prepare an amortization schedule for the lessee covering the six-quarter term of the lease. Assume $6,930 is a bargain price.
2. Give the lessor's entries at the inception of the lease and at the time of the sixth payment if the lessee exercises the purchase option. Assume a direct financing lease.

SUPPLEMENT 19–A: EXERCISE 19–11

Exercise 19–11

Lansing Leasing, Inc., leased a machine to Blue Company for a five-year period beginning January 1, 19A. Lansing acquired the machine at a cost of $250,000, paying $50,000 cash, and borrowing the remainder at 8% per annum. The loan agreement provides for four equal annual payments starting on December 31, 19A.

Blue agreed to pay five equal annual year-end rents of $64,273. Lansing will realize a 10% investment credit the first year and will depreciate the machine (which has no residual value) by the double-declining-balance (DDB) method over its five-year life. Lansing has extensive income from other sources and pays income tax at a 40% rate; any losses on a single phase of its operations result in a 40% income tax saving.

Required (round amounts to the nearest dollar):

1. Prepare a loan amortization schedule for this leveraged lease.
2. Prepare a cash flow analysis similar to Exhibit 19–11.

PROBLEMS

PART A: PROBLEMS 19–1 to 19–6

Problem 19–1

On January 1, 19A, Starr, Inc. rented an office to Moon Corp. for an annual rental of $1,200 due each January 1. In addition, an advance payment of $4,587 was required. The lease was for a three-year period. The advance amount represented three annual rentals that would have been payable each December 31; thus, the $4,587 was somewhat less than the sum of the three annual payments that would have been made in addition to the normal rent of $1,200. This is an operating lease to both parties.

Required (round to the nearest dollar):

1. Give all entries, excluding closing entries, for both the lessor and lessee assuming *(a)* both parties' fiscal years end December 31 and *(b)* a 9% interest rate is appropriate for amortization purposes. Utilize interest method amortization and present the two sets of entries in parallel columns. Show all computations.
2. Show amounts that would be reported on the income statement and balance sheet for each year for both the lessor and lessee.

Problem 19–2

In lieu of making four $10,000 rent payments spaced at one-year intervals with the first payment due at the end of the first year of the lease term, the lessee and lessor agree that the lessee can make a single initial payment of $? at the start of the four-year lease term. This amount was calculated on the basis of an agreed 16% annual interest rate.

Required (round all amounts to the nearest dollar):

1. Show how the lump-sum initial payment amount was calculated.
2. Prepare an amortization schedule for the lessor covering the entire lease term. Show the lessor's entries to reflect receipt of the initial payment and adjusting entries at the end of the first, second, and last years if the lease year and fiscal year of the lessor coincide. Entries are to be based on the amortization schedule.
3. On the assumption the lessee amortizes the prepayment on a straight-line basis, give the lessee's entries to record the initial payment and year-end adjustments if the lease year and lessee fiscal year coincide.
4. Has the lessor or lessee adopted a more realistic approach to recognition of the periodic effects of the lease? Explain.

Problem 19–3

A lessor and a lessee began negotiations which would have provided that the lessee would pay six semiannual $8,000 rents for the use of property with the first payment to be at the beginning of the lease term. However, after agreeing that money was worth 14% per year at the time, the parties finally agreed that the lessee would instead pay $? at the outset and that this single advance payment would be in lieu of all other rents for the three-year term. Assume an operating lease.

Required (round to the nearest dollar):

1. Show how the advance payment was calculated and prepare an amortization schedule covering the entire term of the lease.
2. Give journal entries for both the lessor and lessee, based on the amortization schedule, which reflect the advance payment and adjusting entries (assuming the lease year and fiscal years of the parties coincide) at the end of years 1 and 3. Lessor and lessee use the interest method of amortization.
3. Instead of using the interest method of amortization as in 2 above, assume that the lessor and lessee amortize the advance payment computed in requirement 1 above by the straight-line method. Give entries for both parties to record amortization at the end of the year if the lease year and fiscal years of the parties coincide.

Problem 19–4

Reep Company uses leases as a means of selling its products. It contracted with Sanders Corporation to lease machinery which had a market value of $110,000 and which cost Reep $78,000 (its carrying value in inventory). A downpayment of $22,961 is to be paid at the inception of the lease, and annually thereafter at the start of each of the next five years similar payments are to be made. Reep's implicit interest rate is 10%. Sander's incremental borrowing rate is 12%, and the lessor's implicit rate is unknown to Sanders.

Required (round to the nearest dollar):

1. Prepare amortization schedules for use by Reep and by Sanders covering the six-year lease term.
2. Give the lessor's and lessee's entries at the inception of the lease. Both the lessor and lessee adjust and close books on December 31 (one day before each payment is due). The lessee uses straight-line depreciation and assumes zero residual value of the asset after six years. Based on these data, give adjusting and closing entries for both parties at December 31 of the first year of the lease term.

Problem 19–5

Select the best answer in each of the following. Briefly justify your choices.

Questions 1 and 2 are based on the following information:

On January 1, 19A, Harris Company entered into a noncancelable lease agreement with Jones Company for a machine which was carried on the accounting records of Harris at $2,000,000. Total payments under the lease agreement which expires on December 31, 19J, aggregate $3,550,800 of which $2,400,000 represents the cost of the machine to Jones. Payments of $355,080 are due each January 1. The first payment was made on January 1, 19A, when the lease agreement was finalized. The interest rate of 10%; Jones's incremental borrowing rate was 15%. The "interest" method of amortization is being used. Jones expects the machine to have a 10-year life, no residual value, and depreciates it on a straight-line basis. The lease agreement should be accounted for as a sales-type lease by Harris and as a capital lease which is in substance a purchase by Jones.

1. What should be the income before income taxes derived by Harris from the lease for the year ended December 31, 19A?
   a. $204,492.
   b. $355,080.
   c. $455,080.
   d. $604,492.
2. Ignoring income taxes, what should be the expenses incurred by Jones from this lease for the year ended December 31, 19A?
   a. $204,492.
   b. $355,080.
   c. $444,492.
   d. $595,080.
3. What is the cost basis of an asset acquired by a capital lease?
   a. The net realizable value of the asset determined at the date of the lease agreement plus the sum of the future minimum lease payments under the lease.
   b. The sum of the future minimum lease payments under the lease.
   c. The present value of future minimum lease payments under the lease (exclusive of executory costs and any profit thereon) discounted at an appropriate rate.
   d. The present value of the market price of the asset discounted at an appropriate rate as an amount to be received at the end of the lease.
4. While only certain leases are currently accounted for as a sale or purchase, there is theoretical justification for considering all leases to be sales or purchases. The principal reason that supports this idea is that—
   a. All leases are generally for the economic life of the property and the residual value of the property at the end of the lease is minimal.
   b. At the end of the lease the property usually can be purchased by the lessee.
   c. A lease reflects the purchase or sale of a quantifiable right to the use of property.
   d. During the life of the lease the lessee can effectively treat the property as if it were owned by the lessee.

5. What journal entry should lessor make on January 2, 19A, if the lease is to be accounted for as an operating lease?

a.	Cash	10,000	
	Unearned rental revenue		10,000
b.	Receivable	35,000	
	Cash	10,000	
	Equipment inventory		45,000
c.	Receivable	48,680	
	Cash	10,000	
	Cost of goods sold	45,000	
	Sales revenue		58,680
	Equipment inventory		45,000
d.	Receivable	70,000	
	Cash	10,000	
	Cost of goods sold	45,000	
	Sales revenue		80,000
	Equipment inventory		45,000

6. Beth Company leased equipment to Wolf, Inc., on April 1, 19A. The lease was appropriately recorded as a sales-type lease by Beth Company. The lease is for an eight-year period expiring March 31, 19I. The first equal annual payment of $500,000 was made on April 1, 19A. Beth had purchased the equipment on January 1, 19A, for $2,800,000. The equipment has an estimated useful life of eight years with no residual value expected. Beth uses straight-line depreciation and takes a full year's depreciation in the year of purchase. The cash selling price of the equipment is $2,934,000. With an implicit interest rate of 10%, what amount of interest revenue should Beth record in calendar 19A as a result of the lease?
   a. $0.
   b. $182,550.
   c. $243,400.
   d. $280,000.
7. On January 1, 19A, The Anson Company leased a machine to Scovil Company. The lease was for a 10-year period, which approximated the useful life of the machine. Anson purchased the machine for $80,000 and expects to earn a 10% return on its investment, based upon an annual rental of $11,836 payable in advance each January 1.

   Assuming that the lease was a direct financing lease, what should be the interest entry on Anson's books on December 31, 19A?

a.	Cash	3,836	
	Interest revenue		3,836
b.	Lease receivable	6,816	
	Interest revenue		6,816
c.	Cash	8,000	
	Interest revenue		8,000
d.	Cash	11,836	
	Interest revenue		8,000
	Equipment		3,836

(AICPA adapted)

Problem 19–6

Hamner Leasing Company leased to Priddy Contractors a new machine that cost $18,000. The lease is a direct financing lease to Hamner and a capital lease to Priddy, who agreed to pay all executory costs and assume other risks and costs of ownership. Hamner sets the rents at an amount which will yield an annual return of 14%, and the lessee, being aware of this rate, also uses it to record the lease and calculate interest expense. The property is expected to have no residual value at the end of the four-year lease term. Both lessor and lessee have fiscal years ending December 31.

Required (round all amounts to the nearest dollar):
1. If the annual rents are payable at the end of each year, complete the following: *(a)* lessor computation of periodic rental payments and *(b)* an amortization schedule for the lessor reflecting interest and recovery of investment throughout the four-year lease term.
2. Assume instead that the annual rentals are payable at the start of the lease and annually thereafter. Complete the same items as for 1 above.
3. Priddy depreciates all assets by the straight-line method. Give entries under 1 above for both lessor and lessee relating to the lease for 19A. This includes adjusting and closing entries.
4. Indicate the asset and liability amounts under 1 above that would be reported on the classified December 31, 19A, balance sheets of the lessor and lessee. *(Related to Part B of the chapter.)*

PART B: PROBLEMS 19–7 to 19–13

Problem 19–7

Given the following data about a noncancelable lease:

Leased asset is new at inception of lease term.

Lease term	5 years
Interest rate implicit in the lease	10%
Lessee's incremental borrowing rate	12%
Amount of each lease payment	$2,000
Lessor's cost of asset	$7,582

Lessee has no way of knowing the interest rate implicit in the lease.

Fair market value of leased asset at inception of lease term	$7,582

Each lease payment occurs at the end of each period, i.e., an ordinary annuity.

Unreimbursable cost uncertainties of lessor	None
Credit standing of lessee	Excellent
Ignore executory cost	—
Depreciation method, if appropriate	Straight line

Required (round to the nearest dollar):

1. What type of lease is this to the lessee? To the lessor? Explain.
2. Make entries in parallel columns for lessee and lessor to record:
   a. The inception of the lease on January 1, 19A.
   b. All entries needed at year-end, December 31, 19A, for both parties to record lease payment (receipt), interest, depreciation, and so forth, including closing entries.

Problem 19–8

Lessor and Lessee agreed to a noncancelable lease which specified the following:

a. Lessor's cost of the asset leased, $22,200. The asset was new at the inception of the lease term.
b. Lease term, four years starting January 1, 19C.
c. Estimated useful life of the leased asset, six years.
d. On January 1, 19C, estimated that the residual value of the leased asset one day after the end of the lease term will be $4,000. The residual value is not guaranteed.
e. Depreciation method for the leased asset, straight line.
f. Lessee's incremental borrowing rate on January 1, 19C, 20%.
g. Bank prime rate of interest on January 1, 19C, 12%.
h. Purchase option price of leased asset exercisable one day after the end of the lease term, $4,500.
i. Title to the leased asset retained by the lessor unless the purchase option is exercised.
j. Market value of leased asset on January 1, 19C, $30,000.
k. Lessor's unreimbursable cost uncertainties, none.
l. Four annual lease rentals due on January 1 of each year during the lease term, with the first payment due at inception of the lease term, $8,441.

Both the lessor and lessee knew all of the above information.

Required (round to the nearest dollar):

1. What was the lessor's implicit interest rate in this lease?
2. What type of lease was this to the lessee? To the lessor? Explain.
3. In parallel columns for the lessee and lessor, record the following:
   a. Entry, or entries, at inception of the lease on January 1, 19C, if appropriate.
   b. Adjusting and closing entries on December 31, 19C.

Problem 19–9

On December 31, 19A, a lessor acquired a machine (for leasing purposes) for $70,000 cash and realized a 10% investment credit (i.e., a reduction of 19A income taxes payable) of 10% on cost. The lessor accounts for the investment credit by the deferral method. The machine was leased on January 1, 19B, for five years under a sales-type lease which required annual payments of $27,180 at the end of each year. At inception of the lease, the fair (i.e., market) value of the leased asset was $115,000. At the end of the lease term the machine will revert to the lessor, at which time the estimated residual value will be $8,000 (none of which is guaranteed by the lessee). The lessor's implicit rate of interest was 10% on the net investment (after taking into consideration the investment tax credit and the residual value).

Required (round amounts to the nearest dollar):

1. Show how the lessor computed the annual rental of $27,180.
2. Prepare a lease amortization schedule for the lessor.
3. Give the following entries for the lessor:
   a. To record acquisition of the machine on December 31, 19A.
   b. To record the investment tax credit on December 31, 19A.
   c. To record the inception of the lease on January 1, 19B.
   d. To record collection of the first rental and recognition of interest revenue on December 31, 19B (end of the fiscal period).
   e. To record, at termination of the lease on December 31, 19F, the last rent, interest revenue, and return of the asset assuming the estimate of residual value remained correct.
4. How would the lessor's entries differ at the end of the lease term assuming the market value of the returned machine was $6,000 (instead of the $8,000 estimated residual value)?

Problem 19–10

McRoberts Leasing Company leased equipment to a lessee over an eight-year term whereby $45,000 rents are paid annually in advance by the lessee. The unguaranteed residual value of the equipment at end of the lease term is $20,000. The interest rate implicit in the lease is 15%.

Required (round to the nearest dollar):

1. Compute the initial investment value of the leased property and the total amount of interest to be earned by McRoberts over the lease term.
2. Immediately after the fifth annual payment, the unrecovered investment value is $114,181. By means of an amortization schedule for the lessor, using the value

determined in 1 above, prove the correctness of this amount.

3. Immediately after the fifth payment, McRoberts determines that the expected unguaranteed residual value, which had been estimated to be $20,000, probably will prove to be zero. This change in accounting estimate would decrease the unrecovered investment value by the present value of the previously estimated residual value. Prepare the journal entry to record this change, and complete the lease amortization schedule from the point of the $114,181 value in the light of this new determination.

Problem 19–11

Brownlee Corporation purchased a machine (for leasing purposes) on December 31, 19A, for $300,000 cash on which it received a 10% investment credit (i.e., a reduction in its 19A income taxes payable equal to 10% of the cost). Brownlee accounts for the investment tax credit by the deferral method. By prior agreement the machine was delivered to Butler Company (lessee) under a direct financing lease whereby Butler paid the first lease rental of $73,516 on December 31, 19A, and agreed to pay three more such annual rentals at each year-end. At the end of the four-year lease term the machine will revert to the lessor, at which time it is expected to have a residual value of $20,000 (none of which was guaranteed by the lessee). The lessor's implicit interest rate was 10% on the net investment (after considering the investment tax credit and the residual value).

Required (round amounts to the nearest dollar):

1. Show how the lessor computed the annual rental of $73,516.
2. Prepare a lease amortization schedule for the lessor.
3. Give the following entries for the lessor:
   - *a.* To record purchase of the machine on December 31, 19A.
   - *b.* To record the investment tax credit on December 31, 19A.
   - *c.* To record inception of the lease on December 31, 19A.
   - *d.* To record collection of the first rent on December 31, 19A.
   - *e.* To record collection of the second rent on December 31, 19B. This is the end of the fiscal period; recognize interest revenue.
   - *f.* To record interest earned on December 31, 19E.
   - *g.* To record return of the machine by the lessee at the termination of the lease term on December 31, 19E. At this date assume the machine has an actual market value of $14,000 (instead of the $20,000 estimated residual value).
4. How would the lessor's entries differ at the end of the lease term if the actual market value of the machine turned out to be $23,000 (instead of the estimated residual value of $20,000)?

Problem 19–12

Lessor Company entered into a lease with Lessee Company on January 1, 19D. The following data relate to the leased asset and the lease agreement:

a. Asset leased—large construction crane.
b. Cost to Lessor, $100,000.
c. Estimated useful life, 10 years.
d. Estimated residual value at end of useful life, $4,000.
e. Lessor's normal sales price, $146,913.
f. Lease provisions:
  (1) Noncancelable; the asset will revert to Lessor at the end of the lease term.
  (2) Estimated residual value at end of lease term, $10,000 (none guaranteed).
  (3) Title does not transfer to Lessee by the end of the lease term.
  (4) No bargain purchase option is included.
  (5) Lease term, seven years starting January 1, 19D.
  (6) Lease payment on each year-end, starting December 31, 19D, $31,200.
g. Lessor's implicit rate of return, 12% (assume Lessee knows this rate).
h. Lessee's incremental borrowing rate, 13% (assumed to evidence a good credit rating for problem purposes).
i. Lessor has no material cost uncertainties.

Required (show computations and round to the nearest dollar):

1. What kind of lease was this to Lessee Company? Give the basis for your response.
2. What kind of lease was this to Lessor Company? Give the basis for your response.
3. For Lessor Company give the entries to record *(a)* the lease at inception date and *(b)* the first rental.
4. For Lessee Company give the entries to record *(a)* the lease at inception date and *(b)* the first rental.

Problem 19–13

Lessor and lessee agreed to a noncancelable lease which specified the following:

a. Lessor's cost of the asset leased, $22,200. The asset was new at the inception of the lease term.
b. Lease term, four years starting January 1, 19C.
c. Estimated useful life of the leased asset, six years.
d. On January 1, 19C, lessor and lessee estimated that the residual value of the leased asset on the purchase option date (see h below) will be $5,577 and zero at the end of its useful life. The residual value is not guaranteed.

e. Depreciation method for the leased asset, straightline.
f. Lessee's incremental borrowing rate, 10%. Lessee has an excellent credit rating.
g. Interest rate implicit in the lease, 10%.
h. Purchase option price of leased asset exercisable on January 2, 19F, $5,000.
i. Title to the leased asset retained by the lessor unless the purchase option is exercised.
j. Market value of leased asset on January 1, 19C, $30,000.
k. Lessor's unreimbursable cost uncertainties, none.
l. Four annual lease rentals due on January 1 of each year during the lease term, with the first payment due at inception of the lease term, $7,526.

Required (round to the nearest dollar):

1. Show how the amount of each annual rental was computed.
2. Is this an operating lease or a capital lease to the lessee? Explain. Compute the lessee's capitalizable cost of the leased asset.
3. What type of lease is this to the lessor? Explain.
4. In parallel columns for the lessee and lessor, record the inception of the lease on January 1, 19C, (if appropriate) and the adjusting and closing entries on December 31, 19C.
5. Prepare the financial statement presentation of all lease-related accounts as they would appear in the financial statements of the lessee at December 31, 19C, and for the year then ended. Note disclosures are not required.

SUPPLEMENT 19–A

Problem 19–14

A lessor arranges financing of property to be leased to a lessee under a leveraged lease contract. The property cost $1,000,000 and is expected to have an eight-year life and zero residual value. It will be depreciated by the lessor by the SYD method. The 10% investment credit will be realized by the lessor in the first year. The lessor has other income as well as from this lease; all income is taxed at a rate of 40% and any losses result in a similar 40% tax saving. The parties agree on eight annual payments of $180,674 each for the use of the property.

The lessor pays $300,000 toward purchase price of the property and borrows the remaining $700,000 at an annual interest rate of 8%. Eight annual payments of $121,810 will amortize the debt and interest.

Required (round all amounts to the nearest dollar): Prepare a schedule similar to Exhibit 19–11 covering the entire lease term. Present a proof reconciling cash flow to net income as in that exhibit.

20

Accounting Changes, Error Correction, and Incomplete Records

ACCOUNTANTS often encounter situations in which changes must be made in accounting, such as a change from one accounting principle to another one, or a change in accounting estimate. Also, accountants sometimes find accounting errors that necessitate correction of the account balances. Because numerous ways were used in the past to account for such changes and corrections (often in a way to manipulate reported income), the accounting profession has developed guidelines designed to attain reasonable uniformity and orderly resolution of them. This chapter discusses those guidelines as follows:

Part A—Accounting Changes

Part B—Correction of Accounting Errors

Supplement 20–A—Preparation of Financial Statements from Single-Entry and Other Incomplete Records

The basic accounting issue in this chapter involves the **comparability (including consistency) principle** (discussed in Chapter 1). Whenever a company makes an accounting change or corrects an accounting error that was made in a prior period, the potential exists for the company's financial statements to lack interperiod comparability because of inconsistency. For this reason, the primary objective of *APB Opinion 20,* "Accounting Changes," is to assure that comparability is not impaired, or if that ideal is not attainable in the circumstances, that the effects of the change or correction are fully disclosed.

Part A: Accounting Changes

Current practices for dealing with accounting changes evolved gradually, and no authoritative body such as the APB dealt with them comprehensively prior to *APB Opinion No. 20,* "Accounting Changes," August 1971. As a consequence, various accounting approaches were used to record and report accounting changes. Prior to *Opinion 20* it was not unusual for changes in accounting, depending on how they were recorded and reported, to result in a particular amount of revenue or expense over time *(a)* "passing through" the income statement more than once or *(b)* completely missing the income statement. Accounting changes were widely used for "doctoring" net income or loss. *APB Opinion 20* narrowed the alternatives available by specifying the accounting for **recording** and **reporting** accounting changes.[1]

CLASSIFICATION OF ACCOUNTING CHANGES AND CORRECTIONS

Because of the diversity of accounting changes and accounting errors, *APB Opinion 20* provides the following classifications:

A. **Accounting changes**
   1. Change in accounting principle. This is the situation when an enterprise adopts a generally accepted accounting principle or procedure that is different from the one previously used. An example would be a change from straight-line to double-declining-balance (DDB) depreciation.
   2. Change in accounting estimate. As more current and improved data are obtained in respect to accounting determinations based on estimates, a prior estimate may be changed. An example would be the following: Based on new information, it is decided during year 6 that the economic life of asset X, which cost $12,000, is 12 years, rather than the 10-year life currently being used for depreciation purposes.
   3. Change in reporting entity. This type of change occurs when the reporting entity changes from the prior period. An example would be the first inclusion in the (or exclusion from) consolidated financial statements for the company of the financial statements of a subsidiary. Detailed discussion of this change is deferred to another course which deals with consolidations and mergers in more depth.

B. **Correction of accounting errors**—discussed in Part B of this chapter.

APPROACHES FOR RECORDING AND REPORTING ACCOUNTING CHANGES

APB Opinion 20 recognizes three approaches by which accounting changes can be **recorded** in the accounts and **reported** on the financial statements. They are as follows:

1. **Current**—The cumulative effect of the accounting change is determined. The "adjustment" for this amount is recorded in the accounts as a special item (similar to an extraordinary item), and is reported in the same manner on the **current** income statement.
2. **Prospective**—The cumulative effect of the accounting change is **not** determined. No "adjustment" is recognized or reported; rather, the effect of the change is spread over the current and future periods; therefore, the approach is **prospective.**
3. **Retroactive**—The account balances affected by the change and the cumulative effect of the change on Retained Earnings is determined. The adjustment for this amount is **recorded** in the accounts as a debit or credit to Retained Earnings and is **reported** by **retroactively restating** all accounts affected by the change to reflect the new method.

Because of the dissimilar characteristics of the three types of accounting changes listed above, the *Opinion* specifies when each of these approaches should be used. Basically, the *Opinion* prescribes the following approach for each type of change (with certain exceptions explained later):

Classification of Change	Accounting Approach
1. Change in accounting principle:	
a. Usual applications	Current
b. Exceptions	Retroactive
2. Change in accounting estimate	Prospective
3. Change in reporting entity	Retroactive

With these fundamentals in mind we can now proceed to a detailed discussion of each of the first two types of accounting changes listed above. In the discussions which follow we will focus on (1) **recording** in the accounts and (2) **reporting** on the financial statements.

CHANGE IN ACCOUNTING PRINCIPLE

A change in accounting principle occurs when a company adopts a generally accepted accounting

[1] Accounting changes are reported often. For example, of the 600 surveyed companies in *Accounting Trends & Techniques, 1980* (New York, 1980), table 1–8, the numbers of accounting changes were: 1976, 153; 1977, 191; 1978, 173; and 1979, 223.

principle different from a previously used one that **also** was generally accepted at the time adopted. *APB Opinion 20* states that the term **accounting principle** includes "not only accounting principles and practices but also the methods of applying them." It excludes the adoption of a principle occasioned by events occurring for the first time or that were previously immaterial in their effect. Examples of a change in accounting principle are as follows:

1. A change from straight line to some other method of depreciation, or vice versa.
2. A change in inventory cost flow, such as from FIFO to average.
3. A change in accounting for long-term construction contracts from completed contract basis to percentage of completion, or vice versa.
4. A change from expensing certain costs to capitalizing the costs and depreciating them, or vice versa.
5. A change in the method of accounting for the investment tax credit.
6. A change from cost to equity for long-term investments, or vice versa.

APB Opinion 20 requires that **most** changes in accounting principle be recognized by the **current approach,** which includes reporting the cumulative effect of the change (often referred to as the "catch-up adjustment") in the net income of the period of the change. For example, if a company changed, at the start of the sixth year of the 10-year life of a machine, from straight-line to SYD depreciation, the cumulative effect of the change would be computed as the cumulative difference between the straight-line and SYD depreciation amounts on the machine for years 1–5.

In addition to this basic rule for changes in accounting principles, *Opinion 20* specifies that a few specific changes in accounting principle should be reported by **retroactively** restating the financial statements of prior periods to reflect the new principle (i.e., method or procedure) adopted. Specific principle changes singled out for accounting by the **retroactive approach** are (1) a change from LIFO inventory to another method (discussed in Chapter 8), (2) a change in the method of accounting for long-term construction contracts (discussed in Chapter 9), and (3) a change to or from "full cost" to another method in the extractive industries (discussed in Chapter 11).[2] The exceptions were deemed advisable to prevent income manipulation because such changes often result in large credit adjustments.

The cumulative effect of a change in accounting principle is computed for all prior periods affected by the change up to the beginning of the period in which the change is made, because the financial statements for the period of change must reflect the newly adopted principle. The amount of the cumulative effect of the change must be reported on the income statement separately **between** Income before extraordinary items and Net income. The *Opinion* states that it is "not an extraordinary item but should be shown in a manner similar to an extraordinary item." Per share amounts should be shown for the cumulative adjustment reported.

The *Opinion* also requires that income before extraordinary items and net income be shown on a **pro forma** basis on the "face of the income statements for all periods presented as if the newly adopted accounting principle had been applied during all periods affected."[3] This requirement is specified to satisfy the **comparability and reporting principles.**

Change in Accounting Principle Illustrated

Exhibit 20–1 illustrates the **current approach,** which is used for most changes in accounting principle, and Exhibit 20–2 illustrates the **retroactive approach** which is used for the specially designated changes in accounting principle.

Current Approach. Exhibit 20–1, Panel B, computes the amount of the pretax catch-up adjustment of $37,600, which is the cumulative difference, up to the beginning of the current year, between the old and the new depreciation amounts. Panel C illustrates the *(a)* catch-up entry to record the change from straight-line to double-declining-balance (DDB) depreciation and *(b)* the entry to record 19D depreciation expense of $20,480. In the catch-up entry, Accumulated Depreciation, Machinery is credited for the

[2] In some cases, the company decides to make these changes; in other cases, *APB Opinions* and *FASB Statements* have required a certain accounting method, which has forced companies formerly using other methods to change to the required method. In some cases, the *FASB Statement* specifies how the change should be accounted for—current, prospective, or retroactive.

[3] **Pro forma** is defined in *Webster's Dictionary* as "for the sake of or as a matter of form." Pro forma statements are "as if" statements; the "as if" assumptions should be clearly stated.

cumulative amount of $37,600 (i.e., $97,600 under DDB − $60,000 under straight line) to reflect the change in book value of assets caused by the accounting change. Because the same depreciation method is used for both accounting and income tax purposes, Income Tax Receivable is debited for the income tax effect (i.e., $37,600 × .40 = $15,040), which would be claimed by the company as a refund on an amended tax return for the years 19A–19C. Adjustment Due to Change in Accounting Principle, Depreciation is debited for the aftertax amount of $22,560 (i.e., $37,600 − $15,040).

Panel D should receive your special attention because of the specific guidelines of *APB Opinion 20* implemented therein. Observe that two sets of income amounts are presented for each year: *(a)* the **basic amounts** reported on the income statement and balance sheet and *(b)* the required **pro forma amounts.** The pro forma income amounts for 19D and 19C reflect restated amounts that would have been reported if the DDB method had been used during both 19D and 19C. On the balance sheet for 19D, machinery is reported on the (new) DDB basis (i.e., $200,000 − $118,080 = $81,920) and for 19C, on the (old) straight-line basis (i.e., $140,000). The adjustment due to accounting change (i.e., $22,560) is reported on the income statement between Income before extraordinary items and Net income, as specified by *APB Opinion 20.*

Retroactive Approach. Exhibit 20–2 illustrates a change from LIFO to FIFO, which is one of the accounting principle changes singled out for **special treatment** by the retroactive approach. For instructional convenience, it is assumed in the hypothetical situation given in Panel A, that the beginning inventory amount of the year preceding the change (i.e., 19B) was the same under LIFO and FIFO. This assumption facilitates the computation of the catch-up adjustment needed to record the effect of the change by focusing on the difference between the (new) FIFO and (old) LIFO amounts of the beginning inventory of the year of the change (i.e., ending inventory amounts for the preceding year).[4] With this assumption, the cumulative pretax effect of the accounting change through the date of change (i.e., January 1, 19C) is computed as the $10,000 difference in the 19B ending inventory between FIFO ($60,000) and LIFO ($50,000). Under the retroactive approach, this $10,000 difference is recorded and reported, net of income tax, as an increase in **retained earnings** at January 1, 19C. The entry in Panel C records the cumulative effect of the change in accounting principle: Inventory is debited for $10,000 to restate it to the FIFO basis; Income Tax Payable is credited for $4,000, the tax effect of the change (up to January 1, 19C); and Retained Earnings is credited for the aftertax effect of the change on prior periods' (i.e., only 19B in this example) net income, $6,000 (i.e., $10,000 × .60). This credit to Retained Earnings, rather than to a gain on the income statement, is a distinguishing characteristic of the **retroactive approach.**

In contrast, under the **current approach** illustrated in Exhibit 20–1, the catch-up adjustment (i.e., the cumulative effect of the accounting change) was recorded as a current-year adjustment and reported on the income statement of the year of change.

Panel D of Exhibit 20–2 presents **comparative** financial statements for the years 19C and 19B. The financial statements of both years reflect the (new) FIFO basis under the **retroactive** approach. The note at the bottom of Panel D indicates that the special change in accounting principle increased 19C reported income by $1,200 (pretax, $2,000). The $2,000 is the FIFO-LIFO inventory difference at the end of 19C, $12,000 (i.e., $80,000 − $68,000) minus the difference at the beginning of 19C, $10,000 (i.e., $60,000 − $50,000).

CHANGE IN ACCOUNTING ESTIMATE

Accounting necessarily requires the use of estimates because future developments and events cannot be known with certainty. For example, the amount recorded for periodic depreciation expense is the result of one known (cost) and two estimates (residual value and useful life). Estimates result from judgments which are based on specific assumptions and projections concerning future events. As the anticipated event or events come closer, usually it is possible to improve on the accuracy of the estimates. As a consequence, the accountant frequently is faced with the problem of what to do about improved esti-

[4] Without this simplifying assumption, the pretax amount of the cumulative effect of the accounting change also would need to consider the difference between FIFO and LIFO amounts of the beginning inventory of 19B, as well as the beginning and ending inventories of all preceding years. In this example, we effectively assume that all such differences are zero.

EXHIBIT 20–1: Change in Accounting Principle—Current Approach (usual situations)

Panel A—Hypothetical Situation:

1. Machinery acquired January 1, 19A; cost, $200,000; estimated useful life, 10 years and no residual value; straight-line (SL) depreciation used for both accounting and income tax purposes.
2. Beginning of 19D, a decision was made to change to double-declining-balance (DDB) depreciation and residual value remains at zero for both accounting and income tax purposes.
3. The fiscal year ends December 31. Average income tax rate, 40 percent.

Panel B—Computation of the Amount of the Catch-up Adjustment:

1. This change is accounted for by the **current approach** (it is **not** a specified exception).
2. Computation of the cumulative effect of the change (i.e., the catch-up and adjustment):

Depreciation based on new DDB method (i.e., twice SL rate = 20%):		
19A: $200,000 × .20	$40,000	
19B: ($200,000 − $40,000) × .20	32,000	
19C: ($200,000 − $40,000 − $32,000) × .20	25,600	$97,600
Depreciation recorded to date, SL method:		
Years A, B, and C: ($200,000 ÷ 10) × 3		60,000
Cumulative effect of accounting change, pretax		$37,600
Cumulative effect, net of income tax ($37,600 × .60)		$22,560

Panel C—Accounting Entries to Record the Accounting Change, Net of Tax:

1. Beginning of 19D, to record effect of the accounting change:

Adjustment due to change in accounting principle, depreciation	22,560	
Income tax receivable ($37,600 × .40)	15,040	
Accumulated depreciation, machinery ($97,600 − $60,000)		37,600

This entry assumes an IRS-approved amended tax return.

2. December 31, 19D, to record annual depreciation:

Depreciation expense [($200,000 − $97,600) × .20]	20,480	
Accumulated depreciation, machinery		20,480

Panel D—Financial Statements for 19D and 19C:

	19D	19C
Balance sheet:		
Machinery (cost $200,000, less accumulated depreciation of $97,600 + $20,480 = $118,080, DDB for 19D; $20,000 × 3 = $60,000, SL for 19C)	$ 81,920	$140,000
Income statement:		
Depreciation expense	$ 20,480	$ 20,000
Income before extraordinary items (assumed net of tax)	$150,000	$130,000
Less: Extraordinary items assumed (net of tax)	10,000	(6,000)
Adjustment due to accounting change ($37,600 less $15,040 tax)	(22,560)	
Net income	$137,440	$124,000
Earnings per share (100,000 shares outstanding):		
Income before extraordinary items	$1.50	$1.30
Extraordinary items	.10	(.06)
Effect of accounting change	(.23)	
Net income	$1.37	$1.24

Pro forma amounts for interperiod comparability (reflects DDB in 19D and 19C):	19D	19C
Pro forma income before extraordinary items:		
19D—as above—there would be no cumulative effect in 19D	$150,000	
19C—$130,000 − [($25,600 − $20,000) × .60 = $3,360]		$126,640
Earnings per share	$1.50	$1.27
Pro forma net income:		
19D—$137,440 + $22,560	$160,000	
19C—$124,000 − [$25,600 − $20,000) × .60 = $3,360]		$120,640
Earnings per share	$1.60	$1.21

Note: At the beginning of 19D, the company changed from SL to DDB depreciation; in the opinion of the management the new method better measures income. The aftertax effect of the change was to increase depreciation expense for 19D by $480 (i.e., $288 after tax) and decrease 19D income before extraordinary items by $22,848 (i.e., the adjustment amount, $22,560 plus the current year depreciation difference, $288); ($.23 per share) and 19C income by $3,360 ($.03 per share). The pro forma amounts have been restated to report income for 19D and 19C as though DDB depreciation had been used in both years.

EXHIBIT 20–2: Change in Accounting Principle—Retroactive Approach (used for special situations)

Panel A—Hypothetical Situation:

1. On January 1, 19C, X Company decided to change the inventory cost method from LIFO to FIFO for accounting and tax purposes. The fiscal year ends on December 31, and the average income tax rate is 40 percent.
2. To provide data for the change, a computer run reflected the following selected data:

	19C—Year of Change		19B	
Item	FIFO	LIFO	FIFO	LIFO
a. Beginning inventory	$ 60,000	$50,000	$ 45,000	$45,000
b. Ending inventory	80,000	68,000	60,000	50,000
c. Income before extraordinary items	176,000		166,000	
d. Retained earnings, beginning balance	187,000		92,000	
e. Extraordinary gains (losses), net of tax	(2,000)		3,000	
f. Dividends declared and paid	88,000		80,000	

Panel B—Computation of the Amount of the Catch-up Adjustment:

1. This particular change in principle is an exception to be accounted for by the retroactive approach as specified in *APB Opinion 20* (par. 27).
2. The pretax cumulative effect of the change (i.e., the catch-up adjustment) on January 1, 19C, is: 19B ending inventory, at FIFO, $60,000, minus, at LIFO, $50,000 = $10,000 (increase).

Panel C—January 1, 19C, Entry to Record the Accounting Change, Net of Tax (the credit to Retained Earnings reflects the retroactive approach):

Inventory, beginning FIFO basis ($60,000 − $50,000)	10,000	
Income tax payable ($10,000 × .40)		4,000
Retained earnings, adjustment due to change in accounting principle ($10,000 × .60)		6,000

Panel D—Financial Statements for 19C and 19B:

	19C, FIFO	19B Restated to FIFO Basis
Balance sheet:		
Inventory (at FIFO, and LCM)	$ 80,000	$ 60,000
Income statement:		
Income before extraordinary items	$176,000	$166,000
Extraordinary items, net of tax	(2,000)	3,000
Net income	$174,000	$169,000
Earnings per share (100,000 shares):		
Income before extraordinary items	$1.76	$1.66
Extraordinary items	(.02)	.03
Net income	$1.74	$1.69
Statement of retained earnings (reports the cumulative effect, i.e., catch-up adjustment, of all accounting principle changes singled out for treatment by the retroactive approach):		
Beginning balance	$187,000	$ 92,000
Add: Cumulative effect of accounting change		6,000*
Add: Net income (per above)	174,000	169,000
Deduct: Dividends declared and paid	(88,000)	(80,000)
Ending balance	$273,000	$187,000

* See Panel C for entry crediting Retained Earnings for this amount.

Note: The 19C inventory valuation is at FIFO, LCM. At the beginning of 19C, the company changed from LIFO to FIFO inventory for accounting and tax purposes because FIFO more realistically measures net income. The aftertax effect of the change on the net income of 19C, considering the effects on both the beginning and ending inventories, was an increase of $1,200 ($.012 per share). Retained earnings at January 1, 19C, was adjusted upward by $6,000. Pro forma amounts are not required by *APB Opinion 20* because the prior years' statements are restated to the new basis, which makes them comparable with the statements of the current year.

mates. For example, during the first few years' life of a company, the estimated loss rate on uncollectible accounts may have a wide range of estimation error because of the lack of experience with collections; as time passes, the estimated rate often can be refined as additional information is developed. Thus, changes in accounting estimates are a **natural consequence** of the accounting process. Because of this characteristic, a change in an accounting estimate is viewed as being basically different from a change in accounting principle. Examples of changes in accounting estimates are:

1. Change in the estimated residual value or useful life of an asset subject to depreciation, amortization, or depletion.
2. Change in the estimated loss rate on receivables.
3. Change in the estimated amortization period of a deferred charge.
4. Change in the estimated time over which revenue collected in advance will be earned.
5. Change in the expected warranty cost on goods sold under guarantee.

When a change in an estimate has been decided upon, the accountant is faced with the dual problem of *(a)* how to **record** the effect of the change of estimate in the accounts and *(b)* how to **report** the change on the comparative financial statements. The accountant presumes that a change in an accounting estimate will be made only when there are sound reasons for doing so, as opposed to intent to manipulate reported income.[5]

Because estimates are necessary in accounting and occur with some frequency, it appears reasonable to account for such changes **prospectively.** This approach means that the **new** estimate should be incorporated in revenue and expense determinations of the current and future periods based on the existing balance in the related accounts when the new estimate is made. On this point *APB Opinion 20* states:

> The Board concludes that the effect of a change in accounting estimate should be accounted for in (a) the period of change if the change affects that period only, or (b) the period of change and future periods if the change affects both.

This approach to accounting for a change in estimate means that no retroactive (or catch-up) adjustment is necessary. Therefore, no entry is needed to record the change itself and the only disclosure required by the *Opinion* is the effect on income before extraordinary items, net income, and related per share amounts of the current period, which usually is disclosed in a note.

In some situations a change in accounting principle and a change in estimate for the same item are made concurrently. When the effects of each change can be separated, two changes should be recognized. However, when the two are indistinguishable, the one that clearly is dominant should be used; if neither clearly is dominant, a change in estimate should be assumed.

Change in Accounting Estimate Illustrated

To illustrate a **change in estimate,** assume an asset that cost $120,000 (no residual value) is being depreciated over a 10-year life. On the basis of new information available after 4 years' use, a 12-year life appears more realistic. The change in the depreciation estimate, starting in the fifth year, would be recognized as follows (assuming straight-line depreciation):

a. To compute annual depreciation for the current and subsequent years (no catch-up adjustment to be made):

Original cost of the asset	$120,000
Accumulated depreciation to date of change in estimate ($120,000 × 4/10)	48,000
Undepreciated balance at beginning of year of change in estimate	$ 72,000
Annual depreciation after change $72,000 ÷ (12 − 4 years)	$ 9,000

b. Recording—no catch-up adjustment.

To record depreciation for year 5:

Depreciation expense	9,000	
Accumulated depreciation		9,000

c. Reporting—income statement for year of change, years 4 and 5:

[5] The definition of a change in estimate assumes that the original estimate and the new estimate both represent realistic and good faith determinations based upon the information available at the time the respective estimates are made. A change in estimate not meeting these criteria must be classified as an "accounting error," as defined and discussed in Part B of this chapter.

	Year 4	Year 5
Depreciation expense	$12,000	$9,000

CHANGE IN REPORTING ENTITY

Changes in reporting entity are recorded and reported through retroactive restatement as illustrated in Exhibit 20–2; that is, they "should be reported by restating the financial statements of all prior periods presented in order to show financial information for the new reporting entity for all periods." *APB Opinion No. 20,* paragraph 12, defines this type of accounting change as follows:

> One special type of accounting change in accounting principle results in financial statements which, in effect, are those of a different reporting entity. This type is limited mainly to (a) presenting consolidated or combined statements in place of statements of individual companies, (b) changing specific subsidiaries comprising the group of companies for which consolidated statements are presented, and (c) changing the companies included in combined financial statements. A different group of companies comprise the reporting entity after each change.

This type of change is discussed in detail in another book in this series.[6]

ACCOUNTING CHANGES AND STOCK MARKET REACTIONS

Because companies have used accounting changes to "doctor" reported earnings, it is possible that the information disclosed could mislead investors, which explains why *APB Opinion 20* specifies such detailed **disclosure guidelines** for accounting changes.

Questions of interest to the accounting profession are: How do investors actually react to accounting changes? Are investors able to interpret the implications of accounting changes realistically? These questions have been addressed in a number of research studies with the following empirical results:

1. Investors do not appear to be fooled by accounting changes that increase the reported income of a company with otherwise weak operating results, when the company willfully makes the accounting change (as opposed to being forced to make the change to comply with an APB or FASB pronouncement). That is, the common stock of such companies does not appear to experience upward price movements when the accounting changes are disclosed publicly.[7]
2. Investors seem to impute real economic significance to an increase in reported income caused by an accounting change mandated by an *APB Opinion* or *FASB Statement* because the company making such a change is not likely to be using the accounting change to manipulate reported income. The prices of the common stock of such companies generally increase when the accounting change is disclosed publicly.[8]
3. Investors bid up the common stock prices of companies that change from FIFO to LIFO even though the change usually decreases reported income.[9] Usually changes to LIFO are made by companies when they are experiencing strong operating results, and the increase in stock price appears to be as much a response to the strong operating results of the companies as to the tax saving caused by the accounting change (companies usually change to LIFO for income tax purposes also).[10]
4. Investors do not seem to distinguish between changes in accounting principles and changes in accounting estimates.[11]

The above findings do not offer concrete implications for the direction of future accounting pronouncements. However, they provide a glimpse of the use investors actually make of accounting disclosures. In summary, they suggest that companies

---

[6] C. H. Griffin, T. H. Williams, and K. L. Larson, *Advanced Accounting* 4th ed. (Homewood, Ill., Richard D. Irwin, Inc.), 1980.

[7] See, for example, R. Ball, "Changes in Accounting Techniques and Stock Prices, *Empirical Research in Accounting: Selected Studies, 1972.* Supplement to *Journal of Accounting Research,* pp. 1–44; R. S. Kaplan and R. Roll, "Investor Evaluation of Accounting Information: Some Empirical Evidence," *Journal of Business,* April 1972, pp. 225–57; and W. T. Harrison, "Different Market Reactions to Discretionary and Nondiscretionary Accounting Changes," *Journal of Accounting Research,* Spring 1977, pp. 84–107.

[8] Harrison, "Different Market Reactions. . . ."

[9] S. Sunder, "Stock Price and Risk Related to Accounting Changes in Inventory Valuation," *The Accounting Review,* April 1975, pp. 305–15.

[10] A. R. Abdel-Khalik and J. C. McKeown, "Understanding Accounting Changes in an Efficient Market: Evidence of Differential Reaction," *The Accounting Review,* October 1978, pp. 851–68.

[11] W. T. Harrison, "Accounting Changes in Principles and Estimates: How Different Are They?" *Economic Consequences of Financial Accounting Standards* (FASB, July 1978), pp. 253–78.

which "doctor" their financial statements cannot thereby manipulate their stock prices, which suggests that the total market is relatively sophisticated in its ability to understand accounting information.

Part B: Correction of Accounting Errors

CLASSIFICATION OF ACCOUNTING ERRORS

An accounting error is defined as the **misapplication** of facts existing at the time an event or transaction is recorded. **APB Opinion 20** states that, "Errors in financial statements result from mathematical mistakes, mistakes in application of accounting principles, or oversight or misuse of facts that existed at the time the financial statements were prepared." Accounting errors are of two basic types: (1) those that occur and are discovered in the **same** accounting period and (2) those that occur in one accounting period and are discovered in a **later** accounting period. When an accounting error is discovered, it should be corrected immediately.

The type of error that occurs and is discovered in the same accounting period is not difficult to deal with because the accounts have not been closed and the financial statements have not been issued. This type of error can be corrected readily either *(a)* by reversing the incorrect entry and then entering the correct entry or *(b)* by making a single correcting entry designed to directly correct the account balances.

In contrast, *APB Opinion 20* deals with errors which affect the financial statements of one period and are discovered in a later period. This type of error is more complex because a past period is involved (and the past financial statements have been issued); also, the current period usually is involved, and often one or more future periods will be affected as well. Because of these complexities, and opportunities to manipulate accounting values by selective ways of correction, the *Opinion* provides specific guidelines for correcting accounting errors.

Examples of accounting errors, as distinguished from changes in accounting principles or changes in estimates, are as follows:

a. Use of an inappropriate or unacceptable accounting principle. Thus, a change from an unacceptable accounting principle to a generally accepted one would require the correction of an error (not a change in accounting principle).

b. Use of an unrealistic accounting estimate, that is, the misapplication in the accounts and on the financial statements of known information at the date of the decision in respect to the estimate. Thus, the adoption of an unrealistic depreciation rate, when discovered later, requires the correction of an error (not a change in accounting estimate).

c. Misstatement of an accounting value, such as for inventory, operational assets, liabilities, or owners' equity.

d. Failure to recognize accruals and/or deferrals.

e. Incorrect classification of an expenditure as between expense and asset.

f. Incorrect or unrealistic allocations of accounting values, such as in the allocation of overhead costs during the construction of operational assets for self use.

g. Failure to record a completed transaction.

h. Mathematical errors involved in the accounting process.

FUNDAMENTALS OF ERROR CORRECTION

APB Opinion 20, (pars. 36 and 37) and *FASB Statement of Financial Accounting Standards No. 16,* "Prior Period Adjustments," provide guidelines for the correction of accounting errors. Fundamentally, correction of errors uses the **retroactive approach.** Thus, errors included in the financial statements of a prior period and discovered in the current period require that all of the cumulative effects of the error be computed up to the beginning of the current period and a correcting entry to Retained Earnings be made on a retroactive basis as a prior period adjustment. The correcting entry is made to correct the current beginning balance of Retained Earnings and all other existing accounts affected by the error. The cumulative effect of an error on the net incomes of prior periods should be recorded in a separate account such as Prior Period Adjustment—Correction of Accounting Error. This account is closed directly to Retained Earnings and serves to correct the beginning balance of that account for the current period.

The prior period adjustment, in accordance with *FASB Statement 16,* is reported on the statement of retained earnings as a retroactive adjustment of the beginning balance. As to disclosure *APB Opinion 20* states: "The nature of an error in previously issued financial statements and the effect of its correction on income before extraordinary items, net income, and the related per share amounts should be disclosed in the period in which the error was discovered and corrected. Financial statements of subsequent periods need not repeat the disclosures." On comparative financial statements, all errors must be corrected for each year presented.

CORRECTION OF ACCOUNTING ERROR ILLUSTRATED

Exhibit 20–3 illustrates the correction of errors that occurred in each of the two prior years. Panel A presents the hypothetical situation; Panel B presents the entry to correct the errors, on a **retroactive** basis; and Panel C presents the reporting on the current year's comparative financial statements. In the exhibit, the correcting entry in the current year (i.e., year of discovery, 19F) is shown in Panel B. It is recorded net of income tax, and because the errors also were on the tax returns, Income Tax Receivable is debited. The accumulated depreciation is corrected, and a prior period adjustment (i.e., retroactive basis) is recorded at the net of tax amount of $6,000.

The **comparative financial statements** for the prior year (19E), shown in Panel C, reflects a prior period adjustment of $3,000 to beginning retained earnings of 19E because the restated 19E income statement corrects for the $3,000 aftertax error of 19E. In particular, note the retroactive restatement of the 19E statements, which is comparable to the restatement procedure illustrated previously for the change in accounting principle, retroactive approach (Exhibit 20–2). Exhibit 20–3 does not show a **pro forma** presentation because it is not needed for comparability purposes in view of the restatement of the prior year's statements. For this reason, *APB Opinion 20* does **not** require a pro forma presentation for error corrections; the only instance in which the pro forma results are presented is for a change in accounting principle accounted for by the current approach.

ANALYTICAL PROCEDURES FOR CORRECTING ERRORS

Efficient analytical procedures should be used for dealing with multiple accounting errors. Correcting entries must be determined and appropriate notes prepared to augment the statement disclosure. This section presents some analytical techniques that are useful for these purposes as well as for problem-solving purposes for students, CPA candidates, and others.

It is helpful to classify errors according to which financial statements are affected. Some errors may affect only the balance sheet. For example, a credit to Retained Earnings that should have been to Contributed Capital would affect only the balance sheet. Correction involves a transfer from one **permanent** account to another **permanent** account. In this case, balance sheets for future periods would be in error until correction of the respective account balances. Other errors affect only the income statement. For example, a credit to the Sales Revenue account instead of Interest Revenue would affect only the income statement. Correction of this error involves a transfer from one **temporary** account to another **temporary** account. In this case, financial reports of future periods would be unaffected whether or not the error is corrected (because all temporary accounts are closed each period and retained earnings is unaffected by this error).

A third and more common type of error affects **both** the balance sheet and the current income statement. This type may be further classified on the basis of the effect on the current and future financial statements as follows:

1. **Counterbalancing error.** This kind of error (also called a self-correcting error) results from failure to allocate properly an expense or revenue item between **two** consecutive accounting periods. There is no **pretax** effect upon the balance sheet at the end of the second period because the total revenue and total expense to that date are correct. No error remains in Retained Earnings or

EXHIBIT 20–3: Correction of Accounting Error—Depreciation

Panel A—Hypothetical Situation:

1. The records of Easie Company reflected the following:

	19F	19E
Sales revenue	$ 480,000	$ 450,000
Cost of goods sold	(310,000)	(300,000)
Depreciation expense	(25,000)	(20,000)
Other expenses	(65,000)	(55,000)
Income tax (40% average rate)	(32,000)	(30,000)
Net income (for year ended Dec. 31)	$ 48,000	$ 45,000
Balance in retained earnings, Jan. 1	$ 165,000	$ 135,000
Dividends declared and paid	17,000	15,000

2. During June 19F, the company discovered that **depreciation expense** for 19D and 19E was **understated** each year by $5,000 for both accounting and income tax purposes.

Panel B—Correcting Entry (retroactive approach):

June 19F—To correct the accounts and record the cumulative effect of the error:

Prior period adjustment, depreciation correction ($10,000 × .60)	6,000	
Income tax receivable, or Income tax payable ($10,000 × .40)	4,000	
Accumulated depreciation ($5,000 × 2)		10,000

Panel C—Reporting on Comparative Financial Statements:

Explanation: The 19E statements must be corrected retroactively, although the correcting entry is made in 19F.

Comparative income statement—for the years ended December 31, 19F, and 19E (restated):

	19F		19E Restated		
Sales revenue		$480,000			$450,000
Cost of goods sold	$310,000			$300,000	
Depreciation expense (see Note)	25,000		$20,000 + $5,000	25,000	
Other expenses	65,000			55,000	
Income tax expense (40% rate)	32,000	432,000	$30,000 − ($5,000 × .40)	28,000	408,000
Net income (see Note)		$ 48,000	$45,000 − ($5,000 × .60)		$ 42,000

Comparative statement of retained earnings—for the years ended December 31, 19F, and 19E (restated):

	19F	19E
Beginning balance (for 19E amount, see Panel A)	$159,000	$135,000
Deduct: Effect of accounting error, 19D ($5,000 × .60)		(3,000)
Balance adjusted		132,000
Add: Net income	48,000	42,000
Deduct: Dividends (Panel A)	(17,000)	(15,000)
Ending balance	$190,000	$159,000

Note: Prior period adjustment—During 19F, an error was discovered in which depreciation expense of $5,000 (aftertax effect on net income, $3,000) was understated each year, 19E and 19D. Accordingly, the 19E income statement was restated to reflect a $3,000 decrease in net income. Also, the 19E statement of retained earnings was restated by (1) a prior period adjustment for the 19D error, and (2) the restated 19E net income; the net effect was to reduce the 19F beginning balance of retained earnings by $6,000, from $165,000 to $159,000.

other balance sheet accounts because the error effect is exactly counterbalanced by an opposite error effect the next period. Examples of counterbalancing errors are as follows:

a. Errors in adjusting for prepaid expenses, accrued expenses, revenues collected in advance, or accrued revenues (revenues earned but not yet collected). Such errors cause an incorrect income statement of the period in which the error was made, with an equal misstatement in the opposite direction on the income statement of the following period. To illustrate, assume the correct amount of accrued wages payable was understated at the end of 19A. Instead, Wage Expense was debited and Cash was credited when these wages were paid early in the next period. The effect of this error is as follows:

19A income statement:
Wage expense understated
Income overstated

19A balance sheet:
Current liabilities (wages payable) understated
Retained earnings overstated

19B income statement:
Wage expense overstated (because Wage Expense was debited when wages were paid)
Income understated

19B balance sheet:
No misstatements

b. Errors in the merchandise inventory. Errors of this type are counterbalancing because the ending inventory of the current period is the beginning inventory of the next period and the beginning and ending inventories have opposite effects on income of the two periods. To illustrate, assume the ending inventory for 19A is understated. The effect of this error is as follows:

19A income statement:
Ending inventory understated
Cost of goods sold overstated
Income understated

19A balance sheet:
Assets (inventory) understated
Retained earnings understated

19B income statement:
Beginning inventory understated
Cost of goods sold understated
Income overstated

19B balance sheet:
No misstatements

2. **Noncounterbalancing error.** This kind of error, which is **not** self-correcting, continues to affect account balances, for a long period of time, if not corrected; therefore, one or more balance sheet accounts continue to be reported in error. Examples of noncounterbalancing errors are as follows:

   a. Over- or understatement of depreciation expense; the accumulated depreciation and retained earnings balances are in error until corrected or until the asset is disposed of or fully depreciated. Also, the income statements are in error for the periods in which incorrect amounts of depreciation expense are recorded.

   b. Recognition of a capital expenditure as an expense, or vice versa, results in incorrect asset balances, expense amounts, and retained earnings until corrected or until the asset is disposed of or fully depreciated.

CORRECTING ENTRIES ILLUSTRATED

Correcting entries vary depending upon *(a)* whether the error is counterbalancing (i.e., self-correcting) and *(b)* the lapsed time since the error was made. To illustrate, six situations are given below which involve both counterbalancing and noncounterbalancing errors. For each situation, the correcting entry is given (assuming no income tax effects). As illustrated in Exhibit 20–3, when an error made in a prior period is corrected, the cumulative effect of the error is reported in the discovery (i.e., current) period as a **prior period adjustment.** Because prior period adjustments are closed to Retained Earnings, the prior period adjustment corrects the **beginning balance** of that account.

Situation 1—Error in merchandise inventory. Assume that the ending inventory for 19A was understated by $1,000.

Case A—The 19A error was found at the end of 19B (before books were closed for 19B).

Analysis: Income for 19A was understated by $1,000; therefore, retained earnings at the start of 19B is understated by this amount. Beginning inventory for 19B is understated by $1,000.

Correcting entry at the end of 19B:

Inventory, beginning	1,000	
Prior period adjustment (retained earnings)		1,000

Case B—19A error was found during 19C instead of 19B:

Analysis: Counterbalanced; income for 19A was understated by $1,000, and income for 19B was overstated by the same amount. Therefore, Retained Earnings and all other balance sheet accounts are correct at the end of 19B. No correcting entry is needed in 19C. Restate 19A and 19B financial statements to a correct basis for all subsequent reporting purposes.

Situation 2—Error in both purchases and inventory. Assume that a $2,000 credit purchase in 19A was not recorded until 19B, when cash was paid, and the goods were **not** included in the 19A ending inventory.

Case A—The two 19A errors were discovered in 19B (before books were closed for 19B).

Analysis: In 19A, both purchases and ending inventory were understated by the same amount; therefore, because they had opposite effects on income, the income for 19A was correct. However, on the 19A year-end balance sheet both inventory and payables were understated by $2,000. In 19B, both inventory (beginning) and purchases are in error.

Correcting entry in 19B:

Inventory, beginning	2,000	
Purchases		2,000

Case B—The two 19A errors were discovered in 19C instead of 19B:

Analysis: Both errors counterbalanced in 19B; therefore, no correcting entry is needed in 19C. Restate 19A and 19B financial statements to a correct basis for all subsequent reporting purposes.

Situation 3—Error in prepaid expense. Assume that a five-year fire insurance policy was acquired on January 1, 19A. The five-year premium of $500 was paid and debited in full to insurance expense in 19A, and no adjustment was recorded to recognize the asset at the end of 19A.

Case A—The error was discovered at the end of 19B (before books were closed for 19B).

Analysis: In 19A, insurance expense was overstated and income understated by $400. Also in 19A prepaid insurance and retained earnings were understated by $400. No insurance expense for 19B has been recorded because the full $500 was expensed in 19A.

Correcting entry at the end of 19B:

Prepaid insurance	400	
Prior period adjustment (retained earnings)		400

(An adjusting entry for $100 insurance expense also must be made for 19B.)

Case B—The error was discovered in 19C instead of 19B:

Correcting entry in 19C:

Prepaid insurance	300	
Prior period adjustment (retained earnings)		300

(An adjusting entry for $100 insurance expense also must be made for 19C.)

Situation 4—Error in accrued expense. Assume accrued property tax of $100 for 19A was not recorded. The tax was paid early in 19B and was recorded as expense when paid.

Case A—The error was found at the end of 19B (before books were closed for 19B).

Analysis: In 19A, tax expense was understated and income overstated. Also, liabilities were understated and retained earnings overstated by $100. Tax expense for 19B is overstated by $100 because of the payment entry in 19B.

Correcting entry at end of 19B:

Prior period adjustment (retained earnings)	100	
Tax expense		100

Case B—The error was found during 19C instead of 19B:

Analysis: The error counterbalanced in 19B because 19A income was overstated and 19B income understated by the same amount. No correcting entry is needed for 19C. Restate 19A and 19B financial statements to a correct basis for all subsequent reporting purposes.

Situation 5—Error in revenue earned but not yet collected. Assume interest receivable of $75 at the end of 19A was not recorded. The interest was collected in 19B and recorded as revenue when collected.

Case A—The error was found at the end of 19B (before books were closed).

Analysis: In 19A, interest revenue and net income were understated. On the balance sheet, receivables and retained earnings were understated. In 19B, interest revenue is overstated because of the collection entry in 19B.

Correcting entry at end of 19B:

Interest revenue	75	
Prior period adjustment (retained earnings)		75

Case B—The error was discovered during 19C instead of 19B:

Analysis: The error counterbalanced in 19B because 19A income was understated and 19B income was overstated by the same amount. No correcting entry is needed in 19C. Restate 19A and 19B financial statements to a correct basis for all subsequent reporting purposes.

Situation 6—Expense capitalized as an asset when incurred. Assume that on January 1, 19A, $500 was expended for ordinary repairs; the $500 was debited to the Machinery account, which was being depreciated 10 percent per year.

Case A—The error was discovered at the end of 19B (before books were adjusted for 19B).

Analysis: For 19A, repair expense was understated, depreciation expense overstated, and income was overstated by the difference. On the balance sheet, assets were overstated and retained earnings overstated by $\$500 \times .90 = \$450$.

Correcting entry at end of 19B:

Accumulated depreciation (for 19A)	50	
Prior period adjustment (retained earnings)	450	
Machinery		500

Case B—The error was discovered during 19C instead of 19B: (before the adjustment for depreciation expense was made for 19C).

Correcting entry during 19C:

Accumulated depreciation (for 19A and 19B)	100	
Prior period adjustment (retained earnings)	400	
Machinery		500

These illustrations indicate the care that must be taken in analyzing and correcting errors. Fundamental to the analysis are the following: (1) a clear understanding of how the **incorrect entry** was made, or whether a needed entry was omitted; (2) a determination of what the **correct entry** should have been, and (3) development of a **correcting entry** to bring the accounts affected by the error into conformity with their correct balances by taking into account all effects of the error between the date of the error and the date of correction (i.e., the current period).

WORKSHEET TECHNIQUES FOR CORRECTING ERRORS

Usually errors can be analyzed and appropriate accounting developed without a worksheet. However, when errors are numerous and complicated, a worksheet approach often is helpful. An efficient worksheet usually can be designed to meet the needs of the particular situation. Of necessity, the worksheet will be unique to the situation; therefore, the accountant should develop an ability to design efficient worksheets for specific problems as they arise.[12] In the remainder of this part, two different worksheets which are used often will be presented.

Exhibit 20–4 illustrates an efficient worksheet useful for *(a)* computing correct income for each of several periods and *(b)* providing data for the correcting entry in the year of correction. Panel A presents the hypothetical situation, Panel B presents the worksheet, and Panel C presents the correcting entry. A separate correcting entry could be made for each of the five errors with the same end result.

WORKSHEET TO RECAST FINANCIAL STATEMENTS

Another group of problems commonly requires recasting of incorrect account balances to develop a correct income statement, balance sheet, and statement of retained earnings. Exhibit 20–5 illustrates

[12] A reasonable skill in worksheet design often is quite helpful in tackling problems on the CPA examination.

EXHIBIT 20–4: Worksheet to Correct Net Income:

Panel A—Hypothetical Situation:

1. The first audit of Company X, covering years 19A, 19B, and 19C, discovered the following errors (the books for 19C, but not 19D, have been closed):

	19A	19B	19C
a. Prepaid expense (i.e. asset) not recognized at year-end (i.e., the amount was incorrectly expensed when the cash was paid one year earlier). Example: Prepaid interest expense	$100	$300	$400
b. Revenue collected in advance at year-end (i.e., the revenue was **incorrectly** recognized as earned when the cash was collected earlier). Example: Rent revenue collected one year in advance	300	500	100
c. Accrued expenses **not** recognized at year-end (i.e., the expense was incurred by year-end but was not recognized until paid the next period). Example: Wages payable	600	800	500
d. Accrued revenue (earned but not collected) not recognized at year-end (i.e., the revenue had been earned by year-end but was uncollected; the revenue was incorrectly recognized as earned in the next period when collected). Example: Rent revenue receivable	500	400	600
e. Depreciation expense understated (i.e., depreciation expense not recorded at year-end)	200	200	200

2. Reported pretax income, uncorrected for the above errors was 19A, $5,000; 19B, $7,000; and 19C, $6,000. The fiscal year ends December 31.

Panel B—Worksheet to Compute Correct Income at Each Year-End:

Item	Income		
	19A	19B	19C
Reported income	$5,000	$7,000	$6,000
Corrections:			
a. Prepaid interest expense not recognized as asset:			
19A	+100	−100	
19B		+300	−300
19C			+400
b. Rent revenue collected in advance not recognized as liability:			
19A	−300	+300	
19B		−500	+500
19C			−100
c. Accrued wages not recognized in:			
19A	−600	+600	
19B		−800	+800
19C			−500
d. Accrued rent revenue not recognized in:			
19A	+500	−500	
19B		+400	−400
19C			+600
e. Depreciation understated:			
19A	−200		
19B		−200	
19C			−200
Correct income	$4,500	$6,500	$6,800

Panel C—Correcting Entry during January 19D, year of correction (books already closed for 19C):

		Debit	Credit
a.	Prepaid interest expense	400	
d.	Rent receivable	600	
*	Prior period adjustment (correction of errors)	200	
b.	Rent revenue collected in advance		100
c.	Accrued wages payable		500
e.	Accumulated depreciation		600

* Since the books have been closed for 19C, the amount ($200) of this prior period adjustment to Retained Earnings is the cumulative effect of all errors through 19C, which did not self-correct. For items *a–d*, the 19A and 19B errors self-corrected in 19B and 19C. However, for item *e*, none of the amounts self-corrected. Therefore, the cumulative adjustment to the January 1, 19D, balance of Retained Earnings would be a debit of $200 [i.e., from Panel B, col. 19C, $400 − $100 − $500 + $600 − ($200 × 3)].

EXHIBIT 20–5: Worksheet to Correct Income Statement, Balance Sheet, and Statement of Retained Earnings, December 31, 19B

Panel A—Hypothetical Situation:

Uncorrected and unadjusted trial balance at December 31, 19B—as shown in first two columns of the worksheet.

Additional data: *(a)* Merchandise inventory, December 31, 19A, overstated, $4,000 (periodic inventory); *(b)* prepaid advertising of $2,000 at December 31, 19B, not recorded; *(c)* prepaid insurance of $2,000 at December 31, 19B, not recognized because the entire premium, paid on June 1, 19B, was debited in full to expense; *(d)* accrued sales salaries of $1,000 at December 31, 19A, not recorded; *(e)* accrued utilities expense of $1,000 at December 31, 19B, not recorded (classify as general expense); *(f)* no provision was made for doubtful accounts—the amounts should have been 19A, $1,000, and 19B, $3,000 (classify as general expense); *(g)* depreciation expense was not recorded for, prior to 19B, $15,000, 19B, $5,000 (classify as general expense); *(h)* cash shortage at end of 19B, $1,000 (classify as general expense); *(i)* premium on capital stock is included in the amount credited to the Capital Stock account; and *(j)* 19B ending inventory correctly determined, $32,000.

Panel B—Worksheet to Correct Income Statement, Balance Sheet, and Statement of Retained Earnings for 19B:

Account	Uncorrected Trial Balance		Correcting and Adjusting Entries		Income Statement		Statement of Retained Earnings		Balance Sheet	
	Debit	**Credit**	**Debit**	**Credit**	**Debit**	**Credit**	**Debit**	**Credit**	**Debit**	**Credit**
Cash	9,000			*(h)* 1,000					8,000	
Receivables	20,000								20,000	
Allowance for doubtful accounts				*(f)* 4,000						4,000
Inventory, beginning*	30,000			*(a)* 4,000	26,000					
Equipment	60,000								60,000	
Accumulated depreciation				*(g)* 20,000						20,000
Accounts payable		5,000								5,000
Capital stock, par $10, 7,500 shares outstanding		76,000	*(i)* 1,000							75,000
Retained earnings, beginning		25,000						25,000		
Prior period adjustments:										
Inventory (CGS) correction			*(a)* 4,000				4,000			
Salary expense correction (19A)			*(d)* 1,000				1,000			
Bad debt expense correction			*(f)* 1,000				1,000			
Depreciation expense correction			*(g)* 15,000				15,000			
Sales revenue		130,000				130,000				
Purchases	90,000				90,000					
Selling expenses	17,000			*(b)* 2,000 *(d)* 1,000	14,000					
General expenses	10,000		*(e)* 1,000 *(f)* 3,000 *(g)* 5,000 *(h)* 1,000	*(c)* 2,000	18,000					
	236,000	236,000								
Prepaid advertising			*(b)* 2,000						2,000	
Prepaid insurance			*(c)* 2,000						2,000	
Utilities payable				*(e)* 1,000						1,000
Inventory, ending*						32,000			32,000	
Contributed capital in excess of par				*(i)* 1,000						1,000
Net income					14,000			14,000		
Retained earnings balance							18,000			18,000
			36,000	36,000	162,000	162,000	39,000	39,000	124,000	124,000

* Other entries could be made for the beginning and ending inventories with the same results.

a worksheet designed for this purpose. It concentrates on the income statement, balance sheet, and statement of retained earnings; a separate worksheet would have to be designed for the statement of changes in financial position (SCFP); discussed in Chapter 23.

This type of worksheet is especially important throughout accounting because (1) it can be adapted to many different problem situations and (2) its built-in debit-credit feature assures a degree of accuracy and completeness difficult to attain otherwise. You should analyze each of the "Correcting and Adjusting Entries" given in the worksheet in Panel B.

Supplement 20-A: Preparation of Financial Statements from Single-Entry and Other Incomplete Records

Most businesses maintain a reasonably complete record of all transactions directly affecting them. Usually complete records are best accomplished through a systematic model based on *(a)* the double-entry concept and *(b)* the accounting model. However, many small businesses, especially sole proprietorships, maintain only a single-entry system that records the "bare essentials."

Single-entry recordkeeping includes all those records, whether kept systematically or not, deemed necessary by the proprietor but which do not record the **dual effect** of each transaction on assets, liabilities, and owners' equity, as expressed in the accounting model. In some cases only records of cash, accounts receivable, accounts payable, and taxes paid may be maintained. No record may be kept, except perhaps in memorandum form, of operational assets, inventories, expenses, revenues, and other elements usually considered essential in an accounting system. However, such incomplete data, plus other information that often can be assembled, usually can be analyzed sufficiently to provide a reasonably complete income statement and balance sheet.

PREPARATION OF BALANCE SHEET FROM SINGLE-ENTRY RECORDS

Because single-entry records usually provide little information about assets (other than cash and accounts receivable), preparation of the balance sheet in such situations involves identification and measurement of various assets and liabilities. The cost of the operational assets must be determined or estimated from such data as are available. Canceled checks, receipts, bills of sale, papers transferring title to real estate, and other similar records provide much of the needed data. Once the cost of each operational asset is determined, depreciation can be computed. The amount of merchandise, supplies, and other inventories on hand may be obtained by actual count. If original cost cannot be determined, merchandise and supplies can be recorded at current replacement cost.

Similarly, notes payable and other liabilities (except accounts payable for which there is generally an invoice from the seller) must be obtained from memoranda, correspondence, and even by consultation with creditors.

Exhibit 20–6 illustrates the preparation of a balance sheet and computation of income or loss for the period in a simple situation. Panel A presents the hypothetical situation, and Panel B presents the balance sheet. Owner's equity was computed as the difference between total assets and total liabilities. Panel C computes the net income or loss for the period as the difference between ending and beginning owner's equity; however, this method of computing net income does not provide detailed revenue and expense amounts needed for the income statement.

If there had been additional investments or withdrawals during the period, these would have to be considered in the computation of net income or loss. The following equation indicates the procedure for determining income when investments or withdrawals have occurred during the period:

Income = Ending owner's equity
− Beginning owner's equity
+ Withdrawals
− Additional investments

Typical examples of the single-entry income state-

EXHIBIT 20–6: Incomplete Records—Preparation of Balance Sheet and Computation of Income (loss)

Panel A—Hypothetical Situation:

1. Brown Company was organized by A. A. Brown on January 1, 19A; on this date the owner invested $4,500 cash in the business. During 19A, no formal records were kept.
2. Additional data for 19A:
   a. December 31, cash on hand and on deposit, $2,345—from count of cash and bank statement.
   b. December 31, merchandise inventory, $1,550—Count made by Brown, costed at current replacement cost since purchase invoices were not available.
   c. Office and store equipment acquired on January 1, 19A, $500—from invoice found in the files.
   d. Brown agreed that a depreciation rate of 5 percent per annum, with no material amount of residual value, was reasonable.
   e. Note receivable, dated December 31, 19A, $50—This note, signed by a customer for goods purchased, was in the files.
   f. December 31, accounts receivable, $90—Brown maintained a Charge Book which listed four customers as owing a total of $90; Brown was positive that the bills were outstanding. You called the customers for verification.
   g. December 31, accounts payable, $240—The "unpaid invoices" file contained two invoices that totaled to this amount; Brown assured you that they were the only unpaid invoices.

Panel B—Balance Sheet Prepared from Incomplete Data:

BROWN COMPANY
Balance Sheet
At December 31, 19A

Assets		
Current assets:		
Cash		$2,345
Accounts receivable		90
Notes receivable, trade		50
Merchandise inventory		1,550
Total current assets		4,035
Property and equipment:		
Office and store equipment	$500	
Less: Accumulated depreciation	25	475
Total assets		$4,510

Liabilities	
Current liabilities:	
Accounts payable	$ 240
Long-term liabilities	None
Total liabilities	240
Owner's Equity	
A. A. Brown, proprietorship ($4,510 − $240)	4,270
Total liabilities and owner's equity	$4,510

Panel C—Income (Loss) Computed:

BROWN COMPANY
Computation of Net Loss
For the Year Ended December 31, 19A

Owner's equity, January 1, 19A	$4,500
Owner's equity, December 31, 19A	4,270
Net loss for period	$ 230

ment computations in which the owner had additional investments and withdrawals are as follows:

	Computation Where There Was	
	An Income	A Loss
Owner's equity, end of period	$8,000	$5,500
Owner's equity, beginning of period	7,100	6,300
Change increase (decrease)	900	(800)
Add: Withdrawals during period	1,200	1,000
	2,100	200
Deduct: Additional investments during period	500	300
Income for period	$1,600	
Loss for period		$ (100)

PREPARATION OF INCOME STATEMENT FROM INCOMPLETE DATA

Income or loss for the period can be computed as shown in the preceding section. However, knowing only the amount of income or loss does not identify the components of income for management, nor does it meet the needs of other interested parties. For example, banks and other credit grantors usually request a statement setting out the details of operations. The Internal Revenue Service requires a detailed statement of revenues and expenses for income tax purposes.

An itemized income statement in the conventional form may be prepared from single-entry records and supplemental data without converting the records to double-entry form. By analyzing the cash receipts and disbursements, much of the needed detail may be obtained. The preparation of an income statement from single-entry data may be illustrated as shown in Exhibit 20–7 for Mercer Company. In Exhibit 20–7, Panel A presents the hypothetical situation, and Panel B illustrates schedules to compute sales revenue, purchases, depreciation, and other expenses, respectively. Panel C presents the related income statement. Also, to facilitate your study of this illustration, Exhibit 20–8 presents the T-accounts related to the computations of Panel B.

EXHIBIT 20–7: Preparation of Income Statement from Incomplete Data—J. R. Mercer Company

Panel A—Hypothetical Situation:

	19A	
	Jan. 1	Dec. 31
Account balances:		
Accounts and trade notes receivable (no doubtful accts.)	$35,000	$48,000
Inventory (per physical count)	6,900	8,700
Building and equipment (appraised at estimated cost less depr.)	17,000	17,400
Prepaid expenses (per memoranda)	100	110
Accounts payable (per files)	8,100	9,200
Notes payable (for equipment per files)		500
Cash on hand (per cash register)	60	110
Liability for accrued expenses (per memoranda)	120	150
Salaries paid		7,000

	19A
Analysis of Bank Statements:	
Bank overdraft, 1/1/19A	$ 2,800
Deposits during year:	
Collections on account	42,000
Additional capital contributions by owner	10,000
Checks drawn during year for:	
Purchases (goods for resale)	26,000
Expenses	6,000
Salaries of employees	7,000
Withdrawals by owner	3,000
Purchase of equipment	340

EXHIBIT 20–7 *(continued)*

Panel B—Computation of Income Statement Items:

1. Sales revenue:		
Accounts and trade notes receivable, 12/31/19A		$ 48,000
Cash collected from customers and deposited		42,000
Increase of cash on hand ($110 − $60)		50
Less: Accounts and trade notes receivable, 1/1/19A		(35,000)
Sales revenue for the year, 19A		$ 55,050
2. Purchases:		
Accounts and trade notes payable, 12/31/19A		$ 9,200
Payments to creditors for purchases		26,000
Less: Accounts payable, 1/1/19A		(8,100)
Purchases for the year, 19A		$ 27,100
3. Depreciation expense:		
Net balance of buildings and equipment, 1/1/19A		$ 17,000
Purchases of equipment during 19A:		
By issue of note payable		500
By cash payment		340
Balance before depreciation		17,840
Less: Net balance on 12/31/19A (after 19A depreciation)		(17,400)
Depreciation expense for the year, 19A		$ 440
4. Other expenses:		
Expenses paid in cash during 19A		$ 6,000
Add: Expenses accrued on 12/31/19A		150
Prepaid expenses on 1/1/19A		100
Deduct: Accrued expenses, 1/1/19A	$120	6,250
Prepaid expenses, 12/31/19A	110	(230)
Other expenses for the year, 19A		$ 6,020

Panel C—Income Statement for 19A:

Income Statement
For Year Ended December 31, 19A

Sales revenue (Panel B, item 1)		$55,050
Cost of goods sold:		
Inventory, 1/1/19A (given)	$ 6,900	
Purchases (Panel B, item 2)	27,100	
Goods available for sale	34,000	
Less: Inventory, 12/31/19A (given)	8,700	
Cost of goods sold		25,300
Gross margin on sales		29,750
Less: Expenses:		
Depreciation (Panel B, item 3)	440	
Other expenses (Panel B, item 4)	6,020	
Salaries (given)	7,000	13,460
Net income		$16,290

WORKSHEETS FOR PROBLEMS FROM SINGLE-ENTRY AND OTHER INCOMPLETE RECORDS

The preceding example (Exhibits 20–7 and 20–8), although simplified, suggests the need for a worksheet approach to reduce clerical work and minimize the possibility of errors and omissions. A worksheet provides several internal checks on accuracy and recognizes each group of transactions in terms of their debit and credit effects. To provide a "track

EXHIBIT 20–8: T-Account Analysis of Exhibit 20–7

1. Sales revenue:

Accounts Receivable

Beg. bal. (Jan. 1)	35,000	Cash collections (deposited)	42,000
a. Sales (amount needed to complete account)	55,050	Cash collections (on hand)	50
		End. bal. (Dec. 31)	48,000
	90,050		90,050
Bal. forward	48,000		

Sales Revenue

		a. From reconstructed Accounts Receivable	55,050

2. Purchases:

Accounts Payable

Cash paid on acct.	26,000	Beg. bal. (Jan. 1)	8,100
End. bal. (Dec. 31)	9,200	*a.* Purchases (amount needed to complete account)	27,100
	35,200		35,200
		Bal. forward	9,200

Purchases

a. From reconstructed Accounts Payable	27,100		

3. Depreciation expense:

Buildings and Equipment (net)

Beg. bal. (Jan. 1)	17,000	*a.* Current yr. depr. (amount needed to complete account)	440
19A purchases:		End. bal. (Dec. 31)	17,400
By note	500		
By cash	340		
	17,840		17,840
Bal. forward	17,400		

Depreciation Expense

a. From reconstructed Bldg. and Equip. (net)	440		

4. Other expenses:

Prepaid Expenses

Beg. bal. (Jan. 1)	100	*a.* Adjusting entry to expense	100
c. Adjusting entry to record end. bal. (Dec. 31)	110		

Liability for Accrued Expenses

b. Reversing entry to expense	120	Beg. bal. (Jan. 1)	120
		d. Adjusting entry to record end. bal. (Dec. 31)	150

Expenses

Paid in cash during 19A (includes beginning accrued expense)	6,000	*b.* Reversing entry from accrued	120
a. Adjusting entry for prepaid	100	*c.* Adjusting entry for prepaid	110
d. End. bal. accrued	150	End. bal. (Dec. 31)	6,020
	6,250		6,250
Bal. closed	6,020		

record," such worksheets should be accompanied by explanations and computations of the analyses involved.

Exhibit 20–9 illustrates a worksheet designed to develop an income statement and balance sheet based on incomplete records. Panel A presents the data available, and Panel B presents the worksheet. The entries on the worksheet should be studied carefully; each one is explained in detail in Panel C of the exhibit.

LIMITATIONS OF SINGLE-ENTRY RECORDKEEPING

Single-entry recordkeeping is employed by a large number of particularly small businesses, by nonprofit organizations, by persons acting in a fiduciary capacity as administrators or executors of estates, and by many individuals relative to their personal affairs. Even some regular systems of recordkeeping recommended for retail outlets by trade associations and by manufacturers are maintained on a single-entry basis. For example, one such system is used by a large number of small retail druggists. Single-entry records are used in the interest of simplicity, and usually are less expensive to maintain than double-entry systems, because they do not require the services of a trained person. In fact, more often than not, single-entry records are maintained by the proprietor or someone closely associated with the activities being recorded.

Single-entry recordkeeping usually is inadequate except where operations are especially simple and the volume of activity is small. Some of the more important disadvantages of single-entry systems are as follows:

1. Data may not be available to the management for effectively planning and controlling the business.
2. Lack of systematic and precise recordkeeping may lead to inefficient administration and reduced control over the affairs of the business.
3. Single-entry records do not provide a check against clerical errors, as does a double-entry system. This is one of the most serious of the defects of single-entry records.
4. Single-entry records seldom make provision for recording all transactions. Many internal transactions (i.e., those normally reflected through adjusting entries), in particular, often are not recorded.
5. Because no accounts are provided for many of the items appearing in both the balance sheet and income statement, omission of important data always is a possibility.
6. In the absence of detailed records of all assets, lax administration of those assets may occur.
7. Theft and other losses are less likely to be detected.

EXHIBIT 20–9: Worksheet to Develop Detailed Income Statement Based on Incomplete Records

Panel A—Hypothetical Situation:

1. Main Company has been in business two years and has kept only incomplete records. An accountant prepared a balance sheet at December 31, 19A, and a balance sheet has been completed by "inventorying all assets and liabilities at December 31, 19B." These balance sheets have been entered on the worksheet shown in Panel B.
2. Additional data for 19B, developed in various ways as follows:
   a. Main kept no record of cash receipts and disbursements, but an analysis of canceled checks provided the following summary of payments: accounts payable, $71,000; expenses, $20,700; and purchase of equipment, $3,700. No checks appeared to be outstanding.
   b. Main stated that $100 cash was withdrawn regularly each week from the cash register for personal use. No record was made of these personal withdrawals.
   c. The $5,000 bank loan was for one year, the note was dated July 1, 19B, and 6 percent interest was taken out of the face amount (cash proceeds, $4,700).
   d. Main stated that equipment listed in the January 1 balance sheet at $900 was sold for $620 cash.
   e. The bank reported that it had credited Main with $4,000 during the year for customers' notes that Main left for collection.
   f. One $400 note on hand December 31, 19B, was past due and appeared worthless. Therefore, this note was not included in the $3,000 notes receivable listed in the December 31, 19B, balance sheet. Assume no allowance for doubtful accounts; bad debts are written off directly to expense because of immateriality.

Panel B—Worksheet to Develop Income Statement (Main Company):

Account	Beginning Balances 1/1/19B	Interim Entries Debit	Interim Entries Credit	Income Statement	Ending Balances 12/31/19B
Debit accounts:					
Cash	10,000	*(c)* 4,700	*(a)* 95,400		22,000
		(d) 620	*(b)* 5,200		
		(e) 4,000			
		(h) 103,280			
Notes receivable	5,000	*(g)* 2,400	*(e)* 4,000		3,000
			(f) 400		
Accounts receivable	61,000	*(i)* 112,680	*(g)* 2,400		68,000
			(h) 103,280		
Inventories	25,000	*(j)* 27,000	*(j)* 25,000		27,000
Prepaid expenses	500	*(c)* 150	*(k)* 500		200
		(k) 50			
Furniture and equipment (net)	10,600	*(a)* 3,700	*(d)* 900		12,400
			(l) 1,000		
Expenses		*(a)* 20,700	*(k)* 50	21,000	
		(k) 500	*(n)* 800		
		(n) 650			
Interest expense		*(c)* 150		150	
Loss on sale of equipment		*(d)* 280		280	
Loss on worthless note		*(f)* 400		400	
Depreciation expense		*(l)* 1,000		1,000	
Purchases		*(m)* 77,000		77,000	
Net income		*(o)* 14,850		14,850	
	112,100			114,680	132,600
Credit accounts:					
Bank loan payable			*(c)* 5,000		5,000
Accounts payable	30,000	*(a)* 71,000	*(m)* 77,000		36,000
Accrued expenses payable	800	*(n)* 800	*(n)* 650		650
Main, proprietorship	81,300	*(b)* 5,200	*(o)* 14,850		90,950
Sales revenue			*(i)* 112,680	112,680	
Income summary					
(inventory change)		*(j)* 25,000	*(j)* 27,000	2,000	
	112,100	476,110	476,110	114,680	132,600

EXHIBIT 20–9 *(concluded)*

Panel C—Explanation of Entries on Worksheet (Main Company):

a. To record cash payments shown by analysis of canceled checks.
b. To record Main's cash withdrawals of $100 per week for 52 weeks.
c. To record bank loan of $5,000 less $300 interest of which $150 was prepaid as of December 31, 19B.
d. To record sale of equipment, cost less depreciation, $900, for $620 cash.
e. To record $4,000 notes receivable collected by bank.
f. To record write-off of bad note, $400.
g. To record notes from customers, computed as follows (data taken directly from worksheet):

Notes collected	$4,000
Note written off	400
Notes on hand, 12/31/19B	3,000
	7,400
Less: Notes on hand, 1/1/19B	5,000
Notes receivable (received on accounts)	$2,400

h. Cash collected from customers (observe that it does not matter whether the collection was at time of sale or on account) is computed as follows from data shown in the Cash account on the worksheet:

Cash paid out ($95,400 + $5,200)	$100,600
Cash balance, 12/31/19B	22,000
	122,600
Cash collected from all sources other than from customers: $4,700 + $620 + $4,000)	9,320
	113,280
Less: Cash balance, 1/1/19B	10,000
Cash collected from customers	$103,280

i. Sales are computed by finding the only "missing entry" in **accounts receivable,** which entry is for sales on account. (Balance in notes receivable has already been reconciled on the worksheet.)

Notes received on account (item *g*)	$ 2,400
Cash collected from customers (item *h*)	103,280
Ending balance of accounts receivable	68,000
Total credits and balance	173,680
Less: January 1 balance	61,000
Total debits for the year (sales revenue)	$112,680

j. To close the January 1 inventory and to record the December 31 inventory (to income summary).
k. To adjust the balance of prepaid expenses and to increase the prepaid expense balance as of December 31 to $200 as given.
l. To set up the depreciation expense for the period. All entries have been made in the Furniture and Equipment account on the worksheet except the 19B depreciation credit. Depreciation is computed as follows:

Furniture and equipment, 1/1/19B	$10,600
Equipment purchased	3,700
	14,300
Less: Equipment sold	900
	13,400
Less: Balance of furniture and equipment, 12/31/19B	12,400
Depreciation expense for the period	$ 1,000

m. Purchases are computed by finding the missing entry in accounts payable on the worksheet as follows:

Payments on accounts payable	$ 71,000
Balance of accounts payable, 12/31/19B	36,000
	107,000
Less: Accounts payable, 1/1/19B	30,000
Purchases for the period	$ 77,000

n. To transfer the beginning balance ($800) of accrued expenses payable to expense and to record accrued expenses payable as of December 31. Note that entry *a* on the worksheet transfers all of the expenses paid in cash during 19B to the Expense account. As a result, the beginning and ending balances of Accrued Expense Payable, respectively, are entered in the Expense account.
o. To close net income to proprietorship. The net income may be computed by analyzing the changes in capital from January 1 to December 31, 19B, as illustrated previously or by extending the balances in the temporary accounts to the Income Statement column and then computing the difference between the debits and credits. One computation serves as a check on the other.

QUESTIONS

PART A

1. Briefly distinguish among the following: *(a)* change in principle, *(b)* change in estimate, *(c)* change in reporting entity, and *(d)* accounting error.

2. What are the three basic alternatives for reflecting the effects of accounting changes and error corrections?

3. Complete the following matrix:

	Method of Reflecting the Effect*		
	(1) ____	(2) ____	(3) ____
a. Change in estimate	____	____	____
b. Change in principle	____	____	____
c. Correction of error	____	____	____

* Identify these three captions; then enter appropriate check on each line.

4. What are *pro forma statements?* Why are they used in respect to some accounting changes?

5. From a *matching* standpoint, evaluate the soundness of the GAAP treatment of changing the estimate of the life and/or residual value of a depreciable asset. Cite both pros and cons.

6. Why are the effects of changes *from* LIFO to other inventory flow methods required to be accounted for retroactively when changes *to* LIFO from another method are reflected as changes in the income of the year the change is made?

7. Other than changing *from* LIFO to another inventory flow method (which must be reflected retroactively), what other types of accounting changes must be accorded retroactive treatment rather than being accounted for as impacting solely on income of the year in which the change is made?

8. *APB Opinion 20* deals with three types of accounting changes in addition to error corrections. The three types of accounting changes involve, *(a)* principles, *(b)* estimates, and *(c)* reporting entities. Using these letters and the letter *(d)* for error corrections, identify each of the following types of change:
   (1) A lessor discovers while a long-term capital lease term is in progress that an expected material unguaranteed residual value of the leased property has probably become zero.
   (2) A corporation with foreign subsidiaries has used the cost method of accounting for its investments in the subsidiary companies since they were acquired because economic conditions in the countries in which the subsidiary companies operate have been unstable and exchange of foreign currency into dollars has been restricted. Under changed, improved conditions, it has become feasible to prepare consolidated statements instead, thereby eliminating the foreign investments from the balance sheet of the corporation.
   (3) After five years of use, an asset originally thought to have a 15-year life is now to be depreciated on the basis of a 20-year life.
   (4) Because of inability to estimate reliably, a contractor began business using the completed contract method. Now that reliable estimates can be made, the percentage-of-completion method is adopted.
   (5) Office equipment purchased last year is discovered to have been debited to Office Expense when acquired. Appropriate accounting is to be applied now.
   (6) A company that has been using the FIFO inventory method now is changing to LIFO.
   (7) A company which used 1% of sales to estimate its bad debt expense discovers losses are running higher than expected and changes to 2½%.

PART B

9. What is the difference between a *counterbalancing* and a *noncounterbalancing* error? Basically, why is the distinction significant in the analysis of errors?

10. Complete the matrix below by entering a plus to indicate overstatement, a minus to indicate understatement, and a zero if no effect.

11. Give two examples of each of the following types of errors.
    a. Affects income statement only.
    b. Affects balance sheet only.
    c. Affects both income statement and balance sheet.

SUPPLEMENT 20–A

12. Briefly explain the differences between a *double-entry* and a *single-entry* system.

13. What are the primary *shortcomings* of a single-entry system? What are the advantages?

(Relates to Question 10)

	Effect of Error on			
	Net Income	Assets	Liabilities	Owners' Equity
a. Ending inventory for 19A understated:				
19A financial statements	____	____	____	____
19B financial statements	____	____	____	____
b. Ending inventory for 19B overstated:				
19B financial statements	____	____	____	____
19C financial statements	____	____	____	____
c. Failed to record depreciation in 19A:				
19A financial statements	____	____	____	____
19B financial statements	____	____	____	____
d. Failed to record a liability resulting from revenue collected in advance at end of 19A; instead, credited revenue in full erroneously:				
19A financial statements	____	____	____	____
19B financial statements	____	____	____	____

DECISION CASE 20–1

This decision case is adapted from an actual situation. It focuses on the change from LIFO to the FIFO method of accounting for inventory. This particular kind of accounting change has received considerable interest because when prices are rising it causes a *credit* (often very large in amount) to be recorded, which if reported on the income statement significantly increases *reported* net income. This case is presented in three parts, each of which has its own requirement.

Part A

Effective January 1, 19C, Kowalski Corporation changed its inventory method from LIFO to FIFO. In its 19C annual report (Kowalski's fiscal year ends December 31), the company disclosed that the change decreased the net loss for 19C by $20 million relative to the net loss that would have been reported if the change had not been made. The 19C net loss, including the $20 million effect from the accounting change, was $7.6 million. The change also increased 19C year-end inventories by $150 million over the LIFO inventory amount at December 31, 19C.

The following tabulation gives the relevant amounts ($ millions):

Year	Purchases	FIFO Ending Inventory	LIFO Ending Inventory
19A	$5,802	$1,372	$1,240
19B	6,040	1,445	1,335
19C	6,199	1,541	1,391

Required:

Present the inventory and cost of goods sold as they should be reported on the comparative balance sheet and income statements for 19B–19C. Show the computation of the cost of goods sold amounts.

Part B

The accounting entry made by Kowalski on December 31, 19C, to record the accounting change from LIFO to FIFO was ($ millions) as follows:

Recording:

Inventory	150.0	
Income taxes payable		76.5*
Adjustments due to inventory change from LIFO to FIFO (closed to income summary)—19C		20.0
Prior period adjustment, inventory change (closed to retained earnings)		53.5

* Assume this tax amount is correct; it is the net effect of numerous tax items. This case does not focus on income taxes.

Required:

Briefly explain the reason for the debit or credit to each account shown in the above entry to record the accounting change.

Part C

Long-term notes and debenture bonds payable of Kowalski Corporation require the company to maintain a current ratio of 1.4 to 1 as a condition for retaining the stated interest rate on the debt. Specifically, for every .01 or fraction thereof by which the current ratio of Kowalski falls below 1.4 to 1, the interest rate on Kowalski's outstanding debt automatically increases by ½% (i.e., .005). Total long-term debt at December 31, 19C, was $791 million. The debt matures, on average, in 15 years.

When Kowalski made this accounting change, the Internal Revenue Code required companies to use LIFO for financial reporting purposes as a condition for being allowed to use LIFO for income tax purposes. Therefore, when Kowalski changed to FIFO for accounting purposes, it also had to change to FIFO for income tax purposes. The change caused a $76.5 million increase in income taxes currently payable.

The following table gives relevant accounts ($ millions):

	Current Assets		Current Liabilities	
Year-End	FIFO Basis	LIFO Basis	FIFO Basis	LIFO Basis
19C	$2,168	$2,017	$1,548	$1,471.5

Required:

1. Based on the above description of this case situation, why does it appear that Kowalski made the accounting change?
2. In terms of cash flows (i.e., the present value of future cash flows, where appropriate) evaluate whether Kowlaski made the correct choice by changing inventory methods. Company accountants conservatively estimate that the annual increase in income taxes due to the change will be $2 million over each of the next 10 years. An appropriate discount rate for all present value computations is 10%. Round current ratios to two decimal places.

EXERCISES

PART A: EXERCISES 20–1 to 20–3

Exercise 20–1

Tony Corporation has been depreciating equipment over a 10-year life using the SYD method. The equipment cost $68,000 (estimated residual value, $13,000). On the basis of an engineering study of its economic potential to the company, completed during the fifth year (19E), management decided to change to straight-line depreciation, effective as of the beginning of the fifth year (19E), with no change in the estimated useful life or the residual value. The annual financial statements are prepared on a comparative basis (two years presented). Net incomes (no extraordinary items) prior to giving effect to this change (i.e., on the old basis) were 19D, $48,000; and 19E, $51,000. Shares of stock outstanding were 100,000. Disregard income tax considerations.

Required:

1. Identify the type of accounting change involved and analyze the effects of the change.
2. Prepare entry, or entries, to appropriately reflect the change in the accounts in 19E (fifth year), the year of the change.
3. Illustrate how the change should be reported on the 19E financial statement, which includes 19D results for comparative purposes.

Exercise 20–2

Stacy Corporation has been depreciating equipment over a 10-year life on a straight-line basis. The equipment cost $24,000 and has an estimated residual value of $6,000. On the basis of experience since acquisition (four years prior to 19E), management has decided to depreciate it over a total life of 14 years instead of 10, and with no change in the estimated residual value. The change is to be effective on January 1, 19E. The annual financial statements are prepared on a comparative basis (two years presented). Net incomes (no extraordinary items) prior to giving effect to the change (i.e., on the old basis) were 19D, $48,000; and 19E, $51,000. Shares of stock outstanding, 100,000. Disregard income tax considerations.

Required:

1. Identify the type of accounting change involved and analyze the effects of the change.
2. Prepare entry, or entries, to appropriately reflect the change in the accounts for 19E (fifth year), the year of the change.
3. Illustrate how the change should be reported on the 19E financial statements, which include 19D results for comparative purposes.

Exercise 20–3

XY Sales Company has made several accounting changes with a view to improving the matching of expenses with revenue. Assume it is at the end of 19H, and that the accounting period ends on December 31. The books have not been adjusted or closed at the end of 19H. Among the changes were the following:

a. Machinery that cost $25,000 (estimated useful life 10 years, residual value $3,000) has been depreciated using the SYD method. Early in the eighth year (19H), it was decided to change to straight-line depreciation (with no change in residual value or estimated life).

b. A patent that cost $8,500 is being depreciated over the legal life of 17 years. Early in the 6th year (19H) since its acquisition, it was decided that the economic benefits would not last longer than 13 years from date of acquisition.

Required (disregard income tax considerations):

1. For each of the above situations, identify the type of accounting change that was involved, and briefly explain how it should be accounted for.
2. Give the appropriate entry to record the change and the 19H adjusting entry in each instance. Show computations and disregard income tax considerations. If no entry is required in a particular instance, explain why.

PART B: EXERCISES 20–4 to 20–7

Exercise 20–4

Dyer Corporation never had an audit prior to 19D, the current year. Prior to the arrival of the auditor, the company accountant prepared a comparative set of financial statements with 19C and 19D shown thereon for comparative purposes. The books for 19D have not been closed. During the audit, it was discovered that an invoice dated January 19A for $9,000 (paid in cash at that time) was debited to operating expenses, although it was for the purchase of equipment. The equipment has an estimated useful life of 10 years and no estimated residual value.

Reported incomes reflected on the comparative financial statement prepared by the company auditor (prior to discovery of the error) were 19C, $30,000; and 19D, $33,000. Shares of stock outstanding, 100,000. Disregard income tax considerations.

Required:

1. Identify the type of item involved and analyze the effects of the change or correction, as appropriate.
2. Prepare the entry, or entries, to appropriately record the change or correction in the accounts for 19D, the year of the change.
3. Illustrate how the change or correction should be reported on the 19D financial statements, which include 19C results for comparative purposes.

Exercise 20–5

Give journal entries to correct the accounts, and the subsequent adjusting entry, for each of the errors listed below assuming (1) the errors were discovered on December 31, 19B, before the books were adjusted or closed; and (2) the errors were discovered in January 19C (after the books for 19B were adjusted and closed). Assume each item is material. Disregard income tax considerations.

a. Merchandise costing $6,000 was received on December 28, 19A, and was included in the ending inventory of 19A, but the credit purchase was not recorded in the purchases journal until January 3, 19B.

b. An entry was made on December 30, 19B, for write-off of organization expense as follows (assume only one year's amortization was justified for 19B; amortization per year, $1,000):

General expense	5,000	
Deferred organization expense		5,000

c. Discount of $3,300 on a long-term bond investment purchased on May 1, 19A, was written off to Retained Earnings on that date. These bonds mature on July 1, 19J. Use straight-line amortization.

d. Machinery that cost $900 was purchased and debited to Repair Expense on June 30, 19A. The depreciation rate on machinery is 10% per year on cost.

Exercise 20–6

You are auditing the accounts of Sun Merchandising Corporation for the year ended December 31, 19B. You discover that the adjustments made in the previous audit for the year 19A were not entered in the accounts; therefore, the accounts are not in agreement with the audited amounts as of December 31, 19A. The following adjustments were included in the 19A audit report:

a. Invoices for merchandise purchased in December 19A, not entered on the books until January 19B and not included in the December 31, 19A, inventory, $6,000.

b. Invoices for merchandise received in December 19A were not recorded in the accounts until January 19B; the goods were included in the 19A ending inventory, $9,000.

c. Allowance for doubtful accounts for 19A understated by $1,000.

d. Selling expense for 19A not recorded in the accounts until paid in January 19B, $2,500.

e. Accrued wages at December 31, 19A, not recorded at that date, $2,000.

f. Unexpired insurance at December 31, 19A, understated by $300. The insurance policy expires on December 31, 19B.

g. Tax for year ended December 31, 19A, not entered in the accounts until January 19B, $1,200.

h. Depreciation not recorded prior to January 19A, $3,000; for year ended December 31, 19A, $1,500.

Required:
Assume you have the uncorrected and unadjusted trial balance dated December 31, 19B. Give the journal entry for each of the above items that should be made to the trial balance before using it for further audit purposes. Disregard income tax implications.

Exercise 20–7

Bowler Company failed to recognize accruals and prepayments since organization three years previously. The pretax income, accruals, and prepayments at year-end are given below:

	Amounts Incorrectly Reported at Year-End		
	19A	**19B**	**19C**
Reported income (pretax)	$4,000	$1,000*	$5,000
Items not recognized at year-end (i.e., no adjusting entry was made for these items):			
a. Prepaid expense†	200	280	109
b. Accrued expense (incurred but not yet paid)	250	225	247
c. Revenue collected in advance but not yet earned‡	325	360	293
d. Revenue earned but not yet collected	275	230	196

* Net loss.
† Insurance premiums debited to Insurance Expense when paid.
‡ Revenue credited when cash collected.

Required (disregard income tax considerations):
1. Compute the correct pretax income for each year.
2. Give entry to correct each item assuming the errors were discovered at year-end 19C (books were not closed for 19C).
3. Give entry to correct each item assuming the errors were discovered during 19D, after the 19C books were closed, but prior to the 19D adjusting and closing entries.

SUPPLEMENT 20–A: EXERCISES 20–8 to 20–13

Exercise 20–8

On January 2, 19A, Star Retail Company was organized. During 19A, the company paid trade creditors $49,062 in cash and had an ending inventory per count (FIFO basis) of $9,563. Balances available on December 31, 19A, were the following: accounts payable, $16,125; expenses, $2,450 (no depreciation); capital (representing beginning balance of cash January 2, 19A), $45,000; accounts receivable, $13,188; and sales, $50,000. There were no withdrawals. All sales and purchases were on credit. The company is not subject to income tax.

Required:
1. Develop a worksheet and complete it to provide information for a corrected income statement and balance sheet. *Hint:* Set up four columns for the following: interim entries debit, interim entries credit, income statement, and balance sheet.
2. Prepare a statement of cash inflows and outflows for the year ended December 31, 19A.

Exercise 20–9

On January 1, 19A, Marylee Doaks invested $5,000 cash in a television repair shop. Memoranda revealed that $50 per week was withdrawn by Marylee for living expenses. Marylee's personal automobile, having a market value of $2,500 at that time, was invested in the business for use as a service car. The shop then paid $500 for body changes on the car to make it suitable for their needs; this amount was capitalized. On January 1, 19A, Danny Brown also invested as a partner. Danny invested equipment valued at $3,000 and $1,000 cash. It was agreed that the partners of Doaks-Brown TV Emporium would share profits equally after January 1, 19A. Danny withdrew $800 cash during the year.

On December 31, 19A, the following assets and liabilities of Doaks-Brown were determined from memoranda and other records: cash, $4,810; equipment (less depreciation), $4,600; receivables, $1,200; car (net of depreciation), $2,250; notes payable, $1,000.

Required:
Prepare a balance sheet showing capital balances for each partner and a separate computation of net income.

Exercise 20–10

Compute the four account balances needed for the 19B income statement from the following data (each item is independent):

a. Wages: amount paid during 19B, $15,000; accrued on December 31, 19A, $1,000; and accrued on December 31, 19B, $2,000.
b. Rent revenue: amount collected during 19B, $8,000; unearned (collected in advance), $500 on December 31, 19A, and $300 on December 31, 19B; earned but not collected, $200 on December 31, 19A, and $600 on December 31, 19B.
c. Total sales: Cash account, balance, December 31, 19A, $26,000; balance, December 31, 19B, $33,000; and total

disbursements for 19B, $39,000. All cash receipts were from customers. Accounts receivable: balance, December 31, 19A, $40,160; and balance, December 31, 19B, $59,000. Accounts written off during 19B as uncollectible, $960.

d. Purchases (before discounts): accounts payable balance on December 31, 19A, $28,320, and on December 31, 19B, $33,000; payments made on accounts during 19B, $46,000; cash discounts taken, $820.

Exercise 20–11

Give the journal entry to account for the missing amount in each of the following situations:

a. Prepaid Insurance: starting balance, $1,400; ending balance, $1,900; amount expired, $1,200.

b. Allowance for Doubtful Accounts: starting balance, $5,000; ending balance, $6,000; bad debts written off, $2,700.

c. Bond Sinking Fund: starting balance, $90,000; ending balance, $102,000; current contribution to sinking fund, $20,000; interest earned on the sinking fund, $10,000.

d. Premium on Bonds Payable: starting balance, $6,000; ending balance, $4,500; no change in bonds payable.

e. Capital Stock: starting balance, $200,000; ending balance, $250,000; stock sold at par during the year, $30,000.

f. Retained Earnings: starting balance, $34,000 (credit); appropriation to reserve for bond sinking fund, $10,000; debit for stock dividend, $20,000; net income, $42,000; ending balance, $36,000 (credit).

g. Accounts Receivable: starting balance, $25,000; collections on accounts, $27,000; bad accounts written off, $1,200; sales returns on account, $900; notes received on accounts, $3,000; ending balance, $25,900.

h. Accounts Payable: starting balance, $17,300; cash paid on accounts, $30,200; cash discounts taken, $600; ending balance, $15,500.

Exercise 20–12

For each account indicate the amount that should be reported on the income statement. Show computations.

			Beginning of Period	End of Period
a.	Interest revenue collected in advance (unearned)		$ 50	$ 75
	Uncollected interest revenue (earned)		65	20
	Interest collected during period, $200.			
	Interest revenue should be reported as $_____			
b.	Accrued wages payable		$ 1,000	$ 1,800
	Prepaid wages		400	200
	Wages paid during period, $12,000.			
	Wages expense should be reported as $_____			
c.	Accounts receivable		$10,000	$14,000
	Notes receivable (trade)		2,000	1,000
	Cash sales	$120,000		
	Collections on accounts	40,000		
	Return sales (on account)	2,000		
	Collection on trade notes	5,000		
	Accounts written off as bad	500		
	Discounts given (on account)	600		
	Gross sales should be reported as $_____			
d.	Accounts payable		$ 5,000	$ 7,000
	Notes payable (trade)		10,000	6,000
	Payments on accounts	$ 40,000		
	Cash purchases	100,000		
	Discounts taken on credit purchases	1,000		
	Purchase returns (on account)	1,500		
	Payments on trade notes	8,000		
	Gross purchases should be reported as $_____			

Exercise 20–13

William Sharp operated a hat shop but had not kept complete business records. The following data were secured from various memoranda and records:

An analysis of canceled checks revealed the following cash expenditures: expenses, $4,800; and accounts payable, $9,200. Sharp stated that money was withdrawn from the cash register from time to time for personal living expenses. These withdrawals were estimated to total $3,600. All receipts were deposited in the bank.

A list of assets and liabilities that was developed follows:

	1/1/19A	12/31/19A
Cash	$ 1,200	$ 900
Accounts receivable	1,000	1,500
Inventories	3,900	4,600
Prepaid expenses	100	60
Equipment (net)	4,200	3,800
	10,400	10,860
Accounts payable	1,100	1,300
Proprietorship	$ 9,300	$ 9,560

Required:
Prepare a worksheet to develop the income statement and balance sheet.

Suggestion: Set up columns for: Balances, January 1, 19A; Interim Entries (Debit and Credit); Income Statement; and Balance Sheet, December 31, 19A.

PROBLEMS

PART A: PROBLEMS 20–1 to 20–4

Problem 20–1

From 19A through 19G, the first seven years of its existence, Hatt Company used SYD depreciation. Early in the eighth year, 19H, management decided income would be more fairly presented if straight-line depreciation were used. Accordingly, for 19H and subsequent years, the latter method is to be used for determining income. Hatt Company's income tax rate is 30%. An analysis reveals that the SYD method used had caused depreciation expense and income, to exceed what depreciation would have been under straight line as follows:

Year	Excess of SYD Depr. over Straight Line	Income Previously Reported
19C and before	$160,000	$510,000
19D	50,000	400,000
19E	40,000	386,000
19F	30,000	380,000
19G	20,000	552,000

Analysis of 19H results (reflecting straight-line depreciation) reveals aftertax income from continuing operations, $425,000; an extraordinary loss (before considering tax effects) of $50,000; and an average of 500,000 shares outstanding.

Required:

1. Prepare the bottom portion of the company's income statement for 19H, starting with "Income from continuing operations."
2. Prepare a pro forma restatement of income for 19D through 19G to show the year-by-year change from income previously reported, starting with "Income from continuing operations."
3. Prepare journal entries to record the change in accounting principle. Previously, the same method was used to determine both taxable income and financial income. For income tax purposes, the SYD method will continue to be used.

Problem 20–2

Wing Company purchased a machine on January 1, 19A, for $240,000. At the date of acquisition, the machine had an estimated useful life of 10 years with an estimated residual value of $20,000. The machine is being depreciated on a straight-line basis, for financial reporting (i.e., accounting) purposes, but for income tax purposes, the SYD method is used because of its cash flow advantage. On January 1, 19D, Wing changed, for financial reporting purposes, to the SYD method of depreciation for this machine.

Required:

1. Compute the book value of this machine that would be included in Wing's balance sheet at December 31, 19D. Show supporting computations.
2. Compute the cumulative effect on prior years of changing to a different depreciation method for the year ended December 31, 19D. Assume that the direct effects of this change are limited to the effect on depreciation and the related income tax provision, and that the income tax rate was 40% in all years. Show supporting computations.
3. Make the entry to record the change in depreciation method, including the income tax effect.

(AICPA adapted)

Problem 20–3

Sometimes a business entity may change its method of accounting for certain items. The change may be classified as a change in accounting principle, accounting estimate, or reporting entity.

Listed below are three independent, *unrelated* sets of facts relating to accounting changes.

Situation I: A company determined that the depreciable lives currently used for its operational assets were too long to fairly match the cost of using the assets with the revenue produced. At the beginning of the current year, the company decided to reduce the depreciable lives of all of its existing operational assets by five years.

Situation II: On December 31, 19G, Gary Company owned 51 percent of Allen Company, at which time Gary reported its investment using the cost method due to political uncertainties in the country in which Allen was located. On January 2, 19H, the management of Gary Company was satisfied that the political uncertainties were resolved and the assets of the company were in no danger of nationalization. Accordingly, Gary will prepare consolidated financial statements for Gary and Allen for the year ended December 31, 19H.

Situation III: A company decides in January 19H to adopt the straight-line method of depreciation for plant equipment. The straight-line method will be used for new acquisitions as well as for previously acquired plant equipment for which depreciation in the past had been provided on an accelerated basis.

Required:

For each of the situations described above, provide the information indicated below.

a. Type of accounting change.
b. Manner of reporting the change under current GAAP including a discussion, for situations I and III only, of how amounts are computed.
c. Effect of the change on the balance sheet and income statement (situations I and III only).
d. Note disclosures which would be necessary.

(AICPA adapted)

Problem 20–4

Prather Construction Company began operations January 1, 19A. During its first four years, operating results were determined on a completed contract basis. As of the start of 19E, the company's management decided that measurement of income on a percentage-of-completion basis would "more fairly" measure income. Column (1) below presents net income for the first four years. Column (2) presents the net income that would have resulted had the company used the percentage-of-completion basis. Earnings per share (EPS) on the completed contract basis are reported in column (3); actual dividends per share declared and paid are in column (4). A change in the number of outstanding shares occurred on January 1, 19C.

(Relates to Problem 20–4)

Year Ended Dec. 31	(1) Net Income, Completed Contract Basis	(2) Net Income, Percentage-of-Completion Basis	(3) EPS, Completed Contract Basis	(4) Dividends Paid per Share
19A	$ 10,000	$ 25,000	$ .50	$ .10
19B	70,000	85,000	3.50	.50
19C	120,000	160,000	4.80	.80
19D	100,000	130,000	4.00	1.00

Prather Company's income is taxed at a 25% rate except for an extraordinary gain which occurred in 19E; that gain is taxed at 20%. There were no other extraordinary items in the company's five-year history.

The following is a summary of pretax data for 19E, which was determined on a percentage-of-completion basis.

Billings on contracts	$1,000,000
Applicable costs of contracts	700,000
General and administrative expenses	140,000
Extraordinary gain	40,000

In 19E, a $2 per share cash dividend was declared March 1, and a 20% stock dividend was declared on July 1.

Required:

Prepare an income statement and retained earnings statement for 19E.

PART B: PROBLEMS 20–5 to 20–10

Problem 20–5 (a review problem of Parts A and B of the chapter)

Midwest Sales Corporation initiated several accounting changes during the year and discovered some errors. The changes and errors are given below. Assume the current year is 19J and that the accounting period ends December 31. The books have not been adjusted or closed at the end of 19J. Disregard income tax considerations.

a. The merchandise inventory at December 31, 19I, was overstated by $10,000.
b. During January 19H, extraordinary repair on machinery was debited to Repair Expense; the $15,000 should have been debited to Machinery, which is being depreciated 15% per year on cost (no residual value).
c. A patent that cost $9,350 has been amortized (straight line) for the past 7 years (excluding 19J) over its legal life of 17 years. It is now clear that its economic life will not be more than 12 years from acquisition date.
d. At the end of 19I, revenue collected in advance of $3,000 was included in revenue. It was earned in 19J.
e. Paid $8,000 during January 19H for ordinary repairs on a machine that was acquired during January 19H. The repairs were erroneously capitalized. The machine has an estimated life of five years and no residual value. Assume straight-line depreciation.
f. The rate used for bad debts has been ½% of credit sales, which has proven to be too low; therefore, for 19J and, thereafter, the rate is to be 1% of credit sales. The amount of the expense recorded per year under the old rate was 19H, $800; and 19I, $1,000 (the amount for 19J has not been entered in the accounts since the adjusting entries have not been made). Sales for 19J exceeded 19I sales by 20%.
g. During January 19H, a five-year insurance premium of $750 was paid, which was debited to Insurance Expense.
h. At the end of 19I, accrued wages payable of $1,800 were not recorded; they were paid early in 19J.

Required:

1. For each of the above situations, identify the type of accounting change or error that was involved and briefly explain how each should be accounted for.
2. Give the appropriate entry to record the change and any subsequent adjusting entry in each instance at the end of 19J. Show computations. If no entry is needed, explain why.

Problem 20–6

On January 3, 19A, Young Sales Company purchased a machine that cost $15,000. Although the machine has an estimated useful life of 10 years and estimated residual value of $3,000, it was debited to expense when acquired. It is now December 19D, and the error has been discovered. The average income tax rate is 45%, and straight-line depreciation is used.

Required:

1. Give the entry to correct the accounts at the end of 19D assuming the books have not yet been closed for 19D, and a second entry for depreciation for 19D. Assume the income tax return was correct; therefore, disregard income taxes.
2. Assume instead that the income tax return also was incorrect because of this error; therefore, additional taxes must be paid, including an 8% penalty for each year on the amount of the tax underpayments less any overpayments. Give the entry to correct the accounts, including the income tax effects, at the end of 19D, and a second entry for depreciation for 19D. Round amounts to the nearest dollar.

Problem 20–7

The accounting department of Virginia Corporation had completed the comparative financial reports for the period ending 19C prior to the initiation of the first audit by an outside certified public accountant. This problem relates specifically to two changes recommended by the CPA after the statements were prepared by the company.

The statements have been summarized for problem purposes; details are provided only in respect to the recommended changes; the statements were as shown in the accompanying tabulation.

(Relates to Problem 20–7)

	19A	19B	19C
Balance sheet:			
Assets:			
Machinery	$ 300,000	$ 300,000	$ 300,000
Accumulated depreciation	(80,000)	(100,000)	(120,000)
Remaining assets	2,280,000	2,290,000	2,420,000
Total	$2,500,000	$2,490,000	$2,600,000
Liabilities	$ 373,000	$ 349,000	$ 410,000
Capital stock (200,000 shares)	2,000,000	2,000,000	2,000,000
Retained earnings	127,000	141,000	190,000
Total	$2,500,000	$2,490,000	$2,600,000
Income statement:			
Sales (all on credit)	$1,000,000	$1,100,000	$1,200,000
Cost of goods sold	600,000	650,000	700,000
Gross margin	400,000	450,000	500,000
Operating expenses	300,000	330,000	360,000
Income taxes (assume 50%)	50,000	60,000	70,000
Income before extraordinary items	50,000	60,000	70,000
Extraordinary items	10,000	(20,000)	14,000
Less income tax effect	(3,000)	4,000	(5,000)
Net income	$ 57,000	$ 44,000	$ 79,000
Earnings per share data:			
Income before extraordinary items	$ .250	$ .300	$ .350
Net income	.285	.220	.395
Statement of retained earnings:			
Beginning balance	$ 100,000	$ 127,000	$ 141,000
Net income	57,000	44,000	79,000
Dividends	(30,000)	(30,000)	(30,000)
Ending balance	$ 127,000	$ 141,000	$ 190,000

On the basis of the examination, the auditor insisted on the following changes:

1. Starting with 19C, change the expected loss rate on credit sales from ½% to ¼%. This change was dictated by collection experience and losses during the past two years. These analyses indicate a drop in expected bad debt losses. The company has initiated a tight control on credit granting and has also intensified collection efforts.
2. On January 1, 19A, a machine costing $20,000 (10-year life, no residual value) was inadvertently debited to Operating Expense at that time. The error was discovered by the CPA at the end of 19C; the machine has seven more years of useful life (after 19C). Assume a 6% per annum tax penalty on net tax deficiencies for 19A and 19B only.

Required:

a. Analyze the nature of each item.

b. Determine the effects of implementing the change or error correction, including income tax effects, on the financial statements assuming they are to be reported on comparative statements covering the three years.

c. Give the entry to effect the change including the correction of 19C entries and the related income tax effects. The books for 19C have been adjusted but not closed.

d. Compute the correct amounts for all items on the financial statements that would be affected for each of the three years.

Problem 20–8

Jackson Company failed to recognize accruals and deferrals in the accounts. In addition, numerous other errors were made in computing pretax income. The incomes for the past three years are given in the accompanying tabulation along with a list of the items that were recognized incorrectly in the recordkeeping.

You are to set up a worksheet to correct income for each year. Set up columns for the following: 19A, 19B, 19C, and accounts to be corrected. Key and briefly identify the errors under the Account column and enter amounts under the respective years as plus or minus so that the last line will report corrected income.

All items are pretax and are material in amount. Disregard income tax effects.

(Relates to Problem 20–8)

		19A	19B	19C
a.	Reported pretax income (loss)	$4,000	$(3,500)	$10,000
	Items not recognized correctly at each year-end:			
b.	Accrued expense	400	250	300
c.	Revenue collected in advance	100		200
d.	Prepaid expense	320	410	120
e.	Revenue earned but not collected	170	140	
f.	Annual depreciation overstated (per year)		1,000	1,200
g.	Annual expense for doubtful accts. understated (per year)	170	200	190
h.	Goods purchased on Dec. 31, included in ending inventory; not recorded until following year	460	210	150
i.	Sales on Dec. 31 not recorded until following year; goods were not included in ending inventory	290	770	390
j.	Ending inventory overstated	130	240	290
k.	Checks written and mailed on Dec. 31 as payment on accounts payable; not recorded until next year	1,100	1,500	1,400
l.	Bad debts that should have been written off to allowance for doubtful accts. by year-end	800	950	1,170

Problem 20–9

L. Long established a retail business in 19A. Early in 19D, Long entered into negotiations with S. Short with the intent to form a partnership. You have been asked by Long and Short to check Long's books for the past three years and to compute the correct income for each year.

The income reported on statements submitted to you were as follows:

	Year Ending 12/31		
	19A	19B	19C
Income	$9,000	$10,109	$8,840

During the examination of the accounts, you found the data in the accompanying tabulation:

(Relates to Problem 20–9)

	Year Ending 12/31		
	19A	19B	19C
Omissions from the books:			
A. Accrued expenses at end of year	$2,160	$2,094	$4,624
B. Earned (uncollected) revenue at end of year	200	—	—
C. Prepaid expenses at end of year	902	1,210	1,406
D. Unearned revenue (collected in advance) at end of year	—	610	—
Goods in transit at end of year omitted from inventory:			
E. Purchase for which the entry had been made (ownership passed)	—	2,610	—
F. Purchase for which the entry had not been made (ownership not passed)		—	1,710
Other points requiring consideration:			
G. Depreciation on equipment had been recorded monthly since acquisition, through 19C, by a debit to expense and a credit to accumulated depreciation account at a blanket rate of 1% of end-of-month balances of equipment account. However, the sale during the early part of December 19B of certain equipment was entered as a debit to Cash and a credit to the asset account for the sale price of	—	5,000	—
(This equipment was purchased in July 19A at a cost of $6,000.)			
H. No allowance had been set up for uncollectible accounts. It is decided to set up an allowance for the estimated probable losses on the outstanding accounts as of 12/31/19C, for:			
19B accounts	—	—	700
19C accounts	—	—	1,500
and to correct the bad debt expense each year so that it will show the losses (actual and estimated) relating to that year's sales.			
Accounts had been written off to expense as follows:			
19A accounts	1,000	1,200	—
19B accounts	—	400	2,000
19C accounts	—	—	1,600

(AICPA adapted)

Problem 20–10

The records of Davis Corporation have never been audited. At the end of 19K, the company prepared the following financial statements (summarized):

Income statement:	
Sales and service revenue	$600,000
Expenses:	
Cost of goods sold	(350,000)
Distribution expenses	(120,000)
Administrative expenses	(60,000)
Pretax income	70,000
Income taxes	21,500
Net income	$ 48,500
Balance sheet:	
Assets:	
Cash	$ 23,000
Accounts receivable (net)	40,000
Inventory (periodic system)	110,000
Property, plant, and equipment (net)	160,000
Patent	8,000
Other assets	9,000
Total assets	$350,000
Liabilities:	
Accounts payable	$ 80,000
Income taxes payable	15,000
Notes payable, long term (8%)	40,000
Total liabilities	135,000
Stockholders' equity:	
Common stock, par $10	145,000
Retained earnings (incl. 19K net income)	80,000
Dividends declared and paid	(10,000)
Total stockholders' equity	215,000
Total liabilities and stockholders' equity	$350,000

The company is negotiating a large loan for expansion purposes. The bank has requested that an audit of the company be performed. During the course of the audit, the following facts were determined:

a. The inventory at December 31, 19J, was overstated by $10,000.

b. The inventory at December 31, 19K, was overstated by $20,000.

c. The property, plant, and equipment was underdepreciated in 19J by $9,000 and in 19K by $12,000 (report as a separate expense).

d. A three-year insurance premium of $900 paid on January 1, 19J, was debited to Administrative Expense at that time.

e. Accrued wages (an element of Administrative Expense) were not recorded as follows: 19J, $800; and 19K, $1,000.

f. The patent, which originally cost $17,000, has been amortized to Administrative Expense over a 17-year life (including 19K). Evidence clearly indicates that its economic life will approximate 14 years from date of acquisition.

g. Service revenues earned but not yet collected were not recognized when earned, as follows: 19J, $5,000; and 19K, $7,500.

h. A delivery truck purchased January 19K, at a cost of $13,000, was debited to Distribution Expense at that time. The truck has an estimated useful life of 10 years and an estimated residual value of $2,000. The company uses straight-line depreciation (report depreciation as a Distribution Expense).

i. Uncollectible account receivable from a bankrupt customer has not been written off, $7,500.

j. Common stock outstanding, 12,000 shares.

Required:

1. Set up a worksheet to develop corrected amounts for the 19K income statement and balance sheet. Complete the worksheet and key your entries. Assume the income tax expense amount is correct despite the above items. Suggestion: Set up pairs of columns for Trial Balance, Entries, Income Summary, Retained Earnings, and Balance Sheet. Also, you will need four lines for property, plant, and equipment; six for retained earnings; and three for administrative expense.
2. Prepare a corrected income statement and balance sheet.

SUPPLEMENT 20–A: PROBLEMS 20–11 to 20–14

Problem 20–11

The December 31, 19B, balance sheet of Ratio, Inc., is presented below. These are the *only* accounts in Ratio's balance sheet. Amounts indicated by a question mark (?) can be calculated from the additional information given.

Assets:	
Cash	$ 25,000
Accounts receivable (net)	?
Inventory	?
Property, plant, and equipment (net)	294,000
	$432,000
Liabilities and stockholders' equity:	
Accounts payable (trade)	$?
Income taxes payable (current)	25,000
Long-term debt	?
Common stock	300,000
Retained earnings	?
	$?

Additional information:	
Current ratio (at year-end)	1.5 to 1
Total liabilities divided by total stockholders' equity	.8
Inventory turnover based on sales and ending inventory	15 times
Inventory turnover based on cost of goods sold and ending inventory	10.5 times
Gross margin for 19B	$315,000

Required:

Complete the above balance sheet.

(AICPA adapted)

Problem 20–12

Designer Hat Shop maintained incomplete records. After investigation the following assets and equities were identified:

Assets	1/1/19A	12/31/19A
Cash on hand	$ 90	$ 160
Cash in bank	1,250	870
Accounts receivable	6,700	6,830
Inventory	3,100	3,800
Equipment (net of depr.)	5,200	5,600
Prepaid insurance	120	60
	16,460	17,320
Equities		
Accounts payable	1,000	2,200
Bank loan		3,000
Accrued expenses payable	90	50
	1,090	5,250
Owner's equity	$15,370	$12,070

An analysis of bank deposits and disbursements showed:

Deposits:	
Collections from customers	$8,900
Proceeds of bank loan	3,000
Additional investment by proprietor	1,200
Checks and charges:	
Payments on account	6,100
Expenses	4,500
Refunds on sales (allowances)	350
Proprietor's withdrawals	1,500
Interest on bank loan	30
Purchase of equipment	1,000

Required:

1. Compute the net income or loss by analyzing the changes in the proprietorship account.
2. Prepare a detailed income statement, including computation schedules.

Problem 20–13

Stanley Company has maintained single-entry records. In applying for a much-needed loan, a set of financial statements was needed. An analysis of the records for 19C provided the following data:

Cash receipts:	
Cash sales	$130,000
Collections on credit sales	43,000
Collections on trade notes	1,000
Purchase allowances	1,500
Miscellaneous revenue	250
Cash payments:	
Cash purchases	84,500
Payments to trade creditors	34,100
Payment on mortgage on 7/1/19C plus prepayment of one year's interest of $1,020 to 7/1/19D	4,020
Sales commissions	7,200
Rent expense	2,400
General expenses (including interest)	14,590
Other operating expenses	29,800
Sales returns ($3,000, incl. $1,000 cash)	1,000
Insurance (renewal 3-year premium, April 1)	468
Operational assets purchased	1,500

	Balances	
	1/1/19C	12/31/19C
Cash	$14,100	$10,172
Accounts receivable	13,000	18,000
Trade notes receivable	2,000	1,500
Inventory	10,000	18,400
Prepaid insurance	39	?
Prepaid interest expense	600	510
Trade accounts payable	26,500	23,800
Income taxes payable		1,984
Accrued operating expenses payable	600	400
Operational assets (net)	35,400	33,290
Other assets	11,861	11,861
Capital stock	40,000	40,000
Mortgage payable (6%, dated 7/1/19A)	20,000	?

No operational assets were sold during the year.

Required:

Prepare a worksheet to provide data for a detailed income statement for 19C and a balance sheet at the end of 19C. Show how the amounts for the various entries were developed. Suggestion: set up columns for Balances, January 1, 19C; Interim Entries—Debit and Credit; Income Statement; and Balance Sheet, December 31, 19C (use a "debits-over-credits" format).

Problem 20–14

The following data were taken from the records of Rooster's Sporting Goods Store:

	Balances	
	1/1/19A	12/31/19A
Accounts receivable	$ 2,300	$ 3,900
Notes receivable (trade)	1,500	2,000
Interest receivable	90	70
Prepaid interest on notes payable	75	60
Inventory	9,255	10,400
Prepaid expenses (operating)	100	130
Store equipment (net)	8,500	8,600
Other assets	—	500
Accounts payable	1,700	1,900
Notes payable (trade)	11,000	11,500
Notes payable (equipment)	—	500
Accrued interest payable	40	30
Accrued expenses (operating) payable	170	210
Interest revenue collected in advance	30	40

An analysis of the checkbook, canceled checks, deposit slips, and bank statements provided the following summary for the year:

Balance, 1/1/19A		$4,200
Cash receipts:		
Cash sales	$23,000	
On accounts receivable	7,600	
On notes receivable	1,000	
Interest revenue	160	
Cash disbursements:		
Cash purchases	11,800	
On accounts payable	2,400	
On notes payable (trade)	500	
Interest expense	560	
Operating expenses	14,130	
Miscellaneous nonoperating expenses	970	
Other assets purchased	500	
Withdrawals by Rooster	2,400	
Balance, 12/31/19A		$2,700

Required:

1. Compute income by analyzing the changes in the proprietorship account.
2. Prepare a detailed income statement with supporting schedules; show computations.

21

Analysis of Financial Statements, Segment and Interim Reporting

THROUGHOUT this book, the focus has been on annual financial reporting to external parties. In various chapters, reference was made to comparative statements and certain financial ratios, such as the working capital ratio and earnings per share (EPS). Approaches to analyzing and interpreting financial statements have been developed by accountants, financial analysts, and others. Accountants often are involved in the analysis and interpretation of financial statements. Two additional aspects of external financial reporting—segment and interim reporting—have been referred to only indirectly. To discuss these topics this chapter is subdivided as follows:

Part A—Analysis of Financial Statements
Part B—Segment and Interim Reporting

Part A: Analysis of Financial Statements

PRIMARY PURPOSE OF ANALYSIS

Analysis of financial statements focuses primarily on the data reported in external financial reports plus supplementary information from other sources such as company management, investment advisors, trade associations, business periodicals, government agencies, and other materials distributed by the company. These latter sources often are particularly important because they may disclose useful information on a more timely basis than the published financial statements. For example, litigation may threaten the profit potential of a company, and sources such as *The Wall Street Journal* may provide timely disclosure of such events.

One of the primary objectives of financial statement analysis is identification of **major changes** (i.e., turning points) in trends, amounts, and relationships and investigation of the reasons underlying those changes. Often a **turning point** may provide an early warning of a significant change in the future success or failure of the business.

In analyzing and interpreting financial statements, you should recognize that financial statements are **organized summaries** of an extensive mass of detailed financial information. For example, the published financial statements (and notes) of a large corporation, such as General Motors, Exxon, or IBM, usually fill from 10 to 15 printed pages, including the supporting notes. It is difficult to imagine the number of transactions, the critical accounting decisions, and the voluminous detail summarized in these few pages. Also, it is difficult to perceive, although it is often true, that a million dollars may be immaterial because it amounts to less than 5 percent of the total base amount of which it is a part. Summarization presents serious communication problems. On the other hand, excessive detail is considered to be undesirable because statement users experience time constraints in analyzing a mass of data.

ANALYTICAL APPROACHES AND TECHNIQUES

The analysis of financial statements is much broader than the mere computation of a few ratios. Analysis involves an organized approach to glean from the totality of the financial statements, selected data that are relevant to the decisions of statement users. Analysis of that data and interpretation of the results are important steps in the evaluation and interpretation of financial statements. The analytical steps are as follows:

1. Examine the auditors' report.
2. Analyze the statement of accounting policies included in the notes to the financial statements.
3. Examine the overall financial statements, including notes and supporting schedules.
4. Apply analytical techniques such as—
   a. Comparative statements.
   b. Horizontal and vertical percentage analyses.
   c. Ratio analyses.
5. Search for important supplemental information not provided by the financial statements.

EXAMINE THE AUDITORS' REPORT

Expert financial analysts often suggest that in evaluating a financial statement, the first basic step is careful examination of the auditors' report (often called the accountants' report). Of course, this presumes that the financial statements are audited. If they are not, one should ascertain their credibility before relying on them. The auditors' report is important because it provides the analyst with information concerning the "fairness" of the representations in the financial statements and calls attention to all major concerns of the auditor that came to light as a result of the auditor's intensive examination.

The auditors' report was discussed in Chapter 4, and it would be advisable to restudy that discussion. An unqualified auditors' opinion is given in the Appendix following Chapter 24.

Of particular importance is the possibility that instead of an **unqualified opinion,** the auditor may give *(a)* a qualified opinion, *(b)* an adverse opinion, or *(c)* a disclaimer of opinion. Each of these three unfavorable opinions must include an explanation by the auditor of the factors underlying the decision to render such an opinion. These unfavorable opinions serve to alert the statement user to major problem areas that should be investigated. An unfavorable auditors' opinion may cause the SEC or the stock exchanges to stop public trading in the stock of the company which in and of itself is considered serious by investors.

Below is a qualified opinion (and related notes) that illustrates the kind of information frequently cited by an auditor.[1] Observe in this situation that the qualification is related to continuation of the business as a **going concern** because of a critical credit situation. This may be one of the single most important bits of information in the financial statements of this company.

To the Stockholders and
Board of Directors of
The Rath Packing Company

We have examined the balance sheet of The Rath Packing Company as of September 29, 1979, and September 30, 1978, and the related statements of operations and accumulated deficit and of changes in financial position for the fiscal years then ended. Our examinations were made in accordance with generally accepted auditing standards, and accordingly included such tests of the accounting records and such other auditing procedures as we considered necessary in the circumstances.

During the fiscal years ended September 29, 1979, and September 30, 1978, the company incurred net losses of $1,485,000 and $6,441,000, respectively. Future working capital requirements are dependent on the company's ability to restore and maintain profitable operations, to restructure its financing arrangements and to continue the present short-term financing or obtain alternative financing as required. It is not possible to predict the outcome of future operations or whether the necessary alternative financing

[1] The Rath Packing Company, Annual Report, 1979, extracted from AICPA, *Accounting Trends & Techniques,* 34th ed. (New York, 1980), p. 393.

can be arranged, if needed. The accompanying fiscal year 1979 and 1978 financial statements have been prepared on the basis of accounting principles applicable to a going concern. Accordingly, they do not purport to give effect to adjustments, if any, that may be necessary should the company be unable to continue as a going concern and therefore be required to realize its assets and liquidate its liabilities, contingent obligations and commitments in other than the normal course of business and at amounts different from those in the accompanying fiscal year 1979 and 1978 financial statements.

As described in Note 5, the company was a defendant in two lawsuits alleging breach of brokerage contracts and claiming compensatory and punitive damages; however, one of the lawsuits was dismissed in August 1979. The ultimate outcome of the other lawsuit is not presently determinable. Accordingly, no provision for liability, if any, has been made in the fiscal year 1979 or 1978 financial statements.

In our opinion, subject to the effects on the fiscal year 1979 and 1978 financial statements of such adjustments, if any, as might have been required had the outcome of the uncertainties referred to in the two preceding paragraphs been known, the financial statements examined by us present fairly the financial position of the Rath Packing Company at September 29, 1979, and September 30, 1978, and the results of its operations and the changes in its financial position for the fiscal years then ended, in conformity with generally accepted accounting principles applied on a consistent basis.—*Report of Independent Accountants.*

ANALYZE THE STATEMENT OF ACCOUNTING POLICIES

Accounting is man-made and must accommodate a wide variety of circumstances. Although accounting principles and their implementation are prescribed primarily by the *ARBs, APB Opinions, FASB Statements,* and by precedent, there is considerable room for judgment by the reporting entity and by the independent accountant with respect to the accounting treatment to be accorded many items. In numerous areas of accounting, several alternatives are acceptable, such as the completed contract and percentage-of-completion methods of recognizing revenue on long-term construction contracts (see Chapter 9). The range of judgments and alternatives permitted make it very difficult to analyze financial statements if the major judgments and alternatives used by the company are not communicated clearly.

In response to the **reporting principle,** *APB Opinion No. 22,* "Disclosure of Accounting Policies," states that "information about the accounting policies adopted by a reporting entity is essential for financial statement users." Accounting policies are the specific accounting policies and methods that have been adopted by a company for preparation of its financial statements. The *Opinion* requires that a statement of these policies be clearly enunciated either in the notes, or preferably "in a separate **Summary of Significant Accounting Policies** preceding the notes to the financial statements or as the initial note." The summary must disclose all important accounting policies including *(a)* selections from acceptable alternatives, *(b)* accounting policies used that are peculiar to the industry, and *(c)* unusual or innovative applications of generally accepted accounting principles. Examples include the basis for consolidated statements, depreciation and amortization methods, inventory costing and valuation (e.g., LCM), translation of foreign currencies, revenue recognition on long-term construction contracts, franchising, and leasing. A statement of accounting policies is shown in the Appendix (following Chapter 24).

The information in the statement of accounting policies is fundamental to understanding, interpreting, and evaluating much of the information reported in the financial statements. It is particularly useful in evaluating the **credibility and quality of the reported earnings,** and in comparing data among companies, industries, and reporting periods.

OVERALL EXAMINATION OF THE FINANCIAL STATEMENTS

After examination of the auditors' opinion and analysis of the summary of accounting policies used by the company, the evaluation and interpretive process should continue with a careful examination of the financial statements in their entirety. This phase of the analysis involves study of each statement in order to gain overall perspective and to identify major strengths, weaknesses, and unusual changes, such as **turning points** in the trend of sales, earnings, asset structure, liabilities, capital structure, and cash flow.

The overall examination should include careful study of all of the statements included and the **notes** referred to in those statements. Each note should be read and evaluated at the point in the statement where it is referenced. Consideration of the notes as a separate activity is not as fruitful, because a specific note is helpful primarily in the context of

EXHIBIT 21–1: Comparative Financial Statements Illustrated (with vertical and horizontal analysis)

Panel A—Vertical Analysis:

WZH CORPORATION
Comparative Balance Sheets
At December 31, 19B, and 19A

	19B		19A	
Assets	**Amount**	**Percent***	**Amount**	**Percent***
Current assets:				
Cash	$ 55,000	12	$ 74,000	16
Investments, short term	4,000	1	10,000	2
Accounts receivable (net of allowance for doubtful accts.)	39,000	8	30,000	6
Inventory (FIFO, LCM)	95,000	20	80,000	17
Prepaid expenses	200	—	1,000	—
Total current assets	193,200	41	195,000	41
Investments, long term	55,000	11	50,000	11
Land, plant, and equipment:				
Land	10,000	2	10,000	2
Plant and equipment	315,000	66	290,000	62
Less: Accum. depr.	(97,000)	(20)	(77,000)	(16)
Total	228,000	48	223,000	48
Intangible assets:				
Patent (less accum. amortization)	1,800		2,000	
Total assets	$478,000	100	$470,000	100
Liabilities				
Current liabilities:				
Accounts payable	$ 40,000	8	$ 55,000	12
Notes payable, short term	5,000	1	8,000	2
Taxes payable	4,555	1	7,000	1
Total current liabilities	49,555	10	70,000	15
Long-term liabilities:				
Bonds payable (less unamortized discount)	99,100	21	99,000	21
Total liabilities	148,655	31	169,000	36
Stockholders' equity:				
Common stock, par $5, authorized 60,000 shares	220,000	46	200,000	42
Preferred stock, 5%, par $10, authorized 10,000 shares	50,000	10	50,000	11
Contributed capital in excess of par, common stock	14,000	3	12,000	3
Retained earnings	45,345	10	39,000	8
Total stockholders' equity	329,345	69	301,000	64
Total liabilities and stockholders' equity	$478,000	100	$470,000	100

* For illustrative purposes only; not usually included on published financial statements. Rounded to nearest 1 percent.

WZH CORPORATION
Comparative Income Statements
For the Years Ended December 31, 19B, and 19A

	19B		19A	
	Amount	**Percent***	**Amount**	**Percent***
Revenues:				
Sales revenue	$400,000†		$370,000	
Investment revenue	4,500		3,000	
Gain on disposal of investments	500			
Total revenues	405,000	100	373,000	100
Expenses:				
Cost of goods sold	265,000	65	250,000	67
Distribution	67,000	17	61,200	16
General administrative	30,000	7	27,000	7
Interest	7,100	2	6,200	2
Total expenses	369,100	91	344,400	92
Pretax operating income	35,900	9	28,600	8
Income tax expense	16,155	4	12,870	4
Income before extraordinary item	19,745	5		
Extraordinary loss (net of taxes, $3,600)	4,400	1		
Net income	$ 15,345	4	$ 15,730	4
Earnings per share:				
Income before extraordinary loss	$0.39			
Extraordinary loss	(0.10)			
Net income‡	$0.29		$0.33	

* For illustrative purposes only; not usually included on published statements.

† Credit sales $345,000.

‡ ($15,345 − $2,500, preferred dividends) ÷ 44,000 = $.29.
($15,730 − $2,500, preferred dividends) ÷ 40,000 = $.33.

EXHIBIT 21–1 *(Continued)*

Panel A concluded:

WZH CORPORATION
Comparative Statements of Changes in Financial Position, Working Capital Basis For the Years Ended December 31, 19B, and 19A

	19B		19A	
	Amount	Percent*	Amount	Percent*
Sources of working capital:				
Income before extraordinary items	$ 19,745		$15,730	
Add (deduct) items not requiring or generating working capital:				
Depreciation	20,000		18,000	
Amortization of bond discount	100		100	
Amortization of patent	200	—	200	—
Working capital provided by operations	40,045	66	34,030	86
Extraordinary loss (net of tax)	(4,400)	(7)		
Total	35,645	59	34,030	86
Other sources:				
Sale of common stock	22,000	36	5,500	14
Prior period adjustment	3,000	5		—
Total from other sources	25,000	41	5,500	14
Total working capital provided	$ 60,645	100	$39,530	100
Uses of working capital:				
Equipment acquired	$ 25,000	59		
Long-term investments	5,000	12	$10,000	56
Cash dividends	12,000	29	8,000	44
Total working capital used	$ 42,000	100	$18,000	100
Difference—net increase in working capital	$ 18,645		$21,530	

	19B	19A
Summary of changes in components of working capital:		
Increase (decrease) in working capital current asset accounts:		
Cash	$(19,000)	$ (6,070)
Investments, short term	(6,000)	10,000
Accounts receivable (net)	9,000	11,000
Inventory	15,000	12,000
Prepaid expenses	(800)	600
Total	(1,800)	27,530
Increase (decrease) in working capital current liability accounts:		
Accounts payable	15,000	(2,000)
Notes payable, short term	3,000	(3,000)
Taxes payable	2,445	(1,000)
Total	20,445	(6,000)
Net increase in working capital	$ 18,645	$21,530

* For illustrative purposes only; not usually included on published financial statements.

Panel B—Horizontal Analysis:

WZH CORPORATION
Comparative Income Statements
For the Years Ended December 31, 19B, and 19A

	Year Ended December 31		Increase (Decrease) 19B over 19A	
	19B	19A	Amount	Percent
Revenues:				
Sales revenue	$400,000	$370,000	$30,000	8
Investment revenue	4,500	3,000	1,500	50
Gain on disposal of investments	500		500	—
Total revenues	405,000	373,000	32,000	9
Expenses:				
Cost of goods sold	265,000	250,000	15,000	6
Distribution	67,000	61,200	5,800	9
General administrative	30,000	27,000	3,000	11
Interest	7,100	6,200	900	15
Total expenses	369,100	344,400	24,700	7

	Year Ended December 31		Increase (Decrease) 19B over 19A	
	19B	19A	Amount	Percent
Pretax operating income	35,900	28,600	7,300	26
Income tax expense	16,155	12,870	3,285	26
Income before extraordinary item	19,745	15,730	4,015	26
Extraordinary loss (net of taxes)	4,400		4,400	—
Net income	$ 15,345	$ 15,730	$ (385)	(2)
EPS (not illustrated).				

the specific statement item to which it is referenced. **The official position of the accounting profession is that the notes are an integral part of the financial statements.**

Concurrent with, or subsequent to, the overall examination of the financial statements under review, application of the analytical techniques discussed in the next section may be quite helpful to the analyst.

APPLICATION OF ANALYTICAL TECHNIQUES

Various approaches are used to enhance effective communication through financial statements, such as ratio analysis, the "letter to the stockholders," graphic presentations, special tabulations, subclassifications of information on the statements, comparative statements, and supplementary information in separate schedules and notes to the statements.

Comparative Statements

Comparative statements involve the presentation of financial information for the current and one or more past periods in a way that facilitates comparison by the statement user. Basically, comparative statements are of two types, viz:

1. Presentation of financial reports for *(a)* the current year and *(b)* the immediately preceding years. There is a strong movement in the accounting profession to require three-year, rather than two-year, comparative financial statements.
2. Presentation of selected financial information for a number of years past (e.g., 5 or 10 years). These often are referred to as **financial** summaries.

Trends in the financial development of a business have particular significance to all users. The comparison of current results with those of one or more prior periods provides an added perspective in evaluating the relationship of current performance with past performance; that is, multiple period results provide one of the useful ways to evaluate progress, improvement, or deterioration. As a result, practically all published financial statements include at least comparative data for the current and prior year. For example, the Quaker Oats financial statements presented in the Appendix following Chapter 24 are comparative.

For illustrative purposes, the financial statements for WZH Corporation are used throughout this chapter. Exhibit 21–1 presents the three comparative statements (condensed for discussion purposes). Observe the form: the current year results are in the first column; and single underscores for dollar amount subtotals facilitate the presentation in a single column for each period. Placing the various items for the two periods in juxtaposition (side by side) in the two columns is preferable to separate statements.

The **long-term summaries** of selected financial information often included in the annual financial report are especially significant. An actual example of such a summary is presented in Exhibit 21–2. Observe in particular the nature of the items selected for inclusion in the summary. These measures of the long-term financial performance of the company are particularly relevant for financial statement analysis: The annual financial statements for one year alone present a limited view of the successes and failures of the company. In contrast, the long-term summary provides a broad overview of where the company has been (financially) in the past and may provide clues as to where it is apt to go in the future. In this regard, the results of one, or even two years may give too limited a view of the potentials of the company. It is for these reasons that analysts are especially interested in long-term summaries.

Percentage Analysis of Financial Statements

Financial information expressed in absolute amounts is the accepted means of conveying accounting information. Conversion of absolute amounts to percentages (of some base amount) reveals basic relationships. The expression of relationships in terms of percentages or ratios sometimes may aid in the interpretation of financial information. There are two common forms of percentage analyses used on financial statements—vertical analysis and horizontal analysis.

Vertical analysis involves the expression of each item on a particular financial statement as a percent of one specific item, which is referred to as the **base.** For example, the component items on the income statement may be expressed as a percent of total revenue (net of any sales returns) as shown in Exhibit 21–1, Panel A. Note that the base amount represent-

EXHIBIT 21–2: Long-Term Financial Summary Illustrated—St. Regis Paper Company and Consolidated Subsidiaries

St. Regis is presenting its financial information on an eight-year basis, 1973 being the earliest year for which figures have been restated for acquisitions.

Dollars in thousands, except per share amounts)	1980	1979	1978	1977	1976	1975	1974	1973
Revenues and Earnings								
Net sales	$2,714,175	$2,498,436	$2,300,154	$1,996,337	$1,798,562	$1,536,387	$1,566,126	$1,269,901
Equity in earnings of nonconsolidated affiliates	14,373	17,437	7,013	6,987	3,492	16,996	16,894	6,232
Gain on sale of land			22,061					
Sales of investments						15,020		
Other, net	43,305	17,883	7,300	18,707	10,000	16,812	(84)	10,592
Total revenues	2,771,853	2,533,756	2,336,528	2,022,031	1,812,054	1,585,215	1,582,936	1,286,725
Cost and expenses	2,519,861	2,295,137	2,124,520	1,848,116	1,650,751	1,409,295	1,400,228	1,169,342
Earnings before income taxes	251,992	238,619	212,008	173,915	161,303	175,920	182,708	117,383
Provision for income taxes	81,500	80,126	85,494	67,129	53,770	69,000	69,743	44,804
Net earnings	$ 170,492	$ 158,493	$ 126,514	$ 106,786	$ 107,533	$ 106,920	$ 112,965	$ 72,579
Financial Position at Year-End								
Working capital	$ 606,936	$ 555,996	$ 546,993	$ 522,134	$ 360,452	$ 345,901	$ 334,414	$ 319,155
Investments	132,953	126,500	118,800	124,319	112,538	96,110	108,610	76,684
Other assets	179,882	167,192	142,278	103,131	107,724	103,635	112,177	123,519
Land, buildings, and equipment, net	1,150,006	892,789	838,759	798,879	793,303	731,615	661,063	572,541
Timberlands and cutting rights, net	192,519	188,744	156,751	157,948	141,766	106,711	104,469	95,864
Total	$2,262,296	$1,931,221	$1,803,581	$1,706,411	$1,515,783	$1,383,972	$1,320,733	$1,187,763
Long-term debt	$ 721,910	$ 515,456	$ 505,493	$ 518,660	$ 425,141	$ 413,108	$ 462,206	$ 422,314
Deferred credits	201,235	188,297	171,007	144,798	116,267	99,556	82,588	74,277
Preferred shareholders' equity			11,250	11,250	11,250	11,250	11,250	11,250
Common shareholders' equity	1,339,151	1,227,468	1,115,831	1,031,703	963,125	860,058	764,689	679,922
Total	$2,262,296	$1,931,221	$1,803,581	$1,706,411	$1,515,783	$1,383,972	$1,320,733	$1,187,763
Total Assets at Year-End	$2,642,236	$2,260,845	$2,111,190	$1,927,425	$1,721,737	$1,601,919	$1,502,093	$1,348,154
Per share:								
Net earnings	$ 5.18	$ 4.87	$ 3.94	$ 3.36	$ 3.43	$ 3.58	$ 3.83	$ 2.47
Net earnings, assuming full dilution	5.17	4.84	3.89	3.30	3.34	3.38	3.59	2.33
Dividends paid on outstanding common shares	2.03	1.85	1.74	1.66	1.55	1.43	1.25	1.16
Common shareholders' equity	41.25	38.11	35.01	32.97	31.03	28.73	26.25	23.42
Analytical Information:								
Percent return on common shareholders' equity	12.73	12.89	11.28	10.29	11.10	12.36	14.69	10.58
Percent return on revenues	6.15	6.26	5.41	5.28	5.93	6.74	7.14	5.64
Percent return on invested capital	7.54	8.21	7.01	6.26	7.09	7.73	8.55	6.11
Ratio of current assets to current liabilities	2.60:1	2.69:1	2.78:1	3.36:1	2.75:1	2.59:1	2.84:1	2.99:1
Debt as a percent of total capitalization	31.9	26.7	28.0	30.4	28.0	29.9	35.0	35.6
Additional Financial Information:								
Funds provided from operations	$ 279,772	$ 258,626	$ 250,462	$ 210,662	$ 193,957	$ 181,187	$ 184,870	$ 136,600
Depreciation, depletion, and amortization	97,835	96,013	91,221	77,127	71,723	67,461	59,150	59,344
Investment tax credit	33,260	17,607	6,953	10,094	17,190	9,383	8,755	3,409
Capital expenditures, excluding timberlands and leased property	337,312	132,534	91,358	70,304	133,037	135,503	145,810	105,462
Wages, salaries, and benefits	677,804	649,120	598,642	530,238	472,968	414,992	410,473	374,081
Research and development expenditures	10,212	9,819	9,050	8,444	7,564	7,394	5,065	5,023

ing 100 percent is divided into each component item to derive the component percentages.

In applying vertical analysis, an appropriate base amount must be selected for each statement. Observe on Exhibit 21–1, Panel A, that the base amounts for the balance sheet are total assets, and total liabilities plus stockholders' equity, respectively; and in Exhibit 21–1, the base amounts for the statement of changes in financial position (SCFP) are total working capital provided and total working capital used, respectively. Financial statements expressed in percentages only are referred to as **common-size** statements.

Horizontal analysis refers to the development of percentages indicating the proportionate change in the same item over **time.** The conversion of absolute amounts of change to percentage changes facilitates interpretation and evaluation of trends. For example, horizontal percentages shown on the comparative income statements in Exhibit 21–1, Panel B, serve to emphasize the trend of each component. When the number for the base year is zero or negative (e.g., a cash deficit) it is improper to express a percent of change in a later year when the latter number is positive.

Note in the example in Exhibit 21–1, Panel B, relating to horizontal analysis, that in computing the percentage change from 19A to 19B, as well as the amounts of increase or decrease, the **base year** is the earlier period.

Ratio (Proportionate) Analysis

The analysis of financial statements generally includes one or more forms of ratio analysis. Ratio analysis involves measurement of the relationship between two amounts from one statement, such as the income statement, or from two statements, such as the income statement and balance sheet. The amounts may represent the balances of two different accounts, the balance of one account and a classification total (such as total assets), or two classification totals.

Ratio analysis can be expressed in a variety of ways. To illustrate, working capital has been discussed and referred to in a number of preceding chapters. The **current ratio** is the relationship between current assets and current liabilities. Assume the following:

Current assets	$5,000,000
Current liabilities	2,000,000
Difference—working capital	$3,000,000

The amount of working capital, $3,000,000, standing alone is a useful figure; however, expression as a ratio adds insight to this relationship, viz:

Current ratio (or working capital ratio)

$$= \$5{,}000{,}000 \div \$2{,}000{,}000 = 2.5$$

Alternatively, this ratio may be expressed as 250 percent; 2.5 to 1; or there is $2.50 of current assets for each $1 of current liabilities.

Ratio analysis is helpful only when the relationship between the selected factors, when expressed as a proportion, sheds additional light on the interpretation of the individual absolute amounts. In view of the large number of ratios that could be computed, it is important to focus on those amounts that are functionally related. For example, the relationship between bad debt expense and credit sales is more meaningful than the relationship between bad debt expense and total sales (including cash sales). In evaluating significance, consideration must be given to the purposes for which the ratios are to be used. Investors, managers, and creditors have essentially different interests and problems; consequently, they often use different ratios. Because a complete study of ratio analysis is beyond the scope of this text, only representative ratios having general application are discussed. The analyses selected for discussion will be explained under the following general headings:

1. Ratios that measure current position.
2. Ratios that measure equity position.
3. Ratios that measure operating results.

Ratios That Measure Current Position. The ratio measurements in this category focus on working capital; they are supplementary to the SCFP, working capital basis. The ratios relate to selected elements of working capital and are designed to assess the short-term liquidity position and the ability of the business to meet its maturing current liabilities. Seven measurements of current position are summarized in Exhibit 21–3. Observe that they are expressed variously as a percent, decimal, fraction, or turnover figure. The analysis of current position in-

EXHIBIT 21–3: Ratios That Measure Current Position

Ratio	Formula for Computation	Significance
Ratios that measure ability to pay short-term obligations:		
1. Working capital (or current) ratio.	Current assets / Current liabilities	Test of short-term liquidity. Indicates ability to meet current obligations from current assets as a going concern. Measure of adequacy of working capital.
2. Acid-test (or quick) ratio.	Quick assets / Current liabilities	A more severe test of immediate liquidity than the current ratio. Tests ability to meet sudden demands upon liquid current assets.
3. Working capital to total assets.	Working capital / Total assets	Indicates relative liquidity of total assets and distribution of resources employed as to liquidity.
Ratios that measure movement of current assets (turnover):		
4. *a.* Receivable turnover.	Net credit sales / Average trade receivables (net)	Velocity of collection of trade accounts and notes. Test of efficiency of collection.
b. Age of receivables.	365 (days)* / Receivable turnover (computed per [*a*] above)	Number of days to collect average trade receivables.
5. Inventory turnover. *a.* Merchandise turnover (retail firm).	Cost of goods sold / Average merchandise inventory	Indicates liquidity of inventory. Number of times average inventory "turned over" or was sold during the period. Indicates possible over- or understocking.
b. Finished goods turnover (manufacturing firm).	Cost of goods sold / Average finished goods inventory	Same as 5*a*.
c. Raw material turnover.	Cost of raw materials used / Average raw materials inventory	Number of times raw material inventory was "used" on the average during the period.
d. Days' supply in inventory.	365 (days)* / Inventory turnover (computed per [*a*], [*b*], or [*c*] above)	Number of days' supply in the average inventory. Indicates general condition of over- or understocking.
6. Working capital turnover.	Net sales / Average working capital	Indicates the effectiveness with which average working capital was used to generate sales.
7. Percent of each current asset to total current assets.	Each current asset / Total current assets	Indicates relative investment in each current asset.

* This number varies in practice; 365, 360, and 300 are used.

volves measures of *(a)* ability to pay short-term obligations and *(b)* movement of current assets.[2]

Working Capital (Current) Ratio. The working capital (or current) ratio has long been recognized as an index of short-term liquidity—the ability of the business to meet the maturing claims of the creditors from the current operating assets. The amount of working capital and the related ratio have a direct impact on the amount of short-term credit that may be obtained. Traditionally, as a rule of thumb, a working capital ratio of 2 to 1 has been considered adequate. However, analysts in recent years have tended to disavow simplistic decision rules such as

[2] There is no single "generally accepted" method of computing specific ratios or of determining the values to be used in their computations. The computation should be determined by (1) the data available and (2) the use and interpretation expected in the particular situation. The formulas presented reflect a general approach.

this one. The working capital ratio figure is unique to the industry in which the business operates, and even to the business itself in the light of its operating and financial characteristics. For example, a ratio of 2 to 1 may be realistic in one situation, but it may be too low or too high in another situation. The peculiarities of the industry in which the firm operates and other factors, such as methods of financing and seasonal fluctuations, also should be taken into account in evaluating a working capital ratio.

The working capital ratio is only one measure or index of ability to meet short-term obligations, and it has certain weaknesses. A high working capital ratio may be the result of overstocking of inventory, and it is influenced by the inventory cost flow method used. A business may have a high current ratio even though it has a cash deficit. Furthermore, a high current ratio may indicate excess funds which should be invested or otherwise put to use. As with all ratios, there is a delicate balance between a ratio that is too high and one that is too low. Determination of the most desirable ratio varies among industries and companies, and determination of the optimum ratio for a particular company poses a complex problem.

Acid-Test Ratio. Cash, accounts receivable, short-term notes receivable, and short-term investments in marketable securities generally represent funds which may be made readily available for paying current obligations. Hence, they are referred to as **quick assets.** Inventories, on the other hand, must be sold and collection made before cash is available for paying obligations. In many cases, particularly where there are raw materials and work in process inventories, the marketability of the inventory involves considerable uncertainty as to the timing of its ultimate realization in cash. In view of these considerations the **acid-test** or **quick** ratio (quick assets divided by current liabilities) is used as a test of immediate liquidity. Traditionally, an acid-test ratio of 1 to 1 (a rule of thumb standard) has been considered desirable. As with the current ratio, the acid-test ratio for a particular company must be evaluated in light of industry characteristics and other factors.

Working Capital to Total Assets. The ratio of working capital to total assets is a generalized expression of the distribution and liquidity of the assets employed after current liabilities have been deducted from the current assets. An excessively high ratio might indicate excess cash, inability to collect receivables, and/or overstocking of inventory, whereas a low ratio may indicate a weakness in the current position.

A related analysis involves a **vertical** percentage analysis of current assets employing **total current assets** as the base (100 percent). This analysis may have some significance in that *(a)* the relative composition of the current asset structure is revealed and *(b)* when compared with similar data from prior periods, important trends may be revealed.

Receivable Turnover. In some businesses, cash sales predominate, whereas in others credit sales predominate. In either case the amount of trade receivables on the average should bear some relationship to the credit sales for the period and the terms of credit. The application of the receivable turnover in these respects may be illustrated by referring to WZH Corporation's financial statements (Exhibit 21–1).

$$\text{Receivable turnover} = \frac{\text{Credit sales, \$345,000}}{\text{Average trade receivables, } \dfrac{\$30,000 + \$39,000}{2}} = 10$$

$$\text{Age of receivables} = \frac{365 \text{ days}}{10} = 36.5 \text{ (average number of days to collect)}$$

If we assume the terms of sale are 1/10, n/30, it appears that collections are lagging terms by six days or more on the average—a suggestion of possible laxity in *(a)* granting credit and/or *(b)* making collections.

The above illustration also points up several technical aspects of the computation, viz:

1. Should the total of cash and credit sales, or credit sales only, be used in the computation? A more stable and meaningful ratio will result if credit sales only are used; otherwise a shift in the proportion of cash to credit sales will affect the ratio, although collection experience is unchanged. For internal purposes, credit sales should be used (since the figure is available or may be reconstructed readily); however, for comparison with other firms the total of cash and credit sales generally must be used because published data seldom provide the credit sales amounts for other businesses.
2. Should the ending balance of receivables or average receivables be used? The average **monthly**

receivables balance generally should be used in order to smooth out seasonal influences. The average should be determined by adding the 13 monthly balances (January 1, January 31, and through December 31) of trade accounts and trade notes receivable, then dividing by 13. In the absence of monthly balances the average of the annual beginning and ending balance or only the ending balance may be used (with a potentially significant loss of information).

3. Receivables should be net of the allowance for doubtful accounts.
4. Trade notes receivable should be included in averaging receivables.

Whether to express the receivable movement as a "turnover" or as "number of days to collect" is a matter of preference. If the company uses a business year that ends with the lowest point in the company's operating cycle, the receivables reported on the balance sheet normally will be quite low, which would cause the turnover to look better than is actually the case.

Inventory Turnover. Inventory turnover is the ratio between the cost of goods sold (or used) and the **average** inventory balance. The procedure for determining the average inventory balance is similar to that discussed above for average receivables.

The merchandise inventory turnover may be expressed as a "turnover" or as "days' supply"; the latter appears more often in current usage.[3] The turnover or days' supply figure has significance in that the amount of inventory on hand normally should bear a close relationship to cost of goods sold. The relationship will vary among industries and businesses; for example, a grocery store normally should expect a high inventory turnover, whereas an antique dealer may expect a low turnover. Also, the ratio represents an average—a generalization that does not reflect how fast particular items are moving, but rather how fast all items on the average are moving. For example, a grocer may have a turnover of 20, yet may have items on the shelves that have not turned over at all for a three-month period. Furthermore, this ratio is influenced by the inventory cost flow method used, which may affect comparison among firms. For example, when prices are rising, firms using LIFO will tend to have higher computed turnover rates than those using other cost flow methods.

Inventory turnover is directly related to profitability. To illustrate, assume that the inventory turnover is 12 (cost of goods sold, $1,200,000; average inventory, $100,000) and that the company realizes a profit of $1,000 each time the $100,000 investment in inventory turns over. A $12,000 profit is indicated. Now assume another company is identical in every respect except that its inventory turnover is 6, indicating a $6,000 profit on a similar $100,000 inventory investment.

Work in process inventory turnover is computed by dividing cost of goods manufactured by the average work in process inventory. With respect to all inventories, turnover computations based on appropriate unit data, when practicable, will provide more reliable results than when based on dollar amount data.

Ratios That Measure Equity Position. The balance sheet reports the two basic sources of funds used by the business: *(a)* owners' equity and *(b)* creditors' equity. The relationships between these two distinctly different equities often are measured because they reflect certain financial strengths and weaknesses of the business; in other words, the long-term solvency of a business and its potential capacity to generate and obtain investment resources. Exhibit 21–4 summarizes seven ratios that commonly are used to measure equity position.

Equity Ratios. The three equity ratios reflect essentially the same relationship, that is, the proportion of total assets provided by *(a)* the owners and *(b)* the creditors. The three equity ratios for WZH Corporation (Exhibit 21–1) for 19B are as follows:

1. $\frac{\text{Owners' equity, \$329,345}}{\text{Total assets, \$478,000}}$ = 69% of the assets were provided by owners
2. $\frac{\text{Creditors' equity, \$148,655}}{\text{Total assets, \$478,000}}$ = 31% of the assets were provided by creditors

   100% total assets provided
3. $\frac{\text{Creditors' equity, \$148,655}}{\text{Owners' equity, \$329,345}}$ = 45% —the creditors' equity is 45% of the owners' equity

Usually only one of the three equity ratios is used because each reflects the same relationship (but in a somewhat different way). The balance between resources provided by debt versus owners' equity is considered critical by analysts. Mathematical

[3] Some analysts prefer to use 250 (5-day workweek) or 300 (6-day workweek) days, as the case may be, as an approximation of the number of business days in the year.

EXHIBIT 21–4: Ratios That Measure Equity Position

Ratio	Formula for Computation	Significance
Equity ratios:		
1. Owners' equity to total assets.*	Owners' equity / Total assets	Proportion of assets provided by owners. Reflects financial strength and cushion for creditors.
2. Creditors' equity to total assets.	Total liabilities / Total assets	Proportion of assets provided by creditors. Extent of leverage.
3. Total liabilities to owners' equity. (Also called the debt-equity ratio.)	Total liabilities / Owners' equity	Relative amounts of resources provided by creditors and owners. Reflects strengths and weaknesses in basic financing of operations.
Other ratios related to equity position:		
4. Operational assets to owners' equity.	Operational assets (net) / Owners' equity	May suggest over- or underinvestment by owners.
5. Operational assets to total equities.	Operational assets (net) / Total liabilities and owners' equity	May suggest over- or underexpansion of plant and equipment.
6. Sales to operational assets (plant turnover).	Net sales / Operational assets (net)	Turnover index which tests the efficiency of management in using operational assets to generate sales.
7. Book value per share of common stock outstanding at year-end.	Common stock equity / Number of outstanding common shares	Number of dollars of common equity (at book value) per share of common stock.

* Total assets is represented by the balance sheet totals (i.e., total assets or liabilities plus owners' equity).

models have been constructed to determine optimal capital structure. The most definitive statement to be made from this body of research is that a judicious use of debt financing can increase the value of the firm; however, the incurrence of debt beyond this optimum can lead to higher interest rates at best, and insolvency and bankruptcy at worst. Therefore, there is no rule of thumb that can be pointed to as a guide for evaluation. A company that has 80 percent debt and 20 percent owners' equity usually would be considered overborrowed (overextended); interest payments must be made regardless of the level of earnings, and the debts must be paid at the fixed maturity dates. In contrast, if debt and owners' equity are 20 percent and 80 percent, respectively, the creditors' position is better and interest payments lower. However, owners' equity usually is more costly than debt from the viewpoints of the entity and its owners. From the standpoint of the expectations of those providing the investment funds (i.e., the investors), a company heavily financed by **stock** issuances is required by its stockholders to earn more income and have a higher stock value than a company financed by half stock and half debt—because stockholders assume a greater risk from holding their investment than do creditors.

In computing the equity ratios, users of financial statements often make adjustments of book values to adapt the ratios to their particular purposes. For example, lenders often require borrowers, as a condition for making a loan, to maintain their (i.e., the borrower's) ratio of total liabilities (or long-term debt) to owners' equity below a certain limit. Usually, these debt covenants are written in terms of **net tangible assets,** that is, owners' equity less intangible assets, because intangible assets may have an indeterminate market value if the borrower were forced to liquidate.

Book Value per Share of Common Stock. Book value per share is computed by dividing total common stockholders' equity by the number of common shares **outstanding.** When more than one class of stock is outstanding, total stockholders' equity must be **allocated** among the various classes in accordance with the legal and statutory claims that would be effective in case of liquidation of the company. Because additional classes of stock typically are preferred stock, the usual situation requires allocation based upon the preferential rights of the preferred stock. Liquidation, cumulative, and participating preferences must be included in the computation.

To illustrate a typical allocation, refer to Exhibit 21–1 and assume the **cumulative preferred stock** of WZH Corporation has a liquidation value of $15 per share and that $5,000 of preferred cash dividends were in arrears at December 31, 19B.

Computation of book value per share of common stock at December 31, 19B:

Total stockholders' equity		$329,345
Allocation to preferred stock:		
Liquidation value—5,000 shares @ $15	$75,000	
Cumulative dividends in arrears	5,000	80,000
Allocation to common stock (44,000 shares outstanding)		$249,345

Book value per share of common stock: $249,345 ÷ 44,000 = $5.67

Although often computed, book value per share of common stock has limited usefulness. It has little, if any, correspondence with the market value per share of common stock. A few investors are particularly impressed with stock that has a book value in excess of the market price because this is construed by many to imply a "good" buy; however, under the cost, matching, and comparability principles, the assets are apt to be carried at amounts significantly different from their market value. In fact, under GAAP, they rarely would be reflected in the accounts at more than their market value on a going-concern basis.

Ratios That Measure Operating Results. The ability of an entity to earn a satisfactory income and return on investment (also referred to as ROI) often is viewed as a more important indicator of good financial "health" than a "solid" balance sheet position. Although ratios relating to income are perhaps of more interest to investors than to creditors, the latter must be concerned about the profitability of their borrowers. A creditor may be unwilling to make loans or grant credit for goods supplied if the prospective borrower has dim profit potentials, even though adequate collateral is available. The principal ratios that measure operating results are summarized in Exhibit 21–5.

Profit Margin. The ratio of net income to net sales, generally referred to as the **profit margin,** is widely used as an index of profitability; however, one significant factor related to profitability—investment—is given no consideration in the ratio. To illustrate, assume the accounts of Conway Company showed the following data: net income, $20,000; net sales, $2,000,000; and total assets, $100,000. In this case the profit margin appears to be very low at 1 percent. However, when profit performance is measured by the 20 percent return on total investment, it appears to be satisfactory. Thus, profit margin considered alone is inadequate as a measure of profitability. The profit margin has value primarily for evaluation of trends and for comparison with industry and competitor statistics.

Return on Investment (ROI). Many accountants consider ROI as the single most important ratio because it incorporates the two fundamental factors that are inherent in measuring profitability: (1) earnings and (2) investment. Fundamentally, ROI is computed by dividing **income by investment.** ROI is referred to variously as capital yield, return on assets employed, return on equity, return on capital, and rate of return. ROI has two important applications in business situations:

1. Evaluating proposed capital additions (not discussed herein).[4]
2. Measuring profitability in relation to investment.

As a measure of profitability, ROI may be computed on the basis of either:

1. Owners' equity; that is, income divided by owners' equity.
2. Total investment; that is, income (with interest expense, aftertax, added back) divided by total investment (i.e., liabilities plus owners' equity).

Analysts may compute both ratios and compare them to measure the effect of **financial leverage** (i.e., trading on the equity). The following data are used to illustrate measures of profitability and leverage.

---

[4] For an excellent discussion, see Harold Bierman, Jr., and Seymour Smidt, *The Capital Budgeting Decision* (New York: Macmillan); or James C. Van Horne, *Financial Management and Policy* (Englewood Cliffs, N.J.: Prentice-Hall).

EXHIBIT 21–5: Ratios That Measure Operating Results

Ratio	Formula for Computation	Significance
1. Profit margin.	$\frac{\text{Net income}}{\text{Net sales}}$	Indicates net profitability of each dollar of sales.
2. Return on investment (ROI). *a.* On total investment (i.e., liabilities plus owners' equity)	$\frac{\text{Income plus interest expense (aftertax)}}{\text{Total investment*}}$	Rate earned on **all resources** used. Measures earnings on all investments provided by owners and creditors.
b. On owners' equity.	$\frac{\text{Income}}{\text{Owners' equity}}$	Rate earned on resources provided by owners (excludes creditors). Measures earnings accruing to the owners.
3. Investment turnover.	$\frac{\text{Net sales}}{\text{Average total assets}}$	Indicates efficiency with which total resources are utilized.
4. Financial leverage	Rate of return on owners' equity minus Rate of return on total investment	Reflects the advantage gained by borrowing at a rate that is lower than the rate earned on total investment.
5. Earnings per share (EPS).	$\frac{\text{Income accruing to common stock}}{\text{Common shares outstanding}}$	Profit earned on each share of common stock. Indicates ability to pay dividends and to grow from within. Discussed in Chapter 22, Part B.
6. Price-earnings ratio (the multiple).†	$\frac{\text{Market price per share}}{\text{Earnings per share}}$	The multiple applied to EPS by investors as a guide to the determination of what they are willing to pay for one share of stock.
7. Dividend ratio.†	$\frac{\text{Dividends per share}}{\text{Earnings per share}}$	Measures the proportion of income (before extraordinary items) paid out in dividends.

* Liabilities plus owners' equity.
† Often referred to as "market" ratios.

XY COMPANY

Balance sheet data:	
Total assets	$100,000
Total liabilities	40,000
Stockholders' equity	60,000
Total investment	$100,000
Income statement data:	
Operating income (before interest expense)	$ 20,000
Interest expense	3,200
Pretax income	16,800
Income taxes ($16,800 × 40%)	6,720
Net income	$ 10,080

ROI for XY Company is computed as follows:

1. **Return on owners equity (ROI_o):**

$$ROI_o = \frac{\text{Income*}}{\text{Owners' equity}} = \frac{\$10{,}080}{\$60{,}000} = 16.8\%$$

* Extraordinary items usually are excluded because of their nonrecurring characteristic.

2. **Return on total investment (ROI_t):**

$$ROI_t = \frac{\text{Income + Interest expense (aftertax)}}{\text{Total investment}}$$

$$= \frac{\$10{,}080 + (\$3{,}200 - \$1{,}280)}{\$100{,}000} = \frac{\$12{,}000}{\$100{,}000} = 12.0\%$$

Difference: Financial leverage (16.8% − 12.0%) ... +4.8%

In computing ROI_t, interest expense (net of income tax) is added back to net income because the interest was paid to creditors of the entity. Because the denominator includes the resources provided by both creditors and owners, the numerator must include the return on both types of equities.

Return on total investment (ROI_t) measures the profitability of the total assets available to the business. It indicates the efficiency with which management used the total available resources to earn income.

Return on owners' equity (ROI_o) measures the return that accrues to the stockholders **after** the interest paid to the creditors is deducted. It does not measure the efficiency with which total resources were used, but rather the **residual** return to the owners on their investment in the business.

More on Financial Leverage. Earlier, the concept of financial leverage, sometimes called trading on the equity, was briefly defined. More comprehensively, financial leverage is the effect on ROI of borrowing versus investment by owners. If the interest rate on debt is lower than the rate earned on total investment, financial leverage will be positive; if the interest rate is higher, financial leverage will be negative. Financial leverage can be measured by subtracting ROI_t from ROI_o.

For XY Company (above), the financial leverage effect was +4.8 percent because the ROI_o was greater than the ROI_t. The 4.8 percent positive effect in favor of owners' equity was due to the fact that the company earned a higher rate of return on total assets than the aftertax rate of interest paid for borrowed resources. Had there been no debt, the rate on total investment and the rate on owners' equity would have been the same.

Investment Turnover. This ratio, also called the asset turnover, is computed by dividing net sales by average total assets for the year. It attempts to measure the effectiveness with which management used the total resources at their disposal. It is similar in concept to inventory turnover. However, a company may have high asset turnover, viewed as a favorable condition, in the face of a net loss.

Market Ratios. Different market ratios often are used by investors and analysts to measure the relationship between investment by the stockholder (i.e., the market value of the shares) and the return from the shares (i.e., earnings or dividends). Two market ratios are given in Exhibit 21–5 (ratios 6 and 7).

1. **Price earnings ratio**—Sometimes called the **multiple;** it is used frequently by analysts and investors for evaluating stock price because it relates the earnings of the business to the current market price of the stock. This ratio changes each time the market price of the stock changes. Several years ago, multiples of 20 or more were not unusual; however, multiples in the range of 5 to 10 currently are more common. The multiple generally should be computed on the basis of EPS before extraordinary items. To illustrate, assuming the common stock of WZH Corporation (Exhibit 21–1) is selling at $6.50 per share on December 31, 19B, the multiple would be as follows:

$$\frac{\text{Market price per share, \$6.50}}{\text{EPS, \$0.40}} = 16$$

(i.e., the stock was selling at approximately 16 times the EPS before extraordinary items)

2. **Dividend ratio**—Computed as dividends per share divided by earnings per share; therefore, it measures, on the average, the proportion of earnings paid out as dividends. Because dividends and changes in dividend payout ratios have been shown to possess significant information content to investors, and because dividends are construed to be a reliable indicator of management expectations, this ratio has particular significance as an analytical tool.

USE AND INTERPRETATION OF RATIO ANALYSIS

Ratio analysis of financial statements is used widely as an adjunct to more sophisticated techniques for making investment and credit decisions because ratios communicate some aspects of the economic situation of an entity better than the absolute amounts reported on the financial statements. Empirical studies have demonstrated that the traditional financial ratios are closely associated with the (unobservable) process by which stock prices are formed.[5] This means that the ratios have information content for investors. As one example, financial ratios have been used successfully in prediction models to project whether a business would fail.[6] Thus, it is not surprising that financial and bank lending officers make wide use of ratio analysis in evaluating the future economic prospects of individual companies.

Ratios covering a period of years (as they must to be very useful) represent average conditions;

[5] W. H. Beaver, P. Kettler, and M. Scholes, "The Association between Market Determined and Accounting Determined Risk Measures," *The Accounting Review,* October 1970, pp. 654–82. For an extension of this work, see W. H. Beaver and J. Manegold, "The Association between Market-Determined and Accounting-Determined Measures of Systematic Risk: Some Further Evidence," *Journal of Financial and Quantitative Analysis,* June 1975, pp. 231–84.

[6] W. H. Beaver, "Financial Ratios as Predictors of Failure," *Empirical Research in Accounting: Selected Studies, 1966.* Supplement to *Journal of Accounting Research,* pp. 71–111; E. I. Altman, "Financial Ratios, Discriminant Analysis, and the Prediction of Corporate Bankruptcy," *Journal of Finance,* September 1968, pp. 589–609; and E. B. Deakin, "A Discriminant Analysis of Predictors of Business Failure," *Journal of Accounting Research,* Spring 1972, pp. 167–79.

therefore, they must be interpreted in light of the "smoothing" effect inherent in any average. However, when viewed over an extended period of time, ratios may signal important **turning points,** either favorable or unfavorable, with respect to the future economic prospects for the business. One writer has suggested that the idea of their use may be conveyed by a comparison with the interpretation of a thermometer reading by a doctor—beyond a certain range the fever reading indicates **something** is wrong with the patient, but not exactly what it is. An unfavorable ratio can be thought of as a red flag—the matter should be investigated. However, one ratio or even several ratios, whatever their values, may not convey a clear message. Consequently, a primary problem confronting the statement user relates to the evaluation of a ratio. For example, is it good or bad that the inventory turnover for a company is 12? In determining what constitutes an unfavorable or favorable ratio for a particular business, the following comparisons are suggested:

1. Comparison of the actual ratios for the current year with those of preceding years for the company. Comparisons of selected ratios for the company over a period of 5 to 10 years often are included in the published financial statements.
2. Comparison of the actual ratios for the company with budgeted or standard ratios developed internally by the company. Unfortunately, this kind of comparison, although relevant, seldom is available to external statement users.
3. Comparison of the company's ratios with those of competitors. The published financial reports of competitors provide information that may make this comparison feasible.
4. Comparison of the company's ratios with ratios for the industry in which the company operates. Industry statistics along these lines may be obtained from the following sources:
   a. Industry trade associations—All major industries support one or more trade associations that generally collect and publish financial statistics relating to the industry.
   b. Bureaus of business research at universities—Many of the major universities collect, analyze, and publish a wide range of regional statistics on the surrounding industries and businesses.
   c. Governmental agencies—Agencies that deal directly with business often publish, or have available as a matter of public record, financial information relating to industries and individual companies. The more prominent ones are the U.S. Department of Commerce, the U.S. Department of the Treasury, and the Securities and Exchange Commission, Washington, D.C.
   d. Commercial sources such as
      (1) Robert Morris Associates.
      (2) Dun & Bradstreet.

Despite the wide use of ratio analysis, this technique has a number of inherent limitations. Because of these limitations, ratios must be interpreted with some skepticism. Some of the more important limitations are as follows:

1. Ratios represent average conditions that existed in the **past;** they are historical data that incorporate all of the peculiarities of the past. Also, they are influenced by the latitude available to companies in selecting accounting methods.
2. When the data on which ratios are based are historical book values, they do not reflect either *(a)* price-level effects or *(b)* real economic values.
3. Because the method of computing each ratio is not standardized, the computations (and hence, the results) can be influenced by data selection choices. Except for the EPS ratio, they are not subject to audit.
4. The use of various alternative accounting methods may have a significant effect on ratios. For example, the previous chapters have indicated the significant effects on financial statement amounts of such alternatives as FIFO versus LIFO, straight-line versus accelerated depreciation, and completed contract versus percentage of completion in accounting for long-term construction contracts.
5. Changes in accounting estimates and principles (such as a change from FIFO to LIFO) may significantly affect the ratios for the year of change. Also, to develop data for long-term trends, it may be necessary to remove from the data, or specifically identify, the effects of unusual or nonrecurring items and extraordinary items.
6. Comparisons among companies are difficult because of different operating characteristics such as product lines, methods of operation, size, methods of financing, and geographical location.

In addition, the use of different accounting methods obscures interfirm comparisons.

7. An insidious limitation is that those relying on ratio analysis sometimes overlook the fact that all other investors have the same data available and can also compute the same ratios. Studies have shown that the market very quickly absorbs this information and that, as a result, it is extremely difficult to consistently earn above-average returns on stock investments by relying on publicly available information.[7] Thus, **excessive reliance** on ratio analysis, or any analysis based upon publicly available information, should be practiced with this limitation in mind.

Although the limitations are formidable, ratio analysis is an important technique for financial statement interpretation because ratios capitalize on the fundamental relationships in an entity. However, as we have indicated, the results must be used with care.

[7] For a summary of this evidence, see E. F. Fama, *Foundations of Finance* (New York: Basic Books, 1976), ch. 5.

THE SEARCH FOR ADDITIONAL INFORMATION

An investor should search for information to supplement that provided by the financial statements. Hearsay is hazardous; one should seek objective data concerning the company—its operations, policies, competitive position, the quality of the management, and other nonquantitative information. Brokerage firms and security analysts typically gather and disseminate this type of information. Periodic reports, by listed companies, filed with the SEC are available; they provide considerable information not included in the annual financial statements.

The financial press is a timely source of financial information. Examples of financial publications include *Fortune, Barrons, The Wall Street Journal, Business Week, Forbes,* and various industry publications; such publications are available in most libraries.

Part B: Segment and Interim Reporting

SEGMENT (OR LINE OF BUSINESS) REPORTING

Many large corporations engage in more than one line of business; in fact, even many smaller corporations have diversified their operations into more than one industry. Investors seeking to assess the relative attractiveness of the stock of a diversified company in the past were faced with the difficult task of analyzing company financial reports which reported aggregated data with no information on the performance of its various "lines of business."

To better understand the problem, suppose you are an investor analyzing General Electric Company (GE). GE produces and sells products ranging from light bulbs to household appliances to aircraft engines. Supply and demand for these three product groups (consumer nondurables, consumer durables, and heavy machinery) react differently during good and bad economic times. For example, consumers will continue to buy light bulbs during depressions as well as during prosperous times. To a lesser extent, consumers also must have kitchen ranges to prepare their meals during hard times; however, they probably will continue to use their old ranges longer than during prosperous times. Thus, demand for kitchen ranges is more elastic than demand for light bulbs. The demand for air travel and the concomitant demand for aircraft engines is even more elastic than the demand for light bulbs. Stated differently, these three industrial groups possess different **risk** characteristics. It is reasonable to suppose that investors who know the relative proportions of company resources committed to operations in these (and other) specific industries can make more informed decisions than investors who only know the aggregate data of the company.

The above reasoning is the basis for requiring companies to report **segment data**. The basis is supported by the results of a number of empirical research studies which have indicated that hypothetical investment decisions based on segment data turn out better than decisions based on aggregated data.[8]

In recognition of these circumstances, the FASB first issued *FASB Statement of Financial Accounting Standards No. 14*, "Financial Reporting for Segments of a Business Enterprise," December 1976, which set out the general principles described above. In November 1977, *FASB Statement 18* was issued; it provided that segment information was not required in statements for **interim periods.** *FASB Statement 21,* issued in April 1978, suspended the requirement of reporting segment information by **smaller and closely held** companies.[9] Finally, *FASB Statement 30* (1979) amended *FASB Statement 14* in respect to certain required disclosures.

Reportable Segment Defined

In the context of *FASB Statement 14*, a **reportable segment** is defined by "(a) identifying the individual products or services from which the enterprise derives its revenue, (b) grouping those products and services by industry lines into industry segments . . . , and (c) selecting those industry segments that are significant with respect to the enterprise as a whole."

An industry segment is one which meets **any one** of the following criteria:

a. Its revenue is 10 percent or more of the combined revenue of all segments of the entity.
b. The absolute amount of its operating profit or loss is 10 percent or more of the greater, in absolute amount, of—
  (1) The combined operating **profit** of all industry segments of the entity that did not incur an operating loss, or
  (2) The combined operating **loss** of all industry segments of the entity that did incur an operating loss.
c. Its identifiable assets are 10 percent or more of the combined identifiable assets of all industry segments (of the entity).

[8] For example, see D. W. Collins, "SEC Product-Line Reporting and Market Efficiency," *Journal of Financial Economics*, June 1975, pp. 125–64. Also D. W. Collins and R. Simonds, "SEC Line-of-Business Disclosure and Market Risk Adjustments," *Journal of Accounting Research*, Autumn, 1979, pp. 352–83; and R. Simonds and D. W. Collins, "Line of Business Reporting and Security Prices: An Analysis of an SEC Disclosure Rule: Comment," *The Bell Journal of Economics*, Autumn 1978, pp. 646–58.

[9] *FASB Statement 21* also eliminated the requirement that EPS must be reported by such companies.

SEGMENT REPORTING REQUIREMENTS

FASB Statement 14, as amended by *FASB Statements 18, 21,* and *30*, requires that the company report for **each reportable segment** the following:

a. Segment revenue.
b. Segment operating income or loss.
c. Identifiable segment assets.
d. Other related disclosures.

Segment revenue includes all product and service sales to unaffiliated customers (i.e., customers from outside the enterprise), intersegment sales, and interest on segment trade receivables. It does **not** include interest revenue on loans to other segments.

Segment operating gain or loss is segment revenue (as defined above) less all operating expenses. Operating expenses for a segment include *(a)* operating expenses that are **directly** related to segment revenue and *(b)* operating expenses incurred by the company which can be "allocated on a reasonable basis" among segments for whose benefit those expenses were incurred. **None** of the following can be added or deducted in computing the operating income or loss of a segment: (1) company revenues not derived from a segment, (2) general company expenses, (3) interest expense, (4) income tax, (5) equity in income of unconsolidated subsidiaries or other equity investees, (6) extraordinary items, (7) minority interests in income, and (8) cumulative effect of an accounting change.

Identifiable segment assets include the tangible and intangible identifiable assets of a segment, which are used (1) exclusively by the segment or (2) jointly by two or more segments (allocated on a "reasonable" basis). Asset valuation accounts, such as Allowance for Doubtful Accounts and Accumulated Depreciation, must be included; also, goodwill that represents part of the company's investment in the segment is included. Assets that cannot be included are (1) those used for general company purposes and (2) loans or advances to other segments.

Other related disclosures for each segment include (1) aggregate amount of depreciation, depletion, and amortization expense; (2) amount of capital expenditures during the period (i.e., additions to property, plant, and equipment); (3) the company's equity in the net income and investment in unconsolidated subsidiaries and other equity investees whose operations are vertically integrated with the segment (including disclosure of the geographic area in which that investee operates); and (4) the effect on the segment of all changes in accounting principle.[10]

In addition, *FASB Statement 14* requires companies to report the following three items for each **foreign operation,** if either (1) revenue from foreign operations is 10 percent or more of consolidated revenue or (2) identifiable assets of the entity's foreign operations are 10 percent or more of consolidated total assets:

a. Revenues.
b. Operating profit or loss.
c. Identifiable assets.

Finally, *FASB Statement 30* (par. 6) states that "If 10 percent or more of the revenue of an enterprise is derived from sales to any single customer, that fact and the amount of revenue from each such customer shall be disclosed . . . but the identity of the customer need not be disclosed. . . ." A group of entities under common control, the federal government, a state government, or a local government each is considered as a single customer. Only the industry segments making the sales are disclosed. Data on these three segment groups—**reportable industry segments, foreign operations,** and **major customers**—are intended to provide investors with the data needed to assess the relative risks of diversified companies.

All of the above required information about a segment may be reported in any of the following ways: (1) within the body of the financial statements (with appropriate note disclosure); (2) entirely in notes to the financial statements; or (3) in a separate schedule. Whichever way is selected, the segment disclosures must be an integral part of the financial statements.

Segment Reporting Illustrated

The Appendix following Chapter 24 illustrates an actual segment report by one well-known company. For instructional purposes, a simplified example is presented in Exhibit 21–6; Panel A gives the fact situation assumed, and Panel B illustrates computation of segment information needed to meet the reporting requirements discussed above. Related data are presented for instructional purposes. Observe in Exhibit 21–6 that careful distinctions were maintained among (1) direct segment information; (2) indirect segment information; and (3) general company revenues, expenses, and identifiable assets. The allocations used in the exhibit for indirect segment information were simplified; on this point *FASB Statement 14* merely states that such indirect segment data be identified with reportable segments "on a reasonable basis." Indications are that investors use segment information and find it useful in their decision-making process.[11]

Disposal of a Segment of a Business (Discontinued Operations)

An important issue in segment reporting involves the disposal by a company of a segment of its business. *APB Opinion No. 30,* "Reporting the Results of Operations," provides reporting guidelines for disposal of a segment of a business that is sold, abandoned, spun off, or otherwise disposed. It requires that any loss or gain on disposal, less the applicable income tax effect, be reported separately as a component of income before extraordinary items. For this purpose the *Opinion* defines **segment of a business** as "a component of an entity whose activities represent a separate major line of business or class of customer." A segment may be a subsidiary, division, department, or other part of the entity provided that its assets, results of operations, and activities can be clearly distinguished physically and operationally, for financial reporting purposes, from the other operations of the entity. The *Opinion* does not apply to the disposal of assets incident to the evolution of the entity's business, such as the disposal of a **part** of a division, subsidiary, or line of business, or the phasing out of product lines, changes in services, the disposal of one or more unrelated assets, or changes due to technological improvements.

To account for the disposal of a segment two dates must be carefully identified. The **measurement date** is the date on which the entity formally commits itself to dispose of a segment. The **disposal date** is the closing date of sale of the assets (i.e., when the

---

[10] Vertical integration refers to the complementary nature of a parent and its subsidiaries' product lines whereby one supplies inputs to the other. An example of vertical integration would be General Motors and Libbey-Owens-Ford or Fisher Body. Another example would be American Telephone and Telegraph and Western Electric (which builds the telephones).

[11] For references, see footnote 8.

EXHIBIT 21–6: Segment Reporting

Panel A—Hypothetical Situation:

1. SEG Company sells products in two industries (i.e., two lines of business), designated segment A (lumber industry) and segment B (paper and allied products). The accounting period ends December 31, and the average income tax rate is 40 percent.
2. Selected financial data for 19E, by segment: sales revenue, A—$480,000, B—$320,000; interest revenue, A—$3,000, B—$2,000; investment revenue on equity securities (cost method), $6,000; operating expenses, A—$240,000, B—$75,000, corporate, $100,000 (allocate equally to segments); depreciation expense, A—$48,000, B—$19,000, jointly, $18,000 (allocate to segments A and B in the ratio, 2 to 1), and general company, $4,000; interest expense, $3,000; general company expenses, $150,000; extraordinary gain, $20,000; cumulative effect of change in accounting principle, $10,000 (debit); assets (tangible and intangible), net of allowances and accumulated depreciation and amortization, at December 31, 19E, segment A—$200,000, segment B—$100,000; used jointly by segments A and B in a 2-to-1 ratio, $90,000; and general company assets, $60,000.

Panel B—Computation of Segment Information to Be Included in 19A Financial Reports (based on *FASB Statement 14,* appendix B):

	Segment A		Segment B		Company
Net revenues:					
Sales (direct)		$480,000		$320,000	$800,000
Interest revenue (direct)		3,000		2,000	5,000
Investment revenue (company)					6,000
Total segment revenue		483,000		322,000	
Total company revenue					811,000
Expenses:					
Operating expenses (direct)		240,000		75,000	315,000
Operating expenses (indirect)	$100,000 × ½	50,000	$100,000 × ½	50,000	100,000
Depreciation expense (direct)		48,000		19,000	67,000
Depreciation expense (jointly)	$18,000 × ⅔	12,000	$18,000 × ⅓	6,000	18,000
Depreciation expense (company)					4,000
Interest expense (company)					3,000
Total segment expense (pretax)		(350,000)		(150,000)	
Total company expense					(507,000)
Segment operating income (pretax)		$133,000		$172,000	
General company expenses					(150,000)
Income tax expense ($811,000 − $507,000 − $150,000) × .40					(61,600)
Income before extraordinary items and accounting changes					92,400
Extraordinary gain (net of tax, $8,000)					12,000
Change in accounting principle (net of tax, $4,000)					(6,000)
Net income					$ 98,400
Segment identifiable assets, tangible and intangible (net of allowances, depreciation, and amortization), at December 31, 19E:					
Used directly		$200,000		$100,000	$300,000
Used jointly	$90,000 × ⅔	60,000	$90,000 × ⅓	30,000	90,000
General company assets					60,000
Total assets at 12/31/19E					$450,000

Note: The company operates in two industries: A, which involves lumber, and B, which involves paper and allied products. Revenue by segment includes sales to unaffiliated customers and intersegment sales. Segment operating income is revenue less operating expenses but does not include general company expenses, interest expense, income tax expense, extraordinary items, and accounting change effects. Total company revenue ($811,000) is more than total segment revenue, by $6,000, because of general company revenue on equity investments (cost method) of $6,000. Total company expense of $718,600 was more than total segment expense of $500,000, because of general company expenses (depreciation, $4,000, interest expense, $3,000, general corporate expense, $150,000, and income tax expense, $61,600). There were no foreign sales nor sales to a single unaffiliated customer or government agency in excess of 10 percent of total revenue.

segment is transferred) or the date that operations cease if the disposal is by abandonment. The measurement date typically precedes the disposal date; however, they may coincide.

On the **measurement date** an estimate must be made of the **total loss or gain** on disposal of the segment (net of income tax effects). The total estimate must include separate estimates of the gain or loss on (1) the segment assets and (2) segment operations between the measurement and disposal dates. When a loss is estimated it is recorded (accrued) on the measurement date; when a gain is estimated, it is not recognized until an actual gain is realized, which ordinarily is the disposal date.

EXHIBIT 21–7: Disposal of a Segment

INTERNATIONAL PAPER COMPANY
Consolidated Statement of
Earnings and Retained Earnings
($ millions)

	Year Ended December 31	
	1979	**1978**
Earnings from continuing operations	$347.8	$223.7
Earnings from discontinued operations prior to sale (less applicable income taxes) (Note 3)	7.5	10.5
Gain on sale of General Crude Oil (less applicable income taxes)	170.0	
Earnings from discontinued operations	177.5	10.5
Net earnings	$525.3	$234.2

Note 3: *Discontinued Operations*—On July 6, 1979, the Company sold to Mobil Oil Corporation substantially all of the oil and natural gas assets of General Crude Oil Company, a wholly owned subsidiary, for $802 million. The Company received $763 million in cash and Mobile assumed $39 million in existing obligations resulting in a pre-tax gain of $248.4 million, and after-tax earnings of $170 million, or $3.55 per common share.

The results of operations for this segment (exclusive of the gain on the sale) are included in the Consolidated Statement of Earnings and Retained Earnings under the caption "Earnings from Discontinued Operations" and include:

($ millions)

	1979	**1978**
Net sales and other income	$ 71.7	$133.9
Costs and expenses	(47.1)	(91.0)
Interest expense	(5.0)	(13.8)
Interest on advances(1)	(7.1)	(10.9)
Provision for income taxes	(5.0)	(7.7)
Earnings from discontinued operations	$ 7.5	$ 10.5

(1) Represents interest expense on advances from the Company, which supported the discontinued oil and natural gas operations.

Source: AICPA, *Accounting Trends & Techniques, 1980,* (New York, 1980) p. 307.

Exhibit 21–7 illustrates reporting the disposal of a segment of the business. It is an excerpt from the 1979 annual report of the International Paper Company.

In Exhibit 21–7, observe that in **1978,** International Paper reported "Earnings from discontinued operations" (prior to sale, less applicable income taxes) of $10.5 million to distinguish those earnings from "Earnings from continuing operations" (i.e., $223.7 million). Then, in **1979,** the company reported two items under Discontinued Operations: (1) earnings from discontinued operations of $7.5 million from January 1 to the disposal date (July 6) and (2) gain on sale of $170 million, which was recognized on the disposal date (July 6). In this actual situation, the **measurement date** may have occurred in 1978, as evidenced by the separate reporting in that year of earnings from discontinued operations.

To comply with *APB Opinion 30,* International Paper had to estimate, as of the **measurement date,** the ultimate outcome of the disposal (i.e., gain, loss, or break-even). If the company had estimated a loss, that estimated loss would have been reported in 1978. The absence of such an amount on the 1978 income statement implies that International Paper estimated the ultimate outcome would be a gain or a break-even situation. As it turned out, the final result was a gain of $170 million, which was reported when the disposal actually occurred in 1979, as explained in Note 3. "Earnings from discontinued operations" (i.e., $7.5 million in 1979 and $10.5 million in 1978) should be traced from the last item in the note to the tabular portion of the income statement.

INTERIM REPORTING

The focus throughout this book has been on annual financial statements. This focus reflects the time-period assumption discussed in Chapter 1, which is based on investors' need for timely financial information. Actually, annual data are not very timely because investors cannot wait until shortly after the end of each fiscal year to make all their investment decisions. They need more timely information. Interim data, usually on a quarterly basis, often are presented by companies to help meet this need. Moreover, empirical research has demonstrated that stock prices reflect the impact of quarterly accounting information.[12]

Because of the wide diversity that had developed in applying GAAP, which focuses on annual financial reports, *APB Opinion No. 28,* "Interim Financial Reporting," was issued in May 1973. That *Opinion* does **not** require interim financial statements; rather, its primary purpose is to provide guidelines for their preparation. Interim reports may be monthly, quarterly, or semiannual (usually they are quarterly) and may take the form of either complete financial statements or only summarized financial data. They may be prepared for each interim period or on a cumulative year-to-date basis, or both.

BASIC NATURE OF INTERIM PERIODS

Preparing interim reports presents inherent difficulties because of a number of unavoidable factors. These include seasonality of revenues, major costs that occur only in one interim period but benefit other interim periods within the same fiscal year, seasonality of production activities, extraordinary items and accounting changes which occur in one interim period but not others, selection of appropriate income tax rates for each interim period, and LIFO inventory liquidation during one or more interim periods but which are restored before the end of the fiscal year. Because of these inherent problems, two opposing views of the nature of an interim period exist, viz:

1. **Discrete view**—each interim period is viewed as a basic accounting and reporting period, which stands separate and alone without considering it as a part of a longer (i.e., the annual) fiscal period. Under this view, revenue and expense recognition, accruals, and deferrals for the interim period follow the same principles and procedures as for an annual period, and there would be no "interim-period" allocations. Thus, an expense incurred in one interim period usually would not be allocated to other interim periods.
2. **Integral-part view**—each interim period is viewed as an inseparable part of the annual fiscal period. Under this view, revenue and expense recognition, deferrals, and accruals are affected by judgments made at the end of each interim period about the results of operations for the remainder of the fiscal year. Thus, an expense incurred in one interim period may be **allocated** among other interim periods within the fiscal year.

APB Opinion 28 states that "each interim period should be viewed primarily as an integral part of the annual period." However, the *Opinion* makes some practical concessions on this point.

GUIDELINES FOR PREPARING INTERIM FINANCIAL REPORTS

APB Opinion 28 gives the following guidelines for preparing interim reports:

1. In general, the accounting principles and practices used by the company in preparing its annual financial statements should be used for interim reports, with certain modifications (discussed below).
2. Revenue from products and services sold should be recognized as earned during the interim period on the same basis as followed for the annual period.
3. Costs and expenses for interim periods are classified as:
   a. Costs that are directly associated with interim revenue (discussed below).
   b. All other costs and expenses that are **not** directly associated with interim revenue (discussed below).

Costs Directly Associated with Revenue

Costs directly associated with revenue, such as cost of goods sold, wages, salaries, fringe benefits, and warranties, should be expensed in the interim period in which the related revenue is recognized with the following exceptions or disclosures:

a. Use of the gross margin method (discussed in Chapter 9) for computing cost of goods sold must be disclosed.

b. If LIFO is used and LIFO inventory is liquidated

[12] R. G. May, "The Influence of Quarterly Earnings Announcements on Investor Decisions as Reflected in Common Stock Price Changes," *Empirical Research in Accounting: Selected Studies, 1971.* Supplement to *Journal of Accounting Research,* pp. 119–63; P. Brown and J. W. Kennelly, "The Information Content of Quarterly Earnings: An Extension and Some Further Evidence," *Journal of Business,* July 1972, pp. 403–15; and G. J. Foster, "Quarterly Accounting Data: Time Series Properties and Predictive-Ability Results," *The Accounting Review,* January 1977, pp. 1–21.

EXHIBIT 21–8: Interim Report (income statement only illustrated)

Panel A—Hypothetical Situation:

1. Interim Company is preparing its summarized interim financial report for the first quarter ended March 31, 19H.
2. Selected financial data relating to the first quarter were as follows: sales of products and services, $500,000; interest revenue, $1,000; extraordinary loss, $15,000; accounting error from 19G, $6,000 (correction is a credit with income tax effect); cost of goods sold, $241,000; operational assets, at cost, $480,000 (10-year estimated remaining life, no residual value, straight-line depreciation); salaries and wages, $89,000; inventory decline, LCM (deemed temporary), $4,000; advertising expenditures, $18,000 (benefits first and second quarters approximately equally); estimated 19H annual property tax, $12,000; annual contribution to United Fund, $6,000; shipping supplies, (beginning inventory, $3,000, supplies purchased, $8,000, ending inventory by count, $4,000); unusual loss, $4,000; estimated 19H average income tax rate, 40 percent.

Panel B—First Quarter Report, with Explanations:

Income Statement
For the Quarter Ended March 31, 19H

	Explanation	Amount
Revenues:		
Sales of products and services	Recognize in full as earned	$500,000
Interest revenue	Recognize as earned on accrual basis	1,000
Total revenues		501,000
Expenses:		
Cost of goods sold	Directly related to interim revenue	241,000
Salaries and wages	Directly related to interim operations, accrual basis	89,000
Depreciation expense	Allocate on time basis, $480,000 × 3/120	12,000
Inventory decline, LCM	Not recognized because deemed temporary	-0-
Advertising expense	Allocate on benefit basis, $18,000 ÷ 2 (defer half to next interim period)	9,000
Contributions	Recognize when incurred, not related to operations nor allocable reasonably	6,000
Property tax expense	Accrual basis, $12,000 × ¼ (time basis)	3,000
Shipping expense	Accrual basis, $3,000 + $8,000 − $4,000	7,000
Unusual loss	Recognized when it occurred, not allocated	4,000
Income tax expense	Accrue on basis of estimated average tax rate ($501,000 − $371,000) × .40	52,000
Total expenses		423,000
Income before extraordinary item		78,000
Extraordinary loss (net of income tax of $6,000)		9,000
Net income		$ 69,000

Earnings per share (30,000 common shares outstanding):

Income before extraordinary items ($78,000 ÷ 30,000 shares)	$2.60
Extraordinary loss ($9,000 ÷ 30,000 shares)	(.30)
Net income ($69,000 ÷ 30,000 shares)	$2.30

Accounting error: Report as prior period adjustment of January 1, 19H, balance of retained earnings: $6,000 × .60 = $3,600 (credit).

during an interim period, and it is expected to be restored by year-end, cost of goods sold for the interim period should be debited for the anticipated replacement cost of the number of units liquidated and an estimated liability is credited.

c. Inventory declines, unless temporary, should not be deferred to future interim periods; recovery in later interim periods should be recognized as gains, but not in excess of the previously recognized losses.

Costs Not Directly Associated with Revenue

All costs not directly associated with revenue should be accounted and reported for interim reporting as follows:

a. Recognize as expense in the interim period in which incurred or allocate among interim periods based on an estimate of time expired, benefit received, or activity associated with the periods.
b. Arbitrary allocation of such costs should not be made; if any costs cannot be reasonably allocated, they should be assigned to the interim period in which incurred.
c. Gains and losses that arise in any interim period, similar to those that would not be deferred at year-end, should be recognized in the interim period in which they arise.
d. Income tax expense for each interim period should be based on an estimate of the annual rate as made at the end of each quarter. Revision of the rate for subsequent interim periods is treated as a change in estimate.

Unusual or nonrecurring items and extraordinary items should be recognized in the interim period in which they occur. Similarly, contingent losses not directly associated with revenue and the related liabilities should be recognized in the interim period in which they occur. Accounting changes are accounted for and reported in essentially the same manner as discussed in Chapter 20 for annual periods.

Disclosure of Summarized Interim Financial Data

When a company reports summarized interim information, the following data should be reported, as a minimum:

a. Sales, income taxes, and net income.
b. Disposal of a segment of a business and extraordinary, unusual, or infrequently occurring items.
c. Primary and fully diluted earnings per share (EPS).
d. Seasonal revenue, costs, or expenses.
e. Significant changes in estimates or provisions for income taxes.
f. Changes in accounting principles or estimates.
g. Contingent items.
h. Significant changes in financial position.

Interim Reporting Illustrated

For instructional purposes, a simplified example is presented in Exhibit 21–8; Panel A gives the hypothetical situation assumed, and Panel B illustrates the interim income statement, with explanations, needed to meet the reporting requirements of *APB Opinion 28.* Observe in the exhibit that careful distinctions were maintained between costs directly related to interim revenue and all other costs not directly related to interim revenue.

The Appendix following Chapter 24 illustrates the interim (quarterly) financial data reported by The Quaker Oats Company and Subsidiaries.

QUESTIONS

PART A

1. Why is the past financial track record of a company important to statement users? What is meant by a *turning point?*

2. Explain why financial analysts and others, in analyzing financial statements, examine the auditors' report and the summary of accounting policies.

3. Explain why the notes to the financial statements should be read carefully in the process of analyzing financial statements. Why are long-term summaries considered important to the statement user?

4. Distinguish between vertical and horizontal analyses. Briefly explain the importance of each.

5. What is meant by *ratio analysis?* Why is it important in the analysis of financial statements?

6. Distinguish between the *current ratio* and the *quick ratio.* What purpose does each serve?

7. Current assets and current liabilities for two companies with the same amount of working capital are summarized below. Evaluate their relative liquidity positions.

	X Company	Y Company
Current assets	$200,000	$900,000
Current liabilities	100,000	800,000
Working capital	$100,000	$100,000

8. X Corporation has an accounts receivable turnover of 15; interpret this figure. What would be the age of the receivables? What does it reveal?

9. Y Corporation has an inventory turnover of 9; interpret this figure. What would be the average number of days of supply?

10. Explain and illustrate the effect of leverage.

11. Compute and explain the meaning of the *book value per share* of common stock of the Craft Manufacturing Company assuming the following data are available:

Preferred stock, par $100, 6%, cumulative, nonparticipating, 200 shares issued and outstanding, liquidation value is par	$ 20,000
Common stock, par value $10, 10,000 shares issued and outstanding	100,000
Retained earnings	7,000

(Three years dividends in arrears on preferred stock including current year.)

12. Explain the circumstances where a company has debt financing and the leverage factor is *(a)* positive, *(b)* negative, and *(c)* zero.

13. Explain the *ROI concept.* Why is it a fundamental measure of profitability?

14. What is meant by *the multiple?* Why is it considered important?

15. What are the principal limitations in using ratios?

PART B

16. What critical variable is the focus of segment reporting? That is, about what characteristics of an entity are segment data supposed to inform investors? Why is this variable important?

17. For which three reportable areas are segment data required to be reported? For what logical reason were these areas identified as segments for separate segment reporting?

18. Contrast the *discrete period* and *integral part approaches* to interim reporting. Toward which approach did *APB Opinion 28* lean?

19. How is *income tax expense* accounted for under the interim reporting rules of *APB Opinion 28?* Does this approach to interim reporting represent the discrete or the integral-part approach? Explain. How are *extraordinary items* reported? Does this approach represent the discrete or the integral-part approach? Explain.

DECISION CASE 21–1

Drift Corporation needs additional funds for plant expansion. The board of directors is considering obtaining the funds by issuing additional short-term notes, long-term bonds, preferred stock, or common stock.

Required:

1. What primary factors should the board of directors consider in selecting the method of financing plant expansion?
2. One member of the board of directors suggests that the corporation should maximize the impact of financial leverage by borrowing additional funds.
   a. Explain how financial leverage affects EPS of common stock.
   b. Explain how a change in income tax rates affects financial leverage.
   c. Under what circumstances should a corporation seek financial leverage to a substantial degree?
3. Two specific proposals under consideration by the board of directors are the issue of 12% subordinated income bonds (secured only by the general credit of the issuer with interest paid each year only if there is income equal to the interest amount) or 9% cumulative, nonparticipating, nonvoting preferred stock, callable at par. In discussing the impact of the two alternatives on the debt to stockholders' equity ratio, one member of the board of directors stated that the resulting debt-to-equity ratio would be the same under either alternative because the income bonds and preferred stock

should be reported in the same balance sheet classification. What are the arguments *(a)* for and *(b)* against using the same balance sheet classification in reporting the income bonds and preferred stock?

(AICPA adapted)

DECISION CASE 21–2

Accounting personnel at Moore Enterprises, Inc., have prided themselves on how soon after the close of each quarter the interim financial statements are ready for distribution. A newly hired assistant controller has suggested an even faster reporting procedure whereby instead of preparing formal statements, photocopies of the worksheet could be issued. The assistant controller points out this would avoid having to prepare statements from the worksheet and eliminate the time required to type and proofread them.

Required:
Comment on the feasibility of the proposal of the new assistant controller. If, as to some recipients and as to some times, the copying idea affords some advantages or causes some problems, identify these and provide supporting explanations.

DECISION CASE 21–3

In the context of interim reporting, items may be (A) recognized in the interim statements of the current interim period, (B) recognized in the current interim period but require special disclosure, (C) deferred in their entirety (i.e., not recognized until some later interim period, or not at all), or (D) amortized or accrued (i.e., recognized partly in the current interim period and partly in subsequent interim periods). A number of items are listed below which require a decision as to how they should be incorporated on interim statements. You are to match the letters given above with the numbered items given below to indicate how each item should be incorporated on the interim statements.

1. Salaries allocable to services rendered during the current period.
2. Inventories estimated by use of the gross margin method.
3. Temporary declines in market value of inventories.
4. Short-term stock investment gains from recoveries of market value (not in excess of previously recognized market declines).
5. Materials and wages allocable to products sold this period.
6. Costs benefiting two or more interim periods.
7. Increase in gross margin due to liquidation of a layer of LIFO base inventory expected to be replenished by year-end.
8. Quantity discounts allowed to customers based upon annual volume of their purchases.
9. Contingencies and other uncertainties which may affect fairness of presentation.
10. Income tax on income of first quarter where total income for the first quarter only puts company in "normal tax" bracket; subsequent operations are expected to be sufficiently profitable that by end of second quarter and thereafter taxable income of company will be in a higher bracket.

DECISION CASE 21–4

The management of most medium-sized and large corporations routinely prepare earnings forecasts for their own internal use. At the same time, relatively few corporations disclose these predictions to anyone outside the company.

Required:
Assume that you are a member of the top management of a large, publicly held corporation. Why would you favor or be opposed to disclosure of the company's earnings forecasts? Whichever position you take, if you find others in the top-management group take an opposing view, what reasons would you expect them to give in support of their viewpoint?

EXERCISES

PART A: EXERCISES 21–1 to 21–8

Exercise 21–1

Fox Trading Company income statements (condensed) for two quarters are shown below.

	First Quarter	Second Quarter
Gross sales	$221,000	$242,000
Returns	(1,000)	(2,000)
	220,000	240,000
Cost of goods sold	(110,000)	(130,000)
Gross margin	110,000	110,000
Expenses:		
Selling	(62,000)	(63,000)
Administrative (incl. income taxes)	(30,000)	(31,000)
Interest (net of interest revenue)	(3,000)	2,000
Net income before EO items	15,000	18,000
EO items (net of tax)	5,000	(3,000)
Net income	$ 20,000	$ 15,000
Shares of common stock outstanding	10,000	10,000

Required:

1. Prepare a quarterly multiple-step comparative income statement including a vertical percentage analysis (round to nearest percent). Use net sales as the base amount.
2. Prepare a single-step income statement including horizontal percentage analysis (round to nearest percent).

Exercise 21–2

The following data were taken from the financial statements of the Walker Company. Based on these data compute *(a)* the working capital, *(b)* the current ratio, and *(c)* the acid-test ratio (carry to nearest 1 percent). Evaluate each change.

	19A	19B
Current assets:		
Cash	$ 30,000	$ 40,000
Short-term investments	10,000	10,000
Trade accounts receivable (net)	60,000	70,000
Notes receivable	6,000	2,000
Inventory	150,000	170,000
Prepaid expenses	4,000	2,000
Current liabilities	90,000	120,000

Exercise 21–3

The condensed financial data given below were taken from the annual financial statements of Tatum Corporation:

(Relates to Exercise 21–3)

	19A	19B	19C
Current assets (incl. inventory)	$ 200,000	$ 250,000	$ 270,000
Current liabilities	150,000	180,000	130,000
Cash sales	800,000	780,000	820,000
Credit sales	200,000	280,000	250,000
Cost of goods sold	560,000	600,000	600,000
Inventory (ending)	120,000	140,000	100,000
Quick assets	80,000	90,000	85,000
Accounts receivable (net)	60,000	58,000	64,000
Total assets (net)	1,000,000	1,200,000	1,400,000

Required:

1. Based on the above data, calculate the following for 19B and 19C; use 365 days for computation purposes. (round to one decimal place):
   a. Current ratio.
   b. Acid-test ratio.
   c. Working capital to total assets.
   d. Receivable turnover.
   e. Age of receivables.
   f. Merchandise inventory turnover.
   g. Days' supply in inventory.
   h. Working capital turnover.
2. Evaluate the overall results of the computations including trends.

Exercise 21–4

The following data were taken from the financial statements of Boston Company:

	19A	19B	19C
Sales—cash	$190,000	$200,000	$220,000
Sales—credit	100,000	120,000	130,000
Average receivables	25,000	34,000	50,000
Average inventory	60,000	70,000	80,000
Cost of goods sold	180,000	190,000	200,000

Required:
What conclusions may be drawn relative to *(a)* inventories and *(b)* receivables? (Use 300 business days in year; credit terms are 90 business days; show computations).

Exercise 21–5

The balance sheets for two similar companies reflected the following:

	Company A	Company B
Current liabilities	$ 30,000	$100,000
Long-term liabilities	70,000	300,000
Stockholders' equity:		
Common stock, par $5	220,000	46,000
Preferred stock, par $10	100,000	20,000
Contributed capital in excess of par, common	20,000	4,000
Retained earnings	60,000	30,000
Net income, included in retained earnings (less taxes, 45%)	49,500	13,000

Required:
1. Compute the three equity ratios listed in the chapter that measure equity position and the leverage factor for each company.
2. Interpret and evaluate each situation. The average interest rate for both companies is 10% (on total liabilities).

Exercise 21–6

Supreme Manufacturing Corporation balance sheet showed the following as of December 31, 19A:

Total liabilities	$100,000
Pref. stock, 7%, par value $50 per share	$200,000
Common stock, nopar, 30,000 shares outstanding	360,000
Contrib. capital in excess of par, pref. stock	40,000
Retained earnings	80,000

Required:
Compute the book value per share of common stock assuming:

1. None of the preferred shares has been issued.
2. Preferred is noncumulative and nonparticipating; liquidation preference value of preferred is par.
3. Preferred is cumulative and nonparticipating (three years' dividends in arrears including current year); liquidation value of preferred is par.
4. Preferred has a liquidation value of $60 per share and is noncumulative and nonparticipating.
5. Preferred has a liquidation value of $60 per share and is noncumulative and nonparticipating, and the Retained Earnings account shows a *deficit* of $30,000, instead of the $80,000 credit balance shown above.

Exercise 21–7

The financial statements for Kellog Corporation for 19C reported complete comparative statements. The following data were taken therefrom:

(Relates to Exercise 21–7)

	19A	19B	19C
Sales revenue	$12,000,000	$13,000,000	$14,000,000
Net income	100,000	120,000	100,000
Interest expense, net of income tax	10,000	12,000	9,000
Stockholders' equity	1,400,000	1,450,000	1,460,000
Shares of common stock outstanding	20,000	20,000	24,000
Total assets	3,500,000	3,500,000	3,700,000
Market value per share	$66.00	$72.00	$45.00

Required:
1. Based on the above financial data, compute the following ratios for 19B and 19C: *(a)* profit margin; *(b)* ROI, total investment; *(c)* ROI, owners' equity; *(d)* the leverage factor; *(e)* EPS; and *(f)* price-earnings ratio. (Carry computations to two decimal places.)
2. As an investor in the common stock of Kellog, which

ratio would you prefer as a single measure of profitability? Why?

3. Explain any significant trends that appear to be developing.

Exercise 21–8

The following data relate to the Fast Printing Company:

(Relates to Exercise 21–8)

	19A	19B	19C	19D	19E
Net income	$ 12,000	$ 15,000	$ 25,000	$ 30,000	$ 40,000
Interest expense (net of tax)	1,000	1,200	2,000	2,200	3,000
Sales revenue	120,000	140,000	180,000	230,000	260,000
Total assets	50,000	72,000	110,000	160,000	190,000
Total liabilities	25,000	30,000	40,000	70,000	80,000

Required:

Evaluate the trend of the company in terms of the *(a)* profit margin, *(b)* ROI, and *(c)* leverage factor. Round to nearest percent.

PART B: EXERCISES 21–9 to 21–11

Exercise 21–9

Refer to the annual financial report of The Quaker Oats Company and Subsidiaries for the year ended June 30, 1981 (Appendix following Chapter 24). Respond to the following requirements related to segment reporting (round to nearest percent):

1. List the five industry segments used by the company.
2. For 1981, which segment reported the highest amount of identifiable assets? What was its percent of the total?
3. For 1981, which segment reported the lowest operating income? What was its percent of the "Total Existing Business"?
4. For 1981, what percent of total sales attributable to the "Total Existing Business" was in Canada?
5. During 1981, Quaker sold some of its operations. In what country were these operations?

Exercise 21–10

Watts Company has engaged you to prepare its interim financial statements for the first and second quarters of its current fiscal year. The complication is that during the second quarter, Watts changed depreciation methods from SYD to straight line. However, the change was made to be effective at the beginning of the current year, which is permitted by GAAP.

Summarized data are presented below, on the old (SYD) basis:

	First Quarter	Second Quarter
Income statement:		
Sales revenue	$100,000	$92,000
Depreciation expense (SYD)	(3,500)	(3,300)
Other expenses	(91,500)	(89,700)
Net income (loss)	$ 5,000	$ (1,000)
Balance sheet:		
Operational assets	$ 36,750	$36,750
Accumulated depreciation (SYD)	(14,000)	(17,300)
	$ 22,750	$19,450

Straight-line depreciation prior to the current year was $6,000.

Required:

Assuming no income tax effects result from the change, present the summarized and unclassified financial statement items shown above as they would appear in the second quarter interim report with the first quarter also reported for comparison. Report the catch-up adjustment due to the accounting change as a first quarter item (essentially this is the pro forma presentation). Ignore footnotes.

Exercise 21–11

Refer to the annual financial report of The Quaker Oats Company and Subsidiaries for the year ended June 30, 1981 (Appendix following Chapter 24). Respond to the following requirements related to interim reporting:

1. What interim periods are reported on by this company?
2. Did the auditors' report cover the interim reports?
3. How often were dividends declared?
4. What period reported the highest EPS in 1981? In 1980?
5. Rank the 1981 quarters in order of *(a)* net sales in dollars and *(b)* net income in dollars and also as a percent of net sales. Use *1* to indicate the highest ranking and *4* to indicate the lowest ranking.

PROBLEMS

PART A: PROBLEMS 21–1 to 21–6

Problem 21–1

The following data were taken from the annual financial statements of Lynch Corporation:

(Relates to Problem 21–1)

	19A	19B	19C
Current assets:			
Cash	$ 10,000	$ 5,000	$ 8,000
Short-term investments	45,000	30,000	20,000
Trade receivables	180,000	170,000	190,000
Less: Allowance for doubtful accounts	(5,000)	(6,000)	(8,000)
Notes receivable (nontrade)	110,000	125,000	100,000
Inventories	298,000	355,000	387,000
Prepaid expenses	12,000	11,000	13,000
Total	$ 650,000	$ 690,000	$ 710,000
Current liabilities:			
Trade payables	$ 70,000	$ 158,000	$ 196,000
Notes payable	90,000	72,000	60,000
Accrued wages payable	72,000	46,000	52,000
Income taxes payable	19,000	23,000	24,000
Deferred rent revenue	2,000	2,000	2,000
Accrued liabilities	17,000	19,000	16,000
Total	$ 270,000	$ 320,000	$ 350,000
Additional data:			
Cash sales	$3,300,000	$3,500,000	$3,200,000
Credit sales	1,500,000	1,700,000	1,800,000
Cost of goods sold	2,500,000	2,900,000	2,800,000
Total assets (net)	6,600,000	7,200,000	7,200,000

Required:

1. Compute the ratios listed in the chapter for each year to measure current position and include a vertical analysis of current assets. In the vertical analysis, round percents to the nearest percent and in the ratio analysis, round the ratios to one decimal place.
2. Evaluate the current position as indicated by the statements and the ratios. What additional information would you need to buttress your evaluation?

Problem 21–2

The financial statements of Davis Manufacturing Company for a three-year period reported the following:

(Relates to Problem 21–2)

	19A	19B	19C
Total assets	$2,000,000	$2,040,000	$1,940,000
Total current assets	368,000	450,000	480,000
Total current liabilities	230,000	150,000	150,000
Operational assets (net)	1,248,000	1,257,600	1,260,000
Total liabilities	1,090,000	1,110,000	900,000
Common stock (par value $100)	600,000	600,000	700,000
Retained earnings	310,000	330,000	340,000
Sales revenue (net)	6,600,000	7,000,000	7,100,000
Net income (after tax)	50,000	70,000	40,000
Interest expense (net of tax)	34,000	38,000	30,000

Required (round to nearest percents, or if a decimal, to two places):

1. Based on the above data, calculate the following ratios to measure the current position for each year.
   a. Current ratio.
   b. Working capital turnover.
   Evaluate the current position. What additional information do you need to evaluate adequately the current position? Explain.
2. Based on the above data, calculate the following ratios to measure the equity position:
   a. Creditors' equity to total assets.
   b. Book value per share of common stock.
   Evaluate the equity position. What additional information do you need to evaluate adequately the equity position? Explain.
3. Based on the above data, calculate the following ratios to measure operating results:
   a. Profit margin.
   b. ROI on total investment.
   c. ROI on owners' equity.
4. Evaluate the operating results. What additional information do you need to evaluate adequately operating results? Explain.
5. Evaluate the financial leverage factor.

Problem 21–3

The following annual data were taken from the records of Tricky Trading Corporation:

(Relates to Problem 21–3)

	19A	19B	19C	19D	19E
Sales revenue	$400,000	$420,000	$450,000	$440,000	$490,000
Net income	15,000	16,000	20,000	5,000	40,000
Total assets (i.e., investment)	200,000*	220,000	230,000	240,000	250,000
Owners' equity	100,000*	110,000	120,000	115,000	140,000
Market price per common share	60	62	55	25	60
Dividends per common share	4	4	4	1	5
Capital stock outstanding (shares)	4,000	4,000	4,000	3,900	3,800
Interest expense (net of tax)	4,000	4,500	4,600	5,000	4,100

* The beginning balance was the same as this year-end balance.

Required (round ratios and percents to two decimal places):

1. Compute the ratios listed in the chapter to measure operating results.
2. Compute the price-earnings and dividend ratios.
3. Evaluate the profitability of the company; pinpoint indicated strengths and weaknesses. What additional information do you need? Explain.
4. Compute the financial leverage factor.

Problem 21–4

The following summarized data were taken from the published statements of two companies that are being compared:

($000)	Company A	Company B
Sales revenue	$3,000	$ 9,000
Cost of goods sold	1,900	6,942
Operating expenses	400	1,600
Interest expense (net of tax)	8	108
Extraordinary (loss), after tax	(22)	550
Income tax (on income before extraordinary item)	240	300
Current assets	1,000	4,000
Operational assets	4,500	19,000
Accumulated depreciation	1,500	7,000
Investments, long term	400	100
Other assets	600	7,900
Current liabilities	900	2,000
Long-term liabilities	100	1,800
Capital stock ($10 par value)	3,000	18,000
Retained earnings	1,000	2,200
Market value per common share	$16.75	$1.50

Compute the one ratio that would best answer each of the following questions (show computations). Justify your choice.

a. Which company probably has the better current position?
b. Which company has the better working capital turnover?
c. Which company is earning the better rate on total investment? On owners' equity?
d. Which company has the advantage in "trading on the equity"?
e. Which company has the better profit margin?
f. Which company has the higher book value per share of common stock?
g. In your overall opinion which stock is the better buy?

Problem 21–5

Alabama Corporation is considering building a second plant at a cost of $600,000. The management is considering two alternatives to obtain the funds: *(a)* sell additional common stock or *(b)* issue $600,000, five-year bonds payable at 8% interest. The management believes that the bonds can be sold at par (for $600,000) and the stock at $10 per share.

The balance sheet (before the new financing) reflected the following:

Liabilities	None
Common stock, nopar	$200,000
Contributed capital in excess of par	100,000
Retained earnings	120,000
Average income for past several years (net of tax)	30,000

The average income tax rate is 45%. Average dividends per share have been 50 cents per share per year. Expected increase in pretax income (excluding interest expense) from the new plant, $100,000 per year.

Required:

1. Prepare an analysis to show *(a)* expected income after the addition, *(b)* cash flows from the company to prospective owners of the new capital, and *(c)* the leverage advantage or disadvantage to the present shareholders of issuing the bonds to obtain the financing.
2. What are the principal arguments for and against issuing the bonds (as opposed to selling the common stock)?

Problem 21–6

Each independent item described below deals with some aspect of the analysis of financial statements. For each item, give the answer and show computations.

1. In its most recent fiscal year, Jax Store bought goods for inventory at a cost of $2,000,000; cost of goods sold for the year amounted to $2,200,000, and year-end inventory was $400,000. What was inventory turnover for the year?
2. At year-end 19A, Royal Company's net accounts receivable were $500,000; at year-end 19B, net receivables were $100,000 higher. Net cash sales for 19B were $200,000. Accounts receivable turnover for 19B was five times. What were Royal's total net sales for 19B?
3. Information concerning product A is as follows:

Sales	$300,000
Variable costs	240,000
Fixed costs	40,000

Assuming that sales of product A increased by 20%, what is net income from product A?

4. For 19C, gross margin of Dumas Company was $97,000 and cost of goods manufactured was $340,000. Beginning inventories of goods in process and finished goods were $28,000 and $45,000, respectively, while ending inventories were $38,000 and $52,000. What were sales of Dumas Company for 19C?
5. Companies A and B began the latest year with identical account balances and their revenues for the year are identical in amount except that A has a higher ratio of cash to noncash expenses. If cash balances of both companies increase only as a result of operations (i.e., no additional financing and no dividends during the year and all sales are for cash), ending cash balance of A as compared to B will be (select one):
a. Higher. *b.* The same. *c.* Lower. *d.* Indeterminate from the data given.
6. The current ratio of E Company is 2 to 1. A transaction reduces the ratio. Compare the *working capital* before this transaction *(X)* to working capital after the transaction *(Y)* (select one).
a. $X > Y$. *b.* $X = Y$. *c.* $X < Y$. *d.* Cannot be determined.
7. D corporation wrote off a $100 uncollectible account receivable against the $1,200 credit balance in its allowance account. Compare the current ratio before the write-off *(X)* with the current ratio after the write-off *(Y)* (select one).
a. $X > Y$. *b.* $X = Y$. *c.* $X < Y$. *d.* Cannot be determined.
8. Trail, Inc., has a current ratio of .65 to 1. A cash dividend declared last year is paid this year. What are the effects of the dividend payment on the current ratio and working capital, respectively? (Select one.)
a. Rise and decline. *b.* Rise and no effect. *c.* Decline and no effect. *d.* No effect on either.
9. Selected information from the accounting records of Vigor Company is as follows (all sales were on credit):

Net accounts receivable at 12/31/19B	$ 900,000
Net accounts receivable at 12/31/19C	$1,000,000
Accounts receivable turnover for 19C	5 to 1
Inventory at 12/31/19B	$1,100,000
Inventory at 12/31/19C	$1,200,000
Inventory turnover for 19C	4 to 1

What was Vigor's gross margin for 19C?

10. Refer to 9. Assuming a business year consisting of 300 days, what was the number of days' sales in average receivables for 19C and the number of days' sales in average inventory for 19C, respectively? (Select one.)
a. 30 and 40. *b.* 60 and 60. *c.* 60 and 75. *d.* 63 and 77.

(AICPA adapted)

PART B: PROBLEMS 21–7 to 21–11

Problem 21–7

Century Company, a diversified manufacturing company, had four separate operating divisions engaged in the manufacture of products in each of the following areas: food products, health aids, textiles, and office equipment.

Financial data for the two years ended December 31, 19B, and 19A, are presented below:

(Relates to Problem 21–7)

	Net Sales		Cost of Goods Sold		Operating Expenses	
	19B	**19A**	**19B**	**19A**	**19B**	**19A**
Food products	$3,500,000	$3,000,000	$2,400,000	$1,800,000	$ 550,000	$ 275,000
Health aids	2,000,000	1,270,000	1,100,000	700,000	300,000	125,000
Textiles	1,580,000	1,400,000	500,000	900,000	200,000	150,000
Office equipment ..	920,000	1,330,000	800,000	1,000,000	650,000	750,000
	$8,000,000	$7,000,000	$4,800,000	$4,400,000	$1,700,000	$1,300,000

On January 1, 19B, Century adopted a plan to sell the assets and product line of the office equipment division and expected to realize a gain on this disposal. On September 1, 19B, the division's assets and product line were sold for $2,100,000 cash resulting in a gain of $640,000 (exclusive of operations during the phase-out period).

The company's textiles division had six manufacturing plants which produced a variety of textile products. In April 19B, the company sold one of these plants and realized a gain of $130,000. After the sale, the operations at the plant that was sold were transferred to the remaining five textile plants which the company continued to operate.

In August 19B, the main warehouse of the food products division, located on the banks of the Bayer River, was flooded when the river overflowed. The resulting damage of $420,000 is not included in the financial data given above. Historical records indicate that the Bayer River normally overflows every four to five years causing flood damage to adjacent property.

For the two years ended December 31, 19B, and 19A, the company had interest revenue earned on investments of $70,000 and $40,000, respectively.

For the two years ended December 31, 19B, and 19A, the company's net income was $960,000 and $670,000, respectively.

Income tax expense for each of the two years should be computed at a rate of 40%.

Required:
Prepare in proper form a comparative statement of income of Century Company for the two years ended December 31, 19B, and December 31, 19A. (AICPA adapted)

Problem 21–8

Interim financial reporting has become an important topic in accounting. There has been considerable discussion as to the proper method of reporting results of operations at interim dates. Accordingly, the Accounting Principles Board issued *Opinion 28* clarifying some aspects of interim financial reporting.

Required:
1. Discuss how revenue should be recognized at interim dates and specifically how revenue should be recognized for industries subject to large seasonal fluctuations in revenue and for long-term contracts using the percentage-of-completion method at annual reporting dates.
2. Discuss how product and period costs should be recognized at interim dates. Also discuss how inventory and cost of goods sold may be afforded special accounting treatment at interim dates. Definitional note: **Product costs** are expenses directly attributable to the production of goods and services. **Period costs** are expenses not directly associated with the production of a particular good or service.
3. Discuss how the income tax expense is computed and reported in interim financial statements.

(AICPA adapted)

Problem 21–9

Refer to the annual financial report of The Quaker Oats Company and Subsidiaries for the year ended June 30, 1981 (Appendix following Chapter 24). Respond to each of the following requirements related to segment reporting (round to the nearest percent):

1. List the five industry segments used by the company.
2. What are the principal products in the Toys segment?
3. Prepare a vertical percentage analysis of segment data for 1981 and 1980 for operating income based upon "Total Existing Businesses." Identify any major shifts indicated. As an interested investor, what concerns would you have?

4. Prepare an industry segment analysis for 1981 and 1980 of *(a)* the ratio of operating income to sales revenue and *(b)* the ratio of operating income to the year-end balance of identifiable assets. Give the interpretation of each ratio, identify any shifts, and indicate your concerns as an interested investor.
5. Were sales among industry segments large in amount? Were such sales separately disclosed?
6. What items were not included in computing operating income?
7. Are the operations of Toddy Business Group included in the 1981 and prior years' segment reports? How is this subsidiary being accounted for?

Problem 21–10

Refer to the annual financial report of The Quaker Oats Company and The Subsidiaries for the year ended June 30, 1981 (Appendix following Chapter 24). Respond to each of the following requirements relating to interim reporting:

1. For what periods were interim data reported in the statements?
2. In what 1981 quarterly periods were the market prices of the company's stock at the highest, and the lowest?
3. Prepare a graph to reflect seasonal trends. Scale time on the horizontal axis and dollars on the vertical axis to reflect sales revenue, cost of goods sold, and net income for 1980 and 1981. Does the graph identify any potential problems for the interested investor?
4. Complete the following matrix for 1981 to reflect a vertical analysis of the results of operations (round to the nearest percent):

(Relates to Problem 21–10)

	1981 Quarters				Year	
Item	**First**	**Second**	**Third**	**Fourth**	**1981**	**1980**
Net sales	100%	100%	100%	100%	100%	100%
Cost of goods sold						
Gross margin						
Expenses						
Net income						

Another important objective of this problem is to familiarize you with actual financial statements and to give you confidence that your knowledge of accounting enables you to understand a major portion of even very complex financial disclosures.

Finally, this provides a comprehensive review of practically everything you have studied in the 24 chapters in this book.

Instructions:

Go to your college library and study the published annual reports of corporations. In particular, read as many annual reports as it takes to locate at least *two* disclosures of each of the 20 types listed below. Some types of disclosures will be contained in almost every financial report you read; others will be hard to find. But don't stop until you have found the 40 required disclosures, or have read a minimum of 12 annual reports, whichever occurs first.

As you study the reports, make notes of *(a)* interesting disclosures and *(b)* questions you may have about the interpretation of specific disclosures. Do not hesitate to be critical of what you find, particularly as to the effectiveness of the notes for communication to statement users (i.e., are they sufficiently clear and understandable as written?). Come to the class meeting for which this problem is assigned prepared to discuss what you have learned and to raise questions. Types of disclosures (find two examples of each):

1. Principles of consolidation.
2. Equity method for long-term investments.
3. Cost (LCM) for both short-term and long-term investments. Note different ways of accounting for market losses.

Problem 21–11

This assignment focuses on financial statement analysis, with special emphasis on the disclosure notes to be found in current financial statements. Intermediate accounting typically does not deal comprehensively with note disclosures as a separate topic; instead, the text has listed disclosure requirements of GAAP, and illustrated some, for specific topical areas. This is an opportunity to assess the practical implementation of the reporting principle of accounting.

4. At least *three* of the ratios discussed in the chapter.
5. Inventory method: LIFO, FIFO, weighted average, or other. Also look for the use of LCM for inventories.
6. Operational assets: useful lives, depreciation method, and amount of depreciation.
7. Long-term debt: interest rates, maturity dates, conversion privileges, call options of issuer, and security agreements.
8. Contingent losses and contingent gains.
9. Income taxes: allocation, and investment tax credit.

10. Leases: capital leases—try airlines because they lease a major portion of their assets; sales type and direct-financing leases—try computer companies; operating leases; and disclosures by both lessor and lessee.
11. Pensions.
12. Treasury stock: cost method, and par value method (you may not be able to locate both of these).
13. Accounting changes: estimate, principle, reporting entity, and error (you may not be able to find all of these).
14. Prior period adjustment—look for restated financial statements of prior year.
15. Stock option plans: compensatory, and noncompensatory.
16. SCFP; working capital basis and cash basis or cash plus short-term investments basis.
17. Goodwill, including amortization.
18. Extraordinary items.
19. Segment reports.
20. Interim reports.

22

Income Recognition and Earnings per Share (EPS)

PRECEDING CHAPTERS have discussed income recognition and earnings per share (EPS), but not separately and in detail. For example, income recognition was discussed first in Chapter 1, Part B, under the headings Revenue Principle and Matching Principle. Likewise, EPS was discussed briefly in Chapter 3, which reviewed the income statement.

The purpose of this chapter is to discuss these two topics more substantively. The chapter is subdivided as follows:

Part A—Income Recognition
Part B—Earnings per Share (EPS)

Part A: Income Recognition

BACKGROUND

Income recognition is one of the most pervasive problems in accounting because it embodies all the revenues, expenses, gains, and losses of an entity during a period, in addition to affecting the resulting asset, liability, and owners' equity balances reported at the end of the period. The numerous lawsuits that have involved claims about misstated income suggest the pervasiveness of the problem of income recognition. For example, the primary issues in the *Ultramares, Bar Chris, Yale Express, National Student Marketing,* and *Equity Funding* lawsuits involved issues of income recognition.

The purposes of this part of the chapter are to discuss *(a)* methods of revenue recognition, *(b)* expense recognition, and *(c)* application of income recognition concepts. These topics are discussed under the following headings:[1]

Basic Principles of Income Recognition
Methods of Revenue Recognition
Expense Recognition
Recognition of Gains and Losses
Overview of Income Recognition Applications

BASIC PRINCIPLES OF INCOME RECOGNITION

Income recognition basically involves the recognition of revenues and expenses because the net of

[1] Because previous chapters discussed the specific display and reporting requirements of each area in detail, they are not emphasized in this chapter. You may find it useful to refer back to those earlier discussions.

these two (i.e., revenues minus expenses) is defined as income. The **revenue principle** defines revenues and governs the timing and measurement of revenues to be recognized in an accounting period. The **matching principle** governs the timing and measurement of expenses to be recognized in the period. These two principles comprise the **theoretical foundation** of this part of the chapter.

Revenue Principle

The revenue principle states that revenue should be recognized (i.e., recorded) when *(a)* an exchange transaction involving the transfer of goods or services has occurred and *(b)* the earning process essentially is complete. In most situations, both of these conditions are met at the time of the sale of products and/or services. In other situations, determination of when the revenue process essentially is complete is difficult. Because most of the illustrations used in preceding chapters assumed that revenue is recognized at the time of sale, the discussions to follow focus on those situations which require special revenue recognition procedures.

Matching Principle

The matching principle states that for any period for which income is reported, revenues should be determined according to the revenue principle; then the expenses incurred in generating the revenue of the period should be recognized for that period.[2] The essence of the matching principle is that, as revenues are earned, certain assets are consumed (e.g., supplies) or sold (e.g., inventory) and services are used (e.g., salaries); the cost of those assets and services used up are recognized and reported as expense of the period during which the related revenue is recognized.

REVENUE RECOGNITION

FASB Concepts Statement 3 (par. 63) defines revenue as follows:

> Revenues are inflows or other enhancements of assets of an entity or settlements of its liabilities (or a combination of both) during a period from delivering or producing goods, rendering services, or other activities that constitute the entity's ongoing major or central operations.

[2] Recognition of gains and losses is discussed in a later section, Recognition of Gains and Losses.

The definition of revenue given above identifies two kinds of revenue—product sales and service sales. Traditionally, product sales have comprised the majority of business activity in the United States; however, in recent years, service sales have surpassed product sales in dollar volume. As a result, the accounting profession currently is developing more definitive accounting guidelines for service sales. These guidelines are suggested in an FASB "Invitation to Comment" entitled *Accounting for Certain Service Transactions.* In respect to product sales, the FASB issued *Statement of Financial Accounting Standards No. 48,* "Revenue Recognition when Right of Return Exists," June 1981. This section discusses accounting methods for recognition of revenue from *(a)* product sales and *(b)* service sales.

Revenue Recognition for Product Sales

Sales Method. The sales method is used to recognize sales revenue at the time of sale. Under this method, sales revenue is recognized when *(a)* a completed exchange transaction transfers effective ownership of the merchandise, *(b)* ultimate collection of the sales price is reasonably certain, and *(c)* the expenses related to the transaction are reliably determinable in the period of sale. These specifications satisfy the two general criteria given above under the heading, Revenue Principle.

For retail sales, such as those made by a grocery store or drugstore, cash usually is collected when products are transferred to the customer and the revenue earning process is completed at that time. Likewise, in many cases in which sales are made on FOB shipping point terms, the revenue earning process is completed when the products are removed from the seller's place of business by the common carrier. In many other cases, however, it is difficult to determine reliably when revenue has been earned and, therefore, should be recorded.

For example, when sales are made on FOB destination terms, the revenue earning process is not completed until the products are delivered to the purchaser's place of business. Technically, revenue should not be recognized before ownership to the products passes at that time. However, as a practical matter, sellers customarily recognize revenue when the products sold leave the seller's place of business.

Other difficulties in applying the sales method are not resolved so easily. For example, companies in many industries sell their products under agreements (either contractual or as a matter of industry or company practice) in which the risks and rewards of ownership do not fully pass from seller to buyer at the time of sale. That is, the seller retains some of these risks or rewards subsequent to the sale. These sales agreements take many different forms. Five different types of agreements, along with the industries in which they are common, are discussed below to illustrate the problem of identifying the appropriate time to recognize revenue from product sales.[3]

Agreements in Which Sales Returns Are Permitted by the Seller. FASB, *Statement of Financial Accounting Standards No. 48,* "Revenue Recognition When Right of Return Exists," June 1981 (pars. 6 and 7), specifies the following:

> If an enterprise sells its product but gives the buyer the right to return the product, revenue from the sales transaction shall be recognized at time of sale only if **all** of the following conditions are met:
>
> *a.* The seller's price to the buyer is substantially fixed or determinable at the date of sale.
> *b.* The buyer has paid the seller, or the buyer is obligated to pay the seller and the obligation is not contingent on resale of the product.
> *c.* The buyer's obligation to the seller would not be changed in the event of theft or physical destruction or damage of the product.
> *d.* The buyer acquiring the product for resale has economic substance apart from that provided by the seller.
> *e.* The seller does not have significant obligations for future performance to directly bring about resale of the product by the buyer.
> *f.* The amount of future returns can be reasonably estimated.
>
> Sales revenue and cost of sales that are not recognized at time of sale because the foregoing conditions are not met shall be recognized either when the return privilege has substantially expired or if those conditions subsequently are met, whichever occurs first.
>
> If sales revenue is recognized because the conditions of [the preceding] paragraph are met, any costs or losses that may be expected in connection with any returns shall be accrued in accordance with FASB Statement No. 5, *Accounting for Contingencies.* Sales revenue and cost of sales reported in the income statement shall be reduced to reflect estimated returns.

In the **record and tape industry,** manufacturers often sell products to wholesalers under agreements which permit the retailer to return products directly to the manufacturer. Returns of sales range from 15 percent to 30 percent, but for a given manufacturer, they are relatively stable and usually can be estimated reliably. For this reason, most record and tape manufacturers recognize revenue and estimated returns in the period of sale, under the **sales method.**

In the **food industry,** perishables, such as bakery products, usually are sold with the right to return stale or excess items. One way to account for such sales returns is to record, at the time of sale, an accrued amount of sales returns by debiting Sales Returns and crediting Allowance for Sales Returns, which is a contra account to Accounts Receivable. Usually, however, sales returns in the food industry are low, and most manufacturers record returns as they occur rather than providing an allowance for sales returns. They record sales revenue as sales are made, that is, under the **sales method.**

Agreements in Which Manufacturers Provide Financing for Dealers and Distributors. Some manufacturers of high-unit-cost items sell their products (e.g., **mobile homes, farm machinery, trucks, and boats**) to retailers under so-called "floor" plans in which the manufacturer guarantees amounts payable to financial institutions for loans they have made to the retailer. Thus, if the retailer cannot sell the products and cannot pay the loans, the manufacturer may grant significant price allowances to boost the retailer's sales, or in other cases, grant refunds or other concessions for products the retailer returns to the manufacturer. In such situations, the factors contributing to the uncertainty of the realization of sales revenue by the manufacturer (i.e., economic recession and changes in consumer preferences) may be beyond the control of the manufacturer. Such a situation may cause the estimated expenses related to sales to be less reliable than if those expenses were due to internal factors, such as the manufactur-

[3] The examples used in the first four types of agreements discussed are based upon AICPA, Accounting Standards Executive Committee, *Statement of Position 75–1, Revenue Recognition When Right of Return Exists* (1975).

er's quality control procedures (discussed below in conjunction with sales subject to warranties). Whenever the uncertainty of the realization of revenue is so great as to render estimates of revenue or the related expenses unreliable, revenue should be recognized by a manufacturer only after the dealer makes sales to ultimate consumers. Usually, however, these uncertainties are not so great, and manufacturers recognize revenue as sales are made to dealers and distributors under the **sales method.** At the time of sale, the seller recognizes estimated sales returns and other related expenses. FASB, *Statement of Financial Accounting Standards No. 49,* "Accounting for Product Financing Arrangements" June 1981 (par. 8.a), states that for special cases in which:

> A sponsor sells a product to another entity and, in a related transaction, agrees to repurchase the product . . . , the sponsor shall record a liability at the time the proceeds are received from the other entity to the extent that the product is covered by the financing arrangement. **The sponsor shall not record the transaction as a sale and shall not remove the covered product from its balance sheet.**[4] [Emphasis added.]

Agreements in Which Manufacturers Provide Warranties. Most manufacturers of **appliances and auto tires** sell their products to independent distributors, or in some cases directly to retailers, subject to product guarantees or warranties. The relative magnitude of warranty expenses is determined largely by the quality control procedures of the manufacturer; consequently, manufacturers can estimate warranty expenses reliably. This reliability supports application of the **sales method** of revenue recognition.[5] Accounting for estimated warranty expense was discussed in Chapter 10.

Agreements in Which the Purchaser Has Unlimited Right of Return. Under some sales agreements in the **publishing, toy, and sporting goods industries,** the retailer is given the unlimited right to return the product to the manufacturer for a full refund. In the publishing industry, for example, returns of sales may be as high as 60 percent for paperback books and as high as 25 percent for hardback books. Some of these sales, in substance, may be **consignments** rather than sales of the products involved.

Under a formal consignment arrangement, the seller (often a manufacturer) retains title to the product until the retailer sells the product to the ultimate consumer. Therefore, when the goods are transferred from the manufacturer to the retailer, the manufacturer records a debit to Consignment-Out, an inventory account, and a credit to Inventory for the same amount; this treatment avoids recognition of revenue at the time of consignment. Then, when the retailer sells the products to ultimate consumers, the manufacturer recognizes revenue (actually gross margin) by *(a)* debiting Accounts Receivable for the final sale amount; *(b)* crediting Consignment-Out for its previous debit balance, which reflected the cost of inventory consigned to the retailer; and *(c)* crediting Gross Margin on Consignment Sales for the excess.[6]

Lease Agreements That Are in Substance Long-Term Credit Sales of the Leased Asset. According to *Fortune,* August 27, 1979, pp. 66–68, "Although the numbers are elusive, the big dollars in leasing . . . are going into data processing equipment, railroad rolling stock, trucks, and aircraft." To satisfy this demand, an industry comprised of industrial lessors, such as GATX Leasing, Tiger Financial Services, and leasing divisions of the major banks, has emerged. Many of the leases are of the **operating** type, which are mere rental agreements under which the **lessor recognizes revenue as the lessee pays the rent.**

The **sales method** of revenue recognition is applied to sales-type leases (discussed in Chapter 19); that is, at inception of a sales-type lease, the lessor debits Lease Receivable and credits Sales Revenue as though the lessor had actually sold the leased asset to the lessee. Under GAAP, a sales-type lease is construed to represent a completed sale transaction. In effect, sales-type leases transfer from the lessor to the lessee the essential risks and rewards of ownership. Consequently, lessors with sales-type leases recognize sales revenue at the inception of

[4] In this quotation, "sponsor" refers to the entity seeking to finance a product to a dealer or distributor pending its future use or resale.

[5] Occasionally, such warranty expenses turn out to be much higher than prior estimates (e.g., recalls of automobiles); this situation requires prospective treatment of the expenses as a change in accounting estimate (actually a realization of expenses that differs from prior estimates); isolated instances do not invalidate use of the sales method for recognizing revenue.

[6] Consignment accounting usually is discussed in detail in a subsequent accounting course.

the lease. Also, they recognize interest revenue on the lease receivable as it accrues during the lease term.

Certain sales in which the seller leases **back** the asset sold are **not** construed by GAAP to represent sales and, therefore, are not accounted for by the sales method. If the seller-lessee is in the same economic position after the sale-and-leaseback as before, no revenue should be recognized at the time of the sale. Instead, any gain or loss on the sale is recognized ratably over the term of the lease, often as an adjustment of depreciation expense, if a capital lease, or as an adjustment of rental expense, if an operating lease.[7] Sale-and-leaseback transactions were discussed in Chapter 19.

Revenue Recognition at Times Other than the Point of Sale

Four alternative methods of revenue recognition, designed to accommodate situations in which revenue is earned at a time other than the point of sale, are discussed below. The methods discussed are divided into two categories:

1. Revenue recognized **prior** to the sale:
   a. Percentage-of-completion method.
   b. Production method.
2. Revenue recognized **after** the sale:
   a. Installment method.
   b. Cost recovery method.

Recognizing Revenue prior to the Sale

Percentage-of-Completion Method. This method is appropriate for certain long-term construction contracts that extend over several accounting periods. In such cases, the revenue recognition methods used are known as **percentage of completion** and **completed contract** (discussed in Chapter 9).

Under the percentage-of-completion method, revenue is recognized as construction progresses (on the basis of costs incurred) to attain a contemporaneous matching of revenues and expenses. Under current GAAP, the percentage-of-completion method can be used when reliable estimates of completion percentages are possible and ultimate collection of the contract price is reasonably certain.

Most companies engaged in long-term construction use the percentage-of-completion method. During 1979, 88 companies included in *Accounting Trends & Techniques, 1980* (table 3–15) used the percentage-of-completion method, while only 11 companies used the completed contract method. Often, most companies within an industry use the same method. For example, in its 1979 annual report, Westinghouse Electric Corporation stated (p. 31), "The percentage-of-completion method of accounting is used for nuclear steam supply system orders with durations generally in excess of five years and certain construction projects where this method of accounting is consistent with industry practices." RCA Corporation also used the percentage-of-completion method during 1979.

Production Method. The **production method** is similar to the percentage-of-completion method. Often, the production method is used for cost-plus-fixed-fee contracts (e.g., the contract price is actual costs incurred plus a "profit" of 10 percent of such costs), in which revenue is recognized on the basis of **production;** that is, prorated portions of the fixed fee are recorded as earned before the project is completed in a manner similar to that used for the percentage-of-completion method. An example of use of the production method appeared in the 1979 annual report of Honeywell, Inc., which stated (p. 33), "Revenue under cost reimbursement-type contracts is recorded as cost is incurred. . . ."

Revenue Recognized after the Sale

Installment Method. Under the **installment method,** revenue is recognized as cash is collected rather than at the time of sale. Under current GAAP, the installment method is used only when the sales method, or another GAAP method, is not appropriate because of the absence of reasonable assurance that the entire sale price will be collected, or the related expenses cannot be determined reliably in the period of sale. These conditions indicate that the earning process is not essentially completed at the point of sale. The installment method has very limited application under GAAP. For instance, it is used to account for sales of real estate in which the down payment is relatively low (less than approximately 25

---

[7] However, when the market value of the asset at the time of the sale-and-leaseback transaction is less than its book value, the seller-lessee should recognize this loss at that time (*FASB Statement 13,* par. 32).

percent of the total sale price) and ultimate collection of the remainder is subject to considerable doubt. However, in most cases the seller can estimate bad debts and other expenses (such as warranties) reliably and, thus, must apply the sales method. The installment method is discussed in most advanced accounting courses.

Cost Recovery Method. The **cost recovery method** sometimes is called the sunk cost method because all of the related costs incurred (i.e., the sunk costs) must be recovered before any revenue or gain is recognized. The cost recovery method should be used only for highly speculative transactions in which the ultimate realization of revenue or gain is completely unpredictable. For example, an investor may purchase bonds for which the interest has been in default for a number of years (referred to as purchasing the bonds "flat"). Usually, the price of such bonds is a small fraction of their maturity amount because of the low probability of realization of the principal and the interest revenue.

Under the cost recovery method, collections of interest would not be recognized as revenue until the original investment cost is fully recovered; collections subsequent to this point would be recognized in full as revenue or gain. The cost recovery method is used by creditors for certain troubled debt restructurings in which the book value of the creditor's receivable at the date of restructure exceeds the total cash payments to be made by the debtor after the date of restructure (discussed in Chapter 17, Part C).

Revenue Recognition for Service Sales

This section reviews the four different methods of revenue recognition for **service sales:** (1) specific performance; (2) proportional performance; (3) completed performance;[8] and (4) collection.

Specific Performance Method. The **specific performance method** is used to account for service revenue that is earned by performing a single act. For example, a real estate broker earns sales commission revenue upon consummation of a real estate transaction; a dentist earns dental service revenue upon completion of an operation to remove a tooth; and a laundry earns laundry service revenue upon completion of the laundering process.

FASB, *Statement of Financial Accounting Standards No. 45,* "Accounting for Franchise Fee Revenue" March 1981, deals with a special example of service sales, franchises, and prescribes the specific performance method to account for franchise fee revenue, which the franchisor earns by selling a franchise to the franchisee. Often, it is difficult to determine the point at which the franchisor has "substantially performed" the service required to earn franchise fee revenue. In this regard, *FASB Statement 45* (par. 5) states:

> Franchise fee revenue from an individual franchise sale ordinarily shall be recognized, with an appropriate provision for estimated uncollectible amounts, when all material services or conditions relating to the sale have been substantially performed or satisfied by the franchisor. Substantial performance for the franchisor means that *(a)* the franchisor has no remaining obligation or intent . . . to refund any cash received . . . *(b)* substantially all of the initial services[9] of the franchisor required by the franchise agreement have been performed, and *(c)* no other material conditions or obligations related to the determination of substantial performance exist. . . . The commencement of operations by the franchisee shall be presumed to be the earliest point at which substantial performance has occurred.

Proportional Performance Method. The **proportional performance method** is used to account for

---

[8] This section on service sales revenue is based in part upon FASB, *Invitation to Comment—Accounting for Certain Service Transactions,* October 1978.

[9] FASB, *Statement of Financial Accounting Standards No. 45,* "Accounting for Franchise Fee Revenue," March 1981, appendix A, defines *initial service* as follows:

> Common provisions of a franchise agreement in which the franchisor usually will agree to provide a variety of services and advice to the franchisee, such as the following:
>
> *a.* Assistance in the selection of a site.
> *b.* Assistance in obtaining facilities, including related financing and architectural and engineering services.
> *c.* Assistance in advertising, either for the individual franchisee or as part of a general program.
> *d.* Training of the franchisee's personnel.
> *e.* Preparation and distribution of manuals and similar material concerning operations, administration, and record keeping.
> *f.* Bookkeeping and advisory services, including setting up the franchisee's records and advising the franchisee about income, real estate, and other taxes or about local regulations affecting the franchisee's business.
> *g.* Inspection, testing, and other quality control programs.

service revenue that is earned by more than one performance act.[10] Under this method, such revenue should be recognized based upon the proportional performance of each act. The proportional performance method of accounting for service revenue is similar to the percentage-of-completion and production methods (discussed above). Proportional measurement of the service revenue is applied differently for different types of service transactions, viz:

1. **Similar performance acts**—Recognize an equal amount of service revenue for each such act. Example: Processing of monthly mortgage payments by a mortgage banker.
2. **Dissimilar performance acts**—Recognize service revenue in proportion to the seller's direct costs to perform each act.[11] Example: Providing lessons, examinations, and grading by a correspondence school.
3. **Similar acts with a fixed period for performance**—Recognize service revenue by the straight-line method over the fixed period unless another method is more appropriate in the circumstances. Example: Providing maintenance services on equipment for a fixed periodic fee.

Completed Performance Method. The **completed performance method** is used to account for service revenue earned by performing a series of similar or dissimilar performance acts, the final act of which is so important in relation to the service transaction taken as a whole that service revenue can be considered earned only after the final act occurs. Example: Packing, loading, transporting, and delivery of freight by a trucking company which earns service revenue only after delivery of the freight.

Collection Method. Under the collection method, revenue is recognized when cash is collected. The collection method is used to account for service revenue when the uncertainty is so high, or the estimates of expenses related to the revenues are so unreliable, as to render meaningless the measurement of income.

[10] The proportional performance method should be used only if performance of the service extends beyond one accounting period.

[11] If the direct cost of each act cannot be measured reliably, the total service sales revenue should be prorated to the various acts by the relative sales value method. If sales values cannot be identified with each act, the straight-line method to measure proportional performance should be used as a last resort.

EXPENSE RECOGNITION

FASB Concepts Statement 3 (par. 65) defines expenses as follows:

> Expenses are outflows or other using up of assets or incurrences of liabilities (or a combination of both) during a period from delivering or producing goods, rendering services, or carrying out other activities that constitute the entity's ongoing major or central operations.

After the revenue of the accounting period has been measured and recognized in accordance with the revenue principle, the matching principle is applied to measure and recognize the expenses of that period as the second step in the process of income recognition (the last remaining step involves the recognition of gains and losses). For this purpose, expenses can be divided into two categories: *(a)* expenses that are directly related to the sales of products or services during the period and *(b)* expenses not directly related to the sales of products or services during the period.[12] This section discusses the recognition of both types of expenses.

Expenses Directly Related to Sales of Products or Services

Expenses Directly Related to the Sales of Products. Expenses **directly** related to the sales of products during the period usually include the following:

1. Costs of materials and labor to manufacture, or the cost to purchase, inventory that is sold during the period (i.e., cost of goods sold).
2. Selling expenses, such as sales commissions, salaries, rent, and shipping costs.
3. Warranty expense on products sold.

Under the matching principle, expenses that are directly related to the sales of products should be recognized as expense when the related sales revenue is recognized. For accounting purposes, certain expenses are difficult to classify in terms of the closeness of their relationship with sales revenue. For example, the reason for advertising and research and development (R&D) expenditures is to enhance the

[12] This distinction also is made in AICPA, *APB Opinion No. 28,* "Interim Financial Reporting" (New York, May 1973), which was discussed in Chapter 21.

marketability of a company's products; however, it is difficult to establish a direct causal link between those expenditures and specific revenues. Consequently, the allocation of such costs usually would be quite subjective, and for this reason, GAAP requires that such costs be expensed as incurred.[13]

Expenses Directly Related to the Sales of Services. Expenses directly related to the sales of services can be classified as follows:

1. **Initial direct costs**—costs that are directly associated with *(a)* negotiating and *(b)* consummating service transactions. They include commissions, legal fees, salespersons' compensation other than commissions, and nonsales employees' compensation that is applicable to negotiating and consummating service transactions.
2. **Direct costs**—costs that have a clearly identifiable causal effect on service sales. Examples include the cost of repair parts and service labor included as part of a service contract.

All **initial direct costs** and **direct costs** should be recognized as expense at the time the related service revenue is recognized under the **specific performance** and **completed performance methods** to attain a contemporaneous matching of revenues and expenses.[14] Thus, initial direct costs and direct costs that are incurred prior to the recognition of revenue from performance of the service should be deferred as prepayments and expensed when the related service revenue is recognized.

For service revenue recognized under the **proportional performance method, initial direct costs** should be expensed as the related service revenue is recognized. However, **direct costs** should be expensed as incurred because of the high correlation between the amount of direct costs incurred and the service revenue recognized under the proportional performance method.

For service revenue recognized under the **collection method,** all initial direct costs and direct costs should be expensed as incurred.

[13] *FASB Statement 2* specifically requires that most R&D costs be expensed as incurred.

[14] FASB, *Invitation to Comment—Accounting for Certain Service Transactions,* October 1978.

Expenses *Not* Directly Related to Sales of Products or Services

Expenses not directly related to the sales of products or services include certain types of advertising expense, compensation that is applicable to the time spent in negotiating product or service transactions that are **not** consummated, and general administrative expenses. Because no objective basis exists for relating such indirect expenses to product or service sales revenue, they should be expensed as they are incurred.

Exhibit 22–1 presents an overview of accounting for service revenues and expenses.

RECOGNITION OF GAINS AND LOSSES

FASB Concepts Statement 3 (pars. 67–68) defines gains and losses as follows (emphasis added):

> **Gains** are increases in [owners'] equity (net assets) from peripheral or incidental transactions of an entity and from all other transactions and other events and circumstances affecting the entity during a period except those that result from revenues or investments by owners.
>
> **Losses** are decreases in [owners'] equity (net assets) from peripheral or incidental transactions of an entity and from all other transactions and other events and circumstances affecting the entity during a period except those that result from expenses or distributions to owners.

Gains and losses result from **peripheral** or **incidental** transactions, events, and circumstances; therefore, they are distinguished from revenues and expenses. **Most gains and losses are recognized when the related transaction is completed.** For example, gains and losses from *(a)* disposal of operational assets, *(b)* sale of investments, *(c)* early extinguishment of debt, and *(d)* restructure of troubled debt are recognized in the specific entry made to record the completed transaction. For example, an entry to record the disposal of a tract of land for cash would reflect a debit to Cash, a credit to Land (for its recorded cost), and a debit to Loss, or Credit to gain, on Disposal.

Estimated **losses,** but **not gains,** are recognized prior to their ultimate outcome. For example, **unrealized** losses on *(a)* write-downs of short-term investments to market value below cost, *(b)* disposal of a segment of the business, *(c)* pending litigation, and

EXHIBIT 22–1: Overview of Accounting for Service Revenues and Expenses

Service Revenue Treatment		Cost Treatment		
Method (Treatment)	**Criteria**	**Initial Direct Costs**	**Direct Costs***	**Indirect Costs**
Specific performance	Performance consists of a single act.	Debited to expense when revenues are recognized.	Debited to expense when revenues are recognized.	Debited to expense as incurred.
Proportional performance	Performance consists of more than one act.	Allocated over the term services are provided in proportion to recognition of service revenue.	Debited to expense as incurred.	Debited to expense as incurred.
Completed performance	Performance occurs on completion of final act because of its significance.†	Debited to expense when revenues are recognized.	Debited to expense when revenues are recognized.	Debited to expense as incurred.
Collection	Revenue realization significantly uncertain.	Debited to expense as incurred.	Debited to expense as incurred.	Debited to expense as incurred.

* Assuming direct costs can be reasonably estimated.
† Also used for services that are to be provided in an indeterminate number of acts over an indeterminate period of time.
Source: Adapted from *FASB Invitation to Comment—Accounting for Certain Service Transactions,* October 1978, appendix A.

(d) expropriation of assets are recognized if they are both (1) probable and (2) can be reasonably estimated (FASB, *Statement of Financial Accounting Standards No. 5* "Accounting for Contingencies," par. 8). If both conditions are not met, the nature and estimated amount of the contingent loss must be disclosed in a note to the financial statements.

In contrast, gains usually are not recognized prior to the completion of a transaction that establishes the existence and amount of the gain [*FASB Statement 5,* par. 17(a)].[15] For example, in the case of a "probable" but as yet unrealized gain on disposal of a segment of the business, *APB Opinion 30* (par. 15) states, "If a gain is expected, it should be recognized when realized, which ordinarily is the disposal date." In some cases, potential gains may be disclosed in notes to the financial statements, provided the notes are written carefully to "avoid misleading implications as to the likelihood of realization" [*FASB Statement 5,* par. 17(b)].

Occasionally, a gain or loss results from purely internal events, such as a change in accounting principle. Such gains and losses are recognized in the period when the change occurs.

In summary, accounting for gains and losses is guided largely by conservatism, which permits losses to be recognized prior to their realization, but forbids the recognition of gains prior to the establishment of a completed transaction or event. Because companies usually can control when to engage in such transactions or events (e.g., disposal of investment securities, disposal of an unprofitable division of the business, early extinguishment of its debt, or a change in accounting principle), they exercise considerable latitude over the net income they report, which explains why GAAP poses stringent disclosure requirements for such gains and losses.

OVERVIEW OF INCOME RECOGNITION APPLICATIONS

Chapters 1–21 of this book discussed and illustrated numerous applications of income recognition in accounting. Indeed, a significant portion of the book has been devoted to income recognition.[16] Exhibit 22–2 summarizes most of the income recognition applications of the various topics covered in this book.

[15] The unrealized gain recognized on short-term investments that formerly had been written down to a lower market value under the lower-of-cost-or-market (LCM) rule is limited to the amount of any previously recorded unrealized loss.

[16] The other side of the accounting "coin" is valuation of assets, liabilities, and owners' equity. The structure of this book (e.g., chapters on cash, investments, inventories, operational assets, liabilities, and owners' equity) conveys this corollary emphasis on the other side of the coin.

EXHIBIT 22–2: Income Recognition Applications—Summarized

		Income Recognition Application	
Chapter	**Topic**	**Revenues and Gains**	**Expenses and Losses**
5	Future and present value	*a.* Interest revenue, as distinguished from return of principal amount of receivable.	*a.* Interest expense, as distinguished from cost of asset purchased with debt.
6	Short-term investments	*a.* Interest revenue. *b.* Dividend revenue. *c.* Unrealized gain on write-up from lower market value to cost. *d.* Gain on disposal.	*a.* Unrealized loss on write-down to lower market value. *b.* Loss on write-down due to permanent impairment of value. *c.* Loss on disposal.
	Receivables	*a.* Sales revenue (products or services). *b.* Interest revenue.	*a.* Bad debt expense. *b.* Interest expense on notes payable incurred from use of receivables to obtain immediate cash (e.g., assigning, pledging, factoring).
7	Inventories	*a.* Sales revenue (products).	*a.* Cost of goods sold. *b.* Unrealized loss on write-down to lower market value.
8	Inventories	*a.* Adjustment (credit) due to change in inventory method.	*a.* Cost of goods sold—FIFO, average, LIFO. *b.* Adjustment (debit) due to change in inventory method. *c.* Cost of goods sold—dollar value LIFO.
9	Inventories	*a.* Long-term construction contracts: (1) Percentage-of-completion method for revenue. (2) Completed contract method for revenue.	*a.* Cost of goods sold: (1) Gross margin method. (2) Retail method—FIFO, average, LIFO.
10	Liabilities	*a.* Revenue collected in advance (i.e., unearned revenue).	*a.* Accruals of expenses. *b.* Payroll tax expense. *c.* Interest expense. *d.* Income tax expense. *e.* Loss contingencies.
	Income tax	*a.* Extraordinary gains on realizations of tax loss carryforwards (Supplement 10–A).	*a.* Income tax expense: (1) Intraperiod tax allocation. (2) Interperiod tax allocation.
11	Operational assets	*a.* Gain on disposal.	*a.* Loss on disposal. *b.* Interest capitalized. *c.* Depreciation expense. *d.* Repairs and maintenance expense. *e.* Extraordinary repairs capitalized.
12	Depreciation and depletion		*a.* Depreciation expense. *b.* Depletion expense.
13	Intangible assets	*a.* Gain on insurance indemnity for casualty.	*a.* Amortization expense. *b.* Insurance expense. *c.* Loss on casualty.
14	Compensatory stock options		*a.* Compensation expense.

EXHIBIT 22–2 *(continued)*

Chapter	Topic	Income Recognition Application: Revenues and Gains	Income Recognition Application: Expenses and Losses
16	Long-term equity investments	*a.* Dividend revenue. *b.* Gain on disposal. *c.* Investment revenue under cost and equity methods. *d.* Consolidation of income: (1) Purchase method. (2) Pooling method. *e.* Unrealized gain under market value method.	*a.* Loss on disposal. *b.* Investment loss under equity method. *c.* Amortization of goodwill through Investment Revenue account under equity method. *d.* Depreciation of excess cost of assets through Investment Revenue account under equity method. *e.* Consolidation of loss: (1) Purchase method. (2) Pooling method. *f.* Unrealized loss under market value method.
17	Bonds (as both investments and liabilities)	*a.* Interest revenue, including amortization of premium or discount on bond investment. *b.* Gain on disposal of investment. *c.* Gain on conversion of: (1) Bond investment into stock investment. (2) Bond payable into common stock. *d.* Extraordinary gain on early extinguishment of debt. *e.* Extraordinary gain on restructure of troubled debt.	*a.* Interest expense, including amortization of premium or discount on bonds payable. *b.* Loss on disposal of investment. *c.* Debt issue expense. *d.* Loss on conversion of: (1) Bond investment into stock investment. (2) Bonds payable into stock investment. *e.* Extraordinary loss on early extinguishment of debt. *f.* Loss on restructure of troubled debt.
18	Pensions	*a.* Actuarial gains.	*a.* Pension expense: (1) Normal. (2) Prior service. (3) Past service. (4) Interest additions or subtractions. *b.* Actuarial losses.
19	Leases	*a.* Rent revenue on operating lease of lessor. *b.* Sales-type lease of lessor: (1) Sales revenue. (2) Interest revenue. *c.* Direct financing lease of lessor—interest revenue. *d.* Gain on termination of lease by lessee and lessor.	*a.* Rent expense on operating lease of lessee. *b.* Capital lease of lessee: (1) Interest expense. (2) Depreciation expense. *c.* Sales-type lease of lessor—Cost of goods sold. *d.* Loss on termination of lease by lessee and lessor. *e.* Sale-and-leaseback by seller-lessee—recognition of gain on sale as decrease in expense associated with the lease (e.g., rent, if operating; depreciation, if capital).
20	Changes in accounting estimates	*a.* Prospective treatment of revenue affected.	*a.* Prospective treatment of expense affected.
	Changes in accounting principles	*a.* Catch-up adjustment (credit).	*a.* Catch-up adjustment (debit).

EXHIBIT 22–2 *(concluded)*

Chapter	Topic	Income Recognition Application: Revenues and Gains	Income Recognition Application: Expenses and Losses
21	Interim reports	*a.* Revenues and gains in interim periods.	*a.* Expenses and losses in interim periods.
	Segment reports	*a.* Revenues attributable to particular segments. *b.* Revenues not attributable to a particular segment.	*a.* Expenses attributable to particular segments. *b.* Expenses not attributable to a particular segment.

Part B: Earnings per Share (EPS)

Earnings per share (EPS) applies only to common stock. For many years EPS amounts were computed and reported in various ways on an optional basis. *APB Opinion No. 9,* "Reporting the Results of Operations" (1966), recommended, but did not require, that EPS be disclosed in the income statement. *APB Opinion No. 15,* "Earnings per Share," was issued in 1969; it changed the recommendation to a requirement. This complex *Opinion* is supplemented by a 186-page *Interpretation.*[17] The discussions and illustrations to follow focus on *APB Opinion 15* and the *Interpretation.*[18]

BASIC DEFINITIONS

APB Opinion 15 defines several terms needed for the discussion and illustration of EPS computations. Basic definitions are as follows (emphasis added):[19]

1. **Cash yield. Cash yield** refers to the relationship or ratio of **cash to be received annually to the market value of the related security** at the specified date without regard to the par or face amount of the security. For example, a security with a coupon rate of 4 percent (on par of $100) and a market value of $80 would have a cash yield of 5 percent.
2. **Common stock equivalent.** A security which, because of its terms or the circumstances under which it was issued, is in substance **equivalent to common stock.** The existence of common stock equivalents preclude a simple capital structure.
3. **Dilution (Dilutive).** A **reduction in earnings per share** resulting from the assumption that convertible securities have been converted or that options and warrants have been exercised or other shares have been issued upon the fulfillment of certain conditions. [**Antidilution** is the opposite effect, that is, **an increase in earnings per share.**]
4. **Earnings per share.** The amount of earnings attributable to each share of **common stock.** For convenience, the term is used in this Opinion to refer to either net income (earnings) per share or to net loss per share. It should be used without qualifying language only when no potentially dilutive convertible securities, options, warrants or other agreements providing for contingent issuances of common stock are outstanding.
5. **Primary earnings per share.** The amount of earnings attributable to each share of **common stock outstanding, including common stock equivalents.**
6. **Fully diluted earnings per share.** The amount of current earnings per share reflecting the **maximum dilution** that would have resulted from conversions, exercises and other contingent issuances that individually would have decreased earnings per share and in the aggregate would have had a dilutive effect. All such issuances are assumed to have taken place at the beginning of the period (or at the time the contingency arose, if later).

TYPES OF CAPITAL STRUCTURE

APB Opinion 15 identifies two different types of capital structures and prescribes different EPS presentations for each, as follows:

---

[17] J. T. Ball, *Computing Earnings per Share,* AICPA, *Unofficial Accounting Interpretations of APB Opinion No. 15.*

[18] FASB, *Statement of Financial Accounting Standards No. 21,* "Suspension of the Reporting of Earnings per Share and Segment Information by Nonpublic Enterprises" (Stamford, Conn., April 1978), suspended the EPS reporting requirement for most closely held corporations.

[19] AICPA, *APB Opinion No. 15,* "Earnings per Share" (New York, May 1969), appendix D.

1. **Simple capital structure**—The stockholders' equity either consists only of common stock or includes no potentially dilutive securities that upon their conversion or exercise could in the aggregate **dilute** (i.e., **decrease**) earnings per common share. For **simple capital structures,** the *Opinion* prescribes a **single EPS presentation** as follows (amounts assumed):[20]

Earnings per common share:	
Income before extraordinary items	$1.50
Extraordinary loss	(.11)
Net income	$1.39

2. **Complex capital structure**—Complex capital structures constitute **all** capital structures except those described above as simple. Such a capital structure is not a simple capital structure if the corporation has outstanding convertible securities or rights that are **potentially dilutive** to EPS; dilutive securities are securities that may be converted to common stock and thus cause an increase in the number of outstanding common shares. Dilutive securities that may increase the outstanding shares of common stock include *(a)* convertible preferred stock; *(b)* convertible bonds payable; and *(c)* stock rights, stock options, stock warrants, and other securities that provide for the conversion into or purchase of common stock. For **complex capital structures,** *APB Opinion 15* prescribes a **dual EPS presentation** that reports the dilutive effects in two sets of EPS amounts as follows (amounts assumed):[21]

	Primary EPS	Fully Diluted EPS
Income before extraordinary items	$1.40	$1.25
Extraordinary loss	(.10)	(.09)
Net income	$1.30	$1.16

Basically, EPS is computed by dividing income by the average number of common shares outstanding. However, depending upon the corporation's capital structure, income (i.e., the numerator) and average number of shares (i.e., the denominator) often must be adjusted for certain items. *APB Opinion 15* provides specific guidelines concerning these items (discussed later).

[20] *APB Opinion 15* does not require EPS amounts for extraordinary items because they may be deduced by taking the difference between EPS for income before extraordinary items and EPS for net income. We present EPS for all three income amounts because the *Opinion* recommends their presentation as a convenience to statement users, and companies usually report all three EPS amounts when they have extraordinary gains and losses.

[21] Ibid.

COMPUTING EPS WITH A SIMPLE CAPITAL STRUCTURE

Based upon the definition given above, **a simple capital structure may include (1) only common stock (including fully paid subscribed common stock) or (2) common stock and nonconvertible preferred stock.** The illustrations given in Chapter 3 involved simple capital structures. In this section we present an example of a simple capital structure which has **nonconvertible** preferred stock. We also consider in some detail computation of the **average** number of shares of common stock outstanding used to compute EPS. For a simple capital structure, computation of EPS may be generalized as follows:

$$\text{EPS} = \frac{\text{Income} - \dfrac{\text{Dividend (or dividend claim) of}}{\text{nonconvertible preferred stock}}}{\text{Average number of common shares outstanding}}$$

Exhibit 22–3 illustrates computation of EPS for a **simple** capital structure. Panel A of the exhibit presents the illustrative data, Panel B gives two preliminary computations required in that particular case, and Panel C illustrates the EPS presentation as it would appear in the financial statements.

To compute the "simple" EPS amounts in Exhibit 22–3, two preliminary computations are made in Panel B—one with respect to the numerator and the other for the denominator.

1. **Numerator—nonconvertible preferred stock dividend claim**—Because EPS relates only to common stock, the dividend claims of any outstanding nonconvertible preferred stock must be recognized in the computation of earnings per common share. In Exhibit 22–3, the preferred stock of JWD Corporation is **nonconvertible.** That portion of the income for the period that is subject to the period's preferred dividend claim must be subtracted from the numerator; two situations are possible:

   a. If the nonconvertible preferred stock is **noncumulative,** the subtraction of only one year's dividend is made if and only if preferred dividends have been **declared** for the current year, because if those dividends are

EXHIBIT 22–3: EPS Computations for Simple Capital Structure

Panel A—Hypothetical Situation—JWD Corporation, 19C:

1. Capital stock:

Common stock, par $1, outstanding on January 1, 19C	90,000 shares
Common stock sold and issued on May 1, 19C	6,000 shares
Preferred stock, par $20, 6%, cumulative, nonconvertible, nonparticipating; outstanding throughout 19C, 2,500 shares	$ 50,000

2. Income data for the year ended December 31, 19C:

Income before extraordinary items	$124,000
Extraordinary gain (net of income tax)	10,000
Net income	134,000

Average income tax rate for 19C, 40 percent.

Panel B—EPS Preliminary Computations:

1. For numerator:
   Preferred dividend claim, for current year only, 19C:
   $50,000 (par value) × 6% (dividend preference rate) = $3,000.

2. For denominator:
   Computation of weighted average number of common shares outstanding during 19C:

Dates	Shares	Months Outstanding	Weighted Shares Outstanding
January 1–April 30, shares outstanding	90,000	×4	360,000
May 1, sold additional shares	+6,000		
May 1–December 31, shares outstanding	96,000	×8	768,000
December 31, shares outstanding	96,000		
Totals		12	1,128,000

Weighted average number of shares outstanding during 19C, 1,128,000 ÷ 12 = 94,000.

Panel C—Earnings per Common Share (for simple capital structure):

Earnings per common share outstanding:

Income before extraordinary items: ($124,000 − $3,000*) = $121,000 ÷ 94,000 shares*	$1.29
Extraordinary gain: $10,000 ÷ 94,000 shares	.10
Net income: ($134,000 − $3,000*) = $131,000 ÷ 94,000 shares	$1.39

* Panel B.

"passed," they are permanently lost to the noncumulative preferred shareholders.

b. If the nonconvertible preferred stock is **cumulative** (the usual case), subtraction of the current year's dividend **must** be made whether preferred dividends are declared or not for the current year, because dividends "passed" are **not** lost by the cumulative preferred shareholders. Regardless of the number of years for which cumulative preferred dividends are in arrears, **only** the current year's preferred dividend is subtracted from income (in the numerator of the EPS computation) because the EPS relates to the operations of only one year (the dividends of prior years were considered in computing the EPS of those prior years). When the year shows a loss, the cumulative dividend requirement for that year is added to the loss to compute EPS.

Exhibit 22–3, Panel A, does not indicate whether JWD Corporation declared the annual 6 percent dividend on the preferred stock. However, because the preferred stock is cumulative, declaration is not required in this case; therefore, the $3,000 preferred dividend is subtracted from income in Panel C.

2. **Denominator—weighted average number of shares outstanding during the year**—The underlying concept of EPS is to relate the income of the period to the common stock outstanding during that same period. Therefore, in both simple and complex capital structures, **the denominator contains the weighted average number of common shares outstanding during the period when the income was earned.** The common shares outstanding are weighted by the fraction of the period during which they were outstanding. If the corporation purchases common treasury stock, or retires some of its common stock during the period, those shares would be included in the EPS computation only for the fraction of the year they were outstanding.

Exhibit 22–3, Panel B, presents the computation of the weighted average number of shares of common stock outstanding during 19C. Observe in computing the average that the 6,000 shares issued on May 1, 19C, were included only for the 8/12 of the year they were outstanding during 19C.

Stock dividends, stock splits, and reverse splits are given special treatment in EPS computations because the new shares of stock they create are mere subdivisions of previously outstanding stock. Therefore, when stock dividends, stock splits, or reverse splits increase or decrease shares outstanding during the period, computation of the average number of shares of common stock outstanding should give **retroactive** restatement to the change in capital structure; that is, the computation should not weight the additional shares of common stock created by the fraction of the period they were outstanding. Instead, the computed average number of shares outstanding is based on the assumption that the additional shares of common stock created by the stock dividend or split were **outstanding throughout the entire period** regardless of when the stock dividend or split occurred.

To accomplish this effect, all actual shares outstanding prior to the issuance of any common shares in a stock dividend or split are restated retroactively, for the effect of any stock dividends or splits, to year-end equivalent shares outstanding. Then the year-end equivalent shares are weighted by the fraction of the period they were outstanding. Stock dividends and stock splits have the same effect on EPS computations; and, therefore, no distinction is made between them for this purpose.

Two cases are presented in Exhibit 22–4 to illustrate computation of the average number of shares outstanding when stock dividends (Case A) or splits (Case B) occur.

In Exhibit 22–4, Case A, the 100 percent stock dividend occurred on June 1; accordingly, each share outstanding **before** that date is restated retroactively to two shares. This restatement enables the corporation to relate its earnings for the year to the current capital structure at the year-end date because financial statement users are interested in the current capital structure. In the computation for Case A, shares outstanding after the June 1 stock dividend are **not** retroactively restated because shares subsequent to that date already reflect the stock dividend.

In Case B, the February 25 stock dividend requires restatement of actual shares outstanding from January 1 through February 24. The November 21 stock split requires restatement of all actual shares outstanding before that date (but not after that date), including the shares restated for the February 25 stock dividend.

COMPUTING EPS WITH A COMPLEX CAPITAL STRUCTURE

Corporations with **complex** capital structures, that is, those that do not meet the definition of a simple capital structure, must present two sets of EPS data with equal prominence on the income statement. *APB Opinion 15* describes these two sets as follows:

1. **Primary EPS** is based on the outstanding common shares and those securities that have a dilutive effect and are in substance equivalent to common shares, called **common stock equivalents.**[22]
2. **Fully diluted EPS** reflects the maximum dilution of EPS that would have occurred if **all contingent issuances of common stock** that would individu-

[22] Any reduction of EPS from dilutive securities of less than 3 percent in the aggregate may, but need not, be considered as dilution in the computation and presentation of EPS discussed throughout the *Opinion*. This optional test is based on materiality and is applied in practice on the "net income" line for EPS. There are two independent tests: (1) the difference between *(a)* EPS ignoring all dilutive securities and *(b)* primary EPS, and (2) the difference between *(a)* EPS ignoring all dilutive securities and *(b)* fully diluted EPS. Example: EPS ignoring all dilutive securities, $1; and primary EPS, 98 cents; the difference is less than 3 percent; the corporation may report either 98 cents or $1 as primary EPS. Fully diluted EPS, 97 cents; difference 3 percent; must report fully diluted EPS of 97 cents.

EXHIBIT 22–4: Computation of Weighted Average Number of Shares of Common Stock Outstanding When Stock Dividends and Stock Splits Occur

Case A—Stock Dividend:

1. Illustrative data for year, 19X:

Event	Shares
Common shares outstanding, January 1–March 31	10,000
April 1, 19X, sold and issued common shares	1,000
Shares outstanding, April 1–May 31	11,000
June 1, 19X, issued a 100% stock dividend	11,000
Shares outstanding, June 1–August 31	22,000
September 1, 19X, sold and issued common shares	2,000
Shares outstanding, September 1–December 31	24,000

2. Computation of the weighted average common shares outstanding (including a stock dividend):

Inclusive Dates	Actual Shares Outstanding	Retroactive Restatement for Stock Dividend on June 1		Year-End Equivalent Shares Outstanding	Months Outstanding		Weighted Shares Outstanding
Jan. 1–Mar. 31	10,000	× 2	=	20,000	× 3	=	60,000
Apr. 1–May 31	11,000	× 2	=	22,000	× 2	=	44,000
June 1–Aug. 31	22,000*		=	22,000	× 3	=	66,000
Sept. 1–Dec. 31	24,000*		=	24,000	× 4	=	96,000
Totals					12		266,000

Weighted average number of shares outstanding: 266,000 ÷ 12 = 22,167.

* These numbers already include the stock dividend.

Case B—Stock Dividend, Treasury Stock, and Stock Split:†

1. Illustrative data for year, 19X:

Event	Shares
Common shares outstanding, January 1–February 24	100,000
February 25, 19X, issued a 5% stock dividend	5,000
Shares outstanding, February 25–March 20	105,000
March 21, 19X, purchased treasury stock	(525)
Shares outstanding, March 21–October 8	104,475
October 9, 19X, sold and issued common shares	10,000
Shares outstanding, October 9–November 20	114,475
November 21, 19X, split the common stock 2-for-1—additional shares issued	114,475
Shares outstanding, November 21–December 31	228,950

2. Computation of the weighted average common shares outstanding (including a stock dividend, treasury stock, and a stock split):

Inclusive Dates	Actual Shares Outstanding	Retroactive Restatement			Year-End Equivalent Shares Outstanding	Days Outstanding		Weighted Shares Outstanding
		Stock Dividend	Stock Split					
Jan. 1–Feb. 24	100,000	× 1.05	× 2	=	210,000	× 55	=	11,550,000
Feb. 25–Mar. 20	105,000		× 2	=	210,000	× 24	=	5,040,000
Mar. 21–Oct. 8	104,475		× 2	=	208,950	× 202	=	42,207,900
Oct. 9–Nov. 20	114,475		× 2	=	228,950	× 43	=	9,844,850
Nov. 21–Dec. 31	228,950‡					× 41	=	9,386,950
Totals						365		78,029,700

Weighted average number of common shares outstanding: 78,029,700 ÷ 365 = 213,780.

† Adapted from J. T. Ball, *Computing Earnings per Share*, AICPA, *Unofficial Interpretation of APB Opinion No. 15*, p. 114.
‡ Already includes effect of stock dividend and stock split.

ally reduce EPS had taken place at the beginning of the period (or time of issuance of the convertible security, etc., if later).

The basic EPS computations for a company with a complex capital structure may be summarized as shown at the top of page 801.

Exhibit 22–5 (page 802) provides the illustrative data which will be used for computing the EPS of a company with a **complex** capital structure. The analyses to support those computations are illustrated in Exhibit 22–6, and the EPS computations are presented in Exhibit 22–7. The remainder of the chapter is organized as follows:

Primary EPS:	**Illustrated in—**
1. Equity contracts treasury stock method to compute CSEs	Exhibit 22–6, Panel A
2. Convertible securities analyzed—Interest rate test to identify CSEs	Exhibit 22–6, Panel B
3. Convertible securities—if-converted method to compute CSE shares	Exhibit 22–6, Panel C
4. Dilution/antidilution (D/A) test applied to identify equity contracts and convertible securities which are classified as CSEs and which, when assumed to be converted to common stock, would cause computed EPS amounts to decrease (dilutive effect) or increase (antidilutive effect)	Exhibit 22–6, Panel D
5. Computation of primary EPS	Exhibit 22–7, Panel A
Fully diluted EPS:	
1. Equity contracts analyzed—CSEs included	Exhibit 22–6, Panel A
2. Convertible securities analyzed—CSEs and nonCSEs included, if dilutive	Exhibit 22–6, Panels B and C
3. Dilution/antidilution (D/A) test applied to convertible securities which are not classified as CSEs, to determine whether their effects on computed EPS amounts are dilutive or antidilutive	Exhibit 22–6, Panel D
4. Computation of fully diluted EPS	Exhibit 22–7, Panel B

Primary EPS

Primary EPS is based on the weighted average of the common shares outstanding (as discussed above) plus all dilutive common stock equivalents (see definition under the preceding heading, Basic Definitions).

Neither actual conversion nor anticipated conversion of the potential common stock equivalent (CSE) security is necessary for a security to be considered as a CSE. The determination of whether a convertible security or a stock right is a CSE should be made **at time of issuance and rarely is changed thereafter.** This classification of whether a security is a CSE is important because for primary EPS all dilutive securities classified as CSEs are assumed to have been converted into common stock at the beginning of the period (or at date of issuance if later).

To determine whether a security or a stock right is a CSE and to compute the average number of equivalent shares for EPS purposes, separate consideration must be given to the following two categories:

a. **Equity contracts**—common stock rights, options, warrants, and other common stock purchase contracts (for convenience, referred to hereinafter collectively as **equity contracts**) and subscribed common stock, if not fully paid.

b. **Convertible securities**—securities convertible to common shares, such as convertible preferred stock and convertible bonds payable.

If either an equity contract or a convertible security is classified as a CSE, that security is treated as a CSE from the beginning of the period or from its issuance date if later. These two distinctly different categories (i.e., equity contracts and convertible securities) must be considered separately because they have different characteristics. As a consequence, their particular effects on the computation of EPS are quite different. However, both categories can result in an increase in the number of shares of common stock used to compute EPS.

Summary of Computation of Primary EPS*

Numerator	Denominator
1. Income before extraordinary items: Income before extraordinary items minus dividend claims of **nonconvertible** preferred stock† and minus dividend claims of **convertible** preferred stock† that is not CSE, and plus interest (net of tax) on convertible **debt** classified as common stock equivalents.	Weighted average number of shares outstanding **plus all common stock equivalents** (CSEs).
2. Extraordinary items: Extraordinary gain or loss (net of tax).	Same as above.
3. Net income: Same as (1) plus or minus extraordinary items.	Same as above.

Summary of Computation of Fully Diluted EPS*

Numerator	Denominator
1. Income before extraordinary items: Income before extraordinary items minus dividend claims of **nonconvertible** preferred stock,† plus interest expense (net of tax) on all convertible debt.	Weighted average number of shares outstanding **plus** all common stock equivalents (CSEs) plus all **other common shares that would be issued on convertible securities.**
2. Extraordinary items: Extraordinary gain or loss (net of tax).	Same as above.
3. Net income: Same as (1) plus or minus extraordinary items.	Same as above.

* Excluding all antidilutive securities.

† If preferred stock is cumulative, subtract the dividends for the current year whether declared or not; if noncumulative, subtract the dividends for the current year only if declared during the current year. If preferred stock is participating, subtract the participation dividend for the current year only to the amount of participation declared during the current year.

Equity Contracts—Treasury Stock Method. Common stock rights, subscribed stock, and other common stock purchase contracts, if exercise is assumed, have two effects on the entity: *(a)* an increase in the number of common shares outstanding, and *(b)* usually an increase in the cash of the corporation because their exercise generally requires a cash payment by the investor. Therefore, to compute the CSE shares associated with equity contracts, an assumption also must be made regarding the "as if" use of the assumed cash inflow. *APB Opinion 15* refers to this assumption as the **treasury stock method.** To compute the increase in the number of common shares caused by the "as if" exercise of the stock rights, the treasury stock method assumes that the corporation would apply any cash proceeds from exercise of the stock rights to purchase treasury common stock (see exception on page 802).

The treasury stock method can be explained by an example. If outstanding stock rights entitled their owners to purchase 2,000 common shares for $20 per share, exercise of these stock rights would generate a $40,000 (i.e., 2,000 × $20) cash inflow. If the market value of the company's common stock is $25 per share (indicating that exercise is likely because the option price is less than the market price), the company could purchase 1,600 (i.e., $40,000 ÷ $25) of its own common shares if the proceeds were used to acquire treasury stock. Under the treasury stock method, the net increase of 400 shares (i.e., 2,000 − 1,600) is the number of CSE shares which is added to the average number of common shares outstanding (that is, 94,000; see Exhibit 22–3, Panel B) to give a denominator of 94,400 shares and, thereby, decrease EPS. This **application of the treasury stock method** to the stock rights of JWD Corporation, based on the data given in Exhibit 22–5, is illustrated in **Exhibit 22–6, Panel A.**

EXHIBIT 22–5: Illustrative Data for Computing EPS for a Complex Capital Structure—JWD Corporation, 19C

Panel A—Hypothetical Situation (repeated for convenience from Exhibit 22–3):

1. Capital stock:		
Common stock, par $1, outstanding on January 1, 19C		90,000 shares
Common stock sold and issued on May 1, 19C		6,000 shares
Nonconvertible preferred stock, par $20, 6%, cumulative, nonparticipating; outstanding throughout 19C, 2,500 shares	$ 50,000	
2. Income data for the year ended December 31, 19C:		
Income before extraordinary items	$124,000	
Extraordinary gain (net of income tax)	10,000	
Net income	134,000	
Average income tax rate for 19C, 40 percent.		

Panel B—Additional Data (for complex capital structure):

1. Stock rights:		
a. Outstanding for common shares		2,000 shares
b. Exercise (option) price per share of common stock	$ 20	
c. Average market price per share of common stock during the reporting period.	$ 25	
2. Convertible securities (in addition to those listed in Panel A):		
a. Convertible preferred stock, nopar, $7 annual dividend per share, cumulative, nonparticipating; each preferred share is convertible to 8 shares of common stock; outstanding throughout the year, 1,000 shares; issue price, $108 per share	$108,000	
b. Series A convertible bonds payable, $200,000, 8% payable annually; each $1,000 bond is convertible to 30 shares of common stock; issue price at par*	200,000	
c. Series B convertible bonds payable, $500,000, 10% payable annually; each $1,000 bond is convertible to 50 shares of common stock; issue price at par*	500,000	
Aa corporate bond interest rate at dates of issuance of all convertible securities	12.6%	

* The bonds were assumed to sell at par for instructional convenience.

In Exhibit 22–6, Panel D, item 2, the stock rights are specified as **dilutive** because they increase the number of "as if" shares outstanding by 400 and no dollar amount to "match" those shares is added to income in the numerator. In contrast, if the average market price of the common stock during the reporting period had been **less** than the option price, the above computation, if made, would have reduced the number of shares outstanding, in which case the effect on the computed EPS amount would have been **antidilutive** (i.e., it would have caused EPS to increase).[23] In that case the stock rights would have been excluded because *Opinion 15* does not permit the use of CSEs in EPS computations if the CSEs have an antidilutive effect.[24] Also, the options would not be exercised by rational investors if the market price were less than the option price.

The *Opinion* specifies a variation of the treasury stock method when the number of shares of common stock obtainable upon exercise of outstanding stock rights exceeds 20 percent of the number of common shares outstanding at the end of the period. In these situations, the "as if" cash inflow would be applied in two steps:

1. First, apply the cash to an "as if" repurchase of common shares at the average market price, but not in excess of 20 percent of the outstanding shares, and then,
2. Apply the balance of the cash to *(a)* an "as if" reduction of any short-term or long-term debt outstanding, and then, to *(b)* an "as if" purchase of investments in U.S. government securities or commercial paper (i.e., debt securities). In these situations the "as if" **net-of-tax interest** effect,

[23] Supplement 22–B considers the situation in which the stock rights must be given additional consideration in the computation of **fully diluted** EPS, regardless of whether they are CSEs for computing primary EPS.

[24] *APB Opinion 15*, par. 36, recommends that assumption of exercise not be reflected in EPS data until the market price of the common stock has exceeded the exercise or option price for substantially all of three consecutive months ending with the last month of the period to which EPS data relate.

which would accompany the reduction of debt and/or purchase of interest-bearing securities, must be added back to income in the numerator of the EPS computation.

In Exhibit 22–6, Panel A, the 2,000 additional common shares that would be issued upon exercise of the rights are less than 20 percent of the 96,000 common shares outstanding at the end of the period (i.e., less than 19,200 shares). Therefore, the full amount of "as if" proceeds from exercise of the rights in this example is applied to the "as if" purchase of treasury stock.

Convertible Securities—Interest Rate Test. Convertible preferred stock and **convertible debt securities** generally provide that the holder, under specified conditions, may convert them to common shares. Thus, they may constitute CSEs when issued. *Opinion 15* states that "convertible securities should be considered common stock equivalents if the **cash yield** interest rate to the holder at time of issuance is significantly below what would be a comparable rate for a similar security of the issuer without the conversion option." To illustrate a convertible security which is a CSE, assume a corporation can sell a new issue of nonconvertible bonds at a 13 percent annual interest rate; however, the same bonds, if convertible to common stock, would be marketable at an 8 percent annual interest rate. The 5 percent difference in interest rates measures the value of the conversion privilege. In this example, the convertible bonds probably would qualify as CSEs.

In actual situations the interest rate without the conversion privilege (e.g., 8 percent in the above example) would not be known; therefore, the APB originally specified reliance upon the prime interest rate to determine whether a convertible security should be considered as a CSE. However, in February 1982, the FASB issued *Statement No. 55,* entitled "Determining Whether a Convertible Security is a Common Stock Equivalent." This new *Statement* discarded the bank prime interest rate and replaced it with the average **"Aa" corporate bond interest rate** as the new benchmark for determining whether a convertible security is a CSE.[25]

Under **this interest rate test,** a convertible security should be considered as a CSE at the time of issuance if, based on its market price, it has a cash yield interest rate which is **less** than 66⅔ percent of the then-current Aa corporate bond interest rate.[26] The "cash yield" interest rate is the amount of stated interest on convertible debt, or cash dividends on convertible preferred stock scheduled to be paid each year, divided by the cash received (i.e., issue price) at date of issuance of the convertible security. The **interest rate test** to determine whether a convertible security represents CSEs is illustrated in Exhibit 22–6, Panel B (based on the data given in Exhibit 22–5, Panel B).

In Exhibit 22–6, Panel B, application of the interest rate test, indicates that the convertible preferred stock and the series A convertible bonds payable are CSEs and that the series B convertible bonds are **not** CSEs. The interest rate test is a pragmatic solution to the problem of defining a CSE for **convertible securities.** Realistically, a convertible security bought to yield less than two thirds of the Aa corporate bond interest rate may well have been acquired more for the potential appreciation of the underlying common stock than for its debt features (e.g., annual cash yield);[27] therefore, its conversion feature was an important element in the total consideration paid for it. If the security was purchased primarily for this conversion feature, then it is reasonable to assume that (at least at the date of its issuance) the security is "likely" to be converted to common stock.

Convertible Securities—If-Converted Method. The interest rate test is used only to determine whether a convertible security is a CSE; it does not measure the number of CSEs. If the interest rate test is met, the **number** of common stock equivalents re-

---

[25] FASB, *Statement of Financial Accounting Standards No. 55,* "Determining Whether a Convertible Security is a Common Stock Equivalent" (an amendment of *APB Opinion No. 15,* February 1982, par. 5, states that "In recent years, the bank prime interest rate has been more volatile than it was in years preceding the issuance of Opinion 15," and in par. 7 that "The phrase 'bank prime interest rate' in paragraph 33 of Opinion 15 is deleted and replaced by 'average Aa corporate bond yield.' " The **average** bond yield is based on bond yields for a brief period of time, such as one week, including or immediately preceding the date of issuance of the security being tested. *FASB Statement 55* became effective for issues after February 28, 1982.

[26] If no market price of the convertible security is available, this test should be based on the "fair" value of the security. If there is a scheduled change in the interest rate or dividend rate during the first five years after issuance, the lowest scheduled rate should be used (*APB Opinion 15,* par. 33).

[27] Note that the cash yield is based on **pretax** yield because the Aa bond interest rate is pretax.

EXHIBIT 22–6: Analysis to Support EPS Computations—JWD Corporation, 19C

Panel A—Equity Contracts—Treasury Stock Method to Compute Common Stock Equivalents (CSEs):

	Shares
Shares that would be issued upon exercise of rights (Exhibit 22–5, Panel B)	2,000
Cash proceeds if rights were exercised, 2,000 rights × $20 (option price) = $40,000.	
Treasury stock shares that could be purchased, $40,000 ÷ $25 (average market price)	1,600
Common stock equivalent (i.e., incremental number of common shares that would be outstanding)	400 CSEs

Panel B—Convertible Securities—Interest Rate Test to Identify CSEs:

Convertible Security	Rate	Decision
1. Aa bond interest rate for comparison (Exhibit 22–5, Panel B), 12.6% × ⅔	8.4%	
2. Cash yield on convertible securities (Exhibit 22–5, Panel B):		
a. Convertible preferred stock, issued at $108: (cash dividend, 1,000 shares × $7) ÷ (issue price, $108,000)	6.5%	Lower, CSE
b. Series A convertible bonds payable, issued at par: (cash interest, $200,000 × .08) ÷ (issue price, $200,000)	8.0%	Lower, CSE
c. Series B convertible bonds payable, issued at par: (cash interest, $500,000 × .10) ÷ (issue price, $500,000)	10.0%	Higher, Not CSE

Panel C—Convertible Securities—If-Converted Method to Compute CSEs:

	Shares:
1. Convertible securities which qualify as CSEs (Panel B):	
a. Convertible preferred stock (Exhibit 22–5, Panel B) (1,000 × 8)	8,000
b. Series A convertible bonds payable (Exhibit 22–5, Panel B): ($200,000 ÷ $1,000) × 30	6,000
2. Convertible securities which did **not** qualify as CSEs (Panel B):	
c. Series B convertible bonds payable (Exhibit 22–5, Panel B): ($500,000 ÷ $1,000) × 50	25,000

Note: CSEs from the convertible preferred stock and series A convertible bonds will be used to compute primary and fully diluted EPS. Series B convertible bonds (if-converted shares, 25,000) will be used only in fully diluted EPS. All are subject to the D/A test shown in Panel D below.

Panel D—Dilution/Antidilution (D/A) Test (data from Exhibit 22–3, Panel B, and Panels A–C above):

1. Net income to **common shareholders** [$134,000 − ($50,000 × .06) − (1,000 shares × $7)] = $124,000.
2. Stock rights are **dilutive** because they increase the number of shares of common stock (denominator) used to compute EPS by 400 shares (Panel A).
3. Tentative EPS [$124,000 ÷ 94,400 shares (94,000 shares, Exhibit 22–3, Panel B + 400 shares)] = $1.31
4. D/A ratios of all convertible securities for ranking:

	Amount	Rank Order for Later Use
a. Convertible preferred stock [(1,000 shares × $7) ÷ 8,000 shares]	$ .88	1
b. Series A convertible bonds [($200,000 × .08 × .60) ÷ 6,000 shares]	1.60	3
c. Series B convertible bonds [($500,000 × .10 × .60) ÷ 25,000 shares]	1.20	2

5. **Primary EPS**—Comparison of D/A ratios to tentative EPS amounts considering **CSEs only** (Panel B):
   a. Convertible preferred stock **dilutive** because D/A ratio ($0.88) is less than Tentative EPS ($1.31); new Tentative EPS [$124,000 + (1,000 × $7)] ÷ (94,000 + 400 + 8,000 shares) = $1.28.
   b. Series A convertible bonds **antidilutive** because D/A ratio ($1.60) is more than the new Tentative EPS ($1.28).
   c. Therefore, the **primary EPS** for net income is **$1.28**
6. **Fully diluted EPS**—Comparison of D/A ratios to tentative EPS amounts, considering **all** convertible securities:
   a. Convertible preferred stock **dilutive** because D/A ratio ($0.88) is less than Tentative EPS ($1.31); new Tentative EPS is same as 5*a* above, $1.28.
   b. Series B convertible bonds **dilutive** because D/A ratio ($1.20) is less than new Tentative EPS ($1.28); new Tentative EPS is [$124,000 + (1,000 × $7) + ($500,000 × .10 × .60)] ÷ (94,000 + 400 + 8,000 + 25,000 shares) = $1.26.
   c. Series A convertible bonds **antidilutive** because D/A ratio ($1.60) is more than new tentative EPS ($1.26).
   d. Therefore, **fully diluted EPS** for net income is **$1.26**

EXHIBIT 22–7: Computation of Primary and Fully Diluted EPS (complex capital structure) JWD Corporation, 19C

Panel A—Primary EPS:

Income before extraordinary items:

$$\frac{\$124{,}000^{(a)} - \$3{,}000^{(b)}}{94{,}000^{(c)} + 400^{(d)} + 8{,}000^{(e)}} = \frac{\$121{,}000}{102{,}400} = \$1.18$$

Extraordinary gain:

$$\frac{\$10{,}000^{(f)}}{102{,}400} = .10$$

Net income:

$$\frac{\$134{,}000^{(g)} - \$3{,}000^{(b)}}{102{,}400} = \frac{\$131{,}000}{102{,}400} = \$1.28$$

Explanation:

(a) Income before extraordinary items (Exhibit 22–5, Panel A).
(b) Dividend claim of nonconvertible preferred stock ($50,000 × 6%).
(c) Average number of common shares actually outstanding during the year (Exhibit 22–3, Panel B).
(d) CSE shares from stock rights (Exhibit 22–6, Panel A).
(e) CSE shares from convertible preferred stock (Exhibit 22–6, Panel C).
(f) Extraordinary gain (Exhibit 22–5, Panel A).
(g) Net income (Exhibit 22–5, Panel A).

Note: Series B convertible bonds were excluded because they were not CSEs based on the interest rate test (Exhibit 22–6, Panel B). Series A convertible bonds were excluded because they were antidilutive (Exhibit 22–6, Panel D).

Panel B—Fully Diluted EPS:

Income before extraordinary items:

$$\frac{\$124{,}000^{(a)} - \$3{,}000^{(a)} + \$30{,}000^{(b)}}{94{,}000^{(a)} + 400^{(a)} + 8{,}000^{(a)} + 25{,}000^{(c)}} = \frac{\$151{,}000}{127{,}400} = \$1.18$$

Extraordinary gain:

$$\frac{\$10{,}000}{127{,}400} = .08$$

Net income:

$$\frac{\$161{,}000}{127{,}400} = \$1.26$$

Explanation:

(a) Panel A. In this example, the CSE securities which were dilutive for primary EPS also were dilutive for fully diluted EPS.
(b) Interest expense (net of income tax) on series B convertible bonds, Exhibit 22–5 ($500,000 × .10 × .60 = $30,000); added back because it was deducted to compute net income.
(c) If-converted shares from series B convertible bonds; not CSE but dilutive (Exhibit 22–6, Panels C and D).

Note: Fully diluted EPS includes *(a)* average common shares actually outstanding, *(b)* all dilutive CSEs, and *(c)* all other common shares that could be issued from dilutive securities (i.e., series B convertible bonds; not CSEs, but dilutive; Exhibit 22–6, Panels B and D).

lated to the convertible security is computed using an **if-converted method.** This method assumes the following:

a. That the convertible security is converted to common shares at the beginning of the period (or at time of issuance, if later); the CSE shares would be added to the denominator and

b. That the "as if" reduction in a convertible **debt** security would cause a reduction in interest expense. Because income was reduced by interest expense on the debt, this assumption requires that the interest, net of income tax, be added back to income (i.e., added to the numerator in the EPS computation).

c. In the case of **convertible preferred stock,** the CSE shares would be added to the denominator. The preferred dividends would **not** be added to income in the numerator because dividends are not deducted in computing income; neither would the preferred dividends be subtracted from income.

Exhibit 22–7, Panel A, illustrates the computation of primary EPS, based upon the above discussions. Supporting details of the computation of primary EPS are provided in Exhibit 22–6.

Fully Diluted EPS

APB Opinion 15 requires companies to present **fully diluted EPS** to reveal the lowest amount of EPS the company would report if all its outstanding equity contracts (e.g., stock rights, options, warrants, etc.) and convertible securities were assumed to be converted to common stock. Thus, **in addition** to CSE securities whose conversion to common stock was assumed for computation of primary EPS, computation of fully diluted EPS also must consider convertible securities which were not classified as CSEs; the purpose of this additional consideration is to show the lowest EPS amount the company could report. Determination of this "lowest possible" EPS amount is related to the concept of dilution/antidilution (D/A), which is discussed next. The procedures involved in the computation of fully diluted EPS, including such supporting computations as the number of if-converted shares and the amount of interest (net of tax) to add back to the numerator of the EPS computation, are essentially the same in the computation of fully diluted EPS as in the computation of primary EPS.

The next, and most technical, topic to be considered in computing EPS for a complex capital structure is the **dilution/antidilution (D/A) test.** At this point we present two complementary discussions of the computation of primary and fully diluted EPS as follows:

a. A comprehensive example of a situation in which there are **both dilutive and antidilutive securities** and a detailed dilution/antidilution (D/A) test which is explained and illustrated (Exhibits 22–6, Panel D, and Exhibit 22–7 for JWD Corporation is shown on page 805).

b. An example of the computation of primary and fully diluted EPS when there are **no antidilutive** securities. This less complex situation is presented in Supplement 22–A for those who do not desire to consider dilution/antidilution (D/A) in depth at this time. Supplement 22–A presents the EPS computations for XYZ Corporation, whose capital structure is identical to that of JWD Corporation ([*a*] above) with only **one** exception. XYZ Corporation does not have outstanding the series A convertible bonds payable of JWD Corporation. The reason for omitting the series A convertible bonds from XYZ Corporation's capital structure is that they turn out to be **antidilutive** (i.e., their assumed conversion to common stock increases the computed EPS amount). Therefore, by omitting them from XYZ Corporation's capital structure, we present, in supplementary form, the EPS computation for a company with a complex capital structure in which there are no antidilutive securities. Should you have difficulty in keeping the D/A test in perspective, reading Supplement 22–A will be helpful.

Dilution/Antidilution (D/A)

Dilution/antidilution (D/A) must be considered **only with complex capital structures. Dilution** means a decrease in EPS amounts resulting from **equity contracts or convertible securities.** The equity contracts and convertible securities that cause this effect are called **dilutive securities. Antidilution** means an **increase** in EPS amounts caused by **antidilutive** equity contracts or convertible securities. **To attain the maximum dilutive effect on EPS (because of conservatism), *APB Opinion 15* requires that all antidilutive securities be excluded in computing both primary and fully diluted EPS amounts.**

Footnote 8 of *APB Opinion 15* identifies one exception to this general rule; it states

> The presence of a common stock equivalent or other dilutive securities together with income from continuing operations and extraordinary items may result in diluting one of the per share amounts which are required to be disclosed on the face of the income statement—i.e., . . . income before extraordinary items, . . . and net income—while increasing another. In such a case, the common stock equivalent or other dilutive securities should be recognized for all computations even though they have an antidilutive effect on one of the per share amounts.

Because of this provision, the D/A test should be conducted on the **higher** of *(a)* income before extraordinary items or *(b)* net income. If the lower amount were used, a security could be labelled erroneously as antidilutive.

Overview of D/A Test

D/A must be considered at two levels in EPS computation as follows:

1. **For primary EPS**—A test based on **CSEs only.**
2. **For fully diluted EPS**—A test based on **all** potentially dilutive securities (i.e., all CSEs and non-CSEs).

D/A Test for Primary EPS. Exhibit 22–6, Panels A and B, indicate that three securities qualify as CSEs: the stock rights; convertible preferred stock;

and series A convertible bonds payable. When there is more than one CSE security (as in this case), the D/A effect of a security often depends on the **order** in which the securities are tested for D/A. As a result, all possible combinations of the securities must be tested for D/A, with the combination yielding the lowest EPS amount selected for use in computing primary EPS.

D/A Test for Fully Diluted EPS. Exhibit 22–6, Panel B, indicates that only one potentially dilutive security (i.e., the series B convertible bonds payable) does **not** qualify as a CSE. Therefore, in conducting the D/A test for fully diluted EPS, the series B convertible bonds payable, in addition to the three CSE securities, also must be considered. For fully diluted EPS, the D/A test must **reconsider** the two convertible securities classified as CSEs for computing primary EPS because a security that was dilutive for primary EPS may turn out to be antidilutive for fully diluted EPS.

Implementation of the D/A Test. A short-cut method has been devised to avoid having to test all the possible combinations for determining whether convertible securities are dilutive or antidilutive.[28] The objective of this short-cut method is to identify the lowest (i.e., most dilutive) amounts for primary EPS and fully diluted EPS. The method can be implemented in six steps as follows:

1. Determine net income to **common stockholders** (i.e., net income minus **all** preferred dividend claims).
2. Determine whether equity contracts (e.g., stock rights, options, warrants) are dilutive.
3. Compute Tentative EPS, that is, EPS based upon net income to common stockholders and assuming the conversion of all dilutive equity contracts to common stock.[29] "Income to common shareholders" used in this computation should be the higher of *(a)* income before extraordinary items or *(b)* net income. Use of the higher amount increases the probability of identifying a dilutive security.
4. Compute the D/A ratio (given below) for each convertible security, and rank the respective D/A ratios from lowest to highest.
5. For **primary EPS,** consider **only** convertible securities which are **CSEs.**
   a. Compare the lowest D/A ratio to Tentative EPS (computed in step 3). This comparison determines whether this first convertible security is dilutive or antidilutive. The security is dilutive if its D/A ratio is less than Tentative EPS; it is antidilutive if its D/A ratio is greater than Tentative EPS. If **dilutive,** assume conversion of the security to common stock, and compute a new Tentative EPS. Compare this new Tentative EPS with the next larger D/A ratio. Repeat this process until an antidilutive security is encountered or until the list of convertible securities is exhausted.
   b. If the security is antidilutive, the D/A test for primary EPS is complete because all remaining convertible securities have higher D/A ratios and, hence, are antidilutive.
   c. Primary EPS is the last Tentative EPS amount computed in step 5*a* above.
6. For **fully diluted EPS,** reperform step 4 above, starting once again with the same beginning Tentative EPS amount computed in step 3. This time, however, the comparison of D/A ratios and Tentative EPS amounts involves all convertible securities (i.e., CSEs and nonCSEs). The D/A test for fully diluted EPS is complete when an antidilutive security is encountered. Fully diluted EPS is the last Tentative EPS amount computed.

The D/A ratio for each convertible security is computed as follows:

$$\text{D/A ratio} = \frac{\text{Effect of assumed conversion on } \textbf{numerator} \text{ of EPS}}{\text{Effect of assumed conversion on } \textbf{denominator} \text{ of EPS}}$$

$$= \frac{\text{\$ Interest expense (net of tax) or \$ preferred dividend amount}}{\text{Number of common shares into which the security can be converted}}$$

---

[28] Without this short-cut method, a company with *n* convertible securities would need to make 2^n calculations to identify the lowest EPS amount; with the short-cut method, only *n* calculations are needed. See S. Davidson and R. L. Weil, "A Shortcut in Computing Earnings per Share," *Journal of Accountancy,* December 1975, pp. 45–47.

[29] Equity contracts are treated differently from convertible securities in the D/A test; that is, the common shares associated with dilutive equity contracts are included in the computation of Tentative EPS because equity contracts usually directly affect only the denominator of the EPS computation; by contrast, the assumed conversion of convertible securities affects both the numerator and the denominator.

The D/A test for the computation of the EPS of JWD Corporation is presented in Exhibit 22–6, Panel D. The end product of the two D/A tests are primary EPS (i.e., $1.28) and fully diluted EPS (i.e., $1.26); this illustrates the broad scope of the D/A test for computing the EPS of a company with a complex capital structure. It may appear that the computational approach illustrated in Exhibit 22–6, Panel D, is inconsistent with the more conceptual approach to computing EPS outlined on page 801. The two approaches are not in conflict; the D/A test occupies a more significant role in the computations than is immediately apparent. That is, the D/A test not only tests for D/A; it also produces the primary and fully diluted EPS amounts.

REPORTING EARNINGS PER SHARE (EPS)

APB Opinion 15, as amended by *FASB Statement 21,* requires that EPS data be "shown on the face of the income statement," for all periods presented by "publicly held" corporations. In addition, the following should be disclosed (paraphrased from *APB Opinion 15,* pars. 19–21):

a. A description, in summary form, sufficient to explain the rights and privileges of the various securities outstanding.
b. A schedule or note to explain the bases upon which both primary and fully diluted EPS are calculated.
c. All assumptions and any resulting adjustments used in calculating the EPS data.
d. The number of shares issued upon conversion, exercise, or satisfaction of equity contracts during at least the most recent annual fiscal period and any subsequent interim period presented.
e. Computations and/or reconciliations as needed to provide a clear understanding of the manner in which the EPS amounts were computed.

The income statement presentation of the EPS of JWD Corporation for 19C is shown in Exhibit 22–8.

EXHIBIT 22–8: Reporting EPS for Complex Capital Structure—JWD Corporation, 19C

JWD CORPORATION
Income Statement (partial)
For the Year Ended December 31, 19C

Income before extraordinary items	$124,000
Extraordinary gain (net of income taxes of $6,667)	10,000
Net income	$134,000
Earnings per share (Note X):	

	Primary	Fully Diluted
Income before extraordinary items	$1.18	$1.18
Extraordinary gain (net of tax)	.10	.08
Net income	$1.28	$1.26

Notes to the financial statements:

Note X. EPS amounts were computed in accordance with the provisions of *APB Opinion 15.* Primary EPS includes all common stock equivalents, that are dilutive, based on stock rights and options outstanding (using the treasury stock method) plus those based on convertible securities (using the "if-converted" method). Fully diluted EPS includes all additional contingent common shares that would be issued for all convertible securities that are dilutive; thus, it represents maximum dilution.

The outstanding stock rights, convertible preferred stock, and series A convertible bonds payable were determined to be common stock equivalents; however, the series A convertible bonds had antidilutive effects on both primary and fully diluted EPS and, accordingly, were excluded from consideration as common stock in all EPS computations. The series B convertible bonds, although not common stock equivalents, were included in the computation of fully diluted amounts. The income amounts were adjusted for the interest (net of income taxes) effects of these securities.

The rights and privileges of the stock rights and the convertible securities are explained in the notes related to those items (refer to the balance sheet).

No shares were issued during the past two years for exercise of stock rights or conversion of convertible securities.

COMPUTATION OF EPS—SUMMARY

When a corporation has a simple capital structure, it presents only one set of EPS amounts. In contrast, when a corporation has a complex capital structure, it presents both primary and fully diluted EPS amounts for (1) income before extraordinary items, (2) extraordinary items, and (3) net income. Primary EPS relates the three categories of income (or loss) to the basic capital structure of the corporation, that is, *(a)* its outstanding common stock and *(b)* all dilutive CSEs. On the other hand, fully diluted EPS reflects the maximum possible dilution; therefore, the number of shares in the denominator of the fully diluted EPS computation includes *(a)* the average number of common shares outstanding, plus *(b)* all dilutive CSEs (i.e., those used in computing primary EPS), plus *(c)* all other contingent issuances of common stock that would reduce EPS. If *(c)* is zero, primary and fully diluted EPS are the same.

Exhibit 22–9 presents an overview of the computation of EPS for a company with a simple capital struc-

EXHIBIT 22–9: Overview of EPS Computations

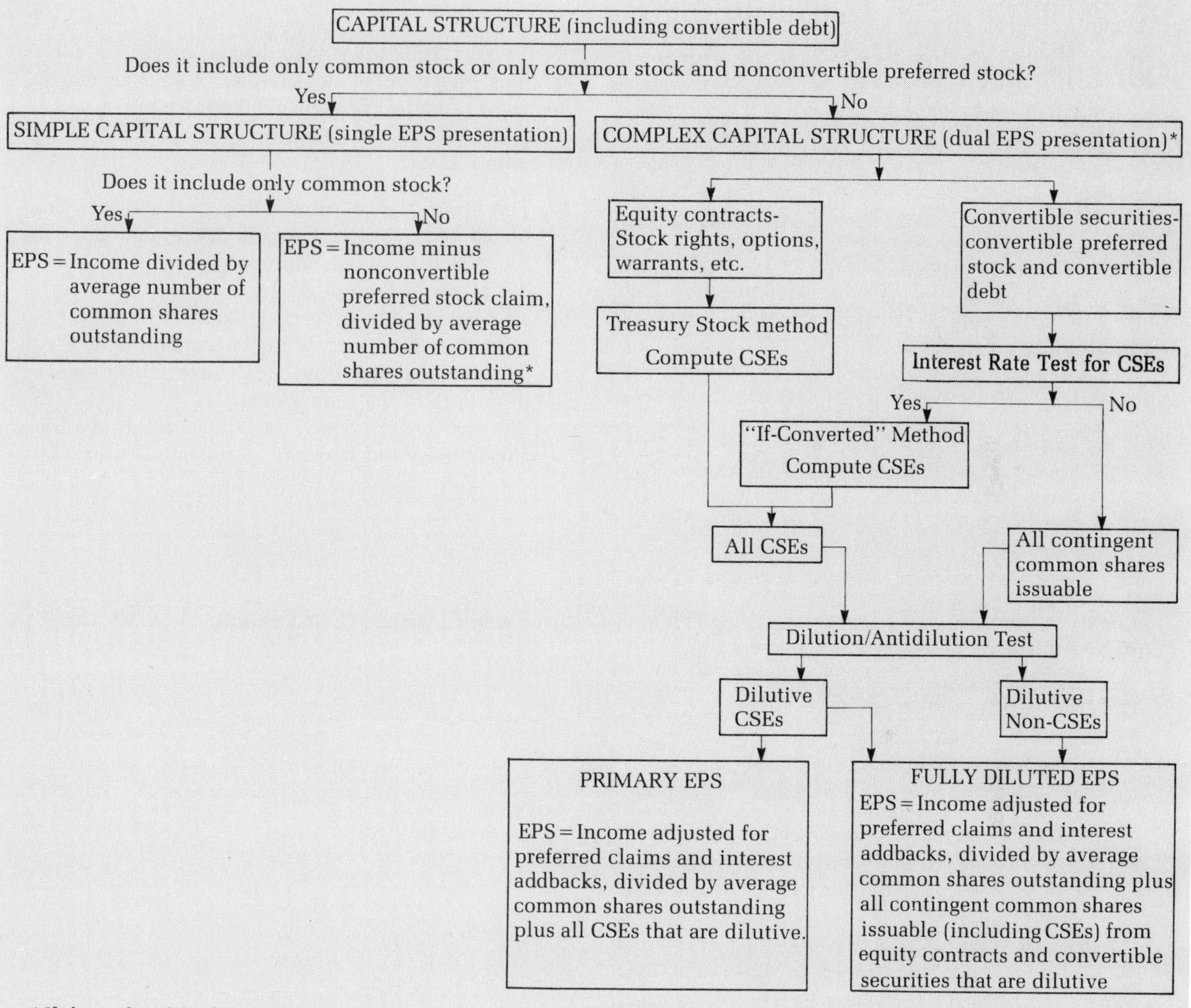

* If the preferred stock is cumulative, deduct the dividends for the current year whether declared or not; if noncumulative, deduct for current year only if declared during the current year.

ture and a company with a complex capital structure (i.e., primary and fully diluted EPS). Supplement 22–B discusses additional issues in EPS computations.

Supplement 22-A: Computing EPS for a Complex Capital Structure in Which There Are No Antidilutive Securities

This supplement presents the computation of primary and fully diluted EPS for a company which has a complex capital structure in which there are **no antidilutive securities.**

This Supplement presents three exhibits as follows:

1. Exhibit 22–10—Illustrative Data.
2. Exhibit 22–11—Computation of CSE shares.
3. Exhibit 22–12—Computation of Primary and Fully Diluted EPS.

These exhibits follow the discussions in the early sections of Part B of the chapter; and each one is designed to be largely self-explanatory.

In respect to D/A securities, note the following in Exhibit 22–12:

a. The **stock rights** are **dilutive** because they increase the number of shares in the denominator (i.e. 400 shares), and **do not** cause any increase of dollars in the numerator.

b. The **convertible preferred stock** is **dilutive** because it added shares in the denominator (i.e., 8,000 shares) but does not cause any increase of dollars in the numerator.

c. The convertible bonds payable are dilutive because they add $30,000 to the numerator and

EXHIBIT 22–10: Illustrative Data for Computing EPS for a Company with a Complex Capital Structure in Which There Are No Antidilutive Securities—XYZ Corporation, 19C

Panel A—Hypothetical Situation:		
1. Capital stock:		
Common stock, par $1, outstanding on January 1, 19C	90,000	shares
Common stock sold and issued on May 1, 19C	6,000	shares
Nonconvertible preferred stock, nopar, preference rate 6 percent, cumulative, nonparticipating; outstanding throughout 19C, 2,500 shares	$ 50,000	
2. Income data for the year ended December 31, 19C:		
Income before extraordinary items	$124,000	
Extraordinary gain (net of income tax)	10,000	
Net income	134,000	
Average income tax rate for 19C, 40 percent.		
Panel B—Additional Data (for complex capital structure):		
1. Stock rights:		
a. Outstanding for common shares	2,000	shares
b. Exercise (option) price per share of common stock	$ 20	
c. Average market price per share of common stock for period outstanding	$ 25	
2. Convertible securities:		
a. Convertible preferred stock, nopar, $7 annual dividend per share, cumulative, nonparticipating; each preferred share is convertible to 8 shares of common stock; outstanding throughout the year 1,000 shares; issue price $108 per share	$108,000	
b. Convertible bonds payable, $500,000, 10% payable annually; each $1,000 bond is convertible to 50 shares of common stock; issue price at par†	500,000	
Aa bond interest rate at dates of issuance of all convertible securities	12.6%	

† The bonds were assumed to sell at par for instructional convenience.

EXHIBIT 22–11: Computation of Common Stock Equivalents CSEs—XYZ Corporation, 19C

Panel A—Equity Contracts—Treasury Stock Method to Compute Common Stock Equivalents (CSEs):

Shares that would be issued upon exercise of rights (Exhibit 22–10, Panel B)	2,000 shares
Cash proceeds if rights were exercised, 2,000 rights × \$20 (option price) = \$40,000.	
Treasury stock that could be purchased, \$40,000 ÷ \$25 (average market price)	1,600 shares
Common stock equivalents (i.e., incremental number of common shares that would be outstanding)	400 CSEs

Panel B—Convertible Securities—Interest Rate Test to Identify CSEs:

Convertible Security	Rate	Decision
1. Prime interest rate for comparison (Exhibit 22–10, Panel B) 12.6% × ⅔	8.4%	
2. Cash yield on convertible security (Exhibit 22–10, Panel B):		
a. Convertible preferred stock, issued at \$108 (cash dividend, 1,000 shares × \$7) ÷ (issue price, \$108,000)	6.5%	Lower, CSE
b. Convertible bonds payable, issued at par (cash interest, \$500,000 × .10) ÷ (issue price, \$500,000)	10.0%	Higher, Not CSE

Panel C—Convertible Securities—If-Converted Method to Compute Number of Common Stock Equivalents:

1. Convertible preferred stock qualifies as CSE (Panel B): (1,000 shares × 8; Exhibit 22–10, Panel B)	8,000 shares
2. Convertible bonds payable did **not** qualify as CSEs (Panel B): [(\$500,000 ÷ \$1,000) × 50; Exhibit 22–10, Panel B]	25,000 shares

Note: CSEs from the convertible preferred stock will be used to compute primary and fully diluted EPS. Series B convertible bonds (if-converted shares, 25,000) will be used only in fully diluted EPS.

EXHIBIT 22–12: Computation of Primary and Fully Diluted EPS (complex capital structure) XYZ Corporation, 19C

Panel A—Primary EPS:

Income before extraordinary items: $\frac{\$124{,}000^{(a)} - \$3{,}000^{(b)}}{94{,}000^{(c)} + 400^{(d)} + 8{,}000^{(e)}} = \frac{\$121{,}000}{102{,}400} = \$1.18$

Extraordinary gain: $\frac{\$\ 10{,}000^{(f)}}{102{,}400} = .10$

Net income: $\frac{\$134{,}000^{(g)} - \$3{,}000^{(b)}}{102{,}400} = \frac{\$131{,}000}{102{,}400} = \$1.28$

(a) Income before extraordinary items (Exhibit 22–10, Panel A).
(b) Dividend claim of nonconvertible preferred stock (\$50,000 × 6%).
(c) Average number of common shares actually outstanding during the year (Exhibit 22–3; Panel B).
(d) CSE shares from stock rights (Exhibit 22–11, Panel A).
(e) CSE shares from convertible preferred stock (Exhibit 22–11, Panel C).
(f) Extraordinary gain (Exhibit 22–10, Panel A).
(g) Net income (Exhibit 22–10, Panel A).
Note: Convertible bonds were excluded because they were not CSEs based on the prime rate test (Exhibit 22–11, Panel B).

Panel B—Fully Diluted EPS:

Income before extraordinary items: $\frac{\$124{,}000 - \$3{,}000 + \$30{,}000^{(a)}}{94{,}000 + 400 + 8{,}000 + 25{,}000^{(b)}} = \frac{\$151{,}000}{127{,}400} = \$1.18$

Extraordinary gain: $\frac{\$10{,}000}{127{,}400} = .08$

Net income: $\frac{\$161{,}000}{127{,}400} = \$1.26$

Explanation:
(a) Interest expense (net of income tax) on convertible bonds (Exhibit 22–10; \$500,000 × 10% × .60 = \$30,000); added back because it was deducted to compute net income.
(b) If-converted shares from convertible bonds; not CSE but dilutive (Exhibit 22–11, Panel C).
Note: Fully diluted EPS includes *(a)* average common shares actually outstanding, *(b)* all dilutive CSEs, and *(c)* all other common shares that could be issued from dilutive securities (i.e., convertible bonds; not CSEs, but dilutive).

25,000 shares to the denominator; this gives a ratio of $1.20, which is **less** than the EPS of $1.28 without their effect [i.e., ($134,000 − $3,000) ÷ (94,000 + 400 + 8,000).

Supplement 22-B: Additional Issues in EPS Computations

This section briefly outlines three additional issues in EPS computations, as follows:

1. Effect of stock dividends and stock splits on the number of shares of common stock represented by stock rights and convertible securities.
2. Application of the treasury stock method for stock rights to fully diluted (but not primary) EPS.
3. Application of the interest rate test and if-converted method to convertible debt securities issued at a premium or discount.

EFFECT OF STOCK DIVIDENDS AND STOCK SPLITS ON THE NUMBER OF SHARES OF COMMON STOCK REPRESENTED BY STOCK RIGHTS AND CONVERTIBLE SECURITIES

When a company issues additional shares of common stock in a stock dividend or a stock split at the time it has stock rights or convertible securities outstanding, the number of shares of common stock represented by the stock rights or convertible securities, as used in EPS computations, must be adjusted for the effect of the stock dividend or split. For example, assume JWD Corporation (Exhibit 22–5, Panel A) had split its common stock 2 for 1 during 19C. In this case, the numbers of shares of common stock represented by the outstanding stock rights and convertible securities of JWD would be doubled as shown below:

The numbers of shares of common stock, given at the bottom of this page, would be used in all EPS-related computations.

APPLICATION OF THE TREASURY STOCK METHOD TO FULLY DILUTED (NOT PRIMARY) EPS

In applying the treasury stock method to compute primary EPS, the **average market price** of the stock always is used. In contrast, for computing fully diluted EPS, the **ending market price** per share of stock is substituted for the average market price per share if the ending market price is higher. Thus, when the ending market price is higher, fully diluted EPS is reduced below primary EPS by use of the treasury stock method.

To illustrate the effect of a higher end-of-period (versus average) price of common stock subject to stock rights or other stock purchase contract, assume the price of the common stock of JWD Corporation at December 31, 19C, was $40 per share[30] (average for the year was $25; Exhibit 22–5, Panel B). This modification would not affect primary EPS. However, it would decrease fully diluted EPS because it would increase the number of shares of common stock added to the denominator in the fully diluted EPS computation, as shown on page 813.

[30] This amount is assumed for instructional convenience.

Security	No. Shares of Common Stock Used in EPS Computations without 2-for-1 Stock Split (Exhibit 22–6, Panels A and C)	Effect of 2-for-1 Stock Split		No. Shares of Common Stock Used in EPS Computations with 2-for-1 Stock Split
1. Common stock (Exhibit 22–3, Panel B)	94,000	× 2		188,000
2. Stock rights	400	× 2	=	800
3. Convertible preferred stock	8,000	× 2	=	16,000
4. Series A convertible bonds payable	6,000	× 2	=	12,000
5. Series B convertible bonds payable	25,000	× 2	=	50,000

Number of CSE shares represented by stock rights for primary EPS (Exhibit 22–6, Panel A)	400
Number of shares represented by stock rights for fully diluted EPS	1,000*

* Computation:

Shares that would be issued upon exercise of rights (Exhibit 22–5, Panel B)	2,000
Cash proceeds if rights were exercised: 2,000 rights × $20 (option price) = $40,000.	
Treasury stock that could be purchased at year-end: $40,000 ÷ $40 (market price)	1,000
Common shares added to denominator in fully diluted EPS computation	1,000

With the above modification, JWD Corporation's fully diluted EPS would be computed using 1,000 common stock equivalent shares added to the denominator of the EPS computation (instead of the 400 shares used for computing primary EPS).

APPLICATION OF INTEREST RATE TEST AND IF-CONVERTED METHOD TO CONVERTIBLE DEBT SECURITIES ISSUED AT A PREMIUM OR DISCOUNT

Debt securities, including those that are convertible, usually are issued at a premium or a discount. When there is a premium or discount, the cash yield on the debt securities is different from their stated interest rate. As a result, the interest rate test used to determine whether convertible debt securities are CSEs must be based upon their cash yield, taking into account the premium or discount on issue of the convertible debt. Also, the D/A ratio used to identify dilutive securities must be based upon the net-of-tax interest expense on the convertible debt, including any related amortization of premium or discount recorded as part of the interest expense on the bonds. Finally, if the convertible debt is dilutive, the net-of-tax interest addback to the numerator in the EPS computation must include the effect of amortization of the premium or discount.

To illustrate the effect of premium or discount amortization on EPS computations, assume the series A convertible bonds payable of JWD Corporation (Exhibit 22–5, Panel B) had been issued at 102 instead of par. This modification would have the following effects on the EPS computations of JWD Corporation:

1. Interest rate test—Cash yield on series A convertible bonds payable:
   ($200,000 × .08) ÷ ($200,000 × 1.02) 7.8%
   Conclusion: Series A bonds are CSEs because their cash yield is less than two-thirds of the Aa bond rate (i.e., 12.6% ×⅔ Exhibit 22–6, Panel B) 8.4%
2. D/A test for series A bonds:
   D/A ratio (Exhibit 22–6, Panel D),assuming straight-line amortization of premium over 10 years)

$$= \frac{\left[\begin{pmatrix}\text{Cash interest,}\\ \$200{,}000 \times .08\end{pmatrix} - \begin{pmatrix}\text{Amort. of premium,}\\ \$204{,}000 - \$200{,}000 \div 10\end{pmatrix}\right] \times .60}{6{,}000 \text{ shares}}$$

$$= \frac{\$9{,}360}{6{,}000} = \$1.56$$

Conclusion: For primary EPS, series A bonds are antidilutive because the above ratio is greater than Tentative EPS used to compute primary EPS, $1.28 (Exhibit 22–6, Panel D, item 5*b*); also greater than Tentative EPS used to compute fully diluted EPS, $1.26 (Exhibit 22–6, Panel D, item 6*c*). Therefore, do **not** treat as common stock in computing primary EPS or fully diluted EPS.

Note: If the series A bonds had been dilutive, in computing primary EPS, $9,360 of aftertax interest expenses would have been added to the numerator and 6,000 shares (Exhibit 22–6, Panel C) would have been added to the denominator.

QUESTIONS

PART A

1. Explain why accretion (such as growing of timber) is not accepted as a basis of recognizing revenue?

2. A corporate vice president said, "If accountants didn't prepare reports at such short intervals, there would be less for them to do." Assume the vice-president was not just alluding to the fact that if reports were prepared twice as often, twice as much effort would be entailed. What are the less obvious implications of the vice president's statement?

3. When is revenue first recognized assuming the—
   a. Completed contract method?
   b. Cost recovery method?
   c. Percentage-of-completion method?
   d. Cash basis?

4. Under which of the following methods is *matching* important?
   a. Completed contract.
   b. Cost recovery.
   c. Percentage of completion.
   d. Cash basis.

PART B

5. What is the difference in EPS computations and reporting as between a *simple* capital structure and a *complex* capital structure?

6. What is a *common stock equivalent?* How do common stock equivalents affect EPS computations?

7. What is the 3% materiality rule in EPS computations and how is it used?

8. Contrast primary EPS and fully diluted EPS.

9. What is the *treasury stock method?*

10. What is the *interest rate test* and when is it used?

11. What is the difference between a *dilutive* security and an *antidilutive* security? Why is the distinction important in EPS considerations?

12. A company split its common stock 2 for 1 on June 30 of its fiscal year ended December 31. Before the split, there were 4,000 shares of common stock outstanding. How many shares of common stock should be used in computing EPS? How many shares of common stock should be used in computing a comparative EPS amount for the preceding year?

EXERCISES

PART A: EXERCISES 22–1 to 22–2

Exercise 22–1

It has been postulated that before the percentage-of-completion method can be used properly the following criteria must be met:

1. There is a written contract executed by buyer and seller which clearly specifies what is to be provided and received, the consideration to be exchanged, and manner and terms of settlement.
2. The buyer can satisfy obligations under the contract.
3. The seller has the ability to perform the contractual obligations.
4. The seller has an adequate estimating process and the ability to estimate reliably both the cost to complete and the percentage of completion of the contract.
5. The seller has a cost accounting system which adequately accumulates and allocates cost to final cost objectives in a manner consistent with the estimates resulting from the estimating process.

Required:

1. Are the foregoing criteria adequate? What, if anything, would you add to or delete?
2. Which *assumption*—separate entity, continuity, unit of measure, or time period—is implied most by criterion 3?
3. Is criterion 4 concerning ability to estimate cost to complete consistent with the *reliability* principle?

Exercise 22–2

At a meeting of the board of directors of Prince Publishing Company, where you are the controller, a new director expresses surprise that the company's income statement reflects that an equal proportion of revenue is earned with the publication of each issue of the magazines the company publishes. This director believes that the most important event in the sale of magazines is the collection of cash on the subscriptions and expresses the view that the company's practice smooths its income and that its subscription revenue actually is earned as subscriptions are collected.

Required:

Discuss the propriety of timing the recognition of revenue on the basis of:

a. Cash collections on subscriptions.
b. Number of magazines delivered each month.
c. Both events, by recognizing part of the revenue with cash collections of subscriptions and part with delivery of the magazines to subscribers. (AICPA adapted)

PART B: EXERCISES 22–3 to 22–9

Exercise 22–3

Morton Corporation's fiscal year is the calendar year. During the three most recent years, its common shares outstanding changed as follows:

	Year 19x3	Year 19x2	Year 19x1
Shares outstanding, Jan. 1	150,000	120,000	100,000
Sale of shares 4/1/x1			20,000
25% stock dividend 7/1/x2		30,000	
2-for-1 stock split 7/1/x3	150,000		
Shares sold 10/1/x3	60,000		
Shares outstanding Dec. 31	360,000	150,000	120,000

Required:

1. For purposes of calculating EPS at the end of each year, *for each year standing alone,* determine the number of shares outstanding.

2. For purposes of calculating EPS at the end of 19x3, when comparative statements are being prepared on a three-year basis, determine the number of shares outstanding for each year.

Exercise 22–4

The records for Boyce Corporation, at year-end, reflected the following:

Common stock, nopar, authorized shares 500,000:	
Outstanding at beginning of year: 100,000 shares	$175,000
Sold and issued during the year, September 1, 3,000 shares	8,000
Preferred stock, 8%, par $10, nonconvertible, cumulative, authorized 20,000 shares:	
Outstanding during the year, 6,000 shares	60,000
Contrib. capital in excess of par, pref. stock	3,000
Retained earnings	150,000
Bonds payable, 6½%, nonconvertible	100,000
Income before extraordinary items	90,000
Extraordinary gain (net of tax)	20,000
Net income	110,000

Required:

1. Is this a simple or complex capital structure? Explain.
2. What kind of EPS presentation is *required?* Explain.
3. Compute the required EPS amounts (show computations).
4. Compute the required EPS amounts assuming the preferred stock is noncumulative and the current year's dividend has not been declared and that the preceding year's dividend was passed.

Exercise 22–5

At the end of 19A the records of Chapman, Inc., reflected the following:

Common stock, par $5, authorized 500,000 shares:	
Outstanding 1/1/19A, 200,000 shares	$1,000,000
Sold and issued 4/1/19A, 1,000 shares	5,000
Issued 10% stock dividend, 11/30/19A, 20,100 shares	100,500
Preferred stock, 6%, par $10, nonconvertible, noncumulative, authorized 50,000 shares, outstanding during year, 20,000 shares	200,000
Contrib. capital in excess of par, common stock	150,000
Contrib. capital in excess of par, pref. stock	100,000
Retained earnings (includes effects of current preferred dividends declared during 19A)	640,000
Bonds payable, 6½%, nonconvertible	500,000
Income before extraordinary items	182,000
Extraordinary loss (net of tax)	(18,000)
Net income	164,000

Average income tax rate, 40%.

Required:

1. Is this a simple or complex capital structure? Explain.
2. What kind of EPS presentation is required? Explain.
3. Compute the required EPS amounts (show computations).
4. Compute the required EPS amounts assuming the preferred is cumulative.

Exercise 22–6

At the end of 19A the records of Raft Wholesale Corporation showed the following:

Common stock, nopar, authorized 200,000 shares:	
Outstanding 1/1/19A, 52,000 shares	$624,000
Purchased treasury shares 4/1/19A, 2,000 shares (at cost)	(50,000)
Issued a 100% stock dividend on 12/1/19A on outstanding shares (50,000 additional shares)	
Preferred stock, par $10:	
Class A, 6%, nonconvertible, noncumulative, outstanding 10,000 shares	100,000
Class B, 7%, nonconvertible, cumulative, outstanding 20,000 shares	200,000
Contrib. capital in excess of par, pref. stock	80,000
Retained earnings (no dividends declared in 19A)	420,000
Bonds payable, 7%, nonconvertible	150,000
Income before extraordinary items	180,500
Extraordinary gain (net of tax)	6,000
Net income	186,500

Average income tax rate, 40%.

Required:

1. Is this a simple or complex capital structure? Explain.
2. What kind of EPS presentation is required? Explain. Disregard the optional 3% materiality test.
3. Compute the required EPS amounts (show computations).

Exercise 22–7

At the end of 19A the records of Chambers Corporation reflected the following:

Common stock, par $10, authorized 100,000 shares; issued and outstanding throughout year, 50,000 shares	$500,000
Stock rights outstanding (all yr. for 10,000 shares of common stock at $15 per share)	100,000
Preferred stock, par $50, 7%, cumulative, convertible into common stock share for share, authorized 25,000 shares; issued and outstanding throughout year, 2,000 shares	100,000
Contrib. capital in excess of par, common stock	30,000

Retained earnings (no dividends declared during the year)	290,000
Bonds payable, 9½%, nonconvertible	90,000
Income before extraordinary items	85,000
Extraordinary gain (net of tax)	35,000
Net income	120,000

Average income tax rate, 40%.
Average market price of the common stock during 19A, $25 per share.
Bank prime interest rate at date of issuance of bonds, 9%.

Required:

1. Is this a simple or complex capital structure? Explain.
2. What kind of EPS presentation is required? Explain.
3. Compute the required EPS amounts (show computations and assume all amounts are material).

Exercise 22–8

At the end of 19A the records of McBeth Corporation reflected the following:

Common stock, nopar, authorized 200,000 shares; issued and outstanding throughout the period to 12/1/19A, 60,000 shares. A stock split issued 12/1/19A doubled outstanding shares	$750,000
Preferred stock, 5%, par $10, nonconvertible, cumulative, nonparticipating, shares authorized, issued, and outstanding during year, 10,000 shares	100,000
Contrib. capital in excess of par, pref. stock	20,000
Retained earnings (no cash or property dividends declared during year)	440,000
Bonds payable, 8%, each $1,000 bond is convertible to 60 shares of common stock (bonds initially sold at par)	200,000
Income before extraordinary items	86,000
Extraordinary loss	(14,000)
Net income	72,000

Average income tax rate, 40%.
Average market price of common stock during 19A, $9.
Aa bond interest rate (at date of issuance of bonds), 15%.

Required:

1. Is this a simple or complex capital structure? Explain.
2. What kind of EPS presentation is required? Explain.
3. Compute the required EPS amounts (show computations, rounded to two decimal places, and assume all amounts are material).

Exercise 22–9

At the end of 19A the records of Lima Corporation reflected the following:

Common stock, nopar, authorized 500,000 shares; issued and outstanding throughout period, 100,000 shares	$850,000
Stock dividend issued, 12/31/19A, 50,000 shares (not included in the 100,000 shares above)	425,000
Retained earnings (includes effect of dividends on all shares)	480,000
Bonds payable, 4½%, each $1,0000 bond is convertible to 80 shares of common stock (bonds issued at par)	60,000
Bonds payable, 6½%, each $1,000 bond is convertible to 90 shares of common stock (bonds issued at par)	300,000
Income before extraordinary items	125,000
Extraordinary gain	12,000
Net income	137,000

Average income tax rate, 40%.
Average market price of common stock during 19A, $13.
Aa bond interest rate at date of issuance: 4½% bonds, 6⅞%; 6½% bonds, 8%.

Required:

1. Is this a simple or complex capital structure? Explain.
2. What kind of EPS presentation is required? Explain. Disregard the optional 3% materiality test.
3. Compute the required EPS amounts (show computations, rounded to two decimal places, and assume all amounts are material).

PROBLEMS

PART A: PROBLEMS 22–1 to 22–4

Problem 22–1

Two schoolmates, Nancy, an accounting major, and Herb, a management major, are discussing the role of accounting in managing an enterprise and reporting on its operating results. Herb says, "When things are so-so or are going badly, current accounting practices portrays the picture reasonably accurately, but when things are going well, these practices sometimes fail to tell the true story." You join their discussion.

Required:

1. Cite some specifics that lend credence to Herb's general line of argument.
2. How can you and Nancy respond to justify current accounting practices in good times as well as bad?

Problem 22–2

York Publishing Company prepares and publishes a monthly eight-page newsletter for an industry in which potential circulation is limited. Because information provided by the newsletter is available only on a piecemeal basis from other sources and because no advertising is carried, the subscription price for the newsletter is relatively high. York recently engaged in a campaign to increase circulation which involved extensive use of person-to-person long-distance telephone calls to research directors of nonsubscriber companies in the industry. The telephone cost of the campaign was $38,000, and salary payments to persons who made the calls amounted to $51,000.

As a direct result of the campaign, new one-year subscriptions at $175 each generated revenue of $164,500. New three-year subscriptions at $450 each generated revenue of $324,000 and new five-year subscriptions at $625 generated $157,500. Cancellations are rare, but when they occur, refunds are made on a half-rate basis (e.g., if a subscriber has yet to receive $100 worth of newsletters, $50 is refunded).

Aside from the two direct costs of the campaign cited above, indirect costs, consisting of such items as allocated office space, fringe benefit costs for calling employees, and supervision amounted to $21,000.

Required:

1. Identify the specific accounting issues involved for York and, for each issue, give the accounting principles that are important in resolving that issue.
2. Assume the campaign was begun and concluded in May, new subscriptions begin with the July issue of the monthly newsletter, and the company's fiscal year ends December 31. How should costs of the campaign be allocated among current and future fiscal years? Show calculations.

Problem 22–3

On July 27, 1977, the Federal Power Commission (FPC) issued a ruling raising the ceiling price on regulated (interstate) gas, but with a "vintaging" system. Gas suppliers could charge $1.42 per thousand cubic feet on "new gas" drilled after January 1, 1975, and $1.01 on gas drilled between January 1, 1973, and December 31, 1974. The old price had been 52 cents per thousand cubic feet and remained there for all "old" gas (i.e., pre-1973 gas). The FPC soon reduced the $1.01 rate to 93 cents and retained the $1.42 rate. As a result of a lawsuit against the FPC seeking a rollback to the old 52-cent rate, a Circuit Court of Appeals decided gas suppliers should go ahead and collect the higher prices provided they would agree to refund the money if the final decision went against the FPC.

Required:

1. If you were part of management of a gas supplier at the time of the Circuit Court decision, what position would you take with respect to recognition of the extra amounts of revenue from the sale of "new" gas? Give reasons for whatever position you take.
2. Disregard whatever answer you gave to 1 above. If the revenue is deferred, how would it be accounted for until a final court decision is rendered? How would the deferred revenue be recognized if the final court decision is delayed until a new fiscal year and then is favorable?

Problem 22–4

The general ledger of Enter-tane, Inc., a corporation engaged in the development and production of television programs for commercial sponsorship, contains the following accounts before amortization at the end of the current year:

Account	Balance (debit)
Sealing Wax and Kings	$54,000
The Messenger	36,000
The Desperado	17,500
Shin Bone	8,000
Studio Rearrangement	7,000

An examination of contracts and records revealed the following information:

a. The first two accounts listed above represent the total cost of completed programs that were televised during the accounting period just ended. Under the terms of an existing contract, Sealing Wax and Kings will be rerun during the next accounting period at a fee equal to 60% of the fee for the first televising of the program. The contract for the first run produced $300,000 of revenue. The contract with the sponsor of The Messenger provides that at the sponsor's option, the program can be rerun during the next season at a fee of 75% of the fee for the first televising of the program. There are no present indications that it will be rerun.

b. The balance in The Desperado account is the cost of a new program which has just been completed and is being considered by several companies for commercial sponsorship.

c. The balance in the Shin Bone account represents the cost of a partially completed program for a projected series that has been abandoned.

d. The balance of the Studio Rearrangement account consists of payments made to a firm of engineers which prepared a report relative to the more efficient utilization of existing studio space and equipment.

Required:

1. State the general principle (or principles) of accounting that are applicable to the first *four* accounts.

2. How would you report each of the first *four* accounts in the financial statements of Enter-tane? Explain.
3. In what way, if at all, does the Studio Rearrangement account differ from the first four? Explain.

(AICPA adapted)

PART B: PROBLEMS 22–5 to 22–9

Problem 22–5

Beamer Corporation is developing its EPS presentation at December 31, 19A. The records of the company provide the following information:

Liabilities

Convertible bonds payable, 7% (each $1,000 bond is convertible to 100 shares of common stock)	$200,000

Stockholders' Equity

Common stock, nopar, authorized 100,000 shares:	
Outstanding 1/1/19A, 59,000 shares	236,000
Sold and issued 10,000 shares on 4/1/19A	40,000
Common stock rights outstanding (all yr. for 4,000 shares of com. stock)	16,000
Preferred stock, par $10, 6%, cumulative, convertible (each share is convertible into ½ of 1 share of common stock) authorized 20,000 shares, outstanding during 19A, 5,000 shares	50,000
Contrib. capital in excess of par, pref. stock	10,000
Retained earnings	380,000
Income before extraordinary items	110,000
Extraordinary gain (net of tax)	20,000
Net income	130,000

Additional data:

a. Stock rights—option price, $4 per share; average market price of the common stock during 19A, $6 (also during last quarter).
b. Convertible bonds—issue price, par.
c. Aa bond interest rate on dates of issuance of all convertible securities, 8%.
d. Average income tax rate, 40%.

Required:

1. Is this a simple, or a complex, capital structure? Explain.
2. What kind of EPS presentation is required? Explain.
3. Prepare the required EPS presentation for 19A. Show all computations.
4. Were there any antidilutive securities? How was this determined?
5. How should antidilutive securities be treated in the computations of EPS? Why?

Problem 22–6

The records of Jarrett Corporation reflected the following data at the end of 19A:

Liabilities

Bonds payable, 5½%, convertible (each $1,000 bond is convertible to 30 shares of common stock)	$150,000

Stockholders' Equity

Common stock, par $2, authorized 300,000 shares:	
Outstanding 1/1/19A, 150,000 shares	300,000
Sold and issued on 10/1/19A, 20,000 shares	40,000
Com. stock warrants outstanding (all yr. for 6,000 shares)	12,000
Preferred stock, 6%, par $5, nonconvertible, cumulative, authorized 100,000 shares, outstanding during 19A, 20,000 shares	100,000
Contrib. capital in excess of par, com. stock	340,000
Contrib. capital in excess of par, pref. stock	60,000
Retained earnings	310,000
Income before extraordinary items	170,000
Extraordinary loss (net of tax)	(20,000)
Net income	150,000

Additional data:

a. Stock warrants—option price, $3 per share; average market price of common stock during 19A, $3.60 per share (also during last quarter).
b. Convertible bonds—issue price, par; Aa bond interest rate at date of issuance of the bonds was 8½%.
c. Average income tax rate, 40%.

Required:

1. Is this a simple, or a complex, capital structure? Explain.
2. What kind of EPS presentation is required? Explain.
3. Prepare the required EPS presentation for 19A. Show all computations. Disregard the optional 3% materiality test.
4. Were there any antidilutive securities? How was this determined?
5. How should antidilutive securities be treated in EPS computations? Why?

Problem 22–7

At the end of 19A, the records of Delano, Inc., showed the following:

Common stock, nopar, authorized 500,000 shares:	
Outstanding 1/1/19A, 200,000 shares	$1,800,000
Treasury shares acquired 6/1/19A, 1,000 shares (at cost)	(12,000)
Stock dividend issued, 11/1/19A, 19,900 shares (10%)	398,000

Stock rights outstanding all yr. for 20,000 shares of common stock at $15 per share.	
Preferred stock, 5%, par $20, noncumulative, nonconvertible, authorized, issued and outstanding throughout the year, 10,000 shares	200,000
Contrib. capital in excess of par, pref. stock	30,000
Retained earnings (no cash or property dividends declared during 19A)	760,000
Bonds payable, series A, 7%, each $1,000 bond is convertible to 20 shares of common stock (bonds issued at par)	50,000
Bonds payable, series B, 6%, each $1,000 bond is convertible to 57 shares of common stock (bonds issued at par)	400,000
Income before extraordinary gain	200,000
Extraordinary gain (net of tax)	20,000
Net income	220,000

Average income tax rate for 19A, 40%.
Average market price of the common stock during 19A (and for the last quarter of 19A), $20 per share.
Aa bond interest rate at date of issuance of: 7% bonds, 12%; 6% bonds, 9%.

Required:

1. Is this a simple or complex capital structure? Explain.
2. Prepare the EPS presentation with all supporting computations.

Problem 22–8

The Big Deal Company balance sheet at December 31, 19D, reported the following:

Accrued interest payable	$ 1,000
Long-term notes payable, 10%, due in 19G	50,000
Bonds payable, 7%, each $1,000 of face value is convertible into 90 shares of common stock; bonds mature in 19M	800,000
Preferred stock, 5%, nonconvertible, cumulative, par value $100	300,000
Common stock, par value $5	700,000
Common stock rights outstanding all yr. entitling holders to acquire 40,000 shares of common stock at $9 per share	200,000
Net loss for 19D	125,000

Additional data:

1. During 19D, 1,000 shares of preferred stock were issued at par on July 1. Dividends are paid semiannually, on May 31 and November 30. Declaration precedes payment by three weeks. On newly issued shares, dividends are prorated from issue date.
2. Aa bond rate of interest was 7¾% when the convertible bonds were issued at par.
3. Average market price of common stock during 19D was $10 (also during last quarter).
4. Income tax rate of Big Deal is 40%.
5. Big Deal earned taxable income of $400,000 during 19A–19C.

Required:
Present the EPS data on the 19D income statement of Big Deal in good form, along with supporting computations.

Problem 22–9

Field Company has a compensatory stock option plan under which options to buy 255,000 common shares were issued in 19A. These options are exercisable during 19B and 19C at $16 per share. In 19B, Field reported net income of $400,000; the company's capital structure remained unchanged that year.

Outstanding stock consists of 1 million common shares which traded at an average price of $20 per share throughout 19B. The company's long-term debt consists of a $2,500,000 bond issue sold at par which pays 12% annual interest and was outstanding throughout 19B. Field had no other indebtedness. Field's average income tax rate is 40%.

Required:

1. Compute primary EPS for 19B.
2. Suppose the facts given in 1 above are modified as follows: Field issued the stock options on July 1, 19B. Per share market price of Field's stock is $20 per share throughout the last quarter of 19B. Compute primary EPS for 19B. Ignore the 3% materiality rule.

23

The Statement of Changes in Financial Position (SCFP)

BACKGROUND

One of the major management problems of practically all companies is planning and controlling the cash inflows and outflows of the business. Cash is a scarce resource in most businesses and is necessary in the day-to-day operations of almost all businesses, and especially in respect to most of the major strategic moves of a company. For example, a 1980 annual financial report stated that "in 1980, Westinghouse directed more than $1 billion in research and development programs which were funded by the Corporation, its customers, and the government through Westinghouse administered contracts." Similarly, the 1980 annual financial report of American Telephone and Telegraph Company reported "Funds Supporting Construction Activity" of $17,300.9 million, and finally, the 1980 annual report of General Motors stated that "our announced intention is to invest $40 billion worldwide during the five years from 1980 through 1984 on product design and plant construction and modernization. . . ." Information such as the above on the inflow and outflow of cash of the business is important to investors, creditors, and other users of financial statements. Investors and creditors pay cash for their investments (equity and debt securities) and expect subsequent cash returns in the form of dividends and interest and cash upon termination of the investments. Because the subsequent cash returns necessarily must be projected by such investors prior to their investment decisions, investors are particularly interested in information that will assist in making realistic projections. The subsequent cash returns that an investor in a business actually will receive are related, in the long term, to the cash inflows and outflows of the business. Therefore, investors and creditors are particularly interested in information which will help them project the future cash flows of the business. Recognizing this need by users of financial statements, the FASB stated that one objective of financial statements is to "provide information to help investors, creditors, and others assess the amounts, timing, and uncertainty of prospective net cash inflows to the related enterprise."[1]

Financial statements, because they are historical in nature, provide a track record of the financial aspects of the company and are useful in projecting future performance. Thus, such statements should

[1] FASB, *Statement of Financial Accounting Concepts No. 1*, "Objectives of Financial Reporting by Business Enterprises" (Stamford, Conn., November 1978), p. viii.

be designed to assist statement users, to the fullest extent practicable, in making predictions of the future flows of funds in and out of a business. The two traditional statements—the balance sheet and income statement—provide, in indirect ways, enterprise information about the sources (inflows) and uses (outflows) of cash and they are not designed specifically for this purpose. In recognition of *(a)* the needs of statement users for better information about resource flows and *(b)* the shortcomings of the balance sheet and income statement in meeting those needs, the APB issued *APB Opinion No. 19,* "Reporting Changes in Financial Position," March 1971. This *Opinion* redesigned the old "funds statement," specified its new title as Statement of Changes in Financial Position (SCFP), and made it mandatory in the following terms:

> The Board concludes that information concerning the financing and investing activities of a business enterprise and the changes in its financial position for a period is essential for financial statement users, particularly owners and creditors, in making economic decisions. When financial statements purporting to present both financial position (balance sheet) and results of operations (statement of income and retained earnings) are issued, a statement summarizing changes in financial position should also be presented as a basic financial statement for each period for which an income statement is presented. These conclusions apply to all profit-oriented business entities, whether or not the reporting entity normally classifies its assets and liabilities as current and noncurrent.

Opinion 19 is particularly noteworthy in that it *(a)* made the statement mandatory, *(b)* required that it be developed on an **all-resources** basis, and *(c)* strongly recommended the title, Statement of Changes in Financial Position (SCFP). This title is used almost exclusively. The significance of the statement, as prescribed by *Opinion 19,* is that it requires the reporting of comprehensive information on the financing and investing activities of the business. The **financing activities** result in inflows of resources, and the **investing activities** result in outflows of resources.

The phrase "changes in financial position" is descriptive of the report because the inflows and outflows of resources are directly related to the changes in the asset, liability, and owners' equity accounts during the period. The statement focuses on reporting these changes.

The balance sheet reports financial position at a **specific point in time;** consequently, it is not a change statement. In contrast, the income statement is a change statement; it reports the change in retained earnings **during** a specified period due to operations. The details on the income statement report the specific factors that underlie net income. Similarly, the statement of retained earnings (or statement of stockholders' equity) is a change statement; it reports all of the changes in retained earnings (or the changes in all stockholders' equity accounts) **during** the specified period. Observe, that none of these change statements reports the **causes** of the changes in assets and liabilities.

The SCFP fills this gap by reporting other changes **during** the specified period. To do this, it reports changes in asset, liability, and owners' equity accounts measured in terms of **funds flow.**

This chapter discusses and illustrates development of the SCFP in conformity with *APB Opinion 19* and is subdivided as follows:

Part A—Basic Characteristics of the SCFP, and the SCFP, Working Capital Basis

Part B—SCFP, Cash Basis

Supplement 23-A—T-Account Approach to Preparation of the SCFP

Part A: Basic Characteristics of the SCFP, and the SCFP, Working Capital Basis

BASIC CHARACTERISTICS OF THE SCFP

The SCFP measures the changes in assets, liabilities, and owners' equity during a specified period in terms of the inflows and outflows of funds. For example, the disposition of an asset or incurrence of a liability causes an inflow or source of funds, and the acquisition of an asset or the payment of a liability causes an outflow or use of funds. In this context, the word **funds** is used broadly to mean cash, cash plus near-cash assets, or working capital.

SCFP All-Resources Concept

The SCFP, as prescribed in *APB Opinion 19* (par. 8) must be based on an **all-resources concept,** viz: ". . . the statement summarizing changes in financial position should be based on a broad concept embracing all changes in financial position," and "each reporting entity should disclose all important aspects of its financing and investing activities regardless of whether cash or other elements of working capital are directly affected." This quotation means that the statement also must include all **direct exchanges** of nonfund items, that is, those transactions that involve neither the direct inflow or outflow of funds. For example, if a business acquires a machine (an asset acquisition) and pays for it in full by issuing its own capital stock to the vendor, there has been no inflow or outflow of funds. Nevertheless, under *APB Opinion 19,* transactions of this type must be reported as *(a)* an inflow of funds (from the issuance of the stock) and *(b)* an outflow of funds (due to acquisition of the asset). This kind of transaction is called a **direct exchange** because it is a "trade" of two **nonfund** items and there is no direct inflow or outflow of funds.[2] Thus, the SCFP must report the following:

1. The **inflows** of all funds during the period, including the effects of direct exchanges, and an identification of these inflows with specific changes in assets, liabilities, and owners' equity.
2. The **outflows** of all funds during the period, including the effects of direct exchanges, and an identification of these outflows with specific changes in assets, liabilities, and owners' equity.
3. The net increase or decrease in funds during the period.

Definition of Funds for the SCFP

In the preceding paragraphs, the terms **cash** and **funds** have been used interchangeably. The inflows and outflows reported on the SCFP are measured in dollars of "funds." For measurement purposes, we must be precise in defining funds. This general term is used throughout financial and accounting literature with diverse meanings.[3] Because of this diversity, and the need for precise measurement, *APB Opinion 19* (par. 11) states:

> The Statement may be in balanced form or in a form expressing the changes in financial position in terms of **cash** or **cash and [short-term] investments combined,** of **all quick assets,** or of **working capital.** (Emphasis supplied.)

Basically, this quotation means that the inflows and outflows of funds may be measured in terms of **either**

1. Cash (or cash plus short-term investments; often called the near-cash basis), or
2. Working capital (i.e., current assets minus current liabilities).

In elaborating upon these two bases for measurement, the *Opinion* (par. 12) states

> a. If the format shows the flow of cash, changes in other elements of working capital (e.g., in receivables, inventories, and payables) constitute sources and uses of cash and should accordingly

[2] Prior to *APB Opinion 19,* these types of transactions were not reported on the old "funds flow statements." This was a significant improvement in meeting the requirements of the reporting principle.

[3] Funds is a particularly troublesome term because of the wide diversity of use. It sometimes is viewed as cash only, cash plus near-cash items (such as short-term investments), working capital (i.e., current assets minus current liabilities), assets set aside for a specific purpose (such as a bond sinking fund), and it has yet another special meaning in governmental accounting.

Item	Increases	Decreases
Cash	**Debit** to the Cash account with a compensating credit to any other account.	**Credit** to the Cash account with a compensating debit to any other account.
Working capital	**Debit** to any current asset or current liability account and **no** compensating credit to any other working capital account.	**Credit** to any current asset or current liability account and **no** compensating debit to any other working capital account.

be disclosed in appropriate detail in the body of the statement.

b. If the format shows the flow of working capital and two-year comparative balance sheets are presented, the changes in each element of working capital for the current period (but not for earlier periods) can be computed by the user of the statements. Nevertheless, the Board believes that the objectives of the Statement usually require that the net change in working capital be analyzed in appropriate detail in a tabulation accompanying the Statement, and accordingly this detail should be furnished.

Format of the SCFP

Because of these specifications, the SCFP typically has the following general formats:

SCFP—Funds Measured as Cash,
or Cash Plus Short-Term Investments

1. Sources of cash, or cash plus short-term investments (inflows).
2. Uses of cash, or cash plus short-term investments (outflows).
3. Net increase or decrease in cash, or cash plus short-term investments.

SCFP—Funds Measured as Working Capital

*Part A**—Sources and uses of working capital:

1. Sources of working capital (inflows).
2. Uses of working capital (outflows).
3. Net increase or decrease in working capital.

*Part B**—Changes in working capital accounts:

4. Net change in current asset accounts.
5. Net change in current liability accounts.
6. Net increase or decrease in working capital.

* The designations "Part A" and "Part B" are not specifically reflected on the statement; they are used here to facilitate explanation.

The *Opinion* permits the use of either approach. However, the specific basis used should be clearly disclosed, for example, "Cash provided from operations" or "Working capital provided from operations."[4]

SIMPLIFIED ILLUSTRATION OF CASH FLOWS VERSUS WORKING CAPITAL FLOWS

The SCFP reports significant differences in results when the flow of funds is measured on a cash flow basis as compared with a working capital basis. The distinction between the cash and working capital bases is important in understanding the analyses and discussions in this chapter.

Exhibit 23–1, Panels A and B, presents an analysis of a series of transactions to illustrate the distinction between the cash and working capital bases.

The analyses in Exhibit 23–1 are based upon the following relationship shown at the top of the page. The resulting SCFP is summarized in Exhibit 23–1, Panel C. This exhibit should be studied carefully.

In Exhibit 23–1, Panel A, observe that the inflow of cash was more than the inflow of working capital in only one of the first three transactions. In item *(d)*, note that total sales caused an increase in working capital, whereas only cash sales caused an increase in cash. Expenses, whether paid or accrued as a current liability, cause a decrease in working capital, whereas only cash expenses cause a decrease in cash. **Depreciation expense does not affect either working capital or cash flow because it does not result from a cash (or working capital) transaction during the period.**

[4] Because cash flows generally are viewed as more critical than working capital flows, and the latter often are larger in amount, there continue to be instances where an entity, by vague terminology, does not clearly disclose whether the statement reflects working capital or cash. The *Opinion* recognizes this problem by stating: "Terms referring to 'cash' should not be used to describe amounts provided from operations unless all non-cash items have been appropriately adjusted."

EXHIBIT 23–1: SCFP—Cash Basis and Working Capital Basis Compared

Panel A—Sources (Inflows) of Funds:

Transaction			Cash (Sources)	Working Capital (Sources)
a. Issued 1,000 shares of common stock during the period, resulting in the following entry:				
Cash	3,000		$ 3,000	$ 3,000
Special receivable (short term)	4,000			4,000
Special receivable (long term)	5,000			
Common stock (par $10)		10,000		
Contributed capital in excess of par		2,000		
Total inflow			3,000	7,000

Observe that working capital increased by the amount of current assets received and not by the selling price, the par value of the stock, or the noncurrent receivable.

b. Sold a plant asset during the period, resulting in the following entry:				
Cash	4,000		4,000	4,000
Notes receivable, short term	5,000			5,000
Mortgage receivable, long term	14,000			
Accumulated depreciation	10,000			
Plant asset		31,000		
Gain on sale of plant asset		2,000		
Total inflow			4,000	9,000

Observe that the working capital inflow was the sum of cash and current receivables recognized and not the amount of the sale price, the gain recognized on the sale, or the noncurrent receivable.

c. Borrowed from the bank, resulting in the following entry:				
Cash	30,000		30,000	+30,000
Notes payable, short term		20,000		−20,000
Notes payable, long term		10,000		
Total inflow			30,000	10,000

Observe that although there was an inflow of cash of $30,000, working capital increased by only $10,000. This was because the increase in current liabilities for the short-term debt "offset" $20,000 of the inflow. Thus, working capital was increased by the amount of the increase in long-term debt.

d. Net income for the period was as follows:				
Sales: Cash	$40,000		+40,000	+40,000
On account receivable	10,000	$50,000		+10,000
Cost of goods sold:				
Goods purchased for cash	18,000		−18,000	−18,000
Goods purchased on account payable	7,000			− 7,000
Decrease in inventory balance	3,000	28,000		− 3,000
Gross margin		22,000		
Expenses:				
Paid in cash	10,000		−10,000	−10,000
Accrued (liability)	2,000			− 2,000
Depreciation	4,000	16,000		
Income from operations		6,000		
Gain on sale of plant asset		2,000		
Net income		$ 8,000		
Total inflow from continuing operations*			12,000	10,000
Grand total inflow for the period (all transactions)			$49,000	$36,000

* The results of this analysis are *(a)* net income of $8,000 on accrual basis converted to a working capital basis is $10,000 and *(b)* net income of $8,000 on accrual basis converted to a cash basis is $12,000.

EXHIBIT 23–1 ***(concluded)***

Panel B—Uses (Outflows) of Funds:

Transaction			Funds Measured as: Cash (Uses)	Funds Measured as: Working Capital (Uses)
a. Purchased a plant asset during the period resulting in the following entry:				
Plant asset	30,000			
Cash		3,000	$ 3,000	$ 3,000
Note payable, short term		7,000		7,000
Mortgage payable, long term		20,000		
Total outflow			3,000	10,000

Observe that working capital used was the sum of the cash paid plus the current liability recognized, not the purchase price or the long-term debt incurred.

b. Cash dividends resulted in the following entry:				
Retained earnings	12,000			
Cash		8,000	8,000	8,000
Dividends payable (current liability)		4,000		4,000
Total outflow			8,000	12,000
c. Payments on debts during the period resulted in the following entry:				
Accounts payable	15,000			−15,000
Notes payable, long term	25,000			
Cash		40,000	40,000	+40,000
Total outflow			40,000	25,000

Observe that although $40,000 cash (and working capital) was used, the decrease in working capital was only $25,000. This was because the $15,000 paid on a working capital debt constituted an "offset." Thus, the working capital used was equivalent to the decrease in long-term debt only.

d. Treasury stock purchased during the period resulted in the following entry:				
Treasury stock (at cost)	8,000			
Cash		5,000	5,000	5,000
Special payable, short term		3,000		3,000
Total outflow			5,000	8,000
Grand total outflow for the period (all transactions)			$56,000	$ 55,000
Increase (decrease) during the period:				
Cash ($49,000 − $56,000)			$ (7,000)	
Working capital ($36,000 − $55,000)				$(19,000)

Panel C—Statement of Changes in Financial Position (summarized)* for the Year Ended December 31, 19X

	Cash Basis	Working Capital Basis
Sources (inflows):		
From continuing operations	$12,000	$10,000
Issuance of common stock	3,000	7,000
Sale of plant asset	4,000	9,000
Borrowing	30,000	10,000
Total inflows	49,000	36,000

	Cash Basis	Working Capital Basis
Uses (outflows):		
Purchase of plant asset	3,000	10,000
Dividends	8,000	12,000
Debt retirement	40,000	25,000
Acquisition of treasury stock	5,000	8,000
Total outflows	56,000	55,000
Net increase (decrease) during the period:		
Cash	$ (7,000)	
Working capital		$(19,000)

* This summarized statement omits some details required for full disclosure. It is summarized in this manner for instructional purposes; detailed statements will be presented subsequently.

In transactions *(a)*, *(b)*, and *(c)*, the differences between working capital flows and cash flows resulted from the **short-term** (current) receivables and payables. In contrast, long-term receivables and payables affect cash flows and working capital flows by the same amounts.

In transaction *(b)* of Panel A, the $2,000 gain on sale of a plant asset does not measure the amount of cash or working capital involved; rather, cash was increased by the amount of the sale price collected during the period and working capital was increased by the amount of the sale price collected in cash **plus** the short-term receivable recorded.

To establish a clear-cut delineation between the two approaches to measuring "funds" and to facilitate discussion, this chapter discusses changes in financial position on a working capital basis separately from changes in financial position on a cash (or cash plus short-term investments) basis.

CRITERIA FOR THE SCFP

APB Opinion 19 specifies certain criteria for developing a SCFP. These criteria may be summarized as follows:

1. The SCFP should be presented as one of three required basic financial statements for each period in which a balance sheet and an income statement are presented.
2. The SCFP applies to all profit-oriented business entities whether or not assets and liabilities are classified between current and noncurrent.
3. The SCFP should be based on a broad concept embracing all changes in financial position (including the effects of direct exchanges). The SCFP should disclose all important changes in financial position for the period.
4. The SCFP should begin with the income or loss before extraordinary items, if any, and add back (or deduct) items recognized in determining income or loss which did not use (or provide) working capital or cash during the period.[5]
5. The items added back (or deducted) in 4 above should be presented clearly to avoid the interpretation that they provided or used funds.
6. The effects of extraordinary items should be reported separately from the effects of normal operating items.
7. The effects of all financing and investing activities, including those which have no direct effect on working capital or cash (i.e., direct nonfund exchanges) should be disclosed **individually.**
8. If the SCFP is prepared on the working capital basis and two-year comparative balance sheets are presented, the detailed changes in working capital accounts must be presented.
9. Working capital or cash inflow or outflow from operations should be appropriately described.
10. If the SCFP is prepared on the cash basis, detailed changes in other working capital accounts should be reported in the body of the SCFP (as adjustments to convert income to a cash flow basis).
11. Terms referring to cash should not be used unless all noncash items have been appropriately adjusted.
12. Flexibility is permitted in format, content, and terminology in the SCFP; flexibility should be used to develop the presentation that is most informative in the circumstances.
13. It is strongly recommended that isolated statistics of working capital and cash, especially on a per share basis, **not** be presented.
14. Stock dividends and stock splits do not have to be disclosed because they do not represent financing or investing activities and they do not affect cash or working capital.

Next we discuss and illustrate the development of the SCFP on the **working capital** basis. Part B discusses the cash basis.

SCFP, WORKING CAPITAL (WC) BASIS

Concepts Underlying the SCFP, Working Capital Basis

Working capital is composed of **positive current** items (cash, short-term investments, receivables, inventories, prepaid expenses, etc.) and **negative current** items (accounts payable, short-term notes payable, accrued liabilities, etc.). Any excess of current

[5] An alternative procedure indicated in *APB Opinion 19* gives the same result. It starts with revenues that increase working capital or cash during the period and deducts therefrom operating expenses that cause outflows of working capital or cash. This approach has the advantage of not suggesting that "adjustments" to net income, such as depreciation expense, cause an increase in working capital or cash.

assets over current liabilities represents a "liquid pool" of net working resources. Transactions that increase working capital are referred to as **sources;** transactions that decrease working capital are referred to as **uses.**

Transactions that involve debits and credits to working capital accounts only, (such as the payment of a current liability, the collection of a current receivable, or the purchase of inventory or short-term investments for cash) neither increase nor use working capital; they merely rearrange the internal **content** of working capital as illustrated in Exhibit 23–1. In contrast, certain transactions that involve debits or credits to **one or more noncurrent** accounts **and also one or more current** accounts, such as the purchase of a **noncurrent asset** with cash or the payment of a **noncurrent debt,** will cause **both** the **content** and the **amount** of working capital to change. This distinction is fundamental in the analysis required to develop a SCFP, WC basis.

An SCFP, working capital basis, necessitates considerable analysis, except in simple situations, because the **accounts** themselves often do not directly provide the required data. Recall from the discussions above that the inflows and outflows of working capital are the result of changes in assets, liabilities, and owners' equity. **Thus, the key to developing the SCFP on a working capital basis is an analysis of the causes of changes in the current asset and current liability accounts. Such an analysis entails a complementary analysis of the noncurrent asset and liability accounts, as well as of the owners' equity accounts.**

Over the long term, the primary source of working capital in a business is from the operations of the business as reflected in "income before extraordinary items." Because the income statement, and the income or loss reported thereon, are based on the accrual concept, an important aspect of the SCFP, working capital basis, is to convert reported income from the accrual basis to a working capital basis. This conversion requires certain adjustments (i.e., additions and subtractions) to **income** for items included on the income statement that did not affect working capital during the period by the same amount they affected income; common examples are depreciation expense, depletion expense, amortization expense on intangibles, income tax expense for which the related credit was to the long-term deferred income tax account, interest expense related to amortization of bond premium or bond discount, and gains or losses on the disposal of long-term investments and operational assets.

To illustrate the adjustment to income related to a loss on the disposal of machinery, assume the disposal was recorded as follows:

Cash	5,000	
Accumulated depreciation—machinery	8,000	
Loss on disposal of machinery	3,000	
Machinery		16,000

In this example, the loss of $3,000 decreased pretax income by $3,000. However, the disposal transaction was a source (i.e., an increase) of working capital in the amount of $5,000. For this reason, on the SCFP the $3,000 loss would be added back to income before extraordinary items to compute "working capital inflow from **continuing** operations." Then, the $5,000 source of working capital would be reported under a separate heading, Other Sources. *APB Opinion 19* (par. 14) appears to permit sources of funds such as this $5,000 source to be reported in either of two ways: (1) as an element in the determination of "working capital from operations" or as Other Sources. In this book we report sources of funds from the disposal of long-term investments and operational assets under the caption Other Sources because the income heading is from **continuing** operations (illustrated in Exhibit 23–2).

Reporting the conversion of income from the accrual basis to a working capital basis is illustrated in the SCFP presented in Exhibit 23–2. In that exhibit, income before extraordinary items is reported as $27,000; however, after reporting the two "conversion" items (depreciation and amortization expenses), the working capital inflow from continuing operations is reported as $35,000. Also, working capital inflows are reported from two other sources—an extraordinary item and other sources (issuance of bonds). Next the uses of working capital are reported. The difference between total sources and total uses is the net increase in working capital during the period ($64,000). This difference must agree with the change in working capital during the period as reported at the bottom of the SCFP. The next section discusses and illustrates how the amounts reported on the SCFP (Exhibit 23–2) were derived.

Preparing the SCFP, Working Capital Basis

The format of the SCFP, working capital basis, was outlined under the previous heading, Format of

EXHIBIT 23–2: SCFP, Working Capital Basis (based on illustrative data given in Exhibit 23–3, and SCFP Worksheet, Exhibit 23–4)

WC CORPORATION
Statement of Changes in Financial Position, Working Capital Basis
For the Year Ended December 31, 19B

Sources (inflows) of working capital:		
Continuing operations:		
Income before extraordinary items	$27,000	
Add (deduct) to convert to working capital:		
Depreciation expense	7,900	
Amortization of discount on bonds payable	100	
Working capital inflow from continuing operations		$35,000
Extraordinary items:		
Sale of land		53,000
Other sources:		
Bonds payable issued for cash		5,000
Total working capital inflow		93,000
Uses (outflows) of working capital:		
Cash dividends declared and paid on common stock	15,000	
Machinery purchased	10,000	
Short-term investment distributed as dividends to shareholders of preferred stock	4,000	
Total working capital used		29,000
Increase in working capital during the period		$64,000
Financing and investing activities not affecting working capital:*		
Common stock issued to retire bonds payable		$21,000
Preferred stock issued to acquire other assets		10,000
Total		$31,000

Changes in working capital accounts:

	Account Balances 12/31/19B	Account Balances 12/31/19A	Working Capital Increase (Decrease)
Current assets:			
Cash	$ 69,000	$ 30,000	$39,000
Investments, short term	8,000	10,000	(2,000)
Accounts receivable (net)	80,000	50,000	30,000
Inventory	30,000	20,000	10,000
Prepaid expenses	2,000		2,000
Total current assets	189,000	110,000	
Current liabilities:			
Accounts payable	55,000	40,000	(15,000)
Total current liabilities	55,000	40,000	
Working capital	$134,000	$ 70,000	$64,000

(The $64,000 increase in working capital and the $64,000 change in working capital accounts: Must Agree)

* Direct exchanges are viewed as concurrent sources and uses (see page 822). Most companies report direct exchanges in this manner; however, some report them twice—once, as a source and also, as a use.

Note: Format and terminology used in this exhibit were selected to facilitate instructional objectives. In actual practice there is considerable variance in both format and terminology.

the SCFP, and its two distinct parts were identified as follows:

Part A—Sources and uses of working capital.
Part B—Changes in working capital accounts.

Exhibit 23–2 presents a detailed SCFP, working capital basis, for WC Corporation. The information reported on the SCFP is classified as follows:

1. Sources (inflows) of working capital.
   a. Continuing operations.
   b. Extraordinary items.
   c. Other sources.
2. Uses (outflows) of working capital.
   a. Detailed by use.
3. Financing and investing activities not affecting working capital.
4. Changes in working capital accounts.
   a. Current assets.
   b. Current liabilities.

The SCFP for WC Corporation given in Exhibit 23–2 was developed using the illustrative data given in Exhibit 23–3. Exhibit 23–2 suggests that an analytical approach is needed. Exhibit 23–4 presents an analytical **worksheet** designed to translate the illustrative data into the SCFP (as shown in Exhibit 23–2). Recall that in Chapter 3 a worksheet was presented to develop the income statement, statement of retained earnings, and balance sheet; the worksheet presented in this chapter serves exactly the same purpose for the SCFP.

SCFP Worksheet, Working Capital Basis. In simple situations (as illustrated in Exhibit 23–1) it is possible to develop an SCFP by direct inspection of the basic data. However, in the typical situation a worksheet usually is used because it is needed to synthesize and analyze the mass of data. The worksheet provides for analysis of the entries that caused changes in the financial position. For instructional purposes, some people prefer a T-account approach, which analytically is exactly the same as the worksheet—only the mechanical format is different (illustrated in Supplement 23–A).

The objective of the SCFP worksheet is to apply an organized approach, which retains the features of the accounting model and the debit-credit concept, in order to analyze and identify all of the sources (increases) and uses (decreases) of working capital to be reported on the SCFP as shown in Exhibit 23–2. This objective can be accomplished on the worksheet by isolating the working capital effects of **all transactions affecting all noncurrent balance sheet accounts** (i.e., all balance sheet accounts except current assets and current liabilities). Also, such a worksheet has the virtue of integrating all of the data in a systematic manner on one schedule. Another important advantage of it is that the formal SCFP, Part A, essentially can be copied directly from the lower portion of the worksheet.[6]

Exhibit 23–4 presents a worksheet designed to develop the SCFP in complex situations. Observe that this worksheet is based on the premise that the **causes** of the changes in working capital can be found only in an analysis of the **nonworking capital accounts.** In contrast, an analysis of **only** the working capital accounts will divulge only changes (as opposed to causes) in the **content** of working capital. The worksheet deals with the **causes** of the changes in working capital; these causes are identified as the sources and uses of working capital. For example, issuance of common stock for cash causes working capital to increase; hence, issuance of common stock is a source of working capital.

The worksheet is set up with four amount columns and six major side headings. The first column (beginning balance) and last column (ending balance) are taken from the two consecutive balance sheets. The two interim columns (debit and credit) are provided for "reconciling through analysis" the beginning and ending balances of each account listed. The six side headings may be explained as follows:

1. Working capital—This heading provides for entering the amounts of working capital at the beginning and end of the period; they are entered on the worksheet **only** for balancing purposes.
2. Nonworking capital accounts—These accounts provide the beginning and ending **noncurrent** balance sheet amounts that must be analyzed in detail. They are grouped by debit and credit balances for convenience in analysis. The amounts were taken directly from the two consecutive balance sheets given in Exhibit 23–3. Sufficient lines should be provided for accounts that usually

[6] For examination and problem-solving purposes by students, a worksheet generally should suffice without having to copy Part A, a formal SCFP. Part B of the SCFP, working capital basis, is purely clerical because it is copied directly from the comparative balance sheets (current assets and current liabilities). For this reason it is redundant; however, it is required by *APB Opinion 19.*

EXHIBIT 23–3: Illustrative SCFP Data for WC Corporation

Comparative Balance Sheet Data

Debits	12/31/19A	12/31/19B
Cash	$ 30,000	$ 69,000
Investment, short term (X Co. stock)	10,000	8,000
Accounts receivable (net)	50,000	80,000
Inventory	20,000	30,000
Prepaid expenses		2,000
Land	60,000	25,000
Machinery	80,000	90,000
Other assets	29,000	39,000
Discount on bonds payable	1,000	900
Total debits	$280,000	$343,900
Credits		
Accounts payable	$ 40,000	$ 55,000
Accumulated depreciation	20,000	27,900
Bonds payable	70,000	55,000
Common stock, nopar	100,000	131,000
Preferred stock, nopar	20,000	30,000
Retained earnings	30,000	45,000
Total credits	$280,000	$343,900

(Amounts Reported at—)

Income Statement Data

	12/31/19B
Sales revenue	$180,000
Cost of goods sold	90,000
Expenses (includes income tax)	55,000
Depreciation	7,900
Amortization of discount on bonds payable	100
Total expenses	153,000
Income before extraordinary items	27,000
Extraordinary items (net of tax):	
Gain on special sale of land	18,000
Loss on bond retirement	(1,000)
Net income	$ 44,000

Additional data; summary of selected transactions for the year:

a. Net income (per above), $44,000.
b. Sales, $180,000 (all on credit); purchases, $100,000 (all on credit).
c. Inventory increase, $10,000.
d. Expenses (including income tax), $55,000.
e. Depreciation expense, $7,900.
f. Prepaid expenses increased during the year, $2,000; paid in cash when originally recorded.
g. Cash dividend declared and paid, on the common stock, $15,000.
h. Common stock dividend issued; retained earnings debited for $10,000.
i. Issued bonds payable for cash, $5,000.
j. Sold land for $53,000 cash, net of tax; book value, $35,000; the gain is assumed to be an extraordinary item for illustrative purposes only.
k. Purchased machinery for cash, $10,000.
l. Purchased short-term investments for cash, $2,000.
m. Declared a property dividend on the preferred stock and paid it with a short-term investment (X Company stock); market value and carrying value are the same, $4,000.
n. Prior to maturity date, retired $20,000 bonds payable by issuing common stock; the common stock had a market value of $21,000 (assumed extraordinary; no tax effect).*
o. Accounts receivable increase, $30,000.
p. Accounts payable increase, $15,000.
q. Acquired other assets by issuing preferred stock, $10,000 (market value).
r. Amortization of discount on bonds payable, $100.

* AICPA, *APB Opinion No. 29,* "Accounting for Nonmonetary Transactions" (New York, May 1973), specifies with certain exceptions that direct exchanges shall be recorded to recognize current market value. FASB, *Statement of Financial Accounting Standards No. 4,* "Reporting Gains and Losses from Early Extinguishment of Debt" (Stamford, Conn., March 1975), specifies that loss or gain on early extinguishment of debt shall be reported as an extraordinary item net of tax. The above amounts are assumed to be net of tax.

EXHIBIT 23–4: Worksheet—SCFP, Working Capital Basis (based on data given in Exhibit 23–3)

WC CORPORATION
Worksheet to Develop Statement of Changes in Financial Position, Working Capital Basis
For the Year Ended December 31, 19B

Item	Beginning Balance 12/31/19A	Analysis of Interim Entries: Debit	Analysis of Interim Entries: Credit	Ending Balance 12/31/19B
Debits				
1. **Working capital**	70,000	*(s)* 64,000		134,000
2. **Nonworking capital accounts:**				
Land	60,000		*(j)* 35,000	25,000
Machinery	80,000	*(k)* 10,000		90,000
Other assets	29,000	*(q–2)* 10,000		39,000
Discount on bonds payable	1,000		*(r)* 100	900
Total	240,000			288,900
Credits				
Accumulated depreciation	20,000		*(e)* 7,900	27,900
Bonds payable	70,000	*(n–2)* 20,000	*(i)* 5,000	55,000
Common stock	100,000		*(h)* 10,000	131,000
			(n–1) 21,000	
Preferred stock	20,000		*(q–1)* 10,000	30,000
Retained earnings	30,000	*(g)* 15,000	*(a)* 44,000	45,000
		(h) 10,000		
		(m) 4,000		
Total	240,000	133,000	133,000	288,900
Classification of items for SCFP:		**Sources**	**Uses**	
3. **Sources (inflows) of WC:**				
Net income		*(a)* 44,000		WC from continuing operations, $35,000
Adjustments to convert to WC basis:				
To remove gain on land			*(j)* 18,000	
To remove loss on bonds retired		*(n–2)* 1,000		
Depreciation expense		*(e)* 7,900		
Amortization of bond discount		*(r)* 100		
Extraordinary items:				
Land sold		*(j)* 53,000		
Other sources of working capital:				
Bonds payable issued		*(i)* 5,000		
4. **Uses (outflows) of WC:**				
Cash dividends declared and paid			*(g)* 15,000	
Machinery purchased			*(k)* 10,000	
Short-term investment distributed as dividend to shareholders of preferred stock			*(m)* 4,000	
5. **Increase in working capital during the period**			*(s)* 64,000	
Total		111,000	111,000	
Grand total		244,000	244,000	
		Financing Activities	**Investing Activities**	
6. **Direct exchanges:***				
Common stock issued to retire bonds payable		*(n–1)* 21,000	*(n–2)* 21,000	
Preferred stock issued for other assets		*(q–1)* 10,000	*(q–2)* 10,000	
		31,000	31,000	

* For instructional convenience the worksheet dual entries for each direct exchange are numbered as follows: "–1" = **source** (i.e. the financing activity) and "–2" = **use** (i.e., the investing activity).

Note. The following items were not entered on the worksheet because they caused no direct change in working capital: *(c), (f), (l), (o),* and *(p)*; *(d)* was subsumed in net income.

EXHIBIT 23–5: Analysis of Entries for Worksheet, Working Capital (WC) Basis (refer to Exhibit 23–4)

Accounts	Original Entry Dr.	Original Entry Cr.	Worksheet Entry Dr.	Worksheet Entry Cr.
a. Net income for the period:				
Income summary	44,000			
Sources of WC (to be adjusted to WC basis)			44,000	
Retained earnings		44,000		44,000

Explanation: Net income for the period is entered as a source of working capital in the same amount and is adjusted to WC basis by the analytical entries to follow.

b.–d. No net effect on working capital (aside from effect on net income, *(a)* above).

Accounts	Original Entry Dr.	Original Entry Cr.	Worksheet Entry Dr.	Worksheet Entry Cr.
e. Depreciation expense:				
Depreciation expense	7,900			
Sources of WC (adjustment of net income)			7,900	
Accumulated depreciation		7,900		7,900

Explanation: Depreciation expense reduced net income; however, it did not reduce working capital during the period. Therefore, it must be added back to net income as an adjustment to derive "working capital inflow from continuing operations."

f. No net effect on working capital.

Accounts	Original Entry Dr.	Original Entry Cr.	Worksheet Entry Dr.	Worksheet Entry Cr.
g. Cash dividend declared and paid:				
Retained earnings	15,000		15,000	
Cash		15,000		
Uses of WC				15,000

Explanation: The use of cash reduced WC.

Accounts	Original Entry Dr.	Original Entry Cr.	Worksheet Entry Dr.	Worksheet Entry Cr.
h. Common stock dividend issued:				
Retained earnings	10,000		10,000	
Common stock		10,000		10,000

Explanation: *APB Opinion 19* specifies that stock dividends, stock splits, and appropriations of retained earnings are not reported on the SCFP. This entry is necessary to reconcile the beginning and ending balances of the accounts involved.

Accounts	Original Entry Dr.	Original Entry Cr.	Worksheet Entry Dr.	Worksheet Entry Cr.
i. Bonds payable issued:				
Cash	5,000			
Sources of WC			5,000	
Bonds payable		5,000		5,000

Explanation: Cash inflow increased WC.

Accounts	Original Entry Dr.	Original Entry Cr.	Worksheet Entry Dr.	Worksheet Entry Cr.
j. Sold land for cash at a gain:				
Cash	53,000			
Sources of WC			53,000	
Land		35,000		35,000
Gain on disposal of land (assumed extraordinary)		18,000		
Sources of WC (negative adjustment of net income)				18,000

Explanation: This transaction increased WC by the cash received, $53,000, rather than by the gain of $18,000. Because net income includes the extraordinary gain and *APB Opinion 19* specifically requires that the SCFP begin with income before extraordinary items, the extraordinary gain must be removed from net income, (this also converts net income from an accrual basis to a WC basis). You should trace this transaction through the worksheet (Exhibit 23–4) and then to the SCFP (Exhibit 23–2).

EXHIBIT 23–5 ***(concluded)***

Accounts	Original Entry Dr.	Original Entry Cr.	Worksheet Entry Dr.	Worksheet Entry Cr.
k. Purchased machinery for cash:				
Machinery	10,000		10,000	
Cash		10,000		
Uses of WC				10,000
Explanation: Use of cash decreased WC.				
l. No net effect on working capital.				
m. Declared and paid property dividend with short-term investments (X Company stock):				
Retained earnings	4,000		4,000	
Investments, short term		4,000		
Uses of WC				4,000
Explanation: Use of short-term investments decreased WC.				
n. Retired bonds payable by issuing common stock, a nonworking capital **direct exchange:**				
Bonds payable	20,000		20,000[2]	
Loss on retirement of bonds payable (extraordinary)	1,000			
Sources of WC (to remove loss from net income)			1,000[2]	
Sources of WC (issuance of stock)			21,000[1]	
Common stock, nopar (issuance)		21,000		21,000[1]
Uses of WC (to retire bonds payable)				21,000[2]

Explanation: This transaction was a **direct exchange** that affected two nonworking capital accounts—Bonds Payable and Common Stock—but did not directly affect WC. The $21,000 issue price of the bonds is an "in-and-out" item that must be reported on the SCFP. Entry 1 is for the financing activity (source), and entry 2 is for the investing activity (use). The extraordinary loss of $1,000 is shown in the worksheet entry as a debit to *(a)* remove it from net income, and *(b)* convert net income from an accrual basis to a WC basis.

Accounts	Original Entry Dr.	Original Entry Cr.	Worksheet Entry Dr.	Worksheet Entry Cr.
o. and *p.* No net effect on working capital.				
q. Other assets acquired by issuing preferred stock:				
Other assets	10,000		10,000[2]	
Sources of WC (issuance of stock)			10,000[1]	
Preferred stock, nopar		10,000		10,000[1]
Uses of WC (to acquire other assets)				10,000[2]

Explanation: This transaction was a nonworking capital **direct exchange** that affected two nonworking capital accounts—Other Assets and Preferred Stock. It is an "in-and-out" item of $10,000 that must be reported on the SCFP similar to entry *(n)* above. Entry 1 is for the financing activity (source), and entry 2 is for the investing activity (use).

Accounts	Original Entry Dr.	Original Entry Cr.	Worksheet Entry Dr.	Worksheet Entry Cr.
r. Amortization of discount on bonds payable:				
Interest expense (discount amortization)	100			
Sources of WC (adjustment of net income)			100	
Discount on bonds payable		100		100

Explanation: This transaction did not affect WC; it affected a nonworking capital account—Discounts on Bonds Payable—and net income (through interest expense). Because interest expense in the amount of this amortization was deducted from income but did not affect WC, it must be added back to net income, similar to depreciation expense, in entry *(e)* above, to convert net income from an accrual basis to a WC basis.

s. This **optional** entry is made simply to balance the worksheet. After this entry, two internal **accuracy checks** should be made: (1) that the beginning and ending balances for each item are reconciled on each line, and (2) that the debits and credits of the "interim" columns are equal.

have high activity during the period (e.g., retained earnings in Exhibit 23–4).

3. Sources (inflows) of working capital—This section, which parallels the SCFP, provides for listing the various "sources" of working capital. The sources under this section are reflected on the worksheet as **debits** (the credits represent offsetting adjustments).[7]
4. Uses (outflows) of working capital—This section, which parallels the SCFP, provides for listing the **uses** of working capital. The amounts under this section are reflected on the worksheet as **credits.**
5. Increase or decrease in working capital during the period (i.e., the difference between total sources and total uses).
6. Direct exchanges—This section parallels the section of the SCFP entitled "Financing and investing activities not affecting working capital." Each **direct exchange** is reflected as *(a)* a **debit for source** (i.e., a financing activity) and *(b)* a **credit for use** (i.e., an investing activity). This **dual effect** of direct exchanges occurs because each exchange is viewed as "in-and-out" item, that is, as a concurrent source and use of working capital.

Completion of the worksheet involves an analysis of each transaction (similar transactions are aggregated) that affected a **nonworking capital account.** Observe that **only** the nonworking capital accounts (but not the working capital accounts) are listed on the worksheet. **Each transaction affecting one or more nonworking capital accounts is entered on the worksheet in essentially the same way as when it was originally recorded in the accounts.** All debits and credits to working capital accounts (such accounts are not on the worksheet) are reflected in the **lower portion of the worksheet—classification of items for the SCFP.** Note on Exhibit 23–4 that the primary classifications (i.e., classifications 3 through 6) are essentially the same as shown on the **SCFP illustrated in Exhibit 23–2.**

The following is a step-by-step approach used in completing the worksheet (Exhibit 23–4) for WC Corporation:

Step 1: Set up the four amount columns and the six major side headings.

Step 2: Compute the beginning and ending amounts of working capital and enter these balances and the other original data from the beginning and ending balance sheets for each nonworking capital (i.e., noncurrent) account.

Step 3: Analyze each listed account; enter on the worksheet under "analysis of interim entries" only those transactions that affected one or more **nonworking capital accounts** so that all differences between the beginning and ending balances of each account are accounted for fully.

Analysis of Interim Entries, Working Capital Basis. The Analysis of Interim Entries columns *(a)* reconcile the beginning and ending balances of each noncurrent account and *(b)* enter on the bottom portion of the worksheet all sources and uses of working capital. Exhibit 23–5 explains the analysis of each entry on the worksheet (Exhibit 23–4). For instructional purposes only, both the original entry and the worksheet entry are shown in Exhibit 23–5; also, for emphasis, the working capital sources and uses are given in **boldface,** and to facilitate cross-reference, the letters to the left are keyed to the illustrative data given in Exhibit 23–3.

---

[7] The word **sources** is used loosely in this context because, for example, depreciation expense and amortization of bond discount are adjustments to income rather than literal "sources" of working capital.

Part B: SCFP, Cash (or Cash Plus Short-Term Investments) Basis

CONCEPTS UNDERLYING THE SCFP, CASH BASIS

Investors and creditors are vitally interested in the debt-paying ability of a company. Traditionally, funds statements have been viewed as providing information that might be useful in assessing the debt-paying ability of a business. Assessing debt-paying ability raises the fundamental issue of whether the SCFP should be on the working capital basis or the cash basis. On this point one writer observed that "many a firm has been known to pay its debts with cash, but no one has been known to draw a check on working capital."[8] More recently, another writer stated that "the emphasis in credit analysis has shifted from analysis of current working capital position to dynamic analysis of future cash receipts and cash payments in much the same way that emphasis in security analysis shifted from static analysis of balance sheet values to dynamic analysis of net income some thirty or forty years earlier."[9]

In view of the advantages of cash-based statements, one may ask why the working capital based SCFP dominates in published financial statements. The answer probably lies in the facts that *(a)* there is no real agreement on the objectives of the SCFP, *(b)* working capital statements represent precedent (which is difficult to change), and *(c)* some businesses (as well as individuals) are very sensitive about revealing their problems associated with cash flows. .[10]

The SCFP on a cash basis can be developed by measuring funds as *(a)* cash only or *(b)* cash plus short-term investments. The total of cash plus short-term investments usually is presented because such investments (by definition) are highly liquid.[11]

PREPARING OF THE SCFP, CASH BASIS

SCFP Worksheet, Cash Basis

Because the general format of the SCFP is similar for the working capital or cash basis, essentially the same worksheet format can be used for either. The the worksheet used to prepare the cash basis SCFP parallels the worksheet format shown in Exhibit 23–4; however, it reflects some changes in terminology (essentially from the words **working capital to cash**).

To illustrate the SCFP, cash basis, worksheet and the statement, we return to the data given in Exhibit 23–3. Exhibit 23–6 presents the cash basis worksheet, and Exhibit 23–7 presents the related SCFP, cash basis, for WC Corporation. This example defines cash as "cash plus short-term investments," which usually is done in actual practice when the SCFP is prepared on the cash basis. The combination of these two items presents no complexities—the two simply are added together (see Appendix following Chapter 24 for such a presentation by The Quaker Oats Company).

To prepare the SCFP worksheet, cash basis, the summarized transactions are analyzed and entered in debit-credit format under the pair of columns headed Analysis of Interim Entries. Observe that, similar to the working capital basis, the original entries are followed with adaptation at the bottom of the worksheet—Classification of items for SCFP—for the original debits and credits to Cash. The worksheet reflects four amount columns—beginning balance, analysis of interim entries (debit and credit), and ending balance. The worksheet reflects six major side headings as follows:

1. Cash—This is the actual cash (or cash plus short-term investments) balance at the beginning and

---

[8] J. W. Coughlan, "Funds and Income," *NAA Bulletin*, September 1964, p. 25.

[9] L. C. Heath, "Let's Scrap the 'Funds' Statement," *Journal of Accountancy*, October 1978, p. 98.

[10] In a few situations the cash basis statement is required, such as in the land development industry and for companies that do not classify assets and liabilities as current (primarily financial institutions). FASB, *Statement of Financial Accounting Concepts No. 1*, "Objectives of Financial Reporting by Business Enterprises" (Stamford, Conn., November 1978) has emphasized cash flow reports because users are concerned particularly with the cash flows of the business under consideration.

[11] Sometimes it is suggested that a simple summary of the Cash account, or a conversion of the income statement to a cash basis, adequately reports cash flows for the period. Both of these approaches would be inadequate and apt to be misleading. In contrast, an SCFP, cash basis, focuses on the changes in assets, liabilities, and owners' equity, on an all-resources basis, measured in terms of cash. Conceptually, the cash basis is identical to the working capital basis except that funds are measured as cash rather than as working capital.

EXHIBIT 23–6: Worksheet—SCFP, Cash Plus Short-Term Investments Basis Plus Short-Term Investments (based on data given in Exhibit 23–3)

WC CORPORATION
Worksheet to Develop a Statement of Changes in Financial Position, Cash Plus Short-Term Investments Basis For the Year Ended December 31, 19B

Item	Beginning Balance 12/31/19A	Analysis of Interim Entries: Debit	Analysis of Interim Entries: Credit	Ending Balance 12/31/19B
Debits				
1. **Cash plus short-term investments**	40,000	(s) 37,000		77,000
2. **Noncash accounts:**				
Accounts receivable (net)	50,000	(o) 30,000		80,000
Inventory	20,000	(c) 10,000		30,000
Prepaid expenses		(f) 2,000		2,000
Land	60,000		(j) 35,000	25,000
Machinery	80,000	(k) 10,000		90,000
Other assets	29,000	(q–2) 10,000		39,000
Discount on bonds payable	1,000		(r) 100	900
Total	280,000			343,900
Credits				
Accumulated depreciation	20,000		(e) 7,900	27,900
Accounts payable	40,000		(p) 15,000	55,000
Bonds payable	70,000	(n–2) 20,000	(i) 5,000	55,000
Common stock	100,000		(h) 10,000 (n–1) 21,000	131,000
Preferred stock	20,000		(q–1) 10,000	30,000
Retained earnings	30,000	(g) 15,000 (h) 10,000 (m) 4,000	(a) 44,000	45,000
Total	280,000	148,000	148,000	343,900
Classification of items for SCFP:		**Sources**	**Uses**	
3. **Sources (inflows) of cash:**				
Net income		(a) 44,000		Cash inflow from continuing operations, $8,000
Adjustments to convert to cash basis:				
Inventory increase			(c) 10,000	
Depreciation expense		(e) 7,900		
Prepaid expense increase			(f) 2,000	
To remove gain on sale of land			(j) 18,000	
To remove loss on bonds		(n–2) 1,000		
Accounts receivable increase			(o) 30,000	
Accounts payable increase		(p) 15,000		
Amortization of bond discount		(r) 100		
Extraordinary items:				
Land sold		(j) 53,000		
Other sources of cash:				
Bonds payable issued		(i) 5,000		
4. **Uses (outflows) of cash:**				
Dividends declared and paid			(g) 15,000	
Machinery purchased			(k) 10,000	
Short-term investments distributed as a dividend to shareholders of preferred stock			(m) 4,000	
5. **Increase in cash during the period**			(s) 37,000	
Total		126,000	126,000	
Grand total		274,000	274,000	
		Financing Activities	**Investing Activities**	
6. **Direct exchanges:***				
Common stock issued to retire bonds payable		(n–1) 21,000	(n–2) 21,000	
Preferred stock issued for other assets		(q–1) 10,000	(q–2) 10,000	

* For instructional convenience the worksheet dual entries for each direct exchange are numbered as follows: "–1 = **source** (i.e., the financing activity) and "–2" = **use** (i.e., the investing activity).

Note: The following items were not entered on the worksheet because they caused no direct change in the sum of cash plus short-term investments: *(b)*, *(d)*, and *(l)*.

EXHIBIT 23–7: SCFP, Cash Plus Short-Term Investments Basis (based on analysis given in Exhibit 23–6)

WC CORPORATION
Statement of Changes in Financial Position,
Cash (Plus Short-Term Investments) Basis
For the Year Ended December 31, 19B

Sources (inflows) of cash:		
Continuing operations:		
Income before extraordinary items	$ 27,000	
Adjustments to convert to cash basis:		
Inventory increase	(10,000)	
Depreciation expense	7,900	
Prepaid expense increase	(2,000)	
Accounts receivable increase	(30,000)	
Accounts payable increase	15,000	
Amortization of discount on bonds payable	100	
Cash inflow from continuing operations		$ 8,000
Extraordinary items:		
Sale of land		53,000
Other sources:		
Bonds payable issued for cash		5,000
Total cash inflow		66,000
Uses (outflows) of cash:*		
Cash dividends declared and paid on common stock	15,000	
Machinery purchased	10,000	
Short-term investments distributed as a dividend to shareholders of preferred stock	4,000	
Total cash outflow		29,000
Increase in cash during the period		$37,000
Financing and investing activities not affecting cash:†		
Common stock issued to retire bonds payable		$21,000
Preferred stock issued for "other" assets		10,000
		$31,000

* This heading does not include the "uses" of cash included in continuing operations (above) because net income subsumes cash used for expenses.

† Direct exchanges are viewed as concurrent sources and uses (see previous discussion, SCFP All-Resources Concept). Most companies report direct exchanges in this manner; however, some report them twice in the SCFP—once as a source and also as a use.

Note: Format and terminology used in this exhibit were selected to facilitate instructional objectives. In actual practice there is considerable variance in both format and terminology.

ending dates; it is entered on the worksheet only for balancing purposes.

2. Noncash accounts—All of the **noncash** accounts from the beginning and ending balance sheets (Exhibit 23–3) are entered on the worksheet for analysis and reconciliation of the beginning and ending balances. Analysis of the transactions affecting the **noncash** accounts identifies the **sources** and **uses** of cash. As with the working capital approach, we can identify the financing and investing transactions that did not directly affect cash.
3. Cash sources (inflows)—This major heading, which parallels the SCFP, is subdivided for net income, adjustments to convert accrual basis income to cash basis income, extraordinary items, and other sources of cash. The **sources,** and related adjustments, are reflected on the lower portion of the worksheet as **debits.**[12]
4. Cash uses (outflows)—This section, which parallels the SCFP, provides for listing **uses,** and the amounts are reflected on lower portion of the worksheet as **credits.**

[12] See footnote 7.

EXHIBIT 23–8: Analysis of Entries for Worksheet, Cash Basis (refer to Exhibit 23–6)

Accounts	Original Entry Dr.	Original Entry Cr.	Worksheet Entry Dr.	Worksheet Entry Cr.
a. Net income for the period, $44,000:				
Income summary	44,000			
Sources of cash (to be adjusted to cash basis)			44,000	
Retained earnings		44,000		44,000

Explanation: Net income for the period is treated as a source of cash in the same amount, to be adjusted to cash basis by the analytical entries to follow.

b. Sales revenue and purchases are not entered on the worksheet because they both are components of net income. The cash flow effects are given in entries *(o)* and *(p)* below.

Accounts	Original Entry Dr.	Original Entry Cr.	Worksheet Entry Dr.	Worksheet Entry Cr.
c. Inventory increase, $10,000:				
Inventory	10,000		10,000	
Cost of goods sold		10,000		
Sources of cash (adjustment of net income)				10,000

Explanation: This entry adjusts net income for the excess of the cash used to acquire inventory over the amount of expense; the remainder of the cash used to acquire inventory will be reflected in entry *(p)* below.

d. Cash expense assumed—not entered on the worksheet because this expense is a component of net income.

Accounts	Original Entry Dr.	Original Entry Cr.	Worksheet Entry Dr.	Worksheet Entry Cr.
e. Depreciation expense, $7,900:				
Depreciation expense	7,900			
Sources of cash (adjustment of net income)			7,900	
Accumulated depreciation		7,900		7,900

Explanation: This is a **noncash expense** which had no effect on cash of this period.

Accounts	Original Entry Dr.	Original Entry Cr.	Worksheet Entry Dr.	Worksheet Entry Cr.
f. Prepaid expenses increased, $2,000:				
Prepaid expenses	2,000		2,000	
Expenses		2,000		
Sources of cash (adjustment of net income)				2,000

Explanation: Expenses already included in net income; this entry adjusts net income on the accrual basis to cash inflow from continuing operations; in this situation cash payments exceeded expenses by $2,000, which was the amount of prepaid expense purchased.

Accounts	Original Entry Dr.	Original Entry Cr.	Worksheet Entry Dr.	Worksheet Entry Cr.
g. Dividends declared and paid, $15,000:				
Retained earnings	15,000		15,000	
Cash		15,000		
Uses of cash				15,000
h. Common stock dividend issued, $10,000:				
Retained earnings	10,000		10,000	
Common stock, nopar		10,000		10,000

Explanation: No direct or indirect cash effects (same as in Exhibit 23–5).

Accounts	Original Entry Dr.	Original Entry Cr.	Worksheet Entry Dr.	Worksheet Entry Cr.
i. Issued bonds payable for cash, $5,000:				
Cash	5,000			
Sources of cash			5,000	
Bonds payable		5,000		5,000
j. Sold land for cash, $53,000; book value $35,000:				
Cash	53,000			
Sources of cash			53,000	
Land		35,000		35,000
Gain on disposal of land (assumed extraordinary)		18,000		
Sources of cash (adjustment of net income)				18,000

Explanation: This transaction increased cash by $53,000 rather than by the amount of the gain. The gain is "removed" from net income because it is not related to continuing operations (also see Exhibit 23–5).

EXHIBIT 23–8 ***(concluded)***

Accounts	Original Entry Dr.	Original Entry Cr.	Worksheet Entry Dr.	Worksheet Entry Cr.
k. Purchased machinery for cash, $10,000:				
Machinery	10,000		10,000	
Cash		10,000		
Uses of cash				10,000
l. Purchased short-term investments for cash, $2,000; not entered on worksheet because cash and short-term investments are combined as "cash."				
m. Declared and paid dividend with short-term investment, $4,000:				
Retained earnings	4,000		4,000	
Investments, short term (S Corp. stock)		4,000		
Uses of cash (includes short-term investments)				4,000
n. Retired bonds payable, $20,000 by issuing common stock (market value $21,000):				
Bonds payable	20,000		20,000[2]	
Loss on retirement of bonds payable (extraordinary)	1,000			
Sources of cash (to remove loss from net income)			1,000[2]	
Sources of cash (issuance of stock)			21,000[1]	
Common stock, nopar		21,000		21,000[1]
Uses of cash (to retire bonds payable)				21,000[2]
Explanation: This is a **direct exchange;** entry 1 is a financing activity (source), and entry 2 is an investing activity (use).				
o. Accounts receivable increase, $30,000:				
Accounts receivable	30,000		30,000	
Sales revenue		30,000		
Sources of cash (adjustment of net income)				30,000
Explanation: This worksheet entry reconciles the beginning and ending balances of accounts receivable and adjusts accrual sales revenue to the cash basis.				
p. Accounts payable increase, $15,000:				
Purchases	15,000			
Sources of cash (adjustment of net income)			15,000	
Accounts payable		15,000		15,000
Explanation: This worksheet entry reconciles the beginning and ending balances of accounts payable and adjusts accrual cost of goods sold to the cash basis.				
q. Acquired assets by issuing preferred stock, market value $10,000:				
Other assets	10,000		10,000[2]	
Sources of cash (issuance of preferred stock)			10,000[1]	
Preferred stock, nopar (issuance)		10,000		10,000[1]
Uses of cash (to acquire assets)				10,000[2]
Explanation: This is a **direct exchange.** Entry 1 is a financing activity, and entry 2 is an investing activity.				
r. Amortization of discount on bonds payable, $100:				
Interest expense (discount amortization)	100			
Sources of cash (adjustment of net income)			100	
Discount on bonds payable		100		100
Explanation: This is a **noncash** expense which had no effect on cash of this period.				

s. This **optional entry** is made simply to balance the worksheet. After this entry, two internal **accuracy checks** should be made: (1) that the beginning and ending balances for each item are reconciled on each line, and (2) that the total debits and credits of the "interim" columns are equal.

5. Increase or decrease in **cash** (or cash plus short-term investments) during the period.
6. Direct exchanges—This section parallels the section of the SCFP entitled "Financing and investing activities not affecting cash"; it reflects the direct exchanges (i.e., those transactions that do not directly affect cash). The **financing activity** (i.e., source) is reflected as a **debit** in this section of the worksheet, and the **investing activity** (i.e., use) is reflected as a concurrent **credit.** This dual effect occurs because direct exchanges are viewed as "in-and-out" items, that is, as **concurrent sources and uses of cash.**

To develop the worksheet (and the related statement), net income on an accrual basis must be converted to a **cash basis** (i.e., cash inflow from continuing operations). Therefore, in Exhibits 23–6 (worksheet) and 23–7 (SCFP), observe the heading, "Adjustments to convert to cash basis." The adjustments under this heading convert income (accrual basis) to "Cash inflow from continuing operations."[13] The cash flows from **extraordinary items** and **other sources** are reported under separate captions as reflected in Exhibits 23–6 and 23–7.

[13] Usual practice is to start with income before extraordinary items and add (or deduct) the "adjustment" items to derive the cash or working capital from continuing operations. Alternatively, some accountants prefer to use a revenue-expense approach rather than an income approach. This approach gives precisely the same cash or working capital from continuing operations. On this point *APB Opinion 19* states: "An acceptable alternative procedure, which gives the same result, is to begin with total revenue that provided working capital or cash during the period and deduct operating costs and expenses that required the outlay of working capital or cash during the period."

Analysis of Interim Entries, Cash Basis. The interim entries reflected on the worksheet for **all transactions affecting cash** (and the direct noncash exchanges) are entered in the pair of columns headed Analysis of Interim Entries. Each debit and credit to Cash is entered in the lower portion of the worksheet—Classification of items for SCFP—and are classified as cash **sources** (inflows) or cash **uses** (outflows). The worksheet is complete when the beginning and ending balances of each noncash account are reconciled by the interim entries.

When the worksheet is completed, the lower portion reflects the SCFP, cash basis. Each entry on the worksheet is analyzed in Exhibit 23–8 for convenience in study. Each transaction is keyed by letters to the illustrative data given in Exhibit 23–3, and the sources and uses of cash are indicated in **boldface** for emphasis.

CONVERSION OF NET INCOME TO CASH BASIS INCOME FROM CONTINUING OPERATIONS SUMMARIZED

Because the conversion of net income to a cash basis income from continuing operations is ponderous, we will summarize the underlying reasons. Exhibit 23–7 reports income before extraordinary items of $27,000 and a net cash inflow (source) from continuing operations of $8,000, which essentially reflects the difference between accrual income and cash basis income from continuing operations. The conversion of accrual income to cash basis income from continuing operations reflected on the worksheet (Exhibit 23–6) and the SCFP (Exhibit 23–7) as "Adjustments to convert to cash basis" can be summarized as follows:

Entry	Item	Amount	Brief Explanation
	Net income, accrual basis	$44,000	
	Adjustments to convert to accrual basis:		
c.	Inventory increase	(10,000)*	Deduct because cash outflow for inventory is **more** than accrual basis inventory cost included in cost of goods sold.
e.	Depreciation expense	7,900	Add because cash outflow is **less** than accrual expense.
f.	Prepaid expense increase	(2,000)	Deduct because cash outflow is **more** than accrual expense.
j.	To remove extraordinary gain on land	(18,000)	Deduct this gain to remove it from income from continuing operations because total cash received, not the gain, measures the cash inflow. The total cash is reported under "Other sources."
n.	To remove extraordinary loss on bonds payable retired	1,000	Add to remove this extraordinary loss from income from continuing operations; same reason as for gain on sale of land.
o.	Accounts receivable increase	(30,000)	Deduct because cash flow from sales transactions is **less** than accrual sales revenue.
p.	Accounts payable increase	15,000*	Add because cash outflow for purchases (and, hence, cost of goods sold) is **less** than accrual purchase cost.
r.	Amortization of discount on bonds payable	100	Add because cash inflow is less than accrual interest expense.
	Cash inflow from continuing operations (Exhibit 23–7)	$ 8,000	

* These two adjustments convert cost of goods sold on an accrual basis to a cash basis. In the above tabulation the combined effect of these two adjustments to convert to cash basis income from continuing operations was a $5,000 **increase** of the cash inflow from continuing operations.

The completed SCFP worksheet, cash basis, shown in Exhibit 23–6, provides all of the information needed to prepare the SCFP, cash basis, in conformity with the general criteria specified in *APB Opinion 19* (see the previous discussion, Criteria for the Statement of Changes in Financial Position). Observe that the SCFP, cash basis (Exhibit 23–7), in comparison with the SCFP, working capital basis (Exhibit 23–2), is not required to include a second section comparable to "Changes in working capital accounts."

SCFP FORMAT SPECIFICATIONS AND TERMINOLOGY

APB Opinion 19, (par. 11) states: "Provided that these guides are met, the statement may take whatever form gives the most useful portrayal of the financing and investing activities and the changes in financial position of the reporting entity." In light of this statement there is a wide variation in the SCFP format and terminology used in practice.

The formats and terminology used throughout this chapter were selected to facilitate instructional objectives. They are consistent with the criteria specified in *APB Opinion 19;* however, no single set of formats and terminology can be said to predominate in practice.

CURRENT STATUS OF THE SCFP

Currently, there exists considerable concern about the objectives, criteria, format, and terminology of the SCFP, and, more specifically, questions about what information would be most useful and how that information should be presented. For example, Ijiri stated that "there has been a serious discrepancy between the way in which investment decisions are made and the way in which results of the decisions are evaluated. In investment decisions the primary factor is cash flow. . . . In performance evaluation the emphasis shifts to earnings." Ijiri believes that often the "decision way" and the "evaluation way" are not reconcilable and therefore "either investment decisions should be based on earnings or performance evaluation should be based on cash flow."[14] On this point Ferrara states that "the economic impact of financial reporting standards plus the notion of a required consistency between decision models and financial reporting are pushing us inevitably toward a greater cash flow orientation in financial reporting. Some accountants still resist this cash flow trend because of the profession's traditionally strong predisposition toward accrual accounting, but the two reasons above may ultimately change their minds."[15]

Because of these important issues about the current practices of reporting funds flow, the FASB has the topic on its current agenda. Consequently, in December 1980, the FASB issued a discussion memorandum, "An Analysis of Issues Related to Reporting Funds Flows, Liquidity, and Financial Flexibility," which lists four main reasons why the FASB is undertaking a comprehensive project on funds flows, viz:[16]

a. Income and funds flow are different—These differences are significant and are particularly important when large price changes occur (discussed in Chapter 24). Investors, creditors, and other statement users are likely to need information about funds flow for assessments of future cash flows.

b. Information about liquidity and financial flexibility is needed for making assessments of future cash flows—**Liquidity** is defined as a measure of the nearness to cash of assets and liabilities; that is, the time interval that will elapse before assets become cash and before liabilities have to be paid. Financial **flexibility** is defined as a measure of the adaptability of a business; it comes from quick access to cash.

c. There appears to be a problem with current practice—Current practice is confusing because it *(a)* compresses too much information in one statement and *(b)* does not focus on a specific definition of funds.

d. A comprehensive foundation relating to resource flows is needed as part of the conceptual framework of financial accounting (discussed in Chapter 1).

This FASB project on the SCFP is important because the value of the SCFPs being presented currently is questionable. The importance the FASB attaches to this project is indicated by the fact that "it will continue through 1982 and probably 1983."

It is difficult to project with any assurance the outcome of the current FASB consideration of the SCFP, except to suggest that significant changes are likely. The following quotation provides additional evidence of a shift to cash basis funds statements:

> The central question in credit analysis today is not whether a company's working capital is "adequate" but whether the cash expected to be received within a given time period will equal or exceed required cash payments within that same period. Analysis of working capital position does not provide that information. A company's principal sources of cash are from sale of its products or services to its customers, from borrowing and from issuance of stock to investors. Its principal uses are payments to employees, suppliers and governments, repayment of debt and purchase of plant and equipment. Most of the cash a company will receive within the following year is not represented by assets classified as current, and most of the obligations it will have to pay are not represented by liabilities classified as current.
>
> The old concept of current assets as the source from which current liabilities will be paid is meaningless under this framework of analysis. Current liabilities are not paid with current assets; they are paid with cash. Whether a company's current or its noncurrent assets were the source of its cash is an unanswerable question. One can no more determine whether current or noncurrent assets provided the cash generated by a company's operations than he can determine which blade of the scissors cut the cloth, because both were clearly necessary.
>
> The rationale for recommending a statement of cash receipts and payments as one of the statements

[14] Y. Ijiri, "Recovery Rate and Cash Flow Accounting," *Journal of Accounting, Auditing and Finance,* Summer, 1978, pp. 331–48.

[15] W. L. Ferrara, "A Cash Flow Model for the Future," *Management Accounting,* June, 1981, pp. 12–17.

[16] FASB, *Discussion Memorandum,* "An Analysis of Issues Related to Reporting Funds Flow, Liquidity, and Financial Flexibility" (Stamford, Conn., December 1980).

to replace the funds statement is implicit in the above discussion. If a financial statement user's primary object of attention is the future cash receipts and payments of a company, then it follows that a statement of past cash receipts and payments would be useful for the same reason that historical income statements are useful in predicting the future income of a company: both provide a basis for predicting future performance.[17]

[17] L. C. Heath, "Let's Scrap the 'Funds' Statement," *The Journal of Accountancy,* October 1978, p. 98.

Supplement 23-A: T-Account Approach to Preparation of the SCFP

The T-account approach to preparation of the SCFP is preferred by some for instructional purposes. It is illustrated below for the SCFP, working capital basis, of WC Corporation (Exhibit 23–2), based upon the data given in Exhibit 23–3.

FUNDAMENTALS OF THE T-ACCOUNT APPROACH

The T-account approach encompasses **five steps** which are illustrated below using the WC Corporation data given in Exhibit 23–3.

Step 1—Compute the change in working capital for 19B; it increased by $64,000 as shown in the "Changes in working capital accounts" section of the SCFP in Exhibit 23–2.

Step 2—Set up the basic format of the SCFP with the headings as given in Exhibit 23–2.

Step 3—Set up T-accounts for each noncurrent balance sheet account with the **beginning** balances (i.e., 12/31/19A) as follows:

Land

Beg.	60,000		

Machinery (net)

Beg.	60,000		

Other assets

Beg.	29,000		

Bonds Payable (net)

		Beg.	69,000

Common Stock

		Beg.	100,000

Preferred Stock

		Beg.	20,000

Retained Earnings

		Beg.	30,000

Step 4—Summarize the **original** journal entries that affected the above noncurrent accounts and post them to the related **noncurrent** T-accounts so that the data needed for step 5 (i.e., completion of the SCFP) are assembled in one place. The completed T-accounts are shown in Exhibit 23–9.

The journal entries reflected in the T-accounts in Exhibit 23–9 are presented below. Working capital accounts are in **boldface type** for emphasis. The letters to the left are keyed to the illustrative data given in Exhibit 23–3 (and also are shown in the T-accounts for reference).

a. To close net income to Retained Earnings:

Income summary	44,000	
Retained earnings		44,000

e. To record depreciation on machinery:

Depreciation expense	7,900	
Machinery (net)		7,900

g. To record cash dividend declared and paid:

Retained earnings	15,000	
Cash		15,000

h. To record common stock dividend issued:

Retained earnings	10,000	
Common stock		10,000

i. To record bonds payable issued for cash:

Cash	5,000	
Bonds payable		5,000

j. To record land sold for cash (gain assumed to be extraordinary for illustrative purposes):

Cash	53,000	
Land		35,000
Extraordinary gain on sale of land		18,000

k. To record machinery purchased for cash:

Machinery	10,000	
Cash		10,000

m. To record preferred dividend paid with short-term investments:

Retained earnings	4,000	
Short-term investments		4,000

n. To record bonds payable retired by issuance of common stock:

Bonds payable	20,000	
Extraordinary loss on retirement of bonds payable	1,000	
Common stock		21,000

q. To record other assets acquired by issuing preferred stock:

Other assets	10,000	
Preferred stock		10,000

r. To record discount amortization on bonds payable:

Interest expense	100	
Bonds payable (net)		100

Explanation of the Analysis

The effects of additional data items *c, d, o,* and *p* are included in net income; the effects of additional data items *f* and *l* (see Exhibit 23–3) did **not** affect any of the **noncurrent** accounts and, therefore, neither group of effects needs special attention in the preparation of the SCFP. In contrast, transactions *a, e, g, h, i, j, k, m, n, q,* and *r* did affect the noncurrent accounts. Therefore, the transaction for each item affecting the **noncurrent** accounts should be analyzed for (1) working capital effects and (2) evidence of financing and investing activities not directly affecting working capital. The working capital analysis involves examination of the entries for effects on working capital. These effects were indicated by the boldface in each of the above entries. For example, in entry *g,* Cash, a working capital account, was credited for $15,000 and Retained Earnings, a noncurrent account, was debited for the same amount. This transaction was a use of working capital in the amount of the cash credit, $15,000.

Similar analysis was used for entries *a, i, j, k,* and *m,* in which the working capital account is in boldface type. In this respect, entry *a* is an anomaly because no working capital account was involved in closing net income into Retained Earnings. Remember, however, that net income is the difference between (1) all revenues and gains less (2) all expenses and losses of the period. Since revenues usually generate cash or accounts receivable, and since expenses require cash or accounts payable (all working capital accounts), it is assumed in the preparation of the SCFP that all revenues and gains and all expenses and losses affect working capital. This is why the SCFP starts with income before extraordinary items, as directed by *APB Opinion 19.*

Nevertheless, certain expenses, as well as some revenues, do not affect working capital of the period. For example, in entry *e,* Depreciation Expense is debited. Depreciation, like all other expenses, reduces income, but the credit side of the entry is a noncurrent account, which has no effect on working capital. Similarly, in entry *r,* Interest Expense is debited for amortization of the discount on bonds payable; this entry decreased income but did not decrease working capital. Starting the SCFP with income or loss before extraordinary items reflects the assumption that all expenses reduced working capital. Because depreciation expense and interest expense for amortization of bond discount do not accord with this assumption, it is necessary to add their two amounts (i.e., $7,900 and $100) back to income. In the WC Corporation example, the sum of income before extraordinary items ($27,000), depreciation expense ($7,900), and amortization of bond discount ($100) is the **working capital inflow from continuing operations** (i.e., $35,000), as shown in the SCFP in Exhibit 23–2. For similar reasons, certain other expenses, such as amortization of patents, amortization of goodwill, and income tax expense for which the taxes payable are deferred to future periods under interperiod income tax allocation procedures, are also added back to income to derive working capital inflow from continuing operations.

On the other hand, revenues for which the seller

EXHIBIT 23–9: T-Account Analysis to Develop SCFP, Working Capital Basis, WC Corporation

Panel A—T-Accounts:

Land

Beg.	60,000	*(j)*	35,000
End.	25,000		

Machinery (net)

Beg.	60,000	*(e)*	7,900
(k)	10,000		
End.	62,100		

Other Assets

Beg.	29,000		
(*q*–2)	10,000		
End.	39,000		

Bonds Payable

(*n*–2)	20,000	Beg.	69,000
		(i)	5,000
		(r)	100
		End.	54,100

Common Stock

		Beg.	100,000
		(h)	10,000
		(*n*–1)	21,000
		End.	131,000

Preferred Stock

		Beg.	20,000
		(*q*–1)	10,000
		End.	30,000

Retained Earnings

(g)	15,000	Beg.	30,000
(h)	10,000	*(a)*	44,000
(m)	4,000		
		End.	45,000

Extraordinary Gain on Sale of Land

		(j)	18,000

Panel B—Summary of Sources and Uses of Working Capital:

Sources of Working Capital

(a) Net income	44,000	*(j)*	18,000
(e)	7,900*		
(i)	5,000		
(j)	53,000		
(*n*–2)	1,000		
(r)	100*		
Total	93,000		

Uses of Working Capital

		(g)	15,000
		(k)	10,000
		(m)	4,000
		Total	29,000

Increase, $64,000

Financing Activities Not Affecting Working Capital

(*n*–1)	21,000		
(*q*–1)	10,000		

Investing Activities Not Affecting Working Capital

		(*n*–2)	21,000
		(*q*–2)	10,000

* Actually an adjustment to income rather than a literal "source."

received a long-term receivable, amortization of bond premium, and deferred income tax expense (from interperiod tax allocation) are deducted from net income to derive working capital inflow from continuing operations. To accommodate this latter category of **deductions,** the heading under income before extraordinary items in Exhibit 23–2 could be expanded to read: "Add or deduct operating items of expense or revenue not affecting working capital in the current period." For each such item, the determination that it should be so treated would be made on the basis of an analysis of the journal entry (to record the item) for its effect on (1) income and (2) working capital. In all cases, except for extraordinary gains and losses (which are accorded special treatment), items affecting income, but not affecting working capital, should be reported in this "addback or deduction" section of the SCFP, immediately under income before extraordinary items.

Transactions *n* and *q* involved **concurrent financing and investing activities** that did not directly affect working capital because each transaction involved a **direct exchange.** This can be determined from the fact that no working capital account was debited or credited in either entry. Nevertheless, because such transactions encompass both financing and investing activities of the enterprise, they must be reported on the SCFP. For example, in transaction *n,* the issuance of common stock was a financing activity and the retirement of bonds payable was an investing activity, although working capital neither increased nor decreased. One way to report such concurrent financing and investing activities is in a separate section of the SCFP captioned "Financing and investing activities not directly affecting working capital," as shown under that heading of the SCFP in Exhibit 23–2.

Now that all of the types of transactions reported on the SCFP have been discussed, we return to the reconciliation of the beginning and ending account balances for the noncurrent balance sheet accounts (the beginning account balances were shown in the T-accounts on page 843). The T-accounts presented in Exhibit 23–9, Panel A, reflect (1) the beginning balances, along with (2) the **postings** of the above journal entries for transactions which affected the noncurrent accounts (keyed by identifying letters), and (3) ending balances which agree with the ending balances on the December 31, 19B, balance sheet given in Exhibit 23–3. Panel B of the exhibit summarizes the **sources** and **uses** of working capital by entering therein the offsetting debit or credit for each entry.

The T-account analysis in Exhibit 23–9 completes the reconciliation of the beginning and ending balances in the noncurrent accounts and provides the necessary assurance that all working capital effects and all financing and investing activities not directly affecting working capital have been identified.

Step 5—Preparation of the SCFP is accomplished by transferring the balances from the summary of sources and uses of working capital (Exhibit 23–9, Panel B) directly to the appropriate captions on the SCFP. The last section of the SCFP titled "Changes in working capital accounts," was taken directly from the comparative balance sheets given in Exhibit 23–3.

QUESTIONS

PART A

1. Briefly explain the objectives and significance of the SCFP.
2. Distinguish between an *investing* activity and a *financing* activity in terms of the SCFP.
3. Explain the *all-resources concept* as applied to the SCFP.
4. Explain the basic measurement distinction between the *cash* basis and the *working capital* basis for the SCFP.
5. Why is it necessary to analyze the changes in the noncurrent accounts, rather than the changes in the current accounts, in developing the SCFP, working capital basis?
6. The income statement for Y Company reported a net loss of $7,000. The statement also showed a deduction for depreciation of $6,000 and amortization of patents of $3,000. In addition, the statement showed amortization of premium on bonds payable of $1,000. Compute the working capital generated by operations to explain why it is different from the net loss.

7. There are two "parts" to the SCFP, working capital basis, and only one part to the cash basis statement. Explain.

8. Give examples of working capital sources involving *(a)* noncurrent assets, *(b)* noncurrent liabilities, *(c)* capital stock, and *(d)* retained earnings.

9. Give examples of working capital uses involving *(a)* noncurrent assets, *(b)* noncurrent liabilities, *(c)* capital stock, and *(d)* retained earnings.

PART B

10. What are the primary advantages of the SCFP, cash basis, compared with the working capital basis.

11. Explain why cash expenditures for merchandise purchased for resale and normal expenses, such as salaries, are not reported under *uses* of cash on the SCFP, cash basis.

12. Explain why a difference between beginning and ending inventories must be included in the analysis to develop an SCFP, cash basis.

13. The income statement for X Company reported a net income of $10,000. The statement also showed a deduction for depreciation of $5,000 and an increase in accounts receivable of $8,000. Give the *(a)* cash and *(b)* working capital inflow from continuing operations and explain why each is different from net income.

14. Assume the sale of an operational asset that cost $50,000 for $5,000 cash plus a $15,000, one-year, interest-bearing note. What was the amount of cash inflow? How much did working capital increase? Explain why an adjustment to the net income for the loss or gain on this transaction is necessary to determine the amount of cash or working capital inflow from operations.

15. Explain why net income is "adjusted" for the depreciation expense amount but not for the estimated bad debt expense amount in determining working capital flow. How do the two expenses affect cash flow?

16. Why is the cash basis often more relevant than the working capital basis for evaluating the financing and investing activities of an enterprise?

DECISION CASE 23–1

The following statement was prepared by the controller of the Clovis Company. The controller indicated that this statement was prepared under the "all financial resources" concept of funds, which is the broadest concept of funds and includes all financing and investing activities.

CLOVIS COMPANY
Statement of Source and Application of Funds
December 31, 19B

Funds were provided by:	
Contribution of plant site by the city of Camden (Note 1)	$115,000
Net income after extraordinary items per income statement (Note 2)	75,000
Issuance of note payable—due 19F	60,000
Depreciation and amortization	50,000
Deferred income taxes relating to accelerated depreciation	10,000
Sale of equipment—book value (Note 3)	5,000
Total funds provided	$315,000
Funds were applied to:	
Acquisition of future plant site (Note 1)	$250,000
Increase in working capital	30,000
Cash dividends declared but not paid	20,000
Acquisition of equipment	15,000
Total funds applied	$315,000

Notes to Financial Statements

1. The city of Camden donated a plant site to Clovis Company valued by the board of directors at $115,000. The company purchased adjoining property for $135,000.
2. R&D expenditures of $25,000 incurred in 19B were expensed.
3. Equipment with a book value of $5,000 was sold for $8,000. The gain was included as an extraordinary item on the income statement.

Required:

1. Why is it considered desirable to present a statement similar to the above in the financial report?
2. Define and discuss the relative merits of the following three concepts used in funds flow analysis in terms of their measurement accuracy and freedom from manipulation (window dressing) in one accounting period:
   a. Cash concept of funds.
   b. Cash plus short-term investments concept of funds.
   c. Working capital concept of funds.
3. In view of *APB Opinion 19,* identify and discuss the weaknesses in presentation and disclosure in the above statement for Clovis Company. Your discussion should explain why you consider them to be weaknesses and what you consider the proper treatment of the items to be. Comment on the accounting treatment Clovis ac-

corded research and development costs, depreciation and amortization, deferred income taxes, extraordinary items, the acquisition of future plant site, and the adequacy of the note disclosures. Do not prepare a revised statement. (AICPA adapted)

EXERCISES

PART A: EXERCISES 23–1 to 23–3

Exercise 23–1

The balance sheets for Sympel Company showed the following information:

	December 31	
	19A	19B
Cash	$ 4,000	$17,000
Accounts receivable (net)	5,000	9,000
Inventory	10,000	12,000
Investment, long term	2,000	
Operational assets	30,000	47,000
Total debits	$51,000	$85,000
Accumulated depreciation	$ 5,000	$ 7,000
Accounts payable	3,000	5,000
Notes payable, short term (nontrade)	4,000	3,000
Notes payable, long term	10,000	18,000
Common stock, nopar	25,000	40,000
Retained earnings	4,000	12,000
Total credits	$51,000	$85,000

Additional data concerning changes in the noncurrent accounts:

a. Net income for the year 19B, $26,000.
b. Depreciation on operational assets for the year, $2,000.
c. Sold the long-term investment at cost.
d. Declared and paid a cash dividend of $7,000.
e. Purchased operational assets costing $5,000; paid cash.
f. Purchased operational assets and gave a $12,000 long-term note payable.
g. Paid a $4,000 long-term note payable by issuing common stock.
h. Issued a stock dividend; $11,000 debited to Retained Earnings and credited to Common Stock.

Required:

1. Prepare an SCFP, working capital basis, for 19B without the benefit of a worksheet.
2. Prepare an SCFP, cash basis, for 19B without the benefit of a worksheet.

Exercise 23–2

The worksheet given at the top of the next page has been set up; you are to complete it in every respect on a working capital basis.

Additional data for 19B:

a. Net income, $23,000.
b. Cash payment to retire bonds payable—at par value, $20,000.
c. Amortization of patent, $300.
d. Purchased long-term investment, $10,000.
e. Purchased operational asset; paid cash, $7,000.
f. Purchased short-term investment, $3,000.
g. Depreciation expense, $8,000.
h. Declared and paid cash dividend, $4,000.
i. Sold and issued stock, 500 shares at $19 per share.

Exercise 23–3

The records of Sampson Company reflected the following data:

Balance Sheet Data

	December 31	
Debits	19A	19B
Cash	$ 34,000	$ 33,500
Accounts receivable (net)	12,000	17,000
Inventory	16,000	14,000
Long-term investments	6,000	
Operational assets	80,000	98,000
Treasury stock		11,500
Total debits	$148,000	$174,000
Credits		
Accumulated depreciation	$ 48,000	$ 39,000
Accounts payable	19,000	12,000
Bonds payable	10,000	30,000
Common stock, nopar	50,000	65,000
Retained earnings	21,000	28,000
Total credits	$148,000	$174,000

(Relates to Exercise 23–2)

WCB CORPORATION
Worksheet, Statement of Changes in Financial Position, Working Capital Basis
For The Year Ended December 31, 19B

Item	Balances 12/31/19A	Analysis		Balances 12/31/19B
		Debit	Credit	
Debits				
Working Capital	30,000			29,800
Nonworking capital accounts:				
Investments, long term				10,000
Operational assets (net)	60,000			59,000
Patent (net)	3,000			2,700
Other assets	7,000			7,000
	100,000			108,500
Credits				
Bonds payable	40,000			20,000
Capital stock, par $10	35,000			40,000
Contributed capital in excess of par				4,500
Retained earnings	25,000			44,000
	100,000			108,500
Sources of working capital:				
Uses of working capital:				
Change in working capital				

Additional data for the period January 1, 19B, through December 31, 19B:

a. Sales on account, $70,000.
b. Purchases on account, $40,000.
c. Depreciation, expense, $5,000.
d. Expenses paid in cash, $18,000.
e. Decrease in inventory, $2,000.
f. Sold operational assets for $6,000 cash; cost, $21,000, and two-thirds depreciated (the loss or gain is not an extraordinary item).
g. Purchased operational assets for cash, $9,000.
h. Purchased operational assets: exchanged unissued bonds payable of $30,000 in payment.
i. Sold the long-term investments for $9,000 cash, net of tax (assume the gain or loss is an extraordinary item).
j. Purchased treasury stock for cash, $11,500.
k. Retired bonds payable at maturity date by issuing common stock, $10,000.
l. Collections on accounts receivable, $65,000.
m. Payments on accounts payable, $47,000.
n. Sold unissued common stock for cash, $5,000.

Required:
Prepare a worksheet to develop an SCFP, working capital basis, for 19B.

PART B: EXERCISES 23–4 to 23–7

Exercise 23–4

On January 1, 19A, Pacific Corporation was organized. During the year ended December 31, 19A, the corporation completed the following transactions:

a. Sold 2,000 shares of common stock, par $10, for $20 per share; collected cash.
b. Borrowed $10,000 on a one-year, 9%, interest-bearing note; the note was dated June 1.
c. On December 31, 19A, purchased machinery that cost

$25,000; paid $5,000 cash and signed two notes: (1) a 60-day, 8%, interest-bearing note, face $15,000; and (2) a one-year, 7%, interest-bearing note, face $5,000.

d. Purchased merchandise for resale at a cost of $40,000 (debited Purchases); paid $30,000 cash, balance credited to Accounts Payable.

e. Declared a cash dividend of $6,000; paid $2,000 in December 19A, the balance will be paid March 1, 19B.

f. Income statement:

Sales:		
Cash	$55,000	
On credit	20,000	$75,000
Cost of goods sold:		
Purchases *(d)* above	40,000	
Less: ending inventory	10,000	(30,000)
Expenses (including income taxes):		
Paid in cash	10,000	
Accrued (unpaid)	17,000	
Depreciation	2,000	(29,000)
Net income		$16,000

Required:

1. Set up a tabulation (similar to Exhibit 23–1, Panels A and B) to derive the fund flows for each item on a *(a)* cash basis and *(b)* working capital basis. Use parallel columns.
2. Prepare a summarized SCFP (cash basis compared with working capital basis for the year ended December 31, 19A, similar to Exhibit 23–1, Panel C).

Exercise 23–5

Use the data given at the top of page 851 to compute *(a)* total cash inflow from *operations* and *(b)* total working capital inflow from *operations*.

(Relates to Exercise 23–6)

Item	Balances 12/31/19A	Analysis		Balances 12/31/19B
		Debit	Credit	
Debits				
Cash plus short-term investments	19,500			32,200
Accounts receivable (net)	34,000			34,000
Merchandise inventory	78,000			85,000
Investments, long term				10,000
Operational assets	168,500			180,500
	300,000			341,700
Credits				
Accumulated depreciation	44,000			34,000
Accounts payable	21,000			19,000
Wages payable	1,500			500
Income taxes payable	2,000			3,500
Bonds payable	100,000			100,000
Premium on bonds payable	4,000			3,700
Capital stock, nopar	120,000			155,500
Retained earnings	7,500			25,500
	300,000			341,700
Sources of cash:				
Uses of cash:				

(Relates to Exercise 23-5)

Transaction	Cash Basis	Working Capital Basis
Net income reported (accrual basis)*	$50,000	$50,000
Depreciation expense, $6,000	______	______
Increase in wages payable, $1,000	______	______
Increase in trade accounts receivable, $1,800	______	______
Decrease in merchandise inventory, $2,300	______	______
Amortization of patent, $200	______	______
Decrease in long-term liabilities, $10,000	______	______
Sale of capital stock for cash, $25,000	______	______
Amortization of discount on bonds payable, $300	______	______
Total cash inflow from operations	______	
Total working capital inflow from operations		______

* Revenues, $190,000; expenses, $140,000.

Exercise 23–6

The SCFP worksheet given on page 850 has been set up; you are to complete it in every respect on a cash basis assuming cash is construed to include short-term investments.

Additional data:

a. Net income, $28,000.
b. Acquisition of operational asset, $30,000; issued 3,000 shares of capital stock in full payment.
c. Depreciation expense, $6,000.
d. Increase in merchandise inventory, $7,000.
e. Decrease in accounts payable, $2,000.
f. Amortization of bond premium, $300.
g. Purchased long-term investment, $10,000.
h. Increase in income taxes payable, $1,500.
i. Decrease in wages payable $1,000.
j. Declared and paid cash dividend, $10,000.
k. Sold operational assets for $5,000 that cost $18,000; accumulated depreciation, $16,000 (not an extraordinary item).
l. Sold 500 shares of capital stock at $11 per share.

Exercise 23–7

Use the data given in Exercise 23–3 to prepare a worksheet to develop an SCFP, cash basis.

PROBLEMS

PART A: PROBLEMS 23–1 to 23–5

Problem 23–1

Some of the following independent items will change working capital or have the potential of doing so. You are to identify the effect of each item on working capital. For those which will, or could, cause an increase, use a plus (+) sign; for those which will or could cause a decrease, use a minus (−) sign; if an item cannot affect working capital, use a 0.

1. Change inventory value from cost to LCM; replacement costs are declining below cost.
2. Change carrying value of short-term investment in equity securities from cost to LCM; market price is declining below cost.
3. Change carrying value of long-term investments in equity securities from cost to LCM; market price is declining below cost.
4. Receive a stock dividend on common stock held as a short-term investment.
5. Receive a cash dividend on common stock held as a long-term investment.
6. Change from the cost method to the equity method of valuing a long-term investment in common stock.
7. Declare and issue a dividend payable in our common stock to holders of our common stock.
8. Declare and pay a dividend payable in the common stock of another company held as a short-term investment.
9. Receive a report of a profitable year from an investee in which we own a 10% common stock interest as a long-term investment.
10. Receive a report of a profitable year from an investee in which we own a 35% common stock interest held as a long-term investment.
11. Accrue interest expense on long-term bonds payable.
12. Record periodic amortization of the cost of computer software classified on our books as a deferred charge.
13. Accrue interest revenue on money-market CDs which we own as a short-term investment.
14. Recognize gross margin for most recent year on long-term construction contract accounted for by the percentage-of-completion method.

Problem 23–2

Accompanying this problem are the comparative statements of financial position of Kenwood Corporation as of December 31, 19B, and December 31, 19A, respectively.

Presented below is the income statement of Kenwood Corporation for the year ended December 31, 19B:

KENWOOD CORPORATION
Income Statement
For the Year Ended December 31, 19B

Sales revenue	$1,000,000
Expenses and losses:	
Cost of goods sold	560,000
Salaries and wages	190,000
Depreciation	20,000
Amortization of patent	3,000
Loss on sale of equipment	4,000
Interest	16,000
Miscellaneous	8,000
Total expenses and losses	801,000
Income before income taxes and extraordinary item	199,000
Income taxes:	
Current	50,000
Deferred	40,000
Income tax expense	90,000
Income before extraordinary item	109,000
Extraordinary item—gain on early extinguishment of long-term bonds payable (net of $10,000 income tax)	12,000
Net income	$ 121,000
Earnings per share:	
Income before extraordinary item	$2.21
Extraordinary item	.24
Net income	$2.45

Additional information:

a. On February 2, 19B, Kenwood issued a 10% stock dividend to shareholders of record on January 15, 19B. The market price per share of the common stock on February 2, 19B, was $15.

b. On March 1, 19B, Kenwood issued 3,800 shares of common stock for land. The common stock and land had current market values of approximately $40,000 on March 1, 19B.

c. On April 15, 19B, Kenwood repurchased its long-term bonds payable with a face value of $50,000. The gain of $22,000 was reported as an extraordinary item on the income statement because the early extinguishment of the bonds payable occurred prior to their maturity date (12/15/K).

d. On June 30, 19B, Kenwood sold equipment costing $53,000, with a book value of $23,000, for $19,000 cash.

e. On September 30, 19B, Kenwood declared and paid a 4 cents per share cash dividend to shareholders of record August 1, 19B.

f. On October 10, 19B, Kenwood purchased land for $85,000 cash.

g. Deferred income tax represent timing differences relating to the use of accelerated depreciation methods for income tax reporting and straight-line depreciation method for financial statement reporting.

Required:
Using the working capital concept of funds, prepare the SCFP of Kenwood Corporation for the year ended December 31, 19B. (Do not prepare a schedule of changes in working capital.)

(AICPA adapted)

(Relates to Problem 23–2)

KENWOOD CORPORATION
Statement of Financial Position

	December 31, 19B	December 31, 19A
Assets		
Current assets:		
Cash	$ 100,000	$ 90,000
Accounts receivable (net of allowance for doubtful accounts of $10,000 and $8,000, respectively)	210,000	140,000
Inventories	260,000	220,000
Total current assets	570,000	450,000
Land	325,000	200,000
Plant and equipment	580,000	633,000
Less: Accumulated depreciation	(90,000)	(100,000)
Patents	30,000	33,000
Total assets	$1,415,000	$1,216,000

	December 31, 19B	December 31, 19A
Liabilities and Shareholders' Equity		
Liabilities:		
Current liabilities:		
Accounts payable	$ 260,000	$ 200,000
Accrued expenses payable	200,000	210,000
Total current liabilities	460,000	410,000
Deferred income tax	140,000	100,000
Long-term bonds (due 12/15/19K)	130,000	180,000
Total liabilities	730,000	690,000
Shareholders' equity:		
Common stock, par value $5, authorized 100,000 shares, issued and outstanding 50,000 and 42,000 shares, respectively	250,000	210,000
Additional paid-in capital	233,000	170,000
Retained earnings	202,000	146,000
Total shareholders' equity	685,000	526,000
Total liabilities and shareholders' equity	$1,415,000	$1,216,000

Problem 23–3

The SCFP worksheet accompanying this problem has been set up; you are to complete it in every respect on a working capital basis:

Additional data for 19B:

a. Revenues, $400,000—expenses (including all gains, losses, and income taxes), $375,000 = net income $25,000.

(Relates to Problem 23–3)

Item	Balances 12/31/19A	Analysis Debit	Analysis Credit	Balances 12/31/19B
Debits				
Cash plus short-term investments	40,000			44,900
Accounts receivable (net)	60,000			52,500
Merchandise inventory	180,000			141,600
Prepaid insurance	2,400			1,200
Investments, long term	30,000			
Land	10,000			38,400
Operational assets	250,000			259,000
Patent (net)	1,600			1,400
	574,000			539,000
Credits				
Accumulated depreciation	65,000			79,000
Accounts payable	50,000			53,000
Wages payable	2,000			1,500
Income taxes payable	9,000			13,400
Bonds payable	100,000			50,000
Premium on bonds payable	5,000			1,700
Capital stock, par $10	300,000			306,000
Contributed capital in excess of par	15,000			18,000
Retained earnings	28,000			16,400
	574,000			539,000
Sources of working capital:				
Uses of working capital:				

b. Depreciation expense, $14,000.
c. Cash dividends declared and paid, $30,000.
d. Increase in current income taxes payable, $4,400.
e. Amortization of patent, $200.
f. Purchased operational asset, cost $9,000; payment by issuing 600 shares of stock.
g. Decrease in wages payable, $500.
h. Payment at maturity date to retire bonds payable, $50,000.
i. Sold the long-term investments for $40,000, net of tax (assume this causes an extraordinary item).
j. Decrease in accounts receivable (net), $7,500.
k. Decrease in prepaid insurance, $1,200.
l. Decrease in merchandise inventory, $38,400.
m. Increase in accounts payable, $3,000.
n. Amortization of premium on bonds payable, $3,300.
o. Error in recording prior years' income taxes; paid during 19B (a prior period adjustment), $6,600.
p. Purchased land, $28,400; paid cash.

Problem 23–4

The balance sheets of Lincoln Company provided the information shown below.

Debits	December 31 19A	December 31 19B
Cash	$ 4,000	$ 11,000
Accounts receivable (net)	9,000	12,000
Inventory	8,000	5,000
Long-term investments	2,000	
Plant	30,000	30,000
Equipment	20,000	22,000
Land	10,000	40,000
Patents	8,000	7,000
	$91,000	$127,000

Credits	December 31 19A	December 31 19B
Accum. depr.—plant	$ 7,000	$ 10,000
Accum. depr.—equipment	10,000	8,000
Accounts payable	8,000	2,000
Wages payable	1,000	
Notes payable, long term	10,000	19,000
Common stock, par $10	50,000	75,000
Retained earnings	5,000	13,000
	$91,000	$127,000

Additional data for 19B:

a. Net income for the year, $12,000.
b. Depreciation expense on plant for the year, $3,000.
c. Depreciation expense on equipment for the year, $2,000.
d. Amortization of patents for the year, $1,000.
e. Increase in accounts receivable, $3,000.
f. Decrease in accounts payable, $6,000.
g. Decrease in wages payable, $1,000.
h. At the end of the year sold equipment costing $8,000 (50% depreciated) for $3,000 cash, net of tax (this was not an extraordinary item).
i. Purchased land costing $10,000; paid $2,000 cash, gave long-term note for the balance.
j. Paid $4,000 to retire long-term notes payable at maturity.
k. Sold $10,000 common stock at par.
l. Purchased equipment costing $10,000; paid half in cash, balance due in three years (interest-bearing note).
m. Issued 1,500 shares common stock (at par) for land that cost $20,000, balance in cash.
n. Sold the long-term investments for $8,000 cash, net of tax (assume this was an extraordinary item).
o. Declared and paid dividends, $4,000.

Required:

1. Prepare a worksheet to develop an SCFP, working capital basis, for 19B. Key your entries.
2. Prepare an SCFP if required by your instructor.

Problem 23–5

The records of Easy Trading Company provided the following summaries and data:

1. Income statement for the month of April 19A:

Sales revenue		$ 80,000
Less: Purchases	$ 40,000	
Increase in inventory	(5,000)	35,000
		45,000
Expenses and losses:		
Depreciation	$ 5,000	
Bad debts	1,000	
Insurance	1,000	
Interest	2,000	
Salaries and wages	12,000	
Other expenses (incl. income taxes)	16,000	
Loss on sale of operational assets	2,000	
Total exp. and losses		39,000
Net income		$ 6,000

2. Balance sheets (unclassified):

	3/31/ 19A	4/30/ 19A
Cash	$ 15,000	$ 31,000
Accounts receivable	30,000	28,500
Allowance for doubtful accts.	1,500*	2,000*
Inventory	10,000	15,000
Prepaid insurance	2,400	1,400
Operational assets	80,000	81,000
Accumulated depreciation	20,000*	16,000*
Land	40,100	81,100
Total	$156,000	$220,000
Accounts payable	$ 10,000	$ 11,000
Wages payable	2,000	1,000
Interest payable		1,000
Notes payable, long term	20,000	46,000
Common stock, nopar	100,000	136,000
Retained earnings	24,000	25,000
Total	$156,000	$220,000

* Deductions.

3. Cash account:

Debits	
Balance	$15,000
Sales	20,000
Operational assets	4,000
Sales	15,000
Notes payable	20,000
Sales	15,000
Accounts receivable	31,000
Common stock	5,000
Credits	
Purchases	$10,000
Salaries and wages	5,000
Accounts payable	4,000
Salaries and wages	2,000
Purchases	5,000
Expenses	6,000
Dividends declared and paid	5,000
Purchases	5,000
Expenses	10,000
Accounts payable	6,000
Land	20,000
Accounts payable	9,000
Salaries and wages	6,000
Interest	1,000

4. Retained Earnings account showed a debit for dividends.
5. Wrote off $500 accounts receivable as uncollectible.
6. Acquired land for common stock issued.
7. Acquired operational assets costing $16,000; gave three-year, interest-bearing note.
8. Paid a $10,000 long-term note at maturity by issuing common stock to the creditor.

Required:

1. Prepare a worksheet to develop an SCFP, working capital basis.
2. Prepare an SCFP if required by your instructor.

PART B: PROBLEMS 23–6 to 23–9

Problem 23–6

Use the data given in Problem 23–3.

Required:

1. Prepare a worksheet to develop an SCFP, cash (including short-term investments) basis.
2. Prepare an SCFP, cash (including short-term investments) basis if required by your instructor.

Problem 23–7

Use the data given in Problem 23–4.

Required:

1. Prepare a worksheet to develop an SCFP, cash basis.
2. If required by your instructor, prepare an SCFP, cash basis.

Problem 23–8

Use the data given in Problem 23–5.

Required:

1. Prepare a worksheet to develop an SCFP, cash basis.
2. If required by your instructor, prepare an SCFP, cash basis.

Problem 23–9

(A review that also emphasizes Chapters 10 and 16.)

The year-end financial statements of Acres Company follow:

(Relates to Problem 23–9)

Balance Sheets, Unclassified
December 31, 19B, and 19C

	19B		19C	
Cash		$ 8,000		$ 9,000
Accounts receivable	$19,000		$16,000	
Less: Allowance for doubtful accounts	1,000	18,000	1,000	15,000
Inventories at lower of cost or market		45,000		44,000
Long-term investment, Jones, Inc., at equity				15,000
Long-term investment, Campbell Company:				
Common stock, at cost	14,000		12,000	
Less: Allowance to reduce to market	2,000	12,000	-0-	12,000
Property, plant, and equipment	60,000		74,000	
Less: Accumulated depreciation	18,000	42,000	19,000	55,000
Total assets		$125,000		$150,000
Accounts payable		$ 6,000		$ 11,300
Income taxes payable		2,000		4,000
Deferred income taxes payable, current		2,000		3,000
Current maturity on serial bonds payable		1,000		1,000
Deferred income taxes payable, long term				1,000
Serial bonds payable, 5%, maturing in $1,000 annual serials beginning 1/1/19A		22,000		21,000
Premium on serial bonds payable		1,100		1,000
Notes payable, long term				4,000
Common stock, par $10		45,000		50,000
Contributed capital in excess of par		3,900		5,000
Retained earnings		44,000		48,700
Unrealized loss on long-term investments		(2,000)		
Total equities		$125,000		$150,000

Income Statement
Year Ended December 31, 19C

Sales revenue		$100,000
Cost of goods sold		65,000
Gross margin		35,000
Operating expenses:		
Depreciation	$4,000	
Interest	1,000	
Income taxes:		
Current payable	8,000	
Deferred, current	3,000	
Deferred, long term	1,000	17,000
Operating income		18,000
Investment revenue (Jones, Inc.)		2,700
Income before extraordinary items		20,700
Extraordinary items (assumed extraordinary for problem purposes only):		
Realized gain on sale of investments (net of tax)	3,000	
Loss on sale of machinery (net of tax)	1,000	2,000
Net income		$ 22,700

Additional information:

1. During 19C, part of the long-term investment in the common stock of Campbell Company was sold for $5,000, which is net of tax. The acquisition cost of these shares was $2,000.
2. During 19C, machinery was sold for $1,000 cash; the cost of this machinery was $5,000; accumulated depreciation to date of disposal was $3,000, which is net of tax.
3. During 19C, Acres Company purchased machinery. The

total cost was paid in cash except for $4,000 which was financed by a long-term note payable.

4. Dividends declared and paid during 19C amounted to $18,000.
5. During 19C, Acres Company issued common stock with a par value of $5,000.
6. As a matter of accounting policy, due to the immateriality of the amounts involved, Acres Company amortizes the premium on the serial bonds payable each year on a straight-line basis (an equal amount each year).
7. Acres's investment in Jones, Inc., is 30% of the outstanding voting common stock of Jones, Inc. The investment was made on January 1, 19C, with a cash outlay of $12,900. On that date Jones, Inc., balance sheet and related data were as follows:

	Book Value	Market Value
Cash	$15,000	$15,000
Receivables (net)	22,000	22,000
Inventories (FIFO)	20,000	23,000
Operational assets (net)	28,000	28,000
	$85,000	$88,000
Liabilities	$45,000	$45,000
Common stock, nopar	30,000	
Retained earnings	10,000	
	$85,000	

During 19C, Jones, Inc., earned net income of $12,000 and declared and paid cash dividends of $2,000. All long-term assets of Jones, Inc., have a 10-year estimated useful life and no residual value. Amortize any goodwill over 10 years.

Required:

Prepare an SCFP for the company on the working capital basis for 19C. You need not prepare the bottom portion of the statement for "Changes in working capital accounts."

24

Financial Reporting and Changing Prices

WHEN the unit-of-measure assumption was discussed in Chapter 1, it was noted that the conventional accounting model, based on historical cost (HC), assumes either a stable monetary unit or that changes in the value of money were not material. During some periods in the history of the U.S. economy, such assumptions were valid. In recent years, however, changing prices have significantly affected financial reporting.

The purposes of this chapter are to:

1. Analyze the effects of changing prices on conventional, historical cost (HC) financial statements.
2. Describe two reporting models designed to report the effects of changing prices on financial statements.
3. Present the reporting requirements specified in FASB, *Statement of Financial Accounting Standards No. 33,* "Financial Reporting and Changing Prices," September 1979.

Three reporting models compared in this chapter are as follows:[1]

Reporting Model	Abbreviation
1. Historical cost	HC
2. Historical cost/constant dollar	HC/CD
3. Current cost/constant dollar	CC/CD

This chapter is divided into two parts as follows:

Part A—Basic Concepts and the Historical Cost/Constant Dollar (HC/CD) Reporting Model

Part B—The Current Cost/Constant Dollar (CC/CD) Model and the Reporting Requirements of *FASB Statement 33*

Supplement 24–A—Worksheet Approach to Preparation of HC/CD Financial Statements

Supplement 24–B—Comparative HC/CD and CC/CD Financial Statements

[1] A fourth accounting model, current cost (without the constant-dollar concept) also could have been included. It is omitted because it clutters the analysis, and the constant-dollar concept adds much to its relevance.

Part A: Basic Concepts and the Historical Cost/Constant Dollar (HC/CD) Reporting Model

BACKGROUND

Since the Great Depression of the 1930s, prices of most commodities and services in the United States (and in most of the rest of the world) have been increasing almost without interruption. Stated another way, the general purchasing power of the dollar (and other monetary units) has been decreasing almost continuously.

A dollar will command a certain amount of **real** goods and services in the marketplace at a given time. As prices change, the value of a dollar changes because it will command a different quantity of real goods and services. **General** purchasing power is the capacity of the monetary unit to purchase some general collection of commodities and services (i.e., a typical "market basket"). When the general level of prices **increases** (i.e., the general purchasing power of the dollar **decreases**), the condition is referred to as **inflation.** When the general level of prices **decreases** (i.e., when the general purchasing power of the dollar **increases**), the condition is called **deflation.**[2]

This part of the chapter concentrates on the historical cost/constant dollar (HC/CD) reporting model. The HC/CD model is designed to report all elements of financial statements (i.e., assets, liabilities, owners' equity, revenues, expenses, gains, and losses) in dollars of constant purchasing power. It also is referred to as the general price level (GPL) reporting model because it requires GPL restatements of the HC amounts reported on the traditional HC financial statements.

[2] Because inflation has been so pervasive, our discussions, illustrations, and assignment material will be primarily in the context of rising prices; however, the concepts discussed also apply to deflation.

EFFECTS OF CHANGING PRICES ON HISTORICAL COST (HC) FINANCIAL STATEMENTS

Historical cost (HC) financial statements add and subtract historical dollar amounts representing assets, liabilities, owners' equity, revenues, expenses, gains, and losses just as though each dollar had the same purchasing power. However, if prices were changing during the periods when those dollars were recorded, such dollars would, in fact, be of unequal purchasing power. For example, assume a building was acquired at a cost of $400,000 in 1967 (say, when the general price level [GPL] index was 100), and another building was acquired at a cost of $900,000 in 1982 (the current year) when the general price index was 200.[3] The total balance in the Buildings account of $1,300,000 (HC dollars) in 1982 would include a mixture of different dollars of different purchasing power, which is akin to adding apples and bananas and treating them as equivalents. In contrast, the historical cost/constant dollar (HC/CD) reporting model, discussed in detail later, would use the two GPL index numbers to compute the HC in constant dollars (abbreviated CDs) of 1982 as follows:

	Restated in 1982 CDs
1982 building (already in 1982 dollars)	$ 900,000
1967 building (restated to 1982 dollars, $400,000 × 200/100)	$ 800,000
Total HC in 1982 CDs	$1,700,000

Note: Accumulated depreciation is discussed later.

The change in prices would affect the depreciation expense on the old building in a similar manner. For example, assume $20,000 annual HC depreciation on the 1967 building; this amount would be GPL restated to 1982 CDs as: $20,000 × 200/100 = $40,000. This $20,000 understatement of expense causes an overstatement of pretax income of a like amount, relative to the HC/CD restated amounts. From this simple

[3] General price level (GPL) index numbers are discussed and illustrated in detail later under the heading, Price Indexes.

example it can be seen that the relevance of many amounts on most HC financial statements suffers from the effects of changing prices. Thus GPL changes cause two basic problems for conventional HC financial statements as follows:

1. Effects on enterprise cash flows—When the GPL rises (i.e., inflation) over an extended period of time, traditional HC financial statements tend to **understate** certain **assets and expenses** because these items were recorded in "old" dollars that had higher purchasing power than today's dollars. Therefore, if the "old" amounts are not **restated** into "current constant" dollars (e.g., restated into 1982 CDs as illustrated above for the 1967 building and its depreciation), there are persistent and undisclosed **understatements** of total assets and a related **overstatement** of HC income relative to their HC/CD equivalents. This overstatement of HC income has significant economic consequences, such as on enterprise cash flows, because **income taxes** and **dividends** paid by the enterprise are based on the overstated income amounts. The economic effect is that *(a)* income taxes paid may be, in part, on permanent capital (rather than on income) and *(b)* dividends paid may be, in part, a return of contributed capital (rather than all from retained earnings). As a consequence, income tax and dividend payments, under such circumstances tend to erode the contributed capital base of many companies, rather than coming exclusively from retained earnings as intended.
2. Comparability—When the GPL changes, the "old and new" dollar amounts reported on HC financial statements are not comparable either *(a)* within the statements of a single period or *(b)* among the statements of different periods. This lack of **comparability** violates *FASB Concepts Statement 2* (i.e., the comparability principle).

Because of the effect of changing prices on financial reporting, the FASB issued *Statement of Financial Accounting Standards No. 33,* "Financial Reporting and Changing Prices," in September 1979. The statement requires certain large companies to report HC/CD and current cost/constant dollar (CC/CD) data as **supplements** to the conventional HC financial statements. The CC/CD reporting model, as well as the reporting requirements of *FASB Statement 33,* is discussed in Part B.

THE HISTORICAL COST/CONSTANT DOLLAR (HC/CD) REPORTING MODEL

The objective of the HC/CD model is to report the HC financial statement **elements** in dollars of equivalent purchasing power (CDs) and, as a result, to make all of the reported amounts comparable. The restatement of each HC amount to its HC/CD equivalent amount is based upon two GPL index amounts as shown on page 859 for the two buildings. In that illustration, the **CD restatement** of the HC of the old 1967 building into CDs of December 1982 (i.e., $800,000) makes it comparable with the HC of the new building acquired in 1982 (i.e., $900,000).

CD restatement is based upon GPL indexes which represent an economy-wide average "market basket"; therefore, each HC/CD amount does not reflect the **current market (sales) value,** nor the current cost (CC) of the item except by chance. Instead, **CD restatement** *(a)* retains the conventional HC relationships reported, and *(b)* for comparability, reports each item on the HC/CD financial statement in CDs (i.e., dollars of equal purchasing power). HC/CD restatement is discussed in detail following discussion of *(a)* **monetary** and **nonmonetary** items, and *(b)* price indexes.

MONETARY AND NONMONETARY ITEMS

The basic distinction in HC/CD reporting (and in CC/CD reporting discussed in Part B) is between **monetary** and **nonmonetary** items. These two terms are defined as follows:

1. **Monetary** items are cash and claims receivable or payable which are stated in a **fixed number of dollars,** and the fixed number of dollars does not change regardless of changes in prices. Examples of monetary items include cash, accounts receivable, notes receivable, and other receivables stated in a fixed number of dollars; and accounts payable, notes payable, bonds payable, and other payables stated in a fixed number of dollars. Thus, neither inflation nor deflation affects the number of dollars to be received or paid for a monetary item.
2. **Nonmonetary** items are those financial statement items which are stated in a number of dollars that is **not** fixed. All items which are not classified as monetary are classified as nonmonetary. Examples of nonmonetary items include inventories, operational assets, investments in stock, and

common stock outstanding. Thus, for these items, the number of dollars they will command in the future will be influenced by price changes.

Exhibit 24–1 presents a list of items and their classifications as monetary or nonmonetary. **Note that the monetary/nonmonetary distinction is not related in any way to whether the item is current or noncurrent.** For instructional convenience in this chapter, we sometimes abbreviate monetary as "M" and nonmonetary as "NM."

The distinction between monetary and nonmonetary items is important in the HC/CD model because the HC of **monetary items** necessarily is equal to their CD equivalents because the number of dollars they will command **does not change when prices change.** Because of the fixed nature of monetary items, their "prices" do not change. Therefore, the HC amounts of monetary items are **not** restated into a different number of CDs on the HC/CD balance sheet.

In contrast, because the numbers of dollars reflected in the HC of **nonmonetary** items can change when their prices change, their CD equivalent amounts may differ from their HC amounts. Therefore, in contrast to the monetary items, the nonmonetary items **must be** restated from their HC amounts to their HC/CD equivalent amounts.

The distinction between monetary and nonmonetary items also is important because of the effect of changing prices on the **purchasing power of monetary items** (but not on nonmonetary items). Nonmonetary items, by their nature tend to fluctuate in price with changes in the GPL. In contrast, monetary items do not fluctuate because of their fixed amounts. Therefore, monetary items experience **purchasing power gains and losses** as the GPL changes. For example, one who holds cash during a period of inflation will lose purchasing power because the number of dollars will not change, but the purchasing power of each dollar will be less. Stated differently, during inflation, a dollar today will buy less than that same dollar would buy a year ago. The same effect will occur if accounts receivable, notes receivable, or other **monetary assets** are held during a period of inflation. By contrast, if a fixed amount of money is owed during a period of inflation, the **debtor** will **gain** in terms of purchasing power because the number of dollars used to pay the debt at maturity will have less purchasing power (i.e., payment will be in cheaper dollars) than the dollars borrowed when the debt was incurred. Therefore, during inflation, **net monetary debtors** (i.e., those whose monetary liabilities exceed their monetary assets) **gain** purchasing power. In contrast, **net monetary creditors** (i.e., those whose monetary assets exceed their monetary liabilities) **lose** purchasing power.

Because of the fundamental difference between monetary and nonmonetary items, a unique feature of both HC/CD and CC/CD reporting is the need to compute the **purchasing power gain or loss on net monetary items** (but **not** on nonmonetary items).

PRICE INDEXES

Preparation of HC/CD financial statements involves the use of GPL index numbers. There are two basic types of price indexes, viz: (1) **general** price level (GPL) indexes and (2) **specific** price level indexes.

A price index is a relative measure of the prices of a specific good or group of goods and/or services at a specific date. As the prices of the components of the index change, the value of the index changes, as shown below for a hypothetical food price index (the base date always is assigned an index value of 100, or, more precisely, 1.00)

Component	Component Prices at— Jan. 1	Dec. 31	Relative Change
Meat (per pound)	$3.00	$3.41	+13.7%
Potatoes (per pound)	.65	.63	− 3.1
Green vegetable (per pound)	.70	.77	+10.0
Beverage (per quart)	.80	.83	+ 3.8
Total	$5.15	$5.64	

Computation of indexes:
Price index: January 1 (base date) 5.15/5.15 = 1.000
December 31 5.64/5.15 = 1.095

EXHIBIT 24–1: Classification of Items as Monetary or Nonmonetary

	Monetary		Nonmonetary
Assets			
1. Cash on hand and demand bank deposits (U.S. dollars)	X		
2. Foreign currency on hand and claims to foreign currency*	X		
3. Investments in securities:			
Common stocks (not accounted for on the equity method): Common stocks represent residual interests in the underlying net assets and earnings of the issuer.			X
Preferred stock (convertible or participating): Circumstances may indicate that such stock is either **monetary** or **nonmonetary.** See convertible bonds.	X	or	X
Preferred stock (nonconvertible, nonparticipating): Future cash receipts are likely to be substantially unaffected by changes in specific prices.	X		
Convertible bonds: If the market values the security primarily as a bond, it is **monetary;** if it values the security primarily as a stock, it is **nonmonetary.**	X	or	X
Bonds (other than convertibles)	X		
4. Accounts and notes receivable	X		
5. Allowance for doubtful accounts and notes receivable	X		
6. Inventories used on contracts: They are rights to receive sums of money (i.e., are monetary) if the future cash receipts on the contracts will not vary due to future changes in specific prices. (Goods used on contracts to be priced at market upon delivery are **nonmonetary.**)	X	or	X
7. Inventories (other than inventories used on contracts)			X
8. Loans to employees	X		
9. Prepaid insurance, advertising, rent, and other prepayments: Claims to future services are **nonmonetary.** Prepayments that are deposits, advance payments or receivables are **monetary** because the prepayment does not obtain a given quantity of future services, but rather is a fixed money amount.	X	or	X
10. Long-term receivables	X		
11. Refundable deposits	X		
12. Most investments in stock of unconsolidated subsidiaries or other investees			X
13. Pension, sinking, and other funds under an enterprise's control: The specific assets in the fund should be classified as **monetary** or **nonmonetary.** (See listings under securities above.)	X	or	X
14. Property, plant, and equipment			X
15. Accumulated depreciation on property, plant, and equipment			X
16. Cash surrender value of life insurance	X		
17. Purchase commitments—portion paid on fixed-price contracts: An advance on a fixed-price contract is the portion of the purchaser's claim to **nonmonetary** goods or services that is recognized in the accounts; it is not a right to receive money.	X		
18. Advances to supplier—not on a fixed-price contract: A right to receive credit for a sum of money; not a claim to a specified quantity of goods or services.	X		
19. Deferred income tax debits*: Offsets to prospective **monetary** liabilities.	X		
20. Patents, trademarks, licenses and formulas			X
21. Goodwill			X
22. Other intangible assets and deferred charges			X

EXHIBIT 24–1: ***(concluded)***

Liabilities	Monetary		Nonmonetary
1. Accounts and notes payable	X		
2. Accrued expenses payable (wages, etc.)	X		
3. Accrued vacation pay: **Nonmonetary** if it is paid at the wage rates as of the vacation dates and if those rates may vary; otherwise, **monetary**	X	or	X
4. Cash dividends payable	X		
5. Obligations payable in foreign currency	X		
6. Sales commitments—portion collected on fixed-price contracts: An advance received on a fixed-price contract is the portion of the seller's obligation to deliver goods or services that is recognized in the accounts; it is not an obligation to pay money.			X
7. Advance from customers—not on a fixed-price contract: Equivalent of a loan from the customer; not an obligation to furnish a specified quantity of goods or services.	X		
8. Accrued losses on firm purchase commitments: In essence, these are accounts payable.	X		
9. Deferred (i.e., unearned) revenue: **Nonmonetary** if an obligation to furnish goods or services is involved. Certain "deferred income" items of savings and loan associations are **monetary.**	X	or	X
10. Refundable deposits	X		
11. Bonds payable and other long-term debt	X		
12. Unamortized premium or discount and prepaid interest on bonds or notes payable: Inseparable from the debt to which it relates—a **monetary** item.	X		
13. Convertible bonds payable: Until converted these are obligations to pay sums of money.	X		
14. Accrued pension obligations: Fixed amounts payable to a fund are **monetary**; all other amounts are **nonmonetary.**	X	or	X
15. Obligations under warranties: These are **nonmonetary** because they oblige the enterprise to furnish goods or services at their future price.			X
16. Deferred income tax credits*: Cash requirements will not vary materially due to changes in specific prices.	X		
17. Deferred investment tax credits: Not to be settled by payment of cash; associated with **nonmonetary** assets.			X
18. Deposit liabilities of financial institutions	X		

* Although classification of this item as **nonmonetary** may be technically preferable, the **monetary** classification provides a more practical solution for the purposes of CD accounting.

Source: Adapted from FASB, *Statement of Financial Accounting Standards No. 33.* "Financial Reporting and Changing Prices" (Stamford, Conn., September 1979), par. 208.

This simplified example illustrates that the prices of all the individual components of an index seldom, if ever, increase or decrease proportionately to each other; therefore, an index for a **group** of components reflects the **average** price movement for that particular group. For example, the price of potatoes decreased while the prices of the other items increased. Overall, food prices, as reflected by this hypothetical index, increased by 9.5 percent during the year. Actual price indexes include a typical collection of goods and services representative of the acquisitions of the group for which the index will be used.

The food price index illustrated above would be characterized as a **specific** price index because it encompasses a single group of goods (i.e., food) from among the broad categories of goods and services available. In contrast, a **general price-level** (GPL) index is designed and computed to be an **average** of the broad category of goods and services available. The most widely known **general price level** (GPL) indexes currently available are the Gross National Product Implicit Price Deflator, the Consumer Price Index, and the Wholesale Price Index. For **CD financial reporting,** the FASB requires the use of the Consumer Price Index for All Urban Consumers (CPI-U), which is published in *Monthly Labor Review* by the U.S. Department of Labor. Annual indexes for the CPI-U are presented below (at the time of this writing, the base year is 1967 = 100).[4]

GPL indexes such as the CPI-U are subject to criticism for several reasons. First, content of the "basket" is changed relatively infrequently; as consumer preferences change, the composition of the index "basket" of goods and services should be changed almost continuously to remain attuned to actual consumer preferences.[5] Second, the CPI-U reflects an average urban consumer and may characterize only a small percentage of the population. For example, persons living in rural areas may have different consumption preferences from those of the average urban consumer. Even within urban areas, many persons differ significantly from the "average." Many businesses purchase goods and services that bear little relationship to the CPI-U basket, and for these businesses, their HC/CD financial statements may not represent a significant improvement over their HC financial statements. This situation would be particularly true for a business operating in an industry in which prices are moving in a direction opposite to the GPL. A recent example of such an industrial group was electronic products. During the 1970s and early 1980s, prices of many electronic products decreased while the GPL was increasing. The HC/CD balance sheets of these companies would have reported their nonmonetary assets at HC/CD amounts in excess of HC amounts.

Year	Annual Average CPI-U Index	Annual Inflation Rate	Year-End CPI-U Index
1950	72.1		
1955	80.2	2.2%*	
1960	88.7	2.0*	
1965	94.5	1.3*	
1967	100.0	2.9*	
1970	116.3	5.2*	
1971	121.3	4.3	
1972	125.3	3.3	
1973	133.1	6.2	
1974	147.7	11.0	
1975	161.2	9.1	166.3
1976	170.5	5.8	174.3
1977	181.5	6.5	186.1
1978	195.4	7.7	202.9
1979	217.4	11.3	229.9
1980	247.3	13.8	258.4

* Annual compound rate for the period specified.

The data presented above indicate that annual inflation rates were low as recently as the 1960s. When annual inflation rates are low, annual differences between such financial statement measures as HC and HC/CD income also are low. Thus, it is not surprising that inflation reporting has been implemented only recently.

Use of Price Indexes in CD Restatements

In HC/CD reporting, CD restatement procedure involves the multiplication of the HC amount by a CD restatement ratio. The numerator of the CD restatement ratio is the GPL index on the date of the financial statements, and the denominator of the GPL restatement ratio is the GPL index that existed on the date of the transaction that caused the item to be recorded. The formula is as follows:

$$\text{HC/CD amount} = \text{HC amount} \times \frac{\text{GPL index at end of current period}}{\text{GPL index on transaction date}}$$

To illustrate, assume plant and equipment were acquired at a cost of $100,000 on January 1, 19A, when the GPL index was 127. The HC balance sheet at December 31, 19F (GPL index, 159), reported the cost of $100,000 and accumulated depreciation of $24,000. The CD restatement would be as follows:

[4] The CPI-U was scheduled to be rebased to 1977 = 100 beginning January 1982. Refer to *CPI Detailed Report* (U.S. Department of Labor, Bureau of Labor Statistics, January 1981), p. 3. However, in 1981, the Bureau of Labor Statistics postponed the "government directive to rebase the Consumer Price Index." As of October 1981, no alternative date for adopting the 1977 reference base had been announced.

[5] In response to this criticism, the Bureau of Labor Statistics announced on October 27, 1981, its intention to revise the CPI-U to consider shelter costs differently. For details, see Consumer Price Index Press Release 81–506, October 27, 1981, U.S. Department of Labor. For specific criticisms of the "old" CPI-U, see the September 1981 issue of *Monthly Labor Review,* which contains three such articles.

Item	HC at 12/31/19F		CD Restatement		HC/CD Restated in 12/31/19F Dollars
Plant and equipment	\$100,000	×	(159/127 = 1.252)	=	\$125,200
Accumulated depreciation ..	(24,000)	×	(159/127 = 1.252)	=	(30,048)

Under the heading, Monetary and Nonmonetary Items, we explained that when the GPL changes, debtors and creditors experience purchasing power gains (losses) on **monetary** items. During periods of inflation, creditors experience purchasing power losses and debtors experience purchasing power gains because the same number of dollars flow at inception and payment dates; however, at payment date each dollar will buy less real goods (i.e., the later dollars are cheaper in the case of inflation). This economic effect may be diagrammed as follows to reflect the **purchasing power gain (loss) on monetary items** held by debtors and creditors:

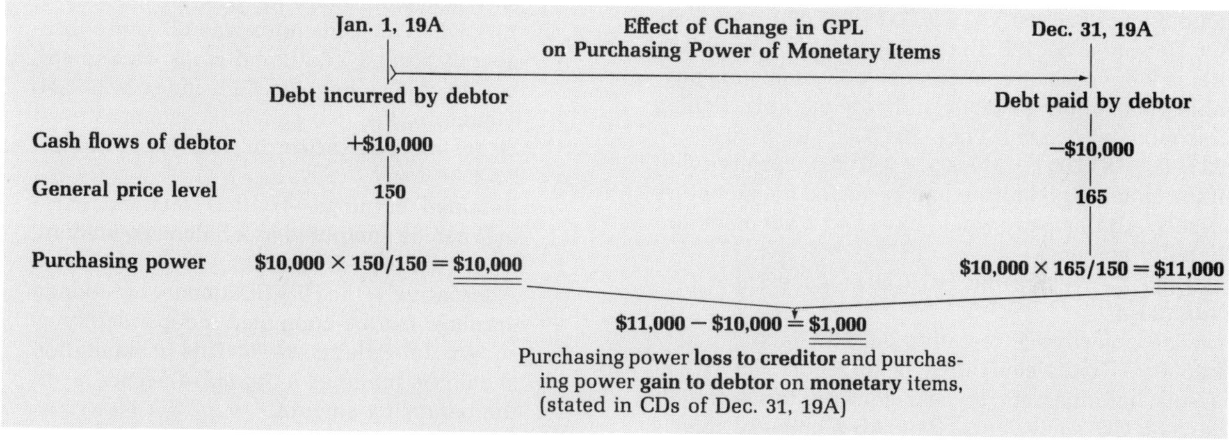

CONSTANT-DOLLAR (CD) RESTATEMENT PROCEDURES

Restatement of HC financial statements into CDs as of the date of the financial statements involves certain procedures to apply the concepts discussed above. To illustrate a comprehensive application of the HC/CD concepts, a hypothetical situation for AB Company is used. The four application steps are as follows:

1. Identify each item on the financial statements as either **monetary** or **nonmonetary** (Exhibit 24–1).
2. Prepare the **HC/CD balance sheet** (Exhibit 24–4).
3. Prepare the **HC/CD income statement** (Exhibit 24–5) and include on it the purchasing power gain (loss) on net monetary items computed in step 4 (Exhibit 24–6).
4. Compute the **purchasing power gain (loss) on net monetary items** (Exhibit 24–6).

Exhibit 24–2 provides relevant GPL indexes needed by AB Company, and Exhibit 24–3 provides the accounting data used in the illustrations; you should trace each of the 19F transactions given in Exhibit 24–3, Panel A, through the 19F worksheet in Panel B of that exhibit. That HC worksheet is provided to establish a foundation for the illustrations throughout the remainder of this chapter.

The four application steps of the HC/CD reporting model outlined above are implemented in the discussions which follow.

Step 1—Identify each financial statement item as either monetary or nonmonetary (Exhibit 24–3, code "M" = monetary).

On December 31, 19E (the **beginning date**), the monetary items were cash, accounts receivable, and

EXHIBIT 24–2: Hypothetical General Price Level (GPL) Index Values for Relevant Dates

Date	GPL Index	HC/CD Restatement Ratio
1/1/19A	127	159/127 = 1.252*
3/31/19B	138	159/138 = 1.152
12/31/19E	147	159/147 = 1.082
3/31/19F	149	159/149 = 1.067
6/30/19F	151	159/151 = 1.053
9/30/19F	154	159/154 = 1.032
12/31/19F	159	159/159 = 1.000
Period		
Average, 4th quarter 19E ...	146	159/146 = 1.089
Average, 4th quarter 19F ...	157	159/157 = 1.013
Average, full year 19F	152†	159/152 = 1.046

* For convenience, the index ratios are rounded in this chapter at the third decimal place. Such rounding generally is precise enough because the index numbers themselves are not all that precise.

† (147 + 149 + 151 + 154 + 159) ÷ 5 = 152.

accounts payable. The beginning **net monetary asset** amount was $20,000 (i.e., $36,000 + $24,000 − $40,000). On December 31, 19F (the **ending date**), the monetary items were cash, accounts receivable, accounts payable, income tax payable, and note payable. Ending **net** monetary assets were $64,000 (i.e., $136,000 + $33,000 − $45,000 − $10,000 − $50,000). Observe that if the monetary liabilities had exceeded the monetary assets, AB Company would have had a **net** monetary **liability** amount.

Step 2—Prepare the HC/CD balance sheet (Exhibit 24–4).

The objective of restating the HC balance sheet into its HC/CD equivalent is to report the HC of assets, liabilities, and owners' equity in terms of their current CD equivalents. (For AB Company this is in terms of December 31, 19F, dollars.) Therefore, the numerator of all GPL restatement ratios is the GPL index as of the balance sheet date and the denominators vary, depending upon when the individual item was acquired (i.e., its transaction date). Thus, for AB Company all numerators are 159, and the denominators vary as discussed below.

1. **Monetary items**—Because monetary items have fixed amounts which are not affected by GPL changes, their HC and CD amounts are the same. Therefore, they do not require restatement on the HC/CD balance sheet. Instead, the purchasing power gain or loss on monetary items is computed in Exhibit 24–6 and reported on the income statement; from there it flows into the balance sheet as retained earnings. For AB Company, the monetary items in Exhibit 24–4 are not restated; however, their purchasing power effects are included implicitly in the "balancing amount" for retained earnings (the accuracy of the "balancing amount" for retained earnings is proved in Exhibits 24–7 and 24–8).
2. Nonmonetary items—The nonmonetary items are restated on the HC/CD balance sheet as illustrated in Exhibit 24–4 because their prices tend to fluctuate as prices change. The restatement ratio for each nonmonetary item uses the GPL index as of restatement date as the numerator and the GPL index at acquisition date as the denominator. The acquisition dates and related GPL index values are summarized in Exhibit 24–4, Panel A. Two items listed there warrant further explanation as follows:
   a. **Common stock, nopar**—AB Company first issued common stock for cash on January 1, 19A, when the GPL index was 127, and subsequently issued additional stock on September 30, 19F, when the GPL index was 154. Therefore, the two separate issuances must be restated as shown in note *(a)* of Exhibit 24–4.
   b. **Retained earnings**—HC/CD retained earnings can be computed as a **balancing amount,** as shown for AB Company in Exhibit 24–4. Alternatively, the HC/CD amount of retained earnings can be computed independently as shown in Exhibit 24–8. This computation should be made as a "proof of accuracy" of the balancing amount.

Step 3—Prepare the HC/CD income statement (see Exhibit 24–5).

The objective of restating the HC income statement into an HC/CD income statement is to report the HC revenues, expenses, gains, and losses in terms of their CD equivalents (for AB Company this is in terms of December 31, 19F, dollars.) Therefore, the numerator of all GPL restatement ratios is the GPL index at year-end (i.e., 159). The denominators of the restatement ratios vary according to when the individual transactions occurred (i.e., when the depreciable assets were acquired or when current expenses were incurred). Thus, for AB Company, all numerators are 159, and the denominators vary as discussed below (for basic data, see Exhibit 24–3, Panel A).

a. **Sales revenue** (all on credit) increased net monetary assets (i.e., accounts receivable) **evenly** during 19F; therefore, the denominator of the CD restatement ratio is the **average** GPL index value for the year, and the numerator is the index at December 31, 19F. Thus, sales revenue is restated by the CD index ratio 159/152.

b. **Gain on sale of investment** [Exhibit 24–3, item *(d)*] requires CD restatement of the HC entry to record the sale on December 31, 19F, when the GPL index was 159, as shown in note *(a)* of Exhibit 24–5. Therefore, the cash received is restated by the CD ratio of 159/159. The HC amount of the investment is restated by the ratio of 159/138 because the GPL index at date of acquisition, March 31, 19B, was 138. The resulting HC/CD gain of $600 is a balancing amount; it reflects a weighted average of the CD equivalents of the cash received and the cost of the investment sold. If the sale and cash proceeds had been $14,000 on December 31, 19F, the sale would have resulted in an HC/CD loss of $400, that is, [$14,000 − ($12,500 × 159/138 = $14,400)]. If the sale had been made on March 31, 19F, for $15,000, the HC/CD gain would have been $1,605, that is, [($15,000 × 159/149 = $16,005) − $14,400].

c. **Cost of goods sold** requires multiple HC/CD restatement as shown in note *(b)* of Exhibit 24–5. Based on the FIFO assumption [Exhibit 24–3, Panel A, item *(m)*], the beginning inventory was acquired during the fourth quarter of the preceding year when the average GPL index was 146 (Exhibit 24–2); therefore, it is restated by the CD ratio, 159/146. Purchases decreased net monetary assets (i.e., increased accounts payable) evenly during 19F; consequently, this amount is restated by the CD ratio, 159/152. Based on the FIFO assumption, ending inventory was acquired evenly during the fourth quarter of 19F, when the average GPL index was 157; this amount is restated by the ratio, 159/157.[6] If AB Company had used LIFO, the denominators of the CD ratios applied to beginning and ending inventory would have been based upon the dates those costs were incurred; in some cases, those dates may have been in the distant past. If AB had used the average cost method for inventory, the denominators of the CD ratios for beginning and ending inventory would have been appropriate average GPL index values for 19E and 19F, respectively. For all three of the inventory cost flow methods, the CD restatement of purchases would be the same because the cost flow method does not affect the timing of purchases.

d. **General expenses** decreased net monetary assets (i.e., decreased cash or increased payables) evenly during 19F; therefore, the HC amount is restated by the average CD ratio for the year, 159/152.

e. **Depreciation expense,** plant and equipment, occurred evenly during 19F; however, the HC/CD amount of depreciation expense is based upon the HC/CD amount of the related asset. For this reason, depreciation expense on plant and equipment is restated by the same ratio applied to plant and equipment, 159/127, because the assets were acquired and decreased net monetary assets on January 1, 19A, when the GPL index was 127.

f. **Depreciation expense,** parking garage, occurred evenly during 19F; however, it is CD restated by the ratio, 159/147, because the garage was acquired, and decreased net monetary assets, on January 1, 19F, when the GPL index was 147.

g. **Income tax expense** decreased net monetary assets (i.e., increased income tax payable) evenly during 19F. Therefore, it is restated by the CD ratio, 159/152. The key concept in identifying the appropriate CD ratio in this case (and in others as well) is identification of when the transaction affected net monetary assets; for income tax expense, this effect occurs when the expense is accrued. In this example, accrual occurred evenly during the year [Exhibit 24–3, Panel A, item (*l*)]. If, during the current year, AB Company had paid all or part of its current year tax liability, the payment would not have affected the CD ratio used because only **monetary** (M) items would have been affected (i.e., debit Income Tax Payable and credit Cash); hence the payment would have no effect on **net** monetary items, and the appropriate GPL index value in the denomi-

[6] These assumptions are reasonably consistent with the inventory turnover for the year, which was 3.56 (i.e., $80,000 ÷ [($20,000 + $25,000) ÷ 2]).

EXHIBIT 24–3: Worksheet, HC Basis—AB Company

Panel A—Summary of Transactions during 19F:

a. Sales of $144,000 were made evenly during the year (assume all on credit).
b. Purchases of $85,000 were made evenly during the year (assume all on credit).
c. The plant and equipment are depreciated 4 percent per year with no residual value; the plant and equipment were bought on January 1, 19A, when the GPL index was 127.
d. The long-term investment in common stock of Smith Company was acquired for $25,000 on March 31, 19B, when the GPL index was 138. On December 30, 19F, when the GPL index was 159, half of these shares (i.e., cost of $12,500) were sold for $15,000 cash.
e. General expenses (including interest) of $20,000 were accrued and paid evenly during the year.
f. Collections on accounts receivable, $135,000, were made evenly during the year.
g. Payments on accounts payable, $80,000, were made evenly during the year.
h. A $10,000 cash dividend was declared at midyear, when the GPL index was 151. It was paid one month later.
i. Parking garage was acquired January 1, 19F, when the GPL index was 147; issued 12 percent note payable, $50,000; interest paid quarterly.
j. Parking garage is depreciated 4 percent per year with no residual value.
k. Issued common stock for cash on September 30, 19F, when the GPL index was 154; cash received, $60,000. The initial $100,000 of common stock was issued on January 1, 19A, when the GPL index was 127.
l. Income tax of $10,000 was accrued evenly during the year. For instructional convenience, assume that all of it will be paid in 19G.
m. The December 31, 19F, inventory was $25,000 (FIFO basis; LCM = cost).
n. Net income for the year ended December 31, 19F, was $30,500.

Panel B—Worksheet HC Basis:

AB COMPANY
Worksheet to Develop Income Statement and Balance Sheet—Historical Cost (HC) Basis
For Year Ended December 31, 19F

	Account	12/31/19E Balances		19F Transactions and Adjustments		19F Income Statement		12/31/19F Balance Sheet	
M	Cash	36,000		(*d*) 15,000 (*f*) 135,000 (*k*) 60,000	(*e*) 20,000 (*g*) 80,000 (*h*) 10,000			136,000	
M	Accounts receivable (net)	24,000		(*a*) 144,000	(*f*) 135,000			33,000	
	Inventory	20,000				20,000	(*m*) 25,000	25,000	
	Investment in common stock of Smith Co.	25,000			(*d*) 12,500			12,500	
	Plant and equipment	100,000						100,000	
	Accumulated depreciation		20,000		(*c*) 4,000				24,000
	Parking garage			(*i*) 50,000				50,000	
	Accumulated depreciation				(*j*) 2,000				2,000
M	Accounts payable		40,000	(*g*) 80,000	(*b*) 85,000				45,000
M	Income tax payable				(*l*) 10,000				10,000
M	Note payable, 12%				(*i*) 50,000				50,000
	Common stock, nopar		100,000		(*k*) 60,000				160,000
	Retained earnings		45,000	(*h*) 10,000		(*n*) 30,500			65,500
	Sales revenue				(*a*) 144,000		144,000		
	Gain on sale of investment				(*d*) 2,500		2,500		
	Purchases			(*b*) 85,000		85,000			
	Depreciation expense, plant and equipment			(*c*) 4,000		4,000			
	Depreciation expense, parking garage			(*j*) 2,000		2,000			
	General expenses (including interest)			(*e*) 20,000		20,000			
	Income tax expense			(*l*) 10,000		10,000			
		205,000	205,000	615,000	615,000	171,500	171,500	356,500	356,500

M = Monetary item.

EXHIBIT 24–4: HC/CD Restatement of Balance Sheet—AB Company

Panel A—Summary of Acquisition Dates and GPL Index Values for Nonmonetary Items:

a. Ending 19F inventory acquired evenly throughout the fourth quarter; GPL index, 157.
b. Investment in common stock of Smith Company was acquired March 31, 19B; GPL index, 138.
c. Plant and equipment were acquired on January 1, 19A; GPL index, 127.
d. Accumulated depreciation, plant and equipment, restated on same basis as related asset account.
e. Parking garage was acquired on January 1, 19F; GPL index, 147.
f. Accumulated depreciation, parking garage, restated on same basis as related asset account.
g. Original issue of common stock, $100,000, on January 1, 19A; GPL index 127. Subsequent issuance of common stock, $60,000, on September 30, 19F; GPL index, 154.

Panel B—Balance Sheet:

AB COMPANY
HC/CD Balance Sheet
At December 31, 19F

	HC (per books)	HC/CD	
Assets			
Cash	$136,000	Monetary	$136,000
Accounts receivable (net)	33,000	Monetary	33,000
Inventory	25,000	159/157 = 1.013	25,325
Investment in common stock	12,500	159/138 = 1.152	14,400
Plant and equipment	100,000	159/127 = 1.252	125,200
Accumulated depreciation	(24,000)	159/127 = 1.252	(30,048)
Parking garage	50,000	159/147 = 1.082	54,100
Accumulated depreciation	(2,000)	159/147 = 1.082	(2,164)
Total assets	$330,500		$355,813
Liabilities			
Accounts payable	$ 45,000	Monetary	$ 45,000
Income tax payable	10,000	Monetary	10,000
Note payable, 12%	50,000	Monetary	50,000
Owners' Equity			
Common stock, nopar	160,000	(a)	187,120
Retained earnings	65,500	Bal. amt.(b)	63,693
Total liabilities and owners' equity	$330,500		$355,813

(a) Original common stock restatement (GPL index at issuance, 127): $100,000 × (159/127 = 1.252)	$125,200
19F common stock issuance restatement (GPL index at issuance, 154): $60,000 × (159/154 = 1.032)	61,920
Common stock restated in CDs	$187,120

(b) For proof of accuracy, see Exhibit 24–8.

nator of the CD ratio still would be the GPL index value when the expense was **incurred.**

h. **Purchasing power loss on net monetary items** of $264 was computed as shown in Exhibit 24–6.

i. HC/CD income of $27,043 is 11 percent less than the conventional HC net income of $30,500.

Step 4—Compute the purchasing power gain (loss) on **net monetary items** for 19F (Exhibit 24–6). The concept which underlies this computation is that the company began 19F with a **net** monetary asset (or liability) amount and during the year engaged in transactions which increased or decreased its monetary assets and liabilities. The beginning net monetary asset amount (i.e., monetary assets minus monetary liabilities), plus the increases and minus the decreases of net monetary assets that occurred during the year, equals the ending **net** monetary asset

EXHIBIT 24–5: HC/CD Restatement of Income Statement—AB Company

AB COMPANY
HC/CD Income Statement
For Year Ended December 31, 19F

	HC (per books)	HC/CD	
Sales revenue	$144,000	159/152 = 1.046	$150,624
Gain on sale of investment	2,500	*(a)*	600
Total revenues and gains	146,500		151,224
Cost of goods sold	80,000	*(b)*	85,365
General expenses (including interest)	20,000	159/152 = 1.046	20,920
Depreciation expense, plant and equipment	4,000	159/127 = 1.252	5,008
Depreciation expense, garage	2,000	159/147 = 1.082	2,164
Income tax expense	10,000	159/152 = 1.046	10,460
Total expenses	116,000		123,917
Net income	$ 30,500		
HC/CD income before purchasing power loss on net monetary items			27,307
Purchasing power loss on net monetary items (Exhibit 24–6)			(264)
HC/CD income			$ 27,043

[a] Entry to record sale of investment (12/31/19F):

	HC		HC/CD		
Cash	15,000		159/159 = 1.000	15,000	
Investment in common stock ($25,000 ÷ 2)		12,500	159/138 = 1.152		14,400
Gain on sale of investment		2,500	Balancing amount		600

[b] Cost of goods sold:

	HC		HC/CD
Inventory, 1/1/19F	$ 20,000	159/146 = 1.089	$ 21,780
Purchases	85,000	159/152 = 1.046	88,910
Goods available for sale	105,000		110,690
Inventory, 12/31/19F (see Exhibit 24–4)	(25,000)	159/157 = 1.013	(25,325)
Cost of goods sold	$ 80,000		$ 85,365

(or **net** liability) amount. When all of these amounts are restated (i.e., beginning balance, increases, decreases, and ending balance) into their CD equivalents at December 31, 19F, the difference between the total *(a)* HC and *(b)* HC/CD **ending** net monetary assets is an **economic** measure of the company's success (a gain), or lack of success (a loss) in using monetary items during the year. This difference between HC and HC/CD ending balances implicitly considers both the amounts and the timing of all net monetary effects on the entity during the period, relative to the changes in prices that occurred during that period. Hence, it is viewed as a measure of the HC/CD **purchasing power gain (or loss) on net monetary items** during the period.

In Exhibit 24–6, AB Company began 19F with $20,000 of net monetary **assets;** on the beginning date, the GPL index was 147. Therefore, because the GPL index at December 31, 19F, was 159, the **total** beginning balance of $20,000 must be restated by using the CD restatement ratio, 159/147. The increases and decreases in all of the monetary items must be restated individually to CDs of December 31, 19F, by using the index at that date (i.e., 159) as the numerator; the denominator must be the index at the transaction date of each item. Sales of goods and services, operational assets, and common stock, whether for cash or on account, cause net monetary assets to increase. In contrast, purchases, expenses, declaration of dividends, and acquisitions of nonmonetary assets, whether for cash or on account, cause net monetary assets to decrease. Exhibit 24–6 illustrates CD restatement of such items. Observe in Exhibit 24–6 that the **purchasing power gain (loss) is computed to be the remainder of the ending HC amount minus the ending HC/CD amount.** A positive remainder signifies a purchasing power gain, and a negative remainder signifies a purchasing power loss. The logic of this relationship can be explained using Exhibit 24–6, in which AB Company transacted business during 19F in such a way that, if AB Company had kept pace exactly with general inflation during the year, theoretically the net monetary assets should have been $64,264 at the end of 19F. However, on December 31, 19F, AB Company actually had net monetary assets of only $64,000. The difference of $264 (i.e., HC, $64,000 minus HC/CD, $64,264) signifies a purchasing power loss. The purchasing power gain (loss) is reported on the HC/CD income statement (Exhibit 24–5); in turn this causes it to be included in the "balancing" amount of HC/CD retained earnings in the HC/CD balance sheet (Exhibit 24–4).[7]

PROOF OF THE ACCURACY OF THE HC/CD FINANCIAL STATEMENTS

Exhibit 24–8 presents an independent computation, which serves as an independent proof of the accuracy of the retained earnings amount computed on the HC/CD balance sheet (Exhibit 24–4). This proof requires preparation of the *(a)* HC balance sheet of the **prior** year rolled forward to ending 19F CDs (Exhibit 24–7) and *(b)* completion of the 19F, HC/CD statement of retained earnings (Exhibit 24–8).[8]

The first step in this procedure is the restatement of the beginning 19F, HC/CD retained earnings balance, which requires rolling forward the entire HC balance sheet of the prior year, 19E, as shown in Exhibit 24–7. This restatement of beginning retained earnings is not detailed because retained earnings "arose," in effect, on the dates relating to the remaining balance sheet items. To illustrate, for AB Company, beginning monetary items (i.e., cash, accounts receivable, and beginning accounts payable) are restated by the CD restatement ratio 159/147, as shown in Exhibit 24–7. Beginning inventory, a nonmonetary asset, was acquired during the fourth quarter of the preceding year when the GPL index was 146. Therefore, it must be restated by the CD restatement ratio, 159/146. To be comparable, in purchasing power with all other items on the 19F financial statements, these items must be rolled forward to their CD equivalents as of December 31, 19F, **without regard to their monetary/nonmonetary classification.** In a similar manner, the HC balances of all other 19E balance sheet items (i.e., investment, plant and equipment, accumulated depreciation, and common stock) must be rolled forward into CDs of December 31, 19F, by using the GPL index of that date (December 31, 19F = 159) as the numerator, and as the denominator the GPL index at their initial transaction dates. The HC/CD equivalent total beginning assets (i.e., $215,660) less the sum of HC/CD equivalent accounts payable and common stock (i.e., $43,280 + $125,200) is beginning retained earnings, stated in CDs of December 31, 19F (i.e., $47,180). An alternative restatement procedure is to "roll forward" the ending HC/CD amounts of the prior year, as illustrated in the top portion of Exhibit 24–7. The HC/CD amount at the end of the preceding year is multiplied by the CD restatement factor of the current year (i.e., for 19F, multiply each prior amount by 159/147).

The last step in the proof is to prepare a 19F, HC/CD statement of retained earnings as shown in Exhibit 24–8, (the source of each amount is shown thereon). Observe that the HC/CD retained earnings balance at the end of 19F ($63,693) agrees with the "balancing amount" shown on the 19F balance sheet in Exhibit 24–4.

HC/CD REPORTING—AN OVERVIEW

HC/CD reporting retains the traditional HC amounts but simply GPL restates those amounts in terms of CDs. Therefore, it affords users of financial statements a basis for comparing HC amounts in a common measuring unit. The HC/CD model also reports the purchasing power gain (or loss) on net monetary items. This gain (loss) is not reported under HC accounting because that model does not measure

[7] *FASB Statement 33* does not take a definitive position on whether the purchasing power gain (loss) is an income statement item or an adjustment of capital. Schedule B of Appendix A to the *Statement* places the gain (loss) **with,** although not **on,** the income statement. *FASB Concepts Statement 3,* par. 60, includes "price changes" as a component of comprehensive income.

[8] The proof of accuracy can be based on total owners' equity instead of retained earnings. The procedures based on total owners' equity would be the same as those illustrated for retained earnings except that the contributed capital accounts would not be restated individually to a CD equivalent on the balance sheet. Instead, total owners' equity would be the "balancing amount"; nevertheless, it still would be necessary to account separately for new issuances of stock and other changes in contributed capital because their effects would be reflected in ending owners' equity but not in beginning owners' equity. Separate treatment of these transactions would be needed for the reconciliation of beginning and ending owners' equity.

EXHIBIT 24–6: Purchasing Power Gain (Loss) on Net Monetary Items—AB Company

AB COMPANY
Computation of Purchasing Power Gain (Loss) on Net Monetary Items
For Year Ended December 31, 19F

	Net Monetary Items-Increases (Decreases)	HC	HC/CD
1.	Total beginning net monetary assets	$ 20,000*	× 159/147 = 1.082 = $ 21,640
2.	Increases in net monetary assets during 19F from:		
	Sales revenue	144,000	× 159/152 = 1.046 = 150,624
	Sale of investment	15,000	× 159/159 = 1.000 = 15,000
	Sale and issuance of common stock	60,000	× 159/154 = 1.032 = 61,920
3.	Decreases in net monetary assets during 19F from:		
	Purchases	(85,000)	× 159/152 = 1.046 = (88,910)
	General expenses (including interest)	(20,000)	× 159/152 = 1.046 = (20,920)
	Income tax expense	(10,000)	× 159/152 = 1.046 = (10,460)
	Cash dividends declared†	(10,000)	× 159/151 = 1.053 = (10,530)
	Parking garage acquisition	(50,000)	× 159/147 = 1.082 = (54,100)
4.	Total ending net monetary assets:		
	HC	$ 64,000‡	
	HC/CD		$ 64,264
5.	Purchasing power gain (loss) on net monetary items; to income statement, HC, $64,000 − HC/CD, $64,264; a positive remainder is a gain and a negative remainder is a loss		$ (264)

* Computation from 19E balance sheet (Exhibit 24–3): Cash, $36,000 + Accounts receivable, $24,000 − Accounts payable, $40,000 = $20,000 (may be positive or negative; positive in this case).

† Declaration date, **not** payment date is relevant to the CD restatement of cash and property dividends because on declaration date, the entity incurs a monetary liability and, hence, decreases net monetary assets. Subsequent payment has no effect on net monetary assets because payment involves monetary items only (i.e., Dr. Dividends Payable; Cr. Cash).

‡ Computation from 19F balance sheet (Exhibit 24–4): Cash, $136,000 + Accounts receivable, $33,000 − Accounts payable, $45,000 − Income tax payable, $10,000 − Note payable, $50,000 = $64,000 (may be positive or negative; positive in this case). This exhibit demonstrates that usually it is not necessary to compute the purchasing power gain (loss) on each separate monetary item; rather they can be combined as in this exhibit.

the loss from holding monetary assets or the gain from owing debt during periods of inflation.

HC/CD reporting does not report current values because the GPL indexes used for HC/CD restatements ignore the specific price changes of the individual assets and liabilities of the entity. Only by coincidence would HC/CD amounts equal the market values (either current sales value or current cost) of the individual assets and liabilities of the entity.[9]

Another characteristic of HC/CD reporting is that during a period of inflation a company can increase its reported purchasing power gain on **net** monetary items by incurring large amounts of debt. The purchasing power gain could imply that more debt may be preferable to less debt **without limit** in a company's financing mix. However, examples abound which illustrate that this inference must be tempered, because for most companies an upper limit exists on the amount of debt such companies can service and remain viable.[10]

[9] This coincidence would be likely to occur only on an aggregate company basis and not on an account-by-account basis and most likely for the type of entity that is so well diversified that changes in the aggregate of the specific price change effects of its individual assets and liabilities paralleled changes in the GPL index.

[10] Often cited examples are: LTV Corporation in the early 1970s; Penn Central in the mid 1970s; Chrysler Corporation and Braniff International in the early 1980s.

EXHIBIT 24–7: Data for Proof of Accuracy of HC/CD Financial Statements—AB Company

AB COMPANY
Data for Proof of Accuracy of HC/CD Financial Statements for 19F
Balance Sheet at December 31, 19E
(stated in CDs of December 31, 19F)

	HC 12/31/19E (Exhibit 24–3)	HC/CD (in CDs of 12/31/19F)	
Assets			
Cash	$ 36,000	159/147 = 1.082	$ 38,952
Accounts receivable (net)	24,000	159/147 = 1.082	25,968
Inventory	20,000	159/146 = 1.089	21,780
Investment in common stock	25,000	159/138 = 1.152	28,800
Plant and equipment	100,000	159/127 = 1.252	125,200
Accumulated depreciation	(20,000)	159/127 = 1.252	(25,040)
Total assets	$185,000		$215,660
Liabilities			
Accounts payable	$ 40,000	159/147 = 1.082	$ 43,280
Owners' Equity			
Common stock, nopar	100,000	159/127 = 1.252	125,200
Retained earnings	45,000	Balancing amount	47,180
Total liab. and owners' equity	$185,000		$215,660

EXHIBIT 24–8: Proof of Accuracy of HC/CD Financial Statements—AB Company

AB COMPANY
HC/CD Statement of Retained Earnings (also Proof of Accuracy)
For Year Ended December 31, 19F

	Source (Exhibit)	HC/CD
Retained earnings, 12/31/19E, stated in CDs of 12/31/19F	24–7	$47,180
Add: HC/CD income, including purchasing power loss on net monetary items, for 19F	24–5	27,043
Deduct: HC/CD dividends for 19F	24–6	(10,530)
Retained earnings, 12/31/19F, in CDs of same date		$63,693*

* Agrees with the balancing amount reported on the 12/31/19F, HC/CD balance sheet (Exhibit 24–4).

Part B: The Current Cost/Constant Dollar (CC/CD) Model and the Reporting Requirements of FASB Statement 33

Fundamentally, current cost (CC) accounting models substitute current costs for HC or HC/CD amounts in the financial statements. Current cost models may be based upon either (1) current costs or (2) current cost in constant dollars (CC/CD). This part of the chapter focuses on the CC/CD reporting model because in our opinion it provides more relevant data than CC for the decisions of most users of financial statements. Also, the "comprehensive statement" reporting specification of *FASB Statement No. 33* is based upon the CC/CD model.

COMPARISON OF THE HC, HC/CD, AND CC/CD MODELS

The CC/CD model can be understood by comparing the information it provides with that of the HC and HC/CD models. During periods of changing prices (either inflation or deflation), the HC model is deficient conceptually because it adds and subtracts dollars with different purchasing powers without adjusting for those purchasing power differences. The HC model does not report the effects of either **general** or **specific** price changes. As a result, the HC model provides neither a current cost measure of income nor specific current cost measures of the company's assets.

The HC/CD model is similar to the HC model except for one major difference. The HC/CD model reports the effects of **general** price level changes on the HC account balances, and by so doing, it does not aggregate dollars of different purchasing power. However, the HC/CD model does not report the effects of **specific** price changes on the enterprise. Therefore, the HC/CD model does not report current cost (CC) measures of income and assets. Many accountants view the CC measures to be closer to "true" amounts and for this reason would characterize the differences between CC amounts and the amounts provided by the HC and HC/CD models as "deficiencies."

The CC/CD model is designed to resolve some of the alleged deficiencies of the HC and HC/CD models by *(a)* reporting income and assets at CC and *(b)* stating them in constant dollars (CDs). The resultant CC/CD amounts then are substituted in the financial statements in place of their corresponding HC amounts; thus, the CC/CD model drops HC reporting and replaces it with combined current cost and constant dollar (CC/CD) amounts. It reports the effects of both **specific** and **general** price level (GPL) changes. The CC/CD model discussed in this part of the chapter is consistent with the supplementary reporting provisions of *FASB Statement 33.*

THEORETICAL FOUNDATION OF THE CC/CD MODEL

The theoretical foundation of the CC/CD model can be traced to the concept of **economic** income, that is, the change in the current (sales) value of an entity.[11] While economic income would be an ideal measure of enterprise income, inherently it is subjective, therefore, it has not been generally accepted by accountants. Under certain conditions, CC/CD income is a close proxy for economic income, and it is viewed as less subjective than economic income.[12]

OBJECTIVES OF THE CC/CD MODEL

One objective of CC/CD reporting is to report distributable income. The latter is the amount which can be distributed in dividends without reducing the future operating capacity (level) of the entity. This goal is operationalized by measuring expenses at the CC of the assets used up in the revenue process.

[11] Two theoretical works on current cost accounting begin with economic income. See E. O. Edwards and P. W. Bell, *The Theory and Measurement of Business and Income* (Berkeley: University of California Press, 1961), chaps. 2–4; and L. Revsine, *Replacement Cost Accounting* (Englewood Cliffs: Prentice-Hall, 1973), chap. 4.

[12] The basic condition for CC/CD income to be a proxy for economic income is a perfectly competitive economy, which implies *(a)* perfect resource mobility, *(b)* the cost of every asset is equal to the discounted present value of the future cash flows the asset can be used to generate, and *(c)* all buyers and sellers have perfect knowledge of prices and buying and selling opportunities. These ideas are developed in Revsine, *Replacement Cost Accounting*, pp. 95–100.

Proponents of CC/CD reporting believe the resultant income (i.e., revenues minus expenses measured at CC, all stated in CDs of the balance sheet date for comparability) measures the **distributable** income of the entity in constant dollars.

The importance of CC/CD income as a measure of distributable income can be seen by comparing it to HC income. During inflation, HC depreciation usually is less than CC depreciation because of the increase in the cost of operational assets. When the lower amount of HC depreciation is matched against revenue, HC income exceeds CC/CD income. A similar effect occurs when the costs of inventory and other nonmonetary assets are expensed. If a company were to distribute all of its HC income, part of the dividends would not be paid from income as intended but instead would erode the contributed capital of the entity. For this reason, *FASB Statement 33* (par. 3d) states that one of the purposes of CC/CD financial reporting is "to help users in . . . the . . . assessment of the erosion of operating capability."

Such erosion appears to be a significant problem. A recent article indicates that the cash dividends of Ford Motor Company, National Steel Corporation, and Standard Brands exceeded their CC incomes by 119 percent, 100 percent, and 87 percent, respectively. Of the 25 U.S. corporations mentioned in the article, 16 (64 percent) paid dividends in excess of their CC income even though none paid dividends in excess of their HC income. Moreover, based on their CC incomes, the median effective income tax rate was 71 percent (versus a maximum statutory tax rate of 46 percent on HC income.)[13]

Another objective of CC/CD reporting is to report assets at the current cost of replacing the assets owned. *FASB Statement 33* (par. 99f) defines current cost as follows:

> **Current cost** is equal to the current replacement cost of the asset owned, adjusted for the value of any operating advantages or disadvantages of the asset owned. **Current cost** differs from **current replacement cost** in that current cost measurement focuses on the cost of the service potential embodied in the asset owned by the enterprise whereas current replacement cost may be a measurement of a different asset, available for use in place of the asset owned. **Current cost** will be less than **current replacement cost** if the service potential of the asset owned is less than the service potential of the asset that would replace it. That may be the case, for example, when the asset owned has a higher operating cost or produces an output of lower quality. Similarly, current cost may be less than **current reproduction cost** if identical used assets are not available for purchase and if acquisition of a new, but otherwise identical, asset would not be worthwhile because that asset is obsolete for the purposes of the enterprise concerned. [Emphasis added.]

FASB Statement 33 (pars. 51–52) provides that when the **recoverable amount** (i.e., net realizable value) of an asset is less than its current cost, the entity should report the asset at the lower recoverable amount. This provision also applies to the CC measures of **expenses** (e.g., cost of goods sold and depreciation); that is, the expenses should be measured on the basis of the current cost of the related asset or its lower recoverable amount, if applicable. Therefore, throughout this chapter all references to CC implicitly include this constraint.[14]

A CC/CD balance sheet reports assets at their CC on the balance sheet date.[15] Consequently, it reports the CC of replacing the service potentials of the entity's assets (or their lower recoverable amount). In this sense, it provides a current value balance sheet.

MEASURING CURRENT COST (CC)

FASB Statement 33 (par. 60) outlines several approaches for developing CC data, as follows:

a. Indexation (use of specific price indexes):
   (1) Externally generated price indexes for the class of goods or services being measured.
   (2) Internally generated price indexes for the class of goods or services being measured.

b. Direct pricing:
   (1) Current invoice prices.
   (2) Vendors' price lists or other quotations or estimates.

---

[13] "Living Off Capital" (Numbers Game), *Forbes*, November 10, 1980, pp. 230–36.

[14] This constraint is ever-present in accounting. It applies to HC amounts in the traditional HC accounting framework, as well as to HC/CD, CC, and CC/CD amounts because under GAAP, assets generally should not be reported at amounts in excess of their net realizable value, and expenses are measured accordingly.

[15] Such CC asset amounts do not require restatement in CDs because measurement of their current costs on the balance sheet date automatically reflects CC in CDs on that date.

(3) Standard manufacturing costs that reflect current costs.

Thus, in the CC/CD model **specific** price indexes often are used to develop CC amounts, whereas a **general** price level index is used to restate amounts into CDs of the fiscal year-end date (as in Part A). **Both specific and general price indexes are used in the CC/CD model.**

Now let's turn our attention briefly to **specific price indexes.** A specific price index relates to a single good or service, or to narrow groups of goods or services. Other than the "size of the basket" represented, the GPL and specific price index concepts are the same. However, the various specific price index numbers do not necessarily change in proportion to, or in the same direction as, the GPL index. To illustrate the magnitude of the divergence of specific prices from general prices, as reflected by the CPI-U, selected price index data are presented below:

	General Index		Specific Index			
	CPI-U		Hardwood Lumber		Particleboard	
Year	Price Index*	Annual Inflation Rate	Price Index*	Annual Inflation Rate	Price Index*	Annual Inflation Rate
1975	161.2		163.6		113.6	
1976	170.5	5.8%	192.0	17.4%	123.7	8.9%
1977	181.5	6.5	231.1	20.4	141.0	14.0
1978	195.4	7.7	286.4	23.9	170.4	20.9
1979	217.4	11.3	331.1	15.6	165.6	−2.8
1980	247.3	13.8	298.1†	−10.0	188.3†	13.7

* 1967 = 100.0.
† Estimated.
Sources: Consumer Price Index—*International Economic Indicators* (Washington, D.C.: U.S. Department of Commerce, December 1980), p. 43. Specific Price Indexes—*Construction Review* (Washington, D.C.: U.S. Department of Commerce, December 1980), p. 45.

The price change data presented above indicate that during 1975–80, the specific price changes for hardwood and particleboard were more volatile than the changes in the CPI-U. This divergence was evident in 1980, when the CPI-U increased by 13.8 percent, but the price of hardwood lumber decreased by 10 percent (the price of particleboard increased by 13.7 percent). Also, see 1979 for similar divergence.

Because specific prices often vary widely, it seems reasonable to conclude that the incidence as well as the magnitude of divergence between specific price changes and changes in the GPL are significant. This conclusion lends substantial support to the importance of CC/CD information, insofar as users of financial statements desire current value information on assets and income.

MEASURING THE EFFECTS OF CURRENT COST PRICE CHANGES

Under the CC/CD model, the following price change effects are measured and reported for the current period:

1. **On monetary (M) items**—Purchasing power gains (losses) on monetary items are discussed and illustrated in Part A of this chapter.
2. **On nonmonetary (NM) items**—For each nonmonetary item, its **total change in current cost** (CC) during the period is the difference between its beginning CC and its ending CC.[16] This total change in CC is subdivided as follows:
   a. **Change in CC of nonmonetary (NM) items due to general inflation** (i.e., the **general** price-level effect), which is the difference between

[16] For assets acquired during the current period, **beginning** current cost is the CC at the transaction date which is the same as the HC on that date. For assets sold or used during the period, ending current cost is current cost on the date the asset is sold or used.

beginning CC and that amount restated to CDs on the year-end date, by using the GPL index, as in Part A.

b. **Change in CC of nonmonetary (NM) items, net of general inflation,** which is measured as the **total** change in current cost **minus** the change due to **general inflation.**

The change in CC of NM items **due to** general inflation is positive in the case of inflation and negative in the case of deflation. The change in CC of NM items **net** of general inflation also can be positive or negative depending on the relationship between the change in the CC of the particular NM item vis-a-vis the change in the CC of that item due to general inflation. These effects of CC price changes outlined above for **nonmonetary** assets may be diagrammed as follows:

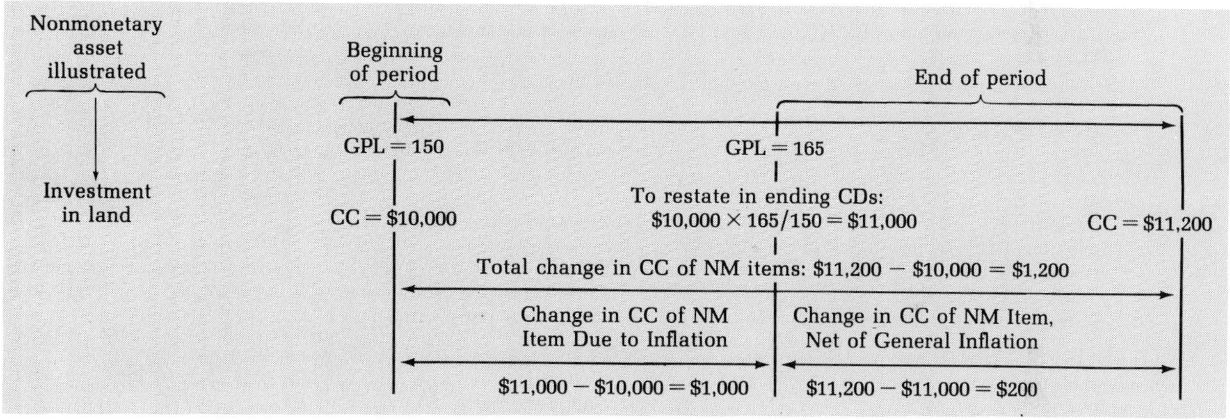

In the above example, the **specific** price of the investment increased during the period faster than the **general** price level. In contrast, if CC had been $10,600, the change in CC of NM items, net of general inflation would have been **negative** $400 (i.e., $10,600 − $11,000).

APPLICATION OF CC/CD CONCEPTS

FASB Statement 33 (par. 52) requires that an enterprise present as a supplement to the HC financial statements either *(a)* specified minimum CC information (par. 52) or *(b)* comprehensive CC/CD financial statements. The discussions and illustrations in the next section assume that **comprehensive** CC/CD financial statements are prepared as **supplements** to the HC statements. This approach establishes a solid foundation for you to learn the concepts and application procedures of the CC/CD model. Also, this approach provides the data needed for the minimum CC/CD reporting requirements of *FASB Statement 33,* which are discussed in the last section of this part of the chapter.

PREPARATION OF CC/CD FINANCIAL STATEMENTS, STATED IN END-OF-PERIOD CDs

Preparation of CC/CD financial statements basically involves measurement of the CC of each financial statement item and restatement of all such CC amounts to end-of-period CDs (as in Part A, but here restating CC amounts instead of HC amounts).

To illustrate a comprehensive application of the CC/CD concepts, the hypothetical situation used in Part A, for AB Company (Exhibit 24–3), is adapted. The five application steps to prepare CC/CD financial statements are:

1. Identify each financial statement item as either **monetary** or **nonmonetary** (exactly as in Part A).
2. Compute the purchasing power gain (loss) on net monetary items (exactly as in Part A).
3. Prepare the CC/CD balance sheet by substituting CC/CD amounts for HC amounts.
4. Prepare the CC/CD income statement and include on it both the *(a)* purchasing power gain (loss) on net **monetary** items (computed in step 2 above) and *(b)* the change in CC of NM items, net of general inflation (computed in step 5).
5. For each **nonmonetary** item, compute the **total**

change in its CC, which is then subdivided into the *(a)* **change in CC of NM items due to general inflation** (i.e., the GPL effect), and *(b)* **change in CC of NM items, net of general inflation.**

The five application steps of the preparation of CC/CD financial statements outlined above are implemented in the discussions which follow. Exhibit 24–9 provides the 19F, CC, and related data in much the same way they would be available in an actual setting. Exhibit 24–9 is divided into three panels:

Panel A—GPL index numbers for relevant dates (see Exhibit 24–2).

Panel B—**Monetary** items are the same in the HC, HC/CD, and CC/CD models.

Panel C—**Nonmonetary** assets, revenues, and expenses by dates. The essential 19F data are: beginning CCs; ending CCs; and revenues and expenses during 19F. Panel C also presents the respective sources of CC data as they could be provided in an actual setting.

Steps 1 and 2—These steps require classification of each financial statement item as either monetary or nonmonetary and computation of the purchasing power gain (loss) on net **monetary** items. These steps were discussed and illustrated for AB Company in

EXHIBIT 24–9: Selected Current Cost (CC) and Related Data—AB Company, 19F

Panel A—General Price Level (GPL) Index Numbers for Relevant Dates (see Exhibit 24–2).

Panel B—Monetary Items—HC, HC/CD, and CC/CD amounts are the same (see Exhibits 24–3 and 24–4).

Panel C—Nonmonetary Assets, Revenues, and Expenses by Dates:

Item	**Source of CC Data**	**Current Cost (In CDs of 1/1/19F)**
December 31, 19E:		
Assets (beginning balances):		
Inventory	From prior period, 19E	$ 20,500
Investment in common stock of Smith Company	From prior period, 19E	33,000
Plant and equipment	From prior period, 19E	175,000
Accumulated depreciation (P&E)	From prior period, 19E	(35,000)
December 31, 19F:		**Current Cost (In CDs of 12/31/19F)**
Assets (ending balances):		
Inventory	Suppliers' price lists	$ 26,000
Investment in common stock	Quoted market price	15,000
Plant and equipment (acquired 1/1/19A)	Indexed, specific	196,000
Accumulated depreciation (P&E)	$196,000 × 24%[a]	(47,040)
Parking garage (acquired 1/1/19F)	Professional appraisal	56,000
Accumulated depreciation (PG)	$56,000 × 4%[b]	(2,240)
During 19F (revenues and expenses occurred evenly throughout the year):		**Current Cost (In average CDs of 19F)**
Sales revenue	HC, Exhibit 24–3	$144,000
Cost of goods sold	Suppliers' price lists	86,000
Depreciation expense (P&E)	Computed[c]	7,420
Depreciation expense (PG)	Computed[d]	2,120
General expenses (including interest)	HC, Exhibit 24–3	20,000
Income tax expense	HC, Exhibit 24–3	10,000

Computations:

[a] $24,000 ÷ $100,000 (i.e., HC depr. ÷ HC) = 24% depreciated to date; $196,000 × .24 = $47,040.

[b] $2,000 ÷ $50,000 (i.e., HC depr. ÷ HC) = 4% depreciated to date; $56,000 × .04 = $2,240.

[c] Current cost depreciation expense for the year based on average current cost of plant and equipment: ($175,000 + $196,000) ÷ 2 = $185,500; $185,500 × .04 (depreciation rate per year) = $7,420.

[d] Current cost depreciation expense for the year based on average current cost of parking garage: ($50,000 + $56,000) ÷ 2 = $53,000; $53,000 × .04 (depreciation rate per year) = $2,120.

Part A. For AB Company the purchasing power loss on **net** monetary items during 19F was $264 (Exhibit 24–6) and was reported on the HC/CD income statement (Exhibit 24–5). This purchasing power loss is reported on the CC/CD income statement immediately below CC/CD income from continuing operations (illustrated in Exhibit 24–11).

Step 3—Prepare the CC/CD balance sheet. The CC/CD balance sheet of AB Company, at December 31, 19F, stated in CDs at that date for all items, is presented in Exhibit 24–10. The reported **monetary** amounts are the **same** at HC, HC/CD, and CC/CD, which is a typical situation. Therefore, they were taken directly from Exhibit 24–3 or 24–4. The 19F ending CC/CD amounts for the **nonmonetary** assets (i.e., inventory, investment, and operational assets) are given in Panel C of Exhibit 24–9. The CC/CD amount for contributed capital is the HC amount restated in end-of-period dollars (same as HC/CD amount reported in Exhibit 24–4). The amount of retained earnings is computed as a balancing amount.[17]

Step 4—Prepare the CC/CD income statement. The CC income statement of AB Company for 19F, stated in CDs of December 31, 19F, is presented in Exhibit 24–11. Sales revenue, general expenses, and income tax expense are the same as in the HC/CD model because their amounts occurred evenly throughout 19F and did not involve **nonmonetary** assets; thus, their amounts are computed as in Exhibit 24–5.

Cost of goods sold and depreciation expense involve **nonmonetary** assets (inventory; plant and equipment and the parking garage, respectively), and their CC amounts are based on the average CCs of those assets during 19F, as shown in Exhibit 24–9, Panel C. To illustrate, the average CC of plant and equipment was $185,500 [i.e., ($175,000 + $196,000) ÷ 2; see Exhibit 24–9], and 4 percent of the asset was used up during 19F. Therefore, CC depreciation on the plant and equipment of AB Company was $7,420 (i.e., $185,500 × .04). CC depreciation on the parking garage is computed similarly.

For cost of goods sold, the company could keep two sets of records, one at HC and the other at CC based on suppliers' price lists. In this comprehensive problem, it is assumed that the CC of goods sold, stated in average 19F dollars, was $86,000. All of the revenue and CC expense measures are multiplied by the CD index ratio, 159/152 = 1.046, to restate them from average dollars of 19F (because they occurred evenly during 19F) to CDs of December 31, 19F, for comparability with all other amounts in the 19F financial statements.

In the CC/CD financial statements, AB Company would report no gain or loss on the sale of the investment in common stock of Smith Company (see Exhibit 24–3) because the sale proceeds ($15,000 in this example) would be the same as the CC of the investment sold at the date of sale. Exhibit 24–9 indicates that the CC of the investment shares at December 31, 19F (or on any date) would be determined by the quoted market price of the shares (this is the typical case); the quoted market price also would determine the sale proceeds, therefore, at CC, no gain or loss would result from the sale.

Income from continuing operations (as defined in *FASB Statement 33*) for AB Company (i.e., $19,309) now can be computed as the difference between CC revenues and CC expenses. The last phase of the preparation of the CC/CD income statement is to enter the *(a)* purchasing power gain (loss) on net **monetary** items during the period and *(b)* the price change effects during the period on the **nonmonetary** assets. For AB Company (Exhibit 24–11), these two amounts are set in a box for emphasis. The fundamental nature of each amount may be summarized as follows:

1. Price change effect of **net monetary** items—The **purchasing power gain (loss)** on net monetary items occurs when monetary assets and/or monetary liabilities are held during a period in which the GPL changes. When such a situation exists, the company will experience a real purchasing power gain (loss) because the number of dollars related to each monetary item is fixed during the period, but the "value" of each of those dollars changes. This kind of gain (loss) was discussed and illustrated in Part A. During 19F, AB Company experienced a purchasing power loss on net monetary items of $264, as computed in Exhibit 24–6.
2. Price change effects of **nonmonetary assets**—Price changes cause two different effects on nonmonetary assets; one is the effect of **general inflation** due to a change in the **GPL**, and the other

[17] Alternatively, total owners' equity can be used as the balancing amount.

EXHIBIT 24–10: CC/CD Balance Sheet—AB Company

AB COMPANY
CC/CD Balance Sheet
At December 31, 19F

	Assets	Source (Exhibit)	CC/CD (in CDs of 12/31/19F)
M	Cash	24–3; 24–4	$136,000
M	Accounts receivable (net)	24–3; 24–4	33,000
	Inventory	24–9	26,000
	Investment in common stock of Smith Co.	24–9	15,000
	Plant and equipment	24–9	196,000
	Accumulated depreciation, plant and equipment	24–9	(47,040)
	Parking garage	24–9	56,000
	Accumulated depreciation, parking garage	24–9	(2,240)
	Total assets		$412,720
	Liabilities		
M	Accounts payable	24–3; 24–4	$ 45,000
M	Income tax payable	24–3; 24–4	10,000
M	Note payable, 12%	24–3; 24–4	50,000
	Owners' Equity		
	Common stock, nopar	24–4	187,120
	Retained earnings	Balancing amount*	120,600
	Total liabilities and owners' equity		$412,720

M = Monetary item; same as HC and HC/CD amount.
* Total assets ($412,720) minus sum of total liabilities and common stock ($45,000 + $10,000 + $50,000 + $187,120) equals $120,600. For proof of accuracy, see Exhibits 24–13 and 24–14.

is the effect of a **price change net of general inflation** related to each individual asset (see the diagram on page 877). Thus, **both** of these price change effects occur when the **specific** price of a nonmonetary asset changes more or less than the change in the **GPL** during the period. Step 5, which follows, explains the analysis of these price change effects.

Step 5—This step relates only to **nonmonetary assets;** it involves computation of the two price change effects related to nonmonetary assets, which must be reported in conjunction with the CC/CD income statement (*FASB Statement 33,* pars. 30 and 56). These two amounts were illustrated on page 877; they are as follows:

a. Change in CC of NM items during the period due to **general inflation** only.

b. Change in CC of NM items during the period, which was more or less than the change in CC due to general inflation. This amount sometimes is called a "holding gain or loss on NM items," due to CC **price changes;** referred to hereinafter as the "change in CC of NM items, net of general inflation."

Exhibit 24–12 illustrates computation of these two price change effects for AB Company. The exhibit uses a standard format illustrated in *FASB Statement 33* (pars. 233–35), which is a short-cut computation that gives a reasonable approximation of the theoretical answers.

The computational format shown in Exhibit 24–12 is the same for each nonmonetary asset. **The reasoning underlying the computations is similar to that applied to compute the purchasing power gain or loss on net monetary assets.** That is, the changes during the period in the CC amount of each nonmonetary asset are analyzed using the beginning balance and the additions and deductions during the period to derive the ending balance, in a manner similar to the first column of the computation of the purchasing power gain or loss on net monetary assets (note the similar formats of Exhibits 24–12 and 24–6).

For inventory, the computed ending CC balance was $19,500 [Exhibit 24–12, column *(a)*]. This CC bal-

EXHIBIT 24–11: CC/CD Income Statement—AB Company

AB COMPANY
CC/CD Income Statement
For Year Ended December 31, 19F

	Source (Exhibit)	CC/CD (in CDs of 12/31/19F)	
Revenues and gains:			
Sales revenue	24–5	$144,000 × (159/152 = 1.046)	$150,624
Expenses and losses:			
Cost of goods sold	24–9	86,000 × (159/152 = 1.046)	(89,956)
General expenses (including interest)	24–5	20,000 × (159/152 = 1.046)	(20,920)
Depreciation expense, plant and equip.	24–9	7,420 × (159/152 = 1.046)	(7,761)
Depreciation expense, parking garage	24–9	2,120 × (159/152 = 1.046)	(2,218)
Income tax expense	24–5	10,000 × (159/152 = 1.046)	(10,460)
CC/CD income from continuing operations			19,309
Purchasing power gain (loss) on net **monetary** items	24–6		(264)
Total change in CC of **nonmonetary** items	24–12	Note A $25,760	
Change in CC of NM items due to general inflation	24–12	Note A 19,482	
Changes in CC of NM items, net of general inflation	24–12		6,278
CC/CD comprehensive income			$ 25,323

Note A: The price change effects of **nonmonetary** assets are as follows (computed in Exhibit 24–12):

Nonmonetary Asset	Change in CC Total	Change in CC Due to General Inflation	Change in CC Net of General Inflation
Inventory	$ 6,500	$ 1,635	$ 4,865
Investment in common stock of Smith Co.	(3,000)	2,706	(5,706)
Plant and equipment	16,380	11,139	5,241
Parking garage	5,880	4,002	1,878
Total	$25,760	$19,482	$6,278

ance reflects CC amounts that occurred at different dates and, therefore, reflects dollars that are not mutually comparable; for example, the CC of beginning inventory (i.e., $20,500) was measured on the beginning date, and each dollar of its amount is **not** comparable with each dollar reflected in the CC amounts of purchases and cost of goods sold, which occurred evenly during the period. Because of this noncomparability, it is necessary to restate each of these three CC amounts to CDs; columns *(b)* and *(c)* provide the restatement to CDs of the year-end date.[18]

To compute the three CC price change effects (i.e., total, general inflation, and net), a series of comparisons is made as illustrated in Exhibit 24–12. Computation of each price change effect is as follows for **each nonmonetary asset** (also refer to the diagram on page 877):

1. **Total change in CC of NM items**—The total change in CC of each nonmonetary asset is computed as the difference between:
   a. Its actual CC at the end of the period, which automatically is stated in end-of-period CDs (i.e., for inventory $26,000), and
   b. Its ending balance at CC when the balance or transaction occurred (i.e., $19,500 for inventory).

   Thus, for inventory the total change in CC during 19F was $6,500 (i.e., $26,000 − $19,500). The general inflation and net of inflation price change effects, explained below, must sum algebraically to this total price change effect.
2. **Change in CC of NM items due to general infla-**

[18] Under *FASB Statement 33,* use of annual average GPL index numbers also is acceptable for the numerator of the CD index ratios, in which case all items on the financial statements would be stated in annual average, rather than end-of-period, CDs.

EXHIBIT 24–12: Computation of the Price Change Effects of Nonmonetary Assets—AB Company, 19F

	Source (Exhibit)	(a) CC at Transaction or Balance Date	(b) Restatement to CDs of 12/31/19F	(c) CC/CD (stated in CDs of 12/31/19F)
Inventory:				
Beginning balance	24–9	$ 20,500	159/147 = 1.082	$ 22,181
Add—purchases during 19F	24–3, 24–5	85,000	159/152 = 1.046	88,910
Deduct—cost of goods sold for 19F	24–9	(86,000)	159/152 = 1.046	(89,956)
Ending balance at CC when the balance or transaction occurred		19,500		21,135
Ending balance at CC of 12/31/19F	24–9, 24–11	26,000	159/159 = 1.000	26,000
Total increase (decrease) in CC ($26,000 − $19,500)		$ 6,500		
Change in CC of NM asset due to general inflation ($21,135 − $19,500)			$1,635	
Change in CC of NM asset, net of general inflation ($26,000 − $21,135)				$ 4,865
Investment in common stock of Smith Co.:				
Beginning balance	24–9	$ 33,000	159/147 = 1.082	$ 35,706
Add—None				
Deduct—sale of half on 12/31/19F	24–3	(15,000)	159/159 = 1.000	(15,000)
Ending balance at CC when the balance or transaction occurred		18,000		20,706
Ending balance at CC of 12/31/19F	24–9	15,000	159/159 = 1.000	15,000
Total increase (decrease) in CC ($15,000 − $18,000)		$ (3,000)		
Change in CC of NM asset due to general inflation ($20,706 − $18,000)			$2,706	
Change in CC of NM asset net of general inflation ($15,000 − $20,706)				$ (5,706)
Plant and equipment:				
Beginning balance (net of depreciation)	24–9	$140,000	159/147 = 1.082	$151,480
Add—None				
Deduct—depreciation during 19F	24–9	(7,420)	159/152 = 1.046	(7,761)
Ending balance at CC when the balance or transaction occurred		132,580		143,719
Ending balance at CC of 12/31/19F (net)	24–9	148,960	159/159 = 1.000	148,960
Total increase (decrease) in CC ($148,960 − $132,580)		$ 16,380		
Change in CC of NM asset due to general inflation ($143,719 − $132,580)			$11,139	
Change in CC of NM asset, net of general inflation ($148,960 − $143,719)				$ 5,241
Parking garage:				
Beginning balance (net of depreciation)	24–9	$ -0-		$ -0-
Add—acquisition on 1/1/19F	24–3	50,000	159/147 = 1.082	54,100
Deduct—depreciation during 19F	24–9	(2,120)	159/152 = 1.046	(2,218)
Ending balance at CC when the balance or transaction occurred		47,880		51,882
Ending balance at CC of 12/31/19F (net)	24–9	53,760	159/159 = 1.000	53,760
Total increase (decrease) in CC ($53,760 − $47,880)		$ 5,880		
Change in CC of NM asset due to general inflation ($51,882 − $47,880)			$4,002	
Change in CC of NM asset net of general inflation ($53,760 − $51,882)				$1,878

tion (GPL)—The change in CC due to general inflation (of each nonmonetary asset) is computed as the difference between:

a. Its ending balance at CC when the balance or transaction occurred (i.e., $19,500 for inventory), and

b. Those amounts restated in end-of-period CDs (i.e., $21,135 for inventory).

Thus, for inventory the change in CC due to general inflation during 19F was $1,635 (i.e., $21,135 − $19,500).

3. **Change in CC of NM items, net of general inflation**—The change in CC, net of general inflation (of each nonmonetary asset) is computed as the difference between:

a. Its actual CC at the end of the period (i.e., $26,000 for inventory), and

b. The ending balance at CC when the balance or transaction occurred (i.e., beginning balance plus additions minus deductions during the period) restated to end-of-period CDs (i.e., $21,135 for inventory). Thus, for inventory the change in CC, net of general inflation during 19F was $4,865 (i.e., $26,000 − $21,135).

Exhibit 24–12 illustrates computation of the three price change effects of CC (i.e., total, general inflation, and net) for each of the **nonmonetary assets** of AB Company. Observe that each computation follows the pattern described above for inventory. Also, the computation for each nonmonetary asset can be diagrammed in the more conceptual manner illustrated on page 877.

During 19F, the current costs of the inventory, plant and equipment and parking garage of AB Company increased faster than did the GPL.[19] Their respective changes in CC, net of general inflation were $4,865, $5,241, and $1,878, as shown in Note A of Exhibit 24–11. During 19F, the CC of the investment in common stock **decreased** from $33,000 to $30,000 (note that half of the investment shares were sold on December 30, 19F). Thus, because the GPL **increased** during 19F, the change in CC, net of general inflation on the investment was **negative** (a loss) $5,706 (i.e., −$3,000 − $2,706). For AB Company during 19F, the total change in CC, net of general inflation of all its nonmonetary assets was $6,278, as shown in Exhibit 24–11 and computed in Exhibit 24–12.

PROOF OF ACCURACY OF THE CC/CD FINANCIAL STATEMENTS

Exhibits 24–13 and 24–14 present an independent computation of the retained earnings amount reported on the CC/CD balance sheet of AB Company at December 31, 19F (Exhibit 24–10), which serves as a proof of the accuracy of the CC/CD financial statements. This procedure consists of *(a)* rolling forward the CC/CD balance sheet of the **prior** year into CDs of the current year-end date (Exhibit 24–13) and *(b)* completion of the CC/CD statement of retained earnings for 19F (Exhibit 24–14). The CC/CD amount of dividends (i.e., $10,530) is the same as the HC/CD amount because the declaration affects net monetary assets in the same way under both models. The CC/CD proof of accuracy is performed in the same manner as for the HC/CD model (see Exhibits 24–7 and 24–8).

USEFULNESS OF CC/CD FINANCIAL STATEMENTS

The usefulness of CC/CD data can be summarized as follows:

1. **CC/CD income from continuing operations** may be useful for assessing future net cash flows of an enterprise.[20] The resulting **CC/CD income from continuing operations** may be a good predictor of future CC/CD income from continuing operations. CC/CD income incorporates more up-to-date information about the current costs of the company's assets used up in production than the corresponding HC or HC/CD amounts.[21] Also, **CC/CD income from continuing operations** is a measure of "distributable income," the maximum amount an enterprise can pay in dividends and maintain its physical operating capacity by retaining sufficient internally generated funds to replace worn-out assets.[22]
2. The **increase or decrease in the CCs** of the non-

[19] For example, reference to Exhibit 24–9 indicates that the CC of plant and equipment (excluding depreciation) increased by 12 percent (i.e., from $175,000 to $196,000), while the GPL index increased by 8.2 percent (i.e., from 147 to 159) during 19F.

[20] This statement is true particularly if the selling price of inventory is related closely to the current cost of inventory at time of sale. See *FASB Statement 33,* par. 117.

[21] Ibid., par. 123.

[22] Ibid., pars. 124–30.

EXHIBIT 24–13: Data for Proof of Accuracy of CC/CD Financial Statements—AB Company

AB COMPANY
Data for Proof of Accuracy of CC/CD Financial Statements for 19F
Balance Sheet at December 31, 19E
Stated in CDs of December 31, 19F

		Source (Exhibit)	CC/CD (in CDs of 12/31/19E)	Restatement to CDs of 12/31/19F	CC/CD (in CDs of 12/31/19F)
	Assets				
M	Cash	24–7	$ 36,000	159/147 = 1.082	$ 38,952
M	Accounts receivable (net)	24–7	24,000	159/147 = 1.082	25,968
	Inventory	24–9	20,500	159/147 = 1.082	22,181
	Investment in common stock	24–9	33,000	159/147 = 1.082	35,706
	Plant and equipment	24–9	175,000	159/147 = 1.082	189,350
	Accumulated depreciation	24–9	(35,000)	159/147 = 1.082	(37,870)
	Total assets		$253,500		$274,287
	Liabilities				
M	Accounts payable	24–7	$ 40,000	159/147 = 1.082	$ 43,280
	Owners' Equity				
	Common stock, nopar	24–7	100,000	159/127 = 1.252	125,200
	Retained earnings	Bal. amount	113,500	Balancing amount	105,807*
	Total liab. and owners' equity		$253,500		$274,287

M = Monetary items; same as HC/CD.
* Computation, $274,287 − $43,280 − $125,200 = $105,807.

EXHIBIT 24–14: Proof of Accuracy of CC/CD Financial Statements—AB Company

AB COMPANY
CC/CD Statement of Retained Earnings (also Proof of Accuracy)
For Year Ended December 31, 19F
Stated in CDs of December 31, 19F

	Source (Exhibit)	CC/CD (in CDs of 12/31/19F)
Retained earnings, 12/31/19E, stated in CDs of 12/31/19F	24–13	$105,807
Add: CC/CD comprehensive income	24–11	25,323
Deduct: CC/CD dividends (same as HC/CD)	24–6	(10,530)
CC/CD retained earnings, 12/31/19F, in CDs of same date		$120,600*

* Agrees with the balancing amount on the 12/31/19F CC/CD balance sheet (see Exhibit 24–10).

monetary assets held by the enterprise may be useful for assessing the future net cash flows of the enterprise because a change in the CCs of an enterprise's assets represents a change in its financial investment. Because an enterprise normally would expect to earn a return on that investment, information on **changes in CCs** may represent one basis for assessing **changes in future cash flows.**[23]

[23] Ibid., par. 122. For a discussion of the contrary position that CC changes **cannot** be used to predict changes in future cash flows, see L. Revsine, *Replacement Cost Accounting* (Englewood Cliffs, N.J.: Prentice-Hall, 1973), pp. 142–64; and R. A. Samuelson, "Should Replacement Cost Changes Be Included in Income?" *The Accounting Review,* April 1980, pp. 254–68.

3. The **separation of CC/CD comprehensive income into its operating** (i.e., income from continuing operations) **and holding** (i.e., increases or decreases in CCs of nonmonetary assets) **components** may be useful information for predicting the future net cash flows of the entity. Specifically, the results of operating and holding activities may be affected differently by economic forces, and these two measures may be used differently in the prediction of future cash flows. It is easier to evaluate the prospective impacts of the various factors affecting operating income and CC changes if the two items are separated than if they are aggregated as in HC and HC/CD accounting.[24]
4. The **CC/CD balance sheet** presents assets, liabilities, and owners' equity at **current** cost (or lower recoverable amount). This provides users with an estimate of the amount required currently to replace the entity's assets in their **present condition** (see definition of current cost on page 875, especially the first sentence).

THEORETICAL FOUNDATION OF THE CC/CD MODEL REVISITED—AN UNRESOLVED ISSUE

An unresolved issue in the CC/CD model is whether to include in income changes in the CCs of the entity's nonmonetary assets. This issue can be addressed in terms of a particular **concept of capital maintenance.**

Two different concepts of capital maintenance underlie the various CC accounting models. The **financial capital** concept holds that capital is maintained when the **money value** of net assets remains intact. A key implication of this concept is that changes in the CCs of assets of an entity should be included as part of its income because they contribute to the maintenance of financial capital. In contrast, the **physical capital** concept holds that capital is maintained when the net assets remain sufficient to produce a **fixed quantity** (as opposed to **money value**) of goods and services. Under the physical capital concept, specific price changes in CCs of assets should not be included in income because the changes in CC do not represent changes in the quantity of goods and services the enterprise can produce.[25]

The FASB did not endorse either concept in *Statement 33*.[26] Instead, *Statement 33* requires companies to disclose the changes in the CCs of their assets separately from CC/CD income from continuing operations. In this chapter, we effectively employ the financial capital concept in the presentation of CC/CD **comprehensive income,** which is consistent with *FASB Concepts Statement 3,* December 1980.[27]

REPORTING REQUIREMENTS OF FASB STATEMENT 33

FASB Statement 33 applies to the annual financial statements of publicly held businesses which, at the beginning of the year, have either *(a)* inventories and tangible operational assets, i.e., property, plant, and equipment (before deducting accumulated depreciation), of more than $125 million or *(b)* total assets of more than $1 billion (after deducting accumulated depreciation). The *Statement* requires that companies make no changes in their primary HC financial statements.

The disclosure provisions are specified in the *Statement* essentially as follows (pars. 29–37):

A. HC/CD basis:
   a. Information on **income from continuing operations** for the current fiscal year on an HC/CD basis.
   b. The **purchasing power gain or loss on net monetary items** for the current fiscal year.
B. CC/CD basis:
   a. Information on **income from continuing operations** for the current fiscal year on a CC/CD basis.
   b. The CC amounts of **inventory and property, plant, and equipment** at the end of the current fiscal year.
   c. Increases or decreases for the current fiscal

[24] Ibid., par. 118. A contrary position (i.e., that operating and holding activities are inseparable and, hence, cannot be evaluated separately) is presented by P. Prakash and S. Sunder, "The Case against Separation of Current Operating Profit and Holding Gain," *The Accounting Review,* January 1979, pp. 1–22.

[25] For a discussion of different concepts of capital maintenance, see L. Revsine, "A Capital Maintenance Approach to Income Measurement" (Education Research Section), *The Accounting Review,* April 1981, pp. 383–89.

[26] *FASB Statement 33,* par. 104.

[27] Changes in CCs of assets constitute "price changes," which *FASB Concepts Statement 3,* par. 60, includes as part of "comprehensive income."

year in the CC amounts of inventory and property, plant, and equipment, net of inflation.

C. Summary of most recent five years:
   a. **Net sales and other operating revenues.**
   b. **HC/CD information:**
      (1) Income from continuing operations.
      (2) Income per common share from continuing operations.
      (3) Net assets at fiscal year-end.
   c. **CC information** (except for individual years in which the information was excluded from the current year disclosures):
      (1) Income from continuing operations.
      (2) Income per common share from continuing operations.
      (3) Net assets at fiscal year-end.
      (4) Increases or decreases in the CC amounts of inventory and property, plant, and equipment, net of inflation.
   d. **Other information:**
      (1) Purchasing power gain or loss on net monetary items.
      (2) Cash dividends declared per common share.
      (3) Market price per common share at fiscal year-end.
      (4) All enterprises shall report, in a note to the five-year summary, the average level or the end-of-year level (whichever is used for the measurement of income from continuing operations) of the CPI-U for each year included in the summary.

D. Format of presentation:
   a. The information required by this *Statement* shall be presented as **supplementary information** in any published annual report that contains the primary financial statements of the enterprise except that the information need not be presented in an interim financial report. The information required by this *Statement* need not be presented for segments of a business enterprise although such presentations are encouraged.
   b. Information on income from continuing operations (on an HC/CD basis or on a CC/CD basis) may be presented either in a **"statement format"** (disclosing revenues, expenses, gains, and losses) or in a **"reconciliation format"** (disclosing adjustments to the income from continuing operations that is shown in the primary income statement). Whichever format is used, such information should disclose, unless they are immaterial, the amounts of adjustments to cost of goods sold, depreciation, depletion, and amortization expense and (in the case of HC/CD income from continuing operations) reductions of the HC amounts of inventory, property, plant, and equipment to lower recoverable amounts.

The disclosures specified above represent minimum reporting requirements; additional HC/CD and CC/CD disclosures and experiments are encouraged. Some disclosures, consistent with the above specifications, are illustrated in the actual set of financial statements given in the Appendix following Chapter 24.

FASB Statement No. 33 (e.g., par. 30) sometimes uses the term "current cost" basis without referring specifically to CD restatement. However, paragraph 52 of the *Statement* states that, "An enterprise that chooses to present comprehensive financial statements on a current cost/constant dollar basis may measure the components of those statements either in average-for-the-year constant dollars or in end-of-year constant dollars." To enhance the instructional content of this chapter, we illustrate **comprehensive CC/CD financial statements presented in end-of-year dollars,** because they represent up-to-date CDs. For example, in a year in which double digit inflation occurs the effects of inflation would be understated considerably if average rather than end-of-year index numbers were used. To convert the CC/CD financial statements illustrated in the chapter to average-for-the-year CDs, simply multiply all amounts shown in Exhibits 24–10 through 24–14 by the following CD restatement ratio: Average-for-the-year GPL index/End-of-year GPL index.

Paragraph 52 of the *Statement* also states that, "An enterprise that presents the minimum information required by this Statement on current cost income from continuing operations shall measure the amounts of *(a)* cost of goods sold . . . at current cost . . . at the date of sale . . . and *(b)* depreciation and amortization expense . . . on the basis of the average current cost . . . of the assets' service potential during the period of use. Other revenues, expenses, gains, and losses may be measured by such an enterprise at the amounts included in the primary (i.e., HC) income statement." This quotation indicates that the resultant CC income from continuing operations essentially is a CC/CD measure because it necessarily would be stated essentially in some form of average-for-the year CDs. It appears that a CD reporting inconsistency is specified in the dual disclosure requirement of *FASB Statement No. 33.* Enterprises that present the "minimum information" must disclose *(a)* CC income from continuing operations stated essentially in average-for-the-year CDs and *(b)* the CCs of inventory and property, plant, and equipment at the end of the current fiscal year (i.e., stated in end-of-year CDs). Again, the CCs of assets stated in end-of-year CDs can be restated to average-for-the-year CDs by multiplying their CCs by the following CD restatement ratio: Average-for-the-year GPL index/End-of-year GPL index. Or, alternatively, the CC income from continuing operations, stated in average-for-the-year CDs, can be restated to end-of-year CDs by multiplying it by the CD restatement ratio (i.e., End-of-year GPL index/Average-for-the-year GPL index). Either CD restatement would produce CC measures stated in the same CDs.

FASB Statement No. 33 stopped short of requiring comprehensive CC/CD financial statements as illustrated in this chapter; its departure from CC/CD reporting is more cosmetic than real. The FASB considers the *Statement* to be experimental and tentative, as stated in pars. 14–15:

> The measurement and use of information on changing prices will require a substantial learning process on the part of all concerned. The Board makes no pretense of having solved all of the implementation problems. Rather, it encourages experimentation within the guidelines of this Statement and the development of new techniques that fit the particular circumstances of the enterprise. This Statement has been written to provide more flexibility than is customary in Board Statements in the belief that those involved will help to develop techniques that further the understanding of the effects of price changes on the enterprise.
>
> The requirement to present information on both a constant dollar basis and a current cost basis provides a basis for studying the usefulness of the two types of information. The Board intends to study the extent to which the information is used, the types of people to whom it is useful, and the purpose for which it is used. The requirements of this Statement will be reviewed on an ongoing basis and the Board will amend or withdraw requirements whenever that course is justified by the evidence. This Statement will be reviewed comprehensively after a period of not more than five years.

Supplement 24–A: Worksheet Approach to Preparation of HC/CD Financial Statements

Preparation of HC/CD financial statements using a series of exhibits was discussed and illustrated in Part A of the chapter. By adapting the traditional worksheet, the information in the exhibits can be synthesized on a single worksheet, which reflects the beginning balances, transactions, income statement, and balance sheet in CDs as of the end of the current period.

Such a worksheet is presented, for AB Company, in Exhibit 24–15, Panel B. The 19F actual transactions are summarized in Panel A. This worksheet is the HC/CD counterpart to the HC worksheet presented in Exhibit 24–3.

The worksheet presents, in transactions *o*–1 through *o*–5, the purchasing power gain (loss) on each monetary item. For example, a purchasing power loss of $5,952 was incurred from holding cash during 19F because the GPL increased by 8.2 percent during 19F (see entry *o*–1 of Exhibit 24–15). The overall purchasing power effect from holding monetary items during 19F was a loss of $264 (i.e., −$5,952 − $2,382 + $3,510 + $460 + $4,100), which also is computed as shown in Exhibit 24–6.

All other account balances and transaction amounts shown in Exhibit 24–15 can be traced back to the respective detailed exhibits where they were derived, the references to which appear in the column headings of Exhibit 24–15. In summary, the worksheet performs its customary tasks: (1) synthesizes all of the activities for a period; (2) facilitates com-

EXHIBIT 24–15: HC/CD Worksheet—AB Company

Panel A—Transactions during 19F (summarized)—see Exhibit 24–2 for CD-restatement ratios:

a. Sales, all on credit, evenly during the year: $144,000 × 159/152 = $150,624.
b. Purchases, all on credit, evenly during the year: $85,000 × 159/152 = $88,910.
c. Depreciation expense, plant and equipment: $4,000 × 159/127 = $5,008.
d. Sold investment for cash on December 30, 19F. See Exhibit 24–5, note a.
e. General expenses (including interest), evenly during the year: $20,000 × 159/152 = $20,920.
f. Collections on accounts receivable, evenly during the year: $135,000 × 159/152 = $141,210.
g. Payments on accounts payable, evenly during the year: $80,000 × 159/152 = $83,680.
h. Declared cash dividend at midyear and paid the dividend one month later: $10,000 × 159/151 = $10,530.
i. Acquired parking garage on January 1, 19F; issued note payable: $50,000 × 159/147 = $54,100.
j. Depreciation expense, parking garage: $2,000 × 159/147 = $2,164.
k. Issued common stock for cash on September 30, 19F, $60,000 × 159/154 = $61,920.
l. Accrued income tax expense, evenly during the year: $10,000 × 159/152 = $10,460.
m. Ending inventory $25,000 × 159/157 = $25,325.
n. HC/CD income, $27,043 (to retained earnings).
o–1. Purchasing power **loss** on cash: amount needed to balance Cash account.
o–2. Purchasing power **loss** on accounts receivable: amount needed to balance Accounts Receivable account.
o–3. Purchasing power **gain** on accounts payable: amount needed to balance Accounts Payable account.
o–4. Purchasing power **gain** on income tax payable: amount needed to balance Income Tax Payable account.
o–5. Purchasing power **gain** on note payable: amount needed to balance Note Payable account.

Panel B—Worksheet to Develop HC/CD Income Statement and Balance Sheet For Year Ended December 31, 19F:

Accounts	12/31/19E HC Balances Restated in 12/31/19F CDs (from Exhibit 24–7)		19F Transactions and Adjustments Stated in 12/31/19F CDs		19F HC/CD Income Statement (same as Exhibit 24–5)		12/31/19F, HC/CD Balance Sheet (same as Exhibit 24–4)	
Cash	38,952		(*d*) 15,000 (*f*) 141,210 (*k*) 61,920	(*e*) 20,920 (*g*) 83,680 (*h*) 10,530 (*o*–1) 5,952			136,000	
Accounts receivable (net)	25,968		(*a*) 150,624	(*f*) 141,210 (*o*–2) 2,382			33,000	
Inventory	21,780				21,780	(*m*) 25,325	25,325	
Investment in common stock	28,800			(*d*) 14,400			14,400	
Plant and equipment	125,200						125,200	
Accumulated depreciation, P&E		25,040		(*c*) 5,008				30,048
Parking garage			(*i*) 54,100				54,100	
Accumulated depreciation, PG				(*j*) 2,164				2,164
Accounts payable		43,280	(*g*) 83,680 (*o*–3) 3,510	(*b*) 88,910				45,000
Income tax payable			(*o*–4) 460	(*l*) 10,460				10,000
Note payable, 12%			(*o*–5) 4,100	(*i*) 54,100				50,000
Common stock, nopar		125,200		(*k*) 61,920				187,120
Retained earnings		47,180	(*h*) 10,530		(*n*) 27,043			63,693
Sales revenue				(*a*) 150,624		150,624		
Gain on sale of investment				(*d*) 600		600		
Purchases			(*b*) 88,910		88,910			
Depreciation expense, plant and equipment			(*c*) 5,008		5,008			
Depreciation expense, parking garage			(*j*) 2,164		2,164			
General expenses (incl. interest)			(*e*) 20,920		20,920			
Income tax expense			(*l*) 10,460		10,460			
Purchasing power loss on net monetary items			(*o*–1) 5,952 (*o*–2) 2,382	(*o*–3) 3,510 (*o*–4) 460 (*o*–5) 4,100	264			
	240,700	240,700	660,930	660,930	176,549	176,549	388,025	388,025

putation of the purchasing power gains (losses) as balancing amounts; and (3) imposes the discipline inherent in the basic accounting model with the debit-credit convention. For these important tasks, the worksheet is invaluable.

Supplement 24-B: Comparative HC/CD and CC/CD Financial Statements

Financial statements usually are presented in a two- (or three-) year comparative format. On such financial statements, the prior year HC/CD amounts are not comparable with the current year HC/CD amounts because the purchasing power of the dollar changed during the current year. For example, for AB Company, the purchasing power of the dollar declined by 8.2 percent during 19F. Therefore, to be comparable with the current year statements, the prior year's HC/CD and CC/CD financial statements must be "rolled forward" into CDs of the current year.

The procedure for rolling forward the prior year's HC/CD financial statements is illustrated for AB Company in Exhibit 24–16. The procedure for rolling forward the CC/CD statements is similar; therefore, it is not illustrated. Exhibit 24–16 is designed to develop the 19E and 19F comparative HC/CD balance sheets.

Column A is the **HC balance sheet** of the prior year (i.e., at December 31, 19E), as given in Exhibit 24–3. Column B incorporates the CD restatement ratios needed to express the December 31, 19E, HC balances into CDs as of that date. Therefore, the **numerator** of all CD restatement ratios in column B is 147, which was the GPL index at December 31, 19E. The denominator of each restatement ratio is the GPL index on the transaction date the item was recorded. Only the **nonmonetary** items are restated in column C. Thus, column C presents the HC/CD balance sheet at December 31, 19E, stated in CDs as of that date.

Column D presents the CD restatement ratios needed to restate the HC/CD balance sheet amounts at December 31, 19E, into ending CDs of the current date, December 31, 19F. Thus, in this "roll forward," the numerator of all GPL restatement ratios in column D is 159, which is the price index at December 31, 19F. In this "roll forward," **both monetary and nonmonetary** items must be restated because, for comparative purposes, both the 19E and 19F balance sheets must reflect December 31, 19F, HC/CD equivalent amounts for all items. The denominator for **all** items in column D is the index at December 31, 19E (i.e., 147) because their HC/CD amounts at that date were stated in terms of the GPL on that date.

Column E represents the culmination of the 19E restatement and "roll forward" needed for the 19E–19F comparative balance sheets. Column F repeats the HC/CD balance sheet at December 31, 19F, from Exhibit 24–4. As a result of the above procedure, both the 19E and 19F balance sheets are stated in CDs of December 31, 19F.

Comparative **income** statements for 19E and 19F, stated in CDs of December 31, 19F, are not developed in the above worksheet. They could be included in the above worksheet or on a separate worksheet. The restatement of the 19E, HC/CD income statement from CDs of December 31, 19E, to CDs of December 31, 19F, is identical to the restatement of the December 31, 19E, HC/CD balance sheet (Exhibit 24–16, Col. D); that is, all items are multiplied by the CD restatement ratio, 159/147.

EXHIBIT 24–16: HC/CD Worksheet for Comparative Statements—AB Company

AB COMPANY
Comparative Balance Sheets—HC/CD Basis
December 31, 19E, and 19F

Accounts	Restatement Procedure				19F Comparative Statements	
	19E				19E	19F
	(Col. A) HC Balance Sheet at 12/31/19E	(Col. B) CD Restatement Ratio at 12/31/19E	(Col. C) HC/CD (in CDs of 12/31/19E)	(Col. D) CD Restatement Ratio at 12/31/19F	(Col. E) HC/CD (in CDs of 12/31/19F)	(Col. F) HC/CD (in CDs of 12/31/19F)
Source	**Exhibit 24–3**	**Exhibit 24–2**	**Col. A × Col. B**	**Exhibit 24–2**	**Col. C × Col. D**	**Exhibit 24–4**
Cash	$ 36,000	Monetary	$ 36,000	159/147 = 1.082	$ 38,952	$136,000
Accounts receivable (net)	24,000	Monetary	24,000	159/147 = 1.082	25,968	33,000
Inventory	20,000	147/146 = 1.007	20,140	159/147 = 1.082	21,780*	25,325
Investment in common stock	25,000	147/138 = 1.065	26,625	159/147 = 1.082	28,800*	14,400
Plant and equipment	100,000	147/127 = 1.157	115,700	159/147 = 1.082	125,200	125,200
Accumulated depreciation	(20,000)	147/127 = 1.157	(23,140)	159/147 = 1.082	(25,040)*	(30,048)
Parking garage						54,100
Accumulated depreciation						(2,164)
Total	$185,000		$199,325		$215,660	$355,813
Accounts payable	$ 40,000	Monetary	$ 40,000	159/147 = 1.082	$ 43,280	$ 45,000
Income tax payable						10,000
Note payable, 12%						50,000
Common stock, nopar	100,000	147/127 = 1.157	115,700	159/147 = 1.082	125,200*	187,120
Retained earnings	45,000	Bal. amt.	43,625	Bal. amt.	47,180	63,693
Total	$185,000		$199,325		$215,660	$355,813

* Rounded to agree with amount in Exhibit 24–7.

QUESTIONS

PART A

1. What is the price phenomenon known as *inflation?* What is the opposite phenomenon called?

2. What indexes measure changes in the general purchasing power of the U.S. dollar? What index has been prescribed for preparation of HC/CD financial statements?

3. In general terms, how much have prices changed in the United States between 1950 and 1980? Why may it be inaccurate to say that prices have changed as much as the percentage of rise in the CPI-U between these dates?

4. "When prices are going up, they all go up; when they drop, they all drop." Comment on this statement.

5. Among sales, cost of goods sold, salaries, and depreciation expense, during an era of rapidly changing prices, which would be on the most nearly current cost (CC) basis under the conventional historical cost (HC) model and which would be on the least CC basis? Give reasons for your response.

6. When prices are changing rapidly, why are financial statements prepared on the HC basis likely to be deficient in some respects?

7. When prices are rising and depreciation expense is computed on the conventional HC basis, what is likely to be true with respect to the availability of resources that would be required for replacement of the depreciable assets?

8. Under the CD restatement approach, financial statement items are classified as *monetary* or *nonmonetary.* Briefly, by which criterion can these two categories be distinguished?

9. Indicate, with explanations where necessary, whether the following items are monetary or nonmonetary: *(a)* stocks held as investments, *(b)* bonds held as investments, *(c)* deposits in domestic banks, *(d)* merchandise inventory, *(e)* allowance for doubtful accounts, *(f)* machinery and equipment, *(g)* accounts payable, *(h)* preferred stock, *(i)* retained earnings, and *(j)* deferred credit related to income taxes.

10. During its most recent fiscal period, XY Company had a larger balance of cash and receivables than monetary liabilities; general prices rose steadily. Would this condition give rise to a purchasing power gain or loss on net monetary items?

11. If prices rise steadily over an extended period of time, indicate whether the following items would give rise to a purchasing power gain, a purchasing power loss, or neither purchasing power gain nor loss on net monetary items:
    a. Maintaining a balance in a checking account.
    b. Owing bonds payable.
    c. Owning land.
    d. Amortizing goodwill.
    e. Holding common treasury stock.

12. If data are available on a quarterly basis rather than on an annual basis, how would this alter the preparation of HC/CD statements at the end of a year?

13. The valuation basis used in conventional HC cost financial statements is—
    a. Market value.
    b. Original cost.
    c. Replacement cost.
    d. A mixture of costs and values.
    e. None of the above. (AICPA adapted)

PART B

14. What are the advantages and disadvantages of CC/CD reporting in relation to HC/CD reporting?

15. What are two ways in which CD restatements can be incorporated into CC financial statements?

16. Why are increases or decreases in the current costs of nonmonetary assets in CC reporting defined in relation to the GPL?

17. How does the recognition of increases or decreases in the CC of nonmonetary assets under the CC/CD model affect the ability of an entity to "manipulate its earnings" by selling selected assets which have increased or decreased in value?

18. Name and briefly describe five recommended ways of estimating CC.

DECISION CASE 24–1

In this situation, HC/CD statements, as supplements to the conventional cost basis statements are presented (inflation has been near double-digit rates). Knowing that you have accounting training, a friend, who owns common stock in several companies, drops their latest annual reports before you with a look that hovers between dismay and bewilderment.

Your friend begins, "I used to think that I understood a little about these reports, but now that the companies have all gone to this price-level accounting, the only things clear to me are the nice pictures of company employees and products!" Upon your inquiry, it develops that the following points bother your friend:

a. Most of the companies reported higher net income on their HC statements than on their HC/CD statements, while at the same time the latter statements showed the assets to be larger in amount.

b. Some of the companies reported general purchasing power gains on net monetary liabilities concurrent with operating gains; others reported general purchasing power losses on net monetary assets concurrent with operating gains; yet all of the companies were subject to the same degree of general inflation.

c. The comparative statements, prepared on an HC/CD basis, showed that even the amount of cash reported for last year had changed. Your friend wonders whether the companies discovered overages or shortages of cash or are somehow "juggling the figures."

d. Your friend realizes that the prices of most things are rising and wonders whether the increased values of certain assets on the HC/CD statements represent what the items are worth. At the same time, your friend noticed that some assets are carried at identical amounts on both sets of statements.

Required:

1. Explain the specifics that are confusing your friend in such a way that a sophisticated layperson (who is not an accountant) can understand them.
2. To cope with the effects of inflation, aside from HC/CD statements, what alternative accounting could be used? Describe them briefly and cite some of their pros and cons.
3. What is your assessment of the usefulness of HC/CD financial statements? Give reasons for your answer.

EXERCISES

PART A: EXERCISES 24–1 to 24–10

Note: Unless instructed otherwise, round all CD restatement ratios to $\frac{1}{10}$%, e.g., 106.3% or 1.063.

Exercise 24–1

Select the best answer in each of the following. Items are independent of one another except where indicated to the contrary. Give the basis, including computations, for your choice.

The following information is applicable to items 1 through 4:

Equipment purchased for $120,000 on January 1, 19A, when the price index was 100, was sold on December 31, 19C, at a price of $85,000. The equipment originally was expected to last six years with no residual value and was depreciated on a straight-line basis. The price index at the end of 19A was 125; 19B, 150; and 19C, 175.

1. HC/CD financial statements prepared at the end of 19A would include:

   a. Equipment, $150,000; accumulated depreciation, $25,000; and no gain or loss.
   b. Equipment, $150,000; accumulated depreciation, $25,000; and a gain, $30,000.
   c. Equipment, $150,000; accumulated depreciation, $20,000; and a gain, $30,000.
   d. Equipment, $120,000; accumulated depreciation, $20,000; and a gain, $30,000.
   e. None of the above.

2. Comparative HC/CD statements prepared at the end of 19B would show the 19A financial statements' amount for equipment (net of accumulated depreciation) at—

   a. $150,000.
   b. $125,000.
   c. $100,000.
   d. $80,000.
   e. None of the above.

   (Relates to Supplement 24–B.)

3. HC/CD financial statements prepared at the end of 19B should include depreciation expense of—
   a. $35,000.
   b. $30,000.
   c. $25,000.
   d. $20,000.
   e. None of the above.

4. The HC/CD income statement prepared at the end of 19C should include—
   a. A gain of $35,000.
   b. A gain of $25,000.
   c. No gain or loss.
   d. A loss of $5,000.
   e. None of the above.

5. If land were purchased at a cost of $20,000 in January 19A when the GPL index was 120 and sold in December 19F when the GPL index was 150, the selling price that would result in no economic gain or loss would be—
   a. $30,000.
   b. $24,000.
   c. $20,000.
   d. $16,000.
   e. None of the above.

6. If land were purchased in 19A for $100,000 when the GPL index was 100 and sold at the end of 19G for $160,000 when the GPL index was 170, the HC/CD statement of income for 19G would show—
   a. A purchasing power gain of $70,000 and a loss on sale of land of $10,000.
   b. A gain on sale of land of $60,000.
   c. A purchasing power loss of $10,000.
   d. A loss on sale of land of $10,000.
   e. None of the above.

7. If the base year is 19A (when the GPL index = 100) and land is purchased for $50,000 in 19C when the GPL index is 108.5, the cost of the land restated to 19A general purchasing power (rounded to the nearest whole dollar) would be—
   a. $54,250.
   b. $50,000.
   c. $46,083.
   d. $45,750.
   e. None of the above.

8. Assume the same facts as in item 7. The cost of the land restated to December 31, 19G, general purchasing power when the GPL index was 119.2 (rounded to the nearest whole dollar) would be—
   a. $59,600.
   b. $54,931.
   c. $46,083.
   d. $45,512.
   e. None of the above. (AICPA adapted)

Exercise 24–2

Select the best answer in each of the following. Give the basis for your response:

1. In preparing HC/CD financial statements, a nonmonetary item would be—
   a. Accounts payable in cash.
   b. Long-term bonds payable.
   c. Accounts receivable.
   d. Allowance for doubtful accounts.
   e. None of the above.
2. In preparing HC/CD financial statements, monetary items consist of—
   a. Cash items plus all receivables with a fixed maturity date.
   b. Cash, other assets expected to be converted into cash and current liabilities.
   c. Assets and liabilities whose amounts are fixed by contract or otherwise in terms of dollars, regardless of price level changes.
   d. Assets and liabilities classed as current on the balance sheet.
   e. None of the above.
3. An accountant who recommends the restatement of financial statements for GPL changes should not support this recommendation by stating that—
   a. Purchasing power gains and losses should be recognized.
   b. Historical dollars are not comparable to present-day dollars.
   c. The conversion of asset costs to a constant dollar basis is a useful extension of the original cost basis of asset valuation.
   d. Assets should be valued at their replacement cost.
4. When comprehensive HC/CD financial statements are prepared, they should be presented in terms of—
   a. The general purchasing power of the dollar at the latest balance sheet date.
   b. The general purchasing power of the dollar in the base period.
   c. The average general purchasing power of the dollar for the latest fiscal period.
   d. The general purchasing power of the dollar at the time the financial statements are issued.
   e. None of the above.
5. During a period of deflation, an entity usually would have the greatest gain in general purchasing power by holding—
   a. Cash.
   b. Plant and equipment.
   c. Accounts payable.
   d. Mortgages payable.
   e. None of the above.
6. The CD restatement of HC financial statements to reflect GPL changes reports assets at—

   a. Lower cost or market (LCM).
   b. Current appraisal values.
   c. Costs adjusted for purchasing power changes.
   d. Current replacement cost.
   e. None of the above.
7. An unacceptable practice for reporting HC/CD information is—
   a. The inclusion of general purchasing power gains and losses on monetary items in the price level income statement.
   b. The inclusion of extraordinary gains and losses in the HC/CD income statement.
   c. The use of charts, ratios, and narrative information.
   d. The use of specific price indexes to restate inventories, plant, and equipment.
   e. None of the above. (AICPA adapted)

Exercise 24–3

Doris Company is preparing financial statements on the HC/CD basis. Selected data are as follows:

1. GPL index data:

1/1/19A	114
12/31/19A	120
6/30/19B	126
12/31/19D	168
Average for 19E	174
12/31/19E	180

2. Property, plant, and equipment acquisition and depreciation data:
   a. Land acquired January 1, 19A, at a cost of $80,000.
   b. Building acquired December 31, 19A, at a cost of $120,000; by year-end, 19D and 19E, respectively, accumulated depreciation on the building amounted to $44,000 and $48,000.
   c. Equipment costing $168,000 was acquired June 30, 19B; by December 31, 19D, accumulated depreciation amounted to $109,200; depreciation recorded for 19E was $8,400.
   d. New equipment added during 19E at a time when the index was at an average value for the year cost $58,000; depreciation recorded on this new equipment for 19E amounted to $4,350.
3. Monetary items: At the start of 19E, total monetary assets amounted to $112,000 while total monetary liabilities amounted to $180,000. At the end of 19E, total monetary assets amounted to $120,000 while total monetary liabilities were $190,000.

Required:
Use the numbers below for identification and compute the amounts for each numbered item. Round conversion ratios to five decimal places.

A. On the HC/CD balance sheet as of December 31, 19E, carrying values for each would be—
   1. Land.
   2. Building (gross amount).
   3. Accumulated depreciation—building.
   4. Original equipment (gross amount).
   5. New equipment (gross amount).
   6. Accumulated depreciation on equipment (original).
   7. Accumulated depreciation on equipment (new).
   8. Total monetary assets.
   9. Total monetary liabilities.
B. On the HC/CD income statement for the year ended December 31, 19E, amounts reported would be—
   10. Depreciation expense (original equipment).
   11. Depreciation expense (new equipment).
   12. Depreciation expense (building).
   13. Sales revenue (if sales of $310,000 were made evenly throughout 19E).

Exercise 24–4

Some items on conventional cost basis financial statements are expressed in current period dollars (or nearly so), while other items are normally expressed in dollars of prior periods.

Required:
1. Name the principal balance sheet items which likely would not be expressed in current period dollars. If any part of your answer depends on the accounting procedures employed, explain.
2. Name the principal items in the income statement which likely would not be expressed in current period dollars (or nearly so). If any part of your answer depends on the accounting procedures used, explain.
3. Name the principal items in the statement of changes in financial position which likely would not be expressed in current period dollars. If any part of your answer depends on the accounting procedures used, explain. (AICPA adapted)

Exercise 24–5

T Company is completing its fifth year of operations (19E). Comparative balance sheets (HC basis) at year-end 19D and 19E are as follows:

	December 31	
	19D	19E
Cash and receivables	$250,000	$325,000
Inventories	187,500	162,500
Future plant site	62,500	62,500
Fixtures	210,000	270,000
Accumulated depreciation	(50,000)	(74,000)
	$660,000	$746,000
Current liabilities	$ 75,000	$137,500
Long-term liabilities	150,000	125,000
Capital stock	400,000	400,000
Retained earnings	35,000	83,500
	$660,000	$746,000

The income statement (HC basis) for the year ended December 31, 19E, follows:

Sales revenue		$1,000,000
Cost of goods sold:		
Beginning inventory	$187,500	
Purchases	625,000	
Goods available	812,500	
Ending inventory	162,500	
Cost of goods sold		650,000
Gross margin		350,000
Expenses:		
Operating expenses except depreciation	120,000	
Depreciation expense	24,000	144,000
Income before taxes		206,000
Income tax expense		87,500
Net income		$ 118,500

A dividend of $70,000 was declared at year-end. At midyear added fixtures costing $60,000 were bought. The annual rate of depreciation on fixtures is 10% of cost. Inventories are on a FIFO basis. When the capital stock was issued and the original fixtures and the future plant site were acquired during the first year of operations, the relevant price index was at 126. Other GPL index data are as follows:

	Index
12/31/19E	163.8
12/31/19D	150
Average for 19E	157.5
Average for 19D	146.25

Assume the beginning inventory was acquired at average 19D prices. Purchases, sales, operating expenses, and income taxes occurred or accrued ratably throughout the year.

Required:

1. Prepare an HC/CD balance sheet as of December 31, 19E, and an HC/CD income statement for 19E. Determine the purchasing power gain or loss on net monetary items and present a separate schedule detailing its computation.
2. Indicate the gross and net carrying values of the fixtures and of the future plant site for the HC/CD balance sheet as of December 31, 19D.

Exercise 24–6

T Corporation sold half of its long-term investment in the common stock of another company (carried at cost) and made the entry shown in Column A below:

	Column A		Column B	
Cash	31,000		31,000	
Investment in stock		25,000		28,750
Gain on sale of investment		6,000		2,250

In preparing HC/CD statements, the transaction of column A was restated as shown in column B.

Required:

1. If the GPL index was at 138 when the transaction recorded above occurred, at what level was it when the stock was acquired? Show computations.
2. Assume the remaining half of the stock is sold later for $30,000 when the GPL index is at 147, give entries paralleling those above in columns A and B.
3. If the stock prices and GPL index values given were unchanged, what other factors, if any, would cause entries reflected in columns A and B to differ at the time of either the first or second sale?

Exercise 24–7

An incomplete computation of purchasing power gain or loss on net monetary items appears below.

	HC	HC/CD
Total beginning excess of monetary assets over monetary liabilities	$121,000	$132,000
Increases during the year:		
Sales revenue	287,500	300,000
Sale of common stock	106,200	108,000
Total increases	393,700	408,000
Total	$514,700	$540,000
Decreases during the year:		
Purchases	$197,800	$206,400
Expenses	33,120	34,560
Cash dividend declared	20,000	20,000
Total decreases	$250,920	$260,960

Added data: Sales, purchases, and expenses occurred evenly over the year. The GPL index at year-end was 120.

Required
(support each answer; show how it was arrived at):
1. What was the index value when the period began?
2. What was the average index value for the year?
3. What was the index value when the stock was sold?
4. Assuming prices rose steadily, when was the dividend declared?
5. What was the purchasing power gain or loss on net monetary items?

Exercise 24–8

The items reflected in the trial balance below were acquired when the relevant price index was 105.

Cash	$27,235	
Land	79,500	
Accounts payable		$ 2,570
Capital stock		100,000
Retained earnings		4,165

The following transactions took place during the first quarter of the current fiscal year:

Date	GPL Index	Data
Oct. 1	110	Purchased machinery costing $9,600 on account.
15	120	Paid for machinery purchased on October 1.
31	135	Billed customers for services rendered, $8,000.
Nov. 15	140	Paid $1,230 of the initial liability balance.
30	145	Collected half of the billed revenue.
Dec. 10	150	Paid general expense of $5,700.
31	160	Recorded three months' depreciation on machinery, which has a five-year life with no residual value.

Required:
1. Enter the initial balances, and then record the transactions for the first quarter directly into ledger accounts; also include, in parentheses, the GPL index number prevailing when each transaction occurred.
2. As of the close of the quarter, prepare both balance sheets and income statements on both the HC basis and the HC/CD basis using the GPL index number procedures illustrated in the chapter. Show calculation of the purchasing power gain or loss on net monetary items. Since no average index value for the period is given, it will be necessary to apply to each transaction, a specific CD restatement ratio. For example, if a $360 transaction occurred when the index was 120, in December 31 terms, this would convert to $360 × 160/120 = $480. Round all calculations to the nearest dollar.
3. Prove the accuracy of ending HC/CD retained earnings.

Exercise 24–9

An investor bought land for $90,000 in 19A when the index measuring general purchasing power of the dollar was 110. Assuming a gain on sale of the land is taxable at a capital gains rate of 25%, at what price would the land have to be sold on each of the following dates for the investor to maintain the equivalent purchasing power after taxes? In each instance the index number on the date of sale was as follows:

	Date of Sale	GPL Index
a.	10/1/19B	121
b.	5/1/19C	129
c.	7/1/19D	143
d.	12/1/19E	154

Round answers to nearest dollar.

Exercise 24–10

Select the best answer in each of the following. Give the basis for your response.

1. The valuation basis used in HC financial statements is—
   a. Market value.
   b. Original cost.
   c. Replacement cost.
   d. A mixture of costs and values.
   e. None of the above.
2. When preparing HC/CD financial statements, it would not be appropriate to use—
   a. Cost or market, whichever is lower, in the valuation of inventories.
   b. Replacement cost in the valuation of plant assets.
   c. The HC basis in reporting income tax expense.
   d. The actual amounts payable in reporting liabilities on the balance sheet.
   e. Any of the above.
3. For comparison purposes, HC/CD financial statements of earlier periods should be restated to the constant dollars of—
   a. The beginning of the base period.
   b. An average for the current period.
   c. The beginning of the current period.
   d. The end of the current period.
   e. None of the above.
   (Relates to Supplement 24–B.)
4. Gains and losses on nonmonetary assets usually are reported in HC financial statements when the items are sold. Gains and losses on the sale of nonmonetary assets should be reported in HC/CD financial statements—
   a. In the same period, but the amount will probably differ.

b. In the same period and the same amount.
c. Over the life of the nonmonetary asset.
d. Partly over the life of the nonmonetary asset and the remainder when the asset is sold.
e. None of the above.

5. A practice for presenting HC/CD information which is not acceptable is the—
a. Use of charts, ratios, and narrative information.
b. Use of GPL indexes to restate inventories, plant, and equipment.
c. Inculsion of purchasing power gains and losses on monetary items in the HC/CD income from continuing operations.
d. Inclusion of extraordinary gains and losses in the HC/CD statement of income.

6. For purposes of restating financial statements for changes in the general level of prices, monetary items consist of—
a. Assets and liabilities whose amounts are fixed by contract or otherwise in terms of dollars regardless of price level changes.
b. Assets and liabilities which are classified as current on the balance sheet.
c. Cash items plus all receivables with a fixed maturity date.
d. Cash, other assets expected to be converted into cash, and current liabilities.

7. Following are four observations regarding the amounts reported in HC/CD financial statements. Which observation is valid?
a. The HC/CD amount reported for an asset usually approximates its current market value.
b. The HC/CD amounts are not departures from historical cost.
c. When inventory increases and prices are rising, last-in, first-out (LIFO) inventory accounting has the same effect on financial statements as HC/CD amounts.
d. When inventory remains constant and prices are rising, LIFO inventory accounting has the same effect on financial statements as HC/CD amounts.

Items 8, 9, and 10 are based on the following information:

The following schedule lists the general price-level index at the end of each of the five indicated years:

197A	100
197B	110
197C	115
197D	120
197E	140

8. In December 197D, the Meetu Corporation purchased land for $300,000. The land was held until December 197E, when it was sold for $400,000. The HC/CD statement of income for the year ended December 31, 197E, should include how much gain or loss on this sale?
a. $20,000 loss.
b. $20,000 purchasing power loss.
c. $50,000 gain.
d. $100,000 gain.

9. On January 1, 197B, the Silver Company purchased equipment for $300,000. The equipment was being depreciated over an estimated life of 10 years on the straight-line method, with no estimated residual value. On December 31, 197E, the equipment was sold for $200,000. The HC/CD statement of income prepared for the year ended December 31, 197E, should include how much gain or loss from this sale?
a. $10,600 loss.
b. $16,000 gain.
c. $20,000 gain.
d. $52,000 loss.

10. An analysis of the Gallant Corporation's Machinery and Equipment account as of December 31, 197E, follows:

Machinery and equipment:	
Acquired in December 197B	$400,000
Acquired in December 197D	100,000
Balance	$500,000
Accumulated depreciation:	
On equipment acquired in December 197B	$160,000
On equipment acquired in December 197D	20,000
Balance	$180,000

An HC/CD balance sheet prepared as of December 31, 197E, should include machinery and equipment net of accumulated depreciation of—
a. $284,848.
b. $360,000.
c. $398,788.
d. $448,000. (AICPA adapted)

PART B: EXERCISES 24–11 to 24–13

Exercise 24–11

The controller of the Robinson Company is discussing a comment you made in the course of presenting your audit report.

". . . and frankly," L. Fisher continued, "I agree that we, too, are responsible for finding ways to produce more relevant financial statements which are as reliable as the ones we now produce.

"For example, suppose the company acquired a finished item of inventory for $40 when the general price level index was 110. And, later, the item was sold for $75 when the general price level index was 121 and the current cost was

$54. We could calculate a 'holding gain' (i.e., an increase in the current cost of the item)."

Required:

1. Explain to what extent and how current costs already are used *within* GAAP to value inventories.
2. Calculate in good form the amount of the "holding gain" (i.e., the increase in the CC of inventory, net of the effects of general inflation) in Fisher's example.
3. Why is the use of current cost for *both* inventories and cost of goods sold preferred by some accounting authorities to the use of FIFO or LIFO? (AICPA adapted)

Exercise 24–12

X Trucking Company transfers freight from its home office in Cleveland, Tennessee, to cities throughout the United States. Thus, it is a service-oriented enterprise and has no merchandise inventory. On January 1, 19C, the HC balance sheet of X Trucking Company was as follows:

X TRUCKING COMPANY
Balance Sheet
January 1, 19C

Assets	
Cash and receivables	$12,000
Trucks	80,000
Accumulated depreciation	(–0–)
	$92,000
Liabilities and Owners' Equity	
Current liabilities	$10,000
Long-term liabilities	30,000
Owners' equity	52,000
	$92,000

Assume for simplicity that all revenues and all expenses occur evenly during the year. The trucks are new on January 1, 19C, are expected to remain in service for five years, and will be depreciated on a straight-line basis with no estimated residual value. GPL indexes were 100 at January 1, 19C, 101 at February 15, 19C, 104 for average of 19C, and 108 at December 31, 19C. Current cost (CC) of the trucks at December 31, 19C, was $88,000.

Historical cost (HC) transactions for 19C included the following:

1. Payment on February 15, 19C, of the $10,000 beginning balance of current liabilities.
2. Service revenue of $100,000, of which $70,000 is collected in cash evenly during the year.
3. Depreciation of $16,000.
4. Other expenses of $75,000, of which $35,000 is unpaid at December 31, 19C. The $35,000 of liabilities are "current."

Required:

1. Prepare the CC/CD balance sheet of X Trucking Company at December 31, 19C.
2. Prepare the CC/CD income statement of X Trucking Company for the year ended December 31, 19C.
3. Prove the accuracy of the ending CC/CD retained earnings for 19C.

Exercise 24–13

Raft Builders International purchased all of the shares of P Corporation (it will be a subsidiary) on January 1, 19D, at a cost of $150,000. P Corporation had cash and receivables of $10,000, finished goods inventory $50,000, building $125,000 with accumulated depreciation $60,000, and land $15,000; all amounts reflect the HC basis. P Corporation had no liabilities at the time of the acquisition, and the GPL index was 109.

It is now December 31, 19D, and the GPL index is 119.9. The December 31, 19D, balance sheet data of the purchased company are as follows, with HC and CC/CD data in comparative form:

P CORPORATION
Balance Sheet—HC and CC/CD
December 31, 19D

	HC	CC/CD
Cash and receivables	$ 15,000	$ 15,000
Finished goods inventory	65,000	75,000
Building	125,000	150,000
Accum. dep.—building	(65,000)	(78,000)
Land	10,000	30,000
Total assets	$150,000	$192,000
Liabilities	$ 25,000	$ 30,000
Owners' equity	125,000	162,000
Total equities	$150,000	$192,000

Required:

1. Which item on the CC/CD balance sheet is reported incorrectly? Why?
2. Does the fact that CC data are presented for the building mean that the building could be sold on December 31, 19D, for $150,000? for $72,000? Explain.
3. Which inventory method (i.e., LIFO, FIFO, average, etc.) would yield an ending inventory cost closest to the CC/CD amount? Closest to the CC/CD amount of cost of goods sold?

Exercise 24–14

Marx Corporation is completing its fifth year of operations (19E). Comparative balance sheets on an HC basis prepared at the end of 19D and 19E were as follows:

	December 31	
	19D	19E
Cash	$ (4,400)	$ 2,500
Accounts receivable (net)	13,000	15,000
Inventory	18,000	20,000
Furniture and fixtures	6,000	8,000
Accumulated depreciation	(2,200)	(3,000)
	$30,400	$42,500
Accounts payable	$ 4,400	$ 7,000
Capital stock	20,000	20,000
Retained earnings	6,000	15,500
	$30,400	$42,500

The income statement for 19E on an HC basis was as below:

Sales revenue		$82,000
Cost of goods sold:		
Beginning inventory	$18,000	
Purchases	43,600	
Goods available	61,600	
Ending inventory	20,000	41,600
Gross margin		40,400
Expenses:		
Depreciation	800	
Salaries	16,000	
Other (including taxes)	10,100	26,900
Net income		13,500
Dividends		4,000
Transferred to retained earnings		$ 9,500

Half of the dividends were declared and paid at midyear, the other half at year-end. Additional fixtures were acquired at the start of the year. Fixtures are depreciated on the assumptions of a 10-year life, and zero residual value under the straight-line method. Expenses were paid uniformly during the year. Purchases and sales occurred uniformly during the year. The ending inventory is assumed to be acquired at year-end prices; the beginning inventory was acquired at year-end prices of the prior year.

When the capital stock was issued and the original fixtures, costing $6,000, were bought May 1, 19A, the price index was at 112. Other GPL index data are as follows:

	GPL Index
12/31/19E	154
12/31/19D	140
Average for 19E and midyear value	146.67

Required:

1. Prepare comparative HC/CD statements as of December 31, 19E, and December 31, 19D, using the statements given and the GPL index data. Determine the purchasing power gain or loss on net monetary items and present a separate schedule detailing its computation.
2. Prove the correctness of the ending HC/CD balance of retained earnings, and present the proof in a separate schedule.

PROBLEMS

Note: Unless directed otherwise, round all CD restatement ratios to ⅒%, e.g., 106.3% or 1.063.

PART A: PROBLEMS 24–1 to 24–10

Problem 24–1

Clara Company is preparing financial statements for 19E on an HC/CD basis. Selected data are as follows:

1. GPL index numbers:

Date	Index
1/1/19A	90
12/31/19A	95
6/30/19B	100
12/31/19B	106
12/31/19D	145
Average for 19E	150
12/31/19E	155

2. From statements—property, plant, and equipment acquisition and depreciation data:

   a. Land acquired January 1, 19A, at a cost of $45,000.

   b. Building acquired December 31, 19A, at a cost of $380,000; by year-end 19D and 19E, respectively, Accumulated Depreciation—Building account reflected balances of $22,800 and $30,400.

   c. Fixtures costing $77,000 were acquired June 30, 19B; on these accumulated depreciation recorded by year-end 19D and 19E amounted to $19,250 and $26,950.

   d. Additional fixtures were bought in midyear 19E for $30,000 when the index was 150; by year-end depreciation recorded on the newest fixtures amounted to $2,250.

3. Monetary assets: At the start of 19E, total monetary assets were $87,000 and total monetary liabilities were $31,900. At the end of 19E, total monetary assets were $96,400 and total monetary liabilities were $33,800.

Required:

Use the numbers given below for identification and compute the amounts that would appear on HC/CD financial statements. Round CD restatement ratios to five decimal places.

A. On the HC/CD balance sheet as of December 31, 19E, the carrying values would be—
   1. Land.
   2. Building (gross amount).
   3. Old fixtures (gross amount).
   4. New fixtures (gross amount).
   5. Accumulated depreciation—building.
   6. Accumulated depreciation—old fixtures.
   7. Accumulated depreciation—new fixtures.
   8. Total monetary assets.
   9. Total monetary liabilities.

B. On the HC/CD income statement for the year ended December 31, 19E, amounts reported would be—
   10. Depreciation expense (building).
   11. Depreciation expense (new fixtures).
   12. Depreciation expense (old fixtures).
   13. Purchases (assume purchases of $285,000 were made evenly throughout 19E).

Problem 24–2

Barden Corporation, a manufacturer with large investments in plant and equipment, began operations in 1940. The company's history has been one of expansion in sales, production, and physical facilities. Recently, some concern has been expressed that the HC financial statements do not provide sufficient information for decisions by investors. After consideration of proposals for various types of supplementary financial statements to be included in the 1982 annual report, management has decided to present an HC/CD balance sheet as of December 31, 1982, and an HC/CD statement of income and retained earnings for 1982.

Required:

1. On what basis can it be contended that Barden's HC financial statements should be restated for changes in the general price level (GPL)?
2. Distinguish between HC/CD financial statements and current market value financial statements. (Relates to Supplement 24–B.)
3. Distinguish between monetary and nonmonetary assets and liabilities as the terms are used in the HC/CD reporting model. Give examples of each.
4. Outline the procedures Barden should follow in preparing the proposed HC/CD statements.
5. Indicate the major similarities and differences between the proposed HC/CD statements and the corresponding HC statements.
6. Assuming that in the future Barden will want to present comparative HC/CD statements, can the 1982 HC/CD statements be presented in 1983 without adjustment? Explain.

(AICPA adapted)

Problem 24–3

CTZ Company prepared the following comparative balance sheets (HC basis) at the close of its fourth year of operations (19D):

	December 31	
	19C	19D
Cash	$ 30,000	$ 41,400
Receivables (net)	74,000	99,000
Inventory	25,000	39,000
Land	100,000	100,000
Building	320,000	320,000
Accum. depr.—building	(38,400)	(51,200)
Fixtures	90,000	120,000
Accum. depr.—fixtures	(40,500)	(58,500)
Total	$560,100	$609,700
Current liabilities	$ 55,000	$ 80,000
Bonds payable	45,000	45,000
Common stock	250,000	250,000
Retained earnings	210,100	234,700
Total	$560,100	$609,700

The income statement (HC basis) for 19D was as follows:

Sales revenue		$950,000
Cost of goods sold:		
Beginning inventory	$ 25,000	
Purchases	584,000	
Goods available	609,000	
Ending inventory	39,000	
Cost of goods sold		570,000
Gross margin		380,000
Expenses:		
Administrative	125,000	
Depreciation—building	12,800	
Depreciation—fixtures	18,000	
Distribution	100,000	255,800
Income before taxes		124,200
Income tax expense		49,600
Net income		$ 74,600

A $50,000 dividend was declared at year-end. Fixtures costing $30,000 were bought on January 2, 19D. Fixtures are depreciated 15% per annum on cost. Inventories are on a FIFO basis; assume the ending inventory was acquired at the average level of prices prevailing during 19D. When the common stock was issued and the land, buildings, and original fixtures were acquired, the GPL was 112.5. Other price index data are as follows:

	GPL Index
12/31/19D	135
12/31/19C	125
Average for 19D	129.8

The beginning inventory was acquired at 19C year-end prices. Purchases, sales, administrative expenses (which include interest), distribution, and income taxes accrued evenly throughout 19D. The building is depreciated over a 25-year life; no residual value, straight-line basis.

Required (round amounts to nearest dollar):

1. Prepare an HC/CD balance sheet as of December 31, 19D, and an HC/CD income statement for 19D; show computation of the purchasing power gain or loss on net monetary items for the year.
2. Indicate the gross and net carrying values of land, fixtures, and building for the HC/CD balance sheet as of December 31, 19C.

Problem 24–4

Eugenia Company prepared the following comparative balance sheets (HC basis) at the close of its 10th year of operations (19J):

	December 31	
	19I	19J
Cash	$ 75,000	$101,000
Receivables (net)	215,000	195,000
Inventory	135,000	127,000
Land	150,000	150,000
Building	240,000	240,000
Accum. depr.—building	(56,000)	(64,000)
Machinery	225,000	280,000
Accum. depr.—machinery	(115,000)	(137,500)
Total	$869,000	$891,500
Current liabilities	$124,000	$137,000
Long-term liabilities	75,000	81,000
Bonds payable	60,000	60,000
Common stock	350,000	350,000
Retained earnings	260,000	263,500
Total	$869,000	$891,500

The common stock was issued, and the land was bought in 19A, when the GPL index was 104. The building was acquired early in 19C when the GPL index was 107; it has an estimated 30-year life and no residual value and is depreciated on a straight-line basis. Machinery is depreciated 10% per annum on cost with no residual value. The first machine was bought at a cost of $50,000 in 19B when the GPL index was 106; a second machine was acquired for $100,000 in 19D when the index was 108.5; a third machine was bought in 19H when the index was 117. A full year's depreciation is taken in the year of acquisition unless the purchase is at year-end. At year-end 19J, machinery costing $55,000 was acquired.

On January 2, 19J, an $85,000 dividend was declared and paid. Assume the beginning inventory was acquired when the GPL index was 107; the ending inventory should be restated to CDs on the assumption the index was 125 when it was bought.

Sales, operating expenses, income taxes, and purchases occurred evenly during 19J. Relevant GPL index data (aside from that already given) are as follows:

	GPL Index
12/31/19J	127
12/31/19I	121
Average for 19J	125

The income statement (HC basis) for the year 19J was as follows:

Sales revenue		$1,275,000
Cost of goods sold:		
Inventory, January 1	$135,000	
Purchases	850,000	
Goods available	985,000	
Inventory, December 31	127,000	
Cost of goods sold		858,000
Gross margin		417,000
Expenses:		
Operating (excl. depr.)	210,000	
Depreciation, building	8,000	
Depreciation, machinery	22,500	240,500
Income before taxes		176,500
Income tax expense		88,000
Net income		$ 88,500

Required (round amounts to nearest dollar):

1. Prepare an income statement for 19J and a balance sheet as of December 31, 19J, on an HC/CD basis. Show computations of the purchasing power gain or loss on net monetary items.
2. Prove the accuracy of ending HC/CD retained earnings at December 31, 19J.

Problem 24–5

When items in the following HC trial balance were acquired, the GPL index was 150.

Cash	$ 7,500	
Equipment	10,000	
Accumulated depreciation		$2,000
Liability		1,900
Capital stock		8,000
Retained earnings		5,600

Transactions during the first half of the current fiscal year follow. GPL index values prevailing at the time are indicated parenthetically.

Jan. 10 A payment of $800 on the liability balance is made (160).

Feb. 15 Revenue for services is billed to customers, $2,500 (175).

Mar. 1 Four fifths of the revenue billed is collected (180).
Apr. 20 Land is purchased for $8,000 cash (190).
May 5 General expenses are paid, $500 (185).
June 30 Recorded six months' depreciation on the equipment which has a 10-year life and no residual value (200).

The index at June 30 was 200.

Required:

1. Enter the initial balances, then record the six months' transactions directly in ledger accounts; also enter the date and the GPL index number parenthetically.
2. At the close of the six-month period, prepare both HC and HC/CD balance sheets and income statements using the CD restatement procedures as illustrated in the chapter. Calculate the purchasing power gain or loss on net monetary items. Since no average for the six-month period is given, it will be necessary to apply, to each transaction and balance, a specific CD restatement ratio. For example, if a $660 transaction occurred when the price index was 165, in June 30 terms (when the index was 200), the restatement would be calculated as $660 × 200/165 = $800. Round all calculations to nearest dollar.

Problem 24–6

Published financial statements of United States companies are currently prepared on a stable-dollar assumption even though the general purchasing power of the dollar has declined considerably because of inflation in recent years. To account for this changing value of the dollar, many accountants suggest that financial statements should be restated for general price level changes. Three independent, unrelated statements regarding HC/CD financial statements follow. Each statement contains some fallacious reasoning.

Statement I: The accounting profession has not seriously considered HC/CD financial statements before because the rate of inflation usually has been so small from year to year that the restatements would have been immaterial in amount. HC/CD financial statements represent a departure from the historical cost basis of accounting. Financial statements should be prepared from facts, not estimates.

Statement II: If financial statements were restated for GPL changes, depreciation expense in the earnings statement would permit the recovery of dollars of current purchasing power and thereby equal the cost of new assets to replace the old ones. GPL restated (i.e., HC/CD) data would yield statements of financial position amounts closely approximating current values. Furthermore, management can make better decisions if HC/CD financial statements are published.

Statement III: When restating financial data for GPL changes, a distinction must be made between monetary and nonmonetary assets and liabilities, which, under the HC basis of accounting, have been identified as "current" and "noncurrent." When using the HC basis of accounting, no purchasing power gain or loss on net monetary assets is recognized in the accounting process, but when financial statements are restated for GPL changes, a purchasing power gain or loss will be recognized on monetary and nonmonetary items.

Required:

Evaluate each of the independent statements and identify the areas of fallacious reasoning in each and explain why the reasoning is incorrect. Complete your discussion of each statement before proceeding to the next statement.

(AICPA adapted)

Problem 24–7

Novo Company's balance sheets (HC basis) at December 31, 19B, and 19C were as follows:

	December 31	
	19B	**19C**
Cash	$ 8,000	$ 7,600
Accounts receivable (net)	19,000	31,000
Inventory	20,000	18,000
Equipment	21,000	29,400
Accumulated depreciation	(11,000)	(17,400)
	$57,000	$68,600
Accounts payable	$24,000	$29,000
Capital stock	25,000	30,000
Retained earnings	8,000	9,600
	$57,000	$68,600

The income statement (HC basis) for the year ended December 31, 19C, was as follows:

Sales revenue		$80,000
Beginning inventory	$20,000	
Purchases	42,000	
Goods available	62,000	
Ending inventory	18,000	
Cost of goods sold		44,000
Gross margin		36,000
Expenses:		
Salaries	15,000	
Other (incl. income tax)	9,000	
Depreciation	6,400	30,400
Net income		$ 5,600

Original equipment was acquired and original capital stock was issued on January 1, 19A, and was not augmented until January 1, 19C. Equipment is being depreciated over a six-year life by the SYD method with an assumed zero residual value. When the first equipment was acquired and the original stock was issued, the GPL index was at 96.

The company uses the LIFO inventory method; the beginning inventory for 19C is below the level at which the company began operations January 1, 19A. Salaries and other expenses were incurred evenly over the year, and purchases and sales occurred evenly over the year. The additional capital stock was sold on June 30, 19C. Dividends were declared and paid at midyear and year-end in equal amounts of $2,000 per payment.

GPL price index data are as follows:

	GPL Index
12/31/19B	120
Midyear 19C and average	126
12/31/19C	132

Required:

1. Using the HC statements and the index data given, prepare a comparative HC/CD balance sheet and 19C income statement. Determine the purchasing power gain or loss on net monetary items for 19C and present a separate schedule detailing its computation.
2. Prove the accuracy of the ending HC/CD retained earnings and present the proof in a separate schedule.

Problem 24–8

Select the best answer in each of the following. Justify your choices.

1. The Chalk Company reported sales of $2,000,000 in 19B and $3,000,000 in 19C made evenly throughout each year. The GPL index during 19A remained constant at 100, and at the end of 19B and 19C it was 102 and 104, respectively. What should Chalk report as sales revenue for 19C, restated for CD changes?
   a. $3,000,000.
   b. $3,029,126.
   c. $3,058,821.
   d. $3,120,000.
2. On January 2, 19C, the Mannix Corporation mortgaged one of its properties as collateral for a $1,000,000, 12%, five-year loan. The mortgage note payable was interest-bearing, and the interest rate was realistic. During 19C, the GPL increased evenly, resulting in a 5% rise for the year.

   In preparing an HC/CD balance sheet at the end of 19C, at what amount should Mannix report the five-year mortgage note?
   a. $950,000.
   b. $1,000,000.
   c. $1,025,000.
   d. $1,050,000.
3. A company was formed on January 1, 19B. Selected balances from its HC balance sheet at December 31, 19B, were as follows:

Accounts receivable	$ 70,000
Accounts payable	60,000
Long-term debt	110,000
Common stock	100,000

   At what amounts should these selected accounts be shown in an HC/CD balance sheet at December 31, 19B, if the general price-level index was 100 at December 31, 19A, and 110 at December 31, 19B?

	Accounts Receivable	Accounts Payable	Long-term Debt	Common Stock
a.	$70,000	$60,000	$110,000	$100,000
b.	70,000	60,000	110,000	110,000
c.	70,000	60,000	121,000	110,000
d.	77,000	66,000	121,000	110,000

4. The HC balance sheet of the Rhuda Company showed the original cost of depreciable assets as $5,000,000 at December 31, 19A, and $6,000,000 at December 31, 19B. These assets' costs are being depreciated on a straight-line basis over a 10-year period with no residual value. Acquisitions of $1,000,000 were made on January 1, 19B. A full year's depreciation was taken in the year of acquisition.

   Rhuda presents HC/CD financial statements as supplemental information to their HC financial statements. The December 31, 19A depreciable assets balance (before accumulated depreciation) restated to reflect December 31, 19B, purchasing power was $5,800,000. What amount of depreciation expense should be shown in the HC/CD income statement for 19B if the GPL index was 100 at December 31, 19A, and 110 at December 31, 19B?
   a. $600,000.
   b. $660,000.
   c. $670,000.
   d. $690,000.
5. If a constant unit of measure during a period of inflation is used, the general purchasing power of the dollar in which some expenses are measured (for assets systematically allocated among several accounting periods) may differ significantly from the general purchasing power of the dollar in which revenue is measured. Which of the following accounting procedures minimizes this effect?
   a. Allowance method of accounting for bad debts.
   b. Income tax allocation.
   c. Accelerated depreciation.
   d. Valuing inventory at the LCM.
6. Land was purchased for $20,000 when the GPL index was at 115. When the index was at 138, the land was sold for $25,000. Ignoring taxes on the transaction, the landowner, for having bought and sold the land, is economically—
   a. Worse off.
   b. Better off.
   c. In the same position.

(AICPA adapted)

Problem 24–9

Skadden, Inc., a retailer, was organized during 19A. Skadden's management has decided to supplement its December 31, 19D, HC financial statements with HC/CD financial statements. The following trial balance (HC basis) and additional information have been furnished:

SKADDEN, INC.
Trial Balance
December 31, 19D

	Debit	Credit
Cash and receivables (net)	$ 540,000	
Short-term investments (common stock)	400,000	
Inventory	440,000	
Equipment	650,000	
Accum. depr.—equip.		$ 164,000
Accounts payable		300,000
6% first-mortgage bonds, due 19V		500,000
Common stock, $10 par		1,000,000
Retained earnings, 12/31/19C ...	46,000	
Sales revenue		1,900,000
Cost of goods sold	1,508,000	
Depreciation	65,000	
Other operating expenses incl. interest	215,000	
	$3,864,000	$3,864,000

a. Monetary assets (cash and receivables) exceeded monetary liabilities (accounts payable and bonds payable) by $445,000 at December 31, 19C.

b. Purchases ($1,840,000 in 19D) and sales are made uniformly throughout the year.

c. Depreciation is computed on a straight-line basis, with a full year's depreciation being taken in the year of acquisition and none in the year of retirement. The depreciation rate is 10%, and no residual value is anticipated. Acquisitions and retirements have been made evenly over each year, and the retirements in 19D consisted of assets purchased during 19B which were scrapped. An analysis of the equipment account reveals the following:

Year	Beginning Balance	Additions	Retirements	Ending Balance
19B	—	$550,000	—	$550,000
19C	$550,000	10,000	—	560,000
19D	560,000	150,000	$60,000	650,000

d. The bonds were issued in 19B, and the short-term investment in common stock was purchased fairly evenly over 19D. Other operating expenses including interest, are assumed to be incurred evenly throughout the year.

e. Assume the values of the GPL index were as follows:

Annual Averages	GPL Index	Quarterly Averages	GPL Index
19A	113.9	19C, 4th	123.5
19B	116.8	19D, 1st	124.9
19C	121.8	2d	126.1
19D	126.7	3d	127.3
		4th and year-end ...	128.5

Required:

1. Prepare a schedule to convert the Equipment account balance at December 31, 19D, from HC to HC/CD amounts.
2. Prepare a schedule to analyze, at HC, the Equipment—Accumulated Depreciation account for the year 19D.
3. Prepare a schedule to analyze, at HC/CD, the Equipment—Accumulated Depreciation account for the year 19D.
4. Prepare a schedule to compute Skadden's purchasing power gain or loss on its net monetary items for 19D (ignore income tax implications). (AICPA adapted)

Problem 24–10

Select the best answer in each of the following. Justify your choices.

For questions 1–4 below, use the following GPL data:

Date	GPL Index
12/31/19A	165
3/31/19B	171
6/30/19B	175
9/30/19B	180
12/31/19B	186
3/31/19C	190
6/30/19C	194
9/30/19C	198
12/31/19C	201

1. On January 1, 19B, P Corporation had as its only asset $7,000 in cash (no liabilities). On March 31, 19B, P Corporation paid $5,000 for a machine which will have a 10-year life and no residual value. On September 30, 19B, P Corporation purchased merchandise inventory on account for $1,000. At an even rate during the three months ended December 31, 19B, P Corporation paid off the $1,000 on the inventory and sold half the inventory for $650 cash. If these are the only transactions P Corporation entered into during 19B, the company will report for 19B a purchasing power gain or loss on net monetary items of—
   a. Loss of $365.
   b. Loss of $426.
   c. Gain of $365.
   d. Gain of $426.
2. On its December 31, 19B, HC/CD balance sheet, P Corporation will report cash of—

a. $1,650.
b. $2,080.
c. $1,285.
d. $2,904.

3. Assume that P Corporation's January 1, 19B, owners' equity consisted of capital stock of $7,000. On its HC/CD income statement for the year ended December 31, 19B, P Corporation will report net income (loss)—*ignoring the purchasing power gain or loss on net monetary items*—of—
   a. $(276).
   b. $(264).
   c. $(255).
   d. $253.
4. You are in the process of preparing the 19C, HC/CD financial statements (assume that you have been given the necessary transaction data involving revenues and expenses for 19C). In particular, you are now "rolling forward" the January 1, 19C, HC balance sheet in order to obtain the January 1, 19C, HC/CD owners' equity balance stated in December 31, 19C, dollars—as a test on the accuracy of your other HC/CD restatements. Assuming that the beginning cash balance arose on the beginning date, the correct January 1, 19C, owners' equity stated in December 31, 19C, dollars would be—
   a. $7,197.
   b. $7,322.
   c. $7,777.
   d. $7,975.
   e. None of the above.
   (Relates to Supplement 24–B.)
5. Which of the following items is a nonmonetary item?
   a. Marketable securities—bonds to be held to maturity.
   b. Accounts receivable.
   c. Accounts payable.
   d. Preferred stock stated at liquidation value.
   e. Unearned revenue.
6. Under HC/CD reporting, purchasing power gains are earned during infaltion on—
   a. Net monetary assets.
   b. Net monetary liabilities.
   c. Nonmonetary assets.
   d. Nonmonetary liabilities.

PROBLEMS

PART B: PROBLEMS 24–11 to 24–14

Problem 24–11

(Note: Problem 24–11 contains questions over theoretical material which is covered only indirectly in the chapter.) In this chapter, changes in the current costs of nonmonetary assets are presented as elements of CC/CD comprehensive income (i.e., on the income statement). Many accountants favor reporting these current cost changes as a direct element of owners' equity, thereby bypassing the income statement. This issue has not been resolved.

Required:
List and discuss arguments for reporting the changes in the current costs of nonmonetary assets on the income statement versus reporting them as separate elements of owners' equity on the balance sheet. List and discuss arguments for reporting the current cost changes on nonmonetary assets as separate elements of owners' equity on the balance sheet.

Problem 24–12

Osgood Bosworth, Inc., is a manufacturing company with a significant investment in machinery and equipment. In recent years HC income has increased dramatically as company products have found increasing consumer acceptance. Bosworth has paid dividends equal to 70% of HC income for the past ten years. Therefore, as income has increased, dividends have risen; as a result shareholders are delighted with their investment in Bosworth. Until the last two years, inflation was a relatively low 2–4% per year. However, during each of the past two years, the general price index rose by 10%. Two years from now, Bosworth machinery will be 10 years old and fully depreciated; as a result it will be replaced at an estimated cost of 300% of the cost (ignoring depreciation) of its existing machinery and equipment. Moreover, it is anticipated that the replacement machinery will offer no technological advantages over the machinery now owned by the company. Replacement costs are expected to rise by 15% during each of the next two years. HC income and straight-line depreciation (also on an HC basis) for the year just ended (today is December 31, end of the current fiscal year) were $200,000 and $120,000, respectively.

Required:
Ignoring inventories, income taxes, the purchasing power effect on the monetary items of Bosworth and changes during the year just ended in the CC of Bosworth's machinery, prepare a schedule to reveal to Bosworth management the extent, if any, to which dividends for the current year represent a return of owners' equity other than current-year income.

Problem 24–13

Eugenia Company prepared the following comparative balance sheets (HC basis) at the close of its 10th year of operations (19J):

	December 31	
	19I	19J
Cash	$ 60,000	$101,000
Receivables (net)	175,000	195,000
Inventory	135,000	127,000
Land	150,000	150,000
Building	240,000	240,000
Accum. depr.—building	(48,000)	(56,000)
Machinery	280,000	280,000
Accum. depr.—machinery	(96,000)	(224,000)
Total	$796,000	$813,000
Current liabilities	$124,000	$137,000
Long-term liabilities	75,000	81,000
Bonds payable	60,000	60,000
Common stock	350,000	350,000
Retained earnings	187,000	185,000
Total	$796,000	$813,000

The common stock was issued, and the land was bought in 19A, when the GPL index was 104. The building was acquired late in 19C when the GPL index was 107; it has an estimated 30-year life and no residual value and is depreciated on a straight-line basis. Machinery is depreciated 10% per annum on cost with no residual value. The machinery was bought late in 19B when the GPL index was 106.

On January 2, 19J, an $85,000 dividend was declared and paid. Sales, operating expenses, income taxes, and purchases occurred evenly during 19J. Relevant GPL index data (aside from that already given) are as follows:

	GPL Index
12/31/19J	127
12/31/19I	121
Average for 19J	125

The income statement (HC basis) for the year 19J was as follows:

Sales revenue		$1,275,000
Cost of goods sold:		
Inventory, January 1	$135,000	
Purchases	850,000	
Goods available	985,000	
Inventory, December 31	127,000	
Cost of goods sold		858,000
Gross margin		417,000
Expenses:		
Operating excl. depr.	210,000	
Depreciation, building	8,000	
Depreciation, machinery	28,000	246,000
Income before taxes		171,000
Income tax expense		88,000
Net income		$ 83,000

Current cost data are as follows:

	December 31	
	19I	19J
Nonmonetary assets:		
Inventory	$160,000	$135,000
Land	185,000	200,000
Building	270,000	270,000
Accumulated depreciation—building	(54,000)	(63,000)
Machinery	300,000	330,000
Accumulated depreciation—machinery	(210,000)	(264,000)

	Stated in Average CDs of 19J
Expenses:	
Cost of goods sold	$897,000
Depreciation expense—building	9,000
Depreciation expense—machinery	31,500
Sales revenue and all other expenses	Same as HC

Required:

1. Prepare the unclassified CC/CD balance sheet of the company at December 31, 19J.
2. Prepare the single-step CC/CD income statement of the company for the year ended December 31, 19J, with all supporting computations.
3. Prove the accuracy of the CC/CD ending balance of retained earnings.

Problem 24–14

Novelle Company began business on January 1, 19A, at which time it acquired plant and equipment at a cost of $200,000; the GPL index at that date was 120. This property is depreciated by the straight-line method based on a 10-year life and zero residual value. At the end of 19D and 19E, the GPL index was 150 and 165, respectively. Estimated current cost of the plant and equipment (gross amounts) at December 31, 19D, and 19E, were $275,000 and $305,000, respectively.

On June 30, 19E, when the GPL index was 157.5, Novelle bought two trucks at a total cost of $40,000; payment was $10,000 cash and a $30,000 interest-bearing note. Depreciation on the trucks on the straight-line method is based on an estimated useful life of five years and no residual value. The average GPL index for the last half of 19E was 161. The current cost of the trucks (gross amount) at December 31, 19E, was $41,500.

During 19B, when the GPL index was at 135, Novelle paid $40,000 cash for an investment in the common stock of Dee Company as a long-term investment carried at cost. On June 30, 19E, half of these shares were sold for $18,000 cash. The quoted market values of the entire block of shares at December 31, 19D, and at December 31, 19E were $38,000 and $34,000, respectively.

The December 31, 19D, inventory was valued at $30,000 (HC); it was acquired evenly during 19D, when the average GPL index was 147.3. The HC value at December 31, 19E, was $32,000. Purchases made evenly over 19E amounted to $130,000. The average GPL index for 19E was 157.5. For purposes of HC/CD and CC/CD statements the 19E ending inventory is assumed to have come from the entire year's purchases. Current cost of the beginning and ending inventories of 19E were $35,000 and $39,000, respectively, and the current cost of goods sold for 19E was $129,523. Sales of $220,000 occurred evenly during the year.

Required:
Based on the information given determine the amounts for each item specified below. Show supporting calculations and, where necessary, round conversion factors to three decimal places. Financial statements are being prepared on both an HC/CD and CC/CD basis. Questions relate primarily to such statements.

1. Book value of plant and equipment on the HC/CD and CC/CD balance sheets as of *(a)* December 31, 19D, and *(b)* December 31, 19E; each amount should be stated in CDs as of its respective date (i.e., not both in CDs of December 31, 19E).
2. Book value of trucks on the HC/CD and CC/CD balance sheet as of December 31, 19E.
3. Depreciation expense related to plant and equipment on the HC/CD and CC/CD income statement for the year ended December 31, 19E, stated in the CDs of that date.
4. Depreciation expense related to trucks on the HC/CD and CC/CD income statements for the year ended December 31, 19E, stated in CDs of that date.
5. Gross margin on the HC/CD and CC/CD income statements for the year ended December 31, 19E, stated in CDs of that date.
6. Gain or loss to be reported on sale of the Dee stock on the HC/CD and CC/CD income statements for the year ended December 31, 19E, stated in CDs of that date.
7. The amount of the total, general inflation, and net of general inflation, changes in CC of the nonmonetary assets to be reported on the bottom portion of the CC/CD income statement for the year ended December 31, 19E, related to *(a)* inventory, *(b)* investment in Dee stock, *(c)* plant and equipment, and *(d)* trucks. State these changes in CC in the CDs of December 31, 19E.
8. The impact on the schedule calculating purchasing power gain or loss on net monetary items for the year ended December 31, 19E, related to *(a)* purchase of the trucks on June 30, 19E, and *(b)* sale of Dee stock on June 30, 19E.
9. Assume a cash dividend of $20,000 was declared December 31, 19E. By what amount would purchasing power gain or loss for 19E be affected?

Appendix

1981 Financial Statements of The Quaker Oats Company (as included in the Annual Report, Fiscal Year Ended June 30, 1981)

This Appendix is included in this textbook for reference and study purposes throughout the 24 chapters.

This particular annual report was selected because (1) it is comprehensive, (2) it includes a broad array of transactions, notes, company programs, and display schedules, and (3) it is characterized by a comparatively high level of clarity and understandable comments.

The Quaker Oats Company and Subsidiaries

Ten-Year Selected Financial Data

Year Ended June 30	1981	1980	1979
Operating Results			
Net sales	**$2,599.5**	$2,405.2	$1,966.3
Gross profit	**848.6**	777.0	635.1
Income before income taxes and minority interest	**190.2**	174.7	150.0
Provision for income taxes	**83.7**	76.7	65.5
Income before cumulative effect of change in accounting principle	**105.2**	96.4	84.5
Cumulative effect of change in method of accounting for investment tax credit	—	—	14.7
Net income	**$ 105.2**	$ 96.4	$ 99.2
Per common share:			
Income before cumulative effect of change in accounting principle	**$ 5.01**	$ 4.55	$ 4.01
Cumulative effect of change in method of accounting for investment tax credit	—	—	.74
Net income per common share	**$ 5.01**	$ 4.55	$ 4.75
Dividends declared:			
Common stock	**$ 31.9**	$ 28.0	$ 23.7
Per share	**$ 1.60**	$ 1.40	$ 1.20
Preference and preferred stock	**$ 4.6**	$ 4.8	$ 4.8
Average number of common shares outstanding (000's)	**20,083**	20,144	19,884
Pro forma amounts assuming retroactive application of the 1979 accounting change:			
Net income	**$ 105.2**	$ 96.4	$ 84.5
Net income per common share	**$ 5.01**	$ 4.55	$ 4.01

(a) *Adjusted for 3-for-2 stock split in fiscal 1973.*

	1978	1977	1976	1975	1974	1973	1972 (a)
					Millions of Dollars Except Share Data		
	$1,685.6	$1,551.3	$1,473.0	$1,389.0	$1,227.3	$ 990.8	$ 795.2
	538.0	479.4	456.8	359.6	312.4	298.1	249.4
	136.6	135.2	110.9	67.3	76.5	85.5	70.6
	63.0	67.6	57.8	36.3	36.6	43.4	35.0
	73.6	67.6	53.1	31.0	39.9	42.1	35.6
	—	—	—	—	—	—	—
	$ 73.6	$ 67.6	$ 53.1	$ 31.0	$ 39.9	$ 42.1	$ 35.6
	$ 3.34	$ 3.01	$ 2.31	$ 1.45	$ 1.91	$ 2.04	$ 1.78
	—	—	—	—	—	—	—
	$ 3.34	$ 3.01	$ 2.31	$ 1.45	$ 1.91	$ 2.04	$ 1.78
	$ 21.4	$ 19.1	$ 17.4	$ 16.6	$ 15.7	$ 14.7	$ 13.0
	$ 1.04	$ .92	$ .84	$ .80	$ .76	$ .72	$ .68
	$ 4.8	$ 5.2	$ 5.2	$ 1.1	$ .4	$ .4	$ .5
	20,623	20,762	20,711	20,699	20,675	20,466	19,760
	$ 75.3	$ 69.2	$ 57.9	$ 33.6	$ 41.5	$ 43.5	$ 36.5
	$ 3.42	$ 3.09	$ 2.53	$ 1.57	$ 1.99	$ 2.11	$ 1.83

The Quaker Oats Company and Subsidiaries

Ten-Year Selected Financial Data

Year Ended June 30 (a)	1981	1980	1979
Financial Statistics			
Current ratio	1.5	1.6	1.8
Working capital	$ 252.4	$ 265.9	$ 250.7
Working capital turnover (c)	10.0	9.3	8.3
Property, plant and equipment—net	$ 633.3	$ 572.8	$ 507.4
Depreciation expense	$ 51.8	$ 46.8	$ 42.6
Total assets	$1,454.1	$1,334.2	$1,131.5
Long-term debt	$ 165.2	$ 151.7	$ 157.5
Redeemable preference stock	$ 46.7	$ 50.0	$ 50.0
Common shareholders' equity	$ 612.6	$ 582.9	$ 513.6
Book value per common share	$ 31.98	$ 28.85	$ 25.94
Return on average common shareholders' equity	16.8%	16.7%	16.3%
Gross profit as a percent of sales	32.6%	32.3%	32.3%
Advertising and merchandising as a percent of sales	12.8%	11.7%	11.3%
Research and development as a percent of sales	1.0%	1.0%	1.0%
Long-term debt ratio (d)	20.0%	19.3%	21.8%
Total debt ratio (e)	36.8%	33.1%	30.7%
Net income as percent of sales	4.0%	4.0%	4.3%
Common dividends to net income available for common	31.7%	30.6%	29.7%
Number of common shareholders	30,418	30,818	31,567
Number of employees worldwide	30,900	31,400	31,400
Market price range of common stock	$ 37¾- $ 25⅞	$ 34½- $ 23½	$ 27½- $ 22

(a) *Financial data presented, where appropriate, reflect pro forma amounts assuming retroactive application of the 1979 accounting change for investment tax credit.*
(b) *Adjusted for 3-for-2 stock split in fiscal 1973.*
(c) *Net sales divided by average working capital.*
(d) *Long-term debt divided by long-term debt plus total equity.*
(e) *Total debt divided by total debt plus total equity.*

Millions of Dollars Except Share and Percent Data

1978	1977	1976	1975	1974	1973	1972
1.8	2.0	2.0	2.4	1.8	2.0	2.1
$ 223.1	$ 233.2	$ 215.5	$ 208.7	$ 184.5	$ 156.1	$ 131.0
7.4	6.9	6.9	7.1	7.2	6.9	6.6
$ 458.0	$ 406.7	$ 373.6	$ 358.2	$ 319.3	$ 272.1	$ 243.9
$ 37.6	$ 33.5	$ 33.0	$ 29.6	$ 24.8	$ 20.1	$ 15.1
$1,008.8	$ 924.3	$ 854.9	$ 765.1	$ 776.4	$ 630.1	$ 532.7
$ 159.4	$ 151.8	$ 148.7	$ 158.3	$ 171.4	$ 123.8	$ 131.5
$ 50.0	$ 50.0	$ 50.0	$ 50.0	$ —	$ —	$ —
$ 461.5	$ 434.3	$ 386.0	$ 350.1	$ 335.2	$ 307.7	$ 252.6
$ 23.13	$ 20.75	$ 18.62	$ 16.91	$ 16.19	$ 14.91	$ 12.73 (b)
15.7%	15.6%	14.3%	9.5%	12.8%	15.4%	15.1%
31.9%	30.9%	31.0%	25.9%	25.5%	30.1%	31.4%
10.6%	9.6%	9.1%	7.9%	6.3%	7.5%	8.6%
1.3%	1.2%	1.3%	1.2%	1.3%	1.4%	1.4%
23.8%	23.9%	25.1%	28.0%	33.4%	28.2%	33.5%
33.0%	30.9%	30.8%	31.5%	45.9%	38.0%	39.8%
4.5%	4.5%	3.9%	2.4%	3.4%	4.4%	4.6%
30.4%	29.8%	33.0%	51.1%	38.2%	34.1%	36.1%
31,853	31,830	24,747	25,064	22,320	21,916	20,524
29,600	27,800	23,900	25,100	25,400	23,300	18,200
$ 26-	$ 27¾-	$ 28⅜-	$ 24⅜-	$ 39⅞-	$ 47½-	$ 46-
$ 20	$ 20⅞	$ 15	$ 11	$ 19¾	$ 31⅜ (b)	$ 25⅞ (b)

The Quaker Oats Company and Subsidiaries

Financial Review

Fiscal 1981 Compared with Fiscal 1980

Operations

Fiscal 1981 sales reached a record $2.6 billion, an 8 percent increase over fiscal 1980. All industry segments contributed to the improvement. This sales increase is principally the result of price increases and favorable product mix. Unit volume gains occurred in International Grocery Products and the Direct-Mail Marketing businesses. Consolidated sales for fiscal 1981 include $43.1 million from the Burry and Needlecraft Divisions, which were divested during the year.

The increase in cost of goods sold of 8 percent is directly related to the increase in sales. Selling, general and administrative expenses increased 12 percent over last year, principally the result of an 18 percent increase in advertising and merchandising expense to support new and existing product lines.

Operating income for fiscal 1981 was up 13 percent to $238.5 million. U.S. Grocery Products' operating income increased 22 percent to $129.1 million, reflecting improved operating income in the Foods Division and Frozen Foods business. International Grocery Products' operating income increased 33 percent to $49.5 million, primarily the result of operating income improvements in England, France, South and Central America, Canada and Mexico. Toys' operating income of $50.6 million was 8 percent below last year. This decline, which was expected, followed a 57 percent improvement over the prior year and was primarily due to the impact of the weak economy on the toy industry. Operating income in Chemicals increased 62 percent, primarily the result of substantial savings in production costs. In the Direct-to-Consumer segment, an operating income decline in the Restaurants Division, due mainly to traffic declines, was partially offset by improved operating income in the Direct-Mail Marketing Division.

Net income increased by 9 percent to $105.2 million in fiscal 1981. The 13 percent increase in operating income was partially offset by significantly higher net interest expense and by foreign exchange losses this year compared to a gain in fiscal 1980. The higher interest expense was due to higher interest rates and increased levels of short-term borrowings. The divestitures of the Burry and Needlecraft Divisions resulted in an aftertax loss of approximately $2.6 million. These losses, plus the expense provisions for the closing of four restaurants, resulted in an 18 cents per share charge against fiscal 1981 earnings. The effective tax rate remained level with last year.

Earnings per common share increased by 10 percent over last year, as a result of the 9 percent increase in net income, lower preference dividends due to the repurchase of 36,020 shares of preference stock during the year, and a slight decline in average common shares outstanding. The growth in earnings per share, both as compared to last year and over the prior five-year period, has been in excess of the rate of inflation, as measured by the GNP Implicit Price Deflator.

Liquidity and Capital Resources

Internally generated funds from operations were the Company's primary source of funds and were adequate to meet capital expenditures and pay cash dividends. During fiscal 1981, such funds amounted to $184.3 million, a 12 percent increase over the prior year.

As of June 30, 1981, the Company had $40.2 million in cash and marketable securities, a 61 percent increase over the comparable June 30, 1980 amount.

The Company maintains domestic and non-U.S. bank lines of credit for future general corporate requirements. At June 30, 1981, the Company had $125 million available in unused domestic bank lines of credit and $98 million in unused non-U.S. bank credit facilities. In addition, the Company has a revolving credit agreement, none of which has been utilized, that provides for $175 million in either domestic or Eurodollar borrowings at the Company's option.

Subsequent to year-end, the Company entered into a transaction in which 287,819 shares of treasury common stock were exchanged for approximately $14 million face value of the Company's outstanding 7.7% sinking fund debentures. This transaction will result in a gain of approximately $4.9 million in the first quarter of fiscal 1982.

Discussion of the impact of Changing Prices, as measured by the requirements of Financial Accounting Standards Board Statement No. 33, is found on pages 63 and 64.

Fiscal 1980 Compared with Fiscal 1979

Operations

Fiscal 1980 sales were $2.41 billion, a 22 percent increase over fiscal 1979. All industry segments contributed to the sales increase. Volume gains, product mix, the full year effect of the acquisition of Chiari & Forti, S.p.A. in March 1979, and fiscal 1980 acquisitions accounted for about half of the increase with the balance due to price increases. U.S. Grocery Products' sales were up 10 percent, principally the result of price increases and product mix. Sales of International Grocery Products increased 41 percent to $726.4 million, primarily due to the inclusion of a full year's results of Chiari & Forti which was acquired in March 1979. Toys' sales rose 32 percent and Chemicals' sales

The Quaker Oats Company and Subsidiaries

increased 8 percent, principally due to increases in unit volume. The sales increase of 33 percent in the Direct-to-Consumer segment was primarily due to the inclusion of Brookstone for the first time in fiscal 1980. Total sales for fiscal 1980 included $92.5 million from the Burry and Needlecraft Divisions which were divested during fiscal 1981.

Total cost of goods sold, which increased 22 percent, is directly related to the increase in sales, while other expenses increased at a higher rate, principally due to a 27 percent increase in advertising and merchandising expenditures.

Operating income for fiscal 1980 was up 17 percent to $211.7 million. Operating income for U.S. Grocery Products increased 8 percent, which was in line with the sales increase. International Grocery Products' operating income increased by 12 percent. Chiari & Forti, the Italian food company acquired by Quaker in March 1979, was the significant factor in the operating income increase. Operating income in Toys increased by 57 percent to $55 million due to strong unit volume sales. Operating income in Chemicals increased 28 percent primarily due to higher sales, particularly in Europe. In the Direct-to-Consumer segment, an operating income decline in the Restaurants Division, due to a $2.5 million expense provision for the anticipated closings of certain locations and to traffic declines, was partially offset by favorable performances in Herrschners and the inclusion this year of the results of Brookstone Company.

Net income, before the cumulative effect of the fiscal 1979 change in the method of accounting for investment tax credit, increased by 14 percent to $96.4 million in fiscal 1980. The operating income increase was partially offset by a significant increase in net interest expense. The higher level of net interest expense was due to significantly higher rates and increased levels of short-term borrowings during the year. Also affecting net income was a foreign exchange gain of $1.8 million in fiscal 1980 compared to a $4.8 million foreign exchange loss in fiscal 1979. The effective tax rate for fiscal 1980 remained level with fiscal 1979 at 44 percent.

Liquidity and Capital Resources

Funds obtained from operations were the Company's primary source of cash funds. During fiscal 1980 such funds amounted to $165.1 million, up 15 percent from the preceding year.

Internally generated funds were adequate to meet capital expenditures for new or existing facilities in fiscal 1980, reduce long-term debt and pay cash dividends. Short-term borrowings were employed to fund increased working capital needs related to the higher level of business activity.

The Quaker Oats Company and Subsidiaries

Consolidated Statement of Income

	Millions of Dollars Except Share Data		
Year Ended June 30	**1981**	1980	1979
Net Sales	**$2,599.5**	$2,405.2	$1,966.3
Cost of goods sold	**1,750.9**	1,628.2	1,331.2
Gross profit	**848.6**	777.0	635.1
Selling, general and administrative expenses	**642.7**	571.7	457.2
Interest expense—net	**36.8**	28.9	17.2
Other (income) expense	**(21.1)**	1.7	10.7
Income Before Income Taxes and Minority Interest	**190.2**	174.7	150.0
Provision for income taxes	**83.7**	76.7	65.5
Minority interest	**1.3**	1.6	—
Income Before Cumulative Effect of Change in Accounting Principle	**105.2**	96.4	84.5
Cumulative effect of change in method of accounting for investment tax credit	—	—	14.7
Net Income	**105.2**	96.4	99.2
Preference dividends	**4.6**	4.8	4.8
Net Income Available for Common	**$ 100.6**	$ 91.6	$ 94.4
Per Common Share:			
Income before cumulative effect of change in accounting principle	**$ 5.01**	$ 4.55	$ 4.01
Cumulative effect of change in method of accounting for investment tax credit	—	—	.74
Net income	**$ 5.01**	$ 4.55	$ 4.75
Dividends declared	**$ 1.60**	$ 1.40	$ 1.20
Average Common Shares Outstanding (in thousands)	**20,083**	20,144	19,884

See accompanying notes to consolidated financial statements.

The Quaker Oats Company and Subsidiaries

Consolidated Balance Sheet

Assets			*Millions of Dollars*
June 30	**1981**	1980	1979
Current Assets:			
Cash and marketable securities	**$ 40.2**	$ 25.0	$ 22.4
Receivables, net of allowances	**339.9**	315.8	242.0
Inventories:			
Finished goods	**189.4**	208.2	179.9
Grain and materials	**109.5**	110.8	91.6
Supplies	**22.7**	23.5	19.3
Total inventories	**321.6**	342.5	290.8
Prepaid expenses	**43.5**	18.6	15.0
Current assets	**745.2**	701.9	570.2
Other Receivables and Investments	**22.5**	9.5	12.1
Property, Plant and Equipment	**920.3**	828.9	717.4
Less accumulated depreciation	**287.0**	256.1	210.0
Properties—net	**633.3**	572.8	507.4
Intangible Assets:			
Excess of cost over net assets of acquired businesses, less amortization	**50.1**	46.7	38.1
Patents, trademarks and designs, less amortization	**3.0**	3.3	3.7
	$1,454.1	$1,334.2	$1,131.5

See accompanying notes to consolidated financial statements.

Liabilities and Shareholders' Equity		Millions of Dollars	
June 30	1981	1980	1979
Current Liabilities:			
Short-term debt	**$ 210.9**	$ 155.1	$ 88.1
Current portion of long-term debt	**7.0**	6.8	4.6
Trade accounts payable	**140.2**	127.6	106.0
Accrued payrolls, pensions and bonuses	**60.3**	63.7	55.7
Income taxes payable	**9.5**	8.8	13.8
Other current payables and accruals	**64.9**	74.0	51.3
Current liabilities	**492.8**	436.0	319.5
Long-Term Debt	**165.2**	151.7	157.5
Other Liabilities	**19.2**	18.5	19.7
Deferred Income Taxes	**111.1**	89.5	71.2
Minority Interest	**6.5**	5.6	—
Redeemable Preference Stock, without par value, $100 stated value, $9.56 cumulative, authorized 1,500,000 shares; outstanding 463,980 shares (net of 36,020 shares held in treasury at cost) in 1981, 500,000 shares in 1980 and 1979	**46.7**	50.0	50.0
Common Shareholders' Equity:			
Common stock, $5 par value, authorized 35,000,000 shares; issued 20,997,349	**105.0**	105.0	105.0
Additional paid-in capital	**22.4**	22.3	22.6
Reinvested earnings	**542.3**	473.6	413.0
	669.7	600.9	540.6
Less treasury common stock, at cost	**57.1**	18.0	27.0
Common shareholders' equity	**612.6**	582.9	513.6
	$1,454.1	$1,334.2	$1,131.5

The Quaker Oats Company and Subsidiaries

Consolidated Statement of Common Shareholders' Equity

Millions of Dollars

	Common Stock	Additional Paid-in Capital	Reinvested Earnings	Treasury Common Stock
Balance at June 30, 1978	$105.0	$22.8	$342.3	$23.3
Net income			99.2	
Dividends on—				
Redeemable preference stock			(4.8)	
Common stock			(23.7)	
Common stock issued for stock options and stock awards		(.2)		(1.0)
Treasury shares acquired				4.7
Balance at June 30, 1979	$105.0	$22.6	$413.0	$27.0
Changes resulting from acquisition accounted for as pooling of interests		(.3)	(3.0)	(6.9)
Net income			96.4	
Dividends on—				
Redeemable preference stock			(4.8)	
Common stock			(28.0)	
Common stock issued for stock options and stock awards				(2.1)
Balance at June 30, 1980	$105.0	$22.3	$473.6	$18.0
Net income			105.2	
Dividends on—				
Redeemable preference stock			(4.6)	
Common stock			(31.9)	
Common stock issued for stock options and stock awards		.1		(2.2)
Treasury shares acquired				41.3
Balance at June 30, 1981	$105.0	$22.4	$542.3	$57.1

See accompanying notes to consolidated financial statements.

The Quaker Oats Company and Subsidiaries

Consolidated Statement of Changes in Financial Position

			Millions of Dollars
Year Ended June 30	**1981**	1980	1979
Sources of Funds:			
Operations			
Net income (1979 excludes the cumulative effect of change in accounting principle)	**$105.2**	$ 96.4	$ 84.5
Depreciation and amortization	**54.2**	48.8	44.6
Deferred income taxes and other items	**24.9**	19.9	14.8
Total from operations	**184.3**	165.1	143.9
Increase (decrease) in short-term debt	**50.4**	67.0	(3.8)
Sales and disposals of property	**27.6**	7.9	2.0
Decrease (increase) in inventories	**27.0**	(51.7)	(45.0)
Proceeds from new long-term debt	**21.2**	3.2	—
Other—net	**3.0**	4.0	3.8
Total funds provided	**313.5**	195.5	100.9
Uses of Funds:			
Additions to properties	**136.4**	112.4	75.8
Acquisition of treasury stock (common and preference)	**44.6**	—	4.7
Cash dividends	**36.5**	32.8	28.5
Increase (decrease) in prepaid expenses	**24.9**	3.6	(1.3)
Increase in receivables	**22.4**	73.8	51.8
Increase (decrease) in other receivables and investments	**14.8**	(2.6)	(5.3)
Cost of acquisitions (excluding working capital)	**10.1**	14.2	11.9
Decrease in long-term debt	**7.2**	11.0	5.8
Decrease (increase) in trade accounts payable and other payables and accruals—net	**1.4**	(52.3)	(51.2)
Total funds used	**298.3**	192.9	120.7
Net increase (decrease) in cash and marketable securities	**$ 15.2**	$ 2.6	$ (19.8)

See accompanying notes to consolidated financial statements.

The Quaker Oats Company and Subsidiaries

Sales and Operating Income by Industry Segment[a]

Year Ended June 30	1981		
	Sales	Operating Income	Sales
U.S. Grocery Products	$1,056.6	$129.1	$ 944.0
International Grocery Products	845.1	49.5	726.4
Toys	384.9	50.6	382.8
Chemicals	131.4	11.0	123.6
Direct-to-Consumer	138.4	1.0	135.9
Total Existing Businesses	2,556.4	241.2	2,312.7
Operations Sold	43.1	(2.7)	92.5
Total Sales and Operating Income	$2,599.5	$238.5	$2,405.2
Less: General corporate expenses		10.8	
Interest expense—net		36.8	
Foreign exchange (gain)/loss—net		.7	
Income before income taxes and minority interest		$190.2	

(a) *Sales between industry segments were not material and are not separately set forth. In computing operating income, none of the following has been deducted from sales: general corporate expenses, net interest expense, net foreign exchange gains and losses, minority interest, and income taxes.*

Segments of the Business
The segments and their principal product lines are:

United States Grocery Products—ready-to-eat and hot cereals; mixes, syrups and corn products; frozen pizza and breakfast products; canned chili; dry, semi-moist and canned dog foods; semi-moist and canned cat foods; and institutional and food service products.

International Grocery Products—food and pet food products in Canada, Europe, Latin America and the Pacific, and household products in Latin America and the Pacific.

Toys—crib and playpen, preschool, audio-visual, dolls, trucks, action figures, plush toys, arts and crafts.

Millions of Dollars

1980 (b)		1979 (b)		1978 (b)		1977 (b)
Operating Income	Sales	Operating Income	Sales	Operating Income	Sales	Operating Income
$106.1	$ 858.1	$ 98.0	$ 781.0	$ 89.3	$ 745.3	$ 96.3
37.2	513.8	33.2	397.1	28.1	356.3	25.8
55.0	290.8	35.0	230.3	27.2	196.0	31.2
6.8	114.5	5.3	112.5	3.0	108.6	(8.2)
3.7	102.5	4.8	83.9	3.9	66.7	3.7
208.8	1,879.7	176.3	1,604.8	151.5	1,472.9	148.8
2.9	86.6	5.2	80.8	8.1	78.4	10.4
$211.7	$1,966.3	$181.5	$1,685.6	$159.6	$1,551.3	$159.2
9.9		9.5		8.5		8.1
28.9		17.2		13.8		12.9
(1.8)		4.8		.7		3.0
$174.7		$150.0		$136.6		$135.2

(b) *Restated to reflect the fiscal 1981 realignment of industry segments.*

Chemicals—furan chemicals (produced from agricultural by-products), which are used in the foundry industry, the refining of petroleum and the processing of a wide range of products, including rubber and plastics.

Direct-to-Consumer—specialty restaurants; mail-order crafts; retail and mail-order specialty tools and gifts.

Operations Sold—Includes the results of the Burry and Needlecraft Divisions for all years presented. See Acquisitions and Dispositions note on page *(928)*.

The Quaker Oats Company and Subsidiaries

Segment Information

Identifiable assets, capital expenditures, depreciation and amortization expense for each industry segment are shown in the following tables. The most significant item included in corporate assets is cash and marketable securities.

Identifiable Assets

June 30	1981	1980*	1979*
			Millions of Dollars
U.S. Grocery Products	**$ 450.2**	$ 395.3	$ 361.5
Int'l Grocery Products	**409.8**	348.7	262.8
Toys	**316.3**	322.2	249.2
Chemicals	**122.3**	118.8	125.2
Direct-to-Consumer	**65.2**	65.8	55.9
Corporate	**90.3**	33.9	36.1
Total Existing Businesses	**1,454.1**	1,284.7	1,090.7
Operations Sold	**—**	49.5	40.8
Total Consolidated	**$1,454.1**	$1,334.2	$1,131.5

Capital Expenditures

Year Ended June 30	1981	1980*	1979*
			Millions of Dollars
U.S. Grocery Products	**$ 41.2**	$ 39.0	$28.7
Int'l Grocery Products	**58.7**	31.3	17.6
Toys	**23.0**	24.6	10.5
Chemicals	**7.1**	2.4	3.6
Direct-to-Consumer	**4.1**	8.8	12.2
Total Existing Businesses	**134.1**	106.1	72.6
Operations Sold	**2.3**	6.3	3.2
Total Consolidated	**$136.4**	$112.4	$75.8

Depreciation & Amortization

Year Ended June 30	1981	1980*	1979*
			Millions of Dollars
U.S. Grocery Products	**$19.1**	$16.7	$16.8
Int'l Grocery Products	**13.9**	11.5	8.3
Toys	**9.9**	8.5	8.9
Chemicals	**5.0**	5.0	4.8
Direct-to-Consumer	**5.0**	5.2	3.9
Total Existing Businesses	**52.9**	46.9	42.7
Operations Sold	**1.3**	1.9	1.9
Total Consolidated	**$54.2**	$48.8	$44.6

**Restated to reflect the fiscal 1981 realignment of industry segments.*

Sales, operating income and identifiable assets by geographic area are shown in the following tables. Sales by geographic areas consist of sales to unaffiliated customers.

Sales

Year Ended June 30	1981	1980*	1979*
		Millions of Dollars	
United States	**$1,524.8**	$1,406.2	$1,216.1
Canada	**143.6**	133.8	117.5
Europe	**579.6**	536.3	371.3
Latin America & Pacific	**308.4**	236.4	174.8
Total Existing Businesses	**2,556.4**	2,312.7	1,879.7
Operations Sold (U.S.)	**43.1**	92.5	86.6
Total Consolidated	**$2,599.5**	$2,405.2	$1,966.3

Operating Income

Year Ended June 30	1981	1980*	1979*
		Millions of Dollars	
United States	**$158.9**	$144.7	$119.7
Canada	**7.6**	5.8	5.5
Europe	**40.6**	35.5	29.4
Latin America & Pacific	**34.1**	22.8	21.7
Total Existing Businesses	**241.2**	208.8	176.3
Operations Sold (U.S.)	**(2.7)**	2.9	5.2
Total Consolidated	**$238.5**	$211.7	$181.5

Identifiable Assets

June 30	1981	1980*	1979*
		Millions of Dollars	
United States	**$ 835.5**	$ 782.8	$ 693.4
Canada	**57.7**	53.6	45.1
Europe	**277.2**	272.7	217.2
Latin America & Pacific	**193.4**	141.7	98.9
Corporate	**90.3**	33.9	36.1
Total Existing Businesses	**1,454.1**	1,284.7	1,090.7
Operations Sold (U.S.)	**—**	49.5	40.8
Total Consolidated	**$1,454.1**	$1,334.2	$1,131.5

**Restated to reflect separately operations sold in fiscal 1981.*

The Quaker Oats Company and Subsidiaries

Notes to Consolidated Financial Statements

Note 1 Summary of Significant Accounting Policies

Consolidation. The consolidated financial statements include The Quaker Oats Company and all of its majority-owned subsidiaries. All significant intercompany transactions have been eliminated. Investments in joint ventures are carried on the equity basis.

Inventories. Inventories are priced at the lower of cost or market, using a first-in, first-out (FIFO) method for the Direct-to-Consumer segment and international toys; last-in, first-out (LIFO) for domestic Chemicals, Toys, and U.S. Grocery Products packaging materials; and average quarterly cost for all other inventories. The percentage of year-end inventories priced using each of the methods is as follows:

June 30	**1981**	1980	1979
Average quarterly cost	**61%**	55%	62%
Last-in, first-out (LIFO)	**25%**	26%	22%
First-in, first-out (FIFO)	**14%**	19%	16%

In fiscal 1980, the Company changed its method of pricing U.S. Grocery Products packaging materials in inventory from average quarterly cost to last-in, first-out, retroactively to the beginning of fiscal 1980. The effect of the change in fiscal 1980 was to reduce earnings by 6 cents per share.

Properties and Depreciation. Property, plant and equipment are carried at cost. Depreciation is computed using the straight-line method and is designed to write-off the cost of the properties over their estimated useful lives. The rates used were:

Buildings and improvements	2% to 10%
Machinery and equipment	5% to 20%
Automobiles and trucks	20% to 33%
Miscellaneous equipment, office furniture and fixtures	5% to 33%

The Company uses the unit method of recording property dispositions which requires that all gains and losses on sales or retirements of property be recognized currently in income.

Maintenance and repairs are charged to expense as incurred. Significant replacements and betterments are capitalized.

Intangibles. Excess of cost over net assets of acquired businesses, including $25.3 million related to acquisitions prior to November 1, 1970 (principally Fisher-Price Toys, Inc.), represents the amounts paid in excess of the fair values of the net assets of such businesses, less amortization. Such costs are considered to represent continuing values and are adjusted only if reduction of such values of underlying businesses is indicated. All such costs resulting from acquisitions after October 31, 1970, are amortized on a straight-line basis over periods not in excess of 20 years.

Costs incurred in acquiring patents, trademarks and designs are amortized on a straight-line basis over their estimated useful lives.

Advertising and Merchandising. Expenditures are charged to expense as incurred.

Income Taxes. Deferred income taxes are provided on timing differences and result primarily from the use of accelerated depreciation methods for tax purposes.

In 1979, the Company changed its method of accounting for U.S. investment tax credits from the deferral to the flow-through method in order to achieve greater comparability with the general accounting practices of most other companies. The flow-through method recognizes credits in income when the assets are placed in service. The cumulative effect of this change, which was made retroactive to July 1, 1978, was to increase 1979 net income by $14.7 million, or $.74 per share.

Except for minor amounts, no U.S. federal income taxes have been provided on the undistributed earnings of non-U.S. subsidiaries, since they are expected to be permanently invested in those countries.

Pension Plans. The Company and its subsidiaries have various plans covering a majority of the employees. The amount charged to income each year is sufficient to cover normal costs of the plans and, for principal plans, amortization of prior-service costs over 30 years. Pension costs are funded currently.

Net Income Per Common Share. Net income per common share is based on the weighted average number of common shares outstanding. Dilution, which would result from the exercise of stock options outstanding, is not significant.

The Quaker Oats Company and Subsidiaries

Note 2
Acquisitions and Dispositions

During fiscal 1981, the Company purchased the Toddy Business Group, a leading manufacturer and marketer of powdered chocolate beverages in Brazil. The Company also acquired the Mellona Company, the leading marketer of honey products in The Netherlands. Both of these acquisitions were accounted for as purchases. Results of operations of the companies acquired have been consolidated from the dates of acquisition. Pro forma data is not presented because the effect is not material.

In fiscal 1981, the Company sold for cash substantially all of the assets of the Biscuit Group of the Burry Division to Burry-Lu, Inc., a unit of Generale Biscuit, S.A. of France. The Company retained the Food Service business of the Burry Division and is now a less than 20 percent shareholder in Burry-Lu. The Company also sold, for cash and notes, the assets and business of the Needlecraft Division to a group of private investors.

On July 1, 1981, the Company acquired Jos. A. Bank Clothiers, Inc. of Baltimore, a marketer of traditional men's and women's clothing and accessories, in a cash purchase transaction. Results will be consolidated beginning in fiscal 1982.

Note 3
Cash and Marketable Securities

Millions of Dollars	**1981**	1980	1979
Cash and cash equivalents	**$37.0**	$22.7	$20.9
Marketable securities*	**3.2**	2.3	1.5
	$40.2	$25.0	$22.4

**At cost, which approximates market*

Note 4
Accounts Receivable Allowances

Millions of Dollars	**1981**	1980	1979
Balance at beginning of year	**$14.2**	$10.8	$ 7.7
Provision for doubtful accounts	**2.4**	3.1	2.4
Provision for discounts and allowances	**13.0**	11.3	9.4
Write-offs of doubtful accounts, net of recoveries	**(.7)**	(.6)	(.7)
Discounts and allowances taken	**(14.7)**	(10.4)	(8.0)
Balance at end of year	**$14.2**	$14.2	$10.8

Note 5 Property, Plant and Equipment

Millions of Dollars	Balance at Beginning of Year	Additions	Retirements and Sales	Acquisitions and Other	Balance at End of Year
1981					
Gross property:					
Land	$ 17.3	$ 5.8	$(.3)	$ 3.0	$ 25.8
Buildings & improvements	271.4	28.6	(11.9)	(22.0)	266.1
Machinery & equipment	540.2	102.0	(42.6)	28.8	628.4
Total	$828.9	$136.4	$(54.8)	$ 9.8	$920.3
Accumulated depreciation:					
Buildings & improvements	$ 56.5	$ 7.9	$(2.9)	$ .4	$ 61.9
Machinery & equipment	199.6	43.9	(21.7)	3.3	225.1
Total	$256.1	$ 51.8	$(24.6)	$ 3.7	$287.0
1980					
Gross property:					
Land	$ 12.8	$ 2.1	$ —	$ 2.4	$ 17.3
Buildings & improvements	230.4	39.9	(3.3)	4.4	271.4
Machinery & equipment	474.2	70.4	(13.5)	9.1	540.2
Total	$717.4	$112.4	$(16.8)	$ 15.9	$828.9
Accumulated depreciation:					
Buildings & improvements	$ 48.4	$ 7.5	$(.5)	$ 1.1	$ 56.5
Machinery & equipment	161.6	39.3	(8.4)	7.1	199.6
Total	$210.0	$ 46.8	$(8.9)	$ 8.2	$256.1
1979					
Gross property:					
Land	$ 10.2	$ 1.2	$(.2)	$ 1.6	$ 12.8
Buildings & improvements	205.7	18.6	(.8)	6.9	230.4
Machinery & equipment	427.5	56.0	(19.0)	9.7	474.2
Total	$643.4	$ 75.8	$(20.0)	$ 18.2	$717.4
Accumulated depreciation:					
Buildings & improvements	$ 43.1	$ 6.3	$(1.0)	$ —	$ 48.4
Machinery & equipment	142.3	36.3	(17.0)	—	161.6
Total	$185.4	$ 42.6	$(18.0)	$ —	$210.0

The Retirements and Sales column in fiscal 1981 includes amounts relating primarily to the sales of the Burry and Needlecraft businesses. The Acquisitions and Other column includes amounts relating to the acquisitions of The Toddy Business Group in Brazil in 1981, The Walbron Group in Colombia, and Brookstone Company, Inc. in 1980, and Chiari & Forti in Italy in 1979. Also included in 1981 and 1980 are various reclassifications relating to previous years.

The Quaker Oats Company and Subsidiaries

Depreciation expense for fiscal 1981, 1980, and 1979 was $51.8 million, $46.8 million and $42.6 million, respectively. Maintenance and repairs were $60.0 million in 1981, $48.8 million in 1980, and $44.8 million in 1979.

Note 6 Intangible Assets

Additions to the excess of cost over net assets of acquired businesses in fiscal 1981 include $5.2 million related to the acquisition of The Toddy Group and in fiscal 1980, $10.5 million related to the acquisition of The Walbron Group.

Note 7 Short-Term Debt

Millions of Dollars	**1981**	1980	1979
Notes payable to banks—			
Non-U.S. subsidiaries	**$ 67.8**	$ 67.3	$44.5
Commercial paper—U.S.			
Dealer placed on the open market	**121.1**	65.8	21.6
Master trust demand notes held by banks	**22.0**	22.0	22.0
	$210.9	$155.1	$88.1
Weighted average interest rates on debt outstanding at end of year—			
Notes payable to banks—non-U.S.	**37.7%**	27.7%	19.4%
Commercial paper	**17.2%**	8.3%	9.7%
Weighted average interest rates on debt outstanding during the year—			
Notes payable to banks—non-U.S. (computed on month-end balances)	**33.4%**	27.2%	17.2%
Commercial paper (computed on daily balances)	**13.0%**	12.3%	9.4%
Weighted average amount of debt outstanding during the year	**$166.4**	$125.2	$78.8
Maximum month-end balance during the year	**$239.8**	$155.1	$95.3

Note 8 Credit Facilities

The Company has a revolving credit agreement, none of which has been utilized, that provides for $175 million in either domestic or Eurodollar borrowings at the Company's option and expires June 30, 1986. The agreement requires a fee of 1/2 of 1 percent for any unused portion.

The Company, in addition to the $175 million revolving credit agreement, has $125 million available in unused domestic bank lines of credit to meet general corporate purposes. The Company's non-U.S. subsidiaries had additional unused lines of credit of approximately $98 million at June 30, 1981.

Note 9 Long-Term Debt

Millions of Dollars	1981	1980	1979
7.80% notes, $3.7 million due annually through 1989 and $3.8 million due annually from 1990 through 1994	**$ 48.6**	$ 52.3	$ 56.0
7.70% sinking fund debentures, $1.8 million due annually through 2000, $6.8 million due 2001 (net of $5.1 million, $5.5 million and $2.8 million held at June 30, 1981, 1980 and 1979)	**35.9**	37.3	41.8
8¾% note, $1.7 million due annually through 1994	**23.3**	25.0	25.0
Industrial revenue bonds due from 1991 through 2009 at rates ranging from 6% to 10¾%	**20.0**	10.1	9.1
8⅜% industrial revenue bonds payable annually through 2002	**8.1**	8.2	8.3
Solid waste disposal revenue bonds— 5½% bonds due 1991	**3.0**	3.0	3.0
6½% bonds due annually from 2000 through 2006	**12.0**	12.0	12.0
6⅝% bonds due annually from 2005 to 2009	**2.0**	2.0	—
Obligations of non-U.S. subsidiaries	**16.0**	4.9	5.0
Obligations of U.S. subsidiaries	**2.0**	2.0	—
Capitalized lease obligations	**1.3**	1.7	1.9
	172.2	158.5	162.1
Less: Current portion	**7.0**	6.8	4.6
	$165.2	$151.7	$157.5

Aggregate required payments of maturities for fiscal 1982 through 1986 on long-term debt are: $7.0 million, $9.2 million, $8.6 million, $9.7 million, and $9.7 million, respectively.

Under the most restrictive terms of the various loan agreements in effect at June 30, 1981, $193.7 million of reinvested earnings is not available for payment of cash dividends and/or certain other distributions to preference and common shareholders, and minimum working capital of $175.0 million must be maintained.

The Quaker Oats Company and Subsidiaries

Note 10 Redeemable Preference Stock

Beginning on July 20, 1981, the Company must make annual payments to a sinking fund and/or repurchase outstanding shares in an amount adequate to retire a minimum of 20,000 shares (maximum 40,000 shares) of preference stock at $100 per share, plus accrued dividends. There were 36,020 shares of $9.56 cumulative preference stock repurchased in fiscal 1981, of which 20,000 shares will be used to meet the July 20, 1981, minimum retirement requirement. The preference stock is redeemable, at the option of the Company, in whole or in part at prices decreasing from $109.56 per share currently to $100 after July 19, 2000.

Note 11 Common Stock

Changes in shares of common stock follow:

	Common Stock	Treasury Common Stock
Balance at June 30, 1978	20,997,349	1,042,456
Stock issued for stock options and stock awards		(44,317)
Shares acquired		200,000
Balance at June 30, 1979	20,997,349	1,198,139
Stock issued for stock options and stock awards		(93,276)
Stock issued in connection with acquisition accounted for as a pooling of interests		(309,012)
Balance at June 30, 1980	20,997,349	795,851
Stock issued for stock options and stock awards		(95,412)
Shares acquired		1,143,514
Balance at June 30, 1981	20,997,349	1,843,953

The repurchase of common shares in fiscal 1979 was for use in the Stock Option Plan. The shares repurchased in fiscal 1981 were for use in the Stock Option Plan and other general corporate purposes.

Note 12
Employee Stock Option and Award Plans

Under the Company's Stock Option Plan, eligible officers and other managerial employees may be granted options for the purchase of common stock at a price not less than the fair market value at date of grant. Options are generally exercisable after one or more years and expire no later than ten years from date of grant. As of the end of August 1981, 408 persons held such options. Changes in stock options outstanding are summarized as follows:

	Shares	Option Price (Per Share)
Balance at June 30, 1978	790,528	$13.13—31.00
Granted	228,690	22.57—23.19
Exercised	(37,392)	15.06—23.44
Expired or terminated	(21,807)	15.06—31.00
Balance at June 30, 1979	960,019	13.13—31.00
Granted	274,245	26.69—26.94
Exercised	(88,981)	13.13—31.00
Expired or terminated	(89,761)	15.06—31.00
Balance at June 30, 1980	1,055,522	15.06—31.00
Granted	248,430	28.32
Exercised	(91,197)	15.06—31.00
Expired or terminated	(45,681)	21.44—31.00
Balance at June 30, 1981	1,167,074	$15.06—31.00

At June 30, 1981, options for 671,519 shares were exercisable, and 687,626 shares were available for future grant.

Since 1977, the Plan has provided for the granting of stock appreciation rights on outstanding options. The exercise of stock appreciation rights accordingly reduces the outstanding stock options. Included in the outstanding stock options at June 30, 1981 are stock appreciation rights for 252,969 shares. 6,420 stock appreciation rights were exercised in 1981, 7,775 in 1980, and none in 1979.

Since 1980, the Plan has also provided for the granting of performance units in conjunction with an equal number of stock options. The ultimate value of each performance unit is dependent upon achieving predetermined financial goals during a subsequent two to five year period and are exercisable only if the goals for the selected period are achieved. Performance units earned expire ten years from the date of original grant. The exercise of earned performance units cancels the related stock options, and the exercise of stock options cancels the related performance units. Included in the outstanding stock options at June 30, 1981 are performance units relating to 477,410 shares. None were eligible to be exercised during the year.

The Quaker Oats Company and Subsidiaries

In connection with the performance units and the stock appreciation rights, expense of $2.4 million was recognized in 1981 and $1.6 million in 1980. Fiscal 1979 expense was not significant.

In 1977, an Employee Stock Award Plan was approved by the shareholders. The Plan provides that all domestic and certain non-U.S. employees will receive five shares of common stock if they complete five years of service prior to January 1, 1982. The maximum number of shares that may be awarded is 60,000. As of June 30, 1981, 59,083 shares have been awarded under the Plan.

Note 13
Pension Plans

Pension expense under all plans was $14.1 million in fiscal 1981, $16.1 million in 1980, and $15.6 million in 1979. The lower expense in 1981 was due to a change in actuarial assumptions made to the Quaker Retirement Plan. The most significant of these changes were an increase in the assumed rate of return from 6.5% to 8% and a change in the salary increase assumptions from 6.25% to 7%.

A comparison of accumulated plan benefits and plan net assets for the Company's domestic defined benefit plans is presented below:

Millions of Dollars	January 1,1981
Actuarial present value of accumulated plan benefits:	
Vested	**$129.8**
Non-vested	**10.2**
Total	**$140.0**
Net assets available for benefits	**$185.9**

The assumed rates of return used in determining the actuarial present value of accumulated plan benefits for the domestic plans ranged from 7 percent to 8 percent. The Company's foreign pension plans are not required to report to governmental agencies pursuant to ERISA and are not required to determine the actuarial value of accumulated benefits. For the foreign plans, the actuarially computed value of vested benefits exceeded the total value of pension funds plus accruals by $1.6 million in 1981 and $.8 million in 1980.

Note 14
Leases

Certain equipment and operating properties are rented under non-cancellable operating leases that expire at various dates through 2062. Subleases are not significant.

Total rental expense under these operating leases was:

Millions of Dollars	**1981**	1980	1979
Minimum rentals (including restaurant rentals of $4.4 million in 1981, $4.3 million in 1980 and $4 million in 1979)	**$25.6**	$24.1	$19.8
Contingent rentals based on restaurant sales	**.6**	.6	.7
	$26.2	$24.7	$20.5

The following is a schedule of future minimum annual rentals on non-cancellable operating leases, primarily restaurants, stores, sales offices and warehouses, in effect at June 30, 1981:

Millions of Dollars	1982	1983	1984	1985	1986	Later	Total
Total payments	$13.7	$10.9	$9.4	$7.5	$7.1	$13.2	$61.8

Capital leases which are included in fixed assets, and minimum lease payments under such leases, are not significant.

Note 15
Long-Term Unconditional Purchase Obligations

The Company is obligated under various contracts to purchase specified goods and services. The contracts expire or become cancellable from 1983 through 1996. The aggregate amount of future required payments at June 30, 1981 is as follows:

Millions of Dollars	1982	1983	1984	1985	1986	Later	Total
Total payments	$13.6	$14.0	$15.1	$16.3	$17.3	$7.2	$83.5

Note 16
Advertising and Merchandising

Advertising and merchandising expenses were as follows:

Millions of Dollars	**1981**	1980	1979
Advertising media and production	**$118.0**	$113.7	$ 87.5
Merchandising	**214.4**	168.4	134.2
	$332.4	$282.1	$221.7

The Quaker Oats Company and Subsidiaries

Note 17 Research and Development

Research and development expenses were as follows:

Millions of Dollars	**1981**	1980	1979
	$27.1	$23.0	$19.7

Note 18 Interest Expense—Net

Millions of Dollars	**1981**	1980	1979
Interest expense on long-term debt	**$12.7**	$12.8	$12.4
Interest expense on short-term debt	**36.2**	24.7	10.7
Interest expense capitalized—net	**(5.8)**	(2.1)	—
Interest income on securities	**(3.3)**	(3.4)	(4.5)
Interest income, other	**(3.0)**	(3.1)	(1.4)
	$36.8	$28.9	$17.2

The Company adopted the provisions of F.A.S.B. Statement No. 34 in fiscal 1980. This statement requires a portion of the interest expense incurred to be assigned to the historical cost of acquired fixed assets.

Note 19 Other (Income)/Expense

Millions of Dollars	**1981**	1980	1979
Net foreign exchange (gains)/losses	**$(25.6)**	$ (1.1)	$ 7.3
Amortization of intangibles	**2.4**	2.0	2.0
Provisions for restaurant closings	**2.0**	2.5	—
Loss on operations sold	**3.2**	—	—
Commitment fees for credit facilities	**.8**	.8	.8
Miscellaneous—net	**(3.9)**	(2.5)	.6
	$(21.1)	$ 1.7	$10.7

F.A.S.B. Statement No. 8 requires that translation gains or losses on inventories, computed based on historical exchange rates, be charged to cost of goods sold, while other foreign exchange gains or losses be reported in other income and expense.

A summary of the exchange and balance sheet translation gains or losses included in other income and expense and the inventory translation gains or losses included in cost of goods sold is as follows:

	Pretax (Gain)/Loss Included In			
	Other Income/Expense	Cost of Goods Sold	Total	Estimated Aftertax Per Share Effect
1981	$(25.6)	$26.3	$ .7	$.12/Share Loss
1980	$ (1.1)	$ (.7)	$(1.8)	$.16/Share Gain
1979	$ 7.3	$ (2.5)	$ 4.8	$.11/Share Loss

Because some foreign exchange items are taxable and others have no tax impact, the estimated aftertax per share effect is not directly related to the pretax result.

Note 20
Provision for Income Taxes

Millions of Dollars	**1981**	1980	1979
Currently payable—			
Federal	**$48.2**	$42.9	$35.6
Non-U.S.	**21.6**	15.1	15.8
State	**7.2**	4.5	3.7
Deferred—net (primarily relating to depreciation)			
Federal	**1.5**	10.0	8.2
Non-U.S.	**4.3**	3.4	1.4
State	**.9**	.8	.8
Total income tax provision	**$83.7**	$76.7	$65.5

See Income Taxes note on page 51 for a description of the change, in 1979, in the method of accounting for the investment tax credit.

The sources of pretax income were as follows:

Millions of Dollars	**1981**	1980	1979
U.S. Sources	**$139.5**	$126.0	$102.5
Foreign Sources	**50.7**	48.7	47.5
Total income before taxes and minority interest	**$190.2**	$174.7	$150.0

The provision for income taxes varied from the "expected" tax provision as follows:

Millions of Dollars Except Percent Data	**1981**		1980		1979	
	Amount	**% of Pretax Income**	Amount	% of Pretax Income	Amount	% of Pretax Income
Computed "expected" tax provision	**$87.5**	**46.0%**	$80.4	46.0%	$70.5	47.0%
State and local income taxes, net of federal income tax benefit	**4.4**	**2.3**	2.9	1.6	2.4	1.6
Non-U.S. tax rate differential	**3.0**	**1.6**	(3.7)	(2.1)	(4.9)	(3.2)
U.S. tax credits	**(7.5)**	**(3.9)**	(3.8)	(2.2)	(3.9)	(2.6)
Miscellaneous items—net	**(3.7)**	**(2.0)**	.9	.6	1.4	.9
Actual tax provision	**$83.7**	**44.0%**	$76.7	43.9%	$65.5	43.7%

At June 30, 1981, total reinvested earnings of non-U.S. subsidiaries amounted to $159.9 million.

The Quaker Oats Company and Subsidiaries

Note 21 Quarterly Financial Data (Unaudited)

Year Ended June 30 — *Millions of Dollars Except Share Data*

1981	First Quarter (Sept. 30)	Second Quarter (Dec. 31)	Third Quarter (Mar. 31)	Fourth Quarter (June 30)	Full Fiscal Year
Net sales	$642.9	$690.3	$645.9	$620.4	$2,599.5
Cost of goods sold	428.1	460.3	436.4	426.1	1,750.9
Gross profit	$214.8	$230.0	$209.5	$194.3	$ 848.6
Net income	$ 22.7	$ 22.4	$ 28.8	$ 31.3	$ 105.2
Preference dividends	1.2	1.2	1.1	1.1	4.6
Net income available for common	$ 21.5	$ 21.2	$ 27.7	$ 30.2	$ 100.6
Income per common share	$ 1.06	$ 1.06	$ 1.37	$ 1.52	$ 5.01
Cash dividends declared per common share	$ .40	$ .40	$ .40	$ .40	$ 1.60
Market price range per common share	34⅝-28¼	31⅝-25⅞	35¼-30	37¾-32⅜	37¾-25⅞

Year Ended June 30 — *Millions of Dollars Except Share Data*

1980	First Quarter (Sept. 30)	Second Quarter (Dec. 31)	Third Quarter (Mar. 31)	Fourth Quarter (June 30)	Full Fiscal Year
Net sales	$574.7	$617.3	$626.5	$586.7	$2,405.2
Cost of goods sold	388.2	417.0	426.8	396.2	1,628.2
Gross profit	$186.5	$200.3	$199.7	$190.5	$ 777.0
Net income	$ 23.9	$ 22.5	$ 28.4	$ 21.6	$ 96.4
Preference dividends	1.2	1.2	1.2	1.2	4.8
Net income available for common	$ 22.7	$ 21.3	$ 27.2	$ 20.4	$ 91.6
Income per common share	$ 1.13	$ 1.06	$ 1.35	$ 1.01	$ 4.55
Cash dividends declared per common share	$ .35	$ .35	$ .35	$ .35	$ 1.40
Market price range per common share	27¾-23½	29⅞-24⅝	31¾-24½	34½-24½	34½-23½

Note 22
Financial Reporting and Changing Prices
(Unaudited)

Financial statements prepared using historical cost accounting principles do not reflect the impact of inflation on a company's financial position and results of operations. In an attempt to measure this impact, the Financial Accounting Standards Board issued Statement No. 33, Financial Reporting and Changing Prices. Accordingly, we are presenting on pages *(941)* and *(942)* selected financial information adjusted for the effect of inflation.

Statement No. 33 requires that historical data be adjusted using two distinct concepts: the "constant dollar method" and "current cost method." The specific financial statement data which must be adjusted using these two methods are cost of goods sold, depreciation expense, inventory and property, plant and equipment. In addition, disclosure of inflation-adjusted information regarding net monetary assets and liabilities, dividends and market price of the common stock is also required.

Because the development of inflation-adjusted data requires the use of estimation techniques and assumptions, caution should be exercised in comparing the financial data presented herein with that of other companies. Also, since the Statement requires that the inflation-adjusted data be developed using the hypothetical assumption that all fixed assets would be replaced in exactly the same state as they currently exist, it does not reflect how the Company would actually replace existing assets. Technological changes, which significantly influence a company's decision regarding fixed asset replacement, are not considered under either of the two methods.

As a result of adjusting pretax earnings for the effects of inflation without adjusting the provision for income taxes (in accordance with Statement No. 33), the effective tax rate for fiscal 1981 is 62 percent using the "constant dollar method" and 73 percent using the "current cost method." This compares with a 44 percent rate in the historical financial statements. The data illustrates that, in general, the tax structures throughout the world tax the income of the Company at a higher than intended rate. We believe that the data will provide a better understanding of how, in an inflationary environment, the current tax laws reduce the amount of cash available for expansion or replacement of existing assets.

Although the data required by Statement No. 33 does not result in a totally accurate or realistic portrayal of the effect of inflation on the financial results of the Company, we recognize the importance of identifying the eroding effect of inflation and support the F.A.S.B.'s initial requirements relating to the disclosure of inflation-adjusted data.

The Quaker Oats Company and Subsidiaries

Constant Dollar Information

The constant dollar method of accounting adjusts historical cost dollars to dollars of equivalent purchasing power by applying the U.S. Consumer Price Index (CPI-U) to selected historical values. The CPI-U is a very broad index that attempts to measure the general rate of inflation and does not give effect to foreign inflation rates or rates that apply to specific types of costs in a particular industry. Accordingly, although this index does provide a uniform and consistent basis of measurement, it does not necessarily reflect the appropriate rate for a diversified company with many locations and products. Therefore, use of this index has limited value in measuring the true impact of inflation on a company and in comparing one company with another.

The adjusted information provided herein, using the constant dollar method, was developed by determining the years the inventory and properties were acquired and adjusting the historical dollar values of these assets as well as the related cost of goods sold and depreciation expense, using the appropriate Consumer Price Index. All data has been restated to reflect the fiscal 1981 Consumer Price Index.

Current Cost Information

The current cost method of accounting adjusts financial data for the effects of specific price changes in goods and services, in order to reflect the current cost of these items. This method follows the logical assumption that inflation does not escalate at the same rate for all items. In developing the current cost data for properties, specific industry indices from sources such as the Construction Cost Index, Producer Price Index, Chemical Engineering Cost Index, or the Factory Mutual Building Cost Index, were used. Current cost amounts for inventories are based on year-end market values of raw materials and current production costs. These adjusted values were then used to compute the related depreciation expense and cost of goods sold. Although this method results in a more meaningful measure of inflation compared to the constant dollar method, it should be recognized that it does require a greater number of estimates and assumptions.

Purchasing Power Gain

Monetary assets such as cash and receivables lose purchasing power during inflationary periods because the same dollars will purchase fewer goods or services, but monetary liabilities such as accounts payable are satisfied with "cheaper" dollars. Since the Company's monetary liabilities exceeded the monetary assets during the period covered in this report, the Company realized a purchasing power gain. In accordance with the provisions of Statement No. 33, this "gain" in purchasing power is not included in income from continuing operations, but is shown separately. It is, however, a significant factor and should be considered when evaluating the inflation adjusted data presented herein.

Consolidated Statement of Income from Continuing Operations Adjusted for Changing Prices

Year Ended June 30, 1981	As Reported in the Primary Statements	Adjusted for General Inflation (Constant Dollars)	Adjusted for Changes in Specific Prices (Current Costs)
		Millions of Dollars	
Net Sales	$2,599.5	$2,599.5	$2,599.5
Cost of goods sold (excluding depreciation expense)	1,708.7	1,735.7	1,751.1
Depreciation and amortization expense	51.8	80.9	85.3
Selling, general and administrative expenses (excluding depreciation expense)	633.1	633.1	633.1
Interest expense—net	36.8	36.8	36.8
Other (income)	(21.1)	(21.1)	(21.1)
Provision for income taxes	83.7	83.7	83.7
Minority interest	1.3	1.3	1.3
Net Income from Continuing Operations	105.2	49.1	29.3
Gain from decline in purchasing power of net amounts owed		34.8	34.8
Total	$ 105.2	$ 83.9	$ 64.1
Increase in current cost of inventories and property, plant and equipment held during the year*			$ 79.5
Effect of increase in general price level			$ 117.2
Excess of increase in the general price level over increase in current costs			$ 37.7

**At June 30, 1981, current cost of inventory was $355.0 and current cost of property, plant and equipment, net of accumulated depreciation, was $1046.0.*

The Quaker Oats Company and Subsidiaries

Five-Year Comparison of Selected Supplementary Financial Data Adjusted for Effects of Changing Prices (a)

Millions of Dollars Except Share Data

Year Ended June 30	1981	1980	1979	1978	1977
Net sales					
—constant dollar	**$2,599.5**	$2,683.5	$2,485.7	$2,330.7	$2,289.0
—historical	**2,599.5**	2,405.2	1,966.3	1,685.6	1,551.3
Net income from continuing operations					
—constant dollar	**$ 49.1**	$ 58.7			
—current cost	**29.3**	26.9			
—historical	**105.2**	96.4			
Net income from continuing operations per common share					
—constant dollar	**$ 2.22**	$ 2.64			
—current cost	**1.23**	1.07			
—historical	**5.01**	4.55			
Gain from decline in purchasing power of net amounts owed	**$ 34.8**	$ 43.8			
Net assets at year-end					
—constant dollar	**$1,001.3**	$1,015.0			
—current cost	**1,058.9**	1,102.9			
—historical	**659.3**	632.9			
Excess of increase in the general price level over increase in specific prices of inventories and property, plant and equipment	**$ 37.7**	$ 1.3			
Dividends declared per common share					
—constant dollar	**$ 1.60**	$ 1.56	$ 1.52	$ 1.44	$ 1.36
—historical	**1.60**	1.40	1.20	1.04	.92
Market price per common share at year-end					
—constant dollar	**$ 34.13**	$ 33.65	$ 28.60	$ 32.87	$ 31.56
—historical	**34.13**	32.12	23.88	24.75	22.12
Average consumer price index (1967 = 100)	**259.4**	232.5	205.2	187.6	175.8

(a) *All constant dollar and current cost amounts are stated in average fiscal 1981 dollars.*

Auditors' Report

To the Shareholders of The Quaker Oats Company:

We have examined the consolidated balance sheet of The Quaker Oats Company (a New Jersey corporation) and Subsidiaries as of June 30, 1981, 1980, and 1979, and the related consolidated statements of income, common shareholders' equity and changes in financial position for the years then ended. Our examinations were made in accordance with generally accepted auditing standards and, accordingly, included such tests of the accounting records and such other auditing procedures as we considered necessary in the circumstances.

In our opinion, the financial statements referred to above present fairly the financial position of The Quaker Oats Company and Subsidiaries as of June 30, 1981, 1980, and 1979, and the results of their operations and changes in their financial position for the years then ended, in conformity with generally accepted accounting principles, applied on a consistent basis subsequent to the change (with which we concur) made as of July 1, 1978, in the method of accounting for investment tax credits as indicated in the Notes to the Consolidated Financial Statements.

Arthur Andersen & Co.

Chicago, Illinois,
August 12, 1981.

Report of Management

Management is responsible for the preparation and integrity of the Company's financial statements. The financial statements have been prepared in accordance with generally accepted accounting principles and necessarily include some amounts that are based on management's best estimates and judgment.

To fulfill their responsibility, management maintains a strong system of internal accounting controls, supported by formal policies and procedures that are communicated throughout the Company. Management also maintains a staff of internal auditors who evaluate the adequacy of and investigate the adherence to these controls, policies and procedures.

The financial statements have been audited by our independent public accountants, Arthur Andersen & Co., who render an opinion as to the fairness and consistency of the Company's financial statements. They obtained an understanding of the Company's internal control systems and performed tests and other procedures to the extent required by generally accepted auditing standards.

The Board of Directors pursues its oversight role with respect to the Company's financial statements through the Audit Committee, which is composed solely of non-management directors. The Committee meets periodically with the independent public accountants, internal auditors and management to assure that all are properly discharging their responsibilities. The Committee approves the scope of the annual audit and reviews the recommendations the independent accountants have for improving internal accounting controls.
The Board of Directors, on recommendation of the Audit Committee, engages the independent auditors, subject to shareholder approval.

Both the independent and internal auditors have unrestricted access to the Audit Committee.

Description of Property

As of June 30, 1981, the Company operated 61 manufacturing plants in 13 states and 14 foreign countries. The number of manufacturing locations utilized by each segment of the business, along with the approximate total manufacturing area, is summarized in the following table:

	Total No. of Mfg. Locations		Total Mfg. Area (In Sq. Ft.)	
Industry Segment	U.S.	Foreign	Owned	Leased
U.S. Grocery Products	13*	—	4,852,000	—
International Grocery Products	—	31	3,847,000	40,000
Toys	5	7	2,124,000	256,000
Chemicals	5*	1	271,000	92,000

**Both U.S. Grocery Products and Chemicals utilize space at Cedar Rapids, Iowa plant.*

Elevator grain storage facilities are located at three plants in the U.S. and 13 plants in foreign countries. Grain storage facilities with capacity in excess of 1.0 million bushels are located in Cedar Rapids, Iowa (10 million bushels), St. Joseph, Missouri (4.5 million bushels), and Peterborough, Ontario, Canada (1.3 million bushels).

As of June 30, 1981, the Company operated 103 restaurants, including 91 Magic Pan, seven Engine House Pizza Co., and five Proud Popover. Brookstone owns a mail-order facility in Peterborough, New Hampshire, and has seven retail stores in various east coast states. Herrschners owns a mail-order facility in Stevens Point, Wisconsin.

The Company also owns a research and development laboratory in Barrington, Illinois, and a pet food nutritional facility in Lake County, Illinois.

In July, 1981, the Company acquired Jos. A. Bank Clothiers, Inc., a marketer of traditional men's and women's clothing and accessories. Bank operates two manufacturing facilities and has 12 retail stores.

Additional 10-K Information

U.S. Grocery Products Description

Quaker, through its U.S. Grocery Products business, is a major participant in the competitive package foods industry in the United States. Quaker is the leading manufacturer in the U.S. of hot cereals, pancake mixes, corn meal and hominy grits and is also among the five largest manufacturers of ready-to-eat cereals and pet foods. Consumers purchase Quaker's grocery products through a wide range of food distributors. Quaker maintains a full-time sales force and has distribution centers throughout the country, each of which carries an inventory of most of the Company's grocery products.

Raw Materials

The raw materials used to manufacture these products include oats, wheat, soy products, corn, rice, sugar, almonds, raisins, beef, shortening, meat by-products and fish, as well as a variety of packaging materials. While most of these products are purchased on the open market, Quaker purchases commodity futures contracts, where possible, in order to assure supply at reasonable prices. This practice has limited commodity price volatility, although raw materials prices have tended to increase over time. Energy availability is important in maintaining production, and costs have escalated in recent years. However, supply has been adequate and continuous.

International Grocery Products Description

Quaker's International Grocery Products business is broadly diversified geographically and by product line. Internationally, Quaker participates in the foods, pet foods and household products markets. Quaker both manufactures and markets these products in Argentina, Australia, Brazil, Canada, Colombia, Denmark, England, France, Italy, Mexico, The Netherlands, Uruguay and Venezuela. The Company markets products in most countries of the free world. Quaker has leading market positions in a number of countries including the following: the Company is the leading hot cereals producer in many countries; the leading edible oil producer in Italy; the leading bar chocolate and chocolate candy producer in Mexico; the leading sardine processor in Brazil; the leading honey company in The Netherlands; the leading scouring pad manufacturer in Colombia; and the second largest pet food company in Continental Europe.

Raw Materials

Raw materials used by the international grocery business are basically the same as for the grocery business in the U.S. but also include corn oil, sardines and cacao beans.

Toys
Description

Fisher-Price is one of the major manufacturers in the highly competitive toy industry in the United States. Fisher-Price also has a growing international business, manufacturing and marketing toys in Mexico, the United Kingdom and Belgium and additionally operating sales offices in Canada, Germany, France, Italy and Australia. In the United States, Fisher-Price has the leading market position in infant and preschool toys.

Consistent with the overall toy industry, Fisher-Price's business is seasonal, as the majority of the year's sales fall in the July-December period due to Christmas demand. Extended payment terms are also customary and this increases the need for short-term financing. Fisher-Price introduced an "Early Shipment Allowance" program in fiscal 1980. This program offers advantageous payment terms in return for orders and shipment early in the year, and this has resulted in a somewhat better balance of production and sales throughout the year.

Raw Materials
Although Fisher-Price is producing toys using a broad range of materials, plastic remains the principal raw material. In line with expectations, plastic resins rose modestly in price during fiscal 1981, and remain in adequate supply.

Trademarks

The Company owns a number of registered trademarks issued by the United States Patent and Trademark Office. Under present law, all such registrations are renewable upon expiration of their present term, and the Company is not aware of any circumstances that could affect its continued use of these trademarks. Among the most important of the grocery products trademarks owned and registered by the Company are *Quaker*, *Cap'n Crunch* and *Life* on breakfast cereals; *Ken-L Ration* on dog foods; *Puss 'n Boots* on cat foods; *Quaker* and *Aunt Jemima* on mixes and corn goods; and *Aunt Jemima* and *Celeste* on frozen foods. Most of the grocery products trademarks owned by the Company are registered in the foreign countries in which Quaker does substantial business. The *Fisher-Price* trademark on toys and the *Magic Pan* name and pan design are also registered trademarks in the U.S. and several foreign countries.

Legal
Proceedings

The Quaker Oats Company is not party to any material pending legal proceedings not previously reported.

Corporate Social Responsibility

With the increased pressures of inflation and changing attitudes toward government-funded social programs, more and more nonprofit organizations are looking to corporations for assistance in meeting the needs of their constituents.

Quaker has long recognized the importance of providing assistance, both through financial aid and human resources, to worthy organizations. The Company has been contributing at a level of about one percent of its annual pretax income to charitable causes. This compares favorably with the industry average which is about one-half of one percent.

Most of Quaker's contributions are channeled through The Quaker Oats Foundation under the guidance of a Contributions Advisory Committee. In fiscal 1981, the Foundation contributed a total of $1.64 million in the form of grants to over 250 different organizations.

The Quaker Oats Foundation operates under guidelines which are designed to encourage participation by individual employees while seeking out opportunities for contributions to innovative programs which respond to the needs of society but are not yet established for traditional support. The Foundation emphasizes contributions in the fields of education, health and welfare. Grants are concentrated primarily in those communities where Quaker has facilities.

The Foundation offers a 3-for-1 Matching Gift Program, which enables Quaker employees to make contributions between $25 and $200 to their favorite educational institutions, hospitals, national health agencies or cultural organizations, and have them matched on a 3-for-1 basis. While matching gift programs are common in many companies, Quaker was the first to offer it on a triple-match basis.

In fiscal 1981, some 1,150 Quaker employees donated a total of 1,453 gifts to 872 organizations. The total matched amount from the Foundation was about $421,000.

Some of the Foundation's major areas of support during fiscal 1981 included over $750,000 to educational institutions; more than $330,000 to the various community funds located in Quaker communities; $180,000 to arts and cultural organizations; $133,000 to health care institutions; and the balance divided among youth programs, urban and civic affairs organizations, and economic/public policy programs.

Quaker also continues to press forward in its affirmative action efforts. During the five-year period ending December 31, 1980, while a small increase (7.5 percent) in total employment was occurring, the representation of women and minority group members moved upward significantly with increases of 15.6 percent and 18.5 percent, respectively. Similar gains were achieved in most job categories. Notable changes occurred in the managerial and professional areas. While total managerial employment increased 15 percent, the gains for women (97.4 percent) and minorities (58.3 percent) were indicative of affirmative efforts in a key area. Similar gains occurred for both groups (61.3 percent and 28.6 percent) in the professional category, while total employment in this category remained static.

Quaker's management has long been aware that, in addition to its responsibility to shareholders, the Company has an overall social responsibility, especially to the communities in which we live, work and do business. Balancing these commitments is no easy task, but it will continue to be an important managerial function and a criterion for measuring our progress as a company and a society.

Index

A

D

Q

R

S

This book has been set by VideoComp in 9 and 8 point Vermilion, leaded 2 points. Chapter numbers are 96 point Onyx, and chapter titles are 24 point Onyx. The overall type page size is 37½ picas by 48 picas.